Patriots
and
Liberators

Ziet, hoe 't heerschzuchtig Hoofd, ô Vrye Batavieren!
Door de Oppermacht des Volks word van den troon geweêrd!
Heil zy die Macht! Door deez' kan Vryheid Zegevieren;
Door deez' Sneer' elk Tiran, die Neêrland overheerd!

J. C. HESPE.

Patriots
and
Liberators

Revolution
in the
Netherlands
1780–1813

SIMON SCHAMA

Alfred A. Knopf · New York · 1977

The frontispiece engraving is taken from Volume II of the *Politieke Kruijer* (*Political Courier*) (1783–87), one of the principal Patriot and anti-Orangist newspapers established in Amsterdam and edited by the publicist and pamphleteer J. C. Hespe (see Chapter 3, pp. 79–80). The verse beneath the figures reads:

> Behold, O Free Bataves, Ambition's Head
> By the Sovereignty of the People is toppled
>   from the Throne!
> Salute its Might! Through which Liberty shall
>   prevail
> And through which every Netherlands' Tyrant
>   shall surely fall!

THIS IS A BORZOI BOOK
PUBLISHED BY ALFRED A. KNOPF, INC.

Copyright © 1977 by Simon Schama
Maps and diagrams Copyright © 1977
by Alfred A. Knopf, Inc.
All rights reserved under International and Pan-American Copyright Conventions.
Published in the United States by Alfred A. Knopf, Inc., New York
Distributed by Random House, Inc., New York. Published in England
by William Collins Sons and Co., Ltd., London.
Manufactured in the United States of America

Library of Congress Cataloging in Publication Data

Schama, Simon.
Patriots and liberators.

Bibliography: p.
Includes index.
1. Netherlands—History—1714–1795.   2. Netherlands
—History—1795–1815.   I. Title.
DJ202.S32   1977   949.2′04   76-20414
ISBN 0-394-48516-5

First American Edition

For
my mother and father

For
my mother and father

Contents

MAPS

Preface

Twenty-three years ago R. R. Palmer published in the *Journal of Modern History* an elegant summary of the politics of the Batavian Republic. Perhaps with a presentiment of the obscurity of the topic, he called it "The Dutch Revolution of 1795: Much in Little." His primary aim was simply to familiarise those ignorant of the vicissitudes of Dutch history at the end of the eighteenth century with their bewildering outline. At the same time he called for more work to be done on the readily accessible collections of printed sources. Lest he think me so churlish in response to the encouragement he gave me in this interest in 1967 as to have ironically inverted the sense of his title, I had better explain how what began as a trim monograph came to assume proportions of such indecent corpulence.

I had originally meant to try to illuminate the relationship between the expansion of revolutionary France and changes in administration and finance in the Netherlands. The major premise of such a study was that the politics of reform in the "client" states was a refracted image of events taking place in France herself. I duly began work on the relevant files both in the Archives Nationales and the Archives des Affaires Etrangères in Paris. It was not long, however, before I was confronted with two stumbling-blocks, one technical, the other methodological. The first was that, while fairly full in ministerial records, the series of cartons AFIV 1726–1832 dealing with Louis Bonaparte's "Royaume de la Hollande" had been subjected, disastrously for the historian, to one of Napoleon's comprehensive exterminations of documents dealing with issues he deemed sensitive or compromising. Much more serious was my growing unease that the French account of events in the Netherlands was evidently based on minimal understanding and even less sympathy for the predicament of their ally, and was conditioned throughout by the crudest exercise of power. This in itself was not, of course, surprising and it afforded some insight into the mentality of conquerors adorning their exploitation with the rhetoric of "liberation." But it gave me no clues as to the springs and motives of Dutch reformers at this time. Reading the reports of French agents and ambassadors was rather like peering through the wrong end of a telescope so that the conduct and motions of men, explicable in their own setting, appeared reduced to an incomprehensible and disordered scuttle of insects.

It thus became necessary to stand my original project on its head. Instead of exploring a small corner of the Greater France, a semi-fief of the "Grande Nation," I set out to try to discover something of the autonomous nature of the revolutionary Netherlands. Rather than elaborate on spurious affinities and analogies, evidently more the product of the lowest common denominators of strategic interest than any profound political kinship, I set myself two tasks. The first was to give an account of the public experience of those on the receiving end of revolutionary fraternity, that "liberty on the points of

bayonets" which Robespierre had warned against; the second to attempt
an elucidation of the changes taking place in the character of Dutch government. To tackle either of these enterprises demanded a mastery of the
language, traditions and manners of a people with whom I then had only the
most superficial acquaintance. In any other country such a proposal might
properly have been regarded as an ambition of colossal impertinence. But
from my very first visit to that most companionable of archives, the Algemeen
Rijksarchief in The Hague, armed with a Dutch that was not so much
double as fractional, I was made to feel that, however eccentric my labours,
I would be furnished with every kindness and assistance.

Without the help and hospitality, not only of the archivists and librarians
of the Algemeen Rijksarchief and Koninklijke Bibliotheek, but also of that
select band of Dutch scholars interested in this period, my efforts at research
would have been prematurely aborted. Above all others I owe an immense
debt to Dr. C. H. E. de Wit whose own work, a decade ago, pioneered renewed
debate on Batavian politics. From a chance encounter at a Brussels "Colloque"
in 1968 where, together with the late Dr. J. Haak, we made a not altogether
successful stand against the massed battalions of the "Grande Nation," Dr. de
Wit has been unstinting in putting at my disposal his library, his immense
store of erudition and research, and his infectious and unblushingly partisan
enthusiasm for the embattled protagonists of the Dutch revolution. While
our accounts do not meet at every point, our long discussions have helped
disentangle what would otherwise have been the unconscionably knotty
problems of political manoeuvres. I hope it is no small tribute to record that
he made me feel at home in Dutch history. I must also thank Dr. Willem
Zappey of the Institute of Social and Economic History at the University of
Amsterdam for urging on my interest in the career of Isaac Gogel, and the
members of the graduate seminar on Dutch history at the Institute of Historical Research for listening to parts of this work presented as papers over the
past five years. In particular I am grateful to Professor Koenraad Swart and
Mrs. Alice Carter for their helpful discussion of many of the points I have
raised. Mrs. Renée Gerson, another member of that seminar group, has been
an invaluable colleague in investigating the byways of Batavian politics, and
her own very penetrating research has refined many of the jejune simplicities
with which I originally examined this period of Dutch history.

The University of Oxford, where research in modern European history is
alive and well, kindly provided me with much-needed opportunities to rehearse
some of my more confused observations, in the graduate seminars convened,
respectively, by Drs. P. G. Dickson and J. M. Roberts, and by Professor
Richard Cobb. To the latter I am especially grateful, not only for the
benevolent interest with which he has followed my peculiar excursions up
the muddy creeks and hollows of the Dutch river estuaries but also for
the inspiration of his inimitable historical genius. A number of colleagues and
friends have helped me, either by reading part or all of the manuscript or
discussing the nature of its content. In particular, I must thank Jonathan
Steinberg for first directing my attention to the Netherlands; Quentin

Skinner and Derek Beales for permitting me to test my notions concerning revolutionary fraternity against the sharp wits of their seminar of 1973; Andrew Wheatcroft and Jane Ward for making valuable suggestions and criticisms during the early stages of the book; and Jacqueline Tammenoms Bakker for rescuing me from elementary and outrageous Dutch solecisms, some of which I fear may have eluded even her vigilant scrutiny.

But for the generosity of the Master and Fellows of Christ's College, Cambridge, I should not, even in the far distant days of the 8 guilder pound, have been able to spend extended periods of research in the Netherlands. Into the bargain, they provided me, for over a decade, with social and intellectual companionship which I still cherish. My thanks are also due to two editors of saintly forbearance and much historical wisdom, Philip Ziegler and Carol Janeway, above all for not despairing on the unnerving discovery that the egg that had taken so long to hatch in their nest had turned out to be a monster cuckoo.

To Professor J. H. Plumb, my teacher and friend, I owe a debt which can only be inadequately expressed in the conventions of such acknowledgements. But the legions of undergraduates, graduates and colleagues who have profited from his incomparable grasp of the historical process; who have taken cheer from his adamant insistence on its centrality to the understanding of human experience; and who have been buoyed up by his sheer intellectual versatility and exuberance, will all know the magnitude of my obligation. From him I learned that history must at least strive to be art before it can pretend to be a science, and in so far as this book serves to demonstrate the severity of that endeavour, the responsibility for its shortcomings rests exclusively with its apprentice author.

Inevitably, even in a work of such presumptuous bulk, I have had to omit certain areas from examination, most conspicuously the repercussions for its colonial empire of the domestic upheavals in the Netherlands. I have, however, tried to avoid the pitfall of assuming that "the Netherlands" and "Holland" are interchangeable historical terms, though my primary sources were principally concentrated in the centre of the country. If, by venturing so rashly into social, political and intellectual history, I have trespassed against the increasingly rigorous demarcations which separate historians from one another, it is a sin to which I willingly own. We are too overcrowded a profession to entrench ourselves in pedantic specialisations, the cliometricians despising the innumerate, the intellectual historians disdaining the artificers of political history. It is time, perhaps, to poke our heads above our several molehills and to take in a view, however nervous and blinking, of the broader historical landscape.

Having unburdened myself of prejudices which may seem more an apology than an explanation, to suggest that what follows merely scratches at the topsoil of its subject must appear to be a joke in poor taste. But that is the fact of the matter. Though interest in this blighted time is gradually reviving, there remain, in the Algemeen Rijksarchief, not to mention its sister Rijksarchieven in the provinces and the innumerable municipal and notarial records available in the Netherlands, massive ranges of as yet unexploited source material. Nothing was more lugubrious than to see files, brimming with documentation, not merely of Dutch politics and society, but by extension of all those European peoples of the north afflicted by the pestilence of war and conquest, raising great dust clouds on inspection, testifying to their long neglect in the depots of the Second Section. Should this study contribute at all to the acceleration of what is already a quickening momentum of research and writing on Europe *outre-France*, then it will have served its turn. In any case no rewards are required, rather a sense of educated gratitude, for having been able to cohabit so long with the congenial ghosts of the Batavian Republic.

Glossary of Dutch Terms
and Historical References

Bataves, Batavian The Germanic tribe to whom sixteenth- and seventeenth-century historians and writers ascribed the founding of "Holland." The revolt against Rome led by Claudius Civilis was regarded as an anticipation of the struggle for national independence against Spain, and the "Batavian Antiquity" as the repository of the classic Dutch virtues. Thus the "Bataves" did duty as ancestral custodians of the "true" constitution in much the same fashion as Saxons for seventeenth-century England or Franks for eighteenth-century France.

"Bijltjes" lit. "little axes," the naval and dockyard workers of the IJ and Amstel, concentrated in Amsterdam, usually fierce partisans of the Prince of Orange

Bijdragen lit. "contributions": volumes or proceedings of a learned society or club

bijlage appendix

burger citizen

burgerij A loose definition, either of the collectivity of citizens (in revolutionary parlance) or of the "middle class"—that large social group excluded from the ruling patriciate and nobility but regarding itself as superior to the urban populace or peasantry.

burgemeester Burgomaster of a town, appointed or elected by the regency. In some towns more than one burgemeester served simultaneously. Amsterdam had four.

convooien en licenten Customs duties imposed by the separate Admiralties of the Dutch Republic. Of the five Admiralties, Amsterdam's was the most important.

driemanschap triarchy

drost Originally sheriff or bailiff, later the chief officer of a governmental district or "county." Under Louis Bonaparte, the approximate equivalent of a French sub-prefect.

"Een- en Ondeelbaar" "One and Indivisible"—the slogan of the Batavian Republic

eendragt union, concord: used in the Batavian Republic to denote national, as distinct from provincial or parochial, sovereignty

fatsoenlijke lieden the well-to-do

federalist those who, during the Batavian Republic, advocated the retention of a loose alliance of sovereign provinces, or at least provincial authority over finance and justice

gemeente the commons, populace

Generality Lands the territories—primarily North Brabant and Flanders on the left bank of the Scheldt—conquered by the armies of the States-General under Maurice of Nassau and thereafter deprived of sovereign provincial status

grachten canals; used, as in "heeren van grachten," to denote the more elegant canals in the centre of Amsterdam where most of the patriciate resided

grauw rabble, mob

grietenij, grietenie jurisdictional subdivision of the Friesland "kwartieren." See p. 664, n. 31.

grond-vergadering primary assembly

heer noble, gentleman

heerlijke rechten seigneurial dues, customary perquisites

huisvrouw housewife

jonkheer landowning noble

landdag provincial assembly/estates

landdrost originally county sheriff; under Louis Bonaparte, the equivalent of a departmental prefect

middenstand amorphous social category of the "middle class"

neringdoen petty-bourgeois, small craftsmen, self-employed tradesmen and shopkeepers

omwenteling revolution

opstootje riot, brawl, fracas

Oranjeklanten supporters of the House of Orange, a mildly pejorative term generally used by their opponents, called, in their turn, "keesen"

Orange-Nassau The dynasty which, under the leadership of William the Silent, united the northern provinces of the Netherlands against Spain in the 1570's. His descendants were made Stadholders in each of the seven provinces of the Union, and Captains- and Admirals-General of the Republic.

Patriot Title adopted by opponents of the Prince of Orange, usually advocates of political reform, in the last quarter of the eighteenth century

Pensionary Originally the legal councillor and advocate of the province, or of a single town. In the seventeenth century, after *Advocate* Oldenbarneveld, the Pensionary of Holland was chief minister of that province. During the "Stadholderless" periods (see chronology) the Pensionary came to exercise a preponderant influence in the formulation and execution of policy, particularly foreign policy.

"Prinsgezind" supporter of the House of Orange

raad council

Raadpensionaris lit. "Council"—more usually Grand Pensionary of Holland. Only when Schimmelpenninck assumed the title in 1805 did it become a national first office of state.

Raad van Staat Council of State (under the United Provinces)

regent member of the governing patriciate of a town

schepen magistrate, sometimes alderman

schout, hoofdschout sheriff, lieutenant of police

schutterij lit. "shooters"; the town watch or militia

Staatsraad Council of State under Schimmelpenninck and Louis Bonaparte

Stadholder Originally "Lieutenant" of the respective provinces, the chief officer responsible for public order and the upholding of the law. After independence from Spain the provincial States appointed their Stadholder, in practice always a Prince of the House of Orange, though in Friesland and Groningen a member of the cadet line of Nassau-Dietz. Only with the accession of William Friso, William IV in 1747, was a Prince of Orange simultaneously Stadholder in all seven provinces. Even before this, however, the Stadholder, as Captain- and Admiral-General of the Union, had been at the centre of a court—if definitely not a monarch, then certainly more than a first minister or commander-in-chief. He also exercised vague but important powers of appointment to local offices, and although

never presiding over the States-General, often dominated the Council of State.

States-General *Not* a national legislature, but an assembly of the delegates of each of the seven sovereign provinces. They could send as many delegates as they wished, each delegation being tightly bound by its respective States, and having equal votes.

stuiver coin, in value one-twentieth of a guilder

tiercering the reduction to a third of the interest payable on the Dutch national debt, imposed by Napoleon in 1810

trekschuit towed barge, the usual means of water-borne passenger transport between towns, especially in Holland

Union of Utrecht The alliance, concluded in 1579, eventually including all the seven northern provinces. It was conceived of as strictly defensive, against Spanish aggression, and bound to uphold local and provincial sovereignties rather than reconstitute them in some new national state.

unitarists the supporters, during the Batavian Republic, of a unified nation state with a single sovereign source of law and government

Vaderland Fatherland

verponding Property tax, based on rental value. After 1805 usually denoting Gogel's national tax introduced in that year.

vrijheid liberty

vroedschap regency, town council

waterstaat Hydraulic service, maintaining dykes, polders, rivers and canals. It was subdivided into innumerable local colleges, councils and the like, sometimes appointed by a regency, sometimes by a local dykegrave, an office which itself could be hereditary. After 1805, referring to the commission or the ministry of hydraulics.

wethouder alderman, after 1807 the appointed councillor of the burgemeester

wijk town district or quarter

wijk-vergadering district assembly

Notes

1. Throughout this book the term "Holland" is used to refer to the province of that name, the national title being "The Netherlands" (even though it is recognised that the southern Netherlands were, except for the period from 1815 to 1830, part of another state). In their successive phases the northern Netherlands were known as:

to 1795	The Republic of the United Provinces
1795–1805	The Batavian Republic
1805–1806	The Batavian Commonwealth (*Gemeenebest*)
1806–1810	The Kingdom of Holland
1810–1813	Departments of the French Empire
1814–1830	The Kingdom of the United Netherlands

2. *Weights and measures.* Until 1820, when the metric system was adopted, the Netherlands used a bewildering variety of denominations, varying from province to province and sometimes even from town to town. I list here, with their modern equivalents, only those units used in the text.

Amsterdam morgen	=	0.8129 hectare
Amsterdam pond	=	494.09 grams
1 scheepslast = 4000 ponden	=	2000 kgs.
1 Dordtse last (fluid)	=	30.04 hectolitres

3. All translations from Dutch and French sources are my own.

1566–68   First revolts in the northern Netherlands, eventually repressed by the Duke of Alva

1572   Capture of Brill by the Sea Beggars; uprising in Holland and Zeeland towns

1579   Union of Utrecht

1581   Forswearing (Act of Abjuration) of allegiance to Philip II

1584–85   Assassination of William I; conquests of Parma in south

1590–94   Conquests of Maurice of Nassau, Stadholder of five of the seven provinces

1609–21   Twelve Years' Truce

1625   Succession of Frederick Henry as Stadholder

1647   Succession of William II as Stadholder

1648   Treaty of Münster; Dutch independence acknowledged by Spain

1650   William II's attempted "coup" in Amsterdam and death

1650–72   Minority of William III in first "Stadholderless" period

1672   William III made Stadholder as French invade the Dutch Republic; Pensionary de Witt murdered

1678   War with France concluded by Treaty of Nijmegen

1702–13   War of the Spanish Succession against France and allies, ended at Treaty of Utrecht

1702–47   Second "Stadholderless" period

1747   Accession of William IV, of the Friesian line

1748–49   Uprisings in Holland and Zeeland, deposition of some regents, protests of the "Doelisten" (see Ch. 2)

1751   Death of William IV, regency of the "Vrouw Gouvernante" Anna

1759   Death of Anna; supremacy of the Duke of Brunswick

1766   Majority of William V; "Act of Consulship"

1780–84   Fourth Anglo-Dutch War

1783–84   Riots in Rotterdam and The Hague; beginnings of the Free Corps

1785   National Assembly of Free Corps at Utrecht

1786   Revolution in Utrecht; expulsion of William V from The Hague garrison

1787   Revolution in Amsterdam; "Battle" of the Vecht; civil war between the Patriot "cordon" and Stadholders' troops. Journey and arrest of Princess Wilhelmina at Goejanversluis; invasion by Prussian troops in October

1787–88   Sacking and plunder of Patriot property throughout the country, exile of Patriots to southern Netherlands and France

1792   Establishment of Batavian Revolutionary Committee in Paris

1793   Participation of the "Free Foreign Legion" in Dumouriez's campaign, culminating in the Battle of Neerwinden

1794   Establishment of a "Committee of Insurrection" in Amsterdam

1795   Successful invasion of the Netherlands by General Pichegru's Armée du Nord; foundation of the Batavian Republic; exile of William V

1796   First Batavian National Assembly

1797   Rejection of the first draft constitution by national electorate

1798   Radical *coup d'état* (January 22); promulgation of the first Dutch constitution inaugurating a unitary state; countercoup in June

1799   Anglo-Russian invasion beaten off

1801   Conservative coup; reversion to federalist form of government

1805   Authoritarian unitarism imposed under the regime of "Grand Pensionary" Schimmelpenninck; first national finance system introduced

1806   Schimmelpenninck removed by Napoleon; replaced by Louis Bonaparte as "King of Holland"

1809   British invasion of Walcheren Island and eventual evacuation

1810   Cession of southern departments of Kingdom to Empire, followed by complete annexation of the Netherlands by France

1810–13   Rule of the "Prince-Governor" Lebrun, intendants and prefects

1813   Collapse of French Imperial power and insurrection in major towns in Holland; landing of the Prince of Orange

1814   William VI and I proclaimed King of Netherlands

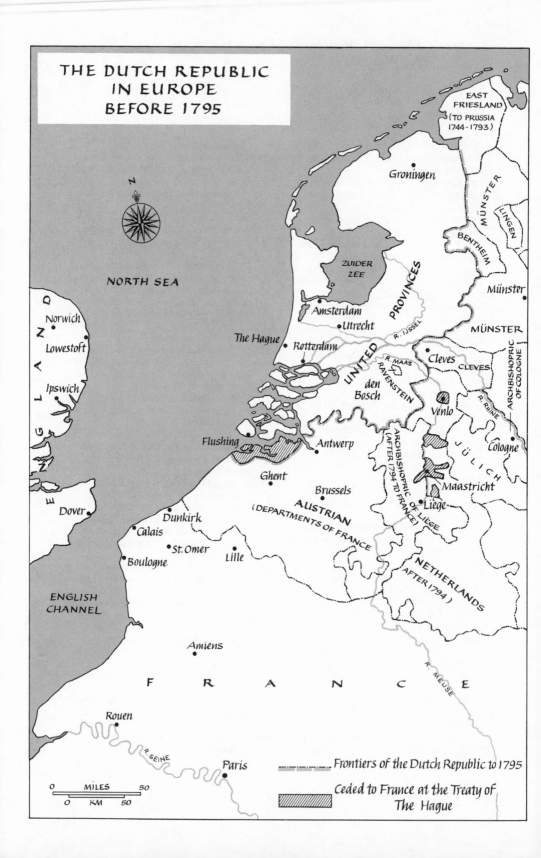

THE DUTCH REPUBLIC IN EUROPE BEFORE 1795

EAST FRIESLAND (TO PRUSSIA 1744-1793)

MÜNSTER

LINGEN

BENTHEIM

Groningen

Münster

ZUIDER ZEE

MÜNSTER

UNITED PROVINCES

NORTH SEA

R. IJSSEL

Amsterdam

Utrecht

The Hague

Rotterdam

Cleves

CLEVES

ARCHBISHOPRIC OF COLOGNE

R. MAAS

RAVENSTEIN

den Bosch

R. RHINE

Venlo

Norwich

Lowestoft

Ipswich

ENGLAND

Flushing

Antwerp

Ghent

JÜLICH

Cologne

Maastricht

Liège

ARCHBISHOPRIC OF LIÈGE (AFTER 1794 TO FRANCE)

Dover

Brussels

AUSTRIAN (DEPARTMENTS OF FRANCE)

Dunkirk

Calais

St. Omer

Lille

NETHERLANDS AFTER 1794)

Boulogne

ENGLISH CHANNEL

Amiens

F   R   A   N   C   E

R. MEUSE

Rouen

R. SEINE

Paris

0   MILES   50

0   KM   50

Frontiers of the Dutch Republic to 1795

Ceded to France at the Treaty of The Hague

❋❋❋❋❋❋❋❋❋

Part
I

❋❋❋❋❋❋❋❋❋

HENDRIK   *Father talks incessantly about the civil discord in our Land. How did that come about?*

FATHER   *Ja, how shall I tell you? Well, sometimes people have very different ways of thinking about things and this was so in respect to the government of our country. The old structure of our government, however good in the opinion of many people, could easily lead to many quarrels and divisions . . . During the War with England there appeared a swarm of writings depicting the shortcomings of the government in the blackest colours; they argued that the power of the Stadholders had to be restricted and that the burghers and inhabitants had as much right to it; a right to decide the appointment of Regents and the government. These writings were greedily read by thousands of people and so the disaffection steadily gained ground and passions were aroused. Burgher societies were everywhere established and powerful petitions sent to the Regents appropriating the honourable title of Patriot to which every well-disposed Fatherlander, whatever his opinions, is surely entitled.*

———*Schoolboek over de Geschiedenissen van ons Vaderland* (Leiden–Deventer–Groningen, 1822), pp. 114, 116.

✳ ✳ ✳ ✳ ✳ ✳ ✳ ✳ ✳ ✳

1

Introduction

Nationality and the French Revolution

John Adams, who knew the Dutch Republic well, once likened its predicament to that of a frog caught between the legs of two fighting bulls.[1] The image was acute if unflattering. While the amphibian wished to be left in peace to order its own disturbed and precarious existence, its croaks of protest were inaudible above the bellowing combat of its neighbours. This book is an attempt to amplify the Dutch complaint and to restore to the events taking place in the Netherlands at the end of the eighteenth century the context of a national revolution.

The term "national revolution" can hardly avoid evoking unsavoury connotations for the twentieth-century reader. Here it is used more innocently to promote the Dutch revolution above its customary station as a footnote to the foreign policy of revolutionary France.[2] It is not astonishing that events in the Netherlands were upstaged by the more arresting drama played out in the great nation to the west. The rebirth of France seemed to coincide with the funeral rites of Dutch power. By the closing decades of the eighteenth century, the Dutch Republic had been consigned to that indeterminate category of states neither truly sovereign nor yet completely subordinate—more than Poland but less than Prussia—whose policy, it was safely assumed by diplomats, was determined outside its own chancelleries. James Harris, the British ambassador who engineered the defeat of the Patriot revolution of the 1780's,[3] took that upheaval to be merely the most spectacular instance of French intrigue.[4] Likewise the restored Prince of Orange—the Stadholder Willem V—and his ministers were assumed by the French to be nothing more than the tools of British strategy. The Batavian Republic (1795–1805), underwritten by the success of French arms, was despised by ally and enemy alike as the mannikin of the Quai d'Orsay. Napoleon had no scruple in writing off the Dutch altogether as a legitimate national entity. The Netherlands, he concluded, were no more than the alluvium formed by "the principal rivers of my empire."[5] For most of the French who were to intrude abruptly into her domestic history Holland was, par excellence, the country of "canaille, canaux et canards."

This account has been written with the presumption that to discount the

[2]

❀❀❀❀❀❀❀❀❀

Part
I

❀❀❀❀❀❀❀❀❀

HENDRIK   *Father talks incessantly about the civil discord in our Land.
          How did that come about?*

FATHER   *Ja, how shall I tell you? Well, sometimes people have very
          different ways of thinking about things and this was so in
          respect to the government of our country. The old structure
          of our government, however good in the opinion of many
          people, could easily lead to many quarrels and divisions . . .
          During the War with England there appeared a swarm of
          writings depicting the shortcomings of the government in the
          blackest colours; they argued that the power of the Stadholders
          had to be restricted and that the burghers and inhabitants
          had as much right to it; a right to decide the appointment
          of Regents and the government. These writings were greedily
          read by thousands of people and so the disaffection steadily
          gained ground and passions were aroused. Burgher societies
          were everywhere established and powerful petitions sent to
          the Regents appropriating the honourable title of Patriot
          to which every well-disposed Fatherlander, whatever his
          opinions, is surely entitled.*

          ————*Schoolboek over de Geschiedenissen van ons Vaderland* (Leiden–De-
          venter–Groningen, 1822), pp. 114, 116.

�֍✾✾✾✾✾✾✾✾✾

1

Introduction

Nationality and the French Revolution

John Adams, who knew the Dutch Republic well, once likened its predicament to that of a frog caught between the legs of two fighting bulls.[1]
The image was acute if unflattering. While the amphibian wished to be
left in peace to order its own disturbed and precarious existence, its croaks
of protest were inaudible above the bellowing combat of its neighbours. This
book is an attempt to amplify the Dutch complaint and to restore to the
events taking place in the Netherlands at the end of the eighteenth century
the context of a national revolution.

The term "national revolution" can hardly avoid evoking unsavoury connotations for the twentieth-century reader. Here it is used more innocently
to promote the Dutch revolution above its customary station as a footnote to
the foreign policy of revolutionary France.[2] It is not astonishing that events
in the Netherlands were upstaged by the more arresting drama played out in
the great nation to the west. The rebirth of France seemed to coincide with
the funeral rites of Dutch power. By the closing decades of the eighteenth
century, the Dutch Republic had been consigned to that indeterminate category of states neither truly sovereign nor yet completely subordinate—more
than Poland but less than Prussia—whose policy, it was safely assumed by
diplomats, was determined outside its own chancelleries. James Harris, the
British ambassador who engineered the defeat of the Patriot revolution of
the 1780's,[3] took that upheaval to be merely the most spectacular instance of
French intrigue.[4] Likewise the restored Prince of Orange—the Stadholder
Willem V—and his ministers were assumed by the French to be nothing
more than the tools of British strategy. The Batavian Republic (1795–1805),
underwritten by the success of French arms, was despised by ally and enemy
alike as the mannikin of the Quai d'Orsay. Napoleon had no scruple in writing
off the Dutch altogether as a legitimate national entity. The Netherlands, he
concluded, were no more than the alluvium formed by "the principal rivers of
my empire."[5] For most of the French who were to intrude abruptly into her
domestic history Holland was, par excellence, the country of "canaille, canaux
et canards."

This account has been written with the presumption that to discount the

[2]

"eighteenth-century Dutch revolution" as the shuttlecock of the Franco-British conflict is to tell less than half the story. Admittedly it is not difficult to see how it has failed to receive serious attention from historians of the period. Even the studied classicism of the nomenclature "Batavian Republic" seems to advertise the spurious credentials of its statehood. Along with "Parthenopean," "Cispadane," and "Rauracian" it joins that gallery of pseudo-republics, established by pseudo-revolutions to serve the interests of French strategy, and discarded as soon as those same interests dictated. Put less brusquely, the Batavian Republic might be seen as just one more stage in the dismal retreat of the first French Republic from its innocent professions of revolutionary fraternity to the habitual practices of *raison d'état*. This depressing history was monumentally chronicled nearly a century ago by Albert Sorel. His *L'Europe et la Révolution française* amounted to an eight-volume indictment of the Revolution, not so much for failing to behave differently from its adversaries, but rather for leading Europe to believe that it would.[6]

Sorel's colossal tour de force reads at times like a morality epic dressed up in the prose of the Académie Française. It overflows with tarnished ideals, forsworn pledges, devious stratagems and counter-betrayals. Hovering over all is the ubiquitous spirit of national ambition and reason of state. Recording their origins, Sorel supplies ample evidence for the most sceptical verdict on the "sister republics." The Helvetic Republic is brought to birth at dinner *chez* Director Reubell, its constitution dictated to its President-designate, Peter Ochs, over coffee. Had it not been for the guns of General Championnet, the Parthenopean Republic would have remained imprisoned in the wishful thoughts of the Neapolitan salon intelligentsia. The Cisalpine (North Italian) Republic was created to decorate Bonaparte's brow with laurels and the Roman to avenge the death of his sister's betrothed. Together their history seems merely a record of political burlesque, the proper complement to the crimes of their protector.

During the period in which the domestic history of the French Revolution was transformed by the assault on the archives led by Alphonse Aulard, and his renegade disciple Albert Mathiez, the history of its expansion remained dominated by the assumptions underlying Sorel's work. The narratives appearing in this period were usually confined to contemplating the triumph and nemesis of the Napoleonic adventure.[7] Interest in, and treatment of, those at the receiving end of French imperialism was perfunctory and continued to be a mirror image of French strategy. The topic of "the French Revolution and Europe" had become interchangeable with French Europe. Not until the publication of studies by Professors R. R. Palmer and Jacques Godechot in the 1950's was there any serious challenge to this orthodoxy.[8] Crudely summarised they argued that, so far from being either a unique and isolated phenomenon, a freak change in the European climate, or the abrupt Romantic reaction against eighteenth-century rationalism, the French Revolution was part of an evolving pattern of political upheavals. Beginning in the 1760's with the rebellion of the Americans, proceeding through Geneva and the Low Countries in the 1780's, this "Atlantic revolution" continued its majestic progress from the Potomac to the Vistula. Viewed from this panoramic perspective, the French Revolution diminishes somewhat from the mountainous place it usually occupies in the foreground of the historical landscape. Rather than the *fons et origo* of the Age of Democratic Revolution, it is its catalyst and most dramatic manifestation. In its several locations the phenomenon, as sketched by Professor Palmer, exhibits a number of common features. It generally begins with the rebellion by patrician or aristocratic "constituted bodies" against the reforming initiatives of the absolute power. As the opposition groups legitimate their disaffection by appealing to these libertarian and historical rights they claim have been violated, their insurrection gathers momentum and recruits popular support. The eventual overthrow of the incumbent authority by the controlled deployment of popular force is then followed by a struggle for power between its legatees: "aristocratic" and "democratic." Of course this typology is not applied indiscriminately, and throughout his work Professor Palmer is concerned to emphasise the importance of local variations. In an introductory chapter he is, if anything, over-diffident in explaining:

all that is necessary or even desirable is to set up a larger framework or conceptual structure in which phenomena that are admittedly different and even different in very significant ways may yet be seen as related products of a common impulse or different ways of achieving under different circumstances and against different degrees of opposition, certain recognisably common goals.[9]

Buried beneath this avalanche of qualifications the original hypothesis of the "common impulse" seems almost lost from sight.

It is not clear, then, whether the "larger framework" is designed to help the historian see events in individual countries and regions in the light of their native history and social experience, or whether, as in the Netherlands, it is a "typical revolution of the era" in that "it reveals on a small and well-lit stage a great many of the phenomena then common to western Europe."[10] Are we, essentially, to deal with the general or the particular? The consequences of the "Atlantic" comparative approach, while seminal for the historiography of the period, have not been without their ambiguities. For if it has encouraged scholars to look more closely at the indigenous revolutions in their own right—in Switzerland, Italy, the Netherlands—in so doing it has robbed the unifying hypothesis of some of its coherence. If the variables of local conditions should, in the end, seem more significant than the political vocabulary yoking them together; if, in other words, the distinctions seem more important than the similarities, then the "democratic revolution" will be only the aggregate of highly distinctive constituent parts—a mosaic, not a single canvas. To be sure, this may be to tax the "Atlantic revolution" with lacking a rigour its historians would not claim for it. But whether the experience of Dutch or Swiss or Italian republicans in this period is to be seen as an integral part of a larger political purpose or simply as the struggle to preserve their own identities is manifestly more than an academic quibble. In one respect at least it goes directly to the heart of the matter. For in the revolutionary redefinition of nationhood, the tension between the two alternative views was most painfully exposed.

The paradox inherent in a fraternity of nations was expressed most pic-
turesquely in Mazzini's analogy of an orchestra of individual musicians, each
playing their separate instruments but by some miracle of natural harmony
ending up playing the same music. Characteristically his romantic optimism
failed to anticipate the possibility of dissonance among the players. And the
simultaneous evolution of democracy and nationality lends support to the
view that the differences between *comparable* revolutions were not merely
incidental variations on the democratic theme but in some cases at least,
most conspicuously the Dutch, proved to be constitutive in their implications. Of course it would be grossly unhistorical to pretend that the revolutions of the eighteenth century were nationalist in the sense in which Mazzini's
messianism demanded. He and his contemporaries of the mid-nineteenth
century saw the consummation of national statehood as the only fit end for
revolutionary activity and the precondition from which all rights and liberties
followed. This was very far from being the case in the 1780's and 1790's, and
it would be anachronistic to suppose that nationality or even territoriality
was the most potent attraction for the common people who rallied, however
uncertainly, to the insurrectionary standard in Europe. Certainly the dimly
transmitted news from France that the peasants there had cast off the burdens
of seigneurial oppression prompted an emulatory effect in many quite dissimilar rural regions. But among the urban lawyers, government officials and
hack writers who supplied the personnel for the revolutionary élites, the desire
for a patriotism reborn was an article of faith scarcely less urgent than the
demand for individual liberty. In the first three constitutions of the French
Revolution national sovereignty and popular sovereignty are virtually co-
terminous. To be sure, the degree of enthusiasm for a revolutionary version
of a nationality of equal citizens varied a good deal from place to place. Even
within France, the Lyonnais or the Bordelais were less keen than the Parisians
to become absorbed into a *patrie* defined by, and governed from, the capital.
But among the flocks of "clubbists," journalists, librarians, *nobles éclairés*, in
Milan, Liège, Naples, Coblenz, who looked to Paris as the centre of their
intellectual world, the hope was that the French would act as the disinterested mentor of their own respective efforts to renew their nationhood.

From the outset, of course, there was much ambiguity involved in these
embryonic aspirations towards nationhood.[11] The Declaration of the Rights
of Man and the French constitution of 1791 used the term "la nation" as a
synonym for political society: that body to which sovereignty had been transferred from the absolute monarchy. In the context of the Old Regime, abbé
Sieyès' apparently truistic definition of the nation as a "body of associates
living under a common law" carried with it subversively egalitarian implications. For put thus bluntly it was the necessary antithesis to a state ordered
around a hierarchy of privilege. And according to the Third Estate of Rennes
at any rate,

It is a disastrous error that what is called the Third Estate, actually comprising
ninety-nine hundredths of the nation has been styled an order and put in balance
with the two privileged orders! This error ought to cease and what has thus far
been called the third in the realm shall henceforth with or without the privileged

orders comprise the people or nation, the only name which accords with the dignity of the people.[12]

So the revolutionary definition of nationhood, as distinct from nationality, was unrelated to the traditional divisions of language, territory and history but was instead based on the assertion of a primary political principle: the equality of the members of a given community. Likewise the axioms "We the people ordain and establish," and "All men are born equally free and independent" were the conditions for the founding of the American nation, and one, moreover, which was to accommodate the most polyglot ethnic elements.

But although nationhood and nationality seem distinct concepts, the act of attaining the one was bound to call in question assumptions about the other. For if the nation was simply that body of free men sharing the same law, and not the traditional division of lordship, parish and custom, who then was to say where the frontiers of liberty should lie? The *philosophes* had commonly referred to a "republic" as a moral rather than a territorial entity[13] and Robespierre, normally a cautious man in such matters, was convinced that "men of every country are brothers and different peoples must come to each other's aid according to their power *as citizens of the same state*."[14] An assault on the liberty of one people was an attack on the freedom of them all. Against this writ of revolutionary fraternity, the treaties which had marked off traditional boundaries could be dismissed as mere parchment, the feudal scrolls of an international seigneurial regime. In settling the frontiers of its democracy, the American Republic was fortunate in its isolation. The rights of Indian or buffalo offered no serious obstacle in the way of the continental progress of a Manifest Destiny. But the jurisdiction of the European "Grande Nation" was bound to be a far more controversial matter. Initially the frontiers inherited from the Old Regime were held to be co-terminous with those of the new France. But even then their authorisation was unorthodox. In 1790, a sign was posted on one of the bridges over the Rhine declaring: "Ici commence le pays de la liberté."[15] The anachronism of papal sovereignty over Avignon was seen to be at odds with the "natural liberty" of the nation, and the see was "reunited" with France in June 1790. Less than two years later, Danton declared the Alps, the Pyrenees and the Rhine to be the "natural frontiers" of the new nation.[16] Doubtless such natural frontiers were most appropriate for a nation constituted from natural law, but their location suggested that more pragmatic interests had not been entirely missing from the announcement. The point at which revolutionary nationhood elided into revolutionary nationalism was, then, very indistinct.

These confusions and ambiguities had important implications for revolutionary enthusiasts living outside France. For if membership of the free nation was to be based on the affirmation of natural rights, it need pay no heed to mere accidents of birth. Those who might have been called "foreigners" could, by a simple act of self-determination, take up their claim to citizenship. The Atlantic crossing provided a simple demonstration of such an intention for those who opted for the liberty of the New World. And in the early years of the French Revolution Paris swarmed with immigrants, visitors and political tourists, some of them men of letters, who had come to claim their membership in a free commonwealth. For not a few, this eighteenth-century reverie was to prove, almost from the outset, a bitter disappointment. But for others the dawn of a fraternal association rose above the inherited anachronisms of race and language. Joachim Heinrich Campe, the Prussian pedagogue, who had travelled to Paris with his young pupil Wilhelm von Humboldt so as to "participate in the funeral rites of tyranny," expressed something of this pleasure: "How to describe all these joyous faces, lit up with pride? I wanted to fold in my arms the very first persons I met. For they were no longer Frenchmen . . . and we were no longer Brandenburgers or Brunswickers; all national differences had disappeared; all prejudices had vanished."[17]

On becoming a Republic in the autumn of 1792, France extended honorary citizenship to a number of distinguished men whose careers or known views were deemed sympathetic to the ideals for which it stood. They included some like Jefferson and Klopstock for whom early appreciation had already given way to resolute hostility, but also such as Tom Paine who, without speaking a word of French, nevertheless came to live in Paris, took his seat in the Convention—and spent time in prison for the honour. Many of the "étrangers, amis de la révolution" became alienated beyond recall by the war, the atrocity of the September massacres, and the violence done to the institution and then the person of the monarchy. But while those Wordsworthian weak stomachs gagged on the more Spartan doses of Jacobin virtue, for a few, the initial promise of fraternity remained an imperishable article of faith. The most passionate and certainly the most extraordinary of such figures was "Anacharsis" Cloots, the self-styled "Orator of the Human Race." His education—committed successively to a Jesuit seminary, the Berlin Military Academy and the Sorbonne—and his half-Dutch, half-German parentage perhaps gave him a vested interest in statelessness. The Revolution was, for Cloots, an event of messianic significance, the heralding of the Last Days of the tyrants; and a titanic battle between peoples and despots in which the victory of the former would be crowned by the establishment of political paradise on earth—the Universal Republic. There the abominations of bureaucracy would be redundant; the postal service would run from Bordeaux to Peking; "there, there will be neither barrier nor walls; neither official nor guard; there will be no more desert and the entire earth will become a garden."[18] In the end, Cloots' eschatological frothings provided him not with a passport to universal citizenship but a pathetic death at the guillotine.[19] But to the last he refused to believe that the interests of France could ever be separated from those of humanity at large, a theme taken up with more nationalist relish by romantics of the next century like Jules Michelet.[20] Other salon cosmopolitans like the marquis de Condorcet had similarly wished the Revolution to herald the democratic millennium. And when two prisoners of the Swiss canton of Freiburg, condemned to the galleys (a service from which the French Old Regime took a useful commission), were presented to the Constituent Assembly, their chains were hung from the rafters of the Église des Prémontrés as a token of the coming emancipation of the slave peoples of the world.[21]

The self-evident utopianism of such assumptions doomed the history of the future "sister republics" to one of truncated expectations. But in 1792 it was thought that if citizenship of the free "nation" could be conferred simply through the express determination of a man to liberate himself from the arbitrary bondage of birth and estate, the same might apply to whole peoples and territories. That was the assigned sense of self-determination and one, for better or worse, which has endured. At that time it was applied, through the means of a doubtfully mobilised plebiscite, to discover the "will" of the Avignonnais to be "reunited" with France. The same went for the Niçois and the Vaudois Swiss after votes recording even less decisive verdicts. Before long the argument was used as a transparent pretext for annexation, as in Mainz, where even a minute and carefully marshalled bunch of presumed sympathisers could not be cajoled or bullied into assenting to the incorporation of the electorate.[22] Thus a principle which began as an extension of self-determination for those peoples awkwardly occupying the margins between the "unnatural" old frontiers and the "natural" new ones, was very quickly transformed into the blunt instrument of national expediency: fraternity on the terms of the biggest brother. It was not at all fortuitous that General Custine's progress of pillage and extortion down the left bank of the Rhine should have been accompanied by a manifesto patronisingly entitled "From the Liberated French to the Oppressed Germans." The citizens of Aachen, at any rate, had the wit (or the innocence) to reply apologetically that, alas, they had no tyrant from whom to be liberated since their city had been free of lordship since the year 1185.[23]

By the end of the first year of war, it was plain that under pressure of attack the ecumenical interpretation of nationhood had retreated before the more imperative defence of the territorial *patrie*: France and the French. It is true that the "Nation in arms" included a number of foreign companies but equally the case that they were subordinated to French command, and that their adherence was always viewed with suspicious misgivings. The state of affairs in which the official resolution to wage what Brissot had called "a universal crusade for liberty"[24] co-existed with a much more pragmatic strategy was exemplified by the two proclamations issued by the Convention at the end of 1792. That of November 19 declared that France would offer assistance to any nation "wishing to recover its liberty," and seemed to offer exactly that disinterested help the European revolutionaries had been led to believe would be forthcoming from the new nation. But less than a month later, on December 15, a second proclamation ordered the generals of the republican armies to proceed forthwith to "revolutionise" the territories occupied in the Austrian Netherlands and the Rhineland. At first glance, it looked like an elaboration of the promises made in November, extending

French laws on the liquidation of the seigneurial regime and the Church and appointing civil commissioners responsible to the Convention for their implementation and for the calling of local elections. Notwithstanding this last provision, the intention of the December decree was less to lay the foundations for a chain of independent republics than to subordinate those areas to the absolute writ of the Convention. In part it had been dictated by the urgent need to bridle the evident rapacity and ambition of the generals, Charles François Dumouriez in particular, who were busy lining their pockets at the same time as they planned to establish bases for their own political power.[25] Nipping that incipient Caesarism in the bud through the civil commissioners thus entailed circumscribing, for example, the Belgians' freedom of action. Instead of underwriting their auto-determination, the December decree imprisoned the foreign partisans of liberty within the requirements of French strategy.

Moreover, the behaviour of the liberators in the territories they occupied made the disparity between promises and fulfilment all the more glaring. Those on the receiving end of republican fraternity might have been pardoned for being unable to distinguish the conduct of its shock troops from that of the mercenaries and tyrants they affected to despise. While Dumouriez announced that the French came as "brothers and friends whose only design is to assure their [the Belgians'] liberty," his troops were stripping the countryside of livestock and corn and the towns of provisions. In Luxembourg, a deputation to the civil commissioners complained that what the French soldiers could not carry off with them they wrecked. And although on December 27 the Convention voted 60,000 livres to indemnify the pillaged inhabitants of the Rhine towns, the gesture was both too little and too late to make good the damage done to the reputation of the armed emancipators. Georg Forster, the most eminent among the handful of Mainz "clubbists," told General Custine that "the inhabitants would have been less cruelly deceived if they had been told from the start 'we have come to take everything.' "[26] Faced with critical shortages of supplies for the immense armies, the French commanders had resorted to extracting them primarily from the most defenceless section of the population—precisely those whom the "war of peoples" was allegedly meant to benefit. Set against the denuding of the countryside, the profession of "Guerre aux châteaux; paix aux chaumières" was exposed as a hollow irony. And on a more rarefied plane, for those intellectuals, club orators and journalists who had enthused over a fraternal community of states sheltering beneath the mantle of French benevolence, the events of 1792 and 1793 came as a rude awakening. Forster died in Paris, outraged at the politics of the Mountain and complaining of the perfidy of his allies. His dreams for the revolutionary birth of a German Republic came to nothing, and when the idea of a Cis-Rhenan Republic was revived in 1795 it was as the fief of General Hoche, its most recent conqueror.

Thus the budding of ecumenical fraternity had always been a most fragile growth. During the spasm of paranoid patriotism from which Jacobin France found the strength to withstand the onslaught of the First Coalition, it perished altogether. There had, in any case, always been a strong tinge of chauvinism within the Revolution. Mistrust of foreigners—especially those near the centre of government, and above all of foreign bankers and financiers, Swiss and Dutch—and a credulous appetite for stories of foreign plots and espionage mirrored the prejudices of the common man far more accurately than flights of cosmopolitan rhetoric from salon reformers like Condorcet. In 1789, rumours of foreign conspiracies hatched by the duc de Broglie and the brothers of the King to open Bordeaux to the British or Paris to the Austrians had helped propagate the "Grande Peur" throughout France and make the resort to arms all the more urgent. Further substance was added to the demonology of the "foreign plot" by the emigration of the aristocracy; by the Queen's collusion with the Swede Axel von Fersen and the abortive flight to Varennes; by the discovery in the Tuileries of documents incriminating the King; and by the defection of Dumouriez to the Austrians in April 1793, until revolutionary propaganda ceased to make any distinction between the enemy without and the enemy within.

The consecutive betrayal of the General and the fall of the Girondins who had, together, been the most effective patrons of the "amis étrangers" and the "foreign legions," meant that henceforth they were stigmatised as at best a nuisance and at worst an insidious fifth column. Some of the Dutch and Belgians who had fought in the campaign which had ended disastrously at the Battle of Neerwinden were greeted on their return with arrest and imprisonment as accomplices of Dumouriez.[27] Others had their property distrained, and all were obliged by the Committee for General Security to carry red identity cards denoting their alien status. Once the honoured guests of the "revolutionary nation," they were now treated as clandestine spies and foreign agents, ready to stab the Republic in the back and all the more dangerous for professing a spurious loyalty. Foreign connections became a stock item in the indictment of political factions. Danton was implicated in corruption charges concerning one Proli, described as "banker to the House of Austria"; a Dutch financier de Kock and the Swiss Clavière were both beheaded; Tom Paine incarcerated; and Cloots guillotined, one suspects, because his politics were too implausibly utopian to be taken at face value. The mere suggestion of "rootless cosmopolitanism" was enough to attract the attention of the revolutionary tribunals. Once the official ideology of the Revolution, it had become, not for the last time in a revolutionary upheaval, a euphemism for treason.

The accusations of foreign plots were not, of course, entirely unhysterical. There were spies in France and at least one major city, Toulon, had already let in the British. But the primary impulse behind the xenophobia was surely the need to externalise objects of fear and hatred. Conspiracy theories were produced like rabbits from a hat by the Committee of Public Safety in order to preserve its own position, unite the country behind its leadership, and deflect demoralisation towards its enemies. The spectacle of a besieged revolutionary state obsessed by these neuroses is not unfamiliar to the modern historian.

Both French and Russian revolutions were made in the name of universal ideals; both provoked military reaction from states concerned to preserve the status quo; both accordingly retreated into a fortress psychology in which patriotism and chauvinism were alarmingly proximate. In both cases, too, the experience of desperate defence wrote *finis* to revolutionary innocence and inaugurated a period in which domestic freedom and international bravura were sacrificed for the sake of security and power. Whether or not this is an inherent feature of the revolutionary process is not our concern here. What, however, was to prove formative in the encounter of the expanding French Republic with its Dutch neighbour was that, for all this regression, there were still those in countries as yet inexperienced in the ways of armed freedom prepared to credit it with the patronage of their own emancipation. From such bewitching illusions the tragi-comedy of the Batavian Republic, like that of other "Peoples' Republics," was to take its cue. And from the eventual dénouement of such miniature dramas there came the paradoxical conflict in which the "Grand Nation" was threatened not only by its own reactionary enemies, but by the persistent insubordination of its own acolytes.

The parallel between French and Russian experience is surely not inapposite. The unsentimental men who survived the revolutionary holocaust were, in both cases, strategic technicians. By the time of the foundation of the Batavian Republic in 1795, the Thermidorian managers of France were no longer, if ever they had been, roused by the altruistic vision of the "crusade for universal liberty." Such ideological flabbiness, as they saw it, had all but cost the Republic its life. War, according to the "Organiser of Victory," Lazare Carnot, who himself managed to survive the dissolution of the Committees and become a Director under the new constitution of 1795 (Year III), was simply: "un état violent; il faut la faire à l'outrance ou rentrer dans ses foyers."[28] It was to be waged without pity or quarter, for the maximisation of power and profit. If the creation of semi-autonomous states served those ends satisfactorily, so much the better; if not, their *raison d'être* could be terminated. The touchstone was always expediency. During the famine-stricken winter of "nonante-cinq" when wolves approached the outskirts of Paris and bark was scraped from trees for soup[29] the priority was for bleeding the occupied territories white so as to ensure supplies of victuals and fodder, first for the troops and then, if anything remained, for the metropolitan centre of France. Thus the image of the French presence was altogether grimmer than in what by comparison seemed the halcyon times of 1792. "Agencies of evacuation" eschewing revolutionary euphemisms, and "military administrations" were established in Belgium, Liège, and on the left bank of the Rhine, which concentrated exclusively on the work of authorised pillage and extortion. The civil commissioners who in 1792 had been appointed to restrain the most flagrant excesses of the military now acted as the principal accomplices in their crimes. A volunteer in the Army of the Rhine wrote to his father that "this land is totally ruined for ten years at least,"[30] and in Aachen a newspaper reported French generals boasting of "leaving the inhabitants only their eyes, so they could weep."[31]

Not infrequently the "sister republics" existed simply as pawns in the elaborate diplomatic games which occupied the hiatuses between campaigns. Bonaparte's cynical bargain with Cobenzl and the Austrians at Campo Formio, when the Venetian Republic was delivered to the Emperor in exchange for the acceptance of the French annexation of Belgium, was only the most spectacular example of assumptions shaping French strategy ever since its armies had taken the counter-offensive in 1794. And it was made clear to those states continuing to live by grace of French military assistance that even their very qualified autonomy had a bill to meet. The Directory told General Jourdan in 1796 that the great art of making war was to live at the expense of the enemy; but the exercise was no less costly for those who liked to count themselves France's friends. Apart from requisitioning everything needed to supply her armies and paying for it, if at all, in depreciating paper *assignats*,[32] the account for "liberation" was submitted to her allies in the form of massive indemnities ranging from the 2.5 million livres levied on Nuremberg to the unconscionable 100 million guilders with which the Batavian Republic was crippled at birth. Henceforth, it was plain, "La guerre nourrira la guerre."

These profit-and-loss computations left little room for the high-minded fraternity of the Revolution's beginnings. And thus far the circumstances surrounding the establishment of the "sister republics" seems to confirm all of Sorel's original scepticism. Certainly they were intended as staging posts for the aggrandisement of what was rapidly turning into a French empire in all but name. But a number of imponderables contrived to sabotage the calculations of the French Directory. First, it had to contend with the ambition of its own military commanders. Dumouriez proved to be merely the first in a long line of generals who saw in the establishment of European republics a power base from which to propel themselves to power in France herself. As the battle was carried further away from France's own frontiers and lines of communication became more extended, the surveillance exercised by the domestic government became correspondingly less effective. Moreover the perpetual disarray of that government, and the deadlock between its legislative and executive branches, brought its authority into disrepute. By contrast, the reputation of the generals who carried the tricolour over the Continent stood high among their compatriots. As a result, a decisive shift of power from the civilian to the military sector occurred at the same time that their invasions were stimulating the activity of European revolutionaries to renewed efforts. Bonaparte's creation of the Cisalpine and Cispadane republics in Italy was perhaps the most important of such manoeuvres, but General Hoche's devious politics in south-west Germany and Switzerland were guided by the same motivation.

The fact that generals rather than civilian commissioners were responsible for the establishment of European republics hardly adds anything to their authenticity as independent states. Indeed, since the relationship between military presence and their political survival was so plain, it is arguable that it was more likely to detract from the possibility of anything approaching an authentic sovereignty. But even the most redoubtable and ruthless of the generals were unable to operate in a complete political vacuum. Invariably they depended for support on the goodwill of indigenous politicians. This was essential if the country they occupied was to remain effectively pacified. Given the virtually endemic recurrence of peasant rebellions in the Po Valley, Calabria, western Switzerland and Brabant, it was necessary to woo a restive population with a confirmation of the end of feudal dues. To ensure the regular administration of day-to-day government as well as the collection of taxes to pay for the army, it was imperative to secure the collaboration of local republicans who could be relied on to regard such tasks, however distasteful, as part and parcel of their revolutionary callings. But the legitimating of *their* authority in turn presupposed at least a rudimentary framework of organised institutions, particularly since the French had no intention of assuming the burden and expense of direct rule wherever their troops happened to hold territory. When combined with a general's wish to preen his vanity by magnanimously offering to his conquered subjects a constitution for their "liberties," these considerations moved the French to establish administrations with domestic autonomy but bereft of military power. In just such a way, for example, Bonaparte's general military administration in Lombardy eventually became the government of the Cisalpine Republic.[33]

This very limited role was not, however, acceptable to many of those who initially came forward to fill positions of political and governmental leadership. Indebted to the French for ridding them of their old regimes, they remained somewhat old-fashioned in their notions of the protectors' disinterest and enthusiastic about setting up republics in their own respective national images. Many of them, like Giuseppe Ranza and Melchiorre Gioia in Italy or Peter Ochs in Switzerland, had been seasoned agitators for just such a cause for years past. And as French strategy had moved further away from the fraternal idealism of the early Revolution, so the republican passions of its putative junior allies were rekindled at the approaching possibility of its realisation on their own territory. Ironically, then, Italians, Dutchmen, Swiss took their constitutions, Church legislation, feudal reform—the whole bag and baggage of revolution—with infinitely more seriousness and good faith than their French contemporaries, for whom the whole exercise was one of a mechanical recitation of shibboleths. The most ardent among them resolved to create states not merely as the passive instruments of the "Grande Nation" but as the inception of their own nationhood. In so improbable a fashion, and with such inauspicious prospects, the birds of the revolutionary nation came home to roost.

The degree to which such fancies might be remotely realistic depended, naturally, on the strength of the several indigenous republican groups. For the most part, this was impressive neither in numbers nor quality. When General Hoche explored the possibility of setting up some kind of German state on the right bank of the Rhine, he was met with such stony apathy that much of his planning was rendered fruitless even before his own death settled the issue.[34] In Switzerland, the enthusiasm for a unitary Helvetic Republic was critically compromised by the fact that many of the grievances which fed insurgence derived from inter-cantonal feuds and the defence rather than the limitation of local liberties. Support for the Republic of 1798 thus depended on a handful of the usual intellectuals, educators, clubmen and the like in Zurich. In Italy, the centres of republican enthusiasm were concentrated on the academies, universities, coffee-house clubs and administrative centres of Naples, Milan, Turin, Bologna and Florence. Most of the urban borghese who stood to benefit from the destruction of the traditional nobilities and patriciates, which had dominated their territories since the sixteenth century, were as yet far too weak to prevail over the opposition of the Church and the unnerving irrepressibility of peasant revolt. And in any event Italian unity or anything approaching it was regarded with suspicion by Directors like Barras, who saw it as a cuckoo in the nest of the "Grande Nation." But however far short the largest— or least spurious—of the Italian republics, the Cisalpine, fell from the ideals of precocious Romantic nationalists like the poet Alfieri, it provided something in the way of what Professor Palmer called "a sketch of the modern state."[35]

The Batavian Republic may well have been the exception which proved the rule so far as the viability of these client states was concerned, but that it *was* an exception ought to be beyond dispute. For it was in the Netherlands that French strategy ran headlong into a robust native tradition of republican politics, and it was here that the fundamental incompatibility between an imperialist connection and the tolerance of a national revolution was most dramatically exposed. However instrumental the French armies may have been in establishing the new regime in that country, there was little chance of them simply imprinting their own desiderata on the yielding matrix of Dutch institutions. The possibility of a Novus Ordo in the Netherlands was ruled out by 200 years of republican freedom, even if latterly in the most degenerated and barely cognizable form. More important still was the fact that the Dutch Republic had undergone a schism of revolutionary proportions five years before the French had begun their own uprising. Even though this had been suppressed by foreign intervention, for not a few of its surviving partisans the inauguration of the Batavian Republic was a matter of resurrecting the democracy nipped in the bud in 1787 by regiments of Prussian grenadiers. Nor was it fortuitous that in that first upheaval, those who had pitted their strength against the reigning House of Orange had annexed to themselves the appellation of "Patriots," as the Americans had done before them and the French were to do afterwards.[36] For their crisis had been, above all, one of national self-esteem, and that indeed was the great theme which continued to dominate Dutch political life right into the first half of the nineteenth century.

So it ought not to have been so surprising that the reputedly docile commonwealth of merchants, the bourgeois society par excellence, should (with the exception of Spain) prove to be the most headstrong, volatile and exasperating of all France's allies during the years of war ahead. Time and again the tiny state, impoverished and bedevilled by domestic divisions of such complication that they addled the wits of those few French agents who attempted to investigate them, stood up to the blandishments and threats of its far more powerful ally. Eventually obliged to accept a brother of the French Emperor as its King, the Dutch succeeded in transforming even Louis Bonaparte into the truculent Dutch patriot Lodewijk I. This obstinacy was not, as Napoleon chose to believe, a streak of incorrigible native deviousness and perversity. On the contrary, it resulted at least in part from the revival of the ideal which France herself had so manifestly abandoned: that of republican self-determination. Because this occurred in a small state and one which, in the last resort, would always need the protection of a senior ally to retain its sovereignty, there is a danger of dismissing the Dutch revolution as merely an interminable and unfathomable squabble between rentiers and men of commerce, Orangists and anti-Stadholderians, landward and maritime provinces, the Reformed Church and dissent—the fag end of an ancient dispute dressed up in the bunting of the French Revolution. All too often, to be sure, the French themselves looked on the Netherlands as little more than a supplementary bank vault or an auxiliary dockyard for their crescent Empire. And some historians have, in this case, been guilty of underestimation. Logically it doubtless ought to have been the case that those states which were most co-operative in doing France's bidding were also those in which the seeds of revolution had taken firmest root.[37] Conversely, those which repeatedly disrupted and aggravated the alliance were those in which the monster counter-revolution remained alert and active. But the Dutch case suggests the very contrary. For the melancholy saga of the Batavian Republic and its successor Kingdom of Holland was in the highest degree an illumination of the classic irreconcilability within a revolution of its two primary constituents: freedom and power.

The Batavian Republic and the Integrity of Dutch History

In the centre of The Hague a monument of massive and triumphal statuary commemorates the liberation of the Dutch "Fatherland" from French hegemony in 1813. The square in which it stands, ringed by embassies, is itself named for that date which, every fifty years, has been celebrated as a day of national thanksgiving. The Batavian Republic has no such memorial. Apart from an alley at the back of the old railway station called after one of its ministers, the only visible evidence of the twenty years preceding 1813 is a plaque on the wall of the dainty Walloon Church, bearing the name of Ludovicus Rex—Louis Bonaparte. It is as if Dutch history had gone into exile along with its Stadholder when the French armies crossed the Waal in January 1795, only to re-emerge eighteen years later, purified by the fires of national revolt. The conventional description of the intervening period as the "French time" (*Franse tijd*) has effectively deleted it from the record of national history. Neglected as a trivial and humdrum episode in European history, Dutch historiography has, for the most part, been content to let it remain shrouded in oblivion.[38] Busken Huet, the nineteenth-century writer, called its "events paltry, its men insignificant and its ideas hackneyed." John Lothrop Motley's collaborator and continuer, William Elliot Griffis, torpedoed what he called "the eighteen unhappy years" by declaring that, "whether under the name of the 'Batavian Republic,' the Kingdom of Holland, or the provinces of the French empire, the French occupation was virtually a French conquest that had little permanent influence on Dutch history or character."[39]

The bitter experience of the Dutch during the Second World War did very little to rehabilitate the "French time." Its themes of occupation, military disaster and foreign domination inevitably seemed an unwelcome anticipation of the contemporary calamity, and in that murky light its leaders were cast as either fools or rogues, the accomplices of the earlier ignominy. Certainly a few writers, perhaps initially drawn by the analogy, arrived at a proper discrimination. The Marxist biographer Theun de Vries and Pieter Geyl, the latter a direct sufferer at the hands of the Germans, both wrote studies explicitly exculpating the eighteenth-century revolutionaries from any lingering taint of treason.[40] But in the popular imagination it was the analogy which proved more persistent than its disclaimer. In 1950 the weekly magazine *Elseviers* still referred to the Batavians by the stigmatising catch phrase of "the NSBers [Dutch Fascists] of the eighteenth century." In the last few years, interest in this period has been showing intermittent signs of life. Yet on either the scholarly or the general level, the historiography remains sparse for a people as preoccupied with their past as the Dutch. The superficial reasons for this neglect are not difficult to surmise. The tag of "satellite" pinned to the Batavian Republic may itself have been sufficient to disqualify it from consideration as an integral part of Dutch rather than French history. And the prospect of immuring oneself amidst the archival evidence of defeat, chaos and poverty has understandably proved an unenticing option for Dutch historians, however dispassionate their native feeling and however stern their professional commitment. No scholar cares much to keep company with calamity for very long. Between 1780 and 1813, after all, the Netherlands was despoiled of its colonies, routed at sea, invaded four times (twice unsuccessfully); driven to the edge of bankruptcy; and finally forced to drain the dregs of its misfortune by becoming mere departments of the French Empire. Little wonder perhaps that the Dutch "time of troubles" has lacked for chroniclers.

Academic gloom, to be sure, is scarcely a sufficient reason for the estrangement of the Batavians from their context in national history. The far more depressing experience of the German occupation has been the object of massive documentation, study and debate. The seemingly irresistible impulse to pick at the scabs and wounds of the last war is not merely attributable to the natural concern of its living witnesses to put their testimony on record or to clarify their recollections. It is also an exercise in national self-reassurance in a way in which the history of the Batavian Republic could never be. For the very weakness of the Dutch Fascists has enabled a clear separation to be made between the unrepresentative few who actively collaborated and the many whose part in defying the Germans is correspondingly projected as more, or less, heroic. The moral odour of those (very many) whose major preoccupation was survival is of small interest beside the dramatic incarnation of the national will to resist in Queen Wilhelmina's exile in London.* The location of national authenticity at that time is in no doubt. But for the earlier period, matters are less clean cut. Willem V, the last Stadholder, also in refuge in England, was denied anything like the unanimous sympathy and allegiance of his people. Conversely, the support which his adversaries could call on was far from negligible. The débacle of the Anglo-Russian invasion in 1799 was caused precisely by the British misapprehension as to where the "natural" allegiance of the Dutch would lie. With heroes and villains so oddly assorted, it has proved awkward to sustain the historical ostracism of one group for the legitimation of the other.

These considerations did not deter the nineteenth-century custodians of national propriety from making just such a simplification. After the failure of the "Kingdom of the United Netherlands" and the traumatic secession of the Belgians, the preservation of national self-respect seemed to demand the cultivation of a more parochial patriotism. In the work of G. Groen van Prinsterer, a version of the past emerged in which its continuity and homogeneity were paramount and in which the destiny of the Fatherland was seen to have been manifest in its founding rebellion. Groen's fundamentalist Orangism drew on the poetry of Willem Bilderdijk for its sentiment, and through him the eighteenth-century epic vapourings of Onno Zwier van Haren. For all three, it had been the reformed religion which had blessed the war against the Spanish anti-Christ with victory and had appointed the Princes of the House of Orange to be its Godly captains.[41] It was, then, axiomatic that the new Republic should be established under their rule. Any subsequent attempt to violate their joint sovereignty incriminated itself as unpatriotic. This comprehensive indictment naturally extended to men like Jan van Oldenbarneveld or the brothers de Witt who had attempted to seduce the burghers of Holland from their proper loyalty. But Groen reserved his most damning anathema for that later rebellion which had tried to destroy both Church and Prince and set up in their place the heathen heresy of democracy. Like the abbé Barruel in France, Groen devoutly supposed the revolution to have been the product of the corrosive notions of the *philosophes*, whose blasphemies had bewitched a normally pious and stiff-necked people into the ways of political iniquity.[42] In so doing they had called down on themselves the chastisements of war, penury and social anarchy until a new Prince, from the old line, could lead them back to their rightful allegiance. Thus the history of the Batavian Republic was turned into a parable of the penalties of revolt and a warning against future temptation. As the title of his Anti-Revolutionary Party implies, its founder made opposition to the hydra-headed menace the criterion of true patriotism.

Not many historians of his generation were prepared to subscribe uncritically to Groen van Prinsterer's Calvinist-Orangist fundamentalism. But there were others like Johan van Vloten who, while taking issue with his ac-

* The monumental histories of Louis de Jong are doing much to revise hitherto simple categories of patriots and collaborators during World War II.

count of the Dutch revolt (just as they disapproved of his arch-conservative politics), were equally conditioned in their assumptions about Dutch nationhood by the prescription of history. If Groen could vulgarly be said to represent a "Tory" view of the Dutch revolt, van Vloten was one of those faithfully transmitting a "Whig" account inherited from sixteenth- and seventeenth-century political theorists like François Francken and Hugo Grotius.[43] They were above all concerned to argue the original sovereignty of the urban regencies and the provincial States. Their version of the "True Liberty" protected by, and vested in, those bodies, was definitively monumentalised by the twenty-volume *Fatherland's History* (*Vaderlandsche Historie*) of Jan Wagenaar—made official historian of Amsterdam in the middle of the eighteenth century. Where the more conservative view had placed the faith militant and its Prince firmly in the foreground, the opposing view established the patriciate, its militia and its chief servant, the Grand Pensionary, as the authentic custodians of national freedom. To their hands the rightful, that is to say, "virtual" (for those of lower social rank were deemed a negligible political quantity) representation was confided and any attempt to encroach on it taken as an act of infamous tyranny.

These rival accounts of the origins of the nation supplied the fuel for the endless contention which so divided the Dutch Republic during its 200 years of independence. But while their content was antithetical, their effect on received ideas of legitimate and illegitimate politics in the nineteenth century was of a like kind. Both provided authorised versions of the founding revolution, a scripture to act as touchstone for what might, and what might not, be invoked in the name of the Fatherland. Such a development was not, of course, unique, to the Netherlands. Seventeenth-century England, eighteenth-century France and nineteenth-century America had treated their "ancient constitutions" in a like manner.[44] And it was surely not fortuitous that the first great English-language history of the Dutch revolt was written by the New Englander John Lothrop Motley, inspired by the saga of another thrifty and resourceful people who had thrown off an imperial yoke in the name of liberty.[45] However grand in style, the influence of both these authorised versions was self-evidently conservative in effect, precluding any politics advancing beyond their terms of reference from being accepted as an integral part of Dutch history.

When those few historians who had not attempted to erase the period from the national memory turned their attention to the relatively recent past of the "French time," they found of course that the Batavian Republic and its successor state had deformed those political institutions celebrated in their histories out of all recognition. In place of the autonomy of corporate communities, and the sovereignty of the seven federated provinces the Republic, at the high-water mark of its republicanism, had attempted to substitute the alien artifice of a unitary state. Instead of the delegated representations of the States-General, they had created a "National Assembly" purporting to represent something called the will of the sovereign people. They had gone so far as to blaspheme against both Prince, stigmatised as a despot, and the ancestral constitution, the Union of Utrecht, derided by some as a "Gothic monstrosity." And despite the fact that men like van Vloten, Busken Huet and their contemporaries all lived in a constitutional monarchy which bore but the faintest resemblance to the polity they respectively revered, they showed no embarrassment about pronouncing on the "un-historical" nature of the revolution which had led directly to its creation.

The heresies for which they held such aversion also convinced the nineteenth-century writers that the roots of the Batavian Republic were to be sought not in the indigenous politics of the Netherlands but in the strategies of its self-interested neighbours. In adopting that view they were mirroring the assumptions arrived at from an opposite perspective, notably by Sorel. When H. T. Colenbrander at the very end of the century launched the first serious attempt at archival documentation, his selection of evidence and some of the deductions he drew from it were very much governed by those presuppositions. In addition to the twelve-volume *Sources for the General History of the Netherlands* (*Gedenkstukken der Algemeen Geschiedenis van Nederland*), he produced a prolific succession of studies and narratives dealing with the period from 1780 to 1840.[46] But although this *oeuvre* made a formidable con-tribution to the materials available for study, one without which any prospec-tive researcher would be irreparably impoverished, Colenbrander's acidulous scepticism (as well as occasional lapses in editing and transcription) in the end tended to diminish rather than enhance the significance of the events he related. While he was prepared to concede to the "Patriot" generation of the 1780's some sincerity of intention, their defeat at the hands of the Prus-sians in 1787 ended for good and all, as far as he was concerned, any possi-bility of an authentically Dutch endeavour for reform.

The whole of the Batavian revolution and the subsequent history of the country until 1813 was, for Colenbrander, merely an ironical postscript to this failure. Borrowing a metaphor from the doggerel poet Gerrit Paape, the exile of the "Patriot" (that is, anti-Stadholderian) fugitives in France between 1787 and 1795 he described as the "High School of the Revolution," where the incompetent and blundering Dutch learned their insurrectionary lessons from the successful French. Properly drilled and tutored, they were then allowed the opportunity to enact a pastiche revolution under the neces-sary auspices of French military power. At no point does Colenbrander deviate from the view that their antics were anything but the crudest extension of French strategy, and rarely are the politics of the Batavian Republic con-sidered within the framework of specifically Dutch interests and conflicts. He upbraids its leaders for both gullibility and pusillanimity, encapsulating his verdict on their importance for Dutch history in the classic image of the "marionetten" jerked along in their clumsy motions by the strings of the French puppet-masters.

The legacy bequeathed by Colenbrander to the study of the eighteenth-century Dutch revolutions was, then, highly ambivalent. While he furnished the groundwork for future archival investigation, his conclusions were so cate-gorical as to preclude much constructive use being made of them. Notwithstanding the vulgar analogy of collaborators, it was in the years following the last war that the beginnings of a more positive approach were announced in the essays of Professors Pieter Geyl, L. G. J. Verberne and L. G. Rogier.[47] Among that generation Geyl, the most renowned to the non-Dutch-speaking world, should have been the least affected by the burden of a Romantic interpretation of the national past. As the *enfant terrible* of Dutch history, he had made his name as its most acute critic. His great work on the revolt against Spain had made short shrift of the epic of a manifest Dutch destiny.[48] But when Geyl came to turn his attention to the Batavian Republic, his attitude toward the continuity of Dutch institutions had mellowed. Unlike Colenbrander, he was prepared to accept the upheavals of the eighteenth century as an intrinsic part of "Fatherland's History" but his conditions for extending, as it were, benefit of naturalisation were such as to deprive the events of any real revolutionary character. Where Colenbrander took revolutionary gestures as a token of Gallomania, Geyl took what he believed to be the authentically Dutch character of those politics as a disavowal of radicalism. Neither conceded the possibility of a revolution which was, at the same time, a new departure in political life and yet also wholly Dutch. Where Geyl described the Batavian Republic as a revolution, he takes care to qualify the category by insisting on it as a "bedaarde revolutie"—a calm and dignified (*deftig*) affair in the best traditions of Dutch moderation.

Such fastidiousness led Geyl to take great pains to sort out the good Dutch quasi-revolutionary sheep from the alien Jacobinical violence-prone goats. As a result, he gives disproportionate weight to the members of the Batavian legislatures expressing "federalist" or "moderate" views on the making of the constitution. These were the men most committed to defending the old loose-bonded alliance of sovereign provinces from absorption into a single national state. Hence he ends up with the paradoxical implication that those who determined to reverse the revolution of 1795–96 were the most representative figures of the new Republic and the genuine tribunes of the popular voice.[49] Conversely, the self-confessed radicals professing a democratic ideology and the rudiments of popular sovereignty are by the same token excluded from Geyl's certificate of national legitimacy. This equivocal attitude toward revolutionary politics was, like so much in Geyl's history, a reflection of his own experience. The suffering he had undergone, and the dread of totalitarian persecution, had produced—in common with other historians outside the Netherlands of the same generation—a marked, though understandable, revulsion from the rhetoric of force. In the excesses of revolutionary zeal he saw the germ of all the tendencies he most abhorred, and his reaction to them led him to occasional exaggeration. For whatever else they may have been, the leaders of the *coup d'état* of January 22, 1798—who introduced the first popular suffrage constitution in the Netherlands but who lasted in power less than six months—were scarcely the unscrupulous manipulators of "party rule" and dictatorial repression that Geyl describes in his account of the event. Had they been so, they might have avoided the woeful blunders which brought about their fall.

It may seem ironic that the historian who had so devastatingly despatched one orthodoxy should have expended such effort into reconciling the Batavian Republic with another. But those who remember Geyl primarily as an iconoclast should bear in mind that the title of his long narrative was *The History of the Netherlands Race*. It was the Dutch state, not the Dutch nation, which he saw as the product of arbitrary military and geo-strategic definition. The people itself, "northern" and "southern" Netherlanders, had in his view been formed not by the capricious chances of war but the evolving processes of a common language, topography and society. And in this respect Geyl was as much a captive of a determined past as his less perceptive predecessors. To have integrated the Batavian Republic in that past necessarily entailed discounting the elements within it which, for whatever reason, sought not an accommodation but a break with it. As a result, the revolution makes a somewhat furtive appearance as one overcome by confusion and shame at its own shortcomings. Only once does Geyl admit the unhistorical truism that, when all is said and done, "The right of the revolution is the right of the future."[50]

That is the crux of the matter. As long as Dutch history remained a prisoner of its nostalgia for the "Golden Century," it would always measure its subsequent progress against that apogee of civilised power which, in historical terms, was very brief, and with every new monograph becomes even briefer.[51] For as prestige and prosperity gradually drained away from the Netherlands, the propensity to indulge in historical immortalisation became more and more marked. Even in the third quarter of the eighteenth century, the stanzas of Simon Stijl's *Rise and Flourishing of the United Netherlands* could present an ecstatically idealised portrait of the Republic as if its greatest qualities had become literally timeless. It was a land where

The richest eschews a vain parade of wealth
And entertains the poor with friendship and with care
. . . Where the farmer so rich . . . the sailor so beloved
The humblest servant as merry as his master?[52]

The tendency to fossilise discussion of the ills of the country within historicist sentiment was common to both pro- and anti-Stadholderian political factions.[53] Adriaan Kluit, a convinced supporter of the Orangist cause and the first Professor of "Fatherland History" at the University of Leiden, rebuked his discontented compatriots for their insufficient appreciation of the freedom and riches for which the Dutch were rightly envied by less fortunate peoples.[54] All that was wrong, the protagonist of either side felt, was that the Republic had departed—temporarily, not irreversibly—from the pure and proper constitution which would restore it to its former splendour. It was only in the actual context of the traumatic war that this cultural self-satisfaction crumbled, generating problems for which the tired platitudes were quite inadequate.

But even in the nineteenth century Potgieter's landscapes, the banal genre paintings, as well as the epic romance-histories, revived the sentimental yearning for a lost commonwealth. It may be that the survival of a small nation in a Europe dominated by machtpolitik invited this cultural introversion. But it is certain that as long as the Dutch saw themselves frozen in the attitudes of Hals' guild deacons and de Hooch's interiors, a maritime community of God-fearing burghers dwelling in piety and liberty, then the Batavian Republic and all its works would inevitably appear a grotesque aberration, an act of patricide unrelated to, and directed against, the integrity of the nation.

Except in its lairs of tourism and in some of the surviving forms of municipal administration, the present Kingdom of the Netherlands is unrecognisable in these terms. Relieved of its empire (or most of it), the Dutch monarchy is a densely populated, highly industrialised state, with a powerful central government and a formidably trained *dirigiste* bureaucracy. Yet there is no question but that the essential traits of Dutch nationhood have survived the most fundamental changes in the character of its governing institutions. Even at the beginning of the eighteenth century there was at least one figure, the Pensionary Simon van Slingelandt, for whom the prospect of laying hands on the sacrosanct federal constitution held no horrors. And during the decades which followed there were a few writers—notably Elie Luzac and L. P. van de Spiegel—who pondered on the reforming potential of an "enlightened Stadholderate." The only drawback was the conspicuous failure of the line of Orange to produce a ruler to fit the bill. It was not until the advent of the Batavian Republic that, through sheer military and fiscal exigency, the inadequacy of inherited institutions could no longer be brushed aside by heroic allusions to the "Golden Age." When that was in its turn eventually replaced by a liberal monarchy, there could be no thought of restoring a political structure once believed indispensable. But only one statesman and historian, J. R. Thorbecke, not only embraced this possibility with enthusiasm rather than wistful reluctance but fully acknowledged the debt that the future owed to the Batavian revolution.

Thorbecke's liberalism derived less from the prescription of immemorial Dutch custom than from contemporary assertions of self-evident natural rights. And he was the principal architect of the constitution which in 1848 embodied most of those rights in a system of representative parliamentary government. In so doing, he brought down the wrath of his arch-rival Groen van Prinsterer for introducing an alien regime likely to subvert the national heritage. But some years earlier Thorbecke had already ruminated on the past and future of the Dutch state and had come to the conclusion that their separation, not their continuity, had been essential for the survival of the nation. Looking back at the period of the Patriot and Batavian revolutions, he saw that division opening. And far from a cleavage cut through the body of the Dutch state by invaders, he concluded it to be a logical consequence of its own terminal weaknesses.[55]

In other words, Thorbecke—as well as those few historians who have followed him, Verberne, J. S. Theissen, Rogier, de Wit—saw change rather than continuity as the key factor in modern Dutch history. And in his purely historical essays he was drawn to those statesmen like himself who had seen that the reality of Dutch society and institutions no longer corresponded to its conventional self-image. Like him, they too had believed drastic surgery to be the precondition of renewal. And his studies of van Slingelandt at the outset, and of Schimmelpenninck at the close of the eighteenth century, both illuminate this favourite theme of the reform of the Dutch state. In common with those two Pensionaries Thorbecke saw reform, even revolution, not at odds with the reaffirmation of his nationality but (to the contrary) as its necessary complement. Thus he was prepared, unlike many commentators before or since, to accept the nomenclature which the first generation of agitators and "Free Corps" militia annexed for themselves—that of "Patriots"—at its face value. In so doing he promoted what had been classified as a dreary and inconsequential episode, the result of foreign incursion, to its rightful place as one of the decisive watersheds in Dutch history: the transition from the first national state to the second.[56]

✻✻✻✻✻✻✻✻✻✻

2

The Dutch Republic in Its Dotage, *1747–1780*

Economy and Society

How far had the Dutch Republic fallen from its state of grace in the "Golden Century"? If the effusions of the self-congratulatory Simon Stijl were to be credited, barely at all. But even more sober spirits like the writer Elie Luzac believed that the blemishes were not so ingrained that with some political amelioration (and a touch of elbow grease) the Republic might not be restored to that arcadia of wealth, wisdom and liberty which had been so rightly eulogised by foreigners.[1] And from their reports it is evident that many visitors to the Netherlands continued to be predisposed to think the best of the nation they had been taught to regard as the cradle of European enlightenment. Diderot, for example, waxed lyrical on the virtues of the bourgeois egalitarian commonwealth: ". . . here everyone is his own master; civil liberty places all the inhabitants on an equal footing; the humble can not be oppressed by the mighty nor the poor by the rich."[2]

But Diderot's stay in Holland lasted only a few months, his information gleaned over convivial dinner tables and on afternoon promenades, and his company was highly select. The subject of the *Voyage de Hollande* is not so much a place as a concept, or rather, a platitude: that of the idealised Republic of Letters, guarding the freedom to publish as sacrosanct. No matter that the Dutch seemed more concerned with the binding or the quality of the paper than with the contents of French publications, or that they were forbidden by their own authorities from reading the dreaded Rousseau, for a *philosophe* the "miracle" would always remain unjaded.[3]

Not all foreign travellers in the Republic were so transported. Despatched to Utrecht to imbibe the education enjoyed by his father, James Boswell had an opportunity at first hand to appreciate the differences between the reputation and the reality of the eighteenth-century Netherlands. Warding off

Boswell senior's persistent exhortations to note the ingenuity of Dutch methods for rendering cow dung inoffensive, James wrote to his friend William Temple:

In such circumstances this trading nation must be in a very bad way. Most of their principal towns are sadly decayed, and instead of finding every mortal employed you meet with multitudes of poor creatures who are starving in idleness. Utrecht is remarkably ruined. There are whole lanes of wretches who have no other subsistence than potatoes, gin, and stuff which they call tea and coffee . . . You see then that things are very different here from what most people in England imagine. Were Sir William Temple to revisit these provinces, he would scarcely believe the amazing alterations which they have undergone.[4]

Boswell's imputation that the qualities for which the Dutch had been so admired were not all they had been was echoed in many other diaristic and journalistic reports, native and foreign. Even the celebrated obsession with cleanliness seemed to be receding. "Batavia insalubris est et brevis aevi," commented Haller. So far from being spick and span, many of the Dutch towns were visibly filthy. Dead cats and dogs were seen floating in the canals of Amsterdam; pigs and cattle grazed happily on the weedy squares of Utrecht. Outsize cuspidors adorned streets overflowing with the refuse from the staple dietary supplements of the common people: tobacco and gin. Some of the moralising journalists feared that medical knowledge and rudimentary hygiene were actually on the retreat. Anxiety was expressed about allegedly increasing fatalities from puerperal fever and the visitations of typhus and cholera. In rural hamlets housewives were seen to clean ordure from their floors by hand before plunging those same hands, unwashed, into churns of milk. A favourite pastime in North Holland and West Friesland was *ganzetrekken*: a competition to see who, at a canter, could best pull the head from a well-oiled live goose, suspended from a wire.[5] Periwig Holland, it seemed, was losing the bucolic serenity conveyed on the canvases of Potter and Ruysdael, or the tranquil, luminous interiors of de Hooch and Vermeer.

Appearances can, of course, be grossly misleading. Happily, the historian need no longer rely on random and literary scraps of evidence from which to piece together an account of Dutch fortunes at this time. Over the past fifteen years a formidable body of research has been undertaken in the Netherlands, much of it avowedly influenced by the quantifying methodology enthroned at the Sixième Section of the École Pratique des Hautes Études in Paris. Its results have disclosed an incomparably more subtle and differentiated picture of the waning of the Dutch economy, and it is not too much to say that the social and demographic history of the country has been transformed by its findings.[6] The progenitor of the work of revision was Dr. Johan de Vries, whose magnum opus *The Economic Decline of the Republic in the Eighteenth Century (De Economische Achteruitgang der Republiek in de Achttiende Eeuw)* has been justly hailed as a dazzling tour de force of analytical scholarship. De Vries was especially concerned to correct the impression of ubiquitous infirmity inherited from the more pessimistic of the

"Patriot" economic commentators of the late eighteenth century. Discovering from the shipping figures supplied by the Admiralties of the Texel and Vlie (North Holland) and Maas and Goeree (South Holland) that the total volume of Dutch trade remained fairly static *throughout* the century, he insisted on the distinction between an absolute and a relative (as well as between a quantitative and qualitative) decline.[7] Given that the level of commercial activity seemed to have remained constant while that of the rest of Europe surged ahead, it was clearly the latter description which was more appropriate for the Netherlands.

Further research has made it evident that neither the eighteenth century as a whole nor the Republic as a whole are meaningful units for generalisation. In many sectors of the economy the trough occurred between 1680 and 1750, or thereabouts, with a subsequent recuperation, strongly marked in the case of agriculture though virtually negligible in most industries.[8] Not only were there significant short-term fluctuations, but the problems affecting the various regions of the country were of a manifestly differing kind and order. According to its historian, Slicher van Bath, the most easterly area of the province of Overijssel, Twente, exactly reversed the demographic experience of Holland. Between 1675 and 1748 its population more than doubled, from some 18,000 to 49,105, relapsing thereafter with the depression of its prematurely-exhausted textile industry.[9] In Friesland, Dr. Faber tells us, those Zuider Zee ports like Hindeloopen connected with the Amsterdam trade managed to hold their own during the period of relative decline. But others like Sneek and Harlingen, embedded within the provincial economy, suffered more seriously. It was only in the 1760's that Sneek began its recovery as a major butter depot of the north.[10]

The phenomenon of economic arrest and stagnation is, then, infinitely more variegated than has hitherto been supposed. But while this massive battery of scholarship has comprehensively disposed of the cliché of a Netherlands sunk in unrelieved gloom, it has not dispelled the overall impression of an economy—or aggregate of sub-economies—in climacteric. If anything, some of the most distinguished recent work, and above all that of Dr. A. M. van der Woude on the Noorderkwartier of Holland, has reinforced the original pessimism. Glimpses at those areas where, in the period of spectacular growth between 1500 and 1650, the Dutch were thought to be strongest reveals that for all the innumeracy of their rhetoric, the Patriot economists did indeed have much to worry about.

The most basic datum of all, that of population, is a case in point. Granted that the correlation between demographic change and economic performance is anything but simple, and that the estimates given in 1965 by Slicher van Bath, *et al.*, were presented merely as "a provisional working hypothesis," they nonetheless offer the clearest possible illustration of arrested growth.[11] That much of the rest of the world, from China to England, was at the same time beginning a massive increase in numbers only serves to make the phenomenon of Dutch stagnation the more striking. Put at its baldest, the population of the Netherlands—which between 1500 and 1650 rose from around 1 million to 1.9 million—thereafter stopped growing altogether for a century. Between 1750 and 1800 there are signs of a localised, very gradual resumption of growth so that by the end of the period covered in this book there were probably a little more than 2 million living in the area covered by the old Republic. But it was only in the nineteenth and present centuries that the Dutch doubled themselves twice over to create, in the Randstad, for example—that straggling monster conurbation between Rotterdam and Amsterdam—one of the most densely peopled areas on the face of the earth. Not all the provinces of the Netherlands, it is true, conformed to this pattern. Overijssel as a whole experienced a gradual growth sustained without either spectacular increase or sharp deceleration, over three centuries.[12] But in Holland Dr. van der Woude has been able to expose dramatic changes:[13]

Number of Inhabitants		Growth Per Period
1514	275,000	
1622	672,000	+ 144%
1680	883,000	+ 31
1750	783,000	− 11
1795	783,000	0

From these figures it is plain that for the first half of the eighteenth century the central urban areas of Holland were depopulating, and that during the latter half those losses were not made good. Again it should be stressed that the process, so far as one may judge—for the first census was not until 1795—was uneven, both chronologically and geographically. But by that date only Amsterdam and Rotterdam, and Schiedam (swollen on gin) and The Hague (swollen on Stadholderian pomp) had retained populations greater than in 1622. In the countryside a late growth in the southern areas and along the river deltas, coinciding with further reclamation, was effectively cancelled out by the shrinkage of population in the rural north behind Haarlem and Edam. But it was in those towns (Amsterdam apart) most intimately associated with the power and prosperity of Holland that the most disastrous evaporation occurred. In the century and a half between 1622 and 1795, Haarlem lost 46 per cent of its population, Leiden—which in the eighteenth century was replaced by Rotterdam as the second city of the Republic—31 per cent, Delft 26 per cent and Gouda some 20 per cent.[14] According to the pioneer of historical demography in Holland, N. W. Posthumus, Leiden's numbers increased to about 60,000 by 1685 and then certainly dropped to *half* that number by the end of the following century. A petition from the burgemeester concerning its poor in 1807 mentions en passant that its population had dropped even further, to around 28,000. And during the period of war and revolution in the 1790's Amsterdam certainly followed this trend as its own numbers dipped below 200,000.[15]

The obvious coincidence of this contraction with the dereliction of traditional industries, in particular cloth-making in Leiden and bleaching and dyeing in Haarlem, inclines van der Woude, among others, to take a gloomier view than de Vries. But this was just one of the marks of dislocation during these years. For if the population in some of the towns of Holland, especially north of the river IJ, was thinning out, Potter's lowing herds were all but obliterated from the Dutch landscape by virulent and repeated attacks of rinderpest. Probably originating in the Balkans, the three major epidemics—1714 to 1720, 1744 to 1754, and 1768 to 1784—took an appalling toll of live-stock herds, particularly in Holland and Friesland. The second epidemic seems to have been the most severe. According to J. A. Faber, more than 70 per cent of the entire cattle stock of the two provinces—in 1744 nearly 200,000 beasts—was wiped out.[16] And in the lush reclaimed polderland of the Schermer east of Alkmaar, 77 per cent of the cattle died during the winter of 1744–45. The third attack was a little less devastating, though in the twelve months from April 1769 to April 1770 Dr. van der Woude has estimated that 55 per cent of the whole stock of Holland perished.[17] Moreover, though gradually ebbing in its ferocity, the third epidemic was drawn out, with sharp recurrences be-tween 1772 and 1773 and 1778–79.

The intervals of the plague were so cruelly spaced that it is difficult to understand how farmers, in a period before livestock insurance was a wide-spread institution, could have had time and means to restock before another visitation laid them low. But, perhaps surprisingly for an economy in which dairying played so major a role, the long-term damage done by the pest seems to have been relatively slight. Figures for cheese production and for the rental value of pasture land show sharp dips, particularly at the time of the first two attacks, but along with the rest of Dutch agriculture resumed a gradual upward momentum by the 1770's at the latest. New strains of cattle were imported; slightly enlarged flocks of sheep grazed vacant pasture, and in Friesland some additional acres were put under clover, flax, potatoes, or the new wonder crop of chicory. More specialised produce—madder in the river lands of South Holland; tobacco on the sandier lands east of Utrecht and Amersfoort; and asparagus around Noordwijk—were all cultivated on a com-mercially successful scale. But there was no significant shift away from pastoral to arable farming. Under the influence of popularising enthusiasts of "English" methods like Geert Reinders, much of the Netherlands shared in the more intensive stock rearing and crop yields that characterised eighteenth-century agriculture in other, relatively prosperous regions of western Europe. A far more compelling influence than the fitful malevolence of nature was the rising level of prices, especially for cereals, which quickened after the middle of the century to scale formidable heights during the great dearths of the war years at the end of the century. Improved market conditions finally brought to an end the protracted depression in Dutch farming which in the earlier decades of the eighteenth century had been critical in Holland. This slowly recovering prosperity was, needless to say, very unevenly distributed. It is well known that agricultural wages lagged considerably behind prices. But with that reservation it seems likely that, whatever strains and stresses were experienced in Dutch towns, the rural background to the political upheavals of the late eighteenth century was one of steadily accumulating well-being.

An altogether different paradigm of Dutch economic activity at this time was their gradual estrangement from the riches of the sea. It would be an absurd exaggeration to suggest that by the mid-eighteenth century the people of the Netherlands were no longer a seafaring folk. Their environment left them very little option in the matter. But laments about the declining numbers (and quality) of mariners, fishermen, shipwrights, anchor-smiths, mast-makers, sailcloth weavers, and the like were becoming commonplace. In the early seventeenth century, it has been estimated (albeit crudely) that there were probably about 80,000 Dutch seamen—or 1 in 10 of the *entire* population. By the 1780's, Admiral Zoutman was complaining of having the utmost difficulty in finding the 3,000–4,000 sailors needed to crew the relatively modest fleet which engaged the British at the Battle of Dogger Bank. Of the last important whaling fleets working the Greenland and Davis Straits' schools, the majority were crewed with Germans, Danes, Norwegians and other foreign mariners. And of the Dutchmen, most came from Groningen or Friesland rather than the traditional catchment areas of Holland. Dr. van der Woude has charted the decline of the maritime population in the single village of Graft, between the North Holland polders of the Schermer and Beemster, plumb in the centre of the region most dependent for its livelihood on marine trades and industries. In 1635, 50 per cent of the male population of Graft— some 500 men—were engaged in seagoing occupations. By 1680, that number had fallen to 32 per cent (100 heads of families), and by 1742 to 8 per cent (or 27 heads of families). In 1811 the prefectoral register listed just three inland boatmen, four fresh-water fishermen, and one pilot.[18]

The decline was qualitative as well as quantitative. The once peerless Dutch superiority in nautical engineering which had produced the swift and versatile fly-boat (*fluit*) was, like their navigational techniques, becoming overhauled by north European competitors. In the middle of the century, Lieutenant-Admiral Cornelis Schrijvers uttered dire warnings were Dutch shipyards to adhere obstinately to old-fashioned methods of construction.[19] Like many such jeremiads, his critique was overwrought in its pessimism. As in other sectors of the Dutch economy, the problem was not that its own skills and products had deteriorated so much as that others had caught up while they stood still. The mere cessation of growth in shipping and fishing necessarily entailed less business for the yards and promoted the emigration of skilled craftsmen, thereby contributing further to the process. The silting of the Zuider Zee and the river mouths compounded the problem (for Dutch dredging techniques were also becoming obsolescent) as merchant vessels of larger bulk tonnage, displacing deeper draught, were obliged to lie off the Pampus or the Marsdiep, discharging their cargo to smaller craft and raising the overall costs of shipment. Unit costs of construction which, through their former supremacy in the Baltic carrying trade of naval materials—timber, pitch, canvas, iron and the like—had artificially favoured the Dutch ship-building industry, no longer applied. Suppliers like the Scandinavians, Germans and, with some Dutch expatriate assistance, even the Russians, either began to build their own merchant fleets or to trade directly with the burgeoning business of the British and French.

By the 1750's, the English companies were taking canvas and sailcloth direct from Danzig and making them up on the Medway, Avon, and Mersey. The Swedes and Russians were exporting their iron ore directly, and though the Dutch St. Petersburg merchants prospered even in the second half of the eighteenth century, exporting tar and timber, caviar, hemp and hides, it was increasingly on terms of trade more favourable to the Russians than to Amsterdam. As suppliers—and even customers—gradually prised themselves free of dependence on that comprehensive staple entrepôt for their market or supplies, they became more aggressively protectionist, imposing formidable duties on the most sought-after commodities. So it is not surprising to find the Dutch share of the Baltic timber trade dropping from over 70 per cent in the 1660's to 65 per cent in the 1730's and just 31.9 per cent in the 1780's.[20] Though the process of contraction was slow and uneven, by the 1750's the United Provinces could certainly not be regarded axiomatically as *the* shipyard of Europe. The yards on the Zaan did not, in fact, reach the zenith of their activity until the 1730's; but their efflorescence had been achieved at the expense of older and smaller centres of the industry: at Hoorn and Edam in North Holland, and Vlaardingen and Dordrecht in the south. Even in Rotterdam, which as an entrepôt for Atlantic merchandise continued to expand, the number of shipyards halved in the century from 1650 to 1750.[21]

In this respect as in so many others, traditional assumptions seem far from ill-founded. When, after the middle of the eighteenth century, the Zaanstreeks in its turn decayed as a centre of shipbuilding, such commissions as were to be had went almost exclusively to Amsterdam.[22] A similar pattern can be detected in the ancillary industries. Krommenie, a few miles north of Zaandam, only succeeded in retaining its sailcloth weaving through the obliteration of that craft in the villages of Wormer, Jisp and Assendelft. It was at this time that the bustling hamlets of the Noorderkwartier turned into stagnant backwaters, their inhabitants emptying into the great sieve of Amsterdam.

The share of Dutch shipping in the Baltic—as measured by the toll books of the Danish Sound—declined from some 53 per cent in the 1660's to 35 per cent a century later.[23] But the fact that this *relative* decline in the carrying trade contributed to the absolute decline in shipbuilding is just one indication that the distinction is anything but clear-cut. At any rate, confronted with the end of Dutch domination over the "mother trade" in Baltic grain at a time when exports west from Riga, Danzig, and Königsberg were expanding, it is not difficult to comprehend why contemporary commentators should have been so ready with their pessimism. For the political historian—and I make no claim whatever here to adjudicate in the economic debate—a potent misapprehension ought to carry as much weight as an accurate diagnosis if it shapes the attitudes of contemporaries towards their situation. The success of the Levant Company in ousting the British (a welcome reversal of roles) from markets for light textiles at Smyrna, Constantinople and Salonika was an inadequate compensation for the loss of the Dutch position as indispensable middlemen in the transit trades between north and south Europe, or between east and west. They had long since ceased to monopolise the carriage of salt from the pans of Setubal in Portugal, still less those of southern France, to the northern states; even in markets regarded as relatively secure, such as the shipment eastwards of Rhine wines, the Dutch share dived from 98 per cent in 1720 to 44 per cent fifty years later. It is true that the Netherlands, and particularly Zeeland and southern Holland, shared in the booming commerce in Atlantic commodities, not the least valuable of which were black humans. After its own humbler fashion, Middelburg became quite as successful a depot for the triangular slave trade as the more celebrated (or notorious) centres of Nantes and Bordeaux, Glasgow and Liverpool. But while the processing and re-export of sugar, tobacco, dyewood, indigo, cotton, and tobacco remained of considerable importance right to the end of the century, Amsterdam dealers had good cause to feel anxious that they were getting less than the lion's share of the business when, between 1760 and 1780, the volume of French colonial shipments east was just about double that of the Dutch.[24]

In another maritime industry commonly held to be one of the foundations of Dutch prosperity, fishing, the decline was absolute as well as relative, quantitative as well as qualitative—simply a decline. The herring may have been assigned a rather grander place in the annals of Dutch economic history than its true value merited, but the demise of the Great North Sea Fishery in the course of the eighteenth century could hardly have been other than a cause for the deepest dismay. At their height in the first half of the previous century, the herring fisheries had sent some 500 busses out to the North Sea and employed some 6,000 to 7,000 men.[25] Competition and protected markets took a decisive toll. In 1748 the first Swedish boats made their appearance off Jutland and Marstrand, and the following decade saw the emergence of the Scots and Irish fishers in force. Hamburg was kept well supplied by boats from Bremen and Altona in Denmark; and the foundation of the Free British Fishery in 1750–52 was rightly seen in Holland as the beginning of the end of the sovereignty of the Dutch herring. By 1761, the number of busses had halved, along with the catch and the work force. Even had catches been greater, the problem of shrinking markets would have remained acute. A poignant epitaph to the erstwhile supremacy of the Great Fishery is provided by the request of the Patriotic Society of Enkhuizen (the port on the west side of the Zuider Zee), forwarded through the good offices of the philo-American politician Baron van der Capellen to George Washington, asking him to note the particular qualities of the salted Dutch herring as evidenced by the crates of samples shipped for his pleasure. A year later, in November 1783, the general was obliged to reply politely but regretfully that though "Your herring, Sir, is undoubtedly of a higher flavour than our own, either to the superior skill of the Hollanders in curing it, or that the fish itself is really richer and more delicious than the same sort with us . . ." he could not, alas, hold out much hope for its prospects in the United States as the Atlantic appeared to teem with inferior but adequate fish.[26]

Other branches of fishing suffered much the same fate. Whaling was even more of a labour-intensive industry, employing at its height in the second decade of the eighteenth century some 10,000 workers and sailors.[27] Although the Dutch had profited enormously from changing course from Spitsbergen to the Davis Straits between Greenland and Baffin Island, their failure to keep pace with harpooning and navigational innovations brought about a sharp decline after the 1740's. From the 250 whalers at work in the 1720's, the total was by 1750 reduced to 160, and 30 years later to just 50. In the second decade of the eighteenth century, when the industry was at its peak, it was extracting on average each year from those great mammalian carcasses some 60,000–70,000 vats of crude blubber. Even in the occasionally prolific years of the 1730's, that volume was dropping to between 30,000–40,000, and by 1780 had shrunk to a mere 8,000 or 9,000 vats.[28] Prices for bone and oil kept up reasonably well throughout the century and there was a minor recovery in the 1770's. But the costs of sending whalers as far away as Greenland were considerable and the estimated returns varied so wildly from year to year, ship to ship, and area to area that to take part in one of the syndicates (rederijen) financing the expeditions became more and more of a speculation against, as it were, whale futures.

The contraction in the number of the rederijen, very marked by the last quarter of the century, was an accurate gauge of the winding down of this once highly profitable industry. There were other, lesser, casualties at the same time. Coastal fishing—at Katwijk, Scheveningen and Egmond aan Zee—had to contend not only with over-fished shoals and legitimate competition from German boats but also with the privateers operating out of Dunkirk who (as we shall see) became an appalling menace by the end of the century. Purmerend had dwindled as the erstwhile international market for the Zaanse and Zuider Zee eel fisheries, and Monnikendam lost much of the prosperity derived from its smokehouses and salting sheds. There were pockets of growth amidst the general dereliction. The fishermen of South Holland were taking a greater rather than lesser share of the Icelandic cod shoals, though here too they were up against British, German and Danish competition. And the silting of the Zuider Zee had had at least one benevolent consequence in multiplying the shoals inside it and introducing, among other varieties, the anchovy fished in quantities by the little boats plying from the ports immediately to the north of Amsterdam—Marken, Durgerdam, Volendam. These waxed as fat then from this lucrative "domestic" fishing as they now do from the shoals of tourists baited, hooked, and landed by studied exhibitions of folk charm. But the exchange of the anchovy for the whale seems a poor bargain. Compared with the virtual destruction of the two major branches of an industry which provided so many livelihoods—for boat-builders, net-makers, curers, salters and driers, as well as fishermen—the paltry bonus hauls of the late eighteenth century were, in every sense, small fry.

This cursory glance at the ailing maritime economy of the Netherlands after 1750 is not, it goes without saying, meant as a contribution to the debate about the degree (and quality) of its decrepitude. We are properly reminded by

Dr. de Vries that what has vulgarly been taken for a net loss was often more in the nature of a shift in the structure of economic resources, or a change in the direction of their distribution. If Holland's traditional trade stagnated, then the coastal shipping of the Friesians and Groningers shared, at least to some extent, in the renascent prosperity of the Hansa ports and Danish Altona—just as Middleburg and Zierikzee in Zeeland, and Dordrecht, Brielle, Maassluis and Vlaardingen in South Holland could not help but benefit from the increasing well-being of Flanders and Brabant, which were now no longer decaying dependencies stranded on the wrong side of the Scheldt. No doubt, as de Vries further argues, the commentary of L. P. van de Spiegel (of whom there is more to be said) in 1782, or that of Cornelis van der Oudermeulen in 1785, both of which took a less stark view of the Dutch economy than the polemics of the "Economic Patriots," were more discriminating in their diagnosis.[29] But, perhaps perversely, I am less concerned here with the reality of the Dutch decline than its appearance. When further research enables a more complete picture of eighteenth-century Dutch society to be drawn, it may well be that appearance and reality converge more closely than the new orthodoxy allows.

Even if the Patriot critics were irresponsibly wide of the mark (and de Vries does not, after all, accuse them of bad faith in their misapprehensions), their express *sense* of decline, especially in those departments of the economy that the Dutch had long assumed to be their forte, surely contributed to the sharpening of disquiet, which in due course grew into rebellion. Seen from the doubtless muddied and unscientific perspective of the political historian, it may well appear that a forcefully expressed misjudgement may count for more in the balance of historical change than a prudently dispassionate truth. It seems unlikely that the economy of the British North American colonies actually turned on the level of imperial excise with which they were burdened. But in the course of an independently conducted argument over constitutional liberties and sovereign prerogatives, it proved no hard thing to transmute economic discomfort into fiscal tyranny. For that matter it was not, perhaps, entirely coincidental that the relatively rosier (or orange-tinged) accounts of van de Spiegel, van der Oudermeulen, and Elie Luzac were all agreed on the remedial value of a reforming Stadholderate.

The fact that, for their part, the Patriot criticisms were conditioned by the habit of making invidious comparisons with neighbouring states may have clouded their judgement in assessing the intrinsic condition of the Dutch economy; but this added to, rather than subtracted from, the potency of their politics. And it is beyond contention that, by the 1770's, the material condition of the Netherlands had become a prime topic for political, even moral, as well as purely economic debate. The impressive range of arguments arrayed to support the 1751 proposals for a limited free port (put to the States-General by the Stadholder Willem IV and then left in abeyance); the running commentaries on the enervation of the Dutch commonwealth published between 1768 and 1776 by Gerrit Bom in his journal *De Koopman* (*The Merchant*); the essay competition set by the Amsterdam business-man Ploos van Amstel in 1771, under the auspices of the Holland Society for Science, on the means required to rejuvenate a flagging economy; the foundation in 1777 by one of the prize winners, H. H. van den Heuvel of "The Economical Branch," devoted to pondering the manifold problems affecting commerce, industry, and agriculture, which enjoyed a prodigious success right up to the Fourth Anglo-Dutch War—all testified to the earnestness with which these matters were considered in governing as well as intellectual and mercantile circles.[30]

Of course there were no simple alignments. Patriots were by no means invariably "pessimists" nor Stadholderian reformers invariably "optimists." Very often just the reverse was the case, for those—in Amsterdam, for example —among the regents most inclined to be anti-Orangist by traditional affiliation could very easily dilate ecstatically on the past and coming glories of the staple market, especially in the wake of the defunct British Empire. But what many of these varied discussions had in common was a shared recognition that there was indeed something decidedly rotten about the state of the Dutch economy, and that an adequate remedy might well have to go beyond the bounds of tinkering with tariffs. Underlying many of the comments was the nagging apprehension formulated by the young Patriot-economist Rutger Metelerkamp as the question: "Has our society reached the limit of its resources or the maximum of its wealth and prosperity?"[31] If that was indeed the case, then more was thought to be at stake than a few bales of buckwheat or a hold full of whale blubber—rather, those special assets which for so long the Dutch had taken for granted and without which, it was feared, not only their wealth but their national freedom would stand forfeit. So that in reviewing the condition of the economy, what will most concern the political historian will be those features which seemed to lend credence to such anxieties, and in so doing further undermined the cohesion of a society never noted for its homogeneity.

What were these elements? To begin with, neither the older nor the newer historiography denies the increasing importance of the Dutch during the eighteenth century in international public finance, nor the development of the Amsterdam capital market to the point at which it ceased to be related to the functioning of the commercial staple market. To borrow the fastidious terminology of Dr. de Vries once more, then, the "relative growth" of the former took place with the "relative decline" of the latter. The expansion of direct trading outside the Netherlands entrepôt and the introduction of finishing industries at the ports of return—at Bordeaux, Liverpool and Hamburg—contributed, as we have seen, to the redundancy of the Dutch middleman. The role of the capitalist, hitherto inextricably linked with trade through the commission business, gradually reverted to more purely banking and broking functions. Attracted by higher rates of interest than those prevailing at home, concentrations of capital detached themselves from the entrepôt and were invested in foreign loans, or lending short with a quick turnaround. Amsterdam thus became predominantly—though by no means exclusively—

a financial centre. This process has been described in detail by Professor Charles Wilson and needs no elaboration here.[32] Suffice it to say that this structural relocation of resources had certain evident political reverberations. Dr. P. W. Klein has sensibly warned against any irrational evaluation of the respective merits or otherwise of commerce as against finance.[33] And it is irrefutable that the growth of the latter, *possibly* at the expense of the former, is not to be taken as necessarily deleterious to the economy as a whole. But it does seem that the process had something of a divisive effect, especially in Amsterdam. For the separation of the financial capitalists from the staple market merchants was to some extent reflected in levels of aggregate capital.

The evolution of the regent oligarchy—from the Tripses and de Geers to the Hopes and Pels—parvenus though the latter were considered by their seniors, did involve some loss of social comprehensiveness. Mrs. Alice Carter, who has pointed out that the level of Dutch investment in the British public debt was lower than often supposed, also observed that inscriptions below 20,000 florins were so minor as to exclude themselves from consideration; further, that the majority of such inscriptions were between 20,000 and 90,-000 florins; and that all such investment originated in less than one-twentieth of the propertied classes of Amsterdam.[34] While the commercial and financial community did not divide into obviously polarised classes, it became more difficult for the merchants and entrepreneurs to make fortunes that could compare with the colossal wealth of the great bankers and financiers. Indeed, the increased penetration of the closed regent oligarchies in Amsterdam by the new super-rich only served to make the distinction more rather than less glaring. As H. R. C. Wright has neatly put it, "a social barrier grew out of a widening economic gulf and the Second Hand was left on the wrong side."[35]

This division, however blurred, was not without its political implications. There was some feeling within the mercantile community that the crises to which the world of acceptance banking seemed periodically prone in turn generated conditions inauspicious for the prospects of trade. The crisis of 1763, when Amsterdam was forced to take goods dumped on an already overloaded market, and to sell at knock-down prices, was a bitter object lesson.[36] More significantly, the close association of Dutch financial operations with the expansion of British power and strength was a sore point with the traditionally Anglophobe commercial lobby in Holland. In the commercial case, the English connexion was necessarily competitive; in the financial case, it was complementary. Mrs. Carter's prudent strictures on the limited number of fortunes, and the limited amount of Dutch capital represented in the British debt, do not weaken the force of a protest at what was alleged to amount to a virtual subsidy for the means of inflicting damage on Dutch shipping, or, at the very least, restraining them from doing lucrative trade with the French and the Americans.

Such objections received dramatic emphasis from the events leading to the Fourth Anglo-Dutch War (1780–84). The Stadholder's preference for "army augmentation" over "fleet restoration" was taken as corroboration of the accusation that those Orangists with strong English connexions—the

Greffier Fagel and the banker Henry Hope, for example—were prepared to subvert the national interest to protect their dividend. In fact, the serious losses carried by the major capitalists suggested that the allegations were over-severe; yet they were not totally bereft of foundation. When the French and their Batavian republican allies entered Holland in January 1795, Hope packed his bags for England with almost as much alacrity as Willem V himself. Even Elie Luzac, who could by no means be counted among the ranks of the opposition to the Stadholder, subscribed to the view that a parasitical dependence on the English economy was tantamount to a form of slow self-strangulation.[37]

Within the capital market itself, those who were the principal victims of what de Vries has called the "eggs in one basket syndrome" often nursed similar grievances. Even if their stake was too trifling to be directly affected by repudiations on the national debt, the dealings of acceptance and discount houses in Holland were so closely tied up with the vagaries of the British money market that their unnerving fluctuations were bound to register across the North Sea. When the Ayr Bank failed in 1772, many investors of "the middling sort" in Holland were swept away in the aftermath. During the Anglo-Dutch War, the Amsterdam Wisselbank was damaged to the tune of some 7,650,000 florins. And while it is true that these periodic fluctuations were never alarming or frequent enough to frighten away Dutch capital from foreign investment, the class of investor after 1773 was drawn from a noticeably more speculative clientèle, many of whom, like Horneca, Hogguer & Co., or Georges Grand, were relatively recent immigrants and certainly newcomers to the regent circles.[38] In some cases (though again not as many as is often assumed), finance houses like the de Neufvilles, which had taken a comprehensive pasting during the crash, salted loan capital away into the French debt, hardly less volatile but apparently more politically logical and certainly with a fetchingly high rate of interest, especially on various kinds of annuities.[39]

It was not until well after the war, however, that movement of capital away from the British debt took on real momentum, and not until 1792 that the "Club of Six" began to subscribe in the attractive new alternative investment of the debt of the American Republic. No simple picture of a political-financial reaction to the vicissitudes of Anglo-Dutch finance can be drawn for the 1780's; but it may be safely said that these difficulties are likely to have contributed to the hardening of "English" and "French" factions in Amsterdam and to division between the trading and financial sectors of the wider economic community.

Complaints over levels of taxation were another favourite theme of Patriot economic propaganda. It was, of course, illogical in the extreme to attribute these burdens to the Orangist-dominated Council of State, since the vast majority of impositions were levied by the treasuries of the separate provinces' States and in by no means all of these Stadholderian placemen had control. Nor had there been any tradition of low taxation during the "Stadholderless" times. But none of these considerations deterred the Patriot journalists from stigmatising efforts to expand the army as wanton and self-interested extravagance, to be paid for by the toil of honest burghers. In any event, the proportion of indirect to direct taxes in Holland—which itself supplied some 60 per cent of Dutch revenue—was of the order of two to one. This was only to be expected in what had been a predominantly mercantile nation; but as was pointed out some time ago, the burden of duties on primary commodities forced up living costs—and therefore labour costs—to ensure that Dutch products became uncompetitive not only on the international but the domestic market.[40]

This fiscal distribution naturally hit the industrial and merchant communities hardest, from entrepreneurs to retailers, and some of their spokesmen were in the van of those pressing for fiscal reform. Most of the formal proposals addressed to the States-General—those of 1751, for example, for a "limited free port" system—were primarily meant as a response to the increasingly menacing protectionism of the Republic's neighbours.[41] But even though the prudence of mid-century Grand Pensionaries like Peter Steyn helped to reduce the weight of interest on the Dutch debt, the disparity between private affluence and the penury of the States' treasury was a favourite theme of popular economic literature. Moreover, until 1748 the burden of high taxes was not made any easier to bear by the fact that much excise was farmed to individuals who were themselves outside the "virtuous" occupations of commerce and industry. Until the fisc was redistributed, the crude imputation that the luxury of the few was maintained at the expense of national impotence and the exploitation of the "middling sort" would always find an attentive audience.

Many of these convictions were grounded in moral prejudice rather than economic principle. The Republic had come a long way since much had been made of the sanctity of honest graft and sober thrift. Yet there was still an underlying animus against the unwholesomeness of moneychanging which, for all the power and prestige of the Amsterdam banks, was liable to surface in incoherent but formidable expressions of anger in times of danger or hardship. Anti-pecuniary diatribes were a stock-in-trade of the increasing number of publicists specialising in nostalgic revivalism, and extolling the virtues of ship and sail, loom and bobbin, against the depraved hoarding of filthy lucre. Some, like van den Heuvel, chose to stress the inherent incompatibility of commercial interests on the one hand, and agrarian and industrial on the other, arguing that trade had had more than its share of favours in the past.[42] But it was far more commonplace to emphasise the fecund interdependence of trade and industry, which had nourished the growth of towns like Leiden where wool imported from Spain (and in earlier days, England) had been woven into bays, says, fustians and serges, and Haarlem, where cloth was bleached and dyed before re-export or sale in the domestic market. Since the only raw material the Dutch provinces could supply to the textile industry was flax, this reciprocity—it could reasonably be argued—was indispensable to the welfare of the towns.[43] So that while it may be academically nice to make a sharp distinction between a "relative decline" in trade and an "absolute decline" in industry, the precision of those categories makes no allowance for the importance to the population of the collapse—for such it was—of labour-intensive enterprises. "Structural unemployment" is an unpleasantly hygienic euphemism peculiar to the twentieth century. It was no consolation to the pauperised textile artisans of Leiden or the unemployed shipwrights of the Zaanstreeks to know that "businesses needing fixed capital such as distilling did rather better than those needing aggregate labour such as textiles."[44] In any process of economic change there is always a social profit-and-loss account to be reckoned, much harder to calculate than arithmetical returns on capital. Dr. van der Woude describes the problem admirably:

An economic recession—even when it is of long duration—does not necessarily involve a decline of all trades. When weighing losses against gains employment should be an important criterion. In this respect a prolonged crisis in agriculture could never be compensated for by greater activities in the stock market, nor could the decline of shipping be made good by increased sales of colonial produce while the employment created by the new spirit industry bore no proportion to the unemployment due to the slump in the brewers trade throughout the province [Holland].[45]

And, as Boswell duly noted, it was the ruin of urban society in Holland, Utrecht, and parts of Friesland which worked the most dramatic changes in the social topography of the Netherlands. For if in the later eighteenth century the Dutch Republic was still able to cling to some of its prosperity, it may be safely conjectured that fewer of its citizens were able to share in that good fortune than at any other time in its history.

The extraordinary economic success of the Dutch, it has often been remarked, rested on exceedingly vulnerable foundations. Their monopoly as the "Middle Persons in Trade," as Defoe called them, necessarily depended to a large extent on the comparative retardation of their suppliers and customers in the techniques of freighting, finishing, and marketing, or from a want of capital to finance those operations. When these deficiencies had been made good, nothing stood in the way of direct trading eliminating the expenses of the intermediary services provided by the Dutch. To complete their misfortune, those ports which successfully developed both direct connections with suppliers *and* their own processing industries—refining, dyeing, bleaching— did so at lower labour costs and, as "late starters," generally with the benefit of improved technology. In this way, flax imported from Germany which had been treated at Haarlem, woven into linen, and exported to England from Amsterdam, was now bleached at Bielfeld and shipped directly to England from Hamburg.[46] From this stage it was but a short time before Dutch manufactures were challenged on their own domestic market. By the 1730's, Scottish and Belfast linens had already encroached on the Dutch market and were even competing with Leiden cloths in an area long deemed a special preserve: the markets of Spain and her colonies. Cost factors in Holland became so prohibitive that it became cheaper to send even Dutch flax abroad to the manufacturing towns of the Austrian Netherlands—Liège and Verviers—and from there import the cloth back into Holland, rather than have it made up at home.

There were no obvious routes out of this quandary. Taxes remained steep because the price of defending the independence of a small Republic with a long, straggling frontier (the first line of which was constituted by the "barrier forts" in the southern Netherlands) was becoming dauntingly expensive. Increases in port duties, the "convooien en licenten," threatened to drive yet more business to the budding German ports. Guild restrictions covered every conceivable occupation from the cradle to the grave, an impediment literally illustrated in 1749 by a demarcation dispute between Amsterdam gravediggers and undertakers' carpenters over the making of coffins. Guild protection naturally sent costs up even higher; but in times of desperately insecure employment, there were few artisans prepared to exchange the imperfect protection and sporadic philanthropy of their guilds for the much more hazardous liberty of the labour market. The Republic in recession seemed to be thrown back increasingly on its own parlously modest resources. Whether it could survive for any length of time on such a basis was, to say the least, an open question.

The industrial impoverishment of the eighteenth century was of such proportions that it overrules any suggestion of catastrophism brought by the polished hindsights of economic history against contemporary critics. De Vries and J. G. van Dillen provide figures which hardly give the impression of a gentle slope.[47] In 1671, Leiden produced 139,000 pieces of textile cloth (*laken*); in 1725, 72,000; in 1775, 41,000; and in 1795, just 29,000. Woollen bays and fustians followed the same pattern. In 1700, there were still some 85,000 pieces produced; in 1750, 53,000; and in 1795, 28,096. In the same city in 1700 there were twenty-nine dyeworks; in 1760, ten; and in 1790, five. At Haarlem the twenty-five bleachworks which had survived in 1700 were reduced to twelve by the middle of the century and to five by 1790. Of the 80 cotton printers left in Amsterdam in 1750, 17 only had survived in 1787; 8 kilns at Delft were all that was left of the ceramic industry by 1780; and over half of the 7,000 inhabitants of Gouda employed in the pipe-making works which were the principal industry of that city were out of work by the end of the century. The figures for soap-boiling in Amsterdam, where both the number of concerns and production were halved between the beginning of the century and the 1780's, suggest that concerns with more fixed capital and less aggregate labour also suffered in the overall slump.[48]

What of those industries which held their own or better during the century? Some were obliged to mark time by adjusting sources of supply and reducing production. Rotterdam, which had become an important centre of the tobacco industry, was obliged to obtain its leaf from Glasgow rather than Essequibo via Amsterdam. Sugar refining was concentrated on Amsterdam but to the loss of Delft, Weesp and Dordrecht.[49] The only industry boasting a success story which others might well have envied was distilling. There were 57 breweries in the Republic in 1787 (27 of which were located in Amsterdam), but this paled into insignificance beside the 200 distilleries in Holland alone: 160 in Schiedam, the remainder in Rotterdam and Delfshaven. Schiedam was the only town to show a very marked increase of population at this time, and its rise to become the gin capital of the country hurt not only the breweries but the provincial distillers in Friesland. Whatever the moral overtones, much dwelt on by evangelical predikants, gin was money in the eighteenth century. Eighty-five per cent of the total production in Holland was exported overseas: to the East and West Indies, England, Scandinavia, and Germany, and not least to the rapidly-expanding American market, which seems to have worked up a significant thirst for the liquor. Yet it is not per-haps an entirely sanctimonious reflection to see the rise in consumption of spirits as a well-known index of impoverishment for the broad mass of the population—outside Schiedam, at any rate. A pattern of trade which imported tobacco, tea and dyestuffs from Britain and sent the vessel back laden with casks of gin was not perhaps the best omen for the health of the domestic economy.

Other industries which kept their heads above the rising tide of failure also suggest economic malaise. Brick-making continued to do well as Dutch clays supplied bricks of high quality to a building trade which, as elsewhere in Europe, was prospering from increasingly elaborate patterns of conspicuous consumption—habits which also kept the Amsterdam diamond-cutting and -polishing trade in business.[50] Some industries, the manufacture of rugs from coarse cow-hair at Hilversum in particular, illustrated a general move away from the older centres of high wages and guild protection to the interior of provinces or to the poorer rural areas of the land provinces. Even under these propitious conditions, success was by no means guaranteed. After enjoying a boom period between 1690 and 1740, the textile industry in the Twente region of Overijssel fell victim to spiralling costs of raw materials and competition from Scotland, Ireland, Münster and Silesia. Enschede, Almelo, and Hengelo thus grew up in the wake of a transient prosperity which in the end left behind more paupers than it had in the first place absorbed.[51]

In Dutch Brabant, for so long a virtual colony of the rest of the Republic and under the direct jurisdiction of the States-General, the textile industry transplanted from Holland achieved a reasonable degree of success. For some time the entrepreneurs of Leiden had been commissioning out work to the cottagers of the Gooi and the Meijerij around 's Hertogenbosch, and by the 1760's the more audacious of them—like Pieter Vreede, who was to become the tribune of the Batavian democrats—had removed their works entirely to Tilburg, Helmond and Eindhoven. Once again this process involved some losses, not so much in the already derelict Leiden as in Hilversum, which had itself fattened on the exodus of work from western Holland.

But all these "new" textiles amounted to very little compared with the earlier success of Leiden cloth. With limited capital and productive capacity, they were at best geared to meeting home demand and trying to stave off the challenge not only from British manufactures but from the ominously budding enterprises in the southern Netherlands and Westphalia. Some of those foreign concerns may even have been established with the help

of expatriate Dutch craftsmen and artisans, for without adequate employment emigration became a real enticement in the eighteenth century. De Vries records some 22,000 cotton-print workers emigrating between 1740 and 1770, and 300 artisans were given employment at Guadalajara, where the Spanish promoters of economic improvement were eager to inaugurate an Iberian textile industry.[52]

What then, are we to make of this depressed but complicated situation? Clearly it would be as misleading to overdo the cheerlessness of the Dutch economic predicament as to discount it altogether. But given the general drift of current historiography, there seems little danger of falling prey to that temptation. It may be acknowledged that trade, and particularly colonial and inland trade, continued to prosper; that Amsterdam remained established as the cash till of Europe, to which states and princes might resort for hand-outs at rates of interest appropriate to their desperation;[53] and that a good deal of cheese and butter got sold at Alkmaar. But I see no reason why, for example, van der Oudermeulen's sanguine expectations for the East India Company (of all corporations) should *necessarily* assume more significance than, say, the mildewed condition of Dutch industry or the termination of its predominance in the Baltic grain trade. I would be prepared to hazard the guess, enlightened or otherwise, that while wealth was being unquestionably generated in the eighteenth-century United Provinces, it was being diffused to a narrower base of population than in the century before 1680. Just what an explanation might look like which argues the contrary is exceedingly hard to suppose. Like France, albeit for different reasons and in a very different fashion, the Republic was becoming simultaneously a richer and a poorer nation.

All this is admittedly in the nature of conjecture. Dr. van der Woude, who on the whole seems to incline to a fairly pessimistic analysis—as historian of the stricken Noorderkwartier he could hardly do otherwise—himself admits that the work of attempting to measure such crucial determinants as unemployment or vagrancy is seriously prejudiced by a lack of reliable, or usable, data.[54] Concerned to supply some sort of social context for the politics of the late eighteenth century, the best that the historian can do is to add to an extrapolation from information about the contraction of labour-intensive sectors of the economy the misgivings registered by contemporaries, and to draw his own, inevitably impressionistic conclusions. I am acutely conscious that to go even so far is to trespass on a whole minefield of historical uncertainty. Nonetheless it seems to me that, given even the most rudimentary information (and for at least some regions of the Netherlands the student is better off than that), it is not outrageously reckless to assume that the dislocations engendered by economic strain, or the animosities sharpened by the contrasts of luxury and penury, would not have made the resolution of conflicts, themselves created by independent *political* tensions, any the easier. All of which is to say nothing more sensational than that there was a social dimension to the Dutch revolutions of the eighteenth century. That this should have been so seems in fact as self-evident as the unlikelihood of those discontents providing a causal explanation of the upheavals.

Perhaps, then, it is possible to proceed to a consideration of social polarisation within the Republic without it entailing any direct correlation with the Patriot or Batavian politics. Unhappily—with the exception of Slicher van Bath's invaluable research on the Twente region of Overijssel, where he has revealed a rural poverty of animal squalor,[55] and the pioneering work of Dr. van den Eerenbeemt on the poor of Dutch Brabant[56]—the historian is as yet without conclusive evidence as to the material distress, numbers, migratory movements, diet, or health of the poor at this time. Even more important, until the Batavian Republic and the Kingdom of Holland took an official interest in the magnitude of the problem, it is impossible to hazard any notions about the growth of the needy during the course of the eighteenth century. In this respect the very excellence of Dutch charitable institutions, quite properly admired throughout the rest of Europe, is the historian's enemy. For by defining as "the poor" those who received relief from the several orphanages, workhouses, hospitals and old age homes with which the major religious denominations and many (though by no means all) of the municipalities were endowed, there is the obvious risk of excluding from consideration the unaccommodated poor—or exactly that section of the needy which may have shown a significant increase. Certainly the prospect of overflowing workhouses and unnumbered battalions of indigent disturbed the composure of mid-century sheriffs and magistrates and supplied excellent copy for the moralising "Spectatorial" press. The *Nederlandsche Jaarboek* complained in 1776 that "the common people are perishing from wretchedness and want: the poor houses lie crammed with their bodies." There are signs, too, in petitions of orphanage deacons and poor-house masters to municipal regents for "additional pennies," that resources were suffering some net depletion; though it was only at the end of the century, with the combination of astronomic food and fuel prices and a massive new army of the needy disgorged by the war crisis, that these strains would threaten to become terminal. What the historian would dearly like to know, but cannot as yet be at all sure of, is whether there was any general deterioration in the standards of life of the petty trades and artisans most likely to have been affected by the gradual economic contraction. In 1773 *De Vaderlander* commented: "Overall, in all the places we have inspected, we have found the unhappy truth confirmed that the well-being from which this [petty-bourgeois] class used to find a living, has entirely fallen off."[57]

It is equally difficult to know whether there was any marked change in habits of dietary consumption. One account, derived from excise receipts, has that very notional figure, the "average" Hollander, eating 75 grams of meat, 40 grams of butter, and 325 grams of bread a day—a spread which would have been regarded as hoggish gluttony by the common people of other European countries.[58] What those gross figures conceal is any alteration of the distribution of these victuals either side of the norm. Writing in the *Letters on Public Prosperity* at the end of the century, Gijsbert Karel van Hogendorp, certainly no radical, affirmed that many of the humbler among the commoner burghers no longer had the means to enjoy a meat, bread and dairy diet.[59] As habitual consumption of adulterated brandies and gin and poor-quality tobacco increased, the poor houses brought in less wheaten flour and more of the poorer rye, together with buckwheat for primitive porridge. And that invaluable cheap substitute of carbohydrates, the potato, seems to have made inroads in areas of the country and society where previously it had been disdained. Not surprisingly the celebrated soup of the Anglo-American philanthropist "Count" Rumford, which combined, it was alleged, maximum nutrition with minimum expenditure, was taken up with enthusiasm by the relief institutions in Holland.

The most wretched areas of indigence may still have been rural, despite the gradual improvement in Dutch agriculture. The mysterious epidemic of dysenteric fever—known as the "Red Death" in the Netherlands—which swept through southern Holland and Brabant in the 1770's was, it seems, partly a product of miserable standards of diet and shelter; and in Twente it has been estimated that between 50 and 60 per cent of the population could be reasonably classified as paupers. Squatters settled on sandy scrub land in Overijssel and Gelderland; peat cutters on the eastern moors attempted to extract a few turves and a minimal subsistence from the exhausted bogs. Their dwellings were rudimentary. Thousands lived in pig-sties, turf huts or sheds some 10 feet long, 8 feet wide and 6 high.[60]

For the first time in the history of the Republic, mendicancy became a matter of publicised concern rather than a social aberration to be kept well out of the way. The periodical *De Borger* remarked that if something drastic was not done, the Republic would before long be reduced to those classes least useful to it: rentiers and beggars.[61] Whether or not that was true, there was a common anxiety that public begging was reaching socially menacing proportions. Gangs of several hundred bandits, vagabonds and vagrants were said to roam the woods of the Neder Betuw in West Gelderland and North Brabant, descending for nocturnal forays to steal food and valuables—such as they were—from isolated farms. On Wednesdays and Saturdays, housewives in the towns of Holland prepared for the public entry of beggars by sorting out small change—"stuivers and duitsers"—to throw from their windows at their approach.[62] In Twente, where it was difficult for even the most fastidious magistrate to distinguish between an inveterate vagabond and a smallholder reduced to begging, many were given casual farm labour and a crust of bread on a day-work basis. Dutch beggars even overflowed beyond the frontiers of the Republic, north to East Friesland, east to Münster and Cleves, and south to Flanders and Austrian Brabant, where they rapidly acquired a notorious reputation for drunkenness and petty pilfering.[63] It is a measure of just how far the realities of the lower depths of Dutch society had ceased to correspond to their popular image abroad as a nation scoured of poverty that the Dutch had become, as it were, the gipsies and Savoyards of East Friesland.

As in England and France in the eighteenth century, the social neurosis generated by public begging often reached irrational proportions. Myths about the size and range of activities of armed vagrant bands not infrequently originated in the terror, on the part of those living just above the level of indigence, of being depressed below it by circumstances for which they could find no adequate explanation. Beggars were accused of poisoning cattle, of carrying the "Red Death"; of soliciting women to act as concubines for their gangs. Retaliation could be hysterical. A general hunt of beggars was decreed around 's Hertogenbosch in 1771.[64] More usually, local authorities would make every effort to deter vagrants from seeking shelter or relief within their jurisdiction, either by force or by making life in the poor houses an even less alluring alternative than the open road. In 1759 the States of Holland reinforced the order dealing with this problem obliging citizens in the principal towns to arm themselves and ring the watch tower bells at the approach of any large gang. Amsterdam took a draconian view of the matter, incarcerating as many beggars as it could physically deal with in a House of Correction where conditions were even more inhumane and malodorous than the common prison.

These were troubles, to be sure, which affected many other societies in eighteenth-century Europe. The picaresque cartoons of Troost found their grim themes reproduced in Hogarth. But it could be maintained that the relative impoverishment of the Dutch was bound to be all the more conspicuous in a society which prided itself on the generosity and disinterestedness of its social philanthropy. It was the finite capacity of those institutions to absorb increasing numbers of the poor which emphasised the vulnerability of the strength and wealth of the whole Republic. By 1808, when the following report was submitted to Louis Bonaparte, then King of Holland, this impression of social weakness was unmistakeable:

. . . In effect, all those who have investigated this matter . . . and who are in a position to make an impartial judgement must recognise that our old institutions concerning the state of the poor, as good as they have formerly been, and quite properly admired not only by the inhabitants of this country but even abroad, can no longer be considered as satisfactory in the present time. The reason is as simple as it is natural. When these institutions were created the nation was increasing in grandeur, work was easy to find and the number of persons who could dispense charity much greater than it is today. Whilst one of the principal points on which these institutions were established, the knowledge of public shame which ensured that recourse to them would only be made in the greatest extremity, has been so lost, that, as has already been attested in many places, one may foresee the total ruin of these Establishments if endeavours are not made to sustain them by means better adapted to present circumstances . . . unexampled calamities . . . and the terrifying increase of the poor are then forcing us to recognise that the measures to be taken for their support have to be of a much greater extent (than heretofore).[65]

Such an acknowledgement, let alone the resolution to act on it, only came about in the depths of the miseries brought on by Napoleon's Continental blockade. But before this crisis—in so many respects a turning point in Dutch history—had been reached, old and well-tried methods were still resorted to.

What problems could not be coped with by the traditional agencies of relief were passed on to neighbouring towns or provinces by local eviction. Learned societies solemnly discussed the establishment of "industry schools," but more with an eye to making the poor pay their way than providing a general level of subsistence. Reform of manners was a substitute for, rather than a prelude to, the reform of society. And as the Republic sank further into the quagmire of insolvency and poverty, the problem of its indigent became not merely a social irritant but a chronic malady. For, unlike her neighbours, the Netherlands had neither great manufactures nor huge armies with which to sponge up the human waste which oozed from the houses of charity into the streets, the patches of waste land and beyond to the moors, peat bogs and woods of the surrounding countryside.

The Alienation of Office

To its critics, Dutch society in the later eighteenth century was evolving towards a situation in which displays of conspicuous affluence by the relatively few were being indulged amidst conditions of increasing impoverishment for the relatively many. The process was held to be all the more offensive for sinning against the cherished self-image of a robust commonwealth of brother-burghers where the distinctions of rank, fortune and status were less formally marked out than in more aristocratic societies. By seeming to become more socially stratified, the Republic was, by the same token, becoming less Dutch. The elaborately beautified Hague, where, in 1777, the tax roll recorded the stabling of between 40,000 and 50,000 "pleasure" and carriage horses, was seen by the upholders of the traditional virtues of plain thrift and honest toil as a cesspool of luxury and foreign manners. French theatre, English riding habits and hats, German porcelain, and the construction of Palladian country villas on the banks of the river Vecht or in the Haarlem Woods outside Amsterdam, all betokened a decadence summed up in the pejorative epithet of "the time of the periwigs" (*pruikentijd*). The "Golden Century"—the "Patriot" moralists insisted—had become adulterated into an age of dross. This is not to say that social animosities, latent or explicit, actually determined the alignments of the political upheavals at the end of the century. Even in France where these polarities were still far more glaring, the Revolution by no means followed a simple scenario of the poor and disfranchised pitting their strength against the rich and privileged. And in the Netherlands a highly idiosyncratic history ensured that the relationship between social and political division would be peculiarly oblique.

Not the least miraculous feature of a Republic notorious for belying its official nomenclature of the "United Provinces" was that it had somehow contrived to remain just about intact, an achievement for which the recurrent threat of extinction, first from Habsburg Spain, later from Bourbon France, must bear a large share of the credit. The classic conflict which defined the wayward course of its domestic politics opposed the House of Orange-Nassau, together with the more militant elements of the Reformed Church and the nobility of the landward provinces, against the mercantile patriciate of Holland without whose wealth the eighty years' war for independence could never have been brought to a successful conclusion. That commercial élite emerged from the war entrenched in the governing offices of the major towns whose delegates made up the States of Holland. They defended their "regent" exclusiveness by claiming that they had been confided with a "virtual" representation of the people as a whole, and that by upholding the sovereignty of town and province, they were championing the "True Liberty" against any encroachment from the Princes of Orange. Naturally the regents of the maritime provinces had a direct interest in conserving at all costs the loose federation enshrined in the Union of Utrecht (1579), whereby the Republic was comprised not as a state but rather an alliance of seven sovereign provinces, their mandated representatives assembled as the States-General. As long as the country was relatively secure from attack by land, the economic paramountcy of Holland, supplying nearly 60 per cent of its total revenues, ensured that the periodic efforts of the Prince of Orange to transform the ill-defined executive office of Stadholder into a quasi-monarchy would be doomed to failure. The clumsy attempt by William II to mount a military coup against the city of Amsterdam in 1650 merely meant that for the next twenty-two years there was no Stadholder at all, and that the foreign policy of the Republic was, to a very large extent, determined by the Grand Pensionary of Holland. It was only when the de Witts' strategy of maintaining an armed commercial supremacy while eschewing expensive Continental alliances foundered in the face of Louis XIV's belligerent ambitions that the Dutch once more turned to the head of the "Princely House" to save the Fatherland from being entirely overrun. Helped on his way by scenes of hysterical and savage rioting directed against the recent élite in general and the de Witts in particular, William of Orange was virtually able to dictate terms for the resumption of his captaincy. A similar pattern of events repeated itself in 1747, following another prolonged "Stadholderless" period, when the Prince of the Friesian branch of the dynasty became installed not only as Stadholder Willem IV but as Captain- and Admiral-General of the Union, all offices which were made hereditary in the male line.

The part played by the Dutch common people in these sharp swings of the political pendulum was confined in times of manifest peril to outbursts of anger inflicted on those held culpable for the national plight. Traditionally, therefore, the *grauw* (an altogether more expressive term of abuse than rabble or *canaille*) of the towns of Holland, Zeeland, and Utrecht were feared by men of property as the volatile auxiliaries of Orangist power. But their spasmodic violence was by no means entirely empty of social implications. It was hardly fortuitous that in 1747, at a time of high taxation and severe material want, the chief bêtes-noires of the rioters who besieged the town halls in Veere and Middelburg in Zeeland and plundered warehouses in Leiden, Haarlem and Amsterdam, should have been the reviled excise men and tax farmers—the "bloodsuckers and carrion" (*kraaiers en verklik-*

kers) of popular jargon. As in comparable manifestations of popular indignation elsewhere (the communal insurrection in Genoa in 1746, the Madrid bread riots of 1766, or the Wilkeite disturbances of the same decade), there was no express intention among the poorer elements of the crowds to assert anything like an independent political identity. On the contrary they were, as they supposed, acting as the instruments of an older and more pristine patriotic morality. The Zeeland fisherfolk who ransacked magistrates' houses and attacked excise men in Veere and Goes professed to believe, as they had been bidden by their Calvinist zealot predikants, that in the Stadholder God had appointed a lieutenant who would smite the foe without and chastise the oppressor within. In this sense the hue and cry of "Oranje Boven" ("Up Orange") had as much, and as little, political content as "Vive le Parlement" or "No Popery." These primitive reactions would remain basically unaltered in the "tumults" of 1784–85 and the "plunder years" of 1787 and 1788.

In the political context, though, what is important is not the unchanging patterns of violent behaviour but the reactions to them of the "middling sort" (*brede middenstand*) in the immediately superior social stratum. In 1748–49, as later in the Patriot and Batavian revolutions, there are, for the first time, indications that it could no longer be assumed that fear of the *grauw* entailed defence of those on whom their fury was being vented. As economic stringencies pressed harder, the attitude of the smaller burgher— the shopkeeper, guildsman or artisan—towards the periwigged oligarchs became decidedly more ambivalent. It would, of course, be grossly unhistorical to see in those disturbances anything remotely like the budding of an "alliance" of the disfranchised commons. But if it remained a truism to accuse Orange agents of lubricating the thirsts of the city poor the better to urge them on against the regent notables, it was as common for the periodical press to accuse the patriciate of a nepotism and venality so flagrant that it could not but contribute to the degeneration of "welfare and order" and even depress the honest citizenry to the level of the mobs they loathed and feared. In so indirect a manner, then, the depredations of the poor could be linked in unholy conspiracy with the corruption of the rich. The Free Corps militia which would be in the van of the Patriot revolution, like the French National Guard, would as a result turn its fire on the poor while using the suppression or containment of that disorder as a lever to force the powerful from office. However implausible, there was evidently some literal belief in the collusion of the wealthy and the indigent—akin to the alarms about brigands in the pay of "aristos" or spies planted in the prisons to promote sedition which excited pathological neurosis in revolutionary France. In the Netherlands nothing so sinister was supposed to be in the offing; but by the 1780's it was not unusual to read an allegation that regent and Orangist, ostensibly at loggerheads, might actually both be conniving to perpetuate hardships from which they, rather than the generality of the people, profited.

In the "Spectatorial" press, the callous sumptuousness of the patriciate was contrasted invidiously with the antique asceticism of republican virtue.

Offices held in trust for the people, it was said, were now abused for pecuniary gain, family promotion, or personal power. Attacks on corruption were, of course, a standard feature of opposition politics in the eighteenth century; but in the United Provinces, the vices of *kuiperij* (literally, "cooperage," but best rendered perhaps as "graft" or "wheeling and dealing") were particularly associated with the decline in national fortune. The members of the Friday Club in Amsterdam, and the editor of *De Denker* (*The Thinker*) Abraham van der Meersch, were especially scathing in their criticism of the falling off of standards in public life. In other similarly vulnerable republics—Venice, Geneva and Genoa—ruling oligarchies were periodically subject to popular harangue or worse for failing to supply adequate defence for the state. And in the Dutch Republic, such failure was associated with a form of grand national peculation—an abrogation of the ethos of heroic republicanism. The blatant disparity between the conventions of national history, of patriotic austerity and sacrifice, and the ornamental nature of much office-holding was bound to supply kindling for those self-appointed tribunes impatient to spark off a new rebellion.

The fact that a Venetian, Andrea Tron, could console his correspondents at home with the observation that "this [the Dutch] republic is, beyond all comparison, worse governed than ours" was in itself an unnervingly damning indictment of how far matters had gone.[66] Yet, by eighteenth-century standards—not, it is true, the most unsullied—the conduct of the Dutch regents was not outrageously scandalous. The corruption of local government in the towns and provinces only appeared lurid when set against the often mythic hagiographies of titans of republican virtue like Oldenbarneveld and the de Witts. In fact office had always been bought, sold and inherited as commodity rather than bestowed as duty. The Council of State and the Receiver-General of the Union had recognised common practice as a necessary evil, and in characteristically Dutch fashion had turned it to public profit by imposing a tax on the traffic. That *ambtgeld* brought a not inconsiderable sum into the treasury of the province of Holland and was abolished only in 1800. In the 1670's William III had secured a loan for Austria by promising offices to prospective subscribers, and it became quite common to reward foreign immigrants, mostly German, with minor offices in the provincial and urban administrations.[67]

As in other European states, large and small, venal office did not necessarily make for incompetent government. Aside from the hated tax farms or the coveted postmasterships there were relatively few sinecures, even in so bloated a metropolis as Amsterdam, from which a fat killing could be guaranteed. The rich paid (either directly or, through matrimonial alliance, indirectly) for an office as town clerk or militia captain in order to qualify for the inner sanctum of the regency. Status rather than fortune was the object of the exercise, though naturally the two frequently went hand in hand. It is true that as the habits of conspicuous consumption among the regents grew more ornate, and the cost of sustaining a regent life style more expensive, the temptation to exploit inherited or transferred offices as exhaustively as possible became correspondingly greater. Often the most rigorous fleecers were *plaats-vervangers* (deputies), who performed the actual function of the office for its titular holder and took as their fee a cut of the perquisites. Others preferred to manage the more commercial posts themselves. The Amsterdam regent Jacob Bicker Raye, who was among other things inspector in chief of the Great Fishmarket, was all the more fervent a supporter of that trade for taking 2½ per cent of all sales—a sum which came to around 500 guilders a month in the 1750's, a handy though scarcely exorbitant bonus.[68]

The "problem," then, of office-holding in the eighteenth-century Dutch Republic was not its intrinsic amorality, for in this respect there is no reason to suppose it was any worse than comparable pockets of venality in England or France. Rather, it was the embarrassment of having to live up to an assiduously cultivated image of public piety and altruism which stared down from every sombre seventeenth-century group portrait of orphanage masters or old age home deacons, and which those outside the charmed circle of the regents were eager to reinstate as the criterion for legitimate authority. It did not help, of course, that those offices most closely connected with the superintendence of the needy were, as the least lucrative, often awarded to cadet recruits, who in their turn regarded them as staging posts to grander styles and grosser pickings. In Gouda, for example, the regent-son van der Hoeve, on succeeding at his father's death to his place in the regency, was immediately presented with the posts of Master and Regent of the Hospice of St. Catherine and the same office at the town's Home for Aged Women (*Oudenvrouwenhuys*).[69] Complaints in the press that absentees, widows and most commonly infant children had been awarded such posts to ensure they remained within a certain family were legion, but then so they had been in the previous century. Their descendants were no more insensitive to the miseries of the poor because they presided over their hostelries in wigs and ribbons rather than linen and lace.

In fact, the decades after 1740 were a time for the foundation of the first public municipal (that is to say non-denominational) poor houses in the better-endowed towns of Holland such as Rotterdam, Amsterdam and The Hague. It was only in the 1790's, as we shall see, that the armies of the poor, freshly mobilised by the war, began to drain off the funds and endowments intended for their upkeep at a much faster rate than they could be replenished. The result was that it became in the end almost impossible to maintain the most elementary functions of municipal government—the preservation of civil peace; the support of religious and philanthropic institutions; and the collection of local taxes—in the leisurely manner decreed by custom. Those unfortunate men, the burgemeesters of the Kingdom of Holland, faced the transformation overnight of an essentially medieval structure of administration into a paternalist bureaucracy—a task which, given the resources of the time, was well beyond their means. Successive ministers of the interior were besieged with begging letters from impecunious officials imploring the national government to help support the burden of relief hitherto born exclusively by private or religious foundations. In 1780, the earliest symptoms of that distress were hardly perceptible. For the most part it was assumed that the duties and dignities of civic office were much as they had always been: the marginal regulation of an inherently tidy society. Even when ordinary local revenues were demonstrably unequal to day-to-day commitments, that predicament in no way invalidated the deep-seated attachment to communal autonomy. And those parochial allegiances, fortified rather than loosened by the revolutions of the 1780's and 1790's, were to prove the most formidable obstacle to well-meaning designs to reform Dutch government root and branch.

It is ironic that as a favourite theme in the litany of criticism of Dutch society, the degree of its venality was surpassed only by complaints of denial to access to its offices. If anything, there were more grounds for the latter allegation. It is one of the hoariest truisms of Dutch history that between 1650 and 1750 the urban oligarchies succeeded in restricting membership of the regencies to an ever-narrowing group of families. Much ink has been spilled, and many computer cards punched, in a strenuous effort to delineate the "aristocratisation" process with some precision.[70] But to date, its findings have done surprisingly little to alter the traditional picture. The indispensable directory of regent careers in Amsterdam compiled by the great genealogist J. E. Elias makes it clear that between 1698 and 1748 just forty regents monopolised the senior offices of the city,[71] intermarrying, inter-contracting, and inter-bartering daughters, posts and chattels with almost masonic exclusiveness. The familiar clans of Hoofts, Trips, Bickers and Dedels constituted at this time the very archetype of an effectively enclosed élite. Outside the metropolis there were less illustrious but no less absolute monopolies. In the North Holland town of Hoorn, the Breedhoff family reigned supreme over the handsomely profitable postmastership as well as the principal magistracies for three uninterrupted generations. Likewise, the Fagel family succeeded in retaining its hold on the office of Greffier to the States-General (a post whose pivotal diplomatic importance was belied by the humdrum title of, literally, "Clerk") virtually from the foundation to the liquidation of the Republic. Even in the towns of the land provinces (the preserve of the landed *Jonkheer* nobility), nepotism was a standard feature of administration. In Zutphen, for example, in 1747 six of the twelve city aldermen belonged to the same albeit extended family.[72] Hereditary succession to nominally appointative posts had become an almost unchallenged rule. When no adult male heirs were apparent, rights of nomination automatically passed to the widow or even minors open to "persuasion" by their relatives.

The techniques for the distribution of offices underwent some refinement during the heyday of this official engrossment early in the eighteenth century. Arrangements known as "contracts of correspondence" provided formal, though covert, agreement between friends, matrimonially linked families, or occasionally regent acquaintances in different towns; these enabled the participants to give reciprocal assistance in promotion and co-option to sought-after offices as and when they became available.[73] Ostensibly, the purpose of the "contracts" was to minimise the friction involved in competing for the most prestigious posts (and the feuding in Amsterdam between rival dynasties had occasionally verged on vendetta). But by the middle of the eighteenth century, the agreements merely reinforced the hereditary claims of a family to a particular post. Such regulatory precautions could be extraordinarily elaborate. Secret agreements in Dordrecht, for example, protected the interests of co-contractors in case of untimely resignation or death without apparent succession—a form of group insurance for the regency, in fact. In cases where disputes were unavoidable, the seniority rule applied. In Amsterdam, regular meetings of the ten most senior regents at the house of the burgemeester constituted an inner cabal within the municipality.

It was also recognised that if any concession at all was to be made to the euphemism of "civil peace," it was judicious to leave some gleanings for those outside the regencies. Middelburg in Zeeland, for example, drew up a comprehensive tariff of offices from their "Commissioned Delegate" to the assembly of the States of Zeeland, down to the "Superintendent of the Fishmarket" and the "Warden of the Butter Barges." That catalogue was further subdivided into four headings: those appointed at the pleasure of the councillors; posts purchasable or auctionable on the open market; those available for regent purchase only; and finally, those transmitted exclusively by bequest and inheritance.[74] To give some notion of the patronage disposable under the first category, over 150 jobs as city bargees and 400 as petty-brokers were in the gift of the burgemeesters of Amsterdam. Postmasterships were especially lucrative and exclusively colonised by the regent élite and their families. Those in Amsterdam—where the revenue was of the order of fl.160–170,000 a year in the early eighteenth century—yielded an income of between fl.16–30,000.[75]

It does not necessarily follow from this enclosure of office that the development of radical politics in the 1780's was the work of frustrated men denied admission to the ruling élite. There is little doubt that in some individual instances real or imagined slights did act as a spur to their indignation. But from what recent research has to tell us, it seems that the tempo of political dispute accelerated at the same time as personnel within the regencies began to shift.[76] Vertical social mobility between 1747 and 1795 seems to have been more, rather than less, pronounced; but as in eighteenth-century France, this was by no means inconsistent with a sharpened demand for reform. For two factors governed the penetration of the old-established élites by new families: money and power.

With the highly mutable money market in Amsterdam destroying some fortunes and making others, it was natural that those plutocrats who survived the crashes of 1763 and 1773 should be accorded a status befitting their often fabulous riches. Whatever their misgivings, relatively straitened circumstances did not allow the Hoofts and Bickers to demur when considering tycoons of the likes of Willem Willink or Theodor de Smeth either as prospective colleagues or matrimonial relations. Likewise, the more combative political atmosphere in the Republic from the late 1770's onwards meant that the supporters of the Stadholder tried to reinforce their preponderance by entrenching themselves in key offices in many of the towns, especially in regions of marginal or divided allegiance like Zeeland and Friesland. But of course neither of these alterations to the old élite would be likely to placate the most trenchant critics of a system of co-option and inherited office. Still less were they reconciled to Stadholderian nomination as a suitable alternative. On the contrary, the admission of new regents on the strength of either their wealth or their partisanship (or both) was almost calculated to alienate those who endorsed neither attribute, and whose own hopes of similar promotion were so remote as to allow them, if nothing else, an outright denunciation of the whole set-up, lock, stock and cooperage.

Intimations of these discontents were first made apparent, albeit in tones of stammering reservation rather than revolutionary boldness, in the agitation of 1747–49 of those known as the "Doelisten"—a nickname taken from the place of their meeting in Amsterdam, the arquebusiers' shooting range (Kloveniersdoelen).[77] Their meetings followed in the wake of the terrorised upheavals in Zeeland and Holland which, with the French overrunning the Scheldt, had brought the Friesian Prince of Orange to power with a suddenness and completeness which had taken everyone—not least the new Stadholder himself—by surprise. In his improbable person were concentrated, whether he liked it or not (and it soon became apparent that he did not), all the grievances which had built up during the decades of economic recession and ossified government by regency. Appropriately enough, the most resented of all venal offices (other than the tax farms), that of the postmasterships, were expropriated from the regents and handed to the Prince who, with lordly magnanimity, delivered them to the States. With characteristic stubbornness, and obviously conscious of its still formidable strength even as all around it were crooking the knee to bits of orange bunting, Amsterdam alone insisted on retaining the profits of its post for the municipal treasury. At the end of 1747 the demands presented to the city by one Daniel Raap, a trader in porcelain (and second-hand ideas), epitomised the admixture of corporate conservatism and popular prejudice on which the anger of these years fed. Together with an hereditary Stadholderate and offices available on the open market, Raap wanted the election of militia officers from the citizenry (a stock feature of the ideology of rebellion in the eighteenth century) and the full restoration of the regulation of the guilds, the last being a traditional response to the hardships come on the industrial centres of Holland.

The following year's dose of violence, directed principally at the tax farmers, produced in its turn the only slightly more radical assertions of the "Doelisten" of Amsterdam in August 1748. The tribunes responsible for their formulation were something of a motley troop: the broker Martini, the surgeon Boekelaar; a pattern-maker from Haarlem, van Gimnig, and a French journalist (without whom such occasions would have been, if not incomplete, then inelegant), Rousset de Missy. They proposed to the Prince that the regents, who "had lost the confidence of the people," should be summarily discharged; that a "free militia council" be elected from the burghers independently of the municipality; and that a parallel citizens' regency be appointed not by co-option but by a body of "free burgher captains" drawn from the militia of the city wards. In Rotterdam and Leiden, where riots had been fierce, similar grievances were expressed; in the latter city, "speakers" of the people, apparently supported by the underemployed textile workers, constituted their own municipal council when the incumbent regents treated their views with disdain.

The efforts of the "Doelisten" could hardly have been blessed with success. To begin with, the contradictions within the anti-regent "coalition" (if so it can be dignified) were ultimately more serious than any temporarily common interests. The leaders of the Amsterdam group bickered with the more aggressively Orangist hero of the Rotterdam populace, the pastry cook Lourens van der Meer. The Rotterdammers in fact were exceedingly reluctant to push their demands at all far and insisted that though offices should be free to the highest bidder, it was necessary that he be a practising member of the Reformed Church. As the violence in the late summer and autumn of 1748 grew more threatening, the more nervous among the petitioners naturally gravitated to the forces of social order. In Amsterdam, after an incident on Dam Square when two looters were hanged and the crowd panicked as troops fired into the air, regent officers were sworn in to the militia once again. In November the Prince's troops entered Leiden, dissolved the "rebel" council and imprisoned two of its "speakers" without more ado.

But the biggest mistake made by the "Doelisten" was to put their trust in the new Stadholder. Admittedly the House of Orange could be relied on to support any attempt to overthrow the power of the regents. It was also reasonable to assume that any such effort would require the backing of the "Eminent Head" to rally the common people to the cause. But it was ingenuous to presume that, once in the saddle, William IV would feel so grateful to those who had helped hoist him there, or that he would incline towards a delegation of his power. The mere contemplation of such a course would have been way out of character for a Prince of Orange, even in the Friesian line of Nassau-Dietz. Instead of becoming the reluctant champion of an aggrieved *burgerij*, William IV reverted to type and became a committed and not unskillful minister of reaction. His troops suppressed the risings in Leiden and Rotterdam, and when in 1749 a group of petitioners from Amsterdam asked for an audience at The Hague he had them summarily incarcerated in the Gevangenpoort prison. Of the purge of regencies hoped for by the more ambitious "Doelisten," just seventeen of the thirty-six Amsterdam regents were removed, only to be replaced by men of identical social timbre—Trips, Hasselaers, van Collens—distinguished from their predecessors only by their greater (if temporary) enthusiasm for the Orange cause. A "free militia council" was accorded—but in name only since the election of officers, at the nub of the radical demands, was discreetly overlooked. By 1751 "Achtenveertiger" ('48er) was a stigma rather than a badge of pride and the unlikely union of "Oranje en Vrijheid" (Orange and Freedom) definitively liquidated.

The settlement imposed by the Stadholder on the Republic equally reflected his wish to leave well alone. Instead of confronting the regencies of Amsterdam and the maritime provinces, he was content with the merest trimming in return for an acknowledgement of his authority as Captain- and Admiral-General and the resumption of his command over The Hague garrison. Gestures were made towards suppressing the most flagrant abuses. Contracts of correspondence were again declared null and void, but since the Prince died in 1751 they remained virtually undisturbed. In any event the practice was too interwoven with the social make-up of the regencies to be eliminated by decree. In June 1748, to draw the sting of the crowds (of whom William had uncomfortably immediate experience in Amsterdam in the autumn of that year), tax farming was abolished. But when the States of Holland were faced with the option of restoring the old excise or introducing a scaled poll tax, they not surprisingly chose the former. Too many vested interests were bound up with the excise duties for them to do otherwise. As head director of the East and West India Companies, the Stadholder was equally complacent in leaving the most obvious venalities in being. Touch one perquisite, he was warned in Amsterdam, and the whole wormy edifice might crumble. In the land provinces, the Prince restored William III's absolutist Règlement of 1672. In consequence not only the armed forces of the States and the town militias, but control over the appointments of magistrates, burgemeesters, aldermen, town councillors, sheriffs and officers of the provincial States passed into his hands. He was as nearly a King of the Dutch as any of his dynasty had been. And while the regents of Holland and Zeeland (the latter, in any case, now committed Orangists) were preserved in their privileges, a swarm of landless Jonkheers, adventurers, foreign mercenaries and courtiers descended on Utrecht, Gelderland, Groningen and Overijssel as well as the Generality Lands, and were there established as dependable agents—party men in the literal sense—of the House of Orange.[78]

The aim of the "Doelisten," then, had proved woefully off-target. Their rising was scarcely more than a semi-articulate protest at the prevailing order and was disarmed with contemptuous ease by the very forces in which they had placed their trust. Even their more radical demands, like the "free militia council" and elected officers of the burgher companies, harked back to a nostalgic mythology of communal liberties. But like so many other urban insurrections in the mid-eighteenth century—in Genoa in 1746, Madrid in 1766, Geneva in 1762 and 1782—the self-consciously historical mode of legitimating protest acted as a trigger for much bolder assertions.[79] And however fumbling in expression, the "Doelisten" marked the departure of Dutch politics from the inherited circumscription of Orangists versus regents. The volte-face of William IV contributed a great deal to this development. Not long before his death in October 1751, Willem Bentinck had warned the Stadholder that the association of the ruling House with both oligarchy and autocracy was bound, in the long run, to damage its standing with the people as a whole.

The foundation of all government is the trust reposed by the people in their governors. At the present [1749] that confidence is entirely extinguished. Complaints are universal and all the complaints fall on the Prince. . . . The nation sees that the Prince did not make proper use of the power given to him. Those persons who almost brought down the state are still in office; they and their allies are well received by the Prince, some continue in the same improper manner as in the days of the earlier anarchy.[80]

This was the lament of an unsatisfied ultra-Orangist, but it correctly pointed to the danger of a nominally omnipotent Stadholderate being held up to ridicule by both its erstwhile supporters and antagonists. As long as that absolutism was held to be in the general interests of the Republic, the Orange cause would still retain its popularity with the common people and "middling sort." But the premature demise of the Stadholder threw this primary assumption in doubt. His widow the "Gouvernante" Anna was a conscientious and reasonably capable Regent, but could hardly prevent the disparity between the office and the person of the infant William V from becoming embarrassingly glaring. Nor was she able to prevent that Stadholderian power from passing into the hands of incompetent or self-interested councillors at the same time as the regents of Holland and Amsterdam recovered their old predominance. And the "interregnum" between Anna's death in 1759 and William V's majority—followed by his manifest incapacity for government—completed the dissociation of the House of Orange from the "national interest" it had traditionally embodied.

Willem Bentinck was a bystander in this gradual degeneration of authority. While William IV was alive, Bentinck attempted to urge on him long-overdue constitutional reforms (also recommended by more dispassionate advocates of a Stadholder-protected "Fatherland Liberty" such as Elie Luzac). In particular, Bentinck proposed the adoption of a cabinet system modelled on English lines in which the Prince would preside over daily meetings of Secretaries of State, the treasurer-general of the Union and his military advisors. There would thus be something like a national administration, with the Prince occupying the place of a constitutional monarch though with rather broader powers than the Hanoverians. The government would be subdivided into ministries, each with senior officers appointed by the Prince but with their own regulations and terms of reference. All that resulted from these suggestions was a consulative "conference" meeting to discuss foreign affairs. After William's death, it is true, that body was the provincial agency in which Anna, in counsel with her closest advisors, decided affairs of state. But paradoxically, since he had originally been appointed on Bentinck's recommendation, it was the marshal Louis of Brunswick-Wolfenbüttel ("fat Louis," as Frederick the Great liked to call him) who came to fill the vacuum left by the death of one Prince and the infancy of his successor.[81]

When it came to mediating between the several interests dividing the Republic, and adopting a realistic attitude towards the Dutch incapacity to man the "barrier forts" in the south, Brunswick showed himself not entirely devoid of statesmanlike qualities. But his reputation as a foreign adventurer of rapacious self-interest was equally based on some foundation. Capitalising on his position at the centre of the court, he became the boy Prince's virtual warder. In 1766 when William attained his majority, he was persuaded to sign away much of his authority by a secret "Act of Advisorship." The act conferred plenary powers of regency on Brunswick, who in practice shared them with a triumvirate of the Greffier Fagel, the Grand Pensionary of Holland (until 1772 the astute Pieter Steyn; afterwards the much less capable Peter van Bleiswijk), and the ancient "secretaire du cabinet" de Larrey.

The regime of the Act of Advisorship sealed the fate of the Stadholderate. Instead of the institutional "regularisation" anticipated by Bentinck, there was a simultaneous regression to the hallowed sovereignty of the Holland patriciate and a resort to the most blatant forms of personal rule and political manipulation in the land provinces. Externally, the *Gouvernante* and Brunswick, guided by Steyn, followed as sensible a course as the narrowing area of manoeuvre would allow: in a word, neutrality. But the attempt to pare down expensive military commitments was in effect only postponing the day when the dispute between the priorities of augmenting the fleet or strengthening the army (upheld respectively by the maritime and the land provinces) would turn into a dangerous confrontation. And although Brunswick's decision to abandon the southern "barrier forts" was designed to reinforce the strength of the army at home, it was represented as an act of capitulation by an Austrian general. The duke was roundly pilloried in the anti-Orangist press in Amsterdam for usurping the Stadholderate and exercising a malign influence on the young prince. The memory of other foreigners who had exploited the Republic for their own advantage—Leicester, Anjou—was invoked to anathematise him. And Burgemeester Groenix of Rotterdam sombrely predicted: "I fear that the Duke will so set the nation against the Stadholderian regime that perhaps our own children may one day send him away."[82] Whatever its redeeming qualities, the government of the Republic appeared to many to be that most odious and most vulnerable of all regimes: an incompetent despotism presided over by a foreign deputy.

As William V ruefully pointed out on more than one occasion, he was not the man supplied by Providence to restore the fortunes of his dynasty and his Fatherland. Physically he was singularly unprepossessing, with pop eyes, fat lips, and a weak chin, something less than the incarnation of military virility. Like his colleague at Versailles he was subject to alternating fits of petulant obstinacy and chronic vacillation and he suffered from the unpleasant malady of spitting bile. No prince of the Ancien Régime can have had a more unanimously damning press, and few such an inauspicious upbringing. Bullied by his mother, subdued by Brunswick, and finally hectored by the wife who had been foisted on him—Princess Wilhelmina, the niece of both Frederick the Great and Louis of Brunswick—his was a classic case of inferiority complex. For over a dozen years he had been drilled by Brunswick and Fagel to believe that his only job was to sign the documents they placed in front of him (and judging from his signature he was not too good at that). Had any questions regarding the policy pursued in his name occurred to him, they would have been met by polite deflection. As a statesman-in-the-making he was deprived of elementary education. Van

Hogendorp, who was to see his son made King, commented that at the age of thirty-eight William V remained a child. In frustration and defeat he threw his hat on the floor and jumped on it.

The best that can be said for him is that he was not a lazy or an unkind man (deposed rulers, indeed, always seem to suffer from misguided hyper-activity). He rose at six and retired often as late as midnight, in between which he crammed lengthy prayers, two audiences, light meals, formal court appearances, and military conferences and reviews. But he remained con-vinced, correctly, that he was basically unequipped to carry out any serious public responsibility. Repressed by the duke, all the cajoling of Princess Wilhelmina was unable to bring him to act with firmness and conviction. Instead, he treated ministers and ambassadors to rambling, incoherent dis-courses on matters of the moment which invariably petered out without any proper conclusion, the Prince usually adopting the view of the last person to speak. Even his military training, he once confessed, fitted him for no higher rank than a corporal. At the most critical moment of his career, he exclaimed that he wished his father had never become Stadholder and that he himself were dead.[83]

The gathering obloquy surrounding the court and the duke gave their opponents among the Amsterdam and Holland patriciate an ideal oppor-tunity to project themselves once more as the authentic guardians of the republican tradition, the lineal descendants of Oldenbarneveld and the de Witts. Indeed, the mangled corpses of the brother-Pensionaries became the object of a fierce polemical tug of war in 1757, in which each of the opposing parties offered rival accounts of present politics dressed up as past history.[84] The regent case was mightily reinforced by the appearance of Jan Wagenaar's massive tomes in the 1750's and 1760's; but it was only in the following decade, with the Republic's neutrality under increasing pressure from both British and French, that the old dogfight took on a new sharpness. Contro-versy again centred on the belated renovation of its armed forces. Bruns-wick had pressed hard for a substantial augmentation of the army, then falling below 30,000, and for the major part consisting of German and other mercenaries. In 1778 Sir Joseph Yorke, the British ambassador, whose inter-est was naturally also in favour of stiffening the anti-French barrier, com-plained:

It is not easy to get recruits for this [Dutch] service, which is too ill-paid and cannot subsist without half being absent on furlough the greater part of the year. . . . The delay in granting furloughs this summer on account of the precarious situation in Europe has already occasioned a desertion which is computed to amount to nearly a quarter of the army.[85]

With the so-called "Scots" regiment recalled by the British to serve in North America in 1775, Brunswick wanted at least 10,000 more troops to make up a sufficient complement. But the States-General, once more dom-inated by Holland's (or Amsterdam's) purse-strings, even if by land province votes, refused to finance what they took to be the blunt instrument of Anglo-

Orangist interests. The maritime provinces were adamant that priority should rather be given to reinforcing the convoys protecting merchantmen in the Atlantic from harassment by British privateers. The regular naval forces, moreover, were in as parlous condition as the army. During the eighteenth century their dockyards and harbours had silted up badly—at its deepest Flushing, for example, drew only 28 feet. At the other end of the Republic the same problem had made the Zuider Zee almost unnavigable at some tides, and even on the Texel large vessels were in frequent danger of running aground. The shores were virtually bereft of adequate batteries; and in 1778 the newest of the Republic's ships-of-the-line was twenty-five years old. Should the two countries ever come to blows, the British outnumbered the Dutch in heavy warships by nearly three to one.

Despite these glaring deficiencies, political polarisation and financial stringency contrived to produce a debilitating stalemate in which almost nothing was done about either army or navy. Hostility to supporting a reinforced army in peacetime—"that costly and expensive bauble," one contemporary commented—was still insuperable in Holland. Memories in Amsterdam went back to 1650, when William II had tried to impose an army on the city by force. And when van Bleiswijk proposed that the province foot half the bill for a new military appropriation, he was turned down flat. So far from acceding to that, the States of Holland recommended a revision in the distribution of fiscal liability—the "Quota"—so as to reduce the 60 per cent of its own portion. Rarely had the inherited governing institutions of the Dutch Republic, once the marvel of Europe, seemed so unequal to the most elementary demands of the country's security. Of course the Pensionaries and regents could hardly be taxed for being unaware how penalised they would be for the years of inertia and factiousness. But the Republic went stumbling into a calamitous war with the British as a state doubly infirm from military incapacity and political feud.

The American Imbroglio

Historians have conventionally located the emergence of Patriot politics in the Fourth Anglo-Dutch War (1780–84) and its immediate aftermath. No doubt that judgement is sound. The pathetic incapacity of William V to act in the manner of his forbears as a true Captain- and Admiral-General, and the inglorious course of the war, only served to parody still further the existence of an omnipotent Stadholderate. Equally, the heroic but pointless battle at Dogger Bank, where Zoutman and van Kinsbergen aroused only faint memories of Tromp and de Ruyter, was overshadowed by the ignominious fiasco of the Brest expedition, when the fleet sent to rendezvous with the French and combine against the British failed to reach its destination and returned in shame and confusion to the Texel. William, for whom war with Britain was tantamout to unnatural practice, was of course suspected of conducting hostilities with at best half a heart and of deliberately blocking naval reinforcement. Amidst the general recrimination for lost

ships, colonies, and money, Brunswick was finally prised out of The Hague and sent to 's Hertogenbosch as Governor, but not before the standing of the Stadholder as a credible Captain-in-Chief had been damaged beyond repair. Yet although the tragi-comedy of the war exacerbated the deepening bitterness between the Orangists and their opponents, it was the American cause more specifically which catalysed the division of the country into two hostile camps.

The support given by Amsterdam to the American rebels seemed to be dictated by economic rationality. It was supposed by a number of the doyens of the economic societies which had grown up in the seventies that the severance of ties between Britain and her colonies would give the Dutch a golden opportunity to recapture a lost market and re-entrench Amsterdam as the major entrepôt of trade between Europe and America. Dutch entrepreneurs were prepared to provide credit necessary for financing a trade which began with very small cargoes out (Leiden cloth, Schiedam gin, Haarlem haberdashery) and larger ladings back (sugar, rice, indigo, coffee, cotton and rum). Ever since the Seven Years' War, the Dutch had been involved in much of the contraband trade between the French and their own Antilles and the North American colonies. St. Eustatius was notorious as a centre for gun running, and at least one entrepreneur, Georges Grand, made a fortune out of the high risks. Other Amsterdammers had bought freely on the land market, up the Ohio and Susquehanna, making sharp and shady killings from speculative investment.[86] But the biggest gamble of all was in American securities. When John Adams arrived in the Netherlands to sound out the possibility of both diplomatic and financial support, he came armed with a list of contacts many of whom were to play a leading part in the Patriot opposition: Nicholas and Jan van Staphorst, Jan de Neufville, the lawyer Hendrik Calkoen, the banking house of de Lalande and Fijnje, and the Pensionary of Amsterdam Engelhart van Berckel.

In 1782 a consortium of houses launched a loan of 5 million guilders at the not exorbitant rate of 5 per cent plus 4½ per cent brokerage commission, payable over fifteen years. Although it was less well subscribed than Adams had hoped, three others followed—in 1784, 1787 and 1788—which supplied in all some 9 million guilders for the prostrated American finances. Part of the attraction of this stock was, doubtless, the possibility of buying cheap and selling at a quick profit to investors less well informed than the brokers as to the state of American credit. But from a list of actual as well as potential subscribers drawn up by the Patriot leader Baron Joan Derk van der Capellen tot den Pol (who himself was marked down for 12,000 guilders), it is plain that support for the American debt was partly a political gesture as well as a financial transaction.[87]

Economic interest by itself may have been strong enough to tie Holland to America. It combined the prospect of commercial revitalisation with the hope of breaking British supremacy in the Atlantic. There was, too, an element of understandable gloating in Amsterdam over the humiliation of the British Empire at the hands of the colonists. But within the Republic there were immediate domestic repercussions. For the Americans' success gave all those in opposition to the Stadholder a chance to crow, vicariously, over their enemy's ally and patron. The emancipation of the Americans was represented as virtually a repeat performance of their own republican epic, complete with tyrannical empire, citizen militia and a taciturn hero as the "father" of the nation. Nor was Adams slow to exploit this echo of lost heroism when in his "Memorial" to the States-General seeking recognition of his credentials, he explicitly set out the affinities between the two republics:

If there was ever among nations a natural alliance, one may be formed between the two republics. The first planters of the northern states found in this country an asylum from persecution. . . . They have ever entertained and have transmitted to posterity a grateful remembrance of that protection and hospitality and especially of that religious liberty they found there having sought them in vain in England. . . . The origins of the two Republics are so much alike that the history of the one seems but a transcript of the other; so that every Dutchman instructed in the subject must pronounce the American revolution just and necessary or pass a censure upon the greatest actions of his immortal ancestors; an action which has been approved and applauded by mankind and justified by the decision of heaven. . . .[88]

America thus became not merely the agent of Britain's undoing but a reminder of the valour of the ancient Bataves. "In America, a holy sun has risen," preached the Patriot predikant François Adriaan van der Kemp, "and it will shine on us if we so will it. . . . America can teach us how to fight against the degeneration of our national character; the debasement of its soul, the corruption of its will to resist . . . how to throttle tyranny and how to restore to health the all but moribund corpse of freedom."[89] The Amsterdam lawyer Hendrik Calkoen showed such interest in the origins of American liberties over dinner with Adams that the emissary undertook to supply him with a comprehensive history—a work which became the *Thirty Questions*.

This euphoric association of the American Revolution with both the chronicled past of Dutch freedoms and their impending rebirth enlisted journalists, pamphleteers, and academics alongside brokers, merchants and regents, in invective broadsides against the Orange establishment. One of Adams' most intimate associates in Holland was Jan Luzac, the cousin of the Stadholderian Elie, and the editor of the *Nouvelles de Divers Endroits* which under its popular title *Gazette de Leyde* had won a European reputation for informed, uninhibited reporting of current affairs, especially those embarrassing to the British interest. Hardly had he arrived than Adams made it his business to provide Luzac with full reports of the constitutional debates in America. On October 3, 1780, the *Gazette de Leyde* carried the first European translation of the constitution of Massachusetts.[90] Two further editions followed in 1781, and other journalists like Marie-Antoine Cérisier, editor of the equally Francophile *Politique Hollandais*, gave the constitutional debate wide publicity. If nothing else, this broadcasting of information would have helped familiarise those at whom the Patriots later aimed their own polemics with the vocabulary of representative democracy.

The engagement of journalists like Luzac and Cérisier in the mobilisation of support for the Americans did more than merely sharpen the edge of political debate within the Republic. For by identifying America with the historical memory of the first Dutch revolt, it stigmatised the British interest not merely as anti-American but anti-Dutch. It was the logical culmination of the resentment which had been building up against Brunswick during the minority of William V, and it spilled over into war in 1780. However disastrous for the Netherlands, that war further enabled the opponents of the Stadholder to annex to themselves their Patriotic credentials. Some of the most self-conscious among them—van der Capellen, in particular—had no compunction about using American political documents to inject a more overtly libertarian strain, grounded on natural right as much as historical prescription, into Dutch political debate. Van der Capellen not only had the Declaration of Independence translated into Dutch, but ordered a copy of the democratic Massachusetts constitution, translated and dedicated to van Berckel on its front page. When a medal was struck in April 1782 to commemorate the recognition of Adams' credentials as ambassador, one side bore the inscription: *"Libera soror,"* the other: *"Tyrannis virtute repulsa."* And at a banquet in 1784 held in Amsterdam to bring together the most prominent Patriot notables and to celebrate the "Tempel der Vrijheid" (Temple of Victory), a toast was drunk, not only to the restoration of "Holland's Might" but also to the "Sovereignty of the People."[91] The American-Dutch cause became, at least in the propaganda of what was emerging as the Patriot movement, a model of republican fraternity.

The war for America and against Britain had as terminal consequences for the Dutch "Old Regime" as it did for the French. It simultaneously bankrupted the treasury and provided the "creditors" of the government—in the Netherlands not only the regents of Holland but countless humbler stockholders below them—with a much more aggressively insurrectionary language with which to verbalise their grievances. The ink was scarcely dry on the Declaration of Independence when the Pensionary of Amsterdam, van Berckel—together with his colleagues, Cornelis de Gijselaar of Dordrecht and Adriaan van Zeebergh of Haarlem—began conducting a secret diplomacy virtually independent of the Stadholderian government and the States-General. While France terminated trade with all Dutch towns, except Haarlem and Amsterdam, in reprisal for the States-General voting against "unrestricted convoy" (that is, armed protection irrespective of cargo or destination), its ambassador the duc de Vauguyon was arranging contact between the three Pensionaries and Franklin. In the same year, 1778, the Amsterdam banker Jan de Neufville met William Lee at Aachen, on van Berckel's instigation, to discuss the terms of a treaty of alliance and commerce between the two republics.

In August van Berckel wrote directly to Lee that, in the event of any permanent settlement with Britain, the United States should promise to make no treaty prejudicial to the commercial interests of the Dutch. This was all the more necessary since, in 1779, receiving no response for help from the Republic under the terms of a treaty of 1678, Britain decided to terminate her own commercial treaty of 1674—or in other words felt free to blockade, attack and eliminate Dutch shipping at will. Such action was made more likely because of the irritation allegedly caused by the Governor of St. Eustatius, de Graaf, using the island as a smuggling depot and sheltering American vessels. Echoes of the old seventeenth-century struggle for a *mare liberum*, for "Free ships, free cargoes" (*vrij schip, vrij goed*) were again heard in the States-General. "Unrestricted convoy" again became a serious issue, and the Dutch made the first manoeuvres, which ended (a few days before the opening of the war) in their joining the Armed Neutrality of the North—the first time for over a century they had joined a deliberately engineered anti-British coalition.

Even before this they were, through the calculated recklessness of the Amsterdammers, seriously compromised. John Paul Jones' squadron with the captured British prize *Serapis* appeared at the Texel, and de Neufville helped refit his ships while he used Dutch ports as a base from which to make raids on British shipping in their own waters. But the ostensibly bluff Captain Jones was a diplomatic agent. At the end of 1779, he wrote to Dr. Bancroft:

The only satisfaction I have is that in spite of the diplomats I have used my position here to strain the relations between Holland and England to a point past mending. Nothing now keeps Holland neutral except the influence of the ship owners, who are doing almost the entire commerce of Europe at enormous rates. . . . But the Dutch people are for us and the war.

After a brush with the British fleet, Jones had still more evidence to suggest the solidarity of the cause: "every day these blessed [Dutch] women came to the ships in great numbers—mothers, daughters, even little girls—bringing with them for our wounded all the numberless little comforts of Dutch homes; a tribute that came from the hearts of the people, and therefore far overlaid in effect all statecraft and all diplomacy against us."[92]

Jones was not far wide of the mark. William V was being dragged into a war against his natural ally, a war provoked by his political antagonists but for which he was unable to disclaim responsibility. Not that the British, in 1780, were particularly keen on preserving Dutch neutrality. War with the Dutch, they calculated, might yield colonial prizes to compensate for the pride wounded so deeply in America. It might also, some thought incorrectly, discredit once and for all the irresponsible opposition to the Stadholder and make him their reliable instrument.

The final rupture was easily enough contrived. Admiral van Bylandt's convoy was apprehended and taken to the Isle of Wight in custody, a direct affront to the States-General and its admiral. Even the Prince showed signs of mortification at the indignity. In September 1780 Henry Laurens, the envoy originally commissioned to follow up the Lee-Neufville negotiations, was taken off *The Mercury* on his way back to the Republic. A chest of documents he threw overboard in a not over-subtle attempt at concealment was recovered and found to contain the text of the proposed draft treaty approved by Pensionary van Berckel. Sir Joseph Yorke, the British ambassador, demanded not only a disclaimer from the Stadholder but the punishment of the man and the city which had treated with the rebels. A rather weak response from Amsterdam attempted to argue that the treaty was contingent on an American-British settlement and that Dutch interests in trade were bound to lie in the Atlantic. This was not calculated to mollify the British. And so before the end of 1780, despite a judgement on van Berckel by the High Court of Holland and William's own attempts at extrication, the two states were at war.

Two years later, John Adams' dogged diplomacy was rewarded with success. The States-General not only accepted his letters of credence but signed an alliance of arms and trade. His coup had marked another stage in the erosion of Stadholderian authority. But, albeit unwittingly, Adams had done more than this. For in his impatience to secure from the States-General a favourable response to his "Memorial," he had gone stumping round the major cities of the Republic addressing its regents and Pensionaries on behalf of the Cause. The immediate result was a vigorous campaign of public meetings and petitions in which an unequivocally pro-American position was urged on the respective provincial States. Adams had set off on his travels in January 1782; on February 26, the States of Friesland voted to accept his letters and instructed their delegates in The Hague to do likewise. By April, all the provinces save the most intransigently Orangist Zeeland had followed suit, and the conclusive vote in the States-General was taken on April 19.

That petitioning campaign was a decisive moment in the development of Patriot politics. Many of its organisers—Jan Luzac in Leiden, de Gijselaar in Dordrecht, Baron van der Capellen in Deventer—were powerful men with access to publicity in one of the most literate states in Europe. For domestic, genuinely Dutch reasons, they were coming to put their faith in some radical change in the whole nature of native political institutions. America had held up a mirror to their own Republic in which they had glimpsed an idealised image of heroic patriotism. From secret diplomacy and maritime war with the British, they passed to further action more directly reminiscent of events on the other side of the Atlantic: public meetings, petition campaigns, and agitation for a citizens' militia. The Dutch were on the point of inaugurating Europe's revolutionary generation.

✿✿✿✿✿✿✿✿✿✿

3

The Patriot Revolt,
1781–1787

The Ideological Context[1]

On the morning of September 26, 1781, copies of a document addressed *To the Netherlands People* were discovered in the streets of all the major towns of the Dutch Republic. The pamphlet was anonymous, bearing only the pseudo-imprint of "Ostend." Its content was inflammatory. It urged its readers to assemble to protest their grievances against the Stadholderian regime; to demand a free press; and to arm themselves. It was, in fact, an unadorned summons to rebellion. *Aan Het Volk van Nederland* had been distributed the previous night by the Mennonite pastor, François Adriaan van der Kemp. He had accomplished this with elaborate secrecy but his precautions were soon vindicated by the response of the authorities. The States of Holland pronounced the pamphlet subversive and forbade anyone to read it. If anything this heightened its oracular effect. Van der Kemp compared its appearance to an electric shock and although the analogy was typically extravagant it was also apt. Such was its power, he suggested, that "although I employed several individuals and thousands of guilders was offered for their discovery . . . no-one betrayed his trust."[2]

The author of this work was never identified by the government, but from a perusal of its declamatory style it might have managed a judicious guess. We are more fortunate. Items of his correspondence reveal it as the work of Baron Joan Derk van der Capellen tot den Pol. Van der Capellen has been described by his biographer as a "burgerbaron," the archetype of renegade aristrocrats, progenitor of a Mirabeau or a Kropotkin.[3] His maternal grandfather had been ejected from the municipality of Arnhem in the province of Gelderland and he had been brought up in the neighbouring province of Overijssel. He had studied jurisprudence at Utrecht, and the early part of his extraordinary career had been spent trying to win admission to the Knightly Order ("Ridderschap") of the States of Overijssel. Ironically, William V, who was to be the butt of van der Capellen's most vehement denunciations, then supported (albeit erratically) his claims against the Ridderschap's exclu-

[64]

sion, since the case could be used to assert the superiority of the Stadholderian prerogative over the order's corporate rights. As a matter of plain fact, van der Capellen lacked the native property qualifications for admission, but he liked to present himself as the "born regent" unjustly denied his birthright.

In 1771 he finally had his way. He then proceeded to use the States as a platform on which to establish his reputation as a political maverick. It was not, after all, usual for a member of that august body of the land province, much less its nobility, to endorse the cause of Amsterdam, America and the fleet. Van der Capellen had the born demagogue's nose for trouble, and exploited the issues coming thick and fast in the 1770's with characteristic élan. He flew to van Berckel's defence, raged over the recall of the Scots' regiment in 1775, and translated and publicised works with pointed relevance to the Dutch situation, in particular Andrew Fletcher's *Discourse of Government with Relation to Militia* (1698) and Richard Price's *Observations on Civil Liberty*, a work which went into eleven editions in 1776. In 1778 he engineered a *cause célèbre* by taking up the polemical cudgel on behalf of the Overijsselaars who paid "drostdiensten"—the vestigial (and commutable) dues owed as a customary perquisite to the local "kwartier" official. "Drostdiensten" could scarcely be represented as grinding the faces of the poor. The sums involved were footling and in many cases lighter than those owed by unfree peasants to their Heer (social, as distinct from public dues) to which the Baron van der Capellen was careful to make no objection. But like *mainmorte* in France, it was often the most redundant practices which could be exploited for maximum political effect. And the fact that the perquisite was inherited with the office gave van der Capellen a chance to launch a general harangue on the degeneration of government, as well as to project himself as the defender of an enslaved people against their petty tyrants.

The baron was not insincere in his advocacy of what he took to be the inalienable rights of the "People" he apostrophised so freely. Like all those who engaged in political argument in the 1770's, he burrowed away painstakingly in the archives and legal records for vindicating precedents and based his case against the "drostdiensten" partly on the fact that the States of Overijssel had themselves abolished the dues in 1631, and partly on the fact that in so doing they had acted in accordance with natural rights. He, the people's baron, was merely bringing this to light. Van der Capellen was an egotist rather than an opportunist. There was something about his obsessive, imperious character which drove him to court political infamy if not martyrdom. When the States expelled him for publishing the "libel" on the diensten, he revelled in the ostracism. He wrote to Benjamin Franklin in April 1778: "You may well imagine, Monsieur, that having, through my birth, the right to vote in the Assembly of the States, I must disdain to accept from my Equals a *permission* of which I had no need, thus I would reject such permission with contempt."[4] His motto, he added, could well be taken from Pope's *Essay on Man*:

Truths would you teach to save a sinking land.
All fear, none aid you and few understand.

Popular acclaim duly came too late for van der Capellen. Having struck the pose of the unheeded prophet who, in the words of *To the Netherlands People*, would lead the Dutch "out of bondage and make of them a free people," he took his Mosaic role over-literally by dying, in 1784, at the age of forty-three within sight of the Promised Land. But his decalogue outlived him. Reflecting all the heroic certainty of its author, it achieved a phenomenal popular success, going through three editions in a year and into immediate translation in French, German and English. As van der Capellen hoped, it succeeded in galvanising hitherto dissociated strands of opposition to the Stadholder, and in giving them a new language of common militancy. It could reasonably be regarded as the *Qu'est-ce que le Tiers État?* of the Patriot revolt. Like Sieyès' pamphlet, its effectiveness as propaganda was due to its reduction of a complicated political situation to a simple description resting on an historical account: on the one hand, the nation; on the other, absolutism and privilege.

Not that van der Capellen thought of himself as an egalitarian, still less an out-and-out revolutionary. On the contrary, he insisted over and again that he was "no friend of pure democracy."[5] What he meant by the "people" was that broad mass of petty traders, artisans, craftsmen, merchants and shopkeepers who could readily identify themselves with the term *"burgerij."* Van der Capellen was, after all, proud to admit to being a born patrician and was deeply suspicious of any appeals to the volatile mob. That he dismissed as low demagoguery worthy only of the viler forms of Orangist intimidation. But neither was he a trimmer. He referred scornfully to the "whigs" of Holland and to the regent colleges, which had been "debased into a sort of aristocracy which appoints itself instead of being annually elected by the Burghers."[6] He was only too ready to associate the landed nobility in Overijssel with the gilded plutocrats of the maritime provinces, who crawled to the Stadholder and who even if in opposition had brought the Republic to decadence and supine weakness. Both groups he anathematised as "privileged," being "aristocrats"; by his definition, both were the enemies of the burghers and thus obstacles in the way of their legitimate aspirations to restore the true self-government.

Though *To the Netherlands People* went through the usual recitation of Stadholderian usurpations—Wagenaar had been an important influence on van der Capellen—it departed from the conventional mode of "Loevesteiner" or "States Party" anti-Orangist polemics. It has often been noted that the baron did not "argue from the enlightenment of the age, of nature and reason or the social contract or human rights in the abstract."[7] The important point is not how closely he proximated to some norm of democratic ideology, but whether or not he contributed decisively to a change in the nature of political argument. And in this respect his seventy-page broadside was of seminal importance. For that matter, both contract and natural rights theories *were* embodied in the pamphlet. At one point the following passage appears:

O fellow countrymen! Arm yourselves, assemble together and take charge of the affairs of the land for these must be your affairs. This land belongs to you—the entire Netherlands people, and not solely to the Prince and his grandees, but to you the descendants of the free Batavians.[8]

The "inheritance of liberty" derived from the "free Bataves" is a stock item in eighteenth-century opposition argument; but in van der Capellen's tract it is used as a justification for representative government: "The people living in this land, its inhabitants, its citizens [burghers], rich and poor, great and humble . . . these are all its true lords and masters, who have the right to say how and through whom they are to be governed. . . ."[9] And when he reverts to the classically Dutch metaphor of a commercial company to emphasise the contractual nature of government, van der Capellen couples it with a ringing if not original declaration of natural equality:

All men are born free. Some are certainly endowed with greater intelligence, stronger will or a greater portion of wealth than others, but that gives them—the cleverer, the stronger, the richer—not the least right to rule over the duller, the weaker, the poorer. God, the Father of us all, has made mankind, without exception, to be happy and so the obligation is laid on us, so far as is possible, to make each other happy.[10]

While the tenor of van der Capellen's language was radical, it is undeniable that both he and the early Patriot agitation had by no means disengaged from many of the traditional, particularly the legal and historical, conventions of anti-Stadholderian polemics. *To the Netherlands People* bears the imprint of a studied manifesto, but it was meant in part to be a reply to a series of withering Orangist tracts written by that party's ablest propagandist, Rijklof Michael van Goens, earlier in 1781.[11] References to the calumnies circulating against van der Capellen as a "misleader of the people" occur more than once in the pamphlet.[12] Though at times the baron found collaboration with the more well-heeled regents in Amsterdam an awkward alliance of convenience, it was axiomatic that in the early stages there could be no thought of the Patriots dispensing with their help. The period between 1781 and 1784 was marked by their co-operation in making the most of the Stadholder's embarrassment during the war. As a consequence the libertarian and egalitarian invective, and the uninhibited appeals to popular sovereignty which would later be aimed as much at the patricians as the Prince, remained for the time being carefully muted by the moderate reformism of such as Jan Luzac and the sober columns of the *Gazette de Leyde*.

On another level, too, the Patriots were by no means liberated from their history. Their ideology looked forward to the *rebirth* of a primitive democracy, but their assumptions as to its content were conditioned by the endless debates on the authentic nature of the early Republic, and the respective constitutional position of Stadholder and States, towns and provinces. That their political language should betray this admixture of historical description and philosophical assertion is hardly astonishing. Exactly the same could be said of the most embattled theatres of French politics—the Parlements—in the same period.[13] And the institutional degeneration of the Dutch Republic was, moreover, a drawn-out affair. It left men clinging to the forms of "burgher government" long after its substance had rotted away. Just as misty ambitions of restoring the commercial grandeur of the Netherlands persisted after they had ceased to be economically feasible, so the peculiar liberties of provincial and municipal sovereignties, the autonomy of the guilds, and the civic virtue of the town shooters continued to condition the political thinking of the Dutch—however "irrelevant" they may have been in solving their most urgent problems. The first Dutch state was not yet dead; it was merely moribund. On its sickbed it experienced that kind of delirious nostalgia in which impending mortality merges with infantile delusion. For a very few democrats its demise would come as a merciful release, a preliminary to the birth of a new Republic; for very many more (less radical spirits), the old Republic was to be rescued from its infirmity and rejuvenated in the image of its heroic beginnings. It was not accidental that the major work of synthesis attempting (not wholly successfully) to reconcile regent and representative views on government was called *The Constitutional Restoration of the Dutch State (Grondwettige Herstelling van Neerlands Staatswezen)*.[14]

It may be accepted, then, that Patriot ideology was a mélange of old and new attitudes towards the Dutch constitution. If I am more concerned here with the new, it is not because they necessarily played a more significant role in the upheavals of 1781–87, but rather because the more self-evidently modern language linked the "first" (Patriot) phase of the Dutch revolution with the second (Batavian) phase in something like a genuine continuity of ideas and practice. By the time the Patriot revolt had reached its climax in 1786–87, the two strands of argument had become sufficiently distinct for their irreconcilability to be apparent. And it was their conflict which has been identified by Dr. de Wit as the leitmotif of Dutch politics over the next half century and which he has called the "struggle between aristocracy and democracy." Less controversially it might be rendered as the antithesis between the first and second Dutch states.

It is an extraordinary reflection of the parochialism of Dutch political preoccupations that, while responsible for printing so many of the major works of the French enlightenment, the influence of its *philosophes* on their debates seems to have passed them by. The prohibition by the States of Holland of Rousseau's *Contrat Social* when it first appeared in Amsterdam in 1762 seems to have been gratuitous, since his works caught the public interest far more for their educational and sentimental content than for any political or philosophical argument.[15] An inferior work like Marmontel's *Bélisaire* (1767) was much more likely to attract controversial attention for impinging on an issue—in this case toleration—on which feeling in the Republic already ran high, with champions of orthodoxy and free thought ranging to do battle over Socrates' credentials for salvation.[16] In common with much of northern Europe, educated Dutch reading tastes, when they were not plunged into antiquarian disputes on the origin and development of their constitution, seem to have inclined more to the German *Aufklärung*, in particular to the work of Christian von Wolff and his disciples, and to the Anglo-Scottish philosophies of Hume, Locke, Hutcheson, Price and Priestley, than to the French *philosophes*. It says little for the discrimination of his printers that Voltaire was favoured in the Netherlands principally for his poetic drama! As a review in the journal *De Rhapsodist* had it: "In poesia magnus; in historia parvus; in philosophiae minimus; in religio nihil."[17]

The glut of works dealing with the national past and the relative paucity of those arguing from first principles means that wherever the more abrasively radical language adopted by the boldest Patriots originated, it was not from the central debates of the French enlightenment. And this obstinate nativism makes it all the more awkward to slot Patriot politics into the niche supplied by an international "democratic revolution." In the same context, the role played by religious and moral doctrine as a medium for the legitimation of political views was very particular to the Netherlands. It is illuminating that Diderot believed the Dutch to be a poor prospect for the diffusion of enlightenment just *because* they remained incorrigibly "superstitieux."[18] Certainly it was true that much intellectual debate in the eighteenth-century Netherlands was surrounded by a dense fog of piety.

Within the conventions of religious dispute, there was still lively enough contention. The yoking of Wolffian rationalism to the Arminian and Remonstrant traditions of heterodoxy produced in the Dutch version of "natural religion" a more aggressive attitude towards toleration and the pluralism of Christian belief. And it was from this peculiarly Dutch amalgam of natural-rights reasoning and popular evangelism that Patriot ideology drew its strong moral ethos. As in France, the most exposed outpost of the old regime, the established Church, drew heavy fire at the same time as the chief executive came under attack. The partnership of the Reformed Church with the House of Orange, sealed in the Synod of Dort in 1618, meant that the sins of the ruling dynasty were visited on its priests. In the middle of the eighteenth century, their ignorance and worldliness as well as their intolerance of dissent once again became the target of critical journalism and university treatises, especially in Holland where the rule of orthodoxy had in fact been least absolute. Just as the principal critics of Marmontel, the predikants Barueth and Hofstede, were trenchant partisans of the Stadholder, so the regent Professor Petrus Burmann and his circle at Santhorst rallying beneath the banner of "Freedom, Piety, Friendship and Toleration" became involved in political opposition. When Dr. Priestley's *Corruption of the Christian Religion* appeared in 1784 it was immediately translated into Dutch and enjoyed wide popularity. F. A. van der Marck, a German jurist and theologian, professed disciple of Wolff, was appointed to the Chair of Public Laws at Groningen by the Gouvernante Anna and for a while enjoyed some immunity for his attacks on established religion. But in 1773 he was finally removed, only to be brought back by van der Capellen ten years later to Deventer. In return, van der Marck obliged the baron by producing a Christian justification for rebellion (though there were, of course such warrants available in Dutch history itself). "The Creator of Nature," van der Marck observed, "has established absolute equality and perfect liberty for mankind, and has ordained that whosoever violates these rights is in a state of sedition with God's lawful society. . . . Every man is obliged to defend these rights against their oppressors."[19]

A critique which had begun with rationalist strictures on toleration was thus, by the 1780's, embracing the doctrine of natural equality without any apparent embarrassment. While the earlier version had appealed to the relatively limited circle of theological disputants and traditional antagonists of Orangism—lawyers, regents, academics, journalists and dissenting predikants —the later evangel was, like van der Capellen's more pungent diatribes, evidently intended for popular consumption. Its revivalist tone was more in keeping with the political sermonising of the previous century, preached at congregations of the *burgerij*, than salon discourse. Exhortative rhetoric had traditionally been an accepted vehicle of political argument in the Netherlands, but like all the major debates concerning the condition of the Republic had relapsed into stereotyped shibboleths during the mid-century hiatus. As that relatively docile period of political calm came to an end in the 1770's, tract readings, sermons and moralising journalism once more became an important means of mobilising the views of the disfranchised. Like the similarly well-rehearsed debates on the Union of Utrecht, the reiteration of the theme of spiritual revival embodied subversive ideas within a conventional Christian framework of expression. The appeal to a purer past sounded an insurrectionary tocsin in a land where the frailties of the elect conferred political disgrace.

Pieter Paulus, a young Pensionary of Rotterdam (later the Patriot director of the Admiralty of the Maas, and later still the first President of the National Assembly of the Batavian Republic), is a perfect sounding board for the testing of political vocabulary. In 1772 when just eighteen, he had taken the opportunity of the birth of a Crown Prince to publish *On the Duty of the Stadholderian Government* (*Het Nut der Stadhouderlijke Regering*), a work which while defending the House of Orange against its historical critics, called on the Prince to introduce necessary and timely reforms in government.[20] Just three years later, his *Elucidation of the Union of Utrecht* represented a perfect ideological somersault since it saw in that "ancient constitution" the consummation of governmental equilibrium and a protection *against* Stadholderian usurpation. Having gone through both Orangist and anti-Orangist phases, it was only to be predicted that Paulus, in 1793, would join a debate, obviously refreshed by events in France, on the "Rights of Man." His work on the Union of Utrecht had been subject to violent tirades by Barueth and the orthodox predikants, and when Paulus came to publish his tract *On the Equality of Mankind* (*Verhandeling over de vraag: In Welken zin kunnen de Menschen worden Gelijk tezijn*), he took some pleasure in extending the primitive doctrine of Christian equality to its most extreme conclusion.[21] Jesus, promoted to be the "the best of men and citizens," was shown to have preached that "the only natural society was a society of liberty and equality," and to have reminded men that one of their greatest gifts from God was their "total independence" or free will.

Paulus' text for the democratic gospel of fraternal love was not the *Contrat Social* but "He who will my Father serve shall be my brother." Only in a true society of fellow citizens (*burgermaatschappij*), where the sacred rights of free speech, assembly, worship and people in arms were properly recognised and guaranteed, could the teachings of Christ be made effective. Paulus' tract has been called "Jacobinism in Christian dress," and no doubt it owed something to the moral sobriety of French republican rectitude. But like other flatly democratic treatises notable not only for their egalitarianism but also for their discarding of the clichés of historical prescription,[22] its roots were firmly planted in the revivalist enthusiasms of radical Patriot politics. It was the culmination of a whole scripture of Christian democracy in which Jesus was described as the "architect of eternal civil rights"; alongside him, Paulus placed the national heroes Claudius Civilis, leader of the Bataves, and Brederode, for demonstrating that "Christ himself preached equality."[23] Through these summonses to the revolt of the righteous, the Stadholder and his "oppressor Church" were transformed from mere political adversaries to morally unclean things, the cohorts of anti-Christ. Van der Capellen was Moses, Joshua and David; William V was Saul, Rehoboam, Nebuchadnezzar, Belshazzar. Only the most drastic action could cleanse the Republic of this Babylonish degradation and restore to it the providential grace forfeited by the crimes of its princes and priests.

Although, in their respective generations, men such as Pastor van der Kemp and Paulus recognised that a specifically Christian version of revolt would be more likely to win adherents in the towns of the Republic than any more sophisticated profession of political principles, theirs was not a cynical observation. Christian rhetoric arose naturally from the culture of Dutch society and from the language of its "brede middenstand." A revolutionary de-Christianising campaign, if it had a mixed success in France,, would never have got off the ground in the Netherlands. It was the strength of both the Patriot and Batavian revolutions that in so far as they were ever able to mobilise popular support, it was through the absorption rather than the repudiation of popular religion. The terminology of Christian patriotic chastisement was immediately accessible to many thousands of the humbler *burgerij* whose prejudices it accurately mirrored. And more ominously, perhaps, it reinforced their alienation from the rich and powerful who, if still entrenched as their regents, had lost the aura of Godly rule.

One of the most effective instruments in the attack on social and moral decadence was the "Spectatorial" journalism of the weekly reviews. By the middle of the eighteenth century, these had gone beyond lampooning the venality and grossness of the Reformed Church and reserved their most scathing tirades for the manners of the regent classes. Their display of opulence in the midst of visible accumulating public squalor seemed all the more indecent since many of the rich derived their titles and offices from an historic commitment to the welfare of the poor. "Luxury" the "tyrantess, the oppressor of good souls," was castigated by the essayists, who lamented the loss of thrift, that most Dutch virtue, as a national fall from grace. "Money,

money, is the idol of all," complained another review. The lavish building in The Hague, Amsterdam and Rotterdam, while the dockyards decayed and the textile looms closed, seemed almost an affront to communal dignity; the exodus of young buck regents from the canals to the newer suburbs of the Harlemmerhout in search of stabling space for their coach horses, an extravagance available to the very few. The great army of domestic servants which resided in the major cities was condemned as the enslavement of a free people. *Bon ton*, the fluctuations of style, were held unbecoming to a free and sober people, fashion damned as Babylonish idolatry. The "theaterprincessen" who thronged the operas and balls, showing off their coiffeur "à l'aile de pigeon," were called little better than whores. The dire fate of all those who pandered to the lure of elegance was recorded in moral parables like *Laura or the Story of a Fashionable Young Lady* published in the *Algemeen Spectator*. No wonder that Richardson's most sentimental epics achieved a popularity in the Netherlands denied to Voltaire or Rousseau. Dutch writers like Betje Wolff and Aagje Deken laboured in much the same vein, producing in *Sara Burgerhart* their paragon of chaste, domestic virtue.[24]

Associated with excessive conspicuous consumption was the slavish pursuit of foreign modes. The *Philosooph* regretted that the national attachment to gabled roofs had been abandoned for poor imitations of the neoclassical façades of Paris. The "theaterprincessen" were scornfully referred to as "French mademoiselles," and the *Nederlandsch Spectator* commented that "men eat, drink, even sniff [snuff] in French."[25] The well-dressed regent would parade in an English coat, French hose, and a German wig. Ysbrand van Hamelsveld, a young predikant who was installed in van Goens' Chair of Theology at Utrecht by the Patriots and who was later a deputy to the Batavian National Assembly, published the most damning indictment of the debasement of national culture under the title *De Zedelijke Toestand der Nederlandsche Natie op het Einde der Achttiende Eeuw (The Moral Condition of the Dutch Nation at the End of the 18th Century)*.

Among other corruptions, van Hamelsveld deplored the sacrifice of a proficient mastery of the native language to the fashionable acquisition of French or instruction in ornamental skills like dancing, singing and versifying. Van Hamelsveld's critique of these retrograde tendencies assumed in places an overtly chauvinist character. In his view, they represented the erosion of Christian ethics and the national character. The corruption of the language by Anglo-French aphorism; the imitation of foreign sartorial habits; the importation of luxury goods in preference to domestic produce were all part of the same process which had seduced men into abandoning their public duties and a livelihood based on thrift and industry for the false gods of luxury and speculative finance. It was no accident, he inferred, that the army had been pawned to an Austrian field marshal and the foreign policy to St. James's. Van Hamelsveld's jeremiad ended with the warning that vice and sloth would, if left unchecked, imperil the very existence of the nation: "Netherlands, Netherlands, you stand on the brink of your own destruction.

Your ruin is inevitable unless reforms which must be as swift as they are necessary can avert the fatal blow."[26]

The reforms van Hamelsveld had in mind were primarily intended to restore virtue and duty to social life: remedial measures in schools, prisons, poor houses. Like comparable reforms discussed in English dissenting circles, they did not in themselves pose any threat to the established political order. In Britain, of course, social radicalism actually served the purposes of the emerging entrepreneurial élite. Similarly, many of the reforming fellowships founded in the 1770's and 1780's like the "Hollandsche Maatschappij voor Wetenschappen" (The Holland Society for Science) at Haarlem, the "Oeconomische Tak" (The Economical Branch), and "Teyler's Genootschap" (Teyler's Fellowship) were primarily interested in social and economic correctives and "instruction in the arts," and were viewed permissively by the States of Holland. But in the charged political atmosphere of the Republic, their evangelism was less innocuous. The resolution to restore the primitive social innocence of the Republic and cleanse it of its most flagrant public inequities was inevitably an accusation against the existing authorities of dereliction of duty. And campaigns on behalf of the poor were indivisible from the wider political purposes of the Patriots. Liberty was a prerequisite of the restoration of civil rights, or, as van Hamelsveld put it, "The free Republican shares his interest along with the general welfare."[27] Its opposite —self-interest—had been erected into a system of government by the regent oligarchies: "When a few patricians are carried away by their lust for power and begin to oppress their fellow citizens, then are opened the many ways to destruction which will deluge the commonwealth as surely as the flood."[28] In other words, the money-changers who were to be driven from the "Tempel der Vrijheid" (Temple of Liberty) were the gentlemen of the *grachten*. Only when this was accomplished would "justice and equality prevail and men of all ranks . . . (freely) practise their professions and perform their duties."

An attack on manners, then, became linked with the authorisation for government. Those who prostituted the virtue of Dutch life were the traffickers in office; the thieves of liberty. The Christian revivalists, like the Yorkshire squires of the parliamentary reform movement in England, urged their congregations to seize back the liberties usurped by borough-mongers and placemen. Their addresses, pamphlets and sermons, emphasising forsworn oaths, religious monopoly, court favouritism and foreign influence; their insistence on the restoration of social good works is still more reminiscent of seventeenth-century English (or New English) puritanism. But all such analogies are inevitably contrived. The style is ineffably Dutch, drawing on a deep well of popular memory and reverence. The Patriot burgher leaders were convinced that they were the true custodians of a national virtue which had been debased by those to whom office had been granted on trust and who had abused that mandate over the generations. They were told that this was at the root of their hardships. The "people" were suffering for the selfish iniquities of the few, and as a consequence the providential dispensation which had blessed the just war against Spain had been withdrawn. Only the overthrow of the guilty would redeem their misfortune. Once Liberty was again seated in her throne, the Dutch returned to the true republican covenant and the rights of the people reclaimed, prosperity and honour would return to the Netherlands.

The doctrine of Christian sociability was in the vanguard of the Dutch revolution. Unlike other regions of Europe, where a democratic ideology was restricted to a diminutive cosmopolitan intelligentsia, in the Netherlands it arose from, and was deeply coloured by, national conditions and the experience of a wider section of the population. Any account which glosses over this consideration will probably underestimate the difficulty with which the Dutch revolution can be fitted into a generalised "democratic" upheaval in the West, much less into a galaxy of petty satellites organised around the interests of the Quai d'Orsay. The Dutch revolution in the 1780's and the 1790's was simultaneously a movement for moral and national revival. It was ironic that Groen van Prinsterer, the arch-Calvinist historian, should, like the abbé Barruel, suppose that revolution is by definition the work of the godless. The truth of the matter in the Netherlands was exactly the reverse. Even the language of its politics was saturated in deep religious conviction, *especially* when directed against the clerical establishment. The paradox of this creed, at once morally intense and politically subversive, is startlingly illustrated by a document which Groen would have undoubtedly condemned as blasphemous. It was, however, devised in all sincerity as a "Patriot catechism" and it was called the *Instruction in the Pure Sentiments of True Netherlanders*. It began thus:

Q: How do you read these articles?
A: I believe in their High Mightinesses, the Heeren States of Holland and West Friesland, the only true governors of this land.
    And the Jonkheer van der Capellen, the true Son of Liberty, conceived from the spirit of the Patriots, born to the Virgin of Freedom; by Prince William wounded, died and buried and on the Third Day risen to a Heavenly Glory, whereon he now sits at the Right Hand of the Fathers of the Nation.[29]

Revolutionary immortality began early in Holland—but it was no more than an intensely sentimental response to the more measured appeal of van der Kemp "to live as Christians, and deal in everything as peaceful burghers, likewise as free people; respect your sovereign dutifully and pray for him. Defend your rights, imbue in your children from their earliest childhood the unquenchable thirst for liberty and independence."[30]

The Character of Patriot Politics

THE LAND PROVINCES

Possibly the most important fact about the Patriot agitation is that it set out to recruit sections of Dutch society for whom active participation in their own government was no more than a memory. Its Christian rhetoric and commonplace pamphlet histories were ideally suited to exploit the contrast between the popular version of the founding of national liberties and their contemporary atrophy. The redress of this grievance eventually became the principal article in the Patriot canon. But even in the early 1780's, the proselytising of the burghers set the Patriots apart from the caucus anti-Orangism of the Holland "whigs."

The expansion of the anti-Stadholderian constituency by the Patriots was geographical as well as social. In contrast to earlier attacks on Orange—and even the "Doelisten" of 1748—the Patriot campaign was not monopolised by the maritime provinces. In fact, the maritime provinces at this time were more than usually divided. Zeeland, where the leading Pensionaries were in conflict with Holland over the administration of the East India Company, was becoming better disposed towards the Prince. Friesland was currently a battlefield for the warring parties of landed nobility and urban patriciate, each seeking to buy up the land which conferred votes for the prized *grietenijen*: the district divisions which controlled representation to the States.[31] Even in Holland itself, opposition to the Stadholder was no longer monolithic. Parties owing favour to Stadholderian favour in towns like Delft and Rotterdam often prevented their coming to the assistance of Amsterdam in States assembly votes. The land provinces were certainly no less factious in their allegiances, but these indications of political life were in themselves remarkable. Provinces which in 1672–74 and again in 1748 had had to submit to the Stadholderian "Règlement" as the price of rescue from the French, had for decades been no more than the pliant instrument of the Orange hegemony. Under the Règlement the Prince acted not only as military commander, president of the orders of nobility (themselves heavily represented in the States), but as dispenser of all magistracies and municipal and judicial offices. Yet in the 1780's, Overijssel actually took the initiative in attacking the misdemeanours of the Stadholder and Brunswick; Utrecht became the cockpit of democratic politics; and two tiny hamlets in Gelderland were brazen enough in their condemnation of William V to provoke the first resort to military subjugation.

Some qualifications must be added to any over-simple impression that the land provinces rose in rebellion against their political enslavement. The disaffected parties *within* the land provinces were located, as it were, at the secondary level of authority. The assemblies of the States of Gelderland and Utrecht remained loyal to the Stadholder throughout the conflict, even when the latter body was ejected from the *city* of Utrecht by the Patriots. Patriot support was confined to dissident urban centres, under-represented in the States and resenting their complete submission to Stadholderian appointments: centres like Deventer, Zwolle and Kampen—the Overijssel triarchy; the city of Utrecht and its immediate hinterland; and the twin cities of Arnhem and Zutphen in Gelderland. In some cases the Patriots were unable to count on the support of all the towns in these provinces. When the Orangist rump of the purged States of Utrecht removed itself from the city, it found a safe refuge in Amersfoort, barely 30 miles away. And despite the presence of a substantial disaffected Catholic population, the Patriots in Nijmegen, by far the biggest town in Gelderland, were unable to dislodge the Orange Party from their control of the Stadholderian garrison stronghold.[32]

With these qualifications in mind, it is nevertheless apparent that the Patriot revolt was deeply coloured by the political situation obtaining in the land provinces. It was these conditions which partly distinguish Patriot from "Loevesteiner" politics, and which inhibited their assimilation within the Holland-orientated background of States-party opposition.

These distinctions are too often overlooked by foreign historians, who tend to equate (even in name) the Dutch Republic with its richest and most illustrious province. In many respects, the societies and constitutions of Gelderland and Overijssel resembled a German duchy more closely than the mercantile commonwealth of Holland. To begin with the most telling dissimilarities, whereas Patriot rhetoric about "Orangist absolutism" and "aristocratic domination" might pass for hyperbole in Holland, where the plaintiff party in reality remained the ruling class, in provinces where the nobility had built-in majorities in the States and where the Stadholder exercised absolute rights of appointment, it had the ring of truth. Those rights, moreover, were more, rather than less, vigorously exercised in the second half of the century. Supernumeraries and placemen filled key positions at both provincial and municipal levels. All nine judges of the provincial court of Gelderland were at the discretion of the Stadholder, and it was not unknown for him to appoint politically reliable laymen rather than doubtful professional lawyers. Town magistracies were divided between parvenus who owed their position entirely to Stadholderian preferment, and cadet members of the noble houses of the eastern provinces. In the first category were professional lackeys like Dr. Hoff, the surgeon of Arnhem who became its bailiff, and a number of men whose origins lent credence to the popular charge, much-aired in *To the Netherlands People*, that the indiscretions of William V had put the Republic in pawn to foreigners. The arch office-monger of Utrecht, for example, Willem Nicolaas Pesters, was not only reputed to be the great-grandson of a coachman, but—as the Patriot press enjoyed reminding its readers—a Limburger who had spent much of his career in Germany and was for good measure probably "a member of the Sheeny race."[33]

There were relatively few in this category able to do the bidding of the Prince with just the right balance of sycophancy and ruthlessness. Many more of the available offices were manned by the scions of the Orange nobility, some of them astonishingly junior. Willem van Lynden van Hemmen dripped with honours. At the age of seventeen he was, among other things, burgemeester of Arnhem and Elburg; bailiff of den Bosch; provincial tax receiver of Gelderland; president of the Council of the Domain and Burgrave of Nijmegen. The earnings from these offices, so the *Politieke Kruijer* reported, came to over 20,000 florins; an impressive income, but small fry compared to the 100,000 florins provided by Burgrave Frans Godard van Lynden's bulging portfolio. Many such posts were of course transparent sinecures. Of the 272 meetings convened by the Zutphen Council between November 1782 and November

1783, the Kamerheer (Chamberlain) of the Prince, Baron Anne Willem Carel van Nagell, attended just 15.[34]

Outside the towns, the domination of the nobility was still more formidable. Powerful dynasties like the van Heeckeren, the Bentincks or the Schimmelpenninck van der Oye provided personnel for all the commanding posts of the military, ecclesiastical and judicial hierarchies. The medieval concept whereby subordinate officers of the nobility were responsible to them in a personal capacity survived in some of the darker recesses of Drente, Gelderland, and Overijssel. In such villages, seigneurs retained the right to present predikancies, schoolmasterships, sometimes even bailiwicks.[35] Often the village *schout* (sheriff) remained the personal dependent of the lord, who would devoutly uphold his hunting rights and graciously receive gift offerings on St. Walburga's Day in lieu of the right to consent to marriage. At the opposite end of the institutional scale, the aristocratic preponderance was reflected in the composition of the assemblies of the States in which they made up three of the four quarters, one only being reserved for the towns. Renegade barons like van der Capellen and his Gelders nephew, Robert Jasper van der Capellen van der Marsch, might upset the voting in a single quarter; but they were never numerically strong enough to disturb the Orange majority.

The very isolation and weakness of the disaffected burghers of the townships proved to be the fuel for their rebellion. Their complete exclusion from power and the remoteness of any change under the Stadholderian Réglement in time developed into a raging sense of grievance. The slightly stilted accusations of nepotism, pluralism and peculation which the Holland Patriots flung at the Stadholder rebounded dangerously close to their patrician allies, who were certainly as much culprits in these matters. But in the more polarized situation of the land provinces, such accusations assumed concrete significance. Unlike the maritime provinces, there was no "alternative" authority of a regent class to offset the pretensions of the Stadholderian regime and to palliate the frustrations of the aggrieved. Consequently, the more hopeless their predicament, the more unrestrained was the protest of the burghers of the little townships of Gelderland, Groningen and Overijssel. It was hardly accidental that two villages of 1,200 and 500 souls, respectively, could by their noisy revolutionary defiance tease the Stadholder into military action.

The offences of Orangism seemed all the more odious to the burghers of the land provinces when they were set against memories of civic liberties which were still relatively fresh. Nothing could be further from the truth than to suggest that these provinces were, in uniform contrast to the mercantile states, obscure backwaters of reaction. The history of Utrecht had long been disfigured by the struggle between the weaving guilds and the massively established authority of the Reformed Church. Although the university had been set up following the Synod of Dort in 1618 as an entrenched ally of orthodoxy, the burghers of the city had until 1672 retained the right to choose their own magistracy and councillors from representatives of the guilds and town watch. In the province of Overijssel, Deventer and Kampen cherished the memory of elected "Burgher Colleges" from whom the city officers were chosen and which acted as a kind of permanent watchdog of civic rights. A body of forty-eight deputies in Arnhem performed similar functions. When, in 1782, Deventer became the first city in the Republic to convene such a representative body, in defiance of the Stadholderian Règlement, it could claim with some reason that it was doing no more than restoring this body to its rightful place in the civic administration.[36] Even in Gelderland, the regents of Zutphen had continued to be elected by the guilds and watch up to 1748; and in still smaller villages like Lochem, Tiel and Doesburg, similar practices had survived into the 1750's.

Many such rights of course existed on paper or in custom in the maritime states, notably in Friesland, where the *grietmannen* had originally been elected on a most democratic franchise. But such rights had long since fallen victim to the manipulation of oligarchies and the restriction of franchises to small numbers of family groups. Paradoxically, in the land provinces where, for economic reasons, no comparable class of regents had developed, the absence of these practices had left surviving medieval liberties less damaged. In this respect they were not unlike some of the Rhineland cities where vestigial burgher rights continued to be respected albeit in restricted forms, and where these islands of civic privileges were surrounded by an ocean of noble estates. That such rights existed alongside a powerful provincial aristocracy in no way diminished their significance for those who, until 1674 or 1748, had continued to exercise them. Given an opportunity, the burghers of Elburg, Schotland, Zwolle and Zutphen were prepared to agitate in the very heartland of the enemy for the restoration of their liberties. And many of those who became most prominent in not only the Patriot but the Batavian revolution—men like Herman Willem Daendels and Rutger Jan Schimmelpenninck—were politically initiated in this way.

If the active Patriots were confined to a minority of the Dutch population as a whole, then the Patriots of the land provinces were a minority within a minority. Yet their very isolation and poverty of numbers stimulated their budding sense of collective identity. The concentration of pockets of Patriots in the smaller towns made for close and easy communication. Meetings of guilds or the resurrection of almost defunct watch companies could provide the institutional framework within which the disaffected could air their grievances. Very often membership of a discriminated Church—Mennonite or Catholic—would add further cohesion. Many of the more militant Patriot leaders in Gelderland were, like Pastors Bergh and Langrate, dissenting predikants. Universities where the students protested against an unpopular professor or, taking the opposite case, against the sacking of a popular academic, were another arena of political discussion, Franeker in Friesland and Utrecht being the most vigorous. Semi-clandestine meetings in the most insignificant hamlets, gathered as a "Patriotic Fellowship" under the presidency of the local surgeon or lawyer, would be encouraged by their very remoteness to seek contact with like-minded burghers in neighbouring towns. Support from a major centre like Kampen or Arnhem not only compensated for local weaknesses; it gave the dissidents enhanced authority when dealing with recalcitrant Orangist magistrates. In January 1783, for example, when the Drost-appointed magistrate of the Overijssel hamlet of Oostmarsum refused to countenance supporting the policy of the new Patriot municipality at Deventer over the Stadholderian conduct of the war, the burghers proceeded to elect their own officers to present grievances directly to Deventer and to meet similarly summoned representatives from neighbouring villages in a spontaneously convened "Diet of Little Twente Towns."[37] The result of these developments was that Patriot burghers from remote parts of the Republic found themselves campaigning for the restoration of local and parochial liberties, but in the process establishing district and even provincial liaisons which gave the movement of protest in 1783 and 1784 something like a national momentum.

THE PATRIOT PRESS

This sense of provincial, if not national, solidarity was of course neither spontaneously generated nor as yet well defined. It ran clean contrary to received assumptions about the sanctity of provincial sovereignties. The primary objective of the Patriots at that time remained the restoration of the rights of self-government to the local community. The rebellion was still against an authoritarian executive. It was to take an extreme polarisation of politics before a burgher from Arnhem, however much a Patriot, could feel more in common with a burgher from Rotterdam than with a "Prinsgezind" of his own town.

Other than the more astonishing blunders of Prince William, the most effective instrument in forging something like a national spirit of revolt was the Patriot periodical press. A bewildering number of journals continued to be printed in the Dutch Republic, especially in Holland; but many, written in French or German, were meant for a foreign or exile readership. The vernacular press by contrast was still in a very docile condition. Only the "Spectatorial" writing contrived to inject some controversy into an otherwise tranquil establishment. In the 1780's, however, two journals signalled the arrival of a full-blooded Patriot press. These were the *Politieke Kruijer* (*Political Courier*), edited in Amsterdam by J. C. Hespe, and the *Post van Neder Rijn*, edited by Pieter 't Hoen and published in Utrecht by Wildt and Paddenburg.[38] The *Post* was perhaps the more outstanding of the two, and duly became the journalistic banner of the Patriots as a whole. Since Utrecht was nicely placed at the crossroads of the land and sea provinces, it was able to cover news from all parts of the Republic, and—perhaps more important—to concentrate national attention on the turbulent politics of Utrecht itself. It was the first Dutch newspaper to adopt an aggressively revolutionary style, which separated it from the more rationalist, eighteenth-century *bon ton* of senior publications like the *Gazette de Leyde*.

Using an earthy vernacular, the *Post* bludgeoned the Stadholderian government with an endless catalogue of its infamy, together with a scriptural account of its rise to despotism. It excelled at reporting the juiciest scandal concerning the more disreputable habits of William V, whom it regularly abused as a sot, a drunkard, a tyrant and an oaf. Brunswick—a commissioned Austrian field-marshal at a time when Joseph II was threatening the frontiers of the Republic—was branded as little more than a foreign spy influencing the hapless Prince to betray his country yet again. In 1784 the *Post* rejoiced euphorically at Brunswick's dismissal. By contrast, van der Capellen was idolised as the father of his people, and events from across the Atlantic as well as in disturbed states like Geneva were avidly reported. The most inflammatory speeches of van der Kemp, snippets from anonymous subversive pamphlets, and the revolutionary songs and poems of the student bard of Utrecht, Jacobus Bellamy, were regularly published in the paper alongside petitions and public announcements by the Patriot leaders. The *Post* was more than another radical periodical; indeed, it could be described as the broadsheet of the Patriot revolution.

Not surprisingly, both the *Post* and the *Kruijer* regularly suffered the penalties of their boldness. Van Paddenburg was once fined as much as 1,000 guilders for allegedly defaming a decree of the States of Utrecht, and both editor and publisher of the *Kruijer* were thrown into jail by the Amsterdam Council when they got around to harrying the regents with as much zeal as they had prosecuted the Stadholder. The risks of the profession were presumably sufficient to deter too many emulators. The only seriously influential radical paper of the second rank was the *Hollandsche Historische Courant*, originally a genteel record, which was rescued from obscurity by the young brother-in-law of Jan Luzac (editor of the *Gazette de Leyde*), Wybo Fijnje. Fijnje was one of the most outspoken of the democrats; and he turned the Delft periodical into a violent polemic, which in 1787 played a significant part in purging the municipality.[39]

Without reliable figures of circulation it becomes impossible to estimate with any precision the influence of the Patriot press on the population at large. Its closeness to the political leadership and its role in disseminating their ideas is beyond question, and it seems obvious that papers like the *Post van Neder Rijn* must have played a formative role in popularising the militant language of the Patriot activists. As much as any other factor the press was responsible for providing Patriot politics with a language independent of the Dutch past.

FROM *Schutterij* TO FREE CORPS

The diffusion of a vulgarised quasi-democratic ideology through the media of Christian evangelism and a radical press mobilised the grievances against the Stadholderian regime into a formidable groundswell of protest. In its initial stages, political action was confined to club meetings and petitions presented to municipal and provincial authorities. But the growing correspondence of hitherto isolated pockets of dissent in the land provinces, together with the much better established and powerful opposition in Holland and Friesland, represented a threat to his authority which the Stadholder could ill afford to ignore. As the Anglo-Dutch war deteriorated from disaster to fiasco, the essential military legitimation for his executive powers disappeared. And when the Republic was forced to turn once more to the French to placate Joseph II's growing belligerence, the "Captaincy-Generalship" of the Prince was further undermined. By 1783, he appeared simply as a tinpot absolutist whose pretensions to power were no longer justified by the protective function of Stadholderate. Nevertheless, until the challenge to the Prince's position had been reinforced by an explicit appeal to arms, it can scarcely be described as even putatively revolutionary. But by the time van der Capellen could write to de Gijselaar: "Liberty and an unarmed people stand in direct contradiction,"[40] it seemed that just such a challenge had been announced.

The principal form this armed initiative assumed was militia. The insistence on the right to recruit and equip a popular military force, commanded independently of the Captain-General, not only threatened the military authority of the House of Orange; it committed its protagonists to the seizure of power.

Like nearly all aspects of the Patriot revolt, the Free Corps simultaneously suggested the heroic past and the militant future. The part played by militia in the American Revolution had been used by van der Capellen to publicise the notion of an armed citizenry as a patriotic duty. But the abiding virtue of promoting militia as the armed wing of Patriotism was that it already commanded a legitimate place in the institutions of the Republic. Under its traditional name, the *schutterij* (shooters) was simply the town watch, the urban guard whose history stretched back to the twelfth- and thirteenth-century communes, was closely intertwined with the guilds, and had acted in the defence of their towns against the Spanish. As part of the national epic, the *schutterij* was celebrated as the embodiment of the people-in-arms in defence of its liberties. Their credentials in respect of both national self-respect and urban liberties were thus impeccable, and their continued existence was intended to symbolise not only the martial vigilance of the people but its dedication to the "True Liberty." During the revolt of the "Doelisten," the more advanced petitioners had concentrated on opening up the burgher companies to election—that is, the militia companies formed later in Dutch history as auxiliary guards and attached more closely to magistrates (often Orange-appointed) than to the town regents. Defenders of the regent supremacy like Wagenaar had been quick to identify the burgher companies as an unhistorical usurpation of the true shooters' rights. But it was an indication of the fertile confusion of the 1780's that in the popular press the two militias became merged as the new "Free Corps."[41]

Whatever the legends surrounding the *schutterij*, the reality was more woebegone. The companies which survived into the eighteenth century lingered on as a mockery of their official history. The many group portraits of well-heeled regents, decoratively posed, testify that even by the later seventeenth century they had deteriorated into another form of social ornament for the ruling élite. Their engagingly picaresque company titles like "Turkiye" and "Bloedkuyl" (Bloodpit) existed only for the purpose of conferring status on their officers, who were, naturally, restricted to members of the regent families or their nominees. The old custom of electing officers was hardly more than a faintly embarrassing memory. Very often officers drew pay for men who existed only on the muster rolls. If this phantom militia was mobilised once a year, it was merely for the ceremonial duty of providing a guard of honour at the swearing in of new commissions. Even then the proceedings were not guaranteed to go with a bang. In 1780, a Rotterdammer complained that whereas in the old days the new captains were greeted with three-gun salvos, the shooters' rifles were in such poor condition that the practice had been abandoned. His troop were fortunate to have rifles at all. Many others were forced to make do with wooden clubs with rusty nails driven in at the end, to be used for drill and solemnly presented for inspection.

Yet as in so many other respects, idealised memory was capable of exerting a greater influence on the Dutch than contemporary fact. Patriot propaganda capitalised on the contrast. The miserable condition of the *schutterij* provided them with new ammunition for the charge that the custodians of the security of the Republic had betrayed their trust. The dispossession of their authority thus became an essential prerequisite for the strengthening of the nation, and the return of its armed corps to the people. As the *Post van Neder Rijn* put it in September of 1782: "Great men [i.e., van der Capellen] have drawn up plans, which, put into action, would reduce to nothing a usurped power. To wit, that each Burgher should be a Soldier, or rather that each Burgher should be a Warrior. This is the lesson of Nature, the lesson of Reason."[42] More specifically, the Patriots promised to open commissions to election; to recruit companies without reference to religious denomination; to promote re-equipment and regular training; to ensure representation of officers on city councils; and to use the militia to defend the rights of free assembly and speech. The restitution of the militia would not only rescue for the Dutch their nearly perished freedoms; it would also provide the Patriots with the means to press their demands on a recalcitrant Stadholder.

Sometimes the transition from *schutterij* to Free Corps was more a matter of political nuance than of outright declaration. In the autumn of 1782, the Oostergo quarter of Friesland put forward a proposal to arm its burghers and farmers as a counter-weight to the strength of the Stadholderian garrison at Leeuwarden. While this was coldly received by the other two land quarters, it is possible that recruitment and some rudimentary drilling went ahead in towns like Sneek and Harlingen. Such manoeuvres, it is true, would have represented not only a response to the provincial agitation against the Stadholder but also the local struggles of provincial factions. But much the same could be said of many of the campaigns of petition and assembly which followed from the military disasters of 1782 and 1783. It was from just such local commotions that the Patriots drew their early support. While Alkmaar in North Holland appears to have been the first municipality to have openly rejected the authority of the Stadholder by appointing its officers independently of his approval, the first explicitly "open" (that is, non-denominational) Free Corps seems to have been established at Dordrecht in January

1783, under the benevolent tutelage of its Pensionary, Cornelis de Gijselaar. About a month later a much larger organisation of two regiments, each of twelve companies—well over a thousand men in all—was set up in neighbouring Rotterdam, to the obvious apprehension of its largely Orangist council. In March the Overijssel burghers followed suit, immediately recruiting numbers of Catholics and Dissenters into their ranks. By the spring, Free Corps units had been organised in the smaller hamlets of Gelderland, on the very doorstep of the Stadholder's garrison.[43] In Utrecht, ancient regimental colours were once more paraded on the Sterrebos park, and under the cautionary euphemism of "exercise societies" clubs like the "Pro Patria et Libertate" helped the old companies—"De Pekstokken" (The Pikes), "Bloedkuyl," "Fortuyn," and "De Zwarte Knegten" (The Black Boys)—to fill out their muster rolls once more.

During the first year of their revival, the activities of the Free Corps remained fairly innocuous. Since the companies were responsible to "Burgher Defence Councils" of the towns and not to their provincial States or the Stadholder, there was nothing the court could do to prevent their formation. Indeed, as the paternal tolerance of councillors in Utrecht, Dordrecht and Haarlem made clear, the regents encouraged and protected their reconstitution as a weapon to be deployed against the Orangists. This, however, turned out to be a dangerous tactic. Historically the claim to revive the shooters was tied up with the principle of electing officers (from among those who exercised the full rights of citizens—*poorteerschap*) and with establishing their proper place in the hierarchy of civic institutions. In actual practice a regent—in The Hague and Utrecht, for example—served as colonel of the shooters; but in Patriot polemics the political relationship was cunningly inverted. Henceforth the mandated representative of the burghers was to be their voice in the city council. Van der Capellen's claim that the principles of rearmament and representation were inseparable was not just another shibboleth filched from the Americans but a fundamental article in the Patriot canon.

Even at the beginning the Free Corps made no attempt to conceal the political implications of their exercises. A draft constitution for a new Training and Drill Society at Leiden—whose founders included Pieter Vreede, the author of some ungarnished democratic pamphlets published as early as 1781–82—declared boldly: "Following the freedom that we naturally possess as inhabitants of a free burgher commonwealth, and which through a public endorsement of . . . our right to exercise in arms is drawing closer to achievement, we shall move to the goal of union in one (shooters') society."[44] The same regulations provided for Sunday evening meetings; a weekly pay of 3 stuivers to troopers, 6 to junior officers and 9 to senior officers; an elected defence committee; and the stipulation that "every man, whatever his station or occupation . . . be he shooter or not, is free to become a member of this society." In Zutphen on July 13, 1783, where five companies of Free Corps had been established, an address on behalf of 300 of them and 105 guild members demanded from the city council "a free and proper vote of the people . . . a legitimate and equitable assembly in accordance with the old constitution."

In Utrecht, the "vaderstad"*—a still more explicit demonstration of popular feeling among the burghers—took place in March 1783, when a petition signed by well over six hundred was presented to the council, urging them to grant full recognition to the reconstituted companies. On July of the same year, the council complied by issuing a new ordinance in place of the neglected order of 1702. The eight companies, one to each city district, were placed on an official footing and put under a new "burgerkrijgsraad" consisting of the colonel, eight captains, eight captains-lieutenant and one under-officer. On October 29, still apparently unwary as to the political implications of the Free Corps, the colonel (who was also one of the leading regents) and the second burgemeester, Petrus van Musschenbroek, inspected a public parade on the Sterrebos.

The political hue of the Free Corps varied from province to province and from town to town. The most aggressive noises came from some of the smallest companies in Overijssel and Gelderland; the weakest bleats from Amsterdam, where until 1786 the *schutterij* remained firmly under the thumb of the city regents and their appointed officers. In Utrecht, where the Free Corps was eventually built up to a force of over 2,000 men, the interest of the burghers was skilfully engaged by an articulate and combative minority. This group revolved around circles of dissident students at the university and the publishers, journalists and booksellers responsible for producing the *Post van Neder Rijn* and similarly subversive literature. Thus the Patriot faction not only formulated its views within a relatively tight-knit group, but also had access to publication. Wall posters, notices concerning public meetings, copies of petitions and petty libels cou'd all be distributed at short notice and with efficient secrecy. To give some continuity to their discussions and to tighten the link between the students and the nascent Free Corps, the "Pro Patria et Libertate" club was established in 1783; by the end of the year it boasted a membership of around 200. Some of the leading members were predikants like Voorda and van Hamelsveld; others were burgher officers of the *schutterij* like Captain Adriaan de Nijs and Otto Dirk Gordon who had seen action in America.

But the dominant figure was the young student Pieter Philip Juriaan Quint Ondaatje.[45] Ondaatje, the son of a Colombo predikant, had been schooled successively at Amsterdam and Leiden, and had come to Utrecht to study law and theology. Before much time elapsed he found himself in furious quarrels with the even younger Professor of Theology, van Goens. Strictly speaking, both van Goens and Ondaatje were "outsiders" in Utrecht, but in 1782 Ondaatje was presented with the prized certificate of citizenship. Henceforth he felt free to act as the spokesman of the burghers of the city. Van

* Lit. "father town" (because the Union of Utrecht had been the founding charter of the Republic in 1579).

Goens, it was bruited, owed his chair to currying favour with the elders of the synod and the Orange cabal in the city. There was good evidence for the allegation, since aside from his very junior years (he was just eighteen on his appointment) he was one of the major contributors to the *Ouderwetsche Nederlandsche Patriot*—a truculently Orangist periodical, set up as a counter-broadside to the *Post*. It was in this latter capacity that van Goens attracted a good deal of odium; and in the summer of 1783, a vituperative campaign for his removal both from the council and from the city was launched. Abandoned by even the Stadholder, van Goens finally left Utrecht for Basel in June. Perhaps it was as well he left when he did. His epitaph had already been prepared for him by his opponents:

Hier onder	Here beneath
Legt een slegten donder	Lies a wicked bully
Een helsch serpent	A hellish snake
Een Hoerjager	A whore-hunting rake
Een goddeloze Vent	A godless cheater
En een verdoemde Burger-plager.	And a damned Burgher-baiter.[46]

Next to van Goens, the man most incriminated by his association with the Stadholderian establishment was Willem Nicolaas ("Klaas") Pesters, the Lieutenant-Stadholder of Utrecht. Through his contacts at court and a thorough exploitation of the terms of the Règlement, Pesters was able to dispose of an immense portfolio of patronage. Naturally, many plum jobs went to his immediate entourage of friends and family; others went to toadies and creditors who were rapidly supplied with the necessary burgher-certificates to qualify them for the desired appointment. In one notorious case in December 1782, Pesters over-reached himself when in the first week of the month he had his servant, Jan Mulder, a Nijmegenaar, appointed to the commissariat of the Great Ferry, and in the last week handed out the job of commissariat of the Rhine shippers to the servant of one of his cronies, a man born in Hanover who had received his certificate just ten days before. The outcry not only among the Patriots but among the old-established regents of the council was spontaneous. One of them, Daunis, complained that it went hard with good burgher families when they saw a man become a citizen one Monday and invested with a profitable post the Monday after.[47]

The Patriots and the regents objected to Pesters' conduct for rather different reasons. To the former, he was the despicable tool of Orangist absolutism; to the latter, the jumped-up parvenu who was able to place his servants, sycophants and creditors in offices which *their* grandfathers had probably assigned in contracts of correspondence not two generations back. However differently they approached the matter, both Patriots and regents were agreed on the importance of ridding Utrecht of Pesters. Attacking his more flagrant acts of corruption was a way of attacking the Règlement and, for that matter, the Stadholder, at one remove. Before very long, the assault became still more direct. In January 1783, a councillor, aloof from Pesters' cabal, attacked the Prince's "recommendatie recht" (nominating rights) to fill city appointments. In August a petition signed by 314 burghers was mobilised by Ondaatje and the *schutterij*, urging that in future the council resist any such interference with their most obvious rights. In this protest they had the support of many of the leading regents and even deputies to the States of Utrecht, who also had much to gain from a decisive curtailment of the Stadholder's powers. The Baron d'Yvoy, no spitfire radical, commented that the Règlement was in blatant contradiction with the Union of Utrecht.[48]

A delegation went to see William V at the Huis ten Bosch, only to be met by a stony insistence on his "due rights." Later, the Prince acknowledged that he had no constitutional right as such to choose city officers, but that he did have a right to inspect the "eligibility" of candidates. Unfortunately for him, the matter shortly ceased to be academic. At the end of the year a member of the council died, and together with van Goens' empty place, two vacancies required filling. A second petition—this time signed by 725 burghers and issuing from a Free Corps and guild meeting—urged the council to take a stand and appoint a successor without reference to The Hague. On January 11, 1784, a hot-air balloon was sent up over the Vaartse Rhine to great popular acclaim. A day later, copies of a splendidly scurrilous pamphlet by the Patriot student Lidth de Jeude were discovered in the city, advertising a further flight to take place on Monday, January 12, at 10:30 a.m. from the town hall, bearing as passengers W. N. Pesters and his supporters. Emboldened by these manifestations of public support, the anti-Pesters regents decided to accept the challenge of a test case. On January 19 they appointed a successor to the vacant place without any application to The Hague, shrewdly selecting a figure acceptable to all parties: Voet van Winssen, a moderate Patriot and a captain of the Paapenvaandel Company. Amidst great public rejoicing he was carried in triumph to the town hall on the 21st, escorted by crowds of burghers and Free Corps.[49]

The autumn of 1783 was the honeymoon of regents and Patriots. In Amsterdam, van der Capellen attended meetings convened by van Berckel and the "Vaderlandsche Regenten" ("Patriot Regents"), and consented in his lordly way to have his health drunk at Hooft's banquet coupled with the "Tempel der Vrijheid." The priority was clearly the reduction of the Stadholder, and in 1782 a "secret programme" had been drawn up by the regents with the express goal of reverting to the status quo ante 1747. By the end of 1783 no serious rift had appeared to divide the Patriots from the Holland regents. Far from regarding the Free Corps as a threat to their entrenched positions in the councils, they valued them as an important asset. The militia would provide the force necessary to persuade the Prince to part with his more obnoxious privileges and if possible to relinquish the military command for which he was so patently unfitted.[50] With the advantage of his Hague garrison offset by Free Corps mobilised in every Holland commune of substance, the Stadholder's bargaining power would be significantly diminished. And there was a second important reason why the militia was tolerated by the regents. Quite apart from their political value, they were a surety against the Prince playing the usual Orange card of mob intimidation.

From the beginning the Free Corps had been intended as a politically aggressive, but socially defensive weapon. While its ranks had been opened to any denomination and its commissions to burghers of relatively modest means, the Corps were by no stretch of the imagination *armées révolutionnaires*. Their rank-and-file were more likely to be tradesmen, small merchants or brokers than the poor of the city streets. With memories of 1748 still fresh in the minds of the Patriot successors of the "Doelisten," the arming of the burghers was a prophylactic against the threat of the very poor. In December 1782, the Prince gave good notice that he would indeed look to the streets for support against the machinations of both regents and Patriots. On the eve of St. Nicholas' Feast, popularly celebrated in the Netherlands on December 6, William addressed a crowd of some hundreds on the Binnenhof at The Hague. Orange cockades were flourished as the Stadholder referred contemptuously to the "libels" circulating regarding his rights and prerogatives. The magistrates of the States of Holland, who had forbidden the demonstrations of oath-swearing to the Stadholder on the grounds that they were inflammatory, were singled out for abuse; a good deal of jenever was passed around; a few fire crackers were set off; and the result was a brawl between the more inebriated members of the crowd and some manifestly unsympathetic Patriots nearby. The incident was not very sensational but it was sufficient to put the regents still more on their guard; to order more city patrols and the prohibition of any public demonstrations of Orangism; and to accelerate the process of rearmament and recruiting among the Holland Free Corps companies.[51]

Between March 1783 and April 1784 a succession of more serious events at Rotterdam seemed to confirm the pessimistic judgements. On the Prince's birthday, March 8, another day of traditional celebration, well-to-do burghers known for their Patriot opinions were molested and in some cases assaulted by a crowd led by one of the notorious "Orange women," Kaat Mossel, who was also alleged to have had a hand in inciting the "opstootje" (brawl) at The Hague a few months before. This incident led directly to further, more violent riots in which Patriot property was sacked and looted, after the pattern of 1748. To combat the threat, Free Corps units took to policing the quarters of Rotterdam, notwithstanding the disapproval of the town council whom the Patriots suspected of a permissive attitude towards the riots. On April 3, 1784, a company of Free Corps ran headlong into an advancing, violently angry crowd. The company was led by a wealthy burgher, one Elsevier, and most of his men were sufficiently well off to be able to afford handsome uniforms and new weapons. In a scene only too familiar a few years later in France, the captain panicked and his men opened fire, killing four and wounding many more.[52] Elsevier was publicly blamed by the council for losing control of his force, but with similarly violent scenes taking place at Haarlem and Leiden, the States of Holland were considerably more sympathetic to the Free Corps. A commission of five members was sent to investigate the disorder, along with two squadrons of horse guards; and despite the initial chastening of the militia, its part in the affair was exonerated. On June 16 a *plakaat* (decree) was issued by the States outlawing all forms of public demonstration and riot, implying strongly that the Orange Party had been responsible for the trouble. A year later, Kaat Mossel was arrested, subjected to a public flogging, and put in The Hague jail until 1787.

There was a good deal of bitter social animosity involved in the conflicts between the Free Corps and the Orangist crowds. Doubtless this is one traditional aspect of Dutch political behaviour which did not change in the 1780's, for all the professions of the Patriots to represent the "people." Like their National Guard counterparts in 1791, enforcing the *limits* of popular sovereignty (and protecting the property of its mandatories) was an integral part of their function. Yet it would be misleading to exaggerate the social cohesion of the Free Corps. "Middle class" is a very comprehensive term of social description in the Netherlands. In Haarlem, where regents had long despised the badly remunerated *schutter* commissions, the revived militia had a more genuinely popular (that is, petty-bourgeois) composition; in Dordrecht, on the other hand, where the city was dominated by the guilds, its character was markedly more affluent. It is probably least helpful, but nearest the truth to describe the Free Corps as sharing a mistrust of both the very rich and the very poor, whom they held to be in collusion to subvert ancient liberties. In this respect too, they were the immediate predecessors of the armed phalanx of the French bourgeoisie: the *gardes nationales*.

The Separation of the Parties: Utrecht, 1784–1786, and the Emergence of Patriot Democracy

The conservative social role of the Free Corps did not restrain them from pursuing revolutionary ambitions regarding a representative form of government. Throughout 1783, the regents remained reasonably confident that they could contain the wilder elements among the Patriots and use the militia exclusively to pressure the Stadholder and repress mob violence. The States and the Council of Utrecht were so secure that early in 1784 they invited their citizens to register freely any objections against the 1674 Règlement. But before long it was to be apparent that they had stirred up a hornets' nest in that city. It may have been significant that on July 19, 1783, van der Capellen paid a visit to Utrecht, for plainly neither he nor the members of "Pro Patria et Libertate" were prepared to contemplate the reduction of the Free Corps to the status of tame auxiliaries of the regents. When the States of Utrecht put proposals for the amendment of the Règlement into commission, the Patriots made it plain that they would be satisfied with nothing less than a completely new constitution.

These views found concrete expression when a 117-article draft constitution for the province was published in the *Utrechtse Courant* on April 23, 1784.[53] The document was divided into five sections, the third and fourth dealing with the government of the city. According to its provisions, the city council was to be an elected body. All burghers, with the exception of those on public relief, were entitled to vote in primary elections. These drew up a list of citizens over twenty, of four years' standing in the city and who paid over 150 guilders a year in taxes, from whom eight men were elected. Together with their co-mandatories from the other seven districts, these men comprised an electoral college of sixty-four which, by a complicated system of ballots and lots, reduced itself to twelve and finally to three men. The council was then entitled to choose from this list of three to fill its vacant place. This rigmarole did not exactly amount to democracy run riot, but at the primary level it did seek to involve in election those whose previous status as citizens had been purely formal. More seriously for the regents, it put the essentially co-optive basis of their power in jeopardy. There were other important novelties in this draft. Section IV provided for a body of sixteen elected burgher representatives to sit in permanent session; these were to hear the grievances of the people against their councillors and magistrates, and to press for their redress. Although purported to be based on a fifteenth-century predecessor, the "Meentemannen," it was rather more uncomfortably reminiscent of the "Burgher College" recommended by van der Capellen and already in shadowy existence in Kampen, Deventer and Zutphen.

The council, so recently liberated from the Stadholderian Règlement, had no intention of allowing itself to be shackled to the Free Corps and a trumped-up version of burgher democracy, however qualified. Rather than lend credibility to the Patriot draft by debating it officially, they proceeded to treat it as one of a possible number of replies to their earlier invitation for suggested revisions to the old Règlement. With some show of flexibility, they declared their readiness to give consideration to all such proposals, and in demonstration of their good faith appointed a commission of ten to report back on these in the autumn. By June, twelve such memoranda had been received, some using the draft constitution as a basis for discussion but omitting either elected councillors or the Burgher College. One of the twelve was a project sent in by a commission from the States which came down firmly for permanently appointed seats on the council and against any burgher institution. This project, which curtailed the powers of the Stadholder without increasing that of the burghers, clearly had the blessing of the council, which had already warned the Patriots that while any proposals could be debated in the city, it was for the provincial body, the States, to give their consent to any scheme which might be agreed upon. In September it went further and declared that if after the elapse of a few weeks no objections to the new scheme had been received, it would be treated as a new draft Règlement for the city.

These manoeuvres finally spurred the Patriots into action. Their original draft was circulated among the Free Corps companies for endorsement, and despite the opposition of one or two senior officers, received 1,215 signatures, appended to a statement of objection to the proposals of the States.[54] A further meeting of the signatories decided to appoint a commission of twenty-four, including Ondaatje and Otto Dirk Gordon, to seek direct negotiations with the council in an attempt to speed up their deliberations and bring them to fruitful conclusion. However narrow the constituency of this committee, it could claim with some truth to represent a broader cross-section of Utrecht's burgher population than any member of the appointed council. It went on, however, to claim much more than this. Calling itself the "Constituted," the committee of twenty-four effectively set itself up as a rival authority to the regency, and proceeded to act as the prototype of the "Burgher College" outlined in the draft. Regular meetings were held in the Stadskelder (city vault), where petitions and requests were heard and in which the council was publicly taken to task for its marathon exercise in prevarication. Impatience at the endless procedural quibbling was growing among the junior officers of the Free Corps, and on January 28, 1785, six companies appeared at the Stadskelder to address the "Constituted." Fourteen weeks had elapsed, they complained, since the "Constituted" were mandated to seek firm assurances from the council, and nothing had been forthcoming. Within a further four weeks, the "Constituted" should demand definite proposals from the council or else take appropriate measures to ensure that the rights of the burghers were respected, for "We do not carry our weapons in support of shadowy privileges."[55] To give their demands more weight, the eight companies shortly after each elected two representatives (all junior officers) to act as spokesmen for the militia and to be known as the "Commissioned."

Despite this proliferation of tribunes of the burghers, negotiations might yet have dragged on through the spring of 1785. The council grudgingly accepted the right of the "Constituted" to act on behalf of 1,215, on February 21, but conceded little else. Unfortunately for them, the active mortality rate of the "vroedschap" intervened to disturb their complacency. Another member of the council died, and on February 28, both the "Constituted" and the "Commissioned" petitioned the regents to appoint a successor from among those known to be interested in the rights of the burghers. Angry at this impertinence, the council promptly went ahead and appointed one of the three men whom the "Constituted" had actually specified as politically undesirable, a certain Jonathan Sichterman.[56] The following day, the "Constituted" and "Commissioned" met in a joint assembly in the Stadskelder. The "Commissioned" proposed a relatively moderate course of action, asking the council to delay Sichterman's swearing in until the new city Règlement was adopted, since they anticipated that the "Burgher College" would almost certainly reject his nomination.

But the "Constituted," led by Ondaatje, took much greater umbrage at the conduct of the council. This, he declared, had been deliberately provocative and the only proper action was to repudiate the appointment. After angry debate, Ondaatje won the vote. On March 7 a delegation of sixteen, representing both bodies, appeared at the town hall. The council agreed to see seven of them and was immediately harangued by Ondaatje, who demanded: "In God's name, most Noble Gentlemen, renounce this appointment of Sichterman. This done, we would ask you to appoint to the vacant place a true friend of the Burghers, a man who has shown with deeds that he is a good and trustworthy Patriot."[57]

The members of the council, however, showed no sign of repenting their choice. If anything, they appeared more recalcitrant than ever, and many of those firmest in their opposition to Ondaatje were those who had led the campaign against the Stadholderian Règlement the previous year. On March 11, at another joint meeting in the Stadskelder, Ondaatje warned those assembled: "If they [the council] persist in their appointment and make Sichterman a councillor, we can throw in the towel once and for all." The intransigence of the council in the face of massive objection, he argued, demonstrated only too well the utter impotence of a "Burgher College" unless drastic action was taken to repair the situation.

The following day such action was taken. With pamphlets urging the burghers to assemble posted around the city, the two bodies passed a resolution demanding an immediate extraordinary meeting with the council that same evening. By seven o'clock the square in front of the town hall was already thronged with people, and such were the fears of social disorder that the council acceded to Ondaatje's demand. The sixteen delegates were almost chaired to the town hall where the crowd was densely packed, among them Free Corps officers haranguing the populace and brandishing sabres and rifles in the direction of the council chambers.

When the seven agreed deputies were received by the council, Ondaatje made his intentions quite plain. The situation, he said, was critical. If the council even now refused to recant, the crowd might get out of hand. The council had to decide whether or not it was to hear the voice of the people. If it remained obstinate he would not be responsible for the "terrible and threatening consequences. . . . 'We are not '48ers,'" he said in a revealing phrase, " 'but '85ers, who understand our rights and liberties well enough. I say again to you we are not '48ers, we are not *canaille.'* "[58] These fine distinctions in the political education of the *burgerij* did nothing to reassure the council members of their personal safety, doubtless just as Ondaatje intended. From their "Green Room" the besieged councillors could see for themselves that they were virtually imprisoned in their own town hall by the dense crowd, becoming steadily more vociferous although as yet non-violent. With great reluctance, van Musschenbroek (the burgemeester) recommended the withdrawal of Sichterman's appointment, and this was accepted by his colleagues. With somewhat belated courtesy, Ondaatje thanked the council for its prudence and wisdom and withdrew. After greeting the news with great and noisy approval, the crowd dispersed without inflicting physical damage on either the person or property of the regents.

The triumph of the burgher tribunes was very short-lived. That same evening, two of the council resigned in protest against having been coerced into acting contrary to their true will. One of the two was Voet van Winssen, who only a year earlier had been escorted by the crowds to the town hall as the people's choice. Within a few days, seventeen more councillors resigned, declaring the proceedings of March 11 illegal. On the 18th, a petition from 125 burghers and the more eminent families of the city repudiated the decision of the 11th and beseeched the States to intervene to restore order in Utrecht.

The States promptly responded with a damning indictment of Ondaatje and his colleagues, and in the *Politieke Kruijer* the Baron d'Yvoy, writing as "*Ultrajectinus,*" castigated his fellow citizens for their disgraceful conduct: "Shame on the people of Utrecht! Nothing can erase the stain on the honour of an assembly which but yesterday showed its repugnance for tyranny."[59]

Alarmed at these *démarches,* the Patriots went on the defensive. Having committed an act of revolutionary coercion they now proceeded, with typically Dutch concern to avoid wounding sensibilities, to apologise for it. On March 23 the "Constituted" and the "Commissioned" wrote to the council that

their intention had never been to offend either the Council as a whole or any individual in particular, but on the contrary, in all their proceedings and especially those of March 11 their only concern had been to free the Council and its members from any possible unpleasantness they might have feared. . . .[60]

Far from harbouring any sinister intentions towards their Very Noble Gentlemen, they wished them nothing but well and hoped that their benevolent motives would be properly appreciated. Instead of relieving political tension, these conciliatory communications invited further counter-attack by the council. The members insisted that no Free Corps officer should in future serve as one of the "Constituted"; and on March 29, professing some reluctance, the nineteen ex-councillors took their places in the town hall. They were not, they insisted, present as councillors, but because they had taken pity on the "well-intentioned and respectable burghers of the city," and because the States of Utrecht had indicated their duty to them.

This civic reticence did not, however, prevent them from launching a furious hunt of recrimination against all those associated with the events of the 11th. Sichterman's place was once more confirmed, but fortunately for the council, the man had had enough of city politics and declined the offer, forestalling any immediate manifestation of public anger. His seat was merely declared vacant and remained unfilled. One hundred ducats were offered for the capture of any of those responsible for the events of the 11th; and proceedings were instituted against Ondaatje as a "disturber of the public peace." D'Yvoy declared with some satisfaction that, after all, he had not been brought into this world to be dictated to by the son of an East India merchant. Faced with this storm of recrimination, Ondaatje surprised both his friends and enemies by bowing to it, resigning both from the "Constituted" and his Free Corps commission.

For the moment the council had the upper hand in Utrecht. But any assumption that it had scotched, once and for all, the possibility of a burgher revolt, would have been unduly premature. What *was* finished was any chance of continuing the alliance between Patriots and regents. The Patriots may have come out of the Sichterman débacle badly bruised, but they had also emerged wiser. Henceforth the full weight of their animus would be turned against their adversaries on the council and in the States. The dramatic appearance in the streets of the city, on the morning of April 3, of a pamphlet whose title as well as method of distribution seemed to owe a lot to van der Capellen's prototype, illustrated most vividly that the spirit of rebellion was far from dead. Entitled *Aan Het Volk van Utrecht*, the pamphlet addressed its readers in tones of shrill warning:

Brave and Valiant People!

You are betrayed and sold. Hardly had you struck off the fetters of a Stadholder than you are handcuffed and branded by an Aristocratic Regime. Already you are forbidden entrance to the Council; you must as Free Burghers no longer assemble in the town hall. In God's name, then, brave and valiant people: You have long been misled and for centuries deprived of your liberties, enduring instead a tyrannical domination. . . . O Burghers of Utrecht. Believe me, God hears and sees . . . there is a sworn conspiracy between your Regents, who have pledged themselves to destroy your freedom; to trample on your rights, arbitrarily to ignore your objections and thus begin to bind, gag and mistreat you.[61]

There was, the pamphlet alleged, a plot afoot to replace the Stadholder with the Princess, who would then be the prisoner of the "Family Regime." Three remedies were open to the burghers if they wished to avert this awful dénouement. First, a general refusal to pay taxes; second, the withholding of recognition from the twenty-one regents who persisted in opposition to the Free Corps; and finally, an approach to the "oppressed" Stadholder, with the proviso that on the one hand the rights of the burghers, and on the other the rights of the Stadholder, would be upheld. Although there was indeed some talk towards the end of 1785 that the Prince might abdicate in favour of his wife, most of the pamphlet's speculation was fanciful. But its strident accusations against the regents accurately mirrored the alienation of the ruling oligarchies from those who sought to replace them with the elected representatives of the *burgerij*.

The notion of a rapprochment with the Stadholder, thus repeating the alignment of 1748, though unlikely, was not out of the question. The *Post van Neder Rijn* made no effort to conceal its scepticism of the chances of wooing the man who very recently had been the object of violent Patriot vilification. Yet there was a doggerel verse then circulating in Utrecht which made the point:

If we needs must live beneath a yoke
Better under One
Than under Forty Gentlemen
Aye much better under One.[62]

Ondaatje, at any rate, was prepared to take the possibility seriously, and undertook several trips to The Hague during May with the object of making such an approach. He may have been encouraged in this by the earlier visit of Pieter Paulus to Utrecht. Paulus had himself once expected great things from a Stadholder who would dare to stand as the champion of burgher rights. But William V was not exactly cut out for this role. He recoiled from the Patriot advances and failed to answer some of their letters. By June it was plain that the affair was unrequited. The Patriots had to stand on their own.

The independent assertion of burgher rights had been touched on by Paulus as early as 1773, when, in his *On the Duty of the Stadholderian Government*, he had complained with some prescience that while two groups monopolised Dutch political life, the third "midden groep" which comprised "many if not most" of the population, counted for nothing at all.[63] Van der Capellen and the Patriot ideologues were to some extent to rescue this Dutch "Third Estate" from its condition of political nullity. But their all-out attack on the "Stadholderian tyranny," as I have already remarked, often submerged their more explicitly democratic claims beneath the inherited vocabulary of oligarchic opposition. It took the disagreeably rude awakening at Utrecht to persuade the Patriots that not only did their interests not coincide with those of the regents, but they were fundamentally in direct conflict. From 1785 to 1787, when this struggle reached its dénouement, the ambitions of Patriot democracy were translated progressively from ideology to action. Divorcing themselves more and more from the burden of the past, the Patriots began to express thier views on representative government in distinctively new, and strikingly radical, forms. Put rhetorically, as the delegate of the Delft Free Corps ecstatically announced:

The Burgher, dear comrades, no longer wanders in the shadows. He can show himself fearlessly in the light of our fiercely breaking dawn. The Sun of his freedom and Happiness shines more strongly from hour to hour, and we can assure you on the most powerful grounds that before she reaches her zenith there will be no more Tyrants of the People to be found in this land. The Armed Freedom will blot out their very name.[64]

The occasions on which this brave new self-consciousness was most confidently flaunted were the assemblies of Free Corps, held at regular intervals from December 1784 onwards, usually in Utrecht. Among its many other lessons, the experience of the battle with the council had taught the Free Corps the penalties of isolation. So apart from the purely charismatic value of ceremonies, parades, orations and salvos, these meetings of Free Corps from all over the Republic were an invaluable means of concentrating numbers and concerting policy. They also made a bold showing under the very noses of the regents, who looked on their activities with increasing perturbation. The second of these gatherings, in February 1785, had gone out of its way to express support for Ondaatje, and later ones publicly exonerated his conduct on March 11. It was in the deliberations of these assemblies that the practical politics of the Patriots was shaped.

The most impressive of the Free Corps assemblies was the third, held in June 1785. Thousands of militia from all the Dutch provinces save Groningen and Zeeland participated in this impressive display of power. But its significance lay in more than its numbers. For on this occasion an "Acte der Verbintenis" (Act of Association) was solemnly sworn by all those present, again in uncanny rehearsal of the almost identical affirmation of the *fédérés* on the Champs de Mars six years later. The act pledged its jurants to defend with the last drop of blood a "true Republican constitution" against all external and domestic violence, to expunge all abuses, and restore the lost or obscured rights of the burghers. It also committed the Free Corps to strive for a "People's government by representation" (*Volksregering bij representatie*). This was the first collective, quasi-national statement of the political aims of the Free Corps. It was an unambiguous declaration for a form of government which excluded both a "freedom-oppressing Stadholderate" (though not a Stadholderate as such) and the "strenuous efforts of an Aristocracy to appropriate to itself the power which rightly belongs to the people . . . and to monopolise for themselves the enjoyment of liberty while they beguile the people with phantoms."[65]

Radical though it was, the Act of Association was by no means the most advanced statement of democratic principles to find expression in these years. A few weeks after the meeting at Utrecht, a smaller assembly of 56 delegates of the 3,780 Free Corps in the province of Holland put its endorsement to a still more revolutionary manifesto. Known colloquially as the "Leidse Ontwerp" (the Leiden Draft), this document was principally the work of the publicists Wybo Fijnje and Pieter Vreede, both of whom were to have a hand in drafting and enacting a democratic constitution for the Batavian Republic thirteen years later. The Leiden Draft was thus the early ancestor of the democratic constitution which eventually became permanent in the Kingdom of the Netherlands after 1848. It also marked a decisive shift, not uncommon in revolutionary declarations, away from historical justifications of liberty towards the more confident affirmation of self-evident natural rights.[66] In line with the revolutionary credo of the time, the first paragraph stated that "Liberty is an inalienable right, adhering to all burghers of the Netherlands commonwealth. No power on earth, much less any power derived truly from the people . . . can challenge or obstruct the enjoyment of this liberty when it is so desired." The preamble made this point even more plainly: "The citizens of a State, above all of a Republic, founded on Liberty, confer this on each of them, head for head." It also insisted on the primacy of popular sovereignty ("the Sovereign is no other than the vote of the people"); the responsibility of elected authorities to their electors (Article III); the abolition of all inherited and venal offices (Article IV); the absolute right of free speech as the "foundation of a free constitution" (Article V); the election of all militia officers by the ranks (Article VIII); and the admission of all citizens to the Free Corps irrespective of denomination (Article XV). And it took the opportunity to complain of the predominance of rentier finance at the expense of trade and industry (one of Vreede's hobby-horses), as well as protesting at the unique combination of crippling taxes and an incompetent military establishment.

The Leiden Draft was the most striking attempt yet to win over the rank-and-file of the Free Corps to the more advanced views of its democratically inclined leadership. With perhaps more optimism than conviction, it declared that "the ideas of a Republican popular sovereignty (*Volks-invloed*) have made so strong an impression and struck such deep roots that it has become impossible to tear them out."[67] However overstated, it was true that their views had gained a wider currency in the Republic by the spring of 1785. Gatherings noticeably less bold but nonetheless radical at towns like Haarlem, Gouda and Dordrecht took place during the year when their Free Corps pressed their respective councils not only to abjure the Stadholderian "recommendatie recht" but also to open their membership to elected representation. Above all, the tone of public declarations on the Patriot side was markedly more hostile to its erstwhile patrons, the regents, now universally dubbed "aristocracies" along with the hangers-on of the Prince of Orange. Indeed, in many instances this "Venetian aristocracy"—as the *Zakboek* (Pocket Book) *van Neerlands Volk* described it—were held to be even more detestable than the Stadholder for having cheated the burghers of their due rights and usurped the name of their representatives.[68] The Leiden Draft had condemned in no uncertain terms the "injurious and improper independence of the Regents from the people whose representatives they should be."[69] It even *defined* their offices in terms of a mandated representative function and underlined the point by emphasising that "There are no other criteria for becoming a Regent than age, property and birthplace, date of civism and membership of the militia."[70] Thus the true regent was no longer an oligarch but, as the *Zakboek* had it, "the representative of each burgher, each inhabitant . . . the Regent has the honour of having entrusted to him the general interest, the execution of the will of the people, and the maintenance of its rights." By contrast, those who claimed to hold the offices at present were no better than the thieves of the people's liberty, or—as described in Gerrit Paape's *De Aristocrat en de Burger* —an almost satanic corrupter of liberty, an unsocial, uncivic being, the very antithesis of a true burgher.[71]

The emancipation of the democratic Patriots from the tutelage of the regents had become, by the end of 1785, an open conflict between the two parties. Van der Capellen, prescient as always, had long recognised the inevitability of this situation. Contemptuous of the slightly fawning flattery of the Holland regents, he had written in June 1782 that "the centuries-old foolish grumbling of the Amstels Fathers will have to come to an end, and then each will receive his due deserts"; but he added judiciously, "the time is not yet ready."[72] A year later he told his nephew van der Marsch: "I think that in the eyes of the nation we both can and will oppose the whole aristocratic party and when the time comes we shall do it openly . . . in the meantime the best plan is to use them and undermine them . . . and eventually bring the whole affair into the open."[73] By the autumn of 1785, the time that van der Capellen had spoken of had arrived, although he had not survived to bear witness to the fulfilment of his prophecies. Without his powerful leadership it remained to be seen whether the Patriots could seize their opportunity and translate their new ideological confidence into political action. Once more the major theatre of their operations was the "vaderstad," Utrecht.

Like their opponents in the Free Corps, the regents on the council of Utrecht had learned some timely lessons from their alarming experiences on March 11, 1785. While determined to resist any future coercion from the militia, they made a bold play to pre-empt further discussion of a new constitution for the city by simultaneously publishing their own draft which made certain concessions to the principle of semi-elected councillors[74] and stiffening the prohibitions on public assembly and petition. Presumably their intention was to divide the Patriots. Instead they divided their own council, as a faction of five regents came out in support of recognising the right of the "Commissioned" to negotiate on behalf of the Free Corps. Still in an offensive temper, the council decided to take the bull by the horns and publicly rejected the credentials of the sixteen "Commissioned." On August 1, a delegation of four were permitted access to the council chamber only to be interrogated—*mirabile dictu*—on the manner of their appointment! Once again the council had pricked the Free Corps beyond endurance. The response of the companies to this ostentatious snub was to summon their militia the next day, when they were asked en masse whether they accepted the "Commissioned" as their accredited representatives and whether they endorsed their protest against the high-handedness of the council. Both questions being greeted with loud affirmatives, the Free Corps marched on the town hall, where the burgemeesters and councillors were duly informed that their "Commissioned" had been appointed, "not by mere notarial act but by the personal affirmation of the burghers." Donning black cockades, the adopted token of the Patriots, and harangued by orators like Pieter 't Hoen (the editor of the *Post van Neder Rhijn*), the Free Corps resolved, as on March 11, to stand their ground until their demands had met with a satisfactory response, and once again the council had no alternative but to capitulate.

Nothing of course would have been simpler than for the council to concede the Patriot demands under pressure and then recant as soon as it was removed. No doubt this is exactly what the members had in mind at the end of 1785. When, in September, a division of cavalry was sent to garrison Amersfoort, the second town of the province, and the naturally apprehensive "Commissioned" urged an emergency strengthening of the city's defences, the council showed a suspicious reluctance to comply.[75] But in any event, the Patriots had lost some of their earlier naïveté. On September 16, a draft which essentially corresponded to their version (with a few relatively insignificant amendments) was officially published. This time they were determined not to let the initiative slip so easily from their grasp. They had slowly awakened to the potency of the weapons the Free Corps had put into their hands, and the demonstration of August 2 merely inaugurated a succession of Dutch revolutionary *journées* which gradually battered the council into submission.

On December 20, 1785, the regents were obliged to abandon their scheme to have the States of Utrecht decide the issue with the Stadholder and to pledge to bring the new constitution into being, unilaterally if necessary, within a period of three months. On March 20, 1786, a massive demonstration standing silently in the heavily falling snow forced the council into permitting its five renegade councillors to forswear their oath to the old Règlement and to the States and take an oath to the new one. Finally, on August 2, after yet more delay, the resisting councillors were replaced by the newly elected choice of the burghers who, together with the forty deputies of the "Burgher College," were sworn in on the Neude.

The distinctly staccato rhythm of the Patriots' progress is some indication of the dogged rearguard action fought by their enemies. At each successive stage of the struggle the pattern of events was repeated. A climactic *journée* on which the council had surrendered to the crowds blockading their town hall was followed first by a period of silence, then one of ambiguous statements, then by nervous subterfuge and finally, emboldened by noises off from the States, by an outright repudiation of the last batch of concessions and total hostility to the next batch of demands. Eventually one of the more foolhardy of the regents would overreach himself, commit some act of needless provocation and vex the Free Corps into action. There was no tocsin in Utrecht, but on the eve of the day of reckoning appointed by the "Commissioned" and the "Constituted," their officers would repair to the *wijk* (town district) on which their company was based. Bills would be copiously distributed and speeches made in public places. (On the eve of December 20, Professor van Hamelsveld spoke from the summit of a giant snowball flanked by two boys holding torches.) The burghers would be summoned to assemble, armed and with their pennants, at their company parade ground early the following morning. When they were gathered, their representative to the "Commissioned" would read aloud their official protest to the council and a statement of the current grievance for the endorsement of those present. Following the acclamation, the company would march towards the city centre, picking up their comrades from other companies at the Goose Market and other points along the route.

Sporting black cockades, ribbons tied in a "V" (for Vrijheid), or even white lilies (*liever Frans dan Prins*), they would finally take up positions in the Oude Kerkhof, surrounding the town hall. The square was large by Dutch standards, but around 2,000 men—and there were often more Free Corps than that present—would suffice to fill the space. The situation must have become chronically familiar to the besieged councillors and burgemeesters. On the one hand they dared not deny the Free Corps spokesmen their demand for an immediate extraordinary meeting (often convened in the evening when the crowd would be supplemented by men coming off work) lest the disturbances in the city get completely out of control. On the other hand, no sooner had they arrived for the meeting than they were virtually imprisoned within the council chamber. Although no direct violence was ever offered to the regents, the veiled threats implied in the militia officers' offers of "protection" communicated themselves plainly enough to the apprehensive councillors.

On December 20, 1785, the "Commissioned" flatly told them that no-one (except for the octogenarian Berger who, in his second flush of youth, was sympathetic to the Patriots) would be permitted to leave the building until they had consented to the Patriots' demands. On a few occasions the more unpopular regents had narrow escapes. The secretary of the council, one Falck, decided to drive his coach bodily through the crowd to his home. He was pursued, harried and before his servants and sons dragged him into his house, had his coat and shirt torn from him. Often the situation was ugly enough to give the council no option but to appease the senior officers in the hope that they would calm down the crowds. By March 10, the day appointed for the institution of the new Règlement, the council was calling on the least radical company, the Handvoetboog, to actually guard the town hall. Once the regents had put themselves in the position of relying on the Free Corps for physical safety, then clearly they had lost control of their own city.

The single-mindedness with which Ondaatje, Lidth de Jeude, Gordon and the rest of the Patriot leaders pursued their goal of an elective government for Utrecht argues an impressive determination. Their exploitation of superiority in numbers and arms was, no doubt, what van der Capellen had had in mind when he called on the Dutch to rise in armed revolt. But it was the Utrecht Free Corps which provided the first experience of how this rhetoric might be translated into practical politics. Professor Palmer has disputed Geyl's contention that the Patriots developed, albeit in a very ad hoc fashion, both an ideology and an organisation; but their ability repeatedly to mobilise armed *attroupements* of between 2,000 and 5,000 people at a time suggests that Geyl's verdict is nearer the truth. The revolution in Utrecht may have been bloodless, but it was nonetheless ruthlessly executed. When their representations were declared illegal, as indeed they were, by the constituted authorities of Stadholder, States assembly and council, the Patriot burghers simply set about creating their own legality, and then ramming it down the throats of those it displaced. In these circumstances, that most overworked category of political description, "revolutionary," seems appropriate.

True to revolutionary form, not all its victims sat in the town hall. In the spring of 1785, when the Free Corps were preparing to enforce the implementation of the new constitution, a thorough purge was carried out in all the Free Corps companies of any doubtful officers. Some were found wanting in their Patriotic zeal and were discharged; others, mostly seniors, resigned of their own accord. Voet van Winssen, now a confirmed reactionary in the council, was removed from his post as Captain-Lieutenant of the Paapenvaandel Company and replaced with a more amenable junior. Called before one of the ad hoc tribunals of investigation, a certain Ravesteyn of the Pekstokken Company complained that "until yesterday I thought that I was living in a free country where no-one could be constrained to swear an oath which his conscience rejected." He was discharged from his commission for "many times giving affront and displeasure to the Watch."[76]

Despite the occasional instances of revolutionary militancy, there was no wish among the Free Corps to appear self-consciously ferocious. The Patriot revolt boasted, if that is the right word, no Marat, and the *Post van Neder Rijn* professed none of the expletive rage of the *Père Duchêne*. Indeed its most celebrated student poet, Jacobus Bellamy, who after the summer of 1783 shared lodgings with Pieter Ondaatje, grumbled that "my head burns with all the bustle and throng at our place. . . . Utrecht has become a battlefield."

Rather unconvincingly, since he was yet to reach his twenty-fifth birthday, he wished that "I could find a little village, far from all this turmoil where I might end my days peacefully."[77]

On the whole, the Patriot revolution was remarkable for its extreme reluctance to resort either to open violence or to punitive measures against its enemies. Moral issues aside, their attitude was eccentrically nice. They were determined to imprison the councillors within the chamber until they had capitulated to their demands, yet provided them with meat, bread and drink to help them through their ordeal. Their power was, in the last resort, based on the coercion of numbers, yet they were obsessed with the legal proprieties of their conduct. After the events of December 20, 1785, for example, the Patriots entered protracted debate with the council and the States as to the legal standing of their proceedings, and of the oath which bound them to the old Règlement. It was like executing the *coup de grâce* and then asking the corpse to declare itself the victim of death by misadventure. The Free Corps demanded nothing more of the councillors than that they should go quietly from their seats of power, and because this was done in the name of "imperishable burghers' rights," they felt the request to be altogether reasonable. When on successive occasions the regents repudiated concessions made under duress and reiterated their hostility to the new constitution, the Patriots registered deep shock and dismay at such dissembling. Under these circumstances, perhaps it is not surprising that their regime was of such brief duration.

For those who measure the success of revolutions in buckets of blood, clearly the Utrecht events were very tame stuff. Indeed, Colenbrander appeared to discount their significance for the lack of appetising sensationalism. But as Pieter Geyl pointed out with some pride, the fact that no guillotine was set up on the Neude nor gibbets on the Oude Kerkhof is scarcely a matter for commiseration. The Patriots had accomplished what they had set out to do in 1784, and, for that matter, many of the objectives first announced in van der Capellen's tract. By the autumn of 1786 there was ample justification for the claim that in Utrecht, "The People's vote is victorious."

The Patriots in Power: The Piecemeal Revolution

Utrecht was now a revolutionary commune. The assembly of the provincial States which had aborted the Patriots' initial attempt at reform but had failed to prevent a successful sequel withdrew to the safety of the Stadholderian garrison at Amersfoort, declaring illegal all the proceedings since December 10, 1785. The new council on its side ordered its deputies to remain in the city, where they were joined by representatives from the neighbouring and similarly revolutionary villages of Montfoort and Wijk-bij-Duurstede in a rival assembly which insisted on its legitimacy as the lawful States. The city itself was governed by a Patriot council with the elected group of fifteen at its core. Its authority was supplemented by a standing commission of burgher tribunes, also elected and closely affiliated to the Free Corps companies from which it had in fact evolved.

In itself there was nothing particularly remarkable or novel about this state of affairs. London, after all, had its Common Hall and Common Council, and was also accustomed to the adroitly managed intervention of the mob to force this issue or that man down the gullets of the aldermen. But the milieu of Utrecht in 1785 was different; Ondaatje was right to insist to the council that "we are not '48ers, not *canaille*." The purposeful organisation in the *wijken*, articulate leadership, the political deliberations of the Free Corps and the marches of the impassive, determined crowds on the town hall all announced a new epoch in Dutch, perhaps in European politics. Unlike the Gordon riots or the Wilkes demonstrations, there were no drunken rampages and no looting. The old duc de Saint-Simon—who had served in the Dutch army, married a Dutch countess and settled in Utrecht—noted the sobriety of the Patriots' conduct and commented that the danger lay in the fact that indeed they were not

vagabonds, libertines, rogues who are armed and led on to pillage; rather, they are magistrates of the towns in opposition to other magistrates . . . peaceful bourgeois, honest merchants, wealthy manufacturers and some of the best soldiers . . . the richest among them supporting the poorest.[78]

The duc's observations on the social constituency of the Patriots is confirmed by the rather random information available to the historian. But he was commenting principally on their leadership, which was only politically, not socially, distinguishable from that of their regent and Orangist opponents. The rank-and-file, however, present a more homogeneous picture. Of the sixteen members of the Utrecht "Burgher College" and the forty electors to the council, not one could really be described as anything except petty-bourgeois. Tradesmen—particularly those in the alimentary trades, bakers, cooks, butchers, grocers, corn chandlers and gin sellers—predominated, with a liberal sprinkling of ironmongers, drapers, haberdashers and the occasional petty-broker, tax collector and even a painter among them. As good as its word, the Burgher College included from the ranks of the Free Corps two Catholics, a Mennonite and an Arminian. While it is dangerous to generalise on these matters, it seems very probable that this social composition was repeated in the Free Corps and Patriot rank-and-file of provinces other than Utrecht, with no doubt a higher concentration of tenant farmers, innkeepers and predikants in the rural areas of Overijssel and Gelderland.

It is harder to provide a confident estimate of the numerical strength of the Patriots. Aside from the imponderable degree of support they may have drawn from the hitherto indifferent majority of the *burgerij*, it is difficult to be sure of the size of even the actively committed phalanx. Colenbrander accepts Saint-Simon's surely conjectural figure of 50,000 as plausible,[79] and this sort of figure finds indirect corroboration in the number of some 40,000 refugees—including women and children—fleeing from the counter-revolution and the unbridled plunder of 1787.[80] Even this number is likely to be misleading as it would certainly have included a number of Patriot regents, office-hunters and substantial property owners who while scarcely Free Corps militants would have been sufficiently associated with the Patriot cause for their persons and property to have suffered in the general mayhem of 1787. Of the 40,000, it is not known how many returned to the Republic within the next two years after the rioting had slowly abated. The number of Free Corps and other militia would surely be smaller. The largest gathering of Free Corps at one place was at Utrecht in August 1786, when 13,517 militia representing the four provinces of Utrecht, Holland, Overijssel and Friesland came together. The fifty-five "Burgher Corps" of Amsterdam almost certainly made up some 2,500 men, and at the point of civil war in July 1787, all troops and militia together at the disposal of the Patriot "cordon" came to 28,000.

However crude these estimates, it is evident that the Patriots constituted a minority of the Dutch population as a whole but equally evident that they were an appreciable portion of that section that was exercised by politics. Man for man they might well have been outnumbered by the poorer and more numerous crowds: the sailors, dockers and carpenters of the Amsterdam and Rotterdam waterfronts, fiercely loyal (and well primed with liquor and money) in their demonstrative Orangism. But like any relatively cohesive political group armed with a new and aggressive ideology, they were able to exercise a political influence out of all proportion to their numbers. Compared to the élite groups of the oligarchies, their support *was* popularly based. Organised in Patriotic societies, disseminating their ideology through press and pulpit, and armed in Free Corps regiments, the Patriots were able to outbid both regents and Orangists for popular allegiance. Like all revolutionary factions of this period which claimed to speak for the "people," the Patriots had just sufficient numbers on their side to make the threat plausible to those who could boast only the prescriptive inheritance of office and the service of a mercenary army on theirs.[81]

The major liability of the Patriots was not weakness of numbers. Nor was it, as Colenbrander often implies, a half-heartedness in pursuit of their professed aspirations to a form of representative government. On the contrary, it was rather an unheeding attachment to the letter and the spirit of those ideas, which diluted the concentration of their strength and compromised the effectiveness of their organisation. For in their determination to reconcile democracy with their mission of national renewal, they were, at least until the eleventh hour, obliged to accept the historical structure of institutions. Politically radical, they remained institutionally conservative. Or, put another way, they aspired to be democratic federalists. The unfortunate paradox of all revolutions, certainly all pre-twentieth-century revolutions—as de Tocqueville pointed out—is the contradiction between liberty and power. Those which inherited a highly centralised and autocratic apparatus of state institutions stood the best chance of survival but also ran the greatest risk of extinguishing the liberties for which the revolution had been undertaken. Such of course was the case in France, and conceivably in Russia a century later.

In the Netherlands there was little enough chance of a revolutionary dictatorship. Until the brink of defeat in summer 1787, not a word was mentioned of any kind of National Assembly, however rudimentary. The federal structure of the Republic and the sanctity of the Union of Utrecht were never at issue in this revolution until its eleventh hour. Indeed, their violation by the Stadholderian Règlements of 1672–74 and 1748 were primary indictments of the House of Orange. The acceptance of this devolution to provincial and even municipal sovereignties signalled a fidelity to promises to restore "imperishable" rights, but in the process dissipated the momentum of the revolution and compromised the effectiveness of the Patriots' organisation. Utrecht was a case in point. Here the Patriots had made the autonomy of the city from the jurisdiction of the States a major principle; the result was the secession of an independent commune, rather than the establishment of a de facto Patriot capital for the whole Republic.[82] Indeed, until the autumn of 1786, when reinforcements for the city's defences were needed and obtained from their comrades in Holland, the Utrecht Patriots (Free Corps assemblies notwithstanding) remained decidedly standoffish towards the Patriots of that province.

It is true that from the correspondence of Patriot clubs, the supra-provincial readership of newspapers like the *Post van Neder Rijn*, and from the assemblies of the Free Corps, something like a crypto-national revolutionary solidarity emerged. But this was no more than an agreed identity of aims, a "programme" in which a greater degree of decentralisation figured prominently. Once again they were impeded by a serious confusion between liberty and liberation. As both the Jacobins and the Bolsheviks saw, power was the precondition of freedom (as well as its potential destroyer), and the Patriots' strategy for its appropriation was improvised rather than planned. Even where the will to assert some kind of national revolutionary sovereignty was present—as it undoubtedly was for men like Pieter Vreede and possibly for van der Capellen—its devolution to so many provincial and municipal offices presented its putative guardians with a problematical task. Seizure of power in Utrecht, as the withdrawal of the States to Amersfoort plainly indicated, in no way guaranteed the adherence of neighbouring cities, let alone the entire province. Similarly the presence of an active Patriot as the Pensionary of Dordrecht failed to persuade Amsterdam to come down on the Patriots' side. In this particular case just the reverse process occurred. By the end of 1786, van Berckel found himself having to choose between the other two members of the "driemanschap" (Zeebergh and de Gijselaar) whose views were moving steadily towards the democrats, and his colleagues on the Amsterdam Council who were retreating in some alarm from the Patriot threats to open the city to an elected government.[83]

Perhaps the institution which most closely approached a repository of national sovereignty was the States-General. But in line with their professed intention to restore the purity of the Union of Utrecht, the Patriots made no attempt to dictate its allegiance by *force majeure*. They were content to wait until they had won the struggle for supremacy within each province, which would then alter its mandated delegation to the States-General and so change its political complexion. This formality of approach had farcical

results in the late spring of 1787, when the States-General alternately resolved and rescinded damning indictments of the Stadholder, according to
which of the two rival delegations from Utrecht had been seated as the accredited representatives of the province. In other provinces allegiances were in
a similar state of flux. Although the Patriots held on grimly to their centres
of power in Zutphen and Arnhem, Nijmegen remained with the Prince,
which meant that with its vote safe, the nobility could continue to command
a solid majority for the Orange cause. In Zeeland—where the Stadholder, as
the Marquis of Veere, counted as the province's only noble and thus automatically commanded its vote—the few isolated centres of Patriot activity
at towns like Flushing were unable to collect sufficient votes to alter its
Orange (that is, anti-Holland) allegiance.

In Friesland, as in Utrecht, the original contest with the Stadholder
which had produced the acceptance of John Adams' credentials had turned
into a triangular conflict between democratic Patriots, the *grietenij*-owning
nobility and the Orangists, with the latter two factions moving towards coalition as the lesser evil, leaving only one of three "quarters," Oostergo, to vote
in the assembly with the Patriots. In Overijssel and Groningen, where the
towns commanded more support from the countryside and its little hamlets,
the reverse situation obtained. Finally, the crucial votes of the States of Holland oscillated between the democratic Patriots and a more conservative regent policy, since the several shades of political affiliation in its cities, and the
confirmed Orangism of councils in Rotterdam, Delft and The Hague, contrived to make the situation in this province extremely complicated.[84]

In this way a struggle at the three levels of city, province and Republic
proceeded simultaneously. Apart from the ensuing chaos, it gave the Patriots'
enemies the chance to recover from the loss of control of a city or even
a province by making good their position elsewhere. The discomfiture of the
regents of Utrecht and Arnhem was the gain of Amersfoort and Nijmegen.
And when the Stadholder found himself the target of violent attack in the
States of Holland, he bowed to this temporary reverse and withdrew to his
stronghold in Gelderland.

The Patriots were seriously handicapped by the lack of a Bastille to
storm or a Tuileries to raze; the nearest they could manage to a demonstrative
victory over their principal enemy was to eject him from his garrison command at The Hague. This city, housing as it did not only the assemblies
of the States of Holland and the States-General but also the Stadholderian
court and Council of State, was virtually an Orangist enclave within Patriot
Holland. But apart from the symbolic implications of the expulsion of the
Prince, it was a matter of some pressing urgency to relieve him of his posts
as Captain- and Admiral-General as in the autumn of 1785, since a war
with the Emperor Joseph appeared to be in the offing. While such a step
would normally have been too draconian for the moderates dominating the
Amsterdam Council and the crypto-Orangists at Rotterdam and Delft, William V, true to form, played into the hands of his antagonists. During
September 1785, he insisted on inspecting his troops on the public square
of the Plein behind the Binnenhof. This bold but rather gratuitous display

generally took place on Sundays, when Free Corps from the neighbouring and distinctively more radical centres of Leiden and Schiedam drifted into the city. Orange and black cockades were flaunted by rival crowds, and on one Sunday the inevitable affray took place after the ceremony. The Hague *schutterij*, by no means uniformly Patriot in their allegiance, were brought on the streets together with some detachments of troops to quell the disturbance. In fact their appearance exacerbated it and the disorder threatened to deteriorate further when a rumour circulated that a plot was afoot to murder the Pensionaries van Berckel and de Gijselaar, who were then travelling between Rotterdam and Amsterdam. This violence failed to materialise. (It was suggested by the Orangists that the rumour, like the riot, had been the work of Patriot *agents provocateurs*.)

Whatever the truth of the matter, it gave the Patriots a good excuse to heap further obloquy on the unfortunate Stadholder and accuse him of acting as "a stoker of discord" and an enemy of civil quiet. Pressure grew to deprive him of his garrison command, although this threat was not made good until the following July and then only by the slenderest majority of one in the States of Holland. The Free Corps, already effectively in charge of civil order in many Holland towns, were given further leave to apprehend anyone suspected of fomenting Orangist riot. Orange was declared the "colour of sedition," and banners and pennants of that hue prohibited from public display; carrots sold with their roots too conspicuously showing were deemed provocative. One foolhardy cook rash enough to use suspiciously lavish helpings of saffron in his cakes was arrested for political subversion.[85]

On September 15 William and the Princess left The Hague, William travelling to Brabant to inspect his garrison at 's Hertogenbosch, the Princess going north to Friesland where she was given a rousing welcome. Joined by the Prince, they finally proceeded to the ancestral castle at Loo near to the stronghold of Stadholderian military power at Nijmegen.

In forcing the Stadholder from his solitary centre of power in Holland, the Patriots had won a signal victory. De Gijselaar, who had led the howls of execration in the States of Holland, proceeded the following March to crown his success by ostentatiously driving his carriage through the Stadhouderspoort in the Binnenhof, a privilege (as its name implies) previously reserved for the Prince. The gesture was an empty one, if less drastic than the guillotine; but it had the similar effect of desacralising the office of Stadholder and removing whatever princely unction remained from the House of Orange and Nassau. This was only the most humiliating of a succession of indignities directed at William V. Subjected almost daily to accusations of virtually criminal and treasonable conduct, he himself plunged into a mood of deep defeatism and melancholy. He spoke to his wife of abdicating and retiring to his estates in Germany. James Harris, the British ambassador, wrote to Carmarthen, the Secretary of State, in November:

They [the Patriots] mean to bring these charges forward with the publicity possible and to terrify him with the idea that his conduct has been so highly criminal against the State that his head is liable to be brought to the block. His imagination is already strongly impressed with this dread and in conversing with me, he has often said the Patriots mean to treat him as the Republicans did Charles the First.[86]

Other than a flight to his family estates and handing over the regency to Wilhemina, two courses of action were open to William V. Through the willing mediation of the French and Prussian ambassadors, he could attempt to negotiate with the more reasonable members of the States of Holland, perhaps offering a modification of the Règlements of 1748 and the Act of 1766 in return for a guarantee of The Hague garrison command. Such a policy might even succeed in driving a wedge between those among his enemies who wanted to settle their grievances quickly and cleanly and those others who wished to press democratic Patriotism to its logical conclusion. His second alternative was to abandon any thought of reconciliation and determine to crush his opponents by whatever means available. Throughout the end of 1785 William vacillated between the two courses, first giving hope to the diplomatic intermediaries, only to disappoint them with shatteringly arbitrary statements of his "due rights and privileges." "Aut Caesar, aut nihil," he was fond of remarking, and like Charles the First or Louis XVI he was temperamentally unsuited to accomplish skilful compromise. That in the end he avoided their fate was not so much due to any of his own qualities as those of the man to whom he entrusted his fortune: James Harris.[87]

Whatever the Stadholder may have lacked in the way of shrewdness, resolution and ruthlessness were compensated for in full by Harris' formidable talents. Egged on by Camarthen, and convinced in his marrow that France was Britain's natural and incorrigible enemy, Harris set about rescuing the Republic from her clutches. He faced an uphill task. Apart from the amicable association of the Patriots and the Amsterdam party with the French, the good offices of Vergennes had just disentangled an unpleasant situation with the Emperor Joseph. As the due reward for a successful negotiation, a treaty of friendship and alliance was signed with Versailles in October 1785 to the applause of the States of Holland. Yet even at this apparent nadir in the Stadholder's and thus the British interest's fortunes, Harris refused to contemplate surrender. Whenever the Prince's resolution faltered, he urged him to reject all thought of compromise. If he agreed to any terms even the more moderate of the Patriots might offer, his office would be reduced to a mere honorific dignity.[88] Indeed, Harris pressed aggressive resistance on the Prince. The alternative, he warned, was to risk losing the Republic by default. "If you still hesitate for any time," he told him, "there will remain no way to rescue the Republic from the French yoke." Until he discovered just how anxious Frederick the Great was to avoid any confrontation with France, Harris had been convinced that an Anglo-Prussian show of strength would be the answer to the Stadholder's problems. He had written to Camarthen that "if England and Prussia were to unite I would be responsible with my own head to drive every Frenchman out of the country and to bring as many Patriots to the block as you should choose."[89]

Harris never ceased to hope that some day, perhaps after Frederick's death, his favoured alignment would materialise. But in the meantime he was obliged to deploy an only slightly less direct strategy. His tactics took two forms. First, armed with generous Secret Service funds—£4,000 a year to the Stadholder alone as a pension with strings—he set about building a strong Orange Party to compete with the Patriots for popular allegiance and to mobilise the crowds in the areas where the Prince was traditionally strong: Gelderland, the Friesian countryside, and above all in Zeeland, where the Pensionary Laurens Pieter van de Spiegel became a close collaborator of the ambassador.[90] Orange "Free Corps" were to be established in the Zeeland towns and its magistrates seduced with promises of a greater share in the direction of the East India Company. Secondly, the more conservative regents in Holland, especially those in Amsterdam, were to be wooed away from the Patriots by intimations of willingness to negotiate the outstanding fiscal and commercial grievances, as well as a modified Stadholderian constitution designed to protect their own privileges. With this in mind Harris even approached Paulus in autumn 1785 but failed to get very far.

Finally, the isolated democrats were to be subjected to sufficient intimidation from crowds, Orange "Free Corps," and the army to reduce their area of manoeuvre to a choice of unconditional capitulation or civil war. Harris aimed, in the long run, to be prepared for either eventuality. And if it should come to blows, he believed neither in the military capacity of the Free Corps nor French professions of intervention. His plan, matured by the spring of 1787, was a collision course plotted with ruthless dedication from which he never veered. Only occasionally when asking Pitt (who shared all his apprehensions over a "French" Netherlands) for yet more funds did he, unconvincingly, admit that "I abhor this dirty work but when one is employed to sweep chimneys one must black one's fingers."[91]

The first decisive action was taken in August 1786. Two small townships in the Veluwe region of Gelderland, Elburg and Hattem, with populations of 1,200 and 500 souls respectively, had followed the lead of larger centres like Kampen and Arnhem in repudiating the Stadholderian right of appointing their magistrates and councillors. In the spring of 1785 they had convened citizens' assemblies and had demanded the restoration of rights of election, in Hattem's case actually surviving into the 1750's.[92] The very fact that towns of this size could mount so bold a show of Patriot principles is itself a startling indicator of how far their ideology had penetrated the inner regions of Dutch society. In May 1786 they formally repudiated the right of both the Stadholder and the States of Gelderland to any jurisdiction in their affairs. Aggrieved at the turn of events in Utrecht but impotent to do anything about it owing to the strength of the city's defences, the Orange Party in the east was impatient for some effective demonstration of its authority. A swift repressive action against virtually defenceless hamlets such as Elburg and Hattem offered just such an opportunity, and in August the States asked the

Stadholder for military assistance in restoring due order to the two townships. Other than bravura, their defence against any serious attack by the army was of course negligible. Hattem had recruited virtually all its male population, men and boys, into an ad hoc militia and had armed half of them with ancient muskets, but this amounted to no more than 200 at the most. When it became known in Patriot circles in the land provinces that the States were bent on military action, Hattem and Elburg became something of a *cause célèbre*. Robert Jasper van der Capellen van der Marsch sent to de Gijselaar in The Hague for help, and received many effusive messages of faith and good-will but only a token number of troops and Free Corps in return. A few more Free Corps arrived from the neighbouring towns of Kampen and Zwolle in Overijssel and Zutphen and Harderwijk in Gelderland. For them, if not for the Holland Patriots, the action against the two towns could well decide the fate of the Patriot cause in the land provinces.

Even with these limited reinforcements, rudimentary earthworks, antique and mostly unfireable batteries were unlikely to detain the troops for very long. Herman Willem Daendels—the son of an ex-burgemeester of Hattem, later destined to serve as a general in the French and Batavian armies, but at this time only twenty-four—attempted to steel the morale of the defenders with talk of fighting to the end. But against two infantry regiments, sixty cavalry and seventy odd artillery, the Patriots were not encouraged to show die-hard resistance. On September 4 and 5 the towns were overrun after a few brief artillery exchanges, and about 500 Patriots fled to safety in Kampen and Zwolle. Plunder, looting and the usual indignities of these occasions took place, including the peculiarly Dutch habit of violating churches known for their Patriot sermons by smearing rancid butter on the pews and tearing up the Bibles. When William was told that the rebels of Hattem and Elburg had been crushed, he was said to have yelled: "Have they been hanged? Hell and damnation! Why not hang Satan's children?"[93]

The attack on Hattem and Elburg and the resolutions of the Landdag (provincial assembly) of Gelderland which authorised the expeditions were taken by the Patriots as a virtual declaration of civil war. They inaugurated a period of repression in that province in which, one by one, the Patriot magistrates and councillors of the towns were isolated and picked off by armed warrants. But if these proceedings were intended to cow the Patriots into an early submission they were badly miscalculated, since their effect was exactly the opposite. The fate of the Gelderland Patriots galvanised their co-partisans into urgent measures for their collective defence and rather tardily brought a measure of unity to the different factions. A "military cordon" was estab-lished, covering Holland, Utrecht and Overijssel, a more or less contiguous stretch of territory in the centre of the Republic dominated by Patriot regimes. The command of the Holland forces, very inadvisedly as it turned out, was entrusted to the Rhinegrave Frederick III van Salm, a professional soldier and a political adventurer who appeared to have the ear of Vergennes. A "National Fund" had been set up in March 1786, and the following October

Amsterdam produced over 30,000 guilders and an undertaking to finance and raise a force of 6,700 men. In the States of Holland, de Gijselaar demanded that the province immediately cut off its quota to the army and call in its troops from the Stadholder's control. This military authority, he said, was in any case illegal since it proceeded from Prince Maurits's refusal to obey an order of Grand Pensionary Oldenbarneveld. De Gijselaar called William "the new Alva . . . a murderer and enemy," and finally threatened to take Dordrecht out of the Union if he were not stripped of his office as Captain- and Admiral-General. And despite an earlier vote on the Amsterdam Council supporting Rendorp's claim that the garrison at The Hague rightly belonged to the Prince, it too was now obliged to join the general obloquy. In August, after the conclusive victory of the democrats at Utrecht, the Amsterdam regents finally signed an act effectively adhering to the Act of Association and proposing a "Government by representation of the People."[94]

Alarmed at the prospect of a siege, Utrecht was turned into an armed camp by its new council. Villas were demolished to make way for strong earthworks, and moats and trenches dug outside city walls. All able-bodied males were conscripted into the militia and a sum of 12 stuivers was paid to all who took regular turns at the watch. The Marquis de Saint-Simon, having his first taste of citizenship in arms, gave a vivid account of its patriotic intensity. He described violent harangues by members of the council before the people in the squares, and remarked with some evident distaste that "the majesty of the people was a word repeated in common speech."[95] He saw the women of Utrecht playing an important part in rallying the spirit of their husbands, taunting those who flagged in their civic duties, some going so far as to run through the streets brandishing knives and threatening to massacre all those who deserted their posts in Utrecht's time of need. Predikants like Bergh took to preaching belligerent sermons dressed in Free Corps uniform from the tops of fruit barrels. In its rehearsal of revolutionary Paris, Utrecht even managed to circulate a rumour of an "aristocratic plot" to let 500 foreign mercenaries into the city. For a while the houses of patricians who had left Utrecht with the Deputies of the States were surrounded by angry crowds.

Yet despite persistent rumors, the threatened siege failed to materialise. By the spring of 1787, the 2,000 Free Corps in Utrecht had been supplemented by about 4,000 troops, some sent from the army of the States of Holland, some from various Free Corps units throughout the "cordon." Of the 6,000, only 500 were cavalry, but this disproportion was not so disadvantageous from the point of view of defence, and in any case was not significantly different in the Stadholder's army. Confidence in their position had greatly increased since the previous September. Learning of the occupation of Vreeswijk, a small canton on the Lek near Amersfoort, the military council in Utrecht decided to send a force against the Prince's troops, led by their colonel, Jan Anthonie d'Averhoult. The encounter was brief. A cannonade from the Prince's troops was met by a musket volley from the Patriots, rifle fire from their sharpshooters and an infantry advance which put the Orange soldiers into a panic-stricken flight, leaving behind eighty dead as well as their arms and baggage. While not the greatest clash of arms, the action at Vreeswijk was hailed as a sensational victory by the Patriots. Certainly it had been the first test of the fibre of the Free Corps on the field of battle, and a successful one, which more than repaired the damage to Patriot morale done by the repression of Elburg and Hattem. God, it seemed, was once more on the side of true Dutch liberty.

Holland Divided, December 1786–June 1787

The skirmish at Vreeswijk in May 1787 had more symbolic than strategic value for the Patriots. No doubt it deterred the Stadholder from any further ill-considered attempts on the defences of the "cordon" and postponed indefinitely any thought of besieging Utrecht itself. It also raised the disturbing possibility that without the troops recalled by the States of Holland, the Stadholder's army might be incapable of inflicting decisive military defeat on the Patriots. But on their side the Patriots had few reasons for celebration. Lack of logistic support had prevented them from exploiting their advantage after Vreeswijk and taking the battle to the enemy. The Orange regiment had returned to Amersfoort with the greater part of its force intact. Further tentative sallies outside Utrecht had come to nothing. Through May and June reports were received of large-scale desertions from the garrisons at Naarden and Woerden. While these losses were to some extent offset by the private legions of van Salm, the inveterate Orangism of both the common soldiers and sailors threw serious doubt on their loyalty in battle. The result of all these uncertainties was a military stalemate in which neither side was able to do much more than defend its territorial base.

In itself this situation was graver for the Stadholder, since it was for him to attempt to recover the military authority over the Union from which all his offices proceeded. The Patriots could afford to sit tight and defend their respective provincial sovereignties. If necessary, as de Gijselaar intimated, the States of Holland and Utrecht should be prepared to annex Dutch Brabant and secede from the union.[96] But the allegiance of even these provinces was by no means unanimous. The withdrawal of the Stadholder from The Hague had not succeeded in stabilising the balance of power within Holland. On the contrary, the shifting coalition of various shades of anti-Stadholderian opinion—ranging from the most cautious Amsterdam regent to the most intemperate Haarlem Free Corps—had been put under severe strain by the military alarms and excursions of autumn-winter 1786. By the turn of the year it was threatening to disintegrate altogether. The activities at Utrecht and the prospect of a siege had raised the temperature of the Patriot agitation to a feverish pitch. Free Corps volunteers and Patriot money were subscribing themselves in advance to an heroic defence of the "vaderstad," and in the face of military action something like an authentically revolutionary militancy was infecting the centres of Patriot radicalism. Meetings of Free Corps in cities like Leiden, Dordrecht and Haarlem were passing resolutions directed against any tenants of city offices not siding publicly and wholeheartedly with the Patriots, and were threatening a repetition of the events at Utrecht. Now that lives seemed to depend on the outcome of the war against the Stadholder, any magistrate or burgemeester considered politically doubtful was treated as a potential fifth columnist, castigated in the press and urged to declare his loyalties. These *démarches* alarmed the regents of Holland. Their reliable *schutterij* appeared to have been transformed into a dangerous armed mob, manipulated by vicious demagogues calling themselves "democrats" for their own ends. Scared off from any more dealings with such men, even when they masqueraded as respectable Pensionaries like de Gijselaar, they began to glance over their shoulders at the Stadholder with slightly less apprehension. Better the devil they knew . . .

Not that the regents of Holland succumbed without a struggle. The character of their institutions assisted their resistance. For however desirable from the Patriots' point of view it may have been to impose a draconian political orthodoxy throughout Holland, their claim to do so in the name of the States of the province was limited by that body's ill-defined jurisdiction. Just as Hattem and Elburg had been able to defy the authority of the Gelderland Landdag until punished for their impertinence with military force, so the little knot of towns around Rotterdam and The Hague (Wassenaar, Delft, Rijswijk and Voorburg) as well as the rural hamlets of Oud Beierland in the extreme south of the province, remained stubbornly Orangist in their affiliation and refused to comply with edicts prohibiting the display of Orange tokens and cockades. It was not until July and August, when similarly arbitrary pressure from Free Corps units and Gerard Mappa's "Flying Legion" succeeded in winkling out recalcitrant magistrates and regents, that this opposition was finally subdued.[97]

The Patriots were unable to command a majority in the States of Holland with any ease. Three degrees of opposition stood between them and the sovereign control they sought with increasing desperation in 1787. First, the outright hostility of towns like The Hague and Delft, where the regencies remained dominated by the traditional oligarchies; second, the wavering sympathies of Rotterdam, whose vote vacillated between more and less conservative groups; and finally and most seriously, the exasperating equivocation of Amsterdam. While insufficiently strong to capture outright control of the States, this "aristocratic" group could generally muster sufficient votes to deny any measures it considered either unduly punitive or unduly radical. In response to these manoeuvres, and with a mounting impatience, the Patriots attempted to redefine the constitution of the provincial States in terms of a more authentically representative assembly. On January 30, 1787, the Pensionary of Haarlem, Adriaan van Zeebergh, put a resolution to the assembly:

. . . whereas the constitution of the province of Holland is in its principles a popular representation, it is necessary that the right of the people be duly ascertained; that the members of the States be rendered responsible to them for their conduct and be precluded from taking any decisive step without their consent. . . .[98]

This was a bold move in the direction of a "democratisation" of the States; but even though Zeebergh was merely proposing the establishment of a commission to "ascertain" the means of implementing the representative principle, his relatively modest proposal was defeated by the opposition of Amsterdam and the moderates. This frustration only stoked the fires of radical reform more powerfully. But such a spurt of activity on the part of the Pensionaries within the States was in part a nervous reaction to the increasingly truculent agitation by Free Corps assemblies to revolutionise the province, root and branch. Their goal was the convening of a genuinely popular assembly with legislative powers, and they were prepared to create it within, or if necessary instead of, the framework of the provincial States. At an extraordinary meeting of the national federation of Free Corps in Utrecht in November–December 1786, proposals for a representative assembly of the whole "Netherlands People" had been mooted and the delegates from Holland had laid special emphasis on the right of resistance to an *"unnatural"* regime. Still more significantly, the publication of a *Deductie van Het Volk van Nederland* (lit., Deduction of the Netherlands People)—in direct parody of Francken's *Deductie*, for so long the charter of the regents' "True Liberty"—explicitly discarded, once and for all, the historical mumbo-jumbo of prescriptive rights, immemorial freedoms and customary liberties allegedly vested in the town regencies. "The Netherlands people," it said, "has long enough borne the yoke of alternating forms of slavery, on which the name of 'Freedom' has been painted. At last the time has come that in fact and not just appearance, the Netherlands will enjoy its full rights and liberties."[99] Sandwiched between this pressure from below and the rigid immobility of regents still in office, the Patriot leaders deflected attention from their predicament by ever more bellicose tirades against the Prince. De Gijselaar, who at the beginning of the Patriot agitation in 1781 had been the moderate colleague of van Berckel, now led the hue and cry for the cashiering of the Stadholder and his permanent exile from the province.

Amsterdam remained by far the greatest obstacle to the achievement of a democratic government in Holland. At the end of 1786, the prospects for its conversion to the Patriot faith seemed bleaker than ever. From its original stance as the principal antagonist of Stadholderian pretensions, Amsterdam had retreated into cautious gloom as the political momentum of the Patriot revolution accelerated. Concerned with its own long-standing grievances and haunted by the nightmare of 1748, the patriciate remained convinced that it could obtain satisfaction from the hard-pressed Stadholder without recourse to a popular revolution which could rebound against its own power and influence. Thus it kept aloof from the wilder nostrums of the Patriot leaders. Van der Capellen's blithe assertion that he would gladly exchange every Dutch colony for the sacred freedom of the press struck the patricians not only as foolhardy but heretical. Their preoccupations remained what they had been at the beginning of the Fourth Anglo-Dutch War: the reform of the navy; subsidies for the ailing East India Company; revision of the tax quota in Holland's favour; abolition of the Act of Consulship and the

Stadholderian "recommendatie recht"; and a foreign policy less inflexibly tied to British interests.

The removal of Brunswick and the French mediation in the Austrian quarrel had marked two notable successes.[100] From the beginning, they had conceived of the Patriot campaign in terms of their limited objectives, and now that they were within sight of success they were loath to have them jeopardised by the hot-headed folly of a few journalists and shopkeepers in uniform. Their flirtation with constitutional reform had been confined to "curtailing" Stadholderian power, much in the manner of the Parlements' intention to de-Bourbonise France. The reversion to the status quo ante 1747 with modest concessions to the representative principle as outlined in the "programme" of 1782 and expanded in the charter known as the Constitutional Restoration (*Grondwettige Herstelling*) was the terminus of their political progress. They had provided an appropriate political organisation to retain control of the movement within traditional circles. The meetings of "Patriot Regents," usually at Amsterdam, were no more than gatherings of thirty to fifty notables, concerned to co-ordinate tactics in their respective provinces of the Republic. Although they included such un-regent-like figures as the van der Capellens and de Gijselaar, it was men like "Father" Henrik Hooft and Abbema who set the tone of moderation.

In marked contrast to the flamboyant publicity of the Free Corps parades at Leiden and Utrecht, these sessions were private, formal and exclusive. Communication was maintained through a "bureau of correspondence" established in 1783, and later by a "Directory" of seven representatives of each of the provinces. But their thunder was stolen by Utrecht. As the revolution of the Free Corps overtook them, the "Patriot Regents" were forced on the defensive. Lagging behind in their gestures toward Patriot democracy they rather apologetically, and a year late, added their adherence to the Act of Association, at the same time making judicious amendments which referred to " . . . government by representation of the people, founded on the basis of the Constitutions and privileges of the individual provinces and cities. . . "[101] With some shrewdness, François Vérac, the French ambassador, advised Vergennes that "those families called 'patrician' will always form the corps of magistrates . . . but in order to win the suffrage of the people they are obliged to make some public profession of their attachment to the system of liberty."[102]

As the conflict with the Stadholder threatened to turn into a full-scale civil war, the equivocal position of the regents became more and more difficult to sustain. The most populous city within the "cordon," and the wealthiest, Amsterdam was naturally looked to to provide the wherewithal to mobilise a Patriot army. But the patricians had not fought a twenty-year struggle with the Stadholder over appropriations for the army only to find themselves saddled with an even more onerous obligation. Why should they help to finance a force raised in the name of an ideology which professed their own destruction? Plainly they had no incentive to become an active party in a conflict in which, whoever proved the victor, they could only lose. Sensing their apprehension, Joachim Rendorp the Orangist burgemeester, and a handful of associates—including the *schutter* colonel and ex-burgemeester Willem Gerrit Dedel, and Hendrik Calkoen, erstwhile friend of that other soured rebel, John Adams—urged a severe attitude toward the excesses of Patriot zeal. Rendorp himself had jailed the printer and editor of the *Politieke Kruijer* in 1785 and fined both 3,000 guilders for "defamatory allegations" concerning the council and the Prince. In March 1786 he had persuaded his colleagues to insist that the garrison at The Hague rightfully belonged to the Stadholder; and while his brand of aggressive Orangism was in a minority on the council, such was the despondency at the activities of the Free Corps that he and Dedel came to call the tune at many of the council meetings early in 1787. James Harris, at any rate, was hopeful that Amsterdam might defect altogether from the Patriot camp. On the other hand, horrified as they were by the "anti-aristocratic" polemics of the democrats, the blood of the Bickers, Abbemas and Hoofts rebelled at too close an association with any Prince of of the House of Orange. Despite encouraging noises from Harris and van de Spiegel, the banker princes of Amsterdam had never before profited from trusting their fortune to a Stadholder and it was difficult now to break the habit. Abandoning the "cordon," recalling the Prince to The Hague, and cutting off monies to the Holland army meant risking the certain fury of the Free Corps for the uncertain prospect of an Orange victory in the ensuing battle. And in the spring of 1787 that was a gamble most of the patriciate felt they could not yet afford.

The result of this confusion was an almost total paralysis of will on the part of the council as a whole. Some of its regents inclined towards Dedel, others towards van Berckel. Most dithered in the middle, glancing nervously over their shoulder at Utrecht. But their very procrastination at a time of impending hostilities only tended to aggravate divisions which were already latent in the city. The generally unfavourable attitude shown by Amsterdam's delegation to the States of Holland towards the democrat resolutions—and particularly those concerned with strengthening the defences of the "cordon" —had antagonised many junior officers in the Free Corps. Such was their discontent at these proceedings that, in February, the precarious tranquility of the city was brusquely interrupted.

The immediate matter of contention was a proposal in the States of Holland to move the Rhinegrave van Salm's legion to The Hague. This would have put the seal on the dispossession of the Stadholder's garrison command. Yet it looked, too, suspiciously like a crude threat not only to the dissident Orange minority in the States of Holland but also to the States General, which was still subject to a majority of Orange votes. The regent faction in Amsterdam looked askance at the proposal, although a massive campaign of petition was mobilised in its support throughout Holland. On February 21, while the council was discussing the matter, a deputation of sixty junior Free Corps officers, led by one van Goedoever, a colonel, appeared at the town hall in a not over-tactful attempt to influence the outcome of the deliberations.[103] Dedel and the regent group were so incensed by this intervention that they immediately moved not only the rejection of the proposal but the dissolution of the legion altogether and a drastic cut in Amsterdam's contribution towards the defence of the "cordon." Once known, this move invited further visits from the officers, in larger numbers on each occasion, until on the 26th they forced an entry into the antechamber of the council room itself. Further brusquer action on their part was only averted by the timely action of old Hooft, who climbed painfully onto a chair and addressed the officers on the justice of their cause and assuring them they had sympathy of the majority of the councillors.

The debut of popular politics in Amsterdam had been abrupt, but it was not so easily pacified. The Free Corps remained restive throughout March and its companies met in Patriot clubs each night to discuss the issues before the council and to object with varying degrees of vehemence to their conservative posture in the States as impatience grew. Petitions streamed to the town hall urging a more positive policy.

On April 3, van Goedoever appeared once more at the town hall, this time with 102 officers, to demand that the city henceforth be represented at the States only by its two Pensionaries, van Berckel and Carel Wouter Visscher, both men trusted by the Patriot rank-and-file. Recognising the seriousness of this new intervention, Dedel acted swiftly. He despatched Calkoen to Nijmegen to make an offer to the Prince. He was to have the full support of Amsterdam in the dissolution of the "cordon," an immediate withdrawal of funds and troops, and the restoration of the Prince to The Hague and to his garrison—all in exchange for the abolition of the "recommendatie recht" and the more stringent provisions of the Règlement of 1748. On his side, the Prince was to put the weight of his name and station behind an attempt to galvanise the "bijltjes" (lit., "little axes")—the mariners, dockyard workers and carpenters of the IJ islands—into action against the Free Corps.

William, of course, showed no sign of conceding anything at all concerning his due rights under the Règlement. But whatever his feelings, the sentiments of the Bijltjes themselves were even more uncompromising, refusing to come to the aid of the regents unless all of the Prince's rights without exception were recognised. Conditioned for generations to regard the "heeren" of the Dam as the enemies of their Prince, they found it impossible to credit the notion that they had suddenly become his loyal allies. Many of the Free Corps soldiers were socially closer to the shipwrights than those who now pretended to be their true patrons. Invited by one Lutteken, a quartermaster in Dedel's pay, to "exterminate some Patriot filth," they replied that while they had great love and respect for the Stadholder, they knew that the aristocracy were detestable tyrants for whom they would not move an inch. As for the Patriots, well, they were fine men in whom they saw nothing much to complain of.[104] Their response to further blandishments remained cool until the sacking of the Orange societies in May, which they took as a direct insult to the Prince. By that time their intervention was too late to save the regents.

On April 20 yet another incendiary pamphlet was discovered on the streets of the city. Called *Het Verraad Ontdekt* (*Treason Unmasked*), it accused Dedel and eight colleagues of actively conspiring with the Prince

to break the "cordon." Its effect traumatized the Patriot burghers. That evening they thronged the halls and galleries of the Patriot societies—particularly
the Vaderlandse and Burgelijke Societies—listening to impassioned denunciations of the culprits and demands for their immediate removal. It was almost
a rehearsal for the aftermath of Necker's dismissal twelve years later. The
"Burgerkrijsraad" (Burgher Defence Council), which provided the effective
command for the fifty-five Free Corps units of the city, assembled late at
night at the Doelen Hall where thirty-nine years before the first programme
of reform of the regencies had been drawn up. On this occasion they were
not to be so easily fobbed off. The following day, on the orders of the committee, a great concourse of burghers, guild brothers and representatives of
the fifty-five companies filled Dam Square in front of the town hall. They
chanted the names of the guilty regents and shouted for their disgrace. Simultaneously in each of the fifty-five districts, meetings of the companies were
convened, the necessary motions passed, and names added to a monster
petition which finished up with over 16,000 signatures. This was the "Act
of Qualification," "emanating from the will of the people," which pressed for
the purge of the regents and their replacement by new and trusted councillors.
As at Utrecht, the crowd on the Dam was noisy but not violent. But it was
plain to the councillors inside that control of the city had passed to the
Burgher Defence Council, which could excite or restrain the crowds at its
will. Certainly it was only too evident that its members had no intention of
leaving their places in the square until their demands had been met. Late in
the afternoon Hooft put the necessary proposal to his colleagues, together with
a whole folio of resolutions passed by the district meetings of the city. With
the rebel caucus discreetly absenting themselves from the meeting, their
permanent exclusion from the council was voted and a new regency proclaimed to the crowd outside. Once more in a major Dutch city, a revolution
by default had succeeded.

Other towns in Holland followed Amsterdam's lead. Outside the province, Free Corps stormed the Orange societies at Deventer. In Rotterdam,
Paulus was engineering the conversion of the Patriot minority into a Patriot
majority on the council. Here the favoured tactic was to press for an "enlargement" of the council from twenty-five to forty members, the new councillors being elected by the *wijken* rather than co-opted by the regents. The claim
had some basis in historical fact. Twenty-five was an unusually small body for
a city of Rotterdam's size, and prior to 1615 there had been a council of forty.
Even when Paulus and his allies had succeeded in dishing the regents, their
representatives at the States made a last-ditch stand, refusing to evacuate their
residence in The Hague and calling on the assembly to declare the proceedings
at Rotterdam illegal. For a while the States hesitated before depriving them
of their seats; it took further evidence of the popularity of the Rotterdam coup
in similar manifestations in Schiedam and Gorinchem before the old guard
was finally ejected. In Amsterdam, resistance to the revolution of April 21 was
bolder still. Letters were written to the new council protesting that signatures

appearing on the Act of Qualification had been forgeries. Newly established Orange Societies mobilised a flood of counter-petitions and attempted to excite the hitherto rather sluggish "Bijltjes" to violent action against their enemies.

At the end of May, with order in the city breaking down, units of Free Corps ran amok in the Orange Societies and sacked the houses of Dedel, Beels, Rendorp, and the leading Orangist regents. Hasty destruction of the bridges connecting the dockyard islands with the centre of the city prevented the intervention of the Bijltjes; and after many days of continuous violence and riot, the council used troops to enforce order and publicly blamed the Orangists for the disturbances. It had become plain that Amsterdam was now an unsafe place for a patrician to keep house; many of the wealthy families, long resident on the *grachten,* evacuated from the "nest of murder" to the comparative safety of the countryside.

Even in the hinterland of the province, though, militant Free Corps officers—egged on by the democratic press—attempted to enforce political uniformity on all occupants of public office. On July 4, the States published further prohibitions on any public expression of sympathy for the Stadholder, including the singing of Orange songs. Violent measures taken by Stadholderian troops in Gelderland against Patriots in Arnhem and Zutphen, and their public humiliation at the hand of "Orange Free Corps" and angry mobs, had persuaded the Holland Patriots to go some way towards retaliating in kind. Rationalising orders to eject any magistrates or councillors known to have sided with the Amsterdam regencies or worse, it was argued that to leave any important posts in the hands of the politically unreliable when exposed to military attack was to invite betrayal. In addition, many magistrates were forcibly removed from office for failing to arrest and prosecute "known disturbers of the peace" (i.e., Orangemen) or for proscribing Patriot clubs in their towns and villages. Often the mere fact of belonging to a family known to have transmitted its tenure of office for some generations was sufficient to warrant deprivation as an "aristocrat." The fact that in the countryside some of the Free Corps were recruited from among the Catholic peasantry added a further edge to the antagonism of the purges.

Sometimes action went beyond mere removal from office. The magistrate and burgemeester of Leerdam who resisted the intrusion of Free Corps was brought back to The Hague as a prisoner, and similar treatment was meted out to officers in Rijswijk and Voorburg. Carts driven to the Maas delta and to Oud Beierland came back laden with Orange flags, rusty sabres and muskets, and pictures of William V. Such were the indignities visited on families that had held positions of public authority that many regents who had originally supported the Patriots repented their allegiance. One of the most prominent of the Patriot aristocracy, the Baron Wassenaar van Starrenburg, commander of The Hague *schutterij,* for a while threatened to march the garrison against the Free Corps but at the last moment hesitated and was himself put in custody and removed from office.

The machinery of this campaign of political duress was necessarily very imperfect. Compared with the counter-repression that was to follow, the number of those ejected from office in the summer of 1787 was relatively few. There was no draconian tribunal; no Jacobin Terror. Only perhaps the "Flying Legion" (*Vliegend Legertje*) of Gerard Mappa, a Free Corps officer from Delft, anticipated the use of militia as political police. Mappa's company consisted of about 300 men armed with rifles, light artillery and about 200 horse. By Dutch standards this amounted to a formidable small regiment, and was at approximately the same strength as the force used to subjugate Hattem and Elburg. Originally, the legion was used to reinforce weak points along the lines of the "cordon," but during August it was employed in the business of enforcing political purges carried out by democrat minorities in the towns of Holland. The most spectacular of these coups took place at Delft itself, where the mere fact of Mappa's camp outside the city was sufficient to persuade eleven recalcitrant regents to depart from office. The purge not only brought Wybo Fijnje, the editor of the *Hollandsche Historische Courant*, and the auto-didact Gerrit Paape to power in the city, but delivered to the Patriots one of the biggest arsenals and magazines in the Republic.

Other towns followed Delft's experience: Leyden and Dordrecht in the south; Alkmaar, Hoorn and Monnikendam in the north. Unfortunately, very little is known of either the social composition or the specific ideological complexion of Mappa's troop. It would be rash to see the legion as a proto-type of the French *armées révolutionnaires* since no more than any other Free Corps unit was it motivated by specifically social or economic antagonisms. Nevertheless the "Vliegend Legertje" was undoubtedly the para-military wing of a political party used not only to ram its ideology down the throats of reluctant admirers but to remove them from office in favour of trusted partisans of the democratic cause.

The Patriot revolution in Holland was relatively late in maturing. Its earlier leadership had been virtually monopolised by the more traditional anti-Orangist regents such as the "driemanschap" of Pensionaries. Only when the conflict had polarised so far that the regents were outflanked in their ideology by the Free Corps were they forced to choose between a volte-face in their relations with the Prince or embarking on the dangerous gamble of revolutionary democracy. In November 1786, François Vérac had noted exactly this "embarras extrême": "On the one hand they fear an accommodation which will not satisfy the bourgeois, and on the other to further inflame the fermentation. The Patriot leaders thus find themselves between Scylla and Charybdis. . . ."[105]

Throughout the Republic in the spring and summer of 1787 the strength of the Patriots was becoming more unevenly dispersed. In the far north, a radical Patriot council clung on to the city of Groningen which through its powerful representation in the Landdag just about retained control over the province. But in practical terms, Groningen was too remote from the Patriot centre and its forces too sparse to offer the democrats much other than a favourable vote in the States-General. Indeed, bordering the territory of East Friesland, Groningen was potentially vulnerable to an easy invasion from that Prussian province. One province to the south in Overijssel, the Patriots retained control of Zwolle' Kampen, and as the receiving centre for refugees from Hattem and Elburg, Deventer had itself become violently democratic in sympathies. The "little towns" governed by the "Burgher Councils" which with the help of Free Corps had taken power in 1785 continued to enjoy their protection. But between them and the now heavily manned Amersfoort garrison there stood only Utrecht. The "vaderstad" had itself received a continuous infusion of men, arms and supplies from Overijssel and Holland since the "Battle" of Vreeswijk, and with a defending force of over 7,000 could afford to be reasonably confident of its capacity to withstand any siege the Orange troops could mount.[106] On the other hand, its few desultory attempts in June to break through the Stadholderian lines to the northeast had failed dismally, so that the forces at Utrecht remained confined merely to the defence of the city.

Further east in Gelderland the Patriots were in terrible disarray. Since September 1786, the Patriot groups in Zutphen and Arnhem had been under continuous threat from Nijmegen; eventually in June, punitive detachments served them with the same notice as Mappa's legion was to hand out to Orangists in Holland. Regents and burghers known for Patriot sympathies were run out of the cities, their houses delivered to the soldiers and mobs for their pleasure. Van der Capellen van der Marsch became a refugee in Kampen before taking up a military commission for the Woerden authorities; and by the end of June, the last resistance to the Stadholder in Gelderland had collapsed. In Zeeland, where the Stadholder had no troops (although detachments could be moved from garrisons in Brabant at 's Hertogenbosch), van de Spiegel had had great success in recruiting "Orange Free Corps" to oppose the pretensions of the few Patriot enclaves at Veere, Goes, Zierikzee and Middelburg.

The sailors and fishermen of Walcheren and South Beveland, always passionately loyal to the House of Orange and in addition socially hostile to the urban patriciate, now availed themselves of an apparently authorised opportunity to ransack their properties and physically assault their persons. One such victim, Lucas van Steveninck, who combined the doubly unpopular professions of shipowner and physician, on July 1 was forced to defend his house in Middelburg from a substantial crowd which had been thoughtfully provided with a cannon by the local garrison commander. According to his own story, he managed to fend them off with the help of only one servant and a copious supply of primitive grenades and rifles before the mob was reinforced by the soldiery and the defenders obliged to beat a rapid retreat over the garden wall, leaving house and more importantly the cellars to the mob. Van Steveninck then hid for three months in a derelict shed before making his way clandestinely to France, where three of his ships lay under embargo in French harbors, while in Zeeland a price of 1,000 guilders was put on his head.[107]

If the counter-revolution had been more or less successfully accomplished in Zeeland and Gelderland by the end of July, in Friesland it ran into some considerable opposition. In 1785, the originally anti-Stadholderian nobility had divided into sharply opposed Patriot and "aristocratic" camps. Taking advantage of its not overwhelming majority in the States, the ruling group subsequently passed a draconian prohibition on all public discussion, petition and assembly concerning the constitution of the province and the Règlement of 1748. Although the Patriot minority included the immensely wealthy Barons van Aylva and a number of other *grietmen*, mostly from the quarter of Oostergo, in the province as a whole the Patriots were outbid in *grietenies*. Consequently they looked to the towns, and in particular to the university centre of Franeker, for support from the burghers and Free Corps. There the dismissal of a Patriot writer and Professor of Laws, Johan Valckenaer, had become something of a *cause célèbre*, and with the help of the students and the guilds the Patriots succeded in gaining control of the Franeker Council. With the adherence of the burgemeesters of other towns such as Sneek and Dokkum and in the now approved revolutionary manner, the Patriot group then authorised their own sovereignty by declaring the decision of the States at Leeuwarden illegal. On July 21, the Patriot minority withdrew from the Leeuwarden Assembly and established their own assembly at Franeker. Under the leadership of Coert van Beijma, the secretary to an Oostergo *grietman*, the Franeker States proceeded to muster forces of Free Corps to defend their secession. According to van Beijma, they were able to command the loyalty of some 2,000 militia in the province and, together with some assistance from Holland, succeeded in surprising the important port of Harlingen and bringing it over to the Patriot side. But almost from the beginning the Friesian Patriots were divided by internecine feuding, which would badly compromise their eventual resistance to the counter-revolution and continue even in their French exile.

By midsummer 1787, the Dutch Republic was deadlocked between rival parties. Three provinces adhered to the Patriots, two to the Stadholder, with two disputed. The ensuing chaos in the States-General where first one, then the other delegation from Utrecht was accredited, and where the Friesian delegation looked to be similarly contested, prompted a new and important departure by the democratic wing of the Patriots. Late in 1786, suggestions had already been voiced in the Free Corps assemblies and in meetings of Patriot societies to convene some kind of National Assembly which would, it was fondly hoped, better represent the majority of the *burgerij*. Although the changed balance of power within the States of Holland had postponed agitation on this matter, for a while the unseemly disarray of the States-General and the renewed sense of solidarity in adversity gave the idea greater currency. On July 26 a meeting of the "Tot Nut van der Schutterij" (The Shooters' Duty) Society proposed constituting a delegation of forty members from throughout the Republic to be sent to Paris as the accredited "Deputies of the People of the Netherlands." The Military Committee at Woerden, alarmed at the threat from Prussia, took up the idea and established an ad hoc commission to draft a list of deputies and settle their terms of reference. At the same time a circular was sent to no less than 126 companies of Free Corps, guild and Patriot societies, enquiring their views on this move. Unhappily, with the exception of the Amsterdam "Vaderlandse Societeit," whose Patriot regents felt the occasion to be inopportune, the replies of these societies are as yet undiscovered. But the original list of members of this "national mission" survives in the important Dumont-Pigalle Collection in the Algemeen Rijksarchief, as a vital illumination of the thinking of the democrats at this eleventh hour of their revolution.[108]

The deputies, rather significantly, were headed by the aristocratic figures of van der Capellen van der Marsch and van der Capellen tot Bysset. But they also included nearly all the outstanding leaders of the Patriot movement: Professor F. A. van der Marck, Gerrit Paape, Marie-Antoine Cérisier; Valckenaer; Amsterdam merchants like Jacob van Staphorst and the banker Johan Koenraad de Kock from Heusden; young Herman Daendels from Hattem and the lawyer Rutger Jan Schimmelpenninck. The list reads like a roll call not just of the Patriot but of the Batavian revolution as well. And in its express determination to represent the "freedom of the nation before the eyes of the whole of Europe," it marks a striking link in the chain between the first Dutch revolution and the second.

So elaborate were the enquiries made by the ad hoc commission to determine whether Patriots all over the Republic approved of the move that very little was done about actually sending anyone to Paris until the end of August. By that time the imminence of an invasion from Prussia had ruled out the possibility of accomplishing the mission, even had the French responded to the overture—in itself a highly unlikely eventuality. The arbitration of an invading army was to postpone for seven years the convention of the National Assembly.

The Failure of Mediation

As die-hard Orangists and Patriot *enragés* rushed towards collision, repeated efforts were made by their respective foreign patrons to restrain them. The neighbours of the Dutch Republic were hardly innocent bystanders to the conflict but, with the conspicuous exception of Britain, all were apprehensive at its development. France could not afford another war with the British; Prussia still hoped to reverse the diplomatic revolution of 1756 and with Count Finckenstein the senior Secretary of State, was keen to avoid any provocation of Versailles. Even as late as June 1787, attempts to mediate were launched from Berlin and Versailles. Pieter Chomel, the Prussian consul at Amsterdam (himself a merchant and insurer) and very much of a Gallomane persuasion, attempted to offer William a settlement in return for the abolition of the Règlements and a curtailed version of his military command. Not surprisingly these terms were unacceptable to the Stadholder, whose political arteries were hardening with every day that passed. In any case, neither he nor the Princess were prepared to pay much attention to proposals from

Chomel. As Hertzberg—the second, much less Francophile Secretary of State at Berlin—pointed out to Frederick William II, Chomel's credentials had been compromised by his membership of the "Vaderlandsche Societeit" and his disreputable associations with many leading Patriots. The previous November he had even entertained a deputation from Woerden, including the infamous Vreede, and had more or less accepted that the abolition of both the 1747 Règlements and The Hague command were a precondition of any guarantee of the Stadholdership by the States of Holland. A man of such sympathies was hardly the one for a business so fraught with obstacles as a last-minute reconciliation between parties accustomed to denouncing each other as traitors.

Even had the negotiator been of better standing than Chomel, it is unlikely that he would have done better. His was only the last in a long and dismal succession of such initiatives, all doomed. The most opportune moments had probably been in late 1785, after the Prince had been ejected from The Hague and the French treaty signed, and in October 1786, when the Prussian minister Baron Graf Johann von Goertz had arrived at The Hague with specific instructions and some arrangements with Versailles for a mediation of the conflict.[109] In both cases there was a faint but distinct possibility of catching William at so low a point in his fortunes that his recurrent defeatism might have prompted him to settle for less than a full restitution of his rights of 1748 and 1766. In both cases, too, the mediators had taken some pains to attempt to accommodate the most serious grievances of both parties. In 1785, Vérac and Thulemeier, the French and Prussian ambassadors, had concocted a compromise whereby the Stadholder's military functions were replaced by a Council including the Princess, the Pensionaries and leading councillors of both the Patriot and Orangist factions. In this way, everyone other than the ultra-democrats would have had a place in power. Since the Stadholder had shown some acknowledgement of his military incapacities, it was hoped that this escape route from unwelcome reponsibilities would appeal to him. But the associated proposal to abolish the Règlements stuck in the Prince's gullet, and without it the Pensionaries would hear of no settlement.

In 1786, von Goertz went even further to preserving William's executive power but at the same time making a gesture towards a representative government. This apparently impossible exercise had been managed by proposing intermediary elections to councils, which would then produce a double list of candidates from which the Stadholder would select his Council of State. This situation in fact already obtained at a provincial level in those States not governed by the Règlement. But Harris, recognising the possibility that William might be tempted by a settlement even after the action at Elburg and Hattem, managed to convince him without too much difficulty that any such concessions would be tantamount to outright capitulation, leaving him a tool of the French party. His anxiety was in any event premature. The Stadholder insisted on an immediate return to The Hague as a precondition of any negotiation, and the Patriots responded by informing him that the

"Sovereign" (the guardian of the people) "does not negotiate with its servant." In May he issued a proclamation in which his full prerogatives were expressed as absolute right.

The terms of *any* hypothetical negotiated settlement were really academic. Short of being welcomed back as the saviour of his people, William was repelled by the idea of bartering his office with his persecutors. On their side the Patriots were convinced, particularly after Hattem and Elburg, that his word was worthless and that his determined policy was one of military repression. Furthermore, the character of any foreign mediation itself posed certain serious problems. Its chances of success obviously depended on two contingencies: the ability of the powers to agree among themselves on a suitable accommodation; and their ability to impose it on their "clients." After Frederick II had brushed off Harris' untimely overtures, France and Prussia were able to reach understanding with surprising ease. But their ability to persuade, cajole or bully their respective protégés into acceptance was always very limited.

This is not a conclusion which recommends itself to the "dismissive" school of Dutch historiography led by Colenbrander. As I suggested earlier, he saw the fulminations of the Patriots as merely the antics of fools deluded into believing they could restore some real measure of sovereignty to the Republic when all the time they were "marionetten" whose strings were being pulled from the chancelleries of Versailles, Potsdam and St. James'. There are some grounds for Colenbrander's view. Certainly the French assumed throughout that the Patriots stood or fell with their support, and even in 1786 Rayneval told Vergennes that "the Patriots . . . have no existence other than that given to them by France."[110] With benefit of hindsight, it seems obvious that if the Patriots pushed the Stadholder to military confrontation, the issue could never have been settled without foreign intervention, perhaps even a general European war. Not all of them were myopic on this point. In 1782, van der Capellen had warned his followers that a successful outcome of their efforts depended on a close collaboration with France, and alliance with that state became written into his programme for the Patriots.[111] On the other hand the baron, who was plainly no innocent in the ways of diplomacy, retained great scepticism on the subject of French interests and was displeased (though not surprised) when France signed a separate peace with Britain in 1783. His insistence on an alliance between the Patriot States and the French was not made in expectation of dependence, but in an attempt to tie the French down to something much more formal in its obligations than vague assurances of goodwill.[112]

The Patriots allowed themselves certain reservations on the value of French support—not only because of the disappointment of 1783 but also because they viewed the nature of their politics in terms quite different from the manoeuvres of international power politics. Indeed, they shared with the Americans before them and the French of 1789 a professed distaste for the devious ways of diplomacy. Those were the gambits of the devil; the impure practices of monarchies and aristocracies, unworthy of a free nation. To the contrary, their revolution stood for the restoration of a moral law of nations proper for the people who had produced Hugo Grotius. Their cavalier disregard for the consequences of drastic action like removing the Stadholder from his command at The Hague merely testified to their confidence in the self-warranting character of revolutionary patriotism. Similarly, the disgrace of Brunswick was viewed not as a move in the game of anti-British diplomacy but as a preliminary to the recovery of true sovereignty. No doubt the British interest was a principal obstacle to the success of their ambition, but only because it insisted on interfering in their domestic politics. Throughout these years, and indeed in the years to follow, both France and Britain underestimated the inherently Patriotic drift of the Dutch revolution. Yet Vauguyon had told Vergennes in 1784: "They [the Pensionaries] have let me know that they regard the present crisis as the time which will determine the prosperity or decadence of the Republic."[113] The Patriots were committed above all else to the restoration of their national standing. Their enemies were those who had brought this into disrepute, beginning with their incompetent Captain-General.

Against this background it was hardly astonishing that attempts to find a settlement through diplomatic intervention were regarded with deep suspicion by the Patriots. The exception was 1785—and then only because war with the Emperor would have offered even more opportunities for foreign intervention than a negotiated settlement. It would also have once more delivered the Republic to the authority of the army and its Stadholder. Even William V had his doubts about the good faith of those who professed to be his friends. He heartily loathed Maillebois, the French noble who had been commissioned to reorganise the Dutch army, and he even took over a year to warm to the admittedly very intrusive ministrations of James Harris.

To add to the confusion, the attitude of France and Prussia towards the Dutch troubles was far from straightforward. On the one hand, neither had much to profit from a war which promised little gain and certain ruin of their much-depleted treasuries. On the other hand, to abandon their protégés meant handing over the Republic on a platter to their rival. Neither prospect was very inviting, and the alternating primacy of each set of motives resulted in vacillating and often flatly contradictory policy. As one would expect, very often the ambassadors closer to the events urged a "forward" policy and firmer support for their clients, only to be fobbed off with cool responses from Vergennes or Frederick II. Vérac was told by his minister: "We have a considerable interest in supporting the leaders of the Republican party because it is due to their courage and perseverance that the King may expect a change in the order in favour of France."[114] Indeed, van Salm's comings and goings at Versailles suggested the adoption of a crypto-military relationship between the states. Yet, a year later, Vérac was reminded: "His Majesty desires that a rupture may be avoided and that instead of pushing matters to extremities, means of conciliation may still be found."[115] Similarly, Goertz's

Instruction from the King on the one hand roundly condemned "the enemies of the House of Orange, who have usurped the name of Patriot," and on the other hand ordered him to "stop the outbreak of a civil war" and to thwart the stratagem of the English minister.[116]

In theory, these directives may not have been so contradictory as they first appear. Both Frederick and Vergennes no doubt wished to press the claims of their respective clients without risking war. In practice, however, their rather disingenuous ambiguity entailed consequences just as serious as a more openly bellicose attitude. For while the powers were seen to restrain with one hand and beckon with the other, their respective protégés heeded only the signals which best accorded with their interests. Thus they were encouraged to pursue reckless policies in the belief that if circumstances went against them, they could always call on their patrons for rescue. In reality no such insurance existed and none had been intended. As the Patriots were to discover to their ruin, a diplomacy of hints and nudges was worse than outright abandonment.

In the end the Prussian word proved sounder currency than the French. But had the old King lived on, this might well not have been so. He was after all the unrivalled exponent of the diplomatic double entendre, as Harris discovered when he went to Potsdam in August 1785 with a plan of joint intervention. There he received the coolest response imaginable from Frederick, who had not the slightest intention of gambling his better relations with France by supporting a Prince whom he plainly regarded as little better than a halfwit. To Wilhelmina's imploring pleas for help, he replied by urging her to convince William to face the realities of a changed power situation in the Republic and forfeit the old Stadholderian Règlement. To Harris' project, he remarked cryptically: "The pear is not yet ripe." But the British minister knew full well that "the King of Prussia's language is a mere mockery . . . and does not proceed from any timidity . . . but from a decided intention to keep at any rate on terms with France."[117]

Frederick's circumspection was matched by a growing nervousness in Versailles about the activities of the more headstrong democrats among the Patriots. All along French support for the Patriots, as Vérac's brief had indicated, had been based on the premise that it was merely following the traditional line of underwriting the "Republican" or "States Party" against their dynastic enemy. When it turned out that they were not merely latter-day de Witts but full-blooded revolutionaries, the French representatives became decidedly apprehensive. The marquis de Rayneval, who had been sent out to negotiate with Goertz, wrote to Vergennes at the end of November that

the ferment here has made terrifying progress and if it is not stopped it is to be feared that it may cause an explosion which will have incalculable consequences. It is the Patriots themselves who are the authors, because they have judged it possible to destroy the Anglo-Stadholderian government only by mobilising the bourgeois. They in their turn are led on by this impetus since they hear only of tyranny on the one hand and liberty on the other.[118]

In the spring of 1787 it seemed to Rayneval that the more sober elements among the Patriots were about to lose complete control of the movement, and he warned that if concessions had to be made to the "bourgeois," there could be no possible "interest in favouring democracy; I would even say that such a government would lose the Republic (for us) or at least render it a useless ally, for it is impossible to undertake anything or concert any-thing with democrats."[119]

That might well have served as the motto of French policy towards the Dutch for the following twenty years. In the 1780's, the French government knew full well that it was one thing to applaud the advent of liberty thousands of miles away across the Atlantic, quite another to foment sedition on the doorstep of their own kingdom. But Rayneval did not go so far as to propose dropping the Patriots altogether. On the contrary, he advised sup-porting at least some of the more reasonable claims of the "système des bourgeois" as the only means of pacifying the Free Corps. Reassured by the Pensionaries, he no doubt believed that it was still possible to work through the moderate Patriots without exciting the Free Corps to go beyond the point of no return in their pursuit of the "aristocraten."

Amid all this vacillation Harris proceeded with his policy of confron-tation with unflinching resolution. After death had removed two of the more formidable obstacles to its realisation—Vergennes and Frederick—he was freer to aggravate the conflict. Between May 13 and 18 a conference was held at Nijmegen, at which the nucleus of the Orangist Party (an Act of Association of Orangists having been drawn up in October 1786) resolved on their strategy. They included Wilhelm van Citters and Baron Hendrick van Kinckel from Zeeland, and the major notables of the land provinces—the burgemeester of Nijmegen and aristocrats like Frans Jan van Heeckeren van Enghuizen and Robert van Heeckeren van Suyderas.[120] Harris himself had managed to commit the British government more deeply than ever. £90,000 had been agreed, nominally as a loan to the States of Gelderland but in fact of course to subsidise the shock troops needed for riots in the cities, the formation of Orange "Free Corps," and the enticement of as many of the Overijssel towns as could be persuaded to rebel against the authority of the Patriots at Deventer. The ambassador at Berlin, Ewart, found Hertzberg, the Secretary of State, in a position of enhanced authority. The new King, on the other hand, was a distinct disappointment. Contrary to expectation, he seemed no more eager to support the Stadholder with military force than had his uncle before him. During the action in Gelderland, Hertzberg had sug-gested that a battalion of the Westphalian regiments be moved up to the Wesel in readiness for a positive response to any appeal for assistance that might come from the States of Utrecht (Amersfoort) or Gelderland. But Frederick William was unhappy about the idea and only token manoeuvres were made. France was still managing to make a show of firm support for the Patriots, and in 1787 French engineers and a few artillerymen were out at the disposal of the commission at Woerden.

The looked-for crisis finally arrived through an adventure in which Harris had no direct part. Emboldened by renewed Orangist activities at The Hague, he had led the Princess to believe that Holland was seething with discontent at the Patriot regime, and given a chance would rise in support of the Prince. Wilhelmina, as audacious as her husband was irresolute, drew the logical conclusion. If the Prince would not, then she would travel to The Hague and raise the Orange flag. Although determined in her own mind, she sent van Hogendorp (the young Orange noble) to reconnoitre the ground, and when he replied: "With one voice, Mevrouw, yes," she set off, on June 28. The ensuing events are well known. She was stopped a few miles short of Schoonhoven, at Goejanversluis, not very far from the border of the "cordon." Escorted to a local inn, she was guarded by soldiers of the Gouda Free Corps, who subjected her and her ladies in waiting to the indignities of naked swords and uninterrupted custody even during the more necessary calls of nature.

The news of the arrest of the Princess was greeted at first with delight by the Patriots and consternation by her supporters. James Harris was so astonished at the news that he was quite put off from his game of cards with the French ambassador. But his dismay, like the Patriots' rejoicing, was very short-lived. The King of Prussia, he learned, was outraged at the indignities done not so much to the Princess of Orange as to a Princess of the House of Hohenzollern. An ultimatum from Berlin to the States-General demanded the immediate liberation of the Princess, her reinstatement at The Hague, and the punishment of all those who had been guilty of the act of *lèse-majesté*. Thus it became rapidly apparent to Harris that the Princess in captivity had been of more use to his cause than ever the Prince had been at liberty. Her obtusely courageous action had given him exactly the occasion and the grounds to draw Prussia firmly to the Stadholder and, backed by overwhelming force, at last call the bluff of the Patriots with the fire of battle.

But the affair was not yet cut and dried. A whole month elapsed between the first and a second ultimatum, during which the King's gallant ardor on behalf of his insulted sister seemed to cool. Having once given an order to march, on learning of the British decision not to intervene, he countermanded the instruction. This hesitation to commit himself irrevocably to military action might have been the result of disquieting information concerning French intentions. It had been discovered that 200 French artillerymen had been smuggled into Woerden, and that this was not by any means the limit of promised French assistance in the event of outside intervention. Indeed Montmorin, Vergennes' successor, although professing to support a mediated settlement of the dispute, had actually indicated that France would back her word with troops should Prussia enforce her ultimatum. In accordance with the wishes of the Woerden military commission, a camp was to be established at Givet at the southern extremity of the Republic. The choice of this site was significant.[121] Situated on the borders of the principality of Liège, Givet could provide a corridor for troops to cross into the Republic via Maastricht without marching through Austrian territory and involving the Emperor in any of the ensuing hostilities. A camp so established looked like more than a token gesture of support; it appeared to be the first step in the practical preparations for a large-scale troop movement. No wonder these reports gave Frederick William pause. When Prussia tried to raise the issue of the Givet camp, her ambassador at Versailles was cut short; and in the Republic, Bourgoing told Thulemeier that it was no longer in the power of France to moderate the actions of the Patriots as they were led by the Free Corps democrats. Thulemeier himself was not above a falsification or two. Paid by Finckenstein, the head of the "Francophile" party in Berlin, he had good reason to try to avert war. So, playing the French game of rumour as deterrent, he relayed false information to the King supporting the most pessimistic reports on the Givet camp.

Even by the standards of eighteenth-century diplomacy, the French were playing a dangerous game. Other than a profound cynicism—since only the Patriots were to suffer—it is difficult to see why Montmorin persisted with a bluff which, if called, he must have known could never have been backed up. Ségur and de Castries had been outvoted in the French Council in July on a policy of intervention, and when Brienne came to power he made it crystal clear that the condition of the royal finances put French military action in the Dutch Republic quite out of the question. At one point in the same month, Montmorin even came near to telling the truth. He informed the British ambassador that the King had no interest at all in going to war with his country over the Dutch, so reciprocating Pitt's anxiety to avoid a needless naval war. The States of Holland were more or less told that if it came to war, they could not expect the King of France to be dragged into hostilities at their bidding, and the recall of Vérac in August seemed to confirm this. But the more optimistic Patriots assumed this to be a canny diplomatic ploy, for at the same time Bourgoing was assuring the Pensionaries that not only would the Givet camp shortly materialise but troops would be landed at Dunkirk and Helvoetsluys for the defence of South Holland. Fabulous figures of 12,000, 25,000, 30,000 men were bandied about by Bourgoing and Montmorin as though already on their way.[122]

Under pressure from the Free Corps—which were becoming increasingly militant, purging municipalities and seizing any available munitions—the Patriot leaders abandoned their original plans voted through the States of Holland for a compromise with the Stadholder and the King of Prussia, whereby mutual troop evacuations from Gelderland and Utrecht would take place under French and Prussian mediation and the Princess be permitted to continue her journey to The Hague. These concessions had been noisily condemned by the Free Corps as capitulation to the King of Prussia; and while the prospect of invasion had prompted the Patriots to attempt to restrain their runaway revolutionaries, the promises whispered in their ear by Bourgoing enabled them to give up trying. As the troops were expected any moment, thousands of livres poured into Holland from Versailles. But this was the Judas kiss.

All along, on the Stadholder's side, there had been some scepticism about the Givet rumours. Wilhelmina had been undeterred by the stories and had urged her brother to invade in July as the camp, if true, could not be ready before August.[123] Harris was still firmer in his disbelief. Throughout he had maintained that

> . . . till France is ready, nothing will provoke her to quarrel with us; and that when she is ready, nothing will prevent it: of course that she would not go to war for the sake of this country [the Republic] and that, if England was to threaten and to threaten seriously, France would shrink from the challenge.[124]

Although Pitt had decided the Cabinet against intervention, Grenville remained an aggressive activist Secretary of State and was more than delighted to let the Prussians do his work. In August he visited the Republic to talk with Harris and determine through spies once and for all the truth of the Givet camp and the possibility of Sluys landings. On the 7th of the month, both rumours were finally exploded as absolutely without foundation. France had made no preparation whatever to come to the Patriots' aid, and it could be reasonably assumed that she was unlikely to do so. Frederick William could be given the go ahead. Just for good measure, and to compound their deceit with crass folly, on September 10, as a last conciliatory measure, the French government informed Frederick William that the Givet camp order had been countermanded. It had the opposite effect. In any case the King had finally made up his mind. The penalty of a French alliance was—not for the last time—to be levied in full on the unfortunate Dutch Patriots.

On September 8 a last ultimatum was received from Berlin at The Hague. It gave the States of Holland four days to reply. Van Berckel remarked that "the note of the King of Prussia was too insulting to deserve any consideration and should only be answered by silent contempt." The States decided instead to send two delegates to Berlin to inform the King of the full facts of the Princess' arrest. The move was by then academic. On the 13th, an army of around 26,000 crossed the frontier under the command of Charles William Ferdinand—Duke of Brunswick and nephew of William V's old minister. Just one month later, he received the final surrender of Amsterdam and installed the Stadholder in The Hague.

Resistance to the Prussian army melted away. Years of parades, drills, Free Corps manoeuvres, and martial ballyhoo simply disappeared in the general terror at the advance of the Prussian armies. While he himself had been against the invasion, Brunswick had taken good care to prepare for it with thoroughness, unlike his future occasions as a counter-revolutionary commander. His army was divided into three divisions, two proceeding west along the rivers Waal and Lek towards South Holland, the third moving past Utrecht to Amersfoort and the Gooi to threaten Amsterdam. Without French help, the prospects for the 9,000 or so Patriot troops was dire. If the two prongs of the advance into Holland were to meet behind Utrecht, the only secure route of retreat for that city's garrison and the most important concentration of defence for Holland would be cut off. Van Salm was faced with an appalling decision, and having made it he has duly gone down in

Dutch history as its most ignominious coward. Just a few weeks after declaring that come what may he would stay in Utrecht and die amidst the rubble, he went to the commission at Woerden on the 14th and asked permission to evacuate the city of its troops. From one angle his action looks like the predictable dereliction of duty of a philandering opportunist and adventurer. But he pointed out quite truthfully that the fortifications of Utrecht had been engineered to withstand a siege from the Stadholderian armies, not a whole division of the Prussians. The city would not, he said, stand for more than three days faced with such an attack. Even the weather conspired against him as an unusually dry Dutch summer had rendered the last-resort action of inundation ineffective. He was listened to with attentive gloom at Woerden. It may be that the commissioners were more concerned with the fate of defenceless Holland than with the traumatic effect of a capitulation at Utrecht. At any rate they granted van Salm his request and ordered him to retire his troops to Amsterdam.

Whether justifiable or not in terms of military tactics, the decision to evacuate Utrecht dealt a shattering body blow to the already demoralised Patriots. The news was so terrible that the city council—men acclaimed as the tribunes of the people just a year before—dared not tell the people. When it was bruited about, hysteria broke out in the city. The Free Corps, who had been preparing themselves for months to "defend" their liberties, now dashed their rifles on the floor of the town hall in disgust or threw them into the canals.[125] Utrecht badly missed a Dutch Danton or a Saint-Just. Burghers were advised to be out of the city before 3 a.m. if they wished to protect their persons, and by nightfall on September 15 the Neude was filled with the pathetic flotsam and jetsam of people who suddenly and inexplicably found themselves refugees. The troops marched out first, followed by the Patriot councillors and the editors and publishers of Patriot newspapers; finally, with handcarts and wagons, came the dispirited Free Corps families and burghers. In the late afternoon of the 16th the Prince's troops and the Prussians marched into the empty city, where a handful of girls and people too poor to pick up and move had hung a few Orange ribbons around the streets. It was a Sunday; the church where van Hamelsveld had fulminated against the aristocratic tyranny was closed, its doors draped with orange. Bells were rung from the Dom tower and the States of Utrecht returned from their exile in Amersfoort. Revolutionary democracy had lasted just one year in Utrecht.

Between the Holland divisions of the Prussian army and The Hague there stood just the two small garrisons at Naarden and Gorinchem. One by one the Patriot camps were abandoned as they fell back on Amsterdam. On the 17th, after a short siege, Gorinchem surrendered. Mappa made a brave show of defending Naarden but once again with the peculiarly Dutch show for legality, receiving orders from the now counter-revolutionised States of Holland, capitulated on the 27th. On the 18th, the order of nobility in the States had taken the initiative prior to the entry of the Stadholder in repealing all the legislation enacted against him since 1784. On the 20th, appropriately accompanied by James Harris and Laurens van de Spiegel, William made his entry unto The Hague. The city was his again. As Professor Cobban observed, it was the only time in his life he managed to be in the right place at the right time.

Amsterdam remained the last bastion of Patriot resistance. The city had become a reception centre for the outcast Patriots of the now occupied provinces. De Gijselaar had fled from Dordrecht, taken on the 18th; Fijnje from Delft, which had fallen on the 19th; van der Capellen van der Marsch from Kampen, already a place of exile for him; van Beijma from Franeker; and the Overijsselaar Patriots from Deventer and Zwolle. Such was the horror of van Salm's action at Utrecht that the Amsterdammers recoiled from his command and appointed instead as their commander de Ternant, an able French soldier. Under him the city was fortified heavily past the central ring of canals, and outlying posts were set up at Halfweg and Amstelveen. Troops were billeted in the houses of patricians who had long abandoned them in the riots of June, and the Free Corps kept up a brave show on the Dam.

On September 17, their last provincial assembly went ahead as planned. With the Prussians closing in on the city, the delegates repeated their final execration of William V and called for a new National Assembly to reconstitute the Republic.[126] This was the last blast on the Patriot bugle. On the 24th, the Prussians crossed the Veluwe and linked up their armies in front of Amsterdam. On October 1, an offer at negotiation from the Pensionary was rejected by Brunswick and the siege of the city began. With a skilful use of night attack on the forward defence posts at Halfweg, resistance began to cave in; on the 10th, after receiving final advice from France that they could expect no help from a relief force, the city surrendered.

At The Hague the Stadholder, restored to the powers not only of 1780 but of 1766, set about eradicating all reminders of his years of humiliation. Harris and the Prussian troops proved able accomplices in this work and clamped a fiercely repressive regime on the ex-rebel provinces. The press was muzzled, all Patriot societies closed down and of course the Free Corps disbanded. Every public body from the States-General down was purged of any elements who had associated with the Patriots, and those who remained were arrested. In the cities of Holland, the Orangist crowds were at last given leave to revenge themselves on the burghers who as Free Corps had lorded it over them for the past four years. Houses were burned, shops and cellars ransacked.[127] Thousands fled in the wake of the plunder. Many went south into the Austrian Netherlands, to either Antwerp or Brussels, where they were welcomed by the emerging "rebel" factions of Vonckist and Statist affiliations. Others proceeded on to France, where they pleaded for asylum at the court which had deserted their cause, and, once received, settled down in Patriot colonies at towns like Dunkirk, Gravelines and St. Omer. Others still, like the pastor van der Kemp, took ship to the United States in hope of finding a society which would live up to the Patriot ideals of democracy. It was perhaps pointedly ironic that the Dutch Republic, celebrated in Europe as the political sanctuary par excellence, should in its turn have created its flight of refugees. It was, wrote Mirabeau, "a day of mourning . . . for Europe."[128] Some had other ideas. Goethe, who was in Rome, wrote to Herder: "It is said here that the Prussians have entered Amsterdam. This should be the first expedition in which *our* century shows its greatness."[129]

The Lessons of Defeat

The Patriots had had their "fédération"; Wilhelmina had given them a "flight to Varenness" (in reverse), and Brunswick an ultimatum. But unlike the French they failed to respond with a levée en masse, a September massacre or a Jacobin Terror. Their revolution perished for want of blood. For those of Geyl's inclinations, this is a matter of much relief; for those of Colenbrander's, an easy target for contempt. Yet the real difference between the two power struggles is not to be measured by depth of political commitment but by a much more mundane factor. For all the heady rhetoric of Danton's oratory (and had the contest in the Netherlands been decided by oratory alone, the Patriots would doubtless have achieved a walkover), the generals of the French Republic inherited from the Old Regime an army of the line without which their volunteers alone would have stood little chance of success. Even had the Free Corps fought to the last man, however, it is inconceivable that they would have prevailed over the larger part of the Stadholder's troops *plus* the invading Prussian divisions.

Once the arbitration of arms had been accepted by Prussia there were, in fact, only two courses open to the Patriots. As Thulemeier requested, they might have attempted to moderate the revolution, disband the Free Corps and accept a Franco-Prussian mediation even if it meant the return of the Stadholder to The Hague. Or, on the contrary, as many in exile observing the course of the French Revolution were tempted to feel, they might have actually intensified the pressure of the revolution, using units like Mappa's "Flying Legion" both to galvanise resistance, conscript defence companies and impose dictatorial submission on the least waverer. But in fact neither course would necessarily have protected the Patriot revolution. It is difficult to imagine the "galvanising" of a population of less than two million, divided by long traditions into seven separate States, half-occupied already by the enemy and accustomed to having its fighting on land done by others. Even had it been politically feasible, a levée en masse in Holland would not have produced very impressive masses. Equally, any measure of conciliation offered to the Stadholder through Franco-Prussian offices would certainly have come to grief on his own paranoid intransigence and the dishonest brokerage of the British ambassador who, all along, had been bent on a counter-revolution supported by military force. Heads and tails the Patriots lost.

The Patriots have been seen as scolded infants who, having played with fire and had their fingers burnt, were obliged to go "to school" in France to learn the true craft of insurrectionary pyrotechnics. From that time onwards, they were doomed to have their French instructors standing over them alternately offering matches and fire extinguishers as their own interests dictated. The evolving relationship of French and Dutch revolutionaries is best left to the chapters which follow, but it would at this stage be an error to dismiss the Patriot revolt out of hand from the ease with which it was crushed by invasion. The Act of Association; the arming of a bourgeois militia; the deployment of crowds to revolutionise local councils at Deventer, Rotterdam, Utrecht and Amsterdam—all announce a political intention far from trivial. Left to themselves the Patriots might well have succeeded in their principal goals, at least within the provinces of the "cordon." But in exile or hiding, their leaders themselves recognised that their disastrous experience in 1786–87 had provided some lessons which they hoped would not be lost on those who received the torch and who would preside over the eventual rebirth of "Batavian Liberty" in 1795.

First, they acknowledged a certain naïveté in matters of power politics. However proper their ambition to restore the lustre and splendour of the Dutch Republic, there was a rueful admission that its position as a power of the second rank would not be changed overnight by the expulsion of the Stadholder and the recovery of republican liberties. Even van der Capellen had seen that the Patriot cause would never prosper without help from a major power for, like it or not, his country had become the cockpit of rival European interests. Since their struggle was waged in the name of patriotic integrity, this was a particularly bitter pill for the insurgents to swallow. For a while the violent turn of events in France and the fraternal professions of its leaders beguiled the Dutch "Patriots" into supposing that Providence had given them an ally whose motives were unsullied by the selfishness of *raison d'état*. But along with other aspirant European libertarians, they very rapidly abandoned that dream for the more sombre realities of machtpolitik. In order to survive, the Dutch revolution was to tread a narrow path between indulging their democracy so uninhibitedly that it risked alienating their protectors (as Rayneval felt happened in 1787) and compromising their principles so far for the sake of security as to do away with the goal of a national rebirth.

The second lesson concerned the Patriots' reluctance to break from the institutional past and the sentiments of republican history. Their rhetoric spilled over with references to the heroic days of the Republic, when the youthful vigour of its liberties had defeated an empire and made it the richest and most civilised place on earth. "Liberty" had been virtually co-terminous with the immortalised "Waare Vrijheid" (True Liberty) of Francken and Grotius, the Union of Utrecht and the sovereign provinces. It seemed unthinkable that those who professed to act as "Patriots" should repudiate that precious patrimony—the very features which set the Republic apart in Europe. But the débâcle of 1786–87 and their observation of the French Republic forced the more perceptive of the exiled politicians like Johan Valckenaer to ruminate purposefully (not so far from some Orangists who remained) on the inadequacy of traditional governing institutions, and the shallowness of an ideology which saw in the Stadholder alone the source of every evil afflicting the Republic. For the Patriot revolt, as a consequence of the anatomy of the state, had been handicapped by its subdivisions not only into provincial but even municipal and village uprisings. As a direct result, its strength had been diffused when the time had come to concentrate on resisting aggression. The belated initiatives, in August and September 1787, made by the Free Corps and Patriot societies towards the creation of some kind of sovereign National Assembly were, in this respect, a profoundly significant turning point.

It is true that the revolutionaries of the 1790's did take stock of the experience of the 1780's. Here their consideration of the immediate past was more important than their view of contemporary events in France in guiding their actions. Indeed, it was the continuation of their national preoccupations which laid up problems in the future in their relationship with the "Grande Nation." It would be mistaken to divide off the two generations of revolutionaries too sharply. Very often they were the same men. Many of those who rose to prominence in the Batavian Republic—Daendels, Paulus, Vreede, van Irhoven van Dam, van Hooff—had played their part in the Patriot revolt, often as more than mere apprentices. Much of their language remained the same. As the title of van der Capellen's pamphlet and many more besides testified, they had formulated that most un-Dutch concept, a "national will," even if it was still far from institutional expression. The stock items of popular sovereignty—*Volksstem; volks-alvermogen*, or the voice; the vote, the will of the people—already recurred in their journalism and public rhetoric. The makings of a political democracy had been beaten out in the Netherlands, even if they had not yet been compressed into the shape of working institutions.

The "people" in the Dutch Republic was as amorphous a sociological entity as its counterpart in America or France. As in those revolutions, it existed more as a politicians' coinage than a social organism. The attitude of the Patriot leaders towards the common people was deeply ambivalent, and the line they drew between "honest folk" and the fickle mob apt to become problematically indistinct. But no more so, perhaps, than Jacobins and rather less so than Thermidorians. If their militia acted first to excite, then to contain, and finally to eliminate the activities of popular protest, they were in this respect merely anticipating the future conduct of *gardes nationales*. And among the newly, if tenuously, politicised popular constituency there is surely little to choose between the independently minded, self-employing tradesmen and craftsmen of the Faubourg St. Antoine; the hatmakers, tailors, carpenters, shoemakers and winesellers who made up the rank-and-file (in so far as there was one) of the sans-culottes, and the grocers, liquor-vendors, bakers, hosiers, school-masters, printers, carriage makers—and carpenters, shoemakers and winesellers—who comprised the "Burgher College" and the Free Corps troopers in Utrecht.

That the Patriots were a minority goes without saying; all revolutionary élites are. Equally, their adversaries in the regencies were without any doubt an even less representative minority. And however inhibited by the conventions of their historical arguments, there can be no question that the direction of Patriot politics was towards a broader, more accessible system of government, an end to the office-mongering and inter-family colonisation of public office, as well as to the military and sovereign prerogatives of the House of Orange. Even the marquis de Rayneval had some inkling of what this presaged for the future, though he could hardly have realised just how prophetic his words were:

> In order to emerge from their state of nullity the bourgeois are asking to take part in government: the most extreme among them wish to participate in all deliberations on public matters, that is to say, they wish to introduce the purest demagogy; the more moderate ask only to be able to elect their regents and to have representatives to watch over the maintenance of their rights and the constitution. . . . The result of this new order of things is as simple as it is certain. The bourgeois, once having become something in the political order will emerge from their apathy and (at the same time) force the populace to return to the most absolute insignificance.

The relationship between the revolutionary élite and its mass constituency in the years ahead was to be fraught with all the problems usually attendant on these upheavals. The content—as distinct from the outline—of a political democracy was to take a very long time to find satisfactory definition. But, ironically, in defeat and humiliation the Patriots were reprieved from judging the implications of these divisions and contradictions. For the time being they lamented the disaster as the subjugation of the "people." Those mobs which ran amok through their houses in Zierikzee, den Bosch, Kampen and Goes were merely the drunken hirelings of a vicious tyrant and a gang of traitors who had opened their country to invasion. Their consolation lay in the still burning conviction that they remained the only true custodians of the national ethos. Left to themselves and granted the blessing of peace, their work of regeneration would reap its due reward. It was a source of pathos rather than bathos that neither condition would be realised in the years which followed.

✽✽✽✽✽✽✽✽✽

Part
II

✽✽✽✽✽✽✽✽✽

FATHER   *We shall now come to a new period in the history of our Fatherland. Hendrik, read what you have written in your essay.*

HENDRIK   *"From 1795 our Fatherland was governed, first by Representatives or Office-holders of the people, who were chosen by the people from amongst themselves." I don't rightly understand, father, what the causes of so great a change were.*

    —— *Schoolboek*, p. 123

4

The Patriots
and the
French Revolution,
1787–1795

The Continuity of the Patriot Revolution

The passing of Patriot liberty was deeply mourned by its survivors. Predictably, they were more concerned with commiseration than with diagnosing the causes of decease. Taking this to be self-evident, they blamed an unholy alliance of treason within and tyranny without: Pitt's gold and Prussian grenadiers.[1] Only the French King, whose ministers had egged them on to revolution and then recoiled at the consequences, was exempt from criticism for the compelling reason that the Patriot émigrés had been reduced to living off his charity. But there were figures in the French opposition, itself going by the sobriquet "Patriot" (though more in recognition of Boston than Utrecht), who were unconstrained by such considerations. In the plight of the Dutch refugees Mirabeau, for example, saw an opportunity not only to unburden himself of yet another homily on liberty but also to let loose a well-aimed shaft at the ministry which had stood idly by while Dutch freedom was done to death.

The most famous lament for the Patriots, Mirabeau's *Aux Bataves sur le Stadhoudérat* amounted to little more than a recapitulation of stock republican Dutch history topped up with exhortations to courage, democracy and revenge.[2] Doubtless it was intended as much for the gossips of the Palais Royal as for the Amsterdam coffee houses. And not for the last time it pressed the Dutch cause into service as the accomplice of French political intrigue. But however grimy the motives, this kind of literature was balm for the smarting morale of the defeated Patriots. It gave them the soothing, if ephemeral, consolation that their sacrifice had exalted them among the ranks of the early martyrs of the democratic era.

Until 1789 it was possible for the Patriot exiles to cocoon themselves in the illusion that they had been the innocent victims of brutal aggression. In this way they avoided any scrutiny of their own deficiencies. But the brilliant light cast by the French Revolution threw their own failure into bolder and more depressing relief. Those who had eyes to see could not help but ruminate on the striking contrast between the triumph of liberty in France and its ignominious rout in the Netherlands. Such a contrast made a particular impression on at least one commentator, Pierre Alexandre Dumont-Pigalle. Dumont-Pigalle had been born in France and had settled in Leiden, first as a merchant and later as a journalist writing for the Patriots. In his middle age he had been abruptly forced to return to his native land to seek asylum. While counting himself an ardent Dutch patriot, Dumont-Pigalle was acutely aware of the foibles of his adopted countrymen and was prepared to lay at least a share of the blame for their defeat at their own door. In 1790, as the French celebrated the anniversary of the fall of the Bastille, he wrote to a young friend in Leiden:

I may dare to say so because I have seen with my own eyes how we gaily frittered away our successes for over three years and let slip the opportunity to triumph. Never can a people have been blessed with so propitious a time to recover their liberties and their rights. But instead of profiting from this our Regents deliberated interminably; some plotting, some gossiping, others betraying us outright. The Patriot people drank, sang, paraded about and played the soldier while our poets spoke only of "Heroes" and "Heroic Deeds." . . . When Mont pigalle [sic] prophesied what would happen they laughed in his face. But in the end the dream disappeared and we awoke to find ourselves in chains.[3]

Dumont-Pigalle was the Cassandra of the Patriots. But his dour irony at their expense injects a refreshing and not inaccurate note of self-criticism into the stream of alibis. His complaint of political levity was one which was taken up with even greater emphasis by Dutch historians like Colenbrander and Geyl. For better or worse—and almost always for the better—they believed that the Dutch were simply not the stuff of which violent revolutions were made. Four years after Dumont-Pigalle's lament, at the height of the Jacobin Terror, an Amsterdam Patriot writing to a correspondent in France made the droll comparison:

The French Patriot seizes his arms and flies to the place where he can use them on behalf of the cause of freedom; the Dutch Patriot, told that his redeemers are at hand on his frontiers, stuffs his pipe full of tobacco and goes peacefully to his back parlour for a quiet smoke.[4]

For such critics the Dutch were virtually congenitally incapable of engineering their own liberty. Talk of revolution was so much hot air from men whose political pulse beat time with the stock index of the Amsterdam Bourse. On this assumption there is no serious problem in evaluating the role of the French Revolution in the development of Patriot politics in the Netherlands. Politically it made grown men of green boys and supplied the practical education required to alert Dutchmen to the seriousness of the enterprise, hence Colenbrander's evident fondness for describing the period from 1787 to

1795 as the "School of the Revolution." Still more important it provided, in the shape of the revolutionary armies, the force necessary to bring down the old Republic and install a version of Patriot freedom in its place. But in this view it is axiomatic that the version was necessarily French. For this period also witnessed the Mephistophelian contract by which the Patriots bought their political redemption at the price of their national soul. And so the French Revolution became not only the necessary condition of the Batavian Republic but also its necessary evil.

Whether this view represents the truth of the matter hinges on a second question, conspicuously neglected by those same historians satisfied with establishing the French pedigree of the Batavian Republic. The French Revolution may indeed have been a necessary condition of the Batavian Republic, but it does not follow from that that it was a sufficient condition. Did it determine the character and career of the new Dutch state so completely that the latter existed merely as a pastiche of its protector? Or did the Batavian Republic retain enough of the matter of Dutch politics to absorb the formative impact of the "Grande Nation" without forfeiting its national identity? This is the question begged by any history of the Batavian Republic but perhaps especially by an account of its genesis. For on it hinges not only an elucidation of the Batavian Republic itself but some explanation of the conflict between French and Dutch republicans which marred their uneasy alliance.

It is a rider of the view which sees the Batavian Republic moulded in the matrix of the French revolution that a clear distinction must be drawn between the upheavals of the 1780's in the Netherlands and those of a decade later. The earlier events are characterised as taking place within the legitimate context of Dutch politics (and are therefore doomed as a revolutionary flop); the later as guided, if not actually dictated, by France (and therefore a qualified revolutionary success). Colenbrander in particular was concerned to describe the Batavian Republic as terrain for new men, new issues and a new manner of political argument, all of which bore the unmistakable imprint of revolutionary France. Even R. R. Palmer, who in many other respects accepts the basic continuity of Dutch history in this period, has drawn attention to an alleged transformation in its political vocabulary.[5] Whereas the Patriot revolt is distinguished by its attachment to historical claims and appeals to restore corrupted institutions to their pristine purity, the second period, exposed to the literature of the French Revolution and the rhetoric of its assemblies, leans heavily towards natural rights egalitarianism and vulgarisations of the General Will.

Random forays into the history of political language with undue regard for the detail of historical context all too often end up as exercises in self-confirmation. The argument set out above is possibly a good example of the genre. If the Constitutional Restoration (*Grondwettige Herstelling*), that interminably dreary tome of the Patriot regents,[6] is taken to be a "typical" document of the Patriots; the Valckenaer proposals for a Dutch constitutional monarchy in 1791 as a fair sample of the thinking of the émigrés; and the

1798 constitution as the paradigm of Batavian democracy, then it is indeed a simple matter to establish a chronology which begins with liberal oligarchy and ends with democracy, with the French Revolution plumb in the middle. But extrapolating from comparably isolated documents—the Leiden democrats' programme of 1785 and the federalist constitution of 1802, for example —exactly the opposite conclusion could be deduced without any difficulty. In the first case, the French Revolution could be seen to be the catalyst of Dutch democracy; in the second case, an inhibiting factor. In actual fact neither deduction would be entirely reliable. For while there was undoubtedly a change of emphasis in the way many of the arguments for reforming Dutch institutions were set out, there is little in the Dutch political literature to suggest that it was the French Revolution alone which accounts for the difference. That literature displays a remarkable degree of autonomy in its discussions of the same matters which preoccupied the Patriots in 1787. It would be possible to read a dozen or so pamphlets in Dutch from 1789 to 1795 without ever seeing a mention of the French Revolution or its manifestoes.

By 1789, the Dutch had already run through the gamut of libertarian arguments from appeals to the ancient constitution to claims of political birthright. The Patriots had produced no Jacobins and they had certainly produced no *enragés*, but in the Leiden Programme, the manifestoes of the Free Corps assemblies at Utrecht, and the writings of publicists like van der Kemp and Fijnje they had expressed the most radical views on elected representation, often alongside Patriot pronunciamentos of a much more conservative hue. A representative assembly based on the "will of the people" (*Volksalvermogen*) was on the agenda of the Amsterdam Patriots through the summer of 1787. And Dumont-Pigalle gave pride of place in his collection to the final number of the *Post van Neder Rijn*, published in Leiden a few days before the Prussians arrived, which urged to the last that councillors, burgemeesters and aldermen should be considered as the directly elected representatives of the sovereign people, invested with the responsibility of safeguarding their rights.[7]

While the *élan vital* of the Patriots was certainly subdued by the disaster of 1787, their defeat in no way stanched the flow of projects, programmes and reform proposals which had issued from their presses in 1786 and 1787. Given that those presses were no longer available for their views and that other presses in St. Omer, Münster, Paris and Geneva had to be hauled into service, the period between 1787 and 1795 was remarkably fecund in political discussion. During this time there was scarcely a single month in which some kind of constitutional project failed to make an appearance.[8] And predictably the satires and broadsides at the expense of William V, William Pitt and van de Spiegel took on an even more vitriolic flavour. In 1789 the émigrés were already offering their account of Patriot democracy "in the late revolution."[9] Others like *The Break in the Form of Government in the Commonwealth of the United Netherlands* (*Verhandelingen over de gebreken in de Regeerings form van het Gemeenebest der Vereenigde Nederlanden*), written by Albert van der Schatte, the former burgemeester of Zierikzee, continued to speculate on the future of the Republic as well as brood on its recent past.[10] Even when this literature paid direct attention to the events in Paris—and a Dutch translation of the *Declaration of the Rights of Man and Citizen* was published in 1790—it sought confirmation rather than edification.[11] The overwhelming preoccupation of the pamphlets, feuilletons and broadsides was with the weighty topic which had engaged them in the period of the Patriot hegemony: the reconstruction of Dutch public institutions in a form more acceptable to their own constituency. From one point of view this may be taken as evidence of incorrigible Dutch parochialism; from another, as the good sense of sober men undistracted from urgent tasks by vapid generalisations authorised by "universal truths." Indeed, when proposals so close to the French view as to be derivative were pressed on the patriot leadership they received very short shrift. Johan Valckenaer, the ex-Professor of Laws at Franeker and Utrecht, and doyen of the émigré circle in Paris, for example, proposed a constitutional monarchy on the lines of the French 1791 constitution designed simultaneously to pander to the vanity of the Stadholder by promoting him to monarchy while shearing away the substance of his power.[12] In many respects this was an intelligent and inventive attempt at compromise, but it plainly mortified his friends in Amsterdam and France who insisted that any plan which preserved "the mortal enemy of liberty" in office, however nominal, was inconceivable to the rank-and-file of those who had sacrificed so much to get rid of him. Dumont-Pigalle, who was himself aghast at Valckenaer's proposal, observed:

If one wishes to make a revolution in that [Netherlands] country it is first necessary to root out the House of Orange and make a new constitution, taking what is good in the French and even in the American constitutions *in so far as they are compatible with the physical and political characteristics of the seven provinces and the character and manners of their people* [author's italics].[13]

To an historian committed to reading it in terms of French politics, much of this literature remains incomprehensibly idiosyncratic. A classic example was the *Sketch for the General Reform of the United Provinces*, published in 1788.[14] The system of government advocated in this pamphlet is described therein as "aristo-democratic," while Colenbrander unhelpfully re-categorises it as "Patriotic-democratic." The hopeless confusion of terminology may itself serve to illustrate the palimpsest-like character of many such documents, half-interested in radical change yet reluctant to abandon the familiar standards of Dutch institutions. Its concern to preserve provincial jurisdiction over finance and its care to restrict the franchise to the substantially propertied appear to mark out the *Sketch* as the logical successor to the conservative *Fundamental Restoration*—a reflection reinforced by the likelihood that the same publicist, Cérisier, had a hand in both documents. But in other important respects the *Sketch* was a good deal more radical. Following on from the Amsterdam meetings of 1787, it accepted the principle of a national representative assembly with a much greater share of sovereignty than that delegated to the traditional States-General. Similarly it endorsed, albeit very warily, a system of elected local councils This matter had been at the heart of the Patriot agitation and it was the undisguised object of this document—termed by Colenbrander "Patriotic-democratic"—to concede some ground on popular influence with the express object of averting the far more disagreeable possibility of an armed burgher democracy. In this respect the *Sketch* appears to anticipate those elastic-sided constitutions in which French revolutionary moderates were to become so thoroughly entangled.

It would, of course, be as absurd to pretend that the French Revolution had no effect on the battle for the Dutch state as it would to see the Revolution as the alpha and omega of the Batavian Republic. Much of what happened in France had the most direct bearing on the fate of the Netherlands and was watched by Dutchmen at home and in exile with attentive anxiety. But few of them, especially among the Patriots who remained at home, looked to the French Revolution for instruction. They were more interested in seeing in its progress the vindication of views they already held and the irresistible advance of the moment when they would be able to set right the unnatural crimes of 1787. As far as they were concerned, the events in France represented not education but expiation.

The Exiles, 1788–1793

Just as Dutch political literature before and after the French Revolution continued to reflect the heterogeneity of Patriot opinion, so the groups of émigrés who congregated in the gloomy towns of French Flanders and Artois mirrored all too accurately the factiousness which, in part, had brought them to that sorry pass. Notwithstanding the high tone of constitutional projects like the *Sketch*, the mood of the rank-and-file was introspective, not visionary. Adversity had not healed their contentions and they remained divided as much by personal animosities as by differences of doctrine. The psychological need to repair their morale by attaching the blame for the débacle on some scapegoat or other created a climate of accusation and counter-accusation which disfigured the early years of the exile. Those suspected of dereliction of duty, military negligence or collusion with the enemy ranked only just below Prussians and Orangists in the role of infamy. Johan Valckenaer, perhaps the most sophisticated of the émigrés, was sufficiently obsessed with incriminating the leadership of the Friesian Patriots to go to the length of compiling an enormous dossier documenting their misdemeanours, winningly filed by Dumont-Pigalle under "Cowardice of Several Friesians."[15] Compared to the consuming need to pick at their scabs, the accelerating momentum of the French crisis seemed to occupy their attention very little.

The most bitter antagonism developed from the circumstances of the emigration itself. Of the few thousand Patriots who fled from Orangist mobs and Prussian soldiers, most departed in small groups or single families. There was no organised exodus and no agreed destination. In the north and east they made for German principalities like Bentheim, Münster and Lingen. In the west, fugitive Patriots from Zeeland and South Holland travelled along the coast to Antwerp; further south, Hollanders and Brabanders made their way to Lier and Brussels in the Austrian Netherlands.[16] And it was in Brussels in March 1788 that the first attempt was made at reconstituting some kind of national representation. A meeting of émigrés, dignifying itself as the "Assembly of Patriots," nominated a commission to "support and defend the interests of the Patriot nation at the court of the King of France and to press with especial vigour for armed assistance to help re-establish the downtrodden liberties of the nation."[17] A year later the commission broadened its membership to seven and appointed officials to act on its behalf at Versailles and St. Omer.

This attempt to put a gloss of authority on the disordered circumstances of the emigration was doubtless laudable in intention but woefully impractical. Given their shabby treatment in 1787 by the French government, the Patriots might well have had reason to feel themselves the moral creditors of the crown; but they were in no position to do anything except beg crumbs off the tables of Versailles. It was, moreover, by no means clear that the Brussels commission was entitled to speak for anyone but itself. Its composition was reasonably representative, ranging from ex-Free Corps officers like Jacob van Haeften from Utrecht to Bernardus Blok, the Enkhuizen lawyer who had been a colleague of Paulus on a Holland Patriots' committee created in February 1787. But its claim to have succeeded in some mysterious way to the sovereignty of the Patriot State assemblies was, as its rivals pointed out, ridiculously far-fetched.[18] The only member with a remotely plausible claim to leadership was Baron van der Capellen van der Marsch. And in 1789 he was persuaded to stand down from the commission by those who were contesting its exclusive right to speak for the Patriot emigration as a whole.[19] These dissenters centered around the laconic and witty figure of Johan Valckenaer. He and his associates had arrived in France, whether from haste or prudence, ahead of the Brussels appointees. One of their number, the merchant Balthasar Abbema, already commanded invaluable contacts in France through his business concern; via these liaisons, Valckenaer was able to persuade the minister appointed by the King to deal with the Dutch refugees that some provision ought to be made for their subsistence.[20] Initially this group worked in harness with the Brussels commission, but fierce rows blew up over the important matter of disbursement of the allocation. Valckenaer and his entourage retired from the committee of administration, withdrawing in high dudgeon to his elegantly decaying Jesuit cloister at Watten in Artois. From this point on the feud degenerated into open war, not only on matters of managing the Patriots' affairs but on competing accounts of responsibility for the defeat.

Valckenaer's group has been misleadingly labelled "Parisian" and identified as wealthier and more patrician than the humbler souls cared for by the commission in Brussels. In fact there was nothing to choose in terms of social position and political views between the rival clans. In Abbema and Jan van Staphorst, the "Valckenisten" had two typical representatives of the Amsterdam mercantile and financial fraternity; but then Johan de Kock on the other side was a lawyer (and ex-Pensionary of Wijk bij Duurstede) whose house in Passy outdid them all for suburban ostentation. J. L. Huber, a member of the commission, was like Valckenaer a Friesian professor, a regent and a member of a family of jurists. J. A. van Hoey of the commission was a physician (a doctor without patients, his enemies said) from The Hague and of uncertain provenance, but Herman Daendels, a colleague of Valckenaer's, was par excellence a soldier of fortune, hungry for recognition and revenge. As for the rest of the exile community—the "oysters of Artois, without warmth or energy," as Dumont-Pigalle observed—they comprised a perfect cross-section of the rank-and-file of the Patriot movement. There were Free Corps officers, predikants, journalists like Dumont himself, university students; petty brokers and shopkeepers and the odd renegade aristocrat like the brothers Aylva, who had jumped on the Patriot bandwagon at the last moment and who with their lands forfeit to the Stadholder had been wanting to jump off ever since.[21]

The man appointed by the commission to manage the funds provided by the French government was particularly galling to Valckenaer. He was Coert Lambertus van Beijma, the erstwhile leader of the Friesian Patriots and already a personal enemy of Valckenaer's. The miserable resistance of the Friesian Free Corps, about 3,000 in all, had persuaded Valckenaer that their nominal leader was in fact scarcely better than a self-interested charlatan. His first lieutenant in St. Omer, named with sublime aptness Rant, was one of those most distinguished in the autumn of 1787 by his cowardice, incompetence and opportunism.[22] Valckenaer and Dumont-Pigalle saw no reason why those to whom they attached a large portion of the responsibility for the débacle were now appointing themselves overseers of what was left of the Patriot cause.

There is no doubt that van Beijma's administration, to put it politely, was both arbitrary and highly irregular. When, in 1790, the books were finally surrendered to the French authorities for their inspection some 29,000 livres remained unaccounted for. Van Beijma had enlarged the relatively limited authority assigned to him by the commission into an office he designated as "Director-General of Refugees."[23] His staff of officials, described with an unhappy sense of timing as "intendants," were divided into "departments" corresponding to the geographical origins of the emigrant. Each "intendant" was not only armed with the power of the purse but also saw fit to exercise a quasi-judicial policing role within the Patriot communities. This officiousness did little to endear the commission to its compatriots. Valckenaer's grievances found support from the flood of letters reaching him complaining of the high-handedness of van Beijma and his confederates. One man alleged that van Beijma had denied him his due subsistence because he was a Catholic; another because he was accused, for reasons unknown to him, of political apostasy; and a woman who turned out to be the estranged wife of the student politician Lidth de Jeude complained that she too had been deprived because of her irregular marital status.[24]

No doubt many of these allegations were scurrilous or else blatantly self-interested. The dismal troop of deposed burgemeesters, dismissed journalists and disarmed militiamen comprised a community which resembled a disorientated transit camp rather than a tight-knit colony of political comrades. Civil delinquency was chronic. Dumont-Pigalle complained of being roughed up by Dutchmen more than once in the streets of St. Omer and on one occasion narrowly missed being thrown in the river. Valckenaer wrote of a former member of the Patriot States of Friesland, one Hogenbrug who, presumably adapting sluggish Friesian manners to the passions of his adopted exile, tried to strangle his mistress in a jealous fit at a St. Omer cabaret. When apprehended minus most of his clothing, he attempted to cloak his dignity by affirming with evident pride that he was a "Regent of the ancient and most noble province of Friesland." "Voilà nos souverains de Franeker," Valckenaer concluded disgustedly.[25] No doubt in this unruly society a measure of policing was required to supplement the meagre resources of the French *maréchaussée*. But through their over-zealous flaunting of authority, van Beijma's officers discredited the pretensions of the commission to provide a unified administration-in-exile, however rudimentary.

The unedifying bickering between the two factions came to a head in the spring and summer of 1789, when both turned to the French government for support. As the Ancien Régime was crashing to the ground around them, the champions of Dutch liberties apparently devoted their energies to the continuing struggle for control over their little enclave. Valckenaer came off the better. He had moved to Paris in April and through social introductions had won the ear of Necker's ministers.[26] But even had the government proved less receptive to his case, it was becoming increasingly exasperated by van Beijma's maladministration of the pensions. It took understandable exception to his insistence that the crown had no right to inspect the registers of émigrés to whom its money was being disbursed. In response to a clumsy attempt to influence Necker directly, the commission received a sharp reproof from Lambert, the Controller-General in charge of these matters. A deadline was imposed after which no new arrivals in France would qualify for assistance and, more humiliatingly, the government demanded a scrutiny of the registers so that they could, if necessary, be "rectified" by its "advisors." Van Beijma and the commission appreciated that those "advisors" included Valckenaer himself. But Lambert's note contained an even more disagreeable shock, as it used the opportunity of arbitration between the factions to remind the commission that it had never accepted its claim to negotiate collectively on behalf of all the refugees. Dismissing any pretension to political authority, Lambert criticised

this pretended authority as Deputies which in no wise can be properly authorised . . . the Dutch refugees in France can only be considered as simple individuals living in the Kingdom under the protection of our laws. If they have been permitted to gather in certain towns of Flanders and Artois, this has been for the convenient administration of their subsistence only and in no sense with the intention of establishing them as a separate entity. . . .[27]

Their asylum, he emphasised, was "a favour granted by His Majesty. He owes it to no-one and may revoke it entirely at his pleasure."

Lambert's note settled the quarrel between the Patriot factions in favour of the more Francophile "Valckenisten." But it also made plain that what divided the two groups was, by 1790 anyway, more than personal antipathies and an historical vendetta. Much of their dispute revolved around the question of how the Dutch should conduct themselves in exile; how they saw their own political position *vis-à-vis* the French; and what was to be their immediate future. Van Beijma and the commissioners continued to think almost exclusively in terms of Patriot retribution. French Flanders and Artois were as close as they could physically approach to the Dutch frontier without actually leaving the territory of the Kingdom. And because they expected their liberation to be imminent at any time, they felt it imperative to maintain an independent and distinctive enclave within France. They considered their exile as a brief, unfortunate hiatus between Prussian invasion and the inevitable overthrow of the House of Orange. They continued to give themselves the airs and graces of the representatives of the "Patriot nation," issuing ukases from St. Omer and Brussels rather than coming, begging bowl in hand, to the French government. And it was this *hauteur*, this refusal to accept their downfall, and their pretension to remain sovereign of their affairs, which the French ministers found so insufferable. In response to Lambert's rebuke, van Hoey, one of the commissioners, retorted that the government looked on the Patriots like "a pack of wild beasts to whom the occasional scrap of bread might be thrown," but in truth they were "the bravest and most honest section of a hitherto free nation."[28]

Van Hoey's indignation was in the best tradition of Dutch defiance of the high and mighty; similar remarks were to be thrown at the French time and again over the next twenty years. The Patriots specialised in biting the hand that fed them. But in 1790, the pretension to be treated as bona fide representatives of the Dutch people struck Valckenaer as not only absurd but just the kind of dangerous illusion which had wrecked the Patriots in 1787. He was less convinced about the imminence of their return to the Netherlands and the wisdom of concentrating the Dutch refugees in one or two settlements in the northeast. It was not that he was defeatist. Originally he had objected not so much to the principle of representation as to those who exercised it. But as the Revolution gathered momentum in France, Valckenaer unlike the majority of his compatriots in Artois came to appreciate its immense significance for their own cause. And as a logical consequence, he came to advocate a closer identification with the politics and principles of the Revolution as strategically desirable. Rather than huddling in St. Omer, he would have preferred a degree of dispersal around the more important cities of France, and particularly in Paris itself. Service in the *gardes nationales*, active participation in the revolutionary clubs, and journalistic endorsement of the progress of the Revolution would, he felt, be the best way to win the confidence of its leaders and its followers and to forge real bonds of alliance between French and Dutch liberty which had proved so fragile in 1787.

The Revolution reconciled these two opposing views—the one assertive, the other self-effacing—only in so far as each side saw in the events of 1789 an endorsement of their respective position. Such contradictions were entirely possible in the euphoria of the First Year of Liberty. The Revolution was regarded not only by Dutchmen but by Frenchmen of extremely diverse interests—peasants, sans-culottes and lawyers—as a bran tub from which each was sure to pull out the prize of his choice. And for revolutionary minorities in Europe, preoccupied as they were with their own business, it had special appeal. Did its leaders not call themselves "Patriots"? Did they not include as their champion the great Mirabeau? The downfall of the Ancien Régime became a providential punishment for the betrayal of 1789, when the good and generous King had been led into iniquity by wicked counsellors. Van Beijma and his associates rallied to the Revolution because they assumed that it would provide redress for the wrongs done to them by the minions of the Old Regime. And they went so far as to attempt to have Valckenaer proscribed as a crony of émigrés and salon aristocrats, and later as an unrepentant monarchist and *Feuillant*.[29]

For their part, Valckenaer and Dumont-Pigalle read in the florid professions of ecumenical fraternity declaimed in the National Assembly the charter not just of French but of European liberty. Taking an active part in revolutionary politics would henceforth be the shortest route to the liberation of the Dutch Republic. And in one not insignificant respect Valckenaer's enthusiasm paid off immediate dividends. For despite ominous noises of retrenchment from the ministry which had inherited the colossal bankruptcy of the Old Regime, the National Assembly in June 1790 agreed to a Patriot petition for a subsidy of 829,000 livres in support of their community. In the spirit of the new order and the acceptance of a more permanent stay in exile, the sum was handed over not as mere charity but to finance the establishment of "useful trades" such as a fishery at Gravelines.[30]

The 1790 petition had been the work of a group comprised exclusively of "Valckenisten," with van der Capellen van der Marsch as its nominal leader. It was this group which now made most of the running in demonstrations of enthusiasm for the Revolution. On his return from Paris in 1790, Valckenaer took a commission in a newly formed company of *gardes nationales* at Watten and persuaded many other Dutch to fill up its ranks. Before long it was indistinguishable from a regiment of Free Corps.[31] He founded a patriotic club at Watten, the "Amis de la Constitution," and to no-one's surprise became its first president. Nosing ahead of events, a "Club des Montagnards" was set up in St. Omer in 1791. Not to be outdone, the "van Beijmanisten" established a rival society, the "Club des Sans-Culottes Bataves," and the two clubs went at it hammer and tongs, complaining at periodic intervals to their respective central clubs in Paris.[32] Presses at Dunkirk, Gravelines and Arras pumped out political literature in both languages, and in 1793 the newspaper *Le Batave* began publication from the cloister of St. Germain l'Auxerrois in Paris. Although principally preoccupied with

French and general European affairs, the indivisibility of Dutch and French causes was emphasised by Dumouriez's campaign in the Low Countries which, until it became catastrophic, was dutifully reported by *Le Batave*.[33]

Finally a number of the Dutch Patriots began to be conspicuous among the throng of European enthusiasts congregating in Paris during these years. De Kock entertained some of the Jacobin tribunes in lavish style at his house in Passy and was to lose his head for being too friendly by half with Hébert. And Valckenaer himself had the seemingly happy knack of managing to be on hand to witness almost every one of the great revolutionary events. In 1789 he watched the July uprising in Paris from an apartment not a stone's throw away from that foyer of subversion, the Palais Royal. And in 1792 he went on a tour of the southern regions of France, arriving in Marseille just in time for the beginning of the march of the *fédérés*.[34]

This bustling participation by the Dutch Patriots in the affairs of the Revolution was much encouraged by the atmosphere of fraternal goodwill generated in its early phase. The grand declarations of the revolutionary assemblies translated the sad fugitives of abortive uprisings in Switzerland, Belgium and the Netherlands into the heroes of the new order of international liberty. Once a burden on the parish, they were now lionised as its most honoured citizens, the expression of the vaunted universality of the Revolution. In July 1790 they were given a special place in the procession of the Fête de la Fédération; but interest in prosecuting the crusade for liberty was very much confined to theatrical gestures. The fêtes galantes showered on its putative heroes, the "étrangers, amis de la révolution," along with other revolutionary festivities, was designed partly with the aim of papering over the cracks in the coalition of groups which together had brought down the old monarchy. It was comforting for legislators and intellectuals to suppose that their Revolution represented a philosophical demonstration or the enactment of self-evident truths, rather than a capitulation to the riot of famished peasants and artisans. But ecumenical egalitarianism was confined to the warriors of the salon like Condorcet, Brissot and Vergniaud. The common people remained untouched by the servitude of Poles or Dutchmen. Their intuitive xenophobia led them to believe ill rather than good of any *étranger*, be he from the next province or a country at the other end of Europe.[35]

The ministers of the constitutional monarchy were themselves sceptical of any attempt to drag France along in the train of the European Patriots. She had, after all, made a "declaration of peace to the world" renouncing conquest and aggression, a measure dictated as much by self-preservation as altruism. For a long time her leaders remained extremely reluctant to express their support for the liberation of France's neighbours beyond carrying wheat-sheaves to the Champ de Mars. The imperatives of the Rights of Man did service as propaganda. Policy was made with an eye to other demands, and it was only the emigration and the criminal folly of the Queen and King which brought France to war and their heads to the guillotine. In 1790, appeals from the Belgian leader Hendrik van der Noot for help against the Austrians went unheeded by the Constituent. The formal presentation of Valckenaer's history of the Patriot revolt to the Legislative Assembly was declined on the grounds that it would needlessly antagonise a power with which France was still at peace. Such restraint was not the monopoly of the moderates. In reply to a Patriot deputation urging an invasion of the Low Countries in May 1791, the president of the Jacobins confirmed that

... despite the absolutely sincere interest that we take in their cause, we will under no circumstances embark on a crusade against Holland and Prussia and so we must be content with expressing our wishes for universal liberty and the true happiness of the entire human race. . . . After all, have we not got sufficient enemies already at this time?[36]

The newly acquired devotion of the Dutch Patriots to the welfare of the French Revolution was, therefore, a sadly unrequited affair. Even the tense diplomatic situation following the abortive flight of the royal family to Varennes in June 1791 gave them little reason for hope. For as the remarks of the president of the Jacobins suggested, if France was to be compelled to defend the Revolution against the tyrants of Austria and Prussia, she had no wish to provoke the additional enmity of Britain and the Stadholder merely to satisfy the grudges of a colony of vagrant bankers and merchants. And in case self-interest showed any signs of flagging before revolutionary fervour, regular communication between the French foreign ministers and the Grand Pensionary, van de Spiegel, was usually able to anticipate any situation which promised to become unduly menacing. The channel of this liaison was provided by the glamorous and entirely self-styled "Baronne" Etta d'Aelders, a double agent of consummate craft who until the war in February 1793 managed to keep herself paid by both Dutch and French governments to look after each of their respective interests at the expense of the other. The Patriots were not the only Dutch lobbyists able to play on official sympathy by expressions of undying loyalty to French liberties. Etta d'Aelders generally outflanked them in the ardour of her Jacobinical egalitarianism. So hotly did she rage for the rights of the people that she entirely won Marat to the view that William V was the true father of his oppressed people, that 1787 had been the blessed revolution, and that those who masqueraded as "Patriots" were no more than a gang of parasitical speculators. Her tirades became so furious that at one stage van de Spiegel felt it necessary to remonstrate with her to moderate her language lest she jeopardise her personal safety.[37] War broke out between the two republics despite her efforts, not because she yielded anything to the Patriots in her advocacy but because the embroilment of France in the political settlement of Belgium made the opening of the Scheldt into a diplomatic *idée fixe*.

However messianic the oratory of the revolutionary assemblies may have sounded, it was never anything more than a veneer for a careful assessment of national interest. Until such interests dictated extending the revolutionary counter-offensive from the Austrian to the Dutch Netherlands, there seemed little prospect of the Patriots realising their dreams of triumphal return. There was, moreover, an additional difficulty involved in a strategy of "engagement" in the Revolution. While it was all very fine for Valckenaer and his friends to present the occasional address of congratulation to the assemblies or go on pumping out printed tirades against the aristocracy to demonstrate their solidarity, the dissolution of a revolutionary consensus in 1792 meant that in practice they were required to identify themselves with one or another of the factions competing for power. In so doing of course they ran the risk of being accused of "intrigue" and, instead of removing suspicion from their lobby, ending up intensifying it. The Swiss, who had founded the "Club Helvétique" (later the "Club Central des Étrangers, Amis de la Révolution") had just experienced this kind of rough justice when, attempting to indict the mutinous Swiss guards for reactionary conduct, they found themselves accused by Marat of arrogance and sabotage.[38]

The Patriots were inevitably associated with the war party in the Legislative Assembly, and with cosmopolitans like Condorcet or actual foreigners like Clavière prominent among the Girondins they became, willy-nilly, part of their baggage train. Similarly, the campaign to raise foreign legions to supplement the regular troops and volunteers was regarded with more suspicion than gratitude. Cloots may have thought of Allobrogian (Swiss) or German legions as the vanguard of the revolutionary millennium but to simpler folk they looked too much like Swiss guard and Hessian mercenaries. As if to confirm them in these doubts, in May Jan Anthonie d'Averhoult, the hero of Vreeswijk (the Patriots' solitary feat of arms), threw in his lot with Lafayette and the Palace guard on August 10, 1792, when the monarchy made its final stand against the Revolution. Rather than be captured alive, d'Averhoult shot himself when apprehended in flight, thereby incurring further opprobrium for his compatriots.[39]

But by far the most compromising factor in the mobilisation of the foreign legions was their association with General Charles Dumouriez. As early as April 1792, Herman Daendels had approached the general with a view to forming a Batavian legion.[40] At that time Dumouriez was already lending his authority to legions of Brabanders and Liègeois who were to assist in the liberation of the Austrian Netherlands and he was inclined to take an interested view of the matter. Through his encouragement the government accepted the proposal, and on July 8 the King announced to the legislative that a Batavian legion would be formed; 700,000 livres were set aside for its finance. But even though France was now at war, such measures failed to win the assent of all revolutionary politicians. Marat announced baldly that Dumouriez wished to make himself Duke of Brabant, and Brissot, certainly no pacifist, declared that the patronage of Belgians and Dutch was an instrument of political adventurism.[41]

These allegations, however wildly expressed, were not altogether wide of the mark. The fate of a Batavian legion was indeed tied up with plans hatched by Dumouriez for the future of territory conquered from the Austrians. A year before, in 1791, a plan to re-unite the Netherlands in a single Republic of seventeen provinces had been given considerable publicity. Even though it entailed a Stadholderate of greatly extended jurisdiction, possibly from the House of Orange, it won endorsement from no less a Patriot than Valckenaer. He assimilated this project into his own constitutional plan for a parliamentary monarchy, to end up with an extraordinary hybrid seventeen-province Netherlands, presided over by an hereditary Stadholder but ruled by an elected legislature and a responsible executive.[42] In actual fact the original project was far removed from either Dumouriez's strategy or Valckenaer's constitutional state. It had been cooked up by the "Statist" conservative wing of the Belgian Patriots to fend off the demands of their democrat opponents for a Belgian Republic based on popular sovereignty. Their plan envisaged the retention not only of provincial autonomy but of the traditional corporate privileges of nobility, clergy and guilds. Moreover, the Statists looked to Britain rather than France for protection—and it was on that side of the Channel that many had sought asylum following the suppression of their revolt by the Austrians in 1790. For these reasons their project was unlikely to commend itself to Dumouriez, who nevertheless hoped to exploit the grievances of both factions and establish himself in a position of arbitration. He wanted a Belgian Republic, but with himself as Protector; it was with this end in mind that he endorsed not only the legion but the creation of a committee of Belgians and Liègeois and the call for a constitutional convention.[43]

Dumouriez's interests in the Netherlands were limited to creating a power base for himself—not in siring the Patriot commonwealth. His memoirs confirm that his intentions regarding the Batavian legion were strictly tactical. He thought of its members primarily as irregulars, who would "supplement the light brigades of the army . . . and who, conversant with several languages, would be of great assistance in divining the intentions of the enemy."[44] In other words, reconnaissance and reinforcement. It is likely that he kept an open mind about the campaign itself. Any territory captured from the Stadholder (should he join the Coalition) would provide a useful bargaining counter in negotiation to guarantee the integrity of Belgium. But beyond that, no political initiatives in the Dutch Netherlands were planned. The Patriots were thus somewhat deluded when they looked to him as their liberator. His provisions for the legion hardly suggested that it was equipped to be the phalanx of Dutch emancipation. It was to consist of just 2,822 men, divided into four battalions of fusiliers, one of cavalry and a couple of artillery companies. With an old-fashioned disregard for the totality of revolutionary war, its arms were to be purchased from London and supplemented by munitions already stored at Dunkirk and St. Omer. Since this was evidently a legion on the cheap, the rather dashing blue and white uniforms originally intended for the whole corps were reserved for the cavalry only, while the fusiliers (much to Daendels' chagrin) had to make do with a black rig of palpably inferior quality.[45] But the economy which most slighted the Dutch was a strictly formal one. Since France was not at war with the United Provinces the government forbade the use of the title "Batavian"—a name, as the Dutch complained, "which was very dear to us . . . since it was the ancient Bataves who were renowned for their courage and for their love of liberty and equality."[46] Instead, they were obliged to go by the thin disguise of "Légion franche étrangère" (Free Foreign Legion), less of a misnomer than the Dutch would have liked to admit since its ranks were liberally supplemented by Flemings and even Swiss. This Falstaff's army was unlikely to strike terror into the heart of the Stadholder. It is hardly surprising that in the autumn of 1792, Etta d'Aelders was still able to assure van de Spiegel that there was scant danger of France and the Dutch Republic coming to serious blows.[47] The legion appeared to be no more than a minor auxiliary of Dumouriez's strategy.

By the close of 1792 that strategy looked to be on the point of making new advances. The general's victory over the Austrians at Jemmapes on November 6 had given him the power to put into execution at least part of his plan for the southern Netherlands. Since his replacement as Minister of War in October by the Jacobin Pache, his reputation had been under a cloud, but the new victory for the Republic re-established his prestige. The Brissotins rallied to him; the Convention seemed to be at his feet, and with the help of his closest ally, the Minister of Foreign Affairs Charles Lebrun, he appeared to have tamed the government into docility. Without more ado he set about calling elections to a Belgian Convention, commissioning contractors to supply the army (to "attach capitalists to our country," as Lebrun disingenuously put it) and operating what amounted to a virtually autonomous foreign policy. In this as in many other respects he was anticipating Bonaparte by five years, but unfortunately for him Dumouriez was not separated from France by the Alps. And in one significant matter he stepped too far out of line with feeling in the Convention. He attempted (with little success) to raise a Belgian army. This was to have been financed by a loan from the Belgian clergy as part of a quid pro quo for preserving their tithes and property intact. In the frenzied atmosphere of the Jacobinising Revolution, such a bargain not only mortified its purists but, worse, appeared to harbour evil intentions towards the French Republic itself. Dumouriez, after all, like other Girondins, was known to have felt queasy about the incarceration of the King; it took little imagination to suppose that he might, if necessary, march on Paris to secure his release. It was in this slightly hysterical atmosphere that the so-called Second Propaganda Decree was enacted by the Convention on December 15. This law put an end to the autonomous authority of the generals, placing them under the control of representatives of the Convention and ordering them to apply the legislation of the revolutionary assembly in any territories captured from the enemy.

This decree succeeded in pulling the rug from under Dumouriez's feet. But it also placed his junior Dutch protégés in a frightful predicament. On the one hand they still supposed (quite rightly) that Dumouriez was likely to prove their most effective, perhaps their only, champion. Yet they had no wish to appear to be a division of a private army, organised in a conspiracy against the French Republic. The decree of December threatened to pre-empt even the remote possibility of a Batavian Republic established on their initiative and according to Dutch rather than French canons of political liberty. In many respects of course these were identical, but the Patriots were by no means reconciled to losing all freedom of manoeuvre for the sake of expediting a revolutionary war. Trapped between complete submission to the dogma of December 15 and the transparent opportunism of Dumouriez, they decided on a modest reaffirmation of their national identity. From the demise of the Brussels commission to the foundation of the legion there had been no collective representation. Following the creation of the legion, a "council of administration" had been established, which included in its members Huber and van Hoey, the commissioners who had fallen foul of the government in 1789. At the end of October, a second body going by the title of Batavian Revolutionary Committee came into being in Paris on the initiative of Dumont-Pigalle.[48] The old bickering threatened to break out again, particularly since the Committee regarded itself as the political guardian of the legion. But the dawning of a new opportunity for liberation reconciled the groups sufficiently to combine their efforts in persuading the French to redeem their promise to "assist all people wishing to recover their liberty."

By the middle of November this Batavian Revolutionary Committee was busying itself with all manner of political activities. Its "Act of Association" had declared its aim to work for the liberation of the Netherlands, the destruction of the Stadholderate, the ejection of the regent aristocracy, and the nullification of the Union of Utrecht, "which has been the cause of so many evils for our Republic." The Committee bent over backwards to be acceptable to French opinion, particularly in the Convention. It hinted that Batavian liberty would be founded "on the bases of the French constitution,"[49] and as Condorcet had recommended in his Avis aux Bataves, the traditional sovereign provinces were to be replaced by departments, further subdivided into districts. The draft constitution produced by the Committee in November (and revised in February prior to the invasion) reflected the intense Francophilia of Valckenaer and Dumont-Pigalle but also incorporated many of the features of the Patriot programme, including directly elected local councils and burgemeesters, a national legislature and an executive directory responsible to it.[50] The Committee produced a large number of pamphlets and broadsides urging war against Britain and the Dutch Republic and made personal approaches to many of the leading figures in the Convention to win them to the cause. In this last enterprise they had mixed success. Thuriot remained opposed to any extension of the war; others like Vergniaud were more encouraging. The only notable convert was Brissot, who had hitherto shown great hostility to the Dutch but, reassured that the legion would remain "foreign" not "Batavian," gave it his blessing. By November 18 Dumont-Pigalle was confident that "the great majority of the Convention was in favour of Batavian liberty."[51]

Yet even before war was declared, the Patriots found themselves in another cleft stick, partly of their own making. Much exercised by the need to appear impeccably revolutionary before the Convention, they were simultaneously concerned to establish the writ of the Committee as a provisional administration in territory occupied by French troops. At the end of November they had sent three of their number, Hendrick Schilge, de Kock and van Hooff, to the front to act as political representatives with the legion. Through their presence they hoped to avoid the worst excesses of occupation currently being visited on the Belgians and Germans.[52] Valckenaer and Dumont-Pigalle were especially concerned that the introduction of the *assignat* paper currency and the anti-clerical legislation of the Convention would irreparably alienate the Dutch people; they had broached the subject many times with Lebrun without getting much in the way of a positive response. Dumouriez, perhaps surprisingly, was more responsive to this special pleading. During the campaign he informed General Miranda that due to the marked differences in "manners, usages and tongue . . . we have only to act militarily in this revolution."[53] But his civilian masters found the pretensions of the Committee to act as a provisional administration less acceptable. The Belgian Committee had already blotted its copybook by showing too much ardour in hounding its political opponents and all too little in securing the population against the Austrians. The Batavian Committee would be no more than an intermediary between the army and the civilian population, soothing the way for efficient requisitions and implementing the instructions of the Convention, until, it was added generously, the sovereignty and integrity of the new Republic could be proclaimed.

On the subject of economic concessions the French were even less forthcoming. Cambon had been particularly concerned over the allegations of graft surrounding Dumouriez's dealings with the Belgian contractors and was resolved to keep authority for supplies firmly within the control of the Convention's representatives. Nor was he keen to sugar the pill by abolishing a wide range of unpopular taxes suggested by Valckenaer. With the campaign bogged down, he was later to consider removing the imposts on bread and beer—a concession through which, he told the Convention, "you will give the Batavian sans-culottes the means to dance the carmagnole around the Liberty Tree."[54] But if at the end of 1792 the French were showing an indecent interest in the "considerable public revenue" of the Dutch Republic, the Patriots were not themselves entirely innocent in whetting their appetite. It was Valckenaer, after all, who presented Cambon with the mouth-watering prospect of "our money, our fleets, our warehouses and our sailors" which would be theirs for the asking (or taking) on the morrow of victory.[55]

Thus there were serious differences between the French and their Dutch protégés over the conduct and indeed the purpose of a campaign against the Stadholder. The more astute among the Patriots were keenly aware of the French reservations about their political future. But for the sake of getting on with the attack on the Netherlands, they were prepared to suppress their misgivings. They played on the French preoccupation with strategy, emphasising the importance of establishing a friendly power to the north and east of Belgium as a guarantor of her integrity. The continuing possibility that the Statists might trump the Belgian republicans by inviting a scion of the House of Orange to become Duke of Brabant gave an additional incentive to be rid of William V. But the one factor most likely to prise the Dutch Republic from its avowed neutrality was the Scheldt, "that cursed river," as Etta d'Aelders said. She might well resent its influence. Until the decree of the Convention on November 16 declaring its navigation open and thus violating the Treaty of Westphalia of 1648, she had achieved considerable success in resolving the major differences between British and Dutch and the French. The British Cabinet had even contemplated recognising the Republic on the basis of the diplomatic status quo. But the opening of the Scheldt, and the threat it posed to Dutch shipping (and thus to British interests) combined with the Propaganda decrees had utterly changed the tone of their diplomacy. Try as she might, Etta d'Aelders could not budge Lebrun on the matter of the river. In reply to an appeal from van de Spiegel, the foreign minister instructed her to inform "the great personage" (for in their triangular correspondence he was never mentioned by name in case the mail should be tampered with) that "French arms have freed this [Belgian] people from feudal servitude and that the pretended rights over the river are thus abolished by this fact."[56]

Yet even at this eleventh hour war was not a foregone conclusion. From Amsterdam, Nicolas van Staphorst wrote that the Patriots were waiting for Dumouriez to plant the liberty tree in The Hague or on the Dam square.[57] But Dumouriez, who had often been criticised for his impetuosity, appeared to be stricken by a mysterious immobility. Rumours circulated that it was not lead but gold in his boots which weighed him down. Lucas van Steveninck wrote to Dumont-Pigalle that he had been paid 1 million florins not to attack the Dutch Republic. Smelling a new procrastination, the Patriots emboldened themselves to remind the French government of its promises. At a joint session of the committees of finance, defence and foreign affairs, a Patriot deputation urged France "at last to assume a role worthy of her. The Bataves are ready. They await you."[58] And perhaps out of fear of a repetition of the volte-face of 1787, a second deputation ended up by alluding to the need to "efface the shameful memory of 1787."[59]

Their reception remained ominously cool. Only two members of the meeting on December 17 could bring themselves to support an immediate declaration of hostilities, and one of those two was the effervescent "Anacharsis" Cloots. It was Cloots who, four days after that bleak encounter, managed to whip up a little more enthusiasm for the Dutch cause at the Jacobins when he referred to the horizontal Dutch tricolour as a happy anticipation of the vertical. More eccentrically still, he felt it necessary to go out of his way to reassure the "opulent Bataves" that as long as they had "the souls of sans-culottes," they could "roll their tons of gold in peace" and still join the march of universal liberty.[60] But after the vapour came the cold water. Cloots was followed at the rostrum by Thuriot, who rejected any invasion of the Netherlands at whatever juncture it might take place, and Robespierre who sneeringly enquired why, since the Dutch were so well off, they could not afford to make a revolution on their own account or at least pay up 100 million to the French for doing it for them (a jibe which was to be taken appallingly seriously by his own successors).[61]

By the turn of the year the Patriots were once again depressed and baffled by the vagaries of French foreign policy. The pledge of November 19 to "assist all those countries wishing to do so to recover their liberty" seemed no more reliable than the bond of the old monarchy. Even before the chilly interview with the committees, Dumont-Pigalle had resumed his familiar pessimism. By not invading Zeeland in October or November the French had missed their best opportunity. In January the exhausted condition of Dumouriez's army and the onset of winter ice around the islands seemed to rule out a swift and conclusive campaign. And as if to reinforce his gloom, the French retained two envoys in London to keep the channels of negotiation open.

But in the new year the attitude of the British government seemed to harden perceptibly. While Pitt remained open-minded and Lord Auckland, the British ambassador at The Hague, conducted a valiant holding operation, both Grenville and van de Spiegel were convinced that war was inevitable sooner or later. The British Secretary of State had been persuaded by Lebrun's intransigence over the Scheldt and by the Propaganda decrees that there was no dealing with the gang of ruffians who had usurped the sovereignty of the French crown.[62] Public feeling in the country was running high over the detention and trial of the King, and in the first week of January Grenville had called the French bluff by sending a naval squadron to Flushing. Plans for the defence of Walcheren and South Beveland were concerted with the Dutch and Prussians. The execution of Louis was almost certainly only the last straw. Etta d'Aelders, desperate to stave off the eclipse of her special commission, attempted to persuade Lebrun that those who urged war were either royalists or else Jacobins intent on creating havoc and massacring Girondins and other Conventionnels.[63] But on January 24 St. James's returned the passports of the French ambassadors, and on February 1 the Convention declared war on the United Provinces and Britain. After so much travail and so much uncertainty it seemed that the Patriots were at last on the threshold of revenge. Naturally they greeted the news of war with transports of pleasure. But their euphoria did not prevent them falling out even at this moment over whether they should, or should not, present their official congratulations to the Convention. In the event, Brahain Ducange read out yet another of the rhapsodies to which the Convention must have been becoming much accustomed. It spoke of the "sacred and common interest of the Patrie which, since the glorious day of the 10th of August, has united us all." Henceforth there was to be one sole object: "the fall of despotism and the triumph of Holy Equality."[64]

In anticipation of their speedy return, the Batavian Revolutionary Committee had established their three deputies at Antwerp. They supplied Dumouriez with a list of reliable Patriots throughout the Netherlands who might present themselves as organisers of a new uprising, and military intelligence on the Stadholder's defences. But the general thought little of either. In his memoirs he remarked drily that the Committee was more notable for its zeal than for the quality of its information.[65] This criticism was not altogether unjust. Daendels, now a lieutenant-major in the "Foreign Legion," insisted that the Dutch Republic was boiling over with sedition. But the only evidence to support this impression were odd reports of a man arrested in Utrecht for singing the *Marseillaise*, another in Zwolle for distributing subversive literature and a third in Haarlem for parading a dummy dressed as the King of Prussia decked out with the tricolour cockade and *bonnet rouge*.[66]

The military advice was not much more helpful. The Committee had counselled a descent on Zeeland and an occupation of the island of Walcheren. This was meant to prevent the junction of the British and Dutch fleets and secure a base from which further operations could be launched. But both Dumouriez and Miranda saw many difficulties in this strategy. The ice around the mouth of the Scheldt had made navigation hazardous, and it was known that both Flushing and Bergen op Zoom were already heavily invested. Dumouriez feared being tied down to Walcheren and immobilised in exactly the way the British were to suffer seventeen years later. An advance on the lower Maas via Dutch Brabant combined with a pincer movement to the extreme south at Maastricht and Nijmegen risked more, as a "frontal" attack, and would involve besieging Breda and Geertruydenberg. But once mastered, this route would give almost direct access to the heartland of South Holland. General Valence was to cover the Belgian flank. The ice which would have proved so treacherous to an amphibious expedition would, it was hoped, be an ally in crossing the rivers further inland.

Dumouriez's calculations were to be vindicated—but by General Pichegru two years later. The French advance stumbled almost as soon as it had begun. Maastricht was occupied without much resistance, but Geertruydenberg put up stubborn fight and Breda took a week's pounding with heavy artillery before capitulation on February 25. Putting a bold face on these limited successes, the Batavian commissioners issued jubilant manifestoes urging their compatriots to insurrection and to refuse any orders from the Stadholder to cut the dykes.[67] "Dumouriez approaches; soon you will be free," annnounced one such proclamation. They had serious hopes of putting into execution the latest version from their now overflowing portfolio of constitutional projects as soon as Dutch Brabant was pacified. In the meantime, Breda received the fruits of fraternal liberty. A liberty tree was solemnly planted in the market place; a Jacobin club was established, and on March 1 elections were held to appoint a new city council. But these modest gestures of political freedom were already being vitiated, not only by the accumulating obstacles of the campaign but by increasingly restrictive instructions from Paris. At the beginning of March, Cambon issued a set of orders curtailing the political authority of the general and forbidding him to take any political action independently of the Convention and the government. Moreover, while the general was exhorted to encourage "Patriotic contributions," his troops were doing rather more than necessary in the way of encouragement. Around Breda and Geertruydenberg the requisitioning was savage, levied indiscriminately on the rural population. The Dutch commissioner at Breda, van Hooff, complained bitterly of these abuses, warning that their continuation could spark off revolt against the French.[68]

His standing challenged, Dumouriez banked his career on one last dramatic throw. On March 18 he accepted battle from Coburg and the Austrians and was disastrously beaten at Neerwinden. The French army fell back in great disorder on Antwerp and their general, vividly aware of his likely reception in France, made a separate peace with the Austrians and accepted the protection of their archduke.

The débâcle of the Dutch campaign abruptly terminated the Patriots' hopes of settling their score with the Stadholder. Yet they clung to the opportunity with almost foolish bravura. In the unorthodox manner which was to become his trademark, Daendels attempted a surprise attack on Dordrecht island which ended disastrously. And as the French retreat turned into headlong flight, van Hooff at Breda found himself marooned behind enemy lines with a light garrison and a battalion of the "Foreign Legion." Yet even as late as March 22 he protested to superiors urging him to evacuate that he could hold out for another six months. His determination to hold on to Breda, that tiny oasis of Batavian liberty, reflected the desperation which he and his colleagues felt as they contemplated a second defeat at the hands of their enemies. "I am devoted to my post," he wrote to Dumouriez before learning of his defection. "Tyrants will never make me tremble. If I have to fall into their hands a second time I will know how to die fighting."[69]

Perhaps Jan van Hooff had more reason than most Patriots to feel desperate about his position. He had been the Patriot burgemeester of Eindhoven in Brabant at the time of the Prussian invasion. Captured by the Prussians, he had been imprisoned twice but had escaped from The Hague in 1790 to reach first Brussels and then France, where he had become a member of the Batavian Revolutionary Committee. One of the first to go to Antwerp, as a native Brabander he was seconded to General Westermann at Breda. Appointed to supervise its administration, he set about his task with the zeal of a model revolutionary commissioner. He marshalled some 200 deserters from the Dutch army into a new militia, organised requisitions and made strong protests about their abuses. Hopelessly short of funds to pay the defending troops, he had advanced 6,000 francs on his own account to finance this, only to have Westermann abscond without ever paying a single coin. Still his faith in the holy alliance of liberty was unshaken. Even when, on March 28, he received his final orders to capitulate from Dumouriez, he refused to believe that the French could abandon a country where they had "been received as brothers," indifferent to the "barbarism to which they now exposed those who were their friends." Rather than undergo this second humiliation, van Hooff resolved to die "buried in the ruins of Breda." But he was to be denied his martyrdom. Although the Prussian officer sent to receive the surrender was sent away baffled by his defiant refusals, his soldiers were markedly less inclined to sacrifice themselves, especially unpaid, for the cause of liberty. They departed of their own accord for Antwerp with van Hooff trailing miserably behind in the rear. On his return to France, he was rewarded for his faith in French integrity by another spell in prison, charged with being an accomplice in Dumouriez's treachery. He remained incarcerated until the 9th Thermidor, Year II, but even this additional hardship failed to break his by now battered optimism. The victories of Fleurus and Wattignies, he said, "justify more than ever the expectation that France will break their [Dutch] chains."[70]

The wretched experience of van Hooff personified the misfortune which befell the Dutch Patriots in the French Revolution. The treason of the general which helped usher in the Terror was an unmitigated disaster for them. The Jacobins, who had never enthused over the war of liberation, pinned the blame for defeats and civil war on "foreign plots." The erstwhile "amis de la révolution" were again demoted to the status of a fifth column and treated as such. In the light of the accumulating disasters of the spring and summer of 1793, the government held responsible for them looked suspiciously cosmopolitan. Brissot and Condorcet had flirted with international revolution; its Minister of Finance had been the Swiss Clavière, and among its generals were the Alsatian Westermann, the Venezuelan Miranda and the Swiss la Harpe.

Many of these forfeited their lives to the violent xenophobic convulsion worked up by the Committee of Public Safety. Others, like van Hooff, were lucky to find themselves merely in prison rather than the tumbril. Active conspiracy was not necessary to qualify for the "republican haircut"; negligence was itself a treason. Sheer physical survival demanded not only dissociation from the criminal incompetence of the Dutch campaign but the axiomatic suppression of all claims to national identity which could possibly be construed to compete with defence of the *patrie*. Thus *Le Batave* became *Le Sans-Culotte* and ceased to deal with Dutch or Belgian affairs. After the guillotining of de Kock, some of the Patriot luminaries in Paris like Abbema and Jan Bicker disappeared across the frontier to Hamburg and Switzerland respectively. Valckenaer, a man with a nose for survival, retired from Paris and lay low in the village of Bièvre-la-Montagne near Versailles to lead a life of exemplary republican patriotism. Crowning the effacement of national identity, he publicly withdrew from his local Jacobin club in compliance with a decree of the Convention prohibiting foreigners from attending patriotic societies. The gesture probably saved his life, for in April 1794 he was exonerated by a revolutionary tribunal for his patriotic zeal, "his adoration of the Supreme Being and his zealous work for the manufacture of saltpetre."[71]

The premature collapse of the Batavian cause owed a good deal to circumstances beyond the control of its partisans. But even had its principal patron's captaincy not been so abruptly terminated, there are grounds for believing that the policy of identification with the French Revolution, taken up by Valckenaer in 1790, had been a failure. Before Neerwinden, it is true, there were a few indications that France might fulfil the role of disinterested liberator cast for her by the Revolutionary Committee. On February 24 Lebrun had assured that body:

The French Republic has no other view and no other interest than to re-establish you in your rights. The principles which form the basis of its existence also form the basis of its relations with its allies. The Republic demands as the price of its numerous sacrifices only the establishment of a free Constitution. This sacred right of independence will be respected in Holland . . . I would like to anticipate the happy results of such a revolution founded on the free and unanimous consent of the Batavian nation. An alliance that the analogy of interests and principles must render indissoluble; the extension of trade of the two peoples; the reciprocal naturalisation of their citizens; the emancipation of the Dutch people.[72]

This remarkable letter coincided in every respect with the hopes of the Batavian Revolutionary Committee. Had it been genuinely representative of the official view of French revolutionary administrations, the work of creating an "analogy of interests" would have been amply vindicated. But it was nothing of the kind. Any interests in common between French and Dutch revolutionaries were based on criteria of utility, not fraternal sentiment. Dumouriez wished to use a Dutch campaign to secure his Belgian dominion; Cambon was interested in what could be extracted from its reputed wealth. Even Cloots saw the new Batavia as a staging post for the Universal Republic. Danton, never a man to mince words, summed up the French interest in liberating the Netherlands when he announced to the Convention: "Prenons Hollande et Carthage est à nous." Conversely, the Batavian Patriots cultivated Lebrun and the Girondins because they saw in them the best chance of extending the war to Britain and the Stadholder. Despite all their lip service to the crusade for liberty, their preoccupations at bottom remained Dutch.

Even on the brief excursion into the Netherlands provided by Dumouriez's campaign, serious differences between patron and protégé arose as to the conduct of the liberation. Cambon's concern to protect the freedom of requisition had already been noted. But there were other sacrifices which the Dutch found hard to swallow. At the outbreak of war an embargo had been placed on all Dutch ships, and those currently lying in French ports were put under distraint. But a good two-thirds of those ninety or so ships belonged to men who, according to the Revolutionary Committee, were true and tried Patriots. As a result they complained bitterly but unsuccessfully to the French government about this arbitrary deprivation.[73] Then there were several issues concerning the status of the future Batavian Republic which remained unsettled at the commencement of the campaign. Was it to be permitted the merciful luxury of neutrality? What indeed was to be the future of the Scheldt, the *casus belli?* Those who were to inherit the burden of the lame Dutch economy were unlikely to relish the prospect of competition from a revived Antwerp any more than their predecessors. The Stadholder's failure to challenge the Emperor

Joseph on just this point had been an important item of the Patriot dispute with him in the 1780's. It was not entirely clear, despite Lebrun's assurance, that there would necessarily be a Batavian Republic at all. Dumouriez's antics with the Belgians had taught the French government to be meaner with their promises than in November 1792. The week that the general crossed into Dutch Brabant, the Belgian provinces were annexed, and those on the left bank of the Rhine were to follow shortly after. On reoccupation in 1794 there was to be no argument over their status as French départements. If they could be conveniently accommodated within Danton's generous definition of "natural frontiers," who was to say where France's north-eastern frontier was to terminate? The Rhine, after all, ran through Arnhem and Leiden. Even before Neerwinden it seemed unlikely that France would accept the establishment of new states on her borders except in the status of satraps. The ordeals of the revolutionary Year II made it abundantly clear to the European "friends of revolution" that France's primary obligation was to her own security.

The sea-change in the relationship between senior and junior revolutionary partner was, in the long run, to be of more serious consequence for the Dutch than even the disgrace of their patron Dumouriez. Henceforth their arrangements with France would be made on a more practical basis, a true marriage of convenience. In 1787 the Patriots had fled from a vindictive enemy to place themselves at the mercy of a fickle friend. They had expected nothing except shelter, subsistence and the freedom to plot revenge. In 1789 they found that, more by chance than design, they had jumped from the Dutch frying pan into a French revolutionary inferno. Their hosts now professed a messianic libertarianism and, having destroyed their monarchy, appeared to be about to practice what they preached. Their obvious course had been to embrace that cause as their own and offer themselves as one of its instruments. The legion, the Committee and the campaign itself were all expressions of that decision. But instead of becoming the beneficiaries of revolutionary war, the Dutch émigrés ended up alongside Belgians and Rhinelanders as its victims. Their punitive treatment under the Terror must have given them abundant evidence that the bonds of revolutionary fraternity were not yet strong enough to contain the more powerful instinct of national survival, and that the frontiers of the true *patrie* looked more like those of the old France than poor Cloots had imagined.

The elimination of the Dutch "lobby" also meant the end of emancipation by remote control. There had always been something cerebral about Valckenaer's revolution planned from a French writing desk. The astonished reaction of his Amsterdam correspondent to the plan to transform William V into a model constitutional monarch suggested just how remote from Dutch political life the émigrés often were. Like the rest of the disaffected European intelligentsia gathered in France, the Patriots were infatuated with the thrilling inspiration of liberty in arms. Its initial successes at Valmy and Jemappes encouraged them to see their own liberation as a phase in a general European struggle, not the resumption of the contest of 1787. And had they remained tantalised by that vision they would have earned historical dismissal. But if, as

Colenbrander insists, the French Revolution was their "school," it was an education in lost illusions. Their miserable experience in 1793 had disabused them sufficiently of their revolutionary innocence to make it plain that any future attempt at reversing the verdict of 1787 would depend on more tangible assets than fraternal goodwill. If it would need the *force majeure* of French arms to alter the situation in the Netherlands, it would also require some kind of Dutch political response to ensure it was changed indisputably in their favour.

Such a response appeared to have been entirely absent during the brief campaign of 1793. But in 1795 the situation in the Netherlands was nothing like so inert. It is, of course, not unimportant that where the first campaign had been an abysmal military failure, the second was at least a qualified success. But for the future of the Batavian Republic it was of more consequence that while in 1793 their leaders had been confined to acting as a front for Dumouriez's adventurism or to inducing submission to requisitions, in 1795 their action followed months of augmenting disturbance within the Dutch Republic. When a new Revolutionary Committee convened, it was not in French Flanders or Artois but in Amsterdam.[74] And it is to the resumed career of Patriot democracy in the Netherlands that the historian must look for the proper context of the foundation of the Batavian Republic.

False Dawn, January–October 1794

Not even the warmest enthusiasts of a Dutch revolution supposed that their efforts were independently capable of removing William V's British and Prussian bodyguards and overthrowing his regime. As long as the French Republic remained on the defensive against the Coalition, differences as to the form the hypothetical Batavian Republic should take were bound to remain strictly academic. Even in the happy contingency of France taking the offensive again, Dutch opinion was by no means unanimous as to the degree of support it could expect from a national uprising. Daendels, always the keenest to get on with the business of revolutionising the Netherlands, was convinced that a golden opportunity had been thrown away very early in 1793. At that time he believed an invasion of Walcheren would have needed no more than a few thousand troops to whom a Patriot militia, 40,000 strong, would have rallied in the Dutch interior. Echoing Jacobin conspiracy theories against Dumouriez, he remained persuaded that "foreign gold" had succeeded in staying the hand of the French until their enterprise was neither militarily nor politically feasible.[75]

While these pipe-dreams of a Patriot army spilling out from the Dutch cities at a given signal were grotesquely far-fetched, other less fevered reports from both French and British sources indicated that there had indeed been some disturbances during the invasion. The secretary at the French legation, Thainville, wrote of Patriot banquets at which Dumouriez's health had been rowdily drunk and François Noël, the ambassador, spoke of men apprehended by the police for enrolling in a clandestine "Batavian Legion." Even Lord Auckland reluctantly observed that "The patriotic party at Amsterdam has laid aside all reserves and is become noisy and impudent. There is scarce a village or alehouse in this province [Holland] in which the language is not seditious at the clubs and frequently (boasts) the accession of a travelling Jacobin."[76]

The calamity of the Dumouriez campaign silenced what agitation there had been in the Netherlands on his behalf. But when Caillard, a French agent, was provided with a false passport and sent into the Dutch Republic to sound out Patriot opinion in December 1793, he was still able to report some cheerful news.

The Patriots [he wrote] form a huge majority in several provinces such as Overijssel and Utrecht. In Holland the Stadholderian sentiment is confined to the regencies which as you know owe their appointment to the Prince. But the body of the nation is generally excellent with the exception of the lowest class of people in The Hague, Amsterdam and Rotterdam. The least certain provinces are Gelderland and Zeeland.[77]

If Caillard and his informants were correct, it would appear that the alignments of 1787 were fundamentally unaltered by the intervening period. But all these fragments of information originated with observers on the periphery of Dutch politics. Others well within the ring remained sceptical about the chances of a spontaneous insurrection. Willem van Irhoven van Dam, the Amsterdam lawyer who made that unflattering comparison between the French sans-culotte and the Dutch Patriot, complained in the same letter to Daendels that "a revolution here is an impossible business. There can be no country in the world where there is more talk of Patriotism but fewer Patriots."[78] His pessimism found corroboration in the long memorandum delivered to the French representatives at Comines in Belgium in February 1794. Its author was Isaac Gogel, a merchant, also of Amsterdam.[79] Gogel was too young to have played any active part in the Patriot revolt. But his head had been turned by the French Revolution against which the failure of the Patriots seemed desperately pallid. He too regarded his compatriots as politically incombustible. They were phlegmatic and complacent. The rich were "egoists," nervous of losing the smallest part of their ill-gotten gains and inured to the perquisites of oligarchy. The very poor were the slaves of Orange, along with the Jews. The Dutch Church was an accomplice in the despotism and the priests of the Roman Church indoctrinated their flock to believe the revolution the work of Satan. "Others who call themselves Patriots gossip a lot, complain a lot and do nothing." There was only one answer. The French would have to bring their revolution with their armies, complete with tribunals and the guillotine. Yet even the fiery young Gogel was prepared to concede that not all the Dutch were utterly beyond redemption. If "we should not flatter ourselves [by expecting] much native support," nor would it be likely that a revolution would meet headlong opposition. In the towns of the land provinces, virtually the entire population was Patriot in sympathy. Artisans, the shopkeeping class and the petty-bourgeois generally, who "have suffered most since the last revolution," would have good reason to applaud revolutionary change. If the fate of Belgium could be avoided; if the Dutch could be guaranteed their religious liberty and granted the fiscal reform they desperately needed, there was still a good chance of rallying popular support.

Thus despite the apparent irreconcilability of the optimistic and pessimistic views of a Dutch revolution, both were agreed on two points. First, that there were those who certainly had cause (if not the will or energy) to rebel against the Stadholder and settle scores with his government. Secondly, that without encouragement from a French invasion they were unlikely to risk coming into the open and taking on not only the police but German and British soldiers. In fact the Orangist authorities had been reasonably successful in discouraging not only Patriot but quite moderate forms of political activity immediately following the invasion. Even at the end of 1792, when war appeared imminent, the French ambassador reported that "the most rigorous inquisition halts every conversation and chills every heart. Even the intimacy of private society affords no shelter from a surveillance worthy of the police of *ancien régime* Paris."[80]

This was to flatter the efficacy, if not the intention, of the Stadholder's officers. Van de Spiegel certainly liked to think himself above the sordid business of political police, but neither Harris nor Bentinck van Rhoon were at all squeamish about using intimidation both as punishment for past misdemeanours and deterrent against renewed resistance. There had been nothing half-hearted about the "Orange terror" of 1787–88, though it had stopped short of spilling blood. The convenient silence of many of the judicial records on the innumerable systematically engineered riots, sackings and plunderings throughout virtually every province of the country makes an accurate estimate of the damage done difficult. But from the Dumont-Pigalle archives and other contemporary sources,[81] much is known of the most notorious episodes. In Zeeland, where the Patriots were isolated amidst a hostile populace and Orangist regents, led by the ruthless burgemeester of Middelburg, Wilhelm van Citters, the treatment was particularly violent. In Gouda 200 houses were looted and sacked in a few days; in 's Hertogenbosch 829, of which 250 were totally obliterated. In Utrecht the bill presented in 1795 for damages done in the aftermath of the Prussian occupation exceeded 1 million guilders! And this kind of treatment, or the threat of it, continued well into 1788, with a "penal expedition" sent against the island of Schouwe in February of that year.

It is virtually impossible to know how many ex-officers of Free Corps forfeited their petty remunerations and posts through the adjudication of sheriffs and magistrates who were the direct nominees of the Stadholderian government. But at the level of the secondary and primary leadership, the penalties were considerably more severe. Some, like de Gijselaar, who after a relatively short and comfortable exile in Brussels returned to Dordrecht, and van Berckel, who vanished discreetly from public life in Amsterdam, managed to evade this punishment. But for the less well-to-do, the traditional sentences of perpetual or hundred-year banishment together with punishing fines and confiscations were commonly imposed. In Utrecht alone, such fines amounted to nearly 100,000 guilders. Ondaatje, van Haeften, Lidth de Jeude and others were permanently banished from the city and declared "publicly infamous." In Rotterdam fourteen members of the regency were similarly treated, and in Delft seventeen. In Friesland and Gelderland many of the punishments were even harsher. And in Amsterdam, seventeen members of the old regency were sentenced variously to deprivation of office, fines and imprisonment. Those deemed to have sided with the militant democrats in 1787 were especially harshly dealt with. Visscher, the Pensionary of Amsterdam, was thrown into jail; Daendels exiled "sword over head" (on pain of death); and van der Capellen van der Marsch condemned to death in his absence.

While a repression on this scale was relatively docile by French standards, it was rigorous enough to inhibit the early re-emergence of opposition to the Stadholder. The exile or imprisonment of able journalists like Pieter 't Hoen, coupled with stringent press laws, succeeded initially in gagging the Patriot organs of opinion. Patriot predikants like Bernardus Bosch, then preaching at Diemen near Amsterdam, thought to abuse their *predik-stoel* for political purposes, were given a dose of Orangist rough-house treatment, and the reinstatement of old prohibitions on petition and public assembly completed the elimination of the means by which the democrats had mobilised their support.

But opposition did survive. For in restoring the status quo ante 1784 van de Spiegel and Bentinck also restored many of the discomforts of the earlier regime. With the democrats driven into exile or underground, the more traditional opposition to the House of Orange—the banking and mercantile interests centred in Amsterdam—felt freer to assert its old antagonism. Hardly had the menace of Patriot democracy been despatched than it became apparent that those who had whole-heartedly collaborated in its destruction were not prepared to repeat the experience of 1748-49. William V's insistence that each province declare the Stadholderate hereditary and intrinsically part of their provincial constitutions met with stony opposition from the regencies; only Gelderland, predictably, submitted to the autocracy without protest.

Van de Spiegel's position was fraught with difficulties. As principal minister of the Restoration, he was automatically committed to strengthening the Stadholderate. On the other hand, by temperament and intellectual inclination he was a reforming, rather than a purely reactionary, Orangist. A parvenu, he had risen to high office as Pensionary of Zeeland via a judicious marriage into a regent family. He was fond of boasting that his own career was an example of Dutch social mobility which gave the lie to the French Revolution's claim to a monopoly on *égalité*.[82] An adopted son of the Zeeland regents, he understood only too well their provincial conservatism and their determination not to cede an iota of sovereignty even to the Prince whose authority they respected. Added to this, van de Spiegel liked to think of himself as a reforming Pensionary in the line of Simon van Slingelandt and Bentinck. An able and prolific contributor to the debate on the economic ills besetting the Republic, he was well aware of the need to overhaul many of its public institutions—above all its taxation. Faced with an accumulating flood of indebtedness, the last Grand Pensionary stood like the proverbial boy with his finger in the dyke. But to tackle these reforms in earnest demanded a period of internal stability and external peace. The ultra-conservative constitution of 1788, together with van de Spiegel's own refusal to contemplate a peace separate from his allies, precluded any such conditions from coming about. In some instances—notably that of the East India Company, by now a national scandal—he even reversed the tentative steps taken by the Patriots to bring it under public scrutiny in favour of Company autonomy.[83]

In the event, all that van de Spiegel managed was some half-hearted tinkering with the quota apportionment of some taxes.[84] With military readiness an urgent priority for his administration, he was obliged to fall back on the traditional much-reviled expedients of forced loans and low interest contributions and stock issues. Living on hand-to-mouth measures, he managed to create maximum alienation with minimum dividends for the government. While intensely unpopular with the various provincial States, his ad hoc measures failed to keep pace with the escalating costs of holding the French at bay. Even those on whom the Grand Pensionary might reasonably have expected to count preferred neither confidence nor cash. Between 1789 and 1791 it was said that Henry Hope the banker had placed some 20 million guilders in lucrative foreign loans. But when approached for a "patriotic contribution," he responded with wringing hands and a show of empty pockets.[85] Van de Spiegel's attempt to emulate the success of the British navy bills by issuing a paper currency redeemable after the peace was bitterly contested by the Amsterdam Bourse. So desperate was he that this chief magistrate of the republic of bankers considered going to the British for a loan!

Much of this obstructionism was politically motivated. The troubles of the Restoration had reactivated the time-honoured rituals of Dutch politics: Holland's interests against Zeeland and Friesland; the East India Company against the West India Company; the land provinces against the maritime, Amsterdam against everyone else. And as more than one commentator writing from afar pointed out, whatever the ostensible disposition of power granted by the 1788 constitution, Holland in fact retained the power of the purse.[86] By 1794 it appeared that Stadholder and regents had learned nothing and forgotten nothing from their narrow escape in 1787.

Yet while the revival of traditional opposition to the House of Orange made life more difficult for its ministers, it scarcely signified the beginnings of revolution. Though the provincial States might feel reluctant to help the Stadholder out of a tight corner, they were even more apprehensive about their own fate at the hands of a Dutch revolution than they had been in 1787. Then there had been no tumbrils. More impressive, and in the long run much more subversive than the conventional pattern of regent opposition, was the re-emergence of radical Patriot literature in the major cities of the Dutch Republic. Much of this was produced clandestinely. But there was more than one way to avoid the unwelcome attention of the police. The pamphlets, which made no attempt at all to disguise their revolutionary contents, usually originated from presses at St. Omer and Dunkirk and were smuggled over the border. They mostly consisted of translations of speeches and decrees of the French revolutionary clubs and assemblies, as well as the propaganda literature of the Batavian Revolutionary Committee.[87] Complete Dutch editions of works like Paine's *Common Sense* and Condorcet's *Avis aux Bataves* also found their way to the alehouses and booksellers; but it was only when the French army made its brief excursion into Dutch Brabant that a propaganda press was actually set up on Dutch territory at 's Hertogenbosch.[88] The pamphlets produced there were also highly derivative of the French genre.

A second category of radical literature was more recognisably Dutch in manner and content. Ostensibly dealing with religious, social and philanthropic issues, it emanated from the religious revival which had begun in the 1760's and which has been described earlier. Preoccupied with the moral disorder of Dutch society, its homilies extended to a multitude of sins— many of them obliquely if not acutely political. One typical product called *Our Duty to the General Good*, for example, made no bones about the implications of its evangel: "As it is our duty as Christians to follow our faith . . . so it is our duty as members of society, united in a social bond, to live as Netherlanders following our constitutional rights, freer than those who have to truckle before despotisms."[89] Many of these pamphlets were doing little more than reviving the traditional Dutch covenant with God and freedom. But many were also written by predikants who had openly identified themselves with the Patriot cause and who continued to follow in the footsteps of van der Kemp by denouncing tyranny and luxury as the dominion of anti-Christ and letting their congregation draw the relevant conclusions. The best known and most explicitly political of such works was Ysbrand van Hamelsveld's *The Moral Condition of the Netherlands People* (*De Zedelijke Toestand van de Nederlandsche Natie* . . .). But not all the crypto-political sermons ran to the length of a treatise. Inexpensive periodicals like *The Simpleton* (*De Zot*) or Bernardus Bosch's *Friend of Mankind* (*Menschenvriend*) comprised the staple diet of the philanthropic and religious societies which mushroomed throughout the Republic in the 1780's and early 1790's.[90] These societies officially eschewed any form of political ideology, advertising themselves as Christian and humanitarian. But their organisers were almost invariably Patriot predikants like Bosch who in any case saw their programme of political change as grounded on fundamental moral authority. The most important of such societies was the Society for the Public Good (*Maatschappij tot Nut van 't Algemeen*), which was founded in 1784 by a predikant from Monninkendam in North Holland. During the Batavian Republic this Society was to play an heroic role in the great Dutch education reforms. But during the Restoration its thirty or so "departments" recruited thousands of petty-burghers, artisans and small shopkeepers who five years earlier would have paraded as Free Corps. The journals, debates and essay competitions offered by the societies provided a platform for an active criticism of the status quo.

It was one such society, Teyler's Society of Haarlem, which gave Pieter Paulus the opportunity to write his famous *Treatise on Equality* (*Verhandeling over de vrage: In welken zin kunnen de Menschen worden Gelijk te Zyn . . . ?*) in 1793.[91] Published at the height of the Terror in France, this was without doubt the most successful attempt to marry the tradition of Patriot evangelism to the revolutionary axiom of natural rights egalitarianism. It set out to supply an emphatically Christian authorisation for natural equality and to assert that the only proper end for a civil society was the guarantee of such equality. That guarantee was to be enshrined in a system of government "in which the members are their own legislators and are administered by a truly elected government." Conversely, regimes grounded on aristocracies of birth or money were moral abominations at war with the providential order. As such, they invited, even demanded, the duty of revolt.

Up to the time he wrote the *Treatise*, Pieter Paulus had hovered on the fringes of the Patriot revolution. A successful lawyer at The Hague, he had passed through virtually every degree of political opinion before arriving at the most radical. As a young man he had penned a vigorous defence of Stadholderian authority, and at university had compiled a massive treatise on the prescriptive and historical authority of the Union of Utrecht. He had secured office as Admiral-Fiscal of the Maas by prudently avoiding identifying himself with extreme democracy, but this had failed to prevent his losing it in 1788 despite a fierce rearguard action on the legal niceties of his dismissal. As has been pointed out, it was of immense importance that the man associated with great expertise on the "Ancient Constitution" of the Dutch should now have put himself at the forefront of those who flatly rejected its primacy.[92] The *Treatise on Equality* made him the acknowledged leader of the Dutch democrats, and even as grudging an admirer as Charles Bentinck was obliged to concede that he

has, with great art and ability, endeavoured to reconcile the people to this (democratic) system by the way he has modified it, by the strain of religious enthusiasm that runs throughout the work, calculated to make a strong impression on a religious people and well adapted to their notions. He endeavours further to recommend this system by the apparent moderation and humanity of every syllable that comes from his mouth or pen.[93]

The *Treatise* also prompted the appearance of a mass of lesser literature of comparable political boldness. As the French Republic emerged from its ordeal to take the offensive against the First Coalition, its Dutch partisans sharpened their attacks. Samuel Iperuszoon Wiselius, the son of an oil merchant in Amsterdam, published three manifestoes expanding Paulus' egalitarian ideas and broadening the attack on privilege to demonstrate the incompatibility of democracy with any form of municipal oligarchy, however far removed.[94]

The success of writers like Paulus and Wiselius in evolving a recognisably Dutch version of egalitarian democracy was perhaps best attested by the character of the opposition put up against them. A few months after the publication of the *Treatise on Equality*, a counter-broadside appeared reiterating the ancient verity that in the Union of Utrecht the Dutch were already blessed with a constitution which comprehensively guaranteed their national liberties and rights.[95] The author of this polemic was Adriaan Kluit, the first Professor of Dutch History at Leiden University—the *alma mater* of both Paulus and Wiselius. Loyal to the spirit in which his chair had been founded, Kluit insisted that revolutionary democracy could be appropriate only for slave nations like France, where for generations liberty had been immured within privilege and monarchical despotism. Ten years earlier. Kluit's remarks would have been shared by many of those writers concentrating on attacking the Stadholder. But by 1793 the political opposition in the Netherlands was less besotted with restoring the purity of the past than pledging the liberties of the future. The strength of this literature, embracing egalitarian ideas in the language of the Dutch Patriots, demonstrates the failure of the attempt to stigmatise democracy as an alien intrusion.[96]

But if the political initiative had passed to men who knew not de Witts or "Loevestein," it would still be misleading to draw too sharp a dividing line between any "first" or "second" generation of Patriots. Paulus' work, it cannot be overstressed, was successful just because it was a synthesis of traditional Dutch debate, perennial evangelism and contemporary democracy. Similarly those who became its advocates were, politically and socially, a very mixed bunch. Some, like Daendels, Paulus himself and van Irhoven van Dam, had in some degree been involved in political action in 1787. Others like Samuel Wiselius had been too young, and only at university in Leiden had founded quasi-political fraternities like the "Infanterie des Cinq Sabres." But not all were young bloods. Those who frequented the successor club to the defunct "Vaderlandsche Societeit," the "Doctrina et Amicitia," or its rival "Felix Meritis," were of moderate views and fat incomes. They included men like Nicolas van Staphorst, whose brother was a member of the Batavian Revolutionary Committee. Associated with them were others of shifting ground whose radicalism was sometimes fashionably, sometimes sincerely held, but never dangerous enough to jeopardise their budding careers. One such character was Rutger Jan Schimmelpenninck, a brilliant young lawyer from a Mennonite family in Overijssel. Schimmelpenninck had made his name in a successful defence of apprehended Patriot moguls like Visscher, and his fortune by joining them in a ring of speculators investing in American land purchases.

All these clubmen professed versions of Patriot democracy; all heartily detested the Stadholderian regime and reserved their most powerful execration for those regents who had sold out to it to save their skins. But many were distinctly queasy at the prospect of a Jacobin republic of virtue. They were not revolutionaries at any price and—as a document that they prepared prior to the campaign of 1794 makes clear—especially not the price of seeing the fragile structure of Dutch credit wrecked by the influx of *assignats* (French paper currency) and heavy requisitioning.[97]

Through its re-emergence in the form of radical literature and the political clubs, it is not difficult to identify the leadership of the political opposition. But this was the tip of the iceberg. How far support for their cause extended into the mass of the *burgerij* as it had obviously done in the Patriot revolt remains necessarily conjectural. Van Irhoven van Dam, always pessimistic, believed he could count committed adherents in hundreds. Others like Caillard, the agent sent to reconnoitre the Republic in December 1793, or Willem Frederik Roëll, a Dutch functionary, later secretary to Louis Bonaparte, described the city as "le foyer révolutionnaire" and assumed a much wider disaffection from the Stadholderian regime. The task of assessing the strength of an opposition is made all the harder by the elimination of the one institution through which such support was easily quantifiable: the militias. The characteristic institution of the pre-Batavian period was one in which numbers fluctuated far more seriously—the *Leesgezelschappen* or reading societies.

Despite the tightened security measures which followed the invasion of 1793, these societies mushroomed throughout the Dutch Republic in the early 1790's. Convened informally for the discussion of literary and social topics, the collective purchase of a library and the organisation of essay competitions on topical matters, these societies were not of course peculiar to the Netherlands. They were the mirror of that "practical" Enlightenment which had disseminated the virtues of philanthropy and education through-out northern Europe. It was precisely for this reason that they were not regarded by the Dutch government as intrinsically subversive. Those most active in the running of the reading societies were, as elsewhere in Europe, middle-class and professional people along with the coffee-house gentry. But even when they recruited their membership from the lower social stratum of the petty-burghers, they were thought to have a civilising, rather than an agitating, effect.

However innocuous their beginnings, the victories of the French at Wattignies (October 1793) and Fleurus (February 1794) nevertheless turned the reading societies into forums of political discussion. In no time at all they became the virtual successors of the old Patriot clubs. Not that the "reading" part of their title was entirely a disingenuous misnomer. For like the clubs of the Paris sections, the "education" of the common man in his civic and political duties formed an important part of their business. When questioned by the police, a bookseller of the Joodbreedenstraat, one Jan van der Heyden (booksellers were always obvious targets of police surveillance), replied that the reading societies had been established to "make the common man more enlightened."[98] But the instruments of their enlightenment were, to say the least, selective. At their meetings there were oral readings from secretly printed newspapers like *The Friend of Man*, satires on William V and his family, and critiques of van de Spiegel and his colleagues. Paulus' *Treatise* was another favoured tract, along with Dutch histories doctored in the approved Patriot manner.[99] When asked what qualifications were needed for membership in these societies, van der Heyden obligingly replied. "None, except that he must be a Patriot."[100] But there is evidence that they were recruiting not only from among the old guard of the Free Corps but from the young. Three members picked up by the police and interrogated were a timber merchant, a wineseller, and a petty broker, all in their early twenties.

By the summer of 1794, the number and organisation of the reading societies presented a distinct threat to the authorities. Caillard reported that there were thirty-four clubs of between sixty and eighty members each in Amsterdam alone. That would have brought the aggregate to around 2,000. By August this figure had risen to over 6,000.[101] While this may not have been an overwhelming percentage of the population of Amsterdam as a whole, it was a very substantial revolutionary nucleus. (Far fewer than that had raised the insurrection in Paris five years earlier.) Their political intentions unambiguous, the reading societies took greater care to conceal their whereabouts, meeting in private houses and changing venues with each meeting. These locations were coded "A-Z and AA-AK." Some ancient musketry and a few more modern rifles were hoarded in a cache in expectation of the great day, and oaths of secrecy and loyalty exacted from all newly inscribed members. Similar clubs were organised in all the old spawning grounds of Patriot democracy: Haarlem, Delft, Dordrecht, Leiden and Rotterdam. In Friesland, student circles once again provided the base for political meetings, as did the guilds in Kampen, Deventer and Zwolle. Predictably, the clubs in Utrecht were the boldest of all. The Duke of Athlone, the commandant responsible for civil order in the city, reported to van de Spiegel that there were nearly 1,000 clubmen armed with a few hundred rifles. Their twelve societies met, as in Amsterdam, in private houses, the largest commanding a membership of some 300 and virtually flaunting its sedition in the face of the city council.

It must have been obvious to even the most complacent of the Stadholder's councillors that if the reaction of 1787 had vanquished the Patriot revolt, it had by no means extirpated it. Barely seven years later, at the mere hint of invasion, the hard core of militant democrats—drilled in the maxims of democracy and inspired by the success of their French heroes—were preparing to revenge themselves for 1787. But although the slogans and pamphlets of the Patriot days were re-appearing with ominous regularity, there were solid reasons why the Stadholder's government should have avoided excessive defeatism. British and Prussian troops were stationed on the Dutch frontiers and there had been strenuous efforts by the Grand Pensionary to overhaul the dismal state of the Generality's army. The French armies of the Sambre and Meuse had beaten the Austrians in the southern Netherlands, but between them and the heart of the Dutch Republic lay the great river estuaries, the formidable fortified strongholds of Brabant, and, in the very last resort, the flood dykes.

The government also knew very well that the leaders of the clubs dared not make a move without the assurance of military help from the French. This assumption was correct. Gogel and van Irhoven van Dam confirmed their reluctance to the French representative at Antwerp and stressed that while the leading group at "Doctrina et Amicitia" had formed a "Committee for Insurrection" (*Raad van Opstand*) it remained wary of any precipitate action, "all fearing a second lesson."[102] The committee had its firebrands, among them Gogel himself and his young business colleague, the assurance broker Johannes Goldberg; but they were restrained by the majority of cooler heads from any impetuousness. The response to a memorandum circularised among Patriot leaders throughout the Republic in March confirmed a policy of cautious expectation. They may have been committed to revolution but they were not ready for it. An overwhelmingly favourable military situation was the precondition for revolt. And in the spring of 1794 such a situation was yet to materialise. Fleurus had checked the Austrians but it had not won the war. The French had taken Belgium before and had lost it again. And among the victims of that disaster had been their Dutch protégés.

On July 10, however, Brussels fell to General Pichegru. Antwerp followed on the 22nd. As a year before, the Dutch frontier fortess at Sluys put up a bold resistance and managed temporarily to detain the French advance. But with the surrender of Ijperen at the end of the month, the whole of Flanders came under French occupation. The Army of the North stood between Boxtel and Doornik—not far from Dumouriez's fatal point of departure fifteen months earlier. With dramatic suddenness the expectations of the Dutch Patriots soared, just as morale among the Amsterdam regency plummeted.[103] On July 31 a clandestine meeting of Patriot leaders was held at one of their favoured taverns, the *Wapen van Amsterdam* (The Amsterdam Arms) in the Harlemmerhout, between Haarlem and Amsterdam. Thirty representatives from the provinces of Holland, Overijssel, Utrecht and Groningen attended to discuss tactics under the able chairmanship of J. G. Hahn, the ex-secretary of Leiden University and a militant democrat.[104]

This meeting was the first collective gathering on any kind of national basis since the collapse of the Patriot revolution in 1787. As if wishing to carry on where they left off, its participants were completely unable to agree on the most important items of discussion, such as whether to arm the mass of the burghers. But some decisions were taken. Two small co-ordinating committees were set up, one for liaising with the French army and with the committees of the Convention in Paris; the other to prepare for an uprising within the Dutch Republic itself. Amsterdam and the major Holland towns were to be its principal theatres of operation, since it was generally agreed that the over-dispersion of Patriot forces throughout the Republic had been a grave source of weakness in 1787. A secret arsenal was set up on Roeters' Island in the IJ harbour, with local depots in the city districts. Forward posts to contact the French were to be set up at Flushing (for the Dutch still assumed the invasion would be by way of Zeeland) and attempts made to remobilise the *schutterij*, a task made more urgent by the ominous overtures currently being made to the dockyard Bijltjes. Finally Gogel and van Irhoven van Dam were to proceed immediately to Brussels to make contact with the commanders of the French army and the representatives of the Convention.

The delegates were allotted two principal directives. They were first to persuade Jourdan and Pichegru that an immediate invasion of the Dutch Republic was not only possible but essential for the success of both parties. This agreed, they were to try to ensure that the campaign would be fought swiftly and cleanly, without the terrible costs to civilians which had been in evidence in Belgium and the Rhineland. Earlier that year a memorandum from "Some Patriots of Amsterdam" had reminded the French representatives that war of liberation was to be waged against the Stadholder and his adherents, not the Dutch people as a whole. Despite this attempt at reinsurance, there were few illusions on either side that the fine distinction between adversaries and tacit allies would be scrupulously respected. After all, a Dutch army as well as a Prussian and British *was* in the field. In any case, when he arrived at Aachen on August 4, 1794, to see the French generals, Gogel found them less than thirsty for combat.

Their hesitation was not entirely due to military considerations. France was then in the throes of the "fournée" of Thermidor which put an end to the Reign of Virtue and the sombre guardianship of the Incorruptible. Before it was clear whose orders he was supposed to be obeying, Pichegru was unlikely to rush into an action which, once begun, could not be reversed without great political cost. Then again the memory of the Dumouriez débacle was a terrible warning against crossing the Scheldt unprepared. Like the previous year, the preliminary campaign had already become bogged down in a succession of sieges. Sluys, Boxtel, Breda and den Bosch all cost dear in lives and time. So that after his conferences, Gogel found to his dismay that the French commanders "nursed wholly ill-founded prejudices as to the difficulty of an invasion of Holland when, following the plans concerted with General Daendels, nothing could be simpler."[105]

Gogel was no strategist. The plans he referred to were basically a rehash of the old Batavian Revolutionary Committee's scheme for a descent on Walcheren Island combined with an attack on Brabant. Daendels, whose pet this was, insisted it would take less time and men and that the initial assault on Zeeland needed a mere 25,000 troops. This was based more on his habitual sanguine than cool logistical assessment, but the Dutch officer was, by this time, almost beside himself with impatience. He had already won a reputation as a military *enfant terrible*, surprising the enemy at Zaandvoort and taking the garrison at Menin with very light losses. In one raid at three in the morning he captured a force of nearly 200 fusiliers and their 4 officers with a handful of men and a mere skirmish.[106] But these were mere diversions. The main business of the advance, he and Gogel insisted, had to be got under way before the autumn rain made the estuaries impassable. Gogel was also concerned by the news that the military commandant of Amsterdam, Golowkin, had at last begun to act against the reading societies, whose activities were rapidly assum-

ing the character of an armed conspiracy. It thus appeared all the more imperative that a major attack should be launched which would rule out any heavy
garrisoning of Amsterdam. If, he warned, this counsel was not followed, it
would result in "the total ruin of Holland; the massacre of their friends and all
those disposed to carry out the revolution."[107]

Thrown into doubt as to the real intentions of the French government,
Daendels went to Paris to try to press the Dutch arguments for action on the
Committee of Public Safety. He attempted to play on the self-interest of
Robert Lindet, the formidable commissioner of food supply, by itemising
the cornucopia that would be available to France after the Dutch Republic
was liberated. But he was received, especially by Carnot, with frosty politeness
and little enthusiasm. The encounter may, however, have been more effective
than Daendels supposed, for on September 1 he received a definite assurance
from the French representative at Antwerp that Pichegru had had his orders
to proceed with the invasion within fifteen days at the most. On the 6th
a draft proclamation was published in which the French Republic promised its
protection to "the Patriot party," and Daendels issued the stern admonition
that "any inhabitant or soldier in the service of Holland who opposes the
orders of the Revolutionary government will be punished by death as a rebel
and traitor to his country."[108]

Like Daendels, Pichegru was expecting a swiftly conclusive compaign.
He was hoping to throw the British well back over the Maas and, after a
decisive battle, penetrate the Holland defences to cut off any investment of
Amsterdam. But the defending forces had no intention of presenting themselves so conveniently. After a skirmish at Boxtel, the Duke of York retreated
over the Maas and locked himself and 28,000 troops up in 's Hertogenbosch.
The Dutch forces, about 22,000 strong, dug in around Breda in front of the
enormously wide Hollands Diep along a line stretching from Geertruydenberg
to Steenberg. These were formidable defensive dispositions. Even if they were
dislodged from their front line, it would be possible to fall back, estuary by
estuary, slowing down the pace of the French advance to a crawl and taking
them further and further from reliable sources of supply. As other invaders
had found to their cost, operating on semi-amphibious terrain demanded
special reserves of military stamina. Even before it began the Dutch campaign, Pichegru's Army of the North was short of arms and supplies.

In spite of these difficulties and the failure of the much-heralded advance
of September 15 to materialise, the Patriots in Amsterdam acted as though the
moment of reckoning was at hand. Six presses were at work day and night
producing an almost incessant stream of posters, pamphlets, feuilletons and
"counter-Proclamations" bearing the imprimatur of the "Secret Committee
for the Revolution Sitting in Holland."[109] The old Patriot refrains complaining that the country was being led to its ruin by a "drunken Prince, a thieving
knavish Pensionary and a debauched aristocracy" were accompanied by an
authentically Dutch contribution to the revolutionary hymnody which,
chanted, promised:

As GOD shall will it, so shall there be
Liberty and Equality![110]

Riots began to occur in a number of towns in the province, and on September 25 Golowkin had to call on his garrison to pacify a violent fracas that had broken out in the Peperstraat between rival crowds of Orange and Batavian partisans.[111] On September 27 Caillard reported to Paris: "Amsterdam is at the point of explosion."[112]

Back in the city from his conferences, Gogel set about mobilising the Revolutionary Committee. Together with the military officer of the Committee, Cornelis Kraijenhoff, he managed to lay his hands on a stock of 800 or so pistols, rifles and sabres on the pretext that they were destined for the Guinea Coast. Even so, the rebels were not exactly armed to the teeth. Nevertheless on October 6 Gogel felt confident enough to write to Representative Bellegarde: "a very large number of good burghers are sufficiently resolved to make themselves masters of the garrison . . . four-fifths of which are from the Plettenburg Regiment," a regiment which, he added, had already shown its disaffection from its officers and was unwilling to make much effort to save William V's skin. As for Utrecht, it was a hotbed of rebellion, where "two thousand men waited from day to day for the order which would make them masters of the city."[113] What was delaying that order? Gogel also reported more circumspectly that on September 29 an Orangist councillor, van Minninghen, had sent word round to the Bijltje leaders to mobilise their men to come to the aid of the Prince should they be called on. Golowkin had increased night patrols, brought cavalry detachments onto the streets, and even approached the Jewish *parnassim* (wardens) for men and money in return for the promise of Jewish emancipation. It was also known that he had for some time been contemplating reinforcing the garrison with British troops, already very unpopular with the Dutch for their appalling conduct in billet towns. Only the extreme reluctance of the Amsterdam city councillors to admit them had prevented this reinforcement from having already taken place. All these factors acted as a dampener on Gogel's enthusiasm. "Nothing," he wrote to the French camp, "is easier for us than to talk of revolution. But we do not want a revolution if we cannot protect our fellow citizens from pillage and murder [in reprisal]. . . . We rest on your promises given to us a month ago. We await your help and will answer with our heads for the success of the invasion."[114] Some of his apprehension was at last relieved when, on October 10, after a long-drawn-out siege, the French finally entered 's Hertogenbosch. On the same day Gogel reported to the Committee that he had informed the French representatives that the insurrection in Amsterdam would break out without fail on the 15th.

But revolutions are not so easily made to order. In the event it was not the revolutionaries but their opponents who took the initiative. Haarlem had already proscribed its clubs and driven the recently resurrected Free Corps underground. On October 14, William V ordered the Amsterdam Council to take the necessary measures for the preservation of civil order and to see that

"the clubbists do not become masters of Amsterdam."[115] This was the license
Golowkin had been waiting for to bring in as many as 4,000 British troops and
to take drastic action against the conspirators. He was nearly too late. On the
same day a petition bearing 3,600 signatures, collated under the auspices of the
"Doctrina et Amicitia," was presented to the town hall by a delegation, including some members of the Revolutionary Committee and the irrepressible
Visscher—a survivor from the days of "driemanschap" of the 1780's. This
was intended to be the signal to revolt, but it was a dismally weak gesture. The
suggestion of the vacillating van Irhoven van Dam (he at least took much of
the blame for its failure), the petition protested strongly against the proposal
to quarter any British troops in Amsterdam and the more alarming threat
to open the dykes should the defence of the city require it. The manner of its
presentation, with crowds processing in public squares like the Turfmarkt and
the Dam, was a copybook repetition of Patriot tactics. But its timing was inept
and its execution half-hearted. There was little or no attempt to mobilise
armed support, and the laborious procedure of inspecting the petition and
awaiting a response gave the council time to rally its own forces.

Forewarned of the action, Golowkin had placed strong guard around the
town hall to avert any threat of a popular siege and had posted cannon and
cavalry at strategic points around the city. The resources available to him even
without British reinforcement were formidable: some 6,000 regular troops
and over 50 purged companies of militia. The crowds assigned by the Revolutionary Committee to impede the progress of the mounted troops were
in the event too thin to do the job properly and merely got viciously kicked
around for their pains. Before any Patriot arms could appear, the combined
forces of order had the city well under control.

Without any signal from Amsterdam the Patriots in other cities bided
their time in some anxiety. The coup had gone off at half cock and the
Patriots had fatally lost the initiative. On October 17 Visscher and Goldberg
were received in the council chamber to hear the rejection of their petition.
Belatedly and with consternation the Committee realised that the petition
had provided the police with a comprehensive directory of its supporters,
whom it now proceeded to round up. On the same day the States of Holland
issued a proclamation banning all public meetings and closing all unlicensed
presses and reading societies.[116] Anyone charged with violating the proclamation would be treated as a "disturber of the public peace and inciter of sedition." In Dijkstraat the club "Den Burg" was physically occupied by the
police, its doors closed and papers confiscated. Others took the hint. And
although the "Doctrina" initially escaped the ban, on November 12 Wiselius
was forced to announce its closure on a magistrates' order to the assembled
members. In a last bid to rally its demoralised supporters, the Committee published a counter-proclamation on the 18th urging open revolt and warning that
"before long, standing with our French friends and allies . . . we will rise as
one man against the tyranny."[117]

This was putting a bold face on defeat. The French were a long way
from Amsterdam, and to make matters worse Pichegru, weakened by poor

supplies and protracted sieges, decided against a frontal assault on the Bommelerwaard. Instead of crossing the Waal he turned southeast to Nijmegen, thus eliminating whatever hopes remained to the Patriots of engineering an effective military diversion in South Holland. On the 18th six of their leaders, including the luckless Visscher, were apprehended by the authorities and the following days saw the completion of their rout. On the 27th, a further proclamation ordered the surrender of all unlicensed arms and before long the Roeters Island cache was duly betrayed. Badly shaken, the remnant of the Committee wrote to the French representatives at den Bosch:

> Death surrounds us on all sides and every moment threatens to turn us into victims for whom there can be no escape. We are made to undergo daily acts of violence and every day our grievances go suppressed. . . . As yet we still stand together, but in a short while . . .[118]

This was a little histrionic, but their situation was certainly bleak. Gogel returned hastily from den Bosch to find the revolutionary organisation shattered, its leaders in jail or in hiding and morale collapsed. A final meeting was held on October 29 in the Beursteeg to see what if anything could be salvaged from the wreckage. The discussion rambled on for nearly eight hours, but even at this parlous time the meeting was unable to agree on a concerted plan. The more militant among the group wanted to break into the prison on the Rokin, which they claimed was guarded by a mere twenty-five soldiers, and liberate their comrades. Others argued for transferring what was left of their organisation, including the presses, to the French army at den Bosch forthwith. According to the contemporary historian Rogge, there was something of a last rallying of spirits but without firm leadership this renewed determination petered out.

On November 19 the arrested rebels received sentences of 6 years, to be followed by 100 years exile from the Dutch Republic. The very last hope of insurrection in Amsterdam disappeared when the Committee's gunsmith, Theodorus van Essen, harassed by the police, finally delivered up his warehouse. Before the authorities could get to them, Gogel had taken flight to Bremen and Kraijenhoff and van Irhoven van Dam to the French headquarters at den Bosch.

The Fall of the Republic, November 1794–January 1795

The miscarriage of the October "uprising" was the second serious mishap to befall the Dutch Patriots in less than two years. But unlike the campaign of 1793, it represented a setback rather than a catastrophe. Though losing momentum, the progress of the French armies was unaffected by the débacle in Amsterdam. As his ministers keenly appreciated, William V had been granted little more than a reprieve. Nevertheless the extreme disarray of the Revolutionary Committee was sufficient to deter any similarly premature efforts to raise rebellion elsewhere in the Republic. In Utrecht and Haarlem the Patriots again laid low. Their helplessness in the face of intimidation confirmed the sceptics among them, and the cynics among the French, that the Dutch people were incapable of spontaneous liberation and would have to await their redemption at the hands of Generals Pichegru and Jourdan. But for their part, some of the Patriot leaders felt resentful at having been egged on to open revolt by their ally, only to be left without military support at the eleventh hour.

Both judgements contained a measure of the truth. What had really happened was that a self-appointed leadership based on the Amsterdam reading societies over-estimated both the speed of the French advance and their own ability to mobilise popular support in a crisis. As a result, they had rashly declared their hand and laid themselves open to counter-measures without adequate means of defence. But whatever the mitigating circumstances, the undeniable fact of their failure left an aftertaste of sourness and suspicion between the revolutionary partners. In the light of the non-event of October, proclamations issuing from the French camp were bound to ring hollow. They urged the "Bataves" to "show Europe, show the whole world, that the blood of your noble forefathers still runs in your veins. Unite your efforts with the French and smash the sceptre of a tyrannical government."[119]

Scepticism about the independent standing of the Dutch revolutionaries was underlined by the devolution of their authority after October to a "National Revolutionary Committee" at den Bosch. This body had been established after the fall of the city in September and enjoyed the direct protection of the French army. Its political pretensions were originally very modest, for it was almost certainly intended by the French to act in much the same capacity as the "central administrations" of Belgium and the Rhineland, that is to say, in arranging for requisitions and the regulation of the *assignat* exchange. Its membership was oddly assorted. Comparatively well-known figures such as Ysbrand van Hamelsveld from Utrecht and the broker Johannes de Fremery from Rotterdam were accompanied by nonentities such as the painter Carel Webbers from Dordrecht or the token Leiden student Jan ten Brink.

But in November the political aspirations of the Committee were much enhanced by the addition of men like Jacob Blauw, the ex-Pensionary of Leiden and a leading Patriot, and a number of distinguished fugitives from Amsterdam: Nicolas van Staphorst, Cornelis Kraijenhoff and van Irhoven van Dam. In its supplemented form the Committee looked upon itself not merely as a bunch of revolutionary sympathisers gathered at random to serve as a liaison committee for the French but as the kernel of a provisional revolutionary government. Blauw in particular was exercised by not only this problem but by the need to think ahead and plan for a properly representative body; others considered the mobilisation of some kind of military force against the Stadholder, conceivably recruited from deserters.[120]

There were also those within the French camp who were unwilling to wait for a Dutch revolution to materialise through some mysterious process of political alchemy, or at the behest of Pichegru. The irrepressible Daendels was straining at the leash for some dramatic gesture which would demonstrate

beyond doubt the integrity of Dutch revolutionary aspirations. His companion
Gerrit Paape wrote:

Daendels is full of fire and zeal. Nothing annoys him more than any sort of
delay. . . . He insists on following the glorious plan whereby the interests of the
French Republic and the interests of his Fatherland will be ordered in the most
exemplary way. If the execution depended on him alone, then we would be in a
free Fatherland in no time at all. . . .[121]

Daendels was unpersuaded by French objections that the campaign had
presented unforeseen military impediments. His own dashing blitzkrieg had
demonstrated his opinion of sluggish French generalship and his arrogance
infuriated his senior officers. Yet his services were indispensable. It had been
his early appearance at Fort St. Crèvecoeur, guarding the approach to 's Hertogenbosch, which had caught the defenders by surprise and greatly abbreviated
the siege. While he regarded Pichegru's decision to call off the frontal attack
on Bommelerwaard as typically pusillanimous, the alternative march northeast to Nijmegen had some special attractions. Once across the Maas this
route would take the army into Gelderland, Daendels' native province and
the scene of his glorious disaster in 1786. He had good reason to suppose that
if any citizens would heed a summons to revolt it might very well be the
burghers of Hattem, Elburg and Arnhem, who had suffered so much from the
troops of William V.

With the prospect before him of settling old scores Daendels acted, not
for the last time in his career, impetuously. On October 21, as the Army of
the North began its attack on Nijmegen, he issued, without any reference to
the French representatives, an astonishing proclamation. In the first place it
was a summons to revolt against the Prince of Orange and to repudiate all his
officers. That much was quite unexceptionable. But it was accompanied by
an appeal to enlist a force of Dutch volunteers—the project which had been
specifically vetoed at den Bosch by the French. Daendels offered these
volunteers a bounty of 35 stuivers a week (25 more than the Prince had felt
able to offer in August); a pound of bread and a pound of meat each week.
Arms were eventually to be issued but prospective soldiers were urged, for
the time being, to use hunting guns and if nothing else were to hand, pitchforks and axes. They were to form companies of 125 men (as in the Free
Corps) and to elect their officers, who were to be "not the richest or the most
elegantly dressed men nor those who speak finely but those who have within
them the most fire." Nor need they fear that once in arms "you will remain
soldiers for many years. No-one will be needed in arms a moment longer
than is necessary to rid this Land forever of Orange and his gilded slaves."

The peroration took the form of an exhortation to revive the spirit of
1787, and in so doing assumed almost the very phraseology of the Patriots
of the eighties:

O my friends! How happy we shall be once our dear Land is scourged of the
brutish aristocracy. . . . There will be no more "drostdiensten" [seigneurial dues];

every man will be free to hunt and to fish as he pleases; taxes and dues will be reduced and no longer fall so heavily on the poor. Our country will be ruled by brave Burghers and Farmers through their public voice.

Zutphen and Arnhem Burghers, you who were first to stand up to the aristocrats and who, on every occasion, have shown your love for your due rights, show now your real feelings and that Gelders blood still courses through your veins. Do not wait for the French to come but be jealous of your freedom. Every righteous Netherlander must, like me, burn to take up arms in his hands to show that we are truly worthy of our French brothers and not as despicable as William of Orange supposes.

Greetings and Fraternity! Long live our inalienable rights.[122]

This extraordinary outburst caught the French authorities at 's Herto-genbosch completely off their guard. They had been themselves continuously urging some kind of uprising in support of the invasion so Daendels had some reason to suppose that they would have welcomed an initiative couched, more-over, in an idiom immediately recognisable to his countrymen. But their re-action was in fact plainly undelighted. They were not averse to insurrectionary propaganda provided that it originated with their own authority. But Daendels' exercise in private revolutionary enterprise, added to his persistent disregard for military discipline, was taken as prima facie evidence of dangerous opportunism. At best it was foolish; at worst treasonable. As good Thermi-dorians the representatives on mission, Bellegarde and Lacombe St. Michel, were hypersensitive to the damage done by inflammatory rhetoric and were convinced that it would be more likely to alienate, than recruit, support for their cause. They were, after all, less interested in settling old Dutch political scores than in easing the progress of the campaign. And so they infinitely preferred a more conciliatory approach if only, as the Committee of Public Safety had pointed out, because "the interest of the [French] Republic is to reassure the Dutch so that they do not emigrate along with their riches. . . . It is necessary to safeguard the rights of property so that Holland will furnish us with our provisions."[123]

Daendels' Dantonesque call to arms, and the spectre of a resurrected Patriot army, threatened to undo this effort to win over the Dutch notability almost before it had begun and to re-awaken all the Jacobinical bogeys which their successors were so anxious to dispel. A drastic dissociation was called for. The culprit was arrested and put in close custody for a number of weeks. The Committee of Public Safety took a very dim view of what looked suspiciously like another episode in the continuing history of Dutch adventurism. But after Representative Lacombe had argued in mitigation of his offence that it was an excess of zeal rather than calculated sabotage which had led Daendels astray, the matter was left there.[124] Ten days after his manifesto had appeared, however, the representatives issued their own reassurance that on no account would any assault be made on Dutch

. . . usages, customs or opinions. For just as it will tolerate no interference by any other people in its own government so the French people will remain faithful to its constitution and refrain from interfering with the government of other peoples . . . property will be respected; the lives of your women and children will be under the safeguard of French honour and the protective laws of humanity.[125]

The French representatives were almost certainly correct in assuming that the best way of winning acceptability as liberators rather than invaders was to reassure the Dutch that their most jealously guarded institutions—religion and money—would not be tampered with. But their Patriot allies, in the van of revolutionary enthusiasm, were bound to chafe at what they saw to be impediments rather than encouragements to their own cause. Thus even before the campaign which was to end in the establishment of the Batavian Republic was properly under way the interests and sympathies of the allies had begun to diverge seriously. Suspicions lingered that if the campaign deteriorated further, the French might actually be tempted to sell them out for the sake of a negotiated peace, which, by ensuring the freedom of the Scheldt and detaching the Dutch Republic from the First Coalition, would preserve all the French strategic interests intact. These fears were by no means baseless. At 's Hertogenbosch an Orangist official, Caspar van Breugel, had made himself available as an intermediary between the French and Grand Pensionary van de Spiegel. Daendels had very unwisely taken van Breugel into his confidence, and it seems likely that the latter's encouragement of his proclamation was meant to discredit the revolutionary party at den Bosch before the representatives and incline them towards truce and negotiation. In the same disingenuous spirit, van Breugel dutifully forwarded Daendels' own "conditions" for a peace to van de Spiegel. These gave more amusement than edification since their terms included the expulsion of the Prince, the elimination of all regencies and noble estates, and the introduction of universally elected administrations —in sum, the cardinal principle of the democratic Patriots.[126]

Of the two representatives, Lacombe St. Michel was the more receptive to van Breugel's overtures. He was acutely conscious that the war had become badly bogged down between the Maas and the Waal, whose waters were already rising with the first winter floods. Some of the fortresses like Grave had proved unexpectedly determined in their resistance, and it was by no means clear that there would be sufficient supplies of fodder and matériel to suffice for a drawn-out winter campaign. Apprehensive of repeating the experience of 1793, and encouraged by van Breugel to believe that in return for peace the Stadholder was prepared to neutralise the Republic and deny its ports to the British navy, Lacombe began to warm to the idea of some exploratory negotiations. Certainly he had no qualms at all about jettisoning such impotent allies as the Patriots should French national interest demand it.

If there were sound reasons why the French should have been contemplating ditching their protégés for a peace, there were even more pressing factors directing the Dutch government to take advantage of this proffered opportunity. The military reverses in Brabant culminating in the fall of 's Hertogenbosch had demoralised an already nervous States-General. The deplorable conduct of retreating British troops and the virtual evaporation of the Austrian army, as well as the open feud between the Duke of York and the Crown Prince of Orange, were all matters of notoriety.[127] The finances of the Republic were in a ruinous condition, and there was a limit to the number of forced loans even van de Spiegel could extort from the grudging Hollanders. The failure of the October agitation had given the magistrates of Amsterdam a breathing space. But it had also rattled them badly and had persuaded the more politically malleable among them that an accommodation with the French on the basis of reciprocal interest was infinitely to be preferred to the revolutionary justice of their domestic adversaries. In discussing the possibility of such negotiations, the regents of Holland thus took an appropriately defeatist view. But it was the assembly of the States of Friesland, always sensitive to the drift of the political wind, which put the matter on an official standing, by drafting a resolution urging preliminary negotiations.[128] The diplomatic committee of the States-General pretended to be outraged at the very suggestion. All the same, it decided to send a mission to St. James to sound out the views of their ally. Officially, this mission was appointed merely to press on the British the urgency of increased financial and military assistance. Unofficially, it was plain that the Dutch government was asking leave of its warder to see what the French had to offer.

Not surprisingly Pitt's ministry offered cold comfort. It too was dismayed by the military havoc but put much of this down to the incompetent generalship and ineffective defensive preparations they had come to expect of the Dutch. Some British ministers cherished the hope that timely remedial measures might yet stave off total collapse; to this end, they urged the appointment of the Duke of Brunswick to command all the Coalition armies in the Republic. But others, while hotly repudiating any thought of settling with men whose hands were still wet with the blood of their King, were resigning themselves to the departure of the Dutch from the alliance. Grenville, not the least pugnacious among the British Cabinet, had already steeled George III to this eventuality. And while King George regretted "any country falling off from the cause of withstanding the principles and conduct of those who tyrannize France," he recognised that "the little vigour shown by the Dutch from the beginning of the contest makes their secession of but little real loss."[129] Even such a doughty champion of the Orange cause as James Harris informed the Prussian King that "the Austrian army is completely disorganised; that the subsidiary treaty with England (of 1787) is broken; and that Holland *would do well to make a separate peace on any terms*."[130] Better, perhaps, a neutral United Provinces than an enemy Batavian Republic! On November 18 Grenville gave Greffier Fagel, the envoy of the States-General, virtual leave to consider French terms, should the military situation deteriorate any further.

So despite van de Spiegel's protests to van Breugel that British objections stood in the way of initiating negotiations, the truth of the matter was that the gravest misgivings lay on the Dutch side of the North Sea. Suspecting, with some justification, that the overtures were merely a ruse to allow time for reinforcement for an attack in strength over the Waal, William V warned that "things look too well not to suspect that an adder lies in the grass."[131] His

Grand Pensionary was similarly sceptical. Like William Pitt, he felt in his marrow that it was not only morally reprehensible but politically injudicious to deal with a revolutionary regime, a creature of the fickle mob for whom today's bond could become tomorrow's treason. Only when a "regular" government was established in France could "a safe and durable" peace (to use Pitt's phrase) be contemplated.[132] When he met van Breugel at The Hague at the beginning of November, van de Spiegel pointed out to him that since the British government had made it clear that under no circumstances short of victory would they contemplate a general pacification, it would be dishonourable to oblige them to shoulder the brunt of the enemy's attack unaided.

But a sudden subsidence on the military front may have helped van de Spiegel to brush aside these scruples. On November 4 the French took Maastricht for the second time in two years, and on the night of November 7–8 they entered Nijmegen, the stronghold of Stadholderian power. The evacuation of Nijmegen by the British had been accompanied by a carnival of pillage, violence and rapine on a scale and with a wanton abandon which more than any Patriot propaganda persuaded the Dutch to defend themselves against their defenders.[133] On the 11th, van de Spiegel drafted preliminary conditions for a peace settlement. Not that he gave much away, for the conditions amounted to a return to the *status quo ante bellum*. In return for a somewhat belated recognition of the sovereignty of the French Republic and a reciprocal pledge of non-intervention in each other's domestic affairs, France was to return *all* territories taken from the United Provinces (including the Flemish bank of the Scheldt). The faint possibility that such terms might be acceptable to the French was based on two unfounded assumptions, both communicated through the doubtful mediation of van Breugel. The first was that the States-General believed it could get away with neutral status, whereas opinion in the National Convention was strongly in favour of the Dutch playing an instrumental role in the downfall of the British. Tallien, for example, spoke of the "Spanish and Dutch ships with whose help we would hasten to the banks of the Thames and destroy the new Carthage."[134] Secondly, van Breugel had misled the diplomatic committee of the States-General into believing that the French representatives at den Bosch had already been authorised to conclude a defensive truce pending the outcome of the negotiations. And it was on the basis of these twin misunderstandings that two emissaries, Gerard Brantsen and Ocker Repelaer, were commissioned to conduct the Republic's case in Paris. The news that negotiations were under way was greeted with immense relief in Holland. The Bourse, whose stock had spiralled downwards with the accumulating military disasters, now picked up again, and the *Gazette de Leyde* looked forward to a period of therapeutic neutrality.[135]

The reaction of the French government to the Dutch overtures was calculatedly circumspect. Van de Spiegel and the Prince had been absolutely correct in suspecting that any offer of negotiation was based less on diplomatic generosity than a short-term reading of the military situation. A complete victory and dictated peace remained, as always, the optimal objective. But by the beginning of December such an outcome seemed less and less likely. Daendels' infuriated urging of a major assault on the Waal and a successful interview with Merlin de Douai on the Committee of Public Safety had resulted in firm orders to Pichegru to proceed with such an attack. But the initial advance against the defences heavily entrenched on the right bank was a miserable flop. Pichegru's divisions had faltered in the face of heavy artillery fire and Daendels' headlong rush at Fort St. Andries had been repelled with serious casualties. Bellegarde's growing gloom at the "extreme penury" of supplies and forage as the deep winter set in was turning to desperation.[136] He was inclined to favour at least a temporary truce if only to reorganise supplies. For, as he explained to the Committee in Paris, some of the most serious logistical problems could be relieved by a more efficient exploitation of the Maas (now French-controlled) in order to transport supplies down river from the huge depots at Maastricht.

To the Dutch Patriots at 's Hertogenbosch the rumoured negotiations looked less like a tactical manoeuvre designed to accelerate the liberation of their country than another French volte-face intended to postpone it indefinitely. Daendels was convinced that Pichegru and Lacombe St. Michel were deliberately sabotaging the campaign in order to give the Stadholder time to come to terms. He complained bitterly to the administration in Brussels that while "the General amuses himself with marches and counter-marches," the cause of liberty went begging.[137] The news of Brantsen and Repelaer's commission seemed to confirm his worst suspicions. Not only would any agreement cooked up between van de Spiegel and the French be in flagrant violation of solemn promises made to the Patriots at the beginning of the campaign and repeated ad nauseam; it would make a mockery of the 's Hertogenbosch Committee's aspiration to represent a provisional revolutionary administration. Had they come almost to the very doors of Holland only to have them slammed in their face by prior arrangement between their enemies and their allies? Gerrit Paape, the Patriot journalist and ex-councillor of Delft, now editor of the new *'s Hertogenbosche Vaderlandsche Courant*, exclaimed that if they were to be told now that they could not be delivered from "the Orange yoke" either by their own efforts or by French arms, they were to reply that they were at last aware that no more sacrifices could be made in the Netherlands on the idle assumption that they would be supported by French help.[138]

So excruciating was the possibility of another desertion that Paape's colleagues on the Committee refused to believe that, whatever the conduct of their generals and representatives, the citizens of the National Convention which in 1792 had promised to "assist all peoples wishing to recover their liberty" would now forswear those vows so casually. To correct any misapprehensions in Paris about the will of the Dutch people, and to challenge the right of Brantsen and Repelaer to speak for that people, the Committee in its turn appointed Blauw and van Irhoven van Dam as its ambassadors. Though they set out optimistically, a decidedly chilly reception from Carnot made it clear that the representatives' temporising had been only too accurate a reflection of their superiors' attitude. Their only chance of redeeming their cause seemed to lie in some dramatic turn of fortune on the war front itself.

This duly happened at the very end of the year. The Patriots had one good friend in December 1794: the weather. For once a change in winter temperature came to the aid of invasion rather than repulsion. In the third week of December the Netherlands was gripped by seventeen degrees of frost, the famous "gelée funeste," as William V was to describe it, which turned the hitherto daunting expanse of the Waal into a great glacial highway over which the French troops could march on the Dutch defences. On the 27th a massed attack was launched simultaneously on Bommel, Boxhoven, Waard, and other key points along the river and together succeeded in penetrating the defensive line. One week later, the major city of Breda and the fortress of Grave, now well behind the French lines, capitulated. Grave had held out for ten weeks. Over 3,000 shells had fallen on the town, reducing most of its houses to rubble. But the tenacity of its resistance was emulated by very few of the Dutch forts. The beginning of the end of the campaign was in sight. The representatives acted appropriately. On the 23rd, Bellegarde informed the States-General that contrary to its assumption, he had never received any authorisation to initiate a truce. Three days later, a communication from the Commitee of Public Safety expressed its astonishment that the Dutch government should have been labouring under the misapprehension that a cease-fire of any kind was in the offing.[139]

The crossing of the Waal proved to be the turning point of the war. Dutch commanders confessed to William V that if that defensive line could not be held there was even less likelihood of standing fast on the Lek. Yet even at this late stage, with Daendels describing the country between Paris and Amsterdam as a "single plain of ice," Pichegru hesitated to press home his advantage. Two routes of advance suggested themselves. The easier lay northeast on the upper Lek, attacking Arnhem and sweeping round to Utrecht from the rear. The alternative, moving due west towards Gorinchem and the forts of the old Patriot "cordon," was more daunting but if successful would yield access not only to the island of Dordrecht but the hinterland of South Holland. Torn between the tempting prospect of liberating his home town of Hattem and participating in the assault on Holland, Daendels urged that whichever route be decided, he be given permission "to begin the revolution in person" as soon as the army crossed the lower Waal.[140]

Pichegru compromised by ordering a forked movement in both directions but invested the major thrust of the advance through Gelderland. At the same time he produced an order posting his truculent Dutch officer to the Army of the Pyrenees! So assured was Daendels that the services of a well-regarded Dutch soldier could not be so lightly dispensed with that he brushed off the order as though it were fictitious. He may even have been right since his commander was forced to keep him on the army staff, though putting him out of harm's way by assigning him to the Holland rather than the Gelderland action. The progress made by his troops was remarkable since on January 6 the first French companies appeared before Werkendam, an outlying village en route to Dordrecht and Gorinchem.

Despite the staccato rhythm of the French advance, the troops of the First Coalition were in terrible disarray. After the crossing of the Waal they had practically ceased to operate as a united army. The Austrians had all but evacuated the Republic, and deprived of regular pay and supplies the British had been reduced to gangs of pillaging bandits. At a depressing conference of commanders at Utrecht on January 7, 1795, Wallmöden informed the Crown Prince that he could not hope to hold any sector of the Waal and added that a retreat behind the Lek would be little more than a token gesture.[141] The Stadholder had asked that, if the worst came to the worst, 8,000 men might be spared to fall back for the defence of Amsterdam and Holland. More concerned to keep the avenues of retreat to Germany open than with futile last stands, the Prussians denied him even this small comfort. The hard truth was that, like his opponents eight years earlier, the army of the Prince of Orange was melting away. Soldiers at Gorinchem threw their rifles away and when asked why they refused to fight declared that they had not eaten for several days. When their bellies were fuller, they said, their hearts would be braver.[142]

A belated attempt by the States of Holland to take a leaf from their enemies' book and call on its burghers for a Dutch levée en masse "for the Fatherland" produced around fifty volunteers. Much of the country was happy to see the backs of Prussians and British for, as the Prussian ambassador later admitted, their brutality had been such that scarcely a single town in Holland would have opened its gates freely to let them enter. Even the traditional last resort of the Fatherland was to be withheld from its last Stadholder, for the ice on the river estuaries was frozen so solid that breaking the dykes was out of the question.

Faced with this host of troubles the States-General began to lose its nerve. On January 6 it voted that if the Lek should be taken, no further resistance should be offered in the province of Holland and steps taken to sue for peace. In other words, it had virtually resigned itself to military defeat. The immediate task was to ward off domestic revolution and (with an eye to the fate of the annexed southern Netherlands) an even worse eventuality! Pieter van Lelyveld, one of the members of the diplomatic committee of the States-General, wrote to a colleague that "whatever the outcome of the negotiations [in Paris] it cannot be *good* for us. But we have before us a major interest—that of our very existence (as a nation)."[143] There then ensued an undignified rush to dissociate themselves from the sins of their allies and so hang on to their political skins. Dyed-in-the-wool Orangists like Volkier Bentinck insisted to Representative Portiez that all Dutchmen heartily loathed the British, who had "ruined our manufactures, devastated our trade and dragged us into a ruinous war contrary to our own interests." Their soldiers, he added,

steal and plunder everywhere. Even I, virtually a relative of the Stadholder, have not been spared. My country house has been ransacked; horses, carriages, everything looted. Such is the hatred which the Stadholder bears towards the English that he is even ready to don the tricolour cockade and unite with you to exterminate this race for whom nothing is sacred.[144]

But if William V had been converted to the tricolour he had concealed the fact remarkably well. In fact the collapse of his army had driven him once more into his old paranoid fantasies of the 1780's. By 1795, the fate of Louis XVI had emphasised in the most dramatic manner what his fate might be should he fall into the hands of the French. Van de Spiegel, who remained touchingly faithful to the end and who now stood as a completely isolated and impotent figure among crowds of defeatists, attempted to console the Prince and revive his drooping spirits. "I asked him," he recalled, "where was the courage he had shown during all our troubles in 1786 and 1787?"[145]

At least William V was not kept waiting long for the dénouement. On January 10 Pichegru's main divisions attacked along the length of the Lek from Arnhem to Rhenen, encircling most of the intermediary garrisons between the two big rivers. At the same time the western defences of the "cordon" were turned, losing Gorinchem and Schoonhoven, beleaguering Heusden (under Daendels' orders), and exposing the whole of South Holland to a virtually unstoppable French advance. In accordance with the planned retreat, Wallmöden withdrew nearly all Prussian troops behind the Yssel, leaving the entire province of Utrecht defenceless. On the 13th, the States of Utrecht voted to send representatives to the French army to treat for terms, and on the 14th and 15th the last British regiment evacuated city and province, taking with them virtually anything that could be moved. On the 16th, General Souham signed the capitulation of the city on the basis of security of person and property, freedom of religion and the *preservation of existing political institutions* pending a general pacification.

The following day, exactly seven years and four months after Brunswick and the Prussians had marched into the deserted city, the French followed in their footsteps. Almost as if the intervening time had stood still, the reading societies and old Free Corps colours paraded on the Neude and listened to speeches applauding the "restoration of liberty in its traditional birthplace." Tricolour streamers festooned the university and cockades were distributed among the crowd. A liberty tree was set up before the town hall and—perhaps in homage to the fall of the Bastille—the municipal House of Correction was sprung open and the baffled but delighted inmates treated to a gin-soaked carousal.

None of the festivities, however, could disguise the sobering fact that it had been the legally constituted body of the States of Utrecht which had signed the capitulation, not a revolutionary assembly or even an insurrectionary committee. The sudden acceleration of the French push forward had put the Batavian Revolutionary Committee on the spot. Since the uprising manqué at Amsterdam they had had no organisation in that city to speak of. But now that liberation finally seemed close it was essential, if they were to retain any pretensions to an independent republican sovereignty, that there should be some semblance of a revolution in Amsterdam in advance of the French troops' arrival.

There had in fact been some timid stirrings among the Patriots following the crossing of the Waal. In cities other than Amsterdam where they had a strong following—Haarlem and Leiden, in particular—they continued to meet to discuss their strategy. And even in Amsterdam the surviving literary and philosophical society, "Felix Meritis," acted as a gathering place for many of the subdued conspirators.[146] On January 2 a group consisting in the main of ex-members of "Doctrina et Amicitia" formed themselves into a second Amsterdam Revolutionary Committee. On the 9th, a meeting of representatives from the Holland clubs was convened at Rotterdam but revealed caution rather than impatience on the part of many delegates.[147] The French were not yet over the Lek and no-one was sure if or when they would be. The Amsterdammers confessed that as yet their new stockpile of arms was very modest, consisting principally of a few hundred pikes, sabres and axes, hardly a match for the 6,000 troops whom the Amsterdam magistrates, more worried by revolution than defeat, ordered to stay put in the city.

The news of the fall of Utrecht on January 17, however, galvanised the Amsterdam Committee into action. Posters and handbills appeared magically overnight in the city and the news was communicated orally around the *wijken* that the following day would see a change of power in the Council. On the 18th, a Sunday, the Committee met at the tavern which had become their secret assembly rooms since the October arrests—the Wapen van Embden (Emden Arms) on the Nieuwendijk. Other meetings to rally support were held at the Groot Keizershof and at the Cherry Tree Tavern in the Kalverstraat, all near the town hall on the Dam. When a substantial number (running into hundreds) of people had assembled, four members were elected, including Gogel, to act as a deputation to the burgemeesters. Throughout the morning there was no attempt to use military force against the rebels nor any show of violence from the crowds. The deputation made its way to the house of President-Burgemeester Straalman to ask for arms "in order to maintain public order." In so doing they were merely following the almost ritual procedure of *coups d'état* whereby the party which has instigated civil disorder then claims the right to arm itself in order to contain it and prevent further riot. But Straalman and his colleagues were not prepared to abdicate their authority without a contest. They still had the garrison and had ordered Golowkin to clear the streets. The Orange militia were quite prepared to carry out this instruction, only Golowkin himself could see that blood would have to be shed if the troops were to make any impression on the crowds. As in so many potentially revolutionary situations, the outcome depended on the decision of one man; Golowkin, with the French a mere 40 miles away, was not anxious to assume the reputation of a butcher.

His mind may have well been made up by the prompt appearance of Dr. Kraijenhoff, the erstwhile military officer of the October Committee and present member of its successor at 's Hertogenbosch, now dressed in the uniform of a French infantry officer. At four o'clock in the afternoon he appeared at the city gates and announced his intention of removing the "illegal" regency forthwith. Much to everyone's amazement and to the burgemeesters' dismay, Golowkin made no effort to eject him and in effect offered him the freedom of the city. However opportunist his conduct, it remains curious that the commandant should have wished to deal with the Patriots rather than the officers of the French army who had shown themselves to be so obliging to the present council in Utrecht. And his behaviour is all the more mysterious since Kraijenhoff came armed with nothing but a scrap of paper bearing van Hamelsveld's signature for the 's Hertogenbosch Committee authorising him to take steps for the independence of the city. Kraijenhoff interpreted this instruction to mean the complete and immediate removal of the regency and it was this demand that he repeated to Straalman, when, supported by an enormous and rowdy crowd, he returned to the burgemeester's house that evening. To judge from the saturnalian scale of the bills (for broken crockery as well as drink) submitted by the proprietress of the Emden Arms to the Committee, the crowds had already been lavishly entertained by the rebels and were in no mood to be cowed by Straalman's insistence on legal proceedings.[148] The scenes outside his house finally became so ugly that he and his colleagues' dependence on Kraijenhoff for their personal safety got the better of their reluctance to part with office. At midnight the president-burgemeester handed over command of the garrison to Kraijenhoff and in effect surrendered power in the greatest city of the Republic to a Committee which, a week before, had barely existed.

At ten o'clock the following morning, January 19, in thick snow, the triumphant Committee made its way by carriage to the Dam. The square was crowded again with people, this time intent on celebration. Carillons rang through the city from the Westerkerk; a liberty tree had been stuck unceremoniously in front of the town hall and tricolour cockades decorated every bonnet and hat. In the chamber of the burgemeester, and then again to the assembled crowd, a proclamation was read declaring the incumbent councillors to have forfeited their offices. But it went much further by declaring those offices themselves abolished. Presently there would be district assemblies of burghers to "decide on the new form of government and a different order of things." For the time being a body of twenty-two men, nominated by the Committee, would exercise the authority of "Provisional Representatives of the People of Amsterdam" and be responsible for the day-to-day administration of the city. Unable to sustain the low emotional key which had characterised the greater part of the proclamation, it lapsed into the florid rhetoric for which Dutch civic officials are justly famed and reviled. "At last," they announced, "that long-wished-for day has dawned on the Batavian horizon when the natural, just, but too long alienated rights of the Netherlands people are restored to them . . ."[149] And in case their audience had not got the message they were assured that "You are all Free! You are all Equal!" But the "Provisional Representatives" were not thirsty for regent blood. They were dominated by Patriot notables like van Staphorst, van Irhoven van Dam and the eminently moderate Schimmelpenninck, their chairman, who after reading the proclamation added his own appeal for calm, order and restraint from any kind of vendetta.

However sober-sided the Amsterdam representatives and however contrived the manner of their inauguration, theirs was the first revolutionary body in a position to make its own peace with their liberators, the French. Having conveniently held up their progress from Utrecht until the political rigmarole had been completed in Amsterdam, the first chasseurs entered the city later on the 19th to great acclaim. Elsewhere in Holland incumbent regents and burgemeesters hastened to pre-empt any revolutionary assumption of power by making their own hurried settlements with the French generals and representatives. At Gouda the magistrates refused to hand over the arms of the city *schutterij* to burgher committees on the grounds that they were still negotiating with the French. On the 17th the States-General itself had bowed to the inevitable by despatching two delegates to treat with the French on terms comparable to those granted to Utrecht the previous day. Their resolution optimistically provided for the maintenance of *all* existing institutions, but none except perhaps van de Spiegel supposed for a moment that the Stadholderate had any chance of surviving the defeat. He continued to beg William V to remain in the Republic to avert revolutionary chaos, and warned that his departure "would be the signal for general confusion the consequences of which it would be hard to foresee."[150]

Somewhat to the Grand Pensionary's surprise, the Prince replied on the evening of the 17th that he had indeed decided to remain in the Republic, since "that is my duty." Only the Princess and their family would be put on board a boat at Scheveningen and carried to safety, either to Zeeland or north to the Texel and thence to England. At eight the following morning Wilhelmina and her children duly departed, praying that the Prince would follow in due course, "for he has no more resources here." The Princess knew her unhappy husband well enough. Overnight his never formidable resolution completely distintegrated. He dictated a message to the States-General declearing that, not wishing to be an obstacle to a peace, he would if required remove himself from the Republic. Towards evening came news from Utrecht that the French had refused the first terms presented by the States-General and would consider no more until the Stadholder had surrendered or forfeited his office.

His fate sealed, William resigned himself to exile. It is said that a fisherman carried him over the beach from where his ancestor kinsman Charles Stuart had sailed to regain his crown. At around midnight on January 18, as Kraijenhoff assumed control of the city of Amsterdam in the name of the Batavian commonwealth, the last Stadholder left the United Provinces for good, bound for Harwich and historical obloquy.

His departure did not quite liquidate the Orange cause. Men whom James Harris and van de Spiegel had placed in office in 1787 or who had resisted the blandishments of the Patriots remained in many towns and provinces. Despite the military occupation there was as yet, as the British ambassador noted, "no appearance of tumult or ill will among the people."[151] Grenville nursed fancies of gathering the remnant of Dutch troops along with the plebeian elements loyal to the Prince into a redoubt on the Zeeland islands. There they would "make a stand with as much assistance as could gradually be sent from hence." Not surprisingly his colleagues' scepticism as to whether such a plan was remotely feasible was shared by Dutch officers themselves. In any event before Grenville's agent, Charles Bentinck, could reach the province the last remaining strongholds there, Bergen op Zoom and Willemstad, capitulated on order from the States-General. The conquest was completed. It remained to be seen whether the revolution would now begin.

The Price of Liberation, January–May 1795

"Never," wrote the Austrian commander Clerfait, with understandable melancholy, "has a revolution been so rapid. Six days have been sufficient to give the enemy possession of all the [Dutch] provinces."[152] It took little more than another six for almost every major town in Holland to follow Amsterdam's example by revolutionising its councils and regencies. Yet this upheaval was not so much a novelty as a resumption of the status quo ante Brunswick in 1787. It was almost as if the intervening passage of time had been a bad dream from which the Patriots had awoken to find themselves once more in full command of the powers and faculties they had assumed seven years before. The same clubs, the same taverns, the same parade grounds, the same pulpits and printing presses took up where they had left off. Men who had traipsed wretchedly into exile that gloomy October now resumed their epic stanzas to the Goddess of Liberty and the liberated Fatherland or their hellfire sermons against the Orange Anti-Christ and his minions. In Friesland a Revolutionary Committee consisting principally of those habituees of the St. Omer cabarets whose disreputable conduct had rattled even the stoical Dumont-Pigalle now struck more becomingly heroic attitudes. They demanded from the Leeuwarden States the immediate repeal of the heinous decree of August 1787 by which petitioning, address and assembly had been proscribed, and the restoration of the old burgher societies and militia. On February 7, with the helpful prompting of General Daendels, the States duly obliged by rescinding not only the objectionable decrees but all sentences passed on political offenders since 1787, and authorised the distribution of arms to the reconstituted burgher companies.

Throughout the towns of Holland, Utrecht and Overijssel a similar political scenario was enacted. Self-convened revolutionary committees, led by the Patriot notability of 1787 or associates of the den Bosch Committee, proceeded to publish a series of demands and present them to the incumbent regency for immediate compliance. They included, inevitably, the surrender of the council's authority to a new provisional administration; the disarmament of the Orange *schutterij* and its replacement by the restored Free Corps companies. With the assistance of clamorous public meetings, belligerent manifestoes and occasionally the discreet appearance of detachments of French cavalry, these demands were pressed on the regents. The ease with which power was transferred naturally depended on the circumstances of local sympathies. But not even ex-Greffier Fagel, reporting to Grenville on these events from his Hamburg retreat, was able to deny the evident popularity of the changes in many of the principal towns of the Republic.[153] In Schiedam crowds, shouting for arms, invaded the council chamber and remained there *à la sans-culotte* until their demands were met. Led by the democrat de Loncq, they declared all those who had held any post whatsoever under the Stadholder to be perpetually barred from public office. A council of twenty-two was summarily appointed by popular acclaim and invested the next day to the strains of the town organ.[154]

In Haarlem elections for the six city districts were rapidly organised, producing a body of electors who provided a municipality almost identical with that deposed in 1787. Other towns were more recalcitrant. In Gouda it took the appearance of troops to persuade the regency to retire gracefully. The Hague, stronghold of Orange strength in the province, was predictably the last of all to bow to the new order. Even the occupation by General Moreau's regiment and its commander's repeated public warnings against Patriot-Orangist collaboration failed to deter the regents from seeking their own accommodation with the representatives of the Convention. They succeeded in remaining in office until February 2, and were not actually replaced by a new council until as late as the 26th of that month.

But The Hague was, as in many other respects, exceptional in Holland for its Orangist affiliations. Events at Leiden offer a better guide to the character of the relatively painless and absolutely bloodless takeover. On the same day that the French entered Utrecht, January 17, the last companies of Hessians evacuated Leiden, departing in a valedictory festival of plunder and riot. At ten o'clock (seemingly the appointed hour for all revolutionary committees in the Netherlands to begin their business) a group of Patriot burghers, many of them reading society members, met at their usual haunt, the Boar's Head Inn. Under the chairmanship of Hahn, the man who had presided over the clandestine meeting in the Harlemmerhout the previous July, they proceeded to constitute a directing committee and draft the usual demands. At ten that evening, accompanied by a suitably substantial and rowdy gathering, they persuaded the regency to hear their demands in a public session of council and to re-arm what was in effect the old Leiden Free Corps. By eleven o'clock nearly a thousand men, many sporting the old black Patriot ribbons along with the new tricolour cockade, paraded near the town hall.

The following day at the Mare Kerk, Pastor Romswinkel sermonised his congregation to conduct itself henceforth as a free people and condemned the regents as no longer fit to govern their affairs. An election of "provisional representatives of the people of Leiden" then took place at the church. More enforced meetings of the council, attended by a gratifyingly shrinking number of regents, followed during the course of the day and more parades of the militia, nominally entrusted with keeping the peace but in fact doing just the opposite. When the new council was finally sworn in that evening it contrived to represent all the major components of the Patriot coalition: known democrats like Hahn; two Roman Catholics and the university rector van Santen; an evangelical predikant Boudwijn van Rees; and the young patrician Frederick van Leyden.[155]

As in Amsterdam, Haarlem, and Rotterdam, the new administration divided itself into sections to deal with finance, police and "General Welfare." Some of these committees showed an impressive burst of energy that their French counterparts would have certainly approved. The Leiden Council issued decrees like a municipal Committee of Public Safety forbidding any exit from the city without special license, ordering all "émigrés" to return within fourteen days on pain of confiscation of their property, and publishing an ad hoc levy on all incomes above a certain level to pay for the disbursement of special relief to the multitudes of Leiden poor. On January 26 some 7,000 guilders were distributed to the poor *without distinction of religious denomination*—a truly revolutionary act in the Dutch Republic. Even the Jews got their share. To round off the coup an impromptu "Festival of Liberty" was celebrated, in which a tree was stuck in front of the town hall to the accompaniment of music and singing; there were dull speeches from the Batavian worthies, processions of small children, and a profusion of tricolour bunting draping houses, trees and roof gables.

Amsterdam enjoyed a celebration in a style proper to that city's dignity. On March 24 a 24-foot column representing the mandatory tree was erected on the Dam and in front of it an altar draped with a cloth embroidered "One Heart for the Fatherland." From thence a procession led by 150 Dutch virgins, clad in white and bearing branches and the proclamation of the new "Representatives of the People of Amsterdam," wound its way down Kalverstraat to the Muntplein. Following them were companies of Patriot *schutters* holding aloft their traditional standards and dressed in their Free Corps uniforms; city councillors, among whom was Burgemeester Carel Visscher, whose career during the past decade seemed to have been punctuated by repeated entrances and exits from jail; more children carrying gigantic flags of the city and the Republic; and finally a mixed company of members of the reading societies and diplomats of friendly powers, Denmark, Sweden and the United States. On arriving back at the Dam a salute of twenty cannon was fired and a fountain turned on, dousing a good section of the spectators and delighting the "Patriotic Children of the Republic."[156]

Despite these revels attending the baptism of the Batavian Republic, the somewhat contrived nature of the revolution and its manifest dependence on French protection left some important questions unanswered. Beneath the liberty tree on the Dam was a plaque inscribed "Through French Help" as if to remind the tribunes of Batavian liberty of the limitations of their new independence. None was so naïve as to suppose that their freedom had been served up gratis. What was as yet unknown was the size of the bill and the means by which it was to be settled. The gravest anxiety was whether the French would—protestations to the contrary notwithstanding—impose a conqueror's peace complete with requisitions, *assignats* and perhaps territorial annexations. By March such an eventuality could still not be ruled out. Liberty trees planted in Brussels and Aachen had not protected their inhabitants from coming to enjoy the rights and duties of French citizenship. Even if the Dutch were to be spared that unhappy fate, it remained unclear what the attitude of their emancipators would be towards their sovereign self-determination.

Not surprisingly, there were differences within the Batavian camp also on this topic. Both "radicals" and "moderates" were however at one in their concern that the French should not adhere too strictly to the letter of the Propaganda decrees of December 1792. The more militant felt that it took too little account of the humiliations of 1787 and of the religious susceptibilities of their burgher constituency. But they welcomed what they took to be a general license to revolutionise the Netherlands. The more moderate Patriots and those regents who, by professing devoted loyalty to the new regime had saved their offices during February and March, hoped that in the men of Thermidor they would find pragmatists like themselves who had left the excesses of democracy behind with the Terror, and who could be persuaded to deal with at least some existing institutions such as the States-General.

The French had in fact given at least three plain assurances that the Dutch would be left at liberty to make whatever political arrangements they pleased (short of retaining the House of Orange), provided they fulfilled their obligations to the army. The proclamation of October 31 which followed Daendels' ukase said as much. And on January 10 (21 Nivôse, Year III) immediately before the assault on the Lek and the first drive into central Holland, the Committee of Public Safety in Paris had assured the Batavian envoys Blauw and van Irhoven van Dam that

from the moment that the revolution breaks out in the interior of Holland and the reins of government have been placed in the hands of a provisionally constituted authority, hostilities will cease and the Batavians, their persons and property will be treated not as enemies but as friends . . . *in no case will the French Republic* interfere with the form of government which the Bataves wish to introduce in their own country.[157]

Finally, on January 20 (1 Pluviôse) upon their entry into Amsterdam the French representatives again promised to respect Dutch persons, property, religions and customs, adding that "only the Batavian people, exercising its sovereignty, can change or modify its form of government."[158]

There seemed to be nothing equivocal about such declarations. But the emissaries of the 's Hertogenbosch Committee, who had had direct dealings with the French government, had good reasons to remain sceptical. Arriving in mid-December, their initiation into the devious ways of Thermidorian politics had been a bruising but timely education. Since the National Convention had itself blessed the Committee as the only rightful representatives of the Batavian people, its delegates Blauw and Van Irhoven van Dam had naïvely supposed that they would be treated accordingly as the only Dutch embassy legitimately accredited to negotiate with the French authorities. They found to their dismay that it was they and not their rivals who were left in the cold, for in December the Waal had not been crossed and the campaign was far from conclusively settled. While it remained in doubt the Committee of Public Safety had no intention of foreclosing its option on the diplomatic victory of neutralising the United Provinces by dismissing its ambassadors and embracing the Patriots. Blauw protested to Carnot about the humiliation of competing for his time with servants of an enemy, but to no avail. The Committee declined to recognise his credentials and ignored his demands for the arrest of Brantsen and Repelaer. The indignant representatives of the Batavian people were sent from the first interview with their fraternal ally with a flea in their ear for having the temerity to question the purity of French republican conduct!

Frustrated in their attempts to win either official recognition from the Committee of Public Safety or a hearing from the Convention, the Batavian envoys made the mistake of fishing for support in the shark-infested waters of Thermidorian politics. In his retrospective *Memoir*, Jacob Blauw insisted that he was an unwitting party to any intrigue that may have been hatched; but the circumstances of his brief (and nearly fatal) flirtation with the Committee of General Security—the executive police body of the Republic—could hardly have been more conspiratorial.[159] One of the survivors of the old Batavian Revolutionary Committee, Bernardus Blok of Hoorn, claimed to be able by means of a French intermediary, Audibert Caille, to introduce the Dutchmen to Courtois—a deputy of the Convention and a member of the Committee of General Security. It was implied that Courtois might be helpful in pressing the Batavian claims on the committees. A rendezvous was arranged at the hotel where the Committee of General Security met. After a long wait, Blauw, Blok, Caille and their secretary Raoul (for with miraculous prescience Irhoven had succumbed to a diplomatic illness) were called into a room where they were confronted not by one Committee member but twenty-five, seated round a table and including notables such as Barras and Legendre, whom Blauw called "the Butcher." Abashed by the unexpected formality of the occasion, the Dutch lost their tongues but were eventually persuaded to recite their complaints against the Orange ambassadors. Soothed by the apparent sympathy of Legendre, and aware that, as Blauw said, "there could be no going back," they agreed to write down their grievances in an eight-point document for the edification of the Convention and added to it an enquiry on the treatment of the occupied Netherlands.

This was, of course, a crude attempt to involve the gullible Dutchmen in an enterprise designed to embarrass the ruling faction on the Committee of Public Safety. It backfired disastrously on its stooges. At two in the morning a panic-stricken Valckenaer (who himself had been coaxing Carnot into a more receptive attitude) burst into Blauw's lodgings, crying: "My God what have you done?"[160] The two committees were apparently in a joint session at which Carnot had accused the Dutch of "sowing la zizanie" between the executive agencies of government. Presumably to cover its tracks, the Committee of General Security joined the chorus of execration and instead of patronizing the two ambassadors sent gendarmes to arrest them two days later. After eight hours of gruelling interrogation in which they were variously accused of being spies, plotters—and for Blauw most mortifying of all—*gens sans aveu* (suspicious vagrants), the "Representatives of the Batavian People" were let out at five in the morning very much the worse for wear.

This was not exactly the protocol they had been led to expect by their brief from the Committee at 's Hertogenbosch, which spoke of negotiating "power to power; republic to republic; friend to friend." Detecting perhaps that Blauw was more fool than knave, the Committee of Public Safety relented to the point of addressing another reassuring statement on the subject of the treatment of occupied Netherlands. But like all such communications, it was an unofficial document; the Committee insisted that in future all exchanges were to be confined to verbal addresses. There was no question, moreover, of recognising the delegates in any capacity other than that of private Dutch citizens residing in Paris.

The attitude of Carnot and the committee smacked of something more ominous than an unrevolutionary regard for diplomatic nicety. Even after the news of the fall of Utrecht became public on January 17 they declined to offer fuller cognizance of the Dutch envoys, nor would they dismiss those despatched by the States-General. Blauw was convinced that their hostility was attributable to misinformation by "the idiot Bellegarde" and his colleagues. "Do they," he added in another appeal, "forget the treachery of 1787?"[161] He persisted in asking for the immediate liberation of all Patriots detained by the Stadholderian authorities; access to the regular diplomatic facilities of couriers and despatches; the expulsion of the rival embassy; and approval of a National Council to include Paulus, Hahn, Visscher and Nicolas van Staphorst to act as a provisional government. If anything his indignities increased rather than diminished. His *carte de sûreté* was withheld, his mail opened and his movements kept under surveillance. He had asked that a deputation be permitted to address the Convention to congratulate them on the victory, but before they were eventually granted the *accolade fraternelle* on January 28 (9 Pluviôse, Year III) they were refused admission three times by the President, each time with a new reason for procrastination. On one occasion they were kept waiting three hours in the petitioners' lobby before being told that the Convention could not, alas, hear their address. This depressing charade merely confirmed Blauw in his view that the Convention remained firmly under the thumb of its executive committees. Even when at length they were allowed, through Valckenaer, to deliver their address, the reception accorded to it was distinctly tepid. Afterwards Blauw observed: "We cannot disguise our feeling that the cool manner in which we were received gave us yet another proof that there is apparently scant support for the Patriot cause here."[162]

However disagreeable, the curt treatment handed out to the Batavian envoys in Paris was a rude awakening. If on his arrival in December Blauw had been shocked at his reception, by the time he reported to Paulus in mid-February he was under no illusions whatsoever that the Batavian Republic would have to battle for its life with its allies as much as with its enemies. From private sources he had gleaned the information that the treaty the French had in mind bore little relationship to their formal effusions of fraternity. It was thought that it would almost certainly include a heavy indemnity; the large-scale supply of military and naval matériels; the continued presence of a French force; and conceivably some unspecified territorial demands. Carnot himself had revealed that he envisaged not a benevolent neutrality but a "defensive alliance," which would obviously involve the new Republic in further military operations.[163] Blauw and van Irhoven van Dam protested that for a nation whose survival depended on commerce and industry, a period of prolonged warfare would be ruinous, whereas a system of armed neutrality which denied the British naval hegemony in the North Sea would suit both French and Dutch interests. But Blauw recognised that his job was to make the very best he could out of a transparently weak bargaining position. He observed to Paulus:

As our country stands in such great dependence on France, I am certain that any action which might alienate the Government here must be scrupulously avoided, for in matters relating to foreign affairs their national pride can be so easily wounded. In Holland the very greatest firmness and circumspection should be used against the Representatives and generals, but in Paris it behoves us better to profess the most heartfelt loyalty and confidence.[164]

The Batavian Republic barely had been born when it put revolutionary innocence behind it.

Blauw had still to establish the indisputable right of the nominees of the National Committee to speak in the name of the Dutch people. Even on February 13, Brantsen and Repelaer reported a "most amicable conversation" with Carnot. Their repeated insistence that dealing directly with the established authorities was the only way of avoiding widespread revolutionary anarchy obviously carried some weight with a Thermidorian regime fending off a resuscitated sans-culotte agitation in Paris. The delegates of the States-General had painted a lurid portrait of a Batavian Terror in full cry, complete with mass arrests, revolutionary tribunals and unnamed but easily imaginable horrors to come. Only when fuller reports from the representatives made it plain that Holland was not awash with blood and that the purges of February had already accomplished a definitive change of regime did all prospects of success for the Orangist mission finally disappear. Their departure on February 26, however, did very little to define the position of their rivals. It was evident to Blauw that the Committee of Public Safety was deliberately postponing recognition as a means of increasing pressure on the Dutch to concede their demands. Nor were reports of French conduct in occupation more reassuring. Appealing to interest rather than altruism, Valckenaer had written in his pamphlet *Le Noeud Gordien Débrouillé* (*The Gordian Knot Untied*) that *if* treated with care and leniency, Holland could be for the French "the hen which lays the golden eggs."[165]

But the scale of French military depredations seemed limited rather by the modesty of the resources the British and Prussians had left behind than by any intentional benevolence. On January 25 the sheriff of the village of Beek near Nijmegen had complained to the representatives that during the two months his hamlet had been occupied by Macdonald's troops they had ransacked the neighbourhood, seized crops as they stood in the granaries; carried off cattle and even dairy cows for meat rations without pausing to settle, even in worthless *assignats*. Jourdan's companies had refrained from pillage but had left their billets removing with them every stick of furniture, "including the beds."[166]

Such conduct augured ill for the character of the peace treaty. But however harsh, the Dutch negotiators assumed that the sovereign independence of the new Republic would be honoured. Belgian Brabant and Liège were not annexed until October of that year, and Blauw saw no reason to suppose that the French would renege so far on their promises as to liquidate the Dutch Republic altogether. The principle division within the committees, he reported, was between those who wished to return *all* conquered territories and those who urged the retention of strategically significant areas like Maastricht and Venlo in the south and Dutch Flanders and Walcheren in the west. Just where the frontiers of the new Republic would lie was to some degree conditional on the outcome of a general peace concluded with the Coalition powers (minus Britain). Blauw assumed that such a peace was in fact in the offing. Rather more optimistically, he believed that this would permit a reduction of military in the Netherlands sufficient to permit the normalisation of economic life.

The economic issues were, as the Dutch negotiators appreciated, very delicate. Their first task was to try to lower the level of French expectations of limitless wealth traditionally associated with the United Provinces. In 1792 Robespierre had asked "why the Batavian Patriots, who have so much money and so great a fortune, cannot make their own revolution, or at least offer a hundred millions to the French nation to carry it out?"[167] Dumont-Pigalle and Valckenaer were especially concerned to educate their mentors in the more impecunious realities of Dutch economic life. In various memoirs addressed to the Convention and the committees they explained the damage war had done to trade and industry; and that their national credit rested not on the capital of a few bloated speculators but the savings of thousands of petty-bourgeois investors. The consequences of introducing any abrupt shocks into this system of credit—such as an uncontrolled paper currency—would, they argued, plunge a vast number of good burghers into complete destitution.[168] Blauw even went so far as to propose the death penalty for speculation in *assignats*, a measure unlikely to appeal to Thermidorians who were themselves accumulating vast fortunes out of just such grubby traffic. Time and again the Dutch memorialists argued that a Netherlands restored to strength and prosperity would be an incomparably greater asset to the republican alliance than one prostrated by war and extortionate depredations. A swift reversal of commercial maritime and colonial alliances could strike a powerful blow against the British, and that arch-fiend William Pitt, whom Valckenaer described as "the most dishonest corrupter of morals" and "the seducer and instigator of crime."[169]

Anglophobia was also a useful instrument for persuading the French to approve the political changes the Patriots had in mind. To guard against the "populicide" plots of Anglomane regents, Valckenaer argued, it was necessary to expel them from all positions of power and influence in the Republic. Dumont-Pigalle had actually drawn up a blacklist of Orangists in each city and province of the Republic, from minor tax collectors in Friesland to the Bentincks and Schimmelpennincks van der Oye of the Prince's immediate entourage. But he had indulged in this Dutch *tricotage* while the Great Terror was at its height in Paris, and in the prevailing atmosphere of the Counter-Terror in the Year III he refrained from urging "fournées" of all the Patriots' political opponents. The Dutch revolutionaries were caught on the horns of a painful dilemma. Encouraged by the fraternal professions of 1792, they had conceived the role of the French as one of disinterested liberation. As Valckenaer put it, they wished to be assisted, like the Americans, to recover their liberty and then left to determine the political form it should take for themselves. This had been duly promised them. But the Patriots were not so numerically overwhelming throughout the Republic as to feel confident of carrying through their revolution entirely without the help, or at least the sanction of force. Denied an instantaneous resurrection of the Free Corps, French arms had to supply that sanction. What they ideally wished for was a degree of coercion sufficient to guarantee the effectiveness of their political enterprise but not so substantial or so enduring as to damage their economy or compromise their sovereignty. Doubtless this was to ask for the impossible. Revolutions, like omelettes, we have been reminded often enough, are not made without breaking eggs. So delicate a balance between dependence and independence asked from the liberators an altruism bordering on the saintly, a quality conspicuous by its absence from French strategy. Such a formula has eluded states far more familiar with the nuances of revolutionary sovereignty than was conceivable at the end of the eighteenth century. That it should have failed to have been realised by the Dutch can scarcely astonish the historian. What is of interest is the persistence and doggedness with which they pursued the unattainable before finally succumbing to the contradictions of geography and power.

The priorities of the Thermidorians were altogether less subtle. They had inherited all the chauvinism of their predecessors with none of their cumbersome ideological baggage. The diplomatic section of the Committee of Public Safety comprised men of serpentine pragmatism like Sieyès, Reubell and Carnot, all concerned that the first interest of the French Republic should be its security, the second its power, and who were convinced that both were better served by judicious exploitation of military success rather than liberal sacrifices which at a later date France might repent. Such views found strong endorsement in the army, already coming to be depended on by the Convention as the principal bulwark of orthodox republicanism. The opinion of General Sauviac, for example, serving with Pichegru, was brutally simple. "Holland," he wrote to the Committee of Public Safety,

has done nothing to avoid being classed among the general order of our conquests. It was the ice, the indefatigable courage of our troops and the talents of the generals which delivered her and not any revolution. It follows from this that there can be no reason to treat her any differently from a conquered country. With a very few exceptions the patriots of this country are all timid adventurers led by ambitious intriguers, avid speculators who never dared to take up arms in our favour.[170]

Such a persuasion, albeit less trenchantly rendered, was commonplace among many deputies of the Convention. While two of its representatives in the Netherlands, Bellegarde and Portiez, were for a relatively lenient approach, the third, Richard, insisted that "this country will heed you only through fear."[171] As for Carnot himself, he was not a supporter of outright annexation. For one thing it interfered with the systematic spoliation of provinces which could be more conveniently handled as under "provisional occupation." He was not averse, moreover, to the occasionally magnanimous gesture, which while appeasing indigenous hostility to requisitions would not in any way impede the overall objective of extracting as much as possible from their national resources. But any concessions were determined by strictly functional criteria. He had no time for patriots, Dutch or any other, who were by and large, he remarked, "so-called patriots, interested only in the expulsion of their personal enemies so that they could replace them in their turn."[172] And he contrived to put a supremely Thermidorian gloss on the fraternal maxim of "guerre aux chateaux; paix aux chaumières," by claiming that the victors were entitled to the disposition of all places and installations urged to wage war against them—a category broad enough to take in not only fortresses and arsenals but granaries, dockyards and warehouses as well.

The question facing the diplomatic section of the Committee of Public Safety was not whether to exploit their victory in the Netherlands but how best to set about it. As a man who set great store by the accumulation of data, Carnot was concerned to undertake a more thorough examination of the assets of the fallen concern to see if in this case a subsidiary arrangement or a full-scale merger would be more appropriate. And to this end he appointed two special commissioners, François Ramel and Charles Cochon de Lapperant, to conduct such an enquiry.[173] Their report back to the Committee and the Convention was not what was expected. Jacob Blauw (in the company of most historians since) supposed that the Convention would be more amenable to discreet reminders of their fraternal obligations than their hard-headed representatives on the spot. But in this case the reverse was true. Far from endorsing the rapacity of the Committee, Cochon and Ramel, echoing the

Dutch memoranda, urged a counsel of prudence and therefore lenience towards the Netherlands. Like Valckenaer they were concerned to correct the impression that the Dutch Republic was lined with bankers' vaults all bulging with gold, and gave a vivid and all too plausible account instead of public and private poverty. Although Cochon—no sentimentalist—observed drily that he had met too many Amsterdammers who claimed to be down to their last change of linen, he advised strongly against a punitive policy, which would ruin the economy, "provide no resources for the future," and "make irreconcilable enemies of the Dutch people for they pardon such injuries very rarely and bad faith never."[174] Ramel, who was notably more temperate than his colleague, concluded his report on a note of striking moderation:

The true resources of the United Provinces consist in the assistance and devotion its citizens can give . . . The means which the French government seeks to dispose of rests for the most part in the hands of private individuals, but to obtain control over them will take time and will above all require winning their confidence.[175]

The two commissioners were not so moved by *égalité oblige* that they were prepared to ask the Committee of Public Safety to throw away all the advantages their Netherlands conquest had won. They both assumed that the Dutch would have to make some contribution towards the cost of their own liberation. On the whole, Ramel preferred the charge of maintaining an army of 40,000 to a once and for all indemnity as a test of republican solidarity. Cochon was more comprehensive. He provided for an indemnity, to be calculated at twice the national revenue for a single year; a loan to the French at a nominal interest; and the cession of limited strategic areas such as Maastricht and Flanders. Equally, both commissioners had assumed that as a return for the beginning of negotiations the French Republic would automatically recognise its new neighbour and treat with its emissaries as ambassadors. It came as something of a shock, even to hardened operators like Charles Cochon, to discover in mid-March that the Committee had no intention of weakening its hand by recognising the Batavian Republic in advance of the settlement of a treaty. Indeed, the condition of such recognition was to be acquiescence in the French terms without demur. The Committee felt on this matter:

that we should place ourselves in such a military and political position that the decrees of the Convention whatever they may be will always be executed with facility. As a consequence we ask you to consider the Batavian petitioners more as a company of merchants than a political power.[176]

Replying with some boldness, the commissioners protested that such proceedings would constitute "a formal disavowal of the public proclamation announced on entry to this country, (an act) of which you were perfectly well aware and have never disavowed."[177]

The Dutch were ill-prepared for this degree of ruthlessness from an ally which barely two months before was continuing to express the most benevolent intentions. Despite his abrupt education in Thermidorian politics, Blauw had remained optimistic about the chances of a satisfactory settlement once the political situation within the Netherlands had been put beyond question. His delegation had been strengthened by the removal of van Irhoven van Dam, whom Blauw complained enjoyed "sitting in an armchair, gossiping on about every conceivable topic and doing nothing about any of them,"[178] and his replacement with Caspar Meijer.

Meijer was a Dutch merchant who had lived in Bordeaux for a number of years and professed familiarity with the devious ins and outs of French politics. Certainly he had a strong interest in pressing for a commercial treaty to be included within the overall settlement with France. The "Instruction" supplied to the negotiators by the reformed States-General was not merely optimistic but ambitious. Apart from the commercial treaty, it was concerned to provide for protection for Dutch colonies and her mercantile fleet from the British navy; for an early evacuation of the Batavian Republic by French troops, and for minimal indemnification in return for generous loan facilities for the French treasury. It even cast covetous eyes on the Prussian province of East Friesland to the northeast and urged the French armies to move their requisitioning agents in that direction—a suggestion which indicated that Dutchmen could be quite as callous about neighbouring territories as French-men were about theirs. If there was no mention in the Instruction of the paramount importance of recognition, it was certainly because it assumed that a guarantee of sovereignty and territorial integrity had been implicit in the proclamation of January 21.

This somewhat buoyant view of Dutch diplomatic prospects received a rude shock when, towards the end of March, the French terms for negotia-tion were made known. They had in fact been decided on at the beginning of the month by Merlin, almost certainly in consultation with Carnot, and passed on in a memorandum to the new member of the diplomatic section, Sieyès, who clearly found its conditions satisfactory. They included an in-demnity of 100 million (or possibly 200 million) florins; a loan of another 100 million at 3 per cent interest; and—worst of all from the Dutch point of view—the cession of substantial tracts of territory. The terrible severity of these terms fell like an axe on Dutch optimism. Their negotiators felt they had been the victims of some profound misunderstanding, or worse, a brutal deception. Meijer wrote to the Committee on March 26 (6 Germinal, Year III):

. . . it is with the most grievous indignation that we have learned of your desire to add to the French Republic a part of our territory, of which *according to your own principles*, the Batavian Republic may not alienate without the freely expressed consent of the inhabitants of that part of the Republic, and of which, certainly the French Republic has no need either for its safety or its grandeur.[179]

But the Committee was unmoved by such reminders of their own fraternal adolescence. They were older and wiser men now. On another occasion when asked how, as the author of the principles of 1789, he could practise such diplomatic extortion, Sieyès replied airily: "Principles are for teachers in school; interests are for statesmen."[180] Nor was he impressed by Meijer's concern to exonerate the Batavian nation from the crimes of its Stadholder, a distinction which seemed to carry a great deal less weight after the conclusion of the campaign than it had during its duration. He pointed out instead that had the Coalition of which the United Provinces had been a member triumphed over France, it would not have scrupled to tear France apart like Poland. They should not now feign outrage if, to make good her safety, France chose to annex parts of those territories on which she had spilt her own blood. In addition to Dutch Flanders and Limburg, it appeared that the imperatives of French security also took in virtually the whole of Zeeland and a number of forts in Brabant, in order "to oppose the Scheldt to the Thames, Antwerp to London and the English tyranny over the seas of the North, Germany and the Baltic with our fleet at Flushing. *Such* are our political views because such is the interest of our Republic."[181]

To bring the Dutch to acquiesce in this act of fraternal mutilation, the Committee of Public Safety subjected its representatives to every conceivable form of harassment and intimidation. They were, of course, still treated as unofficial petitioners rather than ambassadors of a "sister republic." But in addition they were denied the most elementary diplomatic courtesies. Their mail was invariably opened and tampered with; they were under constant police surveillance and without *cartes de sûreté* were liable to be apprehended at will. On more than one occasion Sieyès and Reubell turned their "interviews" with the Dutchmen into a passable replica of a revolutionary tribunal. At one meeting Sieyès shouted that however they tried to avoid it, he *would* have his hundred million; at another, when delegates from the States of Zeeland asked for admission to the Committee to discuss the possible annexation of their province, Reubell threatened to walk out should they so much as show their noses round the door. When Blauw and Meijer attempted to go some way to meet the French demands by offering as a maximum an indemnity of 60 million and the cession of Flanders and Limburg, Sieyès told his representatives: "It is not for them to cede; it is for us to take."

The Committee blankly refused to discuss the issues of recognition, indemnity and frontiers separately, but insisted on presenting its demands as an indivisible ultimatum to which a direct "yes" or "no" was required.[182] To their credit, although in a pitifully weak bargaining position the Dutch withstood the storms of imprecation and abuse, refusing to be bludgeoned into submission. Exasperated by their obstinacy, Sieyès and Reubell began to contemplate more drastic coercion and the use of force within the Netherlands to seize what would not be ceded. On March 21 (11 Germinal) Sieyès told the two more leniently inclined representatives, Portiez and Bellegarde, "We have thought, more than once dear colleagues, that if by an obstinate refusal we were obliged to have recourse to more rigorous means of persuasion, you would charge our colleague Cit. Richard to direct these strictly in accordance with French interests."[183]

But Richard, normally at least as militant as the Committee in riding roughshod over the Dutch in the interests of the *patrie*, was on this occasion apprehensive about using force to break the deadlock. He communicated his

disquiet to the Committee, drawing their attention to a stiffening of resistance in the Dutch Republic, partly due to over-harsh requisitioning
and partly to the general anxieties over the outcome of the negotiations in
Paris. Pieter Paulus had threatened his resignation more than once and the
dissolution of the National Council if the Dutch were to be bullied into an
extortionate treaty. Blaauw later commented that he would rather prefer the
law of a conqueror to such abasement. On March 25 the States-General passed
a secret resolution determining to demand recognition of frontiers as a condition for negotiating any indemnity. Drawing on the traditional rhetoric of
Dutch history, the resolution reaffirmed:

The inhabitants of the Batavian nation, convinced that their country cannot exist
without liberty and that without those efforts and heroic sacrifices of which only
free men are capable it would long ago have succumbed to the waters, consider
freedom the supreme good for which they would sacrifice all that they hold dear.

On a more ominous note it added the warning:

Should the unfortunate hiatus in negotiations not cease immediately they may
find themselves beyond a state of being able to procure for the French troops the
subsistences and other necessities they require, a situation which can only lead
to a total want of vital supplies.[184]

These were not empty threats. The Army of the North was in a dire
condition. Afflicted with desertions and near to famishing, it depended—as
Cochon's reports had made clear—on what the Dutch could provide. Even if it
were to resort to outright pillage, taking what it could get, the practicalities of
the situation meant that such undisciplined provisioning would take time and
brutal effort. Even then there could be no guarantee that it would feed the
whole army. It would, moreover, be certain to alienate the Dutch, who
Richard thought were on the brink of a new rebellion. He had already noted
with some alarm "the seeds of fermentation and discord" in the Dutch cities.
Public unrest seemed to be mounting to threatening proportions. Further
delay over the treaty risked "exposing this country to the errors of Jacobinism"[185]—an argument not lost on a Convention then prone to be gripped by
anti-Jacobin panics. There were, moreover, still some 25,000–30,000 Dutch
troops not yet demobilised. In the event of a national uprising they could still
prove a dangerous force and a potent focus of national allegiance.

It was such reflections which threw a sinister light on the application of
officers like Daendels and Dominique van Damme to be transferred from
French to Dutch commissions, and made Sieyès insist that the organisation of
a Batavian army, like its recognition, be held up until the treaty had been
signed. On April 18 many of these suspicions found dramatic vindication in
another resolution of the States-General, which declared that under no
circumstances could it be empowered by its constitution to alienate the territory of a constituent province, and that such a proceeding would be

in contradiction to all those principles of the Rights of Man which the French
Nation itself, in opposition to its Oppressors, has duly declared . . . and that this
would also be against the true interests of the French Republic to render through

the removal of an important part of its territory, its ally impotent and impoverished. . . .[186]

This was a rousing act of defiance which surprised the French almost as much as the Dutch themselves. And the threat to counter an ultimatum with a refusal to supply the Army of the North gave the Committee some pause in its harassment of the Dutch. Other factors were pressing the French government to conclude their negotiations. The Committee of Public Safety was itself in some disarray after the uprising of Germinal (April 1) and the Convention was looking for a second treaty to match that signed at Basel on April 5 with Prussia. On May 2 the Convention voted to despatch two members of the diplomatic section, Reubell and Sieyès, to The Hague to conclude the negotiations directly with the Batavian government. In some respects this was a back-handed acknowledgement of the Dutch claim to negotiate Republic to Republic, and of the fact that the French would never have their way simply by bullying Blauw and Meijer in the Paris committees. But Dumont-Pigalle, like many others, had no illusions that the two French negotiators were coming to the Netherlands in a spirit of largesse. "I must warn you," he wrote to Pieter Paulus,

that a bear [Reubell] and a fox [Sieyès] depart today for The Hague to conclude the negotiations. . . . Be on your guard against the claws of the former and the wiles of the latter. The more opinionated they become the firmer you must be. Reason, honour and equity are on your side. Moreover I know from a reliable source that while they will begin their case brusquely they have been enjoined to moderate their arguments should they encounter too much opposition.[187]

Dumont-Pigalle's advice was as astute as ever. The fox and the bear had by no means abandoned their major objectives but in a final effort to break the deadlock were prepared to make some concessions to Dutch national pride and to pare their demands down to the essential interests. These were the use of Dutch naval resources in the war against the British and in particular the use of the harbour of Flushing guarding the entrance to the Scheldt; recompense on a substantial scale for the Dutch war; and finally special access to the money market to finance future military commitments.

From the beginning the negotiations at The Hague were conducted with a greater sense of urgency and realism than had been displayed throughout the ill-tempered and theatrical proceedings in Paris. Reubell and Sieyès were joined by the four French representatives to confront the Dutch team, led by Paulus, with as imposing an authority as possible. Discussion began at eleven in the morning on May 11 and lasted until four in the afternoon. Much to Sieyès' disgust the negotiations were not resumed that day "as these 'gentlemen' would not work this evening." All the same the proceedings, by Dutch standards, were remarkably expeditious. Agreement on the major points was reached on the 13th, signatures appended to a draft on the 15th, and the news of the treaty officially announced on the 16th, on the expiry of the last ultimatum decided by the Committee of Public Safety a fortnight before. Some concessions had been made by both sides, though the Dutch had not got off lightly. In return for the reciprocal recognition of the two Republics and pledges of non-interference in domestic affairs, the Dutch had agreed to an indemnity of 100 million guilders, to be paid off in instalments, as well as a huge loan to France discounted at a trifling rate of interest. The French were to take Maastricht, Venlo and Dutch Flanders, and to have the "barrier forts" dismantled on their frontier. But they abandoned their claims on the Zeeland islands and on the Brabant towns, agreeing instead on co-sovereignty in Flushing harbour—a measure as ill-fated in practice as it was ingenious in conception. Nothing specific was said of a commercial alliance, although protection was to be given to Dutch colonies and merchant shipping.

With some justification, the French greeted the news of the Treaty of The Hague as a milestone in the establishment of their Republic in Europe. It also brought much-needed relief to a beleaguered Convention. One happy supporter of the Plain confidently declared: "The Jacobins would never have brought us such a peace as this." For Sieyès it was a personal triumph. He returned from The Hague to enjoy his success, storming into the Committee of Public Safety and thumping a fistful of guilders on their table with the remark, "I have brought you a hundred million of these."[188]

For their part the Dutch rejoiced as best they could, their negotiators nervously concealing in a secret clause their commitment to maintain a French army of 25,000 until the peace. A special delegate of the States-General, Carel van Grasveld, rhapsodised to a bemused Convention: "Is this merely the sweet illusion of free spirits? No, it is the reality of an alliance cemented in liberty, applauded by the French and blessed by the Bataves."[189] But the blessings were very mixed. The political sovereignty of the Batavian Republic had at last been acknowledged by its own ally, yet at a price which placed upon it from the beginning the most crushing burdens.

More important than any specific articles, the Treaty of The Hague set the seal on an arduous process of political re-education about the character of the French Revolution. Initially the Dutch Patriots had seen their own much-admired image in the brilliance of its reflection and had projected on to it many of their own political desiderata. Similarly, they saw the war in 1792 as a providential expiation for the betrayal in 1787 of its wicked predecessor, the Bourbon monarchy. So despite their exile in France and their first-hand witness of the Revolution, the Patriots' understanding of the events taking place around them progressed astonishingly little distance beyond their parochial preoccupations in St. Omer and Dunkirk. On the contrary the messianic advertising of the Revolution helped to falsify their own history, which they began to see as the first blood in the European combat between liberty and despotism, and to reinforce illusions about the character of a fraternal alliance. The débacle of 1793 and the repression which followed effectively wrecked many of these preconceptions, transferring the centre of Patriot politics back to the Netherlands where they properly belonged.

Despite the humiliations, frustrations and excruciatingly slow progress of the campaign of 1794–95, the most dedicated patriots like Paulus remained

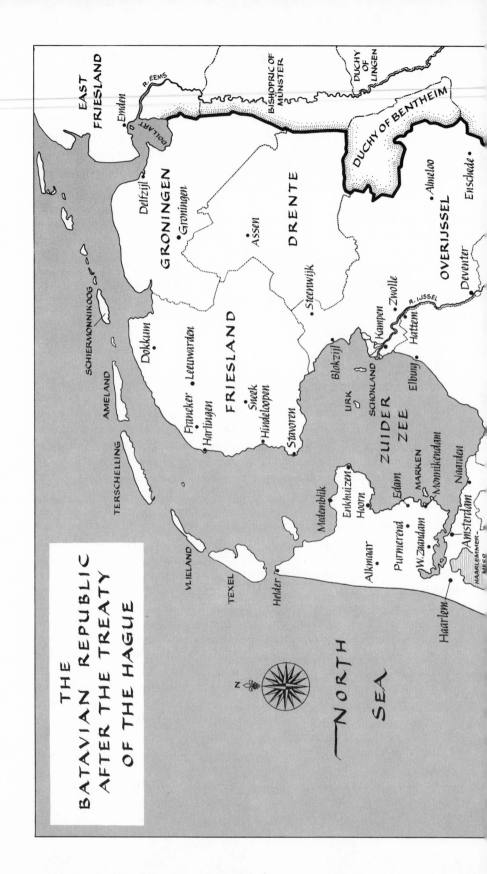

THE
BATAVIAN REPUBLIC
AFTER THE TREATY
OF THE HAGUE

NORTH
SEA

N

EAST
FRIESLAND

Emden

R. EEMS

BISHOPRIC OF
MÜNSTER

DUCHY
OF
LINGEN

DUCHY OF BENTHEIM

Almeloo

Enschede

DOLLART

Delfzijl

GRONINGEN

Groningen

Assen

DRENTE

OVERIJSSEL

Deventer

SCHIERMONNIKOOG

AMELAND

Dokkum

Franeker Leeuwarden

FRIESLAND

Harlingen

Sneek

Hindeloopen

Stavoren

Steenwijk

Zwolle

Kampen

R. IJSSEL

Hattem

Elburg

TERSCHELLING

Blokzijl

URK

SCHOKLAND

ZUIDER
ZEE

VLIELAND

Medemblik

Enkhuizen

Hoorn

Edam

MARKEN

Monnikendam

Naarden

TEXEL

Helder

Alkmaar

Purmerend

W. Zaandam

Amsterdam

HAARLEMMER-
MEER

Haarlem

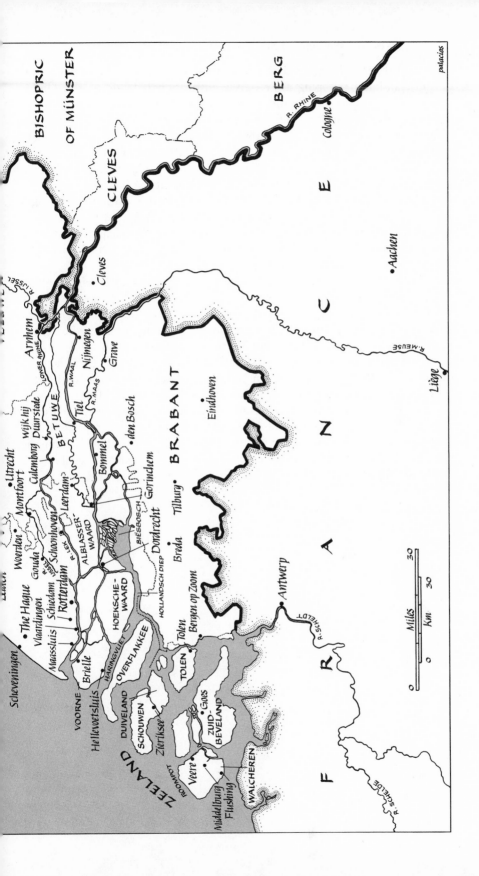

BISHOPRIC

OF MÜNSTER

CLEVES

BERG

R. RHINE

Cologne

Aachen

R. MEUSE

Liège

CLEVES

Cleves

Arnhem

R. IJSSEL

Nijmegen

Grave

BRABANT

Eindhoven

F R A N C E

Utrecht

Montfoort

Wijk bij Duurstede

Culemborg

Woerden

Gouda

Schoonhoven

Tiel

R. WAAL

R. MAAS

LOWER RHINE

BETUWE

Bommel

den Bosch

Leerdam

Gorinchem

R. LEK

Schiedam

Rotterdam

ALBLASSER-WAARD

BIESBOSCH

Dordrecht

Tilburg

Breda

HOLLANDSCH DIEP

HOEKSCHE-WAARD

Maassluis

Vlaardingen

The Hague

Scheveningen

Brielle

VOORNE

Hellevoetsluis

HARINGVLIET

OVERFLAKKEE

Bergen op Zoom

Tolen

TOLEN

Antwerp

R. SCHELDT

DUIVELAND

SCHOUWEN

Zieriksee

Goes

ZUID-BEVELAND

ROOMPOT

Veere

WALCHEREN

Middelburg

Flushing

ZEELAND

R. SCHELDE

Miles

Km

30

30

0

0

palacios

convinced that the foundation of a new Republic, the exorcism of the ghosts of 1787, and the sweeping away of the institutional debris of the United Provinces would provide the foundations for a resurgence of national vigour and even national prosperity. Drawing on the traditional terminology of Dutch history, van Grasveld prophesied that "each generation of Frenchmen and Bataves, fraternising anew, would present to an astonished Europe the striking and brilliant tableau of a hitherto fabulous Golden Century." But if their bruising encounter with the "Grande Nation" had taught the managers of the new Dutch state anything, it was that their future association was fraught with problems. Not least was the paradox that the inauguration of Batavian democracy was to be celebrated at the precise moment when revolutionary enthusiasm in France was cooling, so that the phantom of "Dutch Jacobins" was to haunt their relations for the next few years.

It was also a hard fact that the resumption of the Dutch reforming enterprise, abruptly broken off in 1787, had been bought at the expense of submission to French strategic interests. For the moment the objective of that reform—strengthening the Dutch commonwealth—complemented the French interest of creating a buffer on the North Sea against British interests. But especially if the war were to continue, there was no guarantee that these interests would always converge. Both Paulus and Blauw were clear that if the verdict of 1795 was to prove more than an exchange of one foreign master for another, it was essential that the Batavian Republic consolidate its emancipation by an assertion of both internal and external autonomy. In keeping with that resolution the ensuing history of the new Dutch Republic was marked by a struggle, often desperate, not only to make its revolution a reality within the Netherlands but to affirm its independence without.

✤✤✤✤✤✤✤✤✤

5

The Revolutionary Fracture,
January 1795–February 1796

There was now a Batavian Republic. But had there been a Dutch revolution? It was obvious to even the most wishful thinkers that the one was not conditional on the other. Pieter Paulus recognised, however grudgingly, that the new Dutch state owed its existence primarily to the "God of Justice who froze up the rivers that Liberty [and Pichegru's troops] might enter our Land unimpeded."[1] In case the Batavians were in any danger of being carried away in the first flush of their victory, their mentors and protectors were always on hand to remind them of their debt. The commissioners appointed to rifle through the scientific, fine art and natural history collections of the *ci-devant* Stadholder and to despatch the choice items to Paris as trophies of war graciously consented to make an exception of items considered special mementos of the Dutch past. Thus de Ruyter's sword and Admiral Tromp's baton were "presented" by the "French nation to the Dutch people" as a token of their fraternity. This generosity did not, however, extend to some 200 cases of treasures, which included among their contents a manuscript of the *Roman de la Rose*; Rubens' *Adam and Eve*; Paulus Potter's *The Pasture*; two live elephants and a stuffed hippopotamus —all of which were meant to serve as a reminder, lest anyone forget, of the "success of the arms of the Republic; of the bravery of its armies and the glory of France."[2]

Yet despite these glancing blows to national amour-propre which so mortified Groen van Prinsterer and the nineteenth-century historians, there was no sense that the Republic had reached its bleakest moment. Nor was the departure of the House of Orange a signal for a national rebellion in defence of Church and dynasty in the manner of the Spanish in 1808. According to many contemporary witnesses the prevailing mood in the spring of 1795 was one of relief at the end of hostilities combined, in not a few cases, with an expectation that the nation was on the threshold of a great rejuvenation. Amsterdam, the journalist-predikant Cornelis Rogge said, was like fair time. And he prefaced his spirited version of the events of 1795 by predicting that they

have given so violent a shock to the established notions, prejudices, customs, indeed the entire National Character of the Netherlanders that I dare say that in the future the present time will, through its visible effects, be remembered as the most important era of all, both for the advancement of politics and of mankind. . . .[3]

This buoyant sense of a new beginning was reflected in the rituals attending the birth of the Batavian Republic. The infamous Act of Guarantee sealing the pact between Britain and the House of Orange was ceremonially burned in the States-General. On January 31 the rights of man and burgher were solemnly proclaimed by the "Provisional Representatives of the People of Holland." Seated in the Knights' Hall, where since the twelfth century the nobility and towns of that province had convened their Estates, the new tribunes of the people swept aside in a few terse paragraphs the whole fabric of the old constitution—councils, corporations, colleges and counting chambers. The religious establishment received even shorter shrift. The Synod of Dort which in 1618 had established the Reformed Church as the guardian of the true Faith throughout the Republic was revoked outright and all disabilities removed from Catholics and Dissenters—though not, as yet, from Jews.[4] In further celebration of the Novus Ordo Humanitas, torture and the gruesome spectacle of wayside gibbets were done away with. Heeren and jonkheeren were deprived of their hunting rights, their bailiwick patrimonial jurisdiction, and the privilege of sporting coats of arms on carriages and church pews.[5] Towns which bore in their names the taint of an aristocratic past were rechristened according to the cult of democratic blandness. Thus 's Gravenhage (the Princes' Hedge) and 's Hertogenbosch (the Duke's Wood) became plain den Haag and den Bosch. Even in the humblest towns and villages of the Dutch provinces the inauguration of the new Republic was celebrated with all due pomp and ceremony. At Steenwijk in Overijssel French infantry were welcomed with fraternal kisses from the "burgher daughters" of the town—but only after the interminable oration of magistrate Strup had been concluded by embracing Captain Garat.[6] At Dokkum in Friesland the regent van Cleffens, who had been in exile since 1787, was given a regal homecoming all the more auspicious since, as the burgemeester put it, "You come not to strike Terror into your vanquished foes but with all the blessings of universal Fraternity."[7] And at the village of Haastrecht in Holland a gathering of twenty-four of the "martyrs" of 1787 declared to their fellow citizens that their experience had proved that "the flame of freedom, once lit, cannot be extinguished by acts of violence or high-handed tyranny. That hellish malevolence [of 1787]," they went on, "may have succeeded in robbing some of our comrades of the very breath of life but never could it pluck from their hearts the craving for Freedom."[8]

All this was no doubt magnificent—but was it revolution? Until very recently, most Dutch historians have thought not. The political theatricals seemed only to underscore the essentially contrived character of the event and to demonstrate the forms rather than the substance of revolution. To be sure, the change of regime in the Netherlands was unscarred by the mass violence associated with revolutionary insurrection. Were the shedding of blood a necessary condition for the classification of popular rebellions, the eighteenth-century Dutch would be unarguably disqualified. Protagonists of as radically different sympathies as Paulus and Schimmelpenninck were at one in urging clemency and reconciliation on their partisans rather than punishment and terror. The well-known declaration of the provisional representatives of the city of Amsterdam on February 15 insisted that

the system of Terror now proscribed throughout the French Republic cannot, for one moment, be tolerated in our little country without destroying it for ever. Our system of government, our domestic circumstances and our dealings in commerce are all too sensitive to survive a repetition of those scenes of violence.[9]

One of his correspondents was able to write to Dumont-Pigalle in Paris and assure him that as yet the revolution in the Netherlands was a "velvet revolution."[10] The only signs of vindictiveness on the part of the new authorities were the somewhat ritualistic incarceration of Bentinck van Rhoon, the arch-instigator of the reaction of 1788, and the less culpable figure of the deposed Pensionary van de Spiegel, both standing in for the absent Liberticide William V.[11] The campaign conducted by Valckenaer, re-installed in the Chair of Public Law at Leiden, for a more general proscription of Orangist regents made relatively little impression on councils where the moderation of men like Paulus and Pieter Leonard van de Kasteele inclined them towards leniency. Despite all the propaganda of its enemies, the Batavian Republic was never likely to countenance a Convention of Blood. Nor, despite the emergence in the district assemblies and popular clubs of the larger towns of a pungently expressed (though incoherently reasoned) social egalitarianism, was there any chance that the Dutch revolution would license an assault on property or even the disparity between poor and rich. Nobles and gentry (heeren) who forfeited their privileges of hunt and toll were appropriately compensated for the hardship and, as in France, some of the most severe sentences handed out by revolutionary courts of law were reserved for those violating in word or deed the sacrosanct rights of property.[12]

But while mass violence and social upheaval may most readily come to mind in identifying modern revolutions, they are not, as recent commentators have been concerned to observe, the indispensable, still less the sufficient, conditions of the phenomenon.[13] The most blood-boltered coup may result merely in a substitution of interchangeable military cliques, while as in eighteenth-century Britain profound social and economic change may take place within a framework which leaves the structure of political institutions relatively undisturbed. The results of much research into societies such as republican France have only served to confirm how little their patterns of behaviour were determined by the events central to the "Revolution." Conversely, the dimension in which the Revolution itself may best be comprehended, remains, as far as the eighteenth century goes, the political.[14] Certainly, in so far as the changes which took place in the Netherlands after 1795 can be described as "revolutionary," they were predominantly political in character. That does not mean, however, that they were any the less far-reaching for those whom they affected. A contemporary pamphleteer in Holland observed that "the word 'Revolution' which originally signified a mere alteration of things in general has, in common parlance, come to mean a complete overturning and upheaval in formerly prevailing beliefs. . . ."[15] There were few among those actively engaged in the work of making the Dutch state anew who would have been unhappy to describe the process in such terms. Paulus himself was satisfied with Paine's definition of a revolution as "a renovation of the natural order of things; a system of principle combining moral happiness with national prosperity."[16] For good or ill that seemed a fitting motto for those who gathered behind the banner of what they, at least, imagined to be a Dutch revolution.

On the other hand it is quite true that not all the beneficiaries of the change of regime in 1795 shared such lofty aspirations. While heartily glad to see the back of the House of Orange, a number of those who, by virtue of their defeat and eviction in 1787, undoubtedly looked on themselves as "Patriots" remained limited in their ends as well as their means. For their part, the "revolution" was restricted to an exchange of élites; a return to the status quo ante Brunswick and the reforming whiggery of the Constitutional Restoration. In spirit they were closer to Burke than to Rousseau, and when they reflected on the dreadful turn events had taken in France those who had been first-hand witnesses like Jan Bicker deeply regretted not only their enthusiasm in 1789 but their earlier reveries in 1786 and 1787. The shrewder among their number like Rutger Jan Schimmelpenninck remained persuaded that institutional reform and even some kind of new national representation were needed to trim the fat from the obese old Republic. Still they had no use for those who wanted to pare all its institutions down to the bone or to put in their place an entirely new creature reared in accordance with fancy theoretical desiderata. Not all those who held such convictions did so to sustain their interests as "Patriot Regents." Some, like Jacob Uitenhage de Mist, were quite as much outsiders to the charmed circles of the plutocracy as more revolutionary figures, but he became one of the most passionate defenders of the historical constitution nonetheless.[17]

Yet conspicuous among the more conservative republicans in 1795 were names which were illustrious in the Amsterdam patriciate: Maarten van der Goes; van Staphorst; Maurits van Hall; Bicker—men who had dominated the Francophile interest in the 1780's and who thought of themselves as the "natural" successors to power on the defeat of their Orangist adversaries. They were not so obtuse as to suppose that the rule of oligarchy in its unconstrained "periwig" dress could continue. Indeed, they preferred to think of their entitlement to govern more in terms of disinterested competence than social rank or birth. But if offices were to be elected rather than in-herited or nominated, then, in common with their French counterparts, they felt sure that such elections had better be confided to men whose fortune and education best fitted them for weighty responsibilities. Unrestrained democ-racy was, they were sure, a certain recipe for social and political disaster.

Had such views gone unchallenged, there would indeed be little point in describing marginal political adjustments as anything remotely approximate to a "revolution." But this was far from the case. Before 1795 was out, it was plain that the Batavian Republic was to be a battlefield on which resolutely opposed versions of the Dutch polity would contest its sovereignty. Far from temporising with those who claimed to stand by the Dutch past, their antagonists branded them as the aristocratic enemies of the Dutch future. What was remarkable about the Netherlands after 1795 was the degree to which this conflict succeeded in bringing about just such an "upheaval of formerly prevailing beliefs." Some of those who pressed the attack were, like Gogel and Wiselius, men who had grown to maturity during the Restoration; but others, like Vreede, Daendels and Paulus, were democrats of a 1786–87 vintage. The concern of both groups was to have done once and for all not merely with the House of Orange but with their rivals, who between them had monopolised power during the two centuries of the Republic's existence. As Gogel's friend J. H. Appelius put it, they were "convinced that the evils had to be attacked at their roots and that the road down which they had wandered in the years before 1787 could never lead to a good end. . . ."[18]

Except in so far as they were attached to a romantic conception of a just and thrifty primitive democracy which they supposed they were restoring to the Netherlands, the more convinced democrats among these politicians turned their backs resolutely on their national past. The institutions of govern-ment and the laws which had won the admiration of so much of Europe and had been seen in the "Golden Century" as the paradigm of republican liberty were consigned by their modern custodians to the historical rubbish dump. The constitution based on the Union of Utrecht was variously reviled as the "Seven-Headed Monster" or the "Gothic Ruin," too worm-eaten to support the sagging weight of a moribund society. In its place would be created a virile new state, transformed root and branch, and grounded on the twin principles of democracy and national unity. Democracy signified that the legitimating condition for any legislative or executive body, national or provincial, was to be its representative character. It was this condition which was cited in the formal act of abolition of the States of Holland. One enthusiast of the new order affirmed that "When the former government is wholly altered in the principles of its constitution we shall have true Liberty and pure Equality; then shall each burgher have an equal right, not only to choose his own representatives but also to *order* a fitting means of representa-tion. . . ."[19] Entailed in this version of political egalitarianism was the eligibility of all male adults, other than those living in receipt of public charity, criminals and bankrupts, to hold office as well as vote in primary assemblies. Office was to become what it had always purported to be in the Netherlands: a station of communal trust, rather than what, for a long time, it had actually been: a form of transferable property.

Both representation and eligibility had been cardinal items of Patriot ideology in the late 1780's. The unification of provincial sovereignties into a single national popular sovereignty was a much more explosive issue. Sovereign indivisibility appeared at the masthead of each French constitution and the Republic had suppressed abortive "federalist" rebellions at Lyons and Marseille with extreme severity. But it was by no means an alien dogma, unfit for Dutch consumption, as Colenbrander and, on occasions, Geyl suggested. For the doctrine which came to be known as "unitarism" had a peculiarly Dutch resonance, arose from Dutch circumstances and, far from subverting, was meant to ensure the independent national identity of the Netherlands. As Thorbecke observed, it was the culmination of a long lineage of initiatives at state reform reaching back to Pensionary van Slingelandt at the beginning of the century. As reiterated in their newspapers and countless speeches in the National Assembly, the democrats saw the dissolution of provincial federalism as a necessary precondition of the national revival to which they pledged their revolution. The "Representatives of the People of Rotterdam" (hardly the wild men of the Republic) declared in 1795:

we hold that without Unity our Republic can never succeed in being either important and valuable for her allies or redoubtable to her foes. Common interest dictates that the whole Batavian nation unite to form a single indivisible Republic.[20]

There were obvious practical reasons—especially fiscal and military— why democrats in Holland should urge the creation of a unitary Republic. But while they held that the old federation could never hope to survive in a *Europe des patries,* they argued with even stronger force that, as practised in the Netherlands, federalism had become an inherently immoral form of ad- ministration. It was in the urban councils and provincial States that they saw patrician power most formidably entrenched and the interests of the national community sacrificed to the interests of the élite. Wiselius waxed indignant at the "odious system of federalism; the provincial assemblies [which are] wet-nurses of self-interest and ambition; the nests from which the aristocracy have been hatched."[21] If the roots of that great jungle of nepotism, oligarchy and venality were not torn out, he and his comrades feared that their vision of a Republic restored to the arcadian virtues of its ancestors would be lost forever. If the great cities and States were left with their powers unimpaired, they would be free to ignore the pronouncements of the people's assemblies just as they ignored those of the Stadholder. Anthonie Willem Ockerse, an ex-predikant and, with Gogel, the editor of the newspaper *De Democraten,* went even further. "Should the old system remain," he warned, "then I swear by God to you that within a few years we shall see a Stadholder back again, for I know of no other counter-weight to the formidable spirit of aristocracy into which the seven Provinces have always and must always degenerate."[22] In short, without the establishment of a unitary sovereignty, "liberty" and "equality" would remain so much hollow cant and the revolution be doomed to a stillbirth.

To the defenders of the old constitution, the idea that federalism—traditionally regarded as the chief bulwark of freedom in the Republic—should now be denounced as tyranny and aristocracy was a symptom of the topsy-turvy world which revolutionaries inhabited. They seemed to be a mixture of infants and savages, bent on destroying every institution, no matter how tried or true, which lay across the path of their precious ideology. Some of them, they remembered, had lived in Paris in 1793 and no doubt their fantasies still seethed with *lanternes* and tumbrils. If permitted, they would wreck the hard-won victory against the Stadholder by pandering to a rabble of illiterate tradesmen and proceed to deface the wisdoms of their fathers with the profane graffiti of Rousseau and Robespierre.

The chances of accommodating viewpoints—so diametrically opposed as these—were, from the start, very slim. The cleavages which before long separated republican from republican were at least as wide as those which had earlier divided Orangists from Patriots. After 1796 those differences would become crystallised in the warring factions of the National Assembly. But in the spring and summer of 1795, the atomisation of the political community in the Netherlands postponed the formation of two great mutually irreconcilable parties of federalists and unitarists. Revolutions are almost never the neat surgical excisions they often appear in historical accounts. Just as in France in 1789, the disruption of constituted authority resulted not in the instantaneous creation of a new order in the Netherlands but in the splintering of the community into its component parts. Instead of a clean break there was a multiple fracture of power. In the towns, villages and hamlets of the Dutch provinces, men assumed revolutionary—that is ad hoc—authority as and when it seemed opportune for them to do so. Unlike France, however, there was no great theatre of events at the centre to which those in the localities could look for guidance and leadership. Instead they had to make their own faltering way to power, with very little consensus of their goals beyond the removal of those still incumbent in office.

Those who took on the responsibility of engineering these changes were very often men who had become acquainted in the claustrophobic intimacy of the clandestine societies of the Restoration. As the advance of the French grew nearer their province, they had gradually become bolder in their meetings, their distribution of pamphlets, and their surreptitious posting of wall libels or appeals to their countrymen to resist William V's recruiting officers. Eventually their "revolutionary committees" had surfaced to stage-manage the deposition of aldermen, councillors and burgemeesters in the church meetings of January and February 1795. In a large city like Rotterdam, district meetings (*wijk-vergaderingen*) came into being, often spontaneously, as often organised by the reading societies to supply the numbers needed to sanction the changes. In smaller urban centres such as Alkmaar two clubs, "Eendracht" (Concord) and "Broederschap" (Fraternity), of a respectively radical and moderate hue competed with each other to organise the depositions. In villages such as Oldemarkt in Overijssel, the passage of authority from one set of men to another was entirely managed by one energetic and ruthless man, Anthonie van Ijsselmuiden, very much the political entrepreneur for whom revolutions offer the perfect main chance.[23]

The nearest that the Batavian Republic in the spring of 1795 approached to any kind of leadership were the assemblies of "Provisional Representatives of the People" which were in reality meetings of delegates from each of the major revolutionary centres in each province. Predictably the Holland Assembly was both the most radical and the most efficiently led. It had originated in an informal meeting called at the Prawn Market in Amsterdam by the National Revolutionary Committee just a week after the revolution in that city. Twenty-four delegates from thirteen Holland towns (the most conspicuous absentee being Dordrecht), many of them Catholics and Dissenters, attended. In what was obviously a direct challenge to the sovereignty of the States, it agreed to transfer its proceedings to The Hague. On January 26, with the number expanded to thirty-two delegates, this assembly constituted itself as the "Provisional Representatives of the People of Holland," and under the astute chairmanship of Pieter Paulus smoothly usurped the authority of the States, establishing a pattern which in due course all the remaining provinces bar Zeeland were to follow.[24]

By a nice paradox, though Holland was, from the outset, strongly committed to the principle of unitary sovereignty, the authority of the Assembly in practice derived from the persistence of devolutionary federalism. For none of the "Representatives" had been *directly* elected, merely nominated by their respective municipalities (themselves revolutionised) to serve at the provincial level. Among their first public acts, however, was the formal abolition of the eighteen urban and one noble delegations which had comprised the old States. For the first time, the rural districts of the province and smaller towns which had hitherto gone unrepresented were admitted to the Assembly. It further proposed—in the teeth of opposition from Amsterdam—that Holland be divided into fifty equal electoral districts in the following year.[25] But the more general question of to whom or to what sovereignty had passed from the Stadholder and the States-General remained very mysterious. To announce that it had passed to the "people" was comforting but unhelpful, since it left unresolved which people exactly could claim the privilege. The people represented at The Hague by the still unreformed States-General (the last Orangist delegations remaining seated until March 13)? Or the people represented in the new Holland Assembly? The people whose guardians the Amsterdam Revolutionary Committee claimed to be, or the people who had signalled their consent to the new Amsterdam *municipality*? There was a similar uncertainty about the relationship between the Committee set up by the States-General to replace the old Council of State and the committees appointed by the Representatives of Holland to administer the finance, police and "General Welfare" of the province. In fact the peculiarly Dutch hodgepodge of overlapping and competing authorities which had so bedevilled the government of the old Republic had not been simplified but actually compounded by the new!

In this confused situation, political contests in the different regions of the Netherlands were bound to take on the character imparted to them by local grievances and ancient disputes. In Nijmegen, for example, the revolution was coloured by sectarian issues. Through the emancipation of the substantial Catholic majority, the garrison town was transformed overnight from what had been an impregnable citadel of Orangist allegiance to a Republican stronghold. Yet the Catholics were not the immediate beneficiaries of the change. The men who filled the places vacated by deposed Orange regents and the Stadholderian court nobility were nearly all drawn from the commercial and professional Protestant circles, which had formed what "opposition" there was in the Patriot days of the 1780's. Their caucuses were based on the rump of the old "College of Commoners," which had switched sides just in time to conserve some of its influence with the French *représentant*, Bellegarde, and the club—formerly the "Fatherland Society," now boasting the republican colours of the "Exemplary Vanguard."

It was this Patriot élite which, protected by the French, proceeded to distribute magistracies and council places amongst its own clientèle, which in many cases had a narrower base than its predecessors. Very few Catholics were admitted to full civic rights, and although these Patriot notables made some gestures to woo the majority they were understandably met with suspicion. It was only after the Catholics had mobilised their own clubs, newspaper presses and political campaigns that their force of numbers began to tell. After a number of stormy meetings punctuated with public demonstrations, they were admitted to all primary assemblies and elected to local office. By the end of the year, half the membership of the city council were Catholics, as well as two of the three powerful town secretaries.[26]

Brabant was another area where Dutch Catholics won important gains from the revolution. Not only were they invested with full civil rights but they were liberated from the compendium of humiliating prohibitions which had made their social and religious ritual—from baptism to burial—a virtually clandestine practice. Education was an issue where feeling ran very high. On October 1, 1795, a provincial ordinance decreed that all primary instruction in Brabant should henceforth be non-denominational and that the Calvinist Heidelberg Catechism instituted by the Synod of Dort should be deleted from daily lessons.[27] But aside from the religious question, Brabant had its own special grievance against the old Dutch regime. Unlike the seven provincial signatories of the Union of Utrecht, it had been brought into the Republic though the military campaigns of Princes William and Maurice, and treated ever since as conquered territory. Denied the sovereign status of the other provinces, it had been governed directly by the States-General as the "Generality." As a consequence—one of its native champions, Jan van Hooff, complained—it had lain "utterly forgotten," its "fertile soil neglected and its lands condemned to the sterility of the centuries."[28] Indeed, until comparatively late in the eighteenth century the province had been a stagnant backwater of the Republic, more akin to Austrian Flanders than its prosperous neighbours to the north. The small, parcelled-out land holdings which covered much of its territory produced little in comparison to the dairy farms of the North Holland peninsula or Friesland but were nevertheless subject to disproportionately high *verponding* or land tax. Even its embryonic light industries in centres like Breda and Tilburg, which had profited more from the lower cost of labour than in the north, had been stunted by the erection of high inter-provincial tariffs to protect the urban markets of Holland and Utrecht.

Under these circumstances it should not be surprising that Brabant produced more than its fair share of political radicals in the 1780's and 1790's. There was little reason for men like van Hooff and de Kock—both members of the original Batavian Revolutionary Committee in Paris in 1792—to feel at all sentimental about the disappearance of the Union of Utrecht. Yet, as not infrequently turns out to be the case, it was an immigrant to the region who proved to be its most passionate champion. Pieter Vreede was a Leidenaar by birth and, somewhat against the odds, had managed to make a success of a cloth manufacture there. Brought up in the traditions of Holland's opposition to Orangist supremacy, he had outgrown his apprenticeship when as "Harmodius Friso" he had been one of the most waspish critics not just of Stadholderian misrule but of the urban patriciate. In 1785 he had emerged as the moving spirit of the Free Corps assemblies in Holland and drafted the celebrated "Programme" of that year which proposed transforming the United Provinces into a unitary democratic Republic. After the defeat he had moved his factory south to Tilburg, both to take advantage of economic conditions and to elude the unwelcome attention of the Orangist authorities.

In 1795, Vreede stepped forward as the convenor of a meeting of representatives from all the major towns in Brabant, initially at Tilburg and later at 's Hertogenbosch. Following Holland's example, this meeting duly constituted itself as the "Provisional Representatives of the People of Brabant" and determined to secure immediate recognition as the equal of the provinces represented in the States-General. But its warm messages of fraternity to the States at The Hague were not sufficiently reciprocated to induce that august body to receive two Brabander delegates without further ado. It merely observed in reply that since its own future was under consideration and since the Brabant Assembly itself acknowledged its "provisional" status, it would be premature to alter existing arrangements. In practice this meant that Brabant remained under the jurisdiction of the Generality, a decision which, however intended, was certainly taken by Vreede and his colleagues as a deliberate affront to their newly found liberty. It was, he argued, an iniquitous violation of the sovereignty of the people which the States had endorsed, since the province was once more "to be ruled by a foreign power [meaning The Hague] which we have not ourselves elected."[29]

As a demagogue and mobiliser of opinion, especially offended opinion, Pieter Vreede had no peer in the Batavian Republic. The upshot of the cool dismissal by the States-General of Brabant's claim was the launching of an impassioned public campaign to force their capitulation. Vreede circularised all clubs and municipal councils in the province, urging them to meet at a special assembly at den Bosch in the most emotive language:

... Conquerors of Philip! You, for whom freedom is dearer than life itself ... do not be deceived by the snare that these (arrangements) are merely temporary. The slavery of a SINGLE DAY is too long for a free soul. Since the Batavians are free, we too must be free.[30]

Under some pressure the States-General consented to despatch a delegation of four commissioners to den Bosch at the end of June, but if anything this body only added insult to injury by treating themselves as the *de iure* administration in Brabant, refusing to recognise the Representative Assembly, and addressing themselves directly to the individual municipalities very much as in the old regime. By midsummer, the clubs in den Bosch, Breda, Grave and Tilburg were urging the arming of their members, the establishment of new revolutionary committees, and the violent ejection of any Brabander guilty of "collaborating" with men from the north. Indeed, the momentum of the protest campaign was accelerating so rapidly that effective control was already slipping from Vreede to men of a more militant and plebeian stamp like Willem Hubert—the timber merchant of den Bosch and doyen of its clubs, beside whom Vreede appeared almost staid.

Alarmed at these developments and reports that the Representative Assembly was considering either outright secession or applying to the French Republic for admission as a department, the States-General finally relented. All along it had agreed that if there were to be no new "National Convention" before the end of 1795, then Brabant would be admitted as a full delegation to the States. Now it simply advanced the date and agreed to recognise the legality of the provisional administration established by the representative assembly. Even this settlement was not without its complications. The Generality insisted on retaining sovereignty over the "military crescent" south of the Hollands Diep and including the forts of Willemstad and Klundert which, it pointed out quite correctly, had never been part of Dutch Brabant. In disputing this jurisdiction the Brabanders used almost identical arguments—the indivisibility of the territory; historical connections; and the "sovereignty of the people"—to those advanced by the States when pressing their tutelage on the whole province.

Just what was meant by the "sovereignty of the people" depended very much on where one stood. It was invoked with equal fervour by provinces against the States-General; by towns against provinces; by villages against towns. Even the polder hamlet of Kamperveen in Overijssel cited it in defence of their "liberation" from the authority of the town of Kamper.[31] The "will of the people" was always the will of the aggrieved to end their subordination to those placed immediately above them. In the same province of Overijssel, the inhabitants of Almelo discovered that the Rights of Man entitled them to abolish forthwith the irksome dues and tolls imposed by the local seigneury. But those same rights emboldened the Dame to protest to the Overijssel representatives that she had been unconstitutionally dispossessed of her rightful private property![32]

It was very rare for the revolution to create new contests for authority; far more often it added an extra dimension of fierceness to old feuds which long pre-dated (and would long post-date) the arrival of the Batavian Republic. In Zeeland and Gelderland, where the sparsely dispersed urban Patriots had struggled in vain against the overwhelming weight of the Orange nobility, the revolution was a precious opportunity to reverse the balance of power. The liquidation of the Gelders aristocracy as a political force delivered the government of the province into the hands of the Patriot clubmen of Arnhem and Zutphen who had been the first victims of the Restoration in 1787. In Zeeland, however, the transition was more drawn-out. Although there were a few clubs in Zierikzee and Flushing, the only lively centre of Patriot politics in the province was Middelburg. Not only the nobility but the fisherfolk were intensely loyal to the House of Orange. This made it easier for the regents of the States of Zeeland to fend off the feeble revolutionary initiatives in January and, after it was clear that no British redoubt on Walcheren could be seriously entertained, to negotiate their capitulation with the French before any insurrectionary committees could usurp their authority. The result was that it took several weeks before the Orangist regime was dislodged from power and Zeeland's delegation to the States-General changed. Even when the new Assembly of the "People of Zeeland" finally met, it bore an uncanny resemblance to the old provincial States. Among its deputies were no fewer than eleven ex-regents who only a few days prior to their election as "Representatives of the People" had been deposed as their "oppressors."[33]

In the land provinces and the countryside of Holland and Utrecht, the old feuds of town and country were rehearsed with new emphasis. In Overijssel, the traditional centres of Patriot politics at Kampen, Deventer and Zwolle naturally supplied the post-revolutionary leadership and dominated the administrative committees, working in uneasy cooperation with the French military authorities. In the rural backwoods, peasant smallholders and the (by no means all poverty-stricken) "serfs" of the Twente domains saw the revolution as a providential release from vestigial but irritating encumbrances of seigneurial dues, hunting rights and the *dienstgeld* paid in commutation of their old feudal bonds. As in the rural areas of Holland and Utrecht, the village Patriots—to whom the fall of "feudalism" in the Netherlands could well mean more than the figure of speech used by their urban counterparts—were often inclined to correspondingly more radical opinions. It was their votes which helped the democrats to prevail over their more patrician rivals in the representative assemblies of Holland, Overijssel and Utrecht. This countryside radicalism was not without its complications. Along with hostility towards patrician élites, old and new, went suspicion of politics and politicians outside the province, so that the most socially aggressive elements in Overijssel and Friesland, for example, were also those least inclined to accept counsels coming from The Hague, however dressed up in the apparel of revolutionary democracy. Even at a more local level, the exactions brought on by French military occupation inflamed feeling against the new revolutionary committees so that by the summer of 1795 the Overijssel countryside was on the verge of (and in some areas well beyond) full-scale revolt against the dominance of the three towns.[34]

A cursory sketch of political conditions in the Batavian Republic in the first half of 1795 reveals an image of almost complete chaos. Filling in the details at the parochial level only deepens the confusion. In Rogge's phrase, the revolution was still "a creation without purpose; a riddle without a solution."[35] Many of the causes advanced as the "will of the people" seemed to be in direct contradiction with each other. Yet, as in France in 1789, this riotous political melée in no way deterred many people from seeing in the revolution an almost magical satisfaction of their particular and private grievances. Their bond was in what the revolution *seemed*, not what it was. The actual complexity of its politics was in marked contrast to the essentially simple way in which it was viewed and the potent jargon used as its stock-in-trade. "Sovereignty of the People," "Liberty," and the "Common Cause" were catch-all slogans able to accommodate the most disparate interests within the general temper of, at times, seraphic optimism. Rogge noted that "Men now speak a language different from that which they have spoken for a hundred years or more. . . . The people understands its rights and feels its true worth. Even the humblest wage-earner feels that he too is a Man, a member of Society and a citizen [burgher] of the State."[36]

As political cement, however, this language proved to be a perishable material. For as in all revolutions its extravagance generated expectations which successive governments and legislatures found impossible to satisfy. Eventually the failure to bring about the utopia promised by the rhetoric led to the disenchantment of earlier enthusiasts and the retreat of many thousands back to the political limbo from which the revolution had snatched them. But in the halcyon days of the Republic the axioms of political and even social egalitarianism were taken at their face value. Those who used them casually as tactical weapons in their own interests found that they could be far more dangerous when placed in the hands of those outside the charmed circle of the Patriot élites.

The promise of political democracy was the fundamental ground on which the Dutch revolution in 1795 was held to stand; consequently it was democratic aspirations which gave the leaders of the Batavian Republic their most trying moments throughout the year. Many of those installed as representatives, councillors or committee members in January and February found, by June and July, that they were having to deal not only with the recalcitrance of old political interests but the impatience of the new. Having assumed the role of tribune of the people in Brabant, Pieter Vreede found himself outflanked by the militant agitation of the clubs at den Bosch which were demanding a more aggressive resistance to the States-General and insurrection against its commissioners. At one point the atmosphere in the city, whipped up by Gerrit Paape's paper the *Brutus Bossche Courant*, became so ugly that

Vreede was forced to leave and return to Tilburg for his own physical safety.[37]

In Overijssel the hue and cry was exacerbated by the persistence of quasi-belligerent conditions. Because of the British retreat through the north-east, the furtive presence of a few French émigré bands around Zwolle, and rumours of an impending counter-attack from Osnabrück, the French canton-ment in the province remained very heavy. Overijssel had already endured an appalling winter in 1794–95. As in Zeeland and Friesland, bombardment had destroyed many of the first defence dykes. Much arable land had been flooded and the vicious frosts of late December and early January had destroyed the potato crop in large areas of the province. What had been left of grain and vegetables had been seized, first by British, then by French troops, so that by April the countryside was denuded of both livestock and crops. In Twente, men were reported to be eating bark and millet. Almost a third of the province's population succumbed to famine conditions. As if this were not enough, the requisitions levied by the French army completed the misery. By March 10 Deventer had had to produce 270,000 pounds of hay; 25,000 pounds of straw; 12,000 guilders' worth of bread; 65,000 pounds of oats; and several hundred head of cattle for the army. On the rare occasions that it was made, payment for such colossal amounts was in worthless *assignats*, well below the official exchange rate. And in case there was not already sufficient reason for hating the French "liberators" quite as heartily as their British and Prussian predecessors, a detachment of troops ran amok at Zwolle (as at Zutphen) pillaging houses and shops and raping three burgheresses of the city.

Inevitably much of the odium for the plight of the province fell on the newly elected "Representatives" who had been nominated at Deventer on the crest of revolutionary enthusiasm. That assembly was in no position to do much about what was fast developing into an economic catastrophe. Most of its delegates were well-heeled. Some, like the de Vos van Steenwijk brothers or van Mulert of Delfsen, came from the Patriot squirearchy which had been discomfited in 1787; others like Gerrit Dumbar, Jacob de Mist and Gerrit van Marle were lawyers, political writers and municipal officers (from Deventer, Kampen and Zwolle respectively). They were by no means insensitive to the appeals flooding in from the countryside but were simply overwhelmed by the enormity of the disaster. Their response was to fall back on the traditional palliatives favoured by Dutch local authorities in hard times. The most stricken areas were made exempt from any direct taxation and were given subsidies with which to buy emergency supplies of grain (illegally if necessary from Friesland and Groningen). However, it was only a short time before the dearth in the countryside caught up with the towns, which in their turn required subsidies to feed not merely the poor but middle-class people desti-tuted by forced levies. The result was a pyramid of hunger and debt. Zwolle ran up a deficit of nearly 100,000 guilders trying to feed its own poor and those of its rural environs. In its turn the provincial treasury beggared itself and then borrowed from Mennonite financiers to ease the load on the munici-palities.[38]

Politically, the dearth in Overijssel brought the province near to dissolution. In July guards from Zwolle had to be sent to Zwartsluis to suppress a riot. In the village of Volte peasants took up firebrands and turf-cutters to demand the equal division of common land, and other similar disturbances were reported at Hasselt, Hengelo, Enschede, Almelo and Oostmarsum. Had it not been for the intervention of radical politicians with a constituency in the urban popular societies, these might have remained isolated incidents of rural despair. But their able and unscrupulous leader, Joos van Vridagh, succeeded in exploiting the appalling economic situation by blaming it on the misrule of the old regime and demanding of the Representative Assembly (of which he was himself a member) a much more punitive policy towards its partisans. Their stipends and perquisites should be examined by a tribunal and a fine levied on the regents to help alleviate the ills which their infamy had brought about. In addition he urged that a penal commission be established to try the most flagrant cases of "oppression" and "plunder," and primary assemblies convened so that direct elections could be held for a new, definitive provincial legislature.

This marriage of popular democracy and punitive politics was an exact reflection of the campaign then being waged in Holland by Gerrit Paape and the popular societies. Like his Holland counterparts, van Vridagh used the petition as the first of his weapons. On September 2 he presented his "programme," supported by a list of 2,000 names, culled from the entire province, to the president of the assembly Carel de Vos van Steenwijk. Neither de Vos nor the conservative majority in the Assembly was ready to capitulate so readily to van Vridagh's blandishments. Relying on the goodwill of locally stationed French troops, they called his bluff later in the month. As it turned out, Deventer proved a safe enough bastion against sporadic sorties by armed militia from Zwolle and, even had the affair not turned into an inter-urban quarrel, it seemed that van Vridagh's influence among the militiamen was significantly less than in the halls of the clubs. At any rate de Vos van Steenwijk succeeded in fending off his campaign until the more abundant harvests of 1795 defused what had threatened to be a second revolution in Overijssel. But though that eventuality had been averted, the episode had demonstrated very effectively how easily matters could get out of control, even in a province as reputedly placid as Overijssel.

The emergence of budding, if still incoherent, forms of popular democracy was an unnerving experience for many of those who had been extolling its virtues without being directly exposed to its effects. The great Free Corps assemblies of the 1780's, which had certainly had their more unruly moments, were by now little more than memories from the heroic past of the Patriots. The reading societies of the 1790's had been relatively genteel affairs, with surreptitious conspirators concealing copies of *Common Sense* or Paulus' tract on *Equality* behind improving editions of *Clarissa Harlow* and Wagenaer's *History*. The instructional function of those societies had been preserved in the Batavian clubs, but had become more explicitly political, and designed to fashion an electorate of vigilant democrats. Gerrit Paape wrote that a

> popular society must provide a school for citizens where through the best, most accessible and direct means they may be educated in the pure doctrine of Patriotism. It must be a meeting place and a focal point for the good-hearted, the right-minded, the intelligent and the able. For it is there that the best forms of government . . . may be learned . . . and the people may learn what can, may and must be done to promote the general welfare.[39]

Given the relative novelty of any form of political participation for the rank-and-file of those who made up the membership of the clubs, the abrasiveness of many of their utterances was remarkably precocious. A meeting at Rotterdam of over a hundred of the societies in Holland in July 1795 conceded nothing to the French *sociétés populaires* in its innocent mangling of Rousseauite nostrums. "The Representatives [of Holland]," it insisted, "are merely the executors of our Will since we have alienated no part of our sovereignty. We, the People, must be sovereigns since we are the industrious part of the Nation on whose peace and well-being the rest depend."[40]

The clubs were the most direct means by which the minority of militant journalists, publicists and orators could come into contact with the republican rank-and-file. But the most effective mobilisation of that constituency took place at *wijk-vergaderingen*: district, ward or quarter meetings. These meetings were, like so much of the emblems of the Patriot revolt, part and parcel of the Dutch communal past. They were best established in the most long-lived communities like Dordrecht and Utrecht, where they had originated as informal meetings of areas of the city to regulate parochial matters such as public refuse or the watch and to collect local dues for pastoral purposes. But like that other venerable Dutch institution the *schutterij*, the *wijk* meetings had been given highly charged political connotations by the revolution. Like the Paris "sections" they were, in their political form, a product rather than a cause of the conflict, but once established made their own contribution to its development. Like the sections too they had been resuscitated for the purpose of electing the new municipalities; but in so doing, they had given men whose relatively humble social station would have ruled out any kind of political activity before 1795 an opportunity to make themselves known as watchdogs of the sovereignty of the people.

The more articulate and able among them such as Pieter Baalde in Rotterdam or Willem Holtrop in Amsterdam spoke of the meetings as the primary cells of the new democracy; the "gatherings of the burghers" to which their elected representatives were axiomatically answerable. They showed themselves, moreover, much keener to punish "aristocrats" or "Orange tyrants" for their sins than their social superiors in the Patriot élite who continued to preach the virtues of magnanimity. Their fieriest tirades were reserved for those who had been permitted to leave office quietly with their ill-gotten gains intact while good Patriots were made to pay for their own liberation. If they were not yet full-fledged social egalitarians, many of their spokesmen nonetheless displayed a violent hostility to luxury, plutocracy, and the manners of patrician society in terms reminiscent of the tone of sans-culotte diatribes. One very important pamphlet, written specifically for the *wijk* meetings of Amsterdam, actually treated the contemptible rich as men "formerly going by the description of 'respectable' [*fatsoenlijk*] but among whom there are many who are far less worthy and able than among those associated with a humbler station. . . ."[41] And in an effort to give them some moral improvement, the author called on the members of this socially useless class to attend their *wijk* meetings diligently where they might rub shoulders with

. . . virtuous artisans and tradesmen [thereby] creating a mutual respect while the so-called Gentleman (a title which can no longer exist, for while there are Gentlemen there must also be Slaves and the Equality of Man is our Gospel) will leave off his imaginary superiority if he attends meetings with due regularity . . . if he be a truly upright man he will recognise that the humbler Burgher is a man of greater understanding and truer principle than those in the circles which he has been accustomed to frequent. . . .

The furore raised by the clubs and *wijk* meetings in the summer and autumn of 1795 put the provincial representative assemblies on the horns of a dilemma. On the one hand they needed the assistance of the rank-and-file to dislodge those recalcitrant regents and councillors who had either refused to budge from office or had crept back into local committees as Patriot notables. They would certainly need their help in the future if a National Assembly was to replace the States-General. At the same time, however, they were acutely sensitive to the dangers of letting the clubs have their head. Many who by their own lights were good democrats were unable to countenance the prospect of incessant interference by irate city crowds in the proper conduct of their administration. The assemblies in Brabant and Overijssel had weathered the agitation against their representatives without too much injury being done to their government. But the situation in Holland was much more threatening. The concentration of population in that province, and in particular in its larger cities, made the potential strength of clubs and *wijk* meetings a more ominous possibility: even were the municipalities able to divert popular pressure in the direction of local regent villains, there was always the chance of the agitation backfiring.

This is exactly what happened at Rotterdam. On June 14 a large, noisy and, according to many witnesses, liberally intoxicated crowd assembled in front of the Stadhuis demanding the arrest of the head sheriff of the city and ex-*wethouder*, one van Staveren, commonly vilified as the arch-reactionary of 1787 and 1788. The crowd also insisted on a purge from top to bottom of every public official who had held a post between 1787 and 1795. For several hours the Stadhuis remained besieged while the municipality sweated within over whether or not to call out the city militia to restore order. In the end their reasonable doubts about the allegiance of that guard got the better of their limited supply of valour and they acquiesced in the arrest of the unfortunate van Staveren. The man was dragged from his house, and though mauled severely by the crowd reached the city jail without any serious hurt. The Rotterdam councillors were aware of the dangerous precedent they had set. As soon as the city had calmed down, they sent a letter to the provincial assembly at The Hague indicating that they had been coerced into making the arrest and that they would not take averse a directive from the superior body saying as much. The Hague Assembly duly obliged by declaring the proceedings of June 14 illegal and a violation of the Rights of Man, when "the sovereignty of the people is so publicly flouted and a mere section of the people seeks to force its will on those to whom the whole people have entrusted with their government. . . ."[42]

But neither this declaration nor the despatch of a delegation to Rotterdam succeeded in cowing the rebellious spirit of the club and *wijk* leaders, who assembled even larger crowds to protest at interference in what they insisted was a purely domestic issue. They added, more ominously, that unless the representatives "hear the voice of the people," the "wrath of the virtuous and right-minded citizenry, provoked beyond endurance, would explode." In the end a compromise was patched up between the commission and the radical leaders by which "unlawful" acts were revoked but van Staveren remained in custody—only at the pleasure of the "People of Holland," not the municipality of Rotterdam. The riots had persuaded The Hague Assembly to make a timely concession to the punitive mood of the urban crowds in order to avoid further challenges to its own still fragile authority. On June 22 it established a commission of twenty-four under the chairmanship of Gerrit Paape, the hero of the clubs and prolific journalist, to investigate the financial misdemeanours of the previous administration—the nearest the Batavian Republic had yet approached to any kind of revolutionary tribunal.[43]

Before the summer was out further interventions from the Holland Assembly were needed to pacify disturbances at Haarlem, Dordrecht and Leiden. In Amsterdam, however, their attitude toward the club and *wijk* meetings was far more permissive. In that city the chief threat to republican sovereignty seemed to be "aristocracy," not "anarchy." More than in any other city in the Republic, the "Representatives of the People of Amsterdam" —elected by acclamation rather than vote on January 19—had shown a marked distaste for any abrupt departure from past habits. Eager as they were to see the backs of men regarded as little more than Orangist puppets, they viewed their return to office as the reversion to the natural order of things. They were certainly not prepared to tolerate a wholesale revolutionising of the government of the city, still less a root-and-branch purge of every official who had continued to function during the Restoration. The latter proposal Professors Cras and van Swinden, both of the Amsterdam Athenaeum, denounced in the Holland Assembly as Jacobinical tyranny. Their *raison d'être* was the strength, independence and prosperity of the "hoofdstad." As they saw matters, they had not rid the city of the Orangist gang to deliver it over to a rival bunch of ne'er-do-wells, incompetents and fanatics on the order of an alleged "revolution." Throughout 1795 the municipal authorities resisted as fiercely as they could the two-pronged attack on their authority from the Holland Assembly at The Hague and from the radical clubs inside the city. Above all they attacked the proposal to redistribute the provincial representation in equal electoral districts so that "the merest village would stand equal with the mighty and populous metropolis of Amsterdam."[44]

The determination of the municipality of Amsterdam to protect its freedom of action drove Pieter Paulus and his colleagues directly into the arms of the city clubs. Obviously, therefore, it was issues of sovereignty rather than issues of democracy which conditioned their response to city politics. Rotterdam, Leiden and Haarlem had been supported in their defence against the clubs because in so doing they had implicitly accepted the authority of the provincial representatives; Amsterdam was attacked because its attitude was quite the reverse. In the free-for-all which characterised the post-revolutionary situation, it seemed imperative to Paulus to reduce Amsterdam's special status if he wished to prevent the Batavian Republic from dissolving into so many independent enclaves. He was fortunate in having allies within the city itself. Samuel Wiselius, the solitary democratic renegade on the Amsterdam delegation at The Hague, had made his enthusiasm for the clubs public and with the city commandant Kraijenhoff had set about mobilising support in the city districts for an attack on the municipality.

The machinery for such a campaign was already to hand, brought into being by the activities of the Revolutionary Committee in December and January. Though there were districts of the city, notably the dockyards on the IJ, where republican politicians were inhospitably received, the "Bijltjes" had ceased, with the revolution, to be a very threatening force. They were, moreover, at least as hostile to the new patricians in the Stadhuis as to their opponents in the clubs, and went their own way making occasional Orangist forays into the Patriot clubs and cafés in the centre of the city. With the exception of three wards on the wealthiest canals, numbers 38, 56 and 57, opponents of the municipality dominated the district meetings.[45] Through the medium of a central bureau they sent delegates to a "General Assembly" of the *wijken*, just as each local club provided representatives for a "Central Society." Thus the forces of popular politics in Amsterdam were organised on a far more sophisticated basis than anywhere else in the Republic (with the possible exception of Utrecht). Holtrop, the chairman of the General Assembly; Dirk Hoitsma, the president of the Central Society; and van Hogendorp van Hofwegen, the senior officer of the burgher militia, constituted a powerful triumvirate on whom Wiselius and Paulus relied for their challenge to the city government.

Even in the first months of the life of the Batavian Republic, those who had coalesced to bring it into existence were at each others' throats over the key issue of sovereignty. On three separate occasions in 1795 the assembly of the "People of Holland" and the city authorities in Amsterdam came into head-on collision. The first such occasion was on March 19, when the municipality rejected the oath which The Hague representatives had demanded of all public officials in the province acknowledging the sovereignty of the people and its investiture in the representative assembly. The Amsterdam Council pointed out that this would constitute an act of deference which they had never made even to the old States of Holland. They not only refused the oath but addressed a counter-remonstrance to the assembly arguing that as a strictly provisional and, for that matter, irregularly convened body, it had no right to dictate to Amsterdam, or indeed to any other city, the conditions on which its own public officers might serve. In other words the municipality was re-stating in a spirited manner the traditional rights of the sovereign cities to autonomy in their own domestic government. The Hague Assembly responded with the weapons of what it asserted to be "popular sovereignty." On the 19th, in collusion with Wiselius, Kraijenhoff and the triumvirate, a commission was admitted to the city. The next day an instant siege of the town hall was conjured up by the Central Society as the commission demanded the acceptance of the oath and the revocation of the offensive remonstrance. As usual on these occasions, however, the leaders of the popular demonstration went further than had been intended by insisting on the dismissal of six members of the municipality they considered most opposed to the oath. Under pressure from the crowds the six duly departed from office, but the rump of the council, refusing to bow to force, continued to reject the oath of allegiance. They were calculating that The Hague commissioners might flinch before they permitted the crowds on the streets to run amok over the centre of the city—and they were proved absolutely right. In the last resort, the fear that the riot might boil over into general mayhem prevailed over the desire to see the councillors humiliated. A compromise was concocted, by which the oath was watered down to please the council, order was restored in the streets, the six expelled members restored to office and the impertinent remonstrance duly rescinded. Face had been saved, but not much else.

On April 11 the municipality drove home their victory by publishing an electoral regulation for the city which was tailor-made to perpetuate the influence of the patrician élite. Electors in the primary assemblies were restricted to men over twenty-five who had paid a specific amount in direct and indirect taxation over the previous years. Added to stringent domiciliary qualifications, these restrictions succeeded in paring down the electorate to all but about 8,000 of the more reliable citizens from the better-off districts. On June 19 the first "College" elected under these regulations was installed in office. Predictably it included Jan Bicker, Nicolas van Staphorst, a van der Hoop and Professor Jan Hendrik van Swinden. Half the new council gave their address as either the Keizersgracht or the Herengracht, the two most sumptuous canals in the city.[46]

Emboldened by its success, Amsterdam assumed the leadership of the conservative opposition to a democratic and unitary Republic. It dissociated itself from the Holland Assembly's proposals for a National Convention to be elected directly throughout the Batavian Republic and to replace the States-General delegations. In October it added its weight to that of Zeeland,

Groningen and Friesland, which were continuing to insist on the preservation of provincial sovereignty. The only threat to this resolute campaign of obstruction came from below, where the clubs and *wijk* meetings were preparing, in collusion with Wiselius, to sabotage the saboteurs. The presence at Osnabrück of the impetuous Prince Frederick with a loyal remnant of the Stadholder's army, moreover, added to their campaign the invaluable asset of a patriotic emergency. Exaggerated rumours of the strength of the Osnabrück Assembly had excited fears that a repetition of the invasion of 1787 might be in the offing. Prussia had made her peace with France but had not yet recognised the Batavian Republic. In actual fact, a secret clause of the Treaty of Basel had ruled out any such independent offensives. But heads as level as Wiselius' were swayed by rumours that Frederick William II had supplied 25,000 troops to his sister, and there were verified agents' reports that Prince Frederick was expecting a rebellion by the Orangist societies to support the invasion when it finally materialised. The circulation of these stories, lent further credence by a pamphlet published by Wiselius' own cousin, was enough to create an atmosphere of panic in Amsterdam bordering on hysteria. Wiselius bemoaned the wretched state of the city's defences and insisted that the citizens' militia be augmented, a step the municipality was exceedingly reluctant to entertain. Throughout September the "General Assembly" of the *wijk* meetings had demanded that any unreliable elements remaining in offices of public trust be weeded out and notorious ex-regents incarcerated immediately as a potential fifth column. The rejection by both the States-General and the municipality of a broadly established National Guard suddenly took on a more dramatic and sinister character amid the mounting apprehension.

On Wednesday, November 4, these tensions snapped. While the members of the municipal council were deliberating, they were interrupted by a large deputation from the clubs and the *wijk* meetings, repeating their demands for the arrest of the most dangerous Orangists, and in particular David Elias, the ex-head sheriff and the arch-villain of 1787.[47] Supported by noisy crowds on the streets they added a demand that the councillors who, as a result of their prevarication, had "lost the trust of the citizens of Amsterdam" should be removed and that a member of the militia who had been arrested for publishing and distributing a seditious pamphlet should be freed. When the council insisted that it could not receive collective petitions, let alone demands, but only requests from individual citizens, the deputation retorted that if that were the case it would be better if the rights of Batavian citizens were entrusted to wiser guardianship!

Although Holtrop, the leader of the deputation, had made no plans for more physical gestures of dissatisfaction, the news of the confrontation at the town hall acted as a stimulant for those among the crowds who had no such inhibitions. Conspicuous among these were units of the infantry and cavalry militia who throughout October had been on the verge of mutiny and had been conducting themselves with dangerous arrogance in the city. Though they were not congregating in very substantial numbers, there were enough of them in an ugly mood to make the keeper of the town hall watch nervous for its inmates and apprehensive lest they seize the city keys. At one point their impromptu leader, a distillery owner called Gerrit van Nes, managed to confront members of the council, who then threatened him with proceedings for riot—an act of boldness which virtually ensured that the disorder would continue through the day. Sure enough the city keys did fall into the hands of the militia, who promptly locked the gates to prevent the exit of the enemy regents.

The following afternoon a platoon of horse guards, led by a bank functionary, a wine-shop assistant and a tobacco stall owner, went on a violent rampage in the centre of the city. After they had broken into a coffee house in the Kalverstraat where a few Jews were sitting peaceably, they roughed up the rooms and put the customers to flight, beating up one of them on the way out. Their next stop was Berckmeyer's coffee house, known as a haunt of Orangists, where they became even more uncontrollable. Before they could be evicted by the waiters and servants, they had slashed one of the customers about the head and face with a sabre and caused general havoc in the house. With conditions in the city rapidly deteriorating, the municipality decided to swallow its pride and call on the Holland Assembly for assistance. Paulus played his hand with calm and tact, despatching General Laurent with the force necessary for the restoration of order but making it clear that the pacification was carried out in the name of the "Representatives of the People of Holland." This de facto imposition of the sovereignty of province over city was further underlined when, after impassioned pleading by Gogel and Wiselius, the provincial High Court at The Hague interfered in the judicial proceedings dealing with the chief rioters. Van Nes, who had been said (predictably, given his profession) to have been "under the influence of fanaticism and strong drink in equal parts," had been given a severe prison sentence and an exile from the city for six years by the Amsterdam court. The provincial court commuted this to three years, and set aside the sentences imposed on the café rioters on the grounds that they should have been subject to the military proceedings of the militia!

As long as the city remained disturbed the powers at The Hague had a useful lever with which to exert influence over the insubordinate councillors of the "hoofdstad." It was understandable, then, that the municipality suspected (not entirely without reason) that Wiselius, who was a member of The Hague Assembly's commission, had been partly responsible for aggravating if not actually inciting the disorder. After yet another fracas on November 23, when a crowd attempting to hunt down the fugitive Elias took his absence from his house on the Keizersgracht as an invitation to ransack it from top to bottom and wreck the fixtures and fittings with great thoroughness, the council deposed Wiselius from its delegation to The Hague. There was even some question of bringing proceedings against him for complicity in the troubles. But although the council presented its action as a stand on its constitutional rights, it was in fact acting *unconstitutionally* since the provincial representatives at the assembly were of course elected by primary meetings and not nominated by the municipality. Their irregular action merely succeeded in hastening the day when, on February 2, 1796, Paulus published the "Regulation" governing the future constitution of the province. In direct opposition to the wishes of Amsterdam, Holland was to be divided into twenty electoral districts, each to be further subdivided into thirty primary constituencies with a franchise embracing all males over twenty independent of public charity.

The see-saw of power between the most powerful province of the old Union and the most powerful city in that province had not yet come to an end. Further spasmodic bouts of crowd hostility and shows of resistance by the municipality were to reach a new climax in May 1796. But the events of the first year of the Batavian Republic had been sufficiently troubled to expose the problem of competing and colliding authorities, historically a peculiarly Dutch dilemma, in their most acute form. By the end of 1795 there was still no centre of gravity to the revolution, no generally recognised institution embodying the sacred "sovereignty of the people" on every politician's lips. As long as the States-General, the rock of the *old* Republic, remained—partly reformed, partly intact, acknowledged "provisional" yet apparently immovable—the situation could only deteriorate further. It was as though the Tennis Court Oath of 1789 had been sworn in separate Estates of clergy, nobility and commons. The anomalies of this predicament had been highlighted at the end of August 1795, when a meeting of representatives of clubs from most of the provinces of the Republic was convened in The Hague. Sitting barely a stone's throw away from both the States-General and the Holland Assembly at the Doelen Hall, this "Central Assembly of the Patriotic Societies of the Fatherland" looked uncommonly as though it were making a bid to be acknowledged as the *true* "representation of the people." The curious reality of the matter was that none of these bodies could legitimate such a claim; all were essentially nominated meetings from competing constituencies. But ever since the great Free Corps assemblies at Utrecht from 1785 to 1787 had claimed representative rights by virtue of their very existence, it was open to any body of delegates from clubs, town meetings or militia to do the same. The States-General had issued several rodomontades against this proliferation of assemblies during the summer when there had been informal meetings at The Hague and at Rotterdam, but the August gathering was the most serious since it was by far the best-organised effort to date to steal the thunder of the senior politicians. The "Central Assembly" appointed a president and a steering committee, and equipped itself with all the paraphernalia of parliamentary regulations. Sessions were to be made open to the public (who were nonetheless to be separated from deputies by a tricolour ribbon).[48] Aware of the accusation that they were infringing the sovereignty of the officially constituted organs of the Republic, the members of the "Central" disclaimed any intention of its being convicted as a "*Ryk* within a *Ryk*." But their disclaimer was not without its ambiguities since at the same time they insisted that their "first and most sacred duty was to see that there is but *one* People's Legislature and but one executive power established in a true and properly elected representation . . . and a good, just and patriotic government. To advance this sacred goal this assembly shall use all lawful means within its power. . . . "[49]

The ostensibly modest language of such declarations and the "Central's" insistence that it was acting merely as a pressure group to "persuade" the people's representatives that their duty lay in convening a National Assembly without further delay did little to ease the anxieties of the States-General. Even if it did not harbour ambitions to become a Convention, it looked sufficiently like a grand conclave of Dutch Jacobins to give them serious qualms. When the "Central" proceeded to present its own plan for the immediate summoning of a National Convention based on the direct votes of primary assemblies, their suspicion that it was acting as the Trojan horse for clubmens' democracy seemed vindicated. On October 18, at the urgent prompting of its more moderate deputies as well as the equally apprehensive French agents, the States finally issued a proclamation declaring the "Central" a danger to liberty. It forbade it to continue proceedings on pain of being outlawed as an "inciter of sedition and public unrest" (the identical formula to that used by the Stadholderian authorities in proscribing the Patriot meetings!). Despite the fact that on September 4, in a public ceremony mimicking the Tennis Court Oath, the "Central" had linked hands in a "knot of brotherhood" and had vowed never to separate until the "sacred goal" of the Convention had been achieved, and despite Gerrit Paape's versified exhortations to "triumph o'er with tongue or hand/The cursed tyrants through the land," the "valiant brothers" backed off from a trial of strength with the States-General.[50] "Adjourning" their deliberations, the delegates repaired to their respective provinces to canvass for the National Convention, using the corresponding bureaux they had established at The Hague and Amsterdam.

By avoiding a sustained show of defiance, a situation comparable to the French crisis of sovereignty in 1789 had been avoided. The analogy, it is true, should not be overworked. The representative credentials of the "Central" were hardly as impressive as the Third Estate; the urban crowds of Holland were never as prone to sanguine violence as their French counterparts, and the Osnabrück Assembly turned out to be an even damper squib than the preposterous buffooneries of the émigrés at Coblentz and Turin. But however marginal the actual danger, the French representatives at The Hague felt that it had been a close call. Richard had been horrified to witness a demonstration of nearly 2,000 calling for the Convention on September 24, and hardly less unnerved by Paulus' apparent indifference to such disorder. "Do you wish to abandon yourselves to all the horrors of anarchy," he had warned the burghers of Utrecht, "and found your government over the corpses of thousands?"[51] His own government would not have been so casual. Only a few months before, the Thermidorian regime had survived the swansong of the sans-culotte sections in the uprisings of Germinal and Prairial.

Now that they were engaged in emasculating what was left of popular protest by liquidating the clubs or reducing them to impotent "constitutional circles," it must have seemed alarmingly quixotic that the Dutch were about to invite disaster by conducting polite discourse with revolutionary clubs located in the very proximity of their governing bodies! To correct these errors of judgment François Noël, the first ambassador to the Batavian Republic, was required by his official "Instruction" to "enlighten the Batavian Patriots on all the experience of our own revolution and defend them against the excesses and miseries from which only the robust constitution of France can prevent them falling victim."[52]

This beginners' course in revolutionary tactics was not provided gratis from purely fraternal motives. The French were concerned that the "revolutionary phase" in the Netherlands should be terminated as quickly as possible so that the new Republic might play its allotted role in the war against the British. The most important priority was the reconstruction of an allied naval power strong enough to turn the balance of power in the North Sea and the Atlantic and, if required, provide support for a landing in Ireland or even closer to the heart of Britain. While they were full of admiration for Paulus' miracle-working in getting twelve ships-of-the-line fitted out and ready for sailing within nine months of assuming power, they remained convinced that only the establishment of a strong and stable constitution would provide the energetic, efficient administration they wanted from their Dutch ally. The least that was needed was an ordered constituent assembly. Quite apart from its constituent function, this would act as a prophylactic against further "anarchy" from the clubs and *wijk* meetings where Noël saw the spawning grounds of neo-Jacobinism. With the weight of an authentic national sovereignty behind it, this would supply the needed authority to keep such disruptive elements in their place.

Anxiety about the continuing instability of Dutch politics was not confined to the French. In a series of written reports, communicated first to Boissy d'Anglas on the Committee of Public Safety and later to Charles Delacroix, the Minister for Foreign Affairs, Jan Bicker sketched a scene of the most abandoned anarchy and lawlessness.[53] Such a state of affairs, he added (no doubt with a shrewd eye to French preoccupations), was not only undermining political and social peace in the Netherlands but crippling the Dutch contribution to the war effort. No doubt, he observed, echoing a fashionable French fantasy, the "Jacobin anarchists" were in the pay of the British, who had a special interest in seeing both republics brought to their knees through domestic in-fighting. Bicker's hope was that if they were persuaded that the democrats and their camp followers in the clubs were the enemies of the alliance, French military support might be coaxed away from Paulus and the Holland Assembly and lent instead to the conservative patrician interests he represented. To flatter their amour-propre he was even prepared to suggest that a forceful intervention and the imposition of the French constitution of 1795 might be what was required to bring the Dutch to their senses. And anticipating objections, he even obligingly supplied a form of words whereby, while disclaiming any intention of violating the Treaty of The Hague by interfering in the domestic affairs of their ally, France would merely point out to the Dutch leadership that it would have to choose between its fondness for the clubs and the interests of the alliance.

The new French Directory, like the committees of the Convention it replaced, was less receptive to Bicker's open-handed invitation than he would have liked. As long as Paulus continued to find the wherewithal to pay the instalments of the indemnity and the maintenance of the French army, and as long as he could keep up his success in refloating the Dutch navy, they were happy to remain disentangled from the intricacies of Dutch politics.[54] But the French were baffled by the apparent inability of their neighbours to equip themselves, even after a year of republican liberty, with a stable National Assembly and a sound constitution. Understandably the French were in the habit of measuring revolutions by the dizzy tempo of 1789 and 1790, beside which the Dutch certainly looked slothful to the point of inertia. As far as they could see, the Batavian Republic still had to agree on the *basis* by which a constituent of some kind might be convened, which could possibly then proceed to hammer out a constitution which could just conceivably prove acceptable to the nation at large. In such matters they found the Dutch preposterously finicky. They attributed the unconscionable delay not only to legendary sluggishness but to a certain pusillanimity among their leaders when it came to dealing with sections of the population who, though confessedly inimical to the new order, were left undisturbed.

In fact, the French would have been the first to take fright had the Dutch resorted to the instruments of Terror to deal with the "aristocrats," "anarchists" and other enemies of the republican peace; yet there was some truth in their suspicions. It was a notable feature of many of the Dutch politicians, not least Paulus himself, that they were concerned to legitimise their actions with the gloss of consent. Admirable no doubt in itself, as the French saw it this was decidedly peculiar in men of an allegedly revolutionary persuasion. Even where they owed their position to the sanction of force, they continued to believe that if they had originally overcome their enemies with might, it was the rightness of their cause that would win them the national mandate on which their government was to be grounded.

The legal fastidiousness shown by Paulus and his colleagues in 1795 has been much applauded by Dutch historians; Geyl, in particular, saw it as the authentic hallmark of the national style. That may or may not be the case. It was patently true that the ingenuous faith that all opposition could be sweetened into submission given time and patience handicapped the protagonists of a new political order. It meant, for example, that Paulus seemed quite content to defer to the States-General in the important matter of deciding the ways and means in which a new constituent might be convened and its terms of reference. To be sure, the States-General had escaped much of the odium which had attached to its Captain-General. Even if it was a traditional institution, indeed the very embodiment of the old constitution, it had not assembled in social ranks like its French counterpart, nor was it an institutional anachronism, sprung from oblivion to help the executive out of a tight corner. In short, it was not thought of as ipso facto "aristocratic." All the same, it was naïve of the Hollanders interested in establishing a unitary sovereign Republic to suppose that a body comprising delegations mandated by provincial assemblies would voluntarily liquidate every vestige of provincial and federal authority.

When its plan for a National Assembly appeared on May 29, it confirmed the worst apprehensions of the shrewder pessimists like Wiselius.[55] For while paying some lip service to the principle of "One and Indivisible" and setting out a complicated scheme of elections, it proposed the retention of both the States-General and the provincial assemblies as sovereign bodies pending the adoption of a new constitution. In case even these suggestions were thought too draconian, it added that a constitutional commission should only go to work if three-quarters of the elected assembly was agreeable. Thus the "National Convention," envisaged by the Holland Assembly as both a legislature and a constituent, had been whittled down to little more than an elected advisory commission, stripped of any powers to delegate to an executive or any semblance of representing the national sovereignty.

Six days later, on June 3, the Holland representatives reacted to that plan by appointing their own commission to draft an alternative to be re-submitted to the States. That commission included four of the ablest politicians in Holland and men who were committed to revolutionary change: Paulus himself; Pieter Leonard van de Kasteele, the ex-Pensionary of Haarlem and a formidable financial administrator; Samuel Wiselius; and George Hahn, another of Paulus' circle and a councillor of Leiden. Other than Wiselius there were no Amsterdammers on the commission, and it was against the fierce opposition of that city that the results of its work were published on July 28. The document amounted to the fullest statement of the aims of the democrats and unitarists in the province.[56] It stipulated that the National Assembly was to be invested with full legislative, executive and constituent powers and that it was to *replace* the States-General. Likewise its executive agencies were to replace the old committees of the States-General and were, moreover, to be empowered to act in areas where the States had had only very limited competence—finance and police being two in point. The colleges of the five "Admiralties" were to give way to single national military authorities, and legal and fiscal systems were to be provided for the whole Republic. Briefly, the provincial autonomy which had been the backbone of the federal Republic was to be written off. Not only were the deputies to the assembly to vote strictly by head rather than province or city; the constitutional draft they were to produce was to be submitted not to provincial assemblies but to the entire national electorate for its assent.

By September 10, when the States-General appointed yet another committee to attempt to draw up a digest of all the schemes so far presented, it was apparent that there were two versions which stood in sharpest opposition to each other. In simplest terms one was conservative, the other revolutionary;

one the culmination of the reformist federalism which the Patriot regents had embraced a decade before in the Constitutional Restoration, the other the fruit of democratic notions of popular sovereignty and nationalist axioms of the monistic state. Initially it seemed that the more cautious approach was bound to prevail. Holland's plan smacked to the French of the notorious document of 1793 in permitting too wide a franchise and too much latitude to the primary assemblies. Of the six remaining provinces only Utrecht, traditionally an ally of Holland, voted in favour of the plan. In Overijssel, the popular societies in the three towns remained embattled with their own representative assembly whose final vote could not be confidently predicted. A similar situation obtained in Groningen, where the nucleus of Patriot force was concentrated in the city but heavily outweighed by the rural and landed interests in the province. Gelderland also remained uncommitted but, like Overijssel, anxious lest political amalgamation carried with it a heavier fiscal burden. Brabant and Drente had not yet been officially admitted to the States and so were out of the reckoning as far as votes went. But the most uncompromising and tenacious opposition came from Zeeland and Friesland.

Both those provinces were, in a very small way, maritime competitors of Holland and resented the latter's casual abolition of their admiralties in the name of some nostrum of national solidarity. Both provinces were steeped in a long tradition of opposition to Holland's periodic assumption of hegemony within the Union, and both had a maritime populace—fisherfolk and dock workers—which remained defiantly Orangist in its political sympathies. They shared, moreover, the land provinces' suspicions in advocating an amalgamation of provincial debts and taxes. By assuming a proportionally larger share of the colossal deficit incurred by Holland over the past century, the lesser maritime and land provinces only stood to lose. For its part, Holland was not at all shy of pointing out that the Republic was obliged to spend 85 million guilders *over and above* the ordinary budgetary provision, simply to meet the first indemnity instalments, the costs of maintaining the French and her own army, and the servicing of the debt arrears of the nation. Under current arrangements Holland alone was obliged to find no less than 50 million guilders. Its provincial debt was then running at around 460 million guilders, over 100 million of it incurred since 1780, compared with a Friesian debt of 32 million, Groningen's of 10 million, and Overijssel's of 9. True, Holland's resources, even in these lean times, were still probably more substantial than all the rest of the Republic's put together; but there was no doubt that its finances were suffering extreme strain. On July 17 the provinces had been obliged to follow van de Spiegel by converting what had been a "voluntary loan" into a forced levy.[57]

More purely political anxieties played their part in hardening the opposition to the Holland plan for a National Assembly based on unitary sovereignty. Two-fifths of the Dutch Republic's population were Hollanders, one-seventeenth only Friesians, and the fear of being swallowed up in a unitary Republic dominated by Holland's wealth and numbers remained very real for Friesland, which spoke its own language and thought of itself very much as a separate and distinct "nation." Moreover, the Patriot notability who still held the upper hand in the representative assemblies of Zeeland and Friesland looked on Holland as an alien threat to their own internal power. They were themselves beginning to come under some pressure from clubs and popular meetings in their towns, and they saw in Holland a province already overrun by Jacobinical scum baying for the blood of aristocrats—a dreadful omen of things to come. Their worst nightmare was an alliance between the radicals of Middelburg and Leeuwarden with the Jacobin Central Assembly at The Hague, a waking dream which seemed to have actually materialised in Amsterdam! A letter from the regents of Zeeland to their colleagues in Groningen and Friesland spoke of

. . . the hue and cry of the Central Assembly and the dogmas of journalists, in which ignorance and rashness compete for pride of place (and) the demands for an amalgamation of the provinces and unity in government are made in the name of that shibboleth of "patriotism."[58]

Despite the likelihood of a complete deadlock over the issue of the assembly, the commission of the States-General charged with finalising a plan made a spirited effort to find some patch of common ground between the antagonists. Indeed, the situation was not quite as hopeless as it seemed. To secure the adherence of the wavering land provinces, Holland was prepared to jettison some of its more militant unitarist principles. On October 14 an amended draft regulation duly appeared, accepting that the States-General would disappear on the debut of the new assembly. On the other hand the new body was to be given legislative, but not effective executive power, which, in respect of the most important areas such as finance, remained in the hands of provincial assemblies and committees. This important concession to provincial sovereignty was underlined by the additional proviso that the constitutional commission would be composed of delegates from the provincial bodies and so arranged that Holland could not claim more than six of the twenty-one members. These qualifications appeared to be enough to induce Overijssel and Gelderland to vote for the regulation. The States-General, however, was determined that all proper formalities should be observed, and gave the provinces until November 25 to "consult" their respective peoples in whatever manner they saw fit.

Holland wasted no time at all. The following day its representatives passed a motion put to them by their president, Wiselius, that the National Assembly be convened no later than February 1796. Their deputies seem to have wanted the best of both worlds since although accepting the States-General's draft regulation, they made it clear that they deeply regretted the retention of provincial sovereignty and would never abandon the keystone principles of unitary sovereignty and popular democracy. More ominously, they declared that if by November 25 no further progress had been made towards the summoning of the new assembly, Holland would invite like-minded provinces to join it in an independent unitary Republic of the Netherlands.

This was moonshine, obviously intended as a threat, not a promise. In any case the dissenting provinces were not to be moved by minatory rhetoric. If anything they appeared to be more entrenched in their federalism. Groningen reported that it wanted *both* a States-General *and* a National Assembly to be convened pending the enactment of the constitution. Zeeland and Friesland, however, were only prepared to permit a commission of two delegates to enquire whether anything at all was wrong with the present constitution. Their statements declared in no uncertain terms that radical changes could only do irreparable injury to the nation. The Zeeland representatives concluded their summons to rally round the Union of Utrecht on an heroic note:

If the noble edifice of this Commonwealth, once a miracle in the eyes of all Europe, is destined to fall through the undermining of its own constitution, shall not we, at least, amid the general ruin, give ourselves the satisfaction of refusing to lend assistance to such acts? This letter will (at least) leave for posterity, in the annals of this erstwhile sovereign province, an imperishable monument to the honour of the Zeeland people.[59]

The impasse was dramatic. Yet again, as in 1787, the Republic had divided into two bitterly hostile camps. Unlike the earlier crisis, the chances of actual civil war seemed remote. But so did any means of reconciliation. On November 25 the States-General did its bounden duty by passing the regulation for the new assembly by four votes to three (the non-voting Brabant and Drente also adding their silent assent). It was a pyrrhic victory, for a "National Assembly" without Zeeland, Friesland and Groningen would scarcely be a credible affair. Moreover, Overijssel was beginning to have second thoughts and to demand better assurances that its financial autonomy would not be compromised by the new body. Despite the Holland ultimatum of October 15, neither Paulus nor Wiselius had any wish to preside over a miserably truncated Batavian Republic with scant chance of surviving as a truly independent state. Obviously the renegades had to be brought round to the view of the majority. Yet to effect this without offending against the canons of legality, until now impeccably observed by the Hollanders, seemed virtually impossible. In fact, by giving encouragement not only to the popular societies in Holland and Utrecht but also to their counterparts in Zwolle, Groningen, Goes, Middelburg, Franeker and Leeuwarden, and urging them to campaign against the intransigence of their respective representative assemblies, the politicians in The Hague had already brought pressure to bear on their opponents. Their age of innocence was more transient than many would have cared to admit. A meeting in The Hague invited representatives from all nine provinces to join discussions on the establishment of a National Guard, and only the most stringent penalties succeeded in preventing delegates from the Friesland towns from attending. As the contest became progressively more polarised, even men of calm tempers and fine principles like Paulus were inclined to discard their scruples and contemplate using the final sanction of force. That, after all, was what revolution was about.

Furthermore, Paulus was encouraged in his growing resolution to break the stalemate by the ambassador of France which, until recently, had been very concerned to restrain the Dutch from any resort to revolutionary force. The new minister, François Noël, married into the Dutch patrician family of the Bogaerts, was completely under Paulus' spell. He had been fully persuaded that obstructions had been placed in the path of the National Assembly by men who posed as Patriots but who in reality were bent on sabotaging the alliance and welcoming the British and their minion the Prince of Orange as soon as possible. Was not the leader of the Friesland representatives, Joha, a predikant? Ergo, their opposition was the fiendish work of aristocrats and priests—a combination immediately comprehensible to any student of French politics in 1795![60] On a purely strategic basis, the rift which had opened in the Batavian Republic had disastrous potential. Friesland and Groningen both lay on the frontier of a Prussian province and were vulnerable to an attack from the northeast. Despite their débacle in the "Zeeland redoubt" in February, might not the British manage a landing at Walcheren from which they could harass the naval base at Flushing and close the Scheldt?

These possibilities persuaded both the Directory and its minister at The Hague that France should lend support to some decisive act which would rule out the perpetuation of these dangerous divisions. On January 2, 1796 (12 Nivôse, Year IV), the Directory sent a new "Instruction" to François Noël in which it commented:

. . . without interfering in the domestic affairs of the Batavian government the Executive Directory owes it, both to its own sworn faith and to the maintenance of the treaties, a frank declaration that it will never recognise any government in Holland other than that which is based on the general will.

Nor did the Directory leave it open to doubt what the "general will" then required:

. . . the wish of the majority of the United Provinces [sic] having been definitively expressed in favour of the formation of a National Convention, the deputies of this majority cannot defer for a moment longer the opening of this Convention without betraying their *patrie*.[61]

The directive could not have been much clearer. And somewhat fortuitously, new opportunities for making a virtue of necessity arose as the pressures on the united front of the three dissenting provinces began to tell. In January 1796 the Patriotic societies of the Zeeland towns, led by the Middelburg society and its chairman J. H. van der Palm—yet another ex-predikant and the editor of a newspaper called *The Friend of the People*—published a declaration warning that the obstinacy of their representatives could lead to a fatal severance from their old allies in the Union. Similar societies in Groningen and in Dokkum and Leeuwarden in Friesland went further by echoing the French suspicion that the opposition to the Convention was the work of a "gang of Orangist aristocrats and hangers-on of the old regime." Defections began to accelerate. Huber, next to van Beijma the most renowned figure among the St. Omer veterans, made a public profession that the conduct of the representatives was both wilful and wrong-headed. Nine deputies of the Friesland Assembly announced that they dissociated themselves from the policy of the majority and that they stood with the four provinces which had voted in favour of the new National Assembly.

The most serious breach, however, was between the provincial administrations and the councillors of their principal cities. Friesland in the first months of 1796 experienced a political contest very similar to that of Holland and Amsterdam, only with the political allegiances exactly reversed. The centre of the storm was Leeuwarden. Like Groningen, Deventer and Utrecht, Leeuwarden was simultaneously the seat of the provincial representation (as it had been of the old States) and the hearth of urban radicalism in the province. Since the beginning of the revolution, there had been friction between the town and the assembly. The representatives had been distressed by the defacing of the tombs of the Friesian line of the House of Nassau in the Great Church;[62] perhaps it was too reminiscent to the havoc wrought by the Parisian sans-culottes to the royal remains in the crypt of Saint-Denis. The representative assembly of the province had also strenuously resisted any attempt to establish a volunteer citizens militia in Leeuwarden. Obviously they had reason to fear that it could be used as a weapon by politically unreliable elements and they preferred (mistakenly, as it turned out) to entrust their safety to a small French garrison. More serious was their attempt to intervene in the domestic politics of Leeuwarden, based on almost identical premises to the rights assumed by Holland over the administration of Amsterdam. The distinction was less one of principle than of power. Not only was the Friesian intervention more inept, but it was supported by weaker force. For whereas the provincial assembly at The Hague had been able to call on large numbers within Amsterdam to assist it in pressing its will on the city, those numbers in Leeuwarden were entirely at the command of the municipality.

Confronted with an increasingly assertive city council, the Friesland Assembly met the challenge head-on by declaring in January that the "Provisional Representation of the People of Leeuwarden" would be terminated at the end of the month. In its place a properly regulated ordinance would provide for future elections to the municipal body—and indeed to all comparable towns in the province. But where the Holland ordinance had been designed to broaden the franchise for municipal elections, the Friesian regulation was tailored so as to exclude all but a politically innocuous base of tax payers and property owners. The Leeuwarden Council demonstrated its view of the new ordinance by ignoring it and holding an early election on January 11 under its unimpaired wide franchise. To no-one's surprise the new council was, if anything, more radical than the old. The victors continued to thumb their nose at the provincial assembly by celebrating their success with a public festival in the streets of the city in front of the town hall, led by officials of the popular societies and *wijk* meetings. In the evening, members of the city *schutterij* and the Fatherland Society used the celebrations as a platform from which to launch a violent tirade against the Assembly, which stood accused of an "aristocratic conspiracy to suppress the rights of the people." Affronted by this demonstration, the Representative Assembly used the weight of its authority. The Provincial High Court declared the elections null and void, and the ringleaders of the festivities were to be arraigned for inciting sedition and riot. Escorted by an armed guard from the garrison, three of the most popular members of the municipality were taken from the town hall and imprisoned in the "Friesian Bastille"—the Blokhuis—to await trial.

This bold show of strength by the Friesian Assembly proved counter-productive, for the hue and cry throughout Holland which greeted the incarceration of the "martyrs of the Blokhuis" gave Paulus and Noël the opportunity they had been looking for. A secret "Committee of Restoration" was established to mobilise popular support for the Leeuwarden councillors, not only in the city itself but in sympathetic towns like Harlingen, Franeker, Sneek and Dokkum. The response was so gratifying that it became obvious to Noël that instead of using troops to effect a coup against the Friesian Assembly it would be a shrewder move to evacuate the soldiers on whom they had been relying for their protection and leave them defenceless against the clubs and *schutterij*. This was duly affected on January 25. No sooner had the troops departed than deputations from the clubs demanded the liberation of the prisoners.

The following day, a meeting of the Landshuis where the Assembly was meeting was invaded by a large crowd. Without much trouble it expelled all but the nine deputies who had supported the National Assembly, and a small rump of others who underwent a dramatic conversion. On the 27th, the real purpose of the coup was underlined when the Friesian delegate at the States-General, Huber, was instructed by the new "Assembly" to change his vote and approve the convening of the National Assembly. As they were meant to, the two other renegade provinces took the hint, almost certainly to avoid the unseating of their representatives. Groningen, which had been on the verge of altering its decision in any case, rapidly confirmed the National Assembly before the city clubs had a chance to rouse themselves. And after some weighty deliberation, Appelius and van der Palm were able to announce to the States-General that the "irrevocable decision of the Zeeland people" turned out, after all, to be revocable and that the province was able to assent to the new Assembly.

This was not, however, the end of the matter. For on February 12 a fraction of the Friesian representatives who had taken refuge from the coup in Groningen returned with the troops of General Dumonceau and turned out the new regime in Leeuwarden. Dumonceau was a Belgian by origin who had joined the *Légion batave* and served alongside Daendels in the Dutch contingent of the French army both in 1793 and 1794–95. He had been given the northern sector command and had been readily convinced by the Leeuwarden fugitives that a gang of Jacobins and anarchists had run them out of the city. Moreover, the "Committee of Restoration" had succeeded in un-doing much of the work of January 25 by making itself thoroughly unpopular in the little towns and villages of the province through a fiercely punitive policy of purges and proscriptions. It required further orders from The Hague and a second evacuation of regular troops before the chaos in the Friesian capital was finally pacified in favour of the radicals. These vacillations, however, did not affect the issue of the National Assembly, for on their brief restoration to power Joha and the conservative representatives decided not to attempt altering the submission to the States-General, even though they annulled all the radical regime's edicts concerning the constitution and powers of the primary assemblies.

The tug of war in Friesland gave a vivid demonstration of the coercive power of the popular societies when the restraining forces of regular troops were removed. It was the power of this weapon which had made it impossible for the dissenting provinces to cling to their provincial autonomy indefinitely. On the other hand, although the Friesian coup marked the end of any kind of political squeamishness on the part of men like Paulus he was well aware that popular force could turn out to be a double-edged sword. The repeated interruptions of popular demonstrations could be at least as unwelcome as the conservative obstructionism of the closing months of 1795 and the experience of the Central Assembly at The Hague had left him with a healthy suspicion of indiscriminate manifestations of the "General Will." In short, Paulus, Wiselius and the rest were serving an awkward apprenticeship in the finesses of revolutionary politics, learning to handle popular coercion so as to dislodge obdurate opposition without exposing themselves to similar hazards. Ultimately they appreciated that success in consolidating the Batavian Republic would depend not merely on neutralising their opponents but on establishing a durable set of working institutions. The object of all their endeavours—the National Assembly—could only legislate the new order into being; it could not, of itself, make it work. In the last resort that would only happen if and when those whom the politicians at The Hague untiringly apostrophized as the "people" were prepared to give it their wholehearted support. Indeed, it was the "people" who would finally decide the issue of the conflict which had been abruptly and artificially terminated in Friesland. For, contrary to many pious hopes in the spring of 1796, the last rites on Dutch federalism had not been said by the convenors of the National Assembly. The final exorcism of the Dutch past was a long time coming.

✽✽✽✽✽✽✽✽✽

6

The Struggle for the Constitution,
March 1796—August 1797

N early fourteen months elapsed between the departure of the Stadholder from Scheveningen beach and the opening of the first National Assembly in what had once been his ballroom. The extended
hiatus had already done severe damage to the precarious unity of the Batavian
Republic. It had also generated expectations which any body of mortals, let
alone the very miscellaneous gathering which came under Pieter Paulus' gavel
on March 1, 1796, would have been hard-pressed to satisfy. So momentous an
event could hardly be permitted to slip past without due ceremony. On March
3 a "Festival" was held in The Hague which, like the "Liberty Feasts" a year
before and the ponderous republican rituals staged in Paris by David, was
stronger on didactic allegory than on fun. Following the usual caravan of
cavalry, military bands, massed presumptive virgins bearing laurels and wheat-
sheaves and processing dignitaries, foreign and native, came tableaux, born on
floats, purporting to represent the various sectors of the Dutch economy which
were about to spring to life under the blessings of equality and freedom. The
crowning moment of bathos arrived when, after the "Chariots of Victory"
decked out in republican bunting, an eighty-year-old man and a four-year-old
child were wheeled past, the first bearing a placard announcing:

All my life have I lived in slavery. Now I rejoice that I shall die in
freedom so that my descendants may taste its fruits[1]

and his junior partner declaring that he, like the infant assembly, was the
"Hope of the Fatherland."

Not all the expectations were benevolent. From his exile at Kew, William
V looked forward with almost indecent impatience to "la belle marmalade"
of the Convention, from whose ensuing débacle the phoenix of his restoration
would arise. But if the former Stadholder was looking forward to a Convention

of Blood, he was to be badly let down. Robert Barclay, a British agent still in the Republic, reported to Grenville that although

the very name of a Convention had spread very general alarm it is now mellowed down to a placid submission by this new title [National Assembly]. A very great majority of the members composing this assembly have been chosen not by the violent party called the clubbists, and among them are many respectable for their integrity and abilities.[2]

Indeed, to any dispassionate observer it must have seemed highly improbable that the Batavian National Assembly was about to abandon itself to an orgy of Jacobinical terrorism. The greater part of its personnel was middle-class, middle-aged and middling of opinion.[3] There were sound reasons why this should have been. Although in principle every Dutch male over twenty was eligible to vote in the primary assemblies, in practice the regulation for the assembly had erected a number of barriers against the more disagreeable consequences of political democracy. All domestic servants, for example, and all those in receipt of public charity were automatically excluded from the franchise. In Holland alone, the first disbarment would have removed some 40,000 from the vote; and the effects of applying the second criterion would have been even more dramatic. In a period of severe economic dislocation the numbers of those, especially in the ports and industrial towns, not wholly indigent but needing occasional relief to supplement subsistence income would have been artificially swollen. In Leiden, for example, nearly a quarter of the population was receiving some kind of relief in 1796.[4]

Even if the humbler burgher did find his name on the poll book of a primary assembly, a two-tier system of indirect election ensured that he stood little or no chance of going forward to the electoral assemblies. Both the electors and the representatives themselves were required to be men of station and substance, paying a certain amount in taxes and with higher age and residence qualifications. Finally, it was predictable that outside the large towns like Amsterdam and Rotterdam, where the popular societies were already well practised in city politics, the expertise of the Patriot notability in managing elections (rehearsed in the 1780's and the 1795 local revolutions) would prove a telling factor. In the land provinces in particular, the first batch of representatives sent to the National Assembly coincided very largely with the heroes and martyrs of 1787.

But if the National Assembly was not the nonpareil of popular sovereignty its more radical protagonists had wished to see, neither was it quite like any other representative institution the Dutch Republic had ever known. To begin with, there were many novices to political life. Only 34 of its 127 deputies had served in a public capacity under the old regime. Although some of the best-known patrician names and faces appeared on its benches—van Hoorn, van Lennep, van Wickevoort Crommelin, Bicker—they did so alongside much less exalted company than in the old States. As Colenbrander noticed from the silhouettes printed in Rogge's history, the elegantly perruqued profile of the Overijssel aristocrat, Carel de Vos van Steenwijk, is cheek by jowl with the altogether more bucolic features of the Friesian peasant farmer Kuiken.[5]

Occupationally the assembly was an odd assortment. There were a few representatives of the social groups which had dominated the States-General and the provincial States: landowners, financiers, wealthy brokers and shippers. But the plutocrats were heavily outnumbered by men, often at least as well-off, from the "Second Hand": manufacturers and distillers like Jacobus Nolet and Vreede; retail merchants like the Rotterdammer Midderigh. The revolutionary intelligentsia—lawyers (Schimmelpenninck; Gerard Bacot, Cornelis van Maanen), academics (Valckenaer, Cornelis de Rhoer, Hahn) and public officials (Paulus, de Mist)—were represented in strength. But the most conspicuous group, which at the same time was a recruiting agency to the revolution peculiar to the Netherlands, was the clergy. Some, like Pieter van de Kasteele and Jacobus Kantelaar, were ex-predikants who nevertheless injected large doses of pious vocabulary into their political rhetoric; others like Ysbrand van Hamelsveld held academic posts while preaching their political gospel; and others again such as Bernardus Bosch and Paulus Bosveld continued their vocation while lending their pulpits to republican dogma.[6] One must beware, however, of attributing any particular ideology to any of these groups. Both Vreede and van Staphorst were shrewd business-men but that was all that they had in common. Even the Assembly's two poets, the appropriately alliterative Pieter Pijpers and the septuagenarian Simon Stijl, occupied opposite ends of the political spectrum. Nor was religion a dependable indicator. Although Catholics (who had special reason to be grateful to the revolution) like the Helmond physician Guljé and the textile merchant Stephen van Langen were both camp followers of Pieter Vreede's brand of democracy, Hugenpoth tot Aerdt, one of the Nijmegen representatives, aligned himself very much with the conservative interests of his city and province and for political purposes was a patrician before he was a Catholic.

It would be overstating the case to suggest that *all* social friction was extruded from the politics of the National Assembly. Indeed as the proceedings became more polarised, those who by their style of life, dress, social manners and even speech identified themselves as regents of the upper crust—"Patriot notables"—were tarred by their opponents as "aristocrats" and therefore enemies of republican freedom. But it was the political contest which determined when and where social demarcations counted, not vice versa. Not that this made much difference to the intense acrimony into which the debates of the assembly rapidly descended. Their acerbity was in stark contrast to the lofty ceremonials attending the inauguration when Appelius had commented that "never had the Netherlands seen so much wisdom gathered under a single roof."[7]

Many others among the Patriot rank-and-file, particularly in Holland, fondly imagined that even if the provinces had been at odds over its convening, once the assembly was established, outstanding differences would be sunk in the common labour of producing the constitution on which the new Republic was to be built. Such illusions were short-lived. Before the first year of its life was out, it was plain that instead of a disinterested forum of the Public Good the National Assembly had degenerated into a battlefield of faction. Instead of blunting the edge of the quarrel between unitarists and federalists, the

Assembly had merely raised it to another plane. Marinus Smissaert, the veteran of the Utrecht Free Corps and a keen advocate of the Assembly in 1795, wrote to his friend Valckenaer a year later that it had been reduced to "a disastrous struggle between two opposed parties, each busy in tearing the other apart," and that he could find nothing in its business but "self-interest, cabals and underhand plots."[8]

While it is true that the virtues of political altruism were in distinctly short supply in the Batavian Republic between 1796 and 1798, it was more serious for its future that the issue between the "two opposed parties" was not just one of political manners. Indeed, even had there been a more impressive degree of goodwill and a common intent to work united for the Greater Good, it is highly doubtful that so fundamental a difference on the constitutive principle of Dutch sovereignty could have been glossed over for the sake of a spurious parliamenatry consensus. What is certain is that the absence of any such consensus made it impossible for the political factions to operate within the framework of a "loyal opposition." Such a genteel situation very rarely happens in the aftermath of a revolution, even one so relatively mild as the Dutch. Because each side had its own particular view of what the Batavian Republic ought to be, each branded the other as not merely misguided but an enemy of the nation, whose success would spell catastrophe. Bicker was not far short of the mark when he commented to Delacroix that the gulf separating federalists and unitarists was wider than that dividing royalists and republicans in France.[9] Not that he himself contributed much to reconciliation by describing Valckenaer, Vreede and the democrats as revolutionary *enragés* hell-bent on the destruction of what was left of the Dutch economy and determined to sabotage the good order of the alliance. If unitarism were adopted to remedy the ills of Dutch government it was certain that the cure would prove fatal to the patient, for, as de Vos van Steenwijk put it, "damage or the ruin of any of the parts would lead, inexorably, to the crippling and final destruction of the whole."[10]

For their part the democrats and unitarists were just as firmly convinced that the precondition for securing the Republic was "unity of power, unity of strength, unity of means." Federalism was, by definition, counter-revolutionary. Gogel's paper *De Democraten*, founded in the summer of 1796, described it as "a system in which lust for power competes with greed and self-interest . . . the great sheet-anchor of the Orange [!] and aristocratic parties, the system beloved of all patrons of provincial power."[11] Was it any wonder, asked Valckenaer's *De Advocaat van Nationale Vrijheid*, that the "will to liberty was flagging" when the "well-disposed" part of the nation was being frustrated by "base slaves of Orange, Aristocrats, despots, political chameleons, fanatical zealots, clerical oppressors, mercenary egotists, reactionary agitators, profiteering merchants, slimy lickspittles . . ."[12] and a whole host of gremlins enumerated in his exhaustive catalogue.

These were scarcely propitious conditions for the National Assembly to function as an effective constituent. For a while in the spring and summer of

1796 it seemed that it would merely travel the short distance from stalemate to absolute deadlock. The reason that this did not, in fact, happen was that while the two wings became rapidly more obdurate in their intention to preserve, or liquidate, the Union of Utrecht in its entirety, they by no means monopolised the allegiance of all the representatives in the Assembly. Between the articulate and verbose orators of the opposed factions—de Mist and van Marle on the one side, Valckenaer and Vreede on the other—lay a middle ground of indeterminate position on which a large number of deputies were attempting to find their feet. Oceans of ink have been pointlessly spilled by historians in an unrewarding attempt to find a way through the complicated politics of the Assembly by identifying clear-cut "parties."[13] In fact, even those individuals who thought of themselves as staunch federalists or democrats were far from being drilled into any kind of collective discipline, much less to responding to instructions from a "leadership." But those who have been tagged as "moderates" were even more amorphous in their identity. Like the "Plain" in the French Convention, their "moderation" turns out to be so semantically versatile a term as to tell the historian virtually nothing about their political beliefs or the way such men might have voted on specific issues. It acts simply as a point of reference in relation to other "less" or "more" moderate members along the ideological spectrum. In short, one man's moderate may turn out to be another's radical. Cornelis van Maanen, the Utrecht lawyer, for example, was convinced by the proposition that the Batavian Republic ought, at some date in the future, to be constituted on the basis of a unitary sovereignty. That presumably made him a unitarist. But he was very far from endorsing the revolutionary *means* to effect this advocated by the popular societies and Pieter Vreede. That was enough in 1798 to identify him as an aristocrat. The same was to be true of George Hahn and Hugo Gevers, who in 1796 were devotees of Pieter Paulus and by any standards to the "left" of the assembly on the key issue of sovereignty.

Conversely, Coert Lambertus van Beijma, the doyen of the Friesian exiles, was the darling of the clubs and militia of his province, and on issues such as the emancipation of the Jews and the abolition of slavery, or measures to deal with the poor, very much a radical voice in the assembly. Yet he was too much of a Friesian (and too sensitive to his own best interests as a representative of the province) to surrender its sovereignty by default to the Holland unitarists. That combination of views presumably made him a "democratic federalist." Jan van Hooff was an even more complicated case. A staunch defender of the interests of Brabant, he was nonetheless an advocate of unitary sovereignty, but simply got on very badly at a personal level with his fellow Brabander, Pieter Vreede. Despite consistently voting for radical amendments throughout the debates on the constitution, his reputation has somehow emerged as "moderate." What is true is that as a result of his experiences and imprisonment at the hands of the radicals in 1798, his views then moved decisively away from popular sovereignty so that in 1806 he ended up as the Minister of Justice to King Lodewijk Bonaparte!

Thus there was no shortage of important issues to divide the members of the Assembly, nor of powerful spokesmen to represent the polarities of view. But for the first two years of its life, the majority of the less committed remained essentially an aggregate of individuals, voting and speaking as reason, conscience and interest dictated. All but a very few were prepared to pay lip service to the heraldic device of "Een- en Ondeelbaar"—"One and Indivisible" —which the unitarists had succeeded in making the catch-phrase of the revolution. But just as many were apprehensive about what it might mean in practice. Very often a "theoretical" unitarist turned out to be a "federalist" when it came to voting on substantive issues such as the amalgamation of provincial debts and taxes. Above all, many of the representatives remained uneasy about a once-and-for-all extinction of the Dutch past. They were still unsure whether their republican duty meant throwing the last clods of earth on its mortal remains or administering the kiss of life. To put the matter briefly, they did not yet know whether they were revolutionaries.

Unfortunately for the Batavian Republic, the one man who might have been able to help them make up their mind was abruptly removed from the scene on March 17. The death of Pieter Paulus, at the age of forty-two and at the height of his powers, was an appalling calamity for the young state. Quite apart from his magnetic personal qualities and intellectual ability, Paulus had been the one figure among the politicians of the Batavian Republic able to command respect and attention from men of radically divergent views—not excluding even his adversaries among the British and Orangist camp.[14] His intellectual evolution from uncritical admiration of the Union of Utrecht to the 1793 *Treatise on Equality* seemed to exemplify his ability to marry the Dutch instinct for legitimacy with the contemporary need for radical institutional change. His sang-froid during the tricky crises in Rotterdam and Amsterdam had shown his purely political skills at their best, while his transformation of the moribund navy had given extra force to his determination to assert the independence of the Republic in the face of both the British enemy and the French ally. Indeed the French minister, François Noël, who had fallen completely under his spell, reproached himself for not having insisted more firmly that Paulus go to Paris to receive the official congratulations of the Convention.[15] Instead, he had presided over the opening session of the National Assembly and, according to Noël, sitting hatless in the March frost and The Hague damp, had caught the cold which unaccountably developed into a lethal dose of pneumonia.

Coming on top of their many other trials, Paulus' demise seemed a monstrously cruel blow to the Dutch. The Batavian Republic was not so rich in men who bore the stamp of leadership that it could afford to dispense with his services. The sorrow which almost universally greeted the news of his death attested to the sense of personal loss shared by many of his countrymen. Fennekol, the mulatto member of the East India Committee, wrote to his friend and colleague Wiselius in terms of typical pathos:

My heart bleeds; all hope for the establishment of the "Good Cause" is gone: every Patriot is bereaved . . . tears course down our cheeks (now that) Pieter

Paulus, our own friend, the friend of the Committee [for the East Indies], the friend of the Fatherland is no more. . . .[16]

No other single figure came as near as Paulus to imposing a peace—or at least a truce—on the quarrelling parties in the assembly. While he had occupied the office there had been some hope that the President's chair might be used a-politically to cement the rifts for the sake of putting through constructive legislation. But once he was gone, it too became sucked into the partisan conflict. The almost unanimous vote which had elected Paulus to the Presidency was never repeated.[17] As his official deputy, van de Kasteele initially filled the vacancy; but he was too preoccupied with attempting to sew up the holes in Holland's finances to give much time to political management. On April 2 the system of rotation provided by the governing regulation produced the first contested election for the Presidency between Valckenaer and Albert de Sitter, a dependable Gelderland federalist. This first trial of strength between the two opposed groups was won hands down by the federalists. Thereafter, the Presidency was virtually enfeoffed to those who were either unsympathetic or actively hostile to the democratic wing of the unitarists.[18]

The doctrinaire federalists like de Mist were not so numerically preponderant in the Assembly as to carry the day by themselves. But they were better placed to attract support from the larger group of patrician and conservative deputies, "men of '87" who evidently believed that the revolution was far too serious a business to be left to the revolutionaries. Ex-regents like Bicker and canny lawyers like Schimmelpenninck rapidly became adept at the parliamentary manoeuvring which kept unitarists, and above all, democratic unitarists, out of any positions of power or influence. Only a select few of the milder spokesmen like Hahn, though susceptible to "persuasion" if the need arose, were permitted the luxury of chairing the assembly's committees. And even when admitted to those bodies, the unitarists were almost always kept in a minority. "Dangerous men" like Vreede, Bosch, Blok and Valckenaer were systematically ignored by the Presidential chair, repeatedly outvoted and obstructed in any attempt to interpret the regulation as a mandate to *legislate* for the nation. In his *Outcry to the Batavian Nation*, Vreede complained:

. . . business is adjourned whenever a carefully prepared opinion of the majority cannot be guaranteed! In this way everything is manoeuvred. Who does not know that appointment to the Presidential chair is impossible without intrigue. By such means the Assembly is mastered; commissions selected and reports concluded according to their [the federalists'] views, and the Assembly forced into discussing matters in such a way that the fate of the People is always decided by recommended opinions of the few. Have the People elected their representatives merely to succumb to the influence of these few? I cannot flinch from saying such things in public; as a Representative of the People I am duty bound to do so; Justice cries out to me not to dissemble![19]

As the instrument of Dutch popular sovereignty, the National Assembly proved a serious disappointment. Instead of the expected means of dismantling the structure of oligarchic government, it seemed to the unitarists to have turned out to be an ideal vehicle for its perpetuation. In their desperate efforts to sway the faltering land provinces to agree to the assembly the Holland unitarists had, as Vreede had warned, sold themselves much too dearly. For far from the governing regulation in which differences might be settled in an orderly, if not exactly amicable, manner it was, in Blauw's phrase, the very "pomme de discorde" in the assembly. *De Democraten* called it: "a tyrannical means, ingeniously devised to cripple the Revolution and hinder it from attaining its great goals . . . the last resort of the old despotism of the provincial government."[20] By perpetuating the provincial administrations, the regulation had in fact cut off vital areas of jurisdiction—finance and the militia, for example—from the competence of the Assembly. Instead of sovereignty devolving from the centre to the provinces the reverse, as in the old Republic, seemed to be the case. It was arguable whether the Assembly was entitled to regard itself as a legislature at all. The regulation seemed to have doomed it to an existence as little more than a national emblem, at best a consultative intermediary between the (provincially appointed) constitutional commission and the mass of the electorate who would be engaged to accept or reject it. Even the composition of that commission underlined the weakness of the reformers. Of the twenty-one members, just four (all Hollanders) could be considered dependable unitarists in their principles. Their number was halved when, galled at being consistently outvoted on amendments, two of them withdrew from the commission at the end of 1796.

Frustrated by their impotence, the bolder among the democrats turned to extra-parliamentary opinion for comfort and support. This was not denied them. The restrictions surrounding the election to the Assembly had, if anything, spurred on the clubs and popular societies to further agitation; and they were encouraged in their waxing militancy by an exceptionally vociferous press. Papers like *De Democraten*, *De Domkop*, *De Advocaat van Nationale Vrijheid* and Bosch's *De Politieke Opmerker* upbraided the "aristocrats" of the Assembly in increasingly immoderate language and were often read aloud at sessions of the larger clubs where their editors were usually well placed on the steering committees.[21]

As for the societies themselves, "the schools of liberty . . . the warehouses of disinterested patriotism," as Vreede called them, they continued to proliferate throughout the Batavian Republic until by the end of 1796 there was hardly a single town of any size without its forum of radical opinion. Corresponding agencies were established in Amsterdam, The Hague, Utrecht, Zwolle and den Bosch, and each of the provincial "head cities" had its "Central Bureau" of delegates from the minor towns and villages. Unfortunately it is impossible to quantify the membership of more than a handful of these clubs since so few of the members' registers have survived. Nor is it possible to provide an analysis of their social composition from the petitions sent to the National Assembly beyond observing that, as one would expect, many such documents were drafted by the educated professional leadership of the societies and signed by the petty-burgher rank-and-file, sometimes amounting to over 100 in cities like Utrecht, Leiden and Rotterdam. However amorphous in identity, it can hardly be doubted that what has been called a "conscious public opinion" had come into existence in 1795 and 1796.[22]

The problem remained of how to make that opinion count in the councils of The Hague. The reiteration in petitions of favoured republican maxims—the indivisibility of sovereignty; the absolute division of Church and state; equality of taxation; free public instruction—were little more than an irritation to the deputies of the assembly. Short of resorting to periodic and repeated demonstrations of public rowdiness, or worse, which even the radicals were loath to countenance, the only lever available to make the assembly more responsive to popular opinion seemed to be the primary assemblies. It was with this in mind that Bernardus Blok, supported by Bosch, Valckenaer and Vreede, introduced a motion in the Assembly on May 2 urging that the primary assemblies "approve" the basic principles on which the constitution was to be grounded. Additionally, they were to vote on the establishment of a National Guard and the amalgamation of provincial taxes. This was an audacious attempt to empower the electorate with the right of "initiative" as well as establishing, de facto, the competence of the Assembly to initiate legislation. As such it was, as Bicker was only too happy to point out, in direct contravention of the governing regulation. Indeed, its authors made no pretence that it was otherwise, arguing instead that in time of "national crisis" it was incumbent on the Assembly, as the sovereign representative body of the nation, to make law, overriding if necessary the provisions of the regulation. Until the nation was provided with its constitution, they argued, what else but a state of "crisis" could obtain? Needless to say, this sophistic treatment of the sacred regulation did not recommend itself to the clutch of lawyers among the deputies. As soon as it was pointed out that granting unwonted freedoms to the primary assemblies was to nudge the Republic to the precipice of direct democracy, the Blok proposal stood no chance of survival.[23]

This seemingly impregnable barrage of conservatism was not without its own hazards. Yielding nothing to the radicals and democrats was, sooner or later, bound to tempt them to take everything. By way of reminder, in the middle of May, a sudden spasm of violence in Amsterdam caught the assembly unawares. The storm had in fact been brewing up ever since the committal of the ringleaders of the November disturbances. Neither the clubs nor the district meetings had taken this rap over the knuckles lightly. Through the winter, the agitation for the release of the jailed men and the removal of the most "aristocratic" members of the municipality had gathered momentum. The February elections had held out a chance of a change by peaceful means, but the results—based on an electorate only minimally expanded from 1795—produced a council which was virtually indistinguishable from its predecessor. By late spring the atmosphere in Amsterdam had grown decidedly ugly, with the companies of volunteer militia, some of whose comrades had been directly involved in the November incidents, leading the hue and cry.

On May 8 three companies of artillery mutinied at Overtoom, just out-side the city boundaries, demanding the liberation of the remaining offenders and the summary discharge of the officers concerned with their detention. Two days later, and from the accompanying throng (with some collusion from the clubs and their comrades within the city), the cannoneers entered Amsterdam to serve their summons on the town hall in person. There were only 700 such "cannoneers" in all, and since a number of their officers had already obeyed the order of the municipality to lay down their weapons, only 200 were armed, principally with sabres and pikes. Nevertheless, the situation was sufficiently alarming for the council to call on the services of their own "Burgher Watch," recruited from the more substantial districts of the city, to disarm the mutineers and pacify the crowd. To their dismay, however, instead of complying with their instructions, the watch began to fraternise with the cannoneers to the delighted cheers of the crowd. Having received short shrift from the council earlier in the day, the cannoneers now proceeded to invade the defenceless Stadhuis. When they reached the council chamber they set on its members with the flat of their swords, roughed up some of its more eminent worthies, and tried out the benches for size themselves. The speed at which events had moved had taken the leaders of the clubs and the *wijk* meetings by surprise; only belatedly did they form an ad hoc committee to present the demands to the council in a more formal style. Without waiting for the council to reply, the committee itself deposed the offending regents and authorised the liberation of the prisoners, since this was obviously the minimum acceptable to the by now thoroughly riotous insurgents.

Once again the eruption of casual disorder had succeeded in throwing the greatest city of the Batavian Republic into a state of virtual insurrection. That, at least, was the way in which the principal officers of the National Assembly and the Holland representatives saw the matter. Since the Assembly was technically in recess it fell to Bicker, its current President, in his capacity as commandant of The Hague garrison (an office inherited from the Stadholder!) to decide on what action was necessary to restore order. Neither Bicker nor the French general commanding the province, Beurnon-ville, had any qualms on this score: they were determined to crush the tumult with as much force as should prove necessary. Initially the provincial authori-ties in Holland (in whose name the troops would have to be employed) showed understandable reserve towards Bicker's eagerness to put on a show of *force majeure*. But the radicalism of the Holland representatives had been diluted by new elections, and the reports of physical violence in the city were enough to extract their consent for a repressive operation. The Haarlem garrison, barely 15 miles from Amsterdam, was alerted; but the arrival of two delegations from the city in The Hague made Bicker hesitate before ordering them into action. Both deputations, one from the ad hoc "Burghers Com-mittee" and the other from the municipal council itself, pleaded with him to refrain from action which might cause bloodshed and put the lives of the remainder of the council in serious jeopardy. It was almost too late. Some of the companies from Haarlem had started out for Amsterdam and on learning the news the cannoneers had seized the cannon at the Haarlemmerpoort to prevent it from falling into the hands of the Holland troops. Whether or not they would have used it must remain an open question since at the eleventh hour the soldiers were turned back; instead, an unarmed commission from The Hague deputed to "investigate" the grievances of the citizens was permitted to enter the city. The closeness of the disaster combined with the gesture of conciliation seemed to defuse the crisis, and the violence and disorder quietened down almost as mysteriously as it had flared up. The Hague commission was received by the "Burgher Committee" and a new watch acting under their joint authority posted around the town. Within a week, small detachments of French troops acting under orders from Beurnonville entered the city without any of the panic which had greeted the news of Dutch soldiers marching on Amsterdam.[24]

After the initial fright and the rough-house inside the town hall, the "uprising" of the cannoneers turned out to be merely another episode in the unruly history of popular disorder in Amsterdam. The readiness of the putative insurrectionary committee to accept the pacification of the situation, instead of exploiting it to bring pressure on the authorities in The Hague and to revolutionise the city, was absolutely typical of the way the Dutch radicals fought their battles with, as it were, one hand tied behind their back. Yet for quite fortuitous reasons the little riot acquired, especially for the French, a far more sinister character. For May 10, 1796, had also been the day when the botched-up plans by Babeuf and the "Equals" in Paris had been uncovered by the police of Charles Cochon—the same Cochon who had prepared the invoice on the Dutch indemnity a year earlier. There was nothing beyond the most wildly circumstantial evidence to connect Babeuf and his henchmen with the fracas on the Dam, but with their evidence hard-stretched to cover all the hundred odd arrestees of the "Conspiracy of the Equals," Carnot and the Minister of Justice, Merlin, were not beyond scratching at the public nerves by suggestion of an "international plot." One of Babeuf's closest collaborators, Buonarroti, was of course an Italian, whose arrival in France was relatively recent. Apart from the coincidence of the date (Cochon's police might easily have moved in on the conspirators a day later or earlier without making any difference), it was learned that Babeuf had actually been in the pay of the "légion batave" for a few months in the spring of 1793.[25] In actual fact he had left because the pay of a quartermaster was too meagre for even his sparse needs, but the small gleaning of circumstance was made to travel a long way in the hyper-suspicious imaginings of the Directory's agents.

More seriously for the Batavian radicals, their adversaries were not below borrowing a leaf from the grimy and dog-eared book of the Directory's tactics to discredit the democrats still further. Their opportunity came when Valckenaer made the mistake of launching a fierce attack on Bicker for having authorised the despatch of the Assembly's troops without bringing it before the representatives. In attacking the President for abusing his official powers,

Valckenaer was merely taking advantage of one of the very few situations when he could put his ex-friend and current enemy on the defensive. He was also doing nothing more startling than reiterating the views he had expressed the previous November that neither Dutch nor French troops had any business interfering with the domestic affairs of the capital of Holland. But drawn to defend the action of the popular societies and of the "Burgher Committee" on May 10 and May 11, he was made to seem to be close to advocating periodic sedition against lawfully constituted authority. Like Wiselius the previous winter, his involvement with the clubs was seen in a murky light. Spicy stories began to circulate. He was said to have been recognised incognito in Amsterdam on May 7, a day before the Overtoom mutiny; he had dined in secret at the "Washington" tavern in the Warmoesstraat, the known haunt of the cannoneer officers; money had been seen to have changed hands. None of this was remotely near the truth, but Valckenaer's clumsy attempts in the Assembly to wriggle off the hook on which Bicker had so neatly caught him were painful to behold.

He may also have been aware that the French Directory had been served with discreet reminders of his past: of his "intimacy" with Robespierre (who had so nearly incarcerated him) and of his unrepentant addiction to Jacobinism and the reign of Terror. Nothing more implausible than the elegant and sardonic figure of the Professor of Law at Leiden succumbing to violent Montagnard impulses could be conjured up by the historian of the period. Yet the fact remains that although Valckenaer, the sophisticate, was the fall guy of the cannoneer uprising, his journalism in the *Advocate* had earned him something of a reputation as an *enfant terrible*, and that despite the formal exoneration of his name, his political career never really recovered from the blow it received in the summer of 1796. Unlike Pieter Vreede, Valckenaer was not, in any case, a man to enjoy for very long the arid virtues of a prophet in the wilderness. By the end of the year he had tired of being perpetually outvoted in the Assembly and accepted the post of ambassador to the court of Spain, a translation which brought his career as the champion of unitary democracy in the Batavian Republic to an unpredicted and mundane close.[26]

Although the National Assembly had successfully weathered the storm of the Amsterdam riot, the experience had jolted the majority out of their complacency and had alerted them to the dangers of completely ignoring the barometer of public opinion. It was obvious to the more pragmatically minded among them that a fine line had to be drawn between dismissing the democrats out of hand and giving them too much latitude. None was more pragmatic, nor more solicitous in his desire to avoid future confrontations, than Schimmelpenninck. Appreciating well enough the tactical value of a timely concession, he introduced a motion on May 23 which, while dwelling long on the interdependence of Dutch prosperity and the old constitution and eschewing any idea of influencing the commission in its work, proposed that the Assembly make an affirmation of its intention to create a state based on the sacred motto of "Een- en Ondeelbaar"—"One and Indivisible."[27]

On the face of it this appeared to be an amazing somersault: a capitulation by the most eloquent of the conservative groups in the Assembly to the fundamental demand of his opponents. And no matter how he glossed it, in its assumption of the authority to lay down principles in advance for the constitution, it was as much a usurpation of the commission's independence as Blok's resolution. But Schimmelpenninck's long and rambling speech was a masterpiece of ambiguity. By the summer of 1796 "One and Indivisible" had degenerated into a Patriot shibboleth, virtually capable of as many interpretations as there were political factions, a synonym for the wishful thought of "unity." Schimmelpenninck said nothing of the liquidation of provincial sovereignties and autonomies; nothing of the embodiment of the "General Will" so highly regarded by the democrats. His concept of "One and In-divisible" had encompassed nothing more sensational than a general allegiance to the national sovereignty of the Republic in areas like the decisions to wage war and peace, and the institution of an effective executive power to replace the Stadholderate. Later in the year he was to draw a sharp distinction between those matters which properly belonged to the representatives of the national community and those which, as "domestic administration," remained the domain of the provinces. In this manner, a harmonious balance between the unitary and the federal might be achieved as it had already been instituted in the United States, henceforth his favourite model of government. If the national executive or legislature were to encroach unreasonably on the competence of local administrations, he warned, it would act "in a spirit of oppression and hegemony and under the flag of so-called unity introduce an Oriental despotism."[28]

Despite its disingenuousness, Schimmelpenninck's manoeuvre was very shrewd. By appealing to a principle which the unitarist minority could hardly repudiate, he planned to steal their thunder and quieten the clubs without really yielding anything of substance. Moreover, he hoped to convince Noël and his masters in Paris that the National Assembly was concerned to introduce a constitution which would create an energetic and competent government, not strikingly dissimilar in fact to their own. Finally, he supposed that by passing such an elastically worded motion he would be able to lay the foundations for a broad republican consensus that would exclude only the most recalcitrant federalists and democrats. Unfortunately for these worthy intentions, he had badly overestimated the gullibility of the opposition. All his patriotic references to republican unity had not been able to disguise from his critics the sobering fact that under his version of "indivisibility," the basic attributes of federalism stayed exactly where they were. When the debate on the motion was resumed on June 16, a procession of unitarist speakers—Hugo Gevers, van de Kasteele, Hahn, van Hooff, van Maanen and, of course, Vreede—all exposed the ambiguities of the man whom Valckenaer in a pointed epithet had called the "arch-moderate." By way of a counteroffensive, they reiterated their unequivocal commitment to a unitary state and the abolition of the old provinces as the Dutch had always known them, and called Schimmelpenninck's bluff by inviting him to support *their* proposal for a detailed act of liquidation.

At this juncture it was obvious to Schimmelpenninck that things had seriously misfired and he beat a hasty retreat. On June 21 he sought to stress once more, in the American sense, the importance of the *division* of powers, and finally moved directly back to square one by invoking the sanctity of the regulation which forbade the Assembly from laying down law to the constitutional commission! Indeed, he added, since the commission had already adopted the general principle of "One and Indivisible," there was surely no real need to proceed further with the matter. Observers of the debate on June 21 might well have been forgiven for disbelieving that they were listening to the same Schimmelpenninck as had spoken on May 23!

Despite his best efforts to retreat in good order, Schimmelpenninck was not to be spared further embarrassment. When, at last, on November 10 the constitutional commission presented the fruit of its labours to the Assembly in draft, it was dismally plain that far from incorporating indivisibility as the keystone of their arch they had barely acknowledged its significance. To say that the draft was a disappointment to the unitarists would be a colossal understatement. The commission had presented them with a titivated version of federalism which had left provincial sovereignty over finance, militia, and a whole range of governmental matters quite intact. Valckenaer did not care for it at all.

Everything [he remarked] is arranged for the regents, magistrates and the constituted powers; nothing for the liberty of the people; everything disposed against rebellion (an absurd word in a Republic) and nothing against aristocracy; everything against popular movements, nothing against the efforts of tyranny. O my Fatherland! Is this the end of the untiring efforts of your heroes? Can this seriously be a constitutional plan, drawn up, after so many have gone before it, at the end of the eighteenth century?[29]

Indeed, the draft was held in such scorn by a growing number of deputies that at the end of the month there seemed a serious likelihood that it would not be accepted as even a basis for debate and amendment, and that the National Assembly might break up altogether. This was partly because opinion among moderate unitarists who had belonged to Paulus' circle like Gevers and van de Kasteele hardened perceptibly in response to Schimmelpenninck's antics in the summer, and partly because the unitarists had been fortified by a mission to Paris in October consisting of van Hooff and Vreede which had succeeded in persuading the Directory to lend its weight to the adoption of a genuinely centralised republican state.

Put on the defensive, the two Amsterdam wizards, Bicker and Schimmelpenninck, proceeded to pull another rabbit from their capacious hat. On November 29, Schimmelpenninck proposed what was in effect a compromise with the moderate unitarists. In return for taking the November draft as the *basis* for discussion, two committees for revision were to be appointed by the Assembly, the first to scrutinise the draft in respect to its adherence to the principle of indivisible sovereignty; the second (an even more dramatic concession) to examine the whole vexed question of fiscal amalgamation and to incorporate its findings in the draft. A final version embodying the amendments of the two committees could then be presented to the Assembly for its inspection. This was a genuinely more handsome offer than the knavery of the summer. It was rewarded on December 2 with a substantial majority, which included virtually every faction bar that of twenty-five or so die-hard federalists. For the first (and last) time, Pieter Vreede managed to swallow his disgust and vote for a proposition of Schimmelpenninck's. This, however, by no means marked the end of resistance to unitarism. On hearing the news, Lestevenon wryly remarked to Valckenaer: "For the moment they have ceded to avoid being broken. But like the Jews of Portugal, they still observe their sabbath."[30]

Though arrived at by a circuitous route, and for a variety of motives, not all of them pure, the resolution of December 2 had fulfilled the more creditable of Schimmelpenninck's intentions by loosing the deadlock which had threatened the Assembly with total disaster. Moreover, it freed the representatives from the inhibitions which had prevented them from acting as though they were a national legislature. Reminded that neither Americans nor Frenchmen had waited for their definitive constitutions before seeing off their old regimes, the Dutch reformers finally set about their own. Needless to say, there was no pell-mell rush to wholesale demolition. That, as Geyl tirelessly reminded his readers, would have been out of character. Nevertheless, the debates of the National Assembly in the latter part of 1796 and the first half of 1797 represent the most radical critique yet of the social and political institutions which had been part and parcel of Dutch life ever since the foundation of the Republic.

The first sacred national cows to be dragged reluctantly before the reformers' knife were the guilds and corporations. The original November draft had carefully avoided all mention of the guilds, but the revising committee of seven under George Hahn saw to it that their draft included a clause abolishing them outright as a clear violation of the principle of "One and Indivisible." The liquidation of corporations had come to be virtually a cliché of republican constitutions since 1791, and there could be little doubt that what were termed "private jurisdictions" offended against the "indivisible sovereignty of the people." On the more purely economic plane, the much-rehearsed eighteenth-century debate had it that state regulation of quality standards, and terms of service and wages, violated the "natural" economic laws of the freedom of the market. The debates in the Batavian National Assembly showed that the laisser-faire champions were sufficiently familiar with Adam Smith to cite him, often *in extenso*, without doing too much violence to the sophistication of his thesis.

But the issue was not merely one of abstract speculation for the Dutch. Both the deplorable condition of their traditional industries and the special place which the guilds had occupied in civic life gave their threatened abolition a peculiarly national resonance. From his own business experience Pieter Vreede, vigorously supported by Brabant Catholics like F. Guljé and Petrus Verhoysen who had special reasons for wishing to see the end of the guilds, argued that they had been responsible for maintaining an intolerably high level of labour costs and for keeping prices at a level which ruled out effective competition with cheaper manufactured goods from abroad. Their opponents —arguing for the renovation rather than the destruction of the guilds—expressed their astonishment that those, like Vreede, who constantly expressed their love for the "people" should now be willing to take from them the mainstay of their social welfare. Jacob de Mist professed disbelief that "with one stroke of the pen" the Assembly really intended to wipe out the guilds, corporations and fraternities which were knit into the very fabric of Dutch society. If they were abolished, who would care for the sick, the widowed, the orphaned and the elderly? And what of the sureties which had been paid to the guilds in return for masters' or artisans' certificates? Were these now to be reimbursed to their purchasers, and was the hard-pressed treasury of the Republic to assume liability for such needless extravagances?[31]

To these well-taken points the abolitionists replied that the Republic should indeed assume the social responsibilities hitherto left to the philanthropy of private organisations. But de Mist had touched on a sensitive spot. For despite the sanguine optimism of the champions of a free economy, there were not a few who shared the misgiving that a time of intense depression and high unemployment was not the most opportune for removing what slight protection its victims had left. True, not all were either insensitive or cautious on these matters. Coert van Beijma, Valckenaer's old enemy from Dunkirk days, insisted that like the ill-fated French constitution of 1793, the Batavian constitution should include an article in which the government of the Republic accepted its obligation to provide work for all the able-bodied and sustenance for those who were too infirm, aged or disabled to take it on.[32] Van Beijma's views were remarkably free from the Calvinist paternalism which regarded the relief of the poor as an onerous duty conferring Christian grace on the donor. On the contrary, he stressed that the poor and needy had a *right* to expect the Republic to come to their assistance. Such aid was not a charity but a "sacred debt owed by the Nation." Since its receipt conferred no social ignominy, there could hardly be any reason to withhold the franchise from its recipients. For "if those to whom the Nation pays this debt are to be stripped of their rights as citizens, then all those who now enjoy any income, salary or pension from the State should be similarly excluded."

This degree of social radicalism did not commend itself to many of van Beijma's colleagues in the Assembly; it was too close to Montagnard doctrines of state welfare for comfort. And the notion that the poor were somehow responsible for their own wretchedness was too ingrained in Dutch morality for it to be instantaneously erased by the revolution. A more conventional response to de Mist's objections was to reiterate that once labour had been freed from the fetters of guild restrictions, large numbers of the unemployed would be absorbed by a buoyant market and the reinvigorated production that would come with the restoration of economic strength and stability.

Rather more disreputable economic considerations got in the way of other humanitarian reforms. Pieter Vreede's motion for an outright emancipation of all slaves in Dutch colonies (as well as the less controversial abolition of the slave trade) won a tepid reception from Schimmelpenninck. While he personally had never soiled himself with slave-owning, he said, he knew that despite the good intentions so ill-judged an action might very well lead to a violent insurrection as bad as anything in Saint Domingue. What was more, it would be bound to bring ruin to many virtuous and patriotic burghers.[33]

It was a similar concern to fend off the excesses of egalitarian zeal which led Schimmelpenninck and Bicker to speak out against any suggestion to expropriate the Reformed Church. Indeed, with so many of the clergy of different denominations present in the Assembly, even the disestablishment of the Reformed Church was bound to be a ticklish business. Some of the debates witnessed the bizarre spectacle of militant but iconoclastic predikants like Bosch urging complete separation while more temperate ex-clergy like Kantelaar took the opposite view. The Batavian Republic must have been the only ally of republican France to have inserted an article into their constitution declaring that religion was "the source of all morality and prosperity which the State is bound to defend and maintain."[34] It was much less clear what such a commitment meant in practice. There was no question but that the privileged position secured by the Synod of Dort in 1618 would have to be done away with. That, as Vreede insisted, had been *assumed* in the States-General's edict of March 4, 1795, guaranteeing freedom of worship to all citizens. But whether this axiomatically entailed a complete divorce between Church and state was a moot point. The most ardent secularists like van Hooff and Pieter de la Court demanded that all stipends, pensions, and revenues accruing from public contributions such as tithes and church dues should cease forthwith, since it was a blatant violation of natural rights to oblige a Mennonite or a Lutheran to contribute to the upkeep of the "oppressor Church" for a single day longer. Others such as Bosveld (another cleric) took the more compassionate view that the Assembly could not suddenly deprive the Reformed clergy of their livelihood by abolishing the tithe without making some alternative provision—if necessary in the form of a state salary.

While there were a few who would have applauded a move to turn the clergy into functionaries of the Republic, there were far more deputies who, in tune with the times, saw this as an insidious device to perpetuate the special position of the Reformed Church. As so often in the Batavian Republic, victory went to compromise. On August 5, 1796, the formal connection between Church and state was severed; at the same time it was decided that *present* incumbents should be continued in their livings for as long as they should require support. It was left to provincial authorities whether or not they wished to wash their hands entirely of their clergy, or to levy an ecclesiastical poll tax which could be used for the upkeep of property and personnel of all churches, *irrespective of denomination.*

The one conspicuous exception to these arrangements was the community of some 50,000 Dutch Jews. Not that their rabbis were in immediate need of support. The *parnassim* (wardens) of both Ashkenazi (German—

but denoting central and eastern European) and Sefardi (Spanish and Portugese) communities saw to the maintenance of Orthodox Jewish education, dietary facilities, the enforcement of the religious law, and the upkeep of synagogues. From their steeply rising number of poor, especially among the Ashkenazim, it appears that their provisions for relief were less adequate.[35] The Jews had enjoyed full rights of autonomy under the old Republic but its condition had naturally been the forfeiture of the civil rights of gentile burghers. Though their disabilities were lenient in comparison to neighbouring states, they still fell a long way short of practical or legal equality. Barred from all guilds and corporations, they were restricted in the occupations they were entitled to practice. The more adventurous had made their mark in the speculative corners of the money and colonial markets, but many more had been reduced to the traditional Jewish trades of hawking, dealing in old clothes, gold- and silver-smithing and the (often illicit) transaction in rough gems. Their places of residence were likewise restricted, the vast majority living in the urban centres of Holland, a few finding their way to the towns of Utrecht, Zeeland and even Friesland. The conditional nature of their domicile was underlined by the payment of an additional head tax in return for the grace of their physical protection.

The States-General's declaration of rights in March 1795 specifically placing *all* citizens on an equal footing might have been thought to have ended this inferior status. But, as in France, it turned out that for Jews, blacks and women, some citizens remained less equal than others. It would need a special act of emancipation before these lesser equals could be promoted in the sight of the law. The first gesture of emancipation was made in January 1796, when Jews were specifically admitted to the primary assemblies electing representatives to the National Assembly. There was no question as yet of the possibility of Jewish deputies, but thirteen Jews were elected to the electoral assemblies in the province of Holland. Despite these gestures of goodwill, there remained special problems associated with their emancipation. Although an energetic minority of Jews, notably those gathered in the Amsterdam club "Felix Libertate," had busied themselves in the Patriot cause and shown themselves eager to propagate the ideals of the revolution amongst their co-religionists, the mass of their people were generally thought of, especially among the petty-burghers, as fierce supporters of the House of Orange. Besides lingering suspicions of an "alien race," there was a fear that the emancipation of thousands of ignorant, squalid and destitute Jews would swamp the labour market for trades and industries which were already in severe distress. But the masses of poor Jews were not the major political or economic threat to middle-class and artisan Patriots. In return for the Stadholder's protection of their communal autonomy, the wealthy and powerful *parnassim* and rabbis had shown themselves his dutiful partisans and had inculcated similar attitudes among those who were subject to their authority. Many of the richest among them, particularly those involved in the money market, had connections of business and family in Britain, and stock in its national debt. As a result, their attitude towards the blessings of freedom was the suspicious side of apprehensive. Its most ardent protagonists were, after all, notorious free thinkers who had tried to disrupt the *Kehillah*. Their vaunted "equality," they felt, was merely a subtle means to undermine the authority of the religious law and seduce the people with the assimilationist heresies of the "Haskalah" (emancipation movement). Better the ghetto than the road to heterodoxy and intermarriage![36]

The opponents of Jewish emancipation in the National Assembly—of whom there were not a few—were able to point to this reluctance as evidence that the Jews prized their closed and separate autonomies above the duties and rights of equal citizenship. Some went further. Professor van Swinden of the Amsterdam Athenaeum had argued in a pamphlet that since the Jews refused to accept the divinity of Christ, it was inconceivable that they should ever be satisfactorily integrated into what had been specifically acknowledged as a Christian society. Fortunately the Jews were not short of advocates in the Assembly. In the debate at the end of August, George Hahn refuted criticism of their economic degradation by arguing in the best philosophe manner that it was the effect, not the cause, of their misfortunes, and to the theological objections of those who echoed van Swinden, Professor van Hamelsveld (himself well equipped to exchange biblical quotations with the best) insisted that it was "simply a question of whether or not fifty thousand men remain slaves or are made free."[37] Even Schimmelpenninck on this occasion spoke out unequivocally, reminding his colleagues that the declaration of rights in March 1795 had been intended to embrace all men, not just Christians. Characteristically, it was his contribution which on September 2 produced the resolution emancipating the Jews on the basis of individual citizenship, not as a separate collective entity. The spirit of Clermont Tonnerre's dictum: "To the Jews as a nation we must refuse everything; to the Jews as individuals we must grant everything," had been duly reproduced in the Batavian Republic.

The separation of Church and state and the emancipation of the Dutch Jews were the outstanding achievements of the National Assembly pending the finalisation of the constitutional draft. But as long as that fundamental matter still hung in the balance, they could be little more than legislative diversions. The political penalties for failing to produce some kind of document to present to the nation and one, moreover, which stood a decent chance of acceptance, seemed appallingly daunting. So that despite the howls of derision from the unitarists which greeted the appearance of the 918 articles of what came to be known as the "Dikke Boek" (the "Thick Book"), the urgency with which the committees of revision set to work suggested a vivid awareness that something respectable had to be salvaged from the débacle. By Dutch standards their work was staggeringly expeditious. The Hahn committee on the unity of sovereignty completed its labours in less than three weeks; that on finance under van de Kasteele took just a fortnight or so longer. That the van de Kasteele group ever managed to produce a report at all, with both Vreede and Schimmelpenninck sitting as members, let alone in smart time, seems little short of miraculous.

The "Thick Book" was made no thinner by the exertions of the revising committees. In an effort to make the draft appear more in conformity with the principle of indivisible sovereignty, the Hahn committee too often preferred insertion to deletion. Thus to the original pronouncement that the Netherlands were no longer to be considered as "a confederate state but as one single sovereign people," the Hahn committee added the gratuitous affirmation that "the Batavian Republic is One and Indivisible, its sovereignty resting in the bosom of the collectivity of all citizens."[38] Moreover, given the necessarily mixed composition of political affiliation on the revising committees, compromises could not be avoided. The original draft, for example, had merely substituted the title of "department" for each of the nine provinces and left it at that. Each departmental administration retained responsibility for a very wide range of business, almost identical with that of the old provinces, and was answerable only to a periodically convened council of delegates from each of the province's districts. The Hahn committee raised the number of departments to eleven (the final version of the constitution raised the number again to fifteen), re-drawing the boundaries to form units of equal population size. This was achieved by the radical step of splitting Holland into five units and Brabant into two. As Vreede could not help but notice, however, these adjustments failed to conceal that within each department the substructure of local power had been left almost untouched. Not a few Hollanders felt aggrieved that their own province had been carved up while the more entrenched federalists of the land provinces had been preserved. Indeed, despite the vote of December 2, the attachment of a number of deputies to the basic axioms of federalism remained apparently unshakeable. The more radical demands such as van Beijma's insistence that only the national legislature be given the competence to make any kind of law, or Vreede's proposal that appeals for redress against local authorities to the National Assembly be written into the constitution, were met with impassioned hostility from such as Herman Vitringa of Gelderland. By way of reply he issued a solemn admonition to the Assembly that if it were to usurp rights which properly belonged to the provinces and seek to enforce them, a Dutch "Vendée" or new civil war might be the result. It took the surprisingly dispassionate Presidency of de Mist to coax a compromise Article 11 from the Assembly providing that only those matters not reserved under the constitution as national should be regarded as the province for subordinate authorities.

If unitarism was poorly served by the revisions, democracy was not much better dealt with. The "Legislative Corps" remained a bicameral rather than a unicameral institution and, like the National Assembly itself, was to be the product of indirect elections. To Vreede, all that had been created was an "electoral aristocracy," and he continued to demand both direct elections from the primaries and a single national chamber.[39] The Hahn committee, it is true, did sharpen the few teeth given to the legislature by the commission of twenty-one. The recesses between sessions were reduced to a maximum aggregate of three months, and the sittings themselves substantially extended from the minimal two months provided in the original draft. The executive was reduced from seven to five members (so that it looked uncannily like a Directory) and made responsible to the legislature. The authority of the lower House or "Great Chamber" was expanded so that both chambers took part in the appointment of the executive and the personnel of the high courts. If the upper "Chamber of Elders" rejected a decree sent up by the lower House, the matter was to be referred to a plenary session of the legislature. Yet despite these random garnishings, the proposed constitution was left looking like a passable version of the French constitution of 1795.

For the convinced democrats, this was a most unsatisfactory outcome. Vreede's visit to France and his experience of the conduct of affairs under the Directory had not left him enamoured of its constitution. He was not eager to see the Dutch duplicate the vices of an irresponsible and intrigue-riddled executive and a factious and impotent legislature. That, as he saw it, was "constitutional anarchy," and he predicted that by pursuing a policy of *divide et impera* the proposed "Council of State" would turn out to be "five little Stadholders." If, he argued, the sovereignty of the Republic was to be made truly indivisible, then its institutions should reflect that cardinal principle and subordinate the executive and even the judiciary to the true embodiment of the popular will: the national representation. The authority of that body should then be upheld by peripatetic agents, acting in its name and seeing that the departmental and local administrations carried out its laws to the letter. All this, of course, was more reminiscent of the French constitution of 1793 than that of 1795, and to the more conservative of his countrymen and the French government it confirmed Vreede's reputation as a tiresome, conceivably dangerous renegade. Both were determined to see that he should never have his way.

The more detailed proposals on finance presented by van de Kasteele's committee fared rather better. The November draft had flatly rejected the amalgamation of provincial debts and treasuries and a further vote of the Assembly had confirmed this. Yet on January 20, 1797, following the recommendations of his report, the Assembly turned about-face and in the teeth of bitter opposition from the federalists decided to incorporate the national funding as a constitutional article.[40] How had this happened? The vote for the resolution was sixty to forty-five, but no less than forty votes came from Holland. This meant that some of the conservative patrician representatives (notably the Amsterdammers) had been induced to vote with democrats and unitarists, with whom on other issues they would have strongly disagreed. Naturally this stamped the measure for the land provinces as a typical act of Hollander arrogance. But van de Kasteele was quite unabashed by such a line of attack. The people of Holland, he reminded the Assembly, were currently paying taxes at approximately ten times the rate liable for Gelderlanders. While he accepted certain disparities of fortune within the Republic, there was no reason to suppose that these necessarily coincided with provincial boundaries. If the Batavian Republic was to enjoy a spirit of real national solidarity, it was essential that the burden be more equitably distributed.[41] By way of sugaring the pill he pointed out that the funding of the debts had to be seen as merely the first step in the establishment of an entirely new system of national finances.

In sketching in the outlines of this system, van de Kasteele was borrowing from a powerfully argued memorandum written and published by Gogel in No. 29 of *De Democraten*, the previous November.[42] Its essential point was the shifting of the weight of the fiscal system from indirect to direct taxation, reimbursing the losses on basic commodities with a steeply scaled tax on property and income. In this way, van de Kasteele pointed out, the less well-off citizens of the land provinces would not bear the brunt of the new taxation since the absolute increase for the province would be absorbed by more substantial proprietors. A number of them below a certain fiscal "floor" would be exempted altogether from direct taxation. (Since most of the representatives of the land provinces were in the wealthier category, they were not moved by these charitable considerations.) The introduction of such a system, both Gogel and van de Kasteele insisted, presupposed the establishment of a national treasury and an orderly system of national budgeting. An extended system of the "Quota" such as van de Spiegel had proposed was merely tinkering with the business. What was needed was a modern system of public account able to cope with the expanding commitments of domestic administration, as well as the soaring costs of defence.

Success in unifying the financial system of the Republic was essential to the whole of the unitarist enterprise. Without the power of the purse, the claims of the national legislature and executive to exercise sovereign authority over the departments would have been so much political window dressing. This was keenly appreciated by the federalists, who mounted a last-ditch resistance to the proposals at the end of January 1797. Once again the abstract arguments were submerged in rival versions, idealised or hypercritical of the old Republic. Federalist orators like de Mist and Vitringa recalled that the principal virtue of the union had been its sensitivity to the needs of local communities. In times of economic or geographical disaster, who could know better than the "fathers" of the town or village what their citizens could offer as taxes? The fiscal gross should be based not on some arbitrarily calculated index of the "needs of the state" but on what the resources of its inhabitants could reasonably yield. That, van de Kasteele replied, was all very well but it conveniently overlooked the outrageous abuses perpetrated by the agents and receivers of the provincial authorities in the name of their "Quota." In reality, the provincial, and especially the rural, poor had not been the beneficiaries of the Quota system but those same patricians who were now complaining of the new burdens. Their sudden concern for the poor was little more than a hypocritical masquerade. Moreover, a unified system of taxes for the whole nation could be amended or changed by its representative assembly, which, as an elected body, would be a good deal more responsive to complaint than the provincial councils in the past. Despite the eloquence of rival orators, at the final vote the alignments were virtually Holland versus the rest. The unitarists prevailed, even though many felt uneasy about alienating fellow republicans in the land provinces.

On May 10, 1797, the Assembly gave its assent to a final version of the constitution. Even its staunchest defenders conceded that it was a curious mish-mash, or as Valckenaer put it, a "harlequin's coat" stitched together with more optimism than skill. It was hardly surprising that the joins were showing since the final article had been pieced together from the original draft of the commission of twenty-one, amendments submitted in debates, revisions made by the two committees, revised amendments and amended revisions. By trying to manufacture a version which somehow would succeed in gratifying everybody, the moderates and the pragmatists had run the serious risk of ending up pleasing nobody. Certainly there could be no guarantee that the elaborate political engineering which had been necessary to produce the final assent in the Assembly could be reproduced in the country at large where, unlike France, the fate of the constitution would be decided.

At the eleventh hour, those most anxious to give the draft an easy passage attempted to modify the regulations by which the plebiscite was to be held. Instead of the rigorous procedure by which majorities in each province had to be secured before the constitution could be accepted, Schimmelpenninck proposed substituting a simple national majority. It was ironic that the federalists, who had first demanded the province-by-province count as a safeguard against any unitarist coercion, now assumed a "national" stance in order to help the relatively tame constitution over its last hurdles. This solicitousness, of course, did not apply to their most recalcitrant ideologues, nor to the democrats. Both Hahn and Lestevenon, lukewarm supporters of the draft, and van Hooff, still undecided, warned that an alliance of arch-federalists and revolutionary democrats would coalesce to defeat it.[48] Their prediction turned out to be only too accurate. The three months between the final arrangements for ratification being completed in May and the vote itself on August 8 gave the two wings of opposition ample time to mobilise all the strength they could command.

In the land provinces, the federalists were able to call not only on their usual constituencies among the landowners and the regents of the towns, but also on many of the urban clubs, where fears of higher taxes as well as suspicions that the "slijmgasten" (lit., trimmers; slippery customers) of the Assembly politicians were in the process of betraying revolutionary democracy combined to swell the opposition. Coert van Beijma, who was a federalist on taxation but a unitarist and a democrat on everything else, had no trouble in reconciling the illogicalities of his position nor in urging them on fellow Friesians. Predikants who took exception to the separation of Church and state which de Mist had called "the National Theft," and who felt threatened by the removal of primary education from their tutelage, directed their congregations to cast out the Satanic work. The unitarists were even better organised for a campaign of rejection. Echoing Vreede's denunciation in the Assembly, their press condemned the draft as a mandate for an electoral aristocracy and a staging-post to the restoration of the old regime. Juicy libels circulated about the interests of the deputies who had been keenest to endorse it. Two of the most influential clubs, "Voor Een- en Ondeelbaarheid" ("For Unity and Indivisibility") in Amsterdam and "Voor Eenheid en Orde"

("For Unity and Order") in The Hague published their detailed objections in pamphlet form. *De Politieke Opmerker* (*The Political Observer*) and *De Democraten* treated the document as almost below contempt, urging their readers to have no truck with it; and meetings of popular societies in Utrecht, Dordrecht, Amsterdam and Rotterdam were convened expressly for the purpose of contradicting it, point by point.

The climax came on August 6, two days before the vote, when Pieter Vreede, along with just eleven of his fellow deputies, among them van Beijma, L. C. Vonck, and the Catholics Stephen van Langen and Hendrik Midderigh, issued an *Address to the Batavian People*. This manifesto of the "twelve apostles," as it became known, asked all good patriots to vote against the constitution and to place their faith in the election of a new Assembly. Only when the notorious "Regulation" was removed could the atmosphere be freer for the drafting of a truly enlightened and republican constitution; one which would guarantee the Batavian people their liberties by a sovereign legislature in permanent session, directly elected and permitting the due rights of petition, redress and recall.[44] Just what damage the manifesto did cannot be estimated. But Vreede had no misgivings. Better, he felt, no constitution at all than a wicked constitution. "The cursed spirit of egoism and federalism knows no patriotic feeling or communal spirit," he wrote to Valckenaer in Madrid;

. . . indeed so far as any principle has been retained [in the draft] it is the spirit of aristocracy. If the people can be so hoodwinked as to let this thing be accepted and the machine of state trundle along like an ox-cart with eight-sided wheels then their freedom is lost. . . . If the nation can be content with such a freedom it had as well bring back the old regime.[45]

Not all of those who thought of themselves as unitarists and even democrats were given to such flights of self-righteousness. Lestevenon reminded Valckenaer that should the draft be rejected, "our country will be in no condition to withstand a prolongation of the kind of interregnum which rules at present."[46] And even Hahn, who had agreed that the draft was indeed a "harlequin's coat," confessed that in the circumstances, "it would be better to put on the harlequin's costume than go about bare-arsed."[47] Valckenaer himself, who fully shared many of Vreede's criticisms and felt at bottom that the draft was a botched compromise with the federalists, appreciated the difficulties of the situation. Just before learning the result of the vote, he wrote to van Langen:

As a minister and public official I must desire that it be accepted, understanding well enough the need that we have for some form of definitive organisation. But as a citizen having to live under such a constitution, I disapprove of it and reject it; I even look upon it as likely to revive the old aristocracy and the Stadholder. As a patriot and calculator of events, knowing the mood of the French and fearing the temper of the Second (National) Assembly, elected by a nation already exhausted, will be more federalist, I would counsel acceptance. I know not if there is some contradiction in all this but this in truth is how I feel.[48]

The sponsors of the constitution were well aware of the complaints brought against their draft—the opposition campaign was hardly clandestine —but they had no means of gauging its strength. Not unreasonably they supposed that the same electorate which had chosen a moderate, patrician, federalist Assembly would now endorse the constitution which had found favour in the eyes of its majority. They also hoped that the few concessions to unitarism and the copious references to "Een- en Ondeelbaarheid" would be sufficient to bring round the more temperate of the popular societies. But it was obvious that even if they were successful the result would be a close thing. Trying to tilt the odds a little more in their direction, steps were taken to publicise the draft, to explain it in simple language and to advertise its virtues as widely as possible. A campaign of political education such as had rarely been seen in the Netherlands was launched. Twenty thousand copies of an abridged version were printed for distribution via provincial, municipal and ecclesiastical authorities during June and July. Instructional pamphlets in the form of conversation pieces ("samenspraaken"), devised not only to explain but to anticipate the principal objections, were likewise distributed at virtually no cost to the purchasers and were often printed by the more conservative pro-constitution press. One such specimen, purporting to be the casual conversation of two pipe-smoking, gin-toting Hollanders, "Pieter en Klaas," turns into a breathless recitation by the better-informed of a catalogue of benefits which the constitution is about to bestow on all good citizens. Dazzled by this show of erudition, all that his partner can reply by way of conclusion is: "I'm amazed you can hold all that information up there in your head."[49]

The French ambassador apparently shared this astonishment. Concerned lest even the most strenuous propaganda efforts of the pro-constitutionalists would be insufficient to guarantee it a majority, and supported by the Directory which wished to see their Dutch ally get the wretched business over and done with, Noël decided to add his weight to the scales. A week or so before the vote he descended from the lofty and rather impartial pedestal on which he had carefully placed the reputation of the "Grande Nation" and issued a public appeal to the Dutch not to reject the opportunity for salvation being held out to them on August 8. This was a big mistake. As the Prussian agent happily reported, it alienated rather than attracted support by identifying the draft as the officially approved "French" version. For in the summer of 1797—with 25,000 troops still stationed in the Republic, eating into the treasuries of local and national officials, and friction growing over the treatment of neutral shipping—the French were not exactly riding the crest of a wave of popularity.

Hahn's worst forebodings were shatteringly vindicated on the day. Put to the Dutch people, the constitution of 1797 was rejected by 108,761 votes to 27,955. As it turned out, however the vote might have been counted, it would have been lost, for the constitution failed to win a majority in any one of the nine provinces! The vote was closest in the smallest electorates of all: Zeeland, Drente and Groningen, though the draft won 14,000 ayes in Holland. In the unitarist strongholds of Utrecht and Brabant the vote was crushingly negative, the proportion of rejections to acceptances being, respectively, 5:1 and 54:1. Even in the land provinces of Gelderland and Overijssel, the ratios were 6:1 and 3:1.

It was a brutal and unequivocal verdict on the eighteen months of temporising, manoeuvre and feud which, following the death of Pieter Paulus, had descended on his National Assembly like a poisoned fog. Above all it demonstrated that the consensus so painfully pieced together by such as Schimmelpenninck and the moderate federalists at the end of 1796, and which seemed to have won an important victory on December 2, had in fact been utterly chimerical. It had merely papered over a fundamental crack in the Batavian Republic as to what form the sovereignty of the new state was to take. Because of the peculiar coalition of forces and interests which had combined to defeat the constitution, it was still not yet clear whether or not the Dutch wanted to see a revolution take place in their forms of government. What was damningly plain was that the noble but doomed effort to by-pass this problem by grounding revolutionary institutions in the legitimacy of consent had come to a miserable conclusion. Henceforth the fate of the new Dutch Republic would be resolved by a trial of strength.

****

7

Forced to Be Free,
August 1797–January 1798

The Unsettled Alliance

The rejection of the 1797 constitution brought the hobbling progress of the Batavian Republic to a dead halt. The national veto had led to an impasse from which there seemed to be no obvious exit. The loose coalition of "moderate" federalists, patrician republicans and tepid unitarists had failed to win the assent of the electorate for its government; but by the same token those who had been shut out of power—obdurate federalists and democrat radicals—were each independently incapable of taking it. Collaboration on anything other than frustrating the designs of the majority was unthinkable. The result of the deadlock was to cast the Republic into a kind of Polish chaos, the end of which no-one dared predict. Pieter Vreede had pinned his hopes on the successor Assembly, in which a strong unitarist majority would be empowered to get on with the work of creating a truly unified democracy, unencumbered by hedging regulations and federal anachronisms. But the elections, held a week before the plebiscite, proved inconclusive. To be sure, the radicals were thicker on the benches than in the first Assembly but they by no means made up a decisive majority. It did not take the most mournful pessimist to predict that the new body might prove to be even more divisive than the last.

More serious even than its disunity was the Assembly's lack of credibility. Patriots who had looked to Paulus' "Convention" as the consummation of the revolution had begun to despair, after two years of factious prattle, of seeing anything positive—such as a constitution—emerge from its deliberations. The spectacle of a tawdry slanging match was not what had been expected from a body inaugurated with such lofty ceremony. Was it so surprising, Rogge asked, that the nation had rejected the constitution when it had witnessed its own representatives heaping abuse on what was, ostensibly, to be the charter of the nation's future?[1]

With every month that passed, the gap between promise and fulfilment

[271]

grew wider. Patriots who had rejoiced at the departure of the Stadholder could
be forgiven for wondering what, exactly, the revolution was supposed to
amount to in 1797. The magical transformation of their private and public
lives had not materialised. They remained subject to municipal councils dominated by men of a superior social stratum, even if they disdained the title of
regent. Taxes were certainly no lighter than they had been; if anything, quite
the reverse. Both at the apex and at the base of government there was the same
hectic jostling for place and power which had disgraced the old regime. Indeed,
it still seemed to be conducted by men who, in Valckenaer's choice phrase,
"held the rudder of State in their hands and the cushions of State beneath
their High and most Mighty Behinds."[2] The same pettifogging jealousies had
got in the way of the common good. Daendels complained to his brother-in-
law Colonel Grasveld that the proper organisation of a national militia had
been retarded because

the burghers in a number of towns and other places are well-armed and drilled
but I have no idea how to unite them. You know our nation. If a citizen officer
in one town has just one more silver button on his epaulette than another, a
great hue and cry arises and the important cause goes by the board. . . .[3]

Naturally there were men of probity and energy like van de Kasteele and
Hugo Gevers manning committees and struggling to keep the Republic afloat
against the tidal waves of debt and military liability which periodically threatened to engulf it. For sheer administrative competence they were no worse, and
very often a deal better, than their old regime predecessors. At the subordinate
levels, indeed, the receivers, excise inspectors and butter-measurers were identical with the pre-revolutionary personnel. But too often the mundane exigencies
facing the Republic were obscured by the extravagant vocabulary with which
the revolution continued to be adorned. Transported by great gusts of rhetoric,
the deputies in the Assembly hardly paused to consider if their resources were
equal to their ambitions. For what *was* revolution if not the triumph of native
virtue; the elixir by which decadence would be arrested and virility restored?
If Gerrit Paape and Bernardus Bosch were to be credited, the wonders wrought
by the young republics of America and France would be humdrum compared
to the magnificence of the reborn Batavia.[4] Even in the summer of 1797, with
an evaporating treasury, a client sovereignty and a vacuum for a constitution,
such hallucinations possessed astonishing potency for those addicted to the
nostrums of revolutionary ideology.

There were friends of the Republic whose political intoxication was
diluted by the exercise of cool intelligence. Both Samuel Wiselius and Johan
Valckenaer retained enough detachment to see in the Dutch revolution not the
spontaneous liberation celebrated in official republican hymnals but the discriminate application of force for the ends of benevolent change. Their correspondence with each other, with Dumont-Pigalle in Paris, and with their
circle of friends supplies an ironic commentary on the more euphoric delusions
of those attempting to control events. Yet it could not have been entirely
fortuitous that their percipience on these matters was in directly inverse rela-

tion to their capacity to do anything about them. Even at his most engaged Wiselius remained on the fringes of power, ruling his little empire in the East India Committee in Amsterdam and surveying the follies of The Hague from his club armchair at "De Uitkijk" ("The Watch"). Peremptorily asked to commit himself to an act of overt force in January 1798, he shied away from the engagement.

Exiled in his Spanish fastness Valckenaer discovered in Godoy, the "Prince of Peace," another fish out of water with whom he could freely communicate his anxieties. For his first year in Madrid he scrutinised his intelligences carefully for any signs of a change in the political climate in the Batavian Republic which might enable him to play a more central role; but repeatedly disappointed, he turned instead to vinegary ruminations on the fecklessness of politics.[5] In the last resort, both Wiselius and Valckenaer were intellectuals rather than politicians. For all their avowed republicanism, they shared a somewhat patrician distaste for the hurly-burly of political life. Less fastidious types, marrying together qualities of resolution and intelligence badly needed in a post-revolutionary situation, were conspicuous by their absence in the Batavian Republic.

This said, eighteenth-century Dutchmen should not be taken to task too severely for wanting an admixture of integrity, resourcefulness and mental clarity which has eluded later more sophisticated generations of revolutionary politicians. The task of finding that golden equilibrium between coercive populism on the one hand and reaction by default on the other has proved notoriously difficult. Moreover, since by definition revolution involves a dramatic intensification of expectation, it also runs a correspondingly greater risk of disenchantment. Yet it was not disillusionment but probably the lack of it which impaired the Dutch revolutionaries' comprehension of what they were up to. It was less the failure to effect a unification of sovereignty or a popular democracy which led them astray than that failure combined with the presumption that such changes should have followed "naturally" on the events of 1795. There was a strong tone of wounded bafflement in van Hooff's observation that "so far from making one single Republic this land has reverted to a state of many little republics of towns and localities."[6]

No self-criticism was entailed in such observations. On the contrary, conspiracy theories stood in for political explanations. If the people had somehow been denied the fruits of the revolution, it was plain that some kind of mischievous intervention was responsible. The "aristocratic" domination of the primary assemblies; the attacks on the vox populi of the clubs and the press; the resistance to the formation of a National Guard—all pointed to malevolent political engineering. Its principal consequence had been the relatively disappointing radical representation in the second Assembly. Instead of the "braeve kaerels" (the Dutch equivalent to the saltier Gallic "bons bougres") demanded by Pieter Vreede, the first Assembly had been packed with "slijmgasten." Those "slippery customers" had manoeuvred their way to power by assuming the guise of Patriots (like all conspiracy theories the language of the radicals is peppered with references to disguise, concealment and cosmetic) and usurping their rightful places. Having tricked the people into electing them, they proceeded to cook up their masterpiece of sophistry, the "Dikke Boek," expressly made to ensure the surrender of the people's sovereignty while persuading them that they were in fact exercising it. If, after the foiling of those machinations, they persisted in frustrating the rights of the people, then their true friends would be not merely entitled but duty bound to counter ruse with ruse, subterfuge with subterfuge and, in the last resort, call on the people to support them in the *enforcement* of their will. It was to be, as Ockerse said, "Mauvais jeu, bonne mine."[7]

Painful alliances of means and ends are not unfamiliar in situations where revolutionary élites seek to reconcile the coercive action of the few with the commitment to democracy proclaimed in their ideology. The consummation of this tendency was duly celebrated in the Batavian Republic on January 22, 1798, when with the assistance of a handful of Dutch troops and in collusion with the French ambassador, a caucus of radicals from the second National Assembly purged the legislature, arrested those whom they took to be their principal opponents and established a revolutionary executive. Though the regime survived for only five months, it left an indelible imprint on the Republic and indeed on its subsequent historiography. Its origins and consequences were minutely dissected by Colenbrander. Geyl made it the tragic terminus of his epic narrative. Since Dr. de Wit's more generous interpretation, the issue has been taken up again by academic combatants.[8] Indeed, the attitudes struck by historians towards the coup of January 22 may be taken as touchstones of their regard for the Batavian Republic as a whole. The act which for Groen van Prinsterer and Colenbrander expressed ignoble deference to the imperatives of French domination and the spinelessness of Dutch republicanism was, for Thorbecke and de Wit, a valiant endeavour to galvanise the Batavian Republic into a democratic nation state. Plainly there can be no way of, nor any reason for, yoking together such opposed interpretations. But what may be asked of both is whether the radical coup was actually the paradigmatic event in which all the essential characteristics of the revolution—good or ill—can be discerned. Pieter Geyl may have overstated the case for understatement by seeing it as little more than an arbitrary interruption in the unfolding continuity of Dutch moderation; but the radical revolution owed more to haphazard circumstance than either of the principal competing historiographies allow.

The "sympathetic" case for making the coup the pivotal event of the Republic's history rests largely on the contribution it is held to have made to institutional change, and in particular to the eventual enactment of a constitution in April 1798. Immediately following the coup, as well as later in their careers, those who had been involved argued that it had been an indispensable precondition of those changes, and the logical response to the bankruptcy of "consensus" politics.[9] The "antipathetic" case holds that the coup was a revelation of the true character of the Republic in so far as its naked dependence on French support finally discarded any pretence at upholding national sovereignty. The 22nd of January was the "Dutch Fructidor," just as the counter-coup on June 12 was the "Dutch Floréal," both made in the image of their protectors.

Both arguments warrant further examination not least because if it is clear that France *caused* the revolution to happen, its ramifications for Dutch politics must be seriously qualified. Moreover, while such a view commands little support from recent research, it would be excessively naïve to suppose that the demands of the alliance played no part in determining the twists and turns of Batavian politics.

Since the forced nuptials of May 1795, the condition of the Franco-Dutch alliance had shown no signs of improvement. On the other hand, despite the colossal dowry the bride had been obliged to bring to the match as the price of her future protection and maintenance, nor had it appreciably deteriorated. This was due in large measure to the sensitive and judicious ministry of the first French agent, François Noël. After the caustic manners of types like Richard, Cochon and Sieyès, the affable easy-going diplomacy of Noël must have come as something of a relief to the hard-pressed leaders of the Batavian Republic. Having married into the Bogaerts, Noël was well suited to the un-hurried ways of Hague society. More than this, he was a sincere believer in the value of the alliance. Carefully managed by men such as himself who combined professional talents and a small fortune with a moderate political temper, he believed that the relationship was capable of supplying for the war effort those assets—primarily ships and money—for which it had been struck. In Paulus, Noël believed he had found the model of a republican notable to whom he looked to produce these dividends. Even though some of the ships were as leaky as the finances which paid for them, he was delighted to be able to report to the Directory early in 1796 that not only would the Batavian Re-public honour its next instalment of the indemnity but it would have three squadrons ready for active service at the Texel in the spring.

Coming so hard on this modest success, Paulus' death struck Noël a grave blow. As the political situation steadily deteriorated through 1796, Noël's reports to Paris reflected his difficulties in treading a fine line between federalist reaction and popular revolution. He appreciated the argument that unitarism was the only means by which the devastated finances of the country might be repaired and that a redistribution of the fiscal burden was long overdue. He also sympathised with the reformers' frustration at seeing their efforts to create a new state pared down into an amended version of the old States-General. But on the other hand he was too much a man of the Directory not to take fright at the prospect of wooing the popular societies, the *wijk* meet-ings and Patriot militia. "General Déjean," he wrote to the Directory in February 1797, "is convinced that we have to fear a federalist reaction. I think, however, that the federalists are much less dangerous than the ultra-revolu-tionaries whose system is one of violence and murder."[10] No doubt that was how he felt about the respective threats of royalism and Jacobinism in France. Were the Batavian Republic to be overwhelmed by the horrors of popular democracy, it would mean the emigration of capital and capitalists without whom the Dutch were a useless ally and the sacrifice of the nation to an Anglophile counter-revolution.

Curiously enough, the seriousness of this problem did not incline Noël to use the weight of his position to "persuade" the Dutch leaders to adopt measures he thought in the best interests of the alliance. On the contrary, it seemed to throw him into a state of paralysed circumspection in which no action was preferable to ill-judged action. In 1797, one of the moderate deputies reported that

last Thursday he [Noël] was so mortified by what has happened here that he cried like a child asking us to indicate to him the means that might be employed to prevent this evil. But when he was advised to present a note to the National Convention [sic] and the government committees and to urge them, in the name of the [French] executive Directory to be stern with the malevolent, Noël absolutely refused, insisting that he had no authorisation.[11]

Noël's fixed position on the fence, surveying the growing chaos of Dutch politics, displeased not only the unitarists who had looked to him for support but the French Directory itself—already accustomed to regard their agents in the "sister republics" as the engineers of an active realpolitik. To impatient busybodies like Reubell their man at The Hague seemed too fastidious by half, actually appearing to believe in the letter of the alliance and insisting that the representatives of the "Grande Nation" should hold themselves "above party." His diplomatic credo, announced in 1796, was endearingly old-fashioned:

The great and overriding rule of all alliances must be that of reciprocal interest. Do we wish to draw from our alliance with this nation those advantages which have been proposed to us [by Ramel and Cochon]? Then let us conceal our influence even as it is exercised, revealing only the hand that protects and not that which constrains, and let us try to bring this nation to a constitutional regime with unity as its base and energy for its principle of action, with the same calm that we have brought to the Convention's government.[12]

Admirable as it was in theory, Noël's principle of unobtrusive tutelage came under severe strain during the cannoneers' riots in May 1796 and then again early in 1797 when the war between the Friesian factions became inflamed. On both occasions Noël reluctantly consented to the use of French troops to restore civil order; but equally he insisted that they had been used, not on behalf of any "party," but simply in support of the Dutch "police." It was only in July 1797 that he stepped from the pedestal of dignified neutrality to give the constitution his official blessing—thus bringing about exactly the coalition of federalist and democrat which his intervention had been concerned to prevent. The lesson he drew from the disaster was not that he should have taken a more direct interest in the shaping of opinion all along but that he had been ill-advised to go even as far as he had. Without actually tampering with the Dutch suffrage, he informed the new Foreign Minister, Talleyrand (for whom such malversations held little terror) that nothing could have been done to affect the unfortunate verdict of August 8. The Dutch were incorrigibly attached to their parochial allegiances, clerical fanaticism and administrative anarchy. All that the agent might do was to revert to his role of passive observation and hope for a more auspicious new Assembly. Otherwise the Dutch should be abandoned to "their own wisdom or their own folly."

Neither Talleyrand nor his superiors on the Directory were prepared to share the stoicism of their agent at The Hague, especially since changes in military and political circumstances had promoted the importance of the Dutch alliance to a new level of significance. Up until the summer of 1797, the Batavian Republic had figured in French plans principally as a defensive buffer: protecting the North Sea coast and the Scheldt estuary against a British naval offensive, and shielding the Belgian *départements réunis* against any signs of an Austrian revival. This auxiliary role had matched a foreign policy not yet irreversibly committed to the doctrine of "grandes limites" nor even to the "natural frontiers" of the Pyrenees, the Alps and the Rhine. The conqueror of the Netherlands, General Pichegru, had shown himself suspiciously limp in his further prosecution of the war across the Rhine, and, like Moreau two years later, was correctly rumoured to be negotiating with the Austrians.

Lazare Carnot, now a Director, was anxious to put his Jacobin past well behind him, and for all the lustre of his reputation as the "Organiser of Victory" was conservative in his appraisal of military objectives. Not without reason, Carnot feared perpetual war as the harbinger of a second Terror and a further dose of revolution. He was additionally convinced that an over-ambitious appetite for annexations would inevitably lead to reciprocally incessant belligerence between France and the Coalition powers. He had been cool towards the creation of the Batavian Republic, tolerating it only as a weapon to use in the settlement with Prussia. Under no circumstances was he prepared to regard it as the first link in a chain of "sister republics" strung out along the "natural frontiers" as a second line of defence, and bound to France by interest and ideology.

Not all of his colleagues shared Carnot's caution. The opinionated Alsatian Jean-François Reubell was eager to pursue the Austrians as far as they would go, gobbling up territories and creating a bloc of dependent states enroute to Vienna.[13] His ambitions were supported by the pontiff of "Theophilanthropy" La Revellière-Lépeaux, and by Barras, manoeuvring between the factions with shark-like rapacity and elegance. Barras and Carnot were at daggers drawn, and in the last resort Reubell's fear and suspicion of Carnot prevailed over his nausea at Barras' noxious licentiousness. More important, Barras was the patron of the men of the hour: the Republic's praetorian guard Hoche, Joubert, Bernadotte, and above all Bonaparte, the saviour of "Vendémiaire."

Although the balance of power within the Directory seemed to veer towards Barras and Reubell, the military situation in the late autumn of 1796 was hardly propitious for their plans. The strategy of sending the two great Armies of the Rhine, and the Moselle and Sambre, through southern Germany and Switzerland to join in an offensive on Austria had misfired badly against the intelligent generalship of the Archduke Charles, Francis II's brother. When Malmesbury arrived in France in October to discuss preliminary negotiations with Delacroix, then foreign minister, he had been instructed by Grenville that the precondition of any formal talks would be the restitution of Belgium, the evacuation of Lombardy and the left bank of the Rhine, and a guarantee that France would never again occupy Dutch Flanders and control the estuary of the Scheldt. This was as near to thumbing their nose at the French Republic as the British could get. It was not well received. Grenville and Malmesbury may well have regretted their temerity, as the brilliant success of Bonaparte's gamble in Italy the following spring transformed the situation out of all recognition. The Directory had intended that the relatively weak Army of the Alps should merely act against the Sardinians in a diversionary capacity, while the main thrust against Austria was carried by the junction of the two great forces to the north. But the defeat of Moreau and Jourdan gave Bonaparte an opportunity not only to harry the outflanked Austrians through Lombardy and Venetia but subsequently to conduct virtually independent diplomacy with Thugut, culminating in the armistice of March 1797. However upset by this impertinence, the Directory could hardly decline the abundance of territories and powers presented to it by the Peace of Leoben in April.

The removal of Austria and the death of Catherine the Great had brought the first Coalition to its final débacle. There remained just one enemy—and that the most intractable. But France was now in a position to turn her attention to that enemy alone, and to revert to that most ancient *idée fixe*: the isolation and reduction of British imperial power. The initial attempts had not been auspicious. A tentative landing on Bantry Bay in December 1796 had ended in fiasco; Spanish and Dutch colonies had dropped to British naval power like ninepins, and in February 1797 the Spanish fleet had received a thrashing from Admiral Jervis. But by the summer matters looked more promising. Reliable intelligences suggested bitter divisions within the British Cabinet; the chronic financial disarray, the mutinies at Spithead and the Nore in July, and the stirrings of rebellion in Ireland all seemed to announce that the long-awaited "campaign of England" was at hand. Earlier in the year Wolfe Tone and Lord Edward Fitzgerald, the leaders of the inappropriately named "United Irishmen," had appeared in Paris to concert plans of invasion with the Directory. General Hoche—for whom an Irish invasion was becoming, despite the setback at Bantry Bay, something of an obsession—was an ardent propagandist for the cause and had made an incognito inspection of the naval establishment at the Texel. The original plan had been for two expeditions, one comprising a Franco-Spanish fleet of forty vessels from Brest and another comprising a smaller Dutch fleet bearing French troops from the Texel. The first was to land in the south of Ireland, the second in the north under the command of Hoche. Tone and Hoche had got as far as conferring at The Hague at the end of June, and the Irish leader had then spent a miserable few weeks bobbing up and down on Admiral de Winter's flagship *De Vrijheid* at the Texel waiting for favourable winds which never came.[14]

As the summer passed, enthusiasm for the expedition waned. Hoche fell ill; the Brest fleet never looked like being ready in time, and the French were suspiciously happy to accede to Daendels' request that the bulk of the troops carried on the Texel fleet be Dutch, not French. July would have been the optimal moment for such an offensive. British morale was at a low ebb, its government turning to neurotic repression and Admiral Duncan's Yarmouth fleet short of men and ships. When Malmesbury returned to Lille for negotiations he was in a very much more chastened and defensive temper than in the previous autumn. The British government was now prepared not only to recognise the Belgian *départements réunis* as French territory but also the annexation of the departments on the left bank of the Rhine. On this occasion it was France's turn to prove obdurate. Emphasising the importance of the Dutch connexion, the French demanded on behalf of their allies the return of all colonies and naval vessels seized by the British.

But it was the domestic situation in France which interrupted the invasion plans most decisively. The April elections to the legislative councils had returned a substantial majority of crypto-royalists, "Clichyens" and moderates whose sympathies were for a speedy end to the war, a *modus vivendi* with Britain, and a repudiation both of territorial annexation and the republican crusade. To press home these views Pichegru was elected President of the upper Chamber, the "Council of Ancients"; Barthélemy joined the Directory as an ally of Carnot; and the anti-republican press issued a torrent of execration at the high-handed "tyranny" of the upstart Caesar in Italy. In the period between Leoben in April and the conclusion of a definitive peace at Campo Formio in October, it was obvious to those at the centre of politics in Paris that another political upheaval, either to the "right" or the "left," was in the offing. Pichegru and the Councils on the one hand and the Directorial "triumvirate" of Barras, Reubell and La Revellière-Lépeaux on the other competed in intrigue and conspiracy.

Not for the last time, it was Bonaparte who acted while others gossiped in corners. Replying in kind to the journalists' tirade, he sent General Augereau to Paris with detailed instructions to cleanse the Augean stables of the royalist dirt. On September 4, managed by Barras, the army and the Directory together carried out their coup against the legislature and the constitution they had sworn to defend. Carnot, Barthélemy and Pichegru were all arrested, along with scores of councillors and ministers, among whom were two others who had been instrumental in creating the Batavian Republic as Carnot and Sieyès had wished: François Ramel and Charles Cochon de Lapperant.

The "18 Fructidor" was not only a victory for republican force over constitutional legitimacy. It also signalled the success of the more belligerent and expansionist foreign policy upheld by Barras and Reubell. One of the first acts of the new regime was the abrupt termination of the discussions with Malmesbury at Lille. Plans for the Irish invasion were taken up yet again. If the war was to be prosecuted further and the conquests "consolidated," it was essential that a solid bloc of territories from Tuscany to Brabant be firmly secured within the orbit of French domination. And if this security required interference in the internal affairs of "sister republics," Barras and Reubell had no scruples. To make the politics of Swiss or Italian or Dutch republicans more intelligible, their protagonists were invariably grouped in factions comprehensible to the Paris Directory. Ligurian "anarchists," Batavian "aristocrats" and Bernese "Clichyens" peopled their correspondence on the "sister republics" with little regard for the geographical nuances of nation or region. Local French agents or their military counterparts suddenly found themselves invested with authority to do as they wished with their allied hosts. Thus Genoese democrats were restored to power through a French military ultimatum; the constitutions of the Cisalpine and Cispadane Republics in Italy engineered to suit the predilections of Generals Bonaparte and Brune, and that of the Helvetic Republic jointly manufactured by the Directors and the Zurich republican Peter Ochs.

The strategic shift resulting from the coup of 18 Fructidor was a distinctly mixed blessing for the Batavian Republic. On the one hand, it whetted the appetite of its few warriors like Daendels hungry for combat with the British. But it also created a situation in which the latitude permitted to the Dutch in the conduct of their domestic politics suddenly appeared exceptional. In this latter respect its position was more nearly akin to Godoy's Spain than to the dependent republics of Switzerland and Italy. How long the French would content themselves with passive observation of their seemingly incurable political maladies was a subject of increasingly nervous speculation by the Dutch. The inheritors of the "moderate" majority in the second Assembly, and particularly those on its federalist wing, were uncomfortably aware of their new vulnerability. Given new heart by the Fructidor coup, the radicals had taken the offensive again. Their clubs and papers were renewing the accusation that those in charge of the government of the Republic were, either through impotence or inclination, shielding the sinister forces of counter-revolution. This was just the sort of allegation in vogue immediately prior to Fructidor in France, but propaganda aside, there seemed no shortage of evidence to suggest that the Batavian authorities were letting things slide. In February an Orangist riot at Collum in Friesland had needed a detachment of guards from Dokkum to pacify it, and later that year troops from what had been the Orange-Nassau Regiment at Schoonhoven rioted in their garrison and had to be disarmed by the militia. Although the act of lèse-république was no doubt committed before 1795, it was discovered that about forty sailors at the Texel had portraits of the Stadholder and the slogan "Oranje Boven" tattooed on their chests.[15]

More seriously for the alliance of the two nations, the French army was becoming deeply unpopular with its "hosts." The conditions under which the paper assignat currency was foisted on to Dutch tradesmen invited both hostility and evasion. The obligation to exchange assignats for special "receipts" created a new, even more rapidly depreciating currency, and the number of whippings, swingeing fines and other sentences for currency violations mounted steeply during the course of 1796 and 1797.[16] Fraud was not the worst of it. French soldiers celebrating 18 Fructidor were murdered by unknown hands (suspected to be French émigrés) on the Lange Voorhout, not a stone's throw from the National Assembly. Both in Brabant and Gelderland there was vigorous resistance to French military command. In Geertruydenberg a squadron of Dutch militia laid down its arms rather than accept the command of a certain Houssaye, whose reputation for arrogance and callousness in Utrecht had preceded him to Brabant. The Gelderland mutiny was still more serious as it was led by a group of junior officers. Before it had been suppressed by Daendels' troops from Zwolle, a whole company had been cashiered, two soldiers executed and others exiled or imprisoned after public humiliations.[17] In response to requests from the Batavian Committee for War that the French honour the Treaty of The Hague and gradually reduce the numbers of their troops, General Déjean baldly stated that their presence in the Republic was not merely a bulwark of the alliance but the only guarantee against complete political and social decomposition.[18]

The experiment in co-territoriality at Flushing was an even greater disaster. Brawls between French and Dutch sailors were an almost daily commonplace, and the imposition of French customs officers on the Scheldt estuary only attracted the attention of smugglers for whom they were scarcely a match. The port became the centre of a bitter dispute between the two allies on the interpretation of the treaty clause dealing with its jurisdiction. The Dutch claimed that they had ceded merely the facility, not the sovereignty, of half the port and that they were therefore entitled to exercise civil jurisdiction throughout. The French on their side demanded to be treated with extra-territorial immunity.[19] Still more alarming, detailed reports of the activities of Robert Barclay and the double agent Breukelman were spiced by the rumour that Prince Frederick had traveled the length and breadth of the country in the summer, disguised as a woman, scouting for support and attempting to influence the primary assemblies against the constitution. Whatever the truth of such stories—and the Directory had swallowed far less plausible ones—this accumulation of irritations did little to inspire confidence that the Dutch were able to manage their responsibilities for keeping counter-revolution off north-west Europe.

It was pressures of this kind which, in the late autumn of 1797, led the Committee for Foreign Affairs into reviving the discarded schemes for an attack on Britain. After the humiliation of the loss of Ceylon and Surinam and the capture of Lucas' fleet at Saldanha Bay at the Cape in December 1796, a naval engagement in the North Sea could be little more than an act of bravura intended to demonstrate to both enemy and ally that the Dutch were still worthy of their national independence. If this was the intention, it rebounded back disastrously on its authors. The time for an attack on Britain's eastern flank had passed with the summer. Hoche was dead; Tone had moved on. Eighty thousand British soldiers were stationed in Ireland; there were little signs of the expected "national uprising" in Scotland, and Duncan's fleet —which had been seriously depleted in July—was now more than adequately victualled and reinforced. All this depressing evidence made little impact on Daendels, who seemed still to be thinking in fantastic terms of a landing at

Harwich or Great Yarmouth from which Dutch troops would move in stately progress either south to London or north to Edinburgh and Glasgow and thence perhaps across to Ireland![20]

The Committee for Foreign Affairs, of which Gevers and Hahn were both members, were not quite as zany; but encouraged by Noël (whose own reputation was at stake), they persuaded themselves that de Winter ought at least to engage with Duncan before winter set in. The admiral himself was deeply pessimistic about the whole enterprise, recognising not only that winds favourable for such an engagement were most unlikely in early October but that Duncan's fleet was by that time considerably superior in both mobility and cannon. After so much effort had been put into patching up a dozen ships-of-the-line, it seemed reckless to commit them to so perilous a gamble. But the Committee for Foreign Affairs smelt victory with the October breezes; on the 5th, despite the strong protests of a minority, it ordered de Winter to sail from the Texel.

Needless to say, Duncan and the Lords of the Admiralty were delighted. They were itching to demonstrate to the government conclusively that the summer mutinies had not impaired the effectiveness of the navy; what better way than to administer yet another drubbing to the hapless Dutch? On October 11 the two fleets met off the Helder in what was to be the last great ritual combat between British and Dutch maritime power: the Battle of Camperdown (Kamperduin). Although much more decisive than Dogger Bank twelve years earlier, like that occasion it was a dignified exit from the ranks of the great European powers. Broadsides were exchanged for hours; the crowds gathered at den Helder could actually make out columns of smoke on the horizon and the low rumble of ships' guns. Outgunned and outnumbered, de Winter's fleet fought with grim steadfastness as if attempting to recapture the ardour and resourcefulness which had taken Dutch ships up the Medway to fire King Charles' fleet a century before. But technology and tactics had changed a great deal and, as in so many other spheres, the Dutch were still living in the past. Superior manoeuvrability and the concentration of thirty-cannon ships firing sixty-eight pounders finally succeeded in cutting the line in two places, a disaster to which the alleged misinterpretation of an order from de Winter to Admiral Story had contributed.[21] The rest was academic. After 1,000 of his 7,000 sailors had lost their lives on the big and cumbersome ships-of-the-line, with his own flagship *De Vrijheid* mastless and surrounded by five British vessels, de Winter finally capitulated. According to the gallantries customary on these occasions he surrendered his sword, his person and what was left of his fleet to Duncan. Magnanimous in their turn, the British repatriated him after a few months' imprisonment. De Winter returned to the Batavian Republic to receive, rather surprisingly, a hero's welcome.

At the time, however, these gestures were lost on the Dutch leaders. Instead of the intended vindication of their national autonomy, Camperdown proved to be the clinching argument for those who insisted that matters could no longer be left to drift on aimlessly; that the defeat had been a direct consequence of the chaos eating away at the heart of Dutch government. The radicals who had actually been most vocal in their demands that de Winter set on the British fleet were now in the van of those blaming the Committee for Foreign Affairs for the disaster. There was no doubt that it was as serious a *political* blow to the viability of the Republic as the Brest fiasco had been for William V in 1784.

Even had the naval battle gone the opposite way there is evidence to suggest that the fructidorian Directory was considering some form of intervention in the domestic government of their Dutch ally. Four days before the engagement, on October 7, Noël despatched a report to Paris which took the form of answers to five questions obviously directed at him at the end of September. Had everything possible been done to induce the Dutch to accept a unitary constitution? Could anything more constructive be expected of the new Assembly than of its predecessor? If not, what further action might be contemplated? How should it be efficiently executed? And to whom should its direction be confided? Noël was hardly innocent of the end to which these questions were leading. He still found the prospect of armed intervention profoundly repugnant, but Fructidor had made his own position shaky and he considered it prudent to take his cue from the pliant Talleyrand and bend with the prevailing wind to avoid being broken as a dangerous arch-moderate.

Yet even while embracing the new orthodoxy, Noël managed to blacken the Dutch radicals by continuing to describe them in his reports as "anarchists" who, like their French counterparts, were accused of being the most extreme outriders of the *counter*-revolution. Since it went without saying that such creatures were wholly unsuitable for operations of great delicacy, he had no difficulty in answering the last of the five questions. If intervention could not be avoided, then the Directory should beware of entrusting it to "a secret agent who would have the disadvantage of treading on unfamiliar terrain." Instead, the direction should be confided to

a minister for whom two years of painful experience have garnered a wide understanding of men and matters and whose reputation for moderation, humanity and disinterest will be able to gloss over the irregularities of what must be a very delicate and ticklish operation . . . and who (moreover) will take great care to eschew measures which are odious and violence which is pointless.[22]

Such a man, in short, as François Noël. This unsubtle self-advertisement doubtless reflected the presentiment that he was being asked to write what was in effect his political testament. As the more aggressive intentions of the Directory came into effect, the necessary changes in its diplomatic personnel were being carried out. It was highly unlikely that it would wish to perpetuate a man who had shown himself so exceedingly dainty in the use of French power. But the defensive tone of his October report, coupled with his repeated vilification of the dreaded "anarchists," also suggests that Noël was feeling harassed by the news that a group of Dutchmen in Paris were campaigning for his and General Beurnonville's disgrace.

Noël had good reason for feeling apprehensive. A trio of self-appointed emissaries of the radicals was indeed busy pressing its suit on the Directory. Lobbies such as these were once again becoming a feature of French politics, as they had been in the previous periods of French expansion in 1792 and 1794. Vreede, van Hooff, Daendels and de Winter had all been to Paris at various times to persuade the government to lend support to a political group or to a military venture. The new wave of republicanisation which followed the Italian campaigns had brought fortune hunters and office-mongers as well as more down-at-heel but reputable Patriots swarming like locusts around Paris. Amid this throng, the "Dutch" faction was conspicuous for the energy and unscrupulousness with which it prosecuted its cause. As ambassadors for the radicals, its principals' credentials were highly doubtful. Only one of three was authentically Dutch. He was Jan Eykenbroek, a distiller from Schiedam who had been prominent among the democratic wing of the Patriots in 1787 and had duly gone into exile in the Restoration. On his return in 1795, he had sat as a "Provisional Representative of the People of Holland" and as a deputy in the "Central Assembly" of clubs. He had continued to frequent the world of the popular societies, notably the "Vaderlandsche Societeit" at The Hague. But his political keenness had not been matched by commercial acumen. From a mediocre distiller he had proceeded to total failure as a tobacco merchant at Dunkirk, and supported himself thereafter by a series of shady speculations and investments, usually in troop supply contracts, the bonanza business of the 1790's.[23] It was partly as a consequence of his latest disaster that he arrived in Paris in September 1797 attempting to recover some of the capital he had squandered on one of these collapsing enterprises. He had not, as he claimed, been "sent" there as an agent for the clubs; but once there he began to send back reports to radicals such as van Langen and Vreede on the political atmosphere around the Directory.

Eykenbroek's luck changed when he met another opportunist who by that time was something of an expert at turning adversity to advantage. The Baron Eberstein was the product of an unlikely match between a dissolute German officer and a daughter of the Friesian aristocrats, the Aylva family. Brought up as a page to the Princess of Orange, he had done her bidding by following the fugitive Patriots to Brussels in 1788 and working there to discredit their cause. Two years later, the abruptly altered political situation and the flirtation of the Stadholder with the "Statist" wing of the Belgian republicans obliged him to warm somewhat to the cause of national liberty and try to promote the notion of a seventeen-province Netherlands under the aegis of the House of Orange. The return of the Austrians suddenly marooned him as Wilhelmina, in a hurry to disown the Statist connection, repudiated all connection with him as an agent of the Dutch government. To escape the Austrians, Eberstein fled to Altona in Denmark, where he received a commission and with surprising alacrity became naturalised Danish. Thereafter he was to be found, as Dumont-Pigalle tartly put it, attached "to whichever party paid the best." He too turned to speculating in army contracts and became quite as successful as Eykenbroek had been an ignominious flop.

The trio was completed by A. H. Bode, a deserter from Prussian service who had once acted as drillmaster and publicist for the Patriots in Arnhem, had later changed his name to "David Esias" to take a lieutenant's commission with the Batavian artillery in 1795, and ended up hunting for pickings in Eberstein's line of trade. It was these two who helped Eykenbroek out of a tight financial corner. In return, they persuaded him to use his political connexions for their mutual profit, adding of course that the successful outcome of their venture could only redound to the greater good of their beloved Fatherland.

Beside a grand predator like Barras, Eberstein was no more than a modest pilot fish, leading his patron to the quarry and hoping for a share when larger appetites had been sated. But in his grubby little way he was an accomplished worker. Scenting his opportunity, he went at the business of persuading the Directory to intervene directly in Dutch politics with a plausible combination of zeal and cunning. Conjuring up all its favourite gremlins, he lent an air of informed authentication to what were, in any case, their own suspicions as to where the responsibility for the ills of the Batavian Republic lay. Claiming to represent the popular societies and the "twelve apostles" who had signed Vreede's dissenting manifesto in August, the trio explained that they had been obliged to make an unorthodox approach to the Directory because the representatives of the French Republic in the Netherlands had, in collusion with aristocrats and federalists, succeeded in gagging the righteous indignation of the Batavian citizenry. Instead of giving strong encouragement to true republicans to attack the crimes and blunders perpetrated by the present regime, Noël and Beurnonville had favoured men of society and station, notorious Anglophiles and capitalists who were more concerned with protecting their investments than with the good of the alliance. The character of the official Dutch emissaries at Paris was an indication of how far matters had gone. Carel de Vos van Steenwijk was an Overijssel aristocrat whose intransigent federalism in the first National Assembly had been notorious. His colleague Maarten van der Goes was a confessed Orangist who had actually served van de Spiegel! In short, they represented the situation in the Netherlands as an emergency which demanded drastic action to forestall widespread anarchy, bloodshed and counter-revolution. They even went so far as to suggest that "the Batavian government is, to some degree, hostile to France since the administration is in the hands of its most determined enemies and since its friends are oppressed and powerless."[24]

The minimal palliative for this dire situation was the replacement of Noël and General Beurnonville by less timorous republicans, who would not be quite so squeamish in dealing with the enemies of the two Republics. Two further notes to Barras, moreover, made it clear that the Batavian Republic could never be properly secured until it had been induced to "imitate" the day of 18 Fructidor.[25] Bode was good enough to draw Talleyrand's attention to the wide discrepancies between the Dutch governing regulation of 1795 and the French constitution of the same year, intimating that his countrymen might be deeply grateful for a constitution which could properly safeguard the immortal axioms of freedom and equality. For good measure he informed Vreede that he had already drawn up a plan providing for strong actions to be taken after the "change" in Dutch government, including a compulsory "oath of hatred" against the Stadholder, a purge of all offices and commissions, penalties for holding funds in enemy stock and the reorganisation of a new National Guard.[26]

Much of this was *folie de grandeur* on the part of a handful of adventurers avid to seize the main chance when it came their way. There was nothing special about this in Directorial France. But Colenbrander has dignified this grimy little enterprise with the dimensions of a grand conspiracy on which the fate of the Batavian Republic truly turned. His intention, of course, was not flattering. In so far as the politics of the Batavian Republic *could* ever be determined by Dutchmen, he implied that it had to be this sort of Dutchman. By identifying the revolution of January 22 with the Paris adventurers, he meant to highlight the delusions of the radicals concerning their freedom of action. But in concentrating so single-mindedly on the "plot"; in scrutinising every item of correspondence, complete with gratuitously elaborate ciphers, Colenbrander paid the conspirators the unintentional compliment of taking their own assessment of their significance at its face value. In so doing he mistook the instruments of the coup for its agents, just as he mistook the occasion for the cause.

The truth was less sensational. Though it acted as a useful channel of information between the Dutch radicals on the one hand and the French Directors on the other, the Eberstein group in no serious respect determined the tactics of the former nor the strategy of the latter. The most that may be said of its part in preparing the ground for the coup is that, as plausible rogues, they succeeded in persuading each side that they held the confidence of the other, and that they amply made good their promise to profit from the role of go-between. This is not to suggest that initiating the liaison was a straightforward matter. In October 1797 Eykenbroek admitted that they had "many enemies" in Paris.[27] Talleyrand, who was well disposed to the official Dutch envoys, was unimpressed with their credentials and refused to acknowledge them in any capacity other than that of individual petitioners from the Dutch clubs. He even turned one of their favourite allegations neatly on its head by accusing them of having been bought by "Bicker's gold."

Led by Reubell, the Directory was equally frosty in its reception. Only Barras, smelling profit in their unsavoury company, extended anything like a welcome and made them a promise to help remove the objectionable Noël and Beurnonville. This was finally accomplished with the assistance of Scherer, the Minister of War, a minion of Barras' who had served with Eberstein in Belgium and who, like the two of them, was later the subject of enquiries about the misappropriation of funds during his tenure in office. On October 21, Merlin informed the group that the Directory had decided to replace its agent and military commander in the Republic with men better able to win the confidence of the Dutch people. But at the same time it made it clear that the military commander was not, as they had hoped, to be Scherer himself, and that they must not, under any circumstances, contemplate "either bloodshed or upheavals or proscription." Instead, they were to "imitate in all respects, the calm, the dignity and the magnanimity of 18 Fructidor."[28]

This was scarcely a blank cheque for a new revolution. Perhaps it was a sly wink, but delivered, as it were, with an auspicious and a drooping eye. Noël's replacement was not able to take up his post until the end of December at the earliest, and in the interim the radicals were to be restrained from any impetuous action. In any case it was difficult to know what to make of the new French agent, Charles Delacroix. In his time he had been both regicide Jacobin and enthusiastic Thermidorian. Eberstein's cipher nicknames him "the Broker" and calls him "tricky but self-possessed," two attributes which turned out to be the exact opposite of the truth. In the event Delacioix was to prove all and more that Eberstein could have wished for; but in October 1797 he was noted principally as Noël's superior in the foreign ministry for two years and the presumed author of the policy of passive conservatism that had been the hallmark of the first agent. Such lukewarm encouragement irked the Paris faction, anxious to proceed with the business of "fructidorising" the Batavian Republic and making their own fortunes. Even in December Eberstein complained that Barras was blowing hot and cold on the whole project and that, in the language of their code, he wished them to return to "Africa" (the Netherlands) and send him some more "corn" (money) so that he might resolve his doubts more satisfactorily.[29] His colleagues on the Directory were also undecided about the viability of the venture and were unwilling to commit themselves before receiving reliable intelligence from their new agent. Whatever the reasons, it was clear that France was not yet ready to slip the conspirators from their leash.

Moreover, if the relations between the Eberstein coterie and the Directory were ambiguous, their claim to be in the thick of radical circles in the Netherlands rested on even slighter foundation. Although Caspar Meijer at the Paris embassy was not unsympathetic to their general political views, he was too canny to be taken in by their expressions of devoted service to the Fatherland. His growing suspicion that they were intriguing with the Directory behind the back of the Batavian Republic's accredited representatives led to a cooling of relations, periodic exchanges of abuse, and a final tragi-farcical dénouement when rival factions fought for territorial possession of the embassy the following March. Nor was their reception in the Republic itself much warmer. On October 30, preceded by two letters to Vreede, Bode arrived in The Hague as the courier of the glad tidings of Noël's recall. Through Nolet—another Schiedam distiller, radical clubman and deputy—he was introduced to Vreede's two closest colleagues at that time, the Leiden Catholic textile merchant Stephen van Langen, and Theodorus van Leeuwen, an Amsterdammer who was a doyen among the popular societies in the less patrician parts of the city. But instead of the expected rapturous enthusiasm Bode was disappointed to find "cool indifference" and, what was worse, a lily-livered reluctance to consider drastic action which he put down to "unforgiveable faint-heartedness."[30] The unwelcome truth was that even those like Pieter Vreede who were most enraged by the constraints of parliamentary procedure and the ubiquitously reviled regulation were not yet prepared to commit themselves to a *coup d'état* when it was still possible that a democratic and unitary constitution might be achieved by peaceful and lawful means.

All these hesitations and misgivings are conspicuously absent from Colenbrander's account, where the plot proceeds nudge by nudge and secret by secret, shrouded in the seductive mysteries of preposterous codes and clandestine encounters. The deletion of the altogether duller proceedings at the centre of the Dutch political life has served to obscure rather than clarify the genesis of the revolution of January 1798. But even had he recorded the meanderings of the "plot" with greater fidelity, Colenbrander's detective methodology would, at best, have succeeded only in revealing the "how" and possibly the "whodunnit" of the coup. For the "wherefore," and indeed for the significance of the coup—its "whence"—it is necessary to turn from the intrigues of Paris back parlours and the Directorial corridors to the less cryptic scenario of politics within the Netherlands itself.

The Unnecessary Revolution

If the outlook for the Batavian Republic following Camperdown was bleak, it was not quite as hopeless as its detractors in Paris made out. Naturally Bode and Eberstein had a vested interest in alarmism. They wished to present the Directory with an emergency in which it would feel that it had no option but to intervene directly to save the Dutch from themselves—and by extension from the British. Thus they painted a portrait of the Netherlands on the brink of terrifying anarchy, carefully echoing the Cassandra-like noises that had been made on the eve of 18 Fructidor. But if the Batavian Republic was certainly no model of harmonious and energetic government, neither had it, as Eberstein alleged, run to the very end of its rope. Compared to the course of the French Revolution, the upheavals in the Netherlands had remained virtually bloodless. So far it had escaped the endemic savagery which had scarred popular politics in the valley of the Rhône or the Vendée. If rioting in the provinces hardest hit by billeting and requisitions had become worse in 1796 and 1797, it had not yet spread into anything like an organised campaign of violent revenge on those held to be responsible. The occasional dagger in the ribs of a French hussar was hardly evidence of the popular fury conjured up in Bode's reports.

Above all, Dutch politics remained obstinately parochial. The only region which seemed to promise violence and counter-violence and where a feud persisted reminiscent of Lyons or the Ardèche was Friesland. As in those areas, much of the local conflict had ancient roots and certainly antedated the Patriot troubles of the 1780's. In Leeuwarden, the democratic tribunes of the popular clubs and militias who now made up the personnel of the municipal and even provincial councils wanted nothing so much as to be left alone by The Hague to conduct their own very thorough purge of the old *grietenies* and the rural "kwartieren." Their support came from those for whom the "aristocracy"—not so much as a political collectivity but in the shape of a particular local villain—had long been a serious bugbear and whose bailiffs and tax collectors they had been fending off for generations. Their champions, however, overstepped the mark. Their tribunals, judicial committees and jails in Franeker, Harlingen, Sneek and Dokkum were the nearest that any region of the Republic approached to a Terror and though hardly in competition with Jacobins were far too alarming for even the torpid Noël to overlook. Periodic intervention by French troops was authorised to put the democrats in their place, but the garrisons were widely dispersed through the province and it proved much harder than they anticipated to keep their clients in power in the towns. In the end it took the unlikely arbitration of a figure acceptable to both sides—Jan van Hooff—to concoct a characteristically silly compromise by which, in the autumn of 1797, a great many of the Friesian radicals remained firmly in power within the province but were represented in the National Assembly by two acceptable moderates: Eduard Marius van Beijma, and Jan Huber, the veteran of the 1792 committee. Not surprisingly it was not very long before this schizophrenic provincial representation ran into difficulties yet again.

Friesland apart, Dutch society suffered in silence. Despite the appalling hardships brought on by the war and the accelerating disintegration of the traditional economy, local institutions, as in other times of adversity, proved just sufficiently resilient to contain social catastrophe. But they were put under extreme stress. In the local townships of North Holland, for example— Edam, Purmerend, Hoorn and Castricum—the traditional agencies of poor relief had virtually abandoned any attempt to disburse charity on the conventional scale, nor had they the means or the room to take into the oudemannehuizen (old age homes) and workhouses all those appealing for alms.[31] In this crisis situation, the philanthropic activities of the various religious communities assumed the utmost importance. The deluge of letters, petitions and pleas which swamped the National Assembly from multitudes of common people as well as predikants and civic officials in the autumn of 1797 bore witness to the general apprehension that, despite denials, the separation of Church and state would be followed by the expropriation of funds and property. In October alone, there were 596 such petitions representing 85,000 souls in Holland, Friesland, Overijssel and Gelderland.[32] They had no cause for alarm. There were too many churchmen in the Assembly itself whose addiction to revolutionary doctrine was tempered by social sensitivity to allow a measure so calculated to exacerbate an already distressed situation.

The apprehension of such social fears was never serious enough to shake the foundations of the new republican order. In the rural areas, communities were too dispersed and still too unfamiliar with the ways and means of political action to organise any effective resistance; in the towns, the *wijk* meetings and clubs soaked up much of the pressure. For both communities the tax collector and the militia officer meant identical hardships, whether inflicted by Patriot regent or Orangist. Throughout the period of the Batavian Republic, the historian has the impression of collective experience proceeding on two separate planes which gradually became further and further divorced from one another. On the "lower" level, the vast majority of the common people struggled to keep their modest capital sums intact or merely to subsist in times of exceptional difficulty. On the "higher" plane, their representative clamoured in the centre of the political arena for their "rights." Paradoxically, it was only when the Republic had virtually run the gamut of political permutations and when the conditions of the alliance made it impossible to continue the experiment that politicians turned instead to socially remedial administration.

But in the later part of 1797, the revolutionary credo that the establishment of unitary democracy would provide a panacea for these ills still held good. Organs of radical opinion like *De Democraten* assumed that good government was contingent on the provision of a "correct" constitution and that, despite all setbacks, that goal had not been lost sight of. Even Vreede, who had more reason than most to despair of constitutional change, believed the situation not to be beyond redemption. In May he had written to Valckenaer of his hopes that if "the Nation has enough energy to reject this monster [the 1796 constitution] and to elect some likely fellows, then I may still console myself that in a short time—perhaps four or five months— everything may be restored."[33]

The results of the new elections did not entirely dash his hopes. He himself was re-elected for five constituencies, and if his "party" had nothing like a clear majority, it had the satisfaction of seeing the weakening of the patrician centre which he most despised. Although re-elected for Amsterdam, Schimmelpenninck declined to take his seat in the second Assembly on the pretext that he had qualms about taking the oath of allegiance. From a memorandum written at the time, it is plain that he had been shaken by the rejection of the constitution and now believed that in order to avert the greater evil of surrendering to the clubs it was necessary for the new Assembly to embrace unitarism whole-heartedly, preserving, if it could, the vital principle of the separation of powers.[34] Men of less pragmatic bent like Bicker were more in the shadows in the second Assembly, and the succession of federalist Presidents who had ruled proceedings in 1796 were replaced by men of a decidedly more unitarist stripe, who were anxious to get on with the interminably postponed business of manufacturing a constitution. Vreede himself was one of the first elected to the Presidential chair; he was followed, among others, by van Hooff, van Langen, Blauw and Midderigh.

As the centre weakened, so the two wings which represented the rejection of the August constitution became correspondingly strengthened. Last-ditch federalists like de Mist, de Sitter, van Beveren, Vitringa and van Marle were all returned as the guardians of the autonomy of the land provinces. Oratorically impressive, they were thinner in numbers than those on the opposite radical flank, largely because of the demographic distribution of constituencies. The radicals included a number of new men who rescued Vreede from his lonely role as the democratic messiah. Two in particular were ideally equipped to communicate those political views most effectively. Both were journalists, ex-predikants and powerful speakers: Jan Konijnenburg, who had worked on *De Democraten* and now published his own paper *De Republiekein*, and Willem Ockerse, Gogel's co-editor. The heirs of the Paulus group

—Hahn, Gevers, van de Kasteele and van Hooff—were not slow to grasp their opportunity. Although they were less in sympathy with the purely democratic radicalism of Vreede and Ockerse, they shared their urgent wish for a rigorously unitarist constitution and were prepared to make concessions to the radicals to obtain it. Such a strategy promised much better than the situation a year earlier when the concessions had all been made in the opposite direction.

Even the ultra-federalists recognised that the balance of political power within the Assembly had shifted decisively towards the unitarists. But they were by no means prepared to capitulate without a good fight. They still had the regulation, tailor-made to preserve rather then erode provincial sovereignties, and which bound this and every other Assembly until it could be replaced by a definitive constitution. Even though all deputies were required to swear an oath of allegiance to the Assembly and to the regulation, it was just such constraints which united radical and moderate unitarists in their determination to find means of circumventing it. Sooner or later, they were convinced, the federalists would have to yield and accept an over-riding republican sovereignty. But it was also true that they assumed that when this breakthrough occurred it would be as the result of the conflict of forces on the chamber floor, not through the "fructidorisation" of armed force. In their concern for legality even the most doughty among their number remained "republican legitimists."

At the outset there were ominous signs that the second National Assembly might be about to repeat the dismal history of its predecessor. Amidst preliminary skirmishing among the factions, a proposal that the Republic officially celebrate 18 Fructidor was received very coolly. On September 27, Coert van Beijma urged that all office-holders be made to take an oath of hatred against "the Stadholder and aristocracy," much as Bode had suggested in his blueprint for enforcement. The Assembly showed its view of this by rejecting it seventy-one to eighteen, figures which elicited from Eberstein the comment that if the Assembly had been asked to swear an oath of hatred against liberty, democracy and unity, it would have been accepted with alacrity![35]

To make the atmosphere a little more tense, the federalists succeeded in holding on to control of the new constitutional commission by a majority of just one over the unitarists. This immediately prompted the unitarists to suggest—on grounds of expedition, of course—that the commission be reduced in size. J. van Lokhorst, the proposer, further argued that the time limit of six months stipulated by the regulation should be held to *include* all the discussions on revisions and amendments. Clinging grimly to the letter of the regulation, the federalists refused to contemplate any pruning of the commission (which would have endangered their hair's-breadth majority), though they raised no objection to the acceleration of its work. Perhaps this was a testimony to their good faith since they naturally had a vested interest in prolonging the unconstitutional situation as long as possible. Soon they were in serious retreat. On October 19 the Assembly voted to establish a small sub-commission of five—on which the unitarists won their first clear majority—to draw up a plan of interim government on the basis of a unified executive, *should the second constitution suffer the same fate as the first.*[36] This went directly against the presumption that in the event of a second veto the regulation would once again apply. Evidently a majority of deputies in the Assembly could not face an indefinite perpetuation of such a state of affairs. Although the terms of reference of the sub-committee were left deliberately vague, it was clear that *whatever* the fate of the constitution it would be possible to fill the executive vacuum. Even if the authority of the new body was, as one deputy suggested, to be "provisional until the peace," no less had been true of the French Committee of Public Safety.

How had this important change of direction come about? It had taken a disaster of the magnitude of Camperdown to persuade the floating "centre" of the Assembly of the necessity for efficient and undivided administration. The Committee for Foreign Affairs had shouldered much of the blame for the loss of the fleet, despite the dissociation of a substantial minority. More significantly, the internecine feuding between different agencies of government characteristic of the Dutch committee system was beginning to be seen as inherently damaging to the viability of the Batavian Republic. In this respect Camperdown had been a salutary trauma. On de Winter's return, Amsterdam had behaved as though he had won the most glorious of victories, mounting a lavish public festival on the Dam and presenting the admiral with a golden sword (much to the amusement of an English correspondent). But the National Assembly, more soberly aware of what the true costs of the defeat were likely to be, was not carried away by celebration. It balked at paying the expenses for the elaborate obsequies accorded to Vice-Admiral Reyntjes, whose body had been brought from England for the occasion, and by what was admittedly the slender margin of a single vote, refused de Winter admission to the bar of the Assembly. This sourness was understandable. All the epic stanzas showered on the fleet could not disguise the fact that the greater part of it had been lost; that the hard work of reconstruction begun in 1795 would have to be undertaken all over again; and that the already belea-guered finances of the state had sustained another crippling blow.

If the losses at sea were to be made good—and whether the Dutch liked it or not, the French would insist that they were—a further dose of "extraordi-nary taxation" was inevitable. Initially, the suggestions for financing the naval work were fairly orthodox. Kantelaar proposed a ½ per cent levy on all property over 1,000 guilders which, he claimed, could yield a figure around 7 million. But the Committee on Finance had much greater ambitions. On November 14 it announced a tax of 8 per cent on *income*, based on a sliding scale and starting with incomes over 300 guilders.[37] Predictably, the proposal met with a mixed reception. Taxes of all descriptions had rained down on the unfortunate Dutch at a torrential rate since the disastrous war of 1780–84. Even before that they had been the most heavily taxed nation in Europe. The price of maintaining the independence of a little Republic was very high and could only be sustained with any ease by the buoyant economy which belonged very much to the Dutch past. Since the 1780's successive regimes, Orange and Patriot, had pledged their administrations to easing the fiscal burden, but had somehow ended up doing precisely the opposite. Falling on a society additionally impoverished by military occupation, the costs of continuing the pan-European war were becoming fiscally traumatic.

From 1797 onwards, each of the regimes in the Netherlands was forced to ask itself how much more its citizens could bear; but in each case, the cause of national survival obliged it to harden its heart and give the fiscal screw just one more turn. The 8 per cent tax, however, was not just another levy. It was as important a challenge to the authority of the regulation as the subcommittee of five. For on the grounds of national emergency—the one loophole in the regulation—it was set out as a *national* contribution, levied without regard to provincial differentiations or through the provincial treasuries. Unlike the old "Quota" system, the provinces were not asked how much they could contribute to a given sum, but were required to collect the appropriate sum off each of their inhabitants falling in the taxable sector. Even under the old regime there were precedents for such a move, but as in 1672, the taxes had been imposed under the aegis of the Stadholder's "captaincy" of the federation. On this occasion a tax was being levied by the National Assembly, exercising its right to order such impositions in the name of its republican sovereignty.

The 8 per cent tax revived all the antagonisms traditional to such disputes between the provinces. Holland had flatly announced that it would never consent to pay *unless* the contribution was levied on a national basis. Overijssel and Gelderland, on the other hand, saw no reason why they should be made to pay for the incompetence of the navy, which had been manned and led by personnel from the maritime provinces! In a counter-attack worthy of the States-General at its most quarrelsome, Coert van Beijma (a devoted federalist when it came to fiscal matters) attacked the *army* estimates, demanding either the reduction of the Dutch force or a modification of the obligation to support 25,000 French troops. How could those who called those who called themselves republicans, he argued, now lend their support to a measure which was almost identical with a proposal they had attacked as "tyrannical" in 1783?[38] Indeed, it was the alignment of the deputies from Friesland with those of the land provinces which contrived to defeat the bill by the narrowest margin of forty-four votes to forty-two. Such a margin, however, was unlikely to withstand a concentrated offensive for very long. For if opposition to the tax had cut right across "revolutionary" loyalties and united such opposites as Coert and Beijma and his brother the apple of the moderates' eye, Eduard Marius van Beijma, by the same token it had rallied conservatives in Holland and Utrecht like Kantelaar and van Maanen to their more radical colleagues.

Moreover, the Committee for Finance used all the means of propaganda at its disposal to advertise the tax as a "patriotic contribution" from which no true patriot could decently withhold consent. Leaflets urging altruism were headed by a banner motto proclaiming: "Voor Vrijheid en Vaderland." In the Assembly van Hooff, who could always be relied on to rise to these occasions, fulminated: "No more discussion. We must have a fleet. Without a fleet the Fatherland cannot be saved." In Amsterdam a group of merchants clubbed together to present an entire ship-of-the-line to the nation; and a wealthy widow in Haarlem publicly engaged to equip and build on her own account a frigate, then running at around half a million guilders.[39] On November 30 the Committee returned to the fray in the Assembly. The original proposition had been slightly amended to give 50 guilders' allowance deductible from income for each child and now offered bonds at 3 per cent against the contributions levied. But in essence it remained an unadorned income tax, imposed the same year as its counterpart in Britain. On December 2, exactly a year after the resolution on unitary sovereignty had been passed, the tax was voted through by fifty-eight to fifty-four.

There was a faint whiff of pyrrhic victory about the vote of December 2, for the Assembly was still obliged to canvass opinion (rather than consent, its proponents emphasized) from the provinces. And few among the Assembly's representatives, pro or con, were in much doubt about what that would register. If and when the inevitable negative was recorded, it would require a further vote of the Assembly to see the tax go through. But, along with the establishment of the committees of five, the vote on the 8 per cent tax was the most significant breach yet in the defensive wall of provincial sovereignty. It had also shown what could be achieved were moderate and radical unitarists to collaborate on the common interest of institutional reform.

Such, at any rate, was the hope of Jacob Blauw, who had returned to The Hague from Italy on November 22, the date of the first vote on the tax, to take up his seat for Gouda. Disappointed by the rejection of the first constitution and edified by his experience of the new Italian republics, Blauw was determined to play a more positive role in Dutch politics, and to cement, if he could, a unitarist alliance capable of exercising effective power. He was not really cut out to be a diplomat. Prudence and patience were not among his more notable qualities and he was temperamentally prone to fits of anger, often for petty reasons. Though he was fiercely patriotic, he suffered from the national vice of pomposity and enjoyed delivering lectures to captive audiences on the virtues of the Dutch commonwealth. After the hectic negotiations over the Treaty of The Hague, his relations with the French Directory had not improved, and in June 1796 they had asked for him to be replaced as head of the legation by the blander, more receptive Meijer.

Blauw's time in Milan, Florence and Bologna had given him a useful education in the perils of dependent sovereignty and the Machiavellianism of French foreign policy. Whilst he was not at all averse to The Hague authorities meddling in the affairs of the provinces—and felt that the revolution in Friesland should have been pressed on the land provinces with greater vigour—he was equally keen to keep the French out of Dutch political life. Consequently, he was determined to avoid at all costs the kind of upheaval which would require French armed support and provide the "Grande Nation" with a lever which they would never willingly withdraw. More than any other prominent politician since Paulus, Blauw clung to the innocent belief that it was still possible to create an independent and regenerated Dutch state, capable of playing its own part "in the great revolution of Europe through which we are living."[40] And it was just this peculiar combination of mulish obstinacy with a versatile tendency to appear all things to all men which recommended him as an ally to the Committee for Foreign Affairs, keen to shore up the position of unitarism without recourse to a *coup d'état*. Even Schimmelpenninck—whose successor as the wheeler and dealer in the National Assembly Blauw had become—thought his heart was in the right place and believed that, despite their differences in political mannerisms, there was an essential community among Blauw, himself and Wiselius as to what the constitution ought to uphold.[41]

Not being the most modest of men, Blauw was the first to recognise his ability to build bridges across the competing factions and the first to engage whole-heartedly in this political engineering. Coming from the Italian republics, where political survival depended on tactical skill and the disposition of arms, he was well aware of the possibilities of violent interruptions. One of his first actions on return was to alert the Assembly to the importance of retaining control of The Hague garrison and to induce it to take advantage of the hiatus between Beurnonville's departure and the arrival of his successor, General Joubert, to change the balance of French and Dutch troops in the south Holland garrisons. His second concern was to see to the restraint of the popular societies by way of ensuring that they did not become the instruments of an armed insurrection against the Assembly. His strenuous efforts in both these departments did not endear him to the professional conspirators whose path he had so expertly crossed. "Coos Blauw," complained Bode from Amsterdam,

has played a role which is absolutely unforgivable. He is a consummate villain; a greater deceiver of the people have we none. The "great man" hangs on both parties and wants to be adored by both . . . he and he alone is holding up what would otherwise be a certainty . . . (if we do not take care) that man will play a tune to which we shall all dance.[42]

Blauw's efforts at this time were not confined to obstructing the means by which a coup might be carried out. By establishing an agreed programme uniting both political wings of the unitarists, he hoped to put them in a position to press their plan on the constitutional commission and so obviate the need—or the pretext—for a *coup d'état*. In so doing he was, as Schimmelpenninck hinted, assuming his role of consensus-patcher, albeit without the equivocation on essential points of unitary sovereignty which had been such a feature of earlier plans. But busy as he was, Blauw's efforts in this direction were partly pre-empted on December 12 when the more uncompromising radicals in the Assembly published a nine-point manifesto which they declared to be the *only* basis on which an acceptable constitution could be drafted. Forty-three names were appended to the manifesto, including the best-known radicals: Vreede, van Langen, van Leeuwen, Nolet, Bosch and Coert van Beijma. Belatedly, with some misgivings at the tenor of the document, Blauw added his own.[43] To those like Hahn who found it altogether too radical a statement, Blauw explained that for tactical reasons he thought it inopportune to lose contact with the radicals at that juncture.

Very little of "the Declaration of 43" (as it was termed) was new. Much of it had originally appeared in De Democraten, both in the paper's original review of the 1796 constitution and later in articles following the veto of August 1797.[44] Nevertheless it was a bold and concise document, stating as baldly as possible the essential position of the Dutch democrats. First and foremost it demanded "an unadulterated popular sovereignty by representation," so that "the form of government will give as little nourishment to anarchy on the one hand as to any kind of aristocracy on the other."[45] The safeguards of the democracy were also by now familiar: triennial revisions; annual elections of a third of the Assembly and annual appointment of a third of the executive; unicameral legislature; primary assemblies established on a permanent footing to which disputed legislation might be referred and which would retain rights of petition and recall. The executive was to be reduced to the mere "executor of the national will" as vested in the legislature, though to please the more administratively minded unitarists strong emphasis was placed on the absolute unification of national sovereignty, not excluding finance. A national treasury was to impose taxes without discriminating between provinces but having regard to the differing circumstances of individual households. In sum, the blueprint for Dutch democracy was a good deal closer to the model of 1793 than 1795.

Needless to say, this did not recommend it to the retiring French agent. Despite his imminent recall and the consciousness that the lines of orthodoxy in France had decisively shifted, François Noël remained obstinately faithful to his own creed. By his lights the declaration of December 12 appeared like the spectre of Jacobinism returning to haunt him in his declining days. By way of a parting riposte, he delivered one of his relatively rare admonitions to the National Assembly, warning them that if they did not mend their ways France might find herself compelled to intervene to ensure an *orderly* transition to constitutional rule.

Since his agency was on its last legs, Noël's pronouncements were unlikely to carry much weight with the radicals. They awaited with some impatience the arrival of his successor, from whom they expected an altogether more benign attitude. Yet the official "Instruction" given to Delacroix on December 2 was hedged with ifs and buts.[46] In many respects it was closer to one of Noël's sermons than an all-out license for revolution. True, it lamented the prevailing chaos at the heart of Dutch government, which, if nothing were done, would reduce the Batavian Republic to a "political nullity, whose weight would [then] fall on the French Republic, which would find itself embarrassed by the burdens of an alliance without the means to recover its benefits." To avert this intolerable situation, the agent was to make it crystal clear to the Dutch leaders that France "is determined to put the Batavian Republic in a condition of being able to act *effectively* in the alliance which she had contracted with her."

In other words, the "Grande Nation" was more concerned with military efficiency than with political rectitude. As Lestevenon remarked, the French Directory would support whichever regime came up with the right dividends. Naturally a constitution was essential. The fact that the Batavians were still haggling over their forms of government was ludicrous. But the agent was merely to "*lead* the Batavian nation with certitude and swiftness to the important goal which, left to its own efforts, its divisions would not allow it to attain." Obviously some form of intervention was anticipated—but nothing so drastic as a violent coup. The Instruction further alluded to a "project" being developed by some "enlightened members of the convention" which was "very similar to our own and, moreover, well-suited to the usages and customs of the country for which it is destined." This seems to be a garbling of Noël's reports on the regular work of the constitutional commission and the informal work of Blauw and George Hahn to produce an agreed unitarist "programme." But the Instruction assumed that whatever emerged from these projects they would, with some assistance from the agent, be put to the nation through the orthodox constitutional channels, rather than imposed on it by force of arms. Of course it was vital that the climate of opinion should be better prepared than in 1797 to avoid the repetition of the first fiasco, and if necessary the despatch of "special agents" to the more sensitive parts of the country such as Friesland and Groningen might help the project on its way. But obviously there were certain bounds which it would be foolhardy to exceed. "To succeed," the Instruction concluded, "he [the agent] will by preference employ the ways of persuasion so as not to alarm a people very jealous of their independence."

Thus Charles Delacroix's terms of reference represented only a very partial repudiation of the general policy laid down by Noël. On his appointment it seems that the Directory, the majority of radicals in the assembly, and the moderate unitarists all had an interest in finding the most direct, painless route to a constitution unequivocally grounded on unitary sovereignty and a degree of political democracy. The Eberstein-Eykenbroek group, on the other hand, was interested primarily in the coup itself as a means to obtain profit and place. For the one group, then, the coup was a last resort; for the other, the essential vehicle of their strategy. For the conspirators, the prospects in December looked poor. Eberstein complained that the French Directory seemed to have cooled completely towards their plans; van Leeuwen in The Hague began to suspect that "we and our friends in Paris have been led by the nose."[47] Barras, it seemed, was still dissatisfied with his shipments of "corn from Africa." And in the Netherlands Eykenbroek found it necessary to stiffen Vreede's resolution not to be beguiled into any bargain with the moderates and to be wary in particular of the wiles of Jacob Blauw. Instead, he urged, their efforts ought to be directed at incriminating the "deceivers of the people" (their euphemism for the moderates), for only then could "the aristocracy be vanquished and the execution of your hearts' desire be made simpler than ever."[48]

Obviously, much depended on the way Delacroix interpreted his somewhat ambiguous Instruction. Lestevenon predicted that he would do virtually anything to avert public disorder, and Gevers had such hopes of his moderation that he saw his arrival as an auspicious moment to speed up the work of the commission.[49] Indeed, the Paris faction were themselves so unsure of his allegiances that they urged Meijer to "brief" the agent on the "true" political situation in the Batavian Republic before his departure. Their concern that Delacroix would find himself hemmed in by balancing interests was, however, quite misplaced. Whatever his virtues, the new ambassador was not the sort of man to be overburdened by excessive prudence. The qualities which had made him such an effective *représentant en mission* in the Marne during the Terror—energy, resolution and patriotic ardour—had, in the less innocent years of Thermidor and the Directory, degenerated into headstrong stubbornness; a petulant refusal to brook the slightest contradiction to his own views; and a colossal vanity. As Minister of Foreign Affairs, he had been accustomed to receive ambassadors and foreign dignitaries dressed in silk robes and slippers decorated with scarlet ribbons, an affectation which had earned him the nickname of "the bishop."[50] Like most dandies he was vulnerable to slight, and the circumstances in which he had been given the appointment at The Hague could have done little to mollify his normally aggressive egotism. For many months in 1797 a tumour growing from his abdomen to his private parts, and according to the unkind (and lavish) publicity it received from the medical press, now of monstrous proportions, had been causing him crippling pain. Delacroix was operated on in the summer, successfully as it turned out, and the surgery acclaimed as a spectacular case of the resources of modern medicine. But it left the minister, who had previously looked like "an ugly old pregnant woman" according to one witness, as indisposed as any such patient could be. Sexual activity, before and immediately after the operation, was out of the question. Unhappily, towards the end of the year Madame Delacroix began to develop an abdominal swelling which very clearly was not due to malignant causes. The wagging tongues of Paris had it that the unfortunate ex-minister had been succeeded in his bed by the man who had succeeded him at his desk, Maurice de Talleyrand. Most recent evidence suggests that the rumour was in fact correct and that the remarkable talents of the genius Eugène Delacroix were fathered by the equally remarkable gifts of the Prince de Périgord.[51] Whatever the truth, it seems certain that Charles was sent away to The Hague to avoid the gossip which rose to a crescendo as the birth became imminent. Coming on top of his grotesque illness, the blow can hardly have put Delacroix in an especially benevolent or equable frame of mind for his new ministry.

At this painful stage of his career it is not surprising that Delacroix should have been susceptible to flatterers. He needed all the comfort he could get. The Eberstein-Eykenbroek circle were only too happy to oblige, but until mid-December there was none among them intimate enough with Delacroix to play the part of sycophant and confidant, a counsel shrewd enough to exercise influence while appearing only to confirm his patron's opinions. This failing was made good by the elegant and noxious presence of Brahain Ducange.

If Eberstein was, by the high standards of the day, a reasonably practised opportunist, Ducange was a past-master. His brand of adventurism, moreover, was uniquely suited to the role of intermediary between Delacroix and the Dutch radicals. "Intriguer and crook," "cajoleur à l'excès," he was not, as Blauw ruefully conceded, without talent. Pursued by scandal and debt from his native Tours, he had become tutor to the children of the duc de Montmorency, and later amanuensis to a rich Jew whom he comprehensively fleeced. Ducange then worked on an Orangist journal before switching sides as the Patriot star rose, assisting Jan Luzac on the *Gazette de Leyde*. His sense of timing deserted him in 1787 and he was obliged to flee with the assorted company of Patriots back to France. After further scandals and frauds, he managed to oil his way into the company of the Paris "Bataves" and became close enough to Valckenaer to collaborate with him on *Le Batave* in the cloister of St. Germain l'Auxerrois.[52] Like the professor, he assumed the stance and speech of an impeccable sans-culotte when it proved essential during the Terror and was rewarded with a commission to the Committee of General Security, whose powers he immediately used to see a large number of his creditors thrown into jail or worse. After Thermidor he moved to Hamburg, where he attempted to attach himself parasitically to the leader of the "Patriots," Heinrich Georg Sieveking. This time his own profligacy with the rich patrician's funds was his undoing. Thus the Dutch adventure was possibly his last chance to make his formidable semi-criminal talents work to his advantage. Proffered the opportunity, he seized it gratefully.

The news of Delacroix's appointment was announced nearly two months before he could take up the post. During the interval Ducange made himself known to the new agent, offering himself as an interpreter, informer and general factotum on all Dutch matters. Ignorance of Dutch on the part of most of the soldiers and diplomats who served in the Batavian Republic put them at a real disadvantage in their dealings with counterparts who were fluent in French. A man whose native loyalty was to France but who was proficient in both tongues and expert on both political scenes was too much of a rarity to reject out of hand. What was more, Ducange was charming, personable and witty. A more suitable courtier for Charles Delacroix could scarcely be imagined. In no time at all he had become his closest friend, his initiator to Dutch politics and the engineer of his political tactics.

The first service performed by Ducange was a long memorandum concocted by himself and Eberstein and presented to the Directory on December 16 under the heading of "General Observations on the Present Political Situation in the Batavian Republic."[53] It said little that was fresh but presented the French government with its choice bêtes-noires served up in terms that were both more dramatic and more subtle than Eberstein's solo effort the previous October. It reiterated the accusation that French blood had been spilled merely to irrigate Dutch greed; that the "base interest of the rich capitalists" had attached the majority of the National Assembly to the English and Stadholderian causes; and that a "liberticide indulgence" combined with an "excess of delicacy" on the part of Noël had brought the Batavian Republic to a situation where it had to be considered "more an enemy than an ally." It was no good hoping to hint, lead or coax the Dutch into acting in their own best interests. Such a nation had to be shoved, hectored and directed —in short, "electrified." As long as the new agent pursued a policy directly contrary to his predecessor, supported and encouraged the "true friends of liberty" and the "true enemies of England," he could be certain that the "second revolution" so indispensable for France could be "carried out without any difficulty."

Ducange carefully avoided any reference to the declaration of December 12 in his memorandum, even though he must have been aware of its publication. There were good reasons for this apparently casual negligence. The "manifesto" of the forty-three deputies was a far more authentic statement of the democrats' views on the constitution than anything cooked up by Eykenbroek and the like. As a direct consequence, Ducange knew full well that its radicalism would prove far too trenchant and daring for even the post-Fructidorian Directory. The French coup, after all, had been carried out *by* the executive *against* the legislature. Was it likely that it would tolerate a plan which made the legislature the supreme authority in the Netherlands, and which was itself vulnerable to the attacks of countless hostile democratic cells in the shape of the primary assemblies? In his reports to Delacroix, Ducange alluded occasionally to the democrats' plans, but in the most patronising manner. "Those good fellows," he said, "collectively taken, do not have their ideas perfectly clear; they lack a common spirit of order." They were also faulted on their poor editing and presentation, but "thanks be to God we can do all that for them."[54]

The kindness Ducange meant was a document which he was himself preparing in conjunction with Delacroix for presentation to the Dutch as a "constitutional symbol." It is not clear whether this "symbol" was intended to be merely a guide to the constitution France would most like to see adopted by the Dutch, or something more ambitious. We can be certain that it was meant to serve in place of the "project" alluded to in Delacroix's Instruction and which Ducange had told him was not yet ready. The "symbol" itself was merely another version of the all-purpose portable constitution designed by La Revellière-Lépeaux around the French constitution of the Year III and which had been hawked around the German, Swiss and Italian satellites. There was no obvious reason why what had been good for them should not satisfy the Dutch, and Ducange gave Delacroix no reason for thinking it would displease them. In fact, it differed substantively from both the dissenting manifestoes of August and December 1797 on a number of key points: a bicameral rather than a unicameral legislature; an independent executive; and strict separation of powers. But of course Ducange made sure that Delacroix was completely in the dark as to the true nature of the democrats' views on the constitution. What he was trying to do was to put together a plan for the seizure of power by radical personnel but made in the name of a moderate "Directorial" constitution. To this end Ducange represented the radicals as happy to go along with all the cardinal points of the "symbol" though in reality they paid it little attention. Conversely, he assured the radicals that despite the odd variation here and there, Delacroix was the man to see their ideology finally come to fruition![55]

Despite the skills of this shadow-boxing, Ducange had one major problem to overcome. Delacroix was by no means committed to staging any sort of *coup d'état,* let alone one managed for the benefit of the popular societies and other "anarchists." He saw the "symbol" not as a threat but as a relatively innocuous text around which all good republicans could rally without doing violence to their principles. Far from it serving as the constitution to be imposed on the Dutch following the coup, it was to be the instrument by which a constitution could be introduced on an impeccably legitimate basis. This, of course, was not far from Blauw's own view, and, at the beginning of his stay in The Hague Delacroix saw no contradiction in sounding out the views of the radicals at the same time as befriending the leaders of the radicals.[56] On the other hand, if a rapprochement was Delacroix's initial aim, then he went about it in a peculiarly undiplomatic fashion, if Blauw's version of events is to be believed. To start with, his manners were not so well attuned to the proprieties of Dutch politics as his predecessor's. From his eminence as Foreign Minister he had become accustomed to deliver dressings-down to captive audiences. Ingratiation was certainly not in his nature. On January 7, 1798, at a dinner at the house of Hahn, and in the presence of not only the Committee for Foreign Affairs but also a group of foreign ambassadors, Delacroix launched into a drunken and incoherent harangue against "those now in charge of government." The climax of the outburst was an expression of astonishment that no member of the "States-General" could be found to plunge a dagger into the breasts of those who had proposed the infamous regulation of November 1795. His audience sat in embarrassed silence, unaccustomed to flights of rhetoric over the dinner table. In the end Delacroix, finally calming down and feeling awkward, clumsily apologised if he had expressed himself over-zealously. His discomfort did not last long. During the course of the *soirée* he had produced the "symbol" which, he insisted, must become the "foundation" of their new constitution.

Two days later, at a more private meeting, the document was once again thrust in the faces of the Committee for Foreign Affairs and the President of the National Assembly, who at this juncture was none other than Blauw. In the brief interval, aware that they were dealing with a highly neurotic and volatile personality, the Committee had deputed Hugo Gevers to try to come to some accommodation with the agent since, in points of *detail,* their views of the constitution were not as far apart as his blustering implied. But on the 9th they were, as a body, presented with a virtual ultimatum. The two federalist members of the Committee—van Beveren and van der Goes—were brave enough to decline outright. Bicker and Hahn expressed their "understanding" of its content and "sympathy" with its general direction, while still more pragmatic characters like van Hooff and Gevers asked if they could consider it further.

That the "symbol" had been given so cool a reception was due not so much to what it contained as to the manner in which it had been presented. The high-handedness of Delacroix's behaviour was thought by the moderate souls on the Committee for Foreign Affairs to be an ominous intrusion into the domestic business of the Republic. Instead of reconciling the essentially common interests of the French Directory and the moderate unitarists, it sundered them more efficaciously than Ducange and his associates had ever dared to hope. In retrospect, the dinner of the 7th seemed to van Langen to have been a "declaration of war" on the moderates. Certainly it made them more prickly where issues touching Dutch sovereignty were concerned. Paramount among these was the hardy perennial which had caused so much trouble to the Stadholder in 1786 and to Bicker ten years later: the command of The Hague garrison. Since the generals commanding the joint armies were mostly French, but the ultimate orders to the garrison were vested in the "national sovereign," the question of dual allegiance arose in an acutely embarrassing form. The Committee was even less likely to place its full trust in General Joubert than it had in Beurnonville and Pichegru, and to safeguard the integrity of the seat of Dutch government it made clear its insistence on the retention of its command.

For Gevers the issue was more than symbolic. Like the disputes at Flushing, not only the sovereignty of the Batavian Republic but the good faith of France to hold to the Treaty of The Hague was on trial. Delacroix, however, was not inclined to see the matter in that light. For his part it was a gratuitous offence, another item in the evidence of the Committee's bad faith and, as Ducange promptly reminded him, a hint that it might be planning some treachery against the alliance. In fact, when the issue was first broached, the agent had not at all determined to use the garrison in any act of force against the Assembly and its committees. But when the bitter quarrel had run its course, the Committee for Foreign Affairs' anxiety had become a self-fulfilling prophecy. In this respect as in so many others, Delacroix's eventual commitment to a *coup d'état* was the consequence, not the cause, of what he called his "tergiversations" with the moderates.

Guided by Ducange, Delacroix now began to meet regularly with an ad hoc committee of radicals, among whom were van Langen and van Leeuwen, Vreede having retired to his sick bed in Tilburg. But the very contradictions of his behaviour offered some hope that this was not yet the end of the road. Although at the meeting on January 9 he had threatened the Committee with the prospect of violence and a new revolution if they refused to embrace the "symbol," his letter to the Directory the following day makes it clear that this was a threat, not a promise. He assured Talleyrand that he had "persuaded" the moderates to his point of view and that action on the constitutional front was imminent. For their part the discussions with Delacroix, welcome as they were, did not commit the radicals to a decisive break with the moderate unitarists. The "symbol" was a long way from representing their own views, and they had no intention of knuckling under to Ducange when it was still possible that an alliance of unitarists in the Assembly would succeed in isolating the federalists and producing a constitution more to their liking. Before his illness, Vreede himself had had conversations with van Hooff and Hahn on exactly such a strategy. Even *after* the declaration of December 12 Konijnenburg wrote to another ex-predikant, Boudwijn van Rees, "if the members of the middle party come in with us, the cause will in all likelihood be successful. Their example will serve to sway many aristocrats and federalists [in acquiescing to a unitarist constitution]. But if they do not, they will have destroyed themselves and very likely the nation too."[57]

By the end of the first week of the new year there were no firm indications that a deadlock was in the offing. On the contrary, the declaration of December 12 had actually gathered further support from the floor of the Assembly so that fifty-five representatives adhered to it: more than many majorities needed in most votes. Certainly the growing strength of the radical bloc was sufficient to deter any of the federalists from attempting a pruning job akin to that of the spring and summer of 1797. Moreover, in contrast to the impression given by Colenbrander's narrative, the radicals on the constitutional commission, led by Willem Ockerse, were themselves not bent on force at any cost. Their copious minutes and committee records bear eloquent witness to the seriousness of their attempt to take account of a wide range of opinion within the unitarists' camp, and to produce as comprehensive a document as possible. Counsel was taken not only from the editor of *De Democraten* but from such disparate sources as the young financier and founder member of the "Voor Eenheid en Orde" club in The Hague,[58] Johannes Goldberg, and the sage lawyer of Utrecht, Cornelis van Maanen.

Little of these deliberations suggests a huddle of conspirators brooding over plans to seize power at a moment's notice. Of course it would be naïve to suppose that such a course of action had not occurred to the radicals. Ockerse himself seemed torn between ploughing on with his constitutional duties and grasping the opportunity which Ducange was temptingly holding out. Nor had any such plans been drawn up by January 10 when colleagues from the East India Committee—Wiselius, Bogislaw von Liebherr and Pieter Quint Ondaatje—arrived in The Hague for talks with Ockerse and his group. Colenbrander of course made much of this and other encounters, taking the discussions as the preparation for the seizure of power. His proof is a document known as the "Agreed Constitutional Points," which *was* later used as the new regulation on the morrow of the coup. But when Wiselius came to discuss the items pertaining to colonial affairs, he was certainly not acting as party to a plot of which he had absolutely no knowledge. The "Points" were, as they appear in Ockerse's memoranda, a recapitulation of some of the essentials of his constitutional draft. Colenbrander's mistake, as Dr. de Wit has pointed out, was to assume that the "Points" (Dutch) and the "symbol" (French) were of the same provenance and that both had been manufactured to license an act of force.[59]

The distaste of men like Blauw and Wiselius for arbitrary political action was not just (or perhaps not at all) a product of what Geyl took to be the national virtue of moderation in all things. True, like Paulus before them, they worried a great deal about the reconciliation of revolutionary and legitimate authority. But in their apprehension about a *coup d'état* they were guided more by realism than idealism. For they understood, better than fierier spirits, that only a minority of their nation, however committed, was really interested in deep structural changes in the institutions of the nation. The vast majority wanted only to be left in peace to cultivate their gardens and be free from the curse of heavy taxation. True, their opponents were in all likelihood an even smaller minority; but in the task of re-shaping the Dutch nation into a unitary state, they would be opposed simply by the dead weight of customary practice and familiar institutions. If they were to stand any chance of success they had to induce the majority to comply with rather than resist the changes. A *coup d'état* engineered by a foreign power and executed by a splinter of a political fragment would parody all the high-flown ideals of unity and de-mocracy, and it would leave an already small party fatally debilitated.

Above all, though, it was difficult to see why there should be any pressing *need* for an act of force. On the commission itself the radicals had the majority and the few federalists left were despondent about the survival of provincial sovereignty. Konijnenburg's hopes that increasing pressure from the moderate unitarists would persuade timid souls into joining the unitarist majority or, at least, silence their opposition seemed to have been prophetic. Not a word was heard from Jan Bicker in January 1798, and he had resigned from the Committee for Foreign Affairs. Gevers and Blauw wanted very much to force the pace of the commission so that they could present Delacroix with a fait accompli as an alternative to any kind of drastic intervention. The major difficulty was that even at the bustling rate that Ockerse's colleagues were proceeding, it seemed unlikely all the details would be ironed out in the Assembly much before March. To get around this and persuade the agent of their good faith, Gevers proposed on January 11 that the Assembly appoint a small sub-committee to enquire from the commission on its progress and to issue a kind of interim report. In response to this, Ockerse appeared before the Assembly on January 15 and addressed it in terms which could have left his audience in no doubt that the battle for unitary sovereignty had been virtually won within the commission. Although the draft could not be com-pleted before February, it would be based on

the rights and duties of man and citizen; on civil liberty and equality; on popular sovereignty by representation; on an energetic and *responsible* executive government; on a fully unified administration for both internal and external policy and for finance; on the amalgamation of the old [provincial] debts; the separation of Church and state and the right of the people to revise their own constitution.[60]

The competence of the primary assemblies—an important point of dif-ference between radical and moderate unitarists—went unmentioned in Ockerse's statement. But in the clear subordination of the executive to the legislature and the general tone of the statement it was obvious that if he was reporting them correctly, the commission was nearer the democrats' declaration of December 12 than the French "symbol." It was in fact a summarised account of the areas of *agreement* between radical and moderate unitarists—not a challenge to the sovereignty of the Assembly. And it was in the knowledge that such a new majority had been established that Ockerse rounded off his statement with a peroration worthy of the most melodramatic moments of the revolution, urging his colleagues to "swear in unity to save the Fatherland or die at our posts."

Hopefully, neither extremity was to be anticipated. It is still unclear whether Ockerse's last words were intended as a mere rhetorical flourish or the overture to some new act. Possibly he had not yet made up his own mind. It was, after all, a standard gambit of the Directorial coups for the *attentistes* to announce that they were taking power in order to preserve the *patrie* from dangers which existed only in the fact of their conspiracy! But even if Ockerse was acting disingenuously, the deputies who thudded their fists to their bosoms in attitudes of classic rectitude were sincere enough. Blauw reckoned that the vital breakthrough had already occurred and merely awaited an opportunity to test the strength of the unitarist "alliance." One day after the Ockerse speech he had his chance. On January 8 it had become known that—*mirabile dictu*—all eight provinces bar Holland had rejected the 8 per cent tax on incomes. (Utrecht had rejected it only by the narrowest of margins and Zeeland had asked for more time to "consider.") In reply, the deputies of the provincial assembly in Holland had declared that they would contribute not one florin more to the defence of the Republic until taxes were brought to an equal footing. In this light the Assembly made up its mind to act decisively as a national legislature. Notwithstanding the provincial objections, it reaffirmed the 8 per cent tax by a majority of sixty-eight votes to forty.

It is true that provincial loyalties cut across political affiliations to produce this majority, but there could be no mistake that, whether from panic at the prospect of a coup or from the gradual erosion of its resistance, the federalist opposition to a unitarist state was dying in the National Assembly. Of course there were heroes who refused to lie down. Outstanding among the spokesmen for Dutch traditions as they saw them were Albert de Sitter and Jacob de Mist. Their best weapon was still the legal status of the regulation. Though thoroughly detested by a majority of the deputies, it could not be denied that this provided that the provinces have the last word over any infringement on their fiscal and financial autonomy. While Blauw was unlikely to take Delacroix's invitation to assassinate those who had been responsible for it seriously, he had made up his mind that to "save" the Assembly from a coup it was imperative that the regulation be rescinded. The choice was either a gentle revolution in their own affairs or revolution *à la Ducange*.

Once resolved, the moderate unitarist went about this in a characteristically artful manner. The terms of reference given to the committee appointed on January 15 under Jean Pasteur to consider the Ockerse address in detail were significantly broadened so that if the Assembly approved of what Pasteur (and thus by extension Ockerse) had to say, his committee was to go ahead forthwith and submit immediate proposals for the establishment of an interim executive government. This was, in fact, reviving the plan of the sub-committee of five the previous November, but its timing now was critical. Quite obviously the appointment of a national executive, responsible to the Assembly, was instituting the basic essentials of the new state *in advance* of the constitutional plebiscite. Even if the popular vote were again to be hostile, such a government would continue in office. In other words, the regulation was de facto repealed and a "constitutional coup" carried out with the minimum of upheaval. The only parties likely to be violently opposed to such a move were the doctrinaire federalists.

So exactly it proved on January 19 when Pasteur's proposal was voted on, along with the Ockerse address. Both received a majority of eighty-six votes to twenty-four. The balance of power between unitarists and federalists obtaining at the opening of the National Assembly in March 1796 had, nearly two years later, been exactly reversed.

Understandably Blauw, Pasteur and van de Kasteele, the architects of what they assumed to be a unitarist coalition, were elated at the outcome of the vote of January 19. Pasteur wrote afterwards that "we were advancing in great strides towards the desired goal . . . without shock or violence."[61] The following Monday his committee was to present the Assembly with a detailed decree, which would legalise the new order and eliminate the regulation once and for all. His "parliamentary revolution" appeared to have been successful. The mere *threat* of a coup had persuaded the uncommitted to submit to the lesser evil. Indeed, Pasteur and Gevers felt themselves in so strong a position as to go and see Delacroix on the morning of the 19th. To avoid the editing services of Ducange they presented him with a copy of the new constitutional orders, already translated into French, and went so far as warning him that, in the circumstances of the new unity of the Assembly, any resort to force would do irreparable damage to the Republic. There was, they reiterated, no necessity now for a revolution.

Charles Delacroix, however, was not the sort of man to take such advice in the spirit in which it was intended. He assured Pasteur in the coldest manner he could assume that there would be no "disorder," but reminded him at the same time that he, the agent of the Republic of France, disposed of a large body of French *and* Dutch troops in case anyone should think of armed resistance. Delacroix had, in fact, been far from overjoyed with the past week's proceedings. Where the sudden unity of the Assembly might have delighted him on his first days in The Hague, its show of independence now mortified him beyond reason. He saw only the cajolery of arch-intriguers like Blauw and Gevers, whose proposal on the 11th had pre-empted his own freedom of action and had sidestepped with some ingenuity the document Ducange had been preparing for Dutch consumption. So far from being grateful to Blauw for fulfilling, almost to the letter, the imperatives of his own Instruction, he saw him as his bitterest enemy, refusing even to talk to him on the afternoon of Friday the 19th. What could Pasteur's concern for the disposition of The Hague garrison mean except that his "clique" were themselves preparing for a seizure of power? All these resolutions were a smoke-screen. Thus it was that during the week of the 12th to the 19th Delacroix finally put aside his reservations and, egged on by Ducange, determined to rid the Batavian Republic of all procrastinators.

The Rubicon had, in fact, been crossed by the radicals on Wednesday the 17th. On that day the Amsterdam representatives of the East India Committee—many of them leading members of "Voor Een- en Ondeelbaarheid" and "De Uitkijk"—met with the Assembly's radicals at the committee's residence, the "Logement van Haarlem" in the Bleijenberg in The Hague, a few paces from the present national archives. Even at this stage Wiselius and his colleagues had no inkling that Wybo Fijnje and Willem Ockerse had finally thrown in their lot with Ducange and engaged themselves to a plan to seize power in the Assembly by force. On learning of the plans, they were dismayed and baffled. Like Blauw, Wiselius saw no compelling need for any such action, particularly since Ockerse himself had charted the way ahead in the Assembly. Blauw, who had never been close to Fijnje, faced with the ruin of all his calculations made a bitter protest—but to no avail. Fijnje retorted contemptuously to his attempts to persuade the company that they were all tired of having to listen to his lectures. Wiselius, who commanded more affection and respect, was no less critical. Scanning the emendations that had been made to the "Agreed Constitutional Points" and which provided for punitive action *after* the coup, he protested most strongly at the suggestion that the property of arrested members of the Assembly should be confiscated. He reminded the meeting of the career of the despicable Ducange, notably his activities as a policeman for the Committee of General Security in Paris. Once committed to arbitrary violence, he warned, no-one could say where it might end.[62] His efforts were unproductive. Seeing that Fijnje, van Langen and Ockerse were determined to go through with the plan, Wiselius and his colleagues decided that they would wash their hands of the whole business. Obviously their position was both dangerous and compromising. They could not bring themselves to denounce their comrades—and more important they had not been kept informed on any details of the plan's execution—but neither could they entertain identifying themselves with it. Yet again their scruples reduced them to utter political impotence at precisely the moment when action was needed.

Jacob Blauw made one last effort to avert the disaster after failing to see Delacroix on the Friday. His dire warnings of what would happen as a consequence had moved the most nervous of those men nominated to serve on the revolutionary "Directory," the Zeeland astronomer Dr. Fokker. An hour's closeted discussion with Blauw on Saturday the 20th produced an amended plan. On Monday the 22nd the regulation would be repealed, but only the handful of federalists who were the most intransigent opponents of the new order would be removed. In the first instance they would not be arrested but "asked to resign." If they proved stubborn, then possibly more severe measures might be contemplated. This "plan" was also translated into French for the benefit of Delacroix—but it had to be relayed to him via Ducange who saw to it that the agent paid no attention to it whatsoever. The views of Jacob Blauw were of no consequence to Delacroix, who already saw himself hailed in Paris as the saviour of the Dutch, the Caesar of the Bataves![63]

The events of the 19th decided both the revolutionaries in the Assembly and Delacroix that any action had to take place on Monday before the moderates could dictate the initative in the Assembly. The Assembly had, on the 16th, obligingly voted a radical, Hendrik Midderigh—the Rotterdam wine merchant and a close crony of van Langen's—to be its next President. Had Blauw known then what he and Wiselius knew on the 17th they might have voted differently. But in fact Midderigh was only taken into Fijnje's confidence at this late stage. He was, however, to prove a willing convert. The "Points," which had been in circulation as a recapitulation and summary of the constitutional commission's work, was now touched up to act as a revolutionary bond for all parties to the plot. Virtually the same number as had signed the declaration of December 12 appended their names. Yet, as van Langen later admitted, apart from the punitive clauses regarding purges of those known as "enemies of their principles" and those who refused the oath of hatred to "Stadholderate, federalism, aristocracy and anarchy," it was hardly dissimilar to Pasteur's own plan for Monday, the 22nd.

The Monday which was to have been the crowning moment of the "unitarist alliance" and the consummation of the "legitimate revolution" was destined for a different history. Over the weekend Herman Daendels, lured by the prospect of acting the Batavian Bonaparte, belatedly rallied to the revolution. For Vreede and Fijnje he remained a deeply devious character. But his presence was crucial, for it was planned to give the coup an air of spurious patriotism by relying on exclusively Dutch troops. On Sunday the 21st Joubert and Daendels sealed off The Hague, preventing all ingress and egress to the city. In the provinces Generals Boekop, Dumonceau and Bonhomme had placed their divisions close to the major urban centres in case of an adverse popular reaction to the coup. Only one figure was missing: Pieter Vreede. Delacroix had insisted on consulting with him before finalising the plans. Summoned by letter on the 19th and overruling the protests of his solicitous wife, Vreede rose from his sick bed in Tilburg. Feverish with excitement rather than a chest-cold he hurried to The Hague, arriving there on the Sunday morning. He saw the French agent, cast an eye over the plans made for the following day, approved them and tried to assimilate the dramatic change in his fortunes. For Delacroix clearly saw Vreede as the true leader of the new revolutionary order—a role he was not so diffident as to decline. The same evening Vreede wrote to his wife reassuring her that he was well; that "impending events" had cured him better than any drug; and signing off, as though addressing history rather than Katje: "All is ready for the battle. Adieu, aristocrats, until the morrow!"[64]

In actual fact the destruction of the first republican regime began that same night, January 21–22, 1798. Like such events in France, it felt obliged to pay lip service to the forms of legality. The list of those to be arrested—including all the Committee for Foreign Affairs (and the resignee Bicker), together with most of the leading federalists and moderates in the Assembly—had been drawn up by the secret Revolutionary Committee appointed in The Hague on the 17th and duly signed by the new President of the Assembly, Midderigh. For the order to be legal, however, it needed the signature of the secretary of the Assembly, R. van der Hoeven, an innocuous little man who was brought in some fright to the "Logement van Haarlem" where he was persuaded to do his republican duty. That same night the members of the Committee for Foreign Affairs were placed under house arrest and guards surrounded the areas adjacent to their homes. This happened between three and four in the morning. Those like van Langen and Fijnje who had already assumed a directorial role stayed up throughout the night. At about half past seven the next morning, as previously agreed, the "rebel" members of the Assembly who had signed the "Constitutional Points" assembled at the Haarlem residence. From there they made their way between two field artillery pieces and under heavily armed escort by Dutch soldiers under Daendels' command to the Binnenhof.

At the Assembly they found that all roads leading to it had been invested with more troops sealing it off from the outside. Twenty-one members who had got wind of what was in store and arriving in advance, had been forbidden access to the chamber and "shown" under protest to an anteroom where they found themselves virtual prisoners. This group included de Mist, van Beveren, de Sitter, van Marle—staunch federalists all—but also more surprising figures such as van Maanen and Coert van Beijma! The rump of the Assembly—about fifty representatives—were now allowed to enter the Assembly proper, where they were addressed by Midderigh. He followed through all the ritual gestures proper to such occasions, declaring the "Fatherland in danger" and urging his comrades and brothers to join him in an oath "sworn on the altar of Liberty" that they would not separate until a "true constitution had been established." Thus their own gathering had been transformed into a Constituent in permanent session. In further gestures of revolutionary solidarity, an oath of hatred for "Stadholderate, aristocracy, federalism and anarchy" was sworn and a declaration made that the apprehended deputies had forfeited their seats and the "confidence of the people." Finally the regulation of 1795—the source of all the frustration—was repealed; all provincial sovereignties annulled; an "Interim Executive Directory of Five" set up (including Vreede, Fijnje and van Langen); and the constitutional commission reduced to seven members (two of whom were Ockerse and Konijnenburg).[65]

At four in the afternoon, delighted at the smoothness of the operation, Charles Delacroix arrived at the now "Constituent" Assembly to offer his fraternal embrace to President Midderigh and his felicitations to the representatives. The same evening he wrote to Talleyrand:

At last the Batavian regeneration has been consummated this very day! An 18 Fructidor as wisely conceived and as happily executed as that which saved France has taken place this morning. The people are perfectly calm. At two o'clock this

afternoon the soldiers were able to return to their barracks and the National
Assembly to pursue its business in peace.[66]

There were those among the Dutch Patriots who were less happy with
the outcome of the day's work and more pessimistic about its consequences.
Jacob Blauw had not been arrested along with Gevers' Pasteur and the rest but
had been forbidden to leave The Hague until permitted by the new Directory.
Like Pasteur he took the coup as a personal hurt, as indeed it was, but he
also believed more objectively that it had been a futile iniquity arranged
simply to suit the perverse whims of the agent and further the ambitions
of a handful of men hungry for power. The intervention of Daendels' bayonets
had done nothing which could not have been achieved by peaceful and
orthodox means. Far from uniting the Dutch in a bond of revolutionary
nationhood, he felt convinced that the day's work would in fact divide them
even more fiercely than before.

While relieved not to have been a party to the dirty work—he had
slipped back to Amsterdam just before The Hague had been sealed off—
Samuel Wiselius was nevertheless prepared to reserve judgement. The coup
itself had been an utterly mistaken move, although if the aftermath was
handled with prudence all might not yet be lost. Yet those to whom the
immediate future had been confided did not inspire confidence; it was impossible to be reassured by the combination of such impulsive characters as
Charles Delacroix and Pieter Vreede. But, being Sam Wiselius, he summed
up his expectations in an ironic verse:

Les jours de Noël sont passés
Nous sommes au pied de la Croix
Et on attend la résurrection. . . .[67]

✿ ✿ ✿ ✿ ✿ ✿ ✿ ✿ ✿ ✿

8

Hubris and Nemesis,
January–June 1798

The Pedigree of the Constitution

The transformation of a revolutionary faction into a revolutionary government is a notoriously hazardous process. Each generation of revolutionaries naturally hopes that theirs will prove to be the conclusive act of liberation. Further expressions of dissent are severely discouraged as representing not the salutary exercise of the popular will but, on the contrary, mischievous attempts to sabotage it. The watchwords of the morrow of the revolution are, more often than not, solidarity, unity, order.

Conscious of the frailty of their position, the victors of the coup of January 22 were no exception to this rule. The proclamation read by Midderigh to the rump of the National Assembly that Monday morning was strewn with references to the need to close ranks, end factional strife and "uncertainty in public life," and to the duty of all "right-minded patriots" to rally to the new regime.[1] In places, the tone of the address was almost painfully defensive, as if the makers of the coup wished to issue an apology to the nation for the inconvenience they had caused. It went out of its way to reassure the people that it was not about to embark on a Dutch Terror, but had undertaken the revolution merely to steer the Republic back to the first principles of 1795 from which the machinations of assorted aristocrats, Anglophiles and crypto-Orangists had deflected it. Those villains had allowed the Republic to languish in a state of constitutional anarchy for nearly three years so that they might profit from its disarray. Their crimes had brought the state to the very brink of the pit of despair ("de jammerpoel"). Even when the nation had flung back their pitiful mock-constitution in their faces in 1797, they had not flinched from attempting to sabotage new attempts to give the people their rightful democracy. All this, the proclamation announced, had been tolerated by the "right-minded" part of the nation with almost saintly forbearance. It was only when the perpetuation of such a state of affairs threatened the very life of the Fatherland that they had been obliged to

[311]

come to its rescue. The people wanted their rightful constitution. It was ready for them. All that had been done was to "clear the obstacles from the path."

This rationalisation of the revolution was determined by didactic needs. To shore up their position, particularly if it seems precarious, revolutionary regimes are prone to begin their government by rewriting the history of the circumstances in which they took power. Depending on whether reassurance or galvanisation is a higher priority, defensive or aggressive notes are variously struck in such an account. Obviously the initial utterances of the Dutch radicals were calculated to neutralise the political situation by playing down the consequences of their action. But such modest attitudes did not suit all the protagonists of the new order. It was virtually unheard of, for example, for an apology to struggle to the lips of Pieter Vreede. When, barely eight months later, following his removal from power, he was called on by a new Legislative Assembly to answer for the conduct of his regime and the manner in which it assumed power, he was anything but defensive.

Unlike Fijnje and van Langen, who were also arraigned, Vreede had not been implicated in criminal malversations.[2] His part in the preparation and execution of the coup itself had been negligible. But he made no attempt to extricate himself from either, nor to understate the significance of what had happened. Instead, a seventy-page reply to his accusers reasserted his pride and conviction that the revolution had been the saving of the Batavian Republic.[3] Could it be denied that the Directory had given the nation the constitution it had so badly missed? Could it be denied that the constitution had received the acclamation of an overwhelming majority of the popular vote on April 23? How could it not be seen that all the measures they had taken had been adopted in the nation's best interests? Far from apologising, the indignation of Vreede's argument seemed to demand from his prosecutors an apology for having presumed to question the wisdom of his administration.

The boldness of his counter-attack was typical of Vreede's political mentality. He found it impossible to temporise over anything so momentous as the revolution of January 22. Such events figured in his mind not as the arbitrary consequence of the shifts and changes of a few politicians but as the solemn outcome of a combat of inexorable historical forces. His victory had been that of justice over wickedness; of liberty over slavery. When he stood with his comrades in the hall of the Assembly vowing to dedicate himself to the good of the Fatherland until death, he, at least, meant every word. Both Vreede's rhetorical flights of fancy and the more assiduously worked rationale of the Proclamation were intended to invest the usurpation with the warrant of patriotic authority. The preoccupation with legitimacy, even among the most ardently professed revolutionaries, has already been remarked on. But while Midderigh's speech at the outset of the radical regime and Vreede's defence at the end of it differed widely in the posture of their argument, both agreed on one fundamental point. Without the action on January 22 there could have been no constitution, and without a constitution the Batavian Republic was doomed to perish. They were able, therefore, to insist that they and they alone had come to the aid of the Fatherland in the nick of time.

It was just this point which was hotly disputed by the rival account of those, like Blauw and Pasteur, for whom the revolution had meant political defeat. Pasteur argued that, so far from doing irreparable damage to the political life of the Republic, further abstention from violent action would have had the reverse effect.[4] He had his special reasons for making such a claim— one which could hardly be tested by empirical verification. But it was a feature of his argument that it in no way sought to question the validity or significance of the constitution *as such*. As he told Delacroix on the eve of the coup itself, he "saw no *necessity* why matters should have had to come to a revolution."[5] The huge majority which had voted in favour of his own motion on the 19th had in effect already licensed the revocation of the regulation which was actually scheduled to take place on the Monday! Following that it would have been a simple thing to have set up an interim national executive and given the commission the most expeditious path possible for the completion of its work. In his view the crucial breakthrough had been the retreat of the federalists from all-out opposition a fortnight before. Far from the regulation acting as a noose around the neck of the Republic, threatening it with strangulation, his version saw it as loosened so much that it could be removed without any hurt whatsoever. Why then had the coup come about? Partly, he affirmed, because the French agent had become deaf to all persuasion following the quarrel over the disposition of the command of the Dutch forces and forts and had been so captivated by his role as the Dutch Caesar. But he also alluded sadly to the incapacity on the part of the radical leaders of overcoming their suspicion and hostility towards those they regarded as "chameleons" and "slimies," responsible for ostracising them from political influence since 1796. Confronted by Ducange's offer of the "head of Medusa" with which to stun their rivals into complete submission, they simply had no strength to desist.[6] It was an act of hubris for which they were to pay the inevitable penalty.

Pasteur's view of the genesis of the revolution, jaundiced as it doubtless was by his own imprisonment at the hands of the new regime, was a good deal less dignified than the majèstic romanticisms of Pieter Vreede. But it was far closer to the truth. If further evidence of its basic rightness were needed, it could be culled in ample supply from the papers of one of the major protagonists of the radicals, Anthonie Willem Ockerse.[7] Recently unearthed in Friesland, the detailed minutes of meetings of the constitutional commission as well as Ockerse's private letters to his colleagues confirm Pasteur's presumption that at the time of the artificially induced schisms between radical and moderate unitarists the constitution was well on the way to completion, more or less on the basis of the democratic-unitarist programme.[8] Indeed Ockerse's own speech to the Assembly on January 15 had made this an open secret. The truth is that during the last two weeks before the coup, he was guilty of playing something of a double game. As the responsible member of the commission, he was happy to respond to Gevers' public invitation to set out the fundamental principles of the new draft;

but as an intimate of Fijnje and van Langen, he could hardly help but associate himself with their plans. In a few minor respects, both he and the commission were the beneficiaries of the coup. Its numbers were reduced from twenty-one to seven, leaving only the hard core of radical unitarists to add the finishing touches, and dispensing with the gruesomely long-winded expatiations of de Mist. Koninjenburg and Petrus van Sonsbeek, both signatories of the "Declaration of 43" on December 12, could now help him to expedite the draft as quickly as possible. But in fact neither the size nor the composition of the reduced commission made the slightest difference to its work. The time-table to which it adhered was designed so that the finished draft might be presented to the Assembly by early March—a schedule identical to that which Ockerse had promised as chairman of the old commission on January 15![9]

All the hard work had been done long before the revolution. As I have already suggested, Ockerse's papers leave us in no doubt that the "Agreed Constitutional Points" arose from the commission's discussions between October 1797 and the middle of January 1798. It was not, as Colenbrander seemed to think, a pre-digested French-manufactured constitution foisted on the radicals as the price for giving them absolute power. His confusion arose presumably from regarding the "Points" and Delacroix's "symbol" in identical terms. After irascibly brandishing it at the moderates on January 7, the "symbol" was discarded by the agent precisely because he was deceived by Ducange into believing that the radicals' document differed from his own only in the most insignificant details. The "Points" were not tailored to meet the approval of the French minister, nor were they intended as an insurrectionary charter. Of the nineteen articles dealing with the intended *competence* of the constitution and the twenty-eight dealing with its *provisions*, there was almost nothing to which the moderate unitarists might not have given their assent, save conceivably the measures set out for purging the primary assemblies prior to ratification.[10] To be sure, the "Points" *became* a kind of revolutionary bond on the 19th and 20th, when the fifty-odd radicals who were to form the nucleus of the new "Constituent" appended their names. But this ad hoc transmutation only took place after the decision to go ahead with the coup had been taken. As we have seen, it was perfectly possible for Wiselius to travel to The Hague to discuss the colonial paragraphs of the draft "Points" without the slightest inkling of the sudden change in radical tactics.

Indeed even at this stage, the preamble added to the "Points" on Midderigh's nomination to the Presidential chair was one capable of wide interpretation, which by no means committed the radicals irreversibly to an act of force. It simply stated that it was the "resolve of the undersigned to take the most efficacious and appropriate measures to establish a free and sage constitution and an energetic government."[11] Following the coup the "Points" became, in effect, the new regulation for the "Constituent" enacted on January 25. It established the authority of the pruned-down commission and the Executive Directory of Five. But those changes, too, had not depended on the coup. Pasteur and Blauw both assumed that after the adoption of their resolution, the consolidated majority in the Assembly would induce the federalists to resign of their own accord rather than face repeated defeat on their cherished cause. In summary, the action which Vreede and Fijnje presented as the indispensable condition of the constitution and the unitary Republic made no difference whatever to their achievement, except for the unintended result that their inauguration would take place in a climate of further bitter in-fighting.

A number of important consequences follow from the documentary disentanglement. First, the essential continuity of the work on the "Points" and on the new constitution itself vitiates the argument that the coup was essential to the success of both. Secondly, it reveals that the constitution of 1798, despite the partisan character of the regime which brought it into being, reflected a broader spectrum of Patriot opinion within the Republic. This was precisely why, after the regime had been deposed in June, their moderate successors were at pains to defend the constitution against any attacks and to dissociate its form of government from the first Directory.[12] Its origins are not to be found in any importation of Delacroix but in the debates on constitutional reform which had been carried on in the Netherlands since 1795. Indeed, its more remote tap roots may be traced even to the speculations of the Artois exiles in 1788–92 and the plans of the "Valckenisten" in 1790–91. Van de Spiegel himself had made a characteristic contribution to the consideration of reform, and before him both the Amsterdam Assembly of September 1787 and the Leiden Programme of 1785—drafted by Pieter Vreede—had looked forward to the day when the Netherlands would become a unified democracy. Finally it is clear that, despite the markedly national flavour of the constitution, the carefully sustained deceit of Ducange had succeeded in persuading Delacroix that the accommodating radicals (unlike the obstreperous and arrogant moderates) were in the process of carrying out his instructions to the letter.

Unfortunately for Ducange, Ockerse himself had the irritatingly forthright habit of pointing out these discrepancies directly to Delacroix. Ducange was forced to allude occasionally to these "little difficulties," but spoke of them as a result of editorial incompetence rather than matters of substance. Yet as the day for the completion of the new constitution drew nearer, it was obvious that Ducange was going to have some awkward explaining to do. Even on January 18, when the commission had brusquely rejected his list of "suggested amendments" to the "Points," he had alluded to their baffling insistence on retaining some items "which they appear to regard as essential and to which they are very much attached."[13] This was to persuade Delacroix to accept the "Points" as the revolutionary warrant on the proviso that it would be a simple matter to iron out the "little difficulties" afterwards. When it became plain that no such ironing out was going to happen, Ducange began to pen apologetic warnings to Delacroix that the French Directory "might not have reason to feel absolutely satisfied" with what the commission was about to produce.

Needless to say, Ducange's glosses and "translations" had been faithfully transmitted by Delacroix to Talleyrand, who also assumed that the Dutch were busy putting the finishing touches to yet another version of the constitution of 1795. At the last post Ducange attempted to hold up the publication of the new constitution in the first week of March so as to give himself time to straighten things out. But Ockerse again proved unhelpful, insisting that if the draft were further delayed the Directory risked the most serious unrest in the country. Just how unenlightened Delacroix remained as to the true spirit and letter of the new constitution may be gauged from the fact that both before and immediately after its passage through the Constituent Assembly, he urged that it not be put to the nation but instead deemed valid by the "tacit approbation" which was to follow its implementation.[14] That, after all, had been good enough for the French Republic in 1795.

In fact, Ockerse and his colleagues seemed remorselessly bent on confronting Delacroix with the true situation. They pointed out, as gently as they could, that although they had been interested to see the agent's reflections on the constitutional draft, they could hardly revise their own since, "as matters turned out, it [the plan for revision] was not submitted to us until after our own plan was very far advanced."[15] There was, however, a more substantive reason why the modifications counselled by the agent could not be accepted by the commission. For, as they explained, "nine-tenths of the voters of the Batavian Republic, with justice or not as the case may be, rejected the plan of 1797 and based their repugnance for that plan precisely on those points on which we differ from the French. . . ."

Those differences boiled down to three essentials, all of which concerned the part which political democracy was to play in the Dutch constitution. First, the commission argued that it was essential that a large measure of power be delegated to the primary assemblies in the procedure of elections to the legislature. With the customary exception of bankrupts, those in receipt of public charity, and criminals, it wanted to provide for a male suffrage stripped of the fiscal qualifications woven into the French constitution of the Year III. A form of mandating electors in the intermediate electoral colleges was meant to proximate the system as nearly as possible to a direct election. Secondly, it affirmed that the primaries not only had the right of accepting or rejecting the constitution itself but the right of revision at quinquennial intervals. The 1797 Dutch provision that a petition from 25,000 voters was necessary before a revision could be demanded was regarded as disreputable, but the French stipulation that only the legislative body could revise the constitution was said to be "absolutely contrary to the Dutch national spirit." Finally, the commission expressed its inability to accept the principle of a bicameral legislature. It reminded Delacroix that in 1797 popular feeling had been incensed by the prerogatives allotted to the "Chamber of Elders." The upper Chamber, whether intended or not, had been seen as an attempt by the oligarchies and regencies to cling to their privileged position in the body politic. For good measure they observed that it was common knowledge that "certain families and groups" had laid plans to dominate that chamber and to make the legislature unworkable by a strategy of incessant conflict with the lower House. The purpose of the new constitution, they added, was finally to extirpate those nests of privilege and private sovereignty, not to give them further opportunities for entrenchment.

This last protest might have led Delacroix to further confusion. For both the "Points" and the final constitutional draft (unlike "the Declaration of 43") had made the concession of a legislature formally divided into two houses. But the difference between the French and Dutch models (which Ducange concealed and Ockerse underlined) was that the latter legislature was to be elected as a whole and then divided by lots, without distinctions of age or competence, into a First and Second Chamber. The very blandness of the titles was intended to signify that the division was one of legislative convenience, not of political authority. In some instances such as finance, the First Chamber was to have the right of initiative; in others, the situation was exactly reversed. In most cases legislation had to come before both bodies before it could be implemented. The essential unity of the legislature as a whole was to be safeguarded by the provision that each year one-third of its entire body was to stand down for re-election.

With some justice Ockerse believed that most of these provisions were more democratic than anything the French Republic had contemplated since 1793. Indeed, there was naturally some anxiety lest the comparison with the constitution of the Year II prove too embarrassing—hence the nominal division of the legislative chamber. But in any case he was not concerned to justify the Dutch constitution on grounds so speculative as the dictates of natural law or the foibles of a *régime censitaire*. His rationalisation was rather that of the specificity of national history and political circumstances. His observations on this matter are yet another demonstration of the convergence of the two senses of the word "patriot" in the Batavian revolution. He begged to remind the minister of France that for two centuries Dutchmen had been accustomed to enjoy a degree of popular liberty unusual elsewhere in Europe, and that by that token the people of the Netherlands were perhaps susceptible to a "greater degree of democracy than would be suitable for the people of France." Furthermore, he argued, there was no need to fear democratic excesses in the Batavian Republic. Usually the Dutch had more need "of the spur than the bridle." He concluded that "the constitutional forms, excellent for the French nation, cannot in every respect be considered appropriate for the Dutch: a tranquil, phlegmatic nation already accustomed to a certain degree of democracy." As a consequence, "one may, indeed one must, in the Dutch constitution, proximate more closely to these democratic forms than would be possible in France."

Doubtless Ockerse was aware that he was treading on dangerous territory in raising such issues, for he phrased his critique in the most tactful language. As was customary, he paid the minister the formal compliment of expecting him to take the civilised view:

The constitutional commission is convinced, Citizen Minister, that these truths will appear to you to be enduring and beyond question. It will not have escaped your attention that the French government itself, convinced that one single constitution cannot hold good for each and every republic, has for that express reason left to the Cisalpine and Ligurian Republics the freedom to establish in their own states and in their own constitutions the modifications which their regional and national characteristics require. This freedom, the constitutional commission is certain, the government of France will equally allow to its Batavian ally, persuaded that the only constitution which will make a people happy is one which is in accordance with its opinions, mores, and customs . . . and which is established by the free will, welfare and satisfaction of all its citizens, or at any rate the great majority.

This was as rousing a statement of the claims of republican pluralism as can be found in the whole history of the Batavian Republic. It may well be that in appealing to a spirit of fraternal generosity in Paris, Ockerse and Konijnenburg were (like those before and those to come after them in the Netherlands) sadly deluded. But the worst that can be said of them is that they were naïve. Such utterances hardly bear out the portrait of feeble collaboration etched in by Colenbrander and repeated subsequently as the cliché of revolutionary historiography.

Moreover, if the constitution itself made few allusions to the specifically national concerns of the Batavian Republic, this was just because its authors saw no inherent contradiction between drafting a document tailored for Dutch needs and lacing it with the nostrums of pan-European republicanism. Predictably enough, its preamble declared that the Republic was to be grounded on the imperishable axioms of the equality of citizens and the indivisibility of their sovereignty.[16] But the constitution was also conspicuous for the attention it paid to those issues which had preoccupied aspirant re-formers of the Dutch state for the previous half-century or longer. Many of its articles were concerned to redefine the nature and obligations of public office—the primary target of the Patriots of the 1780's and one of van der Capellen's favourite cockshies. Article XV of the "General Principles" de-clared unequivocally that henceforth office could be regarded neither as transferable nor hereditary—a revolutionary truism but one that would not bear omission from such a document. Article XLV declared that all unneces-sary offices and sinecures were to be abolished; Article LXVI that every office had to be accountable to public surveillance for its salaries and expenses; Article LVIII that pensions and gratuities were to be granted only to those whom sickness or old age had removed from their duties; and Article XL of the constitution proper stipulated that any public servant suspected of con-verting public funds could be summarily charged before a tribunal of the National High Court of Justice.

Another abiding concern of reformist literature reflected in the con-stitution was the condition of the Dutch economy. Like their counterparts in France, the Batavian republicans were divided between mercantilist and laisser-faire remedies; but it was the latter group that had the upper hand as far as constitutional reforms were concerned. Article LII abolished all internal imposts and tolls; Article LIII all guilds—an item which was to elicit an angry response—freeing every citizen to take his labour or his capital any-where in the Republic he judged opportune. Article LI acknowledged the decline in skilled labour by offering encouragement to the immigration of foreigners able to contribute to the depleted national pool. Predictably, many of the articles were given over to the thorny problems of finance on which, it was generally appreciated, the future of the nation vitally depended. The decisions of February and November 1797 to introduce nationally levied taxes had made important breaches in the traditional "Quota" system, and in addition the National Assembly had voted to institute a "new system of general taxation, both for the securing of the needs of the State and for the payment of annual interest and redemptions of the debt." An elaborate system of receivers and accountants was written into the constitution, in addition to the national superintendence of the new "Agent of Finance." It was further stipulated that such a system should come into effect not later than two years after the adoption of the constitution. (Since the administrative details were left to those unfortunates who would be responsible for making it work, this provision proved decidedly over-optimistic. Not until 1805 was the fiscal structure of the old Republic finally and decisively altered.)

Apart from the introduction of the five-man "Interim" Executive Direc-tory, the remodelling of the executive was shaped round eight national "Agencies" appointed by and responsible to the Directory. They were to deal, respectively, with Foreign Affairs; Police and the Interior; Justice; Finance; War; the Marine; National Education; and National Economy. In skeleton the Agencies were obviously akin to the position of the French ministries, though the last two were the peculiar innovation of the Batavian Republic. But they also reflected the Dutch preoccupation with governmental burdens hitherto shouldered by provincial and local bodies whose resources were now unequal to the task of sustaining their responsibilities. In March 1798 this ambitious administration programme was little more than a few offices, a meagre staff of clerks and inadequate supplies of paper and ink.[17] Yet over the following decade, they and their successor bodies were to succeed in shifting the fulcrum of Dutch government from the provinces to the centre, and by so doing to patch together the makings of a new state. Like all such embryonic bureaucracies, they ran the risk of operating within a structure too remote from the painful realities of social life to appreciate the limitations of a centralised administration. A hard apprenticeship was still to come. But even in 1798, the framers of the constitution did not mean the executive Agencies wholly to replace the traditions of civic charity and voluntary service which in the "Golden Century" had been one of the great virtues of the old Republic. On the contrary, the evangelical zeal with which many of the revolutionary predikants pursued their vision of a cleansed common-wealth was expressed in the insistence that it be grounded four-square on the bedrock of civic morality. Article VII of the "General Principles" stated that "no-one can be a good citizen unless he fulfills those domestic duties which are incumbent on his social station and unless he honours all his obliga-tions to society." Not the least significant articles of the constitution were

LX and LXI, which required the legislature to make the necessary arrangements whereby the "National Character may be reformed and its morals and understanding enlightened."

The constitution of 1798 was neither a spuriously doctored license for an act of crude usurpation nor merely a certificate of good conduct awarded by the protecting power. Essentially it was an attempt (by no means comprehensive) to grapple with the major issues which had been exercising reformers and revolutionaries over the past two decades. Its central aim was to change the nature of the Dutch state and to bind its new institutions into the framework of an electoral democracy. But this in its turn created new problems. For although the authors of the constitution assumed the compatibility, even the inter-dependence, of democracy and unitarism, they had no means of knowing whether in practice freedom and order could be so simply accommodated. Experience was to provide harsh instruction.

From the beginning, the outlook was overcast. Political leaders in the provinces most affected by the liquidation of sovereignty were not prepared to go quietly. If radicals like Joost van Vridagh in Overijssel counselled compliance with the edicts from The Hague, others such as Gerrit Dumbar, van Mulert and Anthonie van Ijsselmuiden all resigned their places on the provincial administration rather than assent to the reduction of their power.[18] In Zeeland two of the members of the provincial government, Willem van Citters and Ermerins, both of them from old regent families, went even further. Declaring on January 28 that only the "people of Zeeland" had the right to revoke their mandate, they proposed summoning the primary assemblies to debate the issue on February 1. This was an astute move, for whatever the verdict of their deliberations, a regime which set so much store by the power of the primaries could hardly refuse to pay attention to their decision, even in so recalcitrant a province as Zeeland. Only in Middelburg were the clubs strong enough to guarantee an outcome in favour of unitarism. At the last minute, riots in Flushing against the French provided a pretext for the Directory and the Agent of Police to insist that the assemblies be "postponed" for fear of general public disorder. On the other hand, Friesland was uncharacteristically quiet, and in Groningen General Dumonceau had been able to carry out a miniature revolution with the minimum of resistance. Charles Bentinck's account of the events in the north noted with much distaste that the executive of twelve placed by the general in charge of the provincial administration "were all taken from the inferior classes and included two clergymen."[19]

On the credit side, the pared-down constitutional commission completed its exertions with unexampled alacrity. On March 7, having expressed polite gratitude to Delacroix for all the "interest" he had shown in their work, Willem Ockerse was at last able to rejoin his family in Rotterdam after six months' hard work. He had left few loopholes and had anticipated almost every political contingency. Of all the radical politicians associated with the new regime, there can be no doubt that his was the most constructive contribution. Since most of the "General Principles" had been made known in advance to the Assembly, both purged and unpurged, a discussion of the individual articles and titles took very much less time than in 1797. To be sure, the degree of political unanimity available in the "Constituent" was also a factor in speeding things up. The President, Theodorus van Leeuwen, expedited the discussions in March with brisk efficiency, allowing very little in the way of procedural niceties to slow things up. Only the manner of the constitution's adoption threatened some delay. To Ducange and Delacroix, the radicals' insistence on a plebiscite rather than "legislating" the constitution through the Assembly bordered on insanity. Even a proposal to count the vote by primaries rather than heads (thought to be likely to benefit the "Ja" vote) was rejected by the Directory and the Assembly. Nothing less than the counting of individual votes would do to give the new constitution its authority, whatever the risks involved.

It was accepted, however, on March 10, that it would be "undesirable" (not to say imprudent) to give declared enemies of the regime—"aristocrats," Orangists and the like—the opportunity of organising a campaign of opposition. Thus only those who swore an oath of hatred to these enemies and allegiance to the revolution of the 22nd were to be entitled to inscription on the franchise rolls. Even then they were to be subject to the scrutiny of political agents, who would oversee the final preparation of the voting lists. This decision, which was to have the most dramatic repercussions for the Directory, was taken almost as an axiomatic piece of common sense and the work involved in the "preparations" held back the date for the vote—fixed for April 23—by only a fortnight. On March 17, to the accompaniment of a band of musicians assembled in the antechamber, and with salvos of artillery fired off in all the principal cities of the Republic, the President's gavel came down on the motion of acceptance. On April 23, 153,913 votes were cast for acceptance against 11,587 for rejection. As 28,154 of the "Jas" were from the military, just 641 people more had voted for acceptance in 1798 than had voted for rejection the year before.[20]

The Undoing of the Revolution

In the general elation which followed the acceptance of the constitution, the scale and significance of the victory were not subject to any critical question. Even though roughly half the eligible franchise had voted, a termination to the drawn-out period of constitutional void was itself enough to dispel any gloomy forebodings about the future. Yet by the time the "National Festival" to celebrate its implementation on May 19 was held, it was already plain that the constitution was not going to be the solvent by which all the divisions that had bedevilled the revolution could be absorbed. Wiselius' friend Jan Brouwer wrote to him: "Today, brothers, is the great day on which the form of the State is to be established . . . to the satisfaction of all true Fatherlanders; but if this day is great, so, alas, is the confusion. . . ."[21] Indeed, the celebrations were by that time totally undermined by ominous fissures which had opened up within the ruling élite. Before another month was out, they were to grow so wide that they swallowed up the men of January.

Obviously the radical leaders had not looked for such troubles. It had been their earnest if naïve hope that the acceptance of the constitution would take some of the heat out of Dutch politics, and that partisans of federal sovereignty would swallow their pride and accept the fait accompli. They had even hoped that the work of the commission and the exceedingly detailed items of the constitution would help erase the stigma attaching to the origins of the regime. This was not so forlorn a hope as it seemed from the retrospect of June 12. Jacob Blauw, no friend of Vreede and his comrades, had acknowledged the priority that had to be given to a workable constitution whatever the political indignities. In his *Memoir* recounting the events of 1798, Blauw maintained that in its capacity as a Constituent the Directory might have called on the allegiance of many moderate unitarists who had initially viewed the revolution of January 22 with more dismay than pleasure.[22] Most Dutchmen, he inferred, were relieved to have done with the constitutional void and prepared to gloss over the means by which it had been brought about. How, then, had it happened that the radical Directory had succeeded in squandering this potential support in so short a space of time? Once again Blauw ascribed much of the trouble to the interference of the French minister and his *éminence grise*, and to the weakness of the Directory in failing to resist his interference. But he also recognised that in many respects the radicals had contributed to their own undoing by needlessly alienating just those sections of the Dutch population on whom the Patriots—of whatever hue—depended for support. Here Blauw was not far wide of the mark. The dismal history of the five months of radical power could almost be written in terms of the auto-destruction of their own power base.

Part of the problem was that, being mere mortals, the new men were either unwilling or unable to regard their custodianship as a temporary arrangement pending the enactment of the constitution. Once in power, the appetite grew with the eating. Indeed, although they continued to lock up federalists on the premise of a national emergency, as Blauw and Pasteur argued it had not been strictly *necessary* for a coup to take place to ensure the passage of the constitution. They had taken power because in their heart of hearts they believed that only they were fit to exercise it. The warrant for their authority was not need, but right. Only a government of the right hue, Vreede insisted, could see that the new constitution would be both effective and just. So it was by no means clear how long their "guardianship" of the nation might continue. It was not hard for the radicals to feel themselves the True Elect. From almost their first days in office, any pangs of remorse were stifled by the euphoria of "democratic" acclamation. A letter written to Fijnje on January 25 expressed the writer's "deep gratitude" for

... the memorable day [January 22] as the result of which Batavians may say "Now we are Free." I rejoice that our Beloved Fatherland, with the trust which the Earthly Powers of the People's Liberty has placed in your person, has invested you (Directors), as true freedom-loving People's Representatives, with the honour of holding the five most auspicious offices of state. . . .[23]

In any case, men such as Vreede and Fijnje took flattery in their stride. As Blauw conceded, Vreede, unlike some of the grubbier beneficiaries of January 22, could not have been further removed from the unsavoury trafficking which disgraced similar regimes in Directorial France. By his side even Reubell looked corrupt. As he later pointed out to those who implied that he had been defiled by his colleagues' misdemeanours, he had started his political career a rich man and ended up if not in the workhouse certainly a man without a fortune.[24] For his part, the revolution was a crusade and he was its prophet. His trials and tribulations would have been suffered in vain if all that was to result from their revolution was a marginal adjustment of administrative or financial sovereignty. Like that of all the Patriot Fathers, his democracy was evangelical—and indeed he was fond of referring to the inspiriting examples of "Father" van der Capellen and the sainted Dr. Price. Fijnje, in his address to the Constituent on the reception of the draft constitution, went even further into the antiquity of Patriotism by summoning the ghosts of the de Witts and Oldenbarneveld to testify for the revolution.[25]

Through the dense screen of their own self-righteousness, the radical leaders were incapable of regarding the action of January 22 as in any reprehensible sense a partisan act. Far from the Directory governing as the rule of faction, they saw themselves as much more truly representative than any of their predecessors. (Indeed there was, at least at the beginning, good ground for supposing they were no *less* so.) It was the quality of such thinking which could lead the radicals to see the purges of the National Assembly, the arrests of the deputies, and the expulsion of members of provincial and municipal administrations not as measures taken to entrench the position of a minority but as an operation designed to remove the obstacles which had hitherto prevented the majority—the true "nation"—from obtaining the government of its choice. In one of his more wretched garblings of Rousseau, Gerrit Paape defined democratically enacted law as "the will of the whole people exercised by the majority of citizens or their representatives."[26] The authorisation by which the radicals came to see themselves as the people's heroes was as rhetorical and mystical as anything offered by the Anabaptists of Leiden. Yet however shaky its foundation in reality, the conviction that they had received the democratic unction invited the further paradox that by reducing the national representation they were in fact *extending* its constituency. That is, those who had usurped that representation were removed to make way for the authentic version—in the fullness of time, naturally. Should this peculiar topsy-turvy of majority and minority, élite and broad constituency, seem especially bizarre, it may not be out of place to observe that it is one to which revolutionary regimes have not in the past shown themselves very resistant.

In practice it meant that the Dutch Directory had no qualms whatever about the men it had arrested, even though among them there were politicians like van de Kasteele and van Hooff whose views on the constitution differed from their own by the merest shade. No matter if the "danger" to the Fatherland took the unmenacing form of Cornelis van Maanen or Jacob de Mist, their incarceration was defended as a matter of life and death for Dutch liberty. It was predictable that a disproportionate number of those arrested

should have come from the land provinces,[27] but much less so that they included Coert van Beijma who, whatever his past peccadilloes, had been rather
more consistently a democrat than a number of his jailors. His source of offence had been opposition to the 8 per cent tax and his determination to defend Friesland's special interests, a stance which earned him the peculiar tag
of "federalist-anarchist."

The only figure among the detainees immediately corresponding to the
stock aristocrat-villain was Jacob Bicker. Despite his prominent part in the
Patriot past, Bicker's wealth, his descent from one of the oldest and most
illustrious of the Amsterdam regent families, his financial back-stairs dealings
and his political ambiguities identified him as everything the democrats most
despised. Moreover, as Valckenaer reminded Pieter Vreede in a letter from
Spain, Bicker had been the man responsible for crushing the cannoneers' rising
in 1796 and who had violated the national representation by despatching
troops to the city. (He had no need to add that he had been responsible for
ending Valckenaer's own career.) [28] Valckenaer was himself not inclined to
clemency. On the contrary, he urged Vreede to take proceedings immediately
not only against Bicker, but against Bentinck and van de Spiegel (still in
detention) and even William V in absentia! In case Vreede had not decided
for himself, Valckenaer—the Professor of Public Law—added that it would
be essential to purge all national institutions of anyone suspected of political
disaffection. In addition he was to deport forthwith any "fanatical predikants"
and declare all church, seigneurial and noble properties as having passed into
the hands of the nation.

Even at a distance it is obvious that the revolution of January 22 had
made Valckenaer giddy with vindictive enthusiasm. Happily, however, the
Batavian Directory was in no temper to inflict anything like a Dutch Terror
on its citizens. The suggestion from Ducange and Delacroix that the prisoners
of state should be sent to Paris, from where they could be safely shipped off to
Cayenne, was not greeted with any interest. Despite the heat of their political
blood, the radicals treated their imprisoned adversaries with exemplary
leniency. Initially both the deputies and the members of the ex-Committee for
Foreign Affairs were kept under house arrest and merely forbidden to leave
The Hague. Within ten days, however, they had been distributed around the
various fortified places of the Republic. Unlike the ailing ex-Grand Pensionary,
none were confined in the wretched hole of The Hague Gevangenpoort for
more than a day or two. George Hahn was permitted to choose his place of
detention from a short list and selected Breda. Bicker went to Zaandpoort, and
Willem Queysen, who in many respects seems to have had a harsher time
than his comrades, was sent to Hoorn. Others went to Woerden Castle, where
the ample bills for victuals, wine, heat and light from the jailor do not
indicate an exceptionally austere custody.[29] As was the custom, even in
revolutionary Republics, gentlemen-prisoners were treated as gentlemen, always provided they paid for their board and keep.

The largest group, which included de Mist, van Marle and others of the
Overijssel faction, ended up at the Huis 't Bosch, the ex-Stadholder's residence

outside The Hague. There they were permitted to keep their servants and, though forbidden conversation, had the freedom of the charming park for two hours every day in the afternoon. They were denied any kind of communication with the outside world (including their families), but the prison officers were ordered that those

under their custody be treated as befits men of their quality and station; that they shall keep a good table . . . be provided with a good breakfast, dinner and supper; tea and coffee shall be supplied to them and nothing which might be necessary to their daily subsistence should be wanting. . . .[30]

There were worse prisons in Europe.

The comfortable treatment afforded to the regime's prisoners might suggest that, in locking them away, the Directory (despite Valckenaer) was not seeking to punish those it regarded as responsible for the Republic's troubles but rather to acquire hostages for the good conduct and acquiescence of what they took to be a putative opposition. Perhaps in addition they hoped that the decisiveness of their action on the 22nd would in itself deter the remnant of moderates from staging any kind of counter-initiative, and would persuade them that their best interests—and those of the nation—lay in rallying to the order. If that was really their expectation, they must have been sadly disabused by the actual course of events. Far from closing ranks behind the Directory, the Constituent split itself into further fractions. In the late afternoon of Monday the 22nd, thirteen deputies, most of them loyal either to the land province faction or to individual politicians like van Beijma, resigned their seats in protest at what had happened that morning. No doubt this in itself was not too alarming to the radicals. It saved them the trouble of having to purge them. But when, the following day, a further twenty-three departed in the same manner, it was plain that the National Assembly was crumbling away. It required no very sophisticated calculations to see that the new regime had utterly failed to win over any of the uncommitted "middle" of unitarists who had voted for Pasteur's motion on the Friday and helped to create his huge majority. The "Constituent" was virtually identical with the fifty-odd men who had signed the amended "Points" after the nomination of Midderigh. The dissenting deputies, moreover, comprised a wide spectrum of beliefs. True, a number like Huber and Wentholt (the Gelderlander who had served on the constitutional commission with Ockerse) were obviously moderates, but there were others who by any criteria were democrats who had simply been appalled by the action of their colleagues. One such man was Pompe van Meerdevoort, the fiscal officer and financier from The Hague who had been a signatory of the Declaration of 43 on December 12, 1797, and was a staunch member of the "Voor Eenheid en Orde" Society who had voted with Vreede on nearly every occasion since the opening of the second National Assembly. Now, he found himself on the side of those unable to give their assent to the arbitration of force.

The dramatic contraction of numbers could hardly do much good for the credibility of the "Constituent" to act as the Republic's legitimate national representation. Only half the original Assembly remained seated, a number which, as Pasteur was quick to point out, was considerably inferior to those voting for his motion. Not surprisingly the hard core which did remain reacted to their predicament rather in the manner of jilted suitors, condemning the "renegades" as "deserters of the posts to which the Batavian people had assigned them." For their misdeeds they were punished by the withdrawal of all rights of active citizenship (including the vote and eligibilty for public office) for a period of not less than three years. To the more inflamed of the radical orators, this was not enough. Bosch, like Delacroix, wanted a general proscription of the maverick deputies, arguing that their desertion was yet more evidence of the need to "weed out" unreliable elements before they had a chance to inflict further damage on the precarious unity of the new order. What Bosch had in mind was the full apparatus of "popular justice": committees of surveillance, revolutionary tribunals and even summary execution. The Constituent of course could not bring itself to consider such measures, although in March and April decrees were issued creating the machinery for surveillance over any person suspected of "collaborating" with the 1787–95 Orangist government. Such suspects were prohibited from leaving their municipality without prior permission and were forbidden to transfer any of their property to a third party. While their own property was considered sacrosanct, the Constituent did discuss means of sequestrating the property of émigrés who had refused to respond to repeated summonses to return to the Republic. More important than these rather haphazard measures was the fact that the action of the rebel deputies released the Directory from any inhibitions it may originally have harboured about reorganising and purging provincial and local administrations. Instead of a marginal contingency, such action became essential to their survival. Thus what, on the 22nd, had been conceived as a short, sharp and decisive action, had in less than a week already set off a chain reaction of intervention, counter-intervention and repression.

There were some among the new regime who had not banked on such an eventuality and found it seriously disconcerting. For Isaac Gogel, the new Agent for Finance, the action of January 22 had been meant to *end* a period of division and friction, not inaugurate a new one. In a powerful address to the "Voor Een- en Ondeelbaarheid" Society in Amsterdam before the coup (which he published after it in *De Democraten*), he had warned against the perils of perpetuating internecine political feuding. He castigated:

. . . a people which desires freedom but knows no order . . . a people which on one day elects its rulers, on the next begins to mistrust them and on the third condemns them; a people devoid of any spirit of fraternity or concession; a people among whom may be discovered a hundred different factions each engaged in abusing the other without the slightest spirit of moderation. . . .[31]

Whether his criticism was directed at the sharp partisanship of the new regime or the obstinacy of their adversaries is uncertain. But Gogel was making a plea—as he himself suspected, in vain—for the abandonment of party warfare in the name of the national interest. He knew how remote were the chances of success, but he was not by nature a pessimist. In 1794 he had been among the very first to see in the fires of revolution a salutary catharsis. And it was only after a long and herculean struggle to keep the Dutch state from public destitution that his spirits became finally darkened with fatigue and despondency. In 1798 his strictures were intended more as admonition than any sibylline prophecy of doom. But his sceptical intelligence enabled Gogel, better than many of his colleagues, to see that if their rhetoric predicated the mass support of the "people," their government in reality rested on much thinner foundations.

Even within the ranks of the radicals there was already something of a division between the élite leadership and the rank-and-file. The former, like any of its opposed groupings, was drawn primarily from the patriot intelligentsia: predikants, doctors, lawyers with the odd business-man or manufacturer. However they glossed over their superior social status, such men were removed by education, social decorum and, in not a few cases, fortune, from those they patronised as the "people." As in the case of the lower echelons of the Patriot Free Corps in the 1780's, the latter were recruited principally from among the strata of petty-burghers in the cities: small tradesmen, petty functionaries and clerks, bargees, vergers and clock-winders, spirit-sellers and the like. They were very rarely wage-earners but equally rarely men of much substance or property. They had been allowed—even encouraged—to crowd the public galleries of the grand clubs in Amsterdam, Utrecht and Rotterdam but rarely if ever were permitted the privileges of the rostrum or the floor. The élite societies like "De Uitkijk" and "Voor Eenheid en Orde" were often given to expressions of armchair egalitarianism but had remained largely the preserve of politicians and intellectuals like Gogel and Wiselius.

The more natural habitat of the rank-and-file was in the primary assembly meetings of the *wijken* and districts; the town guard in the more distant towns like Goes, Zutphen and Zwolle; and the newer, less disciplined clubs in the suburbs of the major cities.[32] To mobilise this support behind the Directory without conceding the leadership to "irresponsible" or even "anarchist" demagogues meant treading a wary path between élitism and popular democracy. The sudden contraction of strength at the centre and the harrying of any remaining moderate unitarists seemed to Gogel to be the blindest folly, for it could only upset this delicate balance and throw the regime into increasing dependence on the popular societies. He, for one, had not accepted office to see the chaos of the National Assembly replaced by the chaos of the clubs.

Nor was he the only member of the regime to harbour such misgivings. Both the Agent for Justice, Tadama, and the Agent for the navy, Spoors, had been virtually press-ganged into accepting posts on pain of forfeiture of their civil rights. Lukewarm to what had happened on the 22nd, and highly suspicious of men like Fijnje, they were alarmed at the prospect of the popular societies being given their head. Indeed, despite the effusions of democratic unity which issued from the Constituent, the relationship between the élite democrats and their constituency was still, as it always had been, highly ambivalent. As long as the radicals had been in the minority in the National Assembly, they had naturally encouraged the clubs in their propaganda and had welcomed the ammunition they provided for their depleted artillery in the legislature. Even then they had occasionally overplayed their hand. In 1795 Pieter Vreede had been embarrassed to have been outflanked in his enthusiasm for liberty by the clubs and feuilletons of den Bosch. And despite the warmth of Paape's advocacy, the radicals in the provisional assembly of Holland took a decidedly cautious view of the activities of the "Central Assembly" that same year. As we have seen, Valckenaer was ensnared into endorsing the cannoneers' riot more from hostility to the repressive action than sympathy with the rebels. As in other revolutionary situations the crowd were welcomed as an auxiliary force in the attempt by radical élites to wrest power from governing authorities. But if they tried to take the political initiative themselves, or to demand a share in the devolution of sovereignty, they usually met with a rebuff.

While they understood that, particularly in the first weeks of the Directory's regime, it would be imprudent to disappoint the expectations of the clubs too severely, the Dutch radical leaders had no intention of making the same mistake as the French Jacobins. Though the number was almost certainly exaggerated, Delacroix reported to Paris that the government had closed down fifteen of the clubs in Rotterdam.[33] What the Directory had actually decided was to render the societies harmless by "reorganisation" rather than outright closure. An order was put through the Constituent permitting only those societies which had sworn their allegiance to the principles of "eenheid-en ondeelbaarheid" to meet; and another signifying that their function was to "edify" citizens on social and political affairs rather than mobilise support for political *actions*. To assist this discipline they were to be encouraged to affiliate to central organisations, which (in the manner of the "société mère" of the Jacobins and the "Constitutional circles" in France) would set the keynote. Both the new constitution and the Directorial orders emphasised that the proper place for voicing objections or forwarding petitions on government action was the primary assembly.[34] On no account were corporate petitions from individual clubs purporting to bear some representative character to be allowed. Such an action, it was pointed out, would be tantamount to an attack on the "sovereignty of the people." In its sensitivity to "subversion" from below, the new regime was hardly less anxious than its predecessor.

What, if anything, had it to fear? Were the clubs, on whom the radicals had depended for so much of their political ammunition, poised to enter a phase of sans-culotte militancy? There is precious little evidence to suggest this. There were, it is true, the occasional utterances of individual pamhleteers and club orators like the ex-warehouseman of the East India Company, Lucas Butot, who had risen to prominence in the Amsterdam popular societies. His "Programme" included a ceiling of 3,000 florins for the salary of every public officer; the express obligation of the government to provide work for the able-bodied indigent and subsistence for the disabled and aged; the graduation of fiscal liability according to income, and, more idiosyncratically, the abolition of all fines since "he who offends against the law must pay for it with his life; then are we all truly equal."[35] Butot's Jacobinical radicalism was, it is true, impressively "advanced" by the general standards of Dutch politics. But his sources were almost certainly less the canons of Marat and Babeuf than the traditional anti-sumptuary journalism of the 1770's and 1780's with which the "Programme," both in style and content, had much in common. On the other hand, it is perfectly true that the tenor of the regime and the wholesale changes operating at the level of provincial and municipal administrations had given an opportunity to men from hitherto oppressed minorities, as well as those from a lower social drawer than the radical intelligentsia, to advance themselves to positions of influence and even power.

In Amsterdam their position was exceptionally strong. On March 4, as a direct result of an order of the Constituent Assembly, the corps of cannoneers dissolved after the fracas of May 1796 was restored. According to some reports, it was rapidly turned into a special guard for the leaders of the radical clubs, rather as the militia had acted in cities such as Zwolle and Leeuwarden. The result was that the eviction of those deemed politically undesirable by the new regime from the municipal administration and their replacement with clients of the clubs was accomplished with the maximum of ease. The same followed throughout the major cities of Holland and Utrecht. The warrant for such changes was often highly arbitrary. The commissions established on March 10 had been authorised to "revise and prepare" the franchise lists as a preliminary to the constitutional plebiscite. In practice, they had assumed revolutionary powers to appoint and depose on report, since it was thought inconceivable that any burgher deprived of the right to vote (and therefore found guilty of disaffection to the "new" Republic) should be permitted to continue in any post of public trust. In Amsterdam, heads rolled—metaphorically, that is, for this was still the Netherlands. Many of the best-known figures among the Patriots—most of them members of the Revolutionary Committee of 1794, founders of "Doctrina et Amicitia," and in some cases supporters of "Voor Een- en Ondeelbaarheid"—were forcibly dispossessed of their offices, just as three years before they had forcibly dispossessed their predecessors the Orangists. Among the departing councillors was Pieter 't Hoen, the ex-editor of the *Politieke Kruijer* and one of the principal "educators" of Dutch democracy; M. C. van Hall and Krayenschot, both lawyers and the latter a publisher of radical literature; and J. Willem van Hasselt, with Schimmelpenninck the leading defender of the Patriot cause when it had been harried by the Stadholder's police in the 1780's and 1790's.

The initiative, however, no longer rested with the élite circles. Excluded by the "East India" group—Wiselius, von Liebherr and Ondaatje—from the inner sanctum of "De Uitkijk," a few of the more militant and more authentically plebeian members hived off at the end of 1797 to form their own clubs elsewhere in the city, notably "Deugd en Kundigheden" ("Virtue and Enlightenment") and "Tot het Nut van 't Vaderland" ("For the Good of the Fatherland"). Where before the coup men like Butot and Nobbe had been prepared to defer to the authority of the Central Bureau of the clubs, dominated by the "Uitkijk" group, by March and April of the following year they began to show a more independent spirit. Jews like Moses Asser of "Felix

Libertate" and H. H. de Lemon—a deputy in the Constituent—and many Catholics were conspicuous in the van of the new societies, emancipated as they were not only from the debilitating restrictions of the old regime but also from the qualified social acceptance of their successors.[36] In Utrecht a Catholic club, "Waarheid en Vrijheid" ("Truth and Liberty") came to dominate at least three of the city's eight *wijken*; and in den Bosch, after a relative lull, the clubmen returned to the fray with all their old unruly vigour. Despite the relative novelty of the new societies, if Bode's assertion is to be credited, by March 1798 they had succeeded in Amsterdam in organising all the clubs under the collective umbrella of the "Friends of Unity and Indivisibility" with an aggregate membership of some 4,000.[37]

On March 15 the purging commission in Amsterdam set to work. Its principal, Anthonie Boeseken, an ex-clerk and a colleague of Butot's and Bode's, wrote to the Directory: "Amsterdam shall be dedicated, reconsecrated entirely to the Fatherland, and the administration placed in the hands of those whom no taint of family interest can divert from their sacred path."[38] Such "reconsecrations" had been known before—at Lyons and at Nantes. This, however, was not to be a fiery baptism. Not that that was much consolation to van Hasselt, Angelus Cuperus and Krayenschot, who were removed from the Committee of Justice—the bête-noire of the clubs—to make way for the grocer Schilderup and the pharmacist-apothecary Dommen. Others on the new Committee were an ex-policeman, a draper's clerk and a man "reputed to be an organist." The municipal council itself did a little better with the able Asser and the lawyer Bouwens joining its numbers, but with Hendrik Nobbe elevated to burgemeester and Bode inserted into the senior councillors, the city began to take on the aspect of a revolutionary commune.

So, at least, it seemed to Gogel and Wiselius, who observed the goings-on in Amsterdam with increasing consternation. The morning after the coup, Samuel Wiselius had written to Fijnje urging that nothing drastic be entertained regarding the government of the city lest its already ailing economic and financial condition be subject to possibly fatal shocks.[39] Gogel, too, was anxious for the economic circumstances of Amsterdam and aware that the credit structure of the city rested on a delicate skein of confidence which clumsy attempts at revolution could break. But his objections to the "second revolution" were both deeper and more complex than those of his friend. Behind the references to "fortune seekers" and "office-mongers," both no doubt true of at least some of the clubbist leaders, there was a strong element of social distaste. Despite his relatively humble origins, Isaac Gogel had been brought up, educated and apprenticed through a circle of highly sophisticated, well-off and educated men whose political aims certainly stopped short at a revolution of fortunes. Indeed, their confidence in self-help, meritocracy and liberty of thought and speech placed them firmly on the side of the coming century's liberalism, not among the more traditional low-Calvinism and guild mentality of the artisans and traders who comprised their "public."

To such men it was axiomatic that, whatever their ostensible egalitarianism, it was, like their counterparts in France, an "égalité des talents." Government—the primary object of their attention—was hard enough already, without confiding it to those whose education (and some, like Lestevenon or 't Hoen, would grudgingly admit their social manners) disqualified them for such onerous tasks. Part of the motive which had led Gogel to embrace political democracy had been the conviction that despicable men, both Orangist and "Loevesteiner," had exploited public office for their own ends and fortunes and had, as a result, contributed to the destruction of his beloved Republic. To cast those same offices before men who had not the least inkling how to manage them was, in his eyes, a crime of comparable villainy. It was to license the *usurpation* of the nation's mandate in the guise of championing the "people's rights." And that, for Gogel, was a double blasphemy. He was possessed, moreover, by an even deeper and more secret anxiety. Beneath the mask of the patriotic collective of the "people" he could not help but detect, as he had in May 1796, the uglier physiognomy of the *grauw*—that fickle and violent mob which had torn to pieces the two great fathers of the commonwealth, cheered the judicial murder of Oldenbarneveld and rallied to the House of Orange in so many of its most notorious acts of tyranny and injustice. Gogel and Sam Wiselius were not alone in their generation in simultaneously appealing to the abstract notion of popular rights and yet recoiling in fear and contempt from their concrete manifestation. But they had, barely behind them, the memory of plundered houses, rampaging mobs and burning wharves of October 1788 to refresh their nightmares.

Gogel's deepening concern about such matters coincided with the end of his career as a journalist. The huge weight of business as Agent for Finance had made it impossible to continue *De Democraten* beyond March, and Jan Konijnenburg had founded his own rather dull journal *De Republikein*, which contented itself with reiterating most of the Directorial platitudes coming from The Hague. Early in the spring, Gogel had expressed some of his fears to his friend Ockerse who, however, thought him unduly alarmist. There were, the latter acknowledged, a few "rabid fanatics" in the party, yet

they can do nothing (of any harm) because the good fellows are present in much greater strength, and the others must perforce follow their lead. I abhor the office-hunters and the crazed ultra-revolutionaries quite as much as you but (surely) they can no longer be restrained at the expense of destroying the nation and keeping the people under the thumb of base despots.[40]

But compared to their successors, Gogel was less inclined to label the old councillors as "despots." By the end of March he could no longer contain his worries within his circle of friends. Vreede was unapproachable—he had never got on with Gogel; and when a letter to Fijnje produced only a curt dismissal in response, he took the drastic step of approaching Delacroix directly. In a long letter Gogel warned the minister that the entire well-being of Amsterdam was threatened by the machinations of

a small band of anarchists, dispersed throughout the country but whose headquarters lie in this city. They may be found in the Constituent Assembly and in the provincial administrations. . . . For some time now they have worked steadily to create disorder and to win office for themselves. . . .[41]

It was this caucus of malevolent and selfish men, perhaps no more than 300 or 400 in all, who by gulling the people had been responsible for the uproar in 1796 which had ruined the good name of at least one honest democrat. True, the "outrageous morals" and the "brazen audacity" of such men in manoeuvring themselves into office would surely undo them in the end; but in the meantime they were in a position to do terrible damage to Amsterdam and to the Republic as a whole. Already they had

set about attacking worthy republicans who, since the revolution, had occupied various posts with integrity and honour for the sake of the public good, who had prepared and contributed to the revolution; who had remained constant to its principles. . . . It is these men who are now depicted as aristocrats, federalists, moderates; egoists, chameleons, adventurers and oppressors of the people.

If this state of affairs were permitted to continue, there could be only one end. Already the new "Committee of Justice" had become the creature of demagogues and been manipulated solely to revoke all those acts of its predecessor designed to keep the city in some kind of order. How long could it be before it slid down the slippery slope towards summary trials, arbitrary persecutions, and "the bloody scenes which froze the hearts of men in the time of Robespierre"? Even now they had succeeded in "augmenting the enemies of the present order" by "creating the spectacle of a melancholy and unhappy people, nursing in its bosom the seeds of anger and hatred against its oppressors."

Even if there was more sheer incompetence and less evil conspiracy than Gogel supposed in the "second revolution," he could see clearer than many of his contemporaries the dismaying vision of the revolution beginning to devour its own children. A world where Hendrik Nobbe took the place of Pieter 't Hoen had to be a world upside-down; but such was the potency of the rhetoric which Gogel himself had contributed that it was almost impossible to convey such apprehensions to his colleagues without himself falling under suspicion. From its embattled and increasingly isolated position the new regime was, like others in similar circumstances, predisposed to see potential traitors lurking behind the most obscurely veiled critique. Delacroix, of course, was no use whatever. While he had no wish to see the Batavian Republic delivered to a gang of Dutch Marats, he was enough of a "fructidorian" to see the principal threat in the shape of counter-, not ultra-revolution. As far as he could see—which was no further than Ducange permitted—the purging commissions were merely the salutary instruments of republican orthodoxy, weeding out pockets of aristocracy amid the backwater federalist provinces. Since he was convinced that these provinces were still in the grip of ancient oligarchies, the only way to prise them loose was to hand them over to men who would, in effect, act as the Dutch version of *représentants en mission*.

The purging commissions in fact displayed all the vices of the French agents and none of their virtues, save a misdirected kind of energy. They were pitifully few in number, equipped with a small clerical establishment, and assigned to cover impossibly large areas of the Republic in an impossibly brief span of time. Within a month of their appointment (the middle of March) they were meant to scour every town, village and hamlet where there was a primary assembly and ensure that there would be no delay with the con-stitutional vote. Given these stringent requirements, together with the over-riding object of ensuring that no repetition of the fiasco of August 1797 oc-curred, it was hardly surprising that theirs was usually a hurried and slapdash job. Virtually none of the commissioners or their deputies were familiar with the areas to which they were assigned. Most were Hollanders associated with the militant wing of the clubs: Rant, Boeseken, Butot, and Tjeerd Halbes were all men excluded from the democrat intelligentsia and hostile to their ambi-ence. Some like Rant nursed old wounds from the Dunkirk days and had long been waiting for a chance to revenge themselves on their "superiors." Their sort—small men with minds to match—who confused ideology with personal grievance, could be reproduced in almost every town in the Republic, often holding the posts of secretary to the local popular society or a low com-mission with the town militia. It was their information on which the com-missioners crucially depended in drawing up their franchise lists and crossing out those who fell to their disapprobation.

While the commissioners' ignorance of the areas to which they had been detailed was an obvious handicap in their work, they had a few simple guidelines to assist them. Any Patriot known locally as a "moderate" (or worse) was to be struck off without more ado; any member who had been on the local council *continuously* since 1795 to be scrutinised with extreme care. Membership in the original Revolutionary Committee in January 1795 was regarded as another warrant for suspicion. In case such identities remained obscure, there were always local informers only too eager to come forward to assist the commissioner or his deputy in his unsavoury work, often in the hope of supplanting those against whom they levelled their accusations. Through the archives of the purging commissions the historian has very complete informa-tion on these processes, and to the student of revolutionary France many of the methods will appear depressingly familiar. In Breukelen in the province of Utrecht, for example, one J. Jong supplied Lucas Butot with a complete directory of the views of his villagers, concentrating particularly on the foibles of those currently in office. A further criterion of patriotism in this instance was the attendance of the individual at primary assemblies *prior* to the January revolution. Thus one man, alas, had "not only *not* attended primary assembly (except perhaps two or three times and then only to register his damned objections) but finally revealed himself as an opponent of the present order." Others in the same village were categorised thus:

Jan Speelman	moderate]
	(lit.) "Slimy" [the conventional euphemism for
Benjamin van Janus	A decided dragon, very dangerous
Dirk van Eyck	Bad Patriot. Lives off his own income; never comes to the meetings for fear that his son will end up on the "lanterne"[42]

Jong went on to express a certain wistful regret that some of his comrades whom he felt to be politically impeccable and true Patriots disqualified themselves from the franchise as having been convicted for petty larcenies of one kind or another, or—in their misguided past—had been supporters of the Prince of Orange. On the other hand, illiteracy was certainly no bar to registration. In both a small village like Batenburg, in Gelderland, and the New Amstel, a suburb of Amsterdam (Districts 9 and 10)—as well as in a provincial city like den Bosch—the number of voters signing with a cross varied between 40 and 50 per cent. In a country where illiteracy, by European standards, was reckoned comparatively low, this meant that the muster books for the polls were being filled by many men of the "Fourth Estate" who could never have played any part whatsoever in the political process before 1798.[43]

Although in a very slapdash way and by a very roundabout route, the leaders of the January revolution were in the process of extending political rights to those who had hitherto been a nullity. On the other hand, one man's sans-culotte was another man's *canaille*—the ignorance and apathy of many of those led to the poll books affirm that the moderates' allegation that their enemies had enfranchised large numbers of ex-Orangists is almost certainly correct. Those whose natural allegiance before 1795 would have been with Prince rather than Patriots now found themselves unwittingly recruited as the stormtroopers of democracy. This is not quite so paradoxical as it might appear. The consistent factor in their feeling was a violent antipathy towards *any* governmental élite; and from their point of view, the "regents" of the Batavian Republic were no better than their predecessors. They had done little to alter their material circumstances. Food was no cheaper and taxes no lower; the craftsmen could find no work and the shopkeeper had been ruined by great tides of *assignats*. Even their latent patriotism had hardly been gratified by the wretched performance of the nation's forces at war. Now they listened to men who spoke and understood their colloquialisms and their grudges; men who were offering them the chance to become cock of the walk in their own back yard. They rarely declined the invitation.

Conversely, as we have already seen in Amsterdam, those who had commanded the rank-and-file of the Patriots since the 1780's were now displaced in the name of the revolution. In the major cities of Holland, it was perhaps possible to evict the more obviously patrician councillors and turn instead to alternative Patriots without completely undermining the strength of the anti-Orange groups. But in the provinces, the majority of those struck out by the pens of the purging officers were, given the dispersion of the Patriots, bound to be humbler sorts. In Friesland and Gelderland, the countryside of South Holland and on the Veluwe, the expelled men were predikants and schoolmasters; rural doctors and lawyers; small-town grain chandlers and petty functionaries; inspectors of weights and measures, peasant free-holders and liquor merchants—the broad *middenstand* of the Dutch petty-*burgerij*. To remove them was to cut the heart out of any popular following for the Batavian Republic itself. The purging commission may have imagined that they were substituting in their place the *genuine* representatives of the "people," but in this they were, like their masters on the Directory, the victims of ideological delusions. The unknown quantity of the Fourth Estate was no satisfactory substitute for those who, until April 1798, had regarded themselves as the body and soul of virtuous republicanism.

The commissions were quite oblivious of these considerations and set to work with a will. Perhaps the best index of their success in destroying the rank-and-file of the Patriots is the immense flood of protest which came pouring in during April to the Constituent and the Directory. The writers of these letters, petitions and complaints comprise virtually an entire cross-section of Dutch republicanism. In Overijssel the commissioners had disregarded the wishes of the Zwolle and Kampen militia officers, companies of which had nearly mutinied against their deposition. When the officers protested that they had been elected, they were promptly replaced by new appointees.[44] One of the bitterest objections came from a captain of a company of Zwolle guard which had distinguished itself in 1787 by going to the defense of Utrecht during the siege. It was the collective memory of such men, their sense of having been part of a crusade, of having served and suffered with the Patriot cause, and their conviction that the Batavian Republic was especially "their" state, that was most deeply wounded by these proceedings. Many were driven to recite their biographies as proof of their republican credentials. A Campenaar narrated his time at Elburg when it had been occupied by the Prince's troops, who had broken up his home and plundered his property; another had been in Amsterdam in the last days of the Patriot Republic in August and September 1787.[45] A Groninger showed off his testimonial signed by Admiral de Winter testifying that

the undersigned has shown himself to be an ardent champion of the rights of Man and Citizen; and has, from the first moments of the revolution of 1795 and on all opportunities attended the primary meetings assiduously and now asks to be permitted to bring his vote. . . [46]

In slightly more exalted circles was a doctor of Monnikendam, who "even before the years 1786 and 1787 had shown himself to be a true supporter of the Liberty of the People"; had been a member (like Wiselius) of the Leiden Student Corps; and, since 1795, had not only served as one of the "Provisional Representatives of the Province of Holland" but had subsequently occupied the post of provincial dykegrave—from which he had now been removed.

Not all these cases were examples of outrageous injustice. Gerrit van Schimmelpenninck, Rutger's brother, had been on the Patriot side in Overijssel in both 1787 and 1795, but as one of the leaders of the provincial gentry in Deventer and a powerful advocate of federal rights could hardly have expected generous treatment from the commission. Yet while such men could not have expected to stay in power, few supposed that the regime would go as far as striking them from the franchise and, in effect, dispossessing them of their civil rights.[47] When it duly happened, the affront upset those who were accustomed to regard themselves as leaders of the Patriot élites in small towns or villages, hayseed replicas of the great van der Capellen or the lamented Paulus. In Harlingen, for example, where the struggle for supremacy between the two rival Friesland assemblies had been in the balance in September 1787, two of those who had then been in the thick of the fight for the Patriots and who had later served on both the Revolutionary Committee and the provisional assembly—Jacobus Roorda and Willem van Nooten— were removed.[48] Franeker, where the Patriots had been very strong and where at least three clubs had been founded since the revolution, was the scene of one of Tjeerd Halbes' most drastic purges. Virtually the entire leadership of the city council was expunged. Adam Lentz, "seeing no reason for his exclusion [from the poll] and . . . professing support for the present order of things," protested, albeit in vain, that it was "the most arbitrary and unjust act." Two eminences from Franeker Academy, the curator Georgius Coopmans —probably the most important man in the town—and the secretary Adrianus Alma, followed Lentz into limbo.

The obvious consequence of these depletions was that the franchise figure in centres like Harlingen and Franeker contracted by about half—to 307 and 336, respectively. The commissioners had to be wary of reducing their polls too substantially since they risked producing an implausibly low vote for the constitution. Aside from unlikely citizens introduced to make up the numbers they were able, after a suitable reform of their local councils, to add to the quota by retrieving obscure backwaters of the province from the political nullity in which they had languished since well before the Patriots had ever been heard of. On the island of Ameland, for example, the commissioners were stupefied to discover that "everything stood on the old despotic [i.e., pre-1795] footing" and that no public officer, not even the occasional tax receiver, seemed to have visited the place since most of the inhabitants could remember. There must have been any number of Amelands, particularly among the coastal islands of the north or deep in the woods of the Veluwe, utterly ignorant of the revolution or even of the departure of the Stadholder, but jerked by the peripatetic inquisitiveness of the government agents into joining the pleasures and sorrows of "the nation." Some, of course, put up a stiff resistance. The commission at the village of Opperdoes in North Holland complained that the ancient aldermen there simply refused to part with their insignia of office (or the keys to the village chest), even under threat of imprisonment, and that no-one thereabouts seemed willing to incur the obloquy of taking it from them. On Oud Beierland at the other end of the province there was an even fiercer struggle. In the outlying areas of Drente and Gelderland to the far east of the Republic, the commissions ran headlong into a growing tax revolt where the impoverishment of the peasantry was always associated with "interference" from The Hague.[49]

This kind of opposition to the centralisation of political authority in the Netherlands was only to be expected. It was highly improbable that, whatever the force of the writ with which the commissioners came armed, the traditional strongholds of provincial federalism would capitulate without a struggle. As their experience testified, it was far easier to get rid of the sovereign assembly of the people of Overijssel than to extricate a single alderman at Oesterbroek.

Many of the local regents remained firm in their conviction that in the long run the concrete allegiances of the community would prove too durable for the spasmodic and weakly supported intrusions of a central government. Living in Friesland it was more than possible to believe that the Rights of Man might come and go but—the sea permitting—Slooten and Boxum would live forever. Thus their opposition to the liquidation of local jurisdiction was one of initial acquiescence in the majority of cases, or a gradual erosion of the will of the government. None was prepared to launch an organised revolt.

What was much more serious for the regime in The Hague was the creation of a political opposition from among those who considered themselves not only Patriots but radicals and democrats—the *true* heirs of the mantle of van der Capellen and Paulus. Such men were, as the Directory was about to discover, able to command a powerful following right in the heart of the major cities of the Republic. If, by removing names like Wiselius from the poll book in Amsterdam, the government believed it was taking strong measures to fortify its position, then it was making a serious error of judgement. What it in fact contrived to do was turn grudging allies or men who were at worst neutrals into intransigent political opponents.[50] Apart from Wiselius himself (then in Paris), most of the East India group—Ondaatje, von Liebherr, Fennekol—had rapidly cooled in their enthusiasm for the new regime. "Voor Een- en Ondeelbaarheid" was open in its hostility, and the press, especially the *Politieke Blixem* (*Political Lightning*), had turned quickly against Vreede and Delacroix. Even Ockerse, certainly no enemy of the Directory, attempted to arrest the squandering of goodwill by urging that the purging commissioners be made more closely answerable to the Constituent to whom they were, in any case, technically responsible.

Three of the Directory's own agents—Isaac Gogel; Reinier Tadama, the Agent for Justice; and Jacob Spoors, the Agent for the Navy—had even graver misgivings about the conduct and consequences of the purges. Judged simply from the tactical viewpoint they believed them to have been seriously misused; judged from their effect on the government of the Republic, they thought them disastrous. The Batavian Republic had not such a bounty of administrative talent that it could afford to squander much of it on the force of dogma. Moreover, the fact that, as a result of the commissioners' efforts, the constitution was voted through did not meet their objections, for Gogel at least believed that it would have survived on its own merits and under freer conditions.

In any event the Directory finally sabotaged its chances of survival with an act of such brazen bad faith that it verged on panache. Up until, and even during, the initial "preparation" of the electorate, unitarist Patriots of the Blauw-Wiselius kind had been willing to go along with the government simply to have the business of the constitution over and done with. In their conviction that it was the linchpin of national regeneration, they were prepared to bridle their displeasure at what had happened on January 22 and to endure a degree of intimidation they might not otherwise have tolerated. But once the constitution had been endorsed by the nation, they imagined that more normal conditions would again obtain. Those prisoners who had been expressly detained "until the promulgation of the constitution is secured" could now be set free and both the executive and legislature, which had been accepted in their Constituent capacities, would stand aside for properly elected bodies according to the constitution's stipulations. True, on March 17 the Constituent had passed an order prolonging the life of the present Directory until "conditions" could be obtained in which it could peacefully transfer its authority to an elected successor. But its fate, of course, depended crucially on the legislature. According to the official *Bataafsch Courant*, elections were due to be held on June 29 for the new "Representative Assembly." But on May 4, surrendering to pressure from Delacroix and responding to the promptings of its own self-preservation, the Directory decreed that instead of creating an entirely new Assembly, only one-third of the present Constituent would be required to vacate its seats for reelection, and one-third of the Directory seek re-appointment.

This was a cynical violation of the constitution which they themselves had made the alpha and omega of their regime. The gloss of legitimacy placed upon the order was transparently fraudulent. The Directory had simply deemed both itself and the legislature to have been *already elected* and therefore applied the normal constitutional rule by which one-third of both bodies came up for annual re-endorsement. Had the manoeuvre been more adroit it might be described as sharp practice. As it was, the clumsy hypocrisy of the measure exposed its authors to a fusillade of political accusation. As the *Blixem* lost no time in pointing out, it was obvious to the greatest fool that if only a third of the legislature was to step down, it was a certain fact that the Directory would use its influence to see that the most expendable section was dissolved. Nor was anyone in much doubt as to which of the Directors would depart since Fokker and Wildrik had been, from the beginning, virtual nonentities in the government. If this principle—or lack of it—were followed, it had to be three full years before there could be a chance of obtaining an Assembly properly elected by the people and an executive of their choice.

The possibility that an entirely fresh legislature could use its constitutional position to attack the executive was exactly what had most alarmed Delacroix. In France that situation had required an 18 Fructidor to set matters straight. As a result, it was the French minister who had pressed the alternative on the Directory and the Constituent on May 3. He had summoned both to a grand meeting at his residence and, appearing in his official dress, had delivered a speech to them demanding that, in the sacred name of the alliance, they should accept his proposal. Whether or not he actually used the magic formula Blauw put into his mouth: "La grande nation le veult," that was certainly the spirit of the occasion.[51] The response from the radical leaders was a mixture of embarrassment, indignation and stoicism. The following day Bosch as good as admitted in the Constituent that the edict violated the constitution but urged its acceptance as a weapon to fight "aristocracy and federalism." Spoors and Gogel were unconvinced by this jaded formula. The former made yet another abortive attempt to resign his Agency; the latter was now fully persuaded that unless drastic means were used to halt the Directory's recklessness, it would play into the hands of a counter-revolution.[52]

Their private apprehensions were given a more public airing in the press. Since the debates on the first constitution of 1797, the tone of much of the political press had grown steadily more astringent. And whatever their numerous failings the radical regime made no attempt to muzzle even the most scurrilous of the newspapers. Not all, of course, were threatening. Under Jan Luzac the *Gazette de Leyde* continued the gracious manners of the eighteenth century, and upheld the traditions of the old Republic against the vices of the new, but its style of journalism was that of gentle and ironical opposition. Far more abrasive were the new publications like J. C. Hespe's *Constitution-eele Vlieg (The Constitutional Fly)*, in which all the considerable talents of the ex-editor of the *Politieke Kruijer* were again put to effective use; the *Politieke Blixem*; and the *Constitutioneele Vraag-al (Constitutional Questioner)*. Though some of the most acidulous journalists like Paape and Bosch now wrote for the government press, even before the edict of May 4 the polemical attacks on the Directory were coming thick and fast. Ducange, who was an obvious and favourite target, was driven in February to complain of the *Blixem* to the Directory. He called it a "production vraiment ordurière," whose very existence constituted a direct threat to the Republic and to the alliance.[53] Both he and Delacroix (known in the paper by the literal Dutch translation of "van der Kruissen") wanted it closed down; but Fijnje, who in his time had known all about the governmental hounding of journalists, refused to contemplate any such move. Thus without doing much to remove the source of its grievances, the Directory doubled its jeopardy by giving its loudest critics the ideal means of attacking it.

Moreover, the press criticism of the government before May 4 was relatively restrained compared to what followed. It was not until May 22, when the political situation had chronically deteriorated, that steps were finally taken to bridle criticism of the government and the Assembly. Until then the opposition papers had a field day. Most of them (unlike the sedate but consistent *Gazette de Leyde*) were at pains not to repudiate the January revolution nor to advocate anything that could be construed as support for a federal Republic. Nor did they find serious fault with the constitution itself, which, after all, had enshrined their own liberty of opinion. On the contrary, their (mostly anonymous) writers presented themselves as the true defenders of the constitution against the attempt by the Directory to pervert it. What point, they argued, had there been in spending months to work out the minutest details if the whole document could be treated in so cavalier a fashion? The Directory, it was insinuated, was betraying the national interest, though again most stopped short of attacking France directly. Ducange, on the other hand, was fair game, and every kind of sinister malice and ingenuity was attributed to his counsel. Moreover the perpetuation of the Directors and the Constituent beyond their proper term was prima facie evidence that behind the masquerade of political democracy this regime, like all its predecessors, was in the business of hunting for offices and perquisites. How else, the

Blixem and the *Vlieg* asked, could a nonentity like Pieter Pijpers, the friend of Fijnje, have wormed his way to become Amsterdam's town clerk (*Stadssecretaris*) or one of Fijnje's sons obtain a post with the embassy in Paris?[54]

As it turned out, a diplomatic post in Paris was more trouble than it could have possibly been worth. It was there that some of the least edifying aspects of the radical regime were starkly exposed. The coalition of interests which had been contrived by Eberstein and his colleagues in anticipation of the coup continued to suffer from internal strains after January 22. Vis-à-vis its senior partner in the alliance this was not something the new regime could easily afford. Its efforts to mitigate the harsh terms of the Treaty of The Hague, both in respect of the maintenance of French troops and territorial indemnification for the loss of Maastricht and the left bank of the Scheldt, were seriously compromised by an unseemly feud within the embassy. The official Dutch minister in Paris remained Caspar Meijer, whose attitude towards the plotters had been, to say the least, equivocal. In March he was seconded by Blauw, who despite his opposition to the coup had remained a member of the Constituent and had gone to Paris as a member of its foreign relations commission. In addition to these two, however, there was also an unofficial deputation consisting of Eykenbroek and Eberstein. The former had a secret Instruction signed by van Langen (the Director in charge of external relations) and Pieter Vreede, authorising him to conduct negotiations for a commercial treaty with France, and to explore the possibility of a reduction in its military maintenance commitment, In his version of events, Blauw suggests (though Vreede denied it) that much of this was a cover for Eykenbroek's attempt to discharge the regime's "obligations" to Scherer, Barras and Talleyrand for services rendered prior to the coup.[55]

If this was indeed the case, it might be a motive for Talleyrand's diversionary manoeuvre of assisting Meijer in getting rid of the embarrassing emissary (once he had pocketed the cash). Certainly there was no love lost between the unofficial and the official representatives. When Eykenbroek attempted to present a memorandum on the relations between the two republics, embodying what were in fact the views of Ducange, the document was intercepted by Talleyrand before it reached the Directory. He then returned it to the embassy with an angry note about the status of its donor. Clearly Meijer was being invited to assert his authority. He made a half-hearted attempt to carpet Eykenbroek but a summons to an interview was ignored. On March 18, more dramatic steps were taken. On Meijer's instructions, the police arrested Eykenbroek and locked him up in the Temple prison as a vagrant. By beating a hasty retreat to The Hague Eberstein avoided a similar fate, and once there was able to anticipate Meijer's own account by giving his own carefully edited version to the Dutch government. The result of his efforts, strenuously abetted by Ducange, was a diplomatic coup. As a reward for his attempts to promote the integrity of Dutch diplomacy, Meijer was recalled from his post in disgrace and Blauw sent to Strasbourg to await further orders. In the interim the secretary of the legation, van der Hoeven, assumed the functions of the minister and was ordered to secure the liberation of Eykenbroek at the earliest opportunity. In due course both Meijer and Eykenbroek returned to The Hague, the first to a frosty, the second to a warm reception from both the Directors and Delacroix.

The imbroglio did not end there. Not content with winning a battle, Eykenbroek rashly attempted to win the war. At the end of April he tried to resume his mission. A new ambassador to Paris had been appointed, Willem Buys, who as Agent for External Affairs had been firmly in the pocket of Ducange and van Langen. An innocuous man, Buys had done his best to refuse the post but like some of his colleagues received an offer from the Directors difficult to decline. On arrival at Paris he assumed a posture of mortal terror, alarmed lest he suffer the same fate as Eykenbroek —or worse. The result was that he almost never poked his nose outside the legation residence and abandoned virtually all intercourse with the French authorities. Eykenbroek's return was a mistake. A few days later Eberstein, also back in Paris, was served with a summons to leave Paris within three days and France within a fortnight on pain of arrest. Eykenbroek would certainly have been locked up for a second time had he not eluded the police by going to ground just in time. He remained in hiding until the end of the year, when he was winkled out and transported back to the Netherlands. There he was sentenced to twelve years and perpetual banishment for diplomatic and financial misdemeanours.[56]

In itself this odious little brawl was of slight significance. Its effects were much exaggerated by the various protagonists who subsequently all wrote their version of the events. It was, to be sure, another episode in the fall from grace of the men of January. But its real importance lay in demonstrating to an expanding group of dissidents in the Netherlands that if, the previous winter, France had been able to exploit divisions within the Batavian camp, the converse was now becoming possible. This was underlined by the coup of 22 Floréal (May 11), when the French Directory again intervened to purge its legislature, this time of neo-Jacobin deputies, shifting the centre of political gravity in Paris back towards the "right." Historians of the Batavian Republic have learned to be wary of crude transpositions, but there can be no doubt that the about-face of French politics served the purposes of the Dutch opposition since many of their misgivings were directed at the havoc wrought by the commissions, which they saw, rightly or wrongly, as virtual agents of the popular societies. Most important of all, both the diplomatic *bagarre* and the Floréal coup undermined Delacroix's position in Paris.

As a past-master in the art of political survival, Talleyrand had anticipated (indeed helped bring about) the change of tack and was ready to ditch social and political embarrassments like Charles Delacroix with as much alacrity as he had disposed of his handsome wife. Suitors for his favour were not long in showing up. Towards the end of April, the East India Committee (a body which had been left intact by the new structure of the Agencies) decided to send two special emissaries to France to negotiate with the French government on the awkward issue of privateering. The latest case involved a Danish merchantman carrying East Indian coffee to the Netherlands, which had been waylaid by French privateers and taken to Malaga as prize. The Company tried to resort to neutral carriers in an effort to circumvent the British blockade. But it had not reckoned with the increasing tendency of French pirates and corsairs to prey on the easy game of neutral and allied shipping in preference to the altogether tougher and better-convoyed opposition of their enemies. For a long time the French refused to concede that there was a problem or that there were pirates or that they were in any way French. But while in no wise conceding any point of principle, Blauw and Meijer discovered, surely not to their surprise, that for an unenumerated but "reasonable" consideration Talleyrand was prepared to see to the liberation of the Danishman and do what he could about the navy's tolerance of privateering.[57] It was this opening which Wiselius and von Liebherr, the two emissaries, were sent to follow up.

Once they had obtained access to the Foreign Minister, they lost no time in enlightening him as to the true state of affairs in the Batavian Republic and the growing discontent felt by a large body of Patriots at the management of the present rulers. Nor did they attempt to conceal from him their view that much of this was directly attributable to the interference of the French minister and his notorious alter ego. Quite apart from the chance to profit from the downfall of a regime whose establishment had lined his pocket, Talleyrand was moved by the agents' strategic arguments. Although just as devoted to national interest as a Reubell or a Carnot, Talleyrand's approach to the "sister republics" had a subtlety of which they were quite incapable. He appreciated, for example, that those interests were better served by discreet and insignificant concessions to national amour-propre, and he had specifically advised Delacroix that at all costs the revolution of January 22 had to be seen to be the work of the "volonté nationale."[58] If, after weighing these considerations, he was still undecided whether or not Delacroix's presence was injuring the alliance, a hint of 300,000 florins did wonders for his resolution.

By the end of April Talleyrand had determined on his unfortunate stooge's recall. It was only the sudden appearance of Eberstein at the beginning of May, combined with the peremptory cancellation of Wiselius' and Liebherr's mission on the orders of the Directory, which delayed the execution. After Floréal Talleyrand's hands were freer and he assigned the secretary of the legation, Champigny-Aubin, to spy on Delacroix and to report directly to himself. So even had Dutch politics not taken a sharp turn for the worse at the end of May, it was obvious that the "Floréaliste" government would attend to the complaints of the Dutch "opposition" with sympathy and, if need be, exert some pressure on the Batavian Directors for their redress.

The latest crisis revolved around the mercurial figure of General Herman Daendels. Temperamentally, Charles Delacroix and the Dutch soldier were remarkably similar: headstrong, sentimental and obstinate. After Daendels' belated involvement in the coup of January 22, it is not surprising that the two men came to dislike each other so heartily. In his retrospective account, van Langen alleged that the General had been disappointed in his profiteering expectations of the January revolution and had resolved to make good his loss from the regime's downfall.[59] While certainly no angel, Daendels was not by the standards of the day startlingly venal (he was later to find adequate recompense as Governor of the Dutch East Indies). Compared to Masséna, he was a model of moral parsimony. What is undeniable is that he felt that his services on the 22nd had not been adequately recognised by its beneficiaries. Perhaps he was expecting a seat on the Directory or the Agency for War. In any event he remained commander of the Batavian army, subordinate only to the commander-in-chief of the allied forces, appointed by the French government.

It was not until the activities of the purging commissions came to his attention that Daendels began to take serious issue with the Directory. By May 4 he was more than ready to join in the chorus of execration at what he obviously took to be a betrayal of the government's mandate. Nor was Daendels alone among the Dutch army in his growing antipathy. General Dumonceau, the son of a French mercenary, had been brought up in Groningen, where his family had settled; had fled from the Restoration in 1787; and had served with Daendels in the ill-fated Batavian *légion franche-étrangère*. Like Daendels, he had returned in Pichegru's army with a French commission and was now commander of the northern sector of the Republic. Responsible for the enforcement of the revolution there, he had been dismayed to find himself embroiled in a full-scale battle between rival factions of the Reformed Church in Groningen, and obliged to keep company with a purging commission which preferred blatant Orangists over the heads of affirmed Patriots who, in that province, were not available in great numbers.[60]

There were other powerful men ill-disposed towards the Dutch Directory. Admiral de Winter had been the target of scathing criticism by the radicals following Camperdown, and it was largely due to their efforts that he was denied the accolade of the National Assembly. Apparently he had also fallen out with the Directors over their understandable reluctance to pay him his salary for the time spent in Britain as a prisoner of war. From the standpoint of the Dutch government, however, their most dangerous enemy was the commander-in-chief of the two armies, General Joubert. Like his predecessor, Beurnonville, Joubert found much to complain about in the inefficiency and slowness with which matters of military supply were handled in the Dutch Republic. Social friction between French troops and their Dutch billets— and often between soldiers of the two armies—created serious disorder in a number of the major cantonments. But the running sore was Flushing. The quarrel there was not only a matter of day-to-day disturbances but a conflict of principle between the two governments. To enforce the French claims to exercise rights of sovereignty in their section of the port, Ramel sent in customs officers—this at a time when a commercial treaty was being discussed in Paris—and Joubert was having continually to use troops and marines to support their work.

In April Joubert's relations with the Directors deteriorated further when a French sailor deserted from the Dutch navy and was sentenced to death by a Batavian court-martial. Joubert protested strongly that Dutch courts had no jurisdiction in the matter of French citizens, even if engaged in foreign service. His rather weak case was not helped by the ostentatious defection of Delacroix, who rebuked the General for being rude to the Directory. In themselves all these disputes were miserably petty affairs, but they took place against the backdrop of preparations under the command of Bonaparte for the vaunted "descent on England." They gave to the disaffected exactly the same arguments which had helped erode the authority of the Committee for Foreign Affairs the previous year: the clinching force of the "alliance in peril."

The second important group of dissidents emerged from within the Batavian government itself. All were, in some way, connected with the military difficulties plaguing Franco-Dutch relations. Neither Spoors nor Gogel had taken on their Agencies with much delight, and the former had on more than one occasion attempted to divest himself of the privilege. Gerrit Pijman, the Agent for War who bore the brunt of Joubert's complaints, was known to be equivocal in his feelings towards the Directors, and the other two agents were the chilly side of cool. Drafted into work of increasingly onerous complexity, the Agencies—which had been established like the French ministries as impotent administrative limbs of the executive—had willy-nilly accumulated in a very short space of time an impressive degree of power. To a large extent this was due simply to the mechanics of a national bureaucracy which was still in its infancy. Without any equivalent of the old "Council of State" or the Collegiate administration of the provinces, initiative in vital matters of government automatically devolved to those who were preoccupied with the details and who therefore had access to, if not mastery of, the relevant data. Thus the Committee of Finance of the two national assemblies, under van de Kasteele, enjoyed a quasi-autonomous role as the de facto financial cabinet of the Republic. As national treasurer, auditor and paymaster-general rolled into one, Gogel was invested with the power of the purse as surely as any treasurer-general of the old States. Similarly, it was the Agents of the War and Marine who controlled the logistics and therefore, with the military chiefs, the security of the state.

This tendency for delegation to grow into disaffection was accentuated by the separation of government and politics within the radical regime. The Directory was increasingly preoccupied with the latter just because its position never seemed sufficiently secure. The work on the constitution; the management of the purges; handling relations with the French government on the one hand and the popular societies on the other; the attempts to establish governmental organs of propaganda—all kept the beleaguered Directors too preoccupied with politics to worry overmuch about the details of administration. From the standpoint of the agents, however, this looked more like dereliction of duty. If power entailed responsibilities, they supposed, the converse was equally true and it worked to erode the authority of the Directory a little more.

In sheer ability, the Directors were no match for those who were supposed to be their subordinates. Johan Fokker and Barend Wildrik were conscientious nonentities; van Langen was up to his ears in debt and intrigue, and of all the Directors was closest to the coterie of Ducange. Only Vreede and Fijnje possessed any talent for government. Curiously enough, Pieter Vreede turned out to be a far less effective and energetic figure in power than he had been in opposition. His health was not of the best and according to Blauw's not very charitable description he was kept from his work by indispositions of various unspecified kinds.[61] He was, in actual fact, a born politician, enjoying the skills of oratory, the penning of broadsides and manifestoes, but somewhat lost when faced with a memorandum on budgetary appropriations for the Waterstaat. Certainly he failed to measure up to the quasi-Presidential leader to whom the Republic looked after January 22.

The real governor of the Batavian Republic between January and June 1798 was Wybo Fijnje, and it is to his austere and complex personality that both the vices and virtues of the regime must be primarily attributed.[62] His energy and virtual omniscience in political matters compensated to some extent for the inadequacies of his colleagues; but even he found the task of mobilising support for the regime while trying not to alienate the traditional ranks of Patriot supporters quite beyond his capacity. In any case, Fijnje was not by nature a compromiser. Even more than Vreede he remained convinced that the Republic would stay firmly in the grip of an élite unless a determined effort was made to root out all oligarchies, with whatever force was necessary to do a thorough job. Like other true revolutionaries of his time, Fijnje equated mere dispossession with the creation of a new social order and such preoccupations blinded him to the disastrous short-term consequences. In this respect he was the diametric opposite of the sober, thoughtful Gogel, weighing up the pros and cons of each and every political measure. As the results of his policies became more and more obvious—the deluge of protest reaching the Constituent could hardly have been ignored even by the Directors—Fijnje retreated into obdurate isolation, deaf to the entreaties of even old friends like Ockerse and Sam Wiselius. All he could see in those stacks of letters and petitions was a conspiracy of the privileged massing to sabotage the rule of virtue.

The murmured opposition to the Batavian Directory finally confronted them point-blank in a scene of rich comedy, the humour of which was understandably lost on its dramatis personae. The occasion was another dinner gathering *chez* Delacroix on May 16. Both Daendels and Ducange were present. Conversation turned to the indiscretions of the Dutch press, and the French minister made some choice remarks on the impertinence of the *Politieke Blixem* and the like. More from a mischievous impulse than elaborately planned forethought, Daendels remarked that its criticisms were trivial compared to those of Hespe's *Vlieg*, and pulling a copy of the latter from his coat, offered to translate the spicier passages for the benefit of the assembly. Taken aback at this typically Daendelian performance, Delacroix retorted that he was stupefied the Dutch government still saw fit to refrain from suppressing such disgusting libels. Daendels replied that on the contrary he thought it very good indeed.

He then proceeded in an altogether more serious vein to warn the minister that matters were going very badly in the country and, turning to Ducange, accused him of being the author "of all our misfortunes." When Ducange asked what he had done to merit the charge, the General went on to accuse him of responsibility for the decree of May 4. Stung by this barrage of abuse, Delacroix interjected that *he* had been behind the edict and that it had been essential for the good of the nation. Daendels now abandoned what few reserves of discretion were usually available to him, describing the Constituent as "sixty villains" and the Directors and Fijnje in particular as despicable men. The evening broke up in disarray, Delacroix restraining Ducange from further argument and ushering the fuming Daendels away. The following day, Ducange made it known that henceforth the General was to be considered an enemy of the Republic and that he should be taken into custody forthwith.[63]

The Directors themselves had not made up their minds what to do about Daendels' outburst. The day after, he was summoned to their presence and interrogated by Vreede and van Langen for over an hour. Joubert, who had accompanied Daendels to the Directors, had been refused admission to the interview, a rebuff which inclined him further to take Daendels' side in the dispute. By the 18th the Directory had still not made up its mind whether to arrest the General or to pardon him in return for a public apology to the French minister and others in the catalogue of his anathema.

Their indecision proved fatal, for the same day, Daendels—armed with a passport signed by Joubert and accompanied by a French adjutant for his protection—fled the country. Four days later he was in Paris. There he received a sympathetic hearing from Talleyrand and the "Floréaliste" Directors. In their eyes he was a model republican. Unlike the prating burghers in The Hague, he had the inestimable advantage of a military reputation in the service of the French as well as the Batavian Republic. He had shown himself one of the keenest advocates of the expedition to England and had been entrusted with the command of the Dutch forces. As Merlin put it to the ambassador Buys, who made a lame effort to have the general arrested and returned to the Netherlands, a hero of the Revolution was not to be sacrificed to the whims of a vile intriguer such as Ducange. Indeed, the whole bizarre incident proved to be the undoing of Ducange. Wanting to avoid any more serious action, Talleyrand felt able to assure Daendels that steps would be taken to get rid of the adventurer. Grounds for his complicity were immediately supplied by Champigny-Aubin, who had himself detested his privileged role in the embassy as Delacroix's pet parasite. On May 20, Daendels was informed that Ducange was to leave the Netherlands immediately and that Delacroix was to cease to have any further communication with him. Five days later, the recall of Delacroix was made official.

The drama of Daendels' dressing-down on the 17th and his flight to

Paris had made him an implacable enemy of the Dutch regime. In his own eyes he was now cast as their exterminating angel and urged their rapid overthrow on both Talleyrand and the French Directors. The latter were, however, far from convinced that such drastic remedies were called for. Delacroix would be replaced by the present consul at Hamburg, Roberjot (Bernadotte having declined the doubtful honour). Even Joubert concurred in the view that it would be imprudent to make any hasty decision before the new minister's arrival at The Hague in the third week of June. Blauw, who in defiance of his orders from the Batavian Directors had remained in Paris, joined his voice to those trying to dissuade Daendels from planning a coup, but was brushed aside with contempt for his pusillanimity. Indeed, Daendels never forgave Blauw his eleventh-hour reconciliation with Buys and in a furious exchange on the Champs-Élysées accused him of being a "traitor" to the cause.[64]

Yet Blauw's view was not very far from that of the French Directory, which wanted to resolve the issue without resorting to another act of *force majeure* at The Hague. Despite his record of brusqueness, Reubell in particular made it clear that he felt it unwise for France to be seen to be continually interfering in the domestic affairs of her allies. He and his colleagues hoped that the asylum given to Daendels, combined with the simultaneous expulsion of Ducange from the Netherlands and Eberstein from France (both met up in Antwerp travelling in opposite directions!), would be sufficient to signal to the Dutch Directory that it must mend its ways and make its peace with Daendels. The tokens of this were to be the liberation of the prisoners of the January 22 coup; the revocation of the offending edicts of March 17 and May 4; and the restoration of the franchise to its unpurged condition. This was, of course, doubly naïve. What they were asking of Fijnje and Vreede was the liquidation of their revolution—perhaps not as it had originally been conceived, but certainly as it had turned out. And in permitting Daendels to leave France of his own accord, they seem to have supposed that he would be content to act as the courier of their intentions to General Joubert and accept the restoration of his military office in a spirit of large-hearted generosity. Obviously there were some queasy *arrière-pensées*, for at his last interview before leaving Paris Reubell specifically and firmly counselled the General to remain at Antwerp until he had heard from Joubert that it was prudent to enter the Batavian Republic.

The likelihood of Daendels being restrained by such earnest injunctions was exactly nil. Talleyrand, at least, was quite aware of this and was already anticipating the possibilities of an imminent "incident" occurring on his return. His instructions to Joubert were deliberately unspecific about the means to be used to "correct" the unfortunate state of affairs prevailing at The Hague. No-one was more expert at passing on responsibility, waiting on events, and then taking credit or steering clear of the disgrace than the Foreign Minister. For Champigny-Aubin the situation was problematic. His despatches at the beginning of June are pessimistic about the possibility of a graceful retreat by the Batavian Directory. It would rather, he said, hack itself to pieces than go back on its action against Daendels.[65] The purges had made it so many enemies and it was itself now so neurotically defensive that it was difficult to see how a reconciliation could be contrived. Moreover, the expulsion of Ducange and the news of Delacroix's recall had whipped up the opposition to new acts of audacity and it was already looking to, and beyond, the downfall of the regime. Indeed, Champigny-Aubin could not help sharing the belief of Gogel and Spoors that since the Batavian Directory seemed already to be a dead duck, the immediate danger came not so much from its dwindling supporters in the radical clubs but from those at the very opposite pole of Dutch politics who might seek to exploit their downfall to engineer a federalist or even an Orangist counter-revolution. The agents had convinced themselves that to forestall such an eventuality it had become imperative that they themselves seize the initiative so as to safeguard the constitution of April and the basic structure of the unitary Republic. They had already corresponded with Daendels in Paris on ways and means of concerting such action. Still more ominously, despite his officially restraining instructions Joubert had provided a secret courier service for what had developed into a fully fledged insurrectionary conspiracy.

If it is a gross over-simplification to see the coup of January 22 as a facsimile of 18 Fructidor, so the coup of June 12 took place *in spite of,* rather than ordered by, French policy. Moreover, like the earlier event, it was far from inevitable. But the Dutch Directors made it considerably more likely by playing into the hands of their enemies with defiant ineptness. The more insecure their position became, the more adamant they were in refusing to yield an inch to those who counselled compromise for survival. Joubert's own admittedly not very practical suggestion that the edict of May 4 be put to popular vote was rejected out of hand, partly because he was already considered the accomplice of the traitorous general. As for pardoning Daendels, this was seen as total capitulation. Indeed, they argued that it was to prevent actions such as his that it had been necessary to pass the "emergency" edict of May 4!

Blauw's advice on resuscitating the coalition of moderate and radical unitarists, discarding only the most *enragé* clubbists and purgers, was treated with similar disdain. Vreede insisted that this would be merely to resurrect all the old cabals and uncertainties that had bedevilled the Republic prior to January 22 and to invite a stalking-horse for counter-revolution.[66] The addiction, as Blauw put it, to "conquer or die," was as potent as ever, only this time the odds were heavily on the latter eventuality. By continuing to listen to Delacroix, whose own days were numbered, and refusing to acknowledge the danger of their position, the radicals perversely courted their ruin. They even made the first military moves by augmenting The Hague garrison and putting their own man, Gelderman, in command without informing Joubert until the business was done. This merely had the effect of further antagonising the French commander and prompting him to reinforce his own garrison at Haarlem in response.

The atmosphere of morbid expectancy hanging over The Hague in the first week of June was broken by the appearance of Daendels on the 10th. To the surprise of no-one he had hardly lingered at Antwerp before proceeding directly to the capital. Urged by Reubell to travel in discreet anonymity, he had instead turned the journey into a triumphal progress. His popularity with the Dutch populace was indisputable and on arriving at The Hague he sought to exploit it as thoroughly as he could. Joubert had obligingly replaced the Dutch guards posted at his house with French sentries, and after seeing the commander he paraded himself in full dress uniform through the city, where—in contrast to deputies of the new Representative Assembly, who had been spat on in public—he was hurrahed around town. Some accounts claim that even the guard posted at the residence of the Directors joined in the acclamation.

The following evening a festive supper was held in his honour at the Oude Doelen. About 160 guests were present, most of them men prominent in the opposition to the government. The nominal hosts were a van Kretschmayr and Pompe van Meerdevoort who, apart from being one of the resignees of January 23, was also a close friend of Spoors. Indeed it was an open secret that the agents, now joined by Gerrit Pijman, the Agent for War, were behind the affair. Others in attendance were Joubert, Champigny-Aubin, Caspar Meijer and Daendels' brother-in-law Colonel Grasveld. Beneath a banner reading "Friends of the Constitution" toasts were drunk to the General and a formal programme drawn up, headed by demands for the revocation of the edicts of March 17 and May 4. The party was evidently a social as well as a political success, for it was not until three in the morning that the revellers broke up, leaving the agents to arrange their tactics for the following days.

The Directory could hardly be expected not to respond to so flagrant a challenge.[67] On the morning of June 12 it had gone into committee with leading members of the Representative Assembly, who were themselves urging strong action on the government. After long debate this was granted them. It was decided by Vreede and van Langen in particular that Joubert should be unilaterally removed from his command of the Batavian army; that the two hosts of the previous evening's entertainment should be arrested for sedition, tried summarily by a tribunal from the Assembly and if guilty, executed that very evening in the courtyard of the Binnenhof. If Champigny is to be credited, plans were also made for the subsequent arrest of the three renegade agents on similar charges. If this dramatically punitive measure was intended to cow the opposition into acquiescence, it had the reverse effect. It may, in fact, have given some among the rebels pause to reflect on their course of action; but Spoors at any rate believed they were now committed to an outright challenge to the Directory and had no option but to see it through. The decision was probably taken out of their hands by the fact that the threat to Kretschmayr and Pompe—who was almost as popular a figure as Daendels himself—had had an inflammatory effect on the people of The Hague.

By mid-morning rumours were circulating that a guillotine had been erected in the palace yard and that more arrests were in train. Crowds milled around the centre of the city and in the middle of the Plein, between the Directory and the Binnenhof, uncertain where to lend their support but awaiting a word from Daendels. In the end, it was Joubert who was the arbiter. Before noon he had gone to see the Directors to demand an explanation from them as to the arrest of the two "commissaires" and to insist that no violence be done to them. Accounts of that last fatal meeting are at total variance, but the more plausible versions suggest that after an initial chill the confrontation thawed into a reasonable exchange of opinions. To the Directors at any rate it seemed that Joubert was concerned to restrain Daendels from any impulsive action and that he was asking for a token of their own good faith. Fijnje and Vreede took him at his word and gave it him. No harm, they agreed, would befall Pompe and Kretschmayr if Joubert would guarantee the peace of the city. This he consented to do. He parted from the Directors with the crisis apparently averted.

What immediately followed is a complete mystery. Either Joubert perjured himself to the Directors as he had done on May 18, when he vouchsafed Daendels' good conduct at the same time as he had given him a passport for Paris; or else, on seeing the disturbed state of the city and reflecting on what he had done, he made a spontaneous decision to renege on his promise. He had, after all, only said that he would maintain the peace among the *populace*. Whatever the reasons, he tipped Daendels the wink to proceed with what was obviously a pre-arranged plan. Two or three companies of grenadiers were rounded up and with Daendels and Grasveld made their way across the Plein to the Directory, where van Langen, Vreede and Fijnje had been dining with Delacroix, relieved that the worst had been averted by the conversation with Joubert. Despite the fact that their own guard had taken oaths of loyalty to the Directors, they made no effort to halt Daendels' party. As soon as it became obvious from the noise that armed men had invaded the building, Vreede and Fijnje with an impressive show of athletics made for the window where they beat a retreat through the garden. Brandishing two pistols Grasveld entered the room—his resolution fortified with Dutch courage—accompanied by soldiers, their swords and bayonets unsheathed.

Van Langen made some attempt to defend himself but was violently roughed up by the soldiers, who liked nothing better than to punch authority directly on the nose, and was frogmarched to the war ministry under arrest. Grasveld and Daendels then read a warrant signed by all five agents. When Delacroix made his solo effort to assert his dignity, he received the muzzle of Grasveld's pistol stuck against his chest. Moved to hysteria by the humiliation, the minister shouted at Daendels: "You scoundrel, you will answer to the government of France for the atrocities you are committing." The General's reply was uncharacteristically curt: "I don't give a damn about you (*je m'en fiche de toi*), tyrant of my country!" As soon as the troops had departed, Delacroix rushed to Joubert's own residence where the General was placidly finishing his own lunch. To the minister's incoherent accusations that he had been the victim of a murderous assault, Joubert replied with classic sang-froid: "Are you hurt then, Citizen Minister? Come, I will send you the first physician of the army. Would you like me to see that you are taken safely back to your house?"[68] Faced with this mask of protesting innocence, all that Delacroix could do was accept Joubert's assurance that no more violence would follow that day and resign himself to a chagrined defeat.

The coup was completed with the invasion of the Representative Assembly. As Blauw pointed out after the event, had the Directors given proper attention to the political logistics of The Hague—with which they above all ought to have been familiar—they would have taken more adequate steps for their own protection. As an enclosed and moated area the Binnenhof is in fact ideally suited for such a holding operation, since the Stadhouderspoort and the gate to the Buitenhof might have been closed, the bridges on the Vijver Lake lifted, and the court turned into a miniature citadel without much difficulty. On the other hand, as Vreede pointed out, the Directory could not be sufficiently sure of its troops to risk real bloodshed in the centre of the city. Indeed, his scepticism was more than justified. On the approach of Daendels' troops, the officer in charge of the defending companies who had been given strict orders to fire on any soldiers approaching the gates merely retreated into the Assembly itself to seek a written order to that effect. This handed Daendels the opportunity to occupy the post, disarm the soldiers (who in any case were busy fraternising with his own men) and to seal off the avenues to the Assembly from further forces.

Inside the hall the intrusion of the troops met with a brave harangue by the President, Visser, but before his oratory could have any effect Spoors' valet, who was with the party, dragged the President's chair from under him, pushed him to the floor and ripped the sash from his coat. Pandemonium followed this first act of violence and deputies fled the chamber as best they could, a remnant being rounded up in a nearby tavern where the list of those to be arrested and the proclamation dissolving the body was read out. Most of those taken into custody were men who had been most eager to mete out the same fate on their enemies: Bosch, Rant, Vonck, Ploos van Amstel, van Rosevelt Cateau, de Lemon, de Beere and van der Hoeven. There were two notable exceptions. The first was Theodorus van Leeuwen, the original President of the Constituent, who among the radicals of January had harboured the gravest misgivings about the subsequent conduct of the regime. The second was Willem Ockerse who, as the architect of the constitution the rebels claimed to be defending, was herded into prison along with those who had disgraced it so notoriously.[69]

Inevitably, the coup of June 12, 1798, has born comparison with the *journées* of the French Revolution. Naturally it has been associated with the events of 22 Floréal a month earlier. It should be clear, however, that while Floréal made June 12 possible it did not, of itself, *entail* it. Indeed, it seems likely that it took place in spite of the serious misgivings of the French Directory. It took no time at all before French and Batavian governments were as much at loggerheads with each other as they had been in the first half of the year, for whatever the political complexion of either regime, it could not disguise cleavages which were inherent in the relationship between the two states.

Other historians have seen the coup of June 12 as a rehearsal for 18 Brumaire, with Daendels anticipating Bonaparte by imposing his will and his ambition on the shambling incompetence of garrulous *politiques*. Yet the most unlikely analogy is probably the most germane: that of 9 Thermidor. Not because Pieter Vreede and his colleagues in any serious respect bore resemblance to Robespierre and the reign of Virtue, but rather because, like Robespierre's government, the Batavian Directory fell because no-one, not even those household troops who had been sworn to defend them to the death, was willing to lift a finger to save them. It was an instructive irony that in both cases those who so assiduously professed to champion the "people" should have fallen victim to their indifference. The unpleasant truth was that, special cases like the cannoneers of Amsterdam aside, Pieter Vreede was far outstripped in popularity by Herman Daendels. Like the Jacobins, moreover, the Dutch radicals—in reality, a small minority of the Patriots who in turn had command of only a section of the nation—deluded themselves into believing that they had won the support of a mass constituency known variously as the "Fatherlanders" or the "right-thinking part of the nation." The vocal support of the clubs, and the plebeian consciously anti-patrician character of their ideology, helped sustain the illusion.

There is no doubt that in some cities traditional ruling élites *were* overturned by well-drilled popular pressure, notably in Haarlem, Leiden, Amsterdam, Rotterdam and Utrecht. But these numerically limited forces were not cut out to be surrogate sans-culottes, nor were they an alternative source of strength to the Patriot rank-and-file of burghers whom the Directory systematically alienated in the spring of 1798. The revolution in the Netherlands was not so strong nor so ubiquitous that it could afford to dispense with those among whom it had first taken fire; those who had given it its language, its political expression, and upon whom any real change in the character of the Dutch state would vitally depend. To such people the re-establishment of political liberty had been cherished, and its violation by those who claimed to be acting for the unrepresented was a bewildering heresy. The only problem was deciding whether those who, like Bentinck and Harris in 1787, had robbed them of their votes and dispossessed them of their offices were fools or knaves. Champigny-Aubin was himself taken aback by the strength of the feeling over such matters and felt it necessary to explain to his superiors in Paris that "the Batavian people attaches a great deal more value than the French to its right to vote, to elect its representatives and other magistrates."[70] To exclude the greater part of the Dutch republican movement from the franchise in favour of the unknown quantity of the great unwashed was, as Gogel, Blauw and Champigny all saw, an exercise in political suicide.

Yet it could be argued that the end of the radical regime was predetermined by its beginnings; that Pieter Vreede and Wybo Fijnje never succeeded in removing the stigma which attached to their original usurpation. For the exaggeration of their constituency derived largely from their justification of the coup of January as a necessary precondition of the enactment of the constitution. When he declined Blauw's proposals for an eleventh-hour coalition, Vreede harked back to those 160,000 votes as the mandate for his Directory. What he failed to ask himself was whether, given the growing consensus for a unitary Republic evidenced by the shifting centre of political gravity in the winter of 1797–98, that figure might not have been *more* impressive without the labours of the purging commissions. Such myopia was not the product of disingenuous calculation, nor, as his enemies later alleged, an insatiable lust for power and place. On the contrary, much of the policing of the Republic was unhappily delegated to subordinates whose scruples in such matters were decidedly suspect. In their heart of hearts, Vreede and Fijnje were still political innocents; for their part, power was merely the opportunity to ground the new Batavia in the immortal axioms of popular sovereignty. Without them, they believed that the Dutch revolution would die. If, in the process, hard knocks had to be given and taken, they believed it was better not to flinch from the consequences. For it was worthier by far to have made the attempt to create in the Netherlands a revolutionary democracy than never to have bothered to try. And despite their blunders and follies their prognosis was, in at least one respect, sounder than that of their opponents. Compromise was to prove just as risky a business as dogma. And for those who, on the morrow of June 12, believed that they could govern a revolutionary Republic through the gentler ways of consent and consensus, the future was to be exceedingly sad.

* * * * * * * * * *

9

The Stunted Growth
of the
Unitary State,
1798–1801

Equilibrium or Compromise?

"What fruits, until now, have the people plucked from the liberty tree, planted in the winter of 1795?" asked the *Politieke Donderslag* (*Political Thunderclap*) shortly after the coup of June 12, 1798. "To tell the truth," it answered tersely, "not much."[1]

This was no more than fair comment. If the trees had blossomed with promises they had remained obstinately barren of achievement. As regime followed regime in bewildering succession, the one distinguished from the other only by its greater zeal to purloin the offices of state and wring the last pennies from the impoverished and long-suffering Dutch, enthusiasm for the revolution withered along with its totems. According to a captive tourist, the Englishman Ralph Fell, by 1800 no less than six liberty trees, planted on the Plein in the centre of The Hague, had perished—either from natural causes or the mischievous attention of Orangists. In Rotterdam four perished before the municipality in its wisdom decided to replace them with a more functional pole, on top of which a Phrygian bonnet was hoisted aloft.[2] To the uncharitable, the mortality of these emblems could not help but be a gloomy augury of the Republic's own chances. The persistent chaos of revolutionary politics was compounded, in the summer of 1799, by the sudden menace of an Anglo-Russian invasion in North Holland. When in the successive winters of 1798–99 and 1799–1800 savage floods broke the sea defences in Overijssel, Friesland and parts of Zeeland and South Holland, the Batavian renascence must have seemed more remote than ever.

The patriotic nostrums with which, in the summer of 1798, the new

[354]

government exhorted the people to rally to its leadership had already been thoroughly devalued by its predecessors. Complaining of the hypocrisy of radical demagogues in Groningen, General Dumonceau warned that, had they remained in power in that province:

those words which announced to the universe the happiness of the human race [liberty and equality] would have been degraded into empty shibboleths used to gull and dazzle the Good People into yielding up to a small clique the lucrative perquisites of office.[3]

It was the hope of those who deposed them that their good faith and disinterested concern for the public good would go some way toward repairing the damaged credibility of the revolution. Their legitimation for what had, after all, been a naked exercise of military force rested on the claim to have rescued the constitution from its violators, to whom they referred as the "unconstitutional Directory and Assembly." But initially the taint of usurpation clung to their authority as it had to their predecessors. The national legislature, which had begun life in August 1797 with 127 members, had been reduced by the January 1798 purges to about half that number and was now whittled down even further as the "Interim Legislative Assembly" to a paltry forty-four, most of them the resignees of January. Moreover, the protector of the new regime, Daendels, was, so to speak, doubly perjured, and, it was believed, fully capable of continuing his habit of making and unmaking regimes as his fancy and interest dictated.

Yet in one important respect the "Interim Directory" was as good as its word. Its proclamation on June 12 had promised that it would relinquish power as soon as properly elected authorities could be installed and it emphasised that, unlike the previous regime, it had no desire to monopolise office. Spoors was even said to have remarked that he would be shot rather than remain a Director.[4] Their decree affirmed that "We regard ourselves as responsible to each and every one of you, to our own consciences and to the Creator of Nature," and for once constitutional obligations were treated seriously. The primary assemblies were called for July 10; the new legislature was elected by July 13 and began its sessions on July 31. By the middle of August, a new Executive Directory had been appointed and the Agents who had engineered the coup reverted to their former positions.*

The second feature by which the new government tried to distinguish itself from its predecessors was the attempt to transcend the partisan feuds which had afflicted the Republic for the past three years and to provide its people with an authentically "national" administration. Schimmelpenninck, whose swift appointment to the embassy in Paris betokened just such an eclectic approach, observed later that the great weakness of the January regime's leaders had been their failure to make their government that of the nation's as a whole. For, he insisted, it was a dependable rule of thumb that "every government which fails to turn aside from petty motives and personal

---

* Pijman, the Agent for War; Spoors, the Agent for the Navy; and Gogel, the Agent for Finance who also provisionally took charge of the portfolio for foreign affairs.

rivalries must fall.["]5 The major priority of the new regime was to show the people that June 12 had been a truly "national event." And Spoors, writing to Wiselius, suggested:

Our policy is altogether new and . . . in the short span of our government we will give ample proof that its object is none other than, with the strictest honesty, to deal a blow to all intriguers, to bring the constitution into full operation, to make it *national* and, once and for all, to destroy all factions on whichever side they may stand."6

The new Directory's proclamation argued that the authenticity of the revolution was not to be measured by the zeal with which the interests of any particular group were prosecuted, but by its success in rallying broad popular support around the constitution and the Republic. Thus it was the radicals who had been the pseudo-revolutionaries, for "their revolution was carried out only in personnel and offices and so resembled all those which, for two centuries, have agitated and worn out our unhappy land"; the proclamation added the rider that "the new governors, ignorant and fanatical, were even more dangerous than their predecessors [as] they ended up flattering every form of popular error and by enthroning the most hideous tyranny of all— Anarchy!" As a direct result, "many of the best citizens were excluded from provincial administrations [though they had constantly and publicly defended the rights of the people] simply because they had shaken off the yoke of faction and refused to bow down before the idols of the day."7

Those wounds inflicted on the revolution, it was implied, would be healed by the restoration of the deserving, and of true Patriots to offices and franchises from which they had been so abruptly removed. Instead of polarisation and alienation, a republican reunion would be consummated *within the framework set out by the constitution of April 23*. Far from reneging on the "spirit of January 22," Gogel and Spoors saw themselves realising its true potential, giving concrete expression to the principles of unitarism and democracy.8

The ideal of a republican reunion—in effect, the resuscitation of the strategy drafted by Blauw and Pasteur before the January coup—was very fine in theory. In practice, it was about as straightforward as squaring the circle. Behind it lay the untested axiom that democracy and unitarism were perfectly complementary. The concept of popular sovereignty encapsulated in the slogan "One and Indivisible" assumed a willing acceptance of unified national authority, providing that it was exercised in the name of the people and through their elected representatives. But what if those representatives should, as it were, defy their own nature and repudiate unitary sovereignty? In that case, the "indivisible" Republic would be put in a situation comparable to Christendom with an heretical Pope. Such a situation was not inconceivable. The experience of France had shown that even in a country which had undergone in the Old Regime a degree of centralisation, the revolutionary implementation of democracy had accentuated the centrifugal devolution of power rather than the reverse. The Committee of Public Safety and even the Napoleonic prefects were to make little difference to this. In the Netherlands, where there had been no intendancies nor any general control and where each township was accustomed to regard itself as autonomous, the introduction of a truly national government was likely to meet the severest resistance. If the elections of 1796 were to be repeated and a body of men chosen quite out of sympathy with the constitution to which they swore allegiance, the Batavian Republic was bound to find itself suffering from the chronic French complaint of a deadlock between the executive and legislative branches.

These considerations gave the custodians of the new order some pause. Almost from the very beginning, their laudable intention to pursue a strictly non-partisan policy was conditioned by the requirements of elementary prudence. One practical consequence was that any hope of the immediate liberation of those incarcerated on January 22 must be for the time being disappointed. Restrictions were relaxed; the prisoners at the Huis 't Bosch were permitted to wander freely around the park and to have visits from family and friends. But complete liberty was still denied them.[9] Two of the Agents, Gogel and Tadama, were strongly of the view that a truly even-handed policy required them either to liberate or to detain *both* sets of prisoners: those of January 22 and those of June 12. The new regime further signified its intention not to revert to the status quo ante January 22 by retaining the "oath of hatred" against "the Stadholder, Aristocracy, Federalism and Anarchy," and by issuing warnings to voters to be wary of "high-born gentlemen who made free with your treasure and condemned the Fatherland to poverty and insignificance" while they held the reins of power.[10] A proclamation on June 25 referred specifically to:

a great number of patricians and unenlightened men among whom there are several families who occupied prominent positions during the absence of the Stadholder. . . . These men, who view the destruction of Stadholderian power with satisfaction, had too much interest in the maintenance of the old institutions of Church and state or were still slaves of old prejudices to render sincere homage to the great truths which make the revolution the cause of all the people. It is for this reason that for three years you have been denied the great advantages which the revolution should have assured for you.[11]

Reconciliation, therefore, was not to mean reaction. But as more and more of the "Patriot notables" with an animus against the radical regime returned to office in the provinces, pressure grew on the new government to release federalists and moderates from confinement. On July 9 the "Interim Legislature" gave in to this pressure and enacted an amnesty for all such prisoners. After a long tussle, the Directory confirmed the order by three votes to two. Champigny-Aubin and General Joubert, who were both watching the progress of the government with some apprehension, were incensed that such a move had been made "without communicating a single word to us."[12] That so dangerous a measure could have been approved on the very eve of the primary election was, they insisted, the height of folly. Armed with these objections, Gogel returned to the fray and belatedly succeeded in having the order rescinded. It was not until July 14 that Queysen, de Mist, van Marle Hahn, Pasteur and the rest were finally set free. Only Bicker and Coert van Beijma, for differing reasons regarded as incorrigibly seditious, remained in custody a little while longer. Of those arrested on June 12 only the most intransigent, Vonck, Bosch, de Beere and van Rosevelt Cateau, remained imprisoned. Their turn came in November when—in the curious company of the dying Grand Pensionary van de Spiegel and the far from moribund Bentinck van Rhoon—they were released under a general amnesty for all prisoners taken since January 1795. Only Fijnje and van Langen (and later Eykenbroek) remained subject to criminal investigation by Procureur-General van Maanen regarding the misappropriation of public funds.[13]

The uncertainties affecting political prisoners exemplified the difficulties involved in maintaining the elusive republican equilibrium. The men of June may have believed that they had behind them the broad support of those still identifying themselves with the Patriot cause, but in reality they were balancing on a perilously slack tightrope. A little too much impulsion from one side or the other and disaster threatened. For all their goodwill, it remained problematic to define their "moderate republicanism" in terms other than their often-reiterated abhorrence of both federalism and "anarchy." Yet the elections to the new legislature might have been worse. Despite the absence of Vreede's phalanx of radicals, the distribution of political allegiances was very much like that of the second National Assembly of August 1797. The political machinery of the primaries (100 to 500 souls) and the electoral assemblies (1 to 40 primaries) had operated satisfactorily to return a substantial body of men of moderate views but for the most part committed to the establishment of a unitary Dutch state. Very many of them belonged to the Patriot élite: those who had stepped into the shoes of departing Orangists in 1795 and, until rudely discomfited in March 1798 by the purging commissions, had remained in power in the provinces and towns ever since. They included van Hooff; J. H. Appelius from Middelburg; François Ermerins, the regent of Tholen (also in Zeeland); Daniel de Leeuw and the republican baron from Utrecht, Strick van Linschoten; van Haeften the commander of the Utrecht Free Corps in the Patriottentijd; Pieter van de Kasteele and Couperus of Gouda, both erstwhile disciples of Paulus; the Catholic Guljé from Helmond; and the two men who had fought tooth and nail against the domination of the radical clubs in Friesland, Eduard van Beijma and J. L. Huber.

There were, of course, a number of dyed-in-the-wool federalists among the superior ranks of the members, such as Gerrit van Schimmelpenninck and Jan Arend de Vos van Steenwijk, both Overijssel barons. But equally the oath against "anarchism" failed to exclude the re-appearance of at least a few radicals of the Vreede stripe. Barend Wildrik, the Zutphen advocate who had been a Director (albeit a stooge figure) between January and June, was re-elected, as were Simon Schermer, a signatory of the radical manifesto of December 12, 1797; Nuhout van der Veen, a member of the "Constituent" and the author of the motion proscribing the moderates; Pieter Linthorst, another Constituent and clubbist; and Dirk Hoitsma, the President of the "Central Assembly" of the Amsterdam clubs in 1795. Subsequent elections in 1799 and 1800 strengthened not only the federalist but the radical wings of the Assembly. Pamphleteers like Werner, F. Govers and J. G. Welsman all found places, and both Ploos van Amstel and Stephen van Langen were elected for no less than three constituencies in 1799 (though the latter's election was annulled by the Directory).

The elections only reflected the relative strengths of the various political groups in the Batavian Republic. As in France, a constitution designed to strengthen the centre and to give some ballast to moderate republicanism was unable to prevent a gradual re-polarisation of parties. If this was a measure of the success of the representative machinery, it further emphasised its incompatibility with the aspiration to governmental unity. Freedom and order were to prove no more reconcilable in the Netherlands than they had in France. Whether or not the re-appearance of old divisions could be contained within the framework of the legislature was a further anxiety. There seemed as yet little to fear from any Orangist revival. The suspect navy had come through Camperdown (Kamperduin) with honour but the dearth of officers resulting from that catastrophe had meant that Spoors, with some reluctance, was obliged to re-commission captains like van Braam and van Capellen who made little secret of their devotion to the Prince. Their disaffection was eventually to prove fatal during the invasion of the following year. Miniature conspiracies were regularly weeded out in traditional strongholds of the Orange cause like Nijmegen, but the most serious problem arose from the overflow of rebel priests and peasants from over the Belgian border. It was not until November 1798 that the republican troops finally mastered the "Peasants' War" in Flanders and Brabant—and even then areas of Limburg and almost the whole of Luxembourg remained in rebel hands. The Abbot of Tongerloo had made Maastricht an operational base; from there it was relatively easy for fugitives to make their way to the Meijerij and Tilburg whence, according to French military authorities, they continued to spread violently anti-republican propaganda.[14]

More serious trouble came from the opposite quarter. Following the coup of June 12, an initial political lull was disturbed by an intensive campaign of petition and address in the Amsterdam and Rotterdam clubs, supported by delegations from smaller radical centres such as Delft and Enkhuizen. To begin with, their activities were restricted to the publication of pamphlets and the continuing vilification of Daendels and the Directors in the radical press.[15] But on August 7 an assembly of 300 to 400 clubbists on the Dam degenerated into the usual riot. On this occasion, however, the Stadhuis' armed guard moved in on the demonstrators, with the result that an open brawl culminated in one death and a number of wounded as the guards with evidently uncertain aim fired "over the heads" of the crowd. In the end it needed cavalry from the French garrison and a doubled watch on all the sensitive points to tranquillise the situation.[16]

As in France, the failure of disorganized protest was followed by an equally abortive attempt at conspiracy. In the event the Dutch effort made Babeuf look almost professional by comparison. On November 20, following the advice of a police spy, a clandestine circle of seven were arrested in Amsterdam together with papers incriminating them in a clumsy endeavour to repeat the experience of January 22. Much depended, as before, on the success of liaisons in Paris with neo-Jacobin circles where the *Journal des Hommes libres*, much to Schimmelpenninck's discomfort, kept up a barrage of abuse against the present Batavian Directory. Among those apprehended was Dirk Hoitsma, who was able to claim immunity by virtue of his membership of the Representative Assembly but in so doing severely discredited his more innocent comrades in the legislature. The remainder were a motley bunch. Ary Voogd was a Schiedammer and had been a member of both the second National Assembly and the rump Constituent; F. W. M. Ruysch had been elected burgemeester of Delft under the radicals and a President of the "Central Assembly" of clubs in 1795; Groeneveld was an apothecary at The Hague and one of its leading clubbists; P. J. de Visser occupied the same rank and status in Leeuwarden. Kaltener and Romijn both ran radical clubs in different parts of Amsterdam. The group was crowned by the presence of Anthonie Boeseken, with Joost Vridagh a purging officer in Utrecht and Gelderland, an intimate of Eykenbroek's, and an essential link between the clubbists and the Paris conspirators in the winter of 1797–98. Boeseken's role gave the Amsterdam plot a sinister enough character which its own efforts hardly warranted. The subsequent proceedings made it pathetically clear that the circle had barely advanced beyond contacting a handful of like-minded cronies in the obvious radical centres, and that they had had no luck at all in winning round the junior army officers without whom (they themselves recognised) any attempt at another coup was doomed to failure.

Yet despite its ignominious end, the very existence of such a conspiracy was enough to put the Directory on its guard against subversion from whatever political quarter. Schimmelpenninck was particularly concerned that the new French agent, Lombard de Langres, should not interfere with proceedings against Eykenbroek and van Langen which he regarded as an essential warning against any further attempts to disrupt the stability of the regime. "Both the Batavian government and the members of the Legislative Assembly," he wrote, "share the greatest repugnance for all acts of revenge and their consequences, but on the other hand they must be very firm, for to do nothing would be incompatible with the dignity of the government and the security of the state."[17]

Schimmelpenninck's neurotic anxiety about "anarchist plots" both in France and the Netherlands and his anger that their agents were freely tolerated in Paris betrayed some interior doubts as to the viability of his own ambition to stabilise the Republic around a "national" constitution. In advertising the good faith of his government, he liked to repeat the claim made by van de Kasteele at the opening session of the Representative Assembly that "the revolutions in the Batavian Republic may be considered as completed."[18] But as Talleyrand—for whom Schimmelpenninck, to his later embarrassment, was lost in admiration—pointed out, revolutions were far easier to start than stop. Indeed, it has become a truism of revolutionary historiography that they are "dynamic" phenomena, advancing or retreating in response to appropriate political impulses but by the same token inherently incapable of that equilibrium Schimmelpenninck so earnestly desired. Thus what passed for statesman-like moderation was in fact a nervous alternation between each of the defined political poles: oligarchy or democracy.

Yet neither Schimmelpenninck nor for that matter Gogel or Wiselius were blessed with analytical expertise as to the nature of political revolutions. When Schimmelpenninck expressed the hope that the Batavian "revolutions" were over, he certainly meant the periodic upheavals of state which had impeded rather than assisted the reconstruction of national institutions. A more radical temperament like Gogel's shared with him the view that it should be possible to use the 1798 constitution as the base from which overdue institutional reforms could be carried out without subjecting the country to yet another *coup d'état*. That they were not realised and that the following three years were largely ones of wasted opportunity, Dr. de Wit puts down to a failure of political nerve; to the fact that what was being operated under the guise of the constitution was a *pseudo*-democracy.

Yet the purely political machinery of the constitution worked as well as could have been expected. For three consecutive years voters assembled in nearly 5,000 primary meetings—with franchises varying from 15 to over 100—to elect the men who elected their legislators. The greater degree of direct democracy which Ockerse had sought to build into the electoral provisions by allotting authority to the primaries to send their own men forward was generally observed, even if its effects were not always to increase the radicalism of the representation. The primary assemblies convened to elect provincial and municipal authorities with impressive regularity, and the press in this period showed no sign of tempering its abrasive criticism of those in power. By any working standards, the Batavian Republic between 1798 and the spring of 1800 was an authentic representative democracy. The reason why so much reforming potential was nonetheless squandered was not that the political apparatus functioned defectively, but from the point of view of the unitarists, only too well. For many of the men it established in positions of authority were unlikely to buckle down to the work of transforming the entire structure of Dutch governing institutions. More important, the social and economic conditions of the time were hardly such as to encourage the cautious in so bold an enterprise. Time and again the historian is forced to the depressing conclusion that the war which made the Dutch revolution possible also supplied the limiting conditions of its chances of fulfilment. From that vicious circle there was to be no escape.

Unitarism Manqué

Given the daunting prospect that the respective branches of the new constitution seemed far from complementary, it was all the more important that the executive at least should be sufficiently effective to see that the unitarist axioms of government had some basis in reality. But even in this department, constitutional niceties got in the way. The clause stipulating that Directors must be over forty years of age excluded from consideration most of the ablest talent remaining in public life. In 1798 Gogel was thirty-three, Schimmelpenninck thirty-seven, Wiselius thirty-five, and Procureur-General van Maanen a mere novice of thirty-one. Thus the list of fifteen candidates presented to the First Chamber of the Representative Assembly was not only short on ability but bore a disconcertingly patrician air. None except van Hooff (whose own radicalism had cooled sharply during his detention at Fijnje's pleasure) could be described as an ardent democrat. All were from the respectable eminences of the Patriot notability. They included men of the timbre of Balthasar Abbema, the Utrecht merchant and financier who had been the companion of Bicker and van Staphorst in the days of the Paris Committee, and Professor van Swinden of the Amsterdam Athenaeum, both redoubtable conservatives.

Those five who were eventually chosen to comprise the Executive Directory had not retreated quite so far from the direction of the revolution. Nonetheless they belonged to that class of "Patriot Regents" which had taken power in 1795 and relinquished it only with the greatest chagrin to the forces of Vreede's populism. The most eminent were François Ermerins, the regent of Tholen in Zeeland, friend of Gogel's and a staunch defender of his province's rights; and J. Willem van Hasselt, the Amsterdam tobacco merchant, who had been among the councillors deposed in the purge of March 15. The remaining places were filled by A. W. Hoeth, the Procureur of Groningen; the former Baron Anthonie van Haersolte, whose family had once been favoured by William V and who had himself held the office of Receiver-General of the kwartier of Zutphen; and very briefly, until his resignation, Montanus Hettema, one of Huber's Friesian colleagues, whose place was taken by van Hooff. The constitutional stipulation by which lots decided that one of the Directors would annually make way for a new appointment also worked in favour of a steadily more conservative executive. Augustinus Besier for van Hasselt (1799), van Swinden for van Hooff (1800), and Pijman for Hoeth (1801) eventually came to make up a Directory which, like that of the last French Directory, was virtually prepared to sign its own death warrant and that of the constitution it had sworn to defend.

It was a sharp irony that a college of Patriot regents had been appointed to serve as what had been intended to be the first sovereign government of a unified nation state. The paradox was not lost on Champigny-Aubin, who gave vent to his dismay to an equally apprehensive Gogel.[19] As before the coup of June 12—though for different reasons—the initiative in the matter of instituting a unitary form of government went by default to the agents. While they themselves were no supermen, beside the mediocrities of the Directory talents such as Gogel, Goldberg, Spoors and van der Palm (the new Agent for National Education) seemed colossi of republican government. At least they were, in circumstances of increasing desperation, resourceful and energetic. They were quite clear in their own minds as to their primary obligation. Goldberg was later to insist that "the commonwealth is no longer to be regarded as seven different nations . . . the whole structure is to be made up of individuals from all departments having the same interests and who have accorded to them the same rights."[20]

Much of the Agents' activities amounted to an onslaught not only on the jurisdictional autonomy of the provinces but on the most deeply rooted of its traditional institutions. In their efforts to pare the old structure down to the level of administrative rationality, even the geography of the provinces was not to be spared. As in the case of the French departments, the re-drawing of departmental frontiers was a deliberate attempt to liquidate the very identity of states which traced their history back to long before the foundation of the Dutch Republic itself. The more strictly federal history of the United Provinces made the attack both more ambitious and less likely to succeed than in France. The principal features of the reorganization were the division of Holland into three parts: Amstel, consisting of Amsterdam and a small hinterland; the Texel, accounting for the major part of North and East Holland; and the Delf, incorporating all the land south of Haarlem and Gouda. Zeeland and a small area of western Brabant made up the Schelde en Maas; the remainder of the Generality Land and some of Gelderland, the Dommel. Utrecht—much to the displeasure of the city—was divided between the Rijn (with the rest of Gelderland) and the Texel. Overijssel and Drente were amalgamated to form Ouden Yssel. But the most daring move was the disappearance of traditional Friesland into the enlarged department of the Eems with Groningen.

As with all such bureaucratically contrived cartography, little attention was paid to social or regional topography; indeed the new shape of the Republic was designed, and taken, to be a deliberate insult to the facts of Dutch history. The new principle was demography and administrative convenience (though those who were appointed to test it might have argued otherwise). Each unit was meant to comprise a specific number of primary assemblies on the cardinal principle of 100 to 500 souls—hence the tripartite division of Holland. Of course outside the files and maps of the functionaries in The Hague or at the "governing centre" of each department, the new departments had little reality. It was no more conceivable that a peasant in the Twente or a fisherman at Veere would stop thinking of themselves as Overijsselaar or Zeelander than it was for a Breton to suppose after 1791 that he was a citizen of the Finistère. Even as effective units of government, they lasted a mere two years. For pending the election of the new departmental administrations in March 1799, the old divisions were maintained and a federal constitution in October 1801 killed them off for good. When unitary sovereignty was reintroduced again in 1805 it was through the old provincial demarcations. Only the over-mighty Holland continued to be divided (even after the Orange Restoration) into a north and south.

Flimsy as it was in reality, the authority for the new hierarchy of powers was at least spelt out unequivocally in the constitution. Article CXLVIII stipulated that the "departmental and municipal administrative bodies are subordinate and responsible to the Executive Directory." While it was not until 1803 that a comprehensive law on local government, introduced to prevent a slide back to *before* 1795, defined more clearly the competence and jurisdiction of local authorities, the constitution assumed that they were to exercise only those powers *delegated* to them by the national executive and legislature. (The same feature obtained in the relationship between provincial and national courts of justice.) Authority was to be devolved from the centre to the periphery, not vice versa as in the traditional Dutch manner. Rigid centralisation was, as in France, tempered by the *election* of departmental as well as municipal authorities—and on a far wider franchise than had been the case with the provincial States. Even in this context, the subordination of local to national authority was emphasised by the power invested in the Directory to appoint new members to any places on departmental administrations vacated by officials found culpable of negligence or misconduct. Moreover, all by-laws and local ordinances required the formal approval of the Directory before taking effect, and the junior authorities were prohibited by special decree from "delaying or contradicting" any statute passed by the national legislature. Annual estimates and accounts were to be submitted to the Agent for Finance, to the Directory and to the legislature for inspection, and any ear-marking of local taxes for public expenditure required further special warrant. The whole *raison d'être* of local administration was to act as the efficient executor of the policies laid down by national government.

So, at any rate, the authors of the 1798 constitution had fondly supposed. It did not, however, require powerful clairvoyance to predict that any attempt to reduce the autonomy of Dutch local government would be met with the fiercest resistance. Indeed, the very comprehensiveness of the constitutional regulations betrayed that concern. In the event, it was fully vindicated. The ten-month hiatus between the June coup and the establishment of the new departments gave a vital breathing space to local notables seeking to re-establish their power after the radical interlude. The local elections held at the end of December did nothing to arrest their return. The departmental administration of the Oude Yssel was dominated by Baron Jan Arend de Vos van Steenwijk; and in the Eems the nominees of the curator of Franeker College, Georgius Coopmans, whose dismissal from office had raised such a furore in Friesland, were established in power. In the Dommel eminences of the Brabant, intelligentsia like Lublink de Jonge from Grave and Pieter de la Court were more to the fore, but the overall pattern of the administrations did not suggest that they were about to take office as the submissive instruments of the Executive Directory. The same situation obtained in the cities. Hendrik Nobbe's successor as elected "mayor" was a figure more in keeping with the patrician style of the city regents of Amsterdam: one van Bleyenburgh, a wealthy merchant and colleague of van Hasselt's. Procureur van Hall, who had been the target of radical excoriation, resumed his duties and had an even stronger guard posted on the Stadhuis. In Utrecht, those who had been in charge of the city administration before the purges of Boeseken and Joost Vridagh were restored to office by the polls.[21]

It would be misleading to suggest that the aftermath of the June coup amounted to a wholesale counter-revolution. Many political figures of an inferior or middling social position who had been thrown into prominence by the politics of the clubs and the *wijk* assemblies, and who before 1795 could not have dreamt of any but the most menial office, survived the reaction. In The Hague, for example, one of the most disaffected cities of the Republic, a counter-purge in July removed the most notorious of the "ultras" like Johannes Velt the barber surgeon, Ary Spijkerman the notary and leader of the most radical club, and Baarne de Baas, a pastry cook (a profession which seems to have attracted more than its fair share of radicals). But others whose identification with democratic politics was only a nuance less enthusiastic but who hailed from a slightly superior social stratum—two of them silversmiths; one, van Ijsseldijk, had been in the council since 1795—retained their places.[22] Leiden was a good example of the new distribution of power. The July council there comprised four men restored from their deposition in the spring; three entirely new members; and six who remained from the radical council of January. Yet the impression that the initiative had been regained by the well-to-do and the moderate was reinforced by the fact that Johan van Leyden Gael—the Stadholderian burgemeester who, in 1795, had been compelled to deposit 20,000 florins in the city treasury as a security against the investigation of alleged malpractices—was now cleared of the charges and, demanding his money back, had the sum promptly restored to him.[23]

Similar evidence from all over the Republic bears out the radicals' contention that the effort to establish a political equipoise was getting in the way of a thorough unification. If the government was to be made "national" in Schimmelpenninck's sense of a reconciliation of all Patriot groups, it seemed that it could not be "national" in Gogel's meaning of a rigorous institutional unity. Moreover, quite aside from the taxing problem of allegiances, the sheer logistics of imposing central authority on the patchwork of parochial councils and committees demanded far more in the way of enforcement machinery than the very modest resources of the Directory could hope to supply. But if they were sometimes guilty of regarding the constitution as a kind of self-regulating machine, it had at least supplied one important new office as a monitor of both political and administrative difficulties: that of the departmental commissioner. Article CLV had provided for one commissioner and up to three assistants in the towns, to see "that the laws are properly executed." The commissioner was a far more significant innovation than that terse summary suggests. He was given the unenviable task of representing the authority of national government in the departments, much like the French *représentants en mission* or the imperial prefects. In the Dutch situation, his primary responsibility was to see that the local authorities did not assume any more power than that delegated to them by the national executive and legislature. But he was, in addition, meant to personify the omniscient justice of the "sovereign nation"—to act as a one-man court of appeal for any citizen finding fault with his municipal or departmental administration. More than any other institution it was the commissioners who came nearest to embodying realistically the true consequences of "One and Indivisible."

The men saddled with this awesome responsibility were by and large both capable and conscientious. Many had had experience in public service both in the Patriot period and even under the Restoration; most were professionals—lawyers, notaries, city secretaries and ex-fiscal officials. As difficulties arose in the execution of their duties, they were inevitably exposed to the accusation of divided loyalties; of over-acquiescence in local demands and interests. But without any very specific instructions from the Directory nor any effective policing power, they were bound to be caught up in the great quagmires of parochial social problems afflicting the provinces. From one perspective (though not that of the Directors or the agents), it was as much a measure of their success as their failure that they succeeded in identifying themselves with the more acute of those problems.

No other approach was possible. Their staff was rudimentary and miserably paid.[24] They were required to undertake lengthy perambulations through the department, which in the case of larger areas like the Oude Yssel and the Dommel exacerbated the already severe problem of efficient communications. Even in relatively quiet times, any communication with local authorities from their departmental office took at least a fortnight to a month for a reply. If that circular concerned a notoriously unpopular subject—the registration of militia or the declarations of gold- and silversmiths—they could be met very often with a blank wall of silence. For a sheriff or a bailiff in some remote corner of the Veluwe, his response on being confronted with yet another printed government circular was to ignore it, in the certain knowledge that it would never be followed up or that within a few months another would follow in precisely the opposite sense. Van Linden van der Heuvel, the able commissioner for the Schelde en Maas, complained:

... in some municipal administrations there still prevails a spirit of opposition to the present order of things, and that, as the examples of Middelburg and Zierikzee show, it is difficult for the old Sovereign [States] to be forgotten. Instead of complying with the orders of higher Constitutional authorities, every possible pretext is used to elude and evade them; indeed, I fear that there is no means that can be found to confront the aristocracy and bring it round to its proper sense of duty and that, finally, the decisions of even the highest authorities will be respected only so far as they meet with their private interests and the sensibilities of local authority.[25]

Blatant disobedience to "higher authority" was a special problem in Zeeland, where the regents of the principal towns, many of them unrepentant Orangists, had clung to power with greater tenacity than anywhere else in the Republic. Commissioner van Linden had his work cut out to induce them to answer his enquiries, let alone faithfully to implement government directives. There was very little, for example, to be done about the complaint of a pastry cook, one van Thienen, that he had been disbarred from practising his trade in Zierikzee despite a constitutional guarantee of the freedom to work anywhere within the Republic.[26] And when the commissioner approached the councils of Veere and Middelburg over the administration of the dykes and polders on Walcheren, he found that notwithstanding an order of the provisional representatives of Zeeland in 1796 abolishing the institution, a body of regents still calling itself the "Heeren Staaten van Walcheren" had preserved the "College of Dykgraves" and was administering it through hereditary officials as though the revolution had never happened. Indeed, as far as Zeeland was concerned, it hadn't.

Zeeland, it is true, was something of a special case. The Directory was understandably loath to press home its authority too aggressively (even supposing it had the means to do so) lest it provoke the regents into outright revolt and present the British with an opportune pretext for an invasion (a mistake the French were duly to commit ten years later). But there were other regions: the Ommeland in Groningen; the islands of Goeree and Overflakee in South Holland; the Veluwe and the Meijerij in Brabant, all of which seemed at least as resistant to the authority of the indivisible Republic as they had to Stadholder and States-General. The *continuity* of parochial and often ancient feuds which the commissioners were called on to arbitrate graphically illustrated how lightly the revolution had impinged on the remoter margins of Dutch society. It was slightly comic that the commissioner of the Delf should find himself having to adjudicate the complaint presented to him by the Dame of Katwijk for the full restitution of the 84 florins which she and the late Heer had enjoyed from the local citizens as their rightful "*Haring pond-geld*."[27] In the Rijn, the commissioner spent an unwonted time arbitrating between Utrecht and its erstwhile satellites of Montfoort and Amersfoort over dues and tolls formerly paid to the "hoofdstad." And in the countryside of the same region, the reduction of eighty "gerechten"—the old arrondissement jurisdictions—to a mere twenty-five provoked the bitterest recriminations from those villagers who felt they had been betrayed to their neighbours. At Veldhuizen (about eighty souls) the peasants complained that, although their village was of a greater extent, they were being sacrificed to the "oppression" of their neighbours at Reijerskop Sint Pieter.[28]

Sometimes fraternal citizens actually came to blows. In February 1800, the commissioner for the Dommel was obliged to intervene after a company of militia from den Bosch had run amok in Breda, having enjoyed themselves on the town. Initially, sinister motives were imputed to the instigators of the fracas; but after due investigation and a sharp reprimand to the officers of the company, the commissioner accepted that the brawl had been due to "local jealousies between the citizens of den Bosch and Breda."[29]

In very many of these cases the commissioner acted simply in the role of an additional local magistrate; a further court of appeal for plaintiffs with a case against local officials. But the acid test of his authority over these administrations was whether his power to appoint and dismiss could be made to stick. Once again there were political constraints. The proclamation of the Interim Directory had stated that all those seeking to be restored to the franchise and to exercise their full rights of citizenship had to be re-inscribed in the voting registers before the end of July 1798. Thus the rush to the town secretaries preceded the appointment of commissioners to vet political credentials by nearly six months. The painful history of the radical purges had in any case made the new regime wary of removing local officials once more unless there was incontrovertible evidence of their disaffection. When this was the case, the government did have the last word. Two bailiffs at Zeist and Cattenbroek in the Rijn and the mint-master at Harderwijk in the same department who had not been restored after the June coup had their final petition declined after investigation of their politics.[30] Hendrik Nobbe's election to the departmental administration of the Amstel was annulled from the opposite point of view. There were many more of the same kind.

Very often the posts presented for consideration by the commissioner were of the humblest kind. Now that the government had taken on the responsibility for pensioning predikants for at least three further years—and had assumed powers to organize the institution of national elementary education—its responsibility for approving public officials went all the way down from the agents to the merest sexton or constable. For thousands of predikants in straitened circumstances, living on pitiful stipends, the undertaking of the government to maintain their income was essential for their subsistence. On more than one occasion the commissioners found themselves glossing over legal niceties to save a man from destitution. In some cases they even responded to the more pathetic cries for help. One Arie "van Wadenoijen," for example, living near Buuren in Brabant, had been a typical victim of the unforeseen calamities of war. Teaching at Oirschot since 1766, he had made what turned out to be an ill-timed visit to relatives in Holland in the autumn of 1794. On his return he discovered that the theatre of war had advanced beyond his home town and that the British military authorities would not permit him to travel into enemy-held territory. During his enforced absence another man had taken his job, and as a result "van Wadenoijen" had been reduced to serious poverty. Some years later he had managed to obtain another post, but at a pittance of 50 guilders a year—about half the cost of keeping a pauper in the Amsterdam workhouse. His petition asked for a supplementary pension. After consideration by the commissioner and the Directory, this was eventually granted as an act of charity.[31]

The power to hire or fire was conditioned as much by financial as political contingencies. Theoretically, the constitution had empowered the central government (Directors and agents) to scrutinise every item of expenditure ordered by every public authority in the Republic and, where it saw fit, to insist on economies. It had been a declared aim of the Patriots to prune back the sinecures which had proliferated in local government during the eighteenth century. But where, in normal circumstances, such interference would have met with the most vigorous resistance, in 1798 the stringencies of economic contraction did much of the government's work for it. So far from commanding the reduction of local offices, it was very often difficult to persuade burgemeesters and councillors, trying to keep their heads above rising tides of debt, to remain at their posts. The vanishing of perquisites, the shrinkage of commission money from commercial offices (such as butter-weighing or fish-inspection) meant that in many cases the offices which had once been the object of unedifying traffic and competition now appeared more onerous than profitable. In 's Gravelduyn Cappel, for example, the burgemeester asked to be relieved of his post as soon as possible as he could no longer afford the expenses of the job. In the Oude Yssel, the commissioner Cramer wished to dismiss the council at Lemsterland for doubtful political allegiance during the 1799 invasion but could nowhere find willing replacements for the offices.[32]

At Tolbert and Lutke Gast in the Groningen Wester-Kwartier, the municipalities asked to be relieved of their duties forthwith and complained that they had only agreed, in July 1798, to act in a "provisional" capacity. They added that as they had received no payment of any kind since their appointment, they had been forced to subsidise the costs of their work from their own pockets and this had now become an intolerable burden. Before the revolution there had indeed been no local administration in the countryside, which had been governed from the city. Now that such authorities had been set up within the department of the Eems, no proper provision had been made for their finance. Like so much else in the Batavian Republic, they were expected to improvise.

It was not the least extraordinary feature of this period of the Republic's career that where under the old regime public office had been coveted as the means of consolidating or even making of a fortune, it now *required* wealth to be able to afford its burdens. This was indeed a revolutionary state of affairs but hardly one from which the executors of the constitution could derive much satisfaction. It was true that dependence on subsidies from departmental and national government dictated a greater degree of complaisance in acceding to a centralised structure of command, but such exigencies more often militated against than on behalf of the cause of reform. Instead of providing, for example, a new and simple system of local finance, approved by the commissioners and vetted by the agents, the Directory was obliged to authorise the resuscitation of ancient, often defunct forms of taxation so that local councils could continue to carry out the comprehensive tasks traditionally assumed in the Netherlands. Such authorisations, moreover, were often sustained over the objections of the committees of "delegated citizens" with whom councils were obliged by the constitution to consult before imposing any new taxes. Indeed, the Directory became besieged with such applications. In a single week in 1799, for example, it received requests from the *schout* of Oostcapelle in Walcheren for the imposition of a 2-stuiver tax on right of way over the causeway to West Capelle in order that it might be repaired and saved from imminent collapse; from the Poor Board of the Reformed Church in The Hague for the reimposition of a 4-stuiver duty on wine and spirits last used in 1763; and from the council of Nieuwcoop and Noorden that new taxes should be found so that a clock-tower could be set up in the middle of their village.[33]

Such trifles were not in themselves significant. Yet they formed the smallest units of debt in a pyramid of hardship and bankruptcy which stretched all the way up to the national government with its debt approaching the awesome figure of a milliard guilders. At the intermediary stage, the penury of the great city administrations of Holland bore sombre witness to a further stage in the destruction of the old Dutch commonwealth. During the year 1798–99 Rotterdam reported a deficit of 84,000 florins, Haarlem one of nearly 60,000 florins; and Middelburg, which from 1774 to 1793 had been running

an annual deficit of around 3,500 florins, had accumulated a debt of over
50,000 guilders.[34] In Friesland, relatively small towns such as Franeker and
Harlingen, which had suffered particularly severely from economic recession,
had no other recourse than to seek help from the departmental treasury to bail
them out. The provincial budget which in the 1780's had run at around 1.4
million florins was as a result virtually doubled by 1800.[35]

The urban treasuries were casualties of desperate circumstances. The
economic contraction caused by the war had vastly increased the numbers of
needy and destitute, but had also reduced the customary means by which
such obligations were financed. Funds for the poor and charitable establishments (whether administered by the municipalities themselves or by the
various church communities) and for the day-to-day work of local authorities
were supplied by interest on a variety of investments, rent from property,
private legacies and donations, and by the appropriation of special taxes earmarked for particular purposes. While interest payments on national stock
were very often in arrears, it was the last source of income which suffered worst
from economic contraction, for the "additional stuivers" were skimmed off
from duties imposed on a range of consumer articles. High prices and lower
real wages had led to a reduction in the turnover in many of those articles and,
with them, the loss in revenue for public authorities. Thus the embarrassment
of their finances was a direct consequence of the general economic dilapidation
of the Republic.[36]

Those communities whose livelihoods had been hardest hit by the war
were also those least capable of making ends meet in their domestic administration. Fishing ports were possibly the most serious casualty of all. The North
Holland fleets—from Enkhuizen, Monnikendam and the island of Urk, for
example—reported to the Agent for the National Economy, Johannes Goldberg, that they dared not venture into the North Sea to the herring shoals for
fear of being taken prize by the British patrols. As a result they were forced
to restrict their activities to fishing for eel and smelt within the Zuider Zee.[37]
But the situation was even worse at the mouths of the Waal, Lek and Maas in
South Holland. Deprived of their herring fishing, whole communities at
Middelharnis, Vlaardingen and Maassluis had been virtually economically
destroyed. In 1793–94 the *French* seized twenty-three boats from Maassluis
and twenty-four from Vlaardingen; since 1795, the British had taken twenty-
five from Maassluis and forty-one from Vlaardingen. In each port the fleets
had been reduced to about one-third and many of those boats lay idle. Of
the 230 households and 5,500 souls in Maassluis, *over half* were being
partially or wholly supported by public relief. In Vlaardingen, Ralph Fell
observed

the most distressing symptoms of impoverishment and decay. The harbour was
crowded with fishing vessels no longer employed and many of them unserviceable
through neglect or the absolute inability of their owners to keep them in repair . . .
the quay was covered in long grass and a melancholy assemblage of beggars
importuned us for relief wherever we walked.[38]

Further up the coast things were quite as bad. Katwijk was destitute and at Scheveningen, Fell met fishermen reduced to selling strings of sea-shells for the odd stuiver.

All that part of the Dutch economy which had gained its livelihood from the sea suffered terribly at the turn of the century. When he visited West Zaandam, Fell discovered that "not one vessel was in course of construction" and that "grass was growing in many of the spots where mighty fleets had been created." Of the seven great shipbuilding firms surviving into the 1780's, only one was left twenty years later. Of ninety saw-mills, all but five were out of action.[39] Subsidiary industries like the sail-making at Schoonhoven, rope-making at Oudewater and anchor-smithing at Purmerend had almost ceased to exist by 1800. Quite apart from the lack of custom for their goods, vital supplies of materials from Norway and the Baltic had been either interrupted or else so impeded as to make their prices prohibitive for the shipbuilders.

The war had created special difficulties elsewhere. The small-scale industries in Zeeland—soap-boiling and flax spinning, for example—had been cut off from their captive markets in Dutch Flanders by the cession of that territory in the Treaty of The Hague. Middelburg, which had acted as a receiving centre for Flemish grain and which had even exported modest cargoes, along with white beans, to Spain and Portugal, was marooned on Walcheren, bereft of market and supply. Its most active industry was the workhouse textile factory, subsidised to the tune of 4,000 guilders a year by the municipality.[40] Another area which had been an important, if subservient, adjunct to the Dutch economy proper had been (Belgian) Brabant. Incorporated into the French Republic, blessed with the newly flourishing entrepôt of Antwerp and protected by very high tariffs, Brabant was prevented both from receiving Dutch manufactures and exporting raw materials. This proved crippling for the survivors. Gouda was deprived of Ardennes clay for its pipe-makers (as of its German markets) and their number halved in five years. The brewing industry was no longer served by cheap Flemish hops, nor the distilleries by Brabant grain and coal for its boilers. Lack of fuel affected other major activities such as soap-boiling and sugar refining. For the ailing textile industries in Holland the scarcity and expense of raw wool and flax was the final blow, and in Leiden, Haarlem and Amersfoort they succumbed to British and Irish imports smuggled in considerable quantities.[41]

The British blockade was also responsible for interrupting important colonial supplies. Dutch industries needed sugar for the refineries of Amsterdam; cacao for its chocolate makers, indigo and dye-wood for the dyeing trade; cotton for the says and bombazeens traditionally exported east; and tea and coffee for domestic consumption. Such was the rise in their price that by 1803 they would more often import them via the smuggling boats of Zeeland and the Dutch islands, and from British vessels moored out at sea, rather than from the limited services provided by neutral carriers. In one important commodity, tobacco, the price rise in American leaf ensured for a while the eclipse of the industry before turning to the cruder produce of Sumatra and Brazil. The difficulty in obtaining Setubal salt and Spanish hides likewise damaged the refineries and tanneries which were basic to the economy of most of the major Holland towns.

Under these conditions it was impossible to manufacture products at competitive prices, and the difficulties which such industries had already been undergoing in the 1770's and 1780's were as a result greatly aggravated. Textiles made in Utrecht, Amersfoort and Nijmegen were all but pushed out by the cheaper goods from Elberfeld and Cleves; only the "Frankfurt ware" made in Arnhem from Winschoten clay was able to resist the onslaught of cheap and attractive Stoke pots. It was a hard moment when Wedgwood made its first appearance in the shops in Delft. There were of course some rays of hope amidst all this tenebrous gloom. The famous mechanised spinning factory at Eindhoven (using British machines) and Vreede's factory at Tilburg both managed just about to hold their own; and the twin ports of Delfzijl and Appingedam at the extreme north of the country continued to do a brisk trade not only with Hamburg and Bremen but with towns like Emden, Papenburg and Lingen down the Ems.[42] Agriculture profited from the difficulty of imports to raise the output of cattle, grain, and above all dairy produce, some of which was exported to France, Germany and (clandestinely) England. But the great mountains of butter and cheese displayed at the markets of Alkmaar and Edam each week were no compensation for the virtual obliteration of the trading and manufacturing economy of the Netherlands. Nor could it do much to stem the swelling tide of the poor.

In some cities that tide had already overflowed. On visiting Amsterdam in October 1800, Goldberg found that 80,000—or three-eighths of its population—were in receipt of relief. One institution alone, certainly not the biggest, the Nieuwezijds Outdoor Poor Almoners, provided support for 2,361 in the summer and 8,600 in the winter. To function adequately it estimated it needed a subsidy of over 120,000 florins.[43] In The Hague, the Poor Board of the Reformed Church had already run up a deficit of over 80,000 guilders. At Alkmaar, the figure was 50,000; at Dordrecht, 40,000.

Nor was the dereliction contained within Holland. In den Bosch and Helmond a third of the cities were on relief; and at Sneek and Franeker in Friesland, the expenditure of the poor commissioners amounted to over double their revenue. Indeed those who were the donors of one day could all too easily find themselves the needy of the next. The 1797 Christmas Collection at Delft produced just 11,000 of the 60,000 guilders needed to feed the quarter of the city that had been reduced to destitution.[44] As the numbers accumulated, the price of basic commodities required for subsistence—rye, buckwheat, peat—all rose sharply even though they were not in scarce supply. Many regents reported that traders would often refuse orders from the poor boards because of arrears owing or the likelihood of fetching better prices later on the open market.[45] One result of this reluctance was the commitment by the larger municipalities to buy bulk loads of grain as soon as the harvest was completed—thus adding to the burden of their own debt. For smaller authorities and poor establishments, such large-scale measures were impossible without substantial subsidies from the departmental and national treasuries.

Vlaardingen received 25,000 florins in this respect and Franeker a comparable sum a year later. Without that help, their charitable institutions would simply have ceased to function.

In the face of this crisis, the legislators of the Representative Assembly resumed the laborious efforts to devise a national system of poor relief. Concern at the growing dimensions of Dutch poverty had been a standard item of the Patriot critique, but the solutions it proposed sprang from evangelical and economic rather than purely political enthusiasms. Much of the discussion by learned societies like the "Oeconomische Tak" or the philanthropists of the Society for the Public Good revolved around the provision of "industry schools" or "poor factories" and the contingent separation of the aged and infirm from the able-bodied indigent. Those among the latter refusing the labour supplied by society could be classed as incorrigible beggars and treated with the contempt their indolence merited.

The seeds of this full-blooded utilitarianism had already been planted long before the revolution; a number of municipalities—Haarlem, Hoorn, Amsterdam, Enkhuizen—had established institutions where the needy were set to work spinning, carding or weaving, in return for subsistence wages per piece.[46] In Haarlem, the city and the "Oeconomische Tak" together supplied 1,500 poor with work in this fashion, and in Amsterdam the new Stadszijde Windhuis provided for 1,650. Not the least attractive aspect of such institutions to those who sponsored them was the feasibility of using cheap labour and the circumvention of guild restrictions to produce goods which might be sold at a competitive price on the home market. Often, a guaranteed contract would be arranged with a dyer and finisher in Leiden or Haarlem so that markets for the product could be determined in advance.

After 1795 such establishments spread throughout the Republic, usually with the assistance of interested local councils. At Grave in Brabant, for example, the municipality with the encouragement of Agent Goldberg established a poor factory for weaving bays, says and kerseys into hose. As elsewhere, most of the work was done, not in a closed institution but at home: 173 worked in this way and an additional 40 in a workhouse. Each worker was paid 5 stuivers for a pair of hose, a price which, after deductions for materials, gave the factory a profit of around 25 per cent! If the bulk of the labour was supplied by children the results could be even more gratifying to the public entrepreneur, although the worthies of the Society for the Public Good ensured that the children received a proper elementary education and decent subsistence in addition to their instruction in the "useful arts."

The fact that many such establishments appear to the modern social sensibility deeply exploitative needs to be set off against the real benefits they conferred on people who would otherwise simply have rotted in the traditional workhouses picking tow and oakum or have scraped along on periodic handouts of charity. It was the traditional notion of such philanthropy that the reformers were most concerned to refute. After the revolution they injected into their "economism" and evangelism a more combative form of egalitarianism. In his 1796 tract *The Poor: The Children of the State (Armen: Kinderen van de Staat*), the Remonstrant predikant Rogge, like contemporaries in France such as Fauchet and Grégoire, insisted that far from being an onerous burden of Christian obligations, society had a civil duty to supply work to the able-bodied and subsistence to the infirm, the orphaned and the aged. This concept of "welfare politics" was taken up by the more radical speakers in the National Assembly—Vreede, van Beijma, van Sonsbeek and van Hooff—and loosely formulated in the proposals of the Floh commission, appointed to investigate ways and means of establishing some kind of national administration.[47]

Because any uniform system presupposed a single nationally levied tax to finance it (as the writer Zillesen recomended), it inevitably came up against the opposition of those who were against any form of unitary finance, however admirable the object. But the 1798 constitution nevertheless embodied the innocuous principle (General Principle XLVII): "Concerned in all things for the welfare of all its members, Society undertakes to procure work for the industrious and support for the needy. The 'willing idle' may have no claim on it. Society demands the most scrupulous prohibition of all begging."

Predictably, it was left to a commission to tackle the thorny problems of finance. The principal exponent in the Representative Assembly of Rogge's social equality was another Remonstrant colleague, Boudwijn van Rees. In his view it was imperative that the state—the collectivity of citizens—should have a monopoly over assistance to the poor. He was convinced that the various church and private foundations in whose hands the overwhelming majority of poor funds were vested should relinquish them in favour of a national hierarchy of poor boards, responsible at their apex to the Executive Directory. Quite apart from the principle of non-denominationally distributed relief, it was an axiom of the unitarist approach that what was corporate, local and private was obnoxious to the dictates of reason and equality. It was also a crime against common sense. For since so many of those institutions, even the better endowed, were (as replies to circulars sent out in September 1798 revealed) in a condition of desperate deficit, they could hardly be left indefinitely to their own devices. As they were, in any case, in receipt of state subsidies, by what right did they continue to insist on the autonomy of their institutions, and the provision of relief to the poor of their community alone? Was it just that one community or one town should be better provided than the next merely because of the disparities in corporate wealth or the state of their past economies? Moreover, the more militant of the unitarists—not least the Remonstrant predikants—were convinced that those unsmiling paragons of the Reformed Church who as almoners, orphanage regents or poor-house deacons had decorated the canvases of Hals and Rembrandt, had, like the guild-brothers and the *schutterij* officers become the dross of a corrupted commonwealth.[48]

Such a wholesale onslaught on one of the most cherished and rightly renowned institutions of the Dutch establishment could hardly fail to meet with stern resistance, even in the reformist gatherings of the Representative

Assembly. Van Rees' opponents argued that while the principle of non-denominational relief was entirely acceptable in *public* institutions, the intent of the constitutional instruction to set up a national poor board had been to provide for those not already supported by existing (church and private) institutions. Under no circumstances could the state assume a monopoly of poor relief, nor could it contemplate the mandatory amalgamation of all funds established for that purpose into a single, nationally administered Poor Chest. Laying hands on the multitude of legacies, endowments, properties and bonds which past generations had allotted for the charity of their own church communities would, it was pointed out, be an attack on the principle of property itself, constitutionally protected. Nor could such an ambition be warranted by common sense. Both Schimmelpenninck in the National Assembly and de Vos van Steewijk in the Representative Assembly pointed to the French experience—where the liquidation, after 1790, of the church establishments for the poor had led to the rapid contraction in the funds available for their support—and held it up as a warning against emulation.[49]

The Representative Assembly, like the commission it had appointed to submit a report on the establishment of a national poor administration, remained paralysed by this irreconcilable difference of opinion. But its moderate *rapporteur*, the Lutheran Lublink de Jonge, a member of a well-to-do Amsterdam family, was in no haste to act impetuously. It is likely that he was influenced by the character of the replies to a circular sent to all poor administrations in the Republic in October 1798 enquiring first, in what manner they were financed, and secondly, whether they would be willing to relinquish any private funds in favour of a state-managed poor board. The vast majority of these replies gave a resounding and often indignant negative to the second question. Some, like the Reformed Poor Board at Breda (where the Catholic and Calvinist funds had been amalgamated in 1792 but repartitioned a little later) even refused to divulge the details of its finance, since "proper respect for the constituted powers does not preclude the protection of the rights and interests of this community."[50] Many others declared that however hard-pressed their finances, they were, and would continue to be, in a position to look after their own, and would never surrender them as "children of the state." The Poor Board of the district of Neder Betuwe in the department of the Rhijn, for example, insisted that

the property which, through their thrift and their orderly management, through their own gifts, legacies and [poor] collections, our fathers vested and indeed greatly appreciated can *never*, except under duress, be relinquished by us, for the reason that it has been intended for the needy members of our own parish community and not for all the poor, and that it is the legal property of our own community.[51]

This was the tone and substance of countless similar replies from Groningen to den Bosch. Only in the most hard-pressed towns, usually of middling or modest means, where economic crisis had already passed the point of no return, was there a more sympathetic response to the invitation to relieve them of their responsibilities. At Sneek and Hindeloopen in Friesland, for example, where the expenditure on the poor had run headlong beyond their means, or in semi-rural communities like Asperen and Apeldoorn in Gelderland where funds were scanty, or in Vlaardingen where they had totally disappeared, the parishes were only too happy to hand over their burden. There were, moreover, some special cases. In almost every town the Lutherans responded affirmatively for the simple reason that, as the poorest of all the church communities and devoid of any special funds for the poor, they had nothing to lose. In most cases, their poor (as occasionally with the Mennonites) were sustained by the crumbs off the relatively well-stocked Reformed Church's table. In Zeeland, the church communities usually administered and distributed the poor relief, but were so heavily dependent on subsidies and taxes provided by the municipal councils that they were already virtually public institutions.

There were a few notable instances of enlightened administration. One of the most impressive was at Deventer, where, since 1797, its amalgamated poor fund had been administered jointly by a combined board of Reformed, Roman, Mennonite, Remonstrant and Lutheran churches under the auspices of municipal officials, and funded by a three-weekly levy to which every citizen contributed according to his means.[52] But these were the exceptions. By and large the wholesale rejection of the invitation to part with a portion or the entirety of private and church funds in favour of the state, and the impossibility of contemplating their forcible expropriation, put an end to the ambition of the unitarist zealots.

The moderate complexion of the commission charged with drafting the final plan ensured that when in the spring of 1800 it came before the two chambers of the Assembly, it bore a very modest character. True, the hierarchy of the "General Poor Administration" was elaborate enough for any republican bureaucrat. At the base were "Under-boards," concerned to manage and inspect the operation of individual public establishments; at the intermediary level the eight departmental boards, to which they were responsible and which themselves approved monthly and annual accounts; and at the apex an "Upper Administration," responsible to the Directory and the Assembly for reporting on progress made to economise, reform and retrench the whole administration. But while the administration exercised direct control over all public institutions, it was quite clear that the churches and other private funds would continue to be managed by their own regents and deacons, and that at most only an indirect surveillance would be permitted to the public authorities.

The difficult problems of towns in which private and public institutions competed for the money of donors was sedulously evaded by the law, but it could be easily imagined which would have first call on limited funds. It was in this "binary" form that the law was finally passed on July 15, 1800. Since even the limited public administration presupposed a unitary government to lend it credibility (and money), with the re-federalising of the constitution in October 1801, it survived a mere year before succumbing to the general fate of the short-lived unitary state.

The fate of the General Poor Law graphically illustrated the scale of the problems confronting the would-be architects of a new Dutch state. In a memorandum on the virtues of governmental unification written some five years later, the erstwhile Agent for the National Economy, Goldberg, compared his own labour to that of a builder attempting to construct an entirely new edifice on top of old, ramshackle but enduring foundations. The resulting structure, he argued, would be unwieldy and unsafe. It was first necessary to rip out those old foundations and lay down the new.[53] Despite setbacks and disappointments there still remained those among the reformers who believed that the task of demolition at least was within their means.

Aside from the parish poor boards, there were few likelier targets for Goldberg's attention than the guilds. Developed as a natural accoutrement of the flourishing, highly competitive micro-economies of the Holland towns, they had latterly degenerated into useless social decorations and shells behind which outmoded craft industries sunk further into atrophy. So at any rate the Patriot economists like Wijnand Koopman, Zillesen and Jan van Heukelom—influenced by Turgot, and more particularly Campomanes, the Spanish advocate of economic liberalism—contended. With some justice they laid many of the ills troubling the Dutch economy firmly at the door of the guilds: the failure to evolve a truly national market; the artificial perpetuation of obsolescent modes of manufacture and production; and the inflation of labour costs, all of which made Dutch products uncompetitive not only abroad but even within the Netherlands. They looked enviously at cities like Liège and Namur where the old guilds had fallen victim to the progress of the factory system, and observed that in the few success stories of the eighteenth century—brewing and textiles in Brabant—guild regulations had either been drastically modified to the point where they were a mere formality or else abandoned altogether. They were, in the Patriot view, the instruments by which the general prosperity of the nation—and the inalienable right, as the constitution proclaimed, of a man to take his labour wheresoever it could find its best price—were ransomed for the maintenance of irrational privilege. Writers like Zillesen and politicians like Gogel and Goldberg were enough proto-liberals to believe that whatever offended their code of moral and political propriety, whatever in fact sinned against economic equality, condemned itself to inefficiency. Conversely what was just, *worked.*[54]

As in other areas where reform was embattled, heroism and villainy were less well defined than the protagonists imagined. Certainly there were conspicuous cases where the guilds had ceased to perform anything other than a negative and restrictive economic function and where they had become part and parcel of the array of local spoils. In Dordrecht, for example, the idiosyncratic institution of the "Goede Lieden van Achten" (the Council of Eight) and the "Goede Mannen van Veertigen" (the Assembly of Forty) had a direct say in the election of the principal municipal officers; and in some of the Gelderland towns—especially Zutphen, Arnhem and Harderwijk—they exercised an even more powerful influence. They had also strengthened the barriers protecting the towns from the produce of rural industries, which in many regions were *gaining* ground in the eighteenth century. Many of the keenest petitions supporting abolition originated from villages and small towns which had gone unrepresented in the States of Holland.[55] On the other hand, the periodic acuteness of industrial crises had often provoked towns like Leiden (in 1770) and Utrecht and Amsterdam (in 1796!) to petition the States—or the National Assembly—for the restitution of older and more rigorous regulations.[56]

Certainly the drive for competition seemed to play very little part in the guilds' reaction to economic malaise. Moreover the campaign for the restoration—not the destruction—of the guilds had played its part in mobilising the petty-burghers of the cities on the side of the Patriots in the 1780's. Like the militia officers, the new guild masters had a strong vested interest in protecting the institutions which through the deposition of regents in 1795 had so recently given them status. Thus in Utrecht in 1795, the new masters of the gold- and silversmiths carried on a running battle with the municipality for the protection of their guild, and in Zwolle the fraternities issued solemn warnings against the anarchy and immorality of the commercial law of the jungle. Finally, there was the complicating factor that the guilds performed a number of important social and philanthropic functions, which in a time of distress could hardly be removed without causing even greater hardships to their present beneficiaries—those who had paid subscriptions to and were now enjoying the fruits of funds for the aged, widows, the sick and in some cases the unemployed. In attacking the guilds, the reformers had to balance off their philosophical convictions against the imminent threat of political antipathy and social distress.

It was the pressure of economic reform rather than the much-recited "equality of labour" and the "right to work" which was responsible for the inclusion of a clause abolishing the guilds in the first constitutional draft of November 1796. Hahn, Vreede and van Hooff all spoke forcefully for abolition, and the usual procession of eloquent federalists—van Marle, Jordens, Queysen, de Mist—duly followed. The 1798 constitution showed some sensitivity to the social implications of any abolition by attempting (Articles LII, LIII) to distinguish between restrictions on labour mobility and the right of every citizen to a "civic certificate," entitling him to practise his trade, and the more delicate matters of quality controls and social philanthropy.

During the second spate of reform after 1805, this distinction was further clarified by preserving "professional and trade association" but opening them to all resident practitioners without exception and with nominal fee—and placing them under public rather than a corporative jurisdiction. But although Rant had discoursed on the details of abolition shortly after the January coup, it was left to the successor Directory to take the bold step of ordering the liquidation of the corporations within eight days from October 5. A proviso was added that municipal councils should report back to the Directory and Agencies within a month on the accomplishment of this measure and on any instances of blatant violation. It would have been more to the point to ask for reports of the rare cases where the instruction was actually complied with. Many local authorities simply refused to supply the information or indeed to enforce the edict. True to form, Middelburg responded by actually putting up the price of its civic certificates to 22 florins, and Utrecht invented a surrogate "warrant" which in all respects but title was identical to the guild certificates. Its butter-makers continued to complain about "foreign" cheese and butter-sellers hawking their wares on the city streets without a license.[57]

Some of the more indignant expostulations echoed the eighteenth-century commonplace that the Republic would be drained of its native skilled labour and in return flooded by inferior foreign workers. The position of the guilds remained very ambiguous. Officially liquidated by the order of October 5, 1798, there was nothing to prevent them continuing as purely private corporations instituted for the "good order" of trades and industries. To be sure, the Directory had ordered the surrender of property to its commissioners, but there was about as much chance of seeing this realised as there was of the appropriation of the goods of the local poor boards. Like the General Poor Law, the edict on the guilds remained largely a dead letter. As "private" institutions the guilds arrogated precisely the same powers that they had exercised before 1798, and most often they were supported by town councils which remained unconvinced that the best way to revive their invalid industries was by subjecting them to a large and bracing dose of free competition. Indeed, during the federalist years of 1801 to 1804 councils reverted openly to the status quo, licensing the practice of occupational "regulatory boards" and upholding the right of such corporations to exclude undesirable labour or goods from a town and to demand a sum for the privilege of practising a trade.[58]

Faced with the obdurate non-co-operation of most local authorities, the Batavian government was helpless to impose its will. Having eschewed the drastic medicine of the purges used by the first Directory, and without the assistance of any kind of armed enforcement, those who may have wished to see a centralisation of authority were obliged to fall back on local magistrates —many of them wholly unsympathetic to the 1798 constitution. By 1800 it was obvious that neither the Directory nor the two chambers of the legislature were prepared to demand submission to their sovereignty at any price. Indeed, the immediate dangers arising from the Anglo-Russian invasion in the summer of 1799 and the possibility of an Orangist uprising in the land provinces ruled out any policy which risked repeating the disastrous division within the Patriot camp that had taken place in the spring of 1798. The Republic was not so firmly established that it could risk the luxury of party warfare for the monopoly of its government. The alternative was the shifts and compromises which, piece by piece, manoeuvred the unitarists from power, and which ensured that their constitution went by default.

The primary reason for this failure to create a new Dutch commonwealth was not so much political bad faith as the absence of any machinery to see that legislation could be enforced where it mattered—in the provinces and municipalities. This could not be created overnight, and certainly the Directory was nervous of any sweeping change in the structure of local government. Too much was placed on the shoulders of the departmental commissioners, who by themselves were inadequate to the requirements of enforcement. This was not, after all, a malady peculiar to the Netherlands. The imposition of central control has been shown by recent research to have been far less thorough in France than was once supposed, and in empires like the Habsburg and Prussian states the war coincided with a reaction *away* from the centralising reforms of enlightened despotism. Even in smaller states than the Netherlands such as Switzerland—which shared with it a history of entrenched federalism—the experiment in unitary democracy was rapidly abandoned in favour of a modified version of the old union.

The ministerial impetus from the centre was less casual in the Batavian Republic than its historians have acknowledged. If the Directory—its members constantly shifting towards compromise and vacillation—made something of a speciality in selling the pass, its own Agencies constituted the nucleus of an authentic national government. The three years of their career was hardly long enough for them to prevail over the powerful forces of Dutch federalism and communal autonomy; but resurrected under Schimmelpenninck and Louis Bonaparte as state secretariats and ministries, they laid the foundations for the more formidable paternalism of King William's "United Netherlands." Unable to weld the parts of the Republic into the single bureaucratic entity of the unitarists' ideal, they nevertheless represented the reformed central administration which eighteenth-century Dutch statesmen from van Slingelandt to Bentinck and van de Spiegel had been urging.

The East Indies Committee (which functioned as a quasi-Agency), and those of War and the Marine, established the unified command which had been so conspicuously missing in earlier Dutch government and which was essential to the stringencies of national survival. But it was the more innovatory Agencies—those of Public Instruction and the National Economy, as well as the omniscient Agency of Finance—which acted as sources of reforming energy and expertise. All three drew on the fund of academic and speculative writing which had been encouraged from the 1770's by voluntary societies such as the "Oeconomische Tak" and the Society for the Public Good. Both transferred the enthusiasms of philanthropists, educationalists and amateur entrepreneurs from the voluntary into the public domain. Jan Kops, the able young man appointed by Goldberg to be his Commissioner for Agriculture, had been a teacher at Haarlem for the local branch of the Society for Public Good, as well as a subscriber to economic societies. J. H. van der Palm, the second Agent for National Education, had been a Patriot journalist of some fire and vehemence while also a preacher at Middelburg, and had edited a paper called *The Friend of the People* before taking the chair of Oriental Languages at Leiden and embarking on a public career.[59]

Throughout the rule of the Directory, the Agencies were kept short of money and staff. The personnel of the Agency for the National Economy, despite its manifold interests, never rose above thirty and on one occasion was reduced to a skeleton of seventeen. Its salaries cost the Republic around 60,000 guilders a year, but Goldberg wanted a generous budget with which to finance his research into the resources of the Netherlands. His estimate was around 400,000 florins; he never got more than 275,000, which in the straitened circumstances of the Republic was perhaps not an over-parsimonious allocation. Within these limitations the work carried out by the Agency was quite remarkable.[60] Its ambitious programme embodied the active social and economic policy which the first national government of the Republic, and the character of its constitution, had outlined. Its voluminous and energetic researches represented the first systematic attempt to measure statistically all the economic resources—agricultural, commercial and industrial—that were left to the nation.

The most successful of these was the survey of agriculture—acreage, crops, livestock and soil—which Jan Kops organised and carried out. Although many of the returns received from local authorities were often unreliable, his own perambulations, combined with first-hand inspection by subordinate staff, produced in 1801 a monumental document on the sector of the Dutch economy least affected by the critical conditions of the war. Goldberg himself, in search of reliable information on trade and industry, and wishing to evaluate the degree of hardship currently experienced by economic enterprises, went on a five-month tour of the Republic from June to October 1800. His journal of this trip lists the trades and industries remaining in each town he visited, together with brief data on each one's poor institutions and his own impressions, plus the recommendations of local entrepreneurs for the revival of their and the nation's fortunes.[61] However imperfect, it remains a comprehensive and essential document for the understanding of the economic and social history of the period. The Agency also began the compilation of essays, dissertations and projects, many of them originally commissioned by the "Oeconomische Tak," which together formed the nucleus of a state economic library. It took over the publication of the *Oeconomische Courant* and, very much conscious of the new economic world being opened up on the other side of the North Sea, put on displays of models of advanced machinery pioneered by the British.

At that time evidence of mechanisation in Dutch industry was exceedingly sparse. Aside from the celebrated spinning jennies in the factory at Eindhoven, which employed some 600 workers, and the odd mechanical loom at Utrecht and Hengelo, Dutch industry stuck obstinately to hand-spinning and weaving and the economies of the putting-out system. Although concentrations of capital were still available in the country at large, precious little of it was hazarded on industrial experiment, particularly at a time when the needs of state finance were becoming ever more voracious. But despite the bleak outlook—and misguided optimism which saw the Netherlands taking Britain's place as a major commercial partner of the United States—such was the confidence with which the agent and his staff endorsed the pursuit of this new science that they pressed for economics to become a standard feature on the curriculum of the secondary schools. More mundane matters also came within his competence: arbitrating inter-urban disputes over rights of passage and tolls, managing the "convooien en licenten" duties, encouraging improvements in transport, providing subsidies for new bridges or polders, and following up complaints about the adulteration of comestibles.

While this hardly added up to monolithic state intervention in the national economy, it was enough to make the few who were obliged to have dealings with it look on it as a nuisance interfering in affairs which were none of its business. The time when government dictated to commerce or finance where its best interest lay was, they assumed, a dark hour in the history of the Netherlands. Yet by nagging persistence; by establishing itself as an informal court of appeal in many economic matters; by giving the hitherto voluntary and learned work of organisations like the "Oeconomische Tak" a distinctly public dimension and granting official patronage to new and reforming enterprises, the Agency was paving the way for the energetic and often inspired economic paternalism of King William I.

But to function effectively, let alone to make any impact on the traditional suspicions of government officials, the Agencies depended on a supply of educated personnel—ex-teachers, predikants and local officials—who were fully and zealously committed to the cause of reform. Needless to say, such paragons were thin on the ground in the Batavian Republic. Only the Agency for National Education, for obvious reasons, was able to launch a comprehensive programme of reform of elementary education resting on these resources. Elsewhere the attempt to bring into being an embryonic national government remained very tentative. From every perspective, the Agency which was the *primus inter pares* and upon whose success or failure the rest depended was the Agency for Finance. Both Goldberg and his colleague Gogel appreciated that any reforming project was doomed to remain academic until the financial basis of a national bureaucracy had been properly secured. That, in turn, demanded the introduction of a national fiscal system in which revenue could be generated to accommodate the needs of a rationally budgeted domestic administration. The agents were caught in a circle of peculiar viciousness. The Republic "One and Indivisible" seemed condemned to languish as a paper entity without an effective bureaucracy to sustain its laws and its constitution—yet it required a unitary system of finance to bring that administration into being!

There could have been few men in the Netherlands more determined or better equipped to break that circle than Isaac Gogel. Unlike more intellectually glittering contemporaries like Valckenaer and Wiselius, Gogel had not been educated in the milieu of law and letters. His background and his apprenticeship, like that of Goldberg, had been served in the business world of Amsterdam. Not that he was a natural member of the banking aristocracy like van Staphorst and Abbema. He had been born at Vught in the Meijerij, the son of a German who had served in the Dutch army, and had worked his way up from a clerk's desk to establish his own partnership when he was just twenty-six. Throughout his life he retained the direct manners and clumsy bearing of the self-made man; but far more than either the plutocrats or the literary revolutionaries, he remained close to the problems and society of the small men of Dutch trade and business.[62] If in his bluntness and optimistic intelligence he recalls the aggressive enthusiasm of a seventeenth-century merchant venturer, the image is not accidental. His virtues were old-fashioned. He believed that the revolution and the Republic were providential opportunities to atone for the vices of the periwig time and restore to an ailing nation the moral strength and economic ebullience of the "Golden Century." But candour and integrity were not highly prized in the Europe of Bonaparte. Gogel's directness made him many political enemies, and it was his remarkable administrative ability and his inextinguishable perseverance in the midst of an impossible financial situation which made him almost indispensable for the rescue of the Dutch treasury.

From the time of his appointment as Agent of Finance to his resignation as King Louis' minister in 1809, Gogel was consumed by one overriding question: how to create that sufficiency of means without which the Dutch state would, in all likelihood, disappear beneath a quagmire of debt, but which at the same time would be least oppressive to the majority of Dutch citizens. The historian is tempted to conclude that he might just as well have gone to search for the philosopher's stone. But, as Louis remarked, Gogel had reserves of tenacity not given to most men. The problem did not appear to him as one of pure bureaucratic mechanics. As the preamble to his own draft law on general taxation in 1805 was to make clear, he himself thought of taxation as a means of redistributing income.

In 1798 his sights were altogether less elevated and his purpose constrained by all manner of pragmatic exigencies. It would have been ideal, for example, had the Agency been staffed by capable young clerks and economists, freshly recruited to government service, and untainted by the corrupt and rapacious manners of the tax farms and the Receivers-General. But that was scarcely possible. As in France, the new functionaries were in many instances identical with the old save for a new-fangled motto at the head of their notepaper. Even as unflinching a disciple of republican rectitude as Gogel himself was known on more than one occasion to overlook the rule-book where common charity demanded. He was prepared, for instance, to grant the office of Collector of the hearth tax at Utrecht to the brother of the incumbent's widow, one Burgher Schroot, so that neither brother nor aged lady should be in distress, even though such a grant was in violation of all his own regulations against nepotism. Nor did he have the heart to deny a pension (withheld by the law for serving in office between 1787 and 1795) to Anthonie Temminck, who at seventy-five had put forty-six years of service behind him as Extraordinary Clerk to the successive Fagels, Greffiers to the States-General.[63]

Despite these shortcomings the Agency of Finance was, in theory and practice, a distinctively different institution from its predecessors responsible to the States-General. For the first time in the history of the Republic, a single omnicompetent office was charged with the accounting and financing of every public function carried out in the name of the government, from servicing the national debt and funding the military estimates to paying the wages of the most obscure sexton in the backwoods of Friesland. It was, in other words, the first Dutch exchequer. Concealed in the terse "Instruction" given to the agent and his staff was a mountainous burden of business, which a small number of officials met with epic fortitude. The files of the Agency offer an extraordinary insight into the range and detail not only presented to his subordinates but landing on the desk of the agent for approval or decision.[64] In one week at the end of 1798, for example, besides working on the plan for general taxation to be presented to the Assembly by July 1799 at the latest, and simultaneously preparing proposals on the reform of currency and the establishment of a National Bank of Discount and Issue, Gogel dealt with the pensions of half a dozen retired functionaries and their wives or widows; the reports from departmental commissioners on the progress of the funding of the provincial debts; the arrears on predikants' stipends in Overijssel; export licenses for an Amsterdam shipper; the budget for the Old Age Home at Naaldwyk; details of the premium for the Vlaardingen Herring Fishery, and the fiscal deductions for the same municipality; and a claim by one Abraham Meinstma for an annuity on a loan, some ten years previous, to the Friesland Orange Regiment![65] Merely keeping the Republic afloat would have been— and was—too much for most men. But wading chest-high into this immense financial morass, Gogel managed somehow to keep his sights set firmly on the goal which he was convinced was indispensable to the unitary state: the system of general taxation.

Under Article CCX of the constitution, the Directory had been commissioned to present, within a year, a new general system of taxes to the Assembly for its consideration. This task was passed on directly to the agent who, although not exactly short of administrative duties, grasped the opportunity to formalise ideas which had been generated in the period between 1795 and 1797 when with van de Kasteele and others he had worked on the finances of Holland, and which he had set out in the pages of De Democraten. Something was urgently needed. Quite apart from the ravages of the war, the legacy of a century of complacent neglect and the tepid response by Dutch statesmen to van Slingelandt's summons in 1716 to put their counting house in order had finally caught up with the Dutch state. The account can be baldly if crudely summarised.[66] The ordinary revenue of the Republic at the end of the eighteenth century amounted on average to between 28 and 35 millions. Since the outbreak of the war in 1793, expenditure had been running at between 40 and 55 millions. The burden of the indemnity of 1795; the costs of maintaining a French force of 25,000 and of rebuilding a fleet *three* times (once in 1796 according to the stipulations of the Treaty of The Hague; once more after the disasters of Saldanha Bay and Camperdown; and yet again after the surrender of Story's fleet in the Texel in 1799) were all responsible for the expense account verging on astronomic levels.

For the year of 1800, the Republic was being asked to find 78 millions to meet its commitments. Normally the deficits had been met by recourse to ad hoc expedients: lotteries; "dons gratuits"; interest-bearing loans, first voluntary then forced; levies on property and income; "extraordinary" *penningen*. But from a steady stream under van de Spiegel, these impositions had begun to cascade and finally deluge the Republic by the turn of the century. In the closing months of 1798, *in addition* to the "regular" taxes, the citizens of the Batavian Republic were asked to contribute to a 4 per cent property tax (for rents over 800 florins), a levy on incomes raised progressively but averaging 5 per cent, and the instalment of the "twenty-five-year tax" falling due in November.[67]

No other nation in Europe, let alone one of a mere 1.8 million citizens, was made to suffer this plague of taxes. Even then, the agent correctly estimated that there would be a deficit on that year's account of nearly 20 millions. By 1800, the announced figure was 50 millions. The natural consequence of these expedients was that the national debt had ballooned to bursting point. The capital figure by 1800 was well over 600 millions (that of the old East India Company alone accounted for 118 millions) and the annual interest touched 25 millions. A few years later it had passed the feared 30-million mark, but even in 1799 there was a real anxiety that a situation would soon materialise whereby the ordinary revenue of the Republic would be insufficient to meet its obligations to the debt before it had begun to pay for either its military or its domestic commitments.

This crisis assumed a more than purely financial dimension. The obligation to honour the state's commitments to its creditors had been written into the constitution—indeed it had been the absolute condition of the amalgamation of the old provincial debts—and no-one was more keenly aware than Gogel that the capacity of the Republic to avoid complete collapse rested on the strength of its credit and the dependability of its services. It was an extraordinary irony that even as the Batavian Republic appeared to be sinking to prostration, foreign governments—Spain and a little later France—continued to seek loans in Amsterdam. But the agent was also aware that if his finger remained plugged fast at the hole of the dyke, without an entirely new system of fiscal defences, the day of total inundation could not be indefinitely postponed.

Gogel's immediate priority was to find ways and means of raising the ordinary revenue of the Republic to a figure approaching 50 millions, so that a foundation would be built from which a regular system of budgeting could at least be attempted. His assumption was that however onerous the obligations of the citizen to the Republic were, the state should be in a position to let him know the worst and assess the *limit* of his contribution. Without such accountability and regularity, and with the citizen exposed to the random threat of sudden and enforced taxes, there could be no hope of any kind of saving nor any real prospect of normal commercial exchange.

A secondary change dictated as much by social as economic considerations was the shifting of the fiscal weight from indirect to direct forms of taxation. The ratio had varied a good deal as between province and province, but in Holland between 1787 and 1794 it had been nearly two to one in favour of indirect taxes.[68] This was quite natural in a trading society, where the state could skim something off the volume of internal and external traffic as well as from a relatively high level of consumption. But as the economic pulse of the Republic beat feebler, so the public share of its wealth grew correspondingly smaller. A great deal of Patriot anger had been expended at the continuous style of patrician ostentation while more frugal burghers were forced to pay inflated prices for items of necessity. The Directory had in fact already assented to the abolition of duties on fish, butter, grits, oil, potatoes, candles and linen; but in the general system Gogel wanted to lower or remove altogether the taxes on a far wider range of primary goods, including fuels such as peat.

The quid pro quo for this change was the heavier emphasis on direct taxation. In Gogel's view, this had the advantage of fulfilling what he had set out in the preamble of the system to be its "fundamental principle"— that contributions should be in strict proportion to means. There were in fact a large number of direct taxes in existence in the various provinces, some of them progressively scaled. Gogel's aim was to standardise them into a national code and to sharpen the scaling. The incidence was increased on death and estate duties (*collateral*); on furnishings and moveables (*mobiliair*); and on "pleasure horses" and other sumptuary items. The stamp tax on commercial and legal transactions in usage in Holland was extended through the Republic and redesigned to correspond to the value of capital involved. All poll and capitation taxes were done away with.

But the central features of the system were the *personeel* tax on rental and some other forms of income, and the *verponding* on the ownership and tenure of property. The *verponding* was a generic term used for a wide variety of property taxes on land and buildings in the provinces, many of them of great antiquity, and all calculated on different bases. Gogel's nationally standardised tax was to be based on rent or rental value, from which deductions were to be made for trading or cultivating overheads or for any natural or other disasters.[69] His "rental value" concept owed a great deal to Adam Smith's definition of the "net product" of a property, but had in his view the twin merit of true progression in assessment and simplicity of administration.

The final consideration was that a system of nationally levied taxes would equalise the burden between departments which, towards the end of the century, had seemed to Hollanders to weigh excessively on their shoulders. Of the 30 or so millions produced by the old "Quota," 25 had been paid by 800,000 souls of that province, a proportion which might once have reflected a corresponding disparity in fortune but with the decline of so much urban wealth, it was argued, had long since ceased to be just. Thus the intention of the general system was to redistribute fiscal liability not only between the different parts of the Republic but between different social groups throughout. Indeed, to the objection of the land provinces that they were now the victims of a system which treated them as though they had the wealth of Hollanders, the unitarists retorted that it was only the rich landowners of those provinces who would suffer, for under the old regime it had been their peasants and townsmen who had borne the brunt of their provincial assessment.

These taxes were to be assessed, collected and audited by a bureaucracy reformed from top to bottom. Tax farming, which despite the general abolition in 1751 had crept back in a number of provinces, particularly Utrecht and Gelderland, was to be done away with. The sacred maxims of publicity, responsibility and accountability, were to be inscribed on the headstone of the new system. Gogel's hierarchy followed the outline of comparable unitary administrations proposed for the Poor Law and the National Education inspectorate. Departmental Receivers-General would be appointed by the Agency, to which they would be responsible. They in turn would supervise the work of a staff of collectors, assessors and auditors, each of whom would have clearly defined areas of responsibility and would be discharged at monthly intervals on the acceptance of a monthly statement of account for their respective districts. Separate from that staff was to be an additional hierarchy of inspectors-general, and inspectors, four or five to a department, responsible for the monitoring of abuses, for recommending culprits, if necessary, to a special tribunal established to deal with fiscal misdemeanours, and for supplying a stream of information and ideas on improving methods of assessment or collection and economising on the costs of the bureaucracy. By such regularity, it was hoped, the national finances could be sufficiently ordered for the executive to estimate with a fair degree of reliability the revenue on which it could depend for the future quinquennium and to adjust its expenditure and policy accordingly. It was not beyond Gogel's wildest dreams that the Republic might some day be in a position to begin the amortisation of the debt![70]

Such was the imposing edifice of the system presented to the Representative Assembly on June 30, 1799. But that body of sober and conservative burghers was a good deal less impressionable than the historian, and it reacted to a wholesale onslaught on the traditional fiscal habits of the nation with apprehensive suspicion. Even though the provincial debts had been amalgamated and financial unity written into the constitution, the departmental commissions of finance had prolonged the separate identity of the old provinces. And so long as there was no new general system, the Assembly had decreed that the old taxes should remain in existence. Thus there was much to be gained from the federalist point of view in resisting the general system to the last, and Queysen and de Mist, both back in the legislature, did their utmost to condemn it to a stillbirth. They received support from a number of Hollanders anxious about the effects of swingeing property and revenue taxes and especially resentful of the stamp tax on their commerce and banking.

The First Chamber of the Assembly proved so hostile to the plan that it commissioned the Zeeland financier Appelius to draft a counter-project, eradicating the more controversial items. Appelius in fact incorporated a great number of Gogel's proposals. But he amended the means of assessment of the *verponding* so as to be more lenient to larger proprietors and to lighten the incidence on urban buildings. The stamp duty virtually went by the board, though sumptuary taxes were in some respects actually increased.[71] The overall character of the Appelius plan was more moderate and less doctrinaire than Gogel's; as such it received a cordial reception in the First Chamber in July 1800. Here, however, the waywardness of the constitution intervened to bring about an almost complete paralysis. For the Second Chamber, to whom the Appelius plan had been sent for debate, on October 30, threw it out and re-adopted Gogel's original scheme. The procedure which followed meant that, on a second vote, Gogel's plan was finally adopted on March 25, 1801, by twenty-two votes to seven.

The laboriousness of the process by which Gogel's plan had finally prevailed cost it dear. For during the last year of its consideration, the premises on which its administration had been based—that of a unitary government—had been undermined from within. By the time that the plan was ready to go into operation in the spring of 1801, the Directory was preparing a constitutional revision which, if accepted, would mean the re-federalising of the government of the Republic, the end of the Executive of Five and of the Agencies, and the dissolution of the precariously sustained unitary sovereignty. In fact, it was another five years before Gogel saw the realisation of his plans, under the aegis first of Schimmelpenninck and then the equally unlikely figure of Louis Bonaparte. In May 1802, the last surviving remnant of his reforms—the plan for a National Bank—was finally discarded by the hostile and vestigial "Legislative Corps."[72]

The thwarting of Gogel's financial reforms was merely the finishing touch to an unhappy succession of legislative failures for the reformers. Despite the enthusiasm of the agents and the zeal of the radical press, the political restrictions imposed by the circumstances in which the regime had been inaugurated militated against their chances of success. It is quite clear from the reports of the departmental commissioners (who were in the best position to know) that the unitary Republic was still very far from the image of sovereignty and uniformity reflected in the constitution. All that had been achieved was the superimposition of a number of resourceful and energetic executive agencies over a patchwork of ancient and tenacious jurisdictions, corporate, municipal and provincial. As long as the latter were required to do little more than pay lip service to the redundant shibboleth of "One and Indivisible" and swear their oath of hatred against the House of Orange, their resistance to the axioms of unitarism was passive. But when some cherished institution—the guilds or the parish poor boards—came under serious challenge, they were capable of raising such a storm of protest that the Directors and legislators were unable or unwilling to press on with the reform.

The campaigns of opposition raised for the reformers the awkward issue of the *popularity* of their projects. Zealots like Gogel were in no doubt whatever that their reforms had been foiled by the machinations of selfish and reactionary cliques, but without adopting the brusque tactics of Fijnje, were at a loss to know how to prevent such men from using the political system to exercise influence and power. Indeed, the rough handling which the general system received at the hands of the Representative Assembly marked the beginning of Gogel's disenchantment with representative democracy. Philosophically he remained as ever a democrat, but in practice he acknowledged reluctantly that there were situations in which elected bodies could be more of an impediment than an aid to the cause of national regeneration.[73] Henceforth the causes of democracy and reform, which until 1801 had been joined at the hip in the slogans of the indivisible Republic, were to go their own way.

The Anglo-Russian Expedition: 1799[74]

Even had the Representative Assembly adopted the style of a patriotic Convention, there seems little likelihood that it would have been granted the luxury of seeing its reforms in action. While the importation of the war on to Dutch soil did something to fortify the waning republicanism of the nation, it also subordinated any long-term ambitions to the immediate business of survival. In Jacobin France, the sheaves of reforms produced by the National Convention and its committees, indeed the constitution itself, were put in abeyance while the country remained on the defensive; but the effects of a comparable situation in the Batavian Republic in 1799 were completely paralytic. Although historians are prone to view the disruption of war as a catalyst of change, the exceptional conditions which it stimulates are not necessarily conducive to the cause of institutional reform. Emergencies produce tyrannies more often than constitutions, and war may act as much as a dissolvent of public authority as the reverse. Those living in its immediate theatre—as in Toulon in 1793 or Hoorn in 1799—were left to fend very much for themselves and to protect themselves by nice judgements of interest and tactic. Above all, an invasion brought into question the staying power of the revolution, of the Republic itself, without which there could be not the remotest chance of controversial measures finding a degree of popular assent. Johannes Goldberg, who more than most desired to see the consolidation of a new state, admitted in October 1799 that

. . . the critical times in which we have lived to see the landing of the enemy and the arrival of the theatre of war on the soil of the Fatherland have in no way made it propitious for the extension of my ministerial functions nor for the introduction of so many worthy and valuable projects which it was the intention of my office to sponsor.[75]

The sheer costs of defence vitiated any thought of undertaking expensive domestic experiments. In the estimates for 1800, no less than 31 millions were appropriated for the army and navy and 9 millions for the whole of domestic administration. Even before the invasion, the commitment to maintain 25,000 French troops was costing the Dutch in the region of 10–12 million guilders a year.[76] The reluctance with which this was supplied was compounded by the notorious knowledge that, at the end of 1798, for example, there were hardly more than 10,000 French troops actually stationed in the Republic. The Directors in Paris, when challenged with this negligence of their treaty obligations, had not blushed to argue that the money had been intended for 25,000 French soldiers wherever they should be stationed, and that the defence of Zurich or the capture of Naples contributed, by crushing the Coalition, as much to the defence of the Netherlands as if the armies were kept on its own territory.

However iniquitous the burden of the alliance with France, the sudden emergency of the spring and summer of 1799 put the Batavian Republic in no position to haggle over the price of its survival. Following the murder of the French emissaries at Rastätt—one of whom was Roberjot, originally destined for the Batavian Republic—the armies of the Second Coalition had succeeded in pushing back the French along a broad front. In southern Germany Jourdan failed to press home an offensive against the Austrians and link up with Masséna in Switzerland. Despite some success at the first Battle of Zurich, Masséna was eventually forced to evacuate the Grisons, leaving the veteran Russian General Suvorov to take Milan at the end of May. After defeating Joubert at the Battle of Novi (the French general was killed at the outset), Suvorov went on to recapture the whole of Piedmont for the Coalition. In the south Macdonald, in his turn, cut off from reinforcement from the north by the Austrians and Russians, was forced to evacuate his armies from Calabria—leaving the "Parthenopean" and Roman Republics to the none too tender mercies of Queen Caroline of Naples and Horatio Nelson.

By midsummer 1799, the momentum of the advance had decelerated. But the British in particular, suspicious of Austria's vacillation, were anxious to press home their advantage by attacks on Switzerland and the Low Countries. Grenville, by this time a passionate counter-revolutionary, envisioned a fierce and co-ordinated assault on the French imperium, "from the Col de Tende to the mouth of the Scheldt!" Switzerland and the Netherlands he considered the weak links in the French chain of dependent alliances which, once mastered, would open the way for a descent through the Franche-Comté and Belgium into the heart of France itself. Supported by Pitt, Grenville found that Dundas, the other Secretary of State, and William Windham, the Secretary for War, were both highly sceptical of his "grand design." They were only silenced (if not much reassured) by the information that a combined campaign against the Batavian Republic had been a condition of the agreement with the Russians the previous December and that, following a landing, a general Dutch insurrection was bound to follow.[77]

In that agreement signed with Admiral Popham, Paul I, who added to his mother's detestation of revolutionary France an exotic pathology that was all his own, had placed 45,000 Russian troops at the disposal of the Coalition. In the event, just 17,500 were available in June 1799 for the Dutch expedition. The British were to supply 13,000 troops, a powerful fleet, a subsidy of £88,000 and an engagement for £40,000 a month for a campaign which as a bridge-head operation was not expected to be very protracted.

From the outset, much to Dundas' disgust, the invasion was not planned as a purely military operation. Grenville had been much gratified by signs of counter-revolutionary enthusiasm all over French-dominated Europe. The Belgian "Peasants' War" in the autumn of 1798; the "Viva Maria" riots in northern Italy; the rebellion of the Sanfedisti in Calabria; and the uprising of the Swiss cantons had revealed a reassuring immunity on the part of the populace of some regions to the revolutionary virus. Moreover, the Swiss and Italian rebellions had been of real assistance to the military effort in those theatres of operation and Grenville assumed that, given the opportunity, the Dutch would do likewise. Once the Orange standard had been raised, he seems to have believed that the Batavian army would go over to the forces of the Coalition to the last man and that its Republic would collapse under the barest pressure.

The intelligence on which his assumptions were based was not the most reliable. Agents like Jan Munniks had an unfortunate tendency to confuse genuine hatred of the French and murmured dissatisfaction with the Directory with a craving for the restoration of the House of Orange. In October 1798, Munniks believed the Dutch to be impatient for such a change and wrote that "the counter-revolution in the Batavian Republic will encounter not the least difficulty."[78] At the end of August, when the invasion fleet was approaching North Holland, he continued to believe that an Orangist volunteer army could be conjured up from the major Dutch cities. Despite this confidence, he had attempted to persuade the British government that a covert approach to the Directors would find an interested response, and that the defection of the Batavian government and its replacement with a reformed Stadholderate was to be preferred to a frontal military assault. But by June when the matter was raised, Grenville was not interested in anything less than a repetition of 1787. Charles Bentinck, who had made a secret reconnaissance trip to the Republic, had swept aside all ifs and buts with a report which indicated that the country was seething with barely suppressed insurrection.[79] He believed that a show of force would ensure—not deter—the defection or capitulation of the Batavian Directors, along with Daendels and the whole of the Dutch army.

The reported weakness of the defending forces confirmed Grenville in his desire to go through with the invasion. On paper there were supposed to be between 20,000 and 25,000 Dutch regulars; 30,000 Dutch National Guard and something like 16,000 French troops. But Bosset, the agent of the smaller German states in The Hague, suggested (wrongly) that the reality was far less impressive.[80] It was common knowledge that the French had dishonoured their treaty obligations; that they were loath to take troops from the Belgian departments to defend their ally; their aggregate at the start of hostilities was perhaps not more than 10,000. The mobilisation of the Batavian National Guard, it was said, had been a fiasco and young men had actually fled their villages rather than be enrolled in the militia. The regular Dutch troops, it was well known, would never fire on the Orange flag.

If this contempt was exaggerated, the verdict on the Dutch chances of survival was not the monopoly of one side. General Brune, the commander-in-chief, was himself none too confident. His way had been made smooth by the brief but invaluable embassy of Joseph Fouché, who had persuaded the Batavian Directory to permit him direct command over the Dutch as well as French army; and it had been Fouché, too, who had given enthusiastic reports to the Directory in Paris on both the resolution and the preparedness of the defenders. Brune was much less impressionable. At thirty-six, as a pupil of Masséna, he was a hardened veteran of the Italian campaigns. In addition, he was a republican of unfashionably Jacobin prejudices, who regarded republican austerity (which did not, however, extend to declining back-handers) as interdependent with military competence. He found neither in the Batavian Republic. The Directory seemed unshakeably complacent about the immediacy of the danger. Gerrit Pijman, the Batavian Agent for War, on hearing of the preparations being made in Britain, replied that he had heard such stories at frequent intervals and that "when the heavens fall to the earth, then shall we have an invasion."[81] The shore batteries at the Helder and on Walcheren were pitifully under-manned and the Dutch author-ities seemed to him to be going out of their way to frustrate any attempts to improve their defences. When he tried to inspect arsenals and magazines in North Holland and Friesland, he was told that even the Stadholder would not have dared to make such a request without first seeking the authority of the States-General. "They must have 'authorisations' for everything and—so—delays for everything," he grumbled.[82] Nor were his own superiors any more helpful. In response to his indignant demands that France honour her treaty obligations—and at the least supplement her forces to a level of 17,000—the Minister for War, Bernadotte, showed the greatest reluctance to transfer any reinforcements from the Belgian departments.

When the invasion had come and gone, all the principals claimed great clairvoyance in anticipating both its strength and strategic direction. Daen-dels' biographer and Pijman in his memoirs both assert that the General and the agent predicted a landing in North Holland would be made and both advised the concentration of defending forces in that quarter.[83] If this was the case, then the certitude of the defenders exceeded that of their enemies. For not until the very last moment did General Abercromby decide to risk an engagement with the Dutch navy by making for the Helder. His original strategy had been to bifurcate the attack north in Groningen and Friesland (with, it was hoped, the assistance of Prussian intervention) and south at the mouth of the Scheldt and Maas. What seems to have decided him in favour of an attack on North Holland was belated intelligence that the Texel fleet was seriously under strength and that at least two of its captains, van Braam and van Capellen, were ready to lead a general mutiny on sight of the Orange ensign.[84]

In addition, there was the strong temptation of a comparatively short march on Amsterdam once the North Holland peninsula was taken. Brune seems to have been concerned to guard against all possibilities. The Franco-Batavian army was divided into four forces. General Desjardins held 8,000 men in Brabant covering the south; General Reubell (a brother of the Director) had a further five thousand French in Zeeland and the south Holland islands; Daendels commanded the first Batavian division in north Holland, and Dumonceau the second (6,000 men) in Groningen and Friesland. Brune himself kept a small reserve force under Gouvion near Utrecht both as a watch on a seaward attack and the possibility of any uprising in the interior. In view of the strategic imponderables, this dissipation of an already weak defending army was comprehensible but brought disastrous results. When Mitchell's fleet hove into view on August 19 off the Helder, Daendels had fewer than 9,000 men with which to face a landing force of around 12,000 and a fleet of 24 heavily armed vessels.

On the 27th, with Admiral Story's puny fleet retreating into the Zuider Zee, the invasion army was disembarked at Keeten, between Callantsoog and den Helder. Though belatedly attacked by Daendels' troops the British division consolidated its beach-head, inflicting heavy casualties on the Dutch with fierce fusillades of musket fire. The very fact of the landing had made the batteries at den Helder virtually useless. The forts could no doubt have held out for a while, but Daendels took the grim decision to evacuate the 3,000 men so as to avoid their encirclement.

The abandonment of den Helder was perhaps justifiable on strategic grounds; but from point of view of morale, already rather jittery, it was a disaster. The sight of Orange pennants waving from the Helder forts did nothing to cheer the Batavian ships in the Zuider Zee. Both the Batavian Directory and the French agent Florent Guiot later concluded that Daendels had either gone off his head or was in the process of committing treason. Brune, who got on well with the General, was inclined to take a more charitable view. Yet he too saw that the evacuation had given the British the chance to dig in at the north of the peninsula and establish strong lines at the Zijpe while awaiting reinforcement from the Russian divisions. With their disembarcation points protected, there was nothing to prevent this combined army from establishing an overwhelming numerical superiority.

However bad this looked for the Dutch, worse was yet to follow. With a flotilla that comprised just eight ships-of-the-line, three frigates and a corvette, Story had been unable to risk an engagement with a British fleet about twice its size, and had retired to the Vlieter to guard the entrance to Amsterdam. Mitchell's ships entered the Marsdiep on August 29. At that point the admiral decided to test the reports of universal disaffection among the enemy. Hoisting the Orange flag, he "invited" the Dutch navy to return forthwith to its rightful allegiance. Story declined the offer but sent one of his least reliable officers, van Capellen, to parley with Mitchell, offering to "stand off" from hostilities pending a decision from the Directory at The Hague. As this initiative was in its turn rejected, there was nothing for it but to give the orders for combat, at which point mutiny duly broke out on most of the leading ships-of-the-line including his own. On the *Washington*, all except the officers and a few of the crew seized the bridge and spiked their guns. On the *Hoezee*, ammunition was thrown in the water. Only, appropriately enough, on the *Batavïer*—commanded by a young officer, van Senden—

did the ship, with just 50 guns and 300 men, prepare for action in good order.

Faced with this catastrophe Story had no option but to surrender his fleet, his 632 guns and 3,690 men to Mitchell, lowering the Batavian tricolour but refusing to have the Orange flag hoisted in its place. This was done for him by mutinous crews, who went on to celebrate their treason by roughing up loyal officers and throwing one from the *Embuscade* to death by drowning. Later the Hereditary Prince of Orange went aboard the *Washington*, Story's flagship, where he received the huzzas of the sailors, and proceeded to ask Mitchell to let the captured fleet serve alongside the British. Mitchell, however, was less than confident about the qualities of the crews who were for the greater part composed of various non-Dutch nationals—itself a bleak comment on the state of that nation's maritime power. Instead they were ordered to Texel Island, where the ships were provisioned by the British until they could be refitted in Britain as part of the Royal Navy.[85]

The disaster of the fleet's capitulation was the first (and in fact the worst) verification of the prediction that the armed forces of the Batavian Republic would shrink from defending a state to which they had ceased to give their allegiance. Even the resistance of the soldiers to the landing had shown they were willing to take heavy fire. If anything, the effect of the invasion was, as Munniks had begun to fear, to unify the divided Republic and to set aside the bitter domestic quarrels while the Fatherland was threatened by the invader. If the Dutch had no love for the French, the memory of British hegemony was no more appealing; those who were politically neutral remembered the miseries of 1787 and 1794 with sufficient vividness to have no illusions about the kind of restoration that awaited them. Although Dundas had urged the Prince to make some concessions to reform and to couch his proclamation in conciliatory language, the arrogance of its tone and its "command" to Dutch subjects to rally to Orange suggested that the House had learned nothing and forgotten nothing from its exile. The only member who had shown qualities of open-mindedness and liberality, Prince Frederik, had been killed in action in Germany the year before. Neither Grenville nor Pitt would settle for less than a full-blooded restoration; and William V, besieged by reform projects of all kinds from well-meaning supporters of the Orange cause, affirmed that he "did not want to be a doge of Holland." "I know," he insisted, "all the faults of the old regime, but I know of no other constitution which I believe better suited to the spirit of the nation."[86]

In these circumstances it was not surprising that the call for a national uprising, made by the Prince from Lingen, beyond the borders of Overijssel, should have met with indifference in just those areas where most support might have been expected. Minor affrays at Deventer and Nijmegen were put down with a few companies of militia and the major débacle occurred on September 4. A motley band of a few hundred Orangist émigrés—armed with sabres, a few muskets, pistols and hunting guns—were put to flight on the Westervoortsche Bridge at the south-eastern approach to Arnhem by a small detachment of the local national guard. A handful of militiamen were killed and a few more wounded as the invading army was taken prisoner along with its improvised banners and weapons.[87] The Batavian militia was, to everyone's amazement, proving a far more useful reinforcement than had been anticipated even by their most loyal officers. On the day that Daendels abandoned the Helder, 500 guardsmen marched out of The Hague (not noted for its patriotic zeal) to join the army in the north. By the end of August companies from Leiden, Haarlem, Amsterdam, Delft, Rotterdam, Zwolle, Campen and Franeker were all serving alongside troops of the line, and Utrecht honoured the tradition of its Free Corps by sending 4,000 fully equipped National Guard to serve under Brune. The commander-in-chief, who in some desperation had originally asked Pijman to order every commune in the Republic to conscript five men, was so satisfied with the number of volunteers that he withdrew the request at the beginning of September.

The nadir of Dutch fortunes was reached on September 10 when Brune, who had assumed command of the central sector, decided to attack the British lines before they had a chance to join with the newly disembarked Russian reinforcements. At this point the two forces were of roughly equal strength: 9,000 Dutch and 6,000 French troops opposing Abercromby's army of 17,000. The Franco-Batavian line was concentrated before Alkmaar, which Brune had ordered defended to the last. But the day went wretchedly. After initial success in forcing the British back at Krabbendam, resistance broke on Daendels' right flank when the counter-attack was pressed home. A panicky rout ensued, with companies of cavalry retreating past Alkmaar as far as Haarlem and Amsterdam, spreading alarm and confusion as they went. Brune's wrath knew no bounds. A mere 500 Frenchmen could have withstood the assault which had broken 2,000 miserable Dutchmen, he complained. The situation was indeed dire. Hoorn, Enkhuizen and now Alkmaar had fallen to the British advance. They were masters of the Zuider Zee and their own lines at Zijpe seemed impregnable. Amsterdam itself was vulnerable, though Brune had taken the drastic but obviously warranted precaution of flooding the dykes at Beemster and Schermer and was pinning his hopes on Bernadotte's promise of 15,000 fresh reinforcements. The French Minister for War was in fact more dilatory than ever so that it was just as well that Brune's naturally aggressive instincts got the better of him.

On September 19 the Duke of York (whose appointment as commander-in-chief of the Allies had been greeted by the Dutch as the one ray of hope in an otherwise murky outlook) decided to exploit the advantage of numerical strength and apply the blow which would open the way to Amsterdam. But with the addition of Dumonceau's division transferred from Groningen, the Batavian army was itself ready to make a real show of resistance. At the battle before Bergen, the Dutch National Guard and Daendels' division not only managed to hold the Russians' offensive but pushed them back towards Koedijk. It was Dumonceau's section which, thrown in on the left by Brune, cut off the Russian retreat and turned the whole of the Allied line. Two thousand of their army were killed, 1,500 taken prisoner (including the Russian General Hermann) and 800 wounded. Over twenty pieces of cannon were taken triumphantly by national guardsmen from Delft and Rotterdam, who sent back

Russian colours to their city halls where they were laid out for inspection at the Stadhuis. The Russian prisoners, who had been led to believe that they would all be guillotined, received a little rough treatment from the crowds at Haarlem but were treated with generosity by their captors. Hermann himself, who shared Brune's table and was then moved to a comfortable billet in Amsterdam, responded by throwing the blame for the defeat on the British and making it clear that something less than perfect harmony reigned between the two Allies.

The Battle of Bergen was the turning point of the campaign. Despite the continuing superiority of Anglo-Russian numbers it was obvious, even to the Duke of York, that the army could proceed no further without a second major engagement. The September rains were slowing down progress, and the peasants and townsmen of North Holland had proved less welcoming than had been anticipated. The usual rough treatment had had to be applied to villages reluctant to yield requisitions. Abercromby ruefully acknowledged: "I really imagine the Hereditary Prince has been deceived in thinking he had more friends than enemies in this country. If we can advance, everyone will be on our side, but there are few who are willing to risk anything."[88] A final effort was made on October 2, when Pulteney and Abercromby succeeded in moving down the coast as far as Egmond aan Zee. Brune, who had lost some men in a poorly organised attempt to impede the advance, took up his position before Castricum (south of Alkmaar) where his and Dumonceau's divisions were joined, with Daendels' blocking the way to Amsterdam, south of Purmerend.

The battle on the 6th was decisive. Brune himself entered the pantheon of the immortals by charging the British lines at the head of his cavalry, two horses shot from under him. Five thousand were killed or wounded. In a rapid counter-advance Alkmaar, Hoorn and Medemblik were re-taken, and by the 9th the Allies had retreated back to the safety of the lines at the Zijpe. It was obvious to Abercromby, who unlike the Duke of York and Grenville had remained realistic throughout, that the expedition was lost. Its supply lines from the coast had been cut; continuous rain had made any military movement almost impossible; and fever and exhaustion had completed what Bergen and Castricum had begun. The naval advantage had proved less of an asset than had been anticipated. No attempt had been made to land troops in the centre of Holland where they might have made some serious impact. The only person to have felt the presence of a stray British frigate which appeared without warning off Scheveningen was the Swedish ambassador, whose constitutional promenade on the beach was interrupted when a burst of shot knocked the hat from his head and alarmed his dog.[89] Brune was able to sit back and wait for the inevitable negotiations, which duly commenced (some said with indecent haste) on October 14. The capitulation signed on the 18th provided for an unmolested evacuation before the end of October and the return of Dutch prisoners—though not the fleet!

After a calamitous beginning, the Batavian Republic had survived its trial by fire. Needless to say, the victory was celebrated in Paris as an exclusively

French triumph which had come about in spite of, rather than with help from, their Dutch ally. Yet throughout the campaign Dutch soldiers had made up over half of the defending troops. On more than one occasion Brune had complimented them for their courage and prowess, even if at other moments he had unleashed abuse worthy of a native of the Corrèze. More significantly, the republican order had stood its test reasonably well. The insurrection promised by the Prince to Grenville and the British Cabinet had utterly failed to ignite. In those towns caught between the cross-fire of the two armies, there had been men who had exploited the situation to their own advantage and taken office under protection from the British. At Hoorn the populace had wanted to fly the Orange flag from the Stadhuis, but unable to find one, had to make do with the somewhat confusing gesture of flying the tricolour upside down.[90] Odd collaborators who had gambled imprudently on the outcome of the campaign were dealt with severely, especially in the land provinces. One van Hees, who had stopped a grain convoy on its way to Haarlem and arrested the militiamen in the name of the Prince, was incarcerated indefinitely; the Baroness Dorth van Holthuijzen was actually shot by firing squad for "betraying the Fatherland." But for the most part the common people had remained either apathetic or loyal. In Enkhuizen, after the evacuation of the British troops, a great bonfire was made of Orange flags and bunting in a grand fête celebrating the "liberation." Florent Guiot's comment was probably the most apt when he remarked that "the people who have suffered much from the revolution have everywhere shown courage and devotion in defending it, while those who have received its fruits have not hesitated to betray it."[91]

It was certainly true that some of those in high office had, during the most critical days, conducted themselves with less than unblemished patriotism. After the nightmare last week of August a group within the government, led by Directors Anthonie van Haersolte and Augustijn Besier and Agents Spoors and van der Goes, had attempted covertly to extricate the Republic from its French commitment. They had come to the fatal conclusion that the Republic was facing extinction and that the only possible escape route was through the mediation of the King of Prussia. The moving spirit behind this ill-conceived initiative was Maarten van der Goes, the Agent for Foreign Affairs. Van der Goes had been the secretary to the old Committee for Foreign Affairs during the National Assembly and was close to and sympathetic towards the politics of Jan Bicker. As a good regent he was drawn towards the revival of the traditional eighteenth-century Dutch diplomacy of neutrality, attempting to play off the two predatory neighbours of the Netherlands rather than allowing the Republic to become their catspaw.

Viewed objectively, there was a great deal to be said for such an attitude. But to pursue it in the midst of a shooting war and in violation of the Republic's most solemn promises was an act of recklessness verging on lunacy. Van der Goes and Besier (who had in his time been the Commissioner for the Admiralty of Amsterdam) were quite prepared to pay a steep political price for their rescue. The House of Orange was to be welcomed back in the shape of the Hereditary Prince (emphatically not the Stadholder). He was to assent to an executive role which would attach his dynasty to a genuinely republican constitution. Van der Goes seems to have had in mind a scheme not unlike that of Dr. Tollius, presented to and rejected by the Stadholder at Hampton Court.[92] The Prince was to become an hereditary President of a federal union, in which the balance of legislative, executive and judiciary would be kept in punctilious separation. This poor imitation of the American constitution resembled a contrived hybrid of what were really two utterly incompatible versions of sovereignty: the federal and the unitary. But the naïveté of its conception was capped by an even more astonishing proviso. For as a gesture of "good faith" regarding Dutch neutrality, van der Goes proposed that a British occupation of North Holland should be balanced off by a French occupation of Zeeland and the Scheldt. It was an eccentric version of independence which proposed to secure its integrity by holding two of its most precious territories in pawn. Even Schimmelpenninck, the ambassador in Paris, who was all for adopting any route to "national reconciliation," had the wit to see that such a scheme would be repugnant to any Dutchman still thinking of himself as a patriot and that its very proposal was a dangerous hazard.

Besier and van der Goes had been tempted into pursuing their folly by the cordiality of the Prussian ambassador Bielfeld and the careful advances of British agents like Munniks and James Crawfurd. Even after Abercromby's troops had landed, Besier told Crawfurd that although he could not negotiate under duress, their "discussions" might decently be resumed after an evacuation. Should the campaign go against the Republic, he added, the issue would in any event be academic.[93] The emissaries for this delicate mission to Berlin were chosen with an eye to their political acceptability. Queysen and De Vos van Steenwijk were figures whose hostility to the Stadholder had been mitigated by an aristocratic pedigree in one case and a record of consistent conservatism in both. But their reception at the Prussian court was no less cool for all that. Frederick William III had no intention of compromising his neutrality by joining the Second Coalition; but neither would he go so far as to betray his family in the House of Orange by recognising the Batavian Republic and negotiating with its officers, still less sanction a hare-brained scheme which involved the mutilation of the Stadholder's powers. After much fruitless diplomacy, De Vos van Steenwijk was sent home with a flea in his ear for having had the temerity to make such an overture.

The failure of the mission immediately put its authors in an uncomfortable position, for it could not be long before the news reached its allies in Paris. Not surprisingly when this happened, the French Directors judged it as yet more proof of the deviousness and pusillanimity of an ungrateful client. Had Frenchmen spilled their blood in 1795 and then again four years later so that those to whom they had granted their liberty might go crawling to their enemies? The very least that could be done as atonement was the immediate eviction of the culprits (including Pijman and La Pierre) from office. Despite a sheepish protest from the Dutch side that this was an interference in their domestic affairs, it seemed that the sacrifices would have to be made. Once again, however, the unpredictable drama of French politics came to their rescue. For on 18 Brumaire, Year VII, Napoleon Bonaparte dissolved both Directory and legislature. All at once it seemed possible that the rift which had opened between the two republics could once more be closed.

The Price of Fraternity

The renewed faith in the Franco-Dutch alliance produced by the defeat of the British expedition was not long-lived. By the beginning of November 1799, all the old troubles had returned to plague their association. General Brune, the hero of the hour, had taken to sulking in his tent like Achilles, denying access and correspondence to the official minister Florent Guiot. He in his turn was angry at the appointment of a second agent, Deforgues, whom he suspected of conspiring along with Brune and Daendels to bring about yet another military coup in the Republic. Brune himself had not scrupled to intervene in the factions of the Cisalpine Republic when the fancy took him, and Florent Guiot suspected him of harbouring Jacobinical notions. He was recalled before he could do any damage, but then indicated that he would be satisfied with more concrete tokens of Dutch appreciation than the poetic tributes showered on him in all the major cities. About a million French livres (half a million guilders), he thought, would take care of it. The Dutch were by this time well inured to the rapacity of French generals and confined their protests to whittling down the price. Brune did well. He left with 80,000 guilders' worth of government stock, which on the giddy exchanges of the French Bourse were still worth their weight in gold.

The news of the misconduct of the Directors most wounded Schimmelpenninck, who had set his heart on the establishment of a better understanding between the two states. Shortly after his arrival in Paris in 1798, following a cordial meeting with Talleyrand, he had expressed the hope that there would be

a good, solid and permanent state of affairs between the French and Batavian governments . . . the Batavian government is absolutely resolved to conduct itself loyally and to adhere inflexibly to the great principles of the revolution; to bring the constitution into operation and to use all the means in its power against the common enemy . . . to quell all domestic disputes and to fulfil its engagements faithfully. On the opposite side, it must be understood that it is not proper for the French government to interfere with our own domestic affairs.[94]

If the abortive mission to Berlin made it doubly difficult for the ambassador to plead the cause of his Republic's integrity, he nonetheless welcomed the coup of Brumaire as a fresh start in the history of the alliance. In retrospect this response may seem ironic. Yet like so many of his contemporaries Schimmelpenninck, whose relationship with Bonaparte was to be close and complicated, fell for the propaganda which proclaimed the Consuls' intention to cleanse the Augean stables of the dirt which had accumulated under the rule of the Directory. It would, he hoped, mark the end of the corruption, hypocrisy and selfishness which had characterised French dealings with the

Dutch since the signing of the Treaty of The Hague. Nor could he have been displeased by the Consular announcement that, as far as France was concerned, the revolution had been finally completed.

While a Patriot regent to his marrow and no friend of the Stadholder, Schimmelpenninck had throughout his life been a man of conservative instincts, deeply nervous of the volatile effects of revolutionary politics. His speech in Amsterdam on the morrow of the revolution in January 1795 had tried to neutralise it as soon as it had done the work of removing the Prince's men, and he had bitterly regretted the perpetuation of a revolutionary atmosphere which brought so many upheavals to the Batavian Republic. Naturally he hoped that a stable France, and one in which all classes but the extreme royalist and the extreme Jacobin could find a home, would set a salutary precedent for her ally. But additionally he hoped that with the end to France's violent revolutionary meanderings, there would also be an end to the inconsistencies in that nation's diplomacy. For it had been the alternating policies of intervention and standing off, of radical or anti-radical support, which as much as anything had bedevilled a satisfactory and stable relationship between the two states.

That inconsistency typified even a single embassy. After the coup of June 12, Champigny-Aubin reassured the "Interim Directory" that "the Batavian Republic has nothing more to fear for its domestic tranquillity or for its independence." The days of Charles Delacroix, in other words, were well and truly over. Yet within a fortnight the equable chargé d'affaires had warned Gogel that the government could "lose his confidence" if it was to persist in its foolish plan to pardon all political prisoners prior to the legislative elections. Champigny, moreover, though always a stop-gap chargé d'affaires, was a reasonable example of those diplomats who took their cue from the ministry of François Noël and assumed a relatively easy-going approach to the alliance. Essentially pragmatic in their outlook, others like Joseph Fouché during his brief ministry in July 1799 and Florent Guiot, his successor, made a serious effort to appreciate the strains imposed by the war on a Republic which was only a shadow of its former power and fortune. Such an attitude was based not so much on any special sympathy for the plight of the Dutch (although both Noël and Champigny became fond of the country) as on a shrewd assessment of how to get the most out of the alliance.

All these men were convinced that it would be a mistake to drive the Dutch so hard that in their desperation they would be brought to outright revolt. Nor would the absolute prostration of the country through endless exploitation profit France much. Talleyrand summed up that view when he repeated the advice of a Dutch emissary who had warned that "there is one principle which must direct France, it is to *manage* us [so that] we may be useful to her . . . it is necessary after all not to kill the hen which lays the golden eggs." A year later, Florent Guiot registered his alarm that yet another coup might be inflicted on the Batavian Republic by insisting that it "would kill this country. In less than ten years it would be reduced to an uninhabitable swamp." The message which Champigny tried to get across to Paris time and again was: "We are involved with a people which is extremely jealous of its independence. It is therefore necessary to gloss over our influence."[95]

The plea was made, more often than not, in vain. Champigny's superior, Lombard de Langres, was himself a classic example of the more doctrinaire school of French diplomacy; stiff with republican rectitude, determined to prosecute French interests with the maximum of ruthlessness and to exploit any advantage over ally or enemy alike to the hilt. Like his predecessor Delacroix, he had no compunction about intervening in the internal politics of the Batavian Republic (never more than a client state) whenever interest dictated. As a young academician, he was given to lecturing its rulers on their duties not only to the alliance and to France but to the ethics of republicanism. He insisted with equal vehemence that the Dutch Directors suspend their proceedings against Eykenbroek and against Fijnje and van Langen as that would be "dishonourable" to their interests, and that the secret "convention" signed by Vreede with Delacroix consenting to French sovereign jurisdiction in their part of Flushing and to a French commander of the Dutch army was legitimate and must be honoured.

Like the unfortunate Delacroix, Lombard was no diplomat of the old school. Headstrong and emotional, he believed in the power of confrontation and was apt to let his feelings run away with his better judgement. When, for example, a few vandals, possibly Orangists, smashed some rather poor busts of Directors Merlin and Barras and Generals Bernadotte, Berthier and Beurnonville in Amsterdam, Lombard took the offence as though it were a declaration of war. He wrote to the Batavian government in the following terms:

Vengeance, Citizen Directors, vengeance! I expect no less from your love of my country; indeed I say more, I demand it in the name of my Republic and in the name of its Directory.

Why, he asked, were there so many Orangists apparently free to do their mischief with impunity? Why were the police so lax? How was it that every day under the eyes of customs officers in Amsterdam goods of British and British colonial origin were unloaded on the wharves? All these observations led him to the conclusion that the Batavian Republic was culpable of betraying the terms by which it had been established in the first place and that its rulers required a timely reminder of the subjection of their place in the scheme of things.

It is not pride which forces me to say this. Indeed I only repeat it here because you have said it yourselves. Yes, Citizen Directors, my Republic can exist without you, but without her there can be no political existence for the Batavian Republic. Since the fate of that State must be identified with the prosperity of the French nation, in the name of your own Country, I say strike them, strike at once those enemies of my Fatherland and of yours.[96]

The brutality of Lombard's message (which appalled Champigny-Aubin) had the merit of candour. It cut right through the often unctuous professions of fraternity which French diplomacy used to conceal the most shameless acts of realpolitik. For although at a toast proposed by de Leeuw in the new Representative Assembly, he asked that "justice take the place of force in our relations and that in the sacrifices to be made to the alliance the principle of proportion [to size and power, etc.] be taken and not that of absolute parity," it was the view of the renegades who had sought Prussia's help that such a reformation of manners and character was not to be looked for from the French. The most serious complaints were economic. In their frequent protests to Paris on the conduct of French soldiers and ministers in the Netherlands, the Dutch asked whether the obligations of alliance could be so abused as to license acts of extortion, fraud and blackmail all in the name of military obligation. Such malpractices were of course part and parcel of the miseries of war, whether they took the form of huge "gratuities" to rapacious generals or forced requisitions in which grain was seized from farmers or comestibles from storekeepers at knife point.

Woe betide any trader who failed to take those threats seriously. The petition rolls to the Batavian assemblies are full of lamentations from shop-keepers and the like who had had their premises smashed to smithereens or their daughters seized for a night's entertainment. Those living on the frontiers of the Republic often seemed to fare worst, for it was there that the military patrols were heaviest, often with some justification. The cities of Venlo and Maastricht, which had been Dutch until 1795, swarmed with refugees from the Belgian rebellion of 1798–99, and there were repeated disturbances at Weert, Rosendaal and Maastricht. Consequently the residents of den Bosch, Breda and Bergen op Zoom were subjected to periodic doses of military occupation and summary justice meted out to likely suspects, more often than not "pour encourager les autres."

The traditional pattern of smuggling around the Scheldt estuary had benefited greatly from the annexation of Dutch Flanders to the French "Department of the Scheldt." Apart from opening up a new avenue of contraband directly into metropolitan France, it had installed French-speaking commissioners and magistrates who were pathetically ill-equipped to deal either with the Flemish-Dutch-Yiddish argot which passed for a lingua franca around the creeks and inlets of Axel, or indeed with the geography of the estuary, which was as near to a smuggler's paradise as Providence could provide.[97] If crime had the upper hand over enforcement in this region, there were others where extortion was the privilege of the occupiers. At the village of Groesbeek, just outside Nijmegen, for example, the peasant farmers complained that French customs guards and soldiers were running an efficient protection racket by which they were obliged, on pain of being shot, to take their goods to Cleves—over the border, and about 7 miles away—instead of to Nijmegen just 3 miles west. Apart from the liberal pickings made available to the border guard, it was then sold cheaply at Cleves market and became vulnerable to requisitions which were more strictly controlled than in the Batavian Republic.[98]

The running sore of Franco-Dutch conflict was, as always, the port of Flushing with its south-eastern half occupied by the French and the northwest, facing out into the North Sea, by the Dutch. Ever since the French had taken over their section, argument had raged over the exact interpretation of Articles XIII and XIV of the treaty. These had stipulated that the port would be divided for "use in common," which the Dutch insisted had not meant *cession* in any part nor the surrender of extra-territorial rights. In practice this meant that when (as happened with great regularity) brawls broke out in the port between French and Dutch seamen and customs guards, the cases ought to be tried before Batavian magistrates even where they concerned a French citizen as principal. According to Daendels' friend Rouget de l'Isle, it had been Reubell (the most ardent imperialist among the Directors) who had been responsible for first placing French customs officers in the port to maintain rights of sovereignty. Reubell had even argued that if the treaty had not explicitly mentioned outright cession it was because this had been understood in the negotiations he and Sieyès had conducted with Pieter Paulus. In any case, it was suggested, the dispute had been made academic by the convention signed between Delacroix and Vreede confirming the French view of the matter. It was Rouget who once again provided the information that this had been done just a few days before the June 12 coup as an obvious attempt to enlist official French support for their rapidly deteriorating political position.[99] The new Batavian Directory, and above all Gogel and Schimmelpenninck, had no intention of confirming as legitimate a document which had so flagrantly betrayed the interests of the Republic and which had never been presented to its properly elected representatives for confirmation.

The row over Flushing was one in which tender feelings about sovereignty and the true status of the Batavian Republic in the eyes of its ally were exacerbated by the economic cost of the "occupation." Apart from becoming notorious as a sink of lawlessness, the French port had turned into a haven for privateers and corsairs whose special predilection for Dutch and neutral shipping was threatening to polish off the last remnant of Dutch commercial life in the south. Outgunned and outsailed by their British counterparts, the ships which Gogel described as "vampires" of the sea found the neutral shipping—American and Danish in particular—on whom the Dutch relied for the transport of colonial goods from the East Indies, an ideal prey. Although French orders officially protected such vessels, it was a simple matter to charge their masters with the possession of "disguised" British colonial produce. This justified the seizure of a prize and the confiscation of vessel and cargo after an appearance before a French tribunal—very often at Antwerp.

Deteriorating relations with the United States in the summer of 1798 further disposed the French government to turn a blind eye to these obviously profitable practices. Such were the double standards obtaining in these matters that it has been estimated that, despite the strictest prohibitions in both republics, France and the Netherlands continued to receive between 12 and 18 per cent of British exports right up to the Peace of Amiens! Nor were the Dutch completely innocent of circumnavigating the embargo, for it was widely known that they were sending dairy exports to Britain. Regular trade had got so bad that some merchants were reported to be secretly chartering *Dutch* privateers to go after their own vessels, in order that they might receive the insurance value after the theft. One captain, Willem Wouters, the skipper of the patriotically named *Eenheid*, was said to have made this line of business his particular specialty![100]

By far the majority of cases, however, were those in which neutral ships bound for Dutch ports were taken on the high seas or even at the mouth of Flushing harbour. Within a single fortnight (August 20 to September 5, 1798) two Swedish ships, both bound for Rotterdam, were taken at the Maas estuary, and a Danish ship, the *Apollo*, from Altona was seized off the Spanish coast on its way to Surinam, stopped again at Cayenne and taken as prize to St. Martin. On that occasion the master, a Captain Claassen, was forced to leave the ship with three of his crew and to make his way in a small boat 26 sea leagues to Cayenne. There, having survived the ordeal, he was greeted by a further stretch of interrogation and imprisonment at the pleasure of the French authorities.

The incident which received most publicity in this period and which brought matters to a head was that of the *Wandelaar*. This was a cutter from Christiansand in Norway (then belonging to Denmark), which arrived in Flushing Sound on July 17, 1798, where it was attacked by a French corsair, the *Cartouche*, commanded by a Captain Tierce. Having made an effort to defend itself, the *Wandelaar* placed itself under the protection of the Dutch frigate *Walcheren*, which decided that it should take responsibility for examining the cargo of the Danish ship. This was duly declared clean, but the captain made the mistake of landing at harbour to take on supplies. The vessel was immediately apprehended on order of the French commandant, Percheron, who insisted that it be taken at once to Ostend and that its master appear before the Antwerp tribunal. The master of the *Walcheren*, supported by the Dutch commissioners, declared that if any attempt was made to sail the Danish ship out of harbour both prize and guard would be fired upon. While the Antwerp court as usual obliged the corsairs by declaring the vessel lawful prize, it remained in Flushing as an acidulous correspondence took place between Gogel and Champigny over the rights and wrongs of the matter.[101]

The affair had reached the stage where Gogel was openly denouncing the French Minister of the Marine, Bruix, whose connivance at the malpractices of the corsairs had been an open secret, when Captain Tierce rashly decided to go ashore at Helvoetsluys. His fame had preceded him and he had the misfortune to be recognised by the skipper of the *Walcheren*, Captain Barnevelt. Providentially offered this unique opportunity to give a pirate a taste of his own medicine, Barnevelt recruited a gang of Dutch sailors who gave Tierce a thorough going over and had even begun to drag him along the ground tied to the tail of a horse before he was rescued by a detachment of troops from the French garrison. He remained in Batavian custody however and was jailed at The Hague for maritime misdemeanours, where he continually claimed the right to French justice—having lived most of his life in the French Antilles.[102]

The fate of the *Wandelaar* and Captain Tierce was but one of many similar instances. It was unusual only in that for once the culprit got his just deserts. But the tough attitude adopted by Gogel and the Directory was a fair indication of the lengths they were prepared to go to put a stop to the crimes committed at Flushing in the name of the alliance and the war. These were not in fact satisfactorily settled until Bonaparte adopted far more stringent and rigorously applied sanctions against privateering in 1800. By then the damage done to the relations between the two nations was virtually irreparable. The Batavian authorities wanted to see the issues separating the two states subject to a general settlement in the form of a properly negotiated commercial treaty, which they hoped would compensate to some extent for the loss of their commerce through the exigencies of war.

Such a treaty had been mooted by Valckenaer as early as 1792, when the first proposals for the future of the liberated Netherlands were being discussed by Dumouriez. It had been subsequently pursued by Blauw and Paulus in 1795, and by Wiselius on his mission to Paris in April 1798. None of these emissaries had got very far, and Schimmelpenninck's reminder to the French that a commercial treaty signed with the United Provinces in 1739 was still in effect was a clumsy piece of diplomacy. It was in fact doubtful whether the French really believed that they *would* benefit more from a strong and prosperous Dutch economy as the Batavian agents argued than from a weak and limping state. Even by 1798 Antwerp, now part of the French Republic, was beginning its commercial comeback at the expense of Amsterdam (a reversal of the process which had taken place in the seventeenth century,) and the French were certainly disinclined to help a nation which they always believed to exaggerate the extent of its impoverishment if that assistance was to be at the expense of their own economic interests.

In short, in a game of naked realpolitik the Dutch had just one good card to play (apart from the threat of a pro-British rebellion). By the spring of 1799 France had been bankrupt several times over and desperately required funds with which to defend her dominion against the offensive of the Second Coalition. The apparently limitless flow of British subsidies and the ease with which Pitt appeared to be able to finance his war effort demanded some kind of comparable arrangement for France. The French government, having run through the indemnity, felt that the Batavian Republic, all protestations to the contrary, was in a position to act in effect as the banker of the republican alliance. The notion was that in return perhaps for a formal, largely meaningless commercial treaty and a few concessions over Flushing, the Dutch could be pressured into supplying huge loans at knock-down rates of interest and with specially easy terms of repayment. With this aim in mind Timothy Lubberts, the son of a Bordeaux merchant with family connexions in the Netherlands, was sent to The Hague in March 1799 to sound out the prospects.[103]

Like so many of the more objective French observers before him (Ramel, Florent Guiot, Rouget de l'Isle), Lubberts was struck by the extent of the damage inflicted by the war on the Dutch economy. Unlike those who had commissioned him, he started from the premise that a revival of the Dutch economy would be in the interests of both states and that, combined, Dutch trade and Belgian industry could create a formidable competition for the influx of British manufactured products. Above all, he attempted to point out to the French government the true state of affairs in the Netherlands. If its present condition were not improved, he maintained, the "Batavian Republic will soon be lost." He continued:

It would be in vain to demand yet more sacrifices from this unhappy country. It would indeed be impossible to obtain them and the few wealthy people who live there would certainly transport elsewhere the debris of their fortune. What, alas, can the partisans of France reply to their enemies? Where, they are continually asked, are the advantages which Holland has drawn from its revolution and our alliance?[104]

It would, he optimistically suggested, be "contrary to our laws" to ask for involuntary sacrifices "commanded by terror or by violence." He recommended the return of its section of Flushing to the Batavian Republic and the establishment of a full customs union between the two states. Only then would the Dutch be forthcoming in providing the finance that could be seen to be invested in a union which was of genuinely common interest and profit.

Lubberts' sincerity and goodwill did him more credit than his grasp of political reality. The bleak fact was that the price that France was willing to pay for substantial financial assistance did not extend to a commercial treaty worth the name, still less to a common customs area. Republican, like Imperial France, was—as she had been under the Old Regime—guided by mercantilist principles. In the war of all against all these were incapable of accommodating Lubberts' empire of free trade stretching from Genoa to Brest, with Amsterdam and Antwerp as its twin entrepôts, On the other hand, her need for funds to pay for military campaigning if anything grew more urgent as 1799 passed. One of the first acts to which Bonaparte directed his attention after coming to power was the extraction of a large loan to pay for his forthcoming Italian campaign. This second initiative began with the advantage that Schimmelpenninck had been swept off his feet by the silky charm of Talleyrand, in whom he had an entirely misplaced confidence, and by the adroitness of Bonaparte's own diplomatic approach. In the first of a series of cordial encounters, both men contrived to blame the misfortunes and misunderstandings on their predecessors in power and looked forward with much reciprocal bowing and curtseying to the cementing of a "fruitful" relationship.[105]

The First Consul's representatives in the Netherlands itself were not quite so accommodating. General Augereau succeeded in setting new standards of rapacity and was less discreet about asserting his authority over the Dutch politicians than either Joubert or Brune. His speech to the Batavian legislature was actually interrupted by Director Ermerins, who corrected his impression that he still had command of the Batavian army. Augereau concluded that the Directors would "rather bury themselves beneath the ruins of their country" than entrust the command to a foreigner except in a time of absolute emergency. He warned Bonaparte to "expect nothing from Batavia; for us it is like one of those burdensome colonies which eat up part of the resources of the metropolis without adding anything to its power."[106] Nor was the new French minister any more sympathetic. The *ci-devant* marquis de Sémonville, in contrast to his predecessors, was a diplomat of the Ancien Régime, a master of the expertly polished lie. Compared to his talent for intrigue and his determination to milk the Batavian Republic for everything it had to offer, the shortcomings of all Sémonville's predecessors pale into insignificance. He was, in fact, the perfect tool of Bonapartism. Two things about the Dutch impressed themselves on Sémonville. The first was that those incompetents and demagogues responsible for most of the miseries of the nation now had the impertinence to blame their troubles on their mentor and ally; the second, that the law of the jungle dictated that if the Batavian Republic was too weak to stand up to its ally or defend itself against its enemies without assistance, then so much the worse for it. More than once he looked forward to the inevitable partition of the Netherlands and determined that France should have as much of the pickings as she could.

For a while, however, Bonaparte himself believed that something could be done to settle matters amicably with the burghers of Amsterdam. He retained the ingrained belief, shared by so many of his countrymen, that the cries of poverty from the Dutch were simply a deceit designed to conceal their immense wealth stowed away in some inaccessible vaults by the canals. In response to a request from Schimmelpenninck for the reduction of the commitment to maintain 25,000 troops, he was shrewd enough not to turn the proposal down but to parry with an account of the extreme penury of the armies in Switzerland and Italy. After some further bouts of elaborate shadow-boxing in February 1800, Bonaparte finally revealed that in return for a "settlement" over Flushing, the suppression of the corsairs, and some reduction of military maintenace (on the signature of the peace!), he would require a sum of around 6 million guilders at a rate of about 1 per cent a month, the security for which was to be provided by the issue of the French *coupe des bois*.[107] Schimmelpenninck replied quite candidly that while he knew his countrymen would dearly love to oblige the First Consul, they were, at this moment, at the end of their financial tether. At that very point two further taxes—3 per cent on capital and 6 per cent on income—had been decreed by the Directory and, in any case, Dutch capitalists could still get 4 per cent on their own government stock. Dutch bonds at the latest quotation stood at around 75 per cent of par, compared with any French stock, which not infrequently sank without trace shortly after its issue.

Bonaparte, however, was not interested in taking no for an answer. To make his "terms" clearer he sent his hatchet man, General Marmont, to Amsterdam to round up all the available money bags. The journey was, as Schimmelpenninck had warned, a waste of time. Though a dozen or so of the leading houses dutifully assembled to hear Marmont's request at the Doelen, they replied that they believed it would be impossible to place the loan. After a month of abortive negotiation it was discovered that only a couple of firms, both relatively minor (one of them Cappel and Zoon, a concern where a close friend of Gogel's managed the funds) were forthcoming. De Smeth, Six, Teyler & Severijn and the big firms all wrung their hands in contrition but declared the task beyond them.

On April 4 Marmont finally admitted defeat. The First Consul was not inclined to be charitable. In a cold and hostile interview he said that "a commercial city which had shown so little zeal to do anything for him had no right to expect anything in return, and that he should not forget this disappointment and that the consequences would be seen in the matter of privateering and the maritime prizes."[108] He was indeed not one to forget such slights. However costly the sacrifice of the loan might have been, the Dutch were to repay ample interest in political penalties. A special effort was made by Admiral de Winter in the summer of 1800 to apprise Bonaparte of the true condition of the Dutch economy. In his deliberately blunt and undiplomatic manner, de Winter tried to succeed with shock tactics where subtle diplomacy had so miserably failed. Were France, he insisted, to tolerate the burdens now thrust on a nation of less than 2 million, her people would be paying 2 milliard, 400 million francs every year to its treasury![109] He made no bones about the injustices heaped on his unfortunate countrymen in the name of the alliance:

I will not recall here all the vexations, all the enmity, all the tyranny which has been committed in the name of the French Republic on Batavia . . . I need not speak of . . . the audacious avidity of the corsairs and the iniquities of the French tribunals, which have given a mortal blow to the languishing remains of our trade and dried up all the resources of our industry; in this respect our ally has done us more harm *than if it had been in open war with us.*

While he understood that this was the work of the Consul's detested predecessors, and expected the inauguration of a better relationship between the two powers, de Winter felt bound to warn him that "speaking every day in a haughtier tone of the treaties [can] only prove to us, in a manner too offensive but too true, that the Batavian Republic is very much more of a tributary province of France than an independent power and ally."

De Winter's approach won him precious little more consideration than Schimmelpenninck's. But the admiral, at least, was incapable of sycophancy. Turning to the authentic rhetoric of traditional patriotism, he warned that though

Force may destroy Batavia, we shall never betray her. We are exhausted. Just two precious treasures remain to us for the future: the credit and the morality of her citizens and of the Batavian people. That must be the true guarantee of the alliance . . . misery we may support but slavery never, *no more that of any state or of any individual than that of a Stadholder.* . . .

Those were fighting words. But they did not conceal from de Winter any more than the government which had sent him to Paris the desperate impotence of their situation. Indeed, as the first news of the peace preliminaries at Lunéville in September 1801 reached the Republic, even Schimmelpenninck, for whom hope sprang eternal, began to assimilate the melancholy truth that the Dutch were not destined to take their place again among the great powers of Europe.

Bonaparte had already revealed his true colours; like it or not, the Batavian Republic was gradually being squeezed to death between the competing unscrupulousness of its two powerful neighbours. All that could be contemplated was the defence of its integrity with as much dignity and shrewdness as their history could confer. All that could be done was to play for time and, as Schimmelpenninck advised, "to save the country from further shocks which might destroy it entirely." Then, "If matters can be faced without confusion and quarrels, there may be some hope for calmer times and the restoration of our former prosperity."[110] By 1801 nothing more was heard of fraternity; precious little of the now embarrassing revolutionary past. Nor was it even a matter of seeking a place in the sun beside the brilliance of Consular France. All that the future held was a fight for national survival.

✳ ✳ ✳ ✳ ✳ ✳ ✳ ✳ ✳

10

Illusions Regained and Illusions Lost, *1801–1805*

1801: The September Coup

War, it has been argued, was the determining condition of the Batavian Republic: of its destruction as of its genesis. The political tensions which had eventually led to the Dutch revolution had not been artificially and externally generated. They were the logical outcome of a century of governmental atrophy. But their dénouement came about in circumstances so inauspicious that the career of the new Republic was deflected further and further from the reforming purposes to which its instigators had originally committed themselves. Six years after the exit of William V and three years after the introduction of a constitution, the Batavian Commonwealth had been reduced to the function of auxiliary implement to an imperialist war machine. Resources which might have been devoted to the difficult work of institutional reconstruction had been enervated in the struggle to stay alive as a nation state.

It was no easy thing for Dutch politicians to adjust their sights to so diminished a set of expectations and to abandon their hopes of forging anew the commonwealth of equal toil and general prosperity. Yet however hard the road, it was not until they had divested themselves of such pieties that the more pragmatic among them were able to take stock of what was still possible within a confined context. En route to this sober moment of truth, some of the more jejune notions—most especially those concerning the good faith of their ally and protector—were finally discarded. Jacob Blauw, usually an incorrigible optimist, wrote from Paris in the summer of 1801 that "we

[410]

can no longer hope to play a role in Europe. We must simply try to avoid suffering the fate of the Venetians."[1]

The only practical chance of rescue lay with a general European peace. Ironic though it might have seemed from the perspective of 1801, the Treaty of The Hague had in fact provided for that eventuality. Its articles stipulated that on a definitive termination of hostilities, the Batavian Republic was to receive proper territorial indemnification for the cessions of 1795; French troops were to be gradually withdrawn, and the burden of Dutch military obligations eased. The *coup de foudre* at Marengo and the undoing of the Second Coalition had brought all that within the realm of credibility. The virtually dictated peace made with Austria at Lunéville on February 29, 1801, included formal recognition of the Cisalpine, Helvetic and Batavian Republics. To be sure, the Austrians had little alternative in the matter and their assent was hedged with all sorts of reservations and suspicions; nevertheless, the acknowledgement was an important step forward. So at least it seemed to Italians, Swiss and Dutch. Writing from Paris, Schimmelpenninck tried to express his own sense of the significance of the times:

. . . after the violent shocks suffered by the different parts of the world during ten years of devastating warfare, unparalleled in history, the old political structure has been destroyed. A new one must be built in its place, resting on foundations strong enough to be able to withstand the assaults of force and oppression.[2]

This was the sort of "realistic" talk that Bonaparte in particular liked to hear. But the path to the "new order" was strewn with stumbling blocks. Recognition of the sovereign status of the new republics—the preliminary agreement signed with the British in October made crystal clear—was conditional on the respect shown by France towards their independence, a respect to be manifested by the prompt evacuation of troops. The First Consul (and his omniscient Minister of Foreign Affairs) did not see matters in quite this light. They envisaged not a chain of truly independent buffer states guaranteed by all the powers but innocuous dependencies tied firmly to French interests by their military impotence. If necessary, their docility was to be engineered by constitutions designed to eliminate not only troublesome domestic conflict but any flashes of impertinent nationalism. Only Switzerland, after 1802, proximated to the status of a genuinely independent Republic, albeit with Bonaparte as Mediator and with the strategic Alpine passes brought under direct French sovereignty.[3] What was presented as a magnanimous withdrawal from the affairs of client states was in fact a license for a further period of interference and domination.

As far as the Netherlands were concerned, any new intervention was not likely to support the strengthening of democracy or unitarism. The political posture adopted by the First Consul in 1800–01 was partly meant to reassure the Coalition powers that in return for assenting to a Caesarian peace, they would no longer be troubled by the revolutionary contagion. Such an approach was, in any case, in harmony with Bonaparte's own inclinations. The greater his success, the more clearly revealed were his despotic and reactionary prejudices. Patriot democracy was a card he played only in adversity when the odds were, for once, stacked against him: in Italy in 1796 at the outset of his career and in the Hundred Days at its close. On the day following the coup of 18 Brumaire (1799) he had announced *ex cathedra* that "The revolution is established on the principles which began it; the revolution is completed." Since his narrow escape from the "machine infernale"—the botched-up attempt to assassinate him on Christmas Eve on the way to the opera—Bonaparte's already decided intolerance of the "metaphysicians," those political prattlers who had ruined France for nearly a decade, intensified to an almost paranoid degree. The querulous Tribunate, last source of permitted opposition, was first emasculated then finished off; presses in Paris and other cities were sealed, editors and printers incarcerated, and police surveillance extended to anyone falling within the ever-broadening compass of those suspected of subversion or dissent. The Concordat, which was meant to put the Church at the service of the French state, was accompanied by a rapprochement with those elements of the émigré nobility (and they were considerable) willing to crook the knee to the Consulate in return for a partial restoration to rank and influence.[4]

Much the same principles were followed in respect to the satellite states. In Switzerland, for example, the political conflict had taken a course superficially analogous to that of the Dutch. The legislative councils had defied the executive; the partisans of unitary democracy were embattled with patrician notables concerned to preserve the autonomy of the cantons (and their own privileges within them). After violent oscillation between the two poles Bonaparte intervened in April 1801, with the "Constitution of Malmaison" restoring the loose seventeen-canton Confederation and confining the franchise to a narrow band of the propertied and well-to-do. After a further year of confusion and dramatic counter-revolution, a slightly modified version of this document was imposed on the Swiss as their "Mediation." As President of the newly reconstituted "Italian Republic," Bonaparte was even freer to mould the state in an authoritarian and socially conservative framework. An omnipotent executive was imposed over a pseudo-representative body of appointed councillors, and the Church restored to much of its traditional dominion.

A similar solution seemed appropriate for the Batavian Republic. Apart from his disgust with electoral democracies, the First Consul had neither forgiven nor forgotten the rebuff of spring 1800 when the Amsterdam bankers had failed to rally to his appeal to help fund the new campaign. For this and for their incompetence at keeping British goods out of a greedy and overly gratified European market, he blamed the Batavian Directory, a body he viewed in much the same light as its unlamented pre-Consular counterpart. If the Lilliputian squabbles of revolutionary and anti-revolutionary factions were compromising the Batavian Republic's utility as a factotum of France, then, clearly, an end would have to be made of its politics. As in France, "union" was called for in place of "division"; authority instead of license;

and a restoration to office of those men best fitted for it by experience, ability *and* social station.

In the practical application of these principles, much turned on the attitude of France's representatives in the Netherlands. And in the former marquis de Sémonville, Bonaparte found an enthusiastic practitioner of the arts of "reconciliation" and "amalgam." Like his patron, Talleyrand, Sémonville's own career had been a signal example of the fruits of pragmatism. After the September coup he was to receive from the new Dutch government a secret *douceur* of some 3,000 florins a month, and throughout his residence at The Hague he made no attempt to disguise his fondness for the company of "men of substance." He was only too pleased to have the opportunity to press on the Batavian Directors the view of the First Consul that "the time has come for the pardon of past errors" and that clemency for political offences was "an obligation owed towards all your fellow citizens . . . to all those animated by a love of their country . . . a measure required by general opinion and by the needs of peace."[5]

The general amnesty was duly proclaimed on March 25, 1801. But to scour the Batavian Republic of all its remaining revolutionary impurities, Sémonville was convinced that the constitution of 1798—a disreputable relic of partisan republicanism—would have to go at the earliest possible convenience. In December 1800 he had informed Talleyrand that "the constitutional edifice of Batavia is crumbling in every part. Profusion of public officials; confusion of powers, quarrelling among authorities . . . exorbitant expenses . . . overall a lack of coherence and plan."[6] Such an account was, of course, calculated to upset the Bonapartist concern for order and rationality with which it had become customary to equate sharp doses of political arbitration. In the past, French complaints of Batavian "incoherence" and the jeopardy in which it was allegedly placing the alliance had heralded fresh interference in Dutch domestic politics. So it proved in the spring of 1801. On February 6, Talleyrand gave the ambassador authorisation to investigate the means of making suitable revisions in the Batavian constitution and to supply him with details of the proposed changes.

The fact that the terms of the 1798 constitution specifically precluded any revision until at least a quinquennium had elapsed was, of course, of little moment in the climate of Consular France, where such constitutions were made and unmade with scant regard for notions of legitimacy. Equally it was true that in his efforts to terminate what remained of an electoral democracy in the Netherlands, Sémonville was able to draw on a fairly broad spectrum of dissatisfaction with the operation of the constitution. The year 1798 had marked a fracture of the Dutch past, but the break had not been clean. The Directory and its agents had not had sufficient power to make the newly proclaimed national sovereignty a reality in the departments and municipalities. On the other hand, the financially enfeebled local administrations were in no position to do any more than obstruct legislation of which they disapproved (such as the abolition of the guilds) and which encroached on their traditional jurisdiction. As a result, the Batavian Republic lingered on in a hiatus between two forms of government—the unitary and the federal—without the issue decided one way or another.

In these circumstances it is perhaps less surprising that even convinced advocates of unitarism like Gogel and Wiselius should have been prepared to contemplate revision. Gogel's memorandum written at the end of 1800 began with the trenchant announcement: "The present constitution is wholly unfitted to assure for the Batavian people a lasting happiness."[7] The greater part of his objections were based on utilitarian criteria, but they cut across the assumptions on which the first legislature had been established in 1796. Gogel argued for a drastic truncation of the representatives to about thirty-five (working on the proportion of 1 member to 60,000 souls), which he insisted was quite sufficient for a nation of under 2 millions. The legislature was to be unicameral, largely deprived of the right of initiative, and meeting not in permanent session but in two three-month terms. Contrary to one of Paulus' most jealously guarded axioms, Wiselius was even prepared to recommend that sessions be closed to public admission.[8] Both men proposed a corresponding extension of the powers of the executive, although both were also careful to eschew any suggestion of a Batavian Consulate, let alone the American-fashion Presidency by which Schimmelpenninck set so much (immodest) store.

Colenbrander saw these changes as clear evidence that even erstwhile democrats had had enough of the nostrums of patriot politics and were turning instead to the greyer, more concrete areas of administrative reform; that, in fact, they had become Bonapartised.[9] The observation has some truth in it. It was his painful experience with the General Tax Plan, delayed for over two years through the bicameral prevarication of the legislature, which had so incensed Gogel against its representatives. In his memorandum he had also complained of the ignorance and incompetence of the subcommittees to which the plenary Assembly entrusted its detailed legislative reports. Given the deteriorating financial crisis, a captious body of partisan factions was to his mind a luxury the Republic could no longer afford. On the other hand it would be misleading to infer from this critique that Gogel had turned his back on any form of democratic representation. On the contrary, he was steadfastly opposed to any tampering with the franchise or the dissection of the unitary state into its federal components.

For others of less radical convictions, though, revision was synonymous with the opportunity to re-federalise the Republic, and to introduce the property or tax franchise designed to restore to the regents and patricians the political monopoly they had lost in 1795. The *Dissertation* of Gerrit Dumbar—the ex-secretary of Deventer and Greffier of the province of Overijssel—which appeared in February 1801 and went through several editions, provided a cogent legitimation for that kind of view. Dumbar borrowed crudely from Montesquieu to demonstrate the necessity of provincial "intermediary" institutions. While disclaiming any intention to revert to the status quo ante 1795, Dumbar thought of himself very much as a Patriot of the

1787 stamp; warned solemnly against the "dangers of an undivided form of government"; and criticised unitary administration and the suppression of provincial jurisdictions as an arbitrary, mechanical form of government rashly superimposed on the historical realities of the Netherlands. The distinction he insisted upon was that between the "indivisibility" of the general sovereignty of the Republic and the "despotism" of a supreme national executive. None of this was new, of course. But it was a powerful reiteration of the basic principles of the Constitutional Restoration of 1784–86—that famous opus which remained the high-water mark of reform for those afraid either of popular sovereignty or unified administration.[10]

The distinction between (desirable) "indivisible sovereignty" and (undesirable and oppressive) "absolute unity" was one which could be deployed by expert casuists like Schimmelpenninck with great dexterity. It enabled him, for example, to profess in a letter to Gogel his commitment to the basic unity of the Republic but to make it clear to Sémonville that he had always viewed the "absolute unity" of finances and taxation as impractical and wrong-headed. While he favoured the reversion to provincial authorities of much that was properly their own domestic administration, he also advocated some constitutional safeguards to see that they could not overrule national bodies in any serious dispute.[11] All this artfulness could not (and doubtless was not intended to) conceal Schimmelpenninck's fundamental belief that a greater degree of federal devolution was what the Republic needed, together with an electoral system which would ensure that the choice of voters "*must* fall" on "independent and well-to-do citizens." Only they, after all, had the means which freed them from partisanship. To this whiggish sentiment Schimmelpenninck added a dash of authentic Bonapartism when he urged an end to the "metaphysical fantasies" which had so damaged the "good name" of the Republic. Government should be "very energetic and very popular"; "sober, simple, Batavian." The only politics that mattered now were those of patriotic unity. The general amnesty for Orangists and any other culprits was, he told the First Consul, a proof of the "moderation which has ever distinguished the Batavian Republic."[12]

Schimmelpenninck's equivocation was entirely in character. It harked back directly to the highly ambiguous version of "One and Indivisible" that he had attempted to steer through the National Assembly in December 1796. From the unitarists' point of view, it was far more ominous that men like Director Besier seemed similarly converted to the re-federalising of the state. Augustijn Besier had been Navy Commissioner at Amsterdam and was a close friend of Spoors'. The two colleagues were, like Schimmelpenninck, on the best of terms with the city's trading and banking interests and were not averse to keeping the company of Willink, van Staphorst, Hodshon and the great plutocrats of Amsterdam finance. Yet as Hollanders and men who had made their public reputations since 1795, they were presumed—by Wiselius at any rate—to be in favour of fiscal unification and democratic republicanism. Besier cleared up his position in a letter to Wiselius on March 12 in which he came out firmly for revision. While "no-one is a greater enemy of the former [that is, pre-1795] state of affairs than I," he confessed à la Dumbar, only a judicious "middle way" could rescue the Republic from its contradictions. Of all the desirable reforms he itemised—extension of executive power; curtailing of the legislature—the most important in his own view was federal devolution. Recognizing the difficulty in distinguishing clearly between the legitimate jurisdictions of provincial, municipal and national authorities, Besier was nevertheless happy to sell the pass on taxes. The provinces were to order their own treasuries, legislate for their internal government, and run the hierarchies of justice and police.[13]

Needless to say, Besier's announced intentions were given a further fillip by the encouragement of the French minister. At the same time that he wrote to Wiselius he was already setting in motion the political machinery needed for revision. This proved a far thornier business than he anticipated. Two of his fellow Directors, neither of them exactly ranting Jacobins— Ermerins and van Swinden—were overtly hostile to the initiative; and even more unpredictably, the Representative Assembly seemed markedly un- willing to do away with itself without a struggle. Since Bonaparte believed that any reform had to be seen to be the work of a Dutch proposal and not French intervention, the revisionist Directors and their allies in the legisla- ture, Appelius and de Leeuw, were obliged to proceed with caution. Their initial motion on March 21 proposing that the primary assemblies be con- vened to register a view on the desirability or otherwise of a revision was in effect rejected when the representatives agreed to do no more than nominate a commission to discuss the whole business with the Directory. The *principle* of contemplating a revision before the earliest stipulated date in 1804 was roundly condemned by the democrats in the Assembly, notably Pieter Linthorst and Nuhout van der Veen, and the initiative was further dis- credited when it became known that Sémonville had relayed the First Consul's comments on proposed changes to the Directors, who had hastened to make all necessary accommodations to meet his criticism.[14]

This first project dutifully followed the French constitution of the Year VIII (1799) by featuring a truncated bicameral legislature appointed by a "National College" (akin to the French Senate) from a list of names pro- duced by the most elaborate forms of indirect election. As the debates con- tinued through April and May, it became apparent that this version in fact gave too little to the orthodox federalists like Queysen to command their support. For, however delighted they were to be rid of the constitution of 1798, they were far from happy about following mechanically in the path of Bonapartist authoritarianism. The thinness of support for the Directorial project was humiliatingly exposed on June 11 when it was finally rejected in the Assembly by fifty votes to twelve.

Thus an issue which had been expected to divide the Representative Assembly down the middle and to produce, with some help from the Directors and Sémonville, a "constitutional" revision, had in the event polarised as a contest between executive and legislature. A Caesarian resolution was the only way out. Gerrit Pijman, the new Director, used a project already written by van Irhoven van Dam (Gogel's colleague on the Insurrectionary Committee of 1794) as the basis of a second constitutional draft. To woo the federalists, the provinces were restored to their traditional frontiers and given wider administrative scope; the threat of a Consular executive was similarly diminished by the provision of a twelve-man body presiding over an essentially collegiate system of government. Even so, Pijman was not prepared to leave matters to the risks of assent, particularly since the two renegade Directors remained impenitently hostile.[15] He sought out General Augereau (something of an expert in these matters) and with him prepared contingency measures in case of resistance.

On September 14, the three revisionist Directors issued a proclamation simply announcing the convening of primary assemblies to register a verdict on the Irhoven constitution. Four days later, faced with this fait accompli, the Assembly ruled the proclamation illegal in a final gesture of defiance. The inevitable then ensued. Augereau's troops sealed its doors and cut the Assembly off from any outside help while its proceedings were summarily dissolved by Directional order. Those who could still do so made tracks for the anonymity of private life, and the minority Directors made their dissent public by opposing the proclamation of the 14th. On the 20th, van Swinden found guards posted at his house to assure him proper "protection."

Despite the general climate of alarm and intimidation which always followed these *coups d'état*, the brief period before the day appointed for the vote—October 1—was taken up with urgent campaigning by both sides. The asperity and vigour with which democrats and even moderate unitarists castigated the action of the three Directors attested to a degree of political freedom unthinkable in France under the same circumstances. Gogel was himself emboldened to write very crisply to Sémonville:

Believing to discover in this constitutional plan offered to the Batavian people by the Directorial majority the seeds of the irrevocable ruin of this unhappy country, as well as the future re-establishment of the House of Orange with the concomitant influence of England, I have thought it my duty to submit to that same people my own remarks on the financial section [of the plan].[16]

His remarks appeared in an issue of *De Heer Politieke Blixem*, edited by J. C. Hespe and devoted to attacks on the Dutch patricians. It set out in sharp relief Gogel's predictions of the consequences of fiscal federalism. Hollanders, he warned, would pay for the preservation of the privileges of the regents and aristocrats of the land provinces; global revenue would decline; the towns would plunge further into ruin; officialdom would wax fat in numbers but not in competence; graft would prosper and the nation as a whole continue to suffer the monstrous scourge of arbitrary extraordinary taxation. The return to collegiate management of finance would bring with it, "the continued domination of a minority over the majority, with no possibility of setting matters aright without recourse to revolutions provoked by feebleness, feuds; faction, hatreds and vindictiveness . . ." The proposed constitution would "complete your destruction and the annihilation of your place among the peoples of the world."[17]

Gogel's overriding concern was with the governmental chaos he saw as unavoidable if the new federal constitution was accepted. Others were at least as exercised by the disappearance of any genuine system of representation. Another writer in the *Blixem* warned:

... In the new [constitution] the influence of the people has almost wholly vanished, so that the recognized sovereignty of the people becomes a mere shibboleth; all that is left is the choosing of an Elector and a Candidate . . . in the new the great republican principle is money—in the present [1798 constitution] it is ability, service, virtue—In the new all power is in the hands of a State Regency [the title of the executive] and sixteen National Electors . . . the new is a mishmash of federalism and unity.[18]

But it was Pieter Vreede, perhaps incredulous at the turn events had taken since his own forlorn attempt to institute the Republic of Free Men in 1798, who was best able to sum up the real significance of the document set before the Dutch people. In a letter to Valckenaer he wrote:

Either the projected constitutional plan annuls all civil liberty, all popular representation, or else I know not what the one and the other may be. The whole revolution is lost for our Fatherland if . . . the barriers are lowered to let in those friends of Orange who were excluded but yesterday. *This ultra-moderatism is in effect a counter-revolution. . . .*[19]

It is well-nigh impossible to gauge with any confidence what effect these philippics, public and private, may have had on those Dutchmen who remained at all concerned with politics. It is less doubtful that the regime of 1798—identified as it was with the perpetuation of the war, the alliance with the detested French, the depression of economic life and crushing taxation— was not popular. But that the same people were not enamoured of the alternative now being offered to them was stunningly demonstrated on October 1 when, out of 416,619 voters, just 16,771 voted in favour and 52,219 *against*.[20] In other words, by far the larger part of the political nation either abstained or rejected the 1801 plan. In Brabant and Holland the figures were even more lopsided. In den Bosch, 630 votes were cast against and just 13 in favour.[21] But a mere defeat in the proportion of three to one was not to deter politicians by now well schooled in plebiscitary manipulation. By a sleight-of-hand that perhaps left something to be desired in the way of subtlety, the Directorial majority announced that, counting the 350,000 plus missing votes and abstentions as "tacit affirmations," their project had been triumphantly endorsed by "the will of the people."

This parody of democratic procedure hammered the last nail in the coffin of the representative system begun in 1795. Yet in terms of deciding the fate of the quavering Republic, it was almost a gratuitous gesture. Both coups of January and June 1798 had arisen not merely from the will of the French but from the real conflicts separating the Dutch themselves. That of 1801, as the pitiful number of votes cast suggests, was an act of transparent constitution-mongering. Far more important than anything happening in the Netherlands itself on October 1, 1801, was the news that Great Britain had signed peace preliminaries with France on the same day, and that the "friend and ally" of the Batavian Republic had just handed over Ceylon as part of the bargain.

The Reaction

"The clubs were shut and the business offices opened."[22] Colenbrander's epitaph for the Batavian Republic was, characteristically, pithy and not quite accurate. The more well-heeled gatherings in Amsterdam like "Doctrina et Amicitia" and "Felix Meritis" continued to function, albeit more as literary than purely political societies. The press still produced waspish papers, stinging the new government as they had the old.[23] On the economic front the commercial revival was not all it seemed. But these complications aside, the description of the political climate in the Netherlands from the autumn of 1801 to the late spring of 1803 is fair enough. It may have been galling for those (like Gogel) who had sweated through an appalling war, trying to salvage something of their reforming ambitions, only to see their political enemies profit from the peace. But, as Pieter Vreede had predicted, the reaction which followed the September coup swept aside all those "moderates" who had subscribed to revision in the hope of merely amending the republican constitution. What was at stake was the political existence of the Batavian Republic.

For those whose intentions were not altogether benevolent, the campaign could be won almost by default. The overwhelming number of abstentions from the plebiscite suggests that what remained of the political nation created in 1795 had become increasingly indifferent as to which of the competing élites held power at The Hague. Exorbitant taxes and the accompanying miseries of war had not been made any more bearable for being asked in the name of the "sovereign people" and patriotic sacrifice. Nor had votes had any tangible effect on the downward spiral of their economic circumstances. No-one expected the new government, the Staatsbewind (Regency of State) to be any great improvement on the Directory; but neither was it imagined that it could do much worse. Only the 50,000 votes cast against the new constitution registered the protest of those who had been the beneficiaries of 1795. For the men who had broken the monopoly of the regent juntas and who had cut from the oligarchies their supporting links of patronage, the restoration of federalism posed a direct threat. Deprived of the (already exiguous) support of the electoral assemblies and of a national government, there was little they could do to obstruct the reassertion of that traditional patrimony.

Their pessimism was well founded. The devisers of the constitution had seen to it that the elective principle was reduced to a formality. In the first instance, the Regency of State itself had been made up of the three revisionist Directors plus four of their nominees, a body which went on to co-opt an additional five. The whole executive then appointed the first thirty-five members of the legislature. As vacancies arose at annual intervals it was agreed that they should be filled, so far as possible, on a provincial rota and according to national quotas of representatives from each province, thus reviving once again the practice of the States-General.[24] Not all of the "Batavians" were eliminated from the new regime. At the core of the ruling personnel were those "Patriot Regents" who had set their face against democracy since 1796 and had persisted in supporting the federalist view in successive legislatures. A number had been the first victims of the purges and imprisonments of January 1798: de Sitter, de Beveren, Bicker, de Vos van Steenwijk and Queysen. A disproportionate group represented the paradoxically twinned interests of the land provinces and Amsterdam (in distinction to those of Holland as a whole). Of the erstwhile unitarists and democrats, only Spoors, Besier and Bijleveld survived on the Regency, while the increasingly supple van Hooff (another of the "prisoners" of the Huis 't Bosch) continued to occupy a place in the shrunken legislature.

Of these figures, the most influential by far was Jan Bicker. In neither his political sympathies nor his social affiliations did he have anything in common with the men who had governed the Batavian Republic since 1795. His personal wealth and the lustre of his family put Bicker on the same standing as the élite dynasties of the other provinces—the Aylva in Friesland or the van Heeckeren van Enghuizen in Gelderland—who had been out of favour since the revolution. He had, it is true, been enough of a Patriot to seek refuge in France in 1787 and had played an important part in constituting, with Abbema and Valckenaer, the Paris circle of the Batavian committee. But he was not and never had been a revolutionary. Together with his caucus of dependents in the legislature—Meinardus Siderius, Johannes Busch, and the man who had apprehended Wilhelmina at Goejanversluis, de Lange van Wijngaarden—he stood for all those who in 1786 and 1787 had enjoyed the brief euphoria of deposing the Stadholder while as yet unharassed by the vox populi. Moreover, his prominence in the new regime made it possible for similar patricians (albeit of more Orangist reputation) to be approached.

Bicker himself had hoped that the banker de Smeth might become associated with the Regency, thereby lending it the necessary social and economic tone to restore its financial credibility. But if de Smeth proved reluctant, others perhaps less distinguished were by no means shy of reconciliation. G. J. van der Heim, H. A. Laan and Gerard Brantsen, the Stadholder's emissary to Paris in January 1795, all accepted places from the new Regency. Its most unlikely recruit was the baron Egbert Sjuck Gerrolt Juckema van Burmania Rengers, formerly *grietman* and *dykegrave* of Wijnbritseradeel, and more importantly burgemeester of Leeuwarden before 1795. His activities both in 1787 and 1794 had earned Burmania Rengers an unsavoury reputation as one of the more enthusiastic bloodhounds of the old regime in Friesland, and given the radical reputation of the city just five years before, it is remarkable that his rehabilitation should have been so swift. His inclusion on the Regency was perhaps the clearest indication of just how far it had come, not only from the palmy days of 1798 and unitarist democracy, but from the dethronings of 1795.[25] No wonder that in November 1801 James Crawfurd reported to London that the Orange Party were, on the whole, "well satisfied" with the new regime, "which verges very rapidly to [sic] an aristocracy."[26]

The restoration of the Orange regents to places on both the departmental and the national administrations proceeded so smoothly that their leaders were emboldened to convene a special meeting in The Hague at the end of 1801 to consider the extraordinary turn in their fortunes. Their host was P. H. van der Wall, a former burgemeester of Dordrecht who, with Brantsen and Hendrik Mollerus (the Heer of Westkerk and Vulpendaal, and ex-secretary of the Council of State), represented the more pragmatic elements among the followers of the Orange House. But others among those attending —Admiral van Bylandt Halt, and the Barons van Lynden van Lunenburg and van Spaen van Voorstonde—were not, after all, on the catholic fringe of the interest. The provincial and court nobility had been the bulwark of the Restoration, many of them more avid to see the Patriots comprehensively punished than Pensionary van de Spiegel. But at the "States of the Kneuterdijk" (as the meeting came to be known, after its host's Hague address), the Orangist leaders reconciled themselves to a provisional mode of pragmatism. Like their French opportunist counterparts, they were prepared to accept the inducements with which the new regime was plying them without for one moment abandoning their eventual aim of restoring the House of Nassau to its traditional primacy. Absolution from the sins of consorting with the enemy was made easier by a letter to Baron van Lynden from the Prince in December 1801, counselling insinuation into official positions the better to manipulate the offices of state and make smooth the way for the Second Coming at Scheveningen.[27] For the time being, then, the Orangists were content to match the Patriot regents in ringing declarations of patriotic union for the sake of ending the vendettas of democracy and revolution.

Only one peculiarly irritating fly threatened to mar the ointment of this regent coalition. Gijsbert Karel van Hogendorp, a precocious Orangist who had been rewarded for his services in 1787 by promotion to the office of Pensionary of Rotterdam, had in 1799 already attempted to make direct overtures to the Prince. Brushed aside by the court clique of the Fagels and Bentincks, he had persevered in his ambition of alerting at least the Hereditary Prince to his true interests. By the end of October 1801, he felt confident enough to publish his remarkable *Declaration to the Regency of State* (*Verklaring aan het Staatsbewind*).[28] This manifesto—for that is what it was—ran directly counter to the "official" policy approved by the notables of the Kneuterdijk. Doctrinally it was Oranger than the Orangists although, characteristically, Princess Wilhelmina gave it her blessing when van Hogendorp sent a copy to England in December. Far from endorsing even a tactical alliance with the Patriot regents, the *Declaration* mounted a frontal attack on the resurgence of oligarchy. Pouring scorn on the plebiscite as a credible legitimation of the new regime, it drew on the tap-roots of traditional Orangist populism by proclaiming the Stadholder as the only viable shield against the "oppression" of the regents. The failure of democracy, he argued, had left the Dutch people with only two alternatives: the selfishness and corruption of the patriciate or the disinterested paternalism of the ruling dynasty. The old-fashioned candour of these sentiments, and van Hogendorp's habit of saying out loud what Orangist leaders might well have privately felt—that, for example, the Reformed Church should be re-established and the Jews disfranchised—seriously embarrassed those trying to present a conciliatory front to the government.

It was even more unfortunately timed for those who had argued for the political amnesty on the grounds that with Britain about to acknowledge the sovereignty of the Batavian Republic in a general peace, the issue of a Stadholderian restoration had become academic. Van Hogendorp must have been either very bold or very obtuse in his assessment of the *Declaration*'s reception, since he despatched specially translated copies to both the Prussian and French ambassadors, then engaged in arranging an indemnification for the Stadholder's property and titular pretensions in the Netherlands. Although the Regency of State had no intention of turning the impetuous author of the *Declaration* into a martyr, Procureur-General van Maanen began to show sufficient interest in its seditious content that van Hogendorp was forced into the patently ridiculous position of claiming it had been published merely for private circulation among his friends.[29]

However ill-judged and premature van Hogendorp's *Declaration* may have been, it contained one important truth. If the overtures made to the more pliable among the Orangists were flattering, and in the context of the moribund revolution a further step in its final demise, they amounted to nothing like an "Orange Restoration." The real legatees of the September coup were just that class on whom van Hogendorp had concentrated his attack: the urban patriciate. Blauw, who (like Gogel) had originally been prepared to accept a limited measure of revision, was aghast at what had actually come about, and compared the situation not to 1786 but to that earlier nadir of regent government, the "Stadholderless" time before 1747.[30] The speed and comprehensiveness of the reaction surprised even those who, like Wiselius, had feared the worst. Writing to de Winter in the summer of 1802 about the elections for the departmental administration in Holland, Wiselius remarked that while

. . . I had expected some Orangists to be appointed—for that after all chimes in with the prevailing System of unity, I had nowise . . . imagined that the numbers of true Patriots might be counted on the fingers of a hand and that those few who have been admitted can only be nonentities amongst that company. . . .[31]

How Spoors and Besier—the unwitting stalking-horses of the counter-revolution—could continue to work with men whose beliefs were fundamentally opposed to the grounds on which the Republic was established, he failed to see. Wiselius himself continued to cling tenuously to his office on the

"Asiatic Council"—the body which, at the end of 1799, had replaced the directorate of the Dutch East India Company, and resisted all attempts by the Company patricians to revert to its traditional autonomy. Individual bureaucrats like Elias Canneman in the treasury were retained for their expertise in spite of manifestly unreliable political views. But by and large it was as if the six years of the Batavian Republic had been merely an ephemeral episode in the continuing history of the patrimony of the regents.

There was indeed a conscious effort to erase the more disagreeable iconography of the revolution. Article 20 of the Constitution paid lip service to the principle of an undivided sovereignty, but not that of a Batavian Republic. Instead it seemed there was to be a Batavian Commonwealth (*Gemeenebest*): a familiar and innocuous synonym for the national community and one bereft of revolutionary associations. The epigraph "Liberty, Equality, Fraternity" (*Vrijheid, Gelijkheid, Broederschap*) which had a-dorned all official communications, was dutifully removed and the last wormy liberty trees taken from their places of honour in front of town halls as offending eyesores. Other hitherto taboo features of traditional Dutch ceremonial began to re-appear. At the celebrations for the signing of the Peace of Amiens, the members of the Regency of State appeared dressed in the gold braid and black satin of the magistrates of the old Republic. To the chagrin of the more Patriot-minded predikants in the city, pews and stalls were once more reserved for the councillors, regents and magistrates of Utrecht and decorated again with the tabards, ripped out when the city assembled in the churches to elect its revolutionary committees in 1795.

All this was merely the flummery of the reaction. Bonaparte had permitted, even delighted in, a reversion to the same ritual nonsense while at the same time retaining control over its patronage. The far greater degree of decentralisation inherent in the Dutch old regime meant that once released, that control was much harder to exercise. And the new constitution made it harder still. The key to the re-establishment of regent autonomy lay with the eight departments. Drente had been amalgamated with Overijssel (not without protests in Assen) but Brabant had been preserved in the rights it had won in 1795. In the context of the 1801 constitution, the departmental administration assumed a double significance. In one direction, they mediated between the claims of local communities—towns and villages—and the national government. In the other direction, their competence itself defined the limits to which the authority of the national executive might be extended. In theory the constitution stipulated that the departments were to have jurisdiction over all "domestic" matters not specifically reserved by the superior authority. But finance aside, this could be held to cover all manner of business—fiscal; juridical; police; public works; philanthropy; education— virtually the entirety of government belonging to the old provinces of the Republic.

Initially, at least, the Regency of State retained important sanctions. It required departmental budgets to be submitted and approved before authorising expenditure; in the first instance, it appointed the ten interim councillors and during 1802 published the regulations governing their competence and future appointment.[32] The provision that two of their number were to retire at annual intervals was meant to guard against the entrenchment of interest and to retain the electoral principle. But in practice, high property and tax qualifications; low attendance at the primary assemblies; liberal use of the traditional habit (especially in the land provinces) of co-option; and above all the dropping of the ineligibility bar for retiring councillors meant that selection of the administrations was confined to a small number of mutually acquainted notables. In Utrecht, where the administration comprised six city patricians and four Orangist regents, two men, Taets van Amerongen and Camps, were due, by lot, to retire in 1803. At the appointed time they let their names go forward for re-nomination and were duly elected without any difficulty.[33]

The first elected President of the departmental administration of Holland —in a convincing vindication of his own tactics—was P. H. van der Wall, the Dordrecht regent who had convened the meeting at the Kneuterdijk. His own preferment made it less surprising that the administration should also have included Collot d'Escury of Enkhuizen, who had been made a Knight of the Chamber by William V for his part in the suppression of the Patriots in 1787, and another staunchly Orangist regent of Rotterdam, H. A. van Bleiswijk. The degree to which surviving Patriots were swamped by more conservative figures was dramatically underlined by the inclusion of Pieter Elias, the former sheriff of Amsterdam (*hoofdschout*) and the bête-noire of the city's clubs and *wijk* assemblies. Just five years before, the Stadhuis had been besieged by crowds demanding his imprisonment or worse. Now his restoration to office was accepted without demur. Indeed the interests of Amsterdam, so often at loggerheads with those of the province as a whole, were far more effectively represented in the post-1801 administration. Of the great patrician families, a Wickevoort Crommelin was elected as member, together with Nicholas Calkoen, the son of the dining companion of John Adams and van der Capellen, but a regent whose coat had turned as soon as the Patriot movement had begun to show democratic tendencies.

In Gelderland and Overijssel it was reported that the traditional ruling families, many of them from the Orangist nobility, had returned to office without serious opposition. Even where they were less than a majority on the councils, their experience of public affairs and their greater social weight told heavily in their favour. In Zeeland just one confessed Patriot, van Doorn, hung on grimly in the company of men like Clijver and Passpoort, respectively regents of Flushing and Middelburg who had "encouraged" the sack and plunder of Patriot property in the Orange riots of 1787.[34] Even more remarkable was the fact that van de Spiegel's son-in-law, J. W. van den Houtte, who had been responsible for bringing the Zeeland towns into line with government orthodoxy in 1788, was appointed to be secretary of the departmental administration in 1802. Not surprisingly he resumed where he had broken off seven years before. In 1804 an anonymous commentator observed that of the departmental officials, "almost none of those chosen [in 1795] by the people remains; only aristocrats and Orangists, plunderers and enemies of France."[35]

Although the Regency of State was responsible for the final approval of all municipal regulations, their detailed drafting was left to the departments. The departments were also given the work of "reorganising" their personnel to conform with the new political order, a task they undertook with unconcealed enthusiasm. As a result, by the time those regulations came to be published in February 1803, the major towns had been brought firmly back within the charmed circles of the regents. Electoral procedure differed according to the size of the population but was everywhere sufficiently elaborate to minimise the effects of the initial votes of the primary assembly. In Utrecht, each of the twelve districts (eight plus the rural suburbs) elected a representative to the intermediary college. This then divided in two; one half nominating a list of putative councillors, the other reducing it by half, and a plenary session supplying the final names, not necessarily from among their own number. Needless to say, the complications of this procedure deterred all but those who had a special interest from bothering to participate. In February 1803, the city's population stood at around 33,000; the number registered for the franchise at 3,500; and the average number actually voting in the elections of 1803 and 1804 about 500.[36] The level of tax and property qualifications fixed by the Regency of State was an even more effective deterrent. To be sent to the electoral college as a candidate required 200 florins in annual city taxes or 300 florins in house rent; 10,000 florins' worth of real estate or 20,000 florins' worth of securities.

Given these kinds of conditions it is hardly surprising that the city councils rapidly reverted to traditional regencies. The Amsterdam Council actually re-adopted the magic number of thirty-six as of old; reassumed the traditional titles of *wethouder* (alderman) and *schepen* (magistrate); and re-divided the administration into colleges of finance; trade and commerce; police and public works. The Committee of Justice, which had been the target of excoriation from both the clubbists and ex-regents, was replaced by the old *Schepenbank* which once more dispensed its very customary forms of justice.[37] Other discredited practices received a new lease on life with the revival of urban autonomy. Councils were again free to distribute patronage on much the same scale as they had been accustomed before 1795 and readily took the opportunity to re-establish the networks of obligation and dependence on which regent power had been based. At Scheveningen the seventy-five-year-old Boudewijn de Wit, who had served as *schepen* uninterruptedly from 1761 to 1768, was restored to his office; and in Utrecht and Amsterdam a host of functionaries, dismissed summarily in 1795 and until recently not even daring to petition for redress, could contemplate with confidence the reversal of that misfortune.

Nepotism and family influence once again became important. It might well have set Fijnje's teeth on edge to recall how savagely he had been attacked after June 12, 1798, for "venally" appointing one of his sons to a minor post in the diplomatic service when the present Minister for Foreign Affairs (van der Goes) had his brother Hendrik made a city councillor at The Hague; when one Baron van Haersolte remained a member of the State Regency and another a member of the legislature; when a Samuel van Hoogstraten (a crony of Bicker's) was also a member of the government and his brother Frederick of the departmental administration of Holland; and when no less than three de Kempenaers occupied high office at The Hague—one as a member of the departmental administration, his half-brother as a city councillor and *his* son as a magistrate on the tribunal of justice.

Enno van Gelder's detailed account of the "Incorrigible Regents" of The Hague illuminates the ease and intricacy with which these family and social relationships once more became the essential buttress of local government.[38] Their practitioners could, after all, draw on a deep well of custom, habit and precedent denied to the democrats, always on the defensive against the capricious nature of elective government. There was still room for the enterprising parvenu who played his social cards shrewdly like the Catholic lawyer from Delft, Anthonie Schiefbaan, who remained on The Hague Council, or Pompe van Meerdevoort who, having run through the entire range of political allegiances, was moving back judiciously to his patrician roots. Among The Hague Council, H. A. Caan had been town secretary before 1795; came from a long-established clan of Rotterdam regents and had married into the van Necks, whose familial ramifications stretched to Amsterdam and beyond and who had been burgemeesters at The Hague earlier in the century. The father of another, A. G. Drijfhout, had been the chief syndic of the City Orphanage and naturally the dispenser of important patronage as a result. Both Drijfhout and Caan were related to Pieter Patijn, the city magistrate, whose family were again long established in the city and whose father Johan had also been a burgemeester. The new burgemeester, Jan Slicher (who was to continue in office until 1808), had, like Calkoen in Amsterdam, originally identified himself with the Patriot regents and had been an officer in the Haagse Schutterij. By steering clear of trouble in 1787, he had avoided recriminations and had been rewarded for his inaction during the crisis with restoration to office in 1791. His wife belonged to the van Kretschmayr clan, which had itself supplied the city with a former commandant of the garrison and a present city councillor.

Similar patterns of relationship and allegiance prevailed in all the major towns of Holland: in Amsterdam, where the Six family (there were two on the council), the Bickers and the Wickevoort Crommelins came into their own again; in Haarlem, Gouda and Rotterdam. Leiden, arguably the city where the Patriot cause had been most popular, was more eclectic in its choice; but the net effect of the changes on its council was also to reverse the transformations of 1795. In 1802 figures like Etienne Luzac, now a keen Orangist, and Adriaan Kluit, the former Professor of Dutch History at the university and an advocate of a "reformed Stadholderate," were admitted to the city council, along with more outré figures such as the patrician Wijckerheid Bisdom and van Leyden Gael, the 1787–88 burgemeester who, like Elias in Amsterdam, had in just five years moved from anathema and the possibility of criminal proceedings to reinstatement.[39] The rehabilitation at this time was so expansive that it could afford to take in both protagonists of the dispute in Utrecht, which twenty years before had set fire to Patriot democracy: Voet van Winssen, the people's hero, and "Klaas" Pesters, the arch-villain, once again going by his Stadholderian title of the "Lord [*Ambagtsheer*] of Cattenbroek."[40] With such jaunty presumption the wheel had surely come full circle.

Masters of their own house again, the regents had no compunction about shrugging off the apparatus of social and economic paternalism foisted on them between 1798 and 1801 by the Directorial government. Even at the best of times that machinery was never robust, and earlier departmental and municipal authorities had had little difficulty in failing to comply with or else completely ignoring orders and regulations to which they took exception. But despite the constitutional changes in their favour there remained some outstanding areas of sensitivity. The guilds, for example, which had been formally abolished in 1798, according to Article 4 of the new constitution were to remain defunct, along with any other comparable corporations and fraternities. Unhampered mobility of labour, and freedom from all locally imposed restrictions on the production, exchange and marketing of goods, struck directly at the traditional concept of the town as a self-contained, self-governing organic community with certain formal customs, rights and privileges inherent in its social organisation. Indeed, such a view was shared by most of those in the national government. The constitution sought merely to uphold the formal indivisibility of the Republic the *better* to encourage local administrations to claim their due share of jurisdiction. Thus the regulations for the departments and the municipalities gave them broad latitude over "the good order and well-being" of their citizens, and this was interpreted in such a fashion as to make the circumventing of the prohibitive edicts a relatively minor problem. Moreover, the complaints of those invoking the abolition of restriction against the action of some particular local authority were, in the first instance, referred to the departmental administration (rather than, as before 1801, to the government-appointed commissioner). Such grievances very rarely got any further.[41]

The period after 1802 witnessed the creeping growth of regulations governing the conditions in which certain trades might lawfully be carried on within city limits; the reimposition of local duties on "foreign" produce; and even the re-establishment of a "registration fee" for any trader, artisan or manufacturer wishing to set up shop for the first time. On May 18, 1802, the "Committee of Welfare" in Amsterdam passed an ordinance forbidding the sale of a wide range of commodities originating from outside the city except on appointed market days and at times and places laid down by the municipality.[42] Even though the Patriot burgemeester of Utrecht, M. P. van Eck, insisted: "It is a myth to believe that by the restoration of the deacons of the corporations and guilds . . . the prosperity and well-being of the city of Utrecht will be restored," he was really resisting what was in fact the popular view. In response to repeated petitions from the bakers, shoe-makers, weavers, and a number of the other craft guilds, the city council re-introduced a barely disguised form of registration money in the form of *poorteerschap* (residential) dues, and at the end of 1803 a "College of Commerce, Manufacture, Trade and Crafts" was instituted in which all those not formerly belonging to a guild were obliged to inscribe.[43]

By the end of that year, the old system had been restored virtually in entirety in Dordrecht, Middelburg, Arnhem, Haarlem, Amsterdam, Leiden and Deventer. The real losers from this reversion were the producers and itinerant traders of the country towns and hamlets, who originally had had no protection against goods produced in the Holland towns but were prohibited from their markets. The tanners, shoemakers and brewers of Brabant and the Friesian distillers, for example—who had enjoyed a brief and welcome heyday on the markets of Amsterdam and North Holland, making use of cheap rural labour costs to undercut the city goods—had once more to overcome the obstacles of steep and rigorously enforced tariffs.

The de facto restoration of the guilds was symptomatic of a general reversion to parochial exclusiveness. Sometimes this took the form of eccentric claims. In a passionate letter to the Regency of State, the burghers of Culemborg complained bitterly that their town, once part of the Duchy of Nassau and "liberated" in 1795, had returned to the slave status of a "conquered province" under the system of unitary sovereignty. "How can the Batavian nation treat Culemborg as a tribute state and send its proconsuls and quaestors to interfere with its domestic affairs?"[44] It went on to demand what amounted to full independence for its citizens from its overbearing neighbours to the west; from the province of Holland; from the national government—from everyone but the regents of Culemborg. And if a little town (the rifle-making centre of the province) of just over 10,000 could assert itself so aggressively, what might Amsterdam or Utrecht not do for their part? In a letter to Talleyrand remarking on the impotence of the government to make an impression on recalcitrant authorities, Marivault, the secretary of The Hague legation, commented that

no-one will cede what they call their privileges and their rights. They have been abolished since the revolution only in appearance not in fact . . . each and every municipality; every tribunal continues to conduct itself according to its ancient prerogatives and peculiar customs. The Directorial government failed to use sufficient force to put an end to such pretensions and at this present moment when the organic system of the government has not yet been completed they are reviving with greater vitality than ever before.[45]

However self-defeating in effect, the need to protect the immediate community (if necessary at the expense of its neighbour) became more intense as resources diminished and competition for the remains accelerated. Even though they were increasingly unable to cope with the rising costs of fuel and alimentation, the regents and syndics of orphanages, old age homes and workhouses were resolute in defending their absolute independence against any encroachment from state institutions like the General Poor Administration, however minimal its power. The private establishments were, in any case, protected from interference, since well before 1801 the legislature had decided that testamentary dispositions, endowments and the rights of trustees had to be sacrosanct. Article XV of the new constitution had further strengthened their hand by declaring the repeal of any revolutionary laws or ordinances which might be construed to impinge on the rights of private property.

But even the public establishments run by the municipalities were confining their obligations as far as possible to the needs of their own community. The old "acts of indemnity"—certificates of the pauper's place of origin, entitling the relieving agency to reimbursement at their expense—done away with by the revolution, were again coming to be demanded before any disbursement of charity was made to those unable to prove continuous local residence.[46] Such restrictions were not altogether the consequence of a selfish hardening of philanthropic arteries. In cities like Rotterdam and Franeker the plight of the charitable institutions had become so desperate that the suppliers of basic fuel, food and clothing were refusing to take orders from the poor houses unless receiving payment in advance.[47] The effect of such local discrimination was, of course, to reproduce the problem in adjacent neighbourhoods as the rejected "floating poor" migrated to wherever rumour indicated the possibility of a warmer reception.

In this battle of all against all, taking place in a vacuum of ill-defined and customarily asserted parochial prerogatives, those authorities did best who managed to pass on the responsibility for unwelcome social burdens while innocently upholding their justice. The indemnification of seigneurial rights is a case in point. The 1798 constitution had divided all such rights into those of patronage and appointment (of petty constabular, church and judicial officers in the villages); and those of dues (tithes, rights in money or kind in return for services and utilities such as milling, smithing, baking and so on). The first had been abolished in 1798 in perpetuity and without any form of indemnification, as had the patrimonial jurisdiction which had survived in some odd corners of the land provinces. But the problem of the dues remained more complex. As in France, much hinged on the distinction between rights arising from a tenurial or proprietorial relationship or those vested in legal and historical claims. The latter counted as "feudal" and illegitimate; the former as rental or contractual and subject to proper indemnification. An additional ordinance in 1800 had converted many of these dues into allodial holdings, thus bringing them within the economic category. As a result, the departmental administrations were inundated after 1801 with letters, petitions and addresses, claiming not only those rights which could be quantified in pecuniary terms but those like portage and cartage which defied reliable assessment. Naturally the departments, which themselves contained not a few nobles interested in the settlement of these claims, passed them upward to the national government for adjudication.

That they received a less sympathetic hearing than might have been anticipated was largely due to the efforts of one official: J. H. van der Palm, the president of the Council of the Interior (the collegiate successor to the Agency for Internal Affairs). Van der Palm was a gifted and energetic administrator, a Zeelander who in his time had edited a spicily radical newspaper called, aptly enough, *The Friend of the People*; had practised as a predikant in Middelburg and had been promoted to the Chair of Oriental Languages at Leiden. Despite his somewhat bumptious approach to petitioners and his not infrequent flights into Ciceronian rhetoric, van der Palm's presence in a socially conservative administration was of real importance for the survival of reform. To be sure, even a Walcheren predikant was incapable of working miracles. He encountered obstruction, "non-compliance" and stubborn resistance from local authorities in exact proportion to the boldness of his plans. His interesting scheme for a Catholic diocese based on Delft or Amsterdam was scotched by the furore it provoked among Reformed Church predikants, who were deeply reluctant to accord any further legitimation to the adherents of the "Romish cult."[48] Indeed, the far less audacious ordinance of the Regency of State requiring all citizens over the age of fourteen to be inscribed in *some* church community and to pay an annual donation for the upkeep of their respective establishments had, as van der Palm saw, been a failure partly because tightly organised communities like the Jews and the Mennonites were accustomed to make such donations in any event, so that the scheme was suspected as a way of avoiding the obligation to make public provision for the now disestablished Reformed Church. Van der Palm was himself not in favour of any such move, but the departmental authorities were in the habit of supplying church wardens with "special" sums on petition and charging it against their annual budget, an indirect method of public patronage meant to nudge the state towards some form of re-establishment.

Van der Palm's other major interest was that of public instruction.[49] He was a member of the Society for the Public Good, which had developed an immensely popular national organisation for the propagation of educational reform, the establishment of teacher-colleges, and the publication of new propaedeutic material. As the second Agent for Public Instruction under the Directory, he had harnessed official support for these efforts and in the law of 1801 had succeeded in establishing the first hierarchy of educational commissions at the level of parish, district and department. They were to maintain and improve teaching standards; examine potential teachers; make regular visits to schools within their jurisdiction and report on progress; ensure a regular supply of modern teaching materials; and make financial recommendations where appropriate.[50] From the government's point of view, the great strength of these commissions was their independence from local authorities. For although at the district level they sat on local "school boards" with a body of parents and teachers, their responsibility was to their senior commissions and in the end to van der Palm. It was just this feature which so infuriated the departmental and municipal authorities. Their view of van der Palm's inspectors and commissioners was of nosey do-gooders interfering in matters which were none of their concern and of which they were profoundly ignorant.

Their resistance was made that much easier by the fact that the law of 1801 laid down a very strict distinction between "public" schools and "private" schools; the second, following the principle of the Poor Law, were outside the government's domain. "Public" was restricted virtually to those institutions established for the poor and run by public authorities. A further law drafted by van der Palm in 1803, and endorsed by the Society for the General Good, changed this dramatically. Henceforth "public" was to apply also to all forms of church foundations—indeed only privately funded and domestic tuition was to be exempt from state surveillance and scrutiny. The response of the local authorities was to ignore the statutory demand that within three months they publish full educational ordinances giving the inspectors their necessary warrant. Holland and Brabant actually petitioned the High Court in The Hague to declare the law unconstitutional, since it contravened those articles covering the domestic business of towns and departments. While this purely legal matter remained unresolved, the sheer obstructionism of the local administrations made it impossible for the law to be implemented. It was his experience of this furore which brought van der Palm around to the view that some form of unitary sovereignty would have to be re-established if anything was to be done about social reform in the Netherlands.

This was still a minority view among those actually in power in 1803, but it was shared by those relatively dispassionate foreign observers who were bemused by the Dutch addiction to particularity. Matteo Galdi, the minister of the Italian Republic, who had an obvious interest in giving close attention to the viability of the government of another client state, was struck by the parochial preoccupations of local regencies even when their administrations faced bankruptcy. His comments become sardonic when describing the tendency of the Dutch regents to ramble nostalgically about the time of Tromp and de Ruyter; to speculate wistfully about the restoration of the staple market and their colonial possessions at the peace; and to nourish wholly unrealistic illusions about the place of their nation in the Europe of the new century.[51] A judgement from an Italian that the Dutch lived too much in the past was criticism indeed. And Galdi underlined the folly of sustaining a form of government which accentuated the already centrifugal tendencies of Dutch society. Even on its own terms, he argued, it was a failure. Despite the abandonment of the paternalist Agencies, the purely domestic budget (excluding military costs) of the government had totalled 3 million guilders *more* than before September 1801. "The present Batavian constitution is demonstrably inadequate and insufficient, and has fallen into the most complete discredit. The government is without confidence and without power."[52]

Nor was the new regime an unqualified success as an agent of political pacification. Both the Prussian ambassador Bielfeld and the British minister (after March 1802) Robert Liston commented in their despatches on the continuing activities and not inconsiderable support for the remnant of the revolutionary democrats in Amsterdam and the major towns. Avoiding the excessive enthusiasm of The Hague mobs, who huzzaed his carriage wherever it was seen, Liston warned his Secretary of State that

> there still exists a formidable faction of the champions of Democracy and the partisans of France. These men, of whom a number were excluded from any share of power at the last change that took place in the constitution, express great dissatisfaction with the government of the day for having admitted to places in the administration a number of those who were employed under the ancient system and who are understood to be firm friends of the Prince of Orange.[53]

Allowing for professional Jacobinophobia, Liston's report had more than a grain of truth to it. Despite attempts to produce effective counter-propaganda for the Regency of State, the blasts of *De Heer Politieke Blixem* were becoming steadily more shrill, its satire more caustic, and its popularity more widespread. Even if its circulation was restricted to the few clubs of the Holland cities and the professional intelligentsia, it unnerved the government to be accused at weekly intervals of every conceivable form of crime and vice. Eventually a number was found with an article that could stand up in court as potentially seditious (since there was a fine line between abuse and treason) and Hespe was sentenced by the High Court of Holland to not less than six years' imprisonment and banished thereafter from the provinces of Holland, Zeeland and Utrecht.

Rumours about democratic conspiracies continued to multiply in the summer of 1802. It was said—quite correctly—that the democrats on the "Asiatic Council" like Wiselius had the ear of ex-Director Louis Gohier, now Commercial Secretary for France in Amsterdam. Even though large sums had been despatched to General Victor and a magnificent sword studded with precious stones to the formidably rapacious Augereau, the loyalty of the French military was always suspect. Galdi reported the existence of a "reform party" at Amsterdam, concerned to reduce the number on the Regency of State, create a President with strong executive powers (Schimmelpenninck?) and introduce a new national plan of taxation.[54] But not for the first time, the figure on whom speculation centered as the possible leader of an uprising was the man who had made that activity something of a speciality: General Daendels. The general had retired Cincinnatus-like to his estates in Gelderland after the mixed fortunes of the 1799 campaign. But he was sufficiently appalled by what had happened since September 1801 to respond favourably to the tentative overtures of Wiselius, who himself believed that "a new January 22" was needed if the Republic and the revolution were to survive. Daendels had no special regrets about the demise of the 1798 constitution—or any constitution—but he did take particular umbrage at the preferment of cronies of the Stadholder who had been responsible for the persecution of himself and many of his friends after the débacle of 1787.

The problem was one of political approach. A sounding-out mission in Paris to see if opinion in the Consulate might be brought round in the democrats' favour had been an abysmal flop.[55] Besier and Pijman were known to be feeling their isolation within the Regency of State keenly, but they too fought shy of anything remotely resembling conspiratorial action. Most implausibly of all, Schimmelpenninck's well-known ambition for some kind of Presidential role in the government was believed to be sufficient bait to tempt him to throw his lot in with a possible coup. His real view will never be known, since events in October 1802 overtook the rather clumsy preparations. An anonymous *Bulletin of the Army* appeared in The Hague and in Amsterdam, purporting to record conversations held between Generals Dumonceau and Daendels and Schimmelpenninck at The Hague with a view to forming an oppositional triumvirate. The piece was almost certainly a cunning forgery distributed by government agents. It was true that such a meeting had taken place in September, when political tactics and the general state of affairs had been discussed in the most nebulous terms. Nothing faintly resembling a revolutionary plot had been got under way, partly because Schimmelpenninck's pious aversion for anything so underhand made it necessary to look elsewhere for a respectable figurehead. The appearance of the pamphlet, however, supplied the Regency with a providential pretext for giving the generals a firm dressing-down. A reward of 14,000 guilders was offered for information leading to the discovery of the author—a safe enough bargain in the circumstances—and an explanation and a retraction demanded from the objects of its commentary.

Schimmelpenninck lost no time at all in denouncing the work as a libellous fiction and in proclaiming his loyalty. He was duly rewarded with the London embassy which, for the time at least, it was supposed might satisfy his vanity. It was well known what satisfied Daendels when neither power nor reputation were to be had. Having duly made his peace with the government, he was fobbed off with an additional estate in his province and a decent gratuity "for services to the nation." Thus the democrats' plot fizzled out before it had ever got under way. There could, in any case, be no alternative. In an interview with the Batavian envoy M. Smits, the First Consul made his own attitude to such commotions more than plain: "It is to be recommended that you keep your peace. Europe has need of rest; governments must not be overthrown. On the contrary, those that exist must be consolidated."[56]

The Peace of Amiens and the Dutch, 1802–1803

A traveller returning to the Netherlands after a prolonged absence might be forgiven for believing that very little seemed to have been changed by two decades of war and revolution. In the maritime provinces, office and power continued to be monopolised by largely self-selecting clans of regents and their dependents. In Friesland, the Aylva had re-established their hold on the *grietenies* of Oostergo and Westergo; and in the land provinces, the patricians of Deventer and Zwolle, Arnhem and Zutphen, deferred to the Orangist entourage of the great nobles like Schimmelpenninck van der Oye and van

Heeckeren van Enghuizen. Dissenters and Jews were nowhere to be found on municipal councils or as officers of the militia, and the odd token Catholic in Nijmegen or den Bosch remained the exception rather than the rule. True, the plague of vagrancy and begging seemed to have worsened, but that blight had always been a fact of Dutch social life, even amidst the affluence of the seventeenth-century Republic. And by the standards prevailing in other European cities, the Dutch old age homes and even workhouses remained models of enlightenment and comfort. Indeed on his arrival at The Hague, the British minister Robert Liston found very few signs of the distress previous reports had led him to expect. On the contrary,

with the exception of a few individuals of the lowest classes in The Hague, who suffer by the absence of the Stadholder's court, the people appear as formerly, well fed, well clothed, busy and at their ease: their dikes are in good repair, their causeways and their pavement in excellent condition and order. In their buildings, public and private, not a brick seems to be out of place.[57]

Even Marivault, who thought of himself as a hard-headed realist, observed in July 1802 that in spite of internal political difficulties,

the situation of Batavia has markedly improved during the last six months. The merchants are beginning to reap the harvest of their sacrifices and of their loyalty; commercial relations are taking on a new activity, numerous voyages have already taken place and others are even now in preparation. Credit has been re-established, confidence reborn and soon Amsterdam will be, as it was before the war, one of the greatest markets of the world—always provided that its industrious citizens are no longer made to empty their capital into the coffers of the State.[58]

These cheerful impressions of roadsteads crowded with vessels and wharves crammed with cargo are a salutary reminder to the historian of this time not to exaggerate the degree of disruption and discontinuity to which the country had been subjected. The trade figures given by van Nierop make it plain that given even a brief respite from the rigours of all-out war, Dutch trade was still capable of an impressive degree of recuperation.[59] Even before 1802, the number of ships entering the Texel and Vlie and the Maas had reached 55 per cent of the 1785–89 average; it was not until after 1804 that the figure was to fall back decisively again.

	Texel and Vlie	Maas and Goeree	Value (in fl. 1,000s from rondemaat duty)
1785–89	2,559	1,621	
1799	121	95	426
1800	1,433	560	363
1801	1,620	735	417
1802	2,967	1,723	567
1803	1,970	817	445
1804	2,189	674	545
1805	1,277	672	–
1806	989	371	(tax abolished)

In what had been the most dangerous and controversial traffic—that of Anglo-Dutch trade, which had been carried on before the peace via neutral carriers, Dutch ships flying neutral flags (Danish, Prussian and American) or outright smuggling—the year 1802 witnessed a powerful spurt.[60] Dutch imports from Britain trebled their 1797 volume, and value and goods going in the opposite direction (principally cheese and butter) almost doubled. Nor, for that matter, ought it to be forgotten that the disintegration of the governmental structure of the Dutch state exposed more clearly the resilience and durability—in appalling financial conditions—of its local, cellular institutions. Whatever regime happened to be in power at The Hague, their counterparts in the towns and villages took care to see that the essentials of a still civilised life as they saw it were duly maintained. The dykes and polders still contained the flood tides; the poor were somehow nourished (if more frugally than in the past); the city watch kept burghers safe in the streets at night; and every Sabbath the churches continued to fill up with dutiful congregations.

Of course this picture of order and well-being was less than impeccable. It would be as misleading to suppose that all was well with the Dutch economy in 1802 as to describe these years exclusively in terms of disastrous impoverishment. Even the conspicuous commercial revival was to some extent deceptive. It did not, as Gogel hoped, herald the revival of the staple market but rather a stage on the way to its final demise. Most of the colonial cargoes arriving in the Netherlands before the peace had been brought in neutral vessels: American, Danish, even Prussian. American ships had also served the clandestine export trade from the Republic to Britain and in many areas had used the war to take over the role of carrying intermediary. Even when conditions permitted Dutch vessels to take cargo direct from Britain, it was as often to Emden or Hamburg as to Amsterdam or Rotterdam. Many agencies were established during these years in the German ports which, like American shipping, were the beneficiary of the difficulties faced by the Dutch. One enterprising butter merchant, Anthonie Hoboken, for example, imported coffee from Plymouth but took it to Emden, from where it was carried down the coastal route to Harlingen and thence to the major distribution centres in Friesland and Holland. Of course there can be no doubt that the conclusion of peace benefited the Dutch ports in their economic see-saw with the North Sea German ports. But this was only a minor interruption of a long-term trend in favour of the Germans. Moreover, the Dutch had to contend with the fact that their re-export monopoly to south and central Germany (let alone further afield) was being challenged by the northern ports. If the estuaries of the Rhine and the Maas continued to offer splendid routes into the European heartland for the distribution of colonial and manufactured goods, Emden's position at the mouth of the Ems was at least as advantageous. The high tariff barriers erected at the behest of both the Prussians and the French put a further obstacle in the way of efficient and competitive Dutch re-exports.

Thus an increasing proportion of imports to the Netherlands remained for the domestic market. And an increasing proportion of their content comprised those British manufactures—textiles, cheap pottery and metallurgical goods—which undercut the home product. The unhappy situation came about whereby in so far as the Dutch continued to have a prominent role as entrepôt, it was shared with Hamburg as the "keyhole" of the all-vanquishing British manufactures in Europe. This naturally led to the rekindling of the ancient dispute between commercial and manufacturing interests.

The revival, then, was less than complete, and entailed some crucial qualitative changes for the Dutch economy. Some losses were never made good. The shipbuilding industry was somewhat slow to respond to the new opportunities, and had, in any case, lost access to cheap monopolies of essential raw materials like Archangel tar. The Great Fisheries, generously subsidised by the government, depended absolutely on safe maritime conditions. Unlike those in commerce, the fisheries could not sustain themselves by indirect means once that security had again broken down. The revival of the Bourse and the commodity market was, to be sure, a sign of genuine health. But paradoxically, the efflux of short-term capital away from state securities and into productive enterprise adversely affected the side of the money market to which thousands of petty- and middle-burghers had entrusted their savings in wartime. That market was now dominated by the domestic jungle of loans, credits, bills and securities to which all public administrations had become mortgaged. Like the trading entrepôt the international side of finance had become reduced, or at least confined, to the inner circle of banking moguls such as Hodshon, Stadnitzki, Willink, and above all Henry Hope, whose re-emergence as a prominent power in Amsterdam set the seal on the re-establishment of regent supremacy.[61]

Whether all this activity, much of it best described as feverish, betokened a real measure of economic vigour it is difficult to say. What Robert Liston and Marivault were observing was really a heavily dosed invalid given a sudden, though no less welcome or necessary, transfusion of business and capital. But this apparent "normalisation" of Dutch society, "The burgher in his business; the regent in his place" (*De burger in zijn zaken; de heeren op het kussen*), was based on very precarious foundations. It could be sustained only so long as the Dutch remained sheltered from the vicissitudes of European politics as they had been in the middle years of the old century. But propped as it was on a great pillow of credit, the Republic in its reincarnation of 1801 could not survive another military trauma. No peace; no regents.

Great things, however, were expected from that peace at the beginning of 1802. With its colonies fully restored and its shipping unencumbered by privateers, it was not inconceivable that the carrying trade might make as decent a showing as it had in the 1790's, particularly across the Atlantic. In return for some form of indemnification for its estates in the Republic, it was expected that the House of Orange could be persuaded to forego its titular claims, and even that the British would then be in a position to recognise the sovereignty of a Republic *sans* Stadholder, whatever it might be called. As far as the French were concerned, the Dutch aim was to liquidate as much of the Treaty of The Hague as was consistent with their security; above all rapidly to pare down their military obligations, ensure the withdrawal of

French troops, bargain for some territorial compensation for the cessions of 1795, and have the whole of Flushing restored to their sovereignty.

It was not very long, however, before Schimmelpenninck, the Dutch plenipotentiary at the Amiens Conference, discovered that the position of Spain and the Batavian Republic as nominal equals and co-allies of France was meant to remain strictly nominal. The preliminaries signed at London the previous October had confronted the minor powers with what was in effect a fait accompli. This was all the more galling to the Dutch since sacrifices had been made on their behalf but without any consultation. They were to cede Ceylon and to guarantee free shipping at the Cape for the British. It was no use Schimmelpenninck forlornly pointing out to Talleyrand that in the Treaty of The Hague France had pledged to act as guarantor of all the Dutch colonies and never to make a separate peace. Those were the terms and there was an end of it. "The whole world," the French minister tartly observed, "has need of peace and your country above all."[62] The First Consul, as was his wont, made the point even more bluntly: "This existence [of the Republic], they hold only from us; we owe them nothing and they owe us everything . . . if France and England make peace, what can a secondary power like Holland do but adhere to it?"[63]

Nor did the actual proceedings at Amiens—such as they were—do much to mollify the Dutch sense of hurt. Neither Cornwallis nor Joseph Bonaparte were anything like a match for Schimmelpenninck's diplomatic skills. But with the cards they held, even the clumsiest performance would have sufficed. And Joseph was on a tight rein from Paris. The First Consul had calculated that the easiest way to secure uncomplaining assent would be to organise separate negotiations between France and Britain, merely ironing out the differences outstanding from the October talks, and then leave Britain to negotiate with each of the minor powers, confronting them with a virtual ultimatum. This stratagem was represented to Schimmelpenninck by Joseph as the express wish of the *British*, and in any event a nice concession to national amour-propre—each power, as it were, negotiating in their own right. Neither the Dutch nor Spanish were fooled for a moment. They refused absolutely to sign any treaty based on negotiations to which they had not been full party throughout. Nor were they surprised when a disarmingly baffled Cornwallis explained that contrary to Joseph's allegation, separate negotiation had all along been a French, not a British demand. Why was it, asked Merry, his secretary, that the French were so gratuitously Machiavellian? Because, replied Schimmelpenninck,

they want to make an abrupt peace and steal from you all that you have gained. That done they will mock at the consequences; they will remain with the Spanish and with ourselves without having provided for our interests; they will then make every kind of demand, exercise every kind of despotism on the two countries. They know very well that by including us in the same treaty, you will give us an importance which can only be harmful to their ambitious and unreasonable views.[64]

Whenever there was any danger of British and Dutch interests converging,

France made sure suitable obstacles were placed in the way. The vessels seized from Story in 1799 were, the Dutch hoped, either to be restored to the Batavian navy or set off against the indemnification of the Prince. But that last obligation, Bonaparte insisted, was to be his, since with the Hereditary Prince sitting at his feet he was in a good position to carry out a diplomatic revolution in relations with the House of Orange. The tortuousness of French diplomacy, however, nearly overreached itself. For in the middle of March, opinion in the British Parliament and in the country, never exactly wild for the peace, suddenly hardened, suspecting that the French were playing a double game and merely winning time for preparations for a new war. So close did the talks at Amiens come to complete rupture that Schimmel-penninck had to come to Joseph's rescue and, contrary to the express orders of the British government, forestall Cornwallis from presenting an ultimatum. While Joseph (who would certainly have borne the brunt of his brother's wrath had the conference broken down) was personally grateful for the Dutch ambassador's mediation, official gratitude did not extend to considering the request that matters such as troop evacuation and the status of Flushing be regulated as part of the treaty itself. Negotiations between allies, Talleyrand reminded Schimmelpenninck, were outside the terms of reference of the settlement.[65]

Although the French minister was correct in making his point, the almost perverse reluctance of his government to come to any clear understanding with the Dutch on the issues outstanding between them did not augur well for a long-term peace. In April, an ominously inconclusive interview took place between the Batavian minister in Paris, Smits, and the First Consul, in which the latter hedged over both the number of French troops to be withdrawn in accordance with the Treaty of Amiens and the chronology of their evacuation. In August, Smits complained that whenever he raised the matter with Talleyrand, the minister brushed the enquiries aside with laconic remarks about the "usefulness" of prolonging their stay. On one occasion he even argued that since the Dutch would have to send so many of their troops to defend the colonies being restored to them, it was essential that some French military —6,000, 10,000?—should be kept for the protection of the Netherlands itself.[66]

As the "interim" period dragged on through the autumn of 1802, tempers began to fray and the Dutch, quite rightly, to suspect the worst. Troop reductions aside, Smits reported from Paris that "there appears to be not the least intention on the part of the First Consul to settle the matter of Flushing with any haste."[67] The French customs posts in the port had been overrun by angry Dutch seamen and traders, and the *Rotterdam Gazette* had published a violent tirade by the city council against the continuing depredations of officials and privateers. For their part, the French were incensed at the substantial quantities of dairy goods exported to Britain from Walcheren—although such trade was now of course perfectly legitimate.[68] Before leaving for London, Schimmelpenninck made a final effort to persuade Bonaparte of the wisdom of restoring to the Batavian Republic those conditions which would be economically therapeutic. Otherwise, he warned, catastrophe could follow. "Ah," replied the First Consul with a smile, "you still have so many resources: the industry of the Batavian nation and its calm and wise character will surely enable it to transcend such difficulties."[69]

Of course the French could, with some justice, point to British failure to evacuate Malta with any promptness. And it was not until February 1803 that the citadel and forts at the Cape were finally returned to the Dutch authorities. But the quibbles about the timing of military disengagement merely glossed over a more fundamental difference of interpretation of the Amiens agreement which seriously jeopardised any chance of a lasting peace. In mitigation it is highly unlikely that Bonaparte all along saw the peace as a breathing space in which to arm for a new campaign. But certainly it was meant to set the seal on a "new order," based on French hegemony in the west and an arrangement with a diminished Austria and Russia in the east. That order, moreover, presupposed the tightening of the French grip on a ring of secondary and client states from Spain on the Atlantic to Switzerland and Italy at the Alps and Dolomites. French power was to straddle the traditional crossroads: down the Rhine on the north-south axis and east-west on the central knot of Alpine highlands right down to the Danubian plain and, if need be, the Adriatic. Needless to say, this was not the British view. The peace they signed had been a bargain extended to France and her vulnerable satellites in return for the reciprocal termination of what Britain judged to be the root causes of her own insecurity. This *necessarily* involved evacuation from, and the neutralisation of, Switzerland and the Netherlands—particularly since Belgium's status as departments of France seemed irreversible and northern Italy had become a French fief. Even the mediation of Switzerland was less than satisfactory, as the Jura and part of the Valais had been hived off to form an "independent" Republic meant to secure for France the Alpine passes to the southeast.

The position of the Netherlands in this scheme of things was important. Whatever the possibilities of a real neutrality might have been in the past, there was no chance that the Dutch would ever again be strong enough to maintain their territorial integrity. Since political nature abhorred vacuums, there was a dangerous possibility that the removal of French power would simply invite the substitution of the British on what had become France's own eastern frontier. This, in turn, begged an even more basic question: that despite the exchange of diplomatic civilities between Talleyrand and Hawkesbury, the Secretary of State, there remained a deep-rooted and mutual conviction that by history, economy and political interest France and Britain were natural enemies. No treaty, no diplomacy was capable of convincing men like Pitt and Grenville that a France without a monarch was ever capable of living by the accepted standards of civilised relations between states.

The Dutch were caught fast in the trap of that irreconcilable enmity just as surely as they had been in the 1780's. Only after 1830, when the axis of European conflict moved well away from the English Channel, would it be possible for the Netherlands to enjoy a quieter life. For the moment, as Sémonville put it, "The problem of the alliance and of Batavian independence is insoluble."[70] What, then, was to be done? Annexation was ruled out by Bonaparte; even had it been politically feasible, he had no wish to saddle

France with the wreckage of Dutch finances, and there was, moreover, a good chance that the burghers could still be made to pay albeit for a phantom sovereignty. Talleyrand had whispered in attentive ears that 50 millions (with suitable bonuses) would be the going rate for the reversion of Flushing and a decent indemnification for Flanders, Venlo and Maastricht. On the other hand, the First Consul had had enough of pandering to the fiction that the Treaty of The Hague had been a contract, freely entered into by the two parties, and that it gave the Dutch certain claims on French policy. When, in the autumn of 1803—after the worst had indeed come to pass and the Dutch were being marshalled for their part in the "descent on England"— Bonaparte saw the Dutch representatives at Brussels, he left them in no doubt whatever as to the future of their country.

"You may pretend to a civil independence," he told them, "but the rest is a chimera. You are tied to me like a satellite to a planet. I am not your enemy, but some force must be applied so that you follow in my step."[71] In the future their independence was to be granted to the Dutch as a favour, not as a right. Its condition was their satisfactory performance of obligations to the new war and to the alliance. That this would, in all likelihood, bring about their final ruin did not trouble him overmuch. The unenviable alternatives, it seemed, were subjugation from without or decomposition from within.

The War Crisis, 1803–1804

It was the peculiar misfortune of the Dutch that strategically as well as politically their territory was pivotal to the next phase of the conflict between French military and British naval power. Until the elaborate plan of invasion, first drafted by Admiral Latouche-Tréville, came to assume Atlantic ramifications, Bonaparte could afford to leave the Spanish in a position of uneasy quasi-neutrality. But defensively or offensively the North Sea coast was far too important to permit a similar luxury to the Batavians. Just when Bonaparte decided that a fatal confrontation with the British was inevitable remains much disputed among scholars.[72] By the late spring of 1803 he was certainly behaving as though he had abandoned any hope of coming to an accommodation over matters such as Malta and the "neutralisation" of either Switzerland or the Netherlands.

Once made, however, no time was wasted on consultation. At the same time that the Regency of State haggled with the French ambassador over the number of troops to be taken out of the country, whole divisions were actually pouring into its southern and western departments. On the patently ludicrous pretext that a British flotilla was cruising the Maas estuary (when it was, in fact, well out in the North Sea), General Monnet declared Walcheren in a state of siege; occupied Veere, Middelburg and Flushing; and, still more provocatively, ordered the Dutch garrisons stationed there to depart forthwith. In Brabant the barrier fortress towns were obliged to receive large numbers of French troops, who lost no time in seizing arsenals, magazines and municipal treasuries altogether in the manner of 1795.

This occupation in all but name excited outraged recrimination from the Dutch authorities, who saw it as a calculated provocation and a characteristic example of French brutality and arrogance. A letter to the First Consul protested at

a direct violation of the independence of this State and one which seems to demonstrate that they [the army] regard a country allied to their own as a land of conquest, by ordering inconceivable requisitions and using violence to seize the magazines and the arsenals.[73]

Local reaction was even more incensed. Nijmegen actually closed its gates to the "invaders" and was threatened with a full-scale siege if it refused to submit; at Breda the French troops were abused and pelted with clods of turf and stones; and, predictably, at The Hague where General Montrichard had presumptuously made his headquarters, a tense situation spilled over into open riot. To make matters worse, the Louisiana expedition, fitted out partly at Helvoetsluys, was prevented from sailing—first by late ice, then by violent storms. Much to the embarrassment of General Victor, its commander, his troops decided to treat the local countryside around Putten and the Hoeksche Waard as free pillage. Schimmelpenninck complained bitterly that "the conduct of the French troops in our country is frightful."[74]

Only too conscious that a new war would, in all likelihood, deliver the *coup de grâce* to the Republic, the Regency made strenuous efforts to avert that grim eventuality. Pontoi, an Amsterdam merchant, was sent to France as a special emissary to explain yet again the precariousness of the Dutch economic position. But since his slight of 1800, Bonaparte was disinclined to listen attentively to the laments of the Amsterdam business community, and refused point-blank to see him. When three more official delegates—Six, Blanken and Jacobson—tried their luck, they were presented with a catalogue of obligations incumbent on the Batavian Republic as a faithful ally to fulfil.[75] By mid-June there was no going back. Before his recall to London, Robert Liston observed that after the initial spasm of anger and despair had spent itself, the Dutch seemed resigned to their fate. "It would be difficult," he wrote to Grenville, "for me to give your Lordship an adequate idea of the grief and consternation which has overspread this country since the people became acquainted with the existing danger of a rupture between Great Britain and France."[76]

The trade figures show that the commercial boom which had flourished since 1801 did not, in fact, disappear overnight and even picked up somewhat in 1804. But the panic which ensued when war looked inevitable was real enough. Ships were ordered home laden or unladen to avoid a repetition of the situation in 1795 when they had fallen forfeit in enemy harbours. The Bourse nose-dived and, according to Marivault, several of the major houses "were only awaiting the hostilities to declare their bankruptcy." "A settled gloom appears on every countenance," Liston wrote; "the inhabitants seem to regard themselves as captives ready to be led to the slaughter."[77]

At the eleventh hour, despairing efforts were made to persuade the British not to regard the Batavian Republic as a willing party to any belligerency. But van der Goes—the exponent of neutrality—knew that such hopes were wildly unrealistic. Hawkesbury's final notes to Schimmelpenninck in London gave him the cold comfort that Britain was going to war to assure for Europe a lasting peace, and that while His Majesty had no wish to extend its calamities to any innocent party, he regretted the impossibility of erring on the side of generosity—unless, that is, France would show her willingness to respect the spirit and letter of Amiens by honouring her commitment to evacuate the Netherlands. For their part, the French set to the work of entrenching themselves in the Batavian Republic amidst manifest popular hostility. General Lacuée wrote to Bonaparte in the later part of 1803: "There is only one single constant and general idea hereabouts—hatred of the French and aversion for dependence."[78]

The new "Convention" signed between France and the Batavian Republic was a signal example of the ruthlessness of the former and the impotence of the latter. The survival of an independent Dutch nation was made contingent on terms which seemed likely, in any case, to ruin her. Dutch obligations to the combined army were fixed at about the same level as in 1795. The French forces were to be brought up to 18,000–20,000 and the Batavian army was to stand at around 17,000; the potential offensive and defensive force could therefore be estimated at some 35,000. In addition, 9,000 Dutch troops would accompany the invasion expedition, although it was possible that some of these might come from the nominally standing force. The naval terms were far more severe. Apart from its commitments under the Treaty of The Hague, the Batavian Republic was required to supply, by December 1803, 5 ships-of-the-line; 5 frigates (all fully crewed and equipped); 100 small gun boats; and 250 flat-bottomed transport craft capable of holding between 60 and 80 men each. In total, the Dutch were meant to provide transport for 25,000 men and 2,500 horses, all the vessels being provisioned for twenty-five days from sailing time. In other words, the Dutch were being asked to provide not only conventional naval power with which to fend off any British counter-attacks or preventive engagements, but a great part of that extraordinary flotilla—extending from Boulogne to the Texel—with which Bonaparte seems, in all seriousness, to have meant to undertake his "descent on England," one moonless, perfect night.[79]

The premature death of Latouche-Tréville, the master-mind of the naval plan and the ideal co-ordinator of the Atlantic and Channel fleets, postponed its execution; forced Bonaparte to think again about its strategy and, perhaps fatally, to reshuffle the naval command. But this "temporary" delay had no effect on the punishing preparations imposed on the Dutch. Captain Karel Verhuell had been appointed to liaise between the naval yards at Flushing and the Texel and the Consul's own military command, but such was his impatience and the strength of his obsession with the "Great Project" that in July he felt impelled to make a personal tour of inspection of the Flemish and Dutch ports. He was none too impressed with what he saw. During the previous war, shipbuilding in South Holland and Zeeland had been run down owing to the difficulty in securing adequate raw materials, in particular timber. Of the stocks obtained during the peace, most had gone north to the Zaan. Skilled labour had migrated elsewhere in the Republic or had even left the Netherlands altogether. Many of the Rotterdam sawmills had gone out of business. It was no easy task, then, to convert the yards at Flushing to pell-mell construction. The boss of the biggest yard, Schuyt, took some pride in these circumstances in informing the First Consul that the first part of the fleet could be ready in three months. The gracious reply he received was a demand to see a ship-of-the-line of seventy-four pieces ready for launching in fourteen days.[80]

Bonaparte was also appalled to learn of the continuing presence in the port of a handful of British families, an imprudence he regarded as verging on the criminally subversive. He insisted that they be expelled within four days or else incarcerated where prying eyes could do no possible harm. On June 15, before his trip, he had already given the special delegation of Willem Six and his colleagues a sombre warning:

I have no wish to interfere in the domestic affairs of Holland . . . it is
necessary that there should be no party in a position to impede all necessary
operations. If you co-operate, before a year is out we will take a stunning revenge
on England. It is in London that England will be vanquished. Only by an
invasion can we succeed in this and it is necessary that this should happen. If you
do not co-operate I will still not lose sight of the great cause to which I am
committed: the cause of the continent of Europe against England. I must pursue
this goal and I will not hesitate in it . . . I have no desire to burden Holland but
I need her ports. It is necessary therefore that you co-operate loyally. *Otherwise
I will be forced to turn you into a French Department.*[81]

On July 29 the ambassadors were carpeted once more and given some more of the same treatment.

But despite this frequent resort to the crudest bullying, Bonaparte was not more than characteristically callous where the Dutch were concerned. Other "soft points" on the North Sea littoral experienced their similar share of military rigour. General Mortier had invaded Hanover from Groningen and East Friesland in the summer, occupying Meppen and Cuxhaven with large garrisons to ensure that the mouth of the Ems was firmly under French control. In October Spain and Portugal were forced, through terse ultimata, to disgorge, respectively, 6 million francs *per month*, and 16 millions as a global sum, as their "donation" to the war effort. And as the naval gambit came to involve the participation of the Toulon and Rochefort fleets in diversionary tactics prior to the actual invasion, so the part to be played by the Spanish navy became correspondingly more significant.

The fact was that Bonaparte's preoccupation with the English expedition was grounded on premises of extraordinary irrationality. He remained deaf to the advice of both military and naval commanders that the expedition should be abandoned and that he turn his attention to the growing threat of Austrian military activity. His interviews with van der Goes and Schimmelpenninck (restored to the Paris embassy on Bonaparte's request) reveal that he was expecting a short, sharp and conclusively victorious struggle with the arch-enemy. A peace would be signed in London from which the Dutch would emerge with credit and honour, and what was more to the point, with Ceylon. Was not Britain on the edge of bankruptcy? Why else would they need an "income tax" to finance the war when he, Bonaparte, had no such problem? "I wish," murmured Schimmelpenninck, "we could say the same." "Oh," the Consul retorted, "the Dutch are so wealthy; they should spill their coffers a little." "We can already see to the bottom," van der Goes interjected. "That's very unfortunate," Bonaparte replied, "but sacrifices are necessary if the matter is to be brought to a satisfactory conclusion."[82] He went on to ask Schimmelpenninck how well he thought the British would fight. "They have a fine shop to defend," he responded, obviously pleasing the Consul, who thought that all to the good since "a rich nation always defends itself badly."

By November his fantasies had become even more extravagant. The "inevitable" consequences of the invasion would be mass desertions in the British army; carefully synchronised uprisings in Ireland, Scotland and Wales (nations to be detached from a truncated England in the new order); mutinies in the militia; panic on the Stock Exchange and in the Bank of England; and perhaps even a coup against the King led by his son, of whom Bonaparte had heard promising things.

What will London do? I imagine that everything will be in the greatest disorder. I presume that I will beat them; that I will have to kill many and to take many prisoners—then disorder will engulf London—there are so many *canaille*; pillage will inflame them.

It was to be Cairo all over again.[83]

Optimists though they were, van der Goes and Schimmelpenninck did not set much store by Bonaparte's assurance that the campaign against Britain would be short and sharp. Nor were they much taken with his suggestion that once the immediate battle was over, the Dutch might economise by reducing their own army to a token force of 3,000 or 4,000, demolishing the "barrier forts" and depending on their friendly neighbour for their defence. In an important and touching letter to the Batavian foreign minister, Schimmelpenninck set aside all illusion. He stressed that he "knew all too well that our political existence is already almost all semblance"; that it was in jeopardy of total eclipse, and that the nation was living off borrowed time. As yet, he added, the circumstances of the war had not led to complete destruction. "How to prevent that last," he wrote, "is the great point." His prescription for salvation was less original:

In God's name let every Dutchman feel the parlous position of the Fatherland, not in order that that feeling should bring him to despair, but so that he may put aside all petty matters of internal division, unite in protection of our national existence and show the whole world that this is our great goal.[84]

Political dissent, in other words, was a luxury which should be out of the question in the present situation; all good men should come to the aid of their government and put the divisions of the revolution firmly in the past. This was merely the reprise of the theme of "unity and reconciliation" which Schimmelpenninck had been intoning ever since he first appeared on the balcony of the Amsterdam Stadhuis in January 1795 to try to calm the mood of the city crowds. It was less than astonishing that he should have added the rider that "for my own part, I have not the least opinion that so far as it concerns domestic government, our present constitution should not undergo any significant alteration."[85]

Unwelcome though yet another debate on the forms of Dutch government may have been, in the drastically altered circumstances of the war, it was unavoidable. As the crisis deepened and the financial condition of the Republic progressively deteriorated, it became apparent to some among the Regency of State like Spoors and Besier, and others on its councils such as van der Palm and van de Kasteele (on the Council for Finance), that a loosely co-ordinated federal administration which might be viable in peace was simply too weak to manage in a major war. François Ermerins, the regent of Tholen and friend of Gogel's, who had said of the French that "they are wholly our masters, are squeezing the last drop out of us and will henceforth treat us like rubbish," saw that it was essential to provide "a good internal government" to save the country from collapse. "But how to arrive at such a good internal administration and who shall establish this unity? Shall the great Bonaparte (who in my view is very far from being great) supply the remedy? He does not want our independence."[86]

The two glosses on "patriotic unity" were, then, quite different. Schimmelpenninck's appealed to a nebulous vision of political harmony: a loose coalition of divergent groups based on the present constitution. Yet, as Ermerins viewed it, that same constitution, far from neutralising opposition, had arrogated power to a smaller circle of men than at any time since 1795. Without a greater degree of institutional coherence, and a far more powerful executive, he believed the Republic would simply disintegrate into its constituent parts. Deficit finance would sooner or later lead to a national bankruptcy and perhaps even to failure to meet the most basic military requirements for the maintenance of independence. This view was shared not only by frustrated reformers like Gogel, and junior officials beavering away in the Council of Finance like Elias Canneman, but also by observers like the Prussian ambassador Baron Caesar. In February 1804 the latter remarked:

Since my arrival [in 1803] it has not been at all difficult to observe that the present Batavian government enjoys neither the authority nor the respect adequate to direct the Republic successfully in a position as difficult and critical as that in which the renewal of war between Britain and France has placed it. Composed of heterogeneous parties, the present government is unable to follow fixed principles or an established system, and its resolutions are usually the individual result of the ephemeral preponderance of one group over the other.[87]

Finance was, of course, the nub of the matter. It was not so much that, on its own terms, the reversion to a form of collegiate administration had been an abject failure, but that it had failed to generate anything like the kind of resources required to meet the situation. It was all too reminiscent of 1793–94, when van de Spiegel had done his honest best to find a way to produce the funds needed for defence but fell back in the end on half-baked expedients and forced levies. True, the enlargement of the unwieldy executive did not help. On occasions a conflict of wills—either between departments; between an individual department and the national government; or between the Council of Finance and the Regency—could lead to near-paralysis. In March 1804, faced with an ordinary revenue of about 30 million guilders, an estimated expenditure for the current year of 73 millions, and a deficit for the previous year of 38 millions, the Council of Finance and the treasurer-general were unable to agree on the immediate means of escape from the quagmire. Canneman wrote to Gogel:

from the indecision which now seems to have seized up everything a total stagnation must surely result. One group wants a forced loan in the manner of 1802, of 4 per cent on property via a quota, and as then as a *don gratuit* [without interest]; others want only 2 per cent as *don gratuit* and 1,120,000 as voluntary; others want a wholly voluntary loan; others again want a wholly forced but interest-bearing loan. Between them all, we sit and sweat.[88]

Given the predicament of the Republic in 1803 and 1804, a degree of nervous indecision on the part of those saddled with the work of financing survival was entirely understandable. Since the abortion of the General Tax Plan it was impossible to raise the ordinary revenue of the state (other than by ad hoc augmentation of certain nationally levied indirect duties) to much more than 30 million guilders. Even the most optimistic assessment of *peace-* time expenditure ran to between 52 and 55 million guilders, and during war was expected to rise to between 70 and 80 millions. The pestilence of loans, levies, "*dons gratuit*" and lotteries which had overtaken the Republic since 1793 had swollen the capital debt to the astronomical figure of 1,126 million guilders.[89] Interest payments ran at nearly 33 millions a year, threatening in fact to consume the entire ordinary revenue of the state. In 1803 the mainten-ance of French troops alone had cost 8 millions, and even with the eventual reduction to something like 18,000 would cost no less than 5.4 millions. In that same year the military account rose to 19 million and that for the navy to 8.2 millions. Willem Six, the Amsterdam financier who had been a member of the ill-fated special mission to Bonaparte in the summer of 1803, put the magnitude of this burden in an illuminating context when he calculated (by what were admittedly pretty rough and ready methods) that during the first year of peace 1802–03, the Dutch deficit had reached the equivalent of 77 million francs—or 11 millions *more* than the debt of the French crown at the time of the summoning of the Assembly of the Notables. On a per capita basis, the Dutch were paying four times as much as their French contempor-aries.

The only way in which it was possible for the Dutch to bridge the crevasse of their deficit and succeed in carrying on any sort of national government while averting a possibly terminal bankruptcy was by resorting to that familiar catalogue of short-term expedients: levies, forced and voluntary on income and property; lotteries; special issues of securities; annuities bearing high rates of interest and short-term bill issues which were in effect secured on anticipation of revenue. Interest rates, which during the past century had been conspicuously low, during these years reached 5 and 5½ per cent. Municipalities reduced in extremis to borrowing to cover recurrent expenditure paid even more savage rates. Both The Hague and Utrecht went to 8 and even 10 per cent in 1805.

Much of this monstrous pyramid of debt was self-perpetuating. Securities were issued, earmarked to redeem earlier loans, and themselves created new pools of debt on worse terms. Gogel pointed out disdainfully that the ambitious loan launched in 1802 for 30 millions, even if it were fully subscribed, which was unlikely, would cost another 20 millions in interest and premiums.[90] The burgher of relatively modest means, placing his savings in government funds, was doubly penalised by the lengthening arrears of interest payments and the *dons gratuit* payments extorted well in advance. The wealthier capital houses—and there were still a good number in Amsterdam—exploited the shell-shocked money market for all it was worth; and since its international horizons had been reduced to a very much more domestic framework, saw to it that the government paid through the nose for their services. Gogel compared the prostrate condition of Dutch finance to a "second East Indies, fit only for men to extort what they can and then pass on to happier hunting grounds."[91]

The problem of making ends converge, let alone meet, was compounded by the technical defects of assessment and collection. Levies on income were, inevitably, self-assessed and based on net income calculated after deduction of allowable overheads such as labourers' wages and costs of freight. But then, as now, the elasticities of such calculations depended on norms of social ethics far from the fiscal ideal. It was notorious that many enterprises evaded their obligations by marking down turnover, valuation of product, cargo or profit; and the quasi-clandestine conditions surrounding the grain trade north to the Ems or the butter ships to England made this all the easier to accomplish. A great part of Dutch trade had, in effect, been turned into smuggling. Levies on property were even more open to fraudulent assessment, based as they were on market values (or in the case of mercantile property, assurance valuation). The recession had depressed the estate market seriously and "stretched" insurance statements are not, to be sure, a contemporary innovation.

The sheer number and complication of the taxes, moreover, put an intolerable burden on the very limited staff assigned to the treasurer-general, the National Chamber of Account and the special staff of national receivers created in 1803 to deal with the extraordinary contributions.[92] In 1802 and 1803 alone, there were *seven* separate extraordinary taxes on property and income to account; and those introduced as an "eight year" and "twenty-five year" contribution (at correspondingly reduced rates) had to be treated as instalments of a single levy. Given the zany elaboration of many of these fiscal devices and the tightness of liquid capital, it is no wonder the yields were piti-fully inferior to their estimates. Indeed, estimating the yield of a newly launched tax or loan became a form of investors' hazard much as it would have been on Bourse subscriptions. In its first quarter, the 2 per cent "eight year" tax on incomes produced in 1803 barely half its fairly modest yield expectation. To escape the mass of ad hoc taxes, not a few citizens who could afford to do so moved to a different region or even out of the Republic altogether. The "emigration" of capitalists was a recurrent nightmare of successive govern-ments; in March 1804, the Regency of State published an ordinance requiring intending travellers to deposit a surety with the treasury for those taxes for which they would fall liable during their absence. There was after all ample reason to depart. Since 1787 it was estimated that some 340 millions had been paid in forced levies on property; 35 millions as *dons gratuit*; 280 millions in interest-bearing paper which by 1804 had depreciated to a figure around 114 millions.[93] The limits of exhaustion could not be too far off.

In what was fast approaching a situation of fiscal anarchy, the dis-abling of the government's powers to collect national taxes came to be an increasingly onerous handicap. Despite the liquidation of the Directorial Agencies, the costs of domestic administration had actually been mounting steadily by about 3 millions a year. Yet the authority of the Regency of State itself and therefore of its minister the treasurer-general were constitutionally hedged around by the financial autonomy of the departments. Willy-nilly, the balance of power was gradually reverting to the 1798–1801 model. The de-partments were themselves deep in trouble financially and were having to bail out impecunious municipalities. Subsidies could only come from national revenue, since there was a limit to the "additional stuivers" which could be added on to local duties and tariffs. Moreover, instead of giving the depart-mental chambers of finance a free hand to supply their global quota in what-ever ways they judged most fitting to their particular circumstances, the treasury specified *that portion of departmental revenues the local authorities would be permitted to retain*. This gave the treasury far more leverage over the departments than the analogous pre-revolutionary Chamber of Account. In many respects, the situation in 1803–04 differed markedly from the "Quota" system of the old Republic. The Council of Finance (through the Regency's scrutiny) came increasingly to exercise control over not only departmental expenditure but even the manner of impositions required to fund them. By December 1803 the national receivers had extended their authority over the administration and collection of a range of nationally imposed "ordinary" revenues such as the "collateral" (estate duty) and the hearth tax, as well as the *verponding* property tax in Holland. The council, including as it did a balance of fiscal conservatives like Appelius and modest reformers like van de Kasteele, and presided over by the pliable if none too expert de Vos van

Steenwijk, was moved to encroach more and more on those autonomies which the constitution had pledged to keep sacrosanct.

As a result, 1804 witnessed recurring disputes between the departments and the national government. The finance commissions in Utrecht and Gelderland took to ignoring any demands for national contributions which cut across their own local needs. Brabant, which since its promotion had shown itself hypersensitive to anything touching its "sovereign rights," had actually mandated its commission to withhold any form of imposition not "registered" by the departmental government. In defiance of the Regency, Groningen put its antique colleges of dykes and polders on an official footing, and Gelderland turned itself resolutely towards the past by resurrecting the three separate financial chambers of Zutphen, Nijmegen and the Veluwe.[94]

The fact that the Regency of State was progressively eroding the basis on which it had itself been established was a measure of the seriousness with which it evidently viewed the Republic's predicament. Certainly it did not proceed from any dramatic change of principle. It is paradoxical that under a constitution drafted to appease the federalists, the state should have extended its authority to areas which even under the unitarist Directory had remained the domain of private or corporate jurisdiction. Elementary education has already been mentioned in this context. But none of the reform projects was entertained by the Regency of State without grave reservations and with all due political precautions. The national postal service, for example, came into being at the beginning of 1803 with a board of seven commissioners, one of whom, George Hahn, had made this reform his special interest. But its implementation was only made possible once an act of indemnification had been passed the previous year, compensating all those private and commercial postmasters (many of them having inherited the offices) who had made substantial fortunes from the business in the eighteenth century.[95]

Any significant advances may be balanced by some equally important retreats. The "Asiatic Council" had commissioned one of its servants, Dirk van Hogendorp (the elder brother of Gijsbert Karel) to draft a plan of reform. He produced a bold plan proposing the abolition of all perquisites and sinecures; the admission of private trade and its separation from all governing functions; permission for native subjects to own private property; substitution of the iniquitous "land levies" by a regulated land tax; and the abolition of all "seigneurial rights" in the colonies.[96] The report was greeted by those democrats like Wiselius and Abraham Vereul (one of the poet-chansonniers of the revolution) who had held their places on the Asiatic Council after 1801 with considerable enthusiasm. But the Regency of State, the Amsterdam municipality and the departmental administration of Holland were all exerting pressure on the Council to be more accommodating to the traditional interests of Company servants. The result was that when the new "Charter" was published for the Indies colonies, van Hogendorp's reforms had been whittled down to only the emptiest trivialities. None of the substantive changes had been accepted. This defeat paved the way for the internal "reorganisation" of the Council in the spring of 1804, which saw the eviction of the rump of democrats and their replacement with dependable men such as Hendrik Mollerus, the mobiliser of Orangist support during the invasion of 1799; Hendrik van Stralen, another Orangist, whom Wiselius described as "the greatest scoundrel in the Republic"; and S. C. Nederburgh, van Hogendorp's arch-opponent, who had himself been sent out to Batavia in 1793 as a reformer but had ended up cosily in the pocket of the "Company men."

Even if, then, the Regency of State was obliged by the exigencies of war to make inroads into traditional prerogatives and privileges, it would be quite false to represent its regime as one hell-bent on reform. It had enough to cope with keeping French demands at arms' length without alienating its natural supporters inside the Republic. It was fortunate that, initially, Bonaparte's government seemed unconcerned about the form of the Dutch state—except in so far as it affected the war effort. There indeed was the rub. For by the turn of 1803–04, French suspicions about the good faith of the Batavian government had begun, once more, to thicken. The colonial establishment seemed particularly prone to what might charitably be put down to "weakness." Fearing a slave rebellion in the style of Saint Domingue, the plantation owners of Surinam had in fact been exceedingly reluctant to see British troops depart when the colony reverted to Batavian sovereignty at the peace. Although a naval squadron under Bloys van Treslong had been despatched to the west Atlantic, British naval superiority remained the decisive factor; as early as September 1803—barely weeks after the renewal of hostilities—Demerara and Essequibo duly fell. The following summer the whole colony capitulated to the British without defence, despite the fact that it had been reinforced with a military force of some 2,000—considerably stronger than the number of marines the British could call on. Not surprisingly the conduct of Governor Berrenger, who had arranged the surrender in 1799, and who had been an officer in Louis XVI's Garde du Corps, was deemed by the French to be highly suspicious.

Similar doubts surrounded the protracted delay before the citadel at the Cape of Good Hope was finally handed over to Commissioner de Mist and Governor Janssens. Jacob de Mist was the man of the hour in this situation; he acted boldly and energetically in trying to bring the corrupt and wayward "Company" establishment firmly under the authority of the Republic's government. In 1795 two districts, Swellendam and Graaff Reinet, had risen against the Company, and since de Mist seemed to be bent on throwing in his lot with the natives, both Boer and Kaffir, it was not surprising that they should have looked to the British for support.[97] Thus here too, there was a legitimate suspicion of sabotage before the colony also fell in 1806.

In the East Indies the subversion seemed even more brazen. Vice-Admiral Pieter Hartsinck, who had been instructed in 1802 to defend Java, decided to turn a blind eye to orders to rendezvous in 1803 with Linois' smaller flotilla and together attack the British China fleet. Sticking to the letter of the 1802 Instruction, which said nothing of unprovoked hostilities against the British, Hartsinck remained off Batavia until 1807. This was more than a merely tactical irritation for the French. For an offensive in the East was to have been part of the "colonial feint" designed to persuade the British that a grand assault was in the offing against their overseas empire, or at the very least to tie down their naval forces far away from the crucial theatre of the Channel. Faced with this act of mulish obstinacy, the democrats were quick to point out to their friends in Paris that the navy had once again become dominated by Orangist officers who had been re-commissioned after the 1801 amnesty and on whom the success of the entire enterprise against England might now depend!

Collusion in breaking the economic sanctions against Britain was another irritant between the two allies. Ostensibly the Regency of State had done its duty in re-applying a strict embargo on British cargoes following the outbreak of war. On July 5 it had issued an order prohibiting the import of all enemy goods and had even taken steps to regulate the freight carried in neutral bottoms—the principal route for disguised British and colonial cargoes to enter the Netherlands. In August it had taken the even more drastic step of banning completely all cheese exports except to France and Spain, a measure designed to eliminate the daily provisioning of British ships from coastal cutters. The storm of protest raised by this, however, persuaded the Regency to relent and in March 1804 to permit dairy exports to the United States, a transparent euphemism for re-opening the trade with Britain. The Americans (and to a lesser extent the Danish) had in fact become the masters of a carrying trade between the Batavian Republic and Britain which remained very substantial. In the years following 1803, the exports of cheese and butter from the Republic actually rose in response to the high prices being fetched in a general scarcity. In 1804, the volume of general exports to Britain from the Netherlands very nearly reached the same level as in 1802 when it had been legitimate—a figure which was, in itself, a substantial advance on the level reached in the 1780's.[98]

In the reverse direction, British goods—colonial produce like unrefined sugar, raw cotton, cocoa, tobacco, indigo and coffee; and manufactured textiles, pottery and metallurgical goods—reached Dutch destinations either via Emden and Hamburg or else as disguised "American cargo." At any rate the Netherlands, along with north Germany, continued to be the "keyhole into Europe" for British shippers and manufacturers until at least 1805.[99] It was exactly the sort of people whom the Regency of State represented who were doing well out of such clandestine business. Little wonder, then, that the Regency did its best to widen the loopholes, and that before long the French (who were themselves not above much the same thing) lost patience with its complaisance.

French scepticism about the good faith of the Batavian government reached a climax with the unsavoury business of the Orange indemnity. It was a mark of the distance Europe had travelled from the years of revolutionary wars that at least three governments—France, Britain and Prussia—should all be falling over themselves to offer a modest consolation prize to the

House of Orange-Nassau for its losses in the Dutch Republic. Britain's traditional role of custodian of the dynasty's interests had been somewhat compromised by the débacle of 1799. Her own enthusiasm had been dimmed by the failure of the promised "Orange insurrection" to materialise during the campaign and the gathering consensus that William V, at least, was a lost cause. Parliament was attempting to limit its liability to either a global sum or a form of fixed pension on terms which neither the Prince nor Princess viewed with much delight. Moreover their heir, the Hereditary Prince, had already begun to form a modest reversionary interest: entertaining reforming plans his father eschewed and, worst of all, going to sit at the feet of the Great Man at St. Cloud in 1802. Bonaparte was shrewd enough to dazzle the Prince with the not unseductive charms of the Consular court and to give him the strong impression that in any future settlement arbitrated by France, he would have claim on French support within a "reorganised" Netherlands.[100]

The linchpin in all these calculations was Prussia. Frederick William had proved as deaf as his predecessor to Wilhelmina's pleas on behalf of the Orange cause. Neutrality had been a great success for Prussia, and as early as 1795 the notion of an indemnity of some sort for the Dutch dynasty had been informally agreed between the two powers. The Peace of Amiens had reiterated the principle; after further negotiations, a Franco-Prussian Convention of May 23, 1802, declared that the House of Orange would be ceded in perpetuity the abbatial domains of Fulda and Corvey in lieu of its Dutch estates and revenues.

As Frederick William tried to make plain to his sister, this was about the best that could be done for William V. But the Prince thought it a dismal bargain. He had hoped, at the very least, for something closer to Dutch territory itself—perhaps in Cleves and Jülich—a factor which had not eluded Bonaparte and for precisely that reason had predisposed him to placing the Prince further off. The First Consul was not, after all, lending his weight to the indemnity out of the milk of human charity (a commodity with which he was not over-blessed) but was attempting to bring about a reversal of alliances. His principal goal was the detachment of the dynasty from its traditional patron and the creation of a new pro-French/German satellite. All this was obvious to each of the parties concerned. What remained perhaps deliberately vague was the *object* of indemnification. As far as Bonaparte was concerned, the cession of Fulda and Corvey was conditional on the liquidation of all titular claims on the Stadholderate and the other hereditary offices claimed by the Prince, as well as an implicit end to Orangist sabotage within the Batavian Republic and the frustration of the anti-British campaign. After all, he conjectured, the Orange regents had already been lavishly bestowed with office and status. Could they not be induced by a proper regard for self-interest to abandon the folly of Anglophilia and their attachment to an anachronistic constitution? If the French émigrés had proved, in large numbers, gratifyingly opportunist, why should their Dutch counterparts not prove much the same?

The view from Kew was altogether different. While William V was not averse to accepting compensation which he regarded as perfectly legitimate for the losses of property and income he had suffered by the confiscation of his Dutch estates, he considered the offer as in no sense contingent on abandoning his historic role and titles. Indeed, he of all Stadholders was no more capable of doing this than shedding his skin. Unlike his feckless son, who was prepared to flirt with all manner of reformed constitutions and liberal monarchies, the old Prince had not budged an inch since the days of his apotheosis in the 1780's. Of him it could be truly said that he had "learned nothing and forgotten nothing." As well as being rigidly doctrinal in his Orangism, he was also greedy, perhaps understandably, since the warmth of British hospitality did not extend to the support of a style to which he had accustomed himself. He was moved, therefore, to seek indemnification not only for property but for the *arrears* of revenue, interest payments, perquisites, salaries, and so on, which would have fallen due since 1795. His own and Fagel's calculations as to what such a sum might have amounted to were spectacularly arbitrary; but put to the test, they were prepared to settle for a lump sum of 4 million guilders.[101]

This was 4 millions too much for the Regency of State. The arrangement reached with the British at Amiens and with the Prussians in May 1802 had specifically relieved—or excluded, depending on viewpoint—the Dutch from all further responsibility in the matter of the indemnity. Bonaparte's insistence on this was only partly a matter of fraternal generosity. He was, at the same time, demanding that all Dutch resources be put at the disposal of the alliance in any future campaign and, in 1803, having to listen to endless laments of poverty from Schimmelpenninck as pretexts, he supposed, for military and financial incompetence.

Given these stringent and clearly understood terms, it is astonishing that van der Goes, the Batavian foreign minister, should have embarked on so foolhardy a venture. After the affair had been brought to light, he claimed that he had believed all along that the *additional* indemnity (as it might be called) had really been Bonaparte's aim, whatever might have been formally claimed. But as Dr. de Wit has argued, van der Goes was not a diplomatic *naïf*. He knew the terms of Amiens and the May "Convention" as well as anyone, and he also knew the strength of Bonaparte's feelings on the matter. Like his colleagues he went into the business as a gamble. The entire enterprise hinged on a fat bribe of half a million guilders, offered (naturally) to Talleyrand by the Prince via his envoy at The Hague, d'Yvoy.[102] In return for their cut, the French minister and his ambassador Sémonville were to keep the First Consul in the dark and were to lend credence to the efforts of van der Goes and Schimmelpenninck to persuade the Regency of State that the additional indemnity really represented official Consular policy.

Schimmelpenninck's part in this squalid confidence trick has been glossed over far too often by the more generous—that is to say, virtually all—of his biographers. The best that can be said on his behalf is that he *may* have believed the scheme helpful in buying off any further Orangist opposition to the sovereignty of the Batavian Republic, and ultimately assisting the political "harmony" with which he was so preoccupied. Perhaps more to the point, such petty frauds were a stock in trade of the political life of the time to which he had long been inured. Even if Talleyrand's dealings were in a bigger league than his Amsterdam patrons', they might be seen as merely a "contract of correspondence" or more properly a "good understanding" compacted for a legitimate end.

The affair went reasonably smoothly until the end of June 1804, when the Patriot rump of the Regency of State—notably Besier and Bijleveld—somehow got wind of the truth. They lost no time in communicating this to their partisans outside the government but were prevented from taking any drastic action for lack of hard evidence that, just possibly, the bribe *was* Bonaparte's real intention. After the failure of the *conspiration-manqué* of October 1802, it was well-nigh impossible for the democrats to obtain direct access to the French government, or to break the iron ring of Schimmelpenninck, Sémonville and Talleyrand. Bijleveld's publicised demand that the emissary of the Prince of Orange, d'Yvoy, be evicted from The Hague was a damp squib since the unofficial ambassador enjoyed the protection of the Prussian embassy. But the plot rested on such precarious foundations that in the end it did not need hard evidence to crack it. Scurrilous rumours, some founded, some unfounded, as to the complicity of this and that politician fomented public opinion to the point at which overt action could no longer be postponed. That the affair had got out of hand was dramatically attested when the legislative corps, sitting in secret, and on most occasions a dependable rubber-stamp of the Regency of State, formally repudiated the additional indemnity as directly contrary to the national interest. Once this had happened the dissidents were able to act with the backing of a public body and, fending off a veiled threat from van der Goes to "think again," word was got to Paris of what had happened.

At that point the roof fell in on the heads of the gamblers. On August 27 a belligerent letter arrived from Bonaparte via Verhuell, ordering the revocation of any initiative in the Dutch legislature, expressing amazement that the allegedly poverty-stricken Dutch could even contemplate such a gratuitous action, and that his name had been used without permission to license an act of quasi-criminal chicanery.[103]

Obiter Dicta, 1804–1805

That Talleyrand could survive the scandal of the Orange indemnity relatively unscathed was a testimony to the value of his talents to France and to Bonaparte. But if Napoleon—as we should now call him—was accustomed to the legendary peculation of his foreign minister, he was no less irked by his propensity to conduct private business with his enemies while compromising the authority of his own name. The credit of the Batavian government, moreover, started from a lower stock. The episode gave proof that, as in the abortive and clandestine "neutrality mission" to Berlin in 1799, the Regency of State was less than candid about its intentions. Even had the conspirators not been caught out, it seems likely that the perpetuation of a Dutch national identity was to be made contingent on the fullest possible exploitation of their resources for the war. If this meant another act of constitutional surgery—at a time when France herself had been transformed into an Empire—then so be it. The patrician regencies and the rule of the "notables," which seemed desirable at a time of peace and consolidation, were rapidly losing their charms in 1804. Such a regime had been part of a modus vivendi with Britain. Now that the immediate and overriding objective was the destruction of that power as a major European force, it seemed foolhardy to entrust such work to men whose loyalties had been exposed as mixed.

The contingency of the Batavian Republic becoming a fifth column in the rear of the Empire, moreover, seemed less remote when it was pointed out to Napoleon that included among the new "Asiatic" councillors were men who had actively collaborated to bring about an Orangist rebellion in 1799. Thus the question aired by Sémonville the previous year, of how far the Dutch could be allowed their independence, became once more topical. The ambassador had more or less assumed that annexation could still be ruled out, and had largely confined himself to the means by which all real attributes of independence could be suppressed while maintaining some of the forms. He brought up the possibility of demolishing the "barrier forts" and reducing the Batavian army to negligible proportions, a proposal Napoleon often urged on Schimmelpenninck. But, stimulated no doubt by his monthly sweetener of 3,000 guilders, Sémonville argued that the Regency and the federal constitution were in France's best interests since they kept the Republic's political institutions weak and divided and of no consequence in the alliance, while appeasing the commercial interests. They were, in other words, the most pliable tools of an informal imperialism.

There came a point when illuminating incidents like the indemnity and the continuing unsatisfactory performance of Dutch military and naval efforts pointed to an alternative solution. By the spring of 1804 Napoleon was again seriously preoccupied with the invasion project and, as a direct consequence, with the price of these failures. His own demanding standards of efficiency seemed to cry out against the irrationality of the Dutch system—or lack of it. The reports he was receiving from his commander at the Zeist camp near Utrecht, General Marmont, seemed to confirm his worst suspicions. Like his predecessors in command, Auguste Marmont arrived in the Netherlands already imbued with a lively contempt for all forms of civilian authority—and especially for that of merchants masquerading as republicans. Like Joubert and Brune, Monnet and Hatry, he bullied and hectored the Dutch into accepting arbitrary requisitions, ad hoc billets, extra-territorial privileges in matters of court judgments on Batavian territory and the usual range of indignities. Witnessing for himself the progress of smuggling from Friesland down to Zeeland and the success of British goods in Dutch shops, he proved especially zealous in reinforcing the growing establishment of the despised French customs men and coast guards on the Scheldt and the IJ. Fortunately for the Dutch, their cupidity and avarice (the general was himself no puritan in this respect) more than compensated for the overbearing nature of their official duties. But when on one occasion the Regency of State saw fit to protest at a particular act of extortion, Marmont summed up in one bald retort his view of their pretensions to sovereignty: "You have your pens, Gentlemen, and I have my bayonets; you write with the one and I will put the other to work!"[104]

Marmont's command at Zeist was of double significance for those disaffected from the Regency of State. First, he seemed particularly receptive to complaints against the government; and secondly, his military functions gave him, along with Verhuell, direct access to Napoleon, superseding the quadruple barrier of Talleyrand, van der Goes, Sémonville and Schimmelpenninck. Beleaguered by the offensive on the "Asiatic Council" which was to end in his deposition, Wiselius approached Marmont with a recitation of all the familiar grievances against the patricians. But he was shrewd enough to formulate them as an "explanation" of how and why the Dutch performance of their military duties was so imperfect:

Why does the government conduct itself so badly? For what reasons are the highest authorities vilified and derided by those of the second rank? Why, finally, has the entire nation lost all energy to the point at which it is feeble or rather completely null in its resources against England, that eternal foe of its prosperity and commerce? . . . First of all, it is important not to confuse the national spirit with that of the faction which presently dominates it. . . .[105]

That "faction," Wiselius confirmed, was more interested in subverting than assisting the struggle with Britain. Indeed, he went even further by implying a link between their passive "counter-revolution" and the royalist plots then being uncovered in France. Carefully aimed, there is little doubt that this particular dart struck home. Further letters at the end of April supplied the general with biographical details of the present rulers of the country (compiled with the help of Gogel and Fijnje). These potted biographies, gingered up with the right kind of political bias, could not help but convey the seriousness of a situation in which Patriots were outnumbered by men of disreputable record.[106] The reports were relayed to Napoleon, who in his turn was eager for further enlightenment, albeit discreetly supplied. Such indeed was the success of the initiative that Marmont met with Wiselius in Amsterdam in mid-April to discuss the ramifications of the upheaval on the Asiatic Council, an incident which played directly into the dissidents' hands. The recapitulatory letter sent to Napoleon on April 21 shows him completely persuaded by Wiselius' arguments. The problems of mobilisation, he wrote, were

the necessary consequence of the unheard-of march of opinion in Holland; of the increase and impudence of the Orange party; that is to say, the party devoted to the interests of England . . . (which) . . . at every step slows down the pace of things under the guise of doing everything possible to expedite the preparations for the English campaign.[107]

On April 27 the Emperor wrote to Marmont that his communications had indeed illuminated "details of which I had been ignorant," and asked for more information on those who could be trusted and those who ought to be suspected. It should be added that despite the intelligences Napoleon was not too adept at sorting sheep from goats, particularly when they had unpronounceable Dutch names, so that he continued to believe that among the Orangist saboteurs was a certain "Spurs" and his confederates. At the same time he indicated through the official channels—Talleyrand and Sémonville—that while he did not like to intervene in the affairs of other peoples,

> I can no longer remain indifferent to everything that has happened [in the Netherlands]. The Dutch army is discontented; the greater part of the people equally so. . . . If, in such a state of affairs peace came about and French troops were to evacuate Holland, we would have an enemy government on our frontiers, despite the fact that the greatest part of the nation, all those who still possess energy, credit and vigour, are favourable to the French system. . . . My intention, therefore, is to intervene in the affairs of this country, and I wish, first of all, to be sure of certain facts. . . .[108]

At that time, of course, the affair of the Orange indemnity had not yet been brought to light. Napoleon was concerned merely to test the information he had received from Marmont against the counsel his officials might offer. But however elliptically expressed, the mere hint of another constitutional upheaval was enough to throw the regents of the Republic into consternation. Their most pessimistic construction was that the Emperor meant, sooner or later, to do away with their national independence altogether. Even if the immediate course was to be less draconian, they were certain that measures were going to be imposed rather than offered. Self-determination, they knew full well, was no longer theirs to command. Just when that erosion of sovereignty had become critical was debatable. For those of one persuasion it had started with the Prussian invaders in 1787; for their antagonists, the invasion of 1795 seemed a more appropriate date. But whatever the historical verdict, the crossroads at which the Republic had arrived gave politicians of every kidney an opportunity to reflect on their plight and the means, if any, of escaping complete dereliction.

In a remarkable letter written on May 13 to Marmont (in reply to an equiry about his views on the constitution), Gogel gave the General an unadorned account of the sufferings endured by his countrymen at the hands of their allies and "brothers." In an almost autobiographical excursion into his own revolutionary past, Gogel recorded the life and death of his political optimism: the freebooting of 1795; the *assignats*; the outrages of the privateers; the adventurism of Delacroix; the endless financial extortion; the running sore of Flushing; the arrogance and brutality of French officials, military and civilian; and to crown it all the intervention of Augereau and Sémonville in the autumn of 1801, which had brought about "the unhappy condition in which the nation presently finds itself."[109]

Considering to whom it was addressed, Gogel's scroll of lamentations was an audacious gesture. But it cut no ice with a soldier whose sensitivities in these matters were about as tender as those of the Emperor he slavishly emulated (and whom he was to betray so decisively). Indeed, it is difficult to read it without feeling that it was written as much to unburden Gogel of his own interior disappointments as to enlighten Marmont. Elsewhere, Gogel confessed to his friend Elias Canneman that he had lost the "beautiful dreams" with which he had set out for the French camp in the winter of 1794.[110] He had not gone back on any of his basic political beliefs. Even though his new "constitutional plan" included a truncated legislature, shorn of the right of initiative, as in his 1801 project, it was meant to be directly elected from a franchise of the 1798 model rather than the pseudo-suffrage of the Bonapartist orthodoxy.[111] But at the same time he appreciated that Napoleon was unlikely to countenance anything looking suspiciously like "Jacobinism" or the work of "metaphysicians." That he was now a more pragmatic politician than the Gogel of 1794 or the Gogel of 1798 is indisputable. But his commitment to institutional reform was, if anything, more, rather than less, profound. "Without a total reconstruction there can be no solidity in the order of things," he told Marmont in September.

The essential issue was to provide the Dutch state with a form of government adapted to its contemporary situation, rather than a nostalgic utopia of regents and merchants. The 1801 constitution was quixotic, "a form of government so distorted and so contrary to all opinions on the science of government that one searches in vain for one so bad among all the nations." Gogel provided Marmont with details of the disproportionate fiscal obligations of the different provinces; of the anachronisms of public finance; of the proliferation and duplication of administrative personnel in the departments, the anarchy of local particularities and sovereignties; in short, a haphazard and irrational form of government incapable of ensuring the safety and welfare of the nation.

I am not [he wrote] a partisan of a large number in the [national] government, but I do not know which is the more preferable, a government composed of several members but sovereign in the country, or a government of a single man with several inferior administrations all having the attributes of constitutional power. . . . The present government succeeds in combining the worst of both systems by having an infinity of governments all endowed with constitutional laws and separate powers, so that the departmental councils dispute with the government and the towns and communes with those first councils. All power is disposed to self-extension; and if subordinate administrations are established and given constitutional powers, it will necessarily follow that the frontiers between those administrative authorities and the sovereign power will soon give rise to a great deal of conflict. . . .[112]

What was required instead was

an energetic government which . . . does not have to be in conflict with subaltern bodies and which is not obstructed by every kind of provincial claim, but is limited only by some rules and may proceed freely so long as it does not infringe them.

This unified government, Gogel was careful to add, should not be authoritarian. A "constitutional act" should affirm the civil equality of rights and duties of every citizen and their eligibility for office, the abolition of all private jurisdictions, and the codification of civil and criminal law. He made the important point that the tax and property franchise qualifications in force in France were unnecessary in the Netherlands since, due to the greater social and political decorum of the Dutch, the dangers of a mobocracy arising from a democracy were merely academic. He also emphasised his opposition to the concentration of executive power in a single man (this, in Year I of the Empire). The country was small enough to dispense with the need for a unifying figurehead, and the Dutch retained a strong distaste for the panoply which went with pseudo-monarchic pretensions. An executive of three or five "decent and modest burghers" would quite suffice.[113]

Gogel was not so rash as to put forward proposals amounting solely to a critique of the French Empire and its sovereign. His strictures on presidential power were meant for another target. For it was Schimmelpenninck who, in the summer and autumn of 1804, was being spoken of as a likely candidate for high office. However exasperated Napoleon may have been with the laxity and incompetence of the Batavian Regency of State, little of his displeasure seems to have rubbed off on their ambassador. Napoleon was actually rather fond of the portly and genial figure who played the plain-speaking burgher for all he was worth. Schimmelpenninck was shrewd enough to realise that Napoleon enjoyed receiving home truths from him in a manner he would never have tolerated from his own ministers. Surrounded by sycophants or languid sharks like Talleyrand, Napoleon saw Schimmelpenninck as the epitome of conscientious, unvarnished, stolid bourgeois virtue. He teased the ambassador about the virtue of his family life and the sedateness of his compatriots while making no secret of his admiration for those very qualities. It was an extraordinary and eccentric relationship. On September 16, 1804, Schimmelpenninck (who revelled in the part of the "simple country squire" on his estates in Overijssel, dressed in leather breeches and walking his dogs) was summoned from his bucolic pleasures to an audience with the Emperor at Cologne.[114] After recovering from his discomposure at being improperly dressed for so daunting an occasion, Schimmelpenninck was treated to a lengthy disquisition on the state, present and future, of the Republic and asked his own opinions. Serving notice of his intention to make radical changes in the constitution, the Emperor finally requested recommendations from the ambassador at the earliest opportunity.

At that stage it was politic for Schimmelpenninck to profess ignorance of Napoleon's intentions, even though he had in fact been put in the picture long since by Talleyrand. But it was only after this interview that he was able both to tip off the Regency of State that their days were, in all likelihood, numbered, and privately to congratulate himself that he was to have the honour of getting the Republic out of its unholy mess. He stepped forward to meet his destiny with an almost theatrical self-consciousness. On November 5 he wrote to his wife:

I feel that not only our land but the whole of Europe is in a state of crisis. I feel that through the concurrence of events, and in spite of my own inclinations it has fallen to my lot . . . to play a weighty role, and whatever the outcome may be I shall take good care that the part I play will not be contemptible. The rest must be left to Providence.[115]

Just what form this "weighty role" was to assume was still unclear. Sémonville had spoken in early October of Schimmelpenninck as a "Grand Pensionary," and to be sure, despite his fondness for the role of an American President, the ambassador was not averse to seeing himself in the line of Oldenbarneveld and the de Witts, though he presumably hoped for a better end. But there were also rumours that a prince of the cadet branch of the old dynasty—Nassau-Weilberg—was to be imported as a ceremonial figurehead, beneath which Schimmelpenninck would exercise executive authority. Both proposals fitted with Napoleon's penchant for dressing up institutional change in the trappings of history.

However the cards finally fell, Schimmelpenninck was confident that he would have a decisive say in the new constitution. And on this topic his views were fundamentally opposed to those set out in Gogel's letters to Marmont. For him, too, the summer of 1804 had been a time of taking stock. But the lessons he had learned were barely different from the maxims he had held in 1795. Just how little he had moved from that position may be gauged from a memorandum, nominally written (and actually edited) by Talleyrand and presented to the Emperor in November, but spectacularly misattributed by Colenbrander to Marmont![116] The error is of more than scholarly implication since the document outlines a version of the Dutch revolution and recommends a prescription for the future diametrically opposed to that presented by Gogel and Wiselius to Marmont and relayed by the General to Napoleon. That the guiding spirit of the Talleyrand memorandum was Schimmelpenninck's there is no longer any doubt. With addenda by Sémonville and Talleyrand, it represented his response to the Emperor's request at the interview of September 16. While de Wit's characterisation of it as a "Programme of Government" is somewhat extravagant, it certainly was a systematic attempt to ensure that the "new" constitution conformed as closely as possible to the ideal of the regents.

Throughout the tone is conservative, even fatalistic. The revolution is seen as a whoring after strange gods, and the constitutions it has produced as "alien in spirit and character to the needs of the Batavian people." The Dutch, it insisted, were incorrigible in their habitual regard for parochial and sectional interests and in their refusal to knuckle under to anything based on the abstract nostrums of popular sovereignty.[117] The Patriot movement of the 1780's, it followed, had really had nothing to do with democracy, a taint which had only latterly infected the bloodstream of Dutch reform and broken out in the corrupting fevers of the clubs—a fever happily confined to the very few. Since "most of the Bataves are attached to federalism in direct proportion to the efforts that have been made to submit them to the regime of unity," it was advisable to retain such a system. This alone could not endear France to the Dutch, for only peace and commerce would do that; but with a form of of government better suited to their tastes and customs, they would at least "better support the evils of war."[118]

On September 23 Gogel and Schimmelpenninck met in Amsterdam. From a letter written by Gogel to Marmont shortly afterwards, it can be gleaned that the encounter was something short of a brilliant success, at least from Gogel's point of view. Although Gogel

had furnished him [Schimmelpenninck] with some reflections on the unity to be introduced in the matter of the finances, he appeared to differ from myself a good deal on this point and our conversation proceeded for some time on its possibility and the justice of its introduction.[119]

Even then Gogel refused to give up hope of persuading Schimmelpenninck. At almost the same time he wrote him a long letter, couched in terms of warmth and candour, setting out in detail the reasons—and the emotions—which moved him to advocate financial unification with such conviction. It is worth dwelling on this a little if only for the clarity and perception which Gogel brought to his justification.

With an eye to Schimmelpenninck's own abiding concern for historical legitimacy, Gogel began with a direct admission of his own position:

I have always been for absolute equality of privileges and obligations. But this is not a new view: the drafters of the Union of Utrecht were of the same opinion and so were many other statesmen after them. Only self-interest, both of individuals and of provinces, frustrated this and left matters on the same footing. . . .[120]

The equalisation of rights and duties was, he emphasized, a matter of natural justice; but Gogel also took pains to point out that that justice operated not merely between provinces but within them. If—for example—Overijssel were to pay a globally larger sum to the national revenues, it would be possible to ensure, through direct taxation, that the heaviest burden fell on the broadest backs. Hence

by an equal obligation . . . every citizen with the same means would pay the same contributions; the common man would not be more heavily imposed on; and after all who now pays most heavily through the means of extraordinary taxes? Always the rich alone. . . .[121]

The liquidation of provincial and local duties would promote internal freedom of trade (which as a mercantilist where external trade was concerned, Gogel vigorously endorsed), and would by the same token do away with the problem of smuggling and make substantial administrative economies possible. The great point was

that in unforeseen or exceptional circumstances, the exceptional burdens placed on the national treasury can be better served by *general taxes* . . . than through new *forced loans*, levies, or as yet undiscovered resources, is surely incontrovertible [author's italics].

Any other way, he insisted, would lead the Republic into still deeper waters. As for a reduction in interest, "a bankruptcy is easily decreed and still more easily carried out," but quite aside from running a multitude of modest creditors of the state, it side-stepped the root problems of the nation's finances.

I believe and am fully convinced, that only forceful measures and not palliatives can restore our unhappy nation and revive its prosperity to a certain degree. . . . The general health and care for the future and the gradual revival of our sources of livelihood must alone be kept in mind.

What now lay before them was a singular opportunity, perhaps the last, to put their house in order. If it were not taken, the Republic would continue to decompose until it finally disintegrated completely, losing its separate identity, or else invited the return of the Prince of Orange as it had traditionally done in its moments of disaster.

At the end, conscious perhaps that he had exposed himself in good faith to someone who might remain basically unsympathetic, Gogel added a mild apologia:

Forgive these unsolicited observations: I owe them to my Fatherland; to myself and to our old friendship. They sum up my feelings about a project far too serious to be lightly glossed over, and they come directly from a sincere sympathy and concern for the happiness and welfare of my fellow citizens.

How far this kind of approach affected Schimmelpenninck's view it is difficult to say. Although there was a strong sentimental streak in his character, and although both Gogel and he shared a passionate commitment to their nation as a community of God-fearing, industrious and virtuous citizens, it seems more likely that Schimmelpenninck would have been swayed by what he discerned as Napoleon's intentions than Gogel's rhetoric. But two days later, Elias Canneman told Gogel that the ambassador was having second thoughts about a federal system and that he was gradually coming round to the unitarist view. Others whom Schimmelpenninck sought out for consultation were strongly of the view that Gogel's tax plan was the precondition of an effective government. Even Hendrik van Stralen showed an unpredictable enthusiasm for the Gogel constitution and wrote pointedly to Schimmelpenninck that, "with an able and active man in the finances and the necessary junior officials the campaign may be opened and I would expect a good success. . . ."[122] Van de Kasteele, who had experienced the frustration of trying to impose some degree of fiscal unity through the Council of Finance, argued that "without the general taxes there can be no unity and without unity no concentration and without this no economies may be implemented . . . with any other project the country is lost."[123]

Despite the apparent unanimity of these opinions, Schimmelpenninck's own attitude remained somewhat equivocal. The report given to Talleyrand and presented in November to Napoleon was, in all likelihood, written *after* these consultations. If, as Canneman told him, any administration was going to have to include Gogel and Goldberg and a unified financial system, Schimmelpenninck continued to insist that any constitutional article to that effect must be avoided since it would give the land provinces the impression of a *diktat*.[124] Moreover, the efforts to retain as much as possible of the old establishment had by no means been abandoned. The Regency of State had sent a special mission to Paris (van Haersolte, van der Goes and Brantsen) to put their case, and on October 20 Schimmelpenninck himself arrived to lend his weight to their arguments. After two lengthy audiences on November 5 and 13, he wrote to his wife in terms suggesting that the Emperor had accepted the broad principles of his view of reorganising the Republic and had left it to Talleyrand and himself to work out the details.[125] It was these "details," together with the politico-historical review of the revolution, which the memorandum was meant to provide. By the end of the year it must have seemed to Schimmelpenninck that he had prevailed and that the Republic of regents, presided over by a powerful executive magistrate—namely, himself—would make up the new regime.

Matters were not, however, that cut and dried. According to Bosset, Schimmelpenninck had not in fact succeeded in dissuading Napoleon from his conviction that a General Tax Plan and a unified administration were what was needed in the Netherlands. To be sure, the Emperor had recoiled just as definitely from including in the regime any personnel who could conceivably be stigmatised as "Jacobin" (for example, Wiselius); but as far as a federal constitution was concerned, it was no longer a viable proposition. Gogel was also included in the list of imperatives—but only for the renown of his financial expertise. Schimmelpenninck's growing nervousness about the Emperor's views received another shock at the beginning of January when he was asked to draft an entirely *new* constitution, based on unitarist principles. Understandably, Schimmelpenninck was baffled by this request since he had assumed all along that the Talleyrand memorandum had amounted to just that. Gradually it dawned on him that whether he liked it or not, the price for his promotion to the highest magistracy in the Republic was to be the acceptance of a system of government, and more particularly of finance, which, since 1795, he had done his utmost to circumvent.

Before this happened, however, he was to have the small, sour gratification of seeing at least some of his opponents—Spoors, Besier, G. H. Gockinga and G. C. Bijleveld—expelled from public office by what, even for those times, was a miserable ploy. The seepage of English goods, especially in 1804 when the figures for the illicit trade reached their highest point, had given rise to increasing indignation among the French authorities in the Batavian Republic. Marmont had been particularly vocal on this matter, and in the middle of November he decided, with approval from Paris, to impose drastic countermeasures on the Dutch. French coastguards and customs men were to take over all responsibility for the surveillance of cargoes at Dutch ports, assisted if need be by detachments of French troops. Gendarmes were to be placed in the harbours at Rotterdam and Amsterdam; were to make regular inspections of all cargoes arriving and departing, and in the case of incoming vessels were to issue certificates of legality before cargo could be landed. Powers of confiscation were given to these officers without reference to the Dutch authorities. It was, in fact, a rehearsal for the Continental system. It so happened at that time that van der Goes, Brantsen and van Haersolte were in Paris, but the remainder of the Regency of State decided on November 23 to respond to this indignity by publishing an order forbidding any Batavian officials to take orders from the French.

It was an act of courageous folly. Bosset, with some reluctant admiration, called it "the last breath of energy" of a dying regime. Talleyrand, on the other hand, saw it as a golden opportunity to remove political undesirables from the Regency. He condemned it as a "monument of perfidy or delirium passing all comprehension." Sémonville referred to those "rebellious poltroons."[126] For years it had been murmured to Napoleon that Spoors and Besier were intriguers against the alliance. Here, at last, was the perfect evidence. The resignation of the disgraced "culprits" was duly extracted, and Schimmelpenninck in effect given a blank cheque to exclude any of their political affiliation from his administration. Van der Goes urged him to surround himself with "noble, good and respectable (*fatsoenlijk*) men," those, of course, innocent of the anathema of Patriot democracy. If Gogel and his bureaucrats were to be foisted on the new Pensionary, he would take care to see that they were outnumbered by men of a more congenial turn of mind.

By the end of February 1805, matters were at last finalised. Schimmelpenninck was indeed to be the "Grand Pensionary"; his ornamental legislators "Their High Mightinesses" though not, collectively, a States-General. His government was to have the trappings of the old Republic but the muscle of a new and vigorously co-ordinated administration. As "Raadpensionaris" he would exercise more absolute power than any Stadholder before him could ever have presumed. He was to be what he had long dreamed: a miniature Bonaparte. No wonder that on March 14 he wrote to his wife: "I can in truth assure you that I feel sounder day by day; my appetite grows daily better and I am sleeping very well."[127]

There were, however, still some odd unbelievers who could not credit that the new reign would prove any more durable than its predecessors. Queysen, another Overijsselaar, wondered out loud whether the Grand Pensionary was indeed the Messiah—or merely John the Baptist.[128]

❋❋❋❋❋❋❋❋❋❋

Part III

❋❋❋❋❋❋❋❋❋❋

DORUS *And how did things go with the new government?*

FATHER *The Stadholderate was abolished, the sovereignty of the separate provinces done away with; the debts of the provinces amalgamated.*

HENDRIK *And did that make the government any better?*

FATHER *Many well-intentioned supporters of that order expected it would but their hopes were disappointed. Many Representatives were too inexperienced in matters of government; others showed more self-interest or ambition than patriotism or love of liberty, so that able and courageous men were hindered from executing the laws best for the welfare of the country.*

———*Schoolboek*, pp. 124–5.

✾ ✾ ✾ ✾ ✾ ✾ ✾ ✾ ✾

11

The Watershed,
1805–1808

The Last Grand Pensionary

H ardly had Schimmelpenninck been elevated to the dignity of Raad-pensionaris than the occlusion in his sight began to degenerate irreversibly into blindness. The almost gratuitous cruelty of this misfortune has inevitably lent an aura of pathos to this last, but arguably most important, of the governments of the Batavian Republic. Yet even if his illness had not given Napoleon the pretext for one further, terminal, interference in Batavian sovereignty, it is unlikely that the Pensionary would have been able to escape from the contradictions inherent in his office. He was not, after all, a mere Swiss *Landamann* appointed to keep the cantons from each others' throats, and to prevent their bickering from menacing French strategy. He had been set at the head of the Dutch state to do the bidding of the Emperor without demur or procrastination—unlike his predecessors on the Regency of State—and, as Talleyrand had made plain in Paris, to mobilise the whole of its naval and military forces in the next phase of the life and death struggle with Britain. But this, in turn, would be bound to impose an intolerable strain on the already prostrated finances of the country and thereby hasten the day of either bankruptcy or loss of national independence or both. There seemed precious little chance that Schimmelpenninck could be other than a "six-month Doge."[1]

This was all the more poignant in that the Pensionary obviously saw himself as the personification of the national will to endure: a paternal figure around whom all those who had the good of the Fatherland at heart might rally. But his approach to establishing such unity of feeling was itself highly paradoxical. For while he readily acknowledged that the predicament in which the Republic found itself demanded a powerful executive, his predilection for political "harmony" led him to encourage the process, under way since 1801, of restoring the traditional regents and patricians. Given the still marked tendency of power in the Netherlands to gravitate away from the centre,

[466]

there was more than an even chance that the pursuit of the first objective would be effectively sabotaged by the second. Nor was it a simple matter to find a consensus in which all political groups and interests other than out-and-out revolutionaries might be accommodated. As Besier remarked to Wiselius, it was much more likely that the tune called by Schimmelpenninck would delight neither Orangists nor Patriots.[2] The former would be satisfied with nothing less than the restoration of a genuine Prince-Stadholder; the latter would be mortified to see old enemies placed in favour and power at their expense.

Indeed, the plebiscite arranged for the approval of the new constitution scarcely reflected any great groundswell of Patriotic enthusiasm. Of the already severely pruned franchise of 353,322, only 14,903 bothered to go through the ritual of recording their "Ja," while 136 brave souls voted in the opposite sense. In Leiden just one-twelfth of the electorate cast a vote, with three citizens only recording a "Neen." Following the now well-established precedent on these occasions of pseudo-democracy, abstentions were duly counted as "tacit affirmatives" and the constitution declared valid by 353,186.[3]

Despite the self-evidently fragile foundation of his power, Schimmelpenninck proceeded to act as if he were the acclaimed hero of the people. A lavish public ceremony in The Hague on May 10, complete with carillons from the Groote Kerk and feasting and fireworks on the Buitenhof, marked his installation in office. Relishing his allotted role as Saviour of the nation, he obviously felt that it was best to face what had to come with manful resolution. In any case, pessimism was foreign to his temperament. If, as he told the new legislative corps, "the burdens with which the State finds itself encumbered are manifold and heavy . . . the first proof of our courage will be to confront them as they truly are . . . the second will be not to despair of the Fatherland."[4] He was buoyed up by reserves of ebullient self-belief which other men in similar situations might have found more difficult to marshal. Marmont characterised him as "a man of broad intelligence, eloquent, full of virtues and candour but perhaps just a little credulous for the times and the circumstances in which he lived."[5]

It was this quality of near ingenuousness—which consorted oddly with his highly developed pragmatism—that allowed Schimmelpenninck to believe that, as both Overijssel landowner and Amsterdam patrician-advocate, Mennonite by origin and Reformed by adoption, he was pre-eminently fitted to embody the interests of the whole nation. Had he not always counselled the middle way; had he not been among the very first in 1795 to urge that the rifts opened by the revolution be closed up for the national good? And had he not always opposed oaths of hatred, purges and the like? This, then, was the opportunity to vindicate his deepest convictions about national unity.

Most of all, perhaps, Schimmelpenninck saw himself as the guardian of the continuity of Dutch history. The critique of Rousseau's *Social Contract* which he had written as his dissertation for Leiden University in 1784 had been concerned to argue, among other things, that the imperatives of the General Will were redundant in a Republic where respect for liberty was still so well entrenched.[6] His reforms were meant to be in keeping with that tradition: the accomplishment of what had been tentatively begun by other Pensionaries before him—by van Slingelandt and van de Spiegel. A sovereign government would be shaped in conformity with the past of the Republic, but so adapted as to ensure that there would *be* a national future. His "Fundamental Act" promised that the new constitution

assures the destinies of a people whose peaceful industry requires a stable and independent order of affairs. It approaches the form of government under which the Republic enjoyed its most flourishing period.[7]

In practice, of course, the balance between conservation and innovation was far harder to sustain. The members of the legislature may have reverted to their old title of "High Mightinesses" but they were in no sense the equal of the mandated delegates of the provinces in the old States-General. So far indeed had the Batavian Republic retreated from its ringing declarations of representative democracy in 1796 that the *nineteen* members of the Assembly, only seven of whom were Hollanders (a lower proportion than ever before or since) were corporately reduced to a vestigial limb of the executive. All right of legislative initiative was removed. Only those projects submitted by the Pensionary for consideration were to be debated. Similarly, while it was given the ceremonial functions of declaration of war and peace, it could do so only at the behest of the Pensionary. Exactly the reverse had been the case under the old Republic. Sessions were to be absurdly brief: from April 15 to June 1 and from December 1 to January 15. Like its counterpart in the French Empire, the corps was really little more than the rubber-stamp of the executive.

Schimmelpenninck's regime proximated more to a quasi-Stadholderate than to the office of a Pensionary. For one who affected the manners of a yeoman squire, and who had recommended to the Regency of State that they conduct themselves in a style that was "sober, simple, *Batavian*," he was not all that averse himself to the more ostentatious displays of state pomp. He took up residence in the Huis 't Bosch and drove daily in state, with postillions before and behind, to the palace in the Noordeinde from where he conducted official business and presided over the Council of State (Staatsraad). Household pages were decked out in red and gold, and a special Life Guard wore braided uniforms reputed to have cost 700 guilders each. Both attracted waspish comments from The Hague gossips, who also learned that Mevrouw Schimmelpenninck (who seemed to revel in the flummery even more than her husband) now occupied the pew in chapel previously kept for Princess Wilhelmina. None of this was exactly calculated to endear the Pensionary to a people with whom he claimed to have so intimate a relationship but so many of whom were coming all the time perilously closer to destitution.[8]

A good deal of this parade was designed to lend a presidential air to Schimmelpenninck's office. There is no doubt that he himself saw it as Washingtonian-paternalist rather than Bonapartist-authoritarian; but in practice his efforts to consolidate a Dutch amalgam of interests and political groups owed not a little to the Consular precedent. In building an administration of "all the talents," some talents were evidently thought more desirable than others. Rigorously excluded were all unrepentant Batavian democrats, while those who had shown both administrative ability and a willingness to bend their principles for the sake of the "Good [patriotic] cause" (*goede zaak*) were given preferment.

An exception to this rule was the most unlikely appointment of all, Wybo Fijnje, rescued from hardship by being given the editorship of the official *Staats Courant*, a job which demanded a degree of sustained subservience to which even a down-and-out former Director (whom Schimmelpenninck had known since their Leiden days in the 1780's) was unequal. When the gazette was transmogrified in 1806 into the *Koninklijke Courant*, Louis Bonaparte lost no time in ridding himself of such spectral undesirables. More typical of the calibre of republican opportunists were van Hooff, Siderius and Busch, all of whom sat in the new legislature. Pijman was retained as Secretary of State (the official title for what were in effect national ministries) for War, and Gogel was of course brought back to Finance. Johannes Goldberg, another of the Pensionary's Amsterdam colleagues, was appointed to the Staatsraad.

At the other end of the political spectrum appointments were, if anything, rather more bold. The process of rehabilitating Orangists had already gone a long way under the previous regime; but in 1805 those with reputations for ministerial ability and political mellowness were hoisted into high office, no matter how deeply implicated they had been in efforts at counter-revolution. The most important of such promotions was Hendrik van Stralen, who had acted as the political agent of the Prince in North Holland in 1799 and who had put his name to proclamations calling on the people to rise against the Republic and the French. Notwithstanding his past, he had become a close confidant of Schimmelpenninck's and was rewarded with the vital post of Secretary of the Interior. His two successors under Louis Bonaparte, moreover, Hendrik Mollerus and Twent van Raphorst, were of a similar background and political pedigree and both were given places by the Pensionary—Twent as head of the Commission on the Waterstaat, Mollerus as a member of the "Asiatic Council." It was an extraordinary indication of how up-ended allegiances had become that the ministry with a major share of responsibility for internal security and police should be confided to three men who had proclaimed their loyalty to the House of Orange.

That loyalty was not, of course, unwavering. Given place and influence it was not immune from reorientation. Karel Verhuell—promoted to be Secretary of the Marine by virtue of his special role alongside the Emperor in organising the Dutch section of the Boulogne flotilla—was, like so many other naval officers, an Orangist by background and loyalties. But his service with Napoleon had made him a passionate devotee of the Emperor and in 1814 he was even to prefer exile to the infamy of betraying his new master by rallying to the old.[9] What was perhaps more remarkable was that men who had taken an *active* part in organising the Orangist repressions of 1787 (van Burmania Rengers in Friesland or van Doorn and van Houtte in Zeeland) and

those like Bentinck van Diepenheim in Overijssel or van Lynden van Lunenburg in Utrecht who were the heads of the provincial Orange nobility, should
have found places either in the legislature or on the councils of the departments and municipalities.[10]

The considerably more vivid Orange hue of the governing personnel of
Schimmelpenninck's regime did not, in fact, reflect any wish on his part to
surround himself with a pseudo-Stadholderian "court party." It stemmed
rather from his whiggish conviction that those who by interest, station,
wealth or experience had a legitimate claim on office, and who had been evicted
from it by the revolution, should be re-instated. Although he had been one of
the signatories to the Leidse Ontwerp of 1785 (along with Fijnje and Vreede!),
which had attacked the networks of money and influence that closed up the
regencies to all but members of the charmed circle, his experiences in Amsterdam since the revolution had opened his eyes to the perils of democratic representation. In 1805 he certainly sympathised with the Frieslander who wrote to
him complaining that, "after the removal of the *Grietslieden* in 1795, the
municipalities and the country districts appointed many simple and ignorant
souls instead of those properly versed in matters of police and justice."[11]

Thus the central core of the regime was composed of men who had done
their utmost to resist the onslaughts of democracy, either as Patriot regents
in 1787 (many of whom had defected to the Stadholder) or as Batavian
federalists after 1795. Schimmelpenninck's own secretary was the son of one
of the most powerful oligarchs in Leiden, van May van Streefkerk. Other
regent notables—Frederick van Leyden van Westbarendrecht and Jan van
Styrum from Holland; Hans Willem van Aylva van Neerijnen from Gelderland and Carel de Vos van Steenwijk from Overijssel—were all members of
the legislature. There was a further paradox in that a number of the members
of the Staatsraad (the institutional embodiment of a united national sovereignty) were Patriot regents and Batavian federalists who, since 1795, had
been steadfastly opposed to any interference by central governments in the
prerogatives and autonomies of provinces and towns. In much the same spirit,
it was the Nederburgh faction of "Company servants" who were firmly in
control of affairs at the "Asiatic Council."[12] Even in a watered-down form, the
van Hogendorp proposals had been largely shelved and their author removed
as far as possible from the scene of the crime by a posting to St. Petersburg.
All, in fact, was designed to accelerate the regent reversion and to restore the
republican propriety by which Schimmelpenninck, at least latterly, had come
to set so much store.

Given, then, the exceedingly patrician character of the regime it was
hardly surprising that van Stralen proposed, in September 1805, that those
seigneurial rights and perquisites officially still abolished but in fact connived
and winked at since 1801 should now be officially endorsed, and their
proprietors receive compensation for any loss of revenue in the interim. A law
to this effect had been already drafted by the Regency of State in May 1804
and was only now retrieved by van Stralen. Article 8 of the new constitution

had in any case voided any act passed since 1795 which touched on rights of property, and pecuniary duties—such as market tithes, fishing dues and the like—fell squarely into this category.[13] On the other hand, the 1804 law had stipulated a definite end to patrimonial jurisdiction and, though vague in its implications, suggested the end of rights of *gezag* and *agrement* (presentment and appointment) to curacies, schoolmasterships, dyke- and polder-masters and the petty offices of police and justice, particularly in rural areas.

It was these customary rights which Hendrik van Stralen sought to restore, and in particular those cases where the patron had lost his *leenregt* (the perquisite paid on appointment to an office) were to be suitably indemnified. Even granted the conservative instincts of the Pensionary himself, this was an ambitious item of social reaction; and it went further, not only to liquidate the revolution but to restore the old regime, than any comparable law which had yet been enacted in the French Empire. Schimmelpenninck was, on the whole, inclined to view it favourably as a minor concession to the amour-propre of a social caste he certainly wished to flatter. But matters were not quite that simple. The constitution, if not the ethos of the new regime approved by Talleyrand and Napoleon, insisted on the integrity of national sovereignty and a concentration rather than a dilution of its authority. The acceptance of the right of private individuals to make appointments to public offices, and indeed to treat such offices as disposable property, flew directly in the face of the state's claim to a monopoly of sovereignty.

It was just such an objection which Johannes Goldberg, as an isolated unitarist democrat on the Staatsraad, picked up and emphasised in his dissenting report to the Pensionary on October 28.[14] His attack on the pretensions of the "seigneurial rights and dues" (*heerlijke rechten*) was shrewdly aimed. For by taking the formal self-description of the regime as a true "Representative Government" (*Volksregeering bij Representatie*), he was able to insist that the upholding of private rights violated the collective rights of the whole people, and indeed those of the Pensionary himself, in whom they were vested by the constitution. Such sovereignty, he argued, was not divisible. Judicial, fiscal or appointative powers could only be conferred by the people on their elected nominees. In the final instance Goldberg referred Schimmelpenninck to the letter of Articles 8 and 9 of the constitution, which were quite plain on the matter. The same document, moreover, specified that a national code of law and a national system of taxation would be brought into being, with which private or corporate privileges would have been quite incompatible. The Pensionary's own license for power lay in upholding that doctrine; to abrogate any part of it, he hinted meaningfully, would amount to a self-disqualification.[15]

Goldberg's artful pedantry put Schimmelpenninck in an uncomfortable position. He himself would have been content to support van Stralen's law, but equally he could see the complications. Nor could he suppose it would be an especially popular measure. In the event he let it lie on the table; in June 1806 it was in any case overruled by a supplementary edict, which stipulated that where private or corporate privileges impinged on, or contravened, the authority of the state and its officers, the latter were in all cases to prevail. Nor does it appear that the government ever paid out indemnities to those many "heeren" and "dames" claiming restitution for lost revenues. Torn as he was by influences pulling in exactly opposite directions, Schimmelpenninck's intuitive pragmatism in the end, and with great distaste, inclined him to follow "la force des choses." Often, however, he was unsure; as a result, a rather schizophrenic portrait has emerged from his several biographers.

For his sympathisers and apologists, not least his son, Schimmelpenninck was a figure acutely alert to the needs of the time, resolved to carry out sweeping reforms, albeit within the context of the Dutch traditions which he continued to hold in respect. For more hostile commentators like Dr. de Wit, he remains essentially the protector and accomplice of the old oligarchy. Both versions have a deal of truth in them; both impulses lived within the same man. There can be no doubt that he found the business of imposing a centralised state machine on the old federal institutions a long way from the looser-jointed forms of government in the American manner, combining presidential authority with states' rights. But he also knew that the cumbersome apparatus of provincial sovereignty was no longer adequate to meet the exceptional tests of prolonged war, and that for the sake of survival it was important to subordinate the plural interests of towns, churches, guilds and provinces to the urgent needs of national mobilisation. Although his address to the legislature on May 15 wore a somewhat apologetic air, and was characteristically redolent with historical allusions, the message it spelled out was only too clear. Emphasising the return of the "old respect for legal authority" and the end of revolution, he nevertheless explained that

without powerful means there can, for the most part, be no hope of salvation. . . . The authority given to the executive power by the constitution is necessary so that those measures which, since the establishment of the Republic, over various periods have been desired by our great statesmen and attempted by some, but which through the conflict of powers and the perpetual quarrels . . . have been disappointed and frustrated . . . may at last be carried through. . . .[16]

Neither this historical legitimation, nor Schimmelpenninck's long record in seeming to support unitarism while actually sabotaging it, concealed from less equivocal guardians of the "Fundamental Restoration" the true significance of the new constitution. They appreciated only too keenly that they were now confronted with an alarming fait accompli: the shift of authority away from its traditional location in the various sovereign bodies which together had made up the United Provinces, and placed instead in some form of central administration purporting to act in the name of the whole people. In May an address signed by twelve of the leading patricians and nobles of Utrecht, many like Strick van Linschoten who thought of themselves as old-fashioned Patriot regents, was sent to the Pensionary and published simultaneously. It protested bitterly that the work of reparation, commenced in 1801, had not been continued but actually thrown into jeopardy by the present constitution. That it provided for a supreme power, above all law, an unrestricted even despotic power vested in a single person . . . under the old title of "Raadpensionaris" . . . a power much greater and fuller than of yore, greater even than that of a constitutional monarch.[17]

In particular, they took issue with the pretension of the Pensionary and his appointed officials to arrogate to themselves an authority undreamed of in the Union of Utrecht and which, they insisted, amounted to final and complete liquidation of the old Republic. Possibly they were correct. From a very different viewpoint Goldberg attached a similar importance to the transition. "The Commonwealth [*Gemeenebest*]," he wrote,

is no longer composed of different nations; no department or town will henceforth have conflicting interests and the whole people, made up of individuals of each and every department, will all have the same interests, will be endowed with the same rights and have laid on them the same obligations.[18]

This vision of a uniform, standardised monistic state, with a spick and span bureaucracy prevailing over the local forces of darkness and reaction, was one of the commonplaces of Napoleonic Europe. Even amid the more stagnant backwaters of aristocratic estates, the fiscal arithmetic of war was making it essential for state bureaucrats—and for that matter state policemen—to extend their powers far beyond anything contemplated by the more self-conscious autocrats of the old regime. What was emerging was the bare bones of the nineteenth-century nation state. The struggle in the Netherlands to become, as it were, more ordinary, was only so intense and protracted because its institutional idiosyncrasies were deeply implanted within the local community. Those who would be the real beneficiaries of a new order, and who had been disadvantaged by the old—under-represented Brabanders; overtaxed Hollanders; discriminated Catholics, Jews and Dissenters—were together nothing like so strong a force as to overcome the resistance, passive or active, of the old élite.

Moreover, the "nation" in 1805 was still such a variegated, complicated entity that even the elementary facts of language and geography remained to be straightened out. There was little chance that Holland's Dutch would penetrate the remoter recesses of Friesland or coarsen the softer fricatives of Brabander dialects; but in 1805, the first officially approved standard spelling book was produced by Dr. Siegenbeek with the government's patronage. The Remonstrant predikant Petrus Weiland's *Nederlandsche Spraakkunst*, an authoritative guide to pronunciation and basic grammar, gave added assistance to the work of standardisation. But since even today a Hagenaar claims to be able to pick out a Rotterdammer in a crowded room, the process can scarcely be said to have been completed. Geographical anomalies, ancient feudal parish or bailiwick boundaries arbitrarily dividing this hamlet from that, or surviving enclaves of entirely independent jurisdiction all proved difficult to iron out according to the bureaucratic cartographers' rational desiderata. The old "schoutampten" (bailiwicks) of Benschop and IJsselstein were eventually incorporated with the department of Utrecht; Leerdam and Vianen with Holland; the isolated little island of Ameland with Friesland; and the border

districts of Wedde and West-Woldingerland with Groningen. Ducal enclaves like the Meijerij and Ravenstein—as well as odd abbatial properties—
became integrated with Brabant. But, doubtless in deference to his native
loyalties, Schimmelpenninck made an exception of the three towns of Overijssel—Deventer, Kampen and Zwolle—all of which remained largely free
from the superior authority of the departmental council.

The centralisation of power was more evident in the principal organs of
state. The Staatsraad—whose members were all appointees of the Pensionary—
was closer to the French Conseil d'État than the old Dutch Raad van State,
which had had only as much power as the States-General delegated to it.
Like its French counterpart, the Staatsraad was essentially the deliberative
body of the executive; responsible for considering and reporting through subcommittees on any project drafted by the Pensionary or his ministers for
eventual submission to the legislative corps. Detailed consideration of draft
legislation meant that the sections of the council had to have at least a
modicum of administrative ability. And while the Staatsraad was hardly
a stronghold of republican commitment, there were among its members fewer
adornments of the patrician nobility and rather more of the Batavian regents
who had appeared again and again in the assemblies and committees of the
Republic: men like van de Kasteele, Queysen, Willem Six and van Royen,
who were not without ability or experience. The Staatsraad, as Gogel was to
discover to his cost under Louis Bonaparte, could be in an excellent position
to snipe at intended reforms; it could also, as in the case of the restoration of
seigneurial rights, hold up retrograde legislation indefinitely. In one of its
manifestations at least the Council was meant to be the watchdog of the
constitution. This meant that on more than one occasion it could come into
conflict either with the executive who acted as its chairman or more likely
with his ministers.

It was the five Secretariats of State—War, Marine, Foreign Affairs, Interior and Finance—which acted as the engine of the administration. They
were modelled closely on the Agencies of the Batavian Directory, both in
function and competence, and like them were appointed by the executive.
Except that a Ministry of Justice was added and a Ministry of Waterstaat
(hydraulics) hived off from the Interior, they underwent little other than
titular change under Louis Bonaparte. Even during the period of the
Regency of State, when the powers of the central administration were more
confined, there had been a continuity of personnel within the embryonic
state bureaucracy, especially at the level of senior secretaries and commissioners. The growing appetite for data and the expertise required to gather it
and process it for executive decisions—the day-to-day work, that is, of any
bureaucracy—was creating niches for specialists in the increasing number of
fields for which the national government was accepting responsibility. Jan
Kops, the agronome who had completed the great land survey of 1800, had
continued after 1801 with the work of measuring the agrarian resources of the
Netherlands, and preparing all manner of memoranda on technical improvements. Schimmelpenninck placed him in charge of a separate Commission

for Agriculture under the auspices of van Stralen's secretariat, and from that office there issued a great flow of dossiers on every conceivable subject from the reclamation of sandy and scrub land to protection against cattle plague, the dissemination of improved fertiliser, and experimenting with livestock breeds.[19]

Christiaan Brunings, the outstanding hydraulic engineer of his day, was given a job at a similar level to Kops, that of Director-General of the new Commission for the Waterstaat. This post, too, was a descendant of the executive inspectorate established by the Batavian Directory in 1800 and over which Brunings had presided. Together they represented the first concerted attempt to provide a unified national service of inspection and maintenance for the dykes, polders, rivers and canals on which the Republic so vitally depended. Both Schimmelpenninck (as Louis Bonaparte after him) and van Stralen, who took over Brunings' supervisory role after the latter's death in 1806, took a keen personal interest in the Waterstaat and established a special department of hydraulic engineering at the Military Academy at Amersfoort to train successive generations of men who could be both technically proficient and administratively competent.

In 1807 the Commission for the Waterstaat which had been under the Ministry of the Interior was given separate ministerial status, and the major projects begun by Brunings—the Katwijk sluices; the drainage works at Mijdrecht and the Nieuwkoop marshes (between Amersfoort and Utrecht); the construction of the Dedemsvaart Canal; and the raising of the Sloter-dyke—were all completed. Some of the most ambitious schemes like the drainage of the Harlemmermeer had perforce to wait until the middle of the nineteenth century before they were finally taken up. Not surprisingly, Brunings' controversial principle of permitting a new flood area on the lower Waal and Maas controlled by new irrigation canals met with a good deal of opposition from those in the areas it would have affected. But the general notion of a national organisation to deal with the Waterstaat, partly because of the financial exigencies affecting the old dijk colleges and local bodies, won acceptance in this period and made an important contribution to breaking down the barriers of parish and province where they were most obstructive.

There were other miniature bureaucracies dealing with specialised areas of administration which under Schimmelpenninck's regime received a national framework of organisation and wide authority to act throughout all departments.[20] One was the "Pharmacopeia Batavia," concerned with the regulation of drugs and the propagation of information on domestic and public hygiene, dietary and obstetric matters—a topic which Louis was later to make something of a compulsive interest. Another was Adriaan van den Ende's Commission for Elementary Education. This had grown out of van der Palm's Agency for National Education, and from the continuing vigilance of the inspectorate established by the laws of 1801 and 1803. Van den Ende had been van der Palm's amanuensis, secretary of the inspectorate and major-domo of the whole system of public scrutiny and support. He bore the major responsibility for the School Law of April 1806 (dealt with in detail later in this chapter), which laid the foundation for a system of public elementary schooling so impressive that it won the reluctant admiration even of the inspectors of the French Imperial University on their tour in 1811.

Building on what had been begun in the period between 1798 and 1801, Schimmelpenninck's government created the basis for the first national public administration experienced by the Netherlands. The times were not exactly auspicious for innovation, and there was no guarantee that in the face of hostility every bit as sharp as after 1798, the bones of the unitary state could be made to breathe. There were, however, some important changes from the earlier period which were bound to strengthen the hand of the executive. First the reduction of the legislature, which during the Directory had been the principal forum of federalist and regent opposition to the government, removed a major obstacle to unitarist reform. Even if those who like Wiselius held firmly to their principles of democratic representation found the evolution altogether regrettable, there were other Batavians, not least Gogel and Valckenaer, who as new *politiques* were not oblivious to the advantages of the situation. Secondly, the hierarchy of authorities, central and local, was much more clearly defined both in the constitution and in a supplementary statute on towns and local councils than heretofore. The departmental and municipal bodies continued to be dominated by the traditional patriciate, even though odd Batavians—such as Krieger, who had sat in the National Assembly of 1796, and was a member of the Brabant Council, and Hugenpoth tot Aerdt, the president of the first post-revolutionary council at Nijmegen in 1795 and of the Gelderland Departmental Council ten years later—managed to intrude into the charmed circle.

By and large, the leading figures on such bodies were either unvarnished Orangists like van Heeckeren van Enghuizen (Gelderland) or patrician aristocrats who had returned to office after 1801. Four of the six members of the Utrecht Council fell into this latter category.[21] But while these notables were on the whole left by Schimmelpenninck undisturbed in control of their parishes, the overall importance of their offices was radically diminished by executive decision. Articles 62 and 63 of the constitution had stipulated that the departments consult with all possible urgency with the Pensionary on ways and means to reduce wasteful expenditure and eliminate sinecures. The July law on local government not only confirmed the power of the executive to appoint or dismiss at will but in effect gave him the power of the purse.[22] Registers of expenditure had to be produced on demand; permission sought to impose local taxes earmarked for specific public purposes; authority of general surveillance given to both the Secretary of State for Finance and for the Interior in matters such as poor relief, public works, the stipends of clergy, schoolmasters and other public servants, which normally would have fallen within the exclusive domain of the department.

The delegation of authority had thus been inverted. Whereas after 1798 the agents of the state were effectively excluded from all those functions traditionally regarded as the business of the local community, after 1805 only those matters not detailed by the state as of national concern fell to the local authority. In any cases of conflict the executive had always the final sanction of individual or even collective summary dismissal, should that become unavoidable.

Increasingly, though, drastic pressure on local authorities to conform to the policies and statutes laid down by the national government was becoming gratuitous. The whole nature of public office in the Netherlands during these harrowing times was undergoing something of a sea-change. Major municipalities like Haarlem, Leiden and Rotterdam were sinking irretrievably into deficit. Taking on the office of a burgemeester or a regent was as likely to bring grief as privilege and certain to incur more expense than profit. Now that the state rather than the city disposed of major offices and stipendiary accounts could be inspected on demand by some snooping clerk from The Hague, the reservoirs of patronage which had lubricated the periwig oligarchies were reduced to the pitiful dispensation of a bargeemastership here or a curacy there. The problem was again one of arithmetic. The resources generated by the general level of prosperity—in Holland and Zeeland in particular—and which had gone to finance those features of urban society (poor relief; care of the aged; the universities and Latin schools; canals, dykes and highways) which had been so universally admired, were shrinking away as the exigencies of the war and the Continental system made themselves felt. As this happened, their custodians were forced either to curtail the scope of their expenditures or look to the departmental and thence the national government for subsidy. Naturally that assistance could be bought only with the loss of their cherished independence. It was these hard facts rather than any political assault on their autonomy which, in the years after 1805, brought them increasingly into a subordinate relationship with the state.

By extension, the Dutch state was itself saddled with colossal liabilities and could only take on new responsibilities if it could generate sufficient revenue to meet the basic requirements of defence and its obligations towards its creditors. Whether any eventual amortisation of the national debt and a little elbow room for additional domestic expenditure could be achieved depended, in the first place, on the success of Gogel's panacea: the General Taxation Plan, enacted in statute in June 1805 and put into operation on January 1 of the following year. In the second place, it depended on containing within reasonable bounds the military commitment of the Dutch to their alliance with France. Whether or not the Emperor—on whose word the Dutch state stood or fell—would countenance any such moderation, whether he would give the Pensionary time and grace to realise even part of his hopes and ambitions, no-one dared predict.

From Republic to Monarchy

June 10, 1805, had been ordained by the Grand Pensionary a "Day of Thanksgiving, Prayer and Penitence." Such solemnities, in which the fate of the nation was linked directly with the assiduousness with which it had followed the paths of virtue, were still part of the ritual of public Calvinism. But on this occasion the rather sombre tone of the festivities was exactly appropriate for the trepidation in which most Dutchmen awaited the outcome of the changes that had taken place yet again in their constitution. Few, other than Schimmelpenninck himself, could have supposed that the present order would endure much longer than its predecessors. Indeed, even before the end of 1805 the ominous scenario, heralding further intervention, was already becoming discernible. Just a week before the prayers for delivery, Napoleon had observed—apropos of another decayed maritime Republic—that "where true naval independence no longer exists for a trading people, it may become necessary for them to become united under a more powerful flag."[23]

Hints, broad and narrow, continued to be dropped. Muttered noises off, not all of them appreciative, concerning the running of the Dutch administration, were sometimes amplified into critical articles in the *Moniteur* or other of the Paris gazettes. New military successes, culminating in Austerlitz, were again creating new "realities" and the need for fresh Imperial "reorganisation." Finally, the continuing deterioration in Schimmelpenninck's eyesight was causing ripples of more than polite concern at St. Cloud and the Quai d'Orsay. The oculist Demours was brought from Franec to see if anything could be done, but merely confirmed the most pessimistic diagnoses. Increasingly the Pensionary was becoming dependent on the assistance of secretaries and amanuenses. Napoleon had, after all, intended him as the driving force of a centralised and effective Dutch state and had certainly not envisaged anyone else for the office. A Batavian commonwealth with a crippled *eminente hoofd* would be likely to prove as much of a drag on the alliance as any of its unlamented predecessors.

Even had Schimmelpenninck's blindness not introduced a special problem for the survival of the Batavian Republic, French reaction to the flurry of reforms announced in The Hague would have been mixed. On the one hand, after years of exhortation, the Dutch did seem finally to have aroused themselves from what had threatened to become a condition of terminal torpor. But on the other hand, the very zeal with which the programme of administration was being tackled betokened a sense of renascent patriotism which, if not carefully contained, could as easily work against the interests of France as for them. Ever since the creation of the Batavian Republic, the optimistic proposition set before the French Directors by Jacob Blauw and Pieter Paulus, that a strengthened Netherlands would be the best asset to the alliance, had always been modified by the more expedient consideration that weakness and even disunity had the merit of excluding serious resistance should full-scale "reunion" ever become strategically desirable. The same kind of reflection operated to perpetuate federalism in Switzerland and stop well short of full unification in Italy. So ambivalent an attitude was hard for someone of Schimmelpenninck's good faith to divine. He had long cherished the assumption that most, if not all, of the troubles which had divided the allies had been the consequence of the feuds and upheavals that had stricken both states. The end of revolution, he had earnestly hoped, would signal the beginning of Franco-Dutch harmony, sealed by the personal understanding he believed he had with Napoleon.

Yet now that political conflict had been all but eliminated from the conduct of Dutch affairs, it was still plain that in many essential respects the interests of the two states diverged. Nor was the French press inclined to be more polite about the national pretensions of the Dutch. On June 17 an article appeared in the *Moniteur* expressing the view that the Dutch language was well on the way to becoming defunct and would before long be reduced to the level of a provincial patois, fit only for sailors, peasants and domestic servants.[24] Flemings and Dutch alike would then assume as their natural tongue the civilising influence of French. Nothing could have been more finely calculated to wound Dutch sensitivities at a time when they were in any case feeling raw. The article caused a furore not only in the salons of The Hague (where French was actually the polished tongue) but in the universities and literary societies of Leiden, Haarlem and Amsterdam where, as in Germany, scholars and men of letters were in the process of "rediscovering" their linguistic heritage and trying to purge it of the Gallic impurities of the age of the "lumières."

By itself the article would have had only the most petty significance, but there were other clouds on the horizon darkening the outlook for Franco-Batavian relations. As he had announced in his inaugural address on May 15, the first priority for the Pensionary was "the introduction of a simpler administration and the implementation of very significant economies."[25] But given the general level of Dutch military obligations—then consuming about 80 per cent of ordinary revenue—it was exceedingly difficult to see where such economies could be safely made. Under the terms of the informal treaty which had put him in power, Schimmelpenninck had committed the Republic to continuing to pay for 25,000 French troops until at least September 1806, after which some reduction might be negotiated (at a price, naturally) in the light of the then prevailing military situation in Europe. The only area for possible retrenchment was to eat further into the already much-depleted stock of regular Dutch forces, army and navy alike. A target of 15,000 infantry and 2,000 cavalry was set, and Generals Dumonceau and Bonhomme commissioned to work out where the axe should fall. But Pijman, the Secretary of State for War, was anxious lest if Dutch troops should be ordered to occupy Westphalia or East Friesland as the second line of an offensive against Prussia, the North Sea littoral from Groningen to Walcheren would be left dangerously exposed.

The preference of the French for Batavian payment for their own troops to a strong Dutch army was treated with the same suspicion as their proposal to demolish the "barrier forts" as a needless expense—commended precisely because it would ease the way for total absorption of the Netherlands within the Greater French Empire. The navy was just as contentious a matter. Even after its commitments to the Boulogne flotilla had been fulfilled, the Batavian fleet at the Texel counted five remaining ships-of-the-line and assorted frigates, corvettes and the like. This was a force sufficient to defend the entrance to the Zuider Zee yet too weak to engage any but the lightest British squadron at sea. Napoleon wanted a Dutch force of sufficient strength to bottle up the whole of the Yarmouth fleet and prevent it from reinforcing the Channel defences.[26] He demanded that the Texel and Hellevoetsluys fleets be brought up to a strength of twelve full ships-of-the-line (expanded even further the following year to twenty), an impossibly tall order even had construction materials been less scarce. At the same time, and with some reason, the "Asiatic Council" was beginning to be perturbed about the balance of naval power in the Indian Ocean and the China Sea. The chances, then, of any significant retrenchment at sea seemed very remote.

The catastrophe at Trafalgar on October 21 seemed to rule out, at least for the foreseeable future, any prospect of an invasion of England. So the Dutch naturally began to make discreet soundings about the possibility of a return of part of the Boulogne flotilla and the decommissioning of some of the crews of the small boats. Equally predictably, the Emperor would have none of it. The plans for the invasion had merely been put into cold storage as far as he was concerned. More immediately, there was an all-out economic war to be waged to bring Britain to her knees. To make that blockade effective, naval strength at full mobilisation capacity was to be essential. Renewed arguments between Paris and The Hague over the excessively zealous patrols of French coastguards and customs men, not always on their side of the border, bore witness to the fresh resolution to make the Continental system water-tight.[27]

Nor did it help much that the one man who might reasonably have been expected to use his good offices to defend the Batavian Republic from the more exorbitant demands of the Emperor, the Secretary for the Navy, Verhuell, had in fact thrown in his lot with the French interest. Karel Verhuell, the son of a Gelderland landowner of fairly modest means, had risen rapidly through the ranks of the Batavian navy (once the bar on Orangist personnel had been lifted after 1801). Given the dismal record of defeats, desertions and mutinies, and the consequently brisk turnover in naval officers, it was no hard matter for a gifted opportunist of his calibre, especially when assisted by an elder brother who had been promoted vice-admiral before him, to make his way. It was in fact that brother's decision to decline the command of the Dutch sections of the invasion flotilla which gave Karel Verhuell the chance he seized with such grateful alacrity. During his stay in France, recognising in the Emperor an adventurist talent even sharper than his own, he became an uncritical devotee and so remained for most of his life. His own real talent in marshalling the Dutch section of the expedition and his success in beating off British attacks on the convoy at Cap Gris Nez—as well as the eloquence and, to French eyes, thoroughly un-Dutch charm he showed in the Imperial entourage—gave him a position of key influence which he proceeded to exploit with cool cynicism.[28] He was well placed to see that Schimmelpenninck's reign was destined to be all too brief, and was himself not unhappy to help it on its way. Returned to The Hague, he conducted a secret correspondence with Talleyrand and Napoleon in which the Batavian administration was criticised as lax, the organisation of the army as defective, the Pensionary as surrounded by English agents and sympathisers and his sight dimming to the point at which before long any effective government would be impossible.

Like all intelligent, self-serving collaborators, Verhuell wrote what he knew his peers wished to read. It was just conceivable that Napoleon's careful enquiries after Schimmelpenninck's health were motivated at least in part by a sincere concern for someone whom he had undoubtedly held in esteem. But, as Verhuell gleaned from Talleyrand, were the Pensionary to be forced by his malady to stand down, the occasion might not be inopportune for a new consideration of the whole position of the Netherlands. Post-Austerlitz "realities" had created in their wake new contingencies. The rationale of the dictated Peace of Pressburg (in so far as there was one) claimed that the unprovoked aggression of the Coalition, which had met its just deserts at Ulm and Austerlitz, had necessitated both the annexation of further territory for the "protection" of the Empire and the reorganisation of buffer states for additional security. Thus the newly annexed territories of Istria, Dalmatia and the Tyrol were to be guarded by the Kingdom of Italy, confided to the Vice-Royalty of Napoleon's stepson Eugène de Beauharnais. Cleves and Berg were to be united under Murat and the strategically crucial Neuchâtel reconstituted as a principality under Berthier. The abbacies, episcopacies and Imperial cities making up the Confederation of the Rhine were to be strengthened by the Kingdom of Westphalia. On January 12, 1806, Napoleon wrote formally to the Senate announcing a number of these changes and observing that new territories, such as Genoa, "are to be taken under the protection of the Imperial eagle . . . the reunion of these states will merely give us the resources we need to defend our frontiers and coasts."[29]

However ominous this sounded to the Dutch, it did not necessarily entail their outright annexation. For although in the same letter the Emperor alluded to a desirable "uniformity of laws" as the foundation for a satisfactory rule of thumb, he also conceded that this ought to apply only in so far as it was compatible with "national usage" and "considerations of geography." Berg, Neuchâtel and the Kingdom of Naples, confided to the amiable but obtuse Joseph Bonaparte, were all meant as examples of such a *juste milieu*. The arrangement, moreover, was not without obvious advantages for the Empire proper. It freed it from the burdens of an over-extension of administrative and financial resources while assuring absolute control over political and military affairs.[30] By bringing such territories within the orbit but not the circumference of Imperial power, it was possible to "harmonise" their institutions yet maintain a façade of national independence, thus holding at bay the threat of an insurrection while bleeding off reserves of men and money for "the Empire of recruitment."

As to whether Schimmelpenninck all along had been a stalking-horse for one of the cadet Bonapartes, the evidence is inconclusive. To be sure, when pondering the alternatives in 1804 Napoleon had, in a casual way, intimated that whatever arrangement was arrived at would be only an interim solution. "Voulez-vous Schimmelpenninc; voulez-vous le Prince de Weil-bourg, voulez-vous, pour une couple d'années le Prince d'Orange? Je m'en fiche . . ." But there were eventualities which even Napoleon could not then have foreseen: the failure of the "descent on England"; Austerlitz; and the Pensionary's illness. The Continental system, which demanded that the Netherlands, notoriously permissive in such matters, be made water-tight against British goods, only emerged as the Emperor's principal weapon in the autumn of 1806. A year earlier, when Louis Bonaparte had arrived in the Batavian Republic as commander of the Armée du Nord, he certainly had no inkling that he was being thought of for a royal promotion. His orders were simply to cover the rear of the Imperial armies against any surprise counter-offensive by the Swedes and Russians, and eventually to occupy Hanover and the Hansa ports. In December Louis made his headquarters at Nijmegen, where he inspected the 10,000 Dutch troops destined to be part of that force (as Pijman had feared); cast a none-too-glad eye over the fortifications at Breda; and was formally received as a *Connétable de l'Empire* by the Sec-retaries of War and Marine.[31] But before the campaign could get under way, news of Austerlitz came through, together with orders to recall the major part of the army back to France. Louis, however, was ordered to remain in the Netherlands. Inevitably, rumours that his visit had a purpose other than purely military began to circulate, all the more so when Louis made visits to Amsterdam, Utrecht and The Hague. But so innocent was he of his brother's evolving intentions that, acutely embarrassed by rumours he presumed to be without any foundation, he took himself off out of the country. It was only when he caught up with the returning Emperor at Strasbourg that he was given to understand the nature of his blunder.

Speculation about the future of the country intensified in the early part of 1806. Initially, Gerard Brantsen, the ambassador in Paris, believed that Murat was to be appointed as some kind of pseudo-Stadholder, a prospect nobody could anticipate with much relish. Schimmelpenninck himself re-fused to credit any such skullduggery. As far as he was concerned, Louis' abrupt departure was proof of the falsehood of the rumours. But throughout January and February 1806 the intelligences in the *Moniteur*, carefully re-layed by Brantsen, grew more pointed. On January 25 the Kingdom of Naples was made known; and on March 5, the Minister of the Interior, Champagny, remarked in the corps législatif that before long Holland, too, "would come under the protection of the Imperial eagle."[32] Schimmelpenninck's mortifica-tion grew, along with his understanding of the realities of the situation. Aware of Verhuell's bad faith, and suspecting that he might be the source of the bad publicity appearing in the French press, he complained to him about the "defamation" of the Batavian government, the false allegations of disarray in the Dutch army and the odious harping on the unfortunate capitulation at the Cape.[33] His own public pronouncements tried, albeit wanly, to stress the importance of Dutch sovereignty and at the same time to reassure France of his nation's commitment to the alliance.

But by the middle of March it was more or less common knowledge that

Schimmelpenninck's fate was sealed. On the 1st of that month Talleyrand had conveyed to Verhuell the gist of Napoleon's intentions; and at an audience on the 14th, the bleak alternatives had been put: either outright annexation, or else a Kingdom (or "Stadholderate," if that would flatter Dutch sensitivities), but in either case with the supreme authority vested in Louis Bonaparte.[34] Two days later, a brutally explicit article in the *Moniteur* announced that the Grand Pensionary had lost his sight without hope of cure; the Dutch commonwealth was now without an executive and was sorely in need of one. Finally, on March 17, Talleyrand was civil enough to write to Schimmelpenninck himself about the "uncertainties" involved in the present situation of the Netherlands, both

in its relations with powers with whom it is at peace and those who are at war with France. Such a manner of proceeding cannot be advantageous and, in the long run, however estimable the character of the nation and however personally admirable the qualities of its First Magistrate, must entail . . . the collapse of everything.[35]

The gravity of their predicament had the effect of concentrating wonderfully the minds of the leading figures in the government on what might be salvaged for some kind of Dutch state. Only the Pensionary himself had so identified the survival of the nation with that of his personal rule that he was incapable of making a rational assessment. He also seemed to believe more and more in the power of his charisma. Showing a re-awakened enthusiasm for the processes of popular consultation, he argued that since his regime and the 1805 constitution had been grounded on the consent of the people (that is, the plebiscite), only some similar form of expressed opinion was entitled to alter it. His colleagues were less fastidious about such matters. They were well aware that since 1801 anyway the vox populi had had precious little say in the constitutional changes the Republic had experienced. Schimmelpenninck's government had arisen from a national emergency; so no doubt would that which followed it. Garat, the French Senator who visited the country later that year, summed up their quandary. "The question for them," he said, "is certainly not how Holland [sic] is to be constituted, but rather how to escape complete ruin and total dependence on some other power."[36]

With the possibility of complete extinction as a separate nation staring them in the face, the members of the legislature, the Staatsraad and the Secretaries of State together convened an extraordinary deliberative body called the "Groot Besogne" (the Grand Commission). They were obliged to determine those features of their national life they were least prepared to sacrifice. These were plain enough: the territorial integrity of the Netherlands (within its Batavian frontiers); the guarantee of the national debt; freedom from conscription; freedom of worship; and the preservation of the *moeder-taal* (mother tongue) and of administrative and judicial autonomy. It seemed self-evident that these items would be best safeguarded by the acceptance of a dependent kingdom, if only, as one member put it, to keep the name of Holland on the map of Europe. Interestingly enough, only Johannes Goldberg was prepared to set more store by economic recuperation than national amour-propre. Since he was of the opinion that sooner or later annexation was likely, it would be better to accept a "reunion" which would end the severe tariff discrimination on both raw materials coming out and finished goods going into France, from which Dutch manufactures had suffered. It would also impose a lighter fiscal burden on the population.[37] But Goldberg was in a minority of one. For the majority there was the cold comfort that, as Brantsen put it, they had experienced "Leicesters" (foreign protectors, patrons and overlords) before and yet survived with their identity intact. As long as whichever Bonaparte was to be foisted on them was prepared to accept the essential features of Dutch identity, there was a reasonable chance that they might still emerge from the rigours of Napoleonic imperialism. In any event, as Brantsen also felt compelled to insist, what use was resistance? For "wrath without strength would be in vain."[38]

As at the beginning of the Batavian Republic, so at the end, its negotiators tried to outface what was an impossibly weak position. The "Instruction" given to the delegates of the "Groot Besogne" sent to Paris included the proviso that in all events "the definitive decision will rest with the Batavian nation," though it did not specify exactly how that decision was to be elicited. Van Stralen, who unexpectedly turned out to be the most patriotic of the members of the Commission, wanted Schimmelpenninck to go to Paris to lend extra weight to the deputation; but the Pensionary, by now rather a poignant figure, was himself acutely aware of the embarrassment such an appearance would cause. Even when van Stralen made the kindly gesture of offering to lead him by the arm, he replied that "the matter is decided by Napoleon. I am blind, and even were I to remain in the government that should still appear to be so." He did, however, take care to include Gogel, known as a reforming democrat-Patriot, in a deputation that would otherwise have been dominated by Orangists and regents. As a group they were instructed to try to dissuade the Emperor from going ahead with some degree of amalgamation, but in the last resort to do everything to protect the vital interests of the nation. They were given no authority to sign any conclusive document without first referring back to the Grand Commission and the Pensionary.

Even this turned out to be an optimistic prognosis. France was well accustomed in such situations to employing the diplomacy of the cudgel to extract what had already been predetermined with a minimum of fuss. Gone were even the most specious references to "liberation," the obligations of fraternity or, indeed, Batavian sovereignty and integrity. France, it was stressed, had magnanimously waived her *rights of conquest* in 1795 as a special grace, but over the years it had become apparent that only by planting a dynasty on Dutch soil was it possible to guarantee the survival of the country in war and the absolute stability of its government. Napoleon refused point-blank to see members of the deputation, whom he regarded as supplicants rather than ambassadors, and communicated to them via Verhuell, who was by now acting less as a Dutch minister and more as an errand-boy of the Emperor.

Nor would there be anything so presumptuous as negotiations over the transition to a monarchy. Talleyrand had been busy drafting a "Treaty" which the delegates were to be induced to sign by the usual combination of carrot and stick. The stick—wielded with some zeal by the intelligencers of the *Moniteur*, and brandished on occasions by Napoleon too—was the prospect, should assent not be forthcoming, of a military administration under some such governor as Marshals Soult or Davoût. As against that, the terms of Talleyrand's "Treaty" went some way to pacifying most of the Dutch anxieties. There would be no union of crowns; no forced conscription; the civil list was fixed at 1.5 million guilders; there was the promise (now ten years old) of a possible commercial treaty in the not too distant future; and the basic freedoms of the country—linguistic, religious, judicial—were to be preserved. Indeed, there were to be few alterations to the constitution of 1805, a document which both the Emperor and his foreign minister had already approved. The titular head of state would change; the Staatsraad was to be expanded from eight to thirteen, and the legislative corps from nineteen to thirty-eight (with a slightly disproportionate increase in representation for Holland). That was all.[39]

Despite the appallingly brusque manner in which it was served up, the arrangement, as Gogel reluctantly admitted, might have been worse. The alternatives did not bear thinking about. "The choice is hard," he wrote to Elias Canneman on April 28, "but what can weakness do against might?" The delegation was not even permitted the face-saving concessions of referring back to The Hague for a decision. Napoleon demanded that they present a formal request to Louis, on behalf of the Dutch people, that he consent to become "King of Holland"—a final self-chastisement which even the arch-pragmatist Brantsen was loath to contemplate. But the charade was, of course, played out. The only last-ditch opposition came from van Stralen and from Schimmelpenninck himself, who refused to ratify the treaty or to accept the post of "permanent President of the Legislative Assembly," a decorative office meant to spare his feelings. His insistence to the last that the treaty must be put to popular plebiscite found no response in the Grand Commission and only earned for him the valedictory epithet conferred by Talleyrand of "un grand fou."[40] His colleagues saw easily enough that were a referendum to go the "wrong" way, the nation would be left defenceless against the worst Napoleon might do. Since Schimmelpenninck remained adamant in refusing to sign his official death-warrant, it perforce fell to Appelius, as President of the Staatsraad, and a minor functionary, Cuypers, the clerk of the legislative corps, to perform the formalities and so deliver the *coup de grâce* to what remained of the Batavian Republic. On June 4 Schimmelpenninck resigned and retired to his estates in Overijssel, where he spent most of the twenty years remaining to him enjoying the reputation of a tragic hero victimised by his times.

On the following day the ceremonial comedy at St. Cloud was duly staged —but not until Napoleon had first received the Turkish ambassador. Verhuell presented the prepared "petition," the Emperor made a speech, and Louis graciously "accepted" the request—seeing that the desire of the Dutch people to have him as their sovereign was so fervent. Napoleon went out of his way to emphasise the debt owed by the Dutch to France, even going so far as to imply that, without French assistance, they would never have won their liberty from Spain in the first place.[41] In any case, the republican system of government was encumbered with far too many "inconveniences" to make it secure against the British menace. The regime of the Pensionary had been, in the words of the *Moniteur*, neither "fish nor fowl, neither republic nor monarchy." The only alternative to the perils of popular sovereignty was a kingdom. Indeed, such a regnum would be the best guarantor of all those freedoms which meant so much to the Dutch people. Despite this reassurance, no-one could be left in any doubt where the final court of appeal would lie. The Family Statute of the Empire of March 30, 1806, had stipulated that all princes would be educated in France during their minority and that the Emperor as *chef de famille* would exercise his avuncular puissance on their behalf. He would, moreover, continue to have residual powers of surveillance, police and general "discipline."[42] Louis ascended his throne promising that "My life and my will belong to you [Napoleon]; I will reign in Holland since the people desire it *and Your Majesty commands it.*"[43]

Despite this evidently tepid show of feeling, the initial impression made by Louis Bonaparte on the representatives of his new subjects was not unfavourable. At least they liked the way he stood, spoke, conducted himself. More than that they could hardly say. But in the Netherlands there was still deep foreboding and intense chagrin at the wound which had been inflicted on what was left of national self-respect. Even by those who knew it was inevitable, the creation of a Bonapartist monarchy was treated as an ignoble form of blasphemy, not only against the historical image of the old Republic but also against the spirit of the Patriot revolution itself, which had been made, above all other causes, for the sake of national rejuvenation. The Patriots had drunk deep of predikant evangelism and had castigated the last generation of periwig regents for the moral decadence which had brought down on the Dutch the fatal indifference of their special Providence. Having struggled manfully to bring the nation back to the ways of righteousness and its government to the whole people, they still seemed to have been deserted, sold into captivity or delivered to a foreign Prince. What then might ensue no-one dared say. Perhaps they would disappear from the face of the earth as a Chosen People; perhaps Napoleon would succeed in doing what generations of tyrants before him had failed to do: obliterate all that had been won by hardship, resourcefulness and courage.

Naturally all these dark ruminations were confined to private doubts and grievances. But there were some bold spirits who made their protest public. Adriaan Loosjes, a bookseller and publisher of Haarlem and a deputy to that first celebratory National Assembly of 1796, printed a pamphlet denouncing the foreign yoke, though it seems unlikely that more than a handful ever got distributed. A young professor at Harderwijk made a similar though less bellicose protest. By far the most defiant voice, though, was female: that of Maria Aletta Hulshoff, the daughter of a Mennonite pastor who had been encouraged by Sam Wiselius—himself bitterly and unrepentantly enraged at what had come to pass—to vent her feelings. She not only upbraided her countrymen for indifference in the face of calamity but appealed to the spirit of "Fatherland in danger" (*Vaderland in gevaar*) to restore the popular democracy which alone would act as the shield of the nation. "The only real remedy for our ills," she wrote, "is to recall to public office the true Bataves; the partisans of unity; the friends of France [sic], and to remove from the headship of State, whoever they are and whatever titles they may have, the oligarchs and the regents who are only tools of England. . . ." Despite her passionate concern for the crusade against the British, Maria Hulshoff's firebrand patriotism was by now decidedly out of fashion, not to say seditious. It suddenly became a pressing matter for her father to pack her off to the United States to avoid the attentions of the Procureur-General.[44]

We may be sure that most if not all of these jeremiads went largely unheeded by the audience to whom they were addressed. The passing of the Batavian Republic was remarkable only for the conspicuous lack of obsequies or ululations from any significant part of the Dutch people. Most were all too preoccupied with the increasingly onerous task of providing for their subsistence. But the misgivings felt by those who had worked for, and lived with, the faltering governments and doomed hopes of the Batavian Republic were nonetheless deep and mournful. Elias Canneman, who was as ready as the next bureaucrat to swallow what "la force des choses" dictated, confided his apprehensions to Gogel on the day that the infamous treaty was signed. On perusing it, he complained:

nowhere have I found a single scrap of hope; nowhere any place to attach my republican principles; nowhere an anchor for the civil rights of the population. Everything is reduced to mere ciphers and empty words. . . . No security against an odious conscription; no guarantee against the aristocracy; no pledge of the evacuation of a foreign army; a commercial treaty only in the air and even then no annulment of the appalling tariff barriers. . . . For myself I can see no chance under this new regime of continuing in my present employment; my heart rebels against it. . . . I hold it impossible to remain any longer in a career where there can be no more duties to fulfil and no further disasters to avert.[45]

In the event, Canneman did stay at his post to play an important role in the implementation of the fiscal system on which he and Gogel had worked so hard and so long. Doubtless he was influenced by Gogel's own resolution, made after much agonising, to remain as Minister of Finance. Gogel too had originally thought of resigning, but on June 3, 1806, wrote to his wife that he had thought better of it, since

among the very first thoughts that the Prince had concerning our affairs was to implore me not to leave my office. I still have some hope and some courage that our finances may be saved, providing that the helmsmen remain at the wheel. . . . I have (already) done so much that I must try to persevere. . . .[46]

In fact, Canneman's worst apprehensions went unjustified. There was not much left of republican democracy, but that had already been the case with Schimmelpenninck. The four-year reign of the Bonaparte Prince did not, as he had feared, mean a violent rupture in the continuity of the nation's history, still less the irreversible alienation of national sovereignty. On the contrary, despite the serious constraints imposed by the use of the ultimate Imperial sanction, annexation, Louis' administration embodied the continuity of the reforming enterprise begun by Schimmelpenninck's government, and the vigorous assertion of Dutch traditions and interests. Instead of subjugation to the French Empire, the Dutch subjects of "Koning Lodewijk" found themselves with a monarch who was almost embarrassingly eager to identify himself with his adopted country, and to shield them from the most damaging effects of his own brother's rule. It was an unhappy irony that it was this streak of stubborn integrity which in the end lost him his throne and his people their separate existence for three years. Doubly ironic that, whatever their general misgivings about what lay in store for them as a Bonapartist kingdom, the members of the Grand Commission had supposed that relations between France and the Netherlands would surely take a turn for the better.

Had Napoleon imagined that instead of establishing an obedient cadet on the "throne" of Holland he was creating a new focus for patriotic loyalties, he would no doubt have paused before deciding on Louis' promotion. But there was nothing in his younger brother's career remotely to suggest the extraordinary chronicle of defiance and insubordination which then followed He was, perhaps, a little morose, on occasions even truculent—a good deal less affable than Joseph and much less shrewd than Lucien. But Lucien had, to Napoleon's regret, a mind of his own; Joseph was none too bright, and Jérôme a mere gadfly. Louis, he knew, was not without a moral earnestness of which he thoroughly approved and seemed impatient for responsibility. That indeed was just the problem. Nine years younger than the Emperor, he had been intensively reared as his protégé; had trotted dutifully along on the Egyptian and Marengo campaigns; and had been groomed for an appropriate combination of martial and political skills.

Unhappily, Louis had neither the talent nor the taste for campaigning. A fall from a horse had damaged joints in his right hand and left leg and both as a consequence became prematurely arthritic. By the end of his reign in the Netherlands—where the climate was less than ideal for his complaint—he could barely move the fingers in his hand. He was in pain for much of his life; not all of his compulsive interest in drugs, medicines, cures, spas and surgery was generated by the hypochondria which unfriendly biographers have attributed to him. Despite the mildly bullying paternalism Napoleon affected with his younger brothers, he had, on the whole, treated Louis reasonably, placing him in command first of the Paris garrison, then, as we have seen, of the Army of the North during the 1805 campaign. Despite this solicitousness, Louis gradually came to harbour an almost paranoid resentment against Napoleon for thrusting him into situations for which he was unsuited. His whole personality, he believed, had been deformed to gratify his brother's image of him as the gifted young cub.

The crowning touch was the disastrous marriage with Hortense de Beauharnais, which had been forced on him to gratify Josephine's latest gambit at family politics. Napoleon, for that matter, was genuinely fond of Hortense. A more generous and gentle presence than her mother, he saw in her the epitome of all the womanly virtues he found so sadly wanting in Josephine. But Hortense and Louis were abominably mismatched. Originally a very handsome man, Louis had become self-conscious about his looks since becoming pock-marked. He too had suffered from Napoleon's interference with a love affair of his own and thereafter was nervous and irritable in his relations with women; an unease doubtless aggravated by the early contraction of syphilis. He could not abide his wife's girlish frivolousness (there was more of her mother in her than Napoleon supposed) and she in turn found his starchy gravity dreary and his tantrums of self-pity both contemptible and absurd.

Until the summer of 1806, Louis had never really contemplated any act of challenge to his brother. The dressing-down he had received at Strasbourg at the end of December 1805 had arisen merely from his innocence of the Emperor's real intentions. And even years later—when the two brothers were in all-out battle and Napoleon was sure that he had nursed a viper in his bosom, that Louis was no better than a calculating, hypocritical scoundrel bent on sabotaging the Continental system—Louis himself never imagined that he had ever gone out of his way to pick a quarrel with his brother, only that he was acting according to the solemn vows he had taken on his accession to be faithful to the interests of his subjects. Indeed, at no time was there any disingenuousness or artfulness in Louis' conduct. On the contrary, candour, moral rectitude and political naïveté he possessed in disarming abundance. What he lacked was the one quality indispensable for survival in Napoleonic Europe: a healthy sense of irony. In many respects he was the Candide of the Bonapartes: an earnest *naïf* who clung to his primitive principles as calamity after calamity descended about his ears. On approaching the Dutch frontier, he tells us in his Memoirs, he replaced his French cockade for a Dutch one and then wept at the loss.[47] In all probability this *was* a traumatic experience, since he was unaccustomed to doffing and donning nationalities like strips of ribbon.

When, in 1808, Napoleon found it expedient to move him on to Madrid since "the climate [in Holland] does not suit you," Louis was appalled at the cynicism and determined to stick at his post come what might. Even at the beginning he displayed a scrupulousness which was most un-Bonapartist. On showing the new King the constitution confected with the minister at The Hague, Dupont-Chaumont, Talleyrand was bemused to receive the reply that Louis could not possibly endorse *en bloc* a document which he had had no part in drafting nor time yet to peruse.[48] Evidently Louis was affronted at the presumption that, as a King in name only, he had no real interest in such matters.

Canneman had warned Gogel: "It will take many a summer in our climate before the new plant is naturalised."[49] Here again he was being over-pessimistic. Temperamentally, Louis was remarkably well suited to the people who had been placed under his sovereignty. Later he was to say that one of his only regrets was that he had not been born Dutch. Verhuell, not entirely in sycophancy, observed that in many respects the King was more of a Dutchman than his predecessor; despite the Latin curls and swarthy complexion, he might well have been one. His heavy moral seriousness and his taste for slightly pompous civic ceremonial were those of any provincial burgemeester; his strict sense of duty to family and to Fatherland and his belief in the redemptive quality of hard work were virtually engraved in the national mores of the Dutch. Even his lugubrious melancholia was at least in keeping with the times. The "throne" of Holland was the ideal opportunity for him to redeem a personality which until then he felt had not properly been his own. By upholding the interests of the country with which he had come to identify, he was actually restoring his own self-respect. It was a classic instance of a public role as private therapy. The four years from 1806 to 1810, both in their fleeting happiness and much more enduring misery, were the central experience of his life. In retirement he was to show that he had some inkling of what its real significance had been. "In Holland," he wrote, "the interests, cares and public affairs occupied me entirely; I brought to my country all the affection which I was not able to find within myself. Perhaps I would, little by little, recover from my condition of physical and moral prostration."[50]

Louis flung himself into his official duties with a zeal which verged on the neurotic. He rose at five in the morning; saw Hultman (the private secretary he had inherited from Schimmelpenninck) for two hours; gave audiences from seven to nine; and presided over the Staatsraad from ten until, if need be, four in the afternoon, finally dining at five. "Everyone," wrote the Prussian ambassador, Caesar, "is astonished at his assiduousness and at the judgement and the sentiments he displays in discussion."[51] The unpretentiousness of Louis' manners, Caesar continued, had already done much to win the respect of the nation at large. Certainly his initial reception had been cool. Behind the triumphal arches hastily erected in The Hague to greet his entry on June 18, he saw shuttered windows and sparse crowds, more curious than enthusiastic to glimpse their first monarch. Perhaps there had been too many lordly exits and entrances in The Hague since 1785.

Louis took pains to surround himself with a Dutch rather than a French entourage. The small court staff he had taken with him from Loo was confined almost exclusively to domestic and ceremonial duties and attending on the already disgruntled Queen. Even some of the formal services such as the Chamberlains, Master of Ceremonies and Master of the Household were given to Dutchmen. Louis was only concerned that at least one of his surgeons and one of his chaplains should be French.

One of the King's first actions was to receive in the Oranje-zaal, in the Huis 't Bosch, a gathering of fifty or so of the old nobility, led by Admiral van Bylandt-Halt—a ceremony such as had not taken place since the days of Willem V. Indeed, it may well be that the death of the old Stadholder in Kew on April 9 helped salve any consciences among the barons now giving allegiance to Napoleon's brother. Louis followed up this gesture by attending to another group conspicuous for its devotion to the House of Orange, the navy. Learning of some discontent and even threats of mutiny among the

Texel squadrons, more at the prospect of the decommissioning of certain vessels than any reluctance to serve a King, Louis went in person to the harbours and yards to address the sailors and officers, and was evidently more of a success than he could have hoped.[52]

Verhuell may have been right in implying that the robes of pseudo-monarchy fitted Louis more becomingly than they had Schimmelpenninck, but in most respects the character of their government was very similar. Like the Grand Pensionary, Louis aimed at a balance of groups and parties with his own personal authority acting as arbitrator. Like him too, he was only partially successful at balancing off competing interests and in practice leaned more towards the traditional élite of regents and nobles than their adversaries. But there were if anything rather more formal Batavian republicans in ministerial office than before. Apart from Gogel, Dirk van Hogendorp was made Minister for War; van der Heim for the Colonies; and Jan van Hooff Minister for Justice—to be succeeded by another long-serving Batavian public figure, Cornelis van Maanen.

The "ministries" were simply Schimmelpenninck's Secretaries of State or the Directory's Agencies in a new titular guise. Indeed, Louis allotted rather more importance to the executive offices than they had had under the previous two regimes, even dressing them up in fancy uniforms of white trousers and blue coats with gold edging,[53] and, more importantly, giving them the right to vote at sessions of the Staatsraad—a weapon that was to be indispensable to Gogel in the battles which lay ahead with the regents on the Council. They also met as a regular group on their own account as the "Ministerraad" (the Council of Ministers), though only when the King was himself presiding. Despite its tentative beginnings, this innovation has been seen as the embryo of a more regular cabinet government in the Netherlands.[54]

The enlarged Council of State retained all the eight councillors of 1805, but its additions meant that it had a majority with decidedly federalist-conservative opinions. Its division into the three "Sections" of finance, war and peace, and interior, however, meant that if a minister concerned with a particular piece of legislation was able even to half-persuade the King and a majority within the appropriate Section (particularly that of finance), there was a decent chance that with his own advocacy and vote at a plenary session he could pick up enough support from the Staatsraad as a whole to overcome opposition. That, at any rate, was the technical means used by Gogel in his efforts to finalise the abolition of the guilds in January 1808.

During the first few weeks of his government, Louis saw to it that this machinery did not rest idle. Two features of the Napoleonic make-up—the bureaucratic and the technocratic—also manifested themselves in his brother to a marked degree. Even before he had set out for the Netherlands, Louis demanded and received from Gogel a full and extensive briefing on the condition of Dutch finance.[55] The awesome predicament of his treasury was to preoccupy him and the Second Section of the Staatsraad for much of the rest of the year; but they did not prevent him from making more general enquiries about the extent of the nation's economic resources. To assist him, he inherited from Schimmelpenninck some massively informed memoranda—that of Jan Kops on the reclamation of waste-land,[56] and a dismaying report from the departmental authorities of Holland on the damage done to the economy of that part of the nation. It presented a catalogue of woes: the stagnation of industry; the virtual obliteration of offshore fishing; a steep rise in pauperism in the major cities (one-third now received relief in Rotterdam and three-fifths in Amsterdam), with the resulting dislocation of municipal finances. The current revenues of the city of Amsterdam for 1806 were estimated at 1,570,000 florins; its expenditure at 2,590,000 florins. The interest on the municipal debt paid in that one year came to 7,000 guilders. Leiden, Haarlem and Gouda were in an even worse state.[57]

These exigencies had serious consequences for the maintenance of the vital Waterstaat. The depredations of the insatiable teredo pile worm, *T. Navalis*, had become so alarming by the end of the century that in some parts of the Holland coast, particularly at the south, the replacement of rotten timbers had become imperative exactly when municipalities and dyke colleges were least able to afford it. The slabs of Norwegian stone which had been used during the previous century to ensure against a repetition of the catastrophic floods of 1731 (when large areas of the Noorderkwartier and West Friesland went under) had become so expensive during the blockade that the cost of the operation was virtually prohibitive. Since thorough renovation or even stop-gap measures would inevitably entail substantial fiscal remissions, the responsibility for the overall condition of the sea defences, like so much else of the crippled government of the Netherlands, was gradually passing from the locality to the centre. This is not to say that there was any haste shown in the efforts to establish a national authority for the Waterstaat.

In 1807, the Commission established by Schimmelpenninck within the Secretariat of the Interior became a ministry in its own right, with Twent van Raphorst as its first chief officer. But he then spent a great deal of time mopping up after local leaks and bursts rather than tackling any large-scale operation, for which there was evidently no money available. The one polder in Schieland, known as "De Eendragt," which had collapsed in 1801 had cost some 60,000 florins to make good, and the finance for *that* had not yet been covered when Twent took over.[58] Ermerins suggested to Gogel that the disentangling of anachronistic patrimonial authority from the upkeep of the dykes was an intrinsic part of the assumption of government responsibilities in this area. In Walcheren, he thought the least that could be done was to divert the traditional gratuities and perquisites, such as the commutation for the "ransom-money" exacted by the heeren of the island, directly towards the upkeep of the dykes and polders.[59]

Louis, who was characteristically fascinated by the perennial struggle against the sea, seeing in it exactly that image of rugged endurance which the Dutch liked to project, was equally beset by the problems of trespassing on local custom and privilege. At the centre all went well. His committee of advisors on hydraulics and marine defences was dominated not by state councillors as under Schimmelpenninck but by professional engineers—Blanken, Kroz, and the celebrated auto-didact colleague of Brunings', F. W. Conrad. Louis himself prepared the regulations by which their commission was given national competence to inspect, report and scrutinise the work of local dyke colleges, and if necessary to recommend the appointment or dismissal of their officers and staff—an intrusion which, for all its paternalist concern, was greeted with hostility in the colleges themselves. Louis determined that the major works begun in 1804–05, such as the Katwijk sluice, the drainage of the Nieuwkoop marshes and the building of the coastal highway between The Hague and Haarlem, would at least be completed. This was duly done under his surveillance.

From his account in the *Documents historiques,* the King seems to have enjoyed playing a Solomonic role in adjudicating between the mutually incompatible interests of the Amsterdam Waterstaat and the inhabitants living to the west below the Sloterdijk, alarmed that their own defences were inadequate to meet the gradually rising level of the sea. For their part, the Amsterdammers were equally anxious that if the Sloterdijk were raised by any appreciable degree, its effect would be to displace that volume of water more threateningly towards their own weakened defences. After a protracted dispute, the King managed to reconcile both parties by permitting the raising of the Sloterdijk by a few feet but allowing the Amsterdammers to raise their own major dykes a certain, though obviously not equivalent, degree. Although a compromise, the improvements to the Sloterdijk proved their worth in the winters from 1807 to 1809 when a succession of enormous tides threatened a grave inundation. And the argument gave the King an insight into the complexities of arbitrating between local institutions and corporations unaccustomed to tolerating interference with what had long been regarded as sovereign matters of administration.[60]

It was this sort of situation, in which authorities of what the King evidently considered miniscule significance would thumb their nose at his elaborately rational planning, which brought Louis to appreciate the merits of the unitarists' case for reform. He shared with Gogel, Goldberg and van Hooff the general assumption that the Netherlands could no longer afford a plethora of public institutions, all competing for shares of a shrinking aggregate of resources and gradually dragged down together by common indebtedness. Henceforth, he believed, a "regent" had to be a public official, responsible to the common good and the Head of State who embodied it. Some of the headstrong attachment to customary notions of local independence had to be sacrificed if the nation as a whole was to remain on the map. In his address to the legislative corps in December 1806, he observed that

each year Holland has been on the verge of losing its political and physical existence; the admirable perseverance of its courageous inhabitants in rescuing it . . . from the shocks of political events, as from the calamities of the elements, has prolonged the existence of the Fatherland. But I cannot conceal from you that it will only emerge safely from this crisis when it has the means to adopt a grand system of amelioration and when we can undertake such an enterprise with calmness and perseverance. . . .[61]

As long as Dutch military commitments were so heavy (and there could be no reason to suppose that fraternal sentiment would succeed where all else had failed), Louis' "grand system" of a more rational disposal of available resources could be no more than a very rough and ready measure adopted to fend off a terminal disaster. But at least the Bonaparte King had given an unequivocal commitment to consolidating what had been begun in 1805 and to shoring up some reserves for the future protection of the nation. As a result, the government bequeathed to William I in 1813—after a three-year interval as departments of the French Empire—was the organ of a paternalist monarchy, radically different to the regime from which his father had made his exit in 1795. That change was one of the decisive transitions in the collective life of the Dutch people. What follows for the remainder of this chapter is an attempt to illustrate the ways in which this came about in three different contexts: taxation, the abolition of the guilds and reform of elementary education.

Gogel and the Reform of Taxation

The fiscal quandary faced by successive Dutch governments was exceptional only in its acuteness, not in the general nature of the problem. That the viability of a state depended as much on the generation of revenue as on its prowess on the battlefield had been a recognised truism of the old century, as of the wars which brought it to an end. Pondering the means of extorting as much taxation for as little administrative cost as possible had become the speciality of writers of financial and bureaucratic memoranda—the van Swietens and the Auget de Montyons—wrestling with the attempt to transform venal farms and private contracts into public services.[62] Even the more grandly styled practitioners of *kameralwissenschaft*—the science of government—had evolved from the grimier requirements of the cameralist counting-house. Such men were the necessary auxiliaries and agents of rulers, obliged by ambitious foreign policies to live continually beyond their means. But the implementation of the mechanical fiscal formulae was never without its dangers. The *vingtième* of 1749; the *subvention territoriale* of 1787; the British-American stamp tax and the Austrian and Prussian land taxes were all triggers of rebellion. Only when a government was desperately hard-pressed, yet found either the financial or the political costs involved in buying short-term credit unacceptably steep, could it steel itself to the fierce resistance from those many sectors whose interests militated against any bureaucratisation of finance or just against another form of imposition. It was a calculated risk, and one which not all controllers-general or lords of the treasury were prepared to take. The 1770's and 1780's were littered with the debris of such good intentions—in Spanish and British America; in Hungary; and in the Austrian Netherlands. But in the two decades which followed, the all-out character of the war with Imperial and republican France impelled the belligerent governments to make yet further demands on their long-suffering taxpayers in the name of patriotic sacrifice.

The response to such appeals was not always gratifying. In 1810 the

Prussian Chancellor, von Hardenberg, was forced to abandon his plans for a land tax by the incensed opposition of the Junker estates. Elsewhere, measures were carried through which in quieter times might have had a rougher ride. Despite a highly flexible system of credit, built around the Bank of England (which the Dutch envied but, much to Gogel's chagrin, were slow to emulate),[63] the British were obliged to issue exchequer bills secured against anticipations of specific revenues and carrying 3 per cent—in effect, a kind of short-term loan. And in 1797 they introduced the abominated income tax.[64] Ten years after an attempt to implement a direct tax which had pre-cipitated insurrections throughout the Habsburg Empire, the Imperial govern-ment enacted the *Classensteuer*, which imposed rather more heavily on both income and land. The only European powers in a relatively relaxed fiscal situation were Russia, where a brutalised peasantry supplied both the con-scripts and the poll taxes needed to sustain a huge army; and France, where external conquests enabled the state to saddle both defeated enemies and client allies with the costs of her expansion. Even here, the gangsterish prac-tice of making states pay through the nose for their own "protection" was inadequate to ambitions of a Napoleonic scale. Especially after 1804, ministers like Mollien, trained under the *contrôle* of the old regime, reverted to indirect duties such as those imposed on tobacco, liquor and salt, administered as the *droits réunis,* and invited private contractors and financiers to help tide the Empire over any short-term exigencies.

The difficulties of financing military operations were, in the Dutch case, magnified into gauging the price to be paid for survival. This was an issue which earlier generations of statesmen had attempted to set squarely before the States-General, but on each occasion they had been defeated by the enormity of the steps to be taken to effect serious financial reform. It was not just that the machinery for fiscal unification was not to hand, nor that the institutions of the financial executive like the Algemene Rekenkamer (the General Chamber of Account) were so limited in competence. The im-pediments to a uniform system of taxation were woven into the very fabric of the Union, so that removing them meant in effect tearing it apart. Even so, van Slingelandt had made an effort to show that the very existence of a Dutch state would be contingent on just such a change. In its petition for reform, the Raad van Staat of which he was Secretary in 1716 had observed:

It must be counted as a miracle of Divine Providence that a Republic which has no firmer foundation than that of the United Netherlands, a Republic which is undermined from within by the extravagances of the Union and from without by shock after shock, is still standing.[65]

Ten years later, as Pensionary, he was moved to put the matter even more forcefully, insisting that, "for the salvation of finances and the conservation of the country, the maintenance of a national authority over a unified system of finance is *indispensable*."[66]

That this urgency failed to make any impression on the divisions and the lethargy that were chronic features of the *pruikentijd* (time of the periwigs) is not surprising. Low interest rates (rarely above 3 per cent) and the careful pursuit of a neutral diplomacy during the middle years of the century enabled the caretakers of the debts of Holland, Zeeland, and the East India Company to keep any dramatic crisis at bay and to honour their obligations with proverbial punctiliousness.[67] Dutch loan capital, especially the "riskier sort," gravitated to those areas—Spain, America, the French life annuity market—where more obvious urgency generated the kind of rates (8, 10, 12 per cent) with which the domestic market could not compete.[68] If the Republic were to be caught short by a sudden military crisis, it was assumed that it would not lack for financial ballast—even if, as van de Spiegel was to discover in 1793, its cost was becoming ominously expensive. As long as a really terminal disaster appeared remote, it was altogether easier to take the line of least resistance and relapse into the inertia characteristic of the time. As Gogel commented drily to Louis Bonaparte, the Dutch were so accustomed to surviving through cultivating the arts of conservation that the notion of an abrupt breach with past usage seemed like encouraging unnatural habits.[69]

Like the economy as a whole, the administration of finance suffered from a relative, not an absolute decline. Perfectly adequate to keep the Republic hobbling lamely through the *bagarres* of the eighteenth century, it was no protection at all against the ferocious and unremitting violence of the wars of the revolution. Anton Reinhard Falck, an Orangist regent who was made Commissioner-General for the Colonies by Louis Bonaparte and went on to serve as one of Willem I's senior ministers, summed up this process neatly in 1807:

. . . everything in that respect [of political and financial institutions] had changed around us. Only Holland remained at the point where it had been in the sixteenth century. Everywhere outside Holland greater simplicity had been introduced into the workings of the administration; greater promptness in deciding on measures; greater vigour in their execution. Eventually we began to feel the inconveniences of a system which was in harmony neither with the needs of the times nor with the progress of our neighbours. We wished to change this, but in a land where so many have the right to air their opinions and where so many interests are bound to collide and have to be reconciled, unanimity can hardly be expected. We were agreed on the evils but differed on the remedies, and amidst this contention of parties the very zeal and energy of the best citizens became damaging to the public interest. Beset by storms, the ship of state held an uncertain course on a sea strewn with wreckage; with an active crew but one divided and exhausted by its fruitless efforts.[70]

Despite the unhappy lapse into nautical metaphor, Falck's version of the experience of the Republic before and after revolution was quite apposite. Until it became clear in the starkest terms that the survival of the Fatherland was conditional on institutional change, regents and federalist Patriots would be bound to maintain that the cure would do more damage than the malady; that the state which would result from the liquidation of provincial financial independence would in no true sense be Dutch, and would not, therefore, be worth rescuing. What, argued Queysen and de Mist, was the point of exhuming a cadaver which had already expired as a distinct and separate nation?[71]

By the spring and summer of 1805, just such a climacteric had been reached. The acute gravity of the crisis was indicated by the breadth of opinion supporting the introduction of a unified system of finance on the lines set out by Gogel in 1799. Apart from Schimmelpenninck, whose lease on power (as Napoleon had insisted) entailed the introduction of such a system, other reluctant converts included most of the members of the old Council for Finance. De Vos van Steenwijk, the erstwhile "treasurer-general" and an Overijssel patrician, had been opposed to Gogel's fiscal unification, but had himself been obliged to assume quasi-national powers for the Council simply to levy the extraordinary taxes required to meet the succession of monstrous deficits accumulating since 1800.[72] When, on May 15 in his address to the legislature, the Grand Pensionary called the "restoration of our finances our most difficult task," he was, for once, understating the matter. The arithmetic of the national balance books left no room for ambiguity, as the following statistics show:[73]

Estimated Expenditure: Aggregate of "Ordinary" and "Extraordinary"		
	1804	*1805*
"General Administration"	1,064,522	1,093,107
Foreign Relations	692,754	615,300
Navy (inc. flotilla)	8,316,175	12,748,616
Army (inc. French)	19,067,487	18,983,897
Finances (inc. nat. debt)	33,715,000	33,832,237
Internal Affairs	369,200	333,485
Waterstaat	1,140,865	845,647
Colonial and Levant admin.	6,780,035	?
	71,146,038	68,452,289
		5,000,000
		(for probable
		colonial expenses)
		73,452,289
Estimated Ordinary Revenues (1804)		
	36,280,000	
Less for departmental expenditures and subsidies	3,355,000	
	32,925,000	
	71,146,038	
Estimated gross deficit for 1804	38,221,038	

The absolute accuracy of state accounting during these chaotic years is bound to be in question. If anything, the deficits were slightly optimised. But the assumption on which any in-coming Minister of Finance had to work was that the gap, or rather gulf, between estimated gross expenditure and all ordinary sources of revenue would be in the region of 40 million guilders and almost certainly never less than 35 million.

Necker had compared the predicament of France before the Revolution to that of a man standing in water up to his neck; a wrong footing or a few more inches of water, and he was lost. To the Dutch, albeit more accustomed to both a watery milieu and eleventh-hour escapes, it must have seemed in 1805 that they were already at the point of total submersion. Moreover, the man with the lifebelt had himself brought a further burden to tie around their necks. For a secret condition of Schimmelpenninck's acquisition of power had been the pledge of a low-interest loan to France of 48 million guilders, payable in quarterly instalments over eighteen months—a gratuitous act of extortion which no doubt gave Napoleon some small sour pleasure for the snub of 1800.[74] In such a situation the options open to his government were only too plain. They might continue to ransack the warehouse of short-term expedients: loans, voluntary and coerced; life, term and permanent annuities; lotteries; levies on property and income. But in so doing there was the certain knowledge that new and deeper pools of debt were being created, and with the calculated risk of driving so many into penury that the possibility of violent revolt might become alarmingly real. Even the Regency of State's Council had made the valedictory confession that the country's economic capacities were "so weakened and enfeebled that there can be no conceivable means of meeting the deficit not offset by the misgivings aroused by the population's impoverishment. . . ."[75]

Schimmelpenninck himself thought reliance on further extraordinary impositions—after 500 million guilders' worth had been drained off in under fifteen years—to be "politically inoperable." A second possibility was to emulate the example of the French Directory of 1797, as Napoleon was constantly urging, and declare a partial repudiation of the national debt, leaving its creditors with a third of their interest intact and "consolidating" the remainder by the issue of new promissory paper which, if the French example was anything to go by, would in no time at all depreciate into insignificance. Even to contemplate such action in the Netherlands was, of course, a form of sacrilege comparable only to the defiling of a church or the sabotaging of a dyke. No administration worthy of the name, it was supposed, could perpetrate such an act of cold-blooded infamy and survive the odium. A bankrupt Netherlands was, after all, no better than an annexed or occupied Netherlands. All that was left, then, was the last hope held out by Gogel's General Taxation plan. If it worked, it might be possible to raise the general level of ordinary revenue (and according to its author, reduce the costs of administration) to the point where the rate of deficitary increase would at least be slowed down and the amortisation of the debt become feasible. If only the waters could be made to stop rising, there was the remote chance that when peace eventually came the Dutch might yet live to see dry land again.

Isaac Gogel addressed himself to this unenviable work with all the fortitude of one destined to enjoy the experience of prolonged pain. He had no illusions that the general system was some sort of philosopher's stone able to transform penury into abundance overnight. If anything, he was less of an optimistic than Schimmelpenninck. But his resolution to act effectively where others had faltered was steeled by convictions which were more political in character than economic or bureaucratic and which he had kept intact through all the vicissitudes of the revolution. He was, and would remain, an uncomplicated social egalitarian. Ever since his days as an Amsterdam conspirator in the early 1790's, he had believed that the troubles which had overtaken the Netherlands had been made much worse by the putrefaction of public administration. From this corruption had sprung the revolution. In 1794 he had written to Pluvinet, his business partner:

When a nation, surcharged with every imaginable imposition, and enjoying in effect only an illusory and precarious prosperity, burdens itself with the yoke of a monstrous government in which two-thirds of the product of taxes are devoured by a multitude of offices, for the most part useless . . . when the most treacherous resources of an abominable policy are resorted to—the secrecy of the post violated—and then, after all, manufactures are still ruined, trading houses bankrupted, and lack of work deprives the workers and artisans of bread; when in the midst of abundance and under the very windows of the palaces inhabited by their oppressors they have to watch their wives and children die, what then will those workers and artisans do? Guess . . .?[76]

The fact that this social apocalypse had failed to materialise had not altered the beliefs on which the prediction was based. The almost fatalistic acquiescence of the poor in their own misery, and the reinstatement of those whom Gogel regarded as having a vested interest in perpetuating such misery, made it even more imperative that government be re-established as the custodian of the common good and the arbitrator between the powerful and the weak. It was this kind of preoccupation which made Gogel something of an eccentric in Dutch politics. Despite the pathos of his end, there was nothing in Schimmelpenninck's rhetoric about the renascence of the Dutch commonwealth that was at all out of keeping with the whiggish historicism that went with the patrician view of government. Gogel's republicanism, by contrast, was less sentimental and more austere. In his view, the regencies were not living evidence of the continuity of Dutch history but parasitical excrescences, to be removed before the nation could be restored to health.

Socially, too, he was an oddity. Though among the leaders of the Insurrectionary Committee of 1794 and one of the best-known members of "Doctrina et Amicitia," Gogel never really belonged to the *monde* of the Amsterdam societies, still less to that of The Hague salons. He lacked the intellectual brilliance of Valckenaer, the incisive wit of Wiselius, and the political adroitness of Schimmelpenninck. He had neither illustrious social connections nor—something he felt keenly—the polish of a Leiden education. In so far as he was part of a milieu, it was that of the petty-broking and merchandising world, the "Second Hand" of the metropolis. Even his relations with the Patriot moguls like van Staphorst were very uneasy. And while Schimmelpenninck, at the end of his career, was able to retire to his estates in Overijssel, Gogel, who finally left office in April 1809 (declining, it is true, all offers to continue), went in 1813 to eke out a miserable subsistence from a starch works at Overveen until his death.

His virtues, then, were those of the self-made man, as were his besetting faults; those of the traditional figure of the Dutch burgher, earthy, self-reliant, domestic and bluff. He was impatient of protocol and suffered no fools gladly. He tended to confront delicate problems head-on, and as his brushes with Lombard de Langres in 1798 over privateering had shown, he was not cut out to play the diplomat. Thin-skinned and emotional to a fault, he nevertheless established with Louis Bonaparte, whose temperament was in some respects similar, a rapport of unusual intensity. Before resigning as Minister of Finance in 1809, he more than once lectured the King for not giving him unqualified support in his battles with the forces of darkness assembled on the Staatsraad. Gogel was surely one of the most remarkable men ever to have held high office in the Netherlands. Even if he remains an awkward candidate for admission to the national pantheon, his endeavours deserve better commemoration than the one dingy back-street near the Hollandse Spoor Station at The Hague which bears his name.

Gogel's speculations on the political economy, it must be said, rarely reached a high level of abstraction. Like another major contributor to the debate on finance, Gijsbert Karel van Hogendorp,[77] he was neither an original nor a particularly profound theorist. His ideas were empirically derived from the everyday realities of the Dutch economy and from the polemical commentaries of Patriot writers like Metelerkamp, rather than from any formal framework. According to their relevance to that situation, he tended to borrow, magpie-like, from all the great texts, from the physiocrats to the utilitarians. Adam Smith he had read carefully and held in high regard. Apart from the strictures on taxation in Book Five of *The Wealth of Nations*, which he dutifully imbibed, he also shared the Scottish philosopher's hostility to restraints on the freedom of capital and labour embodied in the corporate monopolies of guilds and local tariffs. He once confessed: "Everyone has their own manner of viewing the political economy; mine is very liberal."[78] More than once he alluded to the "necessary evil" of *all* governments. In 1804 he informed Marmont:

I have always found that men are happiest where governments interfere least with their actions; effectively I believe that government should occupy itself only with what the general interest requires and what is necessary for the repression of crime and the safety of morals.[79]

Despite his belief that, in an ideal world, government should be confined to the minimal functions of defence, police and finance, Gogel was far from a simple prototype of the nineteenth-century liberal. In his approach to the social ramifications of taxation, he was a paternalist; and his scepticism concerning the durability of Dutch political institutions proclaimed him in this respect a utilitarian. Certainly he believed that as soon as it had ceased to function adequately as the guardian of the whole community within the several provinces, the machinery of the federal Republic had outlived its usefulness. Vapourings about the Union of Utrecht and the purity of the "Constitutional Restoration" he dismissed as sanctimonious claptrap, designed to protect the interests of the élite few against the unprivileged many. In one of the memoranda he submitted to Louis Bonaparte in the summer of 1806 reviewing the recent history of the Republic, he poured scorn on the bickerings, not only of the separate provinces, but of rival communes within each province, "each governed after its own manner; each jealous of the other and having a financial interest in concealing its true situation from that of its neighbour."[80] Elsewhere, he decried the

lethargy, and pusillanimity which enlightens them [the regents] only to their own interests and which never gives them the energy to attack the evil at its source and regenerate the administration by overturning the obstacles that attachment to old prejudices and unjust prerogatives might put in the way of so noble an enterprise.[81]

It was not a Bonapartist compulsion for order and uniformity that was offended by the inchoate debris of the Dutch past, in Gogel's view. Rather, he felt that those who had had a purchase on its public institutions and long enjoyed its profits had no right to mortgage the future of the rest of the nation merely in order to cling to an unjust monopoly. If there was to be a Dutch future, it was imperative that a government invested with national authority restore to itself the unqualified exercise of sovereignty. Short of this, further chaos was bound to follow. Taxation, he was well aware, was one area where the requirements of utility and of justice—of solvency and of equity—necessarily coincided.

Few Dutchmen could have been more aware that his countrymen had already endured dreadful fiscal punishment during the decade between 1795 and 1805 than the minister about to inflict an even heavier dose on them. In his general economic lamentation to Marmont at the end of 1804, Gogel had pointed out that going on for a hundred houses were being sold up each *week* in Amsterdam to meet tax arrears.[82] But given that an interest payment of some 35 million guilders on the national debt was likely for 1806, there could be no way around the attempt to raise the level of ordinary revenue from 30 to 50 millions; or, as he put it to Louis Bonaparte, "It is necessary to levy in permanent impositions from the Dutch people a sum amounting to one and a half times as much as they paid under the old."[83]

In this unhappy situation Gogel felt that he owed it to the people to observe three fundamental principles: the equalisation of liability; public accountability for all financial transactions and a reasonably accurate estimate of personal liability; and a maximum economy in administrative costs. These, he felt, were the minimal conditions under which a higher aggregate could be demanded, without subjecting the population to the kind of bureaucratic tyranny that was usually not only odious but incompetent. Self-evidently, all three could only be served by a regulated system of national taxation.

The attempt to redistribute the fiscal burden more justly, particularly in time of war, was gaining wider acceptance towards the end of the eighteenth century. Gogel himself gave prominence to Adam Smith's maxim that

the subjects of every state ought to contribute to the support of the government as nearly as possible in proportion to their abilities, that is in proportion to the revenue which they enjoy under the protection of the state.[84]

In 1818, in a private memorandum written at the behest of King William I, he spelled out what had in effect been his guiding principle during the years of extremity:

When a Government finds itself in the calamitous circumstances where it must needs tax its people *heavily*, it behoves it, so far as possible, to see that all those who are liable pay according to their means, and that a proper assessment is made of them. In this way, the middle class is not taxed in order to spare the rich, nor the poor so much more burdened that they no longer have any possibility of improving their condition; labour is encouraged and industry not deterred; trade remains free and restricted as little as possible; and as far as possible taxes are levied on objects which go beyond necessity, coming under the category of luxuries, and are therefore conditional on the choice of the people. . . .[85]

Such views had no pretensions to constituting anything like a fiscal philosophy. They were merely an effort to reconcile the claims of pecuniary emergency and social fairness. To the modern taxpayer, of course, they appear as a minimal truism. But at the end of the eighteenth century they represented an inversion of the ancient assumption, preserved in much of central and eastern Europe despite the French Revolution, that the lower a man's place in the socio-legal hierarchy, the *greater* his fiscal obligation, since it stood in effect as a commutation of a personal bond. In the Dutch Republic there had been a general hue and cry against the weight of taxation throughout the eighteenth century; but it had been directed, as in 1748, more against the abuses of collection and farming than against incidence, or, as in the 1780's, against the inequities of the provincial "Quotas." Only under the intense strains of the war did views about where the onus of rescuing the Republic from destitution lay become more sharply focussed. Gogel's files, both as Agent and later as Secretary of State for Finance, bulge with projects and memoranda—mostly unsolicited and many of them exceedingly intricate— for raising the revenues of the state. Some, like those of Hubert Horkhausen of Cologne and the ingenious lottery-technician Meyer Hertog of Amsterdam, concentrated on trying to manipulate the capital market more efficiently than hitherto. Bankers or correspondents like George Crawfurd, who carried on a long exchange with both Schimmelpenninck and Gogel, had rather the same idea.[86]

But by far the greater number dealt with direct taxation, taking into account not just the requirements of fiscal mechanics but the general economic and social condition of the population. Rent taxes; house taxes on sliding scales (one project from The Hague only really imposed on houses with sixteen rooms and up!); income tax tariffs like the 1796 scheme implemented in Leiden—all rained down on the minister. One such proposal even anticipated a "pay as you earn" form of contribution, in which the master or employer set aside a portion of his worker's daily earnings for the state and added his own sum based on the number of employees and the size of his concern.[87] Even Gijsbert Karel van Hogendorp, whose general economic and fiscal views were far from harmonising with Gogel's, stressed in his *Gedagten over 's Lands Finantien* (*Considerations on National Finances*) the desirability of an income tax, possibly on the British model.

More usually, however, the need to devise ways of meeting the financial emergency which would be both adequate and fair divided "conservatives" from "innovators." Van Hogendorp, whose booklet was published specifically as a critique of the proposals for general taxation, continued to place his trust in the abiding verities of the Dutch economy. The staple market, he argued, would revive once the war had abated and eventually supply the state with a healthy customs and excise revenue. Impositions on the everyday commodities of life such as grain, fish, meat and sugar were indispensable to the treasury just because they constituted so predictable and regular a flow of revenue.[88] Like Crawfurd, he too was concerned about the possibility of an emigration of capital and capitalists from the country if taxation on sumptuary objects or real estate or market negotiations became too severe. Nor was he over-embarrassed about the polarities of wealth and poverty. On the contrary, he regarded them as both natural and necessary in any economy, and as a salutary stimulus to honest toil and creative enterprise.[89] In taking these views, van Hogendorp was not being especially inhumane or insensitive. Just as he continued to believe in the importance of a full-scale reversion to the autonomies and sovereignties of the old republican constitution, so he was incapable of comprehending the dimensions of the calamities which had befallen the country and which were likely to get worse as the economic struggle with Britain intensified.

To be sure, the more recent economic historiography of the late eighteenth century has taught us that the gloom of the Patriot economists was greatly exaggerated, at least for the period up to 1793. Yet there can be no question that theirs was the more realistic appraisal of the economic landscape after 1805. In the context of a national debt of a capital sum approaching 1200 million guilders, with nearly half the population of Amsterdam on poor relief and most of the fishing fleets of South Holland and Zeeland rotting in the harbours, Metelerkamp's strictures on the social incidence of taxation do not seem out of place. Compared to the obesely complacent effusions of van Hogendorp, they strike a note of refreshing indignation. It was, he said,

outrageous and a great inequality that those who already enjoy the greatest advantages from society and who therefore have the greatest interest in its maintenance should also be relieved from taxation while it is drawn instead from the more useful section of the nation. . . . The more well-endowed members can, through a relatively smaller portion of their income, support the state far more substantially than can the common man from his, for the most part, dearly earned wage; while in so doing the latter are now reduced to a condition where they want for the most elementary necessities of life. . . . The most fitting, indeed the only proper means to provide for the requirements of state are taxes, introduced on sound financial foundations, drawn from all classes of society in proportion to their means; and this, so far from damaging industry, will even serve to strengthen it.[90]

Considerations of social equity aside, the national system of taxation was also meant to alter, albeit to a necessarily unknown degree, the distribution of inter-departmental liability. It went without saying that the removal of arbitrary disparities from province to province and even town to town would also eliminate the expenses of bureaucratic duplication (as well as a solid block of traditional patronage). But it was also meant to meet the long-standing criticism in Holland, Zeeland and Utrecht that the differentials enshrined in the autonomies preserved by the Quota system no longer took account of changes in the relative wealth of the respective provinces. Here again it was the change in the intended function of the tax which, retrospectively as it were, created the anomaly. As long as it was meant to furnish the limited, and widely varying, requirements of local treasuries, there was no reason at all why the customary rates of estate duty (the "collateraal") should not have been set at 2, 3, 5, and 7 per cent in the respective kwartieren of Gelderland, but at 10 per cent in Holland.[91] But once this tax was converted into a source of *national* revenue, there could clearly be no justification for a differential rate. Similarly Gogel was fond of reiterating, first to Marmont, then to Louis Bonaparte, the complaint that Holland, a province of some 800,000 souls, was being obliged to supply nearly two-thirds of the aggregate revenues of the entire state, or some 25 million guilders in *ordinary* impositions. The same province, it was claimed, was the exhausted milch-cow for the endless succession of levies and forced loans, Amsterdam having paid more in such sums than the other eight departments put together.[92] Conversely, under the Regency of State, Holland had been permitted to retain just 5 per cent of its departmental revenues for domestic purposes, against 24–26 per cent for Overijssel and Drente and 18–20 per cent for Friesland.[93]

The insistence of the maritime provinces that the balance of wealth had shifted away from them, and that as a result they were fiscally punished with disproportionate severity, was nonetheless an impression rather than a quantifiable estimate. If it was true that the northern coastal trade between the Hansa ports and Harlingen and Delfzijl, as well as the river traffic down the Ems, continued to prosper while the staple Baltic and Atlantic commerce with Amsterdam and Rotterdam languished, it was equally true that the other conspicuously successful sector of the economy—agriculture—did as well (if not better) in the Holland countryside as it did in the land provinces. If the textile industries of Haarlem and Leiden were in a semi-derelict condition, those of Tilburg were, by 1805, not much better off.[94] With good reason the representatives of the land provinces feared that the "equality" of the general taxation system would merely mean a disproportionate share of the general misery: a topping up of the overall level of impositions to that of Holland.

Indeed, Gogel made no attempt to conceal that Groningers, Frieslanders, and the like would be contributing towards a larger global sum than under the old Quota, one, he argued, that would be more in line with the shrinking differentials between provinces. But he was also at pains to point out that this was not just a form of Quota revision; that the nature of a system based on individual contributions, irrespective of residence, meant that the burden ought to be more equitably distributed *within* the respective departments; and that the poorer of the land provinces would be more likely to end up paying less than under the old system, where they were subject to a whole range of quasi-feudal and customary dues. Nor would assessments of the individual's taxable income and assets overlook regional disparities of rent, wages, or the costs of physical reclamation and dyke maintenance. The preamble to the General Tax Law acknowledged that

he who resides in the less fortunate regions of the Republic and earns a given annual income, but who because of his situation has a more restricted enjoyment of it, will pay less than someone earning the same income in the better-off parts of the Republic.[95]

For the tax system to register all these variations of liability with any sensitivity, it was obviously essential that the greater part of the *additional* revenue be drawn from direct sources. The major item in this category was the *verponding*—the property tax. On the face of it this seemed to bear out most of the fears of the land provinces, since the *verponding* was to be set at the Holland rate of 25 per cent of rental value, a higher rate than anywhere else in the Republic. The pattern of land and property taxes throughout the old provinces was historically exceedingly diverse. As with all other taxes and imposts, they had grown up arbitrarily in response to the accidents of history and geography. Some, like the Friesland *floreen renthe*, had partially evolved from the tribute owed to sovereign lords, in this case the Dukes of Saxony who had ruled the province at the beginning of the sixteenth century. Others reflected not only the discrepancies between provinces but between country-side and town, or quarter and quarter within them. In Overijssel, where property taxes made up nearly half the total provincial revenues, the hearth tax on urban property in towns like Deventer and Zwolle was rather lower than the land tax; whereas in Groningen, the house-and-hearth tax was set at 20 per cent, a higher rate than, for example, in Utrecht and much higher than the rural equivalent.[96] In Zeeland and Utrecht, it was largely left to individual towns to decide how much and in what manner such taxes should be levied, although the Utrecht *oudschildgeld* remained a constant feature of the provincial revenues. And in the three Gelderland kwartieren—Nijmegen, the Veluwe and Zutphen, each with its own separate hierarchy of assessors, receivers and auditors—there were the most elaborate variations of rates, allowances and tithes.

From the bewilderingly complicated and miscellaneous information available to him, Gogel made the admittedly rough-and-ready estimate that on average all the various land and property taxes together had yielded around 8.75 million guilders, of which Holland had supplied around half. His object was to try to augment that total to between 10 and 11 millions, and at a much reduced administrative cost. Assessment was to be based on rental valuation taken over a period of ten years. In the case of rented property, urban or agricultural, the legal rent certificates provided an easily verifiable documentation. But unrented property, whether residential or commercial, meant that until a new and comprehensive property survey could be carried out the government would be dependent on the assessments used in the old *verponding*—in Holland's case dating back to 1732.

In the event, the cadaster commissioners completed their labours with exemplary urgency, working from December 4, 1807, to November 3, 1808. But this in effect meant that only in 1809 was the "real" *verponding* actually in operation. Moreover, as in other countries, the land surveyors and assessors, with their teams of clerks and measurers, met with great hostility and suspicion not only from those whose property they invaded but from local authorities who saw in them the spies of foreign authorities. As in 1800, Appelius (very much Gogel's combatant in fiscal matters) argued that an average market value taken over a period of fifteen years would be a fairer, more reliable base for assessment than rental values (as distinct from rental income). But Gogel treated the proposition as an obvious subterfuge, designed to extend the area of self-assessment, and, with markets for property so depressed in the major centres, an invitation to under-valuation. His concern was to impose on those areas of "dead" fixed capital which, he believed, contributed little or nothing to the productive sectors of the economy but merely expressed the purchasing or consuming power of accumulated wealth. Many of the substantial estate owners, particularly in Holland, Utrecht and Groningen, were urban regents content to enjoy a rental income rather than take any interest in the agrarian development of their tenancies.

It is certainly also true that Gogel had a puritan resentment of those who so conspicuously neither toiled nor spun. In his 1820 Memoir, he wrote that

rich men, and above all proprietors of tenanted estates and holders of stock who practice no other profession than what the price of their money can raise, are incomparably less worthy citizens than a trading or working man . . . especially when the proprietor enjoys that income in the great towns. . . .[97]

Conversely, for those who were actively engaged in some economic enterprise, a system of allowances against the gross assessment was planned to cover overheads such as the upkeep of polders and dykes; the maintenance of irrigation canals; periods of non-productivity due to physical calamities like flood or requisition; or even the artificial inflation of seed, manure or livestock prices owing to short-term dearth. The same care was shown with public or philanthropically endowed institutions, such as hospitals, schools, churches, old age homes and poor houses, all of which were exempt from the tax.

All these complications meant that the *verponding* was not such a straight-forward tax to recover. It needed 104 commissioners, divided into 14 *verponding* districts, working under the direction of a national commission. It says much for Gogel's foresight that he chose as chief commissioner one of the most experienced of his bureaucrats, Caspar van Breugel—even though he had been the man who had acted as not entirely disinterested liaison between the Batavian Revolutionary Committee at den Bosch and the Stadholder's government in 1794.[98]

The overriding principle of "taxing in just proportion," as the preamble to the law had it, was observed in a number of the other principal impositions. The *successie* (death duty) was also levied at the relatively high Holland rate of 10 per cent (it had been 1 per cent in the Zutphen kwartier), but was adjustable according to the degree of relationship to the deceased and the general pecuniary circumstances of the family. Provision was made, for example, that a widow, prematurely losing a sole bread-winner, would not be abruptly deprived by the tax receiver of goods she might have to sell for subsistence. As with the *verponding*, the commissioners were instructed to go to extraordinary lengths to establish all the facts of a situation, requiring from all undertakers and morticians monthly lists of the deceased, together with next of kin and any likely beneficiaries.[99] Similarly the *mobiliair*, the tax on movable property—furniture, jewellery, tapestry, linen and the like—stipulated that household goods to the value of 500 guilders in any one dwelling would be free of tax. The distinction between necessities and luxury was also written into the servant tax (*dienstboden*), which graduated sharply upwards from one and two domestics, and the differential taxes for work-horses on the one hand and coach and luxury horses on the other.[100] The *hardesteen* (hearth tax), where two hearths, notionally one for heating and one for cooking, were allowed free in every dwelling, was one of the clearest instances of the official intention to discriminate in favour of the modest burgher and against the opulent household. In his 1820 Memoir, Gogel explained that he had never intended the tax as one on cooking or heating but on "luxury or comfort," since "four-fifths of the people cook with their pots and warm themselves with just one or two hearths, and in the strictest sense the householder has no need of any more."[101] This, he believed, was a better indicator of household luxury, at least in the Netherlands, than any comparable duty on doors or windows such as had been imposed in the French Empire.

The most idiosyncratic of these taxes and the one which was Gogel's own innovation was the *personeel*. This was not, as inferred in some recent studies,[102] a flat-rate tax on all property and income, but a tax on rent *paid* by tenants, attached again to a sliding scale of contributions. It was therefore in effect a surcharge on rent and, in some respects, for all Gogel's humane intentions, a characteristically insensitive exercise in utilitarian fiscal engineering. The attribute which recommended it so much to the minister was that, unlike income taxes, it could be ascertained and verified through rent with the minimum of investigatory problems and expense. He also presupposed that the tenant would automatically gravitate to the level of rented accommodation, or acreage, which his general income could support, and that that rent would thus provide a reliable impression of his economic situation in terms of gross outgoings. But it took no account of a situation, presumably not uncommon, where a tenant could be doubly penalised by an inflated rent which would then carry with it an artificially high rate of *personeel*. Gogel's presumption that the correspondingly higher rate of *verponding* for which the landlord would fall liable would act as a sufficient deterrent was perhaps a touch disingenuous. Clearly the two taxes were reverse faces of the same coin; either way they fell neatly into the coffers of the state.[103]

The general tax system has been criticised[104] for failing to tap the sources of Dutch capital at the very point where they were most prolific: mercantile and financial deposits and transactions. The argument runs that humble farmers were flayed in order to spare the skins of rentiers, bankers and the like, and that a system based on a land tax in the manner of the French *impôt foncier* was wholly inappropriate for a country where the economy was so geared to trade, finance and manufacture. Quite aside from the fact that it would be a crude misconception to categorise either the *verponding* or the *personeel* as "land taxes" pure and simple, it was precisely because Gogel was concerned with the general economic ramifications of the fiscal system that he forbore to lean more heavily on active enterprise. The whole of the tax operation was, when all is said and done, only a matter of making good by bureaucratic means what could not be generated through investment and credit—or at least not at a price that was tolerable. The conviction that this could be done more cheaply, and with greater social equity, than by the traditional expedients was at the heart of the difference between the old and the new systems.

But Gogel was not so blinkered by fiscal administration that he was eager to impose gratuitous penalties on finance capital. That would be to cut off his own nose to spite his face. Hence he was reluctant to impose an additional duty on interest payments on the state debt, except once in 1806 as an emergency measure. The three-month arrears in interest payments—deplorable though Gogel himself conceded it was—amounted to a de facto premium on government credit. But he was crucially concerned not to bear at all heavily on trading and industrial capital at a time of severe depression and (as the doldrums of the Bourse graphically illustrated) a dearth of investment capital except at exorbitant rates. He much preferred, as we have seen, to tax capital assets, particularly when located in items of conspicuous consumption or real estate.

At a time when high agricultural prices were making investment in land particularly attractive for the urban capitalist—a process, moreover, which had been going on since at least the middle of the seventeenth century[105]— the emphasis on property taxes made good fiscal and economic sense. Moreover, while the urban building trade was depressed, there was certainly no falling-off in the building, selling and exchanging of the elegant palladian summer villas which adorned the banks of the Vecht between Amsterdam and Utrecht. Finally, it should be noted that mercantile and finance capital were of course *not* free of taxation at all. The extension of the *klein zegel* stamp duty—introduced in Holland in 1624 and common in a number of the other provinces—to all commercial, financial, legal and official transactions meant that the government was provided in effect with a turnover tax related to the value of the transaction. There is almost nothing that the historian of this period can touch—passports, contracts, playing cards, newspapers, letters, bills of exchange, stock certificates, even tickets for the theatre, a subscription concert or the race course—which do not bear the inevitable *klein zegel* in one corner. As the following table of receipts of indirect taxes for 1806 (the first full year of the new system) indicates, the three stamp duties, particularly that on legal acts and "patents,"* made a significant contribution to the total.[106]

The care taken to establish a revenue system which had regard for social equity and administrative simplicity; which was cheap to collect, based on verifiable sources of information, and which did as little damage to the general economic structure of the country as was compatible with the fiscal emergency, was also reflected in the arrangements made for indirect taxation. Gogel had often referred to the problems generated by high rates of excise on basic commodities. That these pushed up wage costs and made Dutch manufactures increasingly uncompetitive was one of the clichés of Patriot economic literature. The proliferation of local tariffs and duties (partly in an effort to keep

Direct Taxes (1806)	Estimate (fl.)	Actual receipt (fl.)
Verponding	11,000,000	9,485,634
Personeel	5,000,000	4,705,366
Servant tax	700,000	766,711
Horse, pleasure-coach and passage tax	800,000	756,544
Livestock tax	600,000	679,381
Mobiliair	600,000	518,434
Successie	3,200,000	2,514,014
"Collective" stamp duty	1,000,000	1,556,950
Acts and patents " "	4,000,000	3,349,471
Trade and luxuries " "	1,000,000	104,857
Total direct taxes	27,900,000	24,437,362
Total net revenues for 1806		42,688,731

pace with the rising costs of public works and local poor relief) and the battalions of receivers, collectors, *gaarders* and excise men exemplified, in the

* The term used to cover the fee required for the practice of all trades, manufactures and professions, as well as financial transactions.

unitarist view, the confusion and waste of the old federalism. The unreformed duties offended against almost all of Gogel's canons. They were expensive to collect, notoriously vulnerable to fraud and the excessive use of force; an invitation to smuggling; absurdly duplicated in tariffs and personnel (in 1791 there were seven classes of tea and coffee tax in Holland alone, four classes of grain tax and two on peat—one at the cutting and transport stage, another on purchase and consumption).[107]

These taxes were also socially indiscriminate in their incidence and a barrier to the free passage of goods within the country which Gogel held to be of such importance. As in the 1799 project, the substitution of national for all local taxes meant the end of all the customary petty duties levied on this or that article according to the accidents of historical need. Henceforth the minister was to grant permission to local authorities, departmental or municipal, to levy "additional stuivers" on one of the approved classes of national duties, and to earmark the receipts for a particular item of local expenditure. Gogel also wanted to whittle down the enormous catalogue of indirect duties—on every conceivable object from plovers' eggs and cochineal to butter beans and elephant tusk—to a manageable and estimable number. As Agent for Finance, he had proposed the outright abolition of a wide range of duties on the "necessities" of life: peat, oil and tallow, soap, salt, sugar and the like. But six years later, the straits in which the Dutch treasury found itself hardly permitted Gogel the luxury of dispensing with what van Hogendorp had rightly categorised as sources of revenue that were both regular and predictable. He did succeed in reducing their number to a standard baker's dozen, abolishing those on beer, sugar, tea, coffee and butter, and lowering the rates of the old Holland tariff on soap and salt. But the valuable revenues on peat and flour, and the dry goods-measure taxes known as *waag* and *ronde maat*, were all necessarily retained. Spirits, which Gogel felt to be unquestionably deleterious to the national anatomy (in 1806 the Dutch managed to get through 70,000 vats of *genever*), was actually raised.[108]

The shift in the balance between direct and indirect revenues which was a definite objective of Gogel's system naturally varied a good deal from department to department. In the old land provinces, where direct taxes on land and property had always constituted a relatively high proportion of a smaller aggregate revenue, the change was naturally less marked. But in Holland, the balance of direct to indirect taxes, which had been about 40 to 60 per cent, was reversed after 1806.[109]

The simplification of the range of taxes was accompanied by a corresponding economy in the bureaucracy itself. Instead of a mass of independent officials, responsible to local councils and competing for the available patronage and perquisites—and with an obvious interest in defrauding their superiors as to the amounts collected—there was to be a single national hierarchy, salaried on a grade related to fiscal turnover, experience and responsibility, and subject to a searching routine of monthly certification and account. The transformation of the departmental "Raden van Finantien" from the deputed councillors of the local authority into ministerial officials salaried by, and removable by, the government at The Hague marked a decisive shift in the power of the purse. When in 1807 the law on municipalities made local accounts subject to the audit of the national ministry, the integration of local with national expenditure was completed.[110] Apart from these appointed departmental financial officials, there were three separate staffs for the whole country. The 200 receivers (and a larger, but unspecified number of sub-collectors) were divided into 21 tax districts, each with its receiver-general, and subdivided into bureaux for direct and indirect taxes. The *verponding*, as we have already noted, was given its own staff—much to the objection of the Council of State. Forty-eight inspectors made up the second staff.

The reforms of 1751, arising out of the tax revolts of two years earlier, had established an inspectorate in Holland but inevitably its competence was severely limited by the jealously guarded independence of the municipalities. The inspectors of 1805 were given formidable powers of surveillance over the operation of the whole system. They were to check on the reliability of estimates and of eventual yields, to report on the efficiency of the national and local personnel, and to make any appropriate recommendations for reform or revision to the minister/secretary of state. Finally there was to be an independent corps of advocate-fiscals, appointed to hear cases of administrative abuse and misdemeanour arising out of complaints lodged by any member of the public against an official.[111] This simple tripartite structure of the working members of a national bureaucracy (those at The Hague and those in the departments; the second-line scrutineers and the reserve of judicial sanctions) was to be the basic framework for other hierarchies in what was the first real national Dutch administration. Some of its features, like the advocate-fiscal tribunals, owed something to the French Bonapartist

Indirect Taxes (1806)	Estimate	Actual Receipt
Salt	900,000	1,182,824
Soap	700,000	736,004
Waag	800,000	922,004
Ronde maat	300,000	388,206
Flour and grain	5,000,000	5,396,298
Livestock	1,500,000	1,870,212
Wines and spirits	5,000,000	3,381,129
Peat	1,800,000	1,683,630
Customs	3,000,000	2,514,014
Coaling fuel	1,500,000	658,035
Total indirect taxes		18,732,356
Total net revenues for 1806*		42,688,731

* The difference between the sum of the tables of indirect and direct revenues and the net total is accounted for by the 4% additional duty levied for municipal expenditures, some 30,464 florins.

model; but the major features were developed both from the earlier experience of the Batavian Directory and from the years of speculation, discussion and dispute which had followed.

Moreover, despite the enormously expanded bureaucracy in The Hague itself, Gogel did his best to make good his promise that over the whole country the new system would be cheaper, not more expensive, to administer. He had claimed that it would cost in the region of half a million guilders against nearer a million guilders (that is, 1 per cent of the yield as against 3 per cent) under the old system. It is difficult, however, to estimate with any hope of accuracy what the saving in numbers of officials really amounted to, since there is no way of quantifying the teams of under-collectors and excisemen employed by the many *kantooren* of the towns and provinces. The regent Keuchenius mentioned a gigantic army of 60,000 under the old regime, but this seems most implausible. Even if that figure were to be divided by a factor of ten, it would still represent a far bigger strength than the numbers employed under Gogel. At the top level, before 1798, there had been nineteen receivers-general for Holland alone, each with his own substantial bureau. After 1805, there were just twenty-one for the whole Republic. No more than a thousand officials were on the books of the Ministry of Finance at The Hague in 1807, including the customs officers at the ports, though excluding the most junior employees of the departmental officers. In 1808 Gogel calculated that the ordinary revenue of around 48 millions was costing 3.8 millions in total administrative expenses, or 8 per cent of the total yield—a figure which compared fairly well with the 17 per cent King William I was to pay ten years later.[112]

Such, then, was the "system" which Gogel presented to the "High Mightinesses" of Schimmelpenninck's legislature on July 14, 1805. It represented the sum of a decade's pondering, calculating, and refining of the grim problems of public finance in the Netherlands. All that Gogel expected it to do in the short term was to give the nation something of a breathing space in which the exhaustion of all resources, capital and commercial, might be arrested and the process of rebuilding for the peace gradually got under way. It could never, he knew, be a sufficient condition of financial renovation. In the last resort that depended on forces outside the control of the Dutch. But he also knew full well that it was a *necessary* condition of staying in business as even a quasi-independent concern. With the public endorsement of the Grand Pensionary and the general knowledge that Napoleon was intent on its introduction, it was a foregone conclusion that the system would pass through the legislature without much difficulty. But it was also predictable, perhaps, that despite Gogel's reassurances about the general distribution of the fiscal load, the deputies from the old land provinces, joined by Utrecht and Brabant, would vote *en bloc* against it. It was a considerable irony that the scheme was carried by the votes of the maritime provinces—Holland, Zeeland and Friesland—so that, far from representing the inauguration of a new era in Dutch government, the division of votes served to confirm the tenacity of old interests.

As for its reception in the country, the silence which had descended on the Batavian Republic as it had become steadily more authoritarian since 1801 makes it impossible to gauge. It seems highly unlikely that *any* new taxes, however benevolently intended, could have excited anything but dismay and apprehension from a people already prostrate from its burdens. There was no way to disguise the fundamental fact that Gogel's system was designed to raise more revenue. There were indeed a few scabrous attacks on the Secretary of Finance, and one denunciatory pamphlet appeared characterising the reforms as an act of satanic tyranny.[113] On January 10, 1806, Goldberg reported to the Staatsraad that there was a pressing need "to dampen down the pronounced displeasure and the beginnings of revolt . . . over the introduction of the general taxes."[114]

Reaction seemed to be most vocal in Brabant, where apprehensions about the *verponding* were especially strong. Early in 1806 disturbances were reported from Dongen, ter Heide and Oosterhout. But the more dangerous response, from the government's point of view, was the quiet indifference of the regents who were, after all, more firmly entrenched in their local places than at any time since 1795. Many of them were convinced that like other earlier attacks on their local establishment, the fiscal onslaught would before long become reduced to a bureaucratic dead letter. From Tholen in Zeeland, François Ermerins warned Gogel and Goldberg late in 1805 that while there was little active resistance to the reforms, the local councillors were going out of their way to avoid co-operating with financial officials, and the implementation of the system was not exactly proceeding "at full gallop."[115]

The creation of the "Kingdom of Holland" less than six months after the introduction of the new system seemed to present an ideal opportunity for the regent élites to water down, or do away with altogether, its most objectionable features as they had in 1801. The new King's evident desire to ingratiate himself with the native aristocracy suggested that he might be amenable to proposals for revision, and it was known that Gogel himself had few friends among the governing circle. On the crucial Second Section of the Staatsraad, Goldberg and van de Kasteele would in all likelihood support the minister but de Vos van Steenwijk, Queysen, Six and Jacobson were more lukewarm, and Appelius distinctly hostile. Van Stralen, who had given Gogel so much support under Schimmelpenninck, had been removed; his successor, Hendrik Mollerus, an altogether more orthodox Orangist, was much less sympathetic.

A great deal, then, depended on Gogel's own relations with Louis and the degree to which he was to be allowed to use the authority which on paper his ministerial position gave him. In fact, his beginnings as minister were quite auspicious. Louis had been impressed both with the briefing at Loo at the end of June, and with the expeditious way in which Gogel furnished him with all the necessary details of the unhappy condition of the Dutch treasury once he had got to The Hague. The secretary of the French legation, Serurier, who had contributed to Gogel's reputation in France—not least by conveying the impression that the new reforms were essentially a carbon copy of the French epitome—was unstinting in his appreciation. "Everyone," he wrote, confirms the eulogies given to the establishment of the new system of taxation. It is, in effect, an exceedingly difficult thing to establish fiscal unity in a country where every province and nearly every town has had its own mode of taxation;

where the privileges of nobility on the one hand conflict with republican liberties on the other; where the noble pays on a different basis from the patrician and the patrician differently from every other section of society. It has required nothing less than constant firmness on the part of M. Gogel, even, dare I say, downright rudeness, to overcome all those obstacles in so short a space of time; to found and consolidate this fine system; and to raise the revenue of the fisc to fifty millions in such unpropitious times. This is a homage paid to him even by those whose interests at the outset have been damaged—a flattering measure of the excellence of his achievement![116]

Despite these tributes, Gogel was not exactly mellowed by the climate of 1806. He took great pains to make Louis aware of how serious the situation was, even after the introduction of the new system. In his *Note sur la situation financière actuelle*, he complained that with so many impossible demands being made on the Dutch treasury, not least by its ally, "is it any wonder that the coffers are always empty and the government reduced daily to the most desperate means to sustain itself from one day to the next?"[117] On July 3, Goldberg gave eloquent support to Gogel in the Staatsraad, warning that without the new system the nation would be virtually doomed to lose its political and even physical identity. By the 14th of that month, when the King addressed the legislature, it was clear that at least for the time being he had been persuaded by the reformers. "We have but one aim," he declared, "and that is the conservation and the security of Holland and the happiness of its inhabitants. . . . It is generally thought, and we do believe, that only the new system of finances can be the foundation and true support of the state. . . ."[118] Louis, it seems, had been won over not only by Gogel's pre-eminent expertise with the minutiae of finance, but by his candour, his serious demeanour and the plainness of his manners amidst an already excessively sycophantic court entourage. When rumours were circulating in November 1806 that the minister was on the point of being discharged, the King went out of his way to show his faith in Gogel, and sent him a portrait of himself, adding: "Believe, then, I pray you, in the permanence of my esteem and confidence."[119]

However confident in the ability and integrity of his Minister of Finance, Louis found precious little to cheer him in the summer of 1806. Schimmelpenninck's transfusion of administrative energy had really come too late to rescue the Netherlands from the magnitude of its calamity. "How can we flatter ourselves with success," Louis asked, "when, because of the continuation of this long war, it seems impossible to curtail armaments and so reduce the principal item of expenditure?"[120] Owing to the teething troubles of the new revenue system, it seemed unlikely that its yield would come up to the 50 millions of Gogel's target; in the end it produced 42.6 million florins net, a third rather than a half again as much as the old product. In subsequent years the figure was to approach closer to Gogel's goal, finally touching the magic mark of 50 millions in 1809.[121] Louis insisted that the gross expenditure for the second six months of 1806 be kept under 10 millions; but in his revised estimates, Gogel could do no better than 14,080,000 florins, a figure which

included 3 millions for the army, 2 for the navy, and 3 to cover all the requirements of the ministries of the interior, justice and Waterstaat.

That was, in the last instance, cutting things dangerously fine. There
were, moreover, new "gratuitous" expenses adding to the burden of the current
deficit. Louis' "civil list," fixed in Paris, cost the nation 1.5 million guilders a
year and the King's patriotic concern did not seem to extend to dispensing with
it. More absurdly, 2.5 millions had been paid to a firm of Amsterdam contractors, Maison Wils, on the authorisation of the "Asiatic Council" (but, it
seems clear, with Schimmelpenninck's knowledge and approval) for the transport of 800 men to Batavia via the Helder. In the contract there had been a
safety clause committing the government to make the payment even should
some "unforeseen" contingency prevent their departure. When the troops were
stopped, on French orders, from embarcation, the money was dully paid over,
a transaction which understandably smacked of foul play to both Gogel and
Louis.[122] Recovery was altogether a different matter.

It was even harder in the case of the 6 millions advanced to France and
which had now fallen due for repayment. There was, of course, little hope of
relief from that quarter. Louis and the Dutch ambassador made some effort to
broach what was obviously a delicate subject, but with no illusions about success. In September 1806 the King confirmed to Gogel that

if we have a war [with Prussia], that will be a great affliction for our finances, and
it would be necessary to consider all eventualities (including a suspension of
interest payments). But we cannot count on France for anything; she will do
nothing for us and can do nothing for us. So do not take partial measures, for
they will be of little account and quickly exhausted.[123]

Yet "partial measures" were needed just to soldier on while avoiding bankruptcy. Interest payments on the debt were deliberately allowed to run on
three months in arrears; the duty paid by foreign creditors or investors in
Dutch securities on their interest was substantially increased; and short-term
augmentations imposed on the liquor and *successie* taxes. Between them, these
expedients were to find a sum which would represent a sufficient capital figure
of the national debt to cover the bulk of arrears interest.[124]

This sort of financial juggling obviously gladdened the hearts of those
who had maintained all along that Gogel's system would be insufficient to
finance the deficit without recourse to traditional expenditures. That much
indeed was manifest. It had done no more in its first year of application than
to cut back the deficit on current account from 40 to something like 28
millions—no mean accomplishment to be sure, but failing to obviate the
need for the loans, levies and the like which it had been designed to relieve.
As long as the Dutch continued to bleed themselves white for the sake of a
shadowy degree of independence, their ordinary revenues, however distributed and however collected, would never be adequate to demand. This
in turn meant that the entrepreneurs of public finance who had been so
prominent during the Regency of State continued to play an important role
in bailing out the treasury, alongside the bureaucracy of Gogel's ministry.

Schimmelpenninck had been a powerful patron of the Amsterdam plutocrats, whose social milieu he had made his natural urban habitat. Louis followed suit by making a number of them members of the Staatsraad or, in their capacity as *wethouders* (a traditional title he revived, albeit in modified form) of Amsterdam, honorary advisors to the crown. The money market of what had been, even late in the eighteenth century, the financial metropolis of the world was far from defunct. True, the bottom had fallen out of the market for the former choice commodities of French life annuities, and there seemed little or no prospect of returns or interest on major negotiations like the Russian debt so long as the war continued. But agents of treasuries in Spain, Naples, Westphalia, even (when possible) Prussia and Austria were queuing up for loans at increasingly high interest rates, corresponding to the increasingly high investment risks.

In March 1807, a major loan of 40 millions for the treasury of the Kingdom of Holland was announced, redeemable in eighteen years and carrying 6 per cent. It was to be serviced from, and redeemed by, calls on the revenues of the city of Amsterdam and managed (in effect, underwritten) by a consortium of the five great moguls of the Herengracht: Severijn, van Brienen, Willink, Hodshon and de Smeth. This was partly a financial contract but partly also a barely disguised forced loan, since its security was the revenue of the "hoofdstad." That it offended against the spirit and the letter of the national taxation system was glaringly clear; but given the sorry condition of the treasury in 1807, there was nothing to be done by the minister except to give his assent with as good a grace as he could muster.

Nor was this the end of such concessions. For a year later, with an estimate of government expenditure for 1807 touching almost 80 millions, a second loan for 30 millions (later reduced, after under-subscription, to 20 millions) was floated, this time to be serviced by an annual appropriation of 3 millions recovered by "Quota" from throughout the country. Needless to say, this measure raised a great hue and cry since it represented precisely that evil from which the general tax system had claimed to spare the poor taxpayer. In fact, alongside the high level of ordinary taxation were perpetuated the several modes of raising revenue which had been castigated by Gogel as the iniquities of the old regime: the ad hoc *verdubbeling* of individual duties; short-term bills secured against the anticipation of earmarked revenues; life annuities, and even the most execrated expedient, the global repartition of a predetermined sum. The alternative, it is true, was partial or total repudiation, and the final collapse of the house of cards as the state defaulted simultaneously on its credit and its military commitments. But for those who were being asked to pay, pay, and pay again, the relative merits of different methods of slow strangulation were of academic interest. On November 26 Gogel wrote to the King in one of his increasingly frequent moods of bleak despair:

Your Minister of Finance must confess to Your Majesty that he is frozen with terror on examining the budget for the War, and must also confess that he knows of no means by which such expenses can possibly be met. . . . The heart of Your Majesty no doubt suffers much from the protests and appeals which are mounting on all sides against the established system of taxes. Your Majesty will be persuaded of the justice of those protests when he considers that a burden without any parallel, unknown even in England, is crushing his good subjects. Yet this burden will be increased even more in the coming year by the series of augmentations or by new taxes which will have to increase the revenue . . . by about a tenth of the total [5 millions]. . . .[125]

From the very beginning, then, Gogel's "system" was forced to operate within constraints which effectively ruled out the realisation of its most ambitious objectives. It was only the most critical instance of the general paradox that the war which had made the creation of a unified Dutch state possible—and necessary—had also sabotaged its immediate viability. Within modest expectations, Gogel had reason to feel fairly satisfied by 1808. He had succeeded in reducing administrative costs and in raising the level of ordinary revenues by 50 per cent in such a way as to avoid inflicting additional suffering on the worst off. A national fiscal bureaucracy, of sorts, had come into being. But the minister was the first to recognise that it was far from being the omnicompetent cadre of benevolent and honest officials, the "children of the minister" as he called them in one startling flight of fancy, of his ideal.

At the local level, those engaged in the thorny work of assessment for direct taxes were still dependent on the degree of collaboration volunteered by often truculent burgemeesters and *wethouders*. And the quality of the bureaucracy itself was not unmixed. Naturally, Gogel would have loved to have inaugurated the new fiscal era with a staff uncorrupted by ancient and time-honoured frauds, yet sufficiently professional to discharge its basic functions competently. At the apex of the hierarchy he could feel quite confident. Each of his major subordinates in charge of the three principal subdivisions of the ministry at The Hague—Elias Canneman, Pieter Quint Ondaatje and Copes van Cattenburgh—were able and energetic young men. Van Breugel's control of the *verponding* commission was exemplary. To some extent, moreover, the basic requirement that all collectors and receivers be between twenty and forty-five, and of proven literacy and numeracy, weeded out the more outrageous cases of pluralism and free superannuation. But recruitment to the necessarily complex work of assessment and auditing still left much to be desired. As in the period after 1798, many of those who had been trained under the old provincial treasuries and local exchequers, providing they had not committed any misdemeanour of very scandalous proportions, were taken back into service after cursory scrutiny. Most of the novices were from a miscellaneous group of occupations, many quite unrelated to the work into which they were thrust by the impatient ministry. Schoolmasters were prominent, as were petty functionaries like town clerks and food inspectors, notaries and procureurs' clerks, and there was always the occasional oddity such as a retired sexton or redundant lamp-lighter.[126]

Despite the strict prohibitions against pluralism, the appalling economic conditions of 1807–10 forced many subordinate officials to supplement what was in any case a bare subsistence with a second job. The formidable sheaves of regulations and ordinances issuing from the bureaux at The Hague were no true measure of either the authority or the competence of the bureaucracy in the parochial context where it mattered. The reports of one of the ablest and most determined of the forty-eight inspectors, Theodorus van Swinderen in Groningen, give a graphic indication that the work of the financial officials was hindered not only by local ill-will but also by the inexperience, laxity, and on more than one occasion drunkenness, of the collectors and assessors themselves. He added the well-taken observation that wages scaled to estimated receipts were an open invitation to falsification and urged instead a more fixed gradation of salaries.[127] Quite obviously there was a long way to go before a bureaucracy equal to the task of managing a national system of finance could be securely established.

There were other assumptions on which the 1805 system had been based which in the event proved to have been unfounded. The redistribution of inter-departmental liability, which had so exercised both advocates and opponents of the new taxes, turned out to be much less significant in a system of per capita imposition than either had anticipated. In 1790, for example, Holland's share of the old Quota had been around 62 per cent, whereas in 1807 the yield of the two departments which had made up the province amounted to about 57 per cent of the national aggregate. An estimate excluding the *verponding*, where the shift was more marked, gives an even closer correspondence:[128]

	Holland	Gelderland	Brabant	Friesland	Overijssel	Groningen	Zeeland	Utrecht	Drente
1790	62%	6%	5%	9%	3%	5%	3%	4%	1%
1807	57	5	5	10	4	5	5	7	1
1808	58	6½	5½	10	4½	6	4	5½	1

It must have been surprising that the two most significant adjustments actually occurred in the portions of those two provinces, Zeeland and Utrecht, which had complained most persistently that they were over-taxed under the old Quota. True, the *verponding* figures reveal a more decisive shift away from Holland's top-heavy liability; but even in this category, the provinces which had fretted most about its effects—Gelderland and Overijssel—were less than brutally punished. Brabant, Friesland and Groningen contributed far more to the relative relief afforded to the two Holland departments:

			Proportion of *Verponding* Receipts for 1807					
Holland	Gelderland	Brabant	Friesland	Overijssel	Groningen	Zeeland	Utrecht	Drente
52%	5.2%	6.2%	12.5%	2%	7%	7%	6%	1%

The overall change in the contribution that Holland henceforth made to the national revenues was not seriously out of line with the complaints that its representatives had been making throughout the eighteenth century. Instead of bearing nearly two-thirds of the burden, its population paid something over one-half, perhaps a fairer reflection of the slight relative decline in the province's economic preponderance.

At the heart of the whole system, the *verponding* worked fairly well for the minister. During the four years of the Kingdom, its receipts never climbed above 11 million guilders and only in fact reached that mark with the addition of Jever and East Friesland after Tilsit in 1807. The promised cadaster took some time to get under way, and so complicated were its calculations that van Breugel imported the French expert land surveyor, Lefebvre de Montigny, to help Professor Aeneae of the Amsterdam Athenaeum with the statistical work. Three qualified assessors worked on each fiscal arrondissement and—at least in principle—co-ordinated their efforts with the guidance of the local financial commission. Each assessor was given an area of not less than 3,000 and not more than 5,000 *morgen,** which they managed to get through with impressive, or possibly suspicious, despatch. In Gelderland—not the easiest department for surveying, one would have thought—the sixty-odd officials claimed to have got over 25,000 *morgen* surveyed, assessed, and checked in under a fortnight![129]

To some extent the general uproar, especially vocal in the land provinces, which followed their work was a back-handed form of flattery. But there is also no doubt that the urgency with which the cadaster officers went about compiling their returns and the rough-and-ready calculations they were prone to use if in danger of being bogged down, whether by the procrastination of local officials or the complications of customary land divisions, often resulted in rough treatment. One group of petitioners in Gelderland claimed that in Zutphen and Nijmergen kwartieren an "old" assessment of a property at 4 guilders, 11 stuivers had now been reassessed as 11 guilders, whereas the "legal" figure was closer to 6 guilders, 7 stuivers.[130] Not infrequently the land-drost of the department was sympathetic to protests about harsh assessment and the intrusion of "foreign [from outside the department] assessors." The landdrost of Drente pointed out: "It is well-known that to establish with any precision the value of a house it is necessary to have the complete details of all its circumstances in one's possession and this cannot possibly be expected of any foreign assessor."[131]

Such was the volume of the protests against the *verponding* assessments, and the anger which they had provoked, that by the spring of 1808 the Staatsraad and the King were obliged to pay some official attention to them. For Gogel, of course, they were merely part of the "tableau of opposition, intrigues and subterfuges which have been organised so as to prevent and impede the implementation of this tax." Nor was he impressed by the reassertion of the Appelian claim to base assessments on average market values; to extend the time permitted for appeal beyond the fourteen days allowed by the law; and to appoint independent arbitrators rather than an ajudication by the landdrost or the financial commissioners of the department. "Some landowners and their official spokesmen" (a mildly abusive dig at Appelius) "have preached this doctrine . . . hoping that the old arguments advanced against it have been forgotten."[132] The King, however, was less persuaded that the complaints were all self-interested, and gave the minister official instructions to see whether some means could not be found to mitigate the more offensive stringencies. Gogel responded with a memorandum in June 1808 simply de-

---

* See note on weights and measures, p. xvii.

fending the position he had always taken. Louis persisted that his intention was "to have these complaints about the taxation of houses and land cease . . . in the present circumstances of the country, it would be barbaric not to give every opportunity to repair the possible vexations or errors [committed by the cadaster] so as to do everything for the best." But the minister remained obdurate, arguing:

Without any interest of my own influencing my actions, I have tried always to reconcile the interests of the Treasury with those of the particular individuals who have reason to complain, which evil can hardly be avoided in any measure executed by mortal men. . . . With the intimate conviction of having acted always with correctness and never having lost sight of the principle of the law, I feel myself incapable of proposing to Your Majesty other means to end these protests and complaints coming from some great proprietors. . . .[133]

The concluding phrase was, of course, the most revealing. Through all the barrage of skilfully mobilised opposition, Gogel saw plainly the hand of wealth and privilege striving (as he believed it always had done) to protect its own interests at the expense of the rest of the nation, no matter how desperate the common danger. The issue was for him as black and white as it could possibly be. Either those charged with the exercise of national sovereignty saw to it that all shared the common sacrifices according to their ability to bear them, or else their authority was in reality null and void. "Great fortunes," he was to repeat in his 1820 memorandum, "are a plague on the state"; and to Louis Bonaparte he spelled out the real nature of his objection to the protests against the *verponding*:

It is necessary, Sire, to levy a tax which weighs equally on all those who are liable. Here, Sire, is the true touchstone, which the grand proprietors would like to evade, but cannot, which is also why their protests redouble the more we succeed in touching the heart of the matter. Their appeal to the people is a mask behind which they conceal their interested designs; they are infuriated because the law admits no distinctions and seeks equality. Even as they continue to bask in luxury and sumptuousness in their little palaces and chateaux, enjoying all the comforts of life which the poor artisans in their miserable hovels must perforce now deny themselves, they still demand that so far as taxation is concerned, their properties should contribute only so much as the meanest dwelling and the solitary field from which the poor labourer must draw his subsistence with the sweat of his brow. Here, Sire, is the nub of the question; the law will not concede such a reprehensible distinction, and I must say that if Your Majesty attends to those seductive addresses which mean to engage him to use means other than those I have had the honour to present to Your Majesty, the law will surely lose all its force, the tax will not produce the estimated yield, and Your Majesty may easily conceive what the consequences of such a disaster may be for the Finances and for the Kingdom.[134]

The full-blown rhetoric of republican social democracy, of which Gogel had never quite divested himself, sounded extraordinarily incongruous in the council rooms of Napoleonic Holland. Certainly Gogel was quite right to see behind the fuss made over the *verponding* the articulate voice of the strong taking advantage of the silence of the weak. But his outburst was also to some extent that of a petulant bureaucrat, incensed at a challenge to his own authority and a slight on his competence, from quarters which he considered both ignorant and ignoble. There was, in fact, a measure of truth in Louis' own retrospective criticism of the ablest of his ministers that

it did not take a long time to know and to appreciate Gogel, an indefatigable worker and so well versed in matters of finance, excellent minister of taxation, an honest patriot and a man of great firmness. Unhappily to these many qualities he added faults which in large measure cancelled them out. The sufferings of individuals and their complaints barely touched him. In the matter of the distribution of public charges he saw only the interest of the fisc and the success of his system; nothing else existed for him. It has been said that he considered the Ministry of Finance, or rather that of Taxation, as a state apart since he could suffer not the slightest reform. . . .[135]

It is difficult to know where to apportion the blame in the rapid deterioration of relations between Louis Bonaparte and Isaac Gogel. Both were in their own manner fiercely obdurate, exceedingly fastidious and hypersensitive to anything that could be taken as a slight on their dignity. But of course one was King and one his servant. Gogel always felt himself socially uncomfortable among the habituees of the court entourage and even on the Staatsraad, where, Goldberg and van de Kasteele apart, he had precious few friends. Among the ministers there were van Maanen and van Hooff, who shared many of his political views but who were in the one case too canny or in the other too self-important to lend support when it was needed. As a result Gogel often went out of his way to make life difficult for those he believed were embattled with him. He stood absolutely on the letter of his *Instructie*, and seeing himself as in effect the paymaster of the other ministries, refused to entertain any ad hoc requests for expenses without (and once or twice even with) the counter-signature of the King. In adopting this attitude Gogel was of course acting with immaculate propriety. Seeing himself as the steward of the public purse, he was determined to make a clean break with the notorious malpractices of the past. Certainly he could never be accused of lining his own pockets. But his sort of rectitude won few friends. When, with good reason, he declined to accept a note from Verhuell for 10,000 guilders, he received a sharp dressing-down from the King for his pains. Ministers, Louis rather absurdly suggested, were not allowed to communicate with each other except through the crown. "Your Majesty will permit me to observe," wrote Gogel with unfeigned exasperation, "that nothing could be more dangerous than to permit the ministers to demand that the Minister of Finance grant and the Chamber of Accounts credit payments unless they are in conformity with the law and with their Instructions. . . ."[136]

As relations became steadily more strained, Louis detached certain functions from the responsibility of Gogel's ministry. A "Director-General of the Treasury" was appointed to take care of the amortisation fund, serviced by an appropriation of 1.5 million guilders from annual revenue; and the customs service (about which Napoleon had made increasingly bitter complaints) returned to its autonomy. Aside from what the minister obviously regarded as the dissolution of the administrative unity he had tried so hard to consolidate, it was over the fundamental issue of the importance of the 1805 system that the rupture finally came. Confronted with a stubborn refusal to contemplate any but the most minimal adjustments to the tax system, Louis on June 26, 1808, appointed a special commission to consider its revision.

Predictably, Gogel took this as an unmerited and inexcusable stab in the back, another "March 1801." On August 23 he again exposed his feelings to the King. After ten years of labour,

after having been persuaded to undertake and complete an enterprise which no-one else dared attempt, am I to be deprived of the sole satisfaction of bringing it to perfection? Such a decision can only serve to destroy the last ambition remaining to me; and, if I may be permitted to say so, I have already suffered much because despite my appeals I have never received from Your Majesty the necessary support, still less from your financial servants [on the Staatsraad], nor the least mark of encouragement or approval—to which, I might add, it is necessary to attribute much of the weakness and laxity of the executive. Nothing would be more agreeable to me than to see the Commission succeed . . . but my duty obliges me to confess frankly to Your Majesty that I cannot persuade myself to be reduced to the role of a subaltern and to furnish them with the information they require. If I should so promise to do so, I would be deceiving Your Majesty—something I am incapable of doing, and even less to render an apparent but really perfidious service. . . .[137]

As well he might be, Louis was somewhat shaken by Gogel's letter, both its tone and its implicit threat of resignation. His initial reply in September was to try to soothe his minister's hurt feelings but urge him at the same time to be a little more dispassionate. He set great store, he promised, by the general tax system, but Gogel had surely damaged his own case by refusing to collaborate with the revising commission. Louis ended crisply by reminding Gogel of their respective places:

. . . on other occasions I have observed that my excessive indulgence has been abused, but this must now cease; you must become accustomed to my wishes and not seek to hinder or to contradict my intentions instead of zealously carrying them out. The most essential thing in my government is that the ministers and heads of departments proceed in the same direction, think and act like myself. . . .[138]

Gogel responded promptly to this correction by offering his resignation, insisting that he had had enough of public life; that it had brought him only anxieties and tribulations, and that the King would be doing him a great service by accepting it. Startled once more by his minister's peevish histrionics and his refusal to do his bidding with a good grace, Louis affected to ignore the resignation but went ahead, albeit a little hesitantly, with the commission. He also took counsel—much of it not very illuminating—from all the leading figures in the government, van Maanen, van der Heim, Appelius, even Hendrik Mollerus, on what was to be done about the financial chaos.[139]

By the spring of 1809, Gogel felt his position becoming increasingly invidious and brought up the question of his resignation once more, this time pleading that he had his own private business interests to look to. Louis had in fact been distressed to learn that a minister who laid so much emphasis on the integrity of public administration should be attempting to run his own enterprises at the same time, but he was not yet ready to part company. On April 25, 1809, he wrote a particularly kind and solicitous letter to Gogel, enquiring about his health and asking him in friendship to tell him candidly about his misgivings. Gogel answered bluntly enough:

Personally I have no grievances at all, but only in my capacity as your official and as a Statesman . . . I do not complain of the detachment of several affairs from my ministry . . . but what wounds me is to see myself mistrusted and to be daily exposed to the effects of a contempt which, if I might say so, does as much harm to your Majesty as to myself. . . . It is to receive inexecutable orders every day, or those which can lead only to incalculable confusion; it is to be responsible every day for actions of third parties or matters out of our own control . . . it is to see everything which concerns the unhappy department of finances ill-judged, ill-considered, without any encouragement, support or consideration for services which have been given; it is to see that Your Majesty apparently attaches no value to the raising of revenues; it is to see the opposition to anything which might lead to their amelioration crowned with success and the introduction of measures which can only indispose the public and introduce confusion and embarrassment into the administration without balancing those evils with an equivalent yield. It is never to be able to see the accomplishment of accountability, of order, of stability and economy. . . .

Nor was he able to take his leave of public office without a further bitter aside:

There would be too much presumption on my part if I were to imagine that I might be of sufficient importance for Your Majesty to alter in the smallest detail his System and mode of government so as to to redress these grievances which are perhaps only the effects of an agitated imagination. . . .[140]

The experience of trying to reconcile a fiscal policy grounded on his social egalitarianism with the political skills of remaining a dutiful and pliant member of a Bonapartist bureaucracy had in the end proved too much for Gogel. He had come to feel so embattled, almost to the point of paranoia, and so identified with the indivisibility of the national treasury he had planned and brought into being that he ceased to think rationally in specific moments of crisis. After the last, sour exchange, Louis finally gave up all attempts at accommodation. He accepted Gogel's resignation on May 22, asking him at the same time to remain a member of the Staatsraad.

That there was to be a real shift from the doctrinaire fiscalism of the first minister was plainly suggested by the appointment of the pragmatic Appelius as his successor. As in 1801, the latter succeeded to an office about which he had grave reservations. But there were only eighteen months left before the remains of Dutch independence were finally to be given the *coup de grâce* by order of the Emperor. During that time the British invasion of Walcheren had to be fended off, and more ready revenues were required.

Whatever Appelius' inclinations, the operation of the 1805 law remained much as Gogel had left it, and his principal co-adjutants were all retained in employment as its mechanics. It was no longer thinkable that each department should be free to make its own arrangements to meet its fiscal commitment, or that there should be a wide margin of discrepancy between an estimate of an annual expenditure and the income then extracted to finance it. Henceforth every guilder and every stuiver of expenditure had to be accounted for in advance. This basic reshaping of the nation's finances, resumed in earnest after 1818, was Gogel's monument. Whether it presaged a happier, or at least a more tolerable future for his country, is harder to say.

The Abolition of the Guilds

There were two aspects to Gogel's unbending determination to unify the government of the Netherlands. First was the simple pragmatic imperative that without fiscal unity and the generation of additional ordinary revenue, there would be no possibility of meeting even the most elementary commitments to allies and creditors alike. Bankruptcy and political liquidation would then have been merely a matter of time. But in the longer term, Gogel meant to use the enhanced authority of a national government to undermine the position of the traditional élite. He aimed to substitute for the autonomy of corporate bodies—be they regency, church or guild—the principle of social equity as the cardinal rule of Dutch public life. In what became a celebrated address on the matter of the guilds, he insisted that

all the inhabitants of the kingdom, wherever they may happen to live, are the children of their prince; all have the same right to enjoy his protection; they must all be equal before the law and equally enjoy its favours; just as all, each one according to his means, must bear the heavy burdens of the state. . . .[141]

At heart Gogel was still an intensely political animal, bent on waging war against the oligarchies he held responsible for the nation's decrepitude, and which had survived a decade of the Batavian Republic to emerge unscathed in their old positions of power and influence. Gogel saw the guilds as part of the oligarchies' apparatus of social economic control. Their pretensions to provide paternalistically for the welfare of the local community he dismissed as so much humbug, a pathetic disguise for the perpetuation of monopolies protecting the interests of the privileged few. In the face of more efficient foreign competition, unencumbered by such anachronisms, they neither provided real protection for manufactures nor sustained the growing numbers of poor which resulted from their debilitation. Gogel thought of them as parasitical, eating away at what remained of Dutch economic strength and arresting any possibility of new growth. In a letter to Louis Bonaparte on the subject in December 1806, he revealed the strength of his feeling on the matter by remarking that "all discussion on this issue must be considered as a struggle between the forces of darkness and those of light."[142]

Gogel was under no illusion that the same forces which had done for the General Tax Law in 1801, and which had exploited the tentative restoration of federalism to wink at the resurrection of the guilds, would not now do their utmost to thwart any attempt at more rigorous measures. With van Stralen's active collaboration, he set about nonetheless to try to close the loopholes. Articles 12–14 of the law on local government (August 22, 1805) deprived the municipalities of the right to establish any economic regulations in contravention of national laws; and the General Tax Law itself ruled out any local tariffs other than those specifically authorised by the national government. But the most effective weapon was the Law of Patents of December 2, 1805. Adapted from a French model, it required all those seeking to practice a trade or profession, or employment in manufactures, to pay an annual fee in return for the "patent" which acted as their license to trade. It was made abundantly clear that while the local authorities were charged with the administration of the law, the collection of the patent fees, and the registration of the various occupations in their respective rolls, it had no right to deny any citizen his patent, irrespective of place of origin or domicile. The right to seek work or set up shop could no longer be withheld simply on the traditionally versatile grounds of "goede politie." The law was meant as a signal example of the practical implications of equality of rights under national sovereignty: it laid down universal obligations and prescribed universal rights.

As such, of course, it was anathema to the champions of communal independence. Three of the most prominent of the Amsterdam regents—Jan van Stirum, Petrus van Boetselaar and Willem Six—published *Eenige vrije reflectiën op het Reglement houdende algemeene bepalingen voor Gemeentebesturen (Some Free Reflections on the Law Concerning the Municipalities)*[143] in the autumn of 1805, rehearsing all the principal objections to the perils of economic liberty. To do away with the hierarchy of the guilds, they insisted, was not only to expose established standards to cheapjack workmen but to devalue the work of those who had served proper apprenticeship. Were they to be reimbursed their masters' fees? To withdraw from the corporations their philanthropic functions would be to throw a new and intolerable burden on the already prostrate public institutions of relief. The same points were made over and again by representatives of the forty Amsterdam guilds in their meeting with Gogel on December 17, and in the petitions which flowed in to The Hague from almost every corner of the Republic. However enlightened or benevolent in intention, the law on patents was certainly not popular—at least with the large numbers of artisans and masters more alarmed by the removal of their protection than excited by the prospects of competing on a free market. Illogical though it may have been, the determination to cling to even a stagnant or shrinking local market, and to protect it from the threat of "foreign" enterprise, became more rather than less intense as economic conditions deteriorated further.

As always, Gogel was unmoved by the fears and complaints of those he regarded as either too enmeshed in their own vested interests to think clearly of the common good, or too gullible to share his vision of the economic future. On August 20, 1806, he presented the King with the final draft of a "law on Corporations," completed with the help of van Stralen and Goldberg the previous year. It neatly circumvented the social and philanthropic professions of the guildsmen by making subscriptions to the new "trade associations" obligatory and earmarking the funds for the maintenance of all the traditional charities—benefits for the sick, pensions for widows and the aged. Local government authorities were to be given some latitude in respect of the size and number of these associations and were to approve the arrangements made for electing officials—in sharp contradistinction to the traditional practices of distributing deaconships among the senior families and masters of the town. The new "corporations" were to continue to uphold standards, particularly in professions like that of the notary or the surgeon where a direct service to the public was involved.

But these minor concessions were merely trimmings on the essential act of stripping the old guilds of all their autonomy and integrating their successors into the general administration of the country. As far as Gogel was concerned, it was another contribution to the creation of a single economic nation, and the sweeping away of the debris of the old parochial markets no longer suited to the conditions of the nineteenth century. Echoing the economists he so much admired, he argued in his supplementary letter to the King: "It is an indifferent matter to society as a whole where and how one of its members earns his bread and provides for his subsistence, as long as he does so without committing any act of disloyalty or crime."[144] Every man must be free to profit from his labour and abilities wherever he could best market them; and by putting artificial barriers in the way of that, the guilds, far from containing poverty and economic disarray, were actually contributing to it. The obsession with insulating a community against neighbouring competition was, he reiterated, myopic and self-destructive. It "is in the overall well-being of the industry, talents and labour of all its inhabitants that the power and prosperity of any state consists."

Like most of the reforms of this period, the chances of the law on corporations succeeding depended on the perseverance of a minority of zealots. With the help of an eloquent defence of the virtues of economic liberty by Goldberg, its initial reception in the Council of State was reasonably friendly.[145] But the King himself remained equivocal. He was attentive enough to the arguments of the reformers, but equally impressed by the fact that not only members of the old regencies but banking moguls like Pieter de Smeth and Willink, men not known for their sentimentality, were implacably opposed to abolition. Petitions continued to pour in. From Amsterdam alone there were fifty on behalf of the guilds towards the end of 1806; thirty-five Leiden guilds made similar representations, Groningen twenty-five and Leeuwarden fifteen. At a full session of the Council on December 8, the opposition was reinforced by the appearance of a deputation of the burgemeesters and regents of the principal cities in Holland.[146] Characteristically, their unity was somewhat compromised by the insistence of the Amsterdammers that they be treated as a metropolis where tens of thousands of workers still earned their livelihood within the orderly framework of the guilds.

Willem Willink, who was himself an "extraordinary Councillor of State," conceded that there might be greater "regularity" in their organisation but defended their traditional virtues. Above all, he insisted, tried institutions ought not to be sacrificed to "metaphysical ideas which are of no use here; only experience should decide such matters, and in this case there is the clearest evidence in favour of the guilds."[147] Others like Thin van Keulen from Amsterdam reiterated the anxiety that the city would be swamped with undesirable hawkers and street vendors peddling adulterated food and shoddy materials. Gogel retorted that the monopoly of the "half dozen or so butchers" in the city was notorious for maintaining high prices for inferior meat. It would, he argued, be better for both the pocket and the health of Amsterdammers if free access were given to country traders in comestibles and processed goods like flour and cheese.[148] Johannes Meerman, the president of the department of Holland, skilfully stood Gogel's declarations about "equity" on their head by arguing that under the new free-for-all, those tradesmen established and domiciled within a particular town would actually be disadvantaged *vis-à-vis* the "outsiders" since in addition to the patent they would be liable for heavy local charges—probably made heavier by the burden of having to support a new weight of "foreign" poor.[149] The peripatetic trader, moreover, could make up his 50-guilder patent simply by resorting to the nefarious practices of under-cutting and adulterating qualities to sell on a high turnover basis; in short, by exploiting the competition which held so many horrors for the protectionists. The result, he warned, would amount to nothing less than the "shaping of a new social order" in the Kingdom of Holland. Was that really what the King wanted? Surely the Sovereign Prince was not indifferent to the "means by which his subjects earned their livelihood"?

The Sovereign Prince remained rather flummoxed. On the one hand, he liked to think of himself as in the van of progress. He was curious about the march of technology in the new vistas of manufacturing, and liked to patronise promising inventions and organise industrial exhibitions.[150] But at the same time he wanted to make the position of men like Severijn and Willink more secure, and was moved by the claim that the abolition would cause suffering among the "honest sort" of his subjects. Not for the last time he decided on indecision and referred the whole matter once more to a sub-committee of the Council of State, presided over by the Minister for the Interior, Mollerus, whose enthusiasm for unitarism and economic liberalism was far more lukewarm than van Stralen's. Since the membership of that committee also included de Smeth, Willink, Meerman and de Mist—with Goldberg defending his corner as the solitary confirmed abolitionist—it is hardly surprising that on January 10 it reported against Gogel's project, fearing that "unlimited freedom . . . will be the ruin of the towns and their citizens."[151]

The ruling of the commission seemed to have killed off the chances of

Gogel's draft becoming law. But he was not one to let the matter go lightly. On October 10, 1807, he returned to the fray with an exposition of the social, political and economic reasons for abolition which displayed his polemical gifts at their most outstanding. "I will commence," he said pointedly,

by stating straight away that I regard myself placed in a position of trust by His Majesty by virtue of being a subject of the King of Holland, belonging, that is, to the whole Kingdom, and duty-bound to consider only the interests of the people as a whole. I give no special consideration to private and often conflicting interests of individual towns; or to some persons within such a town; or to the arguments of some magistrates (who) . . . have not yet forgotten that they once were invested with the representation and sovereignty which made them see their duty towards only the inhabitants of their town and to treat all the rest as "foreign."[152]

The word "foreign," he remarked, has a peculiar significance in the Netherlands, meaning "in the language of monopoly" everything found outside the city walls. But there was no reason whatever why those who produced inefficiently should be protected from the consequences of their incompetence by artificial regulation and tariffs. "To see on all sides the imperfect products, the fruit of the mediocre capacities of our artisans, by the side of the more polished and well-finished products of our neighbours" was an illuminating and distressing experience. How could the Dutch ever hope to modernnise their economy if they continued to shelter behind these anachronisms? "When one sees to what extent the majority on the commission has extended that system into the draft law, it is difficult to believe that we are living in the nineteenth century." As for their much-paraded concern for the poor,

I simply cannot conceive, how in time of such misery, the unfortunate can be deprived of the means to sustain themselves. . . . Man must live; that is to say he must eat, drink, clothe himself and be lodged. But what may be his fate if he is actually prevented from providing for these needs? To let him die of hunger out of a concern to protect a monopoly—that is altogether too much to ask of him. . . .

To substitute relief for the derelict for work opportunities was simply to encourage moral as well as physical stagnation; to feed the roots of crime and pauperism and deprive the state of labour. Why, moreover, should the country be held in thrall to the great entrepôts of Rotterdam and Amsterdam, whose goods flooded the rural hinterland while they erected formidable barriers against country manufactures? The days of the monopoly of the "hoofdstad" were gone just as surely as the time when it could depend on the closure of the Scheldt to protect it from the competition of Antwerp.

There is little doubt that Gogel's stirring reprise had some effect on the Council, not least on Louis himself. At the meeting of January 14, 1808, the opposition made a last effort to amend the law out of effective existence by inserting the requirement of the traditional "burgherschap" certificate of civic residence—"a miserable addition to local charges," said Gogel, which "is of no consequence to the well-off but imposes greatly on the humble." Provided they abided by the law and paid their taxes and patent, all the inhabitants of the Kingdom were ipso facto citizens, wherever they happened to live; they had no need of a scrap of paper to award them the "right." The commission's amendments, he insisted, were in fact not only economically anachronistic; they presupposed a divisible sovereignty and private jurisdiction which fundamentally contravened the unity of the monarchy—an argument carefully tailored to appeal to Louis' amour-propre.

In the event, the commission's revisions were rejected by seven votes to four in the financial section of the Council. When, therefore, the original Gogel project was once more placed on the table, it was adopted by thirteen votes to eight—the whole of the finance section voting in favour.[153]

On January 30, 1808, it was enacted by the legislature as the law of the land. But as in 1798, the opportunities for non-compliance at the local level were impossible to eradicate entirely. The very rigour of the provisions by which the landdrost of each department had to be provided with corporation rolls for scrutiny and had to approve each of their regulations, meant that long delays were inevitable, during which the old guilds could proceed to go their own way very much as before. Moreover, even in the final act it was stipulated that no "outsider" might be supported from the charitable funds set up by subscriptions. The duties delegated to the local burgemeester and his council meant the broadest possible interpretation being put on the letter of the law.

There is no dearth of evidence to suggest that the familiar prohibitions continued. One Jacob Isaacs who, for obvious reasons, had been disbarred from guild membership under the old regime (Gogel was very concerned to integrate the Jews into the economic life of the country) and who had duly paid his patent and qualified for membership of the Amsterdam Glass and Porcelain Traders Corporation, as well as that of the Mineral Water Sellers, complained to the minister that he had still been disbarred from trading as a "foreigner" by the city.[154] Sail-makers, rope-makers and ship-smiths, many from the hard-hit smaller centres like Monnikendam and Enkhuizen, wanting to find work in Amsterdam, complained of their continued exclusion. From Utrecht, Haarlem, Leiden and Rotterdam there came reports of the de facto regulation of employment, and further afield in the Overijssel towns of Zwolle, Deventer and Kampen the old guilds remained virtually untouched.[155] When, in 1811, the prefect of what had become the Imperial department of the Zuider Zee came to review the situation, he found it well-nigh impossible to distinguish between the old (illegal) guilds and the new (legitimate) "corporations." In any event, from the beginning of 1812 the French law on corporations took effect.[156]

Was the law of 1808, then, a "great fiasco" as it has been described by a Dutch economic historian?[157] There can be little doubt that its enforcement was subject to the same obstacles as any legislation enacted in The Hague. Yet Gogel's barrage on the guilds had not been without effect. On the eviction of the French in November 1813 there was, as Wiskerke—the historian of the abolition—observes, general expectation that the guilds would be fully restored to the situation obtaining before 1798. Petitions once more flooded in from the major urban centres and the governors of North Holland and Zeeland were particularly strong in their conviction that restoration was desirable, both socially and economically. Equally important was the fact that those parts of the country which for the first time had enjoyed a measure of freedom vis-à-vis the central departments were much less enthusiastic. Drente was firmly against restoration; the governor of North Brabant upheld serious reservations and was completely opposed to the restoration of the apprentice system; and even Utrecht conceded that the guilds, at the end of their life, had been a decidedly mixed blessing. In October 1818, after a period of indecision, William I finally decided to terminate the existence of the old guilds once and for all, an act which added a dash of liberalism to his firmly paternalistic notions on the economy.

"Knowledge Is Virtue": The Reform of the Elementary Schools

It is difficult not to admire the doggedness with which Gogel persevered in the cause of reform even in the face of daunting odds. He was the last person to shrink from a set-to with the champions of institutional orthodoxy. More than once, in the Council of State, he invited a confrontation between what he took to be the old and the new ideas of how the Dutch commonwealth should be constituted and governed. Nor did he take comfort in the illusion that, once measures like the General Tax Law or the abolition of the guilds had become binding, the battle to establish a unified administration in the Netherlands had been won. Gogel never made the mistake of underestimating the power and the tenacity of his opponents. As time went on, his comments on their stratagems if anything grew more trenchant. Behind the campaign to "revise" the verponding he detected an attempt to "departmentalise" the finances of the state and warned the King that appeasing it would amount to "the triumph of federalism; the old power of the magistrates and (for they do not bother to conceal it) the periwigs of Amsterdam."[158] The King was surrounded by sycophants who would not scruple to conceal their real aim of subverting the authority of the government by cloaking it in the garb of disinterested counsel.

Louis, however, was unmoved by histrionic appeals of this kind. The conflict with "the forces of darkness" he felt to be largely of Gogel's own making, and he was always unwilling to give his minister the blank cheque authority he sought. Yet without that unqualified support, Gogel was never able to come to grips with the problems of enforcement inherent in a country which for two centuries had had no experience of sovereign authority beyond that of town or province. Moreover, to uphold the authority of the national government Gogel was obliged to depend on a staff of officials that was still a far cry from the professional bureaucracy with time and loyalty equally undivided which he wished to see come into being. In any contest of wills between those officials and local magistrates or burgemeesters, it was never a foregone conclusion who would prevail. In practical matters like the *verponding* cadaster, the minister was forced to seek the co-operation of just those regents he affected most to despise. Though the two local government acts of 1805 and 1807 had given the executive untrammelled powers to appoint and dismiss local councillors, *wethouders* (aldermen), and burgemeesters as they saw fit, in practice it was virtually unheard of for a landdrost to recommend anyone other than an already well-established regent to such positions. It was a piquant irony that Gogel, who had ceased to place much faith in electoral democracy on largely utilitarian grounds, should have discovered to his cost that there was no more effective way of removing those who stood in the way of change.

We may be sure, then, that in the three years after 1805, Gogel's dismantling of the old administrative structure was far from complete. On the other hand it would be misleading to dismiss the reforms of this period as so much cosmetic. The Dutch state, after all, never did revert to the federal paradigm of the Constitutional Restoration—not even in 1813, when the hopes of the regents, both Orange and Patriot, were at their highest. If there were ever a time when the outlines of a new Dutch state became dimly apparent, it was surely at this juncture. There were still two sets of institutions, not really compatible with each other, operating in curious parallelism: the reformed and the unreformed; the national and the local; those sanctioned by legislation and those by usage and prescription. As economic realities began to exert their own inexorable pressure, the one came gradually to subsume the other. But the process was always slow, halting, and confused. Where there was least retreat and most resistance was at precisely those points which most mattered to the Minister of Finance—those which bore directly on the attributes of sovereignty, like the collection of revenue and the corporate organisation of economic life.

Yet there were other, greyer zones of governmental activity where the lines of battle were less obviously marked out. Matters such as the relief of the poor; the maintenance of the dykes and polders; and the education of the young had traditionally been quite as much within the domain of the local community as the guilds. But static or shrinking resources meant that they were coming increasingly to depend on subsidies from superior administrations to sustain them. It was the incapacity of local communities in the Netherlands to maintain these traditional tasks unassisted, as much as the reforming zeal of ministers, which shifted the centre of gravity of Dutch government progressively from the periphery to the centre. A national Ministry of the Interior was, after all, the creation of this time. In 1802 the Council's budget had been a measly 200,000 guilders. In 1807, it had already reached 5 millions.[159] Of this sum, it is true, approximately 3 millions are accounted for by the transfer of what had been the separate domestic budgets of the departments to the national exchequer; but the amount in itself was over *double* the aggregate appropriation for all the departmental budgets of 1802. The administration of the new national Waterstaat was costed at around 1 million guilders, a sum which in the years that followed proved almost always too modest to meet the needs of intermittent disasters; and the costs of administrating the Ministry of Justice and Police at a further 1.25 million. Moreover, much of the work which came under the Ministry of the Interior's auspices —medical welfare; poor relief; education; the encouragement of the arts and sciences—was regarded as politically innocuous. Whereas the defenders of the guilds characterised the abolition of 1798 as a typical revolutionary folly, they forbore to make the same kind of remarks about the Agencies for Education or the National Economy. Yet arguably the changes introduced by the national administration in these spheres had no less a part in reshaping public life in the Netherlands.

One of the best documented areas of governmental concern after 1805 was elementary education. It is perhaps the more interesting for not being among those imperatives demanded by the continual economic and military emergency through which the Dutch were living. But it was a topic which excited enthusiasm across a broad spectrum of political and social groups. That enthusiasm had its roots embedded in the social evangelism and Pietism of northern Europe rather than the world of the French Revolution; its pedagogy and propaedeutics came from Campe, Basedow and Pestalozzi rather than from Rousseau or Lepeletier.[160] This is not to say that the work of educational reform was untouched by political considerations. On the contrary, its concern to mould a young citizenry embodying the virtues of Christian sociability was almost bound to bring it into conflict with the orthodox custodians of that work—the synods of the established Church.

But it was the practical work of the reformers which created a partly political dispute, not vice versa. Among the active propagandists for the new schooling and members of the Society for the General Good there were to be found Orangists like Admiral van Kinsbergen; Patriot regents like Bicker and Elie Luzac; and staunch Batavians like Kraijenhoff, van Maanen, Kops and Bernardus Bosch.[161] However much these men may have diverged in their political beliefs, they may be presumed to have shared the central moral conviction of the Society—that Dutch society had become fatally engrossed with the besetting sins of luxury, venality, decadence and corruption. This critique of manners, verbalised with a fundamentalist gusto that was peculiarly Dutch, had begun to make itself felt through the Spectatorial writings and the like far back in the eighteenth century and has been discussed in an earlier chapter. But as well as feeding into the mainstream of Patriot rhetoric, the moral revivalism which was the counter-face of the periwig time also produced a small number of practical philanthropic achievements. Cities like Amsterdam (1747) and Rotterdam (1774) set up schools for the poor run and financed by the municipality, although both were more concerned to act as a social prophylactic by indoctrinating the unwanted young in the discipline of subservience than to provide a training academy for model junior burghers.

Of far greater significance was the principal agency of Christian sociability, the Society for the General Good.[162] Quite apart from its independent importance as a disseminator of new educational and philanthropic ideas, the

"Nut" (*Maatschappij tot 'Nut van 't Algemeen*) was instrumental in supplying exactly those squadrons of dedicated enthusiasts needed by the state to staff its Agencies and provide some reinforcement against local indifference and hostility. The Society was different, both in kind and degree, from the other learned societies which mushroomed in the Netherlands towards the end of the century and from which the Batavian Republic had drawn many of its leaders. Founded in 1784 by the Monnikendam predikant Martinus Nieuwenhuizen, it remained less a gentlemen's club or debating society than a kind of social church. It had no truck with the finer points of Latin poetry, French drama or even Scottish philosophy. Its literature was vernacular, earthy and simple, preoccupied with the ethics of everyday life and designed to catch the imagination of the "brede middenstand" who were the principal victims of the events which overtook the Netherlands after 1780. Nor was it shrouded in masonic secrecy. On the contrary it courted publicity, using its own printers and publishers to distribute its material. It meant, above all, to be *popular*. And so indeed it was. By 1800 it could number its "departments" into well over a thousand, extending not only throughout the country but also to its colonies from Paramaribo to Batavia.

Within the Netherlands, the Society's centres of activity were located not only in the predictable regions of North Holland and Zeeland, but in the remoter areas of Groningen to the north and Brabant to the south, where the zeal of a few passionate enthusiasts like Bosch or Hendrik Wester proved infectious. In Groningen in 1797 there were already 255 members; a circulating library; a school; and the *Weekblad voor de Gemeenen Man* (*Common Man's Weekly*). At a small town like Bergen op Zoom, 150 pupils attended the "Nut" school; and the library at The Hague, established in 1800, had by 1805 600 readers.[163] The "Nut" was also the means through which the new techniques of teaching children, on the more humane lines recommended by Basedow and Pestalozzi, became known. It produced the first alphabet book; the exemplary *Schoolbook of Patriotic Duties* (*Schoolboekje van Vaderlandse Deugden*); and manuals like the *Reading Book for Dutch Children* (*Leesboek voor de Nederlandsche Jeugd*) combining instruction in slate and chalk, illustrations and printed language, to get across the rudiments of literacy in an easily palatable form. Above all, it was concerned to train a generation of teachers who were not only versed in the new techniques but prepared to treat their charges as something other than small animals, kept in order only by regular doses of brutal punishment and the most mechanical forms of learning by rote. The "Nut" prohibited virtually all forms of corporal punishment in its schools and frowned on the crude utilitarianism of the Bell-Lancaster monitorial system. Its own major institutions at Edam, Rotterdam and Amsterdam not only flourished as models of the new teaching but also set up as normal schools, turning out the first cadre of "Nut" teachers, inspectors and examiners.[164]

Given the progress made by the Society for the General Good, there were some grounds for supposing that the principle embodied in the 1796 constitution that "throughout the whole Republic without exception instruction shall be given to all those needy children not already provided for from a poor fund"[165] might be more than a pious hope. After the setting up of the Agency for National Education in 1798, the work of the "Nut" and of the state organs became closely interwoven. This had already happened at a local level. In towns like Haarlem, The Hague, 's Hertogenbosch and Groningen, where the municipal authorities were strongly sympathetic to the work of the "Nut," official encouragement and sometimes even subsidy had been given to their efforts to establish schools, libraries, printing presses and the like. In Amsterdam where, by 1800, there were three major branches in the city, the regents paid them the compliment of seeking advice on how best to run its own poor school. But though the "Nut" could and did achieve a great deal from its own resources, the logical end of its work was to persuade the state to adopt a comprehensive programme for public elementary education throughout the Netherlands. The *General Reflections on National Education (Algemeene Denkbeelden over de Nationale Onderwijs)* (1796) was a manifesto inviting the Batavian National Assembly to undertake this enterprise. The two bodies were mutually inter-dependent. The Republic needed the "Nut" to supply its first corps of officials and to sustain the momentum of propaganda for reform. The "Nut" needed the state to lay down authorised minimum standards of educational proficiency for teachers and to help improve their miserable pay and despised status. Subsidies were needed if the remoter regions of the country were to be provided not only with adequate staff but with cheap and prolific teaching materials, and decent working conditions rather than the tallow-lit, clinker-floor hovels in which many country schools were housed.[166] If funds were short, the "Nut" suggested, the revenues from the expropriated domains of the Prince of Orange might be wisely used to establish a national School Fund from which such needs might be catered.

The second Agent for National Education, J. H. van der Palm, embodied most of these aspirations in the official instructions and ordinances issued by his office, in his own celebrated *Memorie* of 1801 which set out the programme as state policy, and in the two school laws of 1801 and 1803. The division of the Republic into "school districts," each with their own local boards and peripatetic inspectors, was arranged in collaboration with the "Nut" and naturally relied heavily on its personnel. Two of the central features of the new establishment—the annual meetings of the inspectors, and the publication of their proceedings together with instructive accounts of new educational ideas and methods known as the *Bijdragen (Contributions)*—were both opportunities for the state and the "Nut" to pool resources. The inspectors passed on many recommendations from the "Nut" departments, which in turn acted as channels for the wider distribution of the *Bijdragen* to teachers and school boards alike.[167] But even in consort, the resources which both bodies could call on were still too slight to make much impression on local authorities that chose to be at best indifferent or at worst actively hostile to their efforts. The number of teachers examined and duly certified under the new regulations had gone from thirteen in 1801, to sixty-one in 1802, to seventy in 1803. But those figures represented the first stream of "Nut" recruits, and only a drop in the ocean of ignorance and circumspection which greeted the attempts to apply the first two school laws.

In the circumstances after 1801, in which federal and local authority was again paramount and the district school boards more often appendages of those authorities than willing participants in the educational hierarchy, it proved particularly difficult to implement the laws with any real rigour. The introduction of the examination system meant that unqualified teachers were meant to be dismissed. But it was a hard thing to turn a man out from a post which he had been accustomed to regard as a part-time extension of more exacting duties like grave-digging or bell-ringing at the local church. Sometimes, as at Utrecht, a venerable but plainly barely literate master like one Meerland of Blauwkapel simply refused to present himself before the local commission for examination, or even to recognise its competence to adjudicate in such matters.[168] In Brabant, at Sint-Oedenrode, it proved well-nigh impossible to remove a barely literate ex-coachman from a post he obviously regarded as no more than a cosy sinecure.[169] Not infrequently such men were appointed by the patronage of the local heer on the same basis of presentment as a predikant or sexton. The other major patron of schoolmasters, the Church, was equally hostile to the intrusive presence of the inspectors and their commissions, even where their staff were local men familiar with the circumstances of the region. Even in the more metropolitan areas of Holland, the deacons of the Reformed Church were intensely suspicious of any deviation from the approved orthodoxy of the Heidelberg Catechism or of attempts to introduce the impressionable minds of the young to ungodly learning.[170]

In the face of such opposition from both Church and regents, it was unlikely that local authorities would be especially keen to play their part in putting the new legislation into practice. Jurisdiction for matters such as education of course fell directly within the provenance of the "domestic" administration allotted under the 1801 constitution to the departmental authorities. Where they could, those authorities delayed, hedged and prevaricated before publishing the "Domestic Regulations" on elementary education for their respective departments.[171] And even then, the authority of the inspectors and school boards was carefully limited to exclusively public institutions.

At their meeting in 1804, the inspectors and van der Palm himself aired their exasperation with the unco-operative attitude of the departments. Describing themselves revealingly as "national civil servants" (*nationale ampten-aren*), they anticipated that sooner or later, further legislation would be needed to resolve the deadlock. What they particularly wanted was an extension of their authority to those semi-private institutions endowed by church or charitable foundations. The chief among their zealots was Adriaan van den Ende, and it was this remarkable man, as reticent and self-effacing as Gogel was ebullient and aggressive, who was to be responsible for laying the foundations of what became a model system of public elementary education and an example for the rest of Europe.[172]

Born into a large family in Delft, van den Ende, like so many others involved in the reform of education, had become a predikant at Rosendaal in Brabant after taking a degree at Leiden. In many respects he was a typical product of the "Nut," passionately concerned with the social, evangel and practical Christianity. He was an admirer of Priestley's *On the Corruption of Christianity* and Paulus' egalitarian gospel *On Equality*. He had also edited William Paley's *View of the Evidences of Christianity*. But in addition to a scholarly inclination towards rationalism and humanism, he was a model bureaucrat who had entered van der Palm's Agency in 1800 and rapidly established himself as an energetic and efficient co-ordinator of the as yet rather unwieldy machinery of inspection, publication and examination.

When van der Palm became chairman of the Council of the Interior under the regime of the Regency of State, it was van den Ende who took over the day-to-day running of the educational establishment at The Hague. He was much more than a cloistered official, though. His special talent lay in being able to identify with and appreciate the routine problems of the working inspectors—he was secretary-general and convenor of their annual conference—and the daily needs of the new teachers, marooned as they often were in the midst of an unsympathetic population. The former, he knew, needed the unqualified support of the state in their efforts to secure proper help and assistance from local authorities; the third, and by far the most important school law of 1806, was framed with this in mind. The teachers needed liaison with each other and a form where the simplicity of their ideas could be explained to suspicious burghers. Van den Ende fostered local societies, patronised jointly by the "Nut" and the school boards, where both needs could be satisfied. In 1803 he published his own *Handbook for Teachers in the Public Schools of the Batavian Republic,* an invaluable addition to this growing literature.

The 1806 Dutch School Law—drafted by van den Ende, and enacted with the interested encouragement of both van Stralen and Schimmelpenninck—was the boldest and clearest statement of the responsibility of a national government towards the primary education, not merely of the poor but of all children between the ages of six and twelve.[173] It stood in marked contrast to the general emphasis in Napoleonic Europe on placing public resources in secondary and higher technical education to produce the engineers, bureaucrats and military men who were the cogs of the Grand Empire. A similar scheme for northern Italy, patronised by General Jourdan in 1802, had been defeated precisely because it was thought not only irrelevant but politically pregnant with subversive egalitarianism. Van den Ende was no revolutionary, but like all those involved in the overhaul of elementary schools in the Netherlands, he was much more concerned to diffuse the basic elements of primary instruction among the broad mass of the population than to provide some kind of streamlined élite of functionaries. This too sprang from the sort of moral conviction about good citizenship which, despite all the vicissitudes that had overtaken his country, was still strongly felt by his countrymen.[174]

The law of 1806 was meant to make a contribution towards the moulding of a new generation of burghers and burgheresses. To accomplish this, it extended the jurisdiction of the inspectorate over all three categories of primary school: private, semi-private (charity and church schools), and public. All were to conform with certain basic standards of educational proficiency; by the same token, no teacher was to be permitted to practice without the proper certificate awarded on examination. So as to avoid any embarrassing mass eviction of aged incompetents, the examinations were divided into three grades, each corresponding to a certain level of instruction for which the certified teacher would then become qualified. Registers of those qualified were to be kept by the local schoolboard and would be published in the *Bijdragen*. The inspectors themselves were increased to fifty-seven (later seventy) and given a more permanent structure of promotion and salary. They were placed firmly at the centre of the local educational establishments, which became much less the nominees of the local authorities and much more the instrument of state education policy.

The thorny issue of religious instruction was dealt with just as severely. No denominational or doctrinal instruction was to be given within regular school hours. It was the business of the respective church communities to provide such instruction, if they so wished, after school or on Sundays. This separation of religious from ordinary elementary education marked an important break with the past—ever since the Synod of Dort in 1618, one of the primary duties of the schoolmaster had been to immunise the faithful against the bacillus of heterodoxy. It also left the way open for public or charitable schools to take pupils from any denomination. It did not mean, however, that Dutch primary education could be characterised as purely secular. Bible stories and scripture provided much of the staple fodder by which the young learned to read, as well as to distinguish virtue from vice. Despite the inclusion of dangerous modern subjects like arithmetic, geography, Dutch language and literature, history and natural history, the teaching was still shot through with that moral earnestness which van den Ende himself believed to be indispensable for the *opvoeding* (literally, the upbringing) of the young citizen.

The system of elementary education set out in the law of 1806 was, by the standards of the time, exceptionally ambitious. Its chances of success were undoubtedly improved by the fact that those who drafted it—unlike the grandiose schemes promulgated by the French revolutionary legislatures, for example—were practical men very much in touch with the detailed problems of implementation. The lessons of 1801 and 1803 had been well learned, and the inspectors and their commissions had had nearly a decade of work in the field from which to draw valuable experience. They themselves were the motor of the system. In 1836 van den Ende told Victor Cousin, who was visiting the Netherlands: "Take care how you choose your inspectors, for they are men for whom you should search, lantern in hand."[175] Of the fifty-six who made up his staff, no less than thirty-six were predikants, pastors or priests of the various denominations, but predominantly of course, from the Reformed Church. Van den Ende was sufficiently sensitive to the religious variations of the country to see that in Brabant, for example, four of the six inspectors were Catholics. Others were recruited from the same sort of middle strata who made up Gogel's fiscal bureaucracy—lawyers, minor functionaries, former teachers, and the odd physician like de Fremerij of Utrecht. The best-known, like Bernardus Spoelstra of Rotterdam, Carel Visscher of Friesland, Teissèdre l'Ange of Utrecht, and par excellence, Hendrik Wester of Groningen, were all important educational writers and publicists in their own right. Through the commissions they gathered to them teams of acolytes and disciples all enthusiastic to pursue the work of bringing enlightenment to the young.

The law of 1806 actually required the inspectors to visit every hamlet and commune within their district, no matter how remote or isolated, at least once a year; and the reports, collated at the departmentad headquarters, provided a basis of information on which van den Ende in The Hague would be able to allocate resources of men and materials as the need arose. Moreover, the fear that the business of examining, grading and certifying teachers for every vacancy would lead to a severe drainage of available staff was shown by 1811 to be quite unfounded. Aged or unsuitable teachers were rarely subject to peremptory dismissal, but they were provided with younger and better qualified "assistants"—whether solicited or not—and retired, sometimes a little prematurely, as soon as a suitable opportunity arose.[176] By 1811, when Cuvier and Noël came to report on the operation of the system for the Imperial University, there were 4,551 elementary schools in the country for a pupil population of around 190,000. Even more impressive was the fact that of this number, 1,775 were fully public schools, 581 fully private, and 281 semi-private endowed institutions, the remainder being made up by miscellaneous establishments like kindergarten, Jewish Talmud Torahs and dame schools for girls.[177]

The geographical distribution was also revealing. In Holland, Amsterdam boasted no less than 239 elementary schools, Rotterdam and The Hague a mere 59 each and Haarlem 29. It was, perhaps, more surprising to discover that Utrecht, with one of the smallest populations in the country, had 131 elementary schools, and that Groningen had 300, of which 183 were public, and 51 were in the city of Groningen alone.[178] Just as the proportion of public to private or endowed schools rose sharply in the land provinces and in Brabant, so the scale of public subsidy rose accordingly. Groningen, before the 1790's one of the more impoverished provinces educationally, had 63 per cent of its elementary budget met from public sources; in Brabant, the figure was nearer 70 per cent.[179] But the proportion of those subsidies coming from the *national* exchequer was, despite van den Ende's strenuous efforts, still piddling. Even in 1815, when the establishment had been expanded, the budget for the lower schools ran at no more than 75,000 florins. By far the greater part of the revenues allocated for these purposes were collected and fed back again at the level of the province or even municipality.[180] That itself was a measure of the convergence of the local authorities and the school boards since the abrasive days before 1806.

The annual reports of the inspectors provide ample evidence of the rise in the quality of teaching given in the schools during the decade following the school laws.[181] More independent corroboration is provided in the admiring remarks made by Cuvier and Noël on their progress in 1811:

We would have difficulty in describing the effect on us of the first elementary school in Holland we entered . . . Two large, light, well-ventilated rooms contained about two hundred children, all cleanly dressed, seating themselves without any disorder, without noise or impoliteness, doing, at agreed signals, all that was asked of them, without the teacher even having to say a word. Not only do they learn, by sound and expeditious methods, to read fluently, to write with a good hand, with no mistakes; to do paper and mental arithmetic; and finally to express quite clearly their own thoughts in little compositions. But the books which are given to them and the pieces which they have to copy out are so nicely graduated, progressing in a carefully thought out order, with skilfully blended precepts and examples, that at the same time these children become versed in all the truths of religion, morality and all the knowledge that can ever be useful to them. . . .[182]

Some of this must be taken with a pinch of salt. No-one who remembers having sat in a class of infant paragons before a school inspector will suppose that such arcadian standards of conduct would last a minute longer than his exit from the schoolroom. The school in question, the municipal poor school at Amsterdam, was, like the remarkable school on the Buitenhof in The Hague, meant to be a model of its kind. There was still an enormous disparity between the best and the worst, and in many corners of the land provinces the polite fun and games of Pestalozzi still deferred to the Heidelberg Catechism and the knobbly stick. But the general impression of both the ambulatory inspectors and foreign visitors to the Netherlands at this time was of an exceptionally advanced and humane kind of elementary education, gradually penetrating the countryside as well as the urban schools. At Oosthorn in Friesland, for example, it was noted that ten-year-old children were already better educated than their parents, and at Ysbrechtum were accustomed to using the newest alphabet and reading-practice books.[183] With the guidance of the popular *Tijdschrift voor School-Onderwijzers* (*School Teachers' Journal*), produced by van den Ende's ministry, the use of wall-charts, arithmetical models and slides, nature projects, and all the now commonplace accompaniments of primary schooling became more widespread. Cuvier and Noël were surprised to find how many teachers had abandoned corporal punishment and had no qualms about mixing boys and girls together in the same classroom.[184]

As van den Ende was the first to admit, not all was perfect in his establishment. Finance, both for teachers' pay and the maintenance or improvement of school buildings, was still woefully inadequate. Now that the general tax system had largely done away with local revenues, the capacity of municipal treasuries to subsidise primary schooling was highly unreliable. The average pay of most teachers in the first two grades, especially outside the larger towns, was so pitiful—perhaps 200 or 300 guilders a year—that despite the enthusiasm of the "Nut" partisans, it remained something of a vocational sacrifice. It was difficult for such men, living in what one inspector called "appalling squalor and distress," not to break one of the sacred rules of the "Nut" by taking other part-time work to supplement their meagre subsistence or by reverting to the frowned-on practice of accepting casual "schoolgeld" from parents.[185] Van den Ende had always wanted to have the pay of teachers established on a proper graded footing, rather as Gogel had done with the fiscal bureaucracy. Both the "Nut" in 1796 and van der Palm in 1801 had suggested that a national "School Fund" be set up with this as one of its first priorities. And in 1809 van den Ende revived the idea more boldly by proposing a flat-rate contribution levied on every family, irrespective of whether they had children of school age or not. The Fund would then issue pay for teachers not otherwise provided for from endowed or private funds, and also for sick payments and pensions for the retired and the widows of teachers.[186]

It was a well-considered and imaginative plan, but 1809 was scarcely a propitious time for proposing additional taxation, on however nominal a scale. Van den Ende's memorandum to the Council of State went forward at almost exactly the same time as the final assault on Gogel and his system was getting under way. Predictably, it was given a sympathetic hearing and then left on the table. The "Commissioner-General" was obliged to soldier on with even his present resources shrinking. On the annexation of the Dutch departments to the Grand Empire, as a result of the lavish praise heaped on his work by the two inspectors of the Imperial University, the Dutch primary system retained almost complete autonomy. Van den Ende kept his post and his system was held up as a model the French might do well to emulate. The only serious difficulties arose in 1812 when (unsuccessful) efforts were made to persuade the Dutch to introduce French as a first language in the primary schools, and when the general financial chaos which overtook the Empire meant that teachers' and inspectors' pay became intermittent to the point of non-existence.[187]

The accomplishments of the Dutch primary schools excited the admiration of almost all the reforming spirits of the nineteenth century. Victor Cousin, who with Guizot was responsible for the first comprehensive French law on elementary education in 1833, conceded: "I have seen no primary schools worthy to be compared, even now, with those of Holland"; and Matthew Arnold, who compared the various approaches then current in states like Prussia, Switzerland and France, took much the same view.[188] The achievement, especially in the circumstances then afflicting the Dutch, was undeniably considerable. To a revealing degree it was the product of a harmonious coalition of voluntary and state agencies that was unique in the history of the reform of Dutch government, certainly not paralleled in, for example, the more embattled zones of finance in which Gogel operated. It must also be said that the zeal and energy so abundantly displayed in the work of overhauling primary education was not matched by a concern for the higher institutions. Cuvier and Noël, and their successors, found as much to criticise in the stagnation and archaism of the Latin schools and the universities as they found to admire in the lower schools.[189] A special commission was set up in 1807 under the chairmanship of the "Director-General of Education, Fine Arts and Sciences" Johannes Meerman, to examine all sectors of education, public and private; two years later it produced a handsomely written and thoughtfully considered report, written almost exclusively by its most distinguished member, Valckenaer.[190] Yet there were neither the funds nor the enthusiasm to extend the root and branch work of reform to middle and higher education.

Plainly, the Dutch were much less interested in broadening the education of their élite than in the kind of evangelical mission which characterised the work of bodies like the "Nut." For the values which lay behind the reform of the primary schools were more than purely pedagogic. They were part of an attempt to rediscover the moral ethos, the loss of which—men like van den Ende felt deeply—had been partly responsible for the plight in which the Dutch found themselves. Seen in this light, the creation of new generations of young citizens cleansed of the dross of the periwig century took on the character of patriotic self-affirmation. That was why, when the statesmen at Vienna yoked together northern and southern Netherlands who, for twenty years, had undergone entirely different cultural and administrative experience, the one area where the Dutch had had undisputed success—education—would cause the most bitter contention in the new Kingdom.[191]

The Discomforts of Monarchy, 1806–1808

By the mid-term of Louis Bonaparte's reign over the Dutch, something not unlike a national administration had come into being. Often, it is true, its sovereignty was more manifest on paper than in action. As in the previous period of unitary government from 1798 to 1801, many of the ordinances and regulations issuing from The Hague were studiously ignored at the level of the town and village where they were meant to have most impact. But even with this reservation, the extension of central authority to virtually every sector of public life in the Netherlands marked an important break with the communal and federal traditions to which the Dutch had clung so tenaciously. There was now almost nothing into which the ministers, councillors and officials of the King might not legitimately intrude, nor any bailiff or burgemeester who might not be removable at his instigation.

The years after 1805 were a bureaucratic heyday. Memoranda, reports, dossiers and laws, both enacted and projected, spewed from the bureaux in the Binnenhof and on the Plein with unremitting regularity. They covered every conceivable topic from the reclamation of sandy waste and the dissemination of cowpox vaccine to the state of jurisprudence in the Dutch universities and the education of young Ashkenazi Jews.[192] But they were never exhaustive or wide-ranging enough to satisfy the omnivorous appetite of the King himself. Presiding over the Council of State, he was at last in his true element, a Bonaparte to the marrow, issuing a great volley of orders and instructions, demanding more information on the condition of the Great Fisheries or the location of the Royal Theatre.[193] In the first three weeks after his arrival he disposed of nineteen major decrees, laws and ordinances. And this fevered rate of activity was punctuated only by the intermittent onset of acute melancholia and sudden flights to the waters at Aachen or Cauterets in the Pyrenees.[194]

Even while he was away, Louis endeavoured to keep his government on a tight rein. His instructions to the ministers on matters pending before his departure were usually very detailed, and with authentically Bonapartist inflexibility he forbade them to initiate new business or even communicate with each other without his specific permission.[195] All the same, it was essential for Gogel especially to arrogate to himself the power to make pressing decisions when they concerned state finances. The centralisation of the government was, for all Louis' royal pretensions, more institutional than personal. Moreover, few of the schemes and projects which his admittedly fecund enthusiasm generated were original. Some, like the plan to drain the Harlemmermeer, based on Brunings' blueprints, were too ambitious for the shrunken public purse to support.[196]

What Louis had in abundance was a nagging talent for driving through projects which had been initiated under the Batavian Republic and allowed to flag by default after 1801. His three major contributions to Dutch culture were realised in just this way. A national archive had first been proposed by H. van Rooijen in the Representative Assembly in 1800; two years later, the Regency of State had got round to appointing the first archivist, van Wijn. Schimmelpenninck had made some moves to establish the archives on a more institutional footing. But it was left to Louis to set them up in The Hague, with a modest staff and appropriation under the surveillance of his "Director-General of Education, Fine Arts and Science," Meerman. The library of the Stadholder, declared "national" in November 1798, had been entrusted to the ex-Sorbonne professor Charles Flament a year later, but was brought to the Mauritshuis in the centre of The Hague and established as the Royal Library only in 1808.

Appropriately, the most important legacy was that of painting. As Agent of Finance, Gogel had seen to it that the collection of the Stadholder had not been sold off but preserved at the Huis 't Bosch, where on May 31, 1800, it was opened for the first time to the public. When Schimmelpenninck moved in, the paintings were taken to the Buitenhof and finally transferred to Amsterdam in April 1808 at the same time as Louis was planning to make the "hoofdstad" his new residence. There were about 450 items in the catalogue, with the occasional Potter or Steen; but for the most part, court battle-and-portrait Italianate painters like Honthorst dominated the great seventeenth-century masters. In August 1808, however, the municipality of Amsterdam bought two of Rembrandt's major works, the *Staalmeesters* and *The Company of Frans Banning Kok* (*The Night Watch*) and placed them in the national collection, thus inaugurating the policy of redeeming the nation's greatest glories and housing them together as the Rijksmuseum—or, as the collection was then called, the "Koninklijke Museum."[197]

Louis was also concerned that the labours on legal codification which had been continuing intermittently since 1798 should be finally completed. Articles 28 and 29 of the January constitution had committed the Republic to this enterprise, but the Representative Assembly got no further than appointing a five-man commission of jurists to ponder the general principles. The pondering continued for some time. It was only in 1803 that a positive decision in favour of at least a new penal code was taken. In October 1804, the Regency of State was presented with an outline code; but oddly enough the ex-advocate Schimmelpenninck passed over the whole matter in silence in 1805. On inspecting the draft Louis found the whole work impressive, although it was more a compilation of juristic principles than a working code. He set up a small commission—Reuvens, the president of the National High Court; van Musschenbroek, a justice of Utrecht; and Elout, a jurisprudence specialist who had been on the original commission of 1798—to undertake the final editing and revisions. By the end of January 1808, just three months after their appointment, they had completed the code, which went into effect from the beginning of 1809.

Although the Dutch code was supplanted by the Napoleonic Penal Code in 1810, it was largely reverted to in 1814 under the Kingdom of the Netherlands. Indeed, it was far from being merely a slavish imitation of the Bonapartist model. In accordance with the practices of Dutch law, for example, justices were given a great deal of latitude in sentencing convicted criminals. Only the *maximum* period of imprisonment was fixed at twenty years. Flogging, torture and deportation with forced labour were all abolished, and if Louis had had his way capital punishment would itself have disappeared from the penal code, clear evidence for his brother that he suffered unduly from a "manie d'humanité." In the end he was persuaded by the members of the commission that for some of the gravest crimes—not least, perhaps, physical *lèse majesté*—it was still indispensable. Even so, it required the unanimous decisions of nine judges before it could be imposed; and, given the opportunity, Louis used his powers of clemency far more liberally than his judges thought either necessary or desirable.

Overall, the first Dutch penal code—as might be expected from a nation with so important a tradition of jurisprudence—was humane, rationally set out and accessible to the layman. It managed to clear away much of the clutter of so many different usages and practices without grafting an artificially uniform "system" on the traditions of Dutch law. Two additional commissions were appointed at the same time, one to deliberate on a civil code and the other to make recommendations on the reform of judicial procedure. The first body was set to work on what was much more like an adaptation of the Napoleonic Code than its criminal counterpart. Even so, the report it produced in 1809 was much castigated by Napoleon himself for maintaining a decorous indifference to matters of matrimonial and divorce law, topics still very sensitive in the God-fearing Netherlands.[198] The procedural changes were in part an attempt to bolster the independence and irremovability of the judiciary *vis-à-vis* the monarch, a principle Louis approved of more in theory than practice. Its proposals to make civil litigation cheaper and more acces-

sible were unexceptionable; but the Council of State, very much at the King's
bidding, declined to establish a High Court in each of the ten departments.
Instead, there were to be four: at The Hague (for "Maasland," Zeeland and
Brabant); at Amsterdam (for "Amstelland" and Utrecht); at Arnhem (for
Overijssel, Gelderland, Drente); and at Groningen (for Friesland, Groningen
and East Friesland-Jever). Together with the forty tribunals of first instance,
dotted around the Kingdom irrespective of department, the final proposals
underlined the unification of the Dutch into one legal group, no longer subject to the vagaries and idiosyncrasies of the customary laws of region, province
and town.

The dismantling of the old provincial sovereignty was further hastened
by the reform of local government in 1807. The groundwork for this had
already been laid by the Gogel-van Stralen law of 1805 through which it had
been made illegal for a local council or regency to contravene, either by omission or commission, ordinances and laws enacted by the national government.
The law of 1807 contributed further to whittling down the competence and
authority of the departmental administrations. While not going so far as the
1798 constitution in actually redrawing the boundaries, it re-emphasised their
function as a strictly administrative subdivision of the country. Holland was
divided into "Amstelland" in the north and "Maasland" in the south, thereby
forfeiting, at least geographically, the immense preponderance it had enjoyed
in the federal Republic. Drente was restored as a full department and East
Friesland-Jever annexed as the tenth, following the arrangements concluded
at Tilsit between Tsar Alexander I and Napoleon.[199]
After the French model, each department was subdivided into kwartieren,
and then again into either rural cantons or urban communes of over or under
5,000 inhabitants. Nominal concessions to historical sentiment were made by
reverting to traditional titles. The major communes were to be administered
through a "burgemeester" and a "vroedschap" of wethouders (aldermen)
whose numbers varied according to the size of the town. But this pseudo-
regency was a far cry from the proudly sovereign bodies of the old Dutch
municipalities disposing independently of places and perquisites. They were
strictly answerable to the representatives of the King, and their appointment
was to be confirmed by him through the landdrost or the Minister of the
Interior. No post was to be hereditary or treated as in any way disposable.
The competence of the new "vroedschappen" was confined to preparing
and submitting estimates of local requirements; they were in fact not much
more than a ways and means committee of the landdrost, who became the
pivotal figure in the government of the departments. The appointee of the
King and the nominee of the Council of State, he was in several respects the
obvious counterpart to the French prefect. But in the scope and function of
his office, the landdrost also owed a good deal to the bruising experience of the
Batavian departmental commissioners. He came rather better armed, however,
to impose state authority on the departments. In each of the kwartieren he
had a "drost" who, like the sub-prefect, was empowered to scrutinise and

report on the deeds or misdeeds of the local bodies. Four or five "assessoren," like the landdrost essentially state officials, helped him with the day-to-day administration of finance, highways, dykes, polders and canals, the upkeep of the ecclesiastical and educational establishments, and the like. By degrees his staff came to replace the departmental committees (or before them the old provincial colleges) as the principal arbiter of local government. It was through the landdrost that urgently needed funds would be disbursed to the communes. With financial control necessarily went patronage, so that—as in the relationship between the "mayor" and the prefect—the burgemeester, instead of being master of his own resources, came to be dependent on a powerful central government, suppliant for a due share of its resources.

By the time that the new system was in operation, these needs had become critical. The estimated expenditure for Leiden for 1809 (333,600 florins) exceeded its revenues by nearly *five* times (67,400 florins).[200] Despite the fairly generous help provided by the government after a disastrous powder-barge explosion in January 1807, and a recurrent subsidy, it was still forced to negotiate loan finance at penal rates of interest, thereby exacerbating its long-term problems. Amsterdam, which was well placed to float new loans, had reached the stage by 1809 when the interest on its municipal debt exceeded 700,000 guilders. Over a third of its annual revenue (about 1.5 million guilders) was committed to relief for the mendicant poor, said to have risen to over 80,000. As the global number of its citizens shrank—to around 200,000—the relative proportion of the impoverished grew. In 1808, when the port was closed by royal decree to all mercantile shipping, its deficit ran to almost a million guilders.[201] Such vexations were only those of any Dutch town at this time, writ very large.

Despite this significant institutional shift in power, it would be wrong to characterise the Kingdom of Holland as simply divided between "court" and "country"; between a freshly minted bureaucracy and a uniformly recalcitrant regency. Both at the apex and at the base of the governing hierarchy, there was a genuine amalgam of elements of the old and the new public service. Paternalist though he was, Louis, like William I after him, was concerned to rally the traditional nobility and patriciate to the crown's government, rather than declare war on them as Gogel would have wished. Hence they were flattered with the royal "Order of the Union" decoration, and invited to the Council of State in extraordinary and advisory capacity; confirmed, where necessary, in municipal dignities, and—more seriously—recruited as land-drosten and drosten. Gogel's favourite rule of thumb, that officials should not be natives of, or have interests in, the area of their jurisdiction, was demonstrably flouted by the appointment of the leaders of the provincial (usually Orangist) nobility as landdrosten. Andringa de Kempenaer served for Friesland; Bentinck van Diepenheim for Overijssel; Baron van Lamsweerde for Gelderland; and, appropriately enough, the man to whom William V's license to infiltrate public office had been addressed in 1801—van Lynden van Lunenburg—for Utrecht.

Louis was by no means completely oblivious to the claims of administrative talent and experience tested by the miserable years of the Batavian Republic. If convinced federalists like Queysen (East Friesland) and de Mist (Maasland) were paradoxical choices to serve as agents of a centralising policy, there were others like Wichers (Groningen), Pieter de la Court (Brabant), and François Ermerins (Zeeland) of whom even Gogel approved. As a group, the landdrosten were in any case largely divorced from their partisan allegiances. Like their prefectoral counterparts in France, they tended to conduct themselves as the severe circumstances of the time required. Taxes had to be collected, the National Guard enrolled, public order preserved, and bridges and polders maintained. By and large they all saw to it that these elementary tasks of administration were carried out as dutifully as befitted a nation with a long tradition of public conscience. At least there was no return to the wholesale commerce in office, to the "contracts of correspondence" which had continued right up to the demise of the old Republic. No more could reasonably have been expected of them. Comforted by their status—and the not inconsiderable stipend—the landdrosten acted as the nucleus of an administrative cadre on which King William I would subsequently base his own version of unifying paternalism.

In the same way, the "vroedschappen" of the municipalities were not so uniformly aristocratic as the reversion to their old title implies. Socially, to be sure, they were drawn from much the same élite—financial, mercantile, landed (in the eastern provinces) and professional—as their authentically regent predecessors. And under Burgemeester Wolters van de Poll, Amsterdam duly returned to the gilded splendours it had last enjoyed in 1794. William V's last principal burgemeester, Joachim Rendorp, even found a place on the council, as did three of the bankers—Severijn, Willem van Brienen and Willink—who had had a hand in declining the "Marengo loan" of 1800. As a token of their devotion to King and Fatherland, they made a not too painful sacrifice by waiving their stipends.

Rotterdam was more typical of the country as a whole in the greater *political* heterogeneity of its municipal officials. Anthonie van der Heim, the burgemeester, was a well-to-do financial official who had served as a magistrate in 1795 but had been ejected by the subsequent revolutionary eruptions in the city and only returned to the council after 1803. He presided over a vroedschap which could include both the inveterate Orangist Marinus Hoog and Richard Brem, a wool manufacturer who had been a municipal councillor since 1796 and even a member of the central *wijk* committee in 1798.[202] While the majority of the Delft municipality comprised regents removed in 1795, they also found room for Arnoldus Schonken, who had been a member of the elected municipality after 1795, and Jan Kruiff, the ex-secretary of Zwartewal, who had been purged in 1787 and returned to office as bailiff in Delft between 1796 and 1803.

Even in The Hague, certainly no bastion of Patriot loyalties, where the Orangist regent Slicher had been made burgemeester, the city treasurer was Franc van der Yves, bailiff of Monster during the revolution, member of the

"Provisional Representatives of the People of Holland" and of the provisional departmental administration of 1798. The drost of the Rotterdam kwartier, H. A. Caan, who was also a member of The Hague vroedschap although of a regent family, had a similar political background. The burgemeesters and *wethouders* of the Kingdom were certainly a far cry from the paragons of civic virtue and unmixed allegiances that Gogel sought and never found. As before, their primary loyalty was to the protection of their own community rather than some nebulous notion of the whole "nation." But neither were they a gang of curmudgeonly office-traders, bent on defeating all reform and obstructing the laws and decrees of the government. At a time when office had lost most of its allure and all of its profit, they simply went about the business of administering their towns, usually on a shortening shoe-string, as best as fiscal and military contingencies permitted.

A much more serious constraint on the refashioning of the Dutch state than the niceties of social and political equilibrium was the predicament of its relationship with the French Empire. Since 1787, the Dutch had suffered quite enough at the hands of French realpolitik not to be aware that any agreement concerning their independence would last just as long as it suited the purposes of French strategy. Deluded as he was in so many other respects, Louis was under no illusion whatever on this score. He understood only too keenly that he was the last inheritor of the classic "Batavian" dilemma and, as he later said, unable "to escape from one of those cruel alternatives—either to put myself in a position of hostility and opposition to France and the Emperor or else take part in a system which had surely to bring about the ruin and the final loss of Holland."[203]

Not unnaturally, Napoleon assumed that by setting his younger brother on the "throne" of Holland—"he whom I had brought up in my politics"—he had disposed of any question of conflicting loyalties. On St. Helena he told Montholon that "in appointing them [the brother-Kings] I considered them merely as viceroys, agents of my policy, whom I could recall to a French position according to the requirements of a general peace or the reorganisation of Europe."[204] But from the very beginning Louis showed no sign of accepting the role of an Imperial subaltern. "He forgot," Napoleon later complained, "that he was French and used all the resources of his reason and the torments of his delicate conscience to persuade himself that he was Dutch." Cruelly sardonic though the judgement was, it was perfectly right. In 1807 Louis-Lodewijk told a gathering of Dutch dignitaries that "from the moment I set foot on the soil of the Kingdom I became Dutch," and in all innocence he protested to the Emperor that "it is by becoming Dutch, by devoting myself above all to the interests and well-being of my new country that I seek to make myself worthy of your name and to prove to you that I have always been a good Frenchman."[205]

This kind of reasoning was altogether outside Napoleon's comprehension. He could better understand the later treachery of Bernadotte, who "became" Swedish and switched alliances from pure self-interest. But Louis' professions of "mission" and "duty" he regarded as preposterously quixotic. It was the *self-delusion* even more than the rank insubordination of the brother he had schooled as a flattering image of himself which mortified him. To have a viper in the bosom of the family was conceivable; to have a self-pitying ninny, outrageous. For his part, Louis drew grim comfort not only from his puritanical dedication to what he took to be his royal duty, but also from a paternal conviction that he might be in a position to stave off the worst of the misfortunes threatening the Dutch: the effacement of their national identity. He could hardly end the war which was at the root of their evils (though later he confessed it had been his secret ambition to secure for them the neutrality which alone could safeguard a peaceful future). But as a patriotic figurehead he meant to mobilise the fortitude necessary for endurance until more auspicious times.

The unlooked-for spectacle of a foreign overlord—and a Bonaparte at that—eager to share in their troubles was certainly flattering for the Dutch. The innumerable scriptures of the pious conduct of *"goede Lodewijk"* have some basis in fact and in that penitential conscience which Napoleon found so irksome. The more sombre the adversity, the more enhanced his reputation among the people. On January 12, 1807, a barge carrying gunpowder from the Amsterdam works to the magazines at Delft exploded while moored on the Rapenburg in the middle of Leiden. The explosion was heard in The Hague, 12 miles distant, and the red glow of the fire seen on the horizon. More than 500 houses in the centre were either totally obliterated or damaged beyond repair. Some had entombed their inhabitants in blazing masonry. Professor Kluit, Jan Luzac and a whole school of children were among the victims. Accounts of the disaster give an impression of a city under modern bombardment: the inhabitants were panic-stricken, desperate to find their families, even to haul them from burning buildings. Amidst this terror and confusion Louis showed to the full the influence of that "manie d'humanité" from which his brother was so conspicuously liberated. That same night he went directly to the centre of the devastation, joined the teams of people working the fire pumps and moving the debris, and with the regents of the city helped organise the evacuation of the injured and homeless to The Hague, Amsterdam and Rotterdam. The Huis 't Bosch was itself made available to shelter those who had suffered from the explosion. The guards of the royal household and regular troops were mobilised to help the city militia, and by working all night the fire was eventually brought under control. Only then, in the morning, did Louis return to The Hague. There he established a special commission to restore the centre of Leiden and appointed an architect to undertake the most important work. The city was exempted from hearth, *personnel* and *mobiliair* taxes for ten years and its debt assumed by the state. A national disaster fund was set up, which eventually contributed more than 1 million guilders to the work of repair. As on all such occasions, safety measures were belatedly adopted involving tight regulation of the movement of all combustible materials and the prohibition of any powder-barges from centres of population.[206]

The familiarity of Louis' style of monarchy may not have recommended itself to Napoleon, who favoured more Imperial attitudes, but it was an uncanny anticipation of the informality adopted by more recent Dutch monarchs. It was almost as if the "King" of so domestic a nation could not but help embrace the bourgeois manners of his subjects. Despite the damp climate he was very pleased with Holland, he told his mother, and he made strenuous efforts to see first hand into every corner of the Kingdom. His tours—which went from Overijssel and Gelderland to southern Brabant— were extraordinary combinations of royal progresses and the casual visits of an inquisitive public functionary. His own journal is tersely revealing of the interest he showed on these trips. At Ravenstein, the old seigneurial enclave in the south, the prison "was an underground dungeon, dark and unhealthy; he [the King, writing in the third person] suppressed it."[207] At Aerle in Brabant in 1809, where a mysterious epidemic of sweating sickness had broken out, he visited the hospitals and private houses where the superstitious population had upturned the furniture, believing them to carry the contagion. Physicians were summoned from all over the department, drugs prescribed and the fever in that notoriously unhealthy year abated.[208] In Zeeland, he attempted (with limited success) to persuade nursing mothers of the virtues of breast-feeding; in Monnikendam, Enkhuizen and Hoorn, he organised naval contract work to try to keep the almost derelict rope-makers, anchor-smiths and ship carpenters in business; and after the floods in Walcheren in 1808 and the Betuwe in 1809, he took charge of the relief work.

Nor was this extraordinary diligence entirely unreciprocated. Gogel's belief that the King had undeniably benevolent intentions (even if misled on occasions by wicked and foolish advisors) testified to a growing indulgence among many at all levels. The old republican Councillor of State Jan Hinloopen, before he died, confessed that, although

I was repelled at having to submit myself to a government imposed by a foreigner . . . you have, Sire, nationalised yourself. I can hardly conceal that the nation is content with its government and does not desire to change it. You are, then, my legitimate King.[209]

The Prussian ambassador Knobelsdorff, who had no reason at all to flatter Louis, also remarked on the warmth with which his tours into the country were received.[210] When, on a visit to Edam in 1807, Louis expressed the hope that one day the Dutch would forget he had not been born in their country, an old man is alleged to have piped up: "Since Leiden, we have already forgotten."[211] All these antics were baffling and infuriating to Napoleon. "You attach too much value to popularity," he wrote to Louis. "The end of all your actions is to seek the applause of shopkeepers while you neglect what is most important for you—energy, energy!" He further warned that "a king who, in the first year of his reign passes for being so good is a prince who will be held in contempt in the second. . . . When it is said of a king that he is a good man, that is a reign manqué."[212] Napoleon brushed aside scornfully the approaches made to him for some repayment of the 6 million guilders owing to Holland on several accounts. The Dutch, he insisted, were the richest people in all Europe; what was needed was a "firm hand" to make them provide for the needs of the treasury. But far from being chastened from these periodic dressing-downs which the Emperor handed out to his relatives like salutary doses of castor oil to naughty children, Louis' wounded dignity became steadily more raw. He began to act not just defensively but aggressively on behalf of the Dutch, more pugnaciously perhaps than a Schimmelpenninck or a Batavian Regency would have dared. Brantsen was replaced as ambassador to Paris by General Dumonceau, of whom the Emperor disapproved, without first informing him. Dutch claims in Flushing were emphasised by rejecting the French nominee for commandant and putting General van Guericke in his place. In case Napoleon should misconstrue the significance of that action, Louis explicitly demanded the recall of General Monnet, an old veteran of the Vendée and Italy, who (following French precedent) had been treating the port very much as his private domain, taking juicy cuts from both the privateering and smuggling trades.[213]

The creation first of Dutch "marshals," later of the "Order of the Union" and, in 1809 of the nobility, prompted paroxysms of wrath from St. Cloud, sensitive no doubt to the devaluing effect of a parody of a parody. Of the "marshals" Napoleon ordered, "First establish conscription and actually have an army."[214] Another source of recurrent friction was the arbitrary and haphazard patrolling of the French border by gendarmes and coastguards along the frontier between Dutch and Belgian Brabant. The area was a magnet for smugglers and notorious for endemic violence of the marine type. On September 15, 1807, the French officers took the calculated step of actually encroaching into Brabant near Breda and Bergen op Zoom and abducting a number of men allegedly suspected of complicity in contraband, one of whom was a septuagenarian. Returning to the country from his stay in Cauterets, Louis went to Antwerp to protest at the "outrage," and sent a note to the Emperor through his ambassador demanding the repatriation of the prisoners. In March 1808, the French Minister of the Interior in authentic Bonapartist style suggested that 50,000 guilders might be a suitable ransom for the men concerned.[215]

But these were merely peripheral skirmishes in a quarrel which deteriorated rapidly into an acrimonious and unrelenting feud between the two brothers. As always they revolved around the men, money and ships for the sake of which alone Napoleon had suspended the death sentence on the Dutch. Louis was above all preoccupied with retrenchment from the autumn of 1806 onwards. To this end he suppressed the Saxe-Gotha and Waldeck regiments, decommissioned part of the Helder fleet, and brought back a squadron of the Boulogne flotilla on the flimsy pretext that it needed refitting in Holland. Napoleon was not deceived. He warned the King: "I will do nothing for Holland [in the way of returning her lost colonies—Curaçao had fallen to the British in 1807] if you insist on reducing your forces at land and sea. There *must* be 50,000 men and 20 ships-of-the-line."[216]

Without conscription, of course, such numbers were purely fantastic. The most that the Dutch could conceivably afford would be 12 ships-of-the-line and, straining matters, 30,000 regular troops. Through the years which followed, Napoleon moderated his demands to 14 ships and 36,000 soldiers. Moreover, Louis was on record several times as pledging himself against the scourge of conscription. Instead he indulged in a great deal of hopeful propaganda about the National Guard, setting up a "Rear Home Guard" of village ancients and striplings to defend the Fatherland in its last peril. A cadet school was founded at Honselaardijk Castle near Utrecht and a harebrained scheme attempted whereby orphans would be recruited or drafted into military service. On each occasion that this was tried, it was greeted not only by outraged protests from the regents of the city orphanages but, in Rotterdam, by a serious riot and in Amsterdam by disturbances in which the militia were themselves participants.[217] Even had Louis contemplated conscription, the problem of paying for 50,000 men would have remained. The Emperor's answer: "Cut down severely on your interest rates" —in other words, cut interest payments, partially repudiate the debt—meant in effect compounding the one national sin with the even greater offence of bankruptcy. Napoleon failed to see why Louis was so exercised on this score. "In any case, *you* cannot save Holland so what do you suppose you are involved in?" If he did not deliver the goods, France would abandon the Netherlands to a spell of British occupation for a few months and see how the people enjoyed that experience. The protection racket was applied remorselessly.

When, in late August 1806, Prussia went to war with the Empire, the arguments over the extent of Dutch military obligations ceased to be academic. Part of the Dutch army, then at a strength of about 26,000, was to act as a division of the Army of the North, covering Marshal Mortier's rear on the Weser, while a number of its regiments occupied the still Prussian province of East Friesland. The crushing victories at Jena and Auerstädt on October 14 and 15 made the outcome of the campaign cut and dried, and increased the likelihood of the kingdom receiving Jever and East Friesland as the long-promised indemnity for the loss of Dutch Flanders. A new treaty between France and Holland in November confirmed this—but with the cession of all Flushing as an extra price. As far as the relations between the two allies went, little that was satisfactory came out of the campaign. Napoleon had asked for 30,000 Dutch troops. He got 20,000, divided into three sections: Louis' division on the Weser; Daendels' at the Ems and Münster; and Dumonceau with the remainder at Zeist, ready to move south or east as required. Given that there seemed a real danger the British might attempt at least a diversionary action in the south, the division of forces was only sensible—but it went against the Napoleonic gamble of concentrating maximum strength.

Louis was also dismayed to discover in Westphalia that Marshal Mortier retained overall command of the army; that each Dutch regiment had been assigned to a French regiment under a French general; and that Napoleon had given Mortier strict instructions as to what his wayward brother was to be permitted to do. The King's reaction was of course to play up the separate identity of his troops as much as he could. East Friesland was occupied specifically in the name of the King of Holland, and the Dutch tricolour flown in the Westphalian territories—Paderborn, Osnabrück, Münster, the Mark—occupied by his troops. Napoleon also wanted Daendels to march northeast to occupy the Hansa ports, allowing Mortier freedom to take Hanover. But Louis was reluctant to leave the Groningen-Friesland coast so exposed to naval attack, and with two-thirds of his army committed to the offensive, he continued to fret about the Scheldt and Maas estuaries. To cover that flank he took the liberty of ordering French detachments north from Antwerp, an action which sent the Emperor into transports of anger. In his customarily magnanimous style, Napoleon had decided that the Elector of Hesse-Cassel should be punished for his presumptuous neutrality during the hostilities and ordered Mortier and Louis to occupy his territories forthwith. The marshal was ready to move but needed reinforcement from the Dutch to maintain his advanced position. Deeply embarrassed by what he regarded as a gratuitously bullying gesture against an innocuous neighbouring sovereign, Louis not only withheld the troops but actually went to the trouble of apologising to an emissary of the Elector for the "inconvenience," dissociating himself from the action.[218] This was not what Europe had come to expect as the Bonaparte style, and Napoleon not surprisingly took it as a personal betrayal—another item to add to the catalogue of such infamies. Later in November he learned that Louis had unilaterally evacuated Westphalia on deciding that the campaign was properly concluded.

If the effect of the Westphalian campaign had been to persuade Napoleon of the juvenility and untrustworthiness of his brother, Louis on his side had been equally disabused. Up to the end of 1806 he retained some notion, however confused and credulous, that the Emperor truly wished him to fulfill the "duty" of protecting his subjects' interests. By the time of the publication of the Berlin Decree on November 21, he had determined to throw in his lot decisively with the losers. Arriving back at The Hague, he told a delegation that

he had been made an expatriate in spite of his own feelings; that he had no great ambition but that he could not be insensible to the honour of leading two millions of his fellow men; that he would make every effort to justify their confidence in him, and to fulfil the glorious destiny of being of service to so estimable a nation; that they could be sure that on arriving at their frontiers he had already become Dutch, and that before all else, and whatever the sufferings of the nation, he would sacrifice his happiness and his glory to alleviate them.[219]

It was during this period from November 1806 to May 1807, when he departed to Cauterets in the Pyrenees to take the waters and attempt a reconciliation with Hortense, that Louis became completely committed to Dutch rather than French interests. A succession of French quasi-spies:

Senator Garat (on the whole a perceptive and sympathetic commentator on the Dutch predicament); the police "expert" Gateau, and ambassadors Dupont Chaumont and then Alexandre, duc de la Rochefoucauld, were all kept at a safe distance and treated with varying degrees of indifference or disdain.[220] When Louis attempted to have de la Rochefoucauld replaced Napoleon refused, apologising that "I have no Englishmen in my service for I know that only the English are welcome in Holland."[221] The French sycophants whom Hortense had brought in her train were banished from the court and replaced by doughty Netherlanders, mostly over sixty, and like Chamberlain van der Dun "looking like Sancho Panza who had swallowed a jumping Jack."[222]

The Queen was wretchedly marooned in a country for which she felt none of the affection mysteriously blossoming in her husband, and a prisoner to a man whom she both despised and feared. Not surprisingly she became another of Napoleon's informants, impatient to leave the country as soon as she could. For a brief period after the death of their eldest son, Napoleon-Charles, early in May 1807, Louis hoped for a reconciliation. But her response to his long nocturnal confessions and monologues was—understandably—fatigue. Despairing of a personal approach, he tried the authentically Napoleonic device of a "Peace Treaty," unilaterally drafted but offering indemnity and oblivion, declaring that both had been at fault and both should now resolve to forget the past and "live for each other and for our children." But Hortense was altogether less keen on the "articles" which bound them not to see any other men or women without the other's consent, gave Louis the disposition of the family purse and, in effect, cut her private lines of communication with the Emperor. She withheld her signature, and from then on the two were virtual strangers to each other. Louis' bizarre combination of Romantic torments and Rousseauan bourgeois chastisement were not at all to her taste. The Beauharnais were not the stuff of which good Dutch huisvrouws were made. Louis, though, made a fair effort to turn himself into a Patriot-King, taking Dutch lessons from the royal librarian Flament and the poet Bilderdijk. By 1807, he could manage elementary but intelligible written Dutch and duly showed it off in a celebrated letter to Secretary Willem Roëll.[223]

The acid test of Louis' commitment to the Netherlands came when the rigours of the Continental system, announced in the Berlin Decree, began to bite. In actual fact that first decree was less severe than Schimmelpenninck's of June 1805, which had extended the prohibitions to neutral shipping with British cargo or that had touched British ports. But it was the mere adoption of the system as the principal weapon of Napoleon's economic war, and the Milan Decree of December 17, 1807, declaring *any* shipping with contact with Britain and any correspondence with that country lawful prize, which was certain to inflict terrible damage on Dutch trade if carried out to the letter. With the Damoclean sword hovering above his neck, Louis was forced officially to observe punctiliously the requirements of the blockade. A ploy by which the decrees were to be introduced in East Friesland and the rest of the country "in so far as their provisions are not already covered by existing legislation" only invited Imperial wrath and the implementation of the full measures. In Paris the King of Holland was reviled as a friend and ally of George III; his wharves were said to be bloated with British cargoes. While the obloquy was extravagant, Napoleon was right to suspect his brother's good faith. Louis had told a group of merchants and business-men: "You know much better than I what has to be done, but I understand that you ought to be freed from impediments; however, I can only open the door; for the rest you must look to it yourselves."[224] Later he pleaded: "One might throw oneself down into a precipice so as to drag down one's enemy with one, but how can anyone responsible for the security and well-being of so many families permit himself to be persuaded by a foreign power to hurl them and theirs into the abyss?"[225] In November 1807 Louis wrote candidly that the Emperor could force him to do anything, even close all the Dutch ports (a measure he was forced to adopt on January 30, 1808), but he would never assent to be the tool by which the Dutch people finally lost their independence.

After a year of violent abuse and hectoring, Napoleon suddenly took a different tack. Adopting an almost airy tone, expressing brotherly considera-tion for Louis' health and peace of mind, he wrote to him on March 27, 1808:

The climate of Holland does not suit you. Moreover Holland will not emerge from her ruins. Amidst the stormy currents of this world, whether there can be peace or not, there are simply no resources by which she can sustain herself. In the circumstances I have thought of you for the throne of Spain . . . can I count on you?[226]

Just let me know, he added, "yes or no." Hardened though he was to his brother's style of realpolitik, Louis gagged at the cynicism. It elicited from him a biting retort, which showed him at the same time cocooned in the mystique of his "kingship" and determined to remain with the Dutch through all their misfortunes:

I am not a governor of a province. There can be no promotion for a King other than that of heaven itself. . . . What possible right could I have to ask for an oath of allegiance from another people if I do not remain faithful to that which I have sworn to Holland when I ascended the throne?[227]

He had cast himself as one of the Netherlands' tragic heroes—an Egmont or an Oldenbarneveld—doomed to destruction for his patriotic sacrifice. He would never, he insisted, desert the sinking ship; rather, he would go down to posterity as the captain saluting from the poop as the vessel went under. It was at this time that Louis began to study with ominous care the geography of the defensive inundations. But at the back of his mind there flickered the dimmest hope that some sort of general peace might yet rescue the Dutch; that, like statesmen before him, he might still play off the mutual rapacity of their neighbours to secure some respite. For the moment, he told his min-isters, "The essential thing is to win some time."[228]

12

Inundations,
1808–1810

DORUS   *And were the people in our Land not bitterly grieved?*

FATHER   *O! Even as I remember it my heart aches with sorrow; everyone felt as though sentence of death had been passed; and
while they regretted their impotence they were forced to
swallow their chagrin—and no wonder—our national freedom
was lost; our flag had vanished, we were struck from the scroll
of peoples . . .*

————*Schoolboek,* p. 133.

"Dus, de Dijk Is Door!"

On July 4, 1810, Marshal Oudinot rode his chasseurs and cuirassiers
through Amsterdam to inaugurate, with the usual Imperial tinsel,
the funerary rites of Dutch independence. The stricken and defunct
had not, however, passed on without protest. During the final doleful days
of his reign Louis Bonaparte—"goede Lodewijk," as he enjoyed being known
—had contemplated the ultimate resort of opening the sluices at the Beemster, Purmer and Schermer and defending his capital to the last. His mortification at the crimes of the brother he referred to as "the invader" brooked
no limits. But there were many among his subjects less keen to drown in the
sea of his troubles. Denied ministerial support for what would plainly have
been a futile act of resistance, Louis abruptly abdicated in favour of his son,
then toddling about the nursery at Malmaison.

On July 1 he took a carriage pell-mell for Töplitz in Bohemia where, apparently still fearful for his life from a hired assassin of Napoleon's, he sought
the hospitality of the Emperor Francis. A week later the whole of the Netherlands north of the Waal (Brabant and Zeeland having already been annexed
in the spring) was incorporated into the French Empire as seven new departments.[1] It was the first time since the summer of 1572 that Holland had been
subjected to a foreign overlord, and the three years which followed are recorded in Dutch history as a Babylonish captivity, a final scourge before the
"redemption" of 1813.

In the period immediately preceding the annexation, as if to augur the impending doom, the Dutch were smitten with all manner of afflictions: the fire of Leiden; the self-mutilating closure of the ports in 1808; the fevers of 1809; and in the summer and autumn of the same year, the occupation of Zeeland by the British who, like Sennacherib's Assyrians before Jerusalem, succumbed to sickness rather than the sword. Of all these calamities none was more familiar or more ominous than the flood. For the Dutch, inundation was more than a periodically unavoidable freak of nature; it was a portent of disaster in the affairs of state. To those who often likened their own destiny to that of the errant Hebrews, the collapse of a dyke or the flooding of an island betokened the chastisement of a disgruntled Providence, just as surely as a defeat at sea or a run on the Amsterdam Bourse.

The perils of physical and political existence, then, were seen to be historically inseparable. At vital junctures in their national life the waters had acted as a shield—in the relief of Leiden in 1574, against the victorious troops of Farnese in 1578, and against Louis XIV a century later. Their toil to reclaim the land from the ooze of the estuaries, their endeavours in building a great mercantile city on the piles of the IJ, had been rewarded with the world's trade and the most fertile alluvial land in Europe.[2] But their amphibi-

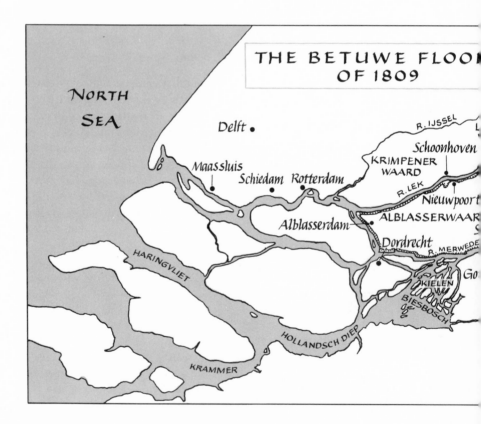

ous relationship with the rivers of northern Europe which tracked across their land had never been easy. For those cottagers living in the *lage landen* below the dykes, sometimes even below the level of the river basins, the prospect of uncontrolled flooding was dreaded. It might be possible to appease the Emperor of the French, however punitive the cost; but a swollen tide could not be accommodated. It too could turn marauder and carry off crops, livestock, houses and families as pitilessly and comprehensively as any of the armies they had endured over the past two decades.

Twice during Louis' reign, these fears were realised. On January 14 and 15, 1808, a violent storm broke up the sea dykes protecting Walcheren and put most of the island under water. Schouwe and Goeree to the north were also affected, but the most serious devastation was in Zeeland where, according to the landdrost, as many as 200 people may have been lost.[3] Middelburg, Veere and Arnemuiden were all partly or wholly submerged, and Flushing, a French port for less than two months, gave the Imperial garrison its first experience of flood conditions. The damage was substantial, though it prompted the King to organise new drainage and reclamation works around Kruiningen which became known as Lodewyks-Polder.[4] A year later another area of the country was flooded on an even worse scale. On this occasion it was not

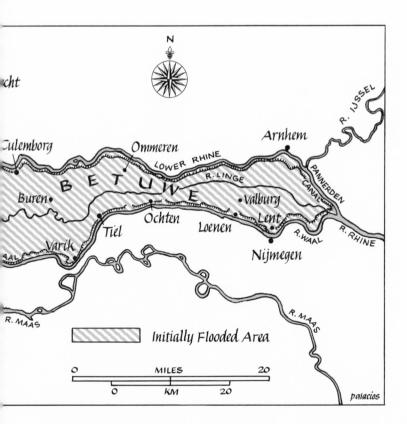

the sea which did the damage but the rivers, swollen with snow, their estuaries part-packed with ice floes, pushing massive volumes of water into channels too narrow to carry them.

By the middle of January 1809, the Rhine had risen so appreciably that Utrecht and Amsterdam were both making contingency plans in the knowledge that only the Lek dykes stood between them and disaster. The real trouble, though, was further south. Before Arnhem the Rhine divides in two. A northern arm travels through the Pannerden Canal and after Wijk-bij-Duurstede becomes known as the Lek. The southern branch, the Waal, flows past Nijmegen towards Tiel and Gorinchem and then out to the Maas estuary around Dordrecht. The almond-shaped island formed by these two rivers is known as the Betuwe, its western sectors as the Vijfheeren Land and the Alblasserwaard. The whole of the Betuwe is fertile agricultural land, rich in dairy pasture and, in the west, ploughed up for prolific grain cropping. Exceptionally cold and wet winters, however, expose the Betuwe to a number of hazards. A tributary of the Waal, the Linge, effectively bisecting the island horizontally, can at that time be transformed by rain and snow and the residue of the saturated marshes from a placid stream into an angry torrent. It joins the Waal itself at Gorinchem, so that in a particularly bad year that town might be besieged on two sides by the major and minor rivers. In the event of the eastern and upper sector of the Betuwe flooding, the Diefdijk had been built behind the town to protect it from the Linge and to shield the more densely populated Alblasserwaard from the waters.

The final problem concerned the estuary itself. To reach the sea, the Waal travelled to the Hollands Diep through the river channel called the Merwede, passing over the area submerged since 1421 and known as the Biesbosch. Between them lie the innumerable little channels—*kielen*—which sieve the water from the Merwede around the mud-flat islands through to the Diep. If these should remain frozen while the Waal upstream begins to thaw, the pressure of water builds up remorselessly—and in less than normal space in which to run its course. A lethal bottleneck is thus created.

This was exactly what happened in January 1809. To make matters even worse, the Pannerden Canal was itself iced up so that the water which would otherwise have fed the Lek flowed back instead into the Waal. Subjected to tremendous pressure, the Waal Dyke broke at two places: at Lent across the river from Nijmegen and at Loenen, 7 miles downstream. The torrents created by the gushing breaches then flowed directly into the interior of the Betuwe, marooning villages and sweeping away farms. They duly fed into the Linge, which in turn burst its banks forming a huge inland sea, kept from the Alblasserwaard only by the Diefdijk behind Gorinchem.

On January 28, Louis arrived at the town to examine the disaster firsthand. Disregarding the apprehensions of his entourage, he went up onto the Diefdijk. There gangs of peasants and townsmen had been mobilised to shore up any suspect crevices almost at the mouth of the Linge, where the flood was most severe. On the one side the town was besieged by the junction of the

Waal and Linge; on the other, as Louis recorded in his memoirs, by the rising lake, lapping at the base of the dyke as if it were a sea wall. The Waal Dyke had been cut near Dalem to try to ease the flow back into the main river; but as long as the damage at Lent and Loenen had not been repaired, this was at best a flimsy expedient. The King tried to travel upstream along the line of the dyke to see what might be done about this but could only get as far as Thiel. Immediately below the dyke was a narrow strip of dry land protecting the river hamlets like Varik and Wadenoijen, but this, as he observed, was no more than "a footpath in the midst of a sea." It was the first time he had seen the reality behind the Dutch obsession with hydraulics: cottages with their roofs just showing above the water; villages cut off from any route to safety; the drifting cadavers of drowned livestock; unknown numbers of people missing.

If one adds to the scene [he wrote] that of misery and the gloomy despair of a crowd of people who have been plunged abruptly from prosperity to a complete want of the most essential things of life; if one imagines the rigours of the season and the difficulty of crossing a terrain, sunken with rain, ice and the debris of disaster, one may have some idea of the spectacle of this desolation.[5]

He managed to return to Gorinchem—now the emergency "hoofdstad" of the department of Maasland—only to find that the water had already started to penetrate the town on the Linge side. Together with Twent van Raphorst, the Minister of the Waterstaat, and his engineers, work was organised by the King in an attempt to stave up the walls with stones, barricaded behind with paving and any other spare materials to hand. But this was a makeshift effort and to no avail. At about noon on January 31 the Diefdijk crumbled near Pedichem, and sent huge floods pouring into the Alblasserwaard right up to Sliedrecht and the delta. Nothing further could be done except to evacuate those living in the freshly flooded area. Vianen and Nieuwpoort were made reception centers, both with their bridges across the Lek intact, and the roads to Utrecht and Schoonhoven respectively still open. Louis continued to make visits to distressed areas, offering ex gratia payments and reimbursements to those who had lost fortunes or even family. He wrote feelingly of the "touching spectacle of the people, gathered around their own houses, or at the entrance to their villages, sadly repeating the words, 'Dus, de dijk is door' [So, the dyke is broken]."[6]

It was impossible to compute the real cost of the Betuwe floods, but the ministers of the Interior and Waterstaat asked for a subsidy of 6 million guilders to make good the damage not only to the water defences but to roads, bridges, canal works, and public and private buildings which had all taken a terrible pounding. The King launched another appeal and seemed gratified by the response. "Once more," he wrote, "the Dutch nation distinguished itself by its generosity. There was no-one who did not wish to contribute to the relief of his compatriots; children were seen to offer their pocket money; soldiers their pay, workers and domestics their wages." But all this spontaneous munificence produced only 687,000 florins of the hoped-for millions. Not the least remarkable feature was that Leiden, which just two years before had been the recipient of such a disaster fund, itself produced 50,000 guilders for the relief of the Betuwe.

Grave though the floods of 1809 undoubtedly were, the historian must be careful not to join contemporaries in investing them with apocalyptic significance. Rather than exposing the fragility of the governing institutions of the Dutch Kingdom, the experience, wretched as it was, showed them in a reasonably flattering light. The conduct of the King had been impeccable, as befitted a ruler with pronounced paternalist inclinations. The energy and practicality displayed by his officials under serious strain to some degree vindicated the claim of the government to act for the nation as a whole. Much of the response had, of course, been entirely traditional: that of a province overwhelmed by a familiar calamity. But equally there is no doubt that the prompt action of Twent van Raphorst, Kraijenhoff and their assistants—working with the burgemeesters of Gorinchem and Nijmegen and the landdrosten of Maasland and Gelderland—did something to mitigate where possible the extent of the tragedy. It was no small achievement to have kept open communications with the isolated villages and farmsteads of the interior long enough to get some food through in small boats, or to have protected Gorinchem as long as they did.

Nor was the government slow to draw lessons from the sombre experience. The special Commission for the Waterstaat established at Utrecht shortly afterwards (presided over by van Swinden, and including the two hydraulic engineers Blanken and Goudriaan), took good care not only to rebuild the Diefdijk on firmer foundations, but also to secure the Lek defences to the north so that they might be able to cope with any threat comparable to what had happened on the Waal. More important, the general principle of *lowering* some of the dykes—particularly on the Rhine and Yssel tributary—so as to permit a better regulation of the water and control its flow to the sea, finally prevailed over the traditional determination to endyke as steeply as possible and await the ordeal if and when it became unavoidable.

Much of the prodigious amount of work undertaken on the Waterstaat —like that in other branches of public administration such as education— presupposed the establishment of a national authority provided with both the power and the funds to make its efforts operative. As always, finance was the major problem. For while the very existence of the ministry and the general commission was a step forward, it was only in 1810 in one of his last edicts that Louis set up the hierarchy of local commissions in which ministerially appointed inspectors and engineers would collaborate with local authorities to ensure that existing defences and polders were in good condition and future improvements planned. By now the national appropriation for the Waterstaat was nearly three times the figure it had been at the start of Louis' reign,[7] but still a long way from making a national hydraulic administration a working reality.

In 1835, when the next major law concerned with these matters was enacted under King William, it preserved the outlines of the establishment of 1810 with a sufficient if not exactly generous financial base. But the times when a municipality or even a province could manage to secure itself against the threat of inundation through its own resources were over.

The Continental System and Dutch Trade

By no stretch of the imagination could the lean years of the Kingdom of Holland be described as a happy, or even painlessly stagnant time for the people of the Netherlands. But neither were they the unrelieved purgatory, when darkness covered the face of the land, commiserated in nineteenth-century historiography. That social and economic conditions were bleak goes without saying. But that very grimness drew from a community which, over the previous twenty years, had pretty well run the gamut of tribulation impressive reserves of tenacity and resilience. It was scarcely remarkable that, following the Edict of Milan (December 17, 1807), the Dutch had to endure serious hardship. There was virtually no part of Europe which, between 1808 and 1814, did not share in the palsied dénouement of the French Imperial adventure. Portugal, Spain, Italy, Austria, Russia, Prussia, Poland, Britain— and in 1811 France herself—all suffered grievously in the economic throes of the war, which ended by consuming both the revolution of the dead century and its enemies.

What was noteworthy was the capacity of Dutch society, frayed and battered as it was, to absorb such punishment without altogether falling apart. For even with extensive impoverishment among wage-earners, probably most of the poor continued to be fed and sheltered, the dykes preserved and, so far as was possible amidst the stringencies of the blockade, business carried on as usual. The year 1809, it should be remembered, was not only a year of flood, fever and invasion, but also one of the most active commercial seasons in the whole period between Amiens and Waterloo. It was only in 1810, after the last turn of the Napoleonic screw when the Netherlands were finally swallowed up in the Empire, that economic life really did threaten to grind to a halt. Until then, the fierce instinct for survival had shown itself in the efforts to evade the brutal cross-fire of the economic war in which they were reluctantly trapped. The commercial data supplied as an appendix to Gogel's *Memorien en Correspondentien*, culled principally from internal excise records, gives an impression of trade which, if not exactly thriving, was evidently not languishing either. Certainly it is at odds with any assumption that these years were a time of unmitigated catastrophe for the Dutch.

Just because the rigid prohibitions of the blockade called for ingenious, and often illegal, methods of procedure if trade was to be carried on at all, the usual indices for measuring levels of commercial activity are not very helpful. It is known, for example, that the number of vessels entering the Texel and Vlie at the north, and the Maas and Goeree in the south, fell dramatically after 1805 from an average of 2,700 (itself some 60 per cent of the prewar numbers), to 1,369 in 1806, and 1,079 in 1807. Thereafter the decline was even steeper, reaching the pitiful figure of 259 ships (144 in the south and 115 and in the north) by 1810.[8] This evidence may help to explain the penury of the Amsterdam and Rotterdam docks and harbours; but it does not supply the value of the cargoes landed, nor does it take account of the "substitute" trade routes which the rigours of the system necessitated. For obvious reasons, figures for contraband cargoes (except where confiscated) must remain imponderable. There is also scant information on the new north-south transit routes, down the Ems from Emden or Delfzijl, or down the Maas from Dordrecht via den Bosch. A good deal of traffic, especially in the more euphemistically designated commodities like "Emden sugar," was carried via the Jahde to Meppel and thence overland through Friesland to Amsterdam and the centres of urban distribution in Holland.

The official gauge of the value of Dutch trade between 1803 and 1809 gives an annual mean average (and there were important short-term fluctuations in single years) of around 175 million florins. Set against the level of 250 million florins for 1750 and about the same for the period between 1787 and 1793 this represents a decline of some 30 per cent.[9] This is substantial but hardly devastating, particularly when the unquantifiable proportion of smuggled goods is taken into account. If the end of the Dutch staple market meant a not only relatively but also absolutely receding share of the world's trade, this was a problem which the vicissitudes of the Continental system would not much affect one way or the other. Indeed since, for a time, the Netherlands became a keyhole for the distribution of colonial and manufactured goods in Europe (along with centres like Hamburg and Tonningen in Denmark), conditions were likely to distort underlying trends in favour of actually maintaining the entrepôt role. Not the least striking of Gogel's figures is his comparison between the "best" year of trade during the war period (1809) and the "best" during the years immediately following the peace (1816). In the latter case, trade rose in value by some 20 per cent, but the increase was exclusively confined to imports. In 1816, the Netherlands actually exported 8½ per cent less goods (in value) than seven years earlier:[10]

	1809	1816
Imports*	fl. 26,807,380	fl. 46,417,254
Exports	fl. 22,919,896	fl. 21,542,673

* Includes transit goods.

The surprising degree of consistency in the trade of many of the major commodities handled by the Dutch is plainly revealed in the per item figures Gogel supplied for the years between 1803 and 1816[11] (omitting of course the three years of the "incorporation"). Naturally there is a good deal of variation between commodity and commodity, but across a fairly broad range of articles there does not seem to have been a very marked disruption following the imposition of the blockade at the end of 1806. Certainly the Milan decree and the extra pressure applied on Louis by his brother do seem to have had some effect, as 1808 is for the most part a "trough" year in the pattern of trade. But in line with the British "boom" of that year, there was a marked recovery in 1809 in almost every commodity, some of which (like cheese and flax) reached an export peak that would not be surpassed in the whole period before 1825. Indeed, taken as a whole the general level of trading in the war period from 1803 to 1809 is not so far below that of the immediate postwar period of 1814 to 1816 as might be expected. True, the implications of this may not be that the Netherlands suffered less during the war than has been supposed but that it suffered so *badly*, in terms of losing the traditional staple market, that any hope of swift recovery was ill-founded. But in either case the causal role of the blockade in accentuating trends that were already latent in the Dutch economy is placed in more accurate perspective.

By far the most prosperous—or least depressed—sector of the Dutch economy was agriculture, and this was duly reflected in the trade figures. While the role of the Dutch as grain carriers was a mere shadow of the past, the production and export of oats is one of the major success stories of this period. The years 1807 and 1809 were both peak ones for this trade; the Netherlands became Britain's third major supplier in oats and seventh in wheat.[12] The wheat trade was more volatile. The harvest varied a good deal, and fairly substantial quantities continued to be imported, especially in 1803 and 1805, mostly from Germany. It was only in 1804, and spectacularly in 1809, that large surpluses were available for export. Supplies of rye—a major cereal of consumption—were derived principally from domestic production and some import, negligible amounts being exported. Dairy produce, as is well known, did especially well during the war. Butter exports (and these, it should be remembered, are official statistics which do not take account of the butter and cheese contraband openly encouraged by the Dutch government) steadily increased, from 5,093,752 *lasten* in 1803 to 9,113,206 *lasten* in 1806. Thereafter they fell back a little, but not so seriously as to damage the thriving trade to any real extent. Sweet-milk cheeses had an even more spectacular record, climbing from 16,757,812 *ponden* in 1803 to the colossal figure of 25,275,204 tons in 1809.

Root crops like madder and flax showed comparable trends: 1804, 1805, 1808, and 1809 were all good years for the export of fine madder, even though the average figure was around a third less than the postwar "norm." Flax was one of the few commodities which showed a dramatic upswing in 1808—the year of the closure of the Dutch ports—a trend which continued the following year. Interestingly, the years of high exports did not coincide with high import years. And as Flemish flax (like hops) became less accessible, the domestic production in the Netherlands itself was contributing proportionately more to this trade. The extensive importation of British manufactured goods is least well represented in this series of figures, partly because only some of the minutely subclassified textiles qualified for duty, and partly, of course, because so much of those wares arrived in the Kingdom as contraband. There are no figures at all for manufactured woollens, and none for linens between

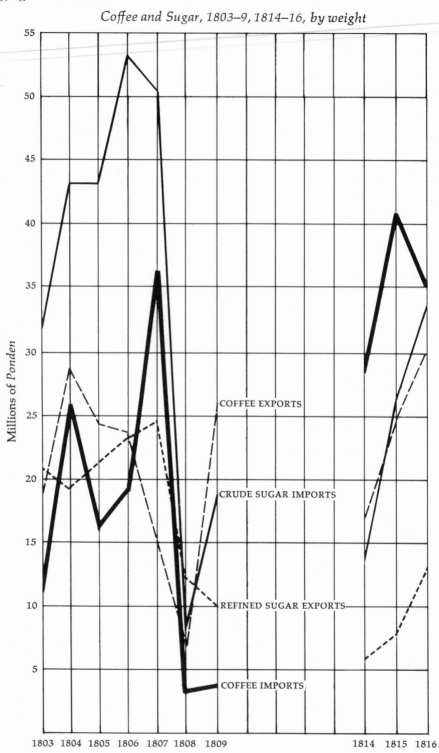

Coffee and Sugar, 1803–9, 1814–16, by weight

COFFEE EXPORTS

CRUDE SUGAR IMPORTS

REFINED SUGAR EXPORTS

COFFEE IMPORTS

Millions of Ponden

1803 1804 1805 1806 1807 1808 1809   1814 1815 1816

Grain, 1803–9, 1814–16, by volume

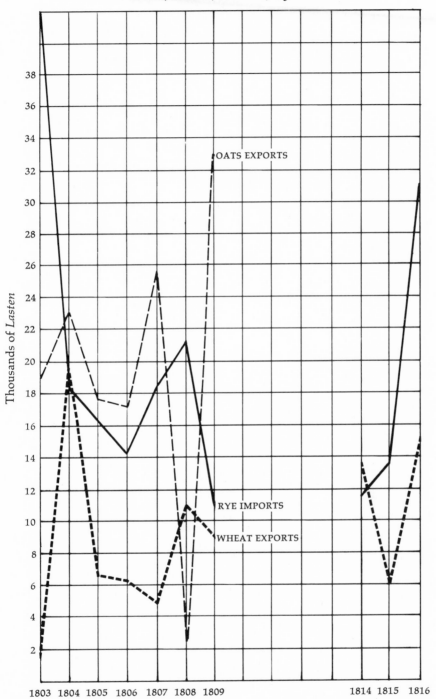

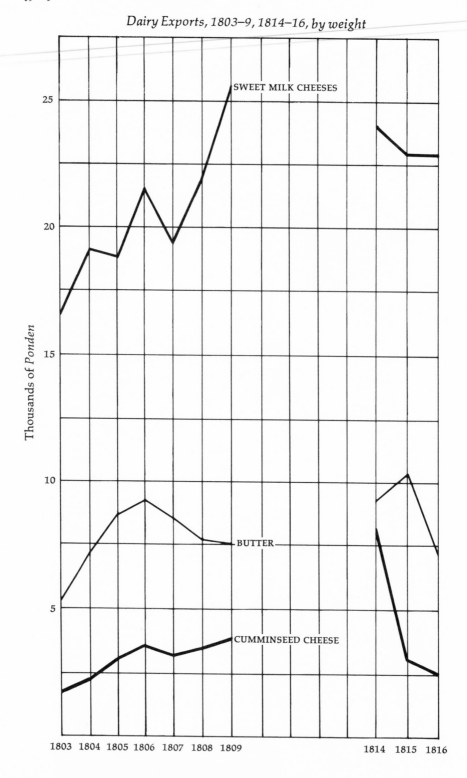

Dairy Exports, 1803–9, 1814–16, by weight

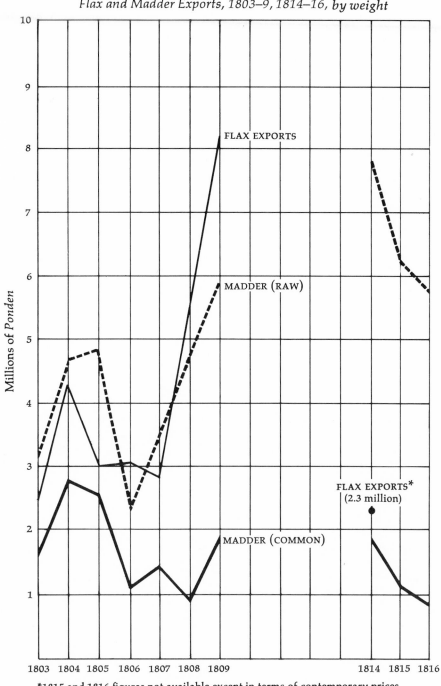

Flax and Madder Exports, 1803–9, 1814–16, by weight

FLAX EXPORTS

MADDER (RAW)

FLAX EXPORTS*
(2.3 million)

MADDER (COMMON)

Millions of *Ponden*

10

9

8

7

6

5

4

3

2

1

1803 1804 1805 1806 1807 1808 1809   1814 1815 1816

*1815 and 1816 figures not available except in terms of contemporary prices

1806 and 1809. Imports and exports of silkstuffs rose appreciably *after* the introduction of the Continental system; imports of manufactured cottons reached a peak in 1804, before falling back somewhat.

Of greater significance than manufactured goods was the trade in the colonial raw materials which the Dutch had traditionally processed and re-exported. Despite the facilities offered by the Americans, and on which Dutch entrepreneurs pinned a lot of hope, imports of raw cotton declined a good deal from their prewar level, rising only gently in 1803 and 1806. Yet imports of crude sugar, mostly from the Caribbean and Surinam, rose spectacularly after 1803, so that in 1806 and 1807 over 50 million pounds were imported, one way or another, into the country. After the loss of both Surinam and Curaçao, the supply dried up; and although it managed a slight recovery in 1809 to some 17,000 pounds, it only reached the earlier peak in the 1820's when the colonies were restored to the Dutch. To keep the picture in perspective, it is worth noting that in 1807 the Netherlands exported three times as much *refined* sugar as in the "boom" year of 1816. Imports of indigo and dyewood show a similar pattern. Though export figures tail off with the more rigorous application of the Continental system, the peaks of 1807 and 1809 reflect the strength of the demand for these goods in the heart of Continental Europe. Finally, the nicely poised balance between wines on the one hand and spirits on the other just about favoured the Dutch. For even without the hidden contraband figure, the exports of gin and *eaux de vie* were, despite the laments of the Schiedam distillers, greater than in any other year between 1802 and 1816.

From this abundance of information it must be apparent that, far from staggering to a dead halt, Dutch merchants were able to adapt their businesses to the rigours of the Continental system at least sufficiently to avoid complete collapse. Of course the pattern was by no means uniform across the board. Small traders who had not the risk capital to chance in highly speculative but highly profitable—and often uninsured—ventures were inevitably the ones who suffered most. A new mercantile geography favoured areas of the Republic which had languished under the old Republic: the mouth of the Ems at Emden and Delfzijl; the southern curve of the Maas past den Bosch; the turn of the Rhine past Arnhem; all became important trading depots. Versatility was essential for survival, and it was a quality at which many of the Dutch were adept. If neither the British nor the French would let a Vlaardingen fisherman earn his living from honest toil at the nets, he could and did turn his expert knowledge of the creeks and inlets of the delta to profit for those who needed to be hidden. The calendar of trade was equally volatile, its rhythms from month to month very staccato, depending on all kinds of political and military imponderables. When the members of the legislature complained to Louis in the late autumn of 1807 that "trade has suffered violent shocks; not to say it is almost destroyed and reduced to insignificant enterprises,"[13] they were not altogether guilty of disingenuous hyperbole. For towards the later part of what had been a fairly healthy year, the government had decided to apply the embargo much more stringently.

American and other neutral vessels had been turned away from Dutch ports and some cargoes even seized. Conversely, while the first half of 1808 was an appallingly barren time for commerce both legal and illegal, British and American traders found that by mid-July there was already a perceptible casualness in the enforcement of the Milan decree. Suspect vessels were being turned away rather than seized; and though the Dutch ports remained firmly fastened, there were always other byways and loopholes through which the precious merchandise could find its way to European markets. It was the embarrassing phenomenon of colonial goods of transparently Anglo-Dutch provenance actually undercutting French contraband in Paris which so galled the Emperor that he sealed off France from all Dutch goods whatsoever on September 16.

Whatever the short-term fluctuations, the one consistent factor in maintaining the quiet momentum of Dutch commerce was precisely that which the blockade was most meant to damage: the liaison with Great Britain. When Napoleon raged to his brother that his Kingdom had become little more than a receiving bay for British goods, and that he must be either a dolt or a villain to pretend otherwise, there was some substance to the charge. The copious evidence available permits only one conclusion: that the Dutch systematically connived at circumventing the Continental system as best they could and that, from the King down to the owner of a small flat-bottomed boat in the reeds of the delta, they all played their part in keeping trade going by *whatever* means were to hand. When, in the celebrated tirade from Schönbrunn in 1809, Napoleon told Louis that the Dutch "have energy all right—for smuggling," he was not so far from the truth. Of course they were not alone in this; *French* exports to Britain in wines particularly rose appreciably after 1807, and the Emperor was not averse to liberality with what he called his "joujoux"—the special trading licenses granted when the occasion arose.

But the fact remains that until the annexation in the summer of 1810, the embargo on British goods in the Netherlands was highly porous. Between 1805 and 1809, the Dutch were Britain's third best individual customer after Russia and Denmark. Around 4.8 per cent of all British exports went to that destination and, more significantly, 16 per cent of her colonial re-exports.[14] On the other hand, during the last year in which Hamburg was available to the British as an entrepôt, 1806, almost six times as much cargo was distributed from there as from either the Maas or Amsterdam stations.[15] Even after the incorporation of the Hansa ports into the Empire, Tonningen on the Jutland coast and later Heligoland, occupied by the British from August 1807, were alternative distribution points to the Netherlands. From the figures below it will be apparent that the fluctuations in British exports were far sharper during these years than those of Dutch imports into Britain, since the latter depended more on the conditions of domestic agriculture than any political or military considerations.[16]

It would be going too far to suggest that the Continental system was so blatantly flouted by the Dutch that it had no effect whatever on the pattern of trade. British exports to the Netherlands never recovered their very high level of 1800–02, the last year representing almost twice the values of the average for the 1789–92 period. But despite the rather jolting tempo of the trade, it remained of considerable importance in the British effort at embargo-breaking. Often, moreover, a sudden deceleration in the number of licenses granted by the British Privy Council for shipments to the Nether-lands reflected anxieties about prospects rather than the reality of a serious interruption. The change of regime in 1805, together with Schimmelpenninck's many public professions that he meant to take the embargo seriously and the mere publication of the May prohibition, did as much to ruffle the feathers of the Anglo-Dutch traders as any effort to enforce it.

The same situation was true in 1807 after the introduction of the Berlin Decree. In the first quarter of the year, only seventeen licenses were issued, whereas in the second and third quarters the numbers were, respectively, eighty-two and sixty-two.[17] Insurance premiums which had stood at 6 guineas

Dutch Imports from Britain. Base 100 (1797)= £1,466,000

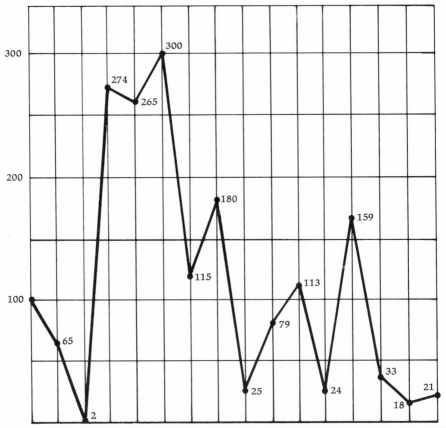

SOURCE: H. R. C. Wright, *Free Trade and Protection in the Netherlands 1816–1830*, pp. 30–1. Cambridge, England, 1955.

at the beginning of 1806 shot up to 10 after the news of the Berlin Decree. But the consternation was brief. At about the same time in the spring of 1807, the American ambassador in Paris, General Armstrong, received an assurance from Napoleon that the neutrality of American ships would be respected, and Louis began to issue special licenses permitting trade through such vessels. By May, the insurance premiums in Britain were down to 7 guineas, and they sank further to 5 and even 4 in the months that followed.[18] On May 19, T. H. van Liender—Boulton and Watt's correspondent in Rotterdam, through whom a steam engine for the Katwijk-Rhine Canal had been ordered—reassured the English firm that "your fears on the subject of this importation based on the strict decrees against the introduction of objects manufactured in England are . . . without foundation."[19] In the event, the machine was shipped directly from Hull to Rotterdam, where it arrived on August 9.

The brazenness with which the prohibitions of the embargo were ignored was extraordinary. Warehouses in Rotterdam and Amsterdam were stuffed with sugar, indigo and coffee that was exceedingly unlikely to have originated

Dutch Exports to Britain. Base 100 (1797)= £530,000

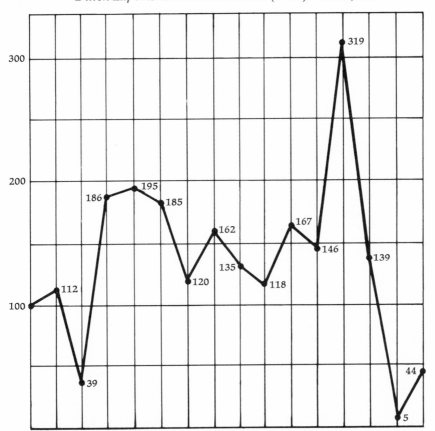

Source: H. R. C. Wright, *Free Trade and Protection in the Netherlands 1816–1830*, pp. 30–1. Cambridge, England, 1955.

in the East Indies as their entrepreneurs devoutly insisted. While large quantities of this colonial produce arrived in neutral bottoms, it was by no means uncommon for British vessels to make for Emden, there receive false papers "Americanising" the ship, and to proceed to their destination unmolested. "Emden," said Sir Francis Baring, is "for Amsterdam what Tonningen is for Hamburg . . . the costs defrayed by a stop in these ports does not exceed 2 or 3 per cent."[20] Should the merchant prefer to err on the side of prudence, it was no trouble to discharge the cargo at Emden, from where it would be transported via Delfzijl, Aurich and the Lemmer to Amsterdam. Back-water harbours and village markets received a new lease of life by their fortuitous placement on the new routes for both legitimate and smuggled goods. Pekela and Winschoten in Groningen were transformed in this way, as was the dairy market at Sneek in Friesland. Further south, Katwijk on the coast between Scheveningen and Zandvoort was virtually an unofficial terminus for the boats from Gravesend, just as the redundant fishing port at Maassluis now made its livelihood through clandestine goods and services (especially correspondence) from Harwich. Whole new ancillary trades proliferated to service the contraband: the highly specialised forging of ships' certificates and lading papers (at which Dutch printing skills proved very handy); nocturnal pilotage around the mudflats and reed-beds of the Maas estuary, or between the sand dune islands off the Friesland coast. There was even an agency specialising in the supply of instant Dutch "sailors," who could be put on board fraudulently certified merchant ships to lend an air of native authenticity should they seem likely to be searched.[21]

None of this could have happened unless not only the Dutch authorities but also a good number of French officers, coastguards and sailors had seen an ideal opportunity to line their own pockets. Even in 1804, the French consul at Rotterdam made no secret of his practice of imposing a private tariff of 3–5 per cent *ad valorem* in return for permitting virtually any cargo to be landed. The corruption of the French marine on Walcheren was a byword amongst the Zeelanders, at least until the end of 1807.[22] Even before the Edict of Milan was published, *Dutch* customs had begun to seize suspect British cargoes; and by September ships were returning to England with their goods undischarged. Insurance rates rose steeply once more, and although some American, Swedish and Danish ships were still taking on cargoes at Liverpool, far more were discharging their own goods in England and abandoning the special Dutch licenses.

The period of real severity lasted from September 1807 to the late spring of 1808. Very little got through then even as contraband, and the smuggling itself became more expensive and more dangerous. The rate for clandestine pilotage around the Texel went up to 20 guilders a day, and secret disembarcation points were necessarily less accessible for shipment of goods on the main routes to central Holland or the Rhine. A middleman at Katwijk who had been accustomed to take a 10 per cent commission in return for guaranteeing freight to Amsterdam, insurance against confiscation included, was himself apprehended by the French. For a while, at any rate, both the King and

Gogel seemed determined, with van Maanen's aid, to enforce the Milan decree in the hope that this would induce Napoleon to permit the free entry of Dutch goods to France and Germany and the lowering of tariffs on needed imports like grain, coal and hops from Flanders. But by the middle of the year it was apparent that the Emperor had no intention of doing anything of the kind, and that the Dutch were now effectively blockaded by sea and by land—a position which Napoleon made official on September 16 when he prohibited the entry of any Dutch goods whatsoever from the Empire.

This was itself a reaction to the evident relaxation of vigilance which had also become apparent to the British by April and May. It may well have been true, in Louis' words, that trying to stamp out smuggling in the Maas estuary was like "preventing the skin from sweating,"[23] but it is also true that after this short spell of enforcement (which after all did have a real impact), the government's attitude reverted to complaisance. Gogel quarrelled with van Maanen, the Minister of Justice, as to which of them should have jurisdiction over the customs police. Van Maanen took exception to the agents the Minister of Finance had posted at Katwijk and Brielle, suspecting them of being less than remorseless in their pursuit of the suspected. In fact Gogel's attitude, like the King's, was very equivocal. He had persuaded Louis in June to grant special "royal licenses" for the export of butter and cheese to "friendly and neutral powers," which in reality meant the resumption of the dairy trade to Britain. His attitude to French privateers, authorised by the Milan decree to take as lawful prize any vessel or goods suspected of British taint, was absolutely unchanged from the summer of 1798 when he personally sought to extirpate them as a species of marine vampire.[24]

La Rochefoucauld had cause on many occasions to complain of the treatment accorded to such ships. The *Poisson Volant*, for example, had taken a ship with English cargo, had then been intercepted by a Dutch frigate and forced to Zierikzee, where the English crew was freed and the privateer arrested! The *Hebe* had caught two small Dutch craft red-handed but had been pursued by two English brigs and obliged to make for the Texel, where it was refused entry to the harbour and its papers confiscated and sent to Gogel. The *Glaneur*, with a prize cargo of smoked salmon (to be sure a Dutch, not a British export), needed to shelter from the weather on the Scheldt roadsteads; but as an English frigate blocked the way it had been forced to Helvoetsluys, from where it hoped to get crew and cargo to Antwerp overland. Once again it was refused permission to dock and, although Gogel was himself more accommodating, the ship was evicted in mid-December.[25] By contrast, when a little American fleet arrived at the Texel on April 20, 1808, (three of whose ships had colonial goods of doubtful provenance aboard), the worst that happened was their expulsion with cargoes undischarged.

For its part the Privy Council was prepared to help the "thaw" along by issuing a number of "general licenses" to small craft, good for any number of trips. Earlier in the year, they had been willing to take advantage of the South Holland fishermen's eagerness to continue trafficking in contraband by issuing special "fishing licenses" permitting them to fish herring in the North Sea and to dry and salt *stokvis*, provided they landed at Yarmouth or Harwich, and took on letters (and no doubt one or two other suitable commodities of a non-piscine nature). It was only the strong objection of the Scottish fisher fleets which put paid to those licenses in June. A further category allowed imports of raw silk—which Gogel's figures show as an important Dutch export—in exchange for British manufactures, but this never developed into a commerce of any significance. The year 1808 was in fact better for Dutch exports to Britain than vice versa—and after Napoleon's draconian prohibition on September 16, Louis was forced to clamp down severely once again in the late autumn.

In December, however, it was still possible for letters and even people to get through from England to the Netherlands in a roundabout fashion. We have an excellent account, reproduced by Professor Crouzet, of one such journey.[26] Having equipped himself with an American passport, the traveller embarked at Gravesend on a boat flying one of the many neutral "flags of convenience"—in this case that of Kniphausen—together with 30 guineas in gold. The boat dutifully did some fishing for cod and sole, making sure that the boxes of sugar and coffee were well stacked under the fish crates. On approaching the Dutch coast, the skipper disguised two of his passengers as sailors, and hid English newspapers (which fetched a good price in Holland), together with a pack of 500 letters, at the bottom of a sack of potatoes. The two disguised men were supplied with aliases as survivors of a shipwreck who had been rescued from a Bremener vessel which had, alas, lost all their baggage and papers. Offshore the boat was searched by a coastguard patrol whose crew, the narrator added, were given a liberal lacing of grog to keep them cheerful, before proceeding to Maassluis. The two "shipwreck" victims were then led to the local customs commissioners, who inspected the ship and removed its papers; having exchanged "that infallible *passe-partout*, some louis d'or" and the signature of a declared purpose of the voyage, the authorisation duly arrived after a comfortable three-day wait. The two men then simply went on their way unhindered to Rotterdam.

The second period of stringency was as short-lived as the first. In the spring of 1809 Louis insisted that "this country can no longer physically sustain the closure or the blockade both by sea and by land . . . I am pressed on all sides to open the ports."[27] On March 31 he duly permitted the export of agricultural produce and textiles, and the import of naval supplies, drugs and a miscellany of raw materials. All, of course, were to be handled strictly by neutrals and none was to be of British provenance. It was in effect a return to the situation obtaining between the Berlin and Milan edicts. But given the tightness of the British blockade in both Europe and the Indies, the notion that any such goods would be "clean" was quite obviously disingenuous. On June 30, moreover, the King authorised landings of American ships in Dutch ports on condition they had not touched British harbours; a further decree specifically licensed the import of rice, quinine, American cotton and "Java" coffee and sugar. These concessions so incensed Napoleon that this brother was obliged to rescind them on July 31. But there had been time enough for the door to be edged, and then pushed wide open, to the old traffic.

Between April and the end of July 1809, the British Privy Council issued 523 export licenses for the Netherlands and 679 import licenses from Holland to Britain. In the third quarter there were 323 export licenses, and even in August–December, when the British were actively involved in the Walcheren campaign, 133 export and 66 import licenses were granted.[28] Efforts were made to compensate for the military fiasco in Zeeland by turning the province into a British entrepôt rather like Heligoland. The Royal Navy was ordered not to molest shipping between Walcheren and the Maas, and re-exports via the island during the relatively brief period of the British occupation were put at £108,000. Imports from the Netherlands reached an unprecedented level of £1,722,000—mostly in cereals and silks.[29] In that year Britain took more grain from the Netherlands than from any other source. So not only did the Dutch contravene the spirit and the letter of the Emperor's economic master weapon; they actually ensured that its intended victim was spared the near certainty of a major dearth in 1810 as a result of this massive transfusion of grain. Moreover, the boom in colonial goods was blatantly obvious in the central depots of Holland. Between October 17 and November 15 the following imports were landed:[30]

Practically all these cargoes had arrived in Dutch ships from the northern

Quay	Goods	Quantity
Harlemmerboom	coffee	1,365,307 Amsterdam pounds
(37 vessels)	sugar	651,885
	indigo	26,855
	cotton	23,075
	dyewood	113,080
Nieuwebrugsboom	coffee	1,235,341
(40 vessels)	sugar	623,810
	indigo	25,280
	cotton	74,080
	dyewood	168,013
Rouaansche-kaai	coffee	979,538
(56 vessels, Oct. 16–Nov. 25)	sugar	797,223
	indigo	24,889
	cotton	5,657
	dyewood	201,936
Kransboom	coffee	1,220,925
(40 vessels, Oct. 22–Nov. 11)	sugar	858,490
	indigo	27,829
	cotton	46,830
	dyewood	129,334

route via Aurich, the Lemmer, Harlingen and Zwolle. The ports from the Jever to Harlingen were very busy as the "Emden circuit" became once more an essential outlet for colonial produce. But the southern route was scarcely inactive. A group of seventy-seven Rotterdam merchants petitioned Gogel to refuse Councillor of State Willem Willink permission to land China tea.[31] Like de Severijn and others among the Amsterdam banking community, Willink had the capital to sink into high-risk, high-profit operations and made, at least for a while, handsome killings on them. Gogel, however, was obliged to point out to the merchants that their own objections stemmed not from any uprightness regarding the embargo laws, but from a fear that Willink might swamp the market in tea and coffee from which they themselves were doing very nicely.

The south was obviously thriving on this kind of business. Even at the end of 1808, the Rotterdam dealer T. T. Cramer reported to van der Heim, the Minister for the Colonies, that 400 bales of coffee had been openly unloaded off the *trekschuit* from Zierikzee and stored in a warehouse in the Bierstraat.[32] Both Zierikzee and Middelburg were reputed to be brimful of colonial merchandise. On January 10, 1809, he reported another consignment of 500 cases of Jamaican sugar in the Besenmakkersteersteeg and 400 bales of coffee at the Jufferstraat. He himself had seen thirty-five cartloads of coffee wheeled over there; it was reliably said there was more to come from Haringvliet and Papendrecht. In March and April he provided even more information about these routes, suggesting that a veritable flotilla (one vessel of which was alleged to have had 1,800 bales of coffee) had docked at Zeeland, from where it had been brought, with gunboat escort, to Rotterdam —to unload with no fuss at all. The situation had become so safe that English ships lying off Goeree could be victualled by small Dutch cutters. Even though such vessels flew odd kinds of flag—or, in accordance with a special order of the Privy Council, the Dutch tricolour (manufactured in Manchester), or even at times the flag of the French marine—no-one supposed that they could be anything other than British.

The year 1809 was, then, a bumper one both for smuggling and for a commerce that was at any rate quasi-legitimate under the generally permissive edicts of the King of Holland. It exemplified the Dutch attitude, which was not that they actively wished to sabotage the French war effort or to be especially friendly towards the British, but rather that business was business. Nothing so trifling as a European war or some madcap design concocted by Napoleon to strangle the British Empire was going to get in the way. It did not, after all, escape the Dutch that the Continental system was meant not only to damage the British economy but to afford especial protection and advantage to the French. Nor that while the Emperor, pillaging half the world, might be able to afford to sacrifice his own Atlantic trade the Dutch could not. That was why his riposte to Louis' communication of the Amsterdammers' complaints— "And do you suppose the merchants of Bordeaux do not also complain?"[33]—cut so little ice. The importance of the staple trade still continued to be proportionately far greater for the Dutch than the French.

And it was, Louis appreciated, all the more vital to cling to whatever they could, since so much of the rest of the Dutch economy—and most conspicuously its manufactures—lay in genuine dereliction.

The Dilapidation of Dutch Industry[34]

It comes as no surprise to discover that the relative buoyancy of Dutch agriculture and the conservation of at least a modicum of trade through all the rigours of the Continental system were not accompanied by any industrial recovery. The interests of the manufacturing and commercial sectors were not necessarily compatible. Where the sensitive issue of tariffs was concerned, their bickering was of long standing—dating back at least to the controversy over the "Free Port" proposals of 1751, and renewed with much acrimony in the reign of William I. The blockade-breaking activities of entrepreneur-bankers like Willink and Severijn threatened already ailing domestic industries by importing cheaper manufactured goods from Britain. Hence the tendency of aggrieved industrialists to appear "law-abiding" and point the finger of accusation at the renegade councillors of state, rather, one feels, to the embarrassment of the Minister of Finance. In Zwolle, for example, button-makers registered bitter complaints to the effect that the market was flooded with cheap British goods; and a hosiery manufacurer who had set up his business at Haarlem on the assumption that the embargo would protect him from British competition was in fact forced under by cheaper imports coming from Amsterdam.[35] There was one industry obviously and directly adversely affected by the constriction of trade: that of shipbuilding, and all its associated crafts such as anchor-smithing, compass and rope-making, and sailcloth weaving. Of all the major traditional Dutch enterprises, this was probably in the very worst condition. The last surviving "Groote Scheep-makkerij" at West Zaandam (even in the 1790's there had been seven) had built exactly one vessel between 1803 and 1808. Its business for the Greenland and St. David's whale fisheries had collapsed with the virtual elimination of that industry; the town itself was rapidly depopulating, and the chain of skills from masters to apprentices which had won the admiration of the world was broken for good. Of the sixty-six sawmills remaining, only a bare handful had any work. In the Amsterdam yards, where in 1800 there had been work for some 2,000, just 500 men were employed 8 years later. The ancillary trades based on Amsterdam and the North Holland yards were likewise in wretched condition. In 1811 the prefect of what had become the "Department of the Zuider Zee," de Celles, reported that of 3,000 sail-makers in North Holland in 1806, only 387 were left in work. Krommenie, which had been one of the principal centres of this trade, had nineteen shops left in 1808. Edam and Enkhuizen had, respectively, five and one carpenters' yards left to them. At Hoorn just three rope-makers remained in business.[36]

The deterioration of what was left of the shipbuilding industry in the Netherlands accelerated after 1806. This was partly because of the scarcity and expense of essential raw materials—pitch, hemp and timber—all of which

came from the Baltic, but also because of the decay of demand brought about
by the loss of almost all the Dutch colonies and the capture of their trade by
the other maritime powers. Even more alarming was the regressive effect
of costly supplies and disappearing markets on those few concerns which
had managed to hold their own up to 1802–03. Production of bombazines at
Amersfoort, for example, between 1804 and 1808 halved from 39,000 pieces to
19,877; and much the same was true of textiles at Almelo and Enschede.[37] At
Eindhoven the manufacturers of bays, says and kerseys, badly hit by the
rise in the price of raw wool, cut back their production by nearly two-thirds.
Other new initiatives were stunted in the same way: the ribbon-makers at
Bolswaard in Friesland, the hosiery-makers in Groningen, and the hatmakers
in Geertruidenberg were all cases in point. On a more esoteric plane, those
highly specialised trades for which Amsterdam was rightly famed virtually
suspended production when they ran out of essential supplies. Jewish diamond
and gemstone cutters out of work added a further burden to the poor of the
Kehillah, and the celebrated Dutch "giraffe" pianos—an extravaganza of
timber of a scale to match local closets and wardrobes—retreated further before the all-conquering Broadwoods.[38] More seriously, those intrepid spirits
who had actually established enterprises during the war like the blue vitriol
works at Deventer found themselves in severe embarrassment during the
Anglo-Danish War of 1807; or, like the promising Rotterdam glue factory,
dependent on adequate supplies of fish waste, collapsed altogether within a
few years of their establishment.

There were a few commodities where raw materials vanished altogether,
such as Setubal salt after 1805 and Merino wool; but more commonly it was
relative scarcity driving up price which made the Dutch manufactures uncompetitive even on the home market. Once again the Dutch dealers often
profited from this. The cotton printers and dyers of Haarlem, New Amstel
and Rotterdam protested about the sharp increase in standard dyes such
as cochineal and indigo which were being exported by Amsterdam traders and
which, up to 1807 anyway, were handicapping the prospects of resisting the
influx of British ready-mades. Extravagant prices charged for tanning and raw
hides for the tanneries, and Baltic grain for the distilleries, drew protests from
the innumerable small producers of these goods throughout the country. The
Imperial prohibition on the export of the much cheaper Flemish grain only
compounded these problems, just as the traditional Brabant lompen shoddy
used for the Dutch paper mills became prohibitively dear, putting the
Dutch paper industry out of business in home as well as foreign markets. The
same factors affected basic fuels. Brabant charcoal timber (what there was of
it) and domestic peat, both subject to penal tariffs and excise duties, helped
send the production costs of a great range of industries with slender margins—
from pottery and brickmaking to distilling and sugar refining—well above the
threshold of competitiveness.

Problems of supply, while severe enough, were not always insuperable.
As elsewhere in Europe, the more enterprising manufacturers met the challenge of the blockade by ingenious substitutions which occasionally proved a

worthwhile long-term economy. Domestic tobacco leaf, particularly the variety cultivated around Amersfoort, began its long and prolific career as American leaf became exceedingly dear. Beet sugar required intensive propaganda by Dutch agronomists and the Prins-Stedehouder Lebrun, Governor-General after 1810, before it was successfully transplanted from northern France to Holland; but with supplies of cane cut off, it eventually won grudging acceptance. The fine-quality clays from Namur and Cologne used for Gouda pipes were replaced with cruder Winschoten clay, which nevertheless produced an acceptable and smokeable commodity. Scottish lead was replaced by Westphalian for the potteries and the paint and whitewash works, shipped up the Rhine from Aachen and Düsseldorf. Even the British monopoly on mustard powder was relieved by the first successful domestic crop raised in South Holland and in Groningen. On the other hand the brewers of Dutch Brabant, by their own account at least, were unable to raise hops for their beer anything like the quality of those they had been accustomed to importing cheaply from Flanders.[39]

In any event, it was the erosion or disappearance of markets which was the decisive blow in demolishing the reveries of a return to the Dutch staple entrepôt entertained alike by both Gogel and Gijsbert van Hogendorp. The reasons for this market shrinkage were principally, but not wholly, exogenous. Contraction in the sales of locally brewed beer, particularly in Zeeland, Holland and Dutch Brabant, was attributed to changes in patterns of consumption and to the lure of those unwholesome beverages tea, coffee and the demon gin. Haarlem brewers even complained that the decline of the custom of plying beer to apprentice ships' masons and carpenters had done untold damage to the local trade—but all such laments had been made long before in the previous century.

The high incidence of domestic taxation on a number of commodities (beer being *freed* of duty in 1805) was also blamed for difficulties experienced by soap-boilers and bleachers obliged to pay the *zeep* excise and, more improbably, by the salmon curers of Schoonhoven (since *zalm* was a most erratically collected tax) for the loss of their trade. More obviously, the general change in purchasing habits among the Dutch urban population (as elsewhere in northern and western Europe) from relatively expensive long-lived garments to lower quality, cheaper manufactured goods—cotton prints and coarse woollen worsteds and kerseys—was taking its toll of even the woebegone remnant of the Dutch textile industry. There were isolated instances of attempts in the Netherlands to use factory methods and sharp entrepreneurial marketing to compete with British and German imports: the black pseudo-jasper ware made in Bergen op Zoom; the splendid patent "Saving Lamp" made by C. F. Schmidt in Utrecht (though his boast that he produced 3,000 in 20 months scarcely suggests streamlined production);[40] a cotton print factory at Zutphen, and a hose and says mill at Harderwijk.

But these were conspicuous exceptions. The rule was a surrender by the Dutch, not just of their neighbouring but of their home markets to the invasion of cheaper imports. And by no means all of these were British. Linens from Namur and Liège and light textiles from a string of mills dotted down the Maas and Rhine—from Elberfeld, Crefeld and Düsseldorf—all found ready markets in the Netherlands, exactly reversing the trade pattern of the seventeenth century. Moreover, those Dutch manufactures which approximated most nearly to the conditions obtaining in Belgium and Westphalia—with cheap labour recruited from the countryside, semi-mechanised production and river-borne freight running north-south as at Eindhoven—stood the best chance of survival.[41]

There can be no doubt that the Dutch were also savagely punished by being the men in the middle of a Franco-British economic as well as military conflict. The British blockade, as we have seen, inflated the price of colonial raw materials; it also robbed the Dutch of colonial outlets for small-scale manufactures. The bottle-makers of Middelburg, for example, perished when their markets in the Antilles, Surinam and the East Indies vanished. But the most severe handicap was imposed by the ruthless French manipulation of tariffs, not merely to bar British goods but more aggressively to capture Continental markets for Imperial goods so as to counter-balance the naval supremacy which so infuriated Napoleon. After September 1808, Dutch finished and semi-processed goods were either prohibited altogether or effectively barred by high tariffs from many of their traditional markets. Tobacco, snuff and sugar from Holland and Groningen lost their best customers in Germany and Switzerland for just this reason. The troubles affecting Gouda pipes on which the working population of that city primarily depended is another illustration of the same process. As a result of their prohibition, first from Britain, then from Prussia and finally from the German and Belgian departments of the Empire, production in that city contracted from 29 ovens at the beginning of the wars to just 12 by the end, and from employment for 7,000 to 2,000.

Perhaps still more extraordinary, the French continued to dangle the possibility of a customs union with the Dutch "sooner or later" at the same time as they were doing their utmost to extrude Dutch products from any Imperial markets. Antwerp and the renascent Belgian towns were, of course, the principal beneficiaries of this policy. To be just, the Emperor was only using his military power to restore the fortunes of that port, just as two centuries earlier the Dutch had used theirs to kill it. Trade up the Rhine, which might earlier have gone to Utrecht and Amsterdam or to Dordrecht and Rotterdam, was now diverted deliberately to the Scheldt and Flanders. Commodities like the wines of the Rhine and Mosel, which for generations Hollanders and Zeelanders had marketed in the southern Netherlands, was now excluded as "bad wine" in favour of French produce, or else handled by Belgian dealers direct. Indeed, it was only when they had been cut off from Flanders, Hainaut and Brabant by prohibitions more rigorous than anything the Spanish or Austrians had ever imposed, that the Dutch appreciated how important a captive market those areas had been—a mercantilism William I would later rather clumsily try to reassert. The Zeelanders were especially upset by the loss of Axel and Cadzand (in *Dutch* Flanders), which had formerly been used as depots for exports to the Flemish hinterland and for those essential imports of flax and hops that no longer materialised. Middleburg salt refineries, which used to export 6,000 vats to Dutch Flanders, as well as their own manufactured soap, shrank to their own local market, so that the early annexation in 1810 which restored those links came as something of a surprise bonus. Before that happened, however, the landdrost of Zeeland, François Ermerins, wrote to the Dutch Minister of the Interior:

The impression given by all the available information is of so miserable and discouraging a condition . . . of the once so prospering trade of the inhabitants of Zeeland, that without a speedy alteration . . . nothing except a total collapse and the annihilation of all sources of prosperity can be foreseen.[42]

The Condition of the People: The Case of "Maasland"

Whatever the variations of Dutch industrial decline—from place to place and industry to industry—one feature struck contemporaries as depressingly uniform: the remorseless growth in the numbers of the poor. This, of course, had been a generally voiced concern throughout the revolution and indeed prior to it. The "augmentation of vagrancy, beggary and pauperdom" had been a recurrent strain in the Spectatorial-philanthropic critique of social manners. It had concerned itself principally with the containment, or rehabilitation, of the habitually destitute. But the terms of reference of this kind of discussion faded into irrelevance in the face of the massive increase in those needing relief to supplement a subsistence which would normally have been provided by regular employment. Hence the note of despondency, and even slight panic, invading the reports made out by burgemeesters to their respective landdrosten in the autumn of 1808. Most of them tabulated the depressed condition of industry *in terms of* the contraction of work. When this employment was normally provided on a putting-out basis (as in most industrial enterprises save processes like soap-boiling and sugar refining), the effect on household economies was particularly severe. In Amsterdam, for example, the diamond cutters complained that owing to the high price of the rough stones and their scarcity, work which could normally have been offered to 600 households now only stretched to a third of that number.[43] Sail-making at Krommenie and rope-making at Schoonhoven had suffered an even more drastic curtailment. In the first case, an industry which would normally have supported some 2,000 artisans barely stretched to 300 or 400. And at Dordrecht, where it was claimed that before the war the refitting yards had had more work than they could handle, just sixteen carpenters, masons, rigging men and the like remained in employment. There is some evidence, moreover, to suggest that the rate of urban depopulation was slightly on the increase. In 1809, Amsterdam dipped below 200,000 and Leiden below 30,000 for the first time since the early seventeenth century. These figures partly reflect the dislodgement of tenants and owners of modest property from residential accommodation for fiscal arrears. In Amsterdam, Valckenaer reported that a string of five houses knocked down that way, which under more normal conditions would have fetched perhaps 150 guilders apiece, barely scraped together 60 between them.[44] Certainly there were precious few buyers on the real estate market at such a time.

Problems of this magnitude imposed an almost insupportable strain on local authorities, unprepared both financially and institutionally to carry it. The independence and social administration of the towns had been one of the most universally admired features of the old Republic, and had testified to the rationality as well as the munificence with which surplus wealth had been redistributed within the community. Social piety had crowned the blessings of the rich and given them added status as deacons and wardens of the several orphanages, old age homes, hospitals and the like. But now that spiralling debts had replaced corporate fortunes, interest payment on state securities which provided current income went unpaid, and whole towns were threatened with massive mendicancy, had this history come to an unhappy end? Were their custodians able to preserve the cohesion of their communities by clinging to what remained of the traditional institutions, or were they obliged to lean on the none too sturdy crutches offered by a monarchy itself better endowed with paternalist intentions than the wherewithal to make them good? I have tried to answer these questions by examining in sharper focus one particular region of the country, always bearing in mind that the several provinces (or "departments") of the Netherlands were not yet so thoroughly homogeneous that what held good for South Holland applied to the same degree elsewhere.

The area known after the local government reorganisation of 1807 as "Maasland" divided the old province of Holland along a line which went from the coast between Zandvoort and Noordwijk due east to Hillegom, south to Gouda and Schoonhoven, and as far into the Betuwe as Culemborg. It was rather broader at its base and narrower at its neck than the present-day South Holland. Its population, which in 1807 numbered some 381,226 souls, was divided into the three kwartieren of Leiden, Rotterdam and Dordrecht, with a "drost" assigned to each. The mixture of sandy loam and highly alluvial, copiously irrigated soils had made for a prolific agriculture, which despite the depression of industry and the restricted conditions of trade had managed to hold its own during the war. Dairying in the Rijnland and near Soeterwoude, in the right and left banks of the Lek in the Albasserwaard and Krimpenerwaard, continued to produce Gouda and Stolwijk cheeses in considerable quantities.[45] Texel sheep were still sent south to Rijnland for fattening, and the horticultural farming—orchard fruit in the extreme southeast around Heusden and cauliflowers at Rijswijk and Voorburg—increased its yield at this time.

Arable farming also prospered in response to both domestic and foreign demand; in the east around Gouda and Bodegraven, some barley and a good deal more oats were grown; mixed grains and beans in the Delfland and Schieland. The more specialised crops needed for manufactures sold to greedy markets starved of raw materials. Thus the hemp which dairy farmers in the Krimpener- and Alblasserwaarden had grown in small plots at the backs of their houses as a supplement for their income assumed far greater importance despite the contraction of rope-making in the traditional centres of that craft industry in Schoonhoven and Gorinchem. With supplies of Flemish and South Brabant flax severely cut back by Imperial protection, the demand for the domestic product cultivated in the saturated soils of the Merwede and Zwijndrechtse was correspondingly more urgent. The same was true of the madder raised on the Hoekse Waard and the island of Voorn and sent to the Rotterdam depot, which despite efforts at French competition still virtually monopolised the European market for this essential dyestuff.

Not all was bucolic serenity in the South Holland countryside. That much is apparent from the bitter complaints registered against the assessment for the 3-million guilder levy (later 2 million) of 1808 and sent to the land-drost.[46] Naturally the incidence of rural poverty was given more than its due the better to appeal for lighter assessment; but even allowing for some exaggeration, the petitions reveal a far more stratified country society than might be conveyed by undifferentiated data of crop or dairy yields. Indeed, the extension of some root and tuber crops requiring little attention for much of the year meant, as in the instance of potatoes covering two-thirds of the acreage around Oegstgeest and Rijnsburg near Leiden, that the seasonal fluctuations in day labour had actually sharpened. The same was true for the sandier and scrubbier land to the northwest around Noordwijk.

Not all of the alterations in Dutch rural society, then, were necessarily for the better. The gap between independent freeholders on the one hand and tenants and wage labourers on the other was probably widening in this period. In 1807, nearly 30 per cent of the working population of the department were listed under the category of day labourers, more numerous even than artisans.[47] At Alkemade to the northeast of Leiden, on the edge of the Haarlemmermeer, not one of the thousand heads of households owned a property of more than 20 *morgen*; just three owned between ten and twenty, four between five and ten, and *sixty* between one and five, many of which were little more than an allotment attached to the house. The remainder were small tenants or labourers. The substantial owners, it was tersely recorded, all lived in Leiden itself or in the well-to-do district of Sassenheim.[48] The real wages of day labour were also becoming steadily depressed. The same village reported that the going rate in 1807 for "labour from the earliest morning to late in the evening" was just 16 stuivers. It is not altogether surprising, then, to find that Alkemade had an unusually high incidence of rural poverty—10 per cent. Tenants were being caught in a trap whereby though the steep rise in rents was to some extent offset by the rising value of their produce, they were still obliged to buy in articles of subsistence at a net loss.

As a result, there are some indications of a regression away from the specialisation of agrarian functions which Jan de Vries has identified as the hallmark of the "golden age of Dutch agriculture." More tenants were taking to polycultural farming as a form of protection against the very high prices of what they themselves were unable to produce and so were *further* undermining their own efficiency against the larger independent farmers. Alongside this trend was another which had been just as foreign to the earlier success of the Holland countryside: the spread of cottage industries such as tanning, brewing, and cole and rapeseed milling, less the specialty of a few rural entrepreneurs than the standby of a hard-pressed "peasantry" against diminishing real income. So that the intricate knot which had formerly tied together a high level of urban industrial and mercantile demand for raw materials with a specialised and commercially orientated farming was, at least on one tier of society, beginning to be unfastened.

These impressions are advanced with all due caution. For if it seems that rural Maasland was a more highly differentiated society than might be expected from a generally prospering sector of the Dutch economy, it is nonetheless true that the incidence of pauperdom (defined as those needing part or whole relief) in the villages was on quite a different scale to that prevailing in the major towns. The data collated by the landdrosten in 1807 and supplemented by further returns in 1808 and 1810 strongly suggests that, with the odd exceptions of the stricken fishing ports of Maassluis and Vlaardingen, where in winter *one in three* souls needed relief, those in receipt of assistance escalated progressively with demographic concentration.[49] Nor should this be so astonishing. For despite the strenuous efforts to restrict relief to their own domiciles, it was well-nigh impossible to seal off towns of middling size like Delft (16,000) or Dordrecht (19,000) from the vagrant poor of their own rural hinterland, nor indeed from feeding their own surplus into the rising sewers of the destitute in Leiden, The Hague and Rotterdam. It was relatively rare for communities of under 1,000 to have more than 9 per cent of their population indigent. There were, however, curious regional variations even within a single kwartier. The villages east of Gorinchem in the Vijfheeren Land *before* the 1809 floods—Vuren, Dalem, Woudrichem, Oosterwijk, Heukelom, Meerkerk, and in a slightly larger category Leerdam and Vianen— all had an incidence running at about half that of hamlets and villages of comparable size further west in the equally prospering Alblasserwaard like Langerak, Lexmond and Lekkerland.

The closer to the more densely populated areas at the mouth of the Lek, Waal and Oude Maas the villages were located, the higher in general the incidence of relief. The two IJsselmonde villages of Portugaal and Roon, both essentially dependent on cottage-spinning the flax grown behind Zwijndrecht in 1807, had an abnormally high rate of 15 and 20 per cent respectively, as the putting-out work retracted into the larger towns. And although it is far from clear whether they were acting as an overflow tank for the cities or as a funnel for the retreat of the migratory poor back into the countryside (probably both), the overgrown villages on the edge of the large towns—virtual suburbs—certainly bore a disproportionate burden of the indigent. Hillegersberg, to the northeast of Rotterdam and a gateway to the Schieland, had 500 of its 3,000 inhabitants on public charity; and at Pijnacker, between The Hague and Delft, the proportion was about the same.[50]

The map below illustrates the radius of pauperdom fanning out from both the larger and middling towns, especially in the southwest of the department, where the crisis in labour-intensive industries which had relied on semi-rural labour was particularly severe. Dordrecht and Delft were serious casualties of this development.[51] Both had been trading centres; Dordrecht at the head of the Rhine-Scheldt-Maas grain and timber trades, with direct connexions to the Swiss and German markets for tobacco and sugar, all of which had been crippled by Imperial diversionary and protective policies. Delft, using Delfshaven, with which it was connected by a good canal, as its port on the Maas, had been one of the principal depots for the East India Company. With the loss of virtually the whole of the Dutch empire— excepting only Java, St. George Elmina (Guinea), Canton and Deshima (off Japan)—and with colonial imports allowed in at Emden and Maassluis by grace of the Royal Navy, Delft's share of the re-export trade had become defunct. The marine industries—sawmills, rope-making, compasses, anchors, masts—had suffered equally. There were still gleanings to be had. If the grain

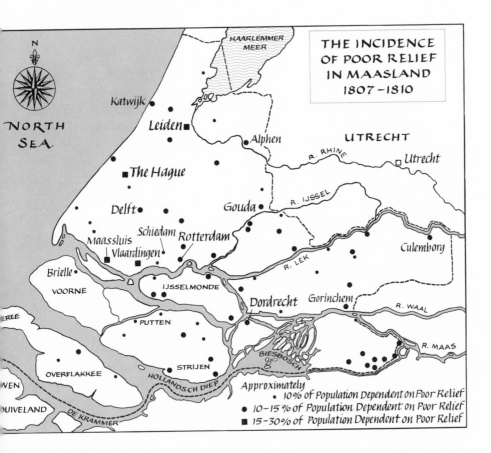

market at Delft and the carrying trade at Dordrecht were largely things of the past, the butter market in the former still prospered and even in 1810 there were thirteen salt works in Dordrecht, salting not only what little fish was to be had but also the more prolific supplies of butter and cheese for the European and British markets.

The potteries in Delft seemed to have undergone some slight adaptation to competing with cheaper Stoke wares (rather than the expensive Wedgwood lines), for at this time there were 7 potteries employing 280 workers. But these morsels scarcely compensated for the surrender of the tanning, milling, oil-pressing and brewing trades to rural small-scale local competition; the contraction of distilling in Delft; and the reliance of woollen textile concerns on military contracts. The poor returns told their own story. In 1807, of 16,779 inhabitants of Delft, 2,570 required public assistance. In Dordrecht the figures were about 19,000 and 3,294: proportions of 1 in 8 and 1 in 6 respectively. The reports of the bailiffs and magistrates of both towns to the Ministry of Justice between 1807 and 1809 are full of anxieties about the threat to public quiet posed by the mounting squadrons of begging poor, who posted themselves in the Markt at Delft and in front of the Oudekerk, across the canal from the Prinsenhof where William the Silent had been struck by his assassin in 1584.

Whole sections of the towns of Maasland were threatened with paupers' blight. The removal of the court and the government bureaux, initially to Utrecht in the autumn of 1807, and in the following spring to Amsterdam, had left The Hague socially and economically threadbare.[52] Its domestic trades—tanning, brushmaking, hosiery-making—had all suffered from the same ills as those of other towns; but its major business, that of government and diplomacy, had been the most serious casualty. Battalions of clerks, scribes, notaries, ushers, porters, gardeners, lackeys, coachmen and the like had all been left marooned by the abrupt departure of the King. The seedy streets at the back of the Groenmarkt and Vismarkt to the southeast of the city had for some time been the haunt of petty hawkers, receivers and peddlers. But the perruqued poor, the unemployed subalterns of court and bureaucracy, congregated alongside the Vijver and under the chestnut trees of the Tournooiveld and the Plein, loitering around the empty warrens of the Binnenhof.

The departmental administration, the office of the receiver-general, the High Court and the garrison had all remained in the city, and Louis had established a military academy for the impoverished young at Honselaardijk Castle on the southern outskirts. But the landdrosten, and in particular the sober-sided Carel Hultman, were concerned to prune back the sinecure and petty offices which had always kept the amiably lethargic Haagenaar *burgerij* in the style to which the Princes' court had long accustomed it. The gardens of the Huis 't Bosch were reopened to the public as they had been before Schimmelpenninck moved in, although the palace itself mouldered away under dust covers, its fixtures and fittings (along with some from Soestdijk) transferred to the unlikely setting of Kampen's Stadhuis on the Dam, promoted (if that is the right word) to be the new "Royal Palace." The theatres, orchestras, opera buffa performers, not to mention sundry cooks, wine merchants and the like, were all sufficiently cast down by the loss of ambassadorial and court custom to organise petitions to the city *wethouders* asking for more publicly sponsored entertainments and functions to keep them going.[53] In 1807, 5,865 needed relief in The Hague out of a total population (including Scheveningen) of 42,000. Moreover, among that number was an unusually high proportion of non-Calvinists who were not catered for by the better-endowed poor establishments: over 1,000 Catholics and another 1,000 Ashkenazi Jews.[54] Burgemeester Slicher—as ancient and crumbling as the "dignified city" over which he presided—grumbled bitterly to van Gennep and Hultman that the town could ill afford to keep up the "Institute for Mendicancy" established there in 1806, even though it was partly subsidised from the national treasury.

Leiden was in even worse shape.[55] Amsterdam aside, it was probably the most derelict of all the cities in the Netherlands at this woebegone time. Of its 30,000 inhabitants,* 6,325—1 in 4 or 5—were receiving public assistance. The disaster in January, like the emigration of the court from The Hague, made Leiden something of a special case but its effects on the domestic economy of the city ought not to be exaggerated. The seeds of its destitution, in the shape of the bankruptcy of the cloth and textile industries, had been germinating throughout the century; and the explosion had in fact brought new capital, in the shape of the national fund, special premiums, and the like, to the town. There were still thirty-four manufactures of woollen yarn and about the same number of carders. But the market for serges, fustians and flannels was virtually non-existent. The industry survived, like that in Delft, leaning on the crutch of guaranteed contracts for the army and navy first proposed in Goldberg's plans for the recuperation of the city after the explosion.[56]

A more reliable index of the real capacity of the town's major industry to survive was the condition of the say and ermine makers, who had once produced 50,000 pieces a year and were now reduced to just under 500.[57] Leiden was really three removes from the world of contemporary textile manufactures. Entrepreneurs like Pieter Vreede had long since gone south to Brabant in search of lower wage costs and cheaper raw material freight; they in their turn had been partly undercut by the Enschede-Almelo manufacturers in the east; and *they* were now suffering from the first buddings of manufactured cottons in the Ruhr. The town was still wrestling with the problems that had brought about the decline of its fortunes a century and more before. P. Klaarenbeek, the Haarlem dyer who submitted a thoughtful and interesting memorandum on the restoration of the Dutch economy to the King in 1807, mentioned the willingness of some of its industrialists to import new British machinery for spinning and printing light cottons, the sort of fabric that could decently compete in the new century for a mass market. But he recorded

---

* The figures vary considerably in different census returns; 1807 gives 28,000, but this was no doubt to dramatize the ratio of poor.

also the bitter hostility of the old guilds and artisans to any device which was likely to distend even further the bloated mass of the Leiden unemployed.[58]

Even the "Spinschool," established in 1796 to teach the orphaned and destitute young the ways of Christian thrift and diligent labour (as well as to cut down on the costs of maintaining them), was in serious difficulties owing to the inflated cost of raw materials. Of the army of poor in the city, over 5,000—80 per cent—were reckoned able-bodied; and of those nearly 2,000 were children, many of course abandoned by their parents themselves in the direst want. A whole generation of destitute was growing up in a city of ruined grace. Some of the urchins, the Curator of the university complained to the *hoofdschout* in The Hague, had been caught stealing berries and fruits (by no means all edible) from the Hortus Botanicus, so desperate were their pangs.[59]

The traditional institutions of philanthropy—by and large those based on the several religious communities—were utterly unequal to the task of stemming this flood tide of indigence. By one of the sour paradoxes in which the history of this time abounds, the very economic phenomena which were creating the legions of the poor were at the same time undermining the capacity of traditional agencies to assist them. For, in common with all other institutional investors dependent on a steady flow of income, their investments in state securities and even the value of their properties (though not, surely, their rents) had depreciated dramatically in terms of the rising costs of their overheads. Thus on contracting real resources they were having to try to meet what must have seemed infinitely expanding commitments. In turn, of course, they passed on the burden to the city. There it stopped. For while the establishment of a General Poor Commission in 1805 by Schimmelpenninck and van Stralen was meant—like exactly comparable institutions dealing with Public Health, Education and the Waterstaat—to contribute to the rationalisation and unification of a highly varied and disorganised miscellany of institutions, its responsibilities did not embrace financing any nationally coordinated system of poor relief. Similarly, the departmental commissions which were responsible to it were confined to overseeing the problems of relief at the local level (which for many burgemeesters meant useless and objectionable interference), and laying down the law about the minimal prescribed standards for assistance. Shelter for the poor who could not be lodged in the institutions had to include at least a tarpaulin or pitch and straw roof of some kind, however rudimentary. For clothes, men should be entitled as of right to two shirts, an upper garment, one pair of breeches, one pair of shoes, two pairs of hose and two jackets; women to two blouses, two pairs of stockings, a pair of shoes and two skirts and petticoats, testifying to the traditional Dutch concern for homely amplitude. Further requirements were light to work by in winter, heat for cooking and body warmth, and a diet which included each week at least some bread, potatoes and *meat*. This would have been considered princely by French standards; in 1811 Baron d'Alphonse, the "Intendant de l'Intérieur" for the Dutch departments, expressed his shock at the unseemly opulence and waste prevailing in Dutch poor institutions. In characteristic Bonapartist style, he recommended a more bracing dose of grinding misery as a tonic for all those idlers crowding the hospices and workhouses.[60]

The departmental commissions, decentralised in much the same way as their counterparts in the ministries of the interior, waterstaat and finance, were also committed to procuring work for the able-bodied poor—especially since it was hoped that useful labour might lead not only to moral redemption but to the restored self-esteem that was at the heart of all Dutch efforts at reform at this time. But as the understandably irritated burgemeester of Brielle put it, the causes of the poverty confronting his municipality were as obvious as the means for dealing with it were lacking.[61] In Leiden, the magnitude of the problem was enough to send any orphanage warden or poor deacon to distraction. Wijckerheid Bisdom had no need of government strictures to let him know what needed to be done; nor Jan Slicher at The Hague, who grumbled that the Instituut voor Bedelarij was costing the town 20,000 guilders a year, or between 300 and 350 florins for every inmate—man, woman and child. In Leiden in 1807, Wijckerheid Bisdom reported to the landdrost that the municipal Huiszittenhuis alone had a deficit of 100,000 florins and a capital debt of *three times* that figure; that the city would need to subsidise all the poor institutions in 1808 to the tune of 266,444 florins; and that the payment merely of interest on loans contracted to provide for these needs was now at 30,000 florins. By 1809, the deficitary gap between ordinary revenues of the town and its expenditure (333,600 florins) was 266,200 florins; the following years, it was 212,000 florins.[62]

There was no alchemist's stone the department could call on to put this unnerving situation to rights. The loan launched by the King had been a success. It was rapidly swallowed up, however, by the costs simply of the physical restoration of the parts of the city which had been destroyed in the explosion, and little was left for current expenditure. Nor did the proffered premiums have much success in attracting new enterprises to Leiden. The city had the smell of death over its economy. What the Ministry of Finance and the Council of State and landdrost could and did do was to authorise the municipality to impose its own special taxes in order to finance the needs of relief, even if these deviated from the rules of thumb laid down in the 1805 Tax Law. In fact, the 1807 edict on the organisation of the poor commissions made it clear that while the general authority of the commissions to supervise relief and encourage improvement was extended, the central government was if anything retreating from any financial responsibilty for the day-to-day and year-to-year administration of these institutions. In effect, it was licensing the *retention* of traditional church and municipal old age homes, workhouses, hospitals and orphanages, while placing the responsibility for their upkeep squarely on the shoulders of the civic authorities rather than the corporate bodies of deacons, churchwardens, regents, and so on. In the case of Leiden, it was necessary to fall back on a depressingly exhaustive catalogue of impositions which almost certainly compounded the evils those funds were intended to obviate. The 250,000 florins for the years 1809–12 were meant to be found as follows:[63]

"Additional stuivers" on national *waag*, cattle and grain taxes	fl. 90,000
Restoration of ancient municipal taxes on coaches, carriages and rights of way	15,700
"*Recognitie geld*" paid on the holding of public offices, as well for the practice of some trades and professions	8,800
Street and bridge taxes—in practice a "rate" based on 5% of the rental value of property	50,000
Local excises on peat, beer, butter, firewood and soap	90,000
	254,500
New loan (in case of a shortfall)	10,000
	264,000

Inevitably, these arrangements were a limp compromise between the nationally financed and directed "General Plan" for poor relief in the Netherlands which had been much rehearsed in the Batavian assemblies, and a simple reversion to the traditional independence not just of each town but of each denominational establishment and each privately endowed institution. As in the case of education, the frail national government was simply devoid of the means (even had it the will) to expropriate the testamentary dispositions of the thousands of poor establishments, and transfer them to the state. Nor was it especially keen to add to its own fiscal problems by attempting to impose the national poor rate which would have been necessary to finance such a scheme. It preferred rather to shift the onus back to the local authorities, restricting its own role to the surveillance of the landdrost and the departmental poor commissions. Needless to say, this arrangement was calculated to lead to frequent clashes between the two sets of officials. Strictly speaking, the burgemeester and his *wethouders* were meant to be agents of the royal government immediately accountable to the landdrost; few saw it that way, however. Since in the last resort they were saddled with the obligation of keeping the town peace, they also demanded latitude in respect of controlling those who might and might not receive assistance, irrespective of poor commission regulations. Whether anything constructive was actually done invariably depended on the attitude of those on the spot.

The experience of Rotterdam is a classic instance. Aside from Amsterdam, it was by far the most energetic and enterprising municipality in its approach to the relief of the needy. True, the problem was not of a scale comparable to Amsterdam or Leiden. In 1807 there were some 5,500 supported by public relief in Rotterdam, scarcely a negligible proportion but about 10 per cent of the total population—an incidence just half that of The Hague and Leiden.[64] Remnants of its traditional economy survived, though mostly to process blatantly contraband goods: 50 tobacco pressers employed over 3,000 men (where before the war they had taken 10,000) and 14 of the 40 sugar refineries remained. There were still eleven bleach-works, two lacemaking shops and a cotton-printing factory employing fifty workers, though barely surviving against German competition. The salt refineries, cement works, glassworks and chocolate factories had all been crippled by the various penalties of the economic war.

Rotterdam's situation, then, was merely miserable rather than critical. But its councillors were neither prepared to try to make do with the denominational institutions nor to await the lumbering efforts of the government agencies. In 1804 a Municipal Poor Administration was established, to provide some kind of overall direction and coordination between the various institutions, both religious and secular. In relating its history Burgemeester van der Heim, a civic worthy of the very best kind (if given to the sort of orotund pronouncements guaranteed to send committees nodding off in their seats), claimed that the objective was not merely to carry out effective economies in the administration but to initiate useful reforms, procure proper employment and provide comprehensive education for the young. He cited the examples of Hamburg and Munich, where similar municipal initiatives had met with some success. Reading between the lines of his report, however, it is apparent that to persuade the regents of the Reformed Church Orphanage, the Catholic Orphanage and the Jewish Lidvarim Tovim Hospital to sit down at the same table together, much less co-ordinate their resources and efforts, had in itself been an uphill battle. Nor was the introduction of the departmental agencies of the General Poor Commission in 1805 seen as an unqualified errand of mercy, since subsequently the Rotterdam administration felt under pressure from two sides: from those commissions laying down the law regarding food, work and the like, and from the regents resisting encroachments in their autonomy.

The decisive change came with the setting up of the municipal poor house in 1806.[65] This was not, of course, the first in the country. Amsterdam had two non-denominational institutions of this kind, and The Hague "Mendicant Institute" which gave Slicher so much worry performed much the same function. But the Rotterdam house, while hardly lavish in its style of accommodation, was something of an advance on most such institutions where the old, the sick, the mad and the orphaned were herded together in malodorous gloom to pick tow or stitch rags. By 1807 about 700 people were housed in the Rotterdam institution, most of them the able-bodied poor and about half under twenty. It was emphatically not a workhouse in the traditional sense (much to the regret of the French inspectors in 1811), though certainly there was a utilitarian provision for sharp treatment (no potatoes; withheld pay) for incidents of wanton sloth or moral degeneracy. The various categories of the needy were all catered for, but separately, according to their particular requirements. The old and infirm were taken in when they were no longer able to earn a living, and the deserted young might stay from five years old to the ripe age of twenty-three. Up to twelve or thirteen they received an education in the rudiments of numeracy and literacy, together with a hefty dose of *burgerlijk* proprieties on approved philanthropic lines. To pay for their keep, they were provided with spinning and weaving and were in addition given some training in other artisan crafts. When employed full-time at work, they received modest payment on a piece-rate basis. The diet of all inmates was based on bread, potatoes, vegetables and a pound of meat per head per week—hard going by Dutch standards, but a subsistence which the indigent of most other European countries would have regarded as sumptuous. Including the purchase of raw materials for the work, the upkeep of the house came to some 87,000 florins a year—a model of what might be done on limited means.

But that was not the end of the Rotterdam poor administration's commitments. There were still 2,000 city poor catered for by the endowed or church establishments. The municipality also kept a school for 500 poor children (not orphaned) offering free education and one square meal a day. Between these obligations and repeated subsidies to the church houses, the total bill came to something like 200,000 guilders every year. As in Leiden, this money had to be found from additional local taxation, specifically authorised by the Minster of Finance. Perhaps in deference to his own views, the burden of this was placed on direct rather than indirect sources so that the de facto poor rate in Rotterdam was more like a fiscal levy than an indiscriminate imposition. In both Leiden and Rotterdam the line between those paying for the succour of the destitute and those joining their ranks was alarmingly shadowy. Yet despite its continuous tales of woe, the "Committee of Superintendence" managing the relief operations in Rotterdam had reason to feel quite satisfied with its progress by 1810. Aside from its practical philanthropy, it had managed to persuade members from different religious congregations (as well as its own regents) that collaboration on these matters was preferable to standing on traditional dignities. It had provided not only food, shelter and education for those who otherwise would have become completely indigent, but free medical and pharmaceutical assistance in addition. As in other areas of social experience in the Netherlands at this time, it was the pressure of misfortune rather than any sudden blossoming of civic altruism and inter-denominational harmony which had removed the most irrational obstacles to making the most of slender resources.

The administration of the department of Maasland was by no means a paradigm of the "new government"; still less a stream-lined, efficient and conscientious salaried bureaucracy. It hobbled along as best it could, with much of the real burden of work placed on the municipality rather than the agents of the crown. But the power of those local dignitaries actually to obstruct the course of administration as they had done after 1798 does seem to have been constrained, both by the rigorous authority assumed by the national ministries and the increasing financial embarrassment in which they found themselves. The preamble to the 1807 Poor Law stated that "If some assistance is not provided through means better adapted to present circumstances, there will be a complete ruin" of the traditional institutions, and that "with the unprecedented calamities which have taken place of late, and the terrifying augmentation of the poor, we are forced to recognise that the measures for their relief must be greatly extended. . . ."[66]

What went for the poor also applied to other basic tasks of administration which would, in more leisured times, have axiomatically been the exclusive business of local and private bodies. Elementary schooling, the care of the waterstaat, local police, and—a particular concern of the mildly hypochondriac King—public health, all had their hierarchies of departmental and local commissions, the last comprising surgeons, physicians, apothecaries and midwives. Whether they liked it or not, the burgemeester and his *wethouders* were increasingly relegated to the role of appointed officials permitted to act only within limits set by the local government statutes and scrutinised by the landdrost. Indeed, in communes of the "second class"—that is, of less than 5,000 inhabitants—the drost virtually acted as burgemeester himself, appointing and dismissing all local commissions and petty officials as he saw fit. Naturally there were many among the tribes of clerks, commissioners, drosten and the like who were determined to enjoy their little brief authority and were unwontedly officious in doing the bidding of the King. In The Hague, the endearingly grumpy Slicher besieged landdrost Hultman with daily protests at the invasion of his jurisdiction: in manning the night watch, cleaning the streets, policing the Haagsche Bosch woods, censoring the press, even licensing balls, theatres and street organs![67] Yet as might be expected, the most efficient landdrosten went out of their way not to act like petty martinets but on the contrary to interpret the edicts and regulations handed down from the Council of State with as much elasticity as befitted local circumstances.

For all the formalities of its criss-crossing hierarchies and multiplying "commissions" on this, that, and the other, the administration of a Dutch department remained obstinately parochial in its preoccupations. In many essential respects this was still the Holland of the stadhuis, the waaghuis and the kerktoren. After all, while Napoleon was weighing the fate of the Continent, his brother was worrying about cow-pox vaccine in East Friesland or the repair of the Ost-Capelle causeway in Zeeland. Nothing less like the bureaucratic automaton which on paper at least characterised Imperial France could be imagined. The Netherlands was undergoing no "revolution in government" but rather the makeshift emergence, in most inauspicious conditions, of a kind of communal fraternalism in which the myriad communities of the country sharing common misfortunes attempted the arduous work of patching and stitching the tattered fabric of their society. The object was never to conform to some set of official rules but simply to prevent a cherished way of life from falling irreparably apart.

Eclipse, 1809–1810

By a quirk of circumstance the month in which Hortense provided Louis with a new Prince, March 1809, was also the time when he made another therapeutic pilgrimage with "Madame Mère" to Plombières—a spa that would have momentous importance for the career of the future

Napoleon III. He was born at a time when the King and Queen were all but formally separated and when Hortense's flirtation with the over-pomaded comte de Flahaut was an open secret at St. Cloud. Historical gossips have chewed long and meatily on the possibilities of Louis-Napoleon's illegitimacy. For all the scandals, imagined and real, it seems virtually certain that the child was Louis' own. Though his sister Caroline, with that winsome delicacy for which the Bonapartes were renowned, exclaimed on viewing the issue: "Oh, quelle tête de Beauharnais," Louis-Napoleon's features, and surely much of his enigmatic and mournful temperament, bore a decidedly Ludovician imprint. In any event, the King's mind was clouded by other less flimsy matters. It was not at all clear that there would be a throne for the royal sprig to inherit. Louis knew that he clung to his sovereignty, as the Netherlands to its independence, by the breadth of the merest fingernail. Internal pressure from the arithmetic of war, finance and external pressure from the Emperor were rapidly taking away what little room there was left for him to manoeuvre. By the summer of that year his two ablest ministers, van Maanen and Gogel, had both left the government, the former warning that there was no secret alchemy which might resolve these dilemmas. He wrote baldly:

It is impossible, financially and politically, to lower expenditure to the level of our revenues in the calamitous times in which we live; and so, however painful and afflicting the idea may be, we must exist from day to day and simply await the outcome of events yet in the making. . . .[68]

There seemed no prospect of relief from the most grave of these troubles. Although, as Louis was not slow to point out, French wines and other goods from within the Empire were reported to be reaching British ports in some quantities, he was not thanked for the intelligence. Napoleon's determination to make the Continental system bite hard, and his conviction that Britain was moving to the edge of ruin, were as fierce as ever. The brief concession made by Louis in allowing American cargoes into the Netherlands on condition they were deposited in officially inspected warehouses was greeted with derisive anger from St. Cloud. Dutch goods were once more prohibited from entering France, and at the end of July the King withdrew the offending edict. Faced with the alternative of either further mutilating Dutch commerce by applying the blockade with maximum force, or risking shutting off French markets for good, Louis oscillated nervously between an excessively rigorous and a casually complaisant approach—neither of which inspired confidence in Paris, or for that matter in Amsterdam. The Kingdom of Holland was becoming fixed in the official French mentality not merely as a liability to the Empire but as a British fifth column on the Continent, all the more insidious for constantly protesting fidelity. On June 18, doubtless at Napoleon's instigation, the *Journal de l'Empire* alleged that

all the bad news, all the rumours that are most unfavourable to France have their source in Holland. It is there that malevolence and calumny seem to have established their residence; there that the falsest and most absurd tales, the product of a feverish hatred for France, find the widest currency.[69]

When Louis called the item a "defamation," Napoleon riposted that it was *he* who had cause for complaint since his brother had turned the Kingdom into "an English province."

Was the press campaign against Louis and the Dutch, sustained at a level of unprecedented vituperation, merely intended to pave the way for annexation? It seems more probable that, as in 1801 and 1805, Napoleon had decided on some sort of change in Dutch status, but waited on the outcome of the next campaign before choosing the form it would take. As his ambassador La Rochefoucauld (not, however, usually known for maxims of any sort) observed, devouring the whole of the Netherlands at one swallow could bring on an attack of acute financial indigestion. Even if the matter of the deficit could be dealt with by partial or total repudiation, the huge costs of administering a nation which Napoleon believed was becoming ungovernable might occasion, at the best, serious discomfort, and at the worst another "Spanish" rebellion. Piecemeal dismemberment was another possibility. The Empire might simply lop off those parts of the country—Brabant, Zeeland and Gelderland to the Waal—which had been proposed to Louis in 1808 as an indemnifiable cession.

Félix Rocquain suggested that in the late summer of 1809 the Emperor deliberately left Louis bereft of troops so as to expose him to British attack and thus provide an unarguable pretext for annexation.[70] This would have been seriously out of character. However preoccupied with the Austrian campaign and resolved to reduce the Dutch to absolute submission, Napoleon was unlikely to have wished a British invasion on his own back door simply to give him a formal reason for taking a course of action he felt open to him at any time. Moreover, he warned his brother not once but many times in the spring and early summer that some kind of British effort, probably in the south, was in the offing, and that conscription or at least the mobilisation of a National Guard was indispensable if his rear was to be adequately covered. For his part, Louis was not oblivious to the military threat; but his resources were paltry, and there was little he felt able to do to withstand an invasion should Napoleon deprive him of substantial reinforcement. As he pointed out, 3,000 of his regular troops were then serving in Spain and another two divisions (6,000) in Hanover at the Emperor's express order. Where, Napoleon retorted, "They are covering themselves with glory by pillaging the countryside."[71] That left, at the most, some 8,000 or 9,000 troops for the defence of the Kingdom itself.

On July 29, the possibility of an invasion ceased to be academic with the appearance off Walcheren of an expeditionary armada.[72] This British force was destined to go down in military history as risibly ignominious; but sighted from Domburg in Zeeland, it looked formidable enough. There were close to 200 sail, including 38 ships-of-the-line, 36 frigates and a substantial complement of gunboats commanded by Sir Richard Strachan. They carried around 40,000 troops, and also their commander, the Earl of Chatham, elder brother of William Pitt, who, it was said, had once "been seen exercising eight or ten thousand men much to his credit." It was, by some way, the largest force to have sailed from Britain since the beginning of the wars.

Despite advance information the timing seemed to catch Louis off guard, for he heard the news at Aachen with his mother. Following Wagram on July 6 and the armistice between Napoleon and the Archduke Charles, Louis had relaxed on the assumption that the transparently diversionary purpose of the expedition would have been vitiated. Certainly, it had been prepared with just that end in view. Had it got under way after the earlier Austrian victory as Essling, it could have changed the character of the whole war of 1809. But it proved so cumbersome in the preparation (like all armadas) that in the end it could not set sail until July 28. Its chances of success at this late stage were highly speculative. Yet once so considerable a commitment of men and money had been made, the campaign generated its own laborious momentum, irrespective of the likely outcome. The altered circumstances, however, did modify strategic objectives. Walcheren was to be used as a base for the seizure of Flushing, the opening of the Scheldt and an attack on Antwerp and the French fleet sheltering in its roads—a glorified version of the Danish expedition of 1807, in fact. The British government was apparently apprehensive at this stage about the possibility of an Imperial naval recovery threatening their naval hegemony, and the Walcheren expedition was meant to nip this in the bud. Even if unable to penetrate very deep into northern France or the Belgian and Dutch departments, there was at least a chance to inflict some serious damage on the arsenals and fortifications concentrated in that region.

At the outset, the defending forces were gravely embarrassed by the suddenness and the scale of the invasion. On July 30 the first troops made landfall between Veere and Oostkapelle on the northern tip of the island. Despite Louis' visit earlier in the year, Veere's defences were not in peak condition (to put it mildly) and after a brief bombardment the port was taken. On the following day Goes and Middelburg capitulated, while another division of the naval force sailed through the Roompot on the Oooster Schelde to Zierikzee, thus occupying the whole of Schouwe and Duiveland. Contrary to past form—and certainly to his brother's expectations—it was the King rather than the Imperial council of ministers who acted decisively in the emergency. Napoleon's men were divided between those, like Cambacérès, conditioned never to so much as blow his nose without the Emperor's permission; the Minister for War, General Clarke, who had misgivings about appointing Bernadotte to take over the defence since the latter seemed to have returned from Austria under an Imperial cloud; and Fouché, Minister of the Interior, preoccupied as he had been exactly ten years before with keeping the British out of the Low Countries. It was on this occasion that Fouché made the fatal mistake of not acting like a stuffed dummy until ukases were handed down from the Imperial eminence and actually seemed to relish organising the *défense de la patrie*. Mobilising the National Guard on his own initiative, handing out ranks and commissions while passing none too flattering comments on the lustre of the Empire, was not calculated to keep Napoleon's temper and proved the prelude to Fouché's disgrace later in the year. While the ministers perspired over the defence of the northern departments, Louis himself went directly to Antwerp, putting Dumonceau in charge of the Amsterdam garrison but gambling on the supposition that there would not be a supporting force landing in the north.

Virtually all the troops Louis had at his disposition were assembled, around 8,000 strong, on Bergen op Zoom opposite South Beveland. Clearly, with the huge disparity of numbers between invaders and defenders, all that could be done was to maintain a holding operation until the Imperial allies could muster sufficient men to bottle up the British. The French naval squadron was moved up to the safety of the guns commanding Antwerp harbour, and Kellermann belatedly ordered to release some of the Paris garrison for the northeast. Later, the marshal was castigated for his delay. "Was he waiting for the English to take him in his bed?" Napoleon asked. Louis' containing operation was, then, crucial. But it was abruptly sabotaged when General Bruce—who had been ordered to hold the strategic fort of Bath at the eastern extremity of Beveland and opposite Bergen—decided on his own account to evacuate, a panic-stricken manoeuvre for which he was cashiered and put in irons for fifteen days by the King. (Napoleon, characteristically, wanted him shot.)

The evacuation of Bath put the Dutch in a dreadful position. The British had overrun virtually the whole of Zeeland in barely a week and were set to threaten Flushing. Provisioned for 6 months and manned with a force of 4,000 the port was, according to Napoleon, "impregnable." But bombarded from both sea and land, should the British have broken out into South Holland or Brabant or moved further up the Scheldt, Flushing would have been *behind* enemy lines. By his prompt concentration of forces, the King had succeeded in forestalling any further advance. He thought that this might have entitled him to the official command of the defending forces. General Clarke, who had deferred to him over Antwerp as "Connétable de l'Empire," thought rather the same. But as in 1806, Napoleon was appalled by the notion. On August 14, Bernadotte was made commander-in-chief of the defence of the Low Countries, and after reviewing troops at Zandvliet, Louis returned in none too sweet a humor to Amsterdam.

The next day, while preparations to celebrate the Emperor's birthday were under way, news came of General Monnet's capitulation at Flushing. Had this unexpected advantage been pressed home with alacrity, the situation could very easily have got out of control. But as in 1799, the incompetence and division within the British camp—principally between the naval and military wings of the expeditionary force—made for a much-needed respite. The delay in attempting to attack the Scheldt estuary by land gave the French and Dutch armies time to build up their strength. While the

British naval officers made feeble sorties against the heavy artillery of the Scheldt forts, troops in Walcheren and South Beveland succumbed in hundreds to the malarial fevers of the islands. The French ships were moved still further upstream above Antwerp and a boom thrown across the mouth of the estuary. By the beginning of September, there were 8,000 Dutch troops deployed on the right bank of the Ooster Schelde—at Bergen op Zoom, on the Dintel, at Tholen, Leur and Willemstad—blocking any possibility of a British advance on the mainland. Thirty thousand French regulars and national guardsmen were concentrated around Antwerp, occupying the left bank of the Scheldt and Zeeland Flanders.

Both armies were being steadily reinforced, the French from Kellermann's Paris garrison and the armies in the east now released from their commitments against Austria; and the Dutch from a division ordered back from Germany. Yet again the British were condemned to waste time, men and munitions without any profit. They had nowhere to go and every day more soldiers buckled and dropped from the sweat and nausea of Walcheren fever. Casualties rose at the rate of 500 a week, and 10,000 of the army had already been immobilised. After another useless sally up the Scheldt, and the recapture of Bath by a Dutch commando force under Coert Heyligers, Chatham decided on September 14 to evacuate all but Walcheren itself and Flushing. He left Eyre Coote with 16,000 men sinking slowly into the Scheldt mud as winter set in on the estuary. On December 24, after destroying as much as he could of the fortifications and harbour, Coote finally abandoned Flushing itself and wrote finis to what, even by British standards of incompetence, had been a stupendous débacle.

Walcheren had not only been inglorious; it had been expensive, and Portland's administration was duly flayed alive in Parliament for the strain it had put on resources that were already tightly stretched. It muddied plots which were as thick on the British as the French side; provoked a duel between Castlereagh (who had supported the plan) and Canning (who hadn't), and ultimately brought about the fall of the British government. Although it gave Napoleon an opportunity to warn the British that a similar fate awaited their efforts in Spain, he showed little pleasure at the way the campaign had been handled on the Imperial side. Initially he had warmed to Fouché's hustle and bustle, elevating him to Duke of Otranto on the Imperial birthday. But before long that very energy came to seem sinister. Why had the minister turned the Empire "upside down" when the threat to it had been so piffling? How could Monnet have abandoned the "impregnable" Flushing so peremptorily? What *was* Bernadotte up to? He was replaced by Marshal Bessières; Monnet court-martialled and Fouché, eventually, "persuaded" to resign. As for Louis and the Dutch, they of course bore the brunt of the Emperor's disquiet and suspicion. In mid-August he had greeted reports of Dutch efforts to contain the invasion with the command to Louis to "finish this comedy," and dismissed the claims to have "recaptured" Bath as ludicrous.[73] Even had Napoleon actually designed the movements of forces in 1809 so as to leave Walcheren undefended, the campaign had given him a powerful pretext for ridiculing Dutch pretensions to sovereignty—and for inserting the French troops necessary to secure an annexation, should that option be taken up.

In a letter to Clarke from Schönbrunn, Napoleon had specifically and confidentially let slip the hint that the invasion was an opportune moment for the occupation of Dutch ports and coastal territory, and that he had no intention of withdrawing them once the war in Holland was over.[74] It was reported to Louis that, on signing the Peace of Schönbrunn, Napoleon had announced: "Here, everything is finished; now we must march on Spain and above all against (*contre*) Holland." With the same chilling ambiguity he told his brother in mid-August that, "through false and feeble measures, you have lost Holland." Knowing in advance that it was hardly likely to meet with a cordial response, Louis made a last despairing appeal to fraternal feeling. On September 6 he wrote:

Sire, I beg you, do not dishonour nor humiliate your brother. How can I not be deeply wounded if Your Majesty truly thinks in the manner in which he writes to me. The names—calumniator, hypocrite—are they really meant for me? Is someone who from duty and inclination defends a good and little nation truly intent on defaming the glory of Your Majesty? . . . No, Sire, you cannot really believe that; but you wrong yourself all the same, for by undermining my position in Holland and treating me as though I were a traitor, you dishonour your own family, the kings of your dynasty, even your own name—and all this will surely rebound, harder than you suppose, on Your Majesty himself.[75]

Napoleon's response to this invitation to do his duty by his kith and kin was in effect a final admission of despair at all the hopes he had once placed in the brother he imagined to be a loyal protégé. It accused Louis of personally betraying him by being seduced by the Dutch, by putting their interests before those of the Empire, and by having the temerity and stupidity to imagine that he held the throne in the Netherlands by virtue of *anything* other than his allegiance to his brother. "What do you want me to tell you?" he asked.

I have told you already a hundred times: you are not a King and you have no idea how to be one. . . . You have neither army nor navy and yet you pretend to be a free and independent state. All your difficulties and anxieties come from your own bad administration and because you have never paid any attention to my advice . . . you would have us believe that the Dutch had great energy and have done all that they can. Yes, they have energy all right—for smuggling. This poor Dutch nation has so much to complain of. Everything it suffers is the result of the instability of your character and the poor judgement of your own measures. I must repeat that my wish is that you refrain from mentioning me, either directly or indirectly, in your harangues, and that there is no mention either of my affairs or of my name. . . . I shall always regret having given you a kingdom where you have merely profited from the reputation of my name to be useful to our enemies. . . . I thank you for the interest you express in my health. I do not believe that that interest can be sincere since I look in vain for the proof of it in your discourses where you calumniate my glory—if that could be possible for such a man as you, who has done nothing in his life. . . .[76]

At a time when his wife had finally deserted Holland for the avuncular refuge of Malmaison; when efforts were being made to prise the Prince Royal from his control by making him Grand Duke of Berg and Cleves, this piercing reproof—all the more wounding since Napoleon had hitherto kept separate their personal and public relations—finally severed what family bonds had been preventing total estrangement.

There is no doubt that Louis felt the blow keenly. By October the worst traits of his old, sour melancholy had returned. He fell ill with scarlet fever and then bronchitis. The arthritis in his hand was so crippling that a pen had to be tied to his fingers in order to sign royal edicts. On some days he stayed incommunicado from his ministers and secretaries for hours on end. His fatalism deepened. There was, he believed, nothing more to be done to repair relations with his brother; if a sacrifice had to be made for the sake of preserving Dutch identity, then he would go through with it. On October 27, and again on November 4, he raised the possibility of his abdication and the creation of a Regency. Far from indicating an unconditional surrender, the gesture was the opening gambit in what Louis knew would be a power game played to the death and in which his brother held all the trumps. But a Regency in the name of his son would mean an effective reversion of power to the Dutch ministers while legitimating his own line in the Netherlands. Needless to say, Napoleon ignored the offer; he would accept it soon enough when the time was ripe.

Louis had just one modest court card in his hand. The Emperor, it was known towards the end of 1809, wanted a divorce from Josephine so as to be able to consummate the Austrian alliance with Marie-Louise, the daughter of Francis I. Strictly speaking, as a principal of the Imperial "Family Council," Louis had the right of withholding his permission for the divorce, and were he, in any case, expecting the worst as far as the future of his own crown was concerned, he may well have felt there was nothing to lose by making the most of this. But there were two snags. First, he had decided, for reasons that were as emotional and moral as Napoleon's were political, that he could no longer stomach his own unhappy conjugal farce. He too wanted a divorce. It would be difficult enough to obtain this from the Emperor, who was not likely to want a general massacre of the Beauharnais women and who was in any case very fond of Hortense, seeing in her virtues enough to compensate for the frailties of her mother. Secondly, any dealings of this sort were bound to require his own presence in Paris. Recalling only too well the circumstances of his last visit in 1807, Louis was not over-enthusiastic about the prospect of a second sojourn. He had a vivid prescience that, with French troops crawling all over the southern departments of the Kingdom, Napoleon threatening to occupy Amsterdam unless smuggling halted forthwith, and his own Dutch soldiers tied up in South Beveland, he might never be allowed to make the return trip.

In the event, he was not given any opportunity to ponder the alternatives. On November 22 Karel Verhuell, the ambassador in France, appeared in Amsterdam with a summons for the King to go to Fontainebleau. Louis was still troubled by the possible consequences of his departure but could hardly decline an invitation couched in terms of an Imperial command. He consulted his ministers on the eventuality of the French army forcing their way into the Kingdom, but only the Minister of War, Kraijenhoff, advised serious defensive preparations. Other less apocalyptic spirits, including most of the ministers and councillors of state, concluded that Louis had no option but to go to Paris, attempt to abate the Emperor's displeasure and play for time— the golden rule of the Kingdom of Holland. What else, after all, could be done? "That moment," Louis later wrote, "was critical . . . it was necessary either to ally with England and play a desperate throw in which the existence of Holland might at least have a glorious end, or else resign ourselves to everything that might happen in order to win some time. . . ."[77] Not for the first or last time Louis was torn between the opposing compulsions of prudence and honour, and ended up by conceding both. He accepted that his holiday in Paris was unavoidable but gave the strictest orders to his commandants in Breda, Bergen op Zoom, Willemstad, and the other Brabant forts not to permit the entry of "foreign" troops under any circumstances, unless they received his written assent.

Arriving in Paris on December 1, he found all his misgivings amply confirmed. He had originally intended to assert his loyalty by residing at the Dutch embassy, but when it was made clear to him that this would not be permitted, he put up instead at the house of "Madame Mère" in the Faubourg St. Germain. The gathering was meant to be something of a family occasion. Louis would be able to see the Prince Royal and try to secure his return to Holland after nearly two years of separation. Celebrations for the victor of Wagram and nuptials for the Imperial marriage were scheduled just as soon as the awkward business of the dissolution could be got out of the way. Jérôme, Joachim Murat, Eugène de Beauharnais, all decorated the court functions along with their ladies. But during what was, by his own report, the worst six months of his life, Louis barely stirred outside the house except to see Napoleon or the ministers (Roëll, Vice-Admiral Bloys van Treslong and Roest van Alkmade) who had accompanied him to France. Throughout the entire period he appeared in public exactly twice: at the "Fête d'adieu" for Josephine and at the official ceremony of the dissolution. Both of these occasions he found repugnant, no doubt because, on December 16, as anticipated, the Family Council denied him a formal separation from Hortense at the same time as it granted Napoleon his divorce from her mother. The balls and parties to mark this occasion, he said ruefully, would have been more appropriate to a general peace than a matter which was "both painful and difficult."

The prospects for Louis' official business did not seem much brighter. In a speech to the corps legislatif, Napoleon alluded to "changes which will become necessary" and described Holland as "the outlet of the principal arteries of my empire."[78] The first confrontation between the two brothers

was frosty rather than turbulent. Napoleon reiterated the self-evident incapacity of the Dutch to sustain their sovereignty, the second scene was altogether more abrasive, with the Emperor declaring: "Holland is an English
province, even more of an enemy to France than England herself." While
Louis made it plain that he would not be bludgeoned into unconditional
abdication, he was nonetheless bruised and battered by the encounters. On
December 6 he wrote to his ministers in Amsterdam in tones of almost incoherent sorrow:

The matter is as good as lost; however it may be through some great sacrifice we
might yet be able to preserve our existence. If that cannot be, well then I will
have done all that I could; even if we are left with Amsterdam alone there may
be some hope—though without it everything is finished. All is not yet lost but it
is desperate; I have nothing left, I am too overborne; grieve for your country then
but grieve also for me, for my cruel destiny. . . .[79]

Inclined as he was to dramatise his predicament, Louis nevertheless
recognised from the outset that there might still be something to play for. He
rightly suspected that with the Austrian marriage in the offing, the Emperor
would want to show his polite front to the old world and avoid an aggrandisement that might be construed as upsetting the power balance once again. His
basic interest was in the stabilisation of the status quo post Wagram. With
Russia, Prussia and Austria reconciled to the Grand Empire, it only remained
to try to come to terms with the recalcitrant British. It was not beyond all
possibility that Napoleon might resume the tactics of 1803 by parading the
threat of an annexation as means of bludgeoning the new British administration into a settlement. At any rate until that possibility had been explored
(however tentatively), it was unlikely that the fate of Holland would be
irrevocably determined.

These slender hopes were given some substance by the fact that the
early interviews between Roëll and Champagny, and in particular the exchange of December 7, concentrated on the cession of Brabant and Zeeland—
a sacrifice which Louis assumed would be compensated by the addition of
territory to the east. Champagny, however, made it brutally clear that in
return for relinquishing a wholesale annexation, the Empire would require
some kind of warranty that the Kingdom of Holland would in future abide
faithfully by the Continental blockade and mend its ways. Just in case the
Dutch should be tempted to stray from the narrow path, French troops would
occupy the coastal territory and the ports and the Dutch customs would be
run by the Imperial service. Roëll was appalled by this further invasion of
sovereignty but, keeping calm, asked the French foreign minister whether
Holland was to be allowed some passing semblance of independence. Louis
then was either overcome by another bout of morose fatalism or else was
trying to call the French bluff. For at their next meeting he informed
Champagny that as King he could not lawfully alienate territory without
indemnity, and that, since it would come sooner or later, the Emperor might
as well depose him and annex the country at one fell swoop. It seems likely
in fact that he was trying to force the French into an explicit repudiation of

annexation and at the same time secure the intercession of the Danish and Russian ministers in Paris. If that was the tactic, it worked. Embarrassed by Louis' outburst, Champagny insisted that Napoleon had never mentioned annexation *tout court* but merely revived the cession proposals of 1808, linked with measures designed to ensure that Holland "was no longer an enemy of France."

On December 17, Louis sent Napoleon a note written in conciliatory terms, explaining once more the unfortunate conflict of loyalties and promising to apply the blockade with all due severity, to cease all intercourse with the British however surreptitious, and to take the necessary fiscal measures to provide for an adequate fleet and army. Napoleon's response was contained in a lengthy letter of the 21st recapitulating his "disappointment" in the King. He had, he wrote:

hoped that, brought up in my *politique*, he [Louis] would have felt that Holland, conquered as it was by my people and owing its independence merely to their magnanimity, weak, bereft of allies, without an army, could and would be subjugated the same day that it put itself in direct opposition to the will of France; that he would never separate his policy from my own. . . . I had, then, hoped that by placing on the throne of Holland a prince of my own blood I had found a median way of reconciling the interests of the two states, uniting them in a common interest and a common hatred of England; but my hopes have been dashed. On ascending the throne Your Majesty forgot that he was a Frenchman and, trying all the paths of reason, tortured by the delicacy of his conscience, persuaded himself that he was Dutch.[80]

He had violated the treaties and agreements they had made, ejected Frenchmen and Francophiles from his councils, promoted unrepentant Anglophiles, and taken advantage of the Emperor's brotherly indulgence and his preoccupation with grand strategy to evade his own military obligations, to sabotage the Continental system and, when American ships were being turned away from French ports, to offer them Dutch harbours in which to unload their illicit cargoes. "I will not hide from you my intention to unite Holland with France, both to complete my territory and as the deadliest blow I can inflict on England.[81]

The Rhine was, after all, the "highway" of the Empire, so that it was only logical that all Dutch territory on its left bank—Zeeland, Brabant and Gelderland to the Waal—should be incorporated forthwith. Nothing was said of any indemnification, but, Napoleon added, so long as Holland complied with "certain absolute conditions," the rest of the country could remain intact. And what were those conditions? Louis was to guarantee the instantaneous and complete cessation of all trade and intercourse with Britain, a fleet of 14 ships-of-the-line and 14 frigates and corvettes; an army of 25,000; and the abolition of the Dutch marshals (who, Napoleon felt, made his own look even more ridiculous than necessary), as well as of the ranks of court nobility which the King had bestowed against his express wishes. If he agreed in principle to this settlement, the details might be worked out with Champagny. In sum, then, "You will find in me a brother if I find in you a Frenchman."

This was bullying taken to the level of a fine art. Napoleon had managed to seem simultaneously absolute and magnanimous. However brutal his methods, there was much substance in his allegations. The proposed solution put Louis in something of a quandary. He had no wish to go down in Dutch history as the dismemberer of the *Vaderland* and, sentiment aside, the loss of the revenues from the south without any corresponding reduction in military obligations did not promise a viable future. But, as he later confessed, he was haunted by the ghosts of Venice and Poland.[82] Half a kingdom was, perhaps, better than none. At all costs he wanted to keep the identity of a separate Dutch nation on the map and pin his hopes on the maritime peace to come.

Like all representatives attempting to parley with senior allies on equal terms (Schuschnigg at Berchtesgaden; Dubček at Bratislava), Louis was obliged to "negotiate" under conditions which only just stopped short of physical intimidation. He was followed and spied on wherever he went. Not only was he denied the request to take his eldest son with him back to Holland, but he was even forbidden to see him except for exchanges of familial civilities. As for his own pleas to be permitted to return, even briefly, to the Netherlands to consult with his ministers, these were contemptuously brushed aside by the Emperor, who continued to pile on public abuse and humiliation until his brother should "see the error of his ways" and, as Champagny, an eager accomplice, warned, "give incontestable proof that you will blindly follow the will of the Emperor."[83]

Wretched though the ordeal was, Louis clung as tenaciously as he could to the bedraggled remnant of his regal dignity, and kept in the back of his mind the possibility of a last-ditch resistance on the dykes. In the last week of 1809, he sent instructions to both van der Heim and Kraijenhoff to go ahead with the defensive preparations discussed prior to his departure. Kraijenhoff then withdrew Dutch troops from Gorinchem, Utrecht and Naarden and concentrated them around Amsterdam, at the same time organising the works needed for the inundation of the city outskirts. Louis' explicit reaffirmation from Paris of the prohibition against any French troops entering Dutch towns was read to the Council of Ministers and endorsed by them all.[84]

This show of defiance was soon put to the test. Three days after the final evacuation of Walcheren by the British, on December 27, General Gilly issued a proclamation to the citizens of Middelburg announcing: "Henceforth your island is part of the French Empire." All Dutch troops, he declared, should remove themselves by January 4 at the latest. But armed with the King's own instructions, the landdrost of Zeeland, Ermerins, together with the burgemeesters of Goes, Veere, Zierikzee and the other major towns, refused to co-operate with the French or recognize their authority. A few days later, news reached Paris that Dutch authorities in Breda and Bergen op Zoom were behaving in a similarly obstreperous manner. Napoleon's ministers were not amused. "In such a manner," declared Clarke to Louis, "Your Majesty has declared war on France and the Emperor." "No bad jokes, I implore you, M. le Duc [de Feltre]," the King replied. "Prisoners cannot declare war."[85]

Napoleon himself ranted and raved that the spineless Oudinot and the craven Dutchmen responsible for the insubordination should all be hanged. "Then," said Louis, with rather impressive sang-froid, "it is I who should be hanged since it is I who gave the orders." Taken aback by the impertinence, Napoleon asked his brother why he should not permit the entry of the French troops, to which the King replied: "So as not to expose my subjects to being dragged from their houses as two years ago you did to the people of Breda who, innocent as they were, were incarcerated in French prisons for months on end. . . ."[86] Louis' show of spirit temporarily disconcerted the Emperor. He had an armed guard put on his brother's residence, both to cow him once more and to ensure against any sudden flight back to the Netherlands to put himself at the head of this ridiculous but irritating gesture of resistance. On January 20 it was announced that an "Army of Brabant" of some 60,000 men was to be raised under Oudinot. Should Louis not, after all, agree to the mutilation of the Kingdom, all-out conquest would swiftly follow. The King began to wilt once more under renewed pressure, having aggravated Napoleon further by informing him loftily that were he forced to abdicate the last thing he would wish to be would be a prince of the French Empire. By the end of January he had reverted to a softer and more wheedling tone: "It is not just to the Emperor that I address myself but to my brother," though adding at the same time that he should be treated "as befits an honest man, not an adventurer."[87]

On February 4, Louis indicated his general assent to the terms and sent instructions to Amsterdam to allow the entry of French soldiers to towns south of the Maas and Waal—though as garrison reinforcements rather than occupying troops, since the cessation had not yet been formally signed. In practice, of course, this nice distinction scarcely signified. On January 24 Oudinot's regiments had in any case entered Breda and Bergen op Zoom, and by February 10 had occupied not only the whole of Dutch Brabant, Zeeland and parts of Gelderland but also South Holland, including Dordrecht. Oaths of allegiance to Napoleon were demanded of burgemeesters, magazines ransacked and militia arsenals destroyed. In general, the French army behaved with the same delicacy that characterised its occupation of any enemy territory. On February 16, in violation of the convention (which itself had not yet been signed), they crossed the Maas. The following day Kraijenhoff persuaded an incensed but fearful Council of Ministers that the preparations for the inundation around Amsterdam and the troop concentrations should be accelerated.

Before the end of the week there were over 5,000 soldiers in or around the city. The Beemster and the Schermer were made ready and arrangements for necessary evacuations finalised. But a clerk in Kraijenhoff's office who had been procured by La Rochefoucauld tipped off the French ambassador, who lost no time in expediting the information to Paris. In another transport of fury, Napoleon demanded that the preparations be stopped at once and that the culpable ministers—Kraijenhoff and the acting foreign minister Hendrik Mollerus—be dismissed. Otherwise, he warned, he would that same day sign the act of "reunion" for the whole country and order Oudinot's army to march on the capital. His brother, he told Fouché, had gone off his head. Louis had no option but to back down—though he kept Kraijenhoff within the Raad, and on April 3 had the burgemeester of Amsterdam, Wolters van de Poll, who had opposed the military defences, discharged for pusillanimity.

Throughout February Louis had resigned himself to the sacrifice of his southern departments. Only one final escape route remained open to him— paradoxically, through England. For even as Napoleon was at the height of his umbrage over the show of resistance, he had abruptly told Louis to despatch a suitable Dutch agent to London to see if, in return for staying his hand in Holland, the British might see reason and come to terms. Like all European dictators, Napoleon could not quite fathom either the intensity or the tenacity of British hostility. Moreover Fouché, who was one of the few real friends Louis had in Paris, was himself strongly in favour of a peace policy and encouraged the Emperor to believe this was conceivable—a bold act in itself since it might rebound in an accusation of "Anglomanie." In December, Fouché had commissioned François Fagan—a royalist ex-officer of Irish descent—to seek out the Marquis of Wellesley (Wellington's elder brother) and see if there was any British willingness for a settlement.[88] It soon emerged that while Spencer Perceval's administration did not have strong views about the changed balance of power on the Elbe or the Oder, the independence of both Spain and Holland were still insurmountable obstacles.

Even before Fagan returned to France, the Dutch effort had got under way. Louis had instructed his Council of State to appoint a reliable business-man; with Fouché's advice Pierre-César Labouchère, the senior partner of Hopes (the bankers) and a son-in-law of the formidable Sir Francis Baring, was selected for the job.[89] Baring was himself close to Richard Wellesley, and, together with Labouchère and the speculator-extraordinary Gabriel Ouvrard (altogether a team of stunning gangsterism), had been involved in a scheme to empty the South American silver mines. Labouchère had also done well out of the major industry of blockade-busting: organising clandestine trade be-tween Murat's Naples and the British via Malta. He turned out to be some-thing of a blunt emissary, but then Wellesley was himself no great believer in courtly protocol. Holland, it emerged, would be incorporated within the Empire, unless the British government saw fit to rescind its orders in council regulating the blockade. Wellesley himself was surprisingly noncommittal but naturally unable to offer the kind of cast-iron assurances Napoleon was after. On February 21 Labouchère returned to the Netherlands, and three days later the Emperor, finally exasperated with all the procrastination, picked up the cudgel again. The *Moniteur* reprinted Champagny's ultimatum of January 24, in which the "recall" of Louis and the immediate occupation of Dutch ports was promised unless the British gave prompt proof of a change of heart.

The "negotiations"—and with them Louis' chances of preserving the Kingdom intact—had run their course. On February 23 Champagny told Roëll that unconditional assent to the two basic terms of the cession was required: the maintenance of a French force of 7,000; and the confiscation of all American goods received during 1809. Despite a 6 p.m. deadline, neither Roëll nor Louis could bring themselves to sign such a document, though they acknowledged capitulation; it remained for Verhuell to provide the response. However painful the sacrifice, it was by no means certain that worse might not yet follow. But as usual, after getting his way, Napoleon instantly assumed an air of brotherly concern at his next meeting with Louis. "Well," he announced, "so our affairs are ordered. I am sorry that I should have had to threaten you, but that was not my fault. You alone are the cause since your Hollanders have been so determined not to follow the French system."[90]

On March 16 the treaty was published. Apart from the points already stipulated, it specified an army of 18,000, one-third French, to be entrusted with surveillance of the coast, customs and the like and, naturally, to be paid for by the Dutch. The naval quota was reduced to 9 ships-of-the-line, 6 frigates and 100 gunboats; the licensing of any special trade was to be authorised from Paris, the debts of the ceded departments to remain a Dutch responsibility, and all colonial wares deposited in 1809 to be rounded up and confiscated— a task which was obviously inoperable since most of it had been already distributed. There was an even more bizarre epilogue to history since, at Compiègne, where the Imperial clan gathered to greet Marie-Louise, Louis attempted a reconciliation with his wife. They returned to the Netherlands together, but after a matter of weeks Hortense made her last exit from Amsterdam, this time never to return.

On April 8 Louis finally crossed the frontier. His relief at escaping the clutches of a brother whom he regarded as a common extortioner may well be imagined. The experience had taken a real toll both of his temperamental stability, never exactly sunny at the best of times, and his physical health. Since the beginning of February he had been continuously sick. The unhappy winter had been a prolonged nightmare. "We have been," he told Roëll as they left Paris together, "in a death-trap."[91]

Even after returning to Amsterdam amidst reciprocated relief and affection, Louis continued to feel insecure. He complained again that he was being spied on by agents of the Emperor, sent away those few Frenchmen remaining at the court, and refused to see La Rochefoucauld, whose vice-regal airs he found a depressing reminder of the Paris ordeal. Compensating for his growing neurosis, he acted the part of Dutch Patriot, wearing his uniform day and night, sporting the decorations of the Royal Guard in his box at the Schouwburg, and avoiding the Théâtre Français at all times. So far from being disgraced, Kraijenhoff was reinstated as Minister for the Waterstaat, a post which, in the fraught circumstances of 1810, had more than purely hydraulic significance. And to complete the effect, doubtless to demonstrate his solidarity with the national cause, Louis took to smoking great wads of tobacco from a Gouda pipe in the middle of official business, to the astonishment of his councillors.

As for the "Treaty" of March 16, Louis rapidly concluded that it was merely putting into abeyance the question of full annexation. All that it had given him and the Dutch was a temporary breathing space.[92] How was it conceivable, given a deficit of 26 millions on the 1809 account, to meet commitments of the current year with two important departments sheared away from the Kingdom? Why sustain the pretence that those colonial goods which had poured into the Netherlands the previous year could be winkled out and confiscated? Where were crews for the navy demanded by his brother to be found? There were 4,500 sailors at present in the Dutch marine; a further 5,000 would be needed just for the ships-of-the-line, if he were to come up to scratch. And most ominously of all, he could hardly be expected to overlook the fact that the French force, stipulated at 6,000 or 7,000, was in fact closer to 20,000. Mile by mile, day after day, it was carrying out what was in effect an invasion by stealth.

By the end of April Oudinot's army had occupied Rotterdam, The Hague, Leiden and Utrecht, where the marshal—the "Duke of Reggio"—made his headquarters. Barely a month after signing a convention allegedly guaranteeing Dutch sovereignty north of the Waal, Louis' effective area of control had been reduced to his own capital and points north. On April 17 he summoned a special consultative meeting of the Council of Ministers, together with the Council of State and representatives of the legislature, once again offering them his abdication. Their unanimous response was to urge him to stay put, since they too knew full well that his own departure would be the signal for the coup de grâce.

Similarly, the relaxation of bitterness between the two brothers which had followed Louis' capitulation was short-lived. Louis complained that even though he had permitted French soldiers and customs men to occupy his ports and river estuaries, France continued to prohibit Dutch goods from the Empire. Napoleon retorted: "Holland must see in you *my* image and understand that it is I who speak through your mouth." Nor was the Emperor over-delighted at a tour of inspection undertaken early in May through the newly "united" territories of the Empire. Jérôme Bonaparte's Queen remarked: "There seems to be no enthusiasm in all these areas ceded by Holland on seeing the passage of the Emperor; the people regrets its sovereign, King Louis —and with good reason."[93] The peasant farmers of Walcheren and South Beveland were disturbed at being cut off from their traditional markets in South Holland, and the benefits which the Brabant manufacturers might have expected from the annexation were offset by the instructions given by Napoleon to the prefects of the Deux-Nèthes that trade down the Maas should be diverted to Antwerp and any necessary traffic down the Rhine to Nijmegen restricted to small river craft.

The Emperor himself made no effort to coax the Zeelanders and Brabanders into an allegiance which he accepted would never be whole-hearted, though he was unpleasantly surprised by the dourness of the Catholic clergy towards their new sovereign. Might was publicly upheld as right. In Flushing he went so far as to inflict an elaborate humiliation on the burgemeester, abusing him as a "traitor" and a "scoundrel," and declining to accept the keys of the port from him for having allegedly been over-friendly towards the British the previous year.[94] Before returning to France, he sent a curious note to Louis which, while signed "Your affectionate brother," in effect served notice of foreclosure on the first Dutch monarchy. He accused Louis of "bizarre" conduct and fancies:

. . . your government means to be paternal—it is only weak. In Brabant and Zeeland I have found only the most incoherent administration. Disabuse yourself. Everyone knows that without me you have no credit; you are nothing. . . . Do you wish to set yourself on the path of a sound policy? Very well then, love France, love my glory—that is the only manner in which a King of Holland can do service. . . .[95]

By the third week of May, Napoleon had almost certainly decided to end the career of the client state. The flimsiest—probably manufactured—incident was excuse enough. With French troops occupying most of the major centres of population in Holland there were regular and repeated affrays, night attacks on customs posts and other fracas testifying to the bad feeling between occupiers and occupied. But the episode which actually brought down the wrath of the French government was another of those challenges to the authority of conquest (like the bust-vandalism of 1798) which rankled precisely because it was so casual. La Rochefoucauld's Dutch coachman, while in his Imperial livery, was assaulted on the Dam. By the time the militia arrived on the scene, the culprits had made good their escape and the memory of assembled bystanders seemed suddenly defective.[96] A broken pate was the most serious consequence. But the ambassador and Napoleon treated the matter as a calculated affront to the Empire. Verhuell, the naval officer whose diplomacy had first prepared the way for Louis' assumption of the throne, was given twenty-four hours to clear out of Paris, and La Rochefoucauld recalled. "The die is cast," Napoleon announced to Louis. "You are incorrigible. Do not address any more of your trite phrases to me, for you have been repeating them for three years now and every moment proving their emptiness . . . this is the last letter in my life I shall ever send you."[97]

That last letter was despatched on May 23. The only decision left for the King was whether he should go quietly or summon his people to make a show of courage, however futile. Serurier, the chargé d'affaires who had remained in Amsterdam after La Rochefoucauld's departure, specifically promised Louis that whatever might seem to be the case it was definitely *not* the Emperor's intention to bring French troops into Amsterdam. But on June 1 Louis learned, without surprise, that Oudinot had orders to make a triumphal progress through the centre of the city. Louis himself had been moving from town to town, one step ahead of the French army, unable to stomach the sight of them acting the conqueror in a land with which by this time he had become obsessively indentified. He took up residence at the Haarlem Pavilion just outside the capital and from there saw to the defences of the city. It was an extraordinary situation—the brother of the French Emperor contemplating a movement of patriotic resistance against the man to whom he owed his sovereignty. But Louis seemed in deadly earnest. On June 20 he drafted nineteen formal "grievances" against France. On June 24, after a French company had been denied entry to the city at the Haarlemmerpoort, Napoleon gave the order for occupation.

The last two days of the month were spent by the King closeted with those councillors who still remained by his side—for Verhuell had made off to his estates in Gelderland and Roëll hovered in agitation between honour and discretion. Once more only Louis, Kraijenhoff and Nicholas Lemmers, the Minister for the Navy, were bent on resistance. The remainder of the ministers and councillors could not bring themselves to face either the consequences of flooding or the military wrath that might follow. Ultimately, de Winter and Dumonceau told the King that Amsterdam was not defensible without help from abroad. Louis buckled. Aghast at the general defeatism, he had the wit to appreciate that he could not in all decency ask a fearful population to fight a war of doomed resistance on his behalf, even if, as he devoutly believed, it was not his crown but their national survival which was at stake. On the other hand, remaining a prisoner in his own palace was out of the question. So on the evening of the 2nd, "convinced that nothing more can be done for your interests or well-being and that I myself am an obstacle to the restoration of good relations between my brother and this land," he signed the abdication order, adding as a parting tribute:

I shall never forget so good and virtuous a people as yourselves. My last thought and my last concern will be for your happiness. . . . Now that I shall be beyond the reach of all malevolence and calumny, I have the just hope that there will finally be an end to all your sacrifices and a proper reward for your uncomplaining steadfastness. . . .[98]

It is tempting to make Louis Bonaparte either ridiculous or heroic. Neither quality fits the case. His personal misfortune lay not only in seeking in his kingship a way to assert his own identity when it had been set up to regularise a condition of dependence, but also in inheriting a political and military situation which could only have deteriorated so long as the war went on. Just as war had created and killed off the Batavian Republic, so it dealt with its successor. The miserable events of 1810 were simply the final culmination of the contradictions between the processes of reform and the obligations of military alliance which had disfigured the Franco-Dutch relationship from the moment the ink had dried on the Treaty of The Hague.

Napoleon was surely mistaken in supposing that "such things would never have happened in the days of Schimmelpenninck."[99] All the diplomatic savoir-faire of the Grand Pensionary would not have been adequate for an equable resolution of these dilemmas. The predicament of the Dutch, trapped in a major European war, had created problems which could not be solved, merely terminated. But perhaps Schimmelpenninck's pragmatism might, in the meantime, have made life a little less painful for himself and the Dutch by bending and flexing where the tactics of survival demanded. Flexibility was not one of Louis' outstanding qualities. And if, in the nature of things, the kingship of "Holland" was bound to be a bed of nails, it is no less true that Lodewijk I leapt upon it with all the masochism of a man impatient for punishment.

****

13

Babylon Undone,
1810–1813

The Makeshift Annexation, 1810–1812

In tearing away the last forlorn shreds and patches of Dutch sovereignty the French, it need hardly be said, were unburdened by remorse. If anything, they saw themselves as performing a salutary service to their enervated and timorous neighbours by exposing them to the realities, however bleak, of a changed world order. In the Napoleonic ethos, the absorption of the Netherlands marked merely another phase in the development of a pan-Continental system of government, beside which the claims of antique and parochial custom shrank to minuscule insignificance. By a circuitous irony, this view was at one with the Orangists in seeing the annexation of 1810 as inherent in the original "forfeiture" of 1795. Pretensions to independence without the military power to make them good were, for the Emperor, a ridiculous sham. All that had happened over the past two decades had been a prolonged exercise in wishful thinking, an expensive masquerade which his economic war could no longer afford to patronise.

What, at the end of it all, had been laid to rest was, then, not a real but an imaginary nationality. The Dutch, it was argued, ought indeed to be grateful to the Empire for releasing them from the inordinate exactions levied in the name of a sovereignty which had long since been spurious. The Procureur-General at The Hague, Jacquinot, one of the least aggressively chauvinist of the French officials who trooped into the new departments, commented:

Wise men of all shades of opinion consider that in the present political state of Europe, Holland must renounce any idea of forming an independent state; indeed it is altogether better for her to be attached to France since in peace-time she [the Empire] will have an interest in restoring [Dutch] trade, whereas England's interest would be in just the opposite direction.[1]

In fact, French economic motives in securing the annexation were quite as predatory as England's in maintaining the blockade. But there were at least some Dutchmen who viewed the "reunion" more as an act of merciful release than a crime of patricide. Johannes Goldberg was quick to point out that even in 1805 he had preferred a full incorporation to the pseudo-independence of the Kingdom, and looked forward to the benefits to be enjoyed by Dutch traders and manufacturers now that the markets of the "Grande Empire" were theirs for the taking.[2]

For Napoleon himself, the annexation was simply a resolution to the conflict of interests and allegiances which had bedevilled his relations with the Dutch ever since the failure of the Marengo loan in 1800. He had long suspected that while perpetually pleading poverty, they were prepared to offer merely token sacrifices in return for military protection. French blood had been spilled, he reckoned, all too cheaply. Perhaps sums might now and again be prised loose from the tightly clenched fists of the Amsterdam bankers, but their "tons of gold" (to which he was fond of alluding) were no longer the issue. The astonishing insubordination of his own maverick brother had convinced him that so devious was that cheesemongering nation in pursuit of its collective interest, nothing short of strict incorporation within his own carefully regulated dominion would suffice to seal off the Continental system from its sabotage.

Nor, since the war with Britain now admitted no quarter, was there anything to be gained from further forbearance. With Imperial coastguards, customs men and police allowed to operate in the Netherlands without let or hindrance, he fully expected to see the stream of smuggling stanched at last —and the long-awaited death-rattle of the British economy to sound across the Channel. He could see no reason why, in the long run, the Dutch should prove any more obstinate in their attachment to anachronistic usages and institutions than, say, Germans or Italians. Eventually, he assumed, their peculiar and cacophonous language would dwindle to the level of a regional patois like Breton—or Corsican. As long as religious liberties were studiously preserved, the combination of political callowness and social pomposity which he took to be their hallmark would incline them to be naturally deferential and loyal subjects of the Empire.

Of course, even Napoleon supposed there might be some wound to national amour-propre occasioned by the end of Dutch independence; and in the summer of 1811, when elaborate preparations were under way for an Imperial progress through the Dutch departments, he was very wary about the project. "I do not know whether or not I shall go to Holland," he wrote; "the important thing is not to be ruined by useless expenditure and to ask only what may be offered from real goodwill."[3] Once actually embarked on the trip, though, many of these reservations were dispelled. Not for the first time in his career, the Emperor was apt to confuse the crook of the knee with enthusiastic greeting and the resplendent civic ceremonies (which the Dutch felt they owed as much to themselves as to the Hero) with affectionate loyalty. In the crowds lining the banks as he toured the Amsterdam canals in an Imperial barge, or pressing in on the Empress when she went to buy Japanese porcelain, he saw not merely curiosity but manifest evidence of the ease with which the Dutch had been won from their old allegiance. He wrote delightedly to Eugène de Beauharnais:

I am extremely happy with Holland: these people have retained the memory of their independence all the better to appreciate the advantages of their reunion and to discover in it a uniformity of laws, moderate taxation and a regular and orderly management of affairs. . . . They are even more French than any other people of the annexed states. . . .[4]

But although the interest of Amsterdammers was naturally excited by the presence of the Emperor in his "third city," it was unwise of him to assume that they had exchanged nationalities with as much facility as altering the Dam to the Place Napoléon. The transports of joy of a people "drunk with happiness"—as the director of police, Devilliers Duterrage, optimistically put it—were about as permanent as the bunting and the arcs de triomphe they laid out in the city for the Imperial couple.[5] A more accurate gauge of the pragmatic temper of the time was supplied by the temerity of a group of merchants and bankers summoned to the "Imperial Palace" to discuss with Napoleon the state of the blockade and the forthcoming collapse of the British economy. Instead of the customary polite echo of his own views, he was regaled with the same litany he had heard from de Winter, Schimmelpenninck and Louis—that until there was peace the Dutch would never enjoy either prosperity or security, and that despite their difficulties the British remained impregnable on the seas and supreme in trade. With "very agreeable moderation" Napoleon replied that no doubt there were still those who might prefer to see King George rather than himself in Amsterdam, but a single year of peace had done more damage to French commerce than the whole of the war; and that whether it took twenty, thirty, fifty years or a whole generation, the struggle would continue until a "just, safe, and honourable peace has been concluded."[6]

The very remoteness of that eventuality was an important constraint on the harmonisation of French and Dutch institutions. Had the assimilation of the Netherlands within the somewhat distended body of the French Empire been as painless as Napoleon suggested, then all those perplexities which had been generated by the embarrassments of a sickly sovereignty would indeed have had their quietus. He certainly meant to convince the Dutch that their new situation was irreversible; that there could be no thought of ever resurrecting the burgher Republic; and at the same time to soothe the hurt by flattering the significance of their joining the Empire. In neither aim was he more than partly successful. For the apparent passivity with which the Dutch seemed to tolerate the effacement of their national identity was conditioned by a presentiment (readily anticipated in the correspondence of Valckenaer, for example) that the fortunes of war might not always run with Caesar. Even at the zenith of Imperial power in 1810–11, there was so little belief in the eternal invincibility of French power that the merest rumour of a reverse in Germany or Russia was enough to send extravagant stories on the wing and license acts of random sabotage that eventually made the Dutch departments some of the least dependable in the Empire. On the other hand, however widespread or genuinely popular the rebellion, it would be unduly flattering to represent it as a courageous blow struck against an oppressor at the height of his powers. Despite the analogies with which the Patriotic doggerel of 1813 was freely sprinkled, the *omwenteling* (insurrection) was neither a repetition of 1572 nor akin to the uprising of Aranjuez in 1808. For the power of the Empire was already more imposing in façade than reality. Even had Napoleon not frittered away two enormous armies in successive years, he would still have had to contend with innumerable troubles arising from within the Empire itself.

While historians have long debated the causes of the severe economic crisis of 1810–11, few have questioned its alarming effects on French trade and manufactures.[7] Even after its recovery, harvest failures and speculative bankruptcies in Paris, Milan and Amsterdam; renewed *chouannerie* in the west; mounting resistance to both conscription and taxation in several departments; and lengthening arrears of salaries for local officials, teachers and priests—all bore witness to the brittleness of government authority once the talisman of military success had gone. To mangle Hanotaux, the Dutch experience of Empire was less one of recruitment than disbandment.

Against this backdrop, it comes as no surprise to find that so far as the Emperor and the Council of State were concerned, the Netherlands, like other territorial acquisitions *outre-Rhin*, were destined primarily to serve short-term logistical needs. The Empire of laws and codes came a poor second to the Empire of recruitment. Ships, naval materials and conscripts were to be wrung from the Dutch, if need be, by glorified press gangs bearing the warrant of the Emperor. At the same time, he instructed General Clarke to "strip Holland of all means of making war so as finally to remove the temptation, one day, to rebel against us."[8] The overriding object was maximum exploitation at minimum expense. Where this suggested not complete but partial integration, then this was the policy adopted in the Dutch *départements réunis*. It was not long before even those Francophile Netherlanders who had urged union on the grounds that it would offer the same rights and privileges as other subjects of "le grand héros de l'époque" discovered that some departments were more uniform than others. They were expected to submit to identical obligations without necessarily enjoying identical benefits.

A case in point was the retention of a prohibitive tariff barrier against not only colonial but Dutch manufactured goods. Even the price of their sovereignty, it seemed, was too cheap to redeem the promise of that elusive customs union promised in 1795. From the French point of view, it would have been quixotic to have given the Dutch an open market since one motive of the Continental blockade, especially inland, was to secure captive markets for their own manufactures and to create what has been called "a vast Un-common market."[9] Napoleon's intention in retaining tariff barriers after the annexation, however, was part penal deterrent; part strategic. It had taken all of Valckenaer's diplomatic arts in Paris to dissuade Montalivet, the Minister of the Interior, from attempting a general confiscation of suspect merchandise, not only from warehouses, but shops, stalls—even private houses. The alternative measure, however, was not much of an improvement: a 50 per cent *ad valorem* duty on all goods entering the "old" Empire from the Netherlands. Had it not been for the intercession of Collin de Sussy, the Director of Customs, the Council of State was prepared, moreover, to calculate the value on the inflated prices then obtaining on the Paris market rather than on value at source. Since the expectation of both Valckenaer and Gogel had been that the somewhat Byzantine commercial diplomacy of the summer of 1810 would eventually result in a 10 per cent *reduction* on duties pending a complete union, the superimposition came as an unwelcome shock. Gogel then did his utmost in correspondence with Montalivet to try to make a case for special concessions, since the Dutch were apparently to be treated in a category of their own. He urged, for instance, that the Imperial prohibition on imported salt be lifted, since the Dutch demand for the commodity for the saltfish industry was so important a feature of their domestic economy.[10] As always, Montalivet responded with the courteous aplomb which indicated sympathy but no more.

Even though the French market was now open to Dutch grain and dairy produce (with the mysterious exception of Friesland butter), it was likewise with the safeguard that should their price rise too far they would again be prohibited. Dutch tobacco was, of course, forbidden to compete with the Imperial *regie* while the latter was given an open door in Holland. The brazenness (as the Dutch saw it) of this manipulative mercantilism was the first serious indication of their real status *vis-à-vis* France. Desperate appeals from the already hard-pressed bombazine manufacturers in Enschede to Gogel and Lebrun warned that the result of closed markets and high tariffs would mean the final dereliction of their trade.[11] The same double standards applied to public finance. While Napoleon's professed long-term aim was fully to integrate the Dutch departments into the Imperial fisc, he was only too susceptible to Minister of Finance Gaudin's reservation that the treasury could not very well afford to do without the 15 million additional francs accruing from the Dutch system of taxation. Hence the Organic Decree of union of October 11, 1810, laid due emphasis on the "complications" (real enough, to be sure) of substituting the French for the Dutch system and retaining the latter until January 1, 1812.

Once again token concessions were made immediately to pacify public feeling. Much to general relief, the irritating stamp duty was done away with, as well as taxes on cattle and movables such as furniture, while the rates on grain and the *personeel* (a tax which the French found bewildering) were reduced. In contrast to the "necessary delays" over introducing the French system of taxes, however, the repudiation of two-thirds of the interest on the Dutch national debt was decreed instantaneously. One Dutch historian of this period called that action "the greatest single act of arbitrary despotism committed by the Emperor against our people,"[12] and certainly its effect in alienating the Dutch from their new rulers was almost comparable to Alva's infamous "tiende penning." There can be no doubt that its effect, not only on the innumerable private individuals for whom state securities represented their only earnings amidst general economic depression, but on corporate and public institutions—schools, churches and poor houses—was quite as disastrous as the most pessimistic prophecies had warned.[13] Ocker Repelaer van Driel suggested to Lebrun that the Dutch would even be willing to bear the burden of Dutch taxes indefinitely, provided they were spared the far more punitive "*tiercering*."[14] And Gogel's old colleague and business associate Jacob Saportas came up with a highly elaborate arrangement by which the whole of the Dutch debt might be divided into a consolidated "active" half carrying interest and properly negotiable, and a "frozen" remainder redeemable at some notional future date—but in practice indistinguishable from worthlessly repudiated bonds.[15]

None of these attempts to circumvent the *tiercering*, clumsy or ingenious, nor the storm of protests and appeals against it, moved Napoleon or his Minister of Finance to reconsider. The Emperor in particular saw no reason why the annexation should actually penalise France by forcing her to assume liabilities which, he believed, had been allowed to augment as the result of incompetent stewardship. When Lebrun, as "Governor-General" of the Dutch departments, passed on the lamentations of the Amsterdam business community, his reply was: "Do the Hollanders take me for a Grand Pensionary Barneveld? I will do just whatever I judge to be suitable for the interests of *my* Empire."[16] Whether outside or inside that Empire, it seemed, the Netherlands were doomed to remain a plunder annexe for the remorseless struggle against the British.

What is striking about the period of the annexation is just how *little* changed in the relationship between France and the Dutch. At a superficial level, the differences might be planed down somewhat. Napoleon ordered the names of new warships being built at the Helder to be changed from the unpronounceable "le Doggerbang [sic], Zoutman et la frégate Kenauhasselaar . . . des noms trop barbare pour moi,"[17] to those which might trip more elegantly off a French tongue; and the *Courrier van Amsterdam* was metamorphosed first into the *Staatkundig Dagblad van het Departement van Zuider Zee* and finally into the bilingual *Journal de l'Amsterdam*. He also seemed to think that lower duties on wine and grain would introduce the Dutch table to the pleasures of bread and wine rather than beer, gin and potatoes.[18] But there were, in fact, very few illusions that they would be rapidly converted into clogged Gauls. Imperial policy towards the seven departments was conditioned by precisely the same divided motives that had characterised its approach to the Batavian Republic and the Kingdom of Holland. On the one hand, logistic and strategic imperatives demanded the absolute subordination of national interests to French direction; on the other, it was orthodox practice in the Imperial administration that political stability and a modicum of efficiency could best be secured by deferring in all non-military matters to local sentiments and prejudices, and by seeking the collaboration of the "natural" ruling élite.[19]

This did not always make for a coherent policy, and the dualism it implied was reflected both in the structure of government (at once centralising and delegated) and the personnel appointed to run it. From one viewpoint, the transplantation of Imperial bureaucracy seemed rigorous enough. The "Architrésorier" of the Empire, Charles Lebrun, duc de Plaisance, was as Governor-General meant to be what Louis had signally not been—the eye of the eagle in Holland. He was to be assisted by a prefect for each department and below them, as elsewhere in the Empire, the hierarchy of sub-prefects, mayors and deputy mayors. But they were also to be supplemented by a Council for Dutch Affairs in Paris, presided over by Gaudin and divided into sections for the Interior-Police, War and Marine, and Finance. In Amsterdam, too, there was to be a further general administration, presided over by two special "Intendants-General," for Finance (Gogel) and Internal Affairs (the Baron d'Alphonse), together with the Directors of Customs, the Treasury, the Public Debt and Police. This last body was, in effect, the inheritor of the old royal Council of Ministers—merely deprived, at least in theory, of independence of action. In practice, however, as elsewhere in the "Grande Empire," it was essential for many decisions to be taken without prior reference to the ministers in Paris and only submitted for "approval" once they had taken effect. Appropriately, the only Director who invariably waited dutifully on instructions from France was Devilliers Duterrage, the chief of police. For purely ornamental purposes a "corps législatif" was retained, stuffed with notables surviving from the reign of Louis: van Lynden van Lunenburg, Mollerus, van Doorn, de Vos van Steenwijk, and the like. The establishment was intended to be a classic Imperial amalgam: an admixture of burghers and barons; a few Dutch officials selected for their proven competence, with French and Belgian bureaucrats in all positions of sensitive security.

As an administrative formula, the arrangement accomplished this purpose. Prefects imported from the Loire and the Vaucluse were responsible, respectively, for North and South Holland, while Carel Hultman was despatched to the Vaucluse in de Stassart's place. The landdrost of Gelderland was moved round to Friesland, and others among his colleagues moved along at intervals just brief enough to prevent them from becoming competently familiar with their parish. To complete the effect, a few token Netherlanders were imported into the government in Paris: Appelius as a full Councillor of State, and the unfailingly orotund Schimmelpenninck as a Senator. This added up to a recipe for confusion rather than equilibrium. Even in the Amsterdam governance there was serious conflict, not (as might be expected) between "old" French and "new" but between those who conceived of their duty (like Devilliers Duterrage) as marshalling Dutch resources for the benefit of the Empire west of the Maas, and those who like d'Alphonse and Lebrun himself took seriously their role of gradually reconciling an independent people to a new allegiance. When this approach—velvet glove rather than mailed fist—prompted Napoleon to criticise Lebrun for mollycoddling his subjects, the Governor, somewhat miffed, replied: "Your Majesty knows me to be of a naturally severe disposition and will do me the honour of believing that neither am I timid; my only ambition is to render this country calm and loyal. I hope to succeed."[20]

Compared with the administration of Berthier in Neuchâtel or Beugnot in Berg, Lebrun's government was on the whole disinterested and lenient. Like Louis, he had his peculiar preoccupations—in this case the cultivation of sugar beet rather than the improvement of hygiene—but as long as he was untroubled by political discontent or social disorder, Lebrun was reasonably happy to delegate most of the active work to his subordinates. Among these, none was quite so inexhaustibly assiduous as the Baron d'Alphonse, one of the authentic prodigies of Napoleonic bureaucracy. The "Intendant de l'Intérieur" operated on the premise that in order to govern a people efficiently, it was necessary to command an encyclopaedic knowledge of their national culture. During his three years in the Netherlands, he tabulated a colossal compendium of information covering every conceivable detail, from the nature of the terrain and climate to the niceties of doctrine separating Arminian from Counter-Remonstrant. Nothing was left to guesswork. His prefects were assailed with circulars requiring details of the state of municipal finances and disbursements to the poor; the condition of the dykes; the content of local diet; the prospects for the madder crop; the history of the Iceland cod fishery; the incidence of pederasty in large towns or bestiality in small villages; the effects of drinking strong tea or weak coffee on the metabolism; the damage done by tobacco to dental hygiene; the numbers of orphans to a bed or schoolchildren to a class.

Wading through the 1,364 pages of the report presented to Montalivet under the beguilingly euphemistic title of *Aperçu sur la Hollande*,[21] the historian is struck not only by its author's cavernous appetite for data, but by his open-minded sympathy for the subject of the examination. The baron seems to have been genuinely liberated from the scornful stereotypes which disfigured previous efforts to penetrate the mysterious idiosyncrasies of the Dutch. Plainly, he admired their struggle with the elements; their attachment to simple liberties and religious toleration. He even had some regard for their language, which "demonstrates the traditional simplicity and sincerity of the nation; possessing few extravagant expressions, it lends itself poorly to flattery or compliment; it is the language of a people who speak what they think."[22] Instead of reducing the complexities of Dutch society to a few readily assimilable clichés, d'Alphonse recognised that its distinctive feature was the extraordinary differentiation of customs, social habits, even dress and diet from region to region, town to town. He noted, with some appreciation, that the women of North Holland seemed less bulky than in the south of the province, "plus svelte," with more animated features and more expressive eyes. In every detail of his domestic circumstances, he observed, the Zeeland fisherman was as different from the Friesland herdsman as from a peasant of another race. Each and every Dutchman it seemed to him "has his own manner of thinking, his own manners and habits, usage and speech." Nor should the French make the fatal mistake of underestimating the Dutch determination to cling to their dearly bought freedoms, for

the love of their country is no less powerful for the Dutch then their love of liberty. . . . Holland may no longer exist, but their native soil has not disappeared and it is to this that all the affection they had for their country is attached. No matter that the terrain is marshy, the sky cloudy, the atmosphere unwholesome; no matter that the misfortune of present circumstances can be seen everywhere. . . . The soil which the Dutchman treads underfoot is the conquest of his fathers; it is their hands which have created it; their sweat which has made it fertile. This is the bond which unites them and which they cannot and will not break. . . .[23]

For Baron d'Alphonse, then, the notion of French Dutchmen was a contradiction in terms. Far from putting them through the mill of Imperial government, there were certain areas—notably in elementary education and the treatment of the aged—where the French might learn from the Dutch example. To be sure, there were also instances where reform would be salutary. The decay of the Latin schools and universities was in marked contrast, he noted, to the enlightenment prevailing in the primary schools. Dutch hospitals were scandalously run down, and "nearly everywhere the prisons are merely narrow cubby-holes, without light or air and nests of infection, crowding together without distinction the detained, the accused and the convicted."[24] Most of the Intendant's remedial proposals were in fact carry-overs from the many memoranda which had lain unattended on Louis' desk as other more urgent matters had distracted his energies. The reform of higher education—and even the closure of Harderwijk and Franeker Universities, which caused much offence to Gelderlanders and Frieslanders respectively—had been anticipated by the Meerman-Valckenaer report of 1809. Van Maanen did not need a French official to detail the miseries of Dutch penal institutions; rather, he needed the funds to do something about them.

For the most part, the Intendant and the prefects were content to keep their departments ticking over rather than launch any grand projects of reform. Even for this they depended to a great extent on the collaboration of men employed by the preceding regime. This was the case at virtually every level of the administration. Without Robert Voûte at the treasury or Elias Canneman in the bureau of direct taxes at The Hague, the fiscal machinery would have been inoperable. There was no thought of displacing Adriaan van den Ende from his presiding scrutiny over the educational establishment set up in 1806. Apart from the endless delays in receiving stipends, the fact that the Dutch school system was officially a department of the Imperial University made no difference to the autonomy of its administration. As the Inspector-General responsible for implementing the requirement laid down by Napoleon that every schoolmaster had to qualify in French before being licensed to teach, van den Ende ensured that the regulation was honoured more in the breach than the observance.

The two most conspicuous intermediaries between French regulations and Dutch ingrained habits were van Maanen and Gogel. Both had accepted office—the former as president of the Imperial High Court at The Hague, the latter as Intendant of Finance—partly under the impression that they would thereby be in a position to cushion their countrymen from the effects of an otherwise over-rigorous application of Napoleonic government. Not that this made them clandestine conservatives, risking their necks for the sake of the

Old Fatherland. Both were genuinely flattered by the appointment, and, like all collaborators, had more faith in the durability of the regime they served than its own native officials. When all the Imperial officials had fled Amsterdam and the customs houses had been razed to the ground, Gogel continued to sign documents with the Imperial seal and despatch them to Paris. His principal concern in accepting the burdens of office (for which, it should be said, Wiselius congratulated him at the time, while later calling him the "arch-scoundrel") was, as always, to try to preserve what he could of the system of 1805. This had become something of an *idée fixe*. Having unsuccessfully pleaded for its retention on the grounds that the financial bureaucracy in the Netherlands could not reasonably be expected to adjust itself for a second time in five years to new *methods*, he ensured nonetheless that those among them whose work he had commended retained their posts.[25]

Gogel did not bother to conceal his personal distaste for some of the French impositions which he regarded as commercially or socially undesirable: in particular, the French *patent* and the tax on doors and windows. If the new order was to mean an unavoidable alteration of his golden rules, then he would—and did—make it his business to see that the Dutch received the benefits rather than the penalties. Given the disaster of the *tiercering*, Gogel believed this to be no less than their due. Quite apart from fiscal affairs, he set himself up as the economic guardian of a besieged community. His correspondence with the Minister of Finance, Gaudin, himself by no means unsympathetic to the Dutch predicament, is crammed with special pleading and requests to make allowances for this city or that industry which had suffered damage from the blockade. Van Maanen was in a comparable position. While the Code Napoléon had become the law of the land in 1810 before the abdication of the King, he had seen to it—and would continue to do so—that it was rendered compatible with traditional Dutch custom and propriety, particularly where cases of divorce and civil litigation over bequests were concerned. In effect it was the Dutch code of 1809 rather than the French which guided the judgements of the magistracy under van Maanen's jurisdiction. When he left The Hague (in some haste) in 1813, Jacquinot, the Procurateur-General, complimented van Maanen not merely on his integrity but on his common sense in making the "Imperial laws" acceptable to his people.

Not all the French officials upholding the Imperial authority in the Dutch departments shared Jacquinot's appreciation. Devilliers Duterrage and the senior officers among the customs men, gendarmes and police took an altogether less charitable view of the concern of Gogel and his Dutch colleagues for the welfare of their compatriots. P.-G. Gateau, the organiser of the political police who had been given short shrift by van Maanen two years earlier, lost no time in offering his judgement of the Dutchmen proposed for official employment. Gogel, he confirmed, was known for his "hypocritical zeal" and his dedication to "amassing thousands of tons of gold." While directing the finances of the Kingdom, he had had three essential goals: to keep himself in office, line his own pockets, and "serve his masters the Orangists."[26] Van Maanen, he graciously acknowledged, had been a reasonably competent Procureur-General but, alas, seemed unable to grasp the important concept of a political crime. Instead of pursuing those real malefactors he spent all his time prosecuting mere murderers, thieves, and men who infringed the common law.

Likewise Devilliers seemed to spend more time in informing his superior in Paris, Minister of Police Savary, of the shortcomings of his colleagues— in particular de Celles, d'Alphonse and even Lebrun ("that irascible old man")—than in sounding out the state of Dutch public opinion. Devilliers reproved those men for what he took to be their naïve leniency in dealing with a population who, it was generally agreed, would never be truly won for the French cause. They had to be mastered rather than indulged. Above all, he was determined to see that the customs and excise men; the gendar- merie; the coastguards and the officials of the *droits réunis* could exercise their authority to search, distrain and confiscate unhampered by the formalities of the law. The predictable results of Devilliers' martinet-like severity were corruption, extortion, nocturnal arrests and gratuitously brutal house searches, all of which ensured that, when the time came, those licensed hoodlums would be the first to be sorted out for popular justice by the irate crowds in Amsterdam and Scheveningen. It also created friction between Devilliers and his subordinates. Both van Maanen (concerned to uphold the integrity of the law) and Gogel were appalled at the crudeness of officials who patently pre- ferred the bayonet to the regulation book to make their authority felt. Gogel took special exception to Pitou, the director of the *droits réunis* (the amalga- mated excise) in Amsterdam. So frequent were the tales of woe, reported to both him and de Celles, of peasants "searched" by having their wagons turned over; of bribes demanded to conceal nonexistent contraband; of wine merchants who, unsurprisingly, were the special target of the protection rackets run by the gendarmes and inspectors (Dutch as well as French)— that even Prefect de Celles, not himself a gentle soul, was moved to echo Gogel's complaints to Gaudin. "The Dutch public," Gogel insisted in Septem- ber 1812, "has always been accustomed to being treated according to the letter of the law." Earlier the same year, he confided to Gaudin,

I must say that matters here might be ordered a good deal better. In general as far as MM. Cuinot, Colomb and other officials are concerned, there is a spirit of bad humour and ill-will towards everything that is Dutch. . . .[27]

The Dutch officials, he observed, were treated so haughtily and with so much abuse that, as Cuinot had publicly acknowledged, it was to be hoped they might be "persuaded" to tender their resignation.

Gogel's mortification at these incidents and at the commonplace viola- tions of hearth and home stemmed from his naïve belief that the authority of the Empire proceeded from a sovereignty which regularised obligations but also guaranteed rights. Despite everything he himself had witnessed, the notion that the warrant of government might indeed rest on the arbitration of brute force was so personally repugnant to Gogel that he turned a blind eye to its reality in the French Netherlands. Others were less deluded. Charles Lebrun may have differed from Devilliers Duterrage, Gateau and Poitou in his attitude towards keeping the peace in the Dutch departments. But in the last resort he, too, knew that the Napoleonic writ ran just as far as its bayonets. In February 1811 he was already showing signs of nervous apprehension, writing to Napoleon:

I told Your Majesty that tranquillity reigns here. I did not then say that there is general contentment. . . . I hope that the enemy will not appear, but should that happen I doubt very much that we could count on the help of the Dutch.[28]

The Rebellion, 1811–1813

"The people," Napoleon instructed his Governor-General, "are never in the right when they begin to revolt."[29] And he was much given to inculpating as anarchists those who through the savagery of their manners rejected the blessings of Imperial government. But when it gathered head and broke, the rebellion in the Netherlands was in no sense a verdict on the wisdom or viability of Napoleonic institutions for, to a large degree, the Dutch departments had remained conspicuously unaffected by them. Rather, it was directed at those aspects of Imperial power which had intruded most aggressively into Dutch domestic life in the form of the armed coastguard, the protected privateer, the inspector of the *droits réunis*, the conscription officer, and the gendarme; the massed battalions, in fact, of the "Empire of recruitment." Since Napoleon and the Dutch were fixed in a relationship of power, not law, the response of the nation state to the majestically decisive events of 1812 and 1813 was correspondingly straightforward and anticipated by all his officials from the Governor-General down. Even in 1811, though, when French hegemony in Europe seemed unassailable, there was some resistance at the points where its demands were most sharply registered. The successful enforcement of the blockade in 1810 and 1811, and the sharp contraction of smuggling, eradicated the livelihood of numbers of fishermen, pilots, receivers, warehousekeepers, chandlers and victuallers—all of whom had been embraced within the community of contraband, which had supported an entire sub-economy on the coasts of Holland, Zeeland and Friesland.

Indeed, it was difficult to disentangle legitimate from illegitimate business. When the cod fishers of South Holland sought special permission through Gogel to fish the Icelandic shoals in 1811, they were denied for the not altogether unfounded reason that such expeditions had become a euphemism for smuggling. Why else would the British let them through? There were other points of economic friction. In 1811 and 1812 there seems to have been a glut of grain in the northern departments, of potatoes in central Holland, and of dairy goods in the Alblasser- and Krimpenerwaarden. The high level of prices which had been sustained throughout the war fell back some way, much to the gratification of the French prefects, who made it as difficult as possible for the Dutch to dump their surpluses in Flanders and points west. With the British market no longer available and the French highly regulated, it seems certain that these two harvests entailed real losses in agrarian income.[30]

By far the most acute source of disaffection, though, was the reaction to conscription. The very fact of Louis' persistent refusal to entertain the idea in the face of his brother's pressure meant that when the breach with tradition was finally made, it seemed (as in the case of the debt repudiation) all the more demonstratively the act of an alien conqueror. This was perhaps never more vividly brought home than when casualty lists of Dutch soldiers in the Grande Armée were published in the Amsterdam press in January 1813. But even in 1811 there had been some trouble in raising conscript quotas. Along with tax rebellion, and desertion, resistance to conscription was a malady affecting metropolitan France as well as the outlying departments after 1810. Whole areas of the southeast and west needed almost as many militia and gendarmes again to secure contingents. And as the demands of a pan-European strategy became more ambitious, so the dependence of the Emperor on non-French allies and auxiliaries also increased. Over half the doomed Grande Armée of 1812 was made up of such regiments, and its fracture was compounded by the defection of Prussians, Austrians, Swedes and Bavarians.

Despite the requirement that the Dutch departments supply their full measure of the "classes" of 1811 and 1812, the Imperial officials were sufficiently aware of the sensitivity of the matter not to press too hard. According to d'Alphonse, between January 1811 and July 1812 only some 17,300 troops were raised from the Netherlands.[31] Even so, desertion rates among the Dutch were high and the practice of buying substitutes, common throughout the Empire, was much indulged in the Holland towns where the families of conscripted "well-to-do persons" (*fatsoenlijke lieden*) were only too ready to buy their children out of service. This only further contributed to the bad feeling engendered by the conscription, which not infrequently spilled over into actual riot in the spring of 1811 when the first lists were posted.[32]

The acts of random violence and disorder which punctuated the conscription drives of 1811 and 1812 were spontaneous attempts, confined for the most part to the poor and lower middle classes, to protect the unity of their families. In almost every recorded instance, the riots were precipitated by the anxiety of women at the departure of their menfolk, both as fathers and breadwinners. In Katwijk in February 1811, the trouble began when a drunken gendarme threatened one of the semi-hysterical women with his sabre, setting off a general melée which needed mounted troops to pacify.[33] In Utrecht the following month, two sergeants of the 326th Regiment, searching a house for deserters and failing to discover them, took the huisvrouw along instead to their commandant to see if she might be persuaded to divulge their whereabouts. As soon as news of the "abduction" filtered through the neighbourhood, a crowd assembled; stones were flung at the soldiers, and a riot ensued in which any Frenchmen in uniform were the targets of indiscriminate attack.[34] Occasionally the scenes were interspersed with tragic farce. On February 25, 1812, in Amsterdam a mother, desperate about the loss of her husband, threw herself and infant child into a canal. In the general anxiety to try to save the woman and baby, there was so much jostling and pushing among the crowd that they succeeded in capsizing a barge on which thirty or so people had thronged to witness the rescue attempt. In the ensuing chaos the mother was dragged alive to the bank but the child had in fact drowned.[35]

The calendar of resistance to conscription ran from February, when the quotas for both the army and navy were made known, through to April and May, when most of the major enrolments for the year had been completed. The early spring was generally the time for the small-town and village riots, especially near the coast where fisherfolk were pressed into the navy. The turn of Rotterdam, Amsterdam, The Hague and the other principal centres of unrest came later, when the Imperial authorities had made their contingency plans in case of resistance and provided enough troops to deal with it. The geography of the disorders was widely dispersed. In 1811 there were affrays in towns as remotely separated as Tilburg in Brabant; Woudrichem in South Holland; and Winschoten, south of Groningen.[36] But there were places which acquired some notoriety and where violence was expected by the local authorities. Virtually all the ports and harbours, inured through their part in contraband to challenging the French officers, put up resistance to inscription in the marine. Brielle, Vlaardingen, Maassluis, Katwijk and Zaandam were all in the van of disorder.

Arguably the most unruly of all was Scheveningen.[37] In the spring of 1812, the entire quota to be furnished by the department of the Bouches de la Meuse (South Holland) was 955. Of that number, Scheveningen was to supply some fifty-nine able-bodied, between the ages of twenty-four and fifty. Given the closure of the smuggling trade and the total dereliction of the fishing port, enlistment in the navy might not have been thought all that disagreeable an alternative to lining for charity meals at the Reformed Almoezeniershuis. But the fierceness of the reaction had little to do with domestic economics. On the appointed day in March the assigned men arrived at the conscription point by the shore, but accompanied by a troop of women, children and most of the local fishing community, all armed with cudgels, knives and boathooks.

Reports of how the fighting started vary considerably, although once again it seems that the richly demonstrative abuse heaped on the gendarmerie by angry women provoked those in the front rank to be over-free with their use of the bayonet. During the fracas some of the soldiers lost their rifles, others their heads, and some shots were fired. Though no-one was seriously injured, the matter threatened at this stage to get out of hand. The prefect, Baron de Stassart, who only a few days before had managed to defuse a dangerous situation at Katwijk, now came to the rescue (by his own not over-modest account). He withdrew the soldiers and gendarmes and faced the people alone:

Even at the very moment when I had force in my hands, I recalled that if I was their prefect, then I was also their father. . . . I let them understand that I would forget their offence so long as they would make it good the same day and show all due obedience and submission. . . .[38]

Just in case this paternal admonition did not have the required effect, Stassart used the hiatus to bring up regular troops from the garrison in The Hague. More prudently, both the date of departure and the route the inscripted men were to take were changed at the last minute so as to thwart any interventions on the road. At the end of the week the men duly left amidst scenes of tearful but peaceful valediction.

The extent and importance of the conscription riots of 1811 and 1812 ought not, then, to be exaggerated. They were a sporadic response to a new additional misfortune for the Dutch common people, and not infrequently took place in some of the most economically blighted towns of the country. Though they caused the French a good deal of anxiety—"As conscription approaches, so irritation augments," observed Lebrun—[39] they nowhere succeeded in actually preventing the departure of the men sooner or later. The more populous incidents in Amsterdam and Rotterdam during April and May did, for the first time, give the French the queasy impression that they were not after all dealing with a people of uniformly bovine placidity. Denied the assistance of the Dutch "National Guard," Lebrun ventured to think, they might be hard-pressed to keep control were there to be the signs of military reverse. Napoleon himself berated the Governor for being altogether too gentle with seditious towns and recommended that a few regents and burgemeesters might be shot *pour encourager les autres*. But at least the French could console themselves that there had been no indications of any political content whatever to the riots. True, the odd shout of "Oranje boven!" had been heard at Katwijk and Scheveningen; but that was a familiar chorus in the sailing towns at any time, and the usual way to be rude to the French. It scarcely betokened the imminence of a national uprising. Lebrun was prone to peaks and troughs of confidence and panic. But during the long, parched summer of 1812, with the *vin du comète* ripening on the stalk, he could write happily enough to the Emperor: "We are in the most perfect tranquility. The government operates without any undue friction; and the police seem to have no anxiety at all."[40]

By the following spring the situation had been transformed. In the arrondissement of Oud Beierland in South Holland, the crowds of peasants involved in the renewal of the riots ran to thousands and there were dead and wounded among the casualties.[41] As elsewhere in Europe, the evaporation of the Grande Armée in Russia had fundamentally changed the credit of Imperial authority in the Netherlands. The losses suffered by Dutch troops, some 14,000 strong, were no more serious in scale than those of the other foreign contingents, but that was bad enough. Of the 500 Dutch members of the élite Imperial Guard, just 40 survived the Russian campaign, few of them with all their limbs intact. The Dutch had been in the thick of all the major engagements and had contributed to the brigades of *pontonniers* who, in the ice floes of the Beresina, managed to build the bridges without which the casualties of the Imperial army would have been even greater. Many of them, as a result, were caught at Studianka on the wrong bank. The 126th Regiment, largely Dutch, which had entered Smolensk with 1,887 men, was reduced to 347 on the retreat and, after defending the Beresina bridges, to the 206 walking cadavers whom the Russians took prisoner on November 28.[42]

Ironically, interest in the campaign in the Netherlands was intense. This was partly because it was the first time thousands of conscripts had been sent away from home to fight in a war with which they only dimly identified, but also because, in expectation of a new string of victories, the French press in Amsterdam and the Holland cities had stoked up enthusiasm by elaborately detailed accounts of the burning of Smolensk and the Battle of Borodino. Towards the end of November, however, the ominous silences of the bulletins began to be punctuated by publication of the Dutch dead and missing in the *Courrier d'Amsterdam*. The prefect de Celles actually encouraged this practice in the misconceived belief that it would excite the anger of the Dutch against the Russians—and by association the British. Instead, of course, it confirmed the demonology of the French as slaughterers of the innocent.

It was the bulletin of December 3, 1812, abruptly announcing the Emperor's return to Paris, which left no-one in doubt as to the fate of the Grande Armée and which turned acts of emotive protest into calculated sabotage and sedition. The prefect of the Bouches du Rhin, Frémin de Beaumont, had tried to put as bold a face on the disaster as he could by reporting widespread relief at the safe return of the Emperor to Paris. But, it was clear, the general demand for copies of the *Bulletin* was not motivated exclusively by concern for his welfare. Later, Frémin de Beaumont admitted that the most alarming stories concerning the misfortunes of the army had spread like wildfire in Nijmegen and den Bosch. In a café in den Bosch a man had openly rejoiced at the destruction of the Imperial troops, arguing that it would bring about a measure of "equilibrium" in Europe.[43] In Zeeland, around Zierikzee, posters describing the retreat in Russia (evidently printed in England) had been pasted up on walls, and during December and January, most of the sniping at the Imperial regime took the form of *affiches*, placards and doggerel versus pinned to doors in public places or scattered in the streets overnight. Early in January one such poster, in the style of a missing persons-deserter notice, appeared in The Hague:

> *Missing: a certain party going by the name of Napoleon.*
> *Anyone providing information assisting in bringing him to justice*
> *will be rewarded with an Orange cockade.*

And in more theatrical style in Dordrecht:

> *Revenge, citizens, revenge! It is all over with the tyrant. Now then,*
> *revolt and revenge!*[44]

By the beginning of February such notices were an almost daily occurrence in all the major cities in Holland, especially in the south, in Dordrecht, Rotterdam and The Hague. Devilliers, who rather prided himself on running an austere regime, complained to Stassart that "incitements to revolt and [seditious] pamphlets are appearing in this department almost without interruption." True, the whole country was far from nearing general insurrection. As Lebrun pointed out to Napoleon, the mayors and councillors of the Dutch towns had responded generously to the appeal for money and horses (though not, significantly, for men) to restock the army in preparation for the German campaign. Nevertheless, as the new conscription season approached, the acts of public impertinence took increasingly vituperative forms. In Dordrecht the *affiches* specifically invoked the holy war against Spain:

Rise up, dear brother citizens! It is for the sake of your children. If you have a fatherly heart then this is the time. The atrocities of the tyrant are shedding too much blood not to excite our vengeance. Citizens, the arms are in your hands; let them serve for our glory; for our Fatherland, for the revenge of our children . . .

Napoleon himself had become not only oppressor but manifestly lunatic:

the man who will die for a tyrant is plainly mad, but the Tyrant himself must be even more crazed to demand such a thing. Cursed, then, is this Arch-Tyrant who does more evil than the Grand Sultan and as much as the Devil himself. Amen![45]

By the beginning of March, areas of the countryside which had at worst been restive were now reported by their prefects as difficult to control. Jever and Groningen in the north and Assen in the east—those sectors nearest to the temporarily liberated Hamburg—were allegedly infested with agents provocateurs, spies and paid rebels of the British and Prussians. Certainly many of the demonstrations were overtly Orangist. The official birthday of the Prince on March 8 provided an ideal occasion to rally traditional loyalties. At Deventer, the public carolling of "Oranjeliederen" was the overture to a major riot which only ended by summoning the garrison. The *trekschuit* from Franeker to Harlingen was boarded by a gang of armed men who "encouraged" the passengers to choruses of anthems, old and presumably well-loved; draped the barge in orange flags; and just in case there were any in doubt about the point of the exercise, distributed cockades.[46] At Arnhem and Harderwijk, crowds roughed up customs men; the same sort of treatment was meted out to isolated companies of gendarmes in Breda, Schoonhoven and Culemborg.

All these incidents were local in origin and incoherent in execution. But they rattled the complacency of the prefects. De Celles sent a gunboat to pacify mobs at Zaandam and Enkhuizen in April, and tried to establish an elaborate network of spies and agents in the estaminets and taverns of Amsterdam where he believed disaffection to be chronic. Even in February he had gloomily concluded: "If the English were to mount any kind of expedition at this time on our coasts, the French troops alone would not be sufficient to maintain order in the towns."[47] The police began to see plots and conspiracies where there were none. Anthonie Santelaar, who had enjoyed a brief celebrity by haranguing the village rioters in Oud Beierland, was rather flattered by his conviction as a paid agent of the British, placed in the Grande Armée to foment mutiny.[48] True, a cache of arms had been found secreted on the Amsterdam-Haarlem *trekschuit,* but the conspiracy theories associated with this were more a product of the imagination of a beleaguered police than of any hard and fast evidence.

The climax of all these incidents, real or imagined, occurred between April 19 and 21 in Leiden. The "drie schoften Oranje boven" (an untranslateable epithet, but loosely meaning the "three marauders for Orange") were celebrated in nineteenth-century accounts as the first blows struck for the freedom of the Fatherland, a Dutch equivalent of the rising at Aranjuez, or the Dos Mayos. But as their sardonic nickname suggests, the whole affair was more a knockabout riot than a patriotic epic.[49] Part of the trouble was that, as the prefects had warned, with disorders occurring simultaneously throughout the Bouches de la Meuse (though nowhere else with the exception of Zaandam), the resources of law and order were simply inadequate to the task of restraining a minor village fracas from spilling over into a major town. On the 19th, Stassart had mobilised most of the mounted troops and militia available for such duties around the area between Dordrecht and Rotterdam where rioting had been most serious and had actually penetrated the city. The same day he received an agitated message from the sub-prefect at Leiden, Gevers van Endgeest, informing him that the whole canton of Alphen was in revolt.

What had actually taken place was that a crowd of peasants variously estimated at 200, 500 or 1,000, including women and children, and armed with the usual pitchforks, cudgels, scythes, skinning knives and the like, had marched on neighbouring villages like Woubrugge and Aarlanderveen doing nothing very much but doing it noisily and with much wagging of orange ribbon. As at Boskoop and Zevenhuizen in the extreme south of the department, the disorder was probably in reaction to the attempt, somewhat mistimed, to enlist men for the Imperial National Guard as a decree had commanded. It is just possible that the ringleaders intended to try to raise the local countryside to the Orange banner, but there was not the least evidence that this was to be the beginning of a planned insurrection. Nor need it have gathered quite so much momentum had the sub-prefect been blessed with even a modicum of sang-froid. The mayors of the villages of Leiderdorp and Nieuwkerk, after all, refused to be intimidated by the crowd into ringing the tocsin and joining the "march" as demanded. But possibly inspired by the stirring example of Baron de Stassart at Scheveningen, Gevers van Endgeest made an abortive attempt to cow the gathering with his official presence at the village of Aarlanderveen. Instead of shuffling about in deferential silence the peasants instantly seized him, danced about and subjected him to various indignities, not the least of which was being released on the order of the Oudshoorn baker van Lee on the grounds that "he was thought to be harmless." Restored safely to Leiden, Gevers van Endgeest decided as a precaution to close the city gates and raise the drawbridge. Intended as a deterrent, this had precisely the opposite effect. On seeing the city barred, the peasants outside assumed that it had been taken from within, as they had been told, and reassured about its safety resolved to "join" the rebellion, hoist the Orange flag and proclaim Leiden for the Prince.

Inside Leiden, apart from the "National Guard" militia (the *schutterij* in Imperial fancy dress), themselves not at all keen to confront the rowdy assembly, were just ten fusiliers mobilised for its defence. When the two leaders, van der Lee and Dirk Klerk, an innkeeper's son, appeared at the Utrechtse Poort asking for "their people" to be admitted, much to their surprise they were arrested and carted along to the town lock-up. But resistance went no further than this, for, summoned by their officer to steel themselves to fight to the death, the militia instantly emptied their rifles of cartridges and together with the mayor, van Heldewier, and his councillors beat a rapid retreat to a fort at the other extremity of the city. In due course the gates of the city were forced and Leiden given over to the scenes of bucolic jollity customary on such occasions: houses pillaged, cellars looted, the gin barrels emptied; the city jail opened and not only the two "rebels" but the other eighty inmates given their liberty.

So general was the merriment that the burghers of Leiden and more particularly their councillors and the student guard were reminded uncomfortably of the plunders of 1787. In the end, a student with the unheroic name of Klopper managed to prise open one of the gates far enough for General Lorcet to charge in with a hundred or so troops, taking the rebels by surprise. After a brief exchange of fire, the leaders were caught and their rank-and-file put to flight, most of them heading for the nearest exit or swimming for it in the canals. Though the number of casualties was never ascertained with any accuracy, Gogel wrote to Gaudin that fifty had been killed or badly wounded in Lorcet's operation. At the end of the month, four of the principals were convicted by court-martial and duly shot.

However inglorious the "invasion" of Leiden may have appeared in retrospect, it unnerved the likes of d'Alphonse to imagine that a city of 30,000 could be mastered and pillaged by a rabble of peasants with such contemptuous ease. Moreover similar incidents had taken place, though with not quite such spectacular effect, at Maassluis, Brielle, Boskoop between Gouda and Woerden, and at Dordrecht where the customs post had been liberally ransacked.[50] In The Hague itself a riot around the Turfmarkt seemed for a time as though it would succeed in demolishing the Prefecture. But it was the very disorderliness of these *attroupements* which came to the aid of the Imperial authorities. For those who saw themselves as the target of a general melée, the spectre of the *plunderjaren* was still too close for them to permit the crowd to have its head. So, as at The Hague, they mobilised the militia and stood firm against the rioters.

In so doing, however, it should have been clear that it was not the authority of the Emperor they were defending so much as their own property and person. Throughout the period, after all, from the time of the Patriots to the turbulent years of 1795 and 1796, the "respectable classes" in the cities had used their guard not only as a political weapon, but as a form of social constraint. So that when Stassart compiled a list of all those Hague worthies who had rallied to his aid in the hour of need, it was not to be supposed that he could count unfailingly on their support in the future. There might well come a time when it would be more prudent to withhold their assistance and avoid the odium of being identified not merely with a tyrant but a fallen one. As yet such eventualities were still in the realm of speculation. But there were those—both among committed Orangists like Gijsbert Karel van Hogendorp and those in the margins of disaffection like the captain of the Amsterdam National Guard, Anton Reinhard Falck—for whom the lessons of the Dutch spring fever were perfectly clear. It was urgent to advance plans for a more organised revolt so that the latent forces of insurrection they had plainly witnessed might be decently canalised for the "good cause," not merely squandered in aimless sabotage and plunder.

For the mass of the Dutch people in the summer of 1813, the way ahead must have seemed unclear. Some doubtless believed the optimistic reports in the press of the "crushing victories" at Lutzen and Bautzen. The legend of Napoleonic impregnability was difficult to kill. But for some among the ruling élite whose loyalty hung in the balance, the subsequent conduct of the French themselves may have helped them make up their minds. For the April riots had convinced Lebrun, alternately severe and vacillating, that he had indeed been too indulgent with the Netherlanders and that doses of corrective medicine would be timely. Hence after May the conduct of customs guards, gendarmes and police was even more pugilistically clumsy and brutal. As in France herself, what was left of the press was subject to harsher censorship. The proceedings against those apprehended during the spring disorders offered an ideal opportunity to mete out exemplary punishment. Six offenders were executed in Zaandam, five in The Hague and three in Rotterdam. Others were deported; two given fifteen-year sentences to forced labour, and many more two or three years. Some managed to be altogether acquitted for want of incriminating evidence.[51] Partly as a result of intelligence gleaned under interrogation, the appetite of the political police grew, as it were, with the eating. In their eagerness to winkle out conspiracies galore, they succeeded in converting many whose earlier attitude towards the regime had been merely pragmatic indifference into outright enemies.

The fact that some of these "plots" embraced men of such different social and political kidney testified either to the increasingly indiscriminate nature of official paranoia, or else more ominously to the growing coalition of those who might agree on nothing else except the desirability of ridding the country of the French imperium. Such indeed seems to have been the case in the curious stratagem involving, plausibly enough, an Orangist naval officer—but in harness with the Jewish physician de Lemon. H. H. de Lemon was a perfect specimen of that section of Amsterdam Jewry which until then the French had regarded as the most dependable element of the population. He was professional, middle-class, semi-assimilated, a member of the reforming club "Felix Libertate," an ex-deputy of the Batavian national assemblies of 1797 and 1798 and one who was clearly amenable to the government-appointed Consistory, antagonistic to the intransigent, obscurantist and (worst of all) Orangist Parnassim and rabbis. The de Lemon plot changed all this. Henceforth the Jews, "cultivated" or "reactionary," were among those most closely scrutinised by Devilliers' men, all the more so after a fracas near the Joodenbreestraat had brought out the militia in June. The result of all this perspiring work in the back alleys of the ghetto was merely to ensure that when the time came, the President of the Consistory—the one man assumed to be steadfast in his loyalty to the Emperor, Jonas Daniel Meijer—was to be found in the van of those leading the Amsterdam uprising, a colleague of Falck's and a member of the provisional administration of November.

The same self-fulfilling prophecy operated in matters of past political allegiance. It was of no avail to de Lemon that he had been a Batavian Patriot and democrat. On the contrary, it confirmed him as a natural fomenter of sedition. Others rounded up in the same category were Johan Valckenaer, classified as "one of the ringleaders [or rather, the elegant anathema *coryphée*] of the Patriots." Valckenaer was released after four days in prison but, as we have seen, he was not a man to take a slight lightly. It is not inconceivable that his retributive Orangism, which was later to border on witch-hunting, dated from the discomforts of this experience.[52] To the French, "Patriot" was in any event virtually synonymous with conspirator or saboteur. In February 1813, de Celles had observed:

It is vain to suppose that the old Batavian Patriot and the Orangist could never conspire together, being old enemies and divided in their opinions and interests; they are in fact all united and tied together by the hatred they share for France and in despair at being subjected to common laws [as the rest of the Empire]. Even the most intelligent personages, while approving of our system of administration and finding it more orderly, more equitable and more economic than their own traditional usages, regret having to be indebted for anything to France and prefer Dutch abuses to the order and regularity of the present arrangements. . . .[53]

The prefect was quite correct in judging that those Dutch who had had experience of politics and government cherished the freedom to be disarrayed in their own fashion more than the symmetrical felicities dispensed by the Napoleonic bureaucracy. But in any event their encounter with Imperial rule in 1813, so far from embodying the principles of "order" and "regularity," seemed on the contrary to reveal an authoritarianism that was both coercive and arbitrary. It was in this climate that many of the men who had viewed a reversion to the House of Orange with no special elation were forced into a position of opting for the lesser evil.

There can be no question that the French themselves accelerated this process of alienating those whose loyalties might otherwise have been more equivocal. Hugo Gevers was a case in point. Like other reasonably well-to-do former Patriots, he had managed to keep his son well clear of the conscription rolls in 1811 and 1812. But the *gardes d'honneur*—a glamorisation of what was generally taken to be a further conscription—was to be without exemptions or substitutions. Indeed it was meant, as the title implied, to be taken as a privilege. Yet all too few youths in the summer of 1813 were keen to bask in a reflected glory which was getting dimmer by the month. The enrolment for the guard recruited to the camp of those hostile to the French exactly the social groups whose support as militia and National Guard officers had been decisive in the spring. Lebrun maintained that the enlistment went off without a hitch. But in his altogether more candid and penetrating analysis of the sudden disintegration of French power in the Netherlands, Procureur-General Jacquinot insisted that it had been a decisive factor.[54]

When Hugo Gevers, a kindly and gentle soul, made so bold as to register a protest not only on behalf of his own son but of others like him who were being transported to military camp (by force if necessary), he was treated to an exhibition of the gratuitous bullying and petty spitefulness that are the hallmarks of insecure imperialism. Gevers complained that his son had been arrested for allegedly resisting conscription without warrant or evidence. But the prefect brushed him aside with a crude threat: "Do you know, Monsieur, that I can confiscate your property?" To which the veteran republican, who with Paulus eighteen years earlier had greeted the legions of General Pichegru as the heralds of liberty, wearily replied: "Do what you want; I have long resigned myself to everything."[55]

His words could serve as the terse epitaph for the Batavian fancy that, liberated from the prejudices of the old world, the armed disciples of the "Grande Nation" might act unlike other men and live up to the professions of their political innocence. Elias Canneman, who had himself been among the devoutest of the believers, and who related this tale of woe to Gogel on June 10, also noted that many others were in a similar predicament to young Gevers: the sons of Gijsbert van Hogendorp and of Donker Curtius, president of the Friesland Court of Appeals, had also been summarily incarcerated. With the sour fatalism that exactly summarised the mood of the summer of 1813 for this shrinking group of stalwarts, Canneman lamented that life had become "bitter and grievous (verdrietig). Had I not a wife and children . . . I would take myself over the border."[56]

To borrow Fouché's verdict on the judicial murder of the duc d'Enghien, the alienation of the old Batavians was worse than a crime; it was a mistake. In the autumn of that year, with his makeshift army jockeying for position in the mud of Saxony against forces overwhelmingly superior in numbers and equipment, Napoleon needed all the friends he could get. But Lebrun's ideas of influencing people were going wildly astray. In July it was learned in North Holland, with some consternation, that lists were being drawn up in Haarlem of eligible brides who, with their male contemporaries in the army, might be shipped off to France (together with ample dowries) as matches for young French gallants. Whatever the truth in the report—and astonishingly it does seem to have had some foundation in fact—it so wounded sexual, religious and patriotic sensibilities that the perfect pretext for righteous indignation had been supplied.[57] Yet another principle held dear by the Dutch, that of the sanctity of property, literally went up in flames when, on August

9, a week before Napoleon's birthday, Lebrun decided to burn nearly 2 million francs' worth of confiscated merchandise on the Dam.

It was the cremation of French power in the Netherlands. Ill-omens then began to crowd in on the Imperial administration like vultures. By the end of August, prefects in Friesland, Ems-occidental (Groningen) and the Bouches de la Meuse were all complaining about the marked reluctance of regents and magistrates to serve on official bodies.[58] Resignations were even being received —and few could match a Dutch regent for the ability to catch the whiff of a political corpse even before it had been laid to rest. To complete the gloom, the "cascade of bankruptcies" in which no less than *eighty-seven* Amsterdam firms had failed at the end of 1812 continued its unhappy momentum. In the wake of a peculiarly malodorous scandal concerning public funds in Paris and Amsterdam, the state cashier Tetterode drowned himself. But along with him he ruined some of the most illustrious pillars of the banking community: Alewijn, Arripé (one of Gogel's old colleagues) and, most traumatic of all, Pieter de Smeth.[59] Of all the dismal auguries this was perhaps the surest sign for those Dutchmen who had not already sensed it, that the centre would not hold. On October 10 the Governor himself suddenly relapsed into a fit of histrionic self-pity. Asking the Emperor if he might not be relieved of his duties forthwith, he confessed that, come what may, "Ma tête est perdue." All that was left to him was a heart profoundly grateful for all the honours and benefits he had had bestowed upon him.[60]

Lebrun's anxiety to depart with dignity while that was still possible reflected a growing nervousness among the French bureaucrats in the Netherlands that, should the gamble in Germany be lost, they would be bereft not merely of power to enforce their authority, but of the most rudimentary defence. The first line of cover for the Dutch departments, confirmed by Napoleon in his tour of inspection in 1811, ran from Delfzijl in the extreme northeast through Coeverden in Drente, Zwolle, Deventer, Zutphen, Arnhem, Nijmegen, Grave, Venlo and Maastricht. Properly manned, munitioned, and provisioned, that chain of forts was meant to provide a *cordon sanitaire* against any attack from the land side. But those arrangements had been made in palmier times when the Emperor could rely on the non-belligerence, if not the true alliance, of most of the major European powers. With the balance of forces swung sharply against him, every man, horse, wagon and gun that could be produced was needed at Leipzig.

Though Napoleon had—rashly as it turned out—allowed Davout to keep 40,000 men stationed at Hamburg, points west were scoured clean of troops and matériel. In his pessimistic review of available resources in early November, de Celles concluded that at least 25,000 *French* soldiers were needed to make the country secure. As it was, General Molitor could count on no more than about 4,000 French, a quarter of them mounted, with perhaps as many again oddments of the "Grande Empire" and its allies. But the mettle under fire of the 1,500 Spanish at the Helder, the 2,000 Swiss at Arnhem, or the few hundred Prussians whose King had already gone over to the Coalition was, to say the least, doubtful. On the eve of the Battle of Leipzig (October 16–19) there were less than 400 gendarmes, regular troops and armed customs men holding Delfzijl, while the fort at Coeverden was manned by exactly 269 veterans. At Deventer the situation was even more parlous, with sixty-seven customs men and eighty auxiliaries for a while the only forces protecting the city. At the most generous count, there were about 1,000 armed men patrolling a frontier stretching over 100 miles and with no major natural barriers to halt a straightforward infantry advance.

All the more ironic, then, that the defence of the Dutch departments should depend so vitally on a handful of those most execrated by its citizens, together with units of the despised Dutch reserve companies and the National Guard. It crossed the mind of French officials like de Celles and Lebrun that the Dutch militia might not actually wish to die in the ditch to save the Napoleonic Empire and that they might find themselves as a result marooned amidst a hostile populace and troops who, defecting en masse, would leave them to an unpleasant fate. For the first time in twenty years they were experiencing the chilly impotence of an authority without muscle; an Empire without clothes. It had been Napoleon himself who, in August 1810, had told a Dutch deputation at St. Cloud: "I hold you by right of conquest and that, to be sure, is the most sacred right of all."[61] By the same token they would stand forfeit to his defeat. Everything, then, turned on the outcome of those few wintry days in Saxony.

By October 20 the dimensions of the catastrophe were apparent to Napoleon's commanders as the battle degenerated into general retreat. He had succeeded in sending yet another huge, if distinctly sub-standard army, scraped with the utmost difficulty from every corner of the Empire, to its doom. Yet he remained irrepressibly sanguine about the chances of extricating himself from disaster, going through the motions of calling up 150,000 men of the class of 1803–14 (which had already supplied 30,000 for Spain) and drawing in advance on 160,000 of the class of 1815. But there was, in fact, not the remotest chance of another Grande Armée coming into being. In the manner of 1799 in Egypt and 1812 in Russia, the human debris of botched-up Napoleonic strategy were left behind to fend for themselves as best they could. Two hundred thousand of them remained in the ice and mud of the German winter as dead, wounded or prisoners of the Coalition. As Vienna and Berlin celebrated with Te Deums, the remnant, wasting away with cold and typhus, and deprived of food and shelter, finally struggled across the Rhine at Mainz on November 2–4. General Griois' verdict on the miserable adventure was coarse but to the point: "*Parbleu!* What a fine piece of work we've carried out. We've been to Moscow to look for the Russians to fetch them back to France."[62]

There was no alternative to evacuating the entire territory between the Rhine and the Elbe. But so sudden and so complete was the vacuum opened up by the annihilation of the Empire in Germany, that the flotsam and jetsam of its authority suddenly found themselves stranded behind enemy lines.

St. Cyr's 20,000 were obliged for that reason to surrender at Dresden on November 11. Only Davout, an automaton of loyalty, kept his 40,000 at Hamburg locked up but militarily useless until ordered to capitulate by Louis XVIII the following May. At the end of October, Marshal Macdonald was forced to fight a rearguard action at Hanau to frustrate a Bavarian-Austrian effort to cut the French retreat. But at the same time, the Kingdom of Westphalia, directly southeast of the Netherlands, had been abandoned by King Jérôme, who had anticipated Napoleon in crossing the Rhine at Coblenz. Cassel was already in the hands of Chernichev's Cossacks when Macdonald was given the thankless task of defending the territory between the Yssel and the Maas. The forces available for what, at best, could only be a holding operation were desperately slight—perhaps 12,000 at the most—and in wretched condition. Macdonald himself was obliged to muster in some strength at the southern end of the sector between Arnhem and Maastricht so as to block off the route through Liège to north-eastern France. General Molitor was promised reinforcements, but in the meantime had to defend the Netherlands with the scanty army on hand. In effect, the invasion of the country by Russian and Prussian divisions of the right wing of the Coalition Armies under Bernadotte was only a matter of time. It was held up, much to British annoyance, by the King of Sweden's interest in throttling the Danes so as to oblige them to disgorge Norway for his own realm's aggrandisement. The liaison between von Bülow's Prussians and the miscellaneous Russian forces of Benckendorff and Chernichev, as usual, left a lot to be desired. But their own frailties aside, there was virtually nothing to bar the Allies' way to Amsterdam.

On November 8 the first Cossacks duly made their appearance at Aurich, catching Hofstede, the Dutch prefect of the Ems-oriental, by surprise and taking him and his staff prisoner. Devilliers even feared that he had been murdered by the Russians. On the 9th Prussian hussars got within 10 miles of Deventer, though the newly reinforced garrison there deterred a serious frontal attack. But the defence line north of the Yssel virtually disintegrated on contact. On the 13th French officials, customs men and gendarmes from Zwolle arrived as fugitives from the *chef-lieu* of the department of Yssel-Supérieure, captured by a tiny force of Russians the day before. The Dutch reserve company had fulfilled all the worst expectations of the French by defecting *en bloc*, and the local Overijsselaars had hailed the Cossacks as liberators and offered them drinks, fruit and hospitality. During the second week of November, moreover, the first signs of serious rebellion declared themselves in the areas adjacent to the Allied advance. At Winschoten, Meppel and Hoogeveen, not far north of Zwolle, there had been violent riots, and attacks on customs posts and gendarmeries. The prefect of the Ems-occidental, Petit de Beauverger, believed the situation north of the Yssel entirely untenable. Within a week both he and the Director of Customs and Excise in Groningen, Dégérando (brother of the *philanthrope* Councillor of State) had taken the coastal route south—for the main road to Utrecht had already been cut.

During the week between November 8 and 15, authority fell away from the French Empire in the Netherlands like dead flesh from a skeleton. The contagion of rumour hastened the process. After Leipzig, anything might be true. It was bruited about in Amsterdam that Napoleon had been deposed by the Senate; that he had been assassinated; that France herself had capitulated unconditionally to Tsar Alexander. The Dutch, in their taverns and coffee houses, at their work benches and shops, could actually watch the "Grande Empire" disintegrating before them as its officials became less and less concerned with the logistics of defence and more with self-protection—in particular, getting themselves and their families back to France while they could. Stories of the treatment allegedly handed out by the dreaded Cossacks only intensified the panic. Women, children and domestic servants bundled into carriages; wagons loaded with furniture, household goods, trunks—as well as anything of value that could be pilfered in one last exercise of Imperial appropriation—began to crowd the roads from Utrecht, Amsterdam, The Hague and Rotterdam, most of them making southwest for Antwerp. As the process of general collapse accelerated, the position of the obedient few who remained at their posts, and above all the detested agents of the economic terror, became steadily more precarious.

The situation rapidly turning into an undignified *sauve qui peut* might have been contained had there been clear and coherent directives from the Emperor himself. But in the miserable period between the defeat at Leipzig and the campaign of France in the new year, Napoleon seemed to retreat into a realm of private self-exoneration, alternately abusing as traitors and numbskulls those he blamed for his predicament, and wildly exaggerating his chances of extricating himself from it. Whole departments of France were already openly defying tax collectors and conscription officers. Disaffection was apparent even within the army, and some of the marshals were expressing dim views of the Emperor's waning powers. Tutored by Talleyrand, the Senate, that dumb creature of Imperial will, was likewise beginning to rediscover its voice. And yet Napoleon persisted in believing in the magic of his destiny. By temporising with Metternich at Frankfurt he might yet divide the Allies and win a breathing space in which to rebuild his military power. Hence his policy towards the Netherlands was simultaneously pragmatic in strategy while unrealistic in tactical detail. Privately, he had already intimated that Holland north of the Maas was to be excluded from the "natural frontiers" to which he was prepared to be reduced. But at the same time he was concerned to frustrate the British design for a Netherlands swollen with Belgium and possibly part of the left bank of the Rhine, ruled over by the Prince of Orange.

It was therefore vital for Napoleon to hang on grimly to the Dutch departments for as long as possible, both as bargaining counters in the peace, and to close off the route through Flanders to north-east France and Paris. But his specific orders betrayed neurotic instability. On one occasion he told Decrès to let Clarke, the Minister of War, understand that by the new year of 1814 there would be "six hundred thousand men on the move."[63] And on the very day that the Amsterdam customs houses went up in flames,

November 15, he informed Molitor that a month hence there would be 60,000 French troops encamped at Utrecht. Two days later he was insisting that 25,000 guardsmen could be raised at the drop of a hat from Ghent, Antwerp and Utrecht.[64] All these figures signified nothing but the fury of his own reveries. It was symptomatic of the apocalyptic egotism which was overtaking his reason that, in the event of a retreat to a second line at Schoonhoven, Naarden and Gorinchem, he insisted that the dykes on the Waal be cut before Gorinchem. Only after Macdonald's remaining troops had been badly mauled by the Russians at Arnhem was he prepared to concede that the line on the Lek had collapsed, and that a withdrawal to the Waal could not be avoided.

Even then, Napoleon could not bring himself to believe the situation in the Netherlands to be irretrievable. Throughout December and January 1814, with the Allied troops simply bypassing French enclaves bottled up in fortresses in Brabant, and with Willemstad evacuated, the Emperor continued to berate General Rampon for not breaching the dykes and flooding the whole of the country between the Scheldt and Waal, so as to make life as difficult as possible for the Allies. This made little military sense, for the conquest of the country from the east and north had already been accomplished and, apart from inflicting a gratuitous catastrophe on the native population, such a flooding was more likely to impede the French retreat than the Allied advance. But Napoleon's instincts during these months between Leipzig and the French campaign (in which many of his old powers reasserted themselves) were not altogether military. Like other dictators confronted with the obliteration of their own power, he found some gratification in forcing his victors to share in the consequences of wholesale destruction.

Many of his officials and generals, notably Charles Lebrun, were more concerned with self-preservation. Failing to obtain authorisation from Napoleon to remove his administration to a safer residence than Amsterdam, the Governor (like other legatees of the Imperial Débacle) was suddenly thrust into the uncomfortable position of having to take the initiative himself when for years he had been conditioned into unquestioning obedience. His situation was unenviable. On the one hand it was essential for Molitor's 2,000 or so regular troops to make some show of resistance on the Yssel; on the other, he knew full well that the evacuation of Amsterdam would be the spark to set off rebellion through central Holland. On November 14, the same day that he assented to have the French soldiers march out of Amsterdam. Lebrun warned Napoleon that "in Amsterdam our withdrawal is (actively) desired; the Cossacks, it is true, are feared, but no-one will lift a finger either for or against us." At The Hague, Dordrecht, and Rotterdam, "everything is ready to receive the Prince of Orange . . . and nowhere is there any force at all either to contain or suppress" such a rebellion.[65] Imperial power, then, simply melted away in the aftermath of major military defeat.

In these circumstances it is less remarkable that the uprising in the Netherlands eventually materialised than that its leaders should have edged towards it with such extreme circumspection. They were, it is true, unsure of the truth of the military situation, and there had been some false starts. On November 8, a mysterious proclamation in The Hague announcing the deposition of the mayor and his replacement with nominees of the Prince had mobilised large crowds near the Stadhuis and on the Plein, who would only disperse on the assurance of the officers of the National Guard that no such event was in fact in the offing. But expectations were at such a level that by the 12th there was a distinct danger of spontaneous and disorderly insurrection, or that the Allies might reach Holland before there had been an opportunity to put on a decent show of auto-emancipation. On the 9th, Gijsbert Karel van Hogendorp summoned a meeting of Orangist notables at his house on the Kneuterdijk, and co-ordinated arrangements with Anton Falck (commandant of the Amsterdam militia) and Job May, a sea captain who was well placed to rouse the shock-troops of incendiarism in the dockyards and taverns along the Amstel and in the Kalverstraat. "I decided," van Hogendorp later wrote, "that the greater danger lay in sitting still; the greater safety in taking action." On November 12 he felt able to let Falck and May know that everything was in order for the uprising.[66]

In more respects than the orthodox pieties of national historiography are prepared to admit, the forms of the rebellion of 1813 were not dissimilar from those of 1795. In both cases there was something of an unseemly haste by largely self-appointed political élites to put a gloss of political authenticity on their regimes before their fate was settled by the arbitration of war. And in both situations it proved more difficult than had been anticipated for that élite to control the disorder it had triggered off. In Amsterdam in particular, in 1813 as in 1795 and 1796, it was necessary for the ad hoc "provisional" authorities to try to damp down the fires of revolt once they had done the necessary work of consuming the old order. As in all demonstrations of Orangist enthusiasm, there was perhaps more reluctance to curb popular violence as long as it was directed at a few selected political adversaries. Moreover, in both cases the work of asserting the legitimacy of revolutionary authority was facilitated by the appalling conduct of a broken and undisciplined army—with the French at Woerden playing the part of the British in Overijssel in 1795. Against indiscriminate assault, pillage, and even rape there seemed nothing for the civilian population but to take up arms in their own urgent self-defence.

Just as the stereotyped view of the Batavian revolution errs on the side of self-criticism; so the mythology surrounding the recovery of national independence is, understandably enough, apt to be somewhat over-self-congratulatory. The massive monument in The Hague square simply bearing the date of the *anno mirabilis* indulges in romantic fancy by having its freedom fighters clustered around the sacred pennant braving the oppressors. On a bas-relief the people of Amsterdam are depicted chasing a grim-faced bunch of *grognards* out of the city with the customs houses burning at their backs. But by the time Job May came to do anything, of course, virtually all the French troops had left. In so far as there were any pioneers of revolt it was, oddly enough, gangs of genial bumpkins from the same area, Alphen, which had caused all the trouble earlier in the spring. Dragging cartloads of orange banners and chorusing "Oranjeliederen," they arrived in Amsterdam on the afternoon of the 14th causing something of a stir, but certainly not sufficient for Molitor to postpone his plans to take the troops to Utrecht that night.

At around eleven the following morning, May learned that the garrison was empty of all but a few gendarmes and customs men. By five the same afternoon he had organised several groups of men, their intentions declared by the buckets of pitch and turpentine and bundles of kindling they were carrying. An hour later, the customs post on the Nieuwe Brug was blazing cheerfully, and before very long all the other emblems of Dutch subjugation—excise houses, Imperial eagles, customs barges, official warehouses—were alight. Surveying his work with justifiable satisfaction, Job May thought: "Never was there a prettier sight than the arc of the city (canals) illuminated by the flames."[67]

With the "hoofdstad" thus given over to gay abandon, the problem confronting Falck's militia—which with evident relief had now removed its Imperial crests and reverted to the more comforting title of *schutterij*—was how to keep the euphoric demonstrations from getting out of hand and providing a general license for arson and plunder. De Celles and Devilliers, both highly unpopular figures, had the wits to secrete themselves well away from their normal residences. But the crowd knew where to seek its special targets: in particular, Dutch gendarmes and customs men and girls known to have enjoyed the favours of French officers. Lebrun himself spent a very sticky night virtually besieged in the "Palace," disappointed by a municipality which "though making protestations of zeal, confessed its impotence in such a situation. It showed itself to be exceedingly weak and without energy," he complained.[68] But with exactly five policemen—aside from a militia committed to the rebellion—more "energy" would of course have been suicidal. An officer of the gendarmes who was courageous (or foolhardy) enough to try to restrain a crowd was roughed up within an inch of his life while the *schutterij* stood back and enjoyed the entertainment. Some of the municipal council under the aegis of the deputy mayor, Charlé, who had presented themselves before Lebrun, attempted to devise tactics by which the situation might be made less emotive. But they were pre-empted by the appearance of Anton Falck, who simply announced the formation of what was plainly not so much a municipal council as a provisional "vroedschap" of twenty-four, under his own chairmanship and including Willem Willink, the two Eliases, and the son of the old Burgemeester Rendorp.[69]

By the morning, when so far from abating the violence seemed to be getting worse, Falck's role in restoring order was obviously indispensable. A number of private residences known to have been occupied by the French had been almost razed to the ground. In the Rokin, where one of the grandest establishments (as well as a large customs house) was situated, the crowd had stoned firemen who arrived to deal with the conflagration and forced them to retire. As the fires burned themselves out, so the retributive appetite of the crowds was gradually sated, without excessive physical injury caused to the few Frenchmen left in the city. But its government was quite manifestly in the hands of Falck and his associates, to whom alone the militia would answer. Lebrun depended for his own personal safety on Falck's goodwill. On the 16th, as he put it, "When I recognised that we had neither the force nor the influence to suppress this rebellion, and that the authority had passed to the control of a faction, I decided to withdraw to Gorinchem." As he did so, with a small cortège of soldiers, unmolested, he passed "the still smoking ruins of the barges and customs posts."[70]

Despite the manifestly insurrectionary power of the "provisional administration," it was typical of the Amsterdammer sense of double insurance that it should have put out feelers both to the Orangist leadership in The Hague and to the General Molitor in Utrecht. To the latter they explained that they had assumed power not as rebels but in an effort to contain and assuage the disorder. From the general they received in reply the remark that if so, he looked forward to their return to their proper allegiance and "the complete re-establishment of the authority of the Emperor."[71] Molitor was, in fact, sorely tempted to descend on the city in a quick sortie and to take hostages for its good conduct, a line of action that Napoleon (though not Lebrun, then at Utrecht himself) would have heartily endorsed. But he appreciated that it might conceivably antagonise the city further and that it could not be done quickly enough to deny the Russians the chance they were waiting for to cross the Yssel. In the event Molitor may have regretted erring on the side of caution, for the Russians managed to cross the river notwithstanding his defences, at Hattem on the night of November 19–20.

In Amsterdam, Falck did his best to hedge all bets and refrained from openly endorsing the cause of the Prince, except when needed to appease an aggressively Orangist crowd. At the same time the last "mayor," the Catholic van Brienen van Groote Lindt, was attempting to persuade Montalivet in Paris that the events in Amsterdam had been so directed as to "keep" rather than lose civic order. This endeavour at studied "neutralism" was again reminiscent of the caution of 1795. Not the least of all these cross-currents and coincidences was that the commandant of the city was Cornelis Kraijenhoff, the officer who, dressed in French uniform, had taken the surrender of Amsterdam from the Prince's officers in January 1795. It was an exquisite irony that the man who, as it were, had acted as page-boy to the long procession of indignities, illusions and injuries visited by the French on their "ally" should now have been given the role of bouncer-in-chief.

The burning of the Amsterdam customs houses was a genuine, if not exactly unprompted, effusion of antipathy towards the authority identified with hardship and tyranny. But it was in The Hague that the shape of things to come announced itself more positively. Van Hogendorp had been given the news of the events in Amsterdam on the night of the 16th, and having sounded out the colonel of the local national guard, was given to understand by him that he would not stand in the way of an efficiently organised, reasonably peaceful assumption of power in the name of the Prince of Orange. The "revolution," however, got off to an unfortunate start when, on setting out from his house on the morning of the 17th bearing all the paraphernalia of proclamations, flags and the like, van Hogendorp was promptly arrested by one of those selfsame guards and ushered unceremoniously back to his house. The second sortie, accompanied by his two principal colleagues, van Limburg Stirum and van der Duyn van Maasdam (both nobles of impeccable Orangist stock), and heralded with fife and drum, was more auspicious. Copies of what has since become the anthem of the "Restoration" were read aloud and posted liberally around the city. The glad tidings were:

Oranje Boven
Holland is free.
The Allies march on Utrecht . . .
The French flee on all sides
The sea is open
Trade revives
All faction has come to an end
All the past is forgotten
And forgiven
All the notables (aanzienlijken) *are in the Government*
The Government calls on the Prince
To His High Office . . .
Every person thanks GOD
The old times have come again
Oranje Boven

   In fact, it was only the following day that the committee of six who constituted themselves as a provisional "General Administration of the United Netherlands" delegated two emissaries to go to London and invite the Prince to assume a (it was not yet clear quite what) sovereign power. Not surprisingly, The Hague responded jubilantly and vociferously to the summons to rally to the Prince. By midday shops, churches and public places on the Plein —courthouses and government offices—were festooned with orange ribbon and flags, and carillons from the Oude Kerk provided suitable accompaniment for the boisterous celebrations. As in April, Baron de Stassart's prefecture was the target of physical as well as vocal menace. Initially, the prefect stood nobly on the crumbling remnant of his official dignity, curtly declining the offer of the ringleaders to pacify the crowds by acknowledging a "provisional regency" for the city. Indeed, he responded with a ringing denunciation of all those who had participated in the uprising, warning that as rebels against the person of the Emperor they would, in due course, pay the appropriate penalty.

   Stassart's last hope of salvaging the situation vanished when the sublimely named General Bouvier des Éclats arrived with 200 troops (mostly Prussian deserters), only to closet them in the military hospital in the Binnenhof, well out of the way of crowds who by that time were drunk not only with delight but copious supplies of *genever*. It was at this point that the prefect, in his turn, took the road for Gorinchem which was fast becoming a reception centre for dislodged Imperial officials. From behind its earthworks he concluded: "The whole of Holland is in revolt and I can see only the fortified places remaining to us if the garrisons there can defend themselves. But granted the manner in which they are comprised, I can have few hopes."[72] On the following day, November 18, having been led from the city by General Bouvier, the Prussians defected—leaving their horses behind in the night but taking themselves and their weapons to be placed at the disposal of the "Governor" of The Hague, van Limburg Stirum. The latter by then could muster something like 1,000 men, mostly volunteers and ex-National Guard; hardly a formidable legion, but enough to deter any punitive expedition from Gorinchem. Lebrun himself now gave up the ghost, writing to Napoleon that he would proceed to Antwerp, "since I believe my presence here in Holland and the neighbouring region to be absolutely useless"—a verdict one imagines the Emperor would not have denied.[73]

During the brief "interregnum" prior to the arrival of the Prince at Scheveningen on November 30, the transfer of authority proceeded somewhat unevenly throughout the country. Troops of either side were present only in small pockets, and apart from a bloody engagement between Macdonald at Arnhem and the Prussians, the only military action was at Papendrecht. Here the unfortunate Bouvier had attempted to redeem himself by marching on Dordrecht with 400 men to recapture a munitions barge from the rebel municipality. Despite subjecting the town to an indiscriminate and futile bombardment, which cost a number of lives and did a great deal of damage, he was unable to recover the barge. But the assault, as well as the orgy of pillage amidst which the French departed from Woerden, succeeded in stiffening resistance in the south, swelling the ranks of volunteer militia, and nudging cautious municipalities towards declaring themselves for the Prince. On November 24, the Amsterdam authorities decided to accept the proclamations of The Hague administration, from which they had so far kept carefully aloof, as lawful and binding; other major towns such as Leiden, Alkmaar and Rotterdam swiftly followed their example. All this could be achieved without any upheaval of personnel, save perhaps a few mayoral figureheads (and not even then invariably), since in its wisdom the Empire had tended to favour exactly the most conservative elements of the old oligarchy likely to desert it with alacrity once the military balance permitted them to do so in safety. Even where there were changes, they were hardly of a revolutionary nature. In The Hague itself, to the surprise of no-one, the provisional administration was entrusted yet again to Jan Slicher, the Orangist of long standing who had managed to keep office under the Batavian Republic, Willem V, Louis Bonaparte, and who might very well with Abbé Sieyès claim to have merely "survived."

Although van Hogendorp's predilection was for a full-blooded return to the status quo ante 1795, even as nostalgic a figure as he recognised the need for a tactical measure of catholicity. Hence the "General Administration" made efforts to recruit to its colours not only men who had served under Louis but even those who had taken part in Imperial government. Both van Maanen and Gogel were approached with a view to ensuring a proper continuity in what were the elementary functions of justice and finance. During the discussions in The Hague on the future constitution, van Hogendorp, as he confessed, saw his dreams for an authentic resuscitation of a States-General of delegations "disappear in smoke."[74] Nor were Elias Canneman's fears of a general purge in the manner of 1787 to be realised. When William took an oath on December 2 to be loyal to "the constitution" (whatever that might be), it was clear from the tone of his utterances that he was seeking an end to the bitter partisanship which had divided the country for thirty years and more. Indeed Canneman himself—though initially stricken by a timely spasm of rheumatism which put him to bed amidst the upheavals in The Hague—decided, after first telling Gogel that he could not stomach any further part in public life, that "God helps those who help themselves," and that Providence pointed to a reconciliation with van Hogendorp and allegiance to the "Sovereign Prince." He himself actually helped van Hogendorp frame the proclamations which urged unity and oblivion beneath the gracious banner of the princely House.[75]

The response of old Patriots and Batavians, some of them still in office, to the disintegration of French power disclosed much about their general attitude to their own career in politics during the years of war and revolution. For Hugo Gevers, installed on the provisional regency at Dordrecht, or Johan Valckenaer, their brush with the brutal face of Napoleonic imperialism had been enough to exorcise what sentiment for the "Grande Nation" might still have lingered within them. Cornelis van Maanen, as his biographer rightly observes, had never really been a revolutionary at all, but always a staunch believer in the supremacy of law, quite independent from the sovereignty in whose name it was being administered. This attitude enabled him at the same time to frown on van Hogendorp's original act of rebellion and even, when invited to join it, to decline association with any disorder unbecoming as he saw it for a high magistrate.[76] But once it became apparent that there *was* no sovereignty, he succumbed to the regency's blandishments. Any temporary discomfort he might have experienced in squaring the circle of allegiances was doubtless soothed by his subsequent appointment to the presidency of the "High Court of the Kingdom of the United Netherlands." Van Maanen's code of justice was nothing if not politically weather-proof.

The one predictable exception in this unseemly rush to transfer allegiance was the perennially prickly Gogel. He had been indirectly sounded out by van Hogendorp via his friend Canneman, whose example he was fully expected (after a decent interval of agonising reappraisal) to follow. On November 21 he received a letter from The Hague administration specifically inviting him to continue to assume supreme responsibility for finance in the Netherlands, pending the formation of a newly constituted government. Whatever might have been obscured by this overture it was apparent that van Hogendorp, who had hardly seen eye to eye with Gogel in the past, was extending a twig if not a branch of the olive. Given the bleakness of his own position—for "Intendant of Finances" for the Empire was not an employment to be widely advertised in 1813—Gogel might have accepted the offer with alacrity. Others in his position had not had the same luxury. Giuseppe Prina in Milan, his counterpart in the Kingdom of Italy, had been torn limb from limb trying to escape from the city mob. During the height of the riots in Amsterdam, Lebrun and de Celles had both been seriously concerned for Gogel's safety. But he was utterly oblivious to all such qualms. Even on November 20 and 21, he continued to write to Gaudin—after Lebrun had abandoned Gorinchem—that the city had calmed down, taxes were being collected, and though it seemed all his French colleagues were "mobile," he would remain at his post come what may.[77]

As ever, in fact, Gogel was the helpless victim of a tyrannical integrity. The temperamental opposite of Cornelis van Maanen, the upheaval going on around him, far from sublimating his political sensibilities, reactivated them with a vengeance. Seeing the orange flags on the church towers, and proclamations signed by survivors of an unholy retinue, revived within Gogel for a final flourish all his old republican austerity. Offered a post of high trust and responsibility in what was evidently going to be the new government of the Netherlands, he wrote proudly to Gaudin: "My choice was not in doubt for one minute."[78] Along with the fugitive excise men, the whores and looters, the deposed prefects and the rags and tatters of the Imperial army, he took the road for Gorinchem, Breda and Paris. His pathetic route march was conditioned not by loyalty to Napoleon, whose shortcomings he was acutely aware of; still less to the France which had made him a Councillor of State, but rather by the revulsion he felt at the return of the House of Orange-Nassau— at the crowning triumph of the periwigs, the regents, the aristocrats, the Anglomanes, the oligarchs whom he believed to have sucked the marrow from the bones of the old Republic.

As his last mildly ridiculous broadside from Paris, signed "Cosmopolite,"[79] revealed, Gogel could not help himself in proclaiming his enmity for men whose governance represented everything he had meant to amputate from the body politic so that its growth might be clean and healthy. Depending on one's point of view, the stiffness of his posture at such a time is either comic or magnificent. Evicted unceremoniously from Paris with the dissolution of the Empire, he was reduced to begging his expenses from Baron Louis, the King's Minister of Finance. Yet no-one wished to see him live in poverty and insignificance so much as himself. Appelius, Anton Falck, Elias Canneman of course—even the King himself—attempted to woo him back into public administration. But the loftiness of his scruples forbade acceptance. He acquired, appropriately enough, a small starchworks at Overveen in South Holland, where he eked out a livelihood until his death in 1821 at the age of fifty-seven. He did agree to emerge from his Timon-like isolation in response to a furtive request from the King in 1818 for advice (at that time sorely needed) on public finance and taxation.[80] The prolific documents and memoranda he supplied on that occasion were later published by his son and comprise a decent memorial. But unlike the Tragic Hero nailed to his rack at St. Helena, Gogel was not cut out to play the persecuted Prometheus in his years of decline. His role had rather been that of Sisyphus, condemned to heave the mountainous burden of Dutch finance up an endless slope, only for it to collapse against his own perspiring efforts.

Gogel was not so fond of the ephemeral attributes of office as to regret any personal deprivation. Rather than strike epic attitudes in the shadow of the Emperor, his whole ambition had been to keep a clean ledger, and in so doing to show how the Fatherland might yet be redeemed according to the gospel of social equity. Doubtless that itself was a mark of the political adolescence from which he may never have fully matured. Aiming to reinfuse an enervated state with the qualities of rigour and *burgerlijk* energy which he took to have been its original hallmarks, he was, perhaps, doomed to fail and fail again. But not to have persevered, Gogel might well have said, would have been culpably un-Dutch.

14

Postscript

The spectacle of Dutch cavalry, their Imperial coats exchanged for the blue serge of the Royal Netherlands Army (putting some overdue trade the way of the Tilburg and Leiden clothiers), may not have struck cold terror into the hearts of the French gunners they faced on the sodden fields of Quatre Bras and Waterloo. But what Motley's collaborator William Griffis ecstatically described as "prodigies of valour" did move as hard-boiled a spirit as Johannes Goldberg to congratulate the King on having revived the "glorious and happy days of [Princes] Maurice and Frederick Henry." It may be that this new-found enthusiasm for the House of Orange-Nassau, coming as it did from a man who had been equally effusive in his welcome for the annexation of 1810, was not wholly unconnected with his government post as Director-General of Trade and Colonies. For, to tell the truth, the Dutch performance in the final campaign of the war left something to be desired as a model of tactical deployment and martial prowess.

There were times, indeed, when their presence seemed to the Allied commanders to be more of a liability than an asset. The Earl of Uxbridge had cause for crisp comment on the virtues of the Dutch horse when he found himself charging solo at the French lines in front of troops who, neither recognising the general nor comprehending his order, declined to follow his beckoning sabre. Having once countermanded a crucial order at Quatre Bras, the twenty-two-year-old Crown Prince of Orange succeeded in decimating the King's Hanoverian Legion (as well as getting himself wounded) at Waterloo by ordering those troops to advance against a massively entrenched French position, apparently under the impression that the cavalry seen standing well behind enemy lines was not French but Dutch. The Prince (later King William II), who was perhaps more notable for his qualities of good cheer and personal courage than any profound grasp of strategy, had been placed in command of some 40,000 assorted Dutch, Belgian and German troops, essentially in courteous recognition that the war was being fought out in what had become his father's southern provinces. But both Princes of Orange, junior and senior, had had greatness somewhat summarily thrust upon them. The position of the "Kingdom of the United Netherlands," like that of its army in June 1815, sandwiched awkwardly between British and Prussians, proclaimed not so much the restoration of the Dutch to the ranks of the sovereign states of Europe, free and independent, as their continued subordination to the interests of its "protectors."

Gogel's observation that his countrymen had been relieved of the French the better to manacle them once more to the Anglo-Prussian connexion was no doubt the remark of a man suffering from an incurable case of sour grapes, but it was not altogether without some truth. For however gratefully William, the "Sovereign Prince," received the Belgian provinces and Luxembourg from the diplomatic platter at Paris and Vienna, it was quite clear that the enlargement of his realm was meant to serve as a buffer against the threat of resurgent French expansionism. It was also in part an emollient for the dynastic losses of Nassau and Fulda, and the British retention of Demerara, Essequibo, Ceylon and the strategically important Cape. Nor was the guarantee for his Kingdom better proof against the swings of the political pendulum than it had been in the previous century. For when, in 1830, the more buccaneering approach of Whig diplomacy judged that unconditional adherence to the letter of the Vienna settlement might actually create more problems than a tame Belgium equipped with the wonders of British engineering and presided over by a Saxe-Coburg, it had no hesitation in wielding the Solomonic sword and slicing the contentious offspring in two.

With a Prince of Orange returned to The Hague, flanked by the supporting powers of Britain and Prussia, the Reformed Church restored to many, if not all, of its former privileges, and the regents of the towns planted more firmly than ever "op het kussen" (on the cushions of office) it may well have seemed that there had been no Dutch revolution at all. The Batavian Republic and the Kingdom of Holland, already shrouded in obscure ignominy, were perhaps merely an arbitrary interruption in the transition from eighteenth-century Stadholderate to nineteenth-century monarchy. The intervening two decades of war, political turmoil, and economic struggle might have been likened to a prolonged and disagreeable reverie from which the Dutch had been finally and gratefully awakened. Once lobotomised from the national memory, it could be classified as an alien episode which, to borrow the Motleyite verdict, "had little permanent influence on Dutch history or character." Yet bitterly though he might regret it, even Gijsbert van Hogendorp knew quite well that the "old times" had *not* come again and that there was no hope of putting back the clock to 1794.

The experiences of the past twenty years, unhappy as they might have been, had wrought irreversible changes in the public life of the Dutch which King William, as much as anyone, acknowledged and legitimised. To some constitutional purists his conduct was such that it seemed "Orange had gone Patriot." This was far from being the case, but certainly any resemblances to the institutions of the old Republic were superficial. The "States-General" established in 1815 was no more than the palest pastiche of the sovereign delegations of the United Provinces, and could be circumscribed with ease by appointed commissions of the King just as the provincial States and municipalities were subject to the vigilant scrutiny of a Governor, the nominated officials of the executive.

In these respects, as in many other features of his administration, William I's principal debt was not so much to the Stadholders, far less the old federal Union, as to the centralised state apparatus introduced under Schimmelpenninck in 1805 and operated, albeit with great difficulty, by Louis Bonaparte. In the provincial governors of the Kingdom of the United Netherlands, it is surely not too presumptuous to see the bureaucratic heirs of the land-drosten of 1807–10 and the departmental commissioners of 1798–1801. Similarly, the ministers and Directors-General of the crown could trace their official paternity back to the Agents of the Batavian Directory. That both sets of government servants were encumbered by an executive figure at once more clumsy and more absolutist than either Schimmelpenninck or Louis in no way invalidates the self-evident truth that the fundamental discontinuity was with the distant, not the immediate, past. To put the matter still more dogmatically, it seems incontestable that the Dutch monarchy of the nineteenth century, conservative before 1848 and liberal after it, was not merely preceded but *caused* by the Batavian Republic and its successor Kingdom. The origins of the second Dutch state are to be found, then, not in the charred remains of the Amsterdam customs houses, nor in the jotting pads of van Hogendorp, memorialised in Rotterdam as the "father of the constitution," but in the travail and tribulations recorded in this history.

That the new regime was not simply to be a reprise of the militant Orangism of 1787–88 was suggested by the men with whom the King surrounded himself. The grandees of the traditional Orangist nobility—the Fagels, Bentincks and Schimmelpennincks van der Oye—were for their comfort during the exile rewarded with offices that were more honorific than functional. William was evidently concerned more with establishing a government than a court. Instead, the councils and ministries of the Kingdom were manned by administrators of proven competence and experience, some of whom had served not only Louis Bonaparte but the Republic before him. Appelius, Canneman, Goldberg, Voûte, van Maanen, and van Stralen all found senior offices in the government, alongside more conservative figures as van Hogendorp and van der Hoop. Wiselius, astonishingly, was made Director of Police in 1814; though much criticised for the appointment the King, reinforced by Anton Falck, stood by it.[1] Naturally, the peculiar mélange of erstwhile Patriots and democrats (become enlightened absolutists), arch-oligarchs and nobles, did not exactly make for smooth government and administrative harmony. Before very long the factionalism that had allegedly been dispelled by the "oblivion" of 1813 crystallised again into reforming and reactionary groups—Canneman and Falck, for example, in bitter opposition to van der Hoop and van Hogendorp.

By no stretch of the imagination could the period be considered one of liberal monarchy. Representative government would have to wait until the bloodless coup of 1848 before becoming finally entrenched in Dutch political institutions. But while in some areas—notably ecclesiastical policy and the restoration of the more innocuous "seigneurial" prerogatives—William was inclined to defer to the most conservative sentiment; in other, perhaps more significant branches of government, he consolidated many of the changes which had taken place since 1798. Despite a storm of lobbying, the guilds remained abolished along the lines of the 1808 law. Greater toleration was extended to Catholics, Dissenters and Jews, one of whom, Jonas Daniel Meijer, played an important part in high office in the early years of the "Restoration." The penal codes compiled by Cornelis Elout, Jan Everhard Reuvens and Petrus van Musschenbroek, and completed in Louis' reign, were made the legal foundation for the Kingdom; van Maanen, the perennial minister, presided over the system which he had played an important part in promoting. The same was true for van den Ende's system of elementary education, established on a firmer financial basis and—with dire consequences—partly extended to the southern provinces.[2] In financial matters the King was more wayward, depending in part on the Appelius tariff of 1810, reinforced with a stiffer dose of neo-mercantilist commercial duties, a direction exactly opposite to that proposed by his grandfather in 1751. He came badly unstuck over the complicated problem of indemnifying those victimised by the *tiercering* of 1810 and tended to grab at fiscal expedients in response to ad hoc needs, rather than consider any overall policy of financial management. Most of the ablest financiers working for the government—Copes van Cattenburgh, Elias Canneman and Johannes Goldberg— parted company with the King on these matters, and it was at their prompting that the penitential overtures were made to the ailing Gogel.

Yet the durability of much of the administrative reforms inaugurated in the Batavian period, and the shift of sovereignty from local to national authorities, stands, in contrast to the impermanence, at least in the short term, of the political revolution. It would be a grotesque misrepresentation of the aims of those who greeted the foundation of the Batavian Republic as an opportunity to build anew—Paulus, Wiselius, Gogel—to suggest that they were *primarily* concerned with replacing an inadequate and defective state machine with a more functional and streamlined one. The mere possibility of contemplating such an overhaul without facing the political implications of a representative electoral system was precisely what separated Paulus the revolutionary from van de Spiegel the conservative—men who had both begun their careers as "enlightened," reforming *Oranjeklanten*. Although the renovation of government was an integral part of what the reformers in the Batavian National Assembly set out to accomplish, the assumption of national sovereignty without popular sovereignty—for democrats like Wiselius, Vreede and Ockerse—would have been to create a political robot, devoid of real animation. If, by 1808, Gogel saw in his tax system the only instrument left to him to affect social inequity at the same time as underpinning the viability of the state, he recognised that it was a far cry from the "beau rêve" he had nurtured in the spring of 1794.[3] The evanescence of that vision of the avenging angel of democracy, and its reduction to bleakly empirical memoranda on the cultivation of sugar beet or the reorganisation of the waterstaat, was then the consequence, not the intention, of the original efforts to rejuvenate a decrepit polity.

But to insist on that distinction is not to imply that the endeavour to establish a more broadly based form of government never took place, or that at best it was but a spectral shadow of the French revolution. By 1799, the "Grande Nation" itself had its offices largely monopolised by an élite of propertied notables, not a few of whom had enjoyed place and status under the old regime.[4] But it would be historically absurd, on those grounds alone, to discount the significance of what had happened previously. The mere *transience* of popular politics, in both their Dutch and French manifestations, did not obliterate their importance for future generations, as the new century was to bear witness. The very fact that for a time the distribution of power was partly determined by the ebb and flow of elections, both locally and nationally—by plebiscites, the formation of burgher militia, the polemics of *wijk* meetings, political clubs and the popular press—ensured that the possibility of more representative government remained an option which at some date in the future might be redeemed.

And in 1848, with rather less blood and more success than in France, that alliance between national sovereignty and constitutional politics first announced in the gusty rhetoric of the Batavian National Assembly was realised. It was not fortuitous that the architect of the new constitution, Johan Thorbecke, explicitly acknowledged his debt to the Batavian precedent. But it was a curious paradox that at the same time that the liberal constitution should have afforded the opportunity for Groen van Prinsterer's Anti-Revolutionary Party to perpetrate the mythology (which very rapidly turned into received orthodoxy) the basis of the new Netherlands had been immanent in the old, and that so far from trying to shore up the defences of the Republic, the Batavians were in fact bent on sabotage, the better to enthrone their godless dogma on its ruins.[5]

At issue between Thorbecke and Groen van Prinsterer was not simply the classic nineteenth-century argument between liberalism and conservatism, but rather the relationship of innovation to the retention of a specifically Dutch identity. That problem—how to change and yet remain the same— was at the heart of Batavian political debate. Such was the condition of the Republic after the Fourth Anglo-Dutch War that it was apparent to all but Stadholderians of the deepest Orange that some degree of institutional reform was essential if the hungry powers lining up to dine off the carcass of the Dutch empire were to be prevented from gratifying their appetite. Within these general terms of reference, all those who participated in the successive attempts to keep the Republic afloat were "Patriots." But in their respective attitude towards the degree of change needed to succeed in this, the division between conservatives and revolutionaries was dramatically plain. For those men to whom Dutch identity was itself inseparable from what, historically, had been the distinguishing marks of the Republic—provincial and municipal autonomy; the sanctity of the guilds; the corporate nature of local government

—only so much change was permissible as would guarantee that in these essentials things would remain the same. Or rather, that given what they considered to be unwarranted intrusions of arbitrarily imposed Stadholderian power, the Republic would *revert* to the "ancient constitution." To imagine a Dutch Republic otherwise was, for both the Patriot regents like "Vader" Hooft and Jan Bicker or Batavian federalists like van Marle or de Mist, quite literally unthinkable.

But for those of bolder principles, the prospect held no terrors at all. Not only were they unprepared to accept as the defining attributes of the Dutch commonwealth those features which they held to be parasitical growths. They argued, on the contrary, that their excision was the precondition for a recovery to health. Those who had postured as the champions of the people—regents, magistrates, burgemeesters—were in reality self-serving "aristocrats," concerned above all to cling to their family monopoly of office. Their vaunted "liberties" of town corporations and guilds were the preserve of the gilded few; and the "old constitution" revered in documents like the Constitutional Restoration the charter of the perpetuation of those abuses. Their goal was to liberate from the encrustations of custom and usage what they took to be a "third" Netherlands. And this they saw as the creature of neither Stadholder nor regents, but made up of the constituency of the "brede middenstand"—tradesmen, artisans, petty-brokers, professional men, Catholic tenant farmers, Jewish physicians—all those, in short, who in times of peace and plenty might have been well content with the "virtual representation" embodied in the old Republic, but who in adversity turned on it with an inflammatory admixture of anger and ambition.

The primitive Dutch virtues to which those promoting a "Patriot" or "Batavian" spirit appealed consisted more of an ethos than an ideology. At its centre was the ascetic, evangelical Christian egalitarianism common to the pulpit harangues of van der Kemp, the elegant tracts of Paulus, the doggerel pieties of Gerrit Paape and the fiery journalism of Bernardus Bosch. Their vocabularly was redolent with scriptural allusions; injunctions to smite down satanic Nebuchadnezzar or the fleshpot Phoenicians who had deserted the ways of the Lord. The notion that it would be harder for a regent to enter the kingdom of Godly democracy than for a camel to pass through the eye of a needle found a ready response in the revivalist atmosphere of the Utrecht Free Corps parades of 1786 and 1787 or the clubrooms of Amsterdam and Rotterdam between 1795 and 1798. The language which had once served the Church as the armour-plating of social and political constraint, as used by predikants who themselves had turned renegade, became a well-honed weapon of rebellion. On a more sophisticated plane, there were those among the new political élite—Samuel Wiselius, George Hahn, Jacob Blauw, Johan Valckenaer, the savants of the revolution—whose notions of republican virtue owed more to the Leiden schoolroom and cullings from Livy and Seneca than to jeremiads of holy wrath.

These two elements were not always coherently assimilated within the various versions of Batavian democracy. But however conflicting the views on how far (and how fast) the blessings of popular sovereignty were to go, they shared a general resolution to attack the whiggery of the historical Republic, the federalism of the "Gothic ruin" of the Union and the received truths of Francken's *Deductie*. Their reborn republican ideals, which had perished with Oldenbarneveld, would be resurrected and reinvested with the vigour of a true commonwealth of burghers. In all these respects, as in their preoccupation with the virtues and duties of right citizenship, the Batavian democrats came closer not so much to the Jacobins of revolutionary France as to the "Levellers of the Netherlands."

This is not to say that they were intent on founding Utopia. For in sardonic commentaries like Valckenaer's and Wiselius', the shortcomings of their enterprise were graphically documented. But to acknowledge that the Batavian Republic was inaugurated in defeat, chaos and a general disintegration of public authority is not to write it off as the stooge revolution of a handful of self-appointed tribunes. The thousands of militiamen of the 1780's and the many thousands of voters of the 1790's seem to suggest otherwise. If that was not exactly to make Jerusalem, then it was at least a new departure for a state whose political alternatives had hitherto been confined to quasi-absolutism and hyper-oligarchy. It is undeniable, however, that politicians who were almost weighed down by the very bulk of their good intentions were further encumbered by one particularly heavy illusion, namely, that simply by virtue of the revolution they would have the freedom of action to refashion their Republic without any undue interference from outside. They were sustained in this pious fiction of course by the official nostrums of the "Grande Nation," whose actual foreign policies sharply diverged from the ostensible promise of self-determination. From the signing of the Treaty of The Hague to the Treaty of Paris in 1814, there was no time when either protagonist in the Franco-British war did not attempt to exploit the vagaries of Dutch politics for their own purposes. And though, by 1805, there were few illusions left, the Batavians were slow to learn their lesson, seeing always in the next regime, Foreign Minister, general or envoy, the possibility of securing fairer treatment. In a famous retort, Napoleon complained that Schimmelpenninck was "too virtuous for the century in which we live." The same might have been said of Blauw, de Winter, Valckenaer, and Daendels—all those who sought in the courts of the powers some precious respite for the invalid state.

If the Batavian enterprise was doomed, then, it was not for any endogenous circumstances but because, after the sealing of the Faustian pact of 1787, when Prussian grenadiers were invited by Wilhelmina and van de Spiegel to settle the affairs of the Dutch for them, there was no escaping the fate dictated by their strategic geography. So the Dutch revolution succumbed to the melancholy circularity which is the lot of all small nations labouring to set their house in order through their own efforts. This, it cannot be overstated, was its fatal flaw: that the alliance and war which had made the Batavian Republic possible was, at the same time, the limiting condition of its viability.[6] To survive among the *Europe des patries*, the Dutch appreciated that they had to alter their institutions of government; but to be able to reform in tranquility required strengths which were not theirs to command.

For this overriding reason, those honest artificers who were prepared to undertake the thankless labour of keeping the Dutch state from foundering amidst debt and invasion were obliged to descend from the lofty heights of Batavian democratic ideals to the pettifogging minutiae of day-to-day, hand-to-mouth administration; from the realm of grandiose declarations of rights to that of tax ledgers, military requisitions, and Rumford soups. Before very long, the exertions of the war enveloped all those partisan allegiances which even a short time before had seemed unbridgeable. Inexorably, their business became not so much that of patriotic revival and dreams of a new Atlantic empire—but simply of survival. The bleak odyssey traversed by the careers of such as Wiselius, Valckenaer, Gogel and Schimmelpenninck, all in their different ways bear witness to the retreat from optimism. It was only those who, from free will or no, withdrew entirely from public life who could afford to preserve their principles intact. Even the arch-tribune Pieter Vreede is to be found in the Kingdom addressing memoranda to Louis Bonaparte on matters as unphilosophical as the revival of the textile industry to which he had returned.[7] Others like Gogel and Goldberg felt that if they were not to be permitted the luxury of seeing the union of democracy and national sovereignty consummated in peace, then neither were they prepared to allow the Dutch state to revert to the impotent oligarchy which, they were convinced, would seal its fate. They were, then, reconciled to swallowing their scruples and working in harness with regents like van de Goes, or even avowed Orangists like van Stralen, men whose principles seemingly represented the vitiation, not the fulfilment, of the revolution.

But this was perhaps less of an apostasy than self-elected purists like Sam Wiselius (who had himself continued in office on the "Asiatic Council" under the Regency of State) were prepared to admit. For though egotism and the almost obsessive desire to see implemented the finance system on which he had lavished so much care certainly played its part, Gogel's motives for accepting the finance portfolio under Schimmelpenninck and clinging to it under Louis were far from opportunist. Responsibility for bleeding the population white was not calculated to win admiration or popularity. Yet Gogel was determined that control of the fisc should not fall into the hands of those less committed than he to the battle, as he saw it, with privilege and obstructionism. If the penalties for staying alive as an independent nation— or even a shrunken satellite—were to be extortionate, he was resolved so to distribute them as to ease the burden for the least fortunate. Privilege in time of plenty, he held, was a sin; in time of want, it was a crime. Clearly, he was far from conforming to the stereotype remorseless bureaucrat concerned with nothing but the balancing of the account. It was his moral truculence which made him so difficult a colleague for the more complaisant and orthodox ministers and councillors of Louis' government.

Gogel was not, of course, alone in his solicitousness. But along with many others who stuck grimly to their work well after the Batavian Republic had withered on the vine, he could see beyond his bureau to a whole commonwealth of the derelict and impoverished, extending down from the grandest cities like Amsterdam to the most miserable hovels in the Veluwe. Most important of all, he realised that arguments over the autonomy of this or that corporation were meaningless when set against their evident inability to pay their way without subsidy from the national treasury. The arrears in interest payments on the national debt; the depreciation of bonds; the steeply rising prices of food, fuel and building materials—all contributed to an inexorable process by which the dereliction of local government was burying the old Netherlands far more completely than the unitarist politicians of the Batavian assemblies could ever have envisaged. What was the civic independence of Rotterdam worth when Burgemeester van der Heim came to the Ministry of Finance with his city keys in one hand and a begging bowl in the other?

The Batavian period and its aftermath was indisputably one of severe discomfort for large numbers of the Dutch people. Whether in public office or private trade, they were all afflicted by the shrinking pains of an obsolescent empire. It was not, of course, for the utterly indigent or for the very well-to-do that the problems of adjustment were most acute. But in the circumstances of the kind of war, and especially the economic war, that France chose to wage in the North Sea, the distress was most marked among exactly that section of the population—the "brede middenstand"—whom the new era was meant to benefit. In the hardships suffered by the fishermen of Maassluis and Vlaardingen; the pipe-makers of Gouda, the Haarlem dyers; the shipwrights and carpenters of the Noorderkwartier ports; the sugar refiners of Amsterdam; the weavers (what was left of them) of Leiden; even the distillers of Schiedam, the nemesis of the revolution found its human documents.

It would not do, though, to exaggerate the pain and calamity. By whatever miracle, the dykes holding the fabric of Dutch society together did *not* break. The waters covering the Betuwe in 1809 eventually receded, leaving that rich alluvium behind which was nature's consolation prize and a real boon to the prolific and, even in the years of war and blockade, successful peasant farmers of south-east Holland. If, at times, whole regions of the country—from the delta of the Maas and Scheldt up to the mouth of the Ems—were reduced to making a living through fraud, evasion and contraband, that too was a way of surviving the ordeal. The resurgent euphoria which greeted the liberation of 1813 and the sudden engorgement of the Netherlands; the perfervid conviction that the mere incantation of "Oranje Boven" would somehow bring back the good "old times"; and the staple market and mercantile splendour, all proved short-lived. Punitive taxation, municipal indigence and, except in the industrialising Belgian towns, a stagnant economy, were to be with the Dutch for some time yet. The process of adjustment to securing a place in the European order that was more modest—and less beleaguered—than that to which the Dutch had been historically accustomed, was in the nature of things bound to be painful, even traumatic.

But what cannot fail to strike the historian, particularly one writing in Britain in the 1970's, is that the fiery baptism of the new Netherlands elicited from its people those qualities of fortitude, endurance, and perseverance which they have always held in high regard. The set-jawed stubbornness, the resolution to survive, impressed itself even on those who, consciously or otherwise, had made the task that much harder. For if, in the ill-starred *mésalliance* between French and Dutch, there were those, like Sieyès, Delacroix and Napoleon, whose ignorance and disdain stereotyped their ally as a smoke-room full of obese cheesemongers and devious bank cashiers, there were also those— François Noël, Louis Bonaparte and the Baron d'Alphonse—who saw in the tribulations of the Dutch a lesson worthy of respect.

Joseph Garat paid his tribute in a memorandum written for the French Senate when, so far from dismissing the Dutch as a national relic, remarkable only for the nuisance they caused the smooth operation of French strategy, he attempted to educate Napoleon in the tenacity of their native feeling:

The Batave is much more Dutch than the Englander is English, the Frenchman French or any other people in the world anything. It is not exactly their patriotism which gives the Bataves this quality of eternal fixity of character; but rather their land, their climate, their whole manner of being and living, all of which resemble nothing else that can be seen on the face of the earth. . . . He who has built his dwelling with his own hands will never leave it; the Dutch built Holland and they have the air of forever saying "What we have done is good," . . . their dazzling but odourless flowers grown beneath the fogs of Haarlem; the wreaths of smoke from their tobacco delight their senses far more than the most exquisite perfume under the most perfect skies. . . . They believe that if this is taken from them they will simply cease to be Bataves; for them it is not just a matter of losing their name; it would be to lose their very lives.[8]

To try to dig themselves in as everything about them sank under war and conquest was in the end the primary endeavour of those Dutchmen who saw their country through its several tribulations. The difficulties they encountered were so formidable that they necessarily reduced the heroic enterprise of rejuvenation announced by van der Capellen and Paulus to the homelier bustle of a chaotic spring-cleaning. To those historians for whom the dimensions of the past must be epic or nothing, the chronicle of a modest nation attempting to survive will always be of trifling consequence. But there are some for whom—amidst all the rites of passage, the extravagant alarums and excursions with which these years are famously crowded—the still small enterprise of tilling God's wet allotment merits at least an honourable mention.

Notes

ABBREVIATIONS

AE: Archives du Ministère des Affaires Étrangères, Paris
AN: Archives nationales de la France
ARA: Algemeen Rijksarchief, The Hague, Afdeeling II (1795–1813)
    BZ: Ministerie van Binnenlandse Zaken (Internal Affairs)
    BuZ: Ministerie van Buitenlandse Zaken (External Affairs)
    DP: Archief Dumont-Pigalle
    GB: Archief der Gewestelijke Bestuur (Holland)
    SB: Archief van Staatsbewind
    SS: Archief der Staatssecretarie van het Koninkrijk Holland
    UB: Archief van Uitvoerend Bewind
    MF: Ministerie van Financiën
    WC: Wetgevende Collegiën
    RAW: Collectie Wiselius
GAA: Gemeente Archief, Amsterdam
GAU: Gemeente Archief, Utrecht
RAU: Rijksarchief, Utrecht

AGN: Algemene Geschiedenis van Nederland (13 vols., 1944–58)
AAG: Afdeling Agrarische Geschiedenis, Landbouwhogeschool, Wageningen
BMHG: Bijdragen en Mededelingen van het Historisch Genootschap
BGZN: Bijdragen tot de Sociale en Economische Geschiedenis van het Zuiden van
    Nederland
DvH: Dagverhaal der Handelingen van de Nationale Vergadering
DH: Louis Bonaparte, Documents Historiques . . .
GS: Gedenstukken der Algemeene Geschiedenis van Nederland van 1795 tot 1840
    (ed. H. T. Colenbrander)
NNBW: Nieuw Nederlandsche Biographische Woordenboek (eds. P. C. Molhuysen
    and P. J. Blok)
MKAW: Mededelingen der Koninklijke Nederlandse Academie van Wetenschappen
O.R.G.: Verslagen en Mededelingen van de Vereeniging tot Beoefening van
    Overijsselsch Regt en Geschiedenis
T.v.G.: Tijdschrift voor Geschiedenis

CHAPTER 1: Introduction

1. Edward Handler, *America and Europe in the Political Thought of John Adams* (Cambridge, Mass., 1964), p. 115.
2. S. S. Biro, *The German Policy of Revolutionary France 1792–1797* (2 vols., Cambridge, Mass., 1957), p. 757, n. 46, citing Lefebvre, calls the Batavian Republic "merely an appendage of France and not a very happy one."
3. Alfred Cobban, *Ambassadors and Secret Agents. The Diplomacy of the First Earl of Malmesbury at The Hague* (London, 1954), *passim*.
4. In an interview with Frederick the Great of Prussia in August 1785, Harris proposed a plan "to recover the Republic from its present subjection to France." H. T. Colenbrander, *De Patriottentijd* (3 vols., 's Gravenhage, 1897–9), I, Bijlagen, p. 311.
5. B. H. M. Vlekke. *The Evolution of the Dutch Nation* (New York, 1945), p. 1.
6. A. Sorel, *L'Europe et la Révolution française*, vol. 1, *Les moeurs et les traditions politiques* (Paris, 1885), pp. 3–6.
7. See, for example, Raymond Guyot, *La Directoire et la paix de l'Europe* (Paris, 1911); Louis Madelin, *Histoire du Consulat et de l'Empire* (Paris, 1932–3).
8. The outstanding works are Jacques Godechot, *La grande nation, L'expansion*

révolutionnaire de la France dans le monde, 1789–1799 (2 vols., Paris, 1956); R. R. Palmer, *The Age of Democratic Revolution* (2 vols., Princeton, N.J., 1959–64).

9. Palmer, *op. cit.*, I, p. 9.

10. R. R. Palmer, "Much in Little: The Dutch Revolution of 1795," *Journal of Modern History*, XXVI (1954), pp. 24, 34.

11. For an important discussion of the origins of these ambiguities, see J. Godechot, "Nation, Patrie, Nationalisme et Patriotisme en France au XVIIIe siècle," *Annales historiques de la Révolution française*, 206 (Oct.–Dec. 1971), pp. 481–501. See also Carlton J. Hayes, *The Historical Evolution of Modern Nationalism* (New York, 1931); Boyd C. Shafer, *Nationalism, Myth and Reality* (New York, 1955).

12. Beatrice Hyslop, *French Nationalism in 1789 According to the General Cahiers* (New York, 1934), p. 70.

13. Voltaire, for example, in the *Dictionnaire philosophique* (1764) in the article on *patrie*, had equated it with that "Republic" providing the best of governments—*Patria est ubicumque bene*. See Godechot, *art. cit.*, pp. 486–7.

14. April 24, 1793. Cited in Alfred Cobban, "The Political Ideas of Maximilian Robespierre During the Period of the Convention," in *Aspects of the French Revolution* (London, 1968), p. 182.

15. Godechot, *op. cit.*, I, p. 73.

16. *Ibid.*, p. 79.

17. Albert Mathiez, *La Révolution et les étrangers* (Paris, 1919), p. 16.

18. *Ibid.*, p. 52. In the debate in the Convention on the 1793 constitution, Cloots proscribed the very concept of foreignness: "L'étranger? Expression barbare dont nous commençons rougir et dont nous laisserons la jouissance à ces hordes féroces que la charme des hommes civilisés fera superâitre sans effort," *ibid.*, p. 132.

19. Cloots was executed on March 24, 1794, with Hébert and sixteen others bundled together in an improbable mélange of *enragés* and *étrangers*.

20. "The Revolution," wrote Michelet in the *Histoire de la Révolution*, "could not accomplish anything unless it made its attempt everywhere. The first condition of its durability was to become universal. The second was everywhere to seize the land and to dig itself in." Quoted in the illuminating essay on "Michelet and the French Revolution" by Pieter Geyl, *Debates With Historians* (London, 1962), p. 96.

21. Ariane Méautis, *Le Club helvétique et les idées révolutionnaires dans la Suisse* (Neuchâtel, 1969), p. 42.

22. See T. C. W. Blanning, *Reform and Revolution in Mainz 1743–1803* (Cambridge, 1974), pp. 267–302.

23. Biro, *op. cit.*, I, p. 141.

24. Speech to the Jacobins, December 30, 1791, cited in Jacques Godechot, "Les variations de la politique française à l'égard des pays occupés," in R. Devleeshouwer (ed.), *Occupants-Occupés 1792–1815* (Brussels, 1970), p. 22.

25. Palmer, *Age of Democratic Revolution*, II, pp. 73–4. See also S. Tassier, *Histoire de la Belgique sous l'occupation française en 1792 et 1793* (Brussels, 1934).

26. Biro, *op. cit.*, I, p. 139.

27. This was the misfortune of J. R. van Hooff, the former burgemeester of Eindhoven and one of the founders of the "Légion batave." See below, Ch. 4, pp. 159–60.

28. Marcel Reinhard, *Le Grand Carnot* (2 vols., Paris, 1950–2), I, p. 106.

29. For an account of the exigencies of this frightful winter, see Richard Cobb, *The Police and the People, French Popular Protest 1789–1820* (Oxford 1970), p. 282. As Professor Cobb makes dramatically plain, an "occupied territory" in this context could as easily be the countryside within France as without.

30. Reinhard, *op. cit.*, I, p. 109.

31. Biro, *op. cit.*, I, p. 206.

32. J. E. Harris, *The Assignat* (London, 1930).

33. Palmer, *op. cit.*, II, pp. 296–8.

34. Biro, *op. cit.*, II, Ch. XXVII. Hoche placed his brother-in-law Durbach in charge of fiscal levies on the right bank of the Rhine and sought to ingratiate himself with the Swabian nobility by ending requisitions in selected areas, restoring prewar taxes and permitting the religious orders to retain their property.

35. Palmer, *op. cit.*, II, p. 310.

36. I. Leonard Leeb, *The Ideological Origins of the Batavian Revolution* (The Hague, 1973), p. 59, n. 1, very properly points out that while in the late eighteenth century the

term meant an anti-Orangist reformer, during the middle of the century it had been their opponents who had applied the title to themselves.

37. This, for example, was the view of Claude Mazauric. See Devleeshouwer, *Occupants-Occupés*, p. 114: ". . . je crois que la rapport 'occupants-occupés' dans un pays comme la Belgique sinon pour tous les pays sous domination française, se réduit simplement au rapport 'Révolution-contre Révolution.' "

38. For the early historiography, see J. Elias, *Bijdrage tot de Kennis van de Historiographie der Bataafsche Republiek* (Leiden, 1906); R. Fruin, *Verspreide Geschriften*, ed. P. J. Blok (10 vols., Leiden, 1900–5). On the later treatment of the period, see C. H. E. de Wit, *De Strijd Tussen Aristocratie en Democratie in Nederland 1780–1848* (Heerlen, 1965), pp. 384–93. This work pioneered the re-assessment of the Batavian period in Dutch history and launched a debate which still continues, albeit intermittently, on the contribution of its politicians towards governmental change in the Netherlands. See also J. van Houtte, *et al.* (eds.), *Algemeene Geschiedenis van Nederland*, vols. VIII, IX (Utrecht, 1955).

39. For Busken Huet, see "De Nederlandsche Letterkunde onder de Bataafsche Republiek," in *Litterarische Fantasiën*, vol. 5 (Amsterdam, 1860), p. 93; also C. H. E. de Wit, "De Nederlandse Revolutie van de 18de Eeuw en Frankrijk," in *Frans-Nederlandse Betrekkingen in de 18de Eeuw, Documentatieblad* (June 1971), p. 29; William Elliot Griffis, *Motley's Dutch Nation* (New York, 1908), p. 898.

40. Theun de Vries, *Rutger Jan Schimmelpenninck, Republikein Zonder Republiek* ('s Gravenhage, 1941); Pieter Geyl, "Patriotten en NSBers," in *Studies en Strijdschriften* (Amsterdam, 1958), pp. 393–430. The care shown by Geyl in the latter essay was the more remarkable in that it originated as a lecture in a prison camp.

41. G. Groen van Prinsterer, *Handboek der Geschiedenis van het Vaderland* (Amsterdam, 1876). Onno Zwier van Haren's motto was: "Orange at heart and no-one's slave." See Leeb, *op. cit.*, pp. 100–1.

42. G. Groen van Prinsterer, *Ongeloof en Revolutie* (Amsterdam, 1903), *passim*; "Staatshervorming in Vaderlandsche Zin," *Verspreide Geschriften*, I (Amsterdam, 1859), pp. 197–202.

43. For the historical legacy of Francken and Grotius, see Leeb, *op. cit.*, pp. 21–9.

44. For the prescriptive use of the "ancient constitution" precedent to assert oppositional arguments, see, in particular, J. A. Pocock, *The Ancient Constitution and the Feudal Law* (Cambridge, 1957); Quentin Skinner, "History and Ideology in the English Revolution," *Historical Journal*, 8 (1965), pp. 151–78. For a comparable use of history, see M. I. Finley, *The Ancestral Constitution* (Cambridge, 1971); E. Carcassonne, *Montesquieu et le problème de la Constitution française au XVIIIe siècle* (Paris, 1927).

45. John Lothrop Motley, *The Rise of the Dutch Republic* (3 vols., London, Glasgow, Manchester and New York, 1889).

46. For example, *De Patriottentijd* (3 vols., 's Gravenhage, 1897–9), *De Bataafsche Republiek* (Amsterdam, 1908). A few other noteworthy studies had paved the way for Colenbrander, especially T. Jorissen, *De Patriotten te Amsterdam* (Amsterdam, 1874) and J. De Bosch Kemper, *Letterkundige Aantekeningen betreffende de Geschiedenis van het Nederlandsche Staatsleven en Staatsrecht* (Amsterdam, 1871).

47. L. G. J. Verberne, *In den Spiegel van het Verleden* (Antwerp-Utrecht, 1947); *Gogel en Uniteit* (Nijmegen, 1945); *Het Sociaal Economisch Motief in de Bataafsche Tijd*; L. G. Rogier, "Rutger Jan Schimmelpenninck, 31 October 1761, te Deventer geboren," in *Terugblik en Uitzicht*, II, pp. 69–112.

48. P. Geyl, *Geschiedenis van de Nederlandse Stam* (3 vols., Amsterdam-Antwerp, 1958–9).

49. P. Geyl, " 'Het Volk' in de Bataafse Revolutie," in *Bijdragen voor de Geschiedenis der Nederlanden*, vol. XIV (1959), No. 3, pp. 202, 214.

50. Geyl, "De Bataafse Revolutie," p. 250.

51. See the suggestive article by I. Schöffer, "Did Holland's Golden Age Coincide with a Period of Crisis?" *Acta Historiae Neerlandicae*, I (1966).

52. Cited in Geyl, *Geschiedenis* . . . (hereafter GNS), III, p. 57.

53. Equally, as Leeb, *op. cit.*, pp. 174–5 argues, there were those liberated from the historical mode of argument on both sides who were prepared to address themselves to remedial reform of the "old" constitution.

54. *Ibid.*, pp. 210–11; de Wit, *op. cit.*, pp. 40–1.

55. See J. R. Thorbecke, "Simon Slingelandt's toeleg om den Staat te hervormen," in *Historische Schetsen* ('s Gravenhage, 1860), p. 82. See also in the same collection,

"Over de Hedendaagsche Staatsburgerschap," and the essays on Wiselius and Schimmel-penninck.

56. For an admirable crystallisation of this theme, see E. H. Kossmann, "The Crisis of the Dutch State 1780–1813: Nationalism, Federalism, Unitarism," in J. S. Bromley and E. H. Kossmann (eds.), *Britain and the Netherlands, vol. IV: Metropolis, Dominion and Province* (The Hague, 1971), pp. 154–71.

CHAPTER 2: The Dutch Republic in Its Dotage . . .

1. See Elie Luzac, *Hollands Rijkdom* (4 vols., Leiden, 1780–84). This work had appeared in French in 1778 under the pseudonym "Jacques Accarias de Serionne." Though the work of a committed partisan of the Stadholder, it was singular for its understanding of the relationship between politics and economics. Leeb, *op. cit.*, pp. 160–75, provides an excellent analysis, though he exaggerates a little in describing Luzac as "the very model of the modern man in the guise of Economic Moralist." In so far as this was true, it was also true for other economic commentators—some of them Patriot.

2. Denis Diderot, "Voyage de Holland," *Oeuvres* (Paris, 1819), vol. VIII, p. 39.

3. For the views of other foreigners, see R. Murris, *La Hollande et les hollandais au 17e et 18e siècles vus par les français* (Paris, 1925); K. W. Swart, *The Miracle of the Dutch Republic in the Seventeenth Century* (London, 1967).

4. Frederick A. Pottle (ed.), *Boswell in Holland* (New York, 1952), pp. 287–9.

5. H. de Peyster, *Les Troubles de Hollande* . . . (Paris, 1905), p. 29.

6. The major works are B. H. Slicher van Bath, *Een Samenleving onder Spanning* (Assen, 1957); J. A. Faber, *Drie Feuwen Friesland* (Wageningen, 1972); A. M. van der Woude, *Het Noorderkwartier* (Wageningen, 1972). An earlier progress report in English may be found in J. A. Faber, *et al.*, "Population Changes and Economic Developments in the Netherlands: A Historical Survey," in AAG *Bijdragen* 12 (Wageningen, 1965), pp. 47–113.

7. Johan de Vries, *De Economische Achteruitgang der Republiek in de Achttiende Eeuw* (Amsterdam, 1959), Chs. I and II.

8. AAG 12 (*art. cit.*), pp. 60–1.

9. *Ibid.*, pp. 73–6.

10. Faber, AAG Bijdragen 12, p. 70.

11. AAG 12, p. 110.

12. *Ibid.*, p. 74. Slicher van Bath estimates the population of Overijssel as 1475: 53,000; 1675: 71,000; 1795: 134,104.

13. *Ibid.*, p. 60.

14. *Ibid.*, p. 56.

15. N. W. Posthumus, *De geschiedenis van de Leidsch laken-industrie*, vol. III ('s Gravenhage, 1939), p. 882; ARA GB 72, 102, 111; in 1803 the population of Amsterdam was estimated by city authorities at approx. 195,000. ARA, SB 231.

16. Faber, *op. cit.*, p. 469; see also the same author's "Cattle Plague in the Netherlands During the 18th Century," in *Mededelingen Landbouwhogeschool Wageningen*, 62 (1962).

17. Van der Woude, *op. cit.*, p. 589.

18. *Ibid.*, pp. 365, 370.

19. J. G. van Dillen, *Van Rijkdom en Regenten* ('s Gravenhage, 1970), p. 542.

20. *Ibid.*, pp. 560–2.

21. de Vries, *op. cit.*, pp. 87–8; van der Woude, *op. cit.*, pp. 470–1.

22. Ibid., pp. 336–8.

23. Van Dillen, *op. cit.*, p. 560.

24. *Ibid.*, pp. 560–5; de Vries, *op. cit.*, p. 40.

25. For the plight of the fishing industry, see van der Woude, *op. cit.*, pp. 400ff. and appendices.

26. W. H. Beaufort (ed.), *Brieven van en aan Joan Derk van der Capellen van de Poll* (Utrecht, 1879), p. 388.

27. See van der Woude, pp. 431, 811.

28. De Vries, p. 137; van der Woude, pp. 421–56, 809.

29. J. de Vries, "Van de Spiegel's 'Schets tot een Vertoog over de Intrinsique en Relatieve Magt van de Republiek,'" *Economisch-Historisch Jaarboek*, XXVII (1958), pp. 80–100. For van der Oudermeulen, see *Recherches sur le commerce* (1778). For another "optimistic" view of the Republic's prospects, even after the Fourth Anglo-Dutch War, see A. Kluit, *Iets over den Laatsten Engelschen Oorlog* . . . (Amsterdam, 1794).

30. J. de Vries, "De Oeconomische-Patriottisch Beweging," *De Nieuwe Stem*, VII, 12 (1952), pp. 723–30; J. Bierens de Haan, *Van Oeconomische Tak tot Nederlandsche Maatschappij voor Nijverheid en Handel* (Haarlem, 1952).

31. R. Metelerkamp, *De Toestand van Nederland in Vergelijking Gebragt met die van Enige Andere Landen van Europa* (2 vols., Amsterdam, 1804), I, p. 251.

32. Charles Wilson, *Anglo-Dutch Commerce and Finance in the Eighteenth Century* (Cambridge, 1941), *passim*.

33. P. W. Klein, "Stagnation économique et emploi du capital dans la Hollande des XVIIe et XVIIIe siècles," in *Revue du Nord*, LII, No. 204 (1970), p. 39.

34. Alice Carter, "Dutch Foreign Investment, 1738–1800," *Economica*, XV (1953), 340, 328.

35. H. R. C. Wright, *Free Trade and Protection in the Netherlands 1816–1830* (Cambridge, 1955), pp. 7–8.

36. J. G. van Dillen "De Beurscrisis van 1763," *T.v.G.* (1922).

37. *La Richesse de lo Hollande* (London, 1778), I, p. 127.

38. Wilson, *op. cit.*, pp. 167, 181.

39. J. C. Riley, "Life Annuity-Based Loans on the Amsterdam Capital Market Toward the End of the 18th Century," *Economisch-en Sociaal-Historisch Jaarboek*, 36, (1974), pp. 102–30.

40. Charles Wilson, "Taxation and the Decline of Empires, An Unfashionable Theme," BMHG, LXXVII, pp. 10–22. For contemporary support, see Metelerkamp, *op. cit.*, I, p. 44.

41. The proposal for a "limited porto-franco" was put forward by the Stadholder William IV himself and was later taken as evidence by Élie Luzac, for example, of the importance of a Stadholder to the repair of government. See, in particular, the outstanding work of J. Hovy, *Het Voorstel van 1751 tot Instelling Van Een Beperkt Vrijhavenstelsel in de Republiek* (Groningen, 1966).

42. H. H. van den Heuvel, *Bloei des Handels, Hollands Welvaart* (Haarlem, 1775). This was one of the three prize-winning answers to the essay competition set by Ploos van Amstel, under the auspices of the Holland Society for Science, on what might be done to revive the Dutch economy. A further competition in 1781 on the revival of industry set by the Utrecht Society also contributed to the debate.

43. Even native flax was in shorter supply. Slicher van Bath, *art. cit.* (AAG 12), p. 86, notes that after 1750 flax growing virtually ceased in Overijssel except in the vicinity of Almelo.

44. Wilson, *art. cit.*, p. 18.

45. Van der Woude, in AAG 12, p. 61.

46. Hovy, *op. cit.*, pp. 72–3.

47. Van Dillen, pp. 540–2; De Vries, pp. 64ff. Further copious data on the condition of these industries by 1800 is to be found in the files of the "Agent for the National Economy," Johannes Goldberg, in ARA, Goldberg 27.

48. In 1686, twenty soap-boilers produced between 35,000 and 40,000 tons; by 1702–11, eleven produced 21,132 tons. De Vries, p. 89. The same trend applied to sugar refining and oil pressing.

49. *Ibid.*, pp. 90, 117.

50. It was in Amsterdam that the drill screw for cutting raw stones was invented and patented, and there too that the Jewish community early established a strong hold on both the importing and finishing of diamonds. See H. I. Bloom, *The Economic Activities of the Jews of Amsterdam in the Seventeenth and Eighteenth Centuries* (Williamsport, Pa., 1937), pp. 40–4.

51. Slicher van Bath, AAG 12, p. 86.

52. De Vries, p. 117.

53. In 1765, for example, the banking firm of Clifford arranged a 10-million guilder loan to the Danish crown; but the big loans, other than to the rather fevered French market, were to the Austrian Empire (Johannes Göll) and Russia (Theodor and Raymond de Smeth). For further details, see van Dillen, Ch. 27.

54. Van der Woude, p. 223, supplies some fragmentary evidence from baptism records of children born to vagrant women and the like. See also J. C. W. le Jeune, *Geschiedkundige nasporingen omtrent den toestand der Armen en de Bedelarij* ('s Gravenhage, 1816).

55. AAG 12, pp. 77, 82–5.

56. H. F. J. M. van den Eerenbeemt, "Armoede en drankmisbruik in de Meierij van 's

Hertogenbosch," *Brabantia, 7* (1958), pp. 310–20; "In het spanningsveld der armoede," *Bijdragen tot de geschiedenis van het zuiden van Nederland* (1968); *Streven Naar Sociale Verheffing in Een Statische Stad* (Nijmegen, 1963). See also the useful study by P. B. A. Melief, *De strijd om de armenzorg in Nederland, 1795–1854* (Groningen, 1955); W. F. H. Oldewelt, "Het antaal bedelaars, vondelingen en gevangenen in tijden van welvaart en crisis," *Jaarboek Amstelodamum*, 39 (1942).

57. See de Vries, p. 170.

58. A. M. van der Woude, "De Consumptie van Graan, Vlees en Boter in Holland op het Einde van de Achttiende Eeuw," AAG 9, p. 140. For diet, see L. Burema, *De voeding in Nederland van de middeleeuwen tot de twintigste eeuw* (Amsterdam, 1953).

59. Wright, *op. cit.*, pp. 48–50.

60. Slicher van Bath, *art. cit.*, p. 85.

61. Quoted in C. H. Boxer, *The Dutch Seaborne Empire* (London and New York, 1965), p. 271.

62. J. Hartog (ed.), *De Spectatoriale Schriften van 1741–1800* (Utrecht, 1872); *De Vaderlander*, III, 329; *De Philosooph*, II, 188.

63. *Ibid.*, p. 186.

64. *Ibid.*, p. 188.

65. ARA, Archief Dassevael, III (50), March 1808.

66. Franco Venturi, *Utopia and Reform in the Enlightenment* (Cambridge, 1971), p. 34, n.3.

67. K. W. Swart, *The Sale of Offices in Europe in the Seventeenth Century* (The Hague, 1949), pp. 73–4.

68. M. G. de Boer (ed.), *Het Dagboek van Jacob Bicker Raye, 1732–1772* (Amsterdam, undated), p. vi.

69. J. Smit, *Een Regenten Dagboek uit de 18de Eeuw* (Assen, 1957), p. 13.

70. See, for example, H. van Dijk and D. J. Roorda, "Sociale Mobiliteit onder regenten van de Republiek," in *T.v.G.* (1971), pp. 306–28. For a concise but illuminating comparative analysis, see Peter Burke, *Venice and Amsterdam. A Study of Seventeenth-Century Elite* (London, 1974), especially pp. 17–61.

71. J. E. Elias, *De Vroedschap van Amsterdam* (2 vols., Haarlem, 1903–5).

72. H. A. Westrate, *Gelderland in de Patriottentijd* (Arnhem, 1903), p. 11.

73. J. de Witte van Citters, *Contracten van correspondentiën . . .* ('s Gravenhage, 1873), *passim*.

74. *Ibid.*, pp. 16–19.

75. J. E. Elias, *De Vroedschap van Amsterdam 1578–1795*, (2 vols., Haarlem 1903–05) I, p. cxl ff.

76. Van Dijk and Roorda, *art. cit.*, p. 320, as one would expect, found from a careful scanning of contemporary politics that the period of "least renewal" in Amsterdam and Zierikzee was 1702–48, and that of a greater entry of new men, 1748–87.

77. See Geyl, GNS, II, pp. 418ff; N. J. J. de Voogd, *De Doelistenbeweging te Amsterdam in 1748* (Utrecht, 1914).

78. Most of the *ambtsjonkheer* nobility in Gelderland were natural or dynastic allies of the Stadholder. In addition to military and provincial "court" offices, the Stadholder had rights of presentment to all judicial and financial offices—and retained the system of tax farming in the three "kwartieren." Individuals thus piled up favours. The seventeen-year-old Willem van Lynden van Hemmen was "landrentmeester generaal" (one of the province treasurers), deputy to the States-General; president of the Domanial Council; burgrave and knight of Nijmegen; and other posts generating an income of some fl.20,000 a year.

79. All these riots and rebellions—as well as other political manifestations in England and France—involved at the same time appeals to "lost" communal liberties, an outraged "moral economy" and the formation of popular militia. I am currently engaged in assembling evidence dealing with these themes.

80. Geyl, GNS, II, p. 421. See also C. van Huffel, *Willem Bentinck van Rhoon, zijn persoonlijkheid en leven* ('s Gravenhage, 1923). Alice Clare Carter, *The Dutch Republic in the Seven Years' War* (London, 1971) argues, convincingly, that Bentinck's influence was slight in these years.

81. The general view of Brunswick has become (improbably) more sympathetic. See N. A. Bootsma, *De Hertog van Brunswick, 1750–59* (Assen, 1962). His grasp of diplomacy

was surer than domestic affairs. Alice Clare Carter, *Neutrality or Commitment, The Evolution of Dutch Foreign Policy 1667–1795* (London 1975), pp. 81–3.

82. "Een Rotterdamsch Gedenkschrift Uit den Patriottentijd en der Dagen der Revolutie" (ed. C. te Lintum), BMHG, XXXI (1910), p. 120.

83. P. Geyl, *De Patriottenbeweging 1780–87* (Amsterdam, 1947), p. 47.

84. P. Geyl, *De Wittenoorlog: een Pennestrijd in 1757* (Amsterdam, 1953); Leeb, *op. cit.*, pp. 86ff.

85. J. Bartstra, *Vlootherstel en Legeraugmentatie* (Assen, 1952), p. 207.

86. See P. J. van Winter, *Het aandeel van den Amsterdamschen handel aan den opbouw van het Amerikaansche Gemeenebest* (Amsterdam, 1927); Wright, *op. cit.*, pp. 15–16.

87. *Brieven van . . . van der Capellen*, p. 620. F. W. van Wijk, *De Republiek en Amerika 1776–1782* (Leiden, 1921), despite ample evidence to the contrary, believes the effect of the Revolution on Dutch politics to have been negligible.

88. Charles Francis Adams (ed.), *The Works of John Adams* (10 vols., Boston, 1851–56), VII, p. 399.

89. J. Hartog, "Een Heftig Patriot," in *Uit der Dagen der Patriotten* (Amsterdam, 1896), p. 58.

90. J. P. Duyverman, "Jean Luzac," in *Kleio*, 5 (1965), pp. 146–9.

91. L. H. Butterfield (ed.), *The Diary and Autobiography of John Adams* (Cambridge, 1961), p. 454, n.2.

92. Van Wijk, pp. 191ff.

CHAPTER 3: The Patriot Revolt . . .

1. There is now available in English an excellent study of Patriot and earlier Dutch political and historical writing, I. Leonard Leeb's *Ideological Origins of the Batavian Revolution*. I have incorporated some of his insights into my own discussion in so far as they concern the practice of politics. But for study of particular texts, references to this work is indispensable. C. H. E. de Wit's stimulating account of the Patriot revolt, and its immediate aftermath, *De Nederlandse Revolutie van de Achttiende Eeuw; Oligarchie en Proletariaat* (Oirsbeek, 1974), appeared too late for me to take careful account of its important reassessment of the "plunder years" of 1787–8.

2. Hartog, *art. cit.*, p. 77. For van der Kemp, see Helen L. Fairchild, *Francis Adrian van der Kemp* (New York, 1903).

3. M. de Jong, *Joan Derk van der Capellen: Staatkundig levensbeeld uit de wordingtijd van de moderne demokratie in Nederland* (Groningen– 's Gravenhage, 1922) remains the definitive biography. For a briefer sketch, see W. F. Wertheim and A. H. Wertheim-Gijse Weenink (eds.), *Aan Het Volk van Nederland, Het Democratisch Manifest* (Amsterdam, 1966). The references in this chapter are to this edition.

4. *Brieven van . . . van der Capellen*, p. 64.

5. *Ibid.*, p. 764.

6. *Ibid.*, p. 463.

7. Palmer, *Age of Democratic Revolution*, I, p. 330.

8. *Aan Het Volk . . .*, p. 65.

9. *Ibid.*, p. 66.

10. *Ibid.*, p. 67.

11. R. M. van Goens, *Politiek vertoog over het waar sistema van de stad Amsterdam, met relatie tot de algemeene belangens der Republiek.* Van Goens had been appointed Professor of History at Utrecht when only eighteen, but was removed for supporting the "tolerationists" in the dispute over Socrates. In 1776 he was appointed to the city's regency by William V and became an active propagandist for the Orangists. His work also invited a counter-attack by W. van Irhoven van Dam, *Missive aan R. M. van Goens* (Kn 19761).

12. *Aan het Volk . . .*, pp. 22, 95.

13. See Carcassonne, *op. cit.*, W. E. Doyle, *The Parlement of Bordeaux and the End of the Ancien Régime 1771–1790* (London, 1974).

14. This "programme" of the Patriot *regents* was misattributed by Palmer to van der Capellen's circle. It has been exhaustively analysed by Kossmann, *art. cit.*; Leeb, pp. 185–97; and de Wit, *De Strijd*, pp. 38ff., emerging as a conservative attempt to absorb the impact of popular sovereignty ideas within a new "virtual" representation. Hence the optimistic formula for an imperium mixtum, "Sovereignty in the People. Government by the most Distinguished, supreme government in the rule of the leaders of the people." It

was only the much more anti-revolutionary Adriaan Kluit who in his *De Souvereiniteit der Staaten van Holland, Verdedigd* (Leiden, 1785), labelled it a "democratic" argument. Judging from the pamphlet literature of the time, the *Grondwettige Herstelling* (2 vols., Amsterdam, 1784–6) has been much more important for historians than for the Patriot rank-and-file.

15. W. Gobbers, *Jean-Jacques Rousseau in Holland* (Gent, 1963), *passim*.

16. The principal champion of "free thought" was Petrus Burman, and the group of scholars and literati around him known from his country residence as the "Santhorst" circle. See Hartog, "Uit de dagen der Patriotten," pp. 1–49. His antagonists included the predikants Petrus Hofstede and Johannes Barueth, whose *De Advocaet der Vaderlandsche Kerk* (Dordrecht, 1771–?) appointed itself the bulwark of orthodoxy.

17. *Spectatoriale Schriften*, pp. 189–90. For eighteenth-century Dutch literature and taste, see O. Noordenbos, "Rationalisme en Romantiek in de Noordelijke Nederlanden," in van Houtte, *et al.*, AGN VIII (Amsterdam-Brussels, 1955), pp. 61ff.

18. *Ibid.*, p. 67.

19. *Redevoering van F. A. van der Marck over "De Liefde tot het Vaderland"* (Deventer-Amsterdam, 1783), pp. 47–9; see also W. P. Goslinga, *De Rechten van den Mensch en Burger* ('s Gravenhage, 1936), p. 41. A number of the German academics to take chairs at Dutch universities had a deep influence on the political education of the new generation—in particular, Professors Trotz and Wesseling at Utrecht and Pestel at Leiden, though, unlike van der Marck, they were careful not to become politically compromised.

20. See Leeb, pp. 110–22.

21. *Verhandeling over de vraag: in welke zin kunnen de menschen gezegd worden gelijk te zijn? En welke zijn de regten en plighten, die daaruit voortvlooien?* (Haarlem, 1793). See Goslinga, pp. 60–73.

22. For a reiteration of the jaded theme that the Dutch had no need of revolutionary freedoms, having had their own "True Liberty" for centuries, see A. Kluit, *De Rechten van den Mensch in Frankrijk, geen gewaande Rechten in Nederland . . .* (Amsterdam, 1793); and for an opposite, exuberantly anti-historical democratic tract, S. I. Wiselius, *Verhandeling over de Burgerlijke Vrijheid en Staatkundige Gelijkheid* (written 1791–3); see de Wit, *De Strijd*, pp. 83–93, Goslinga, pp. 48–50.

23. Goslinga, p. 76. For another, much earlier harangue in the same evangelical tone, see *Wat Het Is, Een Vry Volk Te Zyn* (1783), p. 307, where Daniel and the story of the fiery furnace trio becomes a parable of the Patriot rebellion.

24. Others in this idiom were *Willem Leevend* and *Julia* by Rhijnvis Feith, a Zwolle tax receiver, both carrying the evangelical gospels of sin, fall and penance in the form of sentimental social parables.

25. *Spectatoriale Schriften*, p. 97.

26. Ysbrand van Hamelsveld, *De Zedelijke Toestand der Nederlandse Natie* (Amsterdam, 1791 edn.), p. 554.

27. *Ibid.*, p. 159.

28. *Ibid.*, p. 72.

29. *Spectatoriale Schriften*, pp. 313ff.

30. Hartog, *Uit de Dagen*, p. 57.

31. See C. J. Guibal, *Democratie en Oligarchie in Friesland tijdens de Republiek* (Assen, 1934), pp. 62–190. The Friesian States (*landdag*) comprised representatives from the towns and from each of the *grietenijen* making up the rural cantons of Oostergo, Westergo and Zevenwouden. Ostensibly, the *grietenij* delegates were elected, thus preserving an ancient democratic right. In actual fact, by the eighteenth century the election of the *grietmannen* had become part of the property of the estate, much as in an English rotten borough. Many of the *grietenijen* had long been colonised by the Friesian nobility— the Aylva, Burmania, Eysinga. By the mid-eighteenth century it was common for the *grietenijen* to be traded between families, or used in marriage settlements, like the regencies in Holland. In 1748 William IV, the Stadholder of the province, tried to use his position to subjugate the great families, but the effort petered out with his death. In 1780 there was a triangular conflict between his supporters, the noble *grietmannen* and Patriots excluded from their charmed circle. The analogy with Brittany, both in terms of intransigent regionalism and fiercely combative domestic politics, is irresistible. See W. A. van der Meulen, *Coert Lambertus van Beyma* (Leeuwarden, 1894).

32. H. A. Westrate, *Gelderland in den Patriottentijd* (Arnhem, 1903), pp. 20, 87–91.

Nijmegen had a population of 12,000; Arnhem and Zutphen about 7,000 each. Within the provincial "landdag," the towns were subjected to a perpetual noble majority and the president and the three "directors" of the assembly equally were noble.

33. See I. Vijlbrief, *Van Anti-Aristocratie tot Democratie* (Amsterdam, 1950), p. 169; A. van Hulzen, *Utrecht in de Patriottentijd* (Zaltbommel, 1966).

34. Westrate, *op. cit.*, pp. 47–8.

35. There were pockets of the land provinces where vestiges of the ancient right of mortmain survived. Unfree tenants had to prove continuous occupation after a head of household's death to prevent reversion of the estate. In some parts of the Veluwe, over half the peasant's livestock might be forfeit in token of the lord's benevolence in not enforcing his right. See I. J. Brugmans, "La fin de feodalité aux Pays-Bas," *Annales historiques de la Révolution française*, 169 (1969), p. 167.

36. Colenbrander, *Patriottentijd*, I, p. 281. In the same week six deputies elected by the Zwolle guilds and six by the amorphous *burgerij* had insisted on a new "Burgher Commission" being elected.

37. See Beaufort, *Brieven van . . . van der Capellen*, pp. 494–6.

38. The *Post van Neder Rijn* began publication in 1781; *Politieke Kruijer*, 1782. The articles by W. P. Sautijn Kluit on the press in the Patriottentijd are a useful survey but no substitute for consulting the sources (*Bijdragen voor Vaderlandsche Geschiedenis en Oudheidkunde*, 1877, 1882).

39. Kroes-Ligtenberg, *Dr. Wybo Fijnje 1750–1809* (Assen, 1957), pp. 76–8.

40. *Brieven van . . . van der Capellen*, p. 629.

41. The position of the *schutterij* had been safeguarded in a reference in Article VIII of the Union of Utrecht. In 1701, the States of Holland had made an effort to put at least the Burgher Companies on more regular footing but that had gone the way of all reforms at that time. See Vijlbrief, p. 17. For a typical paeon on the "new" militia as a rejuvenation of the old, see *De Politieke Kruijer*, 30, (Feb. 1783), pp. 300–1 ("An armed *burgerij* is the pillar of national freedom").

42. Te Lintum, *art. cit.*, p. 152.

43. Westrate, pp. 165ff. Harderwijk, a university town, was one of the centres of Patriot activity, as were other academic towns in the more distant provinces—Franeker in Friesland and Groningen.

44. *Programma . . . van de Societeit van Wapenhandel opgericht binnen Leiden* (Leiden, 1783) (KN 20655). Pieter Vreede was a prolific publicist as well as a well-off textile manufacturer. As "Harmodius Friso" and "Frank de Vrij" he was in the van of the most vehement democrats. See his *Aanspraak aan Willem de V . . .* (1581–1781) and the *Brief over de ware oorzaak van 's lands ongeval . . .* (1782) and the thesis on his career to 1787 by A. H. Hussen in the Leidsch Bibliotheek.

45. See C. M. Davies, *Memorials and Times of Pieter Philip Juriaan Quint Ondaatje* (Utrecht, 1870).

46. Van Hulzen, *op. cit.*, p. 81.

47. See *Iets zakelijk voor Utrechtse burgeren* (Utrecht, 1783) (KN 1174); Hulzen, p. 47.

48. Geyl, *GNS*, III, p. 157.

49. Vijlbrief, p. 177.

50. As early as December 1782, the "Patriot Regents" meeting in Amsterdam had agreed on a secret programme in which the militia was to be used to coerce the Stadholder into relinquishing his military and appointative powers. See H. T. Colenbrander, "Aanteekeningen Betreffende de Vergaderingen van Vaderlandsche Regenten te Amsterdam 1783–1787," in *Bijdragen en Mededelingen van het Historisch Genootschap te Utrecht*, X (1899), p. 86.

51. W. W. van der Meulen, "De Betekenis van de Haagsche Opstootjes in de Patriottentijd," *Die Haghe* (1909), pp. 79–112; Colenbrander, *Patriottentijd*, I, pp. 403–4.

52. Geyl, *GNS*, III, pp. 151ff.

53. Vijlbrief, pp. 187ff.

54. A few months later this increased to 1,368 or about one-seventh of the adult male population of the city.

55. Van Hulzen, p. 110. The account which follows relies heavily on this work and on the version given by Vijlbrief.

56. Sichterman's sin had been to sign a counter-draft to the Patriot address. Van Hulzen, p. 96.

57. *Ibid.*, p. 121.
58. *Ibid.*, p. 126.
59. *Ibid.*, pp. 131ff.
60. *Ibid.*, p. 135.
61. *Ibid.*, pp. 142–3.
62. Vijlbrief, p. 222.
63. *Het Nut der Stadhouderlijke Regering Aangetoond by Gelegenheid der Geboorte van Willem Frederik* (1773), pp. 15, 115, 127–9, 166–7. This was coupled with an appeal to the "Eminent Hoofd" to reassert the martial independence of the Republic.
64. De Bosch Kemper, *op. cit.*, pp. 259–60.
65. *Ibid.*
66. For the text, see Colenbrander, *Patriottentijd*, I, Bijlagen, pp. 282–4; de Bosch Kemper, p. 261. For similar expressions of popular sovereignty theory applied to the Dutch situation, see *Wat Het Is, Een Volk Vry Te Zyn* (1783); *Politieke Bedenkingen over de Vryheid* (Amsterdam, 1783).
67. "Leidse Ontwerp," p. 29.
68. "Demophilus" (Vreede?), *Zakboek* (pocketbook) *van Neerlands Volk* (Dordrecht, 1785). This very important little polemic argued that "a people which is truly free . . . is ruled only by laws of its own making . . . it recognises no-one as its lord or master for its sovereignty rests in the bosom of the People, which then elects its regents from among its own number. . . . Liberty is the very soul of its life and the anchor of its state" (pp. 19, 21, 25). It went on to insist that "a proper people's government is one which the People itself has assembled and through which the people can govern itself and decide all matters by a majority of its votes" (p. 29).
69. "Leidse Ontwerp," p. 15.
70. *Ibid.*, p. 46.
71. KN 21046 (Rotterdam 1785).
72. Colenbrander, *Patriottentijd*, I, p. 76, n.1.
73. Colenbrander, *Aanteekeningen*, p. 101, n.1. Van der Capellen's inferiority complex *vis-à-vis* the nobility remained with him all his life. He had remarked that "their High Mightinesses the Gentlemen of Holland reckon it beneath their dignity to admit to their council tuppeny-happeny squires from hayseed provinces like van der Marsch and me," *Patriottentijd*, I, p. 76.
74. The council accepted the principle of an elected short-list but retained permanent tenure and said nothing of a "Burgher College."
75. One of the Free Corps captains, van Haeften, was also a member of the "Patriot" group of regents who had divided the council. It was he who, on August 29, demanded a doubling of the watch and a force of at least eighty men placed at each city gate. Van Hulzen, pp. 165–6.
76. *Ibid.*, p. 210.
77. *Ibid.*, p. 174.
78. Colenbrander, *Patriottentijd*, II, Bijlagen IV, pp. 354–5.
79. *Ibid.*, II, p. 218; III, Bijlagen, pp. 89–97.
80. *Nieuw Nederlandsch Jaarboek*, 1787. On a rather rough-and-ready basis, de Wit, *Nederlandse Revolutie*, p. 68, estimates the number of burghers and artisans volunteering for the Free Corps as around 35% of the whole.
81. Rayneval, the special emissary sent from Versailles to attempt a mediation with the Prussian ambassador von Goertz, warned Vergennes that such was the impact of the armed bourgeois that "the tranquillity and even the existence of the Republic as such demands a change, and this change must be the adoption of a modified system (put forward) by the bourgeois. The result of this new order of things is as simple as it is certain. The bourgeois must become something in the political order"—a prophecy the French might well have taken to heart.
82. The effectiveness of any action taken in Utrecht depended on upholding their autonomy *vis-à-vis* the States. This in turn involved the allegiance of other dependent towns. In April 1786, the defeated regents of Wijk-bij-Duurstede appealed to the States against their expulsion, which duly ordered their reinstatement. The Wijk democrats then turned to the Utrecht Patriot Council, which affirmed that the States had no authority to interfere in the affairs of Utrecht, Wijk-bij-Duurstede or any other town of the province. See van Hulzen, pp. 211–12.
83. Colenbrander, *Patriottentijd*, III, pp. 39ff.

84. The Amsterdam delegation, for example, was evenly split between the minions of, respectively, the Patriot Pensionary van Berckel and the Orangist burgemeester Rendorp, who would vote automatically according to their patron's line.

85. See G. Ellis, *History of the Late Revolution in the Dutch Republic* (London, 1789), p. 113.

86. Colenbrander, *Patriottentijd*, II, Bijlagen, pp. 324–5.

87. See, apart from Cobban, *op. cit.*, *The Diaries and Correspondence of James Harris, First Earl of Malmesbury* (4 vols., 1844), II; de Wit, *De Nederlandse Revolutie*, Chs. V–VI.

88. Harris had a formidable ally in Princess Wilhelmina, who was aghast (as she wrote to Hertzberg, the Prussian Secretary of State) at the Patriots' wanting to "introduce a type of democracy." Colenbrander, *Patriottentijd*, II, Bijlagen, p. 314.

89. Cobban, p. 52.

90. See F. van Dijk, *Mr. Laurens Pieter van de Spiegel, Raad en Burgemeester van Goes* (Assen, 1963).

91. Cobban, p. 111.

92. Westrate, pp. 187ff.

93. *Ibid.*, p. 243.

94. Colenbrander, *Aanteekeningen*, pp. 115–16.

95. Colenbrander, *Patriottentijd*, II, p. 358.

96. *Ibid.*, III, p. 59.

97. De Wit, *Nederlandse Revolutie*, p. 189, takes the more generous view and calls Mappa's force a "burgerlijke observatie corps," established to safeguard the Holland towns like Gouda which had already been subject to general pillage.

98. Ellis, p. 161.

99. De Wit, *Nederlandse Revolutie*, p. 67.

100. The dispute with Joseph II over the Scheldt had proved embarrassing for the regents of Amsterdam. On the one hand they could not possibly permit a direct threat to their commercial interests, but on the other hand were suspicious that William V might provoke a war so as to catapult the Stadholder into the seat of military power as in 1672 and 1747–8.

101. Colenbrander, *Aanteekeningen*, pp. 115–6, n. 2.

102. AE (Corr. Hollande 563).

103. P. Geyl, *De Patriottenbeweging 1780–1787* (Amsterdam, 1947), p. 166; Elias, *De Vroedschap*, I, p. clxvii.

104. Geyl, *Patriottenbeweging*, pp. 176–92.

105. *Ibid.*, p. 176.

106. Colenbrander, *Patriottentijd*, III, Bijlagen, lists 7,051 men in September, including 723 cavalry and 347 officers.

107. For the events at Middelburg, see ARA, Archief Dumont-Pigalle ZZZZ (July 1791) OOOOO. Steveninck blamed the local Organist regents, the van Citters clan, for inciting the mob, among whom he numbered large numbers of "foreigners"—Flemings and Brabanders. For Friesland, see Dumont-Pigalle AAAAA.

108. In particular see Dumont-Pigalle QQQQ. De Wit, *Nederlandse Revolutie*, pp. 149–62, makes full use of this evidence, calling the gathering of representatives from 200 guilds "burgher corporations" and Free Corps a "burgher parliament."

109. Colenbrander, *Patriottentijd*, III, p. 49. Hertzberg had failed in his persistent efforts at this stage to persuade William V to produce a counter-accommodation to pre-empt the French.

110. *Ibid.*, II, p. 88.

111. *Brieven van . . . van der Capellen*, p. 416.

112. *Ibid.*, p. 719. Van der Capellen had been very bitter at what he considered the betrayal of France's separate peace with Britain in the American War and (*ibid.*, p. 497) had warned, "never will the Dutch trust the French."

113. Colenbrander, *Patriottentijd*, I, p. 422.

114. *Ibid.*, II, pp. 281–3.

115. *Ibid.*, II, p. 329.

116. *Ibid.*, III, p. 49.

117. *Ibid.*, III, pp. 311–12.

118. *Ibid.*, III, pp. 313–14.

119. *Ibid.*, III, p. 118.

120. See de Wit, *Nederlandse Revolutie*, pp. 84–94.
121. Cobban, p. 145.
122. Colenbrander, *Patriottentijd*, III, Bijlagen, p. 180.
123. Cobban, p. 152.
124. Colenbrander, *Patriottentijd*, III, p. 56.
125. Van Hulzen, pp. 295–6.
126. ARA, Dumont-Pigalle QQQQ.
127. For an account of the systematic plunder inflicted on Patriot property both before and after the invasion, see de Wit, *Nederlandse Revolutie*, pp. 172–238.
128. Le Comte de Mirabeau (Honoré Gabriel de Riqueti), *Aux Bataves sur le Stadhoudérat* (Amsterdam and Paris, 1788), p. 1.
129. Colenbrander, *Patriottentijd*, III, pp. 90–1.

CHAPTER 4: The Patriots and the French Revolution . . .

1. See, for example, *De Lotgevallen der Nederlandsche Burgers welke door de Troupen
van Zijne Prussische Majesteit in de Maand September van het Jaar 1787 zijn Krijgs-
gevangen Gemaakt* (Brussels, 1788), Institute of Historical Research, London (hereafter
referred to as IHR), Pamphlet No. 21741; *Les Prussiens dénoncés à l'Europe* (Paris 1789),
KN 21843.
2. De Bosch Kemper, *op. cit.*, p. 254, ascribes the authorship to a joint effort in
which a Walloon predikant, Marron, supplied the Dutch history and Mirabeau the libertarian trimmings.
3. Dumont-Pigalle to Etienne Luzac, May 18, 1790. See Sillem, *Het Leven van Mr.
Johan Valckenaer, 1759–1821* (2 vols., Amsterdam, 1883), I, p. 82. For a brief biography of Dumont-Pigalle, see de Bosch Kemper, *op. cit.*, p. 254. In this priceless documentary collection, history is indivisible from autobiography. Apart from shedding light
on the character of the "exile," they describe an old and impoverished man, living
largely on the charity of friends in frugal circumstances, anxious only that "the beating clock of death" should not prevent him from recording the crimes and follies of the
Patriots' defeat. Otherwise, he wrote, "our unhappiness and the infamy of our Tyrants will
be buried in perpetual oblivion." Despite his efforts, his history only just escaped such
oblivion. After the Batavian Republic had been established, he remained in Paris and in
extreme poverty sold his collection to the Batavian ambassador Schimmelpenninck in 1800
for fl.12,000 and a pension of 5,000 to his widow on his death. He died that same year.
Schimmelpenninck, who had no interest in the documents but had merely supposed he was
giving Dumont-Pigalle some charity for his past services, left them at the embassy in Paris
where they remained until 1855. In that year the new Royal National Archives were established at The Hague, and the Dumont-Pigalle collection was finally housed there, where
it remains today.
4. Van Irhoven van Dam to Daendels, Jorissen, *De Patriotten te Amsterdam in 1794*,
p. 41.
5. *Age of Democratic Revolution*, *op. cit.*, II, p. 182.
6. See the remarks of Kossmann, "The Crisis of the Dutch State," *art. cit.*, pp. 166–7.
7. Dumont-Pigalle CC, September 15, 1787.
8. From the Knuttel catalogue, 1790 appears to be the only "silent" year of the
Dutch presses in France and the Netherlands.
9. KN 21842.
10. KN 22059. See also H. Swildens, *Kort Begrip van het geheele hervorming der
republiek behelzende de fundament en voornaamste hoofdzaken eener verbeterde reger-
ingsvorm* (1787); Baron de Loe, *Recherches sur la vraie cause de nos troubles* (Münster,
1789); *Brieven aan Eenige Vaderlandsche Gezinden* (1792), KN 22065; *Catechism of
True Liberty* (Dunkirk, 1792), KN 22061; *Notes historiques pour servir d'introduction aux
développements des bases de la nouvelle constitution de la République Batave*, KN 22064;
and many more.
11. KN 21975.
12. Johan Valckenaer was dismissed from his Chair of Law at Franeker as a result of
his participation in the Patriot revolt against the Stadholderian Règlement. When the
Patriots won control of Utrecht, they elected him professor at that university, but he had
scarcely time to take up his chair in September 1787 before the Prussians invaded. His
constitutional plan was based on an indirect electoral system with a household franchise.

Later Valckenaer came to endorse much more directly democratic systems. For the constitutional plan, see Dumont-Pigalle LLLL; GS, I, pp. 23ff.

13. De Bosch Kemper, *op. cit.*, pp. 299–300.

14. Dumont-Pigalle NNNNN.

15. Dumont-Pigalle AAAAA. Valckenaer reserves particular blame for the officers of the 2,260 Friesian Free Corps who failed to show any resistance at all to the invaders. His dossier includes a rogues gallery of incompetents and villains who had led the Patriots, including one Feico Lemkema, "a miserable and cowardly old man who liked to drink too much and when even sober had no common sense," and a D. Zylstra, described as "bon père, bon citoyen, fameux faiseur d'Enfants, *lapidum Caput ut Cerebrum non habet.*"

16. GS, I, pp. xxxi–xxxii.

17. Dumont-Pigalle H.

18. The Brussels commission had issued a "Procuration nationale," which they delivered to the French government as their credentials. In actual fact this was merely a certificate of self-authorisation issued by those who happened to have been present at the original meeting. In a letter to Dumont-Pigalle in November 1789, Valckenaer referred scornfully to the "Prétendue Procuration nationale," and spent a good deal of time discrediting it to the French authorities.

19. *Ibid.*, May 1789. Brought round to Valckenaer's view, van der Capellen came to the conclusion that the deputation could only "pourrir la zizanie et le désordre." Dumont-Pigalle H.

20. See Colenbrander, *De Bataafsche Republiek* (Amsterdam, 1908), p. 16.

21. Dumont-Pigalle AAAAA. The Aylva were one of the oldest and richest families in the province. Valckenaer calculated that the elder Aylva alone had lost at least fl.10,000 a year from the forfeiture of his *grietenie.*

22. Dumont-Pigalle K. Rant had been commandant of the Free Corps at Heusden— the home town of Valckenaer's friend Abbema. On the approach of the Prussians he not only failed to mobilise the Corps but, waiting till night had fallen, fled the city with a few of his men, taking the keys of the city with him. It was sacked on September 21 and 22.

23. *Ibid.*

24. *Ibid.* The refugees usually arrived in St. Omer armed with a letter of introduction from the Brussels commission. This document constituted their entitlement to the standard allowance of 14 livres laid down by the commission. But van Beijma, who had been delegated an essentially administrative authority, had taken it on himself to scrutinise the applicant's credentials and if unsatisfied, to make arbitrary deductions from the allowance or to refuse it altogether.

25. Dumont-Pigalle AAAAA; Sillem, *Valckenaer*, I, p. 122.

26. Sillem, *Valckenaer*, I, p. 145

27. Dumont-Pigalle H (December 6, 1789).

28. *Ibid.* Van Hoey's burst of blunt speaking was rewarded with an order (later set aside) to leave France within four months.

29. *Het caracter van den Heer J. Valckenaer uit zijn eigene daaden en woorden opgemaakt* (St. Omer, 1792), *passim.*

30. KN 21919.

31. Sillem, *Valckenaer*, I, pp. 130–1.

32. In an address to the Jacobins, van Beijma attempted to have his version of the Patriot revolt accepted as the authentic one. He suggested that its principal objective had been the establishment of democratic government and its characteristic instrument the use of armed citizenry. See KN 21983.

33. The main function of Le Batave was not to act as a propagandist for Patriot views (with the exception of the agitation for war with the Stadholder) but to establish, like Cérisier's Gazette Universelle, a Dutch-owned newspaper at the centre of the revolutionary theatre.

34. Sillem, *Valckenaer*, I, pp. 162–3.

35. Cobb, *The Police and the People*, p. 130.

36. GS, I, p. 116.

37. *Ibid.*, p. 174.

38. Méautis, *op. cit.*, pp. 109–10.

39. GS, I, p. 39, n. 1.

40. *Ibid.*, p. 35. With help from Abbema, Daendels and his Gelderland colleague Gelderman, later the quartermaster of the Batavian legion, had secured the purchase of

4,000 rifles for the Brabant and Liège legions, badly needed after the declaration of war in April. See AE Holl. 583, Abbema-Dumouriez, June 13, 1792; Dumont-Pigalle O, 21.

41. *La Vie et les mémoires du général Dumouriez* (Paris, 1822–3), p. 137.

42. See de Bosch Kemper, *op. cit.*, pp. 298–304; GS, I, pp. 23ff. Valckenaer intended that the executive Directory swear an oath to the constitution, not to the Stadholder.

43. Palmer, *Age of Democratic Revolution*, II, pp. 73–4.

44. Dumont-Pigalle O (19).

45. The committee of administration of the legion promised the French government that it would repay it for the cost of equipping and fighting the campaign. See Mendel, *op. cit.*, p. 30, n. 1.

46. Dumont-Pigalle O (19).

47. GS, I, p. 185.

48. Dumont-Pigalle OOOOO; GS, I, pp. 40–1.

49. Dumont-Pigalle OOOOO; GS, I, p. 53. It is interesting that only in their communication to Dumouriez did the Committee explicitly refer to the "adoption of the base of the French constitution." Elsewhere it cited the more judicious "liberté républicaine."

50. GS, I, pp. 55–7. According to Dumont-Pigalle, this plan was the joint work of Abbema and van der Capellen. Among its articles was a clause prohibiting the execution of any capital sentence without the express consent of the Minister of Justice—a radical step in Dutch penology.

51. *Ibid.*, p. 60; Dumont-Pigalle A; OOOO.

52. GS, I, pp. 65–6. From the remarks of van Hooff, it appears that old rivalries still persisted and that Huber of the *administrative* committee had been greatly shocked by the independent mission of the Antwerp delegates.

53. *Ibid.*, p. 112.

54. *Ibid.*, p. 103.

55. Colenbrander, *Bataafsche Republiek*, p. 32; GS, I, p. 96, n. 1.

56. GS, I, p. 194.

57. *Ibid.*, p. 49.

58. Dumont-Pigalle OOOO; GS, I, p. 200, n. 1 (Steveninck to Dumont-Pigalle).

59. GS, I, p. 84.

60. *Ibid.*, p. 81, n. 1.

61. *Ibid.*, n. 2.

62. See Harvey Mitchell, *The Underground War Against Revolutionary France, The Missions of William Wickham, 1794–1800* (Oxford, 1965), pp. 27–8.

63. GS, I, p. 193.

64. *Ibid.*, pp. 95–6.

65. Dumouriez, *op. cit.*, p. 8.

66. Dumont-Pigalle OOOOO.

67. *Ibid.* (February 12, 1793).

68. *Ibid.* (March 22, 1793).

69. *Ibid.* (March 23, 1793).

70. *Ibid.*, 19 Ventôse, Year II (March 9, 1794).

71. Sillem, *Valckenaer*, p. 191.

72. GS, I, p. 101; Dumont-Pigalle OOOOO.

73. Dumont-Pigalle OOOOO (Steveninck to Dumont-Pigalle); GS, I, p. 124, n. 2.

74. There was a rump committee formed in Boulogne after the failure of the campaign of 1793, but unlike its predecessor it made no attempt to impress itself on the French government as the representatives of a provisional Batavian administration.

75. Mendel, *op. cit.*, p. 30.

76. GS, I, p. 286.

77. *Ibid.*, pp. 316–17.

78. Jorissen, *De Patriotten te Amsterdam in 1794*, p. 20.

79. For an acceptable, if dated biography of Gogel, see J. A. Sillem, *De Politieke en Staathuishhoudkundige Workzaamheid van I. J. A. Gogel* (Amsterdam, 1864) which, however, passes very briefly over Gogel's activities on the Revolutionary Committee of 1794.

80. GS, I, p. 257.

81. See, in particular, Dumont-Pigalle R, QQQQ, ZZZZZ, De Wit, *De Nederlandse Revolutie*, pp. 187–9, 199–239. For the Utrecht fines, see KN 21751, *Naamlyst van alle personen door de geheele Republiek welke na de gezegende omwenteling van 1787 om*

hun gehouden gedrag daar den wettige en competente rechter na verdienste zyn gestraf
(Arnhem, 1788?).

82. GS, I, p. 133; A. J. van der Meulen, *Studies over het Ministerie van Van de
Spiegel* (Amsterdam?, 1905), p. 11.

83. See de Wit, *De Strijd*, pp. 50–5. The history of the East India Company following the Anglo-Dutch War of 1780–84 was one of perennial financial crisis, and an increasing burden of subsidy falling on the States of Holland and the city of Amsterdam. In
return for these public guarantees, a greater measure of public supervision was urged (as
in comparable British legislation in the same period). During the Patriot period, a commission was established to provide this regulation, but was killed off by the Restoration
in 1788.

84. Van der Meulen, *op. cit.*, p. 240. From 1792 to 1794, only 70% of the official
Quota was paid in by provincial treasuries, so that in reforming the fiscal distribution, the
Grand Pensionary was possibly doing no more than recognising the de facto situation.

85. Theodorus Jorissen, *De Overgave van Amsterdam in Januari 1795* (Amsterdam,
1884), pp. 46–7.

86. IHR, No. 21842, *Twee Belangrijk Brieven over de Omwenteling in Holland*
(Geneva, 1789), pp. 46ff.

87. See, for example, IHR, No. 22107, *Aanspraak aan de Bataaven* (Dunkirk, 1792),
or KN 22213, *Aanmerkingen op den getrouwen raad aan mijne Landgenooten* (Dunkirk,
1793) (te Dordrecht verspreid), January 10, 1793.

88. KN 22205 (B. Bosch), *Vrijhart aan het Volk van Nederland over de waare Constitutie* (Holland [sic], 1793). This pamphlet proposed an elaborately decimalised hierarchy
of public authorities in place of the traditional provincial divisions. A "neighbourhood"
was to comprise ten families; ten neighbourhoods one commune, ten communes one
wijk (canton); ten *wijken* one ban, ten bans, one district and finally, as in France, ten
districts to one department. Each department was to send fifty representatives to a national
Dutch Convention.

89. IHR, No. 22344 (B. Bosch), *Onze Verpligting om tot Nut van 't Algemeen te
Werken* (Zaandam and Amsterdam, 1794); see also No. 21991, *De Eer der Nederlandsche
Patriotten verdedigd door het Gezelschap Christenen* (Holland, 1791).

90. This much was confirmed by the unsympathetic but well-informed source of the
police reports of the *hoofdschout* of Amsterdam. See GS, I, p. 393.

91. See above, Ch. 3, pp. 70–71. Paulus dedicated the work to Teylers' "Godgeleerde"
Fellowship, but clearly intended it for a wider audience than the devotees of the new
version of Dutch Pietism. It became a best-seller, going through three editions before
1798.

92. De Wit, *De Strijd*, p. 83. For a brief sketch of Paulus' career, see Surinagar, *Biographische Aantekeningen betreffende Mr. P. Paulus*.

93. GS, II, pp. 409–10.

94. S. I. Wiselius, *De Staatkundige Verlichting der Nederlanden in een Wijsgerig-
historisch verhaal geschetst* (1793); *Proeve over de Verschillende Regeeringsvormen, in derzelver betrekking tot het maatschappelijk geluk* (Amsterdam, 1831) (written 1793). For
a discussion of these works, see de Wit, *De Strijd*, pp. 86–93.

95. Kluit, *De Rechten van den Mensch in Frankrijk*.

96. See, for example, "Amator Patriae," *Brieven aan eenige Vaderlandsche gezinde
Vrienden* (KN 22065).

97. *Examen des vrais intérêts de la France relativement à la Hollande* (Paris, 1793);
GS, I, pp. 382–90.

98. GS, I, pp. 392–3.

99. One of the most popular Dutch "libelles" of this time was *Apenland*, written in
exile by Pieter 't Hoen, the ex-editor of the *Post van Neder Rhijn*, which took the form
of a parody-travelogue describing a land of apes ruled over by a malicious and cynical
tyrant. Another similar tract was *Het Leven van Willem V, bijgenaamd den bederver van
zijn vaderland* (*The Life of William V, Known as the Corrupter of His Fatherland*).

100. GS, I, p. 392.

101. *Ibid.*, pp. 344ff. The later figures were given by Athlone directly to the police
official Vosmaer and are cited by Colenbrander, GS, I, p. 394.

102. *Ibid.*, p. 379.

103. See the letter from the burgemeesters of Amsterdam to William V urging
greater efforts at organising defence, GS, I, pp. 471–2.

104. *Ibid.*, I, p. 370; Jorissen, *De Patriotten*, p. 65.
105. GS, I, p. 408.
106. Mendel, *op. cit.*, p. 41.
107. Jorissen, *De Patriotten*, p. 69.
108. *Ibid.*, p. 73.
109. KN 22324, *Poster-Resolutiën van het Geheim Commite van Revolutie zitting houdende in Holland* (October 6, 1794).
110. KN 22356, *Aanspraak van eenen Verheugden Patriot aan zijne Nederlandsch Medeburgers.*
111. GS, I, p. 416.
112. *Ibid.*, p. 360.
113. *Ibid.*, p. 412.
114. *Ibid.*, p. 413.
115. *Ibid.*, p. 420.
116. The Haarlem city council had already taken the initiative by closing its clubs as early as the end of August. See C. Rogge, *Tafereel van de geschiedenis der jongste omwenteling* (Amsterdam, 1796), p. 136.
117. Jorissen, *De Patriotten*, pp. 88–9.
118. Rogge, *Tafereel*, pp. 142–3.
119. This was the proclamation which attempted to assuage Dutch fears by assuring them that "on entering your territory we come not to impose laws on you, but convinced that you will show yourselves worthy of the people who tore you from your oppressors and who will give you a proper government for the re-establishment of your liberty." Most revealing of all was the patronising promise that "you too will soon have a *patrie!*" Rogge, *Tafereel*, pp. 151–2; also GS, I, pp. 424–5.
120. There had originally been a meeting of club representatives at Leiden after the Amsterdam débâcle. It appears that at this stage it was the Leiden rather than the Utrecht group of Patriots which took the initiative. Jorissen, *Patriotten*, pp. 140–3; GS, I, p. 427. See also for an account of the activities of the den Bosch Committee, ARA, Archief Wiselius 28.
121. Mendel, *op. cit.*, p. 46.
122. Rogge, *Tafereel*, pp. 159–62; Jorissen, *op. cit.*, p. 123.
123. GS, I, p. 423.
124. Of the two *représentants en mission* at den Bosch, much the more sympathetic to Daendels' political aspirations was Bellegarde. Lacombe St. Michel had shown throughout an altogether more opportunist temper and was deeply involved in van Breugel's undertaking. Doubtless he had much to lose from a thorough investigation into the Daendels affray and his pleading may therefore have not been entirely disinterested. Certainly he combined with his plea for leniency a request that the troublesome soldier be put out of harm's way by a transfer to another theatre of the war.
125. GS, I, p. 424.
126. *Ibid.*, p. 499.
127. "As long as the Duke of York remains commander," William V wrote to van de Spiegel, "there can be nothing but the greatest misfortunes to be expected." GS, I, p. 503.
128. GS, I, p. 489. The proposal was brought to the States-General on October 7 although, as Colenbrander points out, it eschewed any mention of a separate peace.
129. GS, I, p. 522.
130. *Ibid.*, pp. 517–18.
131. *Ibid.*, p. 503.
132. Fagel's interview with Pitt, November 10, 1794, GS, I, p. 513.
133. Tinne, the second Clerk of the Secretary to the States-General, wrote to his superior, Fagel, "It would be impossible to convey to you any idea of the universal indignation which the circumstances of this disastrous evacuation have excited . . . a person of distinction, until now known as a partisan of England, told me in so many words that only a traitor to the Fatherland could possibly at this moment find anything to say in favour of the English. . . ." GS, I, pp. 503–4.
134. *Ibid.*, p. 528, n. 1.
135. Tinne, who seems to have been in the habit of using much paper and ink to "find it impossible to describe" this and that, on this occasion found it impossible to portray "the joy and relief that the beginnings of this negotiation . . . has given to the public once the news became known." GS, I, pp. 536–7.

136. *Ibid.*, p. 540.
137. Mendel, *op. cit.*, pp. 59–60.
138. GS, I, p. 551.
139. *Ibid.*, p. 538, n. 3.
140. *Ibid.*, p. 554.
141. *Ibid.*, pp. 565–6.
142. Rogge, *Tafereel*, p. 201.
143. GS, I, p. 565.
144. Volkier Bentinck had actually seen service with the British army in the Seven Years' War (1756–63). GS, I, p. 574.
145. *Ibid.*, p. 558.
146. See *Archief Felix Meritis*, Amsterdam Gemeente Archief.
147. Jorissen, *De Patriotten*, pp. 152–3. For the coup in Amsterdam, see Jorissen, *De Overgave*, pp. 65ff.
148. The bills presented to the Committee charged them for wine, liquor, heat and light from January 9 to 14, which suggests that they had been in continuous session a good ten days before the coup took place. And the bill for the 18th to the 21st charged up fl.2,000 just for food provided for around a *thousand* people—and another fl.1,300 for wine. Jorissen, *De Overgave*, p. 65, n. 1. Breakage of crockery, lamps, stools, windows and stoves cost these revolutionaries another 300 guilders—the total bill coming to some fl.5,650.
149. Rogge, *Tafereel*, pp. 274ff.
150. GS, I, p. 584.
151. *Ibid.*, pp. 580–1.
152. *Ibid.*, p. 588.
153. Grenville Papers, HMC Report (Dropmore), III, p. 41.
154. Rogge, *Tafereel*, p. 303.
155. *Ibid.*, pp. 263–9.
156. *Ibid.*, p. 299.
157. GS, I, p. 437.
158. *Ibid.*, p. 592.
159. Blauw wrote his own account of these events in the "Memorie van Instructie"; cf. Jorissen, *De Patriotten*, pp. 131–3; GS, I, pp. 428–30.
160. Together with Dumont-Pigalle, Staphorst and de Witt, Valckenaer had tried to maintain the liaisons with the Committee of Public Safety since the fall of Robespierre. It was to him that Blauw first went for assistance, and Valckenaer was preparing the way for a more auspicious debut before the CPS when Blauw took his unofficial initiative with Courtois. See Verzameling Valckenaer (Luzac), Leidsche Bibliotheek, January 1795.
161. GS, I, p. 430.
162. *Ibid.*, p. 454.
163. *Ibid.*, p. 463.
164. *Ibid.*, pp. 462–3.
165. *Le Noeud gordien débrouillé ou solution d'un grand problème politique* (Paris, Year III), KN 22465, p. 16; Sillem, *Valckenaer*, I, p. 202.
166. GS, I, p. 591, n. 2.
167. *Ibid.*, p. 81.
168. Sillem, *Valckenaer*, I, pp. 202ff.; Dumont-Pigalle YYYY.
169. Sillem, *Valckenaer*, pp. 206–7.
170. GS, I, p. 595.
171. Colenbrander, *Bataafsche Republiek*, I, p. 65.
172. GS, I, p. 601.
173. For the career of Charles Cochon Lapperant, see Richard Cobb, *Reactions to the French Revolution* (London, 1972), pp. 94–7.
174. GS, I, p. 619. Cochon added that if the Netherlands were to be treated as conquest territory and annexed to France, they "will perhaps submit out of necessity and force of circumstance to the conditions you dictate, but this will not be done in good faith and they will neglect no opportunity to throw off the yoke you will have imposed on them." GS, I, p. 620.
175. GS, I, p. 613. Ramel noted at the very end of his report that the [French] Republic should take as its maxim the adage, "Nothing can be useful unless it be just." GS, I, p. 617.
176. *Ibid.*, p. 625.

177. *Ibid.*, p. 629.
178. *Ibid.*, p. 459.
179. AE, Corr. Hollande 586, fol. 288 (6 Germinal, Year III).
180. The secret resolution of the States-General on March 25 also endeavoured to find a form of words which would emphasise the dissociation of the Batavian nation from the acts of war done by their former Stadholder. More aggressively still, it made the point that it had only been on the strict understanding that the French Republic was to recognise Dutch sovereignty and independence that the revolutionary authorities had permitted them peaceful entry to so many Dutch cities. GS, I, p. 673.
181. AE, Corr. Hollande 586, fols. 213, 252; GS, I, p. 632.
182. GS, I, pp. 675–8.
183. *Ibid.*, p. 635.
184. "Mémoire au Comité de Salut Public," delivered in reply to the ultimatum, March 31 (11 Germinal, Year III), GS, I, pp. 680–1.
185. *Ibid.*, pp. 637, 645.
186. *Ibid.*, p. 685.
187. *Ibid.*, p. 647.
188. *Ibid.*, p. 654.
189. *Ibid.*, p. 655, n. 3.

CHAPTER 5: The Revolutionary Fracture . . .

1. De Wit, "La République Batave," in *Occupants-Occupés, 1792–1815*, p. 146.
2. F. Boyer, "Le Transfert à Paris des collections du stathouder (1795)." *Annales historiques de la Révolution française*, 205 (July–September 1971), p. 393.
3. Rogge, *Tafereel*, p. iii.
4. See M. E. Bolle, *De Opheffing van de autonomie der Kehilloth in Nederland 1796* (1960); J. Hartog, "De Joden in de Eerste Jaar der Bataafsche Vrijheid," in *Uit de Dagen der Patriotten*, pp. 195–238. For an adequate if not entirely punctilious account in English, see Raphael Mahler, *A History of Modern Jewry 1780–1815* (London, 1971), pp. 78–103.
5. Geyl, GNS, III, p. 314; Rogge, *Tafereel*, pp. 477ff.
6. J. Theunisz, *Overijssel in 1795* (Amsterdam, 1943), pp. 42–3.
7. Geyl, GNS, III, p. 316.
8. *Ibid.*, p. 315.
9. G. W. Vreede, *Bijdragen tot de Geschiedenis der Omwenteling van 1795 tot 1798* (2 vols., Amsterdam, 1847–51), II, pp. 9–10; Colenbrander, *Bataafsche Republiek*, I, p. 77.
10. GS, II, pp. 481–2.
11. Van de Spiegel was arrested on February 4, 1795, and Bentinck van Rhoon a day later. They were taken initially to the Kastelany van Hof in The Hague and later in October of that year to the Huis 't Bosch, the Stadholder's palace, where they were kept in detention until 1801. The grounds for their arrest were not their service under the Stadholder per se—for the logical extension of that principle would have meant (as the radical clubs hoped) the apprehension and imprisonment of thousands throughout the Republic. The case against them was based on their alleged role in the tumults of October 1787 and their complicity in a design to permit the unlawful invasion of the Republic by the Prussian army in that month. In his defence, van de Spiegel maintained that the Prussians had been *called in* by the rightful authority of the Republic and opposed only by those who had usurped that authority, and that he had been innocent of any violence done to life or property in 1787 and 1788.
12. As in France, it was often debatable whether certain exiguous seigneurial rights had been held as property and/or rent, or in fief. Only in the latter comparatively rare case was abolition immediate and straightforward. Proprietors of estates on which dues were payable were to be found among the Patriots as well as their opponents, so it is hardly surprising that there were delays in the extinction of Dutch "feudalism." For an illuminating account of these matters, see I. J. Brugmans, "La Fin de la feodalité aux Pays-Bas," and J. Haak, "Tentatives bataves de régler la question des droits seigneuriaux," both in *Annales historiques de la Révolution française*, 196 (April–June 1969), pp. 163–184.
13. For a discussion of the aetiology and identification of revolutions, see Isaac Kramnick, "Reflections on Revolution: Definition and Explanation in Recent Scholarship," in *History and Theory*, XI, (1972), No. 1, pp. 26–63; John Dunn, *Modern Revolutions* (Cambridge, 1972), pp. 1–22.

14. See the remarks of Alfred Cobban, *The Social Interpretation of the French Revolution* (Cambridge, 1964), p. 162.

15. *Missive Behelsende Eenige Bedenkingen over het Provisioneel Rapport van de Commissie van Vierentwintig . . . tot Het Onderzoek na het Politicq en Finantieel Gedrag der Leden en Ministers van het Voorig Bestuur* ("Een Waare Vaderlander") (Haarlem, 1796), p. 8.

16. Cited in Kramnick, *art. cit.*, p. 31.

17. See Fehrmann, "Mr. Jacob Abraham Uitenhage de Mist 1749-1823," in *Overijsselse Portretten*, pp. 143-94; A. H. Murray, *The Political Philosophy of J. A. de Mist*, (Cape Town, 1960).

18. J. H. Appelius, *De Staatsomwenteling van 1795 in haren loop en Gevolgen Beschouwd* (Leiden, 1801), p. 10. In his address to the "Provisional Representatives of the People of Holland" on January 29, 1795, Paulus emphasised the "aristocratic" nature of the old system of government and the importance of establishing the exercise of popular sovereignty in the institutions of the new Republic. See *Verzameling van Authentique Stukken kunnende dienen tot Bijlagen voor de Nieuwspapieeren van het Jaar(en) 1793-1796* (5 vols., Amsterdam, 1796-), II, p. 81.

19. *Raad Aan Myner Medeburgers welken aan de Oude Constitutie zyn toegedaan* KN 22358; see also (Abraham Vereul), *Redevoering over de Gelijkeid der Menschen* (1795), KN 22594. On the reform of office see, for example, *Bedenkingen van Eenige Burgers op een Voorstel betreffende het Afgezeten van Ambtenaars door de Burgervergadering in den Raad der Gemeente Leyden* (Leiden, 1795), KN 22677.

20. Vreede, *op. cit.*, II, p. 38.

21. Cited in de Wit, *De Strijd*, p. 129 (ARA, Archief Wiselius 14).

22. Vreede, *op. cit.*, II, pp. 32-3.

23. For Alkmaar, see C. W. Bruinvis, *Uit Alkmaar's Verleden, Politieke Afstraffing en zuivering in 1795-1798*, (Alkmaar, n.d.), *passim*; for Oldemarkt, Theunisz, *op. cit.*, p. 31.

24. Rogge, *Tafereel*, pp. 329-43; Geyl. GNS, III, pp. 311-13. The revolution at Dordrecht was held up by a courageously stubborn regency refusing to relinquish its offices until January 24. At the other extreme of political reaction the regents and councillors of Edam, no doubt more concerned with self-preservation than political altruism, collaborated in its own dismissal by politely asking the citizens' committee for nominations to replace it.

25. This number was reduced to thirty in a later provincial regulation in 1796.

26. See A. G. Pikkemaat, *Bataafse Vrijheid in Nijmegen 1794-1795* (Nijmegen, 1963), Bijlage III.

27. *De Vrijwoording van Noord-Brabant in 1795* (Preface, G. W. Vreede) ('s Hertogenbosch, 1859), p. 8.

28. *Ibid.*, p. 23.

29. *Ibid.*, p. 41.

30. *Ibid.*, p. 45. See also Geyl, GNS, III, p. 372.

31. Theunisz, *op. cit.*, p. 72.

32. *Ibid.*, p. 70.

33. GS, II, p. 261.

34. Theunisz, *op. cit.*, p. 57. Steenwijk, a small town in the north of the province, made a special protest against the removal of the representative assembly from Zwolle, where the popular societies and militia were relatively strong to the more patrician Deventer, but its petition was studiously ignored by the provincial administration.

35. Rogge, *Tafereel*, p. 553.

36. *Ibid.*, pp. 7-8.

37. *Ibid.*, p. 562. The most powerful of the den Bosch clubs, the "Bosse Vaderlandse Societeit," abetted by the *Brutus Bossche Courant*, launched a vitriolic attack on the leader of the provisional administrative committee of Brabant, Donker Curtius, who came from one of the province's best-known and most well-to-do families. See *Vrijwoording, op. cit.*, Bijlage 1.

38. Theunisz, *op. cit.*, pp. 50, 98, 115. Hasselt received fl.1,600; Kampen and Deventer fl.8,000 each. See C. L. Vitringa, *Gedenkschriften van de Revolutie te Campen, 1795-8* (Kampen, 1798), *passim*.

39. *Leven en Ervaring van Gerrit Paape. Bijdrage tot de kennis van het Volks leven op het Laatst der Achttiende Eeuw* (Amsterdam, 1857), p. 26.

40. Rogge, *Tafereel*, pp. 560-1.

41. ("W. Bataavus"), *Vertoog over de Ware Bedoelingen der Wyk-Vergaderingen* (Amsterdam, 1795), KN 22613, p. 7.

42. ARA, Archief Wiselius (hereafter RAW). 14; Geyl, GNS, III, p. 348.

43. Geyl, GNS, III, pp. 353–5.

44. M. G. de Boer, "Het Amsterdamsche Stadsbestuur in Moelijkheden," *T.v.G.*, vol. 46, No. 31, p. 6.

45. RAW 5. In particular see the correspondence between Gogel, Hahn and Wiselius on the contests between the *wijken* over the attempted proscription of Wiselius.

46. de Boer, *art. cit.*, p. 12.

47. *Ibid.*, p. 20

48. Geyl, GNS, III, pp. 355–7; Rogge, *Tafereel*, pp. 577–92. See also the *Reglement der Algemeene Centrale Vergadering van alle Patriottsche Genootschappen in de Bataafsche Republiek* (1795), KN 22522; RAW 5 (Hahn-Wiselius); GS, II, p. 493.

49. Rogge, *Tafereel*, p. 583.

50. Gerrit Paape, *De Onverbloemde Geschiedenis van het Bataafsch Patriottismus* (Delft, 1799), p. 257.

51. GS, II, p. 3.

52. *Ibid.*, p. 8.

53. *Ibid.*, pp. 487, 495–6.

54. A former official of the Admiralty of the Maas, Paulus had married his formidable organisational skills to his naval expertise to renovate the Dutch navy with remarkable results. By the spring of 1796, fifty-two vessels were ready for active service, four ships-of-the-line with 70–6 pieces, twelve with 60–8 pieces; six with 50–6 pieces, and thirty frigates. The army—a much more daunting proposition—had been put in Daendels' hands. Fears of mass desertion and mutiny after the revolution had not been realised, but the paying off of Swiss and German mercenaries, in accordance with the doctrine of the "nation in arms," had not been compensated by a corresponding recruitment in native troops. So the strength of the Batavian army had been reduced from about 40,000 in 1792 to something like 25,000 in 1795. See C. N. Fehrmann, *Onze Vloot in de Franse tijd* (The Hague, 1969), p. 23; Rogge, *Tafereel*, pp. 443–6; Mendel, *op. cit.*, pp. 82ff.

55. Rogge, *Tafereel*, pp. 569–70. The plan was exceedingly comprehensive, setting out elaborate regulations governing the franchise, and procedure for the convening and conduct of primary and electoral assemblies.

56. Geyl GNS, III, pp. 345–6.

57. GS II, pp. 702–3; Rogge, *Tafereel*, pp. 461–70. Holland's deficit had been aggravated by the provincial assembly's acceptance of the old States' debts. On the other hand, being a revolutionary gathering did not extend to repudiating inherited deficits, and the common practice for the post-January municipalities had been to honour their predecessors' obligations. Had they reneged on them, quite apart from the principle involved there was a general fear, shared by Gogel among others, that it would have been impossible to secure credit for future commitments. The financial disarray inherited by the Holland Assembly was, however, so alarming that its Committee for Finance called a conference in The Hague in April under the general auspices of the States-General in an abortive attempt to find ways of simply continuing to meet military and domestic obligations without crediting repudiations or forced levies.

58. Geyl, GNS, III, p. 360.

59. *Ibid.*, p. 358.

60. GS, II, p. 30.

61. *Ibid.*, pp. 27–8.

62. For a more detailed account of the revolution in Friesland, see the *Nieuw Nederlandsch Jaarboek*, 1796, pp. 1249, 2010.

CHAPTER 6: The Struggle for the Constitution . . .

1. C. Rogge, *Geschiedenis der Staatsregeling voor het Bataafsche Volk* (Amsterdam, 1799), pp. 429–34. The second volume of Rogge's remarkable contemporary history, the *Geschiedenis* is an indispensable guide through the meandering and often exceedingly verbose proceedings of the National Assembly. The verbatim reports were published in the *Dagverhaal der Handelingen van de Nationale Vergadering Representeerende Het Volk van Nederland* ('s Gravenhage, 1796-8).

2. GS, II, p. 360.

3. According to Rogge, the average age of the deputies was between thirty-five and

forty. The electoral regulation of November 1795 stipulated that the minimum age for a representative was thirty. One primary assembly had been provided for every fifty voters (though in practice a "turn-out" could vary from five to seventy-five); and thirty primary assemblies to each electoral constituency. Thus the final electoral ration was approximately 1:1,500, giving a total franchise of around 180,000 in a total population of 1,800,000. This was evidently a long way short of total democracy, but it was nonetheless the most representative "provincial" assembly to have been convened in the Netherlands.

4. ARA, Agentschap van Inwendige Politie, pp. 195–6.

5. Colenbrander, *Bataafsche Republiek*, p. 88.

6. See H. F. J. M. van den Eerenbeemt, "Bernardus Bosch: Nutsfiguur, schrijver en politicus," *De Gids* (1971), No. VIII, p. 495.

7. Appelius, *op. cit.*, p. 43.

8. GS, II, p. 508.

9. *Ibid.*, p. 60.

10. Vreede, *Bijdragen*, p. 76.

11. ARA, Archief Gogel 173, *De Democraten*, November 10, 1796, p. 172.

12. De Bosch Kemper, *Letterkundige Aanteekeningen*, p. 332.

13. See, for example, H. de Lange, "Revolutie en democratie," in *De Gids* (1971), No. VIII, pp. 476–8.

14. The Prussian agent Bosset wrote: "The whole nation recognised in him not only the most notable leader of the revolution but also its pivot and the principal wheel on which the machine turned, an excellent mind, a man full of knowledge and a true patriot." GS, II, p. 268, n. 1.

15. *Ibid.*, p. 48. With some foreboding Noël added that "he leaves no-one who may begin again," and observed that while van de Kasteele was an able man, he was not in Paulus' class as a statesman and military expert.

16. ARA, RAW 5 (Fennekol-Wiselius, March 17, 1796).

17. He had received eighty-eight of the ninety votes cast. The remaining thirty-seven members of the Assembly were from the Friesian and Zeeland delegations, which had not yet taken their seats.

18. See the list given in Vreede, *Bijdragen*, p. 63. Of the thirty-seven presidents of the first National Assembly, only five (Hahn, de la Court, Hartogh, Blok and van de Kasteele) could be described as in sympathy with the unitarist principle. The remainder were all federalists or patrician conservatives. Bicker and Schimmelpenninck both had two terms of office during the eighteen months. Van de Kasteele was given a full term in addition to his deputisation for Paulus.

19. Vreede, *Bijdragen*, II, pp. 45–6.

20. ARA, Gogel 173.

21. Gogel and Ockerse, the co-editors of *De Democraten*, were luminaries of the club "Voor Een en Ondeelbaarheid" and, a little later, of the club-cum-corresponding bureau "De Uitkijk" (The Watch). Bosch had already edited two papers, *De Vaderlandsch Praat-al* in 1793 and *De Wereldbeschouwer* in 1795. In addition to his championship with Paape of the "Central Assembly" in 1795, he also played a prominent part in Hague clubs such as "Voor Eenheid en Orde." See van den Eerenbeemt, *art. cit.*, p. 495.

22. H. de Lange, "De politieke actie van een bewuste publieke opinie," *De Gids* (1971), No. VIII, pp. 506, 508–9.

23. Rogge, *Geschiedenis*, pp. 78–81.

24. *Ibid.*, pp. 82–5.

25. See J. Godechot, "Unita Batava e Unita Italiana," in *Archivo Storico Italiano*, 1955, pp. 341–51. Babeuf had been recruited into the business of liberating other peoples by Makketros, one of de Kock's colleagues at a moment of desperate poverty, having failed to get a commission in Fournier's legion of the "Defenders of the Republic." His association with the cause of Dutch freedom had lasted just one month—April 1793—the month that the Batavian cause was crashing to the ground with Dumouriez's fiasco.

26. For Valckenaer's involvement, see ARA, RAW 3 (Spoors-Wiselius, April 15, 1796); Sillem, *Valckenaer*, I, pp. 312–28.

27. G. Graaf Schimmelpenninck, *Rutger Jan Schimmelpenninck en Enige Gebeurtenissen van Zijnen Tijd* (2 vols., Amsterdam and 's Gravenhage, 1845), II, pp. 75–6.

28. *Ibid.*, p. 97; see also Rogge, *Geschiedenis*, pp. 109–10.

29. GS, II, pp. 513–14.

30. *Ibid.*, p. 515.

31. For the debates on the guilds, *Dagverhaalen*, IV, 255–61, see also C. Wiskerke, *De Afschaffing der Gilden in Nederland* (Amsterdam, 1938), pp. 104ff.

32. *Dagverhaalen*, IV, pp. 331–2.

33. Graaf Schimmelpenninck, *op. cit.*, I, p. 138.

34. Rogge, *Geschiedenis*, pp. 134, 312.

35. J. de Bosch Kemper, *Geschiedkundige onderzoek naar de armoede in ons vaderland* (Haarlem, 1851), Bijlage XI.

36. Mahler, *op. cit.*, p. 93.

37. *Dagverhaalen*, V, 529ff.

38. For the original draft of the constitution, presented on November 10, 1796, see ARA, Wetgevende Collegiën, 462; KN 22703, *Plan van Constitutie voor Het Volk van Nederland*. The "Dikke Boek" restricted electors to property owners of tenants with an income of at least fl.50–200 (depending on the size of the commune). For the Hahn amendments, see *Dagverhaalen*, V, 529ff.

39. Rogge, *Geschiedenis*, pp. 256ff.

40. Article 401 of the "Dikke Boek" had provided the ambiguous clause that "each Province or Department is charged with the finance of its own domestic affairs separately from that of the Republic as a whole." On the other hand, it did provide for a "National Chamber of Finance" of seven as well as a treasurer-general and secretary-general—much as the old Generality. This was to have jurisdiction "over all the finances of the Republic" (Art. 482) although the precise demarcation between provincial and national competence remained deliberately blurred. A "National Chamber of Account" (Art. 529) was to act as a national exchequer.

41. *Dagverhaalen*, III, 683–93. For the details of van de Kasteele's proposals and his defence of a redistribution of the fiscal apportionments, see KN 22704, *Advies van den Burger P. L. van de Kasteele op het Overgegeven Plan Eener Constitutie voor 't Volk van Nederland*.

42. ARA, Gogel 173, *De Democraten*, November 10 and 24, 1796, *Iets over de Een en Ondeelbaarheid der Financien in de Bataafsche Republiek*, pp. 179–84. The article cited the respective provincial debts as: Holland fl.460m (van de Kasteele gave a more precise figure of fl.453,985,724 *capital*; 12,501,824 cumulative interest Friesland fl.32m; Overijssel 9m, Groningen 10m. *De Democraten* No. 29 gave detailed statistics of Holland's contributions to the finances of the Republic since the Peace of Breda and argued that "all members of the commonwealth who enjoy (equally) its rights and privileges must also be duty bound to assume its obligations or there can be no more true equality."

43. *Dagverhaalen*, VI, 185.

44. *Beoordeeling van het Ontwerp van Constitutie voor het Bataafsche Volk . . . door eenige Burgers, zijnde Representanten van het Volk van Nederland* (Leiden, 1797). The twelve were H. L. van Altena, H. Midderich, J. Nolet, P. Vreede, M. H. Witbols, H. Quesnel, L. C. Vonk, J. Koene, P. van Zonsbeek, S. J. van Langen, C. L. van Beijma, B. Bosch. Their conclusion anticipated the obvious criticism by insisting: "We have been painted *as Revolutionaries* and *Terrorists*; the Nation will judge if we are anything other than true Republicans, friends of the Fatherland, and supporters of a regular Liberty." See Rogge, *Geschiedenis*, pp. 379–82; also Dumont-Pigalle PPPPP.

45. GS, II, pp. 528–9.

46. *Ibid.*, p. 523.

47. *Ibid.*, p. 520.

48. *Ibid.*, p. 531.

49. KN 22851. *De Zaakelijke Inhoud van het Ontwerp van Constitutie Bij Wijze van Samenspraak tusschen Twee Burgers onder de Naamen Pieter en Klaas* (Amsterdam, 1797).

CHAPTER 7: Forced to Be Free . . .

1. Rogge, *Geschiedenis*, p. 383.

2. Geyl, GNS, III, p. 441.

3. Mendel, *op. cit.*, pp. 94–5.

4. See, for example, Gerrit Paape's "Staatkundige Opera," *Het Verloste Nederland* (Delft, 1796).

5. Sillem, *Valckenaer*, II, pp. 95–100.

6. Geyl, GNS, III, p. 465.

7. GS, II, p. 585.

8. See, for example, H. de Lange, "Revolutie en democratie," *De Gids* (September 1971), pp. 470–82.

9. Although before the coup Gogel, like Wiselius, was unsure of his sympathies and sceptical of its results, Nos. 90 and 93 of *De Democraten*, published afterwards, argued that a situation had arisen which "without a shock could not be ameliorated; so that such a shock was necessary and, without it, nothing good could be expected." See de Lange, "De politieke actie . . .", *art. cit.*, pp. 513–14.

10. Mendel, *op. cit.*, p. 128.

11. *Ibid.*

12. GS, II, pp. 49–50.

13. Sorel, *op. cit.*, vol. IV, *Bonaparte et le Directoire 1795–1799* (Paris, 1903), p. 8.

14. Fehrmann, *op. cit.*, pp. 35–7. Tone was angry at losing the most opportune moment for an Irish sailing through unfavourable winds. On July 18, 1797, he wrote in his journal: "Hell! Hell! Hell! Allah! Allah! Allah! I am in a most devouring rage."

15. For the Collum riot, see Rogge, *Geschiedenis*, p. 445; for the Texel and Schoonhoven disturbances, see GS, II, pp. 258, 293.

16. For the unpopularity of *assignat* exchanges, see GS, II, p. 412; also ARA, BuZ, pp. 208–9.

17. For Geertruydenberg, see GS, II, pp. 281; the Zwolle executions, GS, II, p. 308.

18. *Ibid.*, p. 535.

19. Articles 13 and 14 of the Treaty of The Hague established merely that "The port of Flushing will be common to the two nations in all franchise." The Directory insisted that "it cannot and will never abandon the rights necessary for the French marine"; the Dutch that their constitution expressly forbade them from alienating any territory without the consent of the nation. See ARA, BuZ 232.

20. *Ibid.*, pp. 393–4; Fehrmann, *op. cit.*, pp. 39–40. There was virtually no chance of a *joint* Franco-Dutch expedition. Hoche had discovered to his dismay how backward preparations were at Brest and Barras later claimed that he had wanted to explain quite candidly to the Dutch that any action they undertook would be essentially their own responsibility. The madcap schemes cooked up by Daendels were dismissed by the Directory as eccentric, and the death of Hoche on September 19 also set back any "grand designs" on Ireland.

21. For Camperdown (Kamperduin), see G. J. Pijman, *Bijdragen tot de Voornaamste Gebeurtenissen voorgevallen in de Republiek der Vereenigde Nederlanden* (Utrecht, 1826); C. N. Fehrmann, "Vice-Admiral J. W. de Winter en de slag bij Kamperduin," in *Kamper Almanack*, 1959–60.

22. GS, II, p. 139.

23. See the biographical sketches in ARA, Wetgevende Collegiën, 509 (partly reproduced in GS, II, p. 539, n. 2); also Dumont-Pigalle QQQQQ.

24. ARA, Wetgevende Collegiën, 509 (227).

25. GS, II, pp. 548–50.

26. *Ibid.*, pp. 547–8.

27. *Ibid.*, pp. 546, 553.

28. *Ibid.*, p. 552.

29. ARA, Wetgevende Collegiën, 509.

30. *Ibid.*

31. ARA, BZ (Binnenlandse Zaken), 195.

32. Rogge, *Geschiedenis*, p. 451. See also ARA, Wetgevende Collegiën, 466, 470, 472–8. Up to January 1798, 1,350 petitions on this matter had been received by the National Assembly.

33. Sillem, *Valckenaer*, II, p. 91, n. 2.

34. GS, II, pp. 559–60; ARA, Wiselius 3 (481–3).

35. ARA, Wetgevende Collegiën, 508.

36. The committee of five were: Vreede, van Maanen, van de Kasteele, Queysen (the solitary federalist) and van Hooff.

37. GS II, p. 331. See also the outline in *De Democraten*, July 18 and November 30, 1796.

38. GS, II, p. 331.

39. Geyl, *GNS*, p. 475.

40. Dumont-Pigalle MMMMM; GS, II, pp. 624–5.

41. *Ibid.*, p. 560.

42. *Ibid.*, pp. 558–9.
43. For the Declaration of 43, see Rogge, *Geschiedenis*, pp. 477ff; Dumont-Pigalle RRRRR.
44. *De Democraten*, Nos. 88–92; de Wit, *De Strijd*, p. 152.
45. Rogge, *Geschiedenis*, p. 477.
46. *Ibid.*, pp. 140–5.
47. *Ibid.*, pp. 561, 574.
48. *Ibid.*, p. 563.
49. *Ibid.*, pp. 583, 585.
50. Sorel, *op. cit.*, IV, p. 25; F. Masson, *Le Département des Affaires Étrangères pendant la Révolution, 1787–1804* (Paris, 1877), pp. 361, 363, 375.
51. See Jean Orieux, *Talleyrand ou le Sphinx Incompris* (Paris, 1970), pp. 270–3.
52. Dumont-Pigalle QQQQQ; GS, II, p. 641.
53. ARA, Wetgevende Collegiën, 508; GS, II, pp. 567–70.
54. Mendel, *op. cit.*, p. 136.
55. For a clear disentangling of the various drafts, see de Wit, *De Strijd*, pp. 160ff.
56. GS, II, pp. 171–7. Even as late as January 10 Delacroix was convinced that he had brought all Dutch republicans together in harmony and told Talleyrand: "I do not fear to state, Cit. Min., that I have succeeded in my ambition by means of persuasion, both on the side of the moderates and those who are known as the 'ultra-revolutionaries.' " He also said, referring to his "symbol," that "I hope to have both the moderates and those who are known as ultra-revolutionaries sign this." See Mendel, Bijlage XII. GS, II, 169.
57. *Ibid.*, p. 571.
58. ARA, Verzameling Ockerse, I–IV; "Voor Eenheid en Orde," despite its slightly severe name, was a centre for the democrat intelligentsia. Gogel and Wiselius, though Amsterdammers, were members, as were the two Jewish deputies of the National Assembly, H. H. de Lemon and H. L. Bromet. See W. Zappey, *De Economische en Politieke Werkzaamheid van Johannes Goldberg* (Alphen aan den Rhijn–Brussels, 1967), pp. 28–9.
59. De Wit, *De Strijd*, pp. 160, 397 (Bijlage II). For Wiselius' account of The Hague meetings, see the "Beknopt Verhaal," ARA, Wiselius 5; GS, II, p. 591.
60. Colenbrander, *Bataafsche Republiek*, p. 122.
61. GS, II, pp. 593–4.
62. GS, II, pp. 625, 642–5; ARA, Wiselius 5.
63. ARA, Wetgevende Collegiën, 508; GS II, p. 587.
64. ARA, Wetgevende Collegiën, 508.
65. The two other members of the "Directory" were the Zeeland astronomer Fokker and Wildrik, a Gelderland lawyer.
66. Mendel, Bijlage XIIB.
67. ARA, Wiselius 4.

CHAPTER 8: Hubris and Nemesis . . .

1. Published in J. W. van der Pol, *Verzameling van Vaderlandsche Wetten en Besluiten, 1798–1810* (Amsterdam, 1840), pp. 1–9.
2. The record of these proceedings was published by the new Executive Directory as the *Authentique Bylagen tot de Geschiedenis der Omwenteling van 22 Januarij 1798 en van het Arrest en Ontslag van 28 leden der Nationaale Vergadering Representerende Het Volk van Nederland* (Amsterdam, 1799). The "malversations" referred to concerned the sums alleged to have been paid to Talleyrand and Barras by Eykenbroek and van Langen and the misconduct of the Paris embassy. Fijnje, whose son had been appointed to a minor post at the embassy, was also implicated and charges were formally made against the two Directors. Partly as a result of pressure from Paris, however, the proceedings against them were discontinued at the end of the year in a general amnesty which also liberated Bentinck and van de Spiegel from detention.
3. *Verandwoording van Pieter Vreede . . . Lid van het Voormalig Uitvoerend Bewind aan de Bataafsche Natie* (October 1798); also included in Dumont-Pigalle QQQQQ.
4. GS, II, pp 593ff., and the much fuller account in *Authentique Bylagen*, pp. 133–40.
5. *Ibid.*, p. 137.
6. GS, II, p. 167. Ducange's own phrase.
7. ARA, *Verzameling Familie Ockerse*; in particular, portfolios i–iv. Ockerse's papers give emphatic support to the supposition that although only just holding the balance

for the unitarists, his committee worked in almost complete autonomy from the National Assembly. Its financial sub-committee, led by Konijnenburg and advised by Johannes Goldberg, produced exceedingly detailed blueprints of a unitarist constitution as early as October–November 1797, well before the possibility of a political coup occurred to Ockerse himself.

8. ARA, Ockerse, Nos. 5, 2, 4 (Constitutioneele Ontwerp). No. 3 deals specifically with lawful means of revising the present regulation for the National Assembly.

9. Dumont-Pigalle RRRRR.

10. De Wit, *De Strijd*, pp. 159–65; Bijlage II, pp. 397–403.

11. De Wit, *De Strijd*, pp. 399–401.

12. Pasteur, on June 19 (a week after the counter-coup), writing to La Revellière-Lapeaux, maintained: "Every good Republican would approve of the *general* result of the revolution of the 22nd of January and I am of this number. It conquered federalism and promptly gave us a Constitutional Act accepted by the people . . ." *Authentique Bylagen*, p. 134. See also the proclamation of June 12, ARA, Wetgevende Collegiën, 509 (I).

13. GS, II, p. 171. Ducange added that these idiosyncrasies were a sign of "the good faith of these men [the radicals]; for they will not sign or commit themselves until they have fought the good fight, just because they intend carrying out to the letter all that has been promised."

14. *Ibid.*, pp. 197–8.

15. *Ibid.*, p. 190; for the following citations from the important letter of March 5, see pp. 190–4.

16. Van der Pol, p. 11. For references to the individual titles of the constitution, see pp. 11–93.

17. ARA, Archieven van Finantiën, Agent voor Finantiën, 47–50 (Memoriën en Voorstellen).

18. For the provincial reaction to the coup, see *Authentique Bylagen*, pp. 268–87.

19. GS, II, pp. 469–71.

20. Colenbrander, *Bataafsche Republiek*, p. 134; Dumont-Pigalle RRRRR; Mendel, *op. cit.*, p. 149. The navy, which remained strongly pro-Orangist in its sympathies, was thought to have voted overwhelmingly negative; while the army, surprisingly, produced the reverse verdict.

21. GS, II, p. 773; Mendel, *op. cit.*, pp. 148–50.

22. GS, II, p. 626. In his deposition to the investigation of the conduct of the January regime, Blauw insisted that the *principles* of the revolution of January "were my principles, even three years ago (1795); but the form and application that they took did not attract me . . ." (GS, II, p. 660).

23. Johan van der Heysen–Fijnje, Januari 25, 1798, ARA, WC, 508.

24. *Verandwoording*, pp. 40–7. Vreede stressed the probity and thrift which had characterised the "first five servants of the Republic," restricting themselves to renting two carriages between them; eating and lodging frugally. The fl.16,000 which the Directory had run through in its five months had been, Vreede insisted, strictly for the entertainment of foreign dignitaries and the *corps diplomatique*.

25. Mendel, *op. cit.*, p. 157.

26. *De Onverbloemde Geschiedenis van het Bataafsch Patriottismus* (Delft, 1799), p. 317.

27. Among them: van Beveren, de Sitter, van Marle, de Mist and Queysen, the leading federalists from Overijssel and Gelderland. See J. L. Rijndorp, "Gerrit Willem van Marle," and Fehrmann, *art. cit.*, in *Overijsselse Portretten*, p. 215.

28. GS, II, pp. 717–18.

29. ARA, BZ (Agent van Politie).

30. *Authentique Bylagen*, p. 103.

31. ARA, Gogel 173.

32. In Utrecht, for example, the tradition of *"wijk* politics" was inherited from the old Free Corps companies of the 1780's (the same went for Zwolle). The eight "captains of burgher companies" became, on January 28, 1795, eight *wijkmeesters*; each *wijk-vergadering* sending two representatives to a "Central Assembly" which acted in a representative capacity *vis-à-vis* the municipality. In Utrecht, at any rate, the *wijk-vergaderingen* had the vague right of "control and advice" of the municipal council, as well as the possibility of demanding an ad hoc general assembly. Much of these arrangements actually followed the plan of municipal government set out by Ondaatje in 1784 and rejected by the

then Orangist regents. Originally the right to vote in *wijk* and/or primary meetings had, as in Amsterdam, been restricted to those in possession of the "burgerrecht"—citizens' franchise—which presupposed a certain amount of property, however modest. Between 1796 and 1798 the clubs attempted to expand that franchise and to use the instrument of the *wijk* meetings as a weapon against the council—as in Amsterdam and Rotterdam. See Savornin Lohman, *De Bestuursinrichting*, pp. 175–94.

33. ARA, BuZ 232.

34. See, for example, Arts. XVII–VIII, where the right of petitioning a deputy or the legislature as a whole was granted to individuals but denied to corporate bodies.

35. His "Programma" insisted on "absolute equality of rights, both for the poorest and for the better-off burgher—thus shall the common man be bound to the Good Cause." In the fashion of the puritanism of the Paris sans-culottes, he reserved his sharpest barbs for the vicious and idle rich, stock-jobbers, rentiers, bankers and merchants, who bled good Patriots to death while gorged on profits from the war. See ARA, WC 508; GS II, pp. 709–10.

36. Bromet and de Lemon had, in fact, been permitted to be members of "Voor Einheid- en Ondeelbaarheid" but this was a fairly unusual dispensation. See H. Italie, "De Emancipatie der Joden in 1796," in *Amsterdam Jaarboekje*, pp. 86–101; "Over de societeit Felix Libertate," *Oud Holland*, V (1898), pp. 79–92; 147–67.

37. GS, II, p. 726, n. 2.

38. *Ibid.*, p. 740.

39. ARA, WC 508; see also 508/119.

40. Ockerse was less concerned about the alleged excesses of democracy and the clubs than what he saw to be the *decline* of popular ardour, "a falling off from (the true) principles and a leaning towards aristocracy and municipal federalism." GS, II, pp. 715–16.

41. *Ibid.*, p. 759.

42. ARA, BZ (Stemrecht), 194. The basic sources for the 1798 purges are to be found in the files of the Ministry of the Interior (Agent van Inwendige Politie).

43. BZ/191/480. In District 9, Nieuw Amstel, thirty-nine voters signed by mark and forty-seven by signature (the character of which suggests that for many this was as far as their literacy went); in District 10, there were twenty-five illiterate to thirty-eight "literates"; in Oude Amstel, Assembly 2, where the Assembly population density was much lower and incomes more substantial, there were only four marks from forty-one voters. For Batenburg and comparable villages in Utrecht and Gelderland, see BZ, 194.

44. *Ibid.*, 186 (April 24, No. 3; May 1, No. 6).

45. *Ibid.*, 190/471.

46. *Ibid.*, 195 (May 8, No. 20).

47. *Ibid.*, 186/23.

48. For the Friesland dossier, see also 186.

49. *Ibid.*, 195, especially No. 55.

50. *Ibid.*, 189/442. On May 6 Wiselius wrote to the Directory upon discovering that he too had been removed from the franchise; his complaint is followed by that of another Amsterdammer who listed his patriotic credentials *in extenso*: membership of the right clubs; contributions to the city's poor schools; an organiser and elector of the primary assembly—in short, the model of the conscientious republican, who saw his exclusion from the vote as both bewildering and spiteful.

51. GS, II, p. 647.

52. RAW 3, 5.

53. WC 508 (328). For an account of the agitation of public opinion in this period, see H. de Lange, *art. cit.*

54. *De Politieke Donderslag*, after the counter-coup, devoted much ink to descriptions of the "Bataafsche Ambtjagers" (office-hunters); parodied their mottos by accusing them of embracing the ideology of "office or death," and referred to a "harvest of offices" to be gleaned from the Directors. Dumont-Pigalle QQQQQ.

55. GS, II, p. 650.

56. WC 509 (Eykenbroek-Eberstein).

57. De Wit, *op. cit.*, pp. 170–1.

58. ARA, BuZ 232.

59. GS, II, pp. 607–8. Van Langen also accused de Winter of seeking to extort money from the Directory "in lieu of the pay denied him while in prison in England" (!) and Joubert of being dissatisfied with the *tafelgeld* (entertainment allowance) given him by the Directors.

60. GS, II, p. 777. See also *Mémoires du General Comte François Dumonceau*, (ed. J. Paraye), (Brussels, 1958) Ch.1; ARA, BuZ 231–2.

61. Although the feelings were by no means reciprocated, Blauw had a certain respect for Vreede, whom he said was "certainly not without talents" and "had fought almost alone for two years against his adversaries; had weathered all the affronts, injuries and disagreements possible, and his heart was very embittered and ulcerous; and his moral and physical resources exhausted. . . ." GS, II, pp. 648–9.

62. WC 508; Dumont-Pigalle QQQQQ.

63. For accounts of the famous dinner, see the Blauw memoir, GS, II, 653; Mendel, *op. cit.*, p. 153; Dumont-Pigalle RRRRR.

64. Mendel, p. 169; 174–5.

65. GS, II, p. 233.

66. WC 508, 345.

67. The most dependable account of the events of June 12 is in Dumont-Pigalle RRRRR, but this is largely based on the details supplied by Steven Dassevael (GS, II, pp. 673–85); and Blauw (GS, II, pp. 653–61).

68. GS, II, p. 659.

69. Among the others arrested were the *enragés* Bosch, Vonck, Nolet and van Rosevelt Cateau from Leiden. See de Bosch Kemper, *op. cit.*, pp. 373–5.

70. GS, II, p. 235.

CHAPTER 9: The Stunted Growth of the Unitary State . . .

1. *Politieke Donderslag*, July 30, 1798 (included in ARA, Dumont-Pigalle QQQQQ). The paper was founded after the coup of June 12 as an organ of the moderate Patriots. Though defending the new government, it did not hesitate to borrow the tone and style of the radical press in order to hound and vilify the evicted Directors and their supporters.

2. R. Fell, *A Tour Through the Batavian Republic during the Latter Part of the Year 1800* (London, 1801), pp. 47, 72. Fell, who was captured off the Yorkshire coast by a French corsair and taken to Brielle, was a lively and by no means unsympathetic commentator on the Batavian Republic. Among the first he met was his pilot at the mouth of the Maas who had had a fishing boat seized and his son made a prisoner of the British. But, though offended by the orange-coloured shawl one of the passengers wore and representing "himself and his countrymen as the bitterest enemies of the English name," his "animosity against our nation was of the mildest kind, it was cordiality of friendship compared with the aversion he expressed to the French" (p. 9).

3. GS, III, pp. 481–2.

4. *Ibid.*, p. 17.

5. This was not automatic, since their appointments had to be confirmed by the new Directors. The first Agent for National Education, Theodorus van Kooten, a friend of Johan Valckenaer's, was replaced by another academic, van der Palm, a Middelburg ex-predikant and Professor of Oriental Studies at Leiden. Gogel, who had acted with great adroitness as provisional Agent for External Affairs, retained Finance, Spoors the Marine, and—for a while—Tadama Justice.

6. GS, III, p. 442, n. 1.

7. ARA, Dumont-Pigalle RRRRR.

8. Gogel assured Champigny-Aubin on June 29, 1798, that the Directors' intention was to "pay a sincere homage to the great principles of January 22" and to "achieve constitutionally the day of June 12, to end the revolutionary shocks, to re-establish the sovereign people in the rights which sacrilegious hands so impudently took from it, to destroy all factions by reuniting all citizens around the constitution . . ." ARA, BuZ 119.

9. The most dangerous federalists—or those considered to be so—Bicker, Hahn (!), van Marle and van Beijma, were still kept under close detention. See *Authentique Bylagen*, pp. 126–7.

10. Dumont-Pigalle RRRRR.

11. *Ibid.*

12. Mendel, *op. cit.*, Bijlage xxxviii, c.

13. There was a matter of about fl.50,000 short in the accounts of the Executive Directory. But the more serious charge was that against Eykenbroek, accused of misappropriating East India Committee funds to pay his debt to Barras, and that about fl.2.5m were allotted in this way to a secret political fund. Van Maanen wanted the ex-Directors detained, along with the direct culprit, as he felt a strong case could be made to show

their responsibility for his misdeeds. See E. M. Kluit, *Cornelis Felix van Maanen tot het Herstel der Onafhankelijkheid 9 September 1769–6 December 1813* (Groningen-Djakarta, 1954), pp. 65ff.

14. ARA, Uitvoerend Bewind (hereafter UB), 360, 384.

15. The *Politieke Blixem* continued publication after June 12 and immediately resumed the polemical role it had made a speciality before January 22. See Dumont-Pigalle QQQQQ.

16. AE, Corr. Hollande 599; GS, III, p. 23.

17. GS, III, p. 447.

18. ARA, BuZ 210.

19. Mendel, Bylage XXXVIII (H), p. 68. Champigny would have preferred Gogel or Schimmelpenninck, who were both under age.

20. ARA, Archief Goldberg 59.

21. ARA, UB 361.

22. H. E. van Gelder, "De Regeering van 's Gravenhage 1795–1851," in *Die Haghe* (1908), p. 225.

23. P. J. Blok, *Geschiedenis eener Hollandsche Stad (Nieuwere Tijd)* ('s Gravenhage, 1918), pp. 64–5.

24. The commissioners usually had two or three deputies and a clerical staff of not more than half a dozen. See ARA, UB 381–4.

25. ARA, UB 382.

26. *Ibid.* (October 13, 1799).

27. ARA, BZ 182.

28. Savornin Lohman, *op. cit.*, p. 310.

29. ARA, UB 382.

30. BZ 182 (August 7, 1799); Wetgevende Lichaam, 361.

31. ARA, Wetgevende Lichaam, 361. The file is full of such pathetic cases.

32. ARA, UB 382.

33. ARA, BZ 182.

34. ARA, Staatsbewind 230–1; UB 381.

35. ARA, UB 360.

36. Not all city treasuries were in absolute penury. If its accounts are to be relied on Utrecht, annually subsidising its own outdoor relief with between 30,000 and 50,000 guilders, only got into serious trouble in 1801 and 1802 and from 1805 onwards. Apart from enjoying revenues from local bridge, road and lock tolls, it still continued to collect money from the rent of municipal offices. See Gemeente Archief Utrecht 284. In Haarlem (Staatsbewind 230), on the other hand, the exigencies of poor relief, the need to use local taxes for extraordinary grain purchases and the supply of army requisitions in the 1799 campaign had reduced the local administration to extreme difficulties. Until their specific abolition in 1805, most municipalities continued to levy local taxes notwithstanding higher directives. They could ill afford to lose any source of revenue. See ARA, Gewestelijke Bestuur 348.

37. Archief Goldberg 27.

38. Fell, *op. cit.*, p. 27; Archief Goldberg 50.

39. Goldberg 27. The same was true for Hoorn, Edam and Monnikendam on a smaller scale.

40. *Ibid.* Veere and Brouwershaven were in similarly miserable condition and, aside from the rival garrisons at Flushing, the port's most thriving trade was smuggling (timber and gin to England and tobacco to Flanders) with French commissioners usually taking a cut.

41. *Ibid.* In Haarlem there had also been a dramatic decline in the brewing industry, seventy breweries reduced to just three in 1800. The Holland (as indeed the Breda) brewers complained of an increasing tendency for small towns and even villages to set up their own local breweries, producing inferior but much cheaper beer for a purely local market.

42. Though by no means well off, Groningen too shared in this *relatively* arrested decline. Goldberg reported on his visit that although its refineries had suffered through the cut in supplies of Portuguese salt, its pottery making red ware (Winschoten clay from the same province), sugar refinery and wool dyers were all in a reasonable condition.

43. ARA, BZ 197.

44. ARA, BZ 195.

45. This was particularly the case in Friesland. See (Franeker) BZ 200; Staatsbewind 230.

46. See the illuminating remarks of H. F. J. M. van den Eerenbeemt, *'s Hertogen-bosch in de Bataafse en Franse Tijd 1794–1814, Bijdrage tot de kennis van de Sociaal-Economische Structuur* (Nijmegen, 1955), pp. 50ff; "Het Huwelijk tussen Filantropie en Economie: Een Patriotse en Bataafse Illusie," in *Economische-en Sociaal-Historisch Jaarboek*, vol. 25 (1972), *passim*; on the efforts to provide a national system, see P. B. A. Melief, *De Strijd om de Armenzorg in Nederland 1795–1854* (Groningen, 1955), Ch. II.

47. Melief, *op. cit.*, pp. 16–18.

48. Rogge, for example, accused the traditional provision for charity of perpetuating "Idleness, wantonness, immorality, superstition, and crookedness" in place of "industry, thrift . . . and piety." See Melief, *op. cit.*, p. 11.

49. This point was made by the *Constitutie nopens het Armen bestuur overwogen*, written by a number of well-to-do burghers from Amsterdam and including Remonstrant, Lutheran and Catholic priests. It was also the objection at the heart of the many petitions responding anxiously to the investigaations of the Committee established by the Assembly in August 1798. See ARA, BZ 203–9.

50. ARA, BZ 204.

51. ARA, BZ 206.

52. ARA, BZ 207.

53. Archief Goldberg 59.

54. See Wiskerke, *op. cit.*, pp. 91–4; L. G. J. Verberne, "De Afschaffing van de Gilden," in *In den Spiegel van het Verleden* (Utrecht-Amsterdam, 1947), pp. 187–206.

55. In 1796, for example, the villages of 's Gravelduyn Cappel and Waspik petitioned the provincial authorities to permit them to sell local wares in the larger urban markets without paying special dues. But it was just such "interloping" which provoked the guilds, in petitions to the National Assembly (see ARA, Wetgevende Colleges 507), to insist that such activity was *unfair* competition since those who came from outside to sell produce were free of local imposts and taxes and therefore could afford to sell at undercutting prices.

56. Initially, the provincial authorities in Utrecht and the revolutionary municipality had acted boldly in declaring public guild regulations redundant. But a storm of protest, culminating in a large majority at the primary assemblies in favour of retaining their protective status, forced the city council gradually to revert to a more conservative position. See the accounts of the Utrecht guilds in GAU, 484–5; for Amsterdam, which experienced a similar history, see M. G. de Boer, "De Ondergang der Amsterdamsche Gilden," in *T.v.G.*, vol. 37 (1932), pp. 225–245.

57. Wiskerke, *op. cit.*, pp. 33–5. The returns to the enquiry on the guild finances and property, due to be placed in the hands of the government-appointed commissioners in October 1798, were very incomplete. See ARA, Wetgevende Lichaam 507. Those that did reach the Assembly and the Directory, however, indicated the extreme difficulty of unravelling the intricate links which bound guilds, like the poor boards, to the whole structure of local government in the Netherlands. The Haarlem gold- and silversmiths, for example (one of the most powerful guilds in the city), based their establishment, including the upkeep of their hall and the pay for their deacons, on the annual contributions of members, the income from certain properties and stock—but also from a traditional sum given by the city from its own tax on peat and firewood. A great many of the guilds received some form of public subsidy in this way. The strength of their monopoly rested of course on the assent of the municipalities in enforcing the protection and exclusiveness of the local market.

58. In den Bosch, for example, while the guilds remained officially abolished, the constitutional provision that each municipality was free to make provision for the regulation of its domestic economy meant that by 1803, the majority of guilds were able to petition for an openly recognised restoration. See van den Eerenbeemt, *op. cit.*, pp. 88–92.

59. Kops was appointed in June 1800, and after the dissolution of the Agency, remained a commissioner, responsible to the collegiate "Councillors for the Interior." See his own autobiography, *Levensberigt Betrekkelijk Mijne Werkzaamheden Voor het Publiek en Hetgeen Hierop Invloed Had* (1839), published in *Economisch en Sociaal-Historisch Jaarboek* 31 (1970), edited by W. M. Zappey; J. Baert, *Jan Kops, pionier van Hollands landbouw* ('s Gravenhage, 1943). For an account of van der Palm, see A. de Groot, *Leven en arbeid van J. H. van der Palm* (Wageningen, 1960).

60. The Agency was, in fact, established a year later than the other seven in April 1799, with the active encouragement of both van de Kasteele and Gogel. For a summary

of its bureau and finance, see Archief Goldberg 59. For an account of its work, see Zappey, *Goldberg*, pp. 32–52; ARA, UB 355, 356.

61. See Goldberg 27; L. van Nierop, "Eene Enquête in 1800. Eene Bijdrage tot de economische geschiedenis der Bataafsche Republiek," in *De Gids*, vol. 77, III (1913).

62. See L. G. J. Verberne, *Gogel en de Uniteit* (Nijmegen-Utrecht, 1948). Throughout his public career, Gogel remained a partner in a business of insurance and finance, and as his private correspondence shows (Archief Gogel 41), he dealt with his own affairs at the same time as those of the government.

63. ARA, UB (Agent van Finantiën) 261.

64. See Archief Gogel 7, 8, 9, 10, 16; Archief van Finantiën 47–50, 51–62; UB 261, 269, 290.

65. ARA, UB 269.

66. The "national account" was never published as such, and estimates for the whole Republic are available only from 1798. The figures given here are synthesised from the following sources: ARA, Archief Gogel 6, 7, 28, 29, 47; Staatssecretarie 514; Ministerie van Financiën 390, 390a; Sillem, *Gogel*, pp. 169–74; W. M. Keuchenius, *De Inkomsten en Uitgaven der Bataafsche Republiek Voorgesteld in Eene Nationale Balans* (Amsterdam, 1803), pp. 89–103; and Metelerkamp, *op. cit.*, II, pp. 68–105.

67. E. van Voorthuijzen, Hz., *De Directe Belastingen* (Utrecht, 1848), pp. 209–13.

68. See the tables in ARA, Archief Gogel 6, 7. Of the approximately fl.20m of revenue in Holland alone, the "ordinary" *verponding* accounted for between 4 and 4.5 millions; and the "personal" *verponding* on the income from property a further 2 millions. The "General Collective Taxes" (most of them indirect) amounted on average to between 10 and 11 millions.

69. F. N. Sickenga, *Geschiedenis der Nederlandsche Belastingstelsel, Tijdvak der Omwenteling* (Amsterdam, 1865), pp. 73–5; ARA, Archief Gogel 8.

70. In fact, during the Agency period he established an amortisation fund, for which it was planned an estimated fl.250,000 should be annually earmarked. See ARA, Archief Gogel 15.

71. Sickenga, *op. cit.*, p. 65; Sillem, *Valckenaer*, p. 24.

72. See Gogel's remarks on the grounds given for the rejection of his Bank reform in Sillem, pp. 330–46.

73. In particular, he felt that a large legislature necessitated the extensive use of select commissions in which "everything depends on the idleness or hard work of the commission; on its knowledge or ignorance of the matters." See ARA, Archief Gogel 5.

74. This brief account of the Anglo-Russian campaign of 1799 was written before the publication of Piers Mackesy's definitive analysis, *Statesmen at War, The Strategy of Overthrow, 1798–1799* (London, 1974). While I am more concerned here with the effects of the campaign on the Batavian Republic and he with British policy and war-making, his massively documented account seems to reinforce the impressions I record in this chapter.

75. ARA, UB 355.

76. The Prussian agent Bielfeld, GS, III, p. 217, put the likely cost of keeping the French troops at around fl.1.5m a month, which was almost certainly exaggerated. The estimates of the government were probably a little optimistic in the reduction of costing from fl.11m in 1799, fl.10m in 1800 to fl.9m in 1801. To some extent they reflected the de facto reduction of the number of French troops well below the treaty apportionment. Before the convention made with Bonaparte in 1801, the Republic had been obliged to pay over for 25,000 irrespective of the real level of troop commitment. See the printed accounts in ARA, Staatssecretarie 514.

77. See Mitchell, *op. cit.*, pp. 233–5; Mackesy, pp. 37–9, 177.

78. GS, III, pp. 351, 374.

79. *Ibid.*, p. 357.

80. *Ibid.*, p. 246.

81. Mendel, *op. cit.*, p. 234.

82. GS, III, p. 65.

83. Mendel, pp. 235–6; G. J. Pijman, *Bijdragen tot de Voornaamste Gebeurtenissen voorgevallen in der Republiek der Vereenigde Nederlanden 1787–1807* (Utrecht, 1826).

84. GS, III, pp. 377, 1026, 1046.

85. See Fehrmann, *op. cit.*, pp. 60ff; ARA, Dumont-Pigalle UUUUU; BuZ 121.

86. GS, III, pp. 961–2.

87. ARA, Dumont-Pigalle UUUUU; UB 381; GS, III, xxvi.

88. GS, III, pp. 1061–2, n. 1.

89. ARA, Dumont-Pigalle UUUUU; Mendel, *Bylagen*, p. 173. At this time The Hague garrison was manned by only 200 French and 1,500 Batavian troops.

90. ARA, UB 381.

91. GS, III, p. 75.

92. *Ibid.*, pp. 869–83. Tollius' plan retained a Captain-General of a federal union of states but substituted a "Council of the Union" for the States-General, to which the Stadholder was to have some degree of responsibility.

93. GS, III, p. 418.

94. *Ibid.*, p. 449.

95. GS, III, pp. 25, 37, 108.

96. ARA, BuZ 232.

97. See Richard Cobb, "La Route du Nord" in *Paris and Its Provinces* (Oxford, 1975), pp. 144ff.

98. ARA, UB 360.

99. GS, III, p. 463.

100. See Fell, *op. cit.*, pp. 40–1.

101. Gogel wrote to Champigny that "all friends of the French Republic view with regret such acts of violence so contrary to the principles of the French Republic . . . they are indignant that so many triumphs may be tarnished by men who succeed in making odious the cherished name of France," ARA, BuZ 119. Schimmelpenninck believed that the French government openly connived at the privateering. He wrote to Wiselius in July 1798: "I am more and more convinced in these unhappy circumstances that the system of French privateering is so organised and in such a formidable and extended state that an announcement of the arrival and landing of a neutral ship . . . is now synonymous with a confiscation." ARA, BuZ 210.

102. For further details of the case of the *Wandelaar* and Captain Tierce, see ARA, BuZ 210, 232, 122, 233.

103. On the Lubberts mission, see ARA, RAW 36; also GS, III, pp. 44–56 (AE, Corr. Hollande 600).

104. GS, III, p. 51.

105. *Ibid.*, pp. 569–78.

106. *Ibid.*, pp. 140, 143.

107. Historians seem as baffled as Schimmelpenninck as to what this form of collateral actually represented. Certainly it was not well enough known in Amsterdam to inspire the open-handedness Bonaparte seems to have expected. GS, III, p. 604.

108. *Ibid.*, p. 611.

109. ARA, UB 482. The extracts that follow are also from this source.

110. ARA, BuZ 210.

CHAPTER 10: Illusions Regained and Illusions Lost . . .

1. ARA, Wiselius 3. Venice had been perhaps the most conspicuous example of French diplomatic cynicism—its revolutionised Republic handed to the Austrians by Bonaparte at Campo Formio in 1797 as part of the exchange for the annexation of the Belgian departments and the satellisation of the Po Valley.

2. Schimmelpenninck to van der Goes, July 1801, ARA, BuZ 123.

3. The Valais was constituted as an independent Republic in May 1802, and the important valley of Dappes ceded directly to France. The "independence" of the Swiss Federation, as it became in 1803, was strictly limited by a defensive alliance with France lasting fifty years, signed on September 27. No standing army was permitted to it, merely cantonal contributions of 4,000 men to the alliance. And even this modicum of neutrality was conditional on the national impotence guaranteed by the restored autonomy of the nineteen cantons.

4. J. Tulard, in "Problèmes sociaux de la France Napoléonienne," *Annales historiques de la Révolution française*, 199 (January–March 1970), pp. 141, 153, has estimated that the nobility recovered more than a quarter of its old patrimony under the Consulate and Empire, and that 22.5% of the Napoleonic nobility were comprised of the Ancien Régime aristocracy—including members of the most illustrious families: Noailles, Montmorency, Turenne, Montesquiou.

5. ARA, BuZ 233; GS, III, pp. 182–3.

6. GS, III, p. 179.

7. *Ibid.*, pp. 643–5.
8. Wiselius to Besier, March (?) 1801, ARA, Wiselius 4.
9. Colenbrander, *Bataafsche Republiek*, pp. 229–30. See also the critical comment of de Wit, *De Strijd*, p. 184.
10. C. W. van der Pot, "Een Ontwerp-Staatsregeling van Gerhard Dumbar," *Vereeniging tot Uitgaaf der Bronnen van het Oudheid Vaderlandse Recht; Verslagen en Mededelingen*, Vol. XI, Nos. 1–3 (1954–8), pp. 439–80.
11. GS, III, pp. 645ff; 650–2; 663. In the first of these letters (to Verbeek), Schimmelpenninck was most concerned to distinguish between acceptable "eenheid" that is of sovereignty, and "volstrekte (absolute) eenheid" with its unpalatable associations of Jacobinical centralisation. Even with a degree of financial autonomy, he assured Sémonville, it would be impossible for local or departmental administrations seriously to impede the "collection of impositions voted by the Republic."
12. ARA, BuZ 123.
13. ARA, Wiselius 4.
14. For the protest of the Nobbe-Linthorst group, see *Aan het Bataafsche Volk* (March? 1801), in ARA, Gogel 5.
15. That neither of the two "dissident" Directors was on the radical wing of Patriot regents gives some indication of the general upset provoked by the proposals for revision. Van Swinden, a Professor of Law at the Amsterdam Athenaeum, had been one of the principal adversaries of the clubbists in 1795–6 and François Ermerins, another lawyer and a friend of Gogel's, was a characteristic product of Zeeland Patriot circles: a lawyer, regent at Veere and Pensionary of Middelburg before 1787. Their staunch resistance, even if it meant making common cause with disreputable democrats in the Assembly, surprised and exasperated Sémonville, who wrote to Talleyrand that "their desire for the public good seems to me to lead them astray as to the means. Most of them believe that the constitution which they created and of which they have been the primary instruments can still be preserved. They refuse to see that circumstances have changed around them." GS, III, p. 199. See also NNBW, IV, 577.
16. GS, III, pp. 713–14, n. 4.
17. *Ibid.*, pp. 713–16; ARA, Gogel 172.
18. *De Heer Politieke Blixem*, No. 4. Bernardus Bosch had been editor of this paper in its earlier 1797–8 manifestation. Hespe took over in 1801 until forcibly closed by order of the Staatsbewind's *Procureur General*, van Maanen, in 1802. This was the second time in his career he had been prosecuted for seditions libel; the first was in May 1785 when editor of *De Politieke Kruijer*. See G. D. Homan, "The Staatsbewind and the Freedom of the Press" *T.v.G.*, 1976, pp. 12–27.
19. GS, III, p. 716.
20.

Dept	Ja	Neen	Franchise	"For"
Ems	2,315	1,189	50,560	49,371
Oud Yssel	3,916	7,707	59,825	52,118
Rijn	4,576	1,908	55,849	53,941
Amstel	1,052	2,999	48,601	45,602
Texel	1,379	3,175	48,638	45,463
Delft	1,546	2,928	48,555	45,927
Dommel	902	26,691	51,909	25,218
Sch. en Maas	1,085	5,622	52,182	46,560
	16,771	52,219	416,119	364,200

Source: De Bosch Kemper, *op. cit.*, p. 398.
21. Van den Eerenbeemt, *'s Hertogenbosch*, p. 88.
22. Colenbrander, *Bataafsche Republiek*, p. 237.
23. *De Heer Politieke Blixem* (the successor to *De Burger Politieke Blixem*) peddled an astringent mixture of political gossip, scandal-mongering exposures of leading public figures, reports from France and the rest of Europe and biting attacks on the post-1801 regime. It was when these attacks were extended to the French minister and the generals that the careers of such papers, already terminated in France, were put in danger. *Blixem* survived longer than most, even after Hespe the editor was arrested and imprisoned in spring 1802, but was gradually watered down in the following year. The government thereafter was pressed to close down papers like the *Gazette de Leyde*, thought to be over-friendly to the British and abusive to France. In October 1804, Bonaparte personally intervened to end the distinguished and long career of this famous newspaper.
24. De Wit, pp. 218–19, notes the important emendations in the constitution which

proved so reactionary in effect. The deletion of any requirement for a "republican declaration" for the franchise let in the Orangists, and this had its due effect on the composition of both the departmental administrations and the Legislative Assembly. The members of that latter body were to be paid fl.4,000 for sessions of no more than three to four months in the year—a salary verging on the perquisites the regents were accustomed to expecting from public office. The legislature in fact had the final say in appointing new members of the Regency of State, but from a list of two prepared by the Regency from departmental nominations of four!

25. For a vivid—if highly coloured—directory of the political careers of those comprising the major administrations of the state, see the information supplied to General Marmont by Wiselius, Fijnje, and Gogel in GS, IV, pp. xliii–lvi; for Rengers, see also NNBW, III, p. 1065.

26. GS, III, p. 319.

27. GS, III, pp. 1191–2.

28. See L. G. J. Verberne, "Gijsbert Karel van Hogendorp en Zijn Verklaring Aan het Staatsbewind 1801," in *Bijdragen voor Nederlandsche Geschiedenis* (1950), pp. 31–62.

29. *Ibid.*, p. 50.

30. GS, IV, pp. 345–6.

31. ARA, Wiselius-de Winter, June 12, 1802 (Wiselius 5); see also the correspondence Wiselius-Besier and Wiselius-Daendels in Wiselius 4, 5.

32. See Arts. 59–61 of the constitution; van der Pol, *op. cit.*, p. 218.

33. Savornin Lohman, *op. cit.*, pp. 135–6.

34. GS, IV, pp. xliii; l–liii.

35. ARA, Wiselius 5; see also *Blixem*, June 1802 (Gogel 172–3).

36. Savornin Lohman, *op. cit.*, pp. 125ff; GAU, Archief van de Secretarie 32, 33.

37. Brugmans, *Het Nieuwe Amsterdam*, pp. 41–2.

38. H. E. Enno van Gelder, "Onverbeterlijke Regenten"; "De Regeering van 's Gravenhage 1795–1851," both in *Die Haghe* (1908), pp. 216–306.

39. Blok, *Geschiedenis van een Hollandse Stad*, pp. 68–73; see also NNBW, IV, 624.

40. Savornin Lohman, p. 335, n. 1.

41. See the remarks on the autonomy of the departmental administration in ARA, Wiselius 4; Gogel 5; and Canneman 13; SB 230–1.

42. Wiskerke, *Afschaffing*, p. 143.

43. GAU, Archief van de Secretarie 442–5.

44. ARA, SB 230 (20 April 1802).

45. GS, IV, pp. 4–5.

46. On "Acts of indemnity" and the situation after 1801, see Melief, *op. cit.*, pp. 70–3.

47. ARA, SB (Gemeente Bestuuren) 230; also GAU 224.

48. GS, IV, pp. lxx–lxxiii.

49. There is a large literature on the subject of educational reform in the Netherlands in this period, not all of it alert to the political implications of the institutional changes that the establishment of a system of public instruction at the elementary level represented. Apart from his diligent work as Agent for National Education (see ARA, BZ 330–2, Agent voor Nationale Opvoeding), one of van der Palm's major contributions to reform was the famous Memorandum of 1801, read to the annual meeting of school inspectors and the general school boards. In it he defined the aim of public instruction as the improvement of quality and salary of teachers; the improvement of teaching methods; the establishment of a publicly organised and financed system of teacher-training and examination; and the provision of subsidy finance, both for the teaching of needy children and for authorities where local finance was deficient. For this and other aspects of the reforms, see, *inter alia*, A. M. van der Giezen, *De Eerste Fase der Schoolstrijd* (Assen, 1937); I. van Hoorn, *De Nederlandsche Schoolwetgeving voor het Lager Onderwijs* (Groningen, 1907), pp. 107ff; pp. 116ff; C. Hentzen, *De Politieke Geschiedenis van het Lager Onderwijs in Nederland* (Nijmegen-'s Hertogenbosch-Antwerpen, 1920), pp. 47ff; R. Turksma, *De Geschiedenis van de opvgeding tot onderwijzers in Nederland aan de Openbare Protestants-Christelijke en Bijzonder-Neutrale Instellingen* (Groningen, 1961); and Simon Schama, "Schools and Politics in the Netherlands 1796–1814," in *Historical Journal*, XIII, 4 (1970), pp. 589–610.

50. The departmental commissions established in 1801 worked in close collaboration with local branches of the Society for the General Good, and often distributed their pedagogic literature among the schools within their jurisdiction. For the work of the early

commissions, see, in particular, the printed *Bijdragen betrekkelijk den staat en der verbeteringen van het schoolwezen in het Bataafsch Gemeenebest* (1801–5).

51. GS, IV, pp. 32–7. See also *Quadro Politico delle Rivoluzioni delle Provincie-Unite e della Repubblica Batava e dello stato attuale del Regno di Olanda* (Milan, 1809).

52. GS, IV, p. 34.

53. *Ibid.*, p. 320.

54. *Ibid.*, p. 37.

55. ARA, Wiselius-Daendels (June 1802); Wiselius 5.

56. GS, IV, p. 388, n. 1.

57. *Ibid.*, pp. 319–20.

58. *Ibid.*, p. 11.

59. L. van Nierop, "Amsterdam's scheepvaart in den Franschen tijd," in *Jaarboek Amstelodamum*, vol. 21 (1924), p. 136. The figures given in Metelerkamp, *op. cit.*, I, p. 124, add some few vessels to the total but give much the same impression.

60. For the volume and value of Anglo-Dutch trade, see Wright, *op. cit.*, pp. 29–31.

61. Hope was a major factor in the American loan floated for the Louisiana Purchase, a well-publicised piece of information which reinforced Bonaparte in his certitude that Dutch capitalism was far from exhausted. See GS, IV, p. 476, n. 1. Marivault (GS, IV, p. 11) also reported that a loan had been advanced to the Austrian Emperor from Amsterdam and that the house of Hope still controlled assets of around 30 million guilders.

62. GS, III, pp. 725–7.

63. GS, IV, pp. 451–2.

64. GS, III, pp. 748–9.

65. *Ibid.*, p. 846.

66. GS, IV, p. 332.

67. ARA, BuZ 231.

68. ARA, BuZ 233, 234.

69. ARA, BuZ 215, 231.

70. GS, IV, pp. 7–8.

71. *Ibid.*, pp. 449–50; 451–2.

72. See, for example, H. C. Deutsch, "Napoleonic Policy and the Project of a Descent Upon England," *Journal of Modern History*, XI (1930), pp. 549–63.

73. ARA, BuZ 124; GS, IV, pp. 200–1, 206.

74. GS, IV, pp. 423–5, 427, 453–6, 465.

75. *Ibid.*, pp. 436–9.

76. *Ibid.*, p. 335.

77. *Ibid.*, pp. 55, 335.

78. *Ibid.*, p. 63.

79. *Ibid.*, pp. xix–xxi, lxv.

80. *Ibid.*, pp. 445, 449–50. In fact, 150 flat-bottomed boats were ready by November 1803. But although "no effort is spared," the shortage of manpower in particular delayed the completion of the second flotilla. It was not until March 1804 that the whole of the first Flushing fleet was transferred to Ostend, followed in May by the second part—encountering a British squadron under Sidney Smith on its way which Verhuell successfully held off.

81. *Ibid.*, p. lxvi.

82. *Ibid.*, pp. 453–6.

83. *Ibid.*, p. 465.

84. *Ibid.*, p. 425.

85. *Ibid.*

86. *Ibid.*, pp. 428–30; see also p. 460.

87. *Ibid.*, p. 223.

88. *Ibid.*, p. 496, n. 2.

89. ARA, Staatssecretarie, pp. 514–17; Gogel 24. For the financial situation in 1803–4, see also the memoranda of van Stralen-Schimmelpenninck in GS, IV, pp. 471–4, using data supplied by Canneman in November 1803; and Schimmelpenninck's own "opstel" (paper) written in the second half of 1803 with the aim of persuading the French to reduce their demands on the Republic: GS, IV, pp. 483–6.

90. GS, IV, p. 346.

91. *Ibid.* (February 16, 1802); see also ARA, Canneman 9.

92. ARA, Gogel 24, 29. The treasurer-general and his councillors were constantly em-

battled with the departmental authorities and in the course of 1803 were complaining to the Regency of State about the habit of Utrecht and Gelderland in particular of assuming exclusive responsibility for their finances. But although in this instance they insisted that "the Constitution nowhere, neither directly nor by inference, gives the Departmental authorities in any respect, however minor, responsibility for the National Impositions" (Gogel 24; April 18, 1803), the local authorities were able to cite the treasurer-general's own *Instructie*, which gave him direction over the "property goods, revenues and duties of the entire Commonwealth *in so far as they have not been confided to any other Persons or Colleges.*" And even though, in theory, the government was entitled to approve budgets as *that portion of departmental revenues freed after the national budget had been met,* the whole balance of the 1801 constitution and the weakness of the national executive institutions weighed heavily in favour of the departments. It is interesting that even so committed a partisan of local interests (and of the land provinces in particular) as Jan Arend de Vos van Steenwijk, on becoming treasurer-general, was forced into adopting highly "unitarist" attitudes to administration.

93. GS, IV, p. 541, n. 2. For a resumé of these problems, see Simon Schama, "The Exigencies of War and the Politics of Taxation in the Netherlands 1795–1810," in J. M. Winter (ed.), *War and Economic Development, Essays in Honour of David Joslin* (Cambridge, 1974), pp. 103–37.

94. ARA, SB 230.

95. On the reform of the post, see E. A. B. J. ten Brink, *Geschiedenis van het Nederlandse postwezen 1795–1810: het ontstaan van een Rijksdienst onder de Bataafse Republiek en het Koninkrijk Holland* (Amsterdam, 1950).

96. I am only concerned here with changes in the Dutch colonies in so far as they reverberated back into politics in the Netherlands itself. But historians of this period are quite rightly taken to task by J. G. Schutte for failing to pay attention to events overseas. His work *De Nederlandse Patriotten en de Koloniën* (Groningen, 1974) makes good this neglect, though it presupposes an over-literal fidelity of the Patriots to what are called "Enlightenment" ideals. For the politics of the East Indies, see also de Wit, pp. 187–93, 231–9; and J. A. Sillem, *Dirk van Hogendorp 1761–1822* (Amsterdam, 1890).

97. Colenbrander, *Bataafsche Republiek,* pp. 262ff. A. H. Murray, *The Political Philosophy of J. A. de Mist,* attempts to foist onto de Mist the burden of having generated a tradition of "pluralism" and "respect for autonomous rights"—as distinct from the natural rights egalitarianism of the French Revolution—thereby legitimising the eventual political development of Boer South Africa! For a less original interpretation of de Mist's career, see Fehrmann, *art. cit.* in *Overijsselse Portretten,* pp. 143–93; also Palmer, *Age of Democratic Revolution* II, pp. 205–7.

98. Wright, *op. cit.,* p. 31.

99. Brugmans, *Pardenmacht,* p. 29, suggests that the imports of textile products alone (finished) between 1790 and 1799 trebled, although some, as with colonial goods, arriving in the Netherlands via Hamburg and Bremen. Wright's figures, therefore, do not necessarily mean a *direct* Britain-Dutch export trade but do illustrate the continuity of the commerce between 1800 and 1805:

1797 base	= £1,466,000	(in the same year, the value
	= 100	of exports to Germany was
		£8,384,000)
1798	65	
1799	2	
1800	274	
1801	265	
1802	300	
1803	115	
1804	159	
1805	25	
1806	79	
1807	113	
1808	24	
1809	168	(year of Walcheren)
1810	33	
1811	18	
1812	21	

Not the least interesting conclusion to emerge from these figures is the inefficacy of the measures imposed by the Berlin Decree in 1806 to prevent British goods being imported to Europe via the Netherlands. Once the country was actually annexed, matters were very different. French chagrin at the overt complaisance of the Dutch in this business was already manifested in 1803–4. Marmont in particular was horrified. See ARA, BuZ 233, 234.

100. For a full account of the affair of the indemnity, see de Wit, pp. 246–51; for the Prince's ecstatic account of life at the Tuileries, GS, IV, pp. 680–1.

101. At the same time, it should be remembered, William V was trying to settle an account with the British by which their obligations would be capitalised, either in a fixed pension-annuity or in a capital sum. The ships taken in 1799 from Story and not declared prize by the British, but in the name of the Prince, were to be set off against *this* sum, not any further Batavian-Orange settlement. GS, IV, p. 671.

102. For the correspondence between Talleyrand and d'Yvoy on this, see GS, IV, p. 744; and AE, Corr. Hollande 608.

103. "I am surprised," Napoleon told Talleyrand on August 20, 1804, "to learn that in the midst of the penury in which the Batavian government finds itself it has the generosity to pay twelve millions to the Prince of Orange . . ." GS, IV, p. xxix.

104. GS, IV, p. 232.

105. ARA, Wiselius 53.

106. GS, IV, pp. xliiiff.

107. "The Batavian government," Marmont wrote, "is without any doubt the feeblest which has ever existed." GS IV, pp. 90–2.

108. *Ibid.*, p. xxv.

109. GS, IV, pp. 504ff.

110. ARA, Canneman 12.

111. ARA, Gogel 5; GS, IV, p. 522, where in his "Points de Constitution" Gogel insisted that "the election of the legislative body is to be made by citizens without distinction." But he added the proviso that they were to do this through nominating those "who contribute, to a certain degree, through direct contributions." See also GS, IV, p. 535.

112. GS, IV, p. 532. This was from the memoranda written for Marmont in 1804. Gogel sent along with it the original memorandum written for Sémonville in 1801 and a copy of the letter on finances he had written to Schimmelpenninck.

113. GS, IV, p. 534 (*ibid.*).

114. GS, IV, pp. 517ff.

115. *Ibid.*, p. 544.

116. *Ibid.*, pp. 122–32. For a further analysis of what he calls a "Programme of Government," see de Wit, pp. 251–62.

117. GS, IV, p. 124.

118. *Ibid.*, p. 129.

119. *Ibid.*, p. 521.

120. *Ibid.*, p. 522.

121. *Ibid.*, p. 523.

122. *Ibid.*, p. 544.

123. *Ibid.*, p. 539, n. 2.

124. *Ibid.*, p. 546.

125. *Ibid.*, p. 548.

126. ARA, BuZ 218; GS, IV, pp. lx, 261–62.

127. GS, IV, p. 591.

128. *Ibid.*, p. 566.

CHAPTER 11: The Watershed . . .

1. GS, IV, p. lxxvii. See BMHG XIII (1892).

2. Colenbrander, *Schimmelpenninck en Koning Lodewijk*, p. 53.

3. For a detailed analysis of the votes recorded, see de Bosch Kemper, *op. cit.*, p. 404. The greatest number of votes cast against the constitution in a single department was the forty-eight in Holland! In Groningen there was just one vote cast in opposition.

4. Graaf Schimmelpenninck, *op. cit.*, p. 130.

5. Legrand, *op. cit.*, p. 336.

6. *De Imperio Populari Rite (Caute) Temperata*; translated as *Verhandeling over eene wel Ingerigte Volksregeering* (Leiden, 1785).

7. ARA, BuZ 113.

8. See ARA, Gogel 40 ("Particuliere Brieven over Publieke Zaken"); Colenbrander, *Schimmelpenninck en Koning Lodewijk*, pp. 52–3.

9. See Q. M. R. ver Huell, *Het Leven en Karakter van Karel Hendrik Graaf Ver Huell* (2 vols., 1847).

10. Burmania Rengers was the Friesian regent who, after sitting on the fence for some time, threw in his lot with the Prince rather than the Patriots. He travelled to Nij-megen to join van de Spiegel's circle planning the counter-revolution, and subsequently became one of the principal orchestrators of Orange crowd violence in his province. As such his reputation was peculiarly odious to those who had been on the receiving end of his pragmatism.

11. ARA, Gogel 40.

12. The other members of the "Aziatische Raad" were: de Mist, P. J. van Ijzendoorn, J. H. Mollerus, H. van Stralen, J. P. Scholten van Asschot, J. J. Keizer, A. H. Brouwer and W. Kist—an almost solid caucus of "Company men" and clients of Nederburgh. Possibly an even more astonishing appointment was that of Gerard Brantsen to the embassy in Paris, since his last diplomatic office had been on behalf of the beleaguered Willem V in January 1795.

13. On the complicated problem of seigneurial dues and rights, see the important material in ARA, Goldberg 59; also J. Haak, "Tentatives Bataves de Régler la Question des droits seigneuriaux," in *Annales historiques de la Révolution française*, 196 (1969), pp. 183–4.

14. ARA, Goldberg 59.

15. Goldberg, throughout this exceedingly eloquent memorandum, had no compunc-tion about referring the Pensionary back to the "great revolution of 1795" and the "establishment of a representative democracy." This, he inferred, was still the basis of the present regime, and had established once and for all the principles of collective, national sovereignty, with which the notion of a private property in office or appointment was self-evidently incompatible. He also emphasised that "most of these rights have been bought for money," and suggested that even if there were any right to restitution, it could only be for the capital sum so expended, not for any allegedly forfeit revenues thereby derived.

16. Graaf Schimmelpenninck, II, p. 133.

17. GS, IV, pp. 594ff.

18. ARA, Goldberg 59: *Consideratiën nopens het doen vervaardigen van sommige Ordonnantiën, als een gevolg van het thans geadopteerde Systhema van Eenheid en Ondeel-baarheid.*

19. See W. M. Zappey (ed.), J. Kops, "Levensberigt Betrekkelijk Mijne Werkzaam-heden voor het Republiek en hetgeen hierop invloed had" in *Economisch-Historisch Jaar-boek*, XXXIII (1970), p. 147, n. 4.

20. For a thorough survey, and assessment of the historical importance of the Schim-melpenninck reforms, see S. J. Fockema Andreae, "Schimmelpenninck's Binnenlandse Bes-tuur," in O.R.G. (1949), pp. 15–182; see also L. Rogier, "Rutger Jan Schimmelpenninck, 31 Oktober 1761, te Deventer geboren," in *Terugblik en Uitzicht*, vol. II (Hilversum-Antwerp, 1965), pp. 69–113.

21. In the old Utrecht Departmental Council there had been four Orangists and six Patriot regents of the new council of six, three of those four—van Lynden van Lunen-burg; Craeyvanger; and Normandie van Schalkwijk—were all retained, as was the secretary Hinlopen who had also been at the Staten van Kneuterdijk in 1801. See Savornin Lohman, *op. cit.*, p. 141.

22. The "General Departmental Regulation" of July 19, 1805, laid down these clear demarcation lines between departmental and central authorities, and clarified the sub-ordination of the former to central control.

23. GS, IV, p. 280 n.1. (Genoa).

24. Ibid., pp. 600–1.

25. Graaf Schimmelpenninck, II, p. 129.

26. GS, IV, p. 608, n. 1; Colenbrander, *Schimmelpenninck*, p. 54. Marmont had been encamped at Driebergen until the summer of 1805 but was about to move south into Germany to join the main weight of the Imperial army moving against Austria. This left just about 6,000–9,000 Dutch troops guarding the North Sea coast against a possible invasion. Napoleon's response to anxious enquiries from Pijman and the Pensionary con-cerning these dispositions was to urge the Dutch, if they wished still to avoid conscription, to organise and mobilise an efficient National Guard.

27. GS, IV, p. 599; ARA, BuZ 166, 167.

28. For Verhuell's own account to Schimmelpenninck of the naval engagement in July 1805, see GS, IV, p. 604; for the correspondence with Paris, see AN, AF IV 1682. On December 22, 1805, he wrote to the Emperor that "since my arrival here [at The

Hague] I have noticed, with great pain, that the organisation of our new government, and the personnel whom the changes have placed in the various civil, financial and military offices, are not at all analogous with the principle of the true interests of Holland or the intentions the Grand Pensionary manifested and on which we were agreed. . . ." Any hope of a change, he said, was ruled out "by an almost total loss of sight with which the Grand Pensionary has been afflicted." GS, IV, p. 152.

29. GS, IV, p. 614, n. 2.

30. Colenbrander, *Schimmelpenninck*, p. 22.

31. GS, IV, pp. 612–13. Paradoxically, Schimmelpenninck's reply to Louis' complaints about the derelict state of defences at Breda and Bergen op Zoom was to echo the Napoleonic commonplace that the Batavian Republic had no need of fortifications along the frontier with her most powerful ally!

32. Colenbrander, *Schimmelpenninck*, p. 70.

33. The capitulation at the Cape was not officially announced until April 16, but rumours about its insecurity were circulating both in Paris and The Hague in March. In his letter to Verhuell of the 14th, Schimmelpenninck made pointed references to the "inaccuracies" of the French press. In particular he referred to malicious stories concerning the loyalties of Governor Janssens at Batavia and the state of the Dutch naval squadron there. GS, IV, p. 619.

34. *Ibid.*, pp. 624ff.

35. *Ibid.*, pp. 622–3.

36. GS, V, p. xxxvi.

37. Zappey, *op. cit.*, pp. 69–70. Goldberg took the opportunity to give lavish praise to Napoleon himself. Dr. Zappey points out that he remained, to the end of his days, an enthusiast and in 1826 reflected on the "sufferings" that the ex-Emperor had had to endure in exile on St. Helena. For his memorandum on the economic unity of the Empire, see ARA, Goldberg 60.

38. GS, IV, p. 621. Brantsen, it should be noted, was already more preoccupied with the dangerous possibility that a new regime, be it Imperial or royal, might admit political or socially undesirable "new men" in place of regents to public office. He wrote to van der Goes that, at all costs, the government should be confined to "respectable men" and (GS, IV, p. 631) was appalled by the inclusion of Gogel on the Paris delegation as signalling just such a contingency. Gogel, he freely admitted, "Je déteste souverainement."

39. GS, V, p. lvii.

40. Gogel attempted to persuade Schimmelpenninck to bow, however reluctantly, to the inevitable. But he insisted that "the majority" had "decided" not to surrender the country to a foreign Prince and he had no option but to withhold his assent from any such arbitrary action. See GS, IV, p. 648. For Talleyrand's reaction, see GS, IV, pp. 649 (Brantsen's reports), 651.

41. For an account of the ceremony and the text of Louis' and Napoleon's addresses, see Louis Bonaparte, *Documents Historiques et Réflexions sur le Gouvernement de la Hollande* (Ghent-Bruges-Amsterdam, 1820) (hereafter DH), I, pp. 128ff; Colenbrander, *Schimmelpenninck*, p. 87.

42. Colenbrander, *Schimmelpenninck*, p. 82.

43. For the original text prepared by Talleyrand, see AN, AF IV 1747; also Colenbrander, *Schimmelpenninck*, pp. 87–8. For these various expressions of protest, see Colenbrander, *Schimmelpenninck*, pp. 79–80; Limburg Brouwer, *Wiselius*, pp. 165–8; (Loosjes) *Brieven over de Tegenwoordig in Omloop Zijnde Geruchten Omtrend Eene Nadere Vereeniging van de Bataafsche Republiek met Frankryk* (Amsterdam, 1806) (KN 23297).

44. GS, IV, pp. 646–7.

45. GS, V, p. lv.

46. For the details of Louis' early life and career, see Colenbrander, *Schimmelpenninck*, pp. 61–2; D. Labarre de Raillicourt, *Louis Bonaparte* (Paris, 1963).

47. DH, I, p. 140.

48. AN, AF IV 1747.

49. GS, IV, p. 647, n. 2.

50. DH, I, p. 124.

51. GS, V, p. 181.

52. *Ibid.*, pp. 227–8.

53. ARA, Goldberg 59.

54. E. van Raalte, "De Ministerraad onder Lodewijk Napoleon in 1807," *T.v.G.*, no. 63 (1950), pp. 12–37.

55. AN, AF IV 1069; GS, V, pp. 215–18 ("Note sur la Situation Financielle de la Hollande").
56. *Ibid.*, pp. 253–4.
57. *Ibid.*, pp. 603–37; Colenbrander, *Schimmelpenninck*, p. 108; GS, V, p. 215, n. 3.
58. ARA, Gogel 40.
59. ARA, Gogel 28.
60. DH, I, pp. 179–80.
61. DH, I, p. 299.
62. For a general discussion of these problems, see C. Morazé, "Finance et despotisme: Essai sur les despotes éclairés," *Annales*, 3 (1948); J. F. Bosher, *French Finances 1770–1795* (Cambridge, 1970), *passim*.
63. See ARA, Gogel 22, in which the 1802 plan for a National Bank was set out in detail.
64. An authoritative account of the financing of the British war effort against France is still awaited, but see P. M. Dickson, *The Financial Revolution in England 1688–1756* (London, 1967).
65. Sillem, *Gogel*, p. 167.
66. ARA, Gogel 24.
67. Adam Smith, *The Wealth of Nations* (1776), I, IX, 38–9, refers to the Dutch rate as 2–3% and has praise for the general dependability of the Dutch capital market. See also Metelerkamp, II.
68. For an illuminating discussion of the role of life annuity loans on the Dutch capital market, see J. C. Riley, "Life Annuity-Based Loans on the Amsterdam Capital Market Toward the End of the Eighteenth Century," in *Economisch- en Sociaal-Historisch Jaarboek*, XXXVI (1974), pp. 102–30.
69. ARA, Gogel 31; see also GS, V, pp. 282–4.
70. *Ibid.*, p. 638, n. 1.
71. ARA, Gogel 28.
72. Even by the winter of 1802 and the spring of 1803, the treasurer-general was trying to impress on the Regency of State and the legislature the desperate extremity of the situation and to establish the clear *national* jurisdiction of the treasury in all fiscal matters. This ran clean contrary to the spirit of the 1801 constitution which had set up his Council, and did not take place without some opposition in the legislature, from van Marle and Six, for example. But on December 20, 1803, the hierarchy of national receivers was set up, responsible for the collection of a wide range of direct taxes. See ARA, Ministerie van Finantiën 390; also Gogel 24, 29; and the letter of December 8, 1803, in which de Vos van Steenwijk set out the critical nature of the finances of the Republic before the Staatsbewind.
73. For the sources for this table, see ARA, Staatssecretarie 514–16; Gogel 29; GS, IV, p. 541, n. 2; and Graaf Schimmelpenninck, *op. cit.*, II, p. 312.
74. Colenbrander, *Schimmelpenninck*, p. 36; ARA, Gogel 28; GS, IV, p. 594. Canneman not unreasonably referred to this new and dreadful burden as "the colossus of 48 millions." It was ironic that in the circumstances Talleyrand should have written on April 2 to Schimmelpenninck that he had "the earnest desire that the new administration which you are establishing and leading will be freed from all the trammels which result from your poor financial position." GS, IV, p. 601.
75. ARA, Gogel 29.
76. Sillem, *Gogel*, p. 14.
77. See, in particular, *Gedagten over 's Lands Finantiën* (Amsterdam, 1802).
78. Sillem, *Gogel*, p. 246.
79. *Ibid.*, p. 42.
80. ARA, Gogel 31.
81. ARA, Gogel 40.
82. ARA, Gogel 31.
83. AN, AF IV 1069.
84. *Wealth of Nations*, II, p. 382.
85. Gogel, *Memoriën en Correspondentiën, Betrekkelijk den Staat van 's Rijk's Geldmiddelen in den Jare 1820* (Amsterdam, 1844), p. 39.
86. ARA, Gogel 29.
87. *Ibid.*
88. Hogendorp, *Gedagten*, pp. 47ff. He naturally regarded the new tax system as deleterious for commercial revival, and the direct taxes as bound to have the effect of reducing real wages rather than the reverse.

89. *Ibid.*, pp. 78–9. "The dislike of the rich man is not," he wrote, "yet politic in our country, nor does it conform to the thinking of the greater part of the Nation."

90. Metelerkamp, II, p. 102.

91. For the various differential rates, see the original report, completed by the Commission for Finance of Holland in 1796; ARA, Gogel 6.

92. GS, IV, pp. 514–17.

93. Sickenga, *op. cit.*, p. 78.

94. In 1800–1, the textile manufacturers at Tilburg were complaining of sharply rising costs of raw materials through French tariff protection and of blocked markets in Italy and Turkey. But the number of enterprises was still considerable—about 40 or 50, employing in all 4,000 or 5,000 workers. By the time of the 1806 and 1808 reports, both the linen and cotton factories were at almost "complete stoppage" owing to the difficulties of supply; much the same was true of the dye- and bleachworks at Breda. Brabant industry largely reverted to processing semi-agricultural goods; in particular tanning hides and brewing. See Ch. 12, pp. 578–9; also ARA, Goldberg 27, 50; BZ 786; Gogel's remarks on inter-provincial fiscal liability and its relationship to economic conditions, see Sillem, *Gogel*, p. 187.

95. ARA, Gogel 8 (in MSS.), 40, 59 (preamble to the tax law); also Sillem, *Gogel*, p. 178.

96. See Sillem, *Gogel*, pp. 150–1 for the diverse evolution of the direct taxes; ARA, Gogel 6.

97. Gogel, *Memoriën en Correspondentiën*, p. 38.

98. For the *Verponding* commission, see ARA, Gogel 59, 60.

99. ARA, Gogel 59; Sickenga, pp. 115ff; Sillem, pp. 204–5.

100. *Sillem*, pp. 212–17.

101. *Memoriën en Correspondentiën*, p. 153.

102. Connelly, *op. cit.*, p. 149, referred to this as a "personal" tax, based on *income* from all sources (10%) whereas the verifiable basis of assessment was not incomings but outgoings.

103. For Gogel's own speculations on the operation of the *personeel*, see ARA, Gogel 40; for the official arrangements, 59.

104. Connelly, p. 150, observes that "he [Gogel] seemed unaware that his one major reform [the land tax] was directed toward the landowners [*this too is a misconception of the objects of the* verponding] and peasants, not the persons who had the greatest wealth, the merchants and the bankers who controlled the legislature, and lent him money he could have taken by taxation." Quite apart from this confusion over the *verponding*, "bankers and merchants" as owners of real estate and often substantial landed estates themselves, were not to be sharply differentiated from urban plutocrats. And of course there were a variety of ways in which non-commercial capital was imposed on very heavily.

105. For a brilliant and definitive account of the inter-relationship of the urban and rural economies, see Jan de Vries, *The Dutch Rural Economy in the Golden Age 1500–1700* (New Haven and London, 1974), *passim*.

106. For the sources for this table, see Gogel, *Memoriën en Correspondentiën*, pp. 520–2 (Bijlagen; PP); ARA, Staatssecretarie 516; Gogel 31–2.

107. ARA, Gogel 6, 7; for the data on the indirect duty tariffs and receipts before the revolution, see Gogel 47–9.

108. *Memoriën en Correspondentiën*, pp. 520–2.

109. *Ibid.*, Bijlagen FF.

110. See ARA, Gogel 60; Sickenga, p. 98.

111. For the jurisdiction of the various sectors of the bureaucracy, see the "Mémoire relativement à l'organisation aux operations du Ministère des Finances," presented to the King by Gogel, the manuscript of which is in ARA, Gogel 40.

112. *Ibid.*; Sillem, *Gogel*, p. 243.

113. *Iets uit de geschiedenis des vaderlands 1795–1805* (Amsterdam, 1806) attacked the tax reform as an act of monstrous tyranny calculated to ruin the nation beyond any hope of restoration.

114. Zappey, *op. cit.*, p. 67; Colenbrander, *Schimmelpenninck*, p. 47.

115. ARA, Gogel 26.

116. GS, V, pp. 31–2.

117. AN, AF IV 1069; GS, V, pp. 215–18.

118. AN, AF IV 1765.

119. GS, V, p. 267.

120. ARA, Staatssecretarie 637; Gogel 78.

121. For the data of the state accounts between 1806 and 1809, see ARA, Gogel 31–5, 142. The diverse outstanding receipts on the 1806 account, collected during subsequent years, brought the aggregate up to around 45 millions. But since the books on each financial year were never finally closed it is difficult to be confident of the final yield figure for revenues. We do know, however, that at *least* for

1806	42.6 millions
1807	46.8
1808	46.8
1809	50.5
1810	44.6

were actually collected (Gogel 142).

122. Louis Bonaparte, DH, I, pp. 178–9.

123. AN, AF IV 1765; DH, II, p. 236.

124. DH, II, pp. 210–16.

125. AN, AF IV 1802, 1807; for an account of the two loans of 1807 and 1808, see DH, II, pp. 80, 234–40.

126. For details of the selection and confirmation of the fiscal personnel, very much a *semi*-professionalised body, see ARA, Gogel 60; also for lists of the receivers-general for each department.

127. ARA, Canneman 13.

128. *Memoriën en Correspondentiën*, pp. 134, 136, Bijlage pp. 520–1, FF, pp. 514–15, CC, pp. 510–11.

129. ARA, Gogel 78, 80. The records of the *verponding* assessors and cadaster surveyors at den Bosch lay down stringent penalties for fraudulent information, but the comments of those engaged in the work make it plain that haste and expedition rather than fine accuracy were the object of much of the work.

130. ARA, Gogel 78 (23).

131. *Ibid.* (17).

132. *Ibid.* (25).

133. *Ibid.* (27).

134. *Ibid.* (29).

135. DH, II, p. 57.

136. Sillem, p. 60.

137. *Ibid.*, pp. 61–2.

138. *Ibid.*, p. 63.

139. See, for example, the rather gloomy comments of Mollerus, GS, V, p. 458, and van Maanen's *obiter dicta* that "in such calamitous times it is simply impossible to reduce the level of expenditure to that of revenues, and that, however difficult and painful the idea may be, it is necessary to continue to live from day to day and to await the outcome of events. . . ." GS, V, p. 265. (October 21, 1808).

140. Sillem, pp. 71–5.

141. ARA, Gogel 112. This dossier is devoted to the last phase of Gogel's efforts to suppress the Dutch guilds and includes the MSS of his addresses to the Council of State, and his correspondence, first with Schimmelpenninck and later with Louis Bonaparte. See also Sillem, *Gogel*, pp. 277–305; and Wiskerke, *op. cit.*, p. 176. My account owes much to these last two narratives.

142. ARA, Gogel 112.

143. See M. G. de Boer, "De Ondergang der Amsterdamsche Gilden," *T.v.G.*, vol. 47 (1932), pp. 230–1.

144. ARA, Gogel 112; Wiskerke, pp. 170–2.

145. See ARA, Goldberg 73.

146. There were delegates from Amsterdam, The Hague, Delft and Leiden—the representative from Alkmaar arriving too late to attend the session of the Council. For their respective comments, see GS, V, pp. 591–606.

147. *Ibid.*, pp. 604–5.

148. ARA, Gogel 112.

149. GS, V, pp. 602–4.

150. On April 19, 1808, Louis opened the first national industrial exhibition in the Netherlands at Utrecht; he also offered prizes for the best inventions and technological advances and was an enthusiast of the experimental work of the Haarlem Society for Arts and Science.

151. Wiskerke, pp. 180–1; ARA, Gogel 112.

152. ARA, Gogel 112; the full text of Gogel's great speech on economic freedom is also in Sillem, *Gogel*, pp. 280–2.

153. Curiously, van der Heim, the Minister for the Colonies, abstained from the final vote, and van Maanen actually cast his vote against, possibly more on the legal grounds of violating the prescriptive nature of the institutions than for any economic conviction.

154. For the details of the operation of the law (and instances of its early abuse), see ARA, Gewestelijke Besturen 85; BZ 731–5.

155. ARA, BZ 731–5; Wetgevende Lichamen 507.

156. For the problems of the corporations under the French annexation, see ARA, BZ 1034; Wiskerke, pp. 190ff. De Celles, the Belgian prefect, found there were still 14,071 members of corporations in Amsterdam, but the experience of all his colleagues was not identical. The prefect of Friesland, Verstolk, reported at the same time that the law of 1808 had been fairly rigorously implemented in that part of the country, and the same comments came from Amersfoort and Arnhem. Even after the French decree was put into operation on January 31, 1812, Amsterdam continued to put up a stiff resistance, demanding that the Emperor give it special exemption, a concession that was in fact made over the head of the prefect de Celles.

157. See Brugmans, *op. cit.*, p. 5.

158. GS, IV, p. 416.

159. AN, AF IV 1765 (Finances); 1805 (Budgets). In 1802, the following sums were earmarked for the domestic administration of the respective departments:

Holland	519,172	Friesland	179,287
Utrecht	220,802	Zeeland	42,930
Gelderland	169,180	Groningen	84,501
Overijssel	108,831	Drente	13,810
Brabant	124,927		

The aggregate was fl.1,463,440, a figure which excluded the costs of the Waterstaat but included those of justice. The comparable figure for 1807 was approximately fl.6,200,000. The 3.5m set aside for departmental government in 1807 thus represented double the earlier appropriation. Between 1806 and 1810, the costs of the national Waterstaat rose nearly fivefold.

160. See, in particular, F. Turksma, *De Geschiedenis van de opleiding tot onderwijzer in Nederland aan de openbare Protestants-Christelijke en bijzonder neutrale instellingen* (Groningen, 1961); N. L. Dodde, *Het Rijks-schooltoezicht in de Bataafse Republiek* (Groningen, 1968); and for an older but very sound view, A. M. van der Giezen, *De Eerste Fase van de Schoolstrijd in Nederland* (Assen, 1937).

161. Other active members included Elias Canneman (but not Isaac Gogel); Pijman, Gerard Brantsen, Pompe van Meerdevoort and Janssens, the Governor of the Cape. See *Archief van Maatschappij: Tot Nut van 't Algemeen*, Gemeente Archief, Amsterdam, No. 211. For Kinsbergen's school, see ARA, BZ 897.

162. For a good account of the "Nut" in the single community of Bergen op Zoom, see H. F. J. M. van den Eerenbeemt, *Streven Naar Sociale Verheffing in Een Statische Stad* (Nijmegen, 1963).

163. For a summary of this progress, see *Gedenkschrift der Maatschappij: Tot Nut van 't Algemeen voor de vijf en Twintig jaren van haar bestaan* (Amsterdam, 1820), p. 112.

164. *Ibid.*; Archief MNA, 1188.

165. ARA, BZ 330–1.

166. See P. L. van Eck, Jr., *Hoe 't Vroeger Was* (Groningen, 1927), *passim*; "Onderwijs Toestand in het laatste der 18de eeuw," *Nieuwen Drentschen Volksalmanac*, 1923; ARA, BZ 331 (Agentschap van Nationale Opvoeding), 1800, Klagten over schoolmeesters. For the *Algemeene Denkbeelden over het Nationale Onderwijs*, see Archief MNA, 1366.

167. ARA BZ 331 (Agentschap van Nationale Opvoeding); I. van Hoorn, *De Nederlandsche Schoolwetgeving voor het lager onderwijs, 1796–1807* (Groningen, 1907), pp. 107ff; *Bijdragen betrekkelijk den staat en der verbeteringen van het schoolwezen in het Bataafsch Gemeenebest* (1801–4).

168. De Groot, *op. cit.*, pp. 72–3.

169. Van der Giezen, *op. cit.*, p. 108.

170. See *Bijdragen* . . . (1803); C. Hentzen, *De Politieke Geschiedenis van het Lager Onderwijs in Nederland* (Nijmegen-'s Hertogenbosch-Antwerp, 1920), pp. 80–2. In Utrecht too the church authorities were especially truculent about the impertinence of

school boards; see ARA, BZ 527. In Groningen, however, where the predikants of the Reformed Church had been traditionally embattled with the provincial gentry and nobility, they tended to support attacks on the seigneurial rights of presentment. For Hendrik Wester's contest with the Heer of Aduard, BZ (September 1805, no. 15).

171. The "domestic regulation" for Brabant was not published until September 1804; Overijssel in December 1804; and Zeeland and Friesland not until March 1805—nearly two years after the law enjoining them to establish their lower school commissions and inspectorates. The local school boards, with just three members, and an inspectorate paid at the rate of just fl.600 a year, were hardly in any position to urge compliance on the powerful departmental councils. See ARA, BZ 527; van der Giezen, op. cit., p. 116.

172. See A. van den Ende, Geschiedkundige Schets van Neerlands Schoolwetgeving (Deventer, 1847); A. A. J. Meylink, Officiele Geschiedenis der Wet van 1806 voor het lager schoolwezen en onderwijs ('s Gravenhage, 1857), pp. i–xii.

173. For an account of its significance, see Schama, "Schools and Politics in the Netherlands," pp. 589–610; see also van den Ende's (unduly modest) version of the law in Geschiedkundige Schets, p. 39 (Aanteekeningen); p. 43.

174. For his general principles, see Geschiedkundige Schets, pp. 50–1; Hentzen, op. cit., p. 47.

175. Cited in Matthew Arnold, The Popular Education of France, with Notices of that of Holland and Switzerland (London, 1861), p. 30; for the composition of the inspectorate, see Meylink, op. cit., pp. 115–17; D. Langedijk, De Geschiedenis van het Protestants-Christelijk Onderwijs (Delft, 1953).

176. In Utrecht department in 1808, half the registered teachers were under the age of thirty-five, but two-thirds of the remainder were over sixty. Once veterans were removed in the course of nature, dramatic improvements could come about. At Renswoude, a school hitherto notorious for its low educational standards was transformed by a young successor to the principal. Before long his pupils were, in the words of the inspector, "able, at twelve, to read, write, to do mental arithmetic," Rijksarchief Utrecht, Archief van School-opzieners 3, 5.

177. See G. Cuvier and F. Noël, Première partie du rapport sur les établissements d'instruction en Hollande (The Hague and Paris, 1816); AN, AF IV 1816; Meylink, op. cit., pp. 358–83.

178. ARA, BZ (Commissioner-General) 2678.

179. ARA, BZ 719 (Groningen); see the same set of files for the "Algemeen Overzigt" (general review) of Utrecht; and Overijssel. For Brabant, see AN, AF IV (Rapport du Préfet du Département des Bouches de la Meuse, 1813).

180. AN, AF IV, 1805. In 1805 the allocation for the "Nationale School-Bestuur" came to just fl.24,100, of which fl.18,800 was accounted for in the salaries of the inspectors. The bulk of expenditures on teachers' wages and such like would have been hidden in the fl.200,000 of "subsidies and premiums" to the departments—though the fact that the Great Herring Fishery alone had a subsidy of fl.90,000 gives an idea of general priorities.

181. See, for example, the printed reports in the Bijdragen (1809), where complaints about the suspicion and reluctance of parents in Gelderland and Overijssel are mixed with enthusiasm for improved teaching methods and attendance in Friesland and Utrecht. See also BZ 719; 796; 797. Even within a single school district the disparities were marked. At Montfoort in 1809–10 there was a school for 130 children in 3 classes receiving tuition of an exemplary standard; whereas at Haastrecht, not far away, very few attended the local school and those that did continued to be "very unruly." There was, however, an impressive degree of unanimity on the improvements in rural schools in unlikely and remote regions of Groningen (BZ 719). See Schama, art. cit., pp. 596–7.

182. Première partie du rapport.

183. ARA, BZ 719.

184. Cuvier and Noël, op. cit., p. 578.

185. In the Bijdragen for 1806, Inspector Visser in Friesland had reported teachers living in dire poverty on 100 guilders a year. The Maatschappij "Tot Nut van 't Algemeen" had recommended that teachers should be paid on a range between 400 and 1,000 guilders a year, depending on their grading, to avoid the necessity of dependence on casual charity or part-time menial work (MNA 1366).

186. Van den Ende also wanted to fix the proportion of schools to the population more exactly at 1:150 children and to provide evening classes for young people from the ages of twelve to eighteen. His report embodying these and other far-sighted ideas was finalised in January 1809 and received by the ministers and Council of State the following month. See van den Ende, Geschiedkundige Schets, Bijlage XII.

187. For a retrospective account of the financial difficulties during the years of the Empire, see ARA, BZ 2645 (Subsidiën).

188. Arnold, *op. cit.*, used Victor Cousin's laudatory account, particularly of the inspectors in the Netherlands, where "in his own district each inspector reigns supreme; local and municipal school committees can only be named with his concurrence, no teacher, public or private can be appointed without his authorisation."

189. ARA, AF IV 1816; the two inspectors recommended that there should be secondary schools established in every principal district town, where mathematics, physics, chemistry, logic, modern languages and agriculture could be studied in addition to or instead of the classical disciplines of the old Latin schools.

190. For the "Valckenaer Report," see AN, AF IV 1816 (13); Collectie Johan Valckenaer, *Leidsche Bibliotheek*, 1034 (draft), a commission which aroused the intense displeasure of his old friend Wiselius, who criticised him for truckling to the "Caesar."

191. For an illuminating discussion of the effects of the Dutch educational system on the Belgians, see M. de Vroede, *Van Schoolmeester tot Onderwijzer* (Leuven, 1970), pp. 109–384.

192. For the business of the Council of Ministers and the Council of State see, respectively, AN, AF IV 1789, 1790. For the various reports on agriculture, industry, waterstaat, etc., see AF IV 1812, 1813, 1817, 1820, 1821. Bilderdijk's report on the condition of the Dutch universities is in GS, V, pp. 220–5, but should be read in conjunction with the much more penetrating "Mémoire sur les Universités" (Valckenaer) in AN, AF IV 1816 (13) and Mollerus' version of the Kops report on the reclamation of waste land, GS, V, pp. 235–243. For medical welfare and education, see ARA, BZ 827; and for the reports of the departmental commissioners on public health, BZ 793. The report on the condition of the Jews, GS, V, pp. 268–76, which Colenbrander cites as the work of an unknown writer, was in fact written by Jonas Daniel Meijer and Karl Asser. These were two luminaries of the *Adat Yeshurun* community, a breakaway group which had rebelled against the traditional prerogatives of the official *Kehilla* over education, ritual slaughtering and butchering, the meat tax and poor relief. Meijer produced a further report on the plight of the poor Jews in GS, V, pp. 284–6, and Asser a memorandum in *ibid.*, pp. 406–13.

193. For the report on the theatres and the proposal for a Royal Theatre, see GS, V, pp. 233–4; for the Great Fishery, pp. 615ff; AN, AF IV 1801.

194. Despite the recurrence of both genuine illness and bouts of hypochondria, Louis' several afflictions did not make him an absentee King. His first trip to Wiesbaden and Aachen lasted under two months. The second, from June to September 1807, occurred after the death of his son from croup and the failure to reconcile with Hortense.

195. AN, AF IV 1740, 1744.

196. Expenditure on the Waterstaat, nominally earmarked at 1m guilders, was difficult to keep in order during these flood years. Such was the inflated cost of even ordinary works that the drainage of the Mijdrecht and Nieuwkoop marshes (a fairly modest project) cost not less than fl.114,000 in 1806. See ARA, Gogel 31, MF 870; AN, AF IV 1806–9; 1817.

197. AN, AF IV 1816; T. Spaans-van der Bijl, *Lodewijk Napoleon, Koning van Holland* (Zaltbommel, 1967), p. 175; L. Brummel, "Lodewijk Napoleon en het Koninkrijk Holland," in the Catalogus for the Exhibition, *Lodewijk Napoleon . . .* (Rijksmuseum, Amsterdam, 1959), pp. 16–18.

198. For a brief account of the law reforms, see Colenbrander, *Schimmelpenninck*, pp. 125–9; see also H. Cohen Jehoram "Wie Geeft de Burgerlijke Wet?" (Deventer, 1967), p. 10, n. 19; Kluit, *Van Maanen*, pp. 184–5; G. A. van Hamel, "Koning Lodewijk en het crimineele wetboek van 1809," in *Tijdschrift voor Strafrecht*, III; and AN, AF IV 1818 for the discussion of the Council of State on both penal and civil codes. Napoleon insisted that "a nation of 1,800,000 souls cannot have a separate legal system," but Reuvens (DH II, p. 424) nevertheless was clear that the Dutch codes had to be adapted to "our institutions, our physical and moral situation, to our manners and customs."

199. East Friesland had been detached from Prussia and awarded to Russia in 1793. The Dutch had long had their eye on it as "idemnification" for the cession of Flanders. The inhabitants, it is clear from the landdrosten's reports, were less enthusiastic about becoming Dutch as that entailed a far higher fiscal burden. GS, V, p. 196.

200. ARA, MF 871.

201. See GS, V, p. 607, n. 1; ARA, BZ 776 suggests that during 1808 additional taxes were levied in Amsterdam to cover the current year's deficit. In that same year the

city spent fl.26,929 on education; fl.468,931 on its poor houses and workshops; and fl.78,-
355 in subsidies to various churches (inclusive of sums for the poor).

202. For the personnel, see GS, V, p. 286, n. 1; ARA, GB 103, Archief Couperus 36.
203. DH, III, pp. 170–1.
204. Labarre de Raillicourt, p. 145.
205. DH, I, p. 254.
206. For the Leiden fire, see DH, II, pp. 12ff; ARA, BZ 833–5.
207. DH, III, p. 87.
208. *Ibid.*, pp. 82–3.
209. Labarre de Raillicourt, p. 262.
210. GS, V, p. 198.
211. DH, II, p. 97.
212. Rocquain, pp. xliv–xlv.
213. DH, I, p. 231.
214. Rocquain, *op. cit.*, pp. xxxix–xli.
215. AN, AF IV 1819.
216. DH, I, p. 230.
217. *Ibid.*, III, p. 121.
218. *Ibid.*, II, pp. 242–9.
219. *Ibid.*, I, p. 253.
220. Gateau (see Kluit, *van Maanen*, pp. 189–206; GS, V, pp. 295–302) had been
sent to Holland with the obvious mission of implanting a political police in the Kingdom,
linked to Fouché's network in France. Van Maanen strongly resisted his efforts to create
a cadre so alien to Dutch traditions, but in any event Louis treated him as little better
than a spy and disregarded his reports. Garat's "Mémoire sur la Hollande," GS, V, xxxvff,
by contrast is sensitive and sympathetic, one of the very best French documents of the
Dutch predicament.
221. Rocquain, p. lxxxii.
222. Jean Hanoteau (ed.) (tr. Arthur K. Griggs), *The Memoirs of Queen Hortense*
(New York, 1927), I, p. 199.
223. Spaans-van der Bijl, *op. cit.*, p. 158.
224. DH, I, p. 196.
225. *Ibid.*, p. 259.
226. *Ibid.*, II, p. 291.
227. *Ibid.*, p. 293.
228. *Ibid.*, p. 63.

CHAPTER 12: Inundations . . .

1. The eight departments (excluding East Friesland, which became a German-speak-
ing department of the Empire) were: Bouches de l'Escaut (Brabant, Zeeland, southern-
most Holland); Bouches de la Meuse (South Holland); Zuider Zee (North Holland,
Utrecht); Bouches du Rhin (Gelderland); Bouches d'Yssel (Amsterdam, Utrecht); Yssel-
Supérieure; la Frise; Ems-Occidental (Groningen).
2. Jan de Vries (no sentimentalist), *op. cit.*, p. 236, writes: "The battles against the
sea and against Spain in a society with a profoundly pacifist culture produced an environment without parallel in the seventeenth century." J. Huizinga likewise in *Dutch Civilisa-
tion in the Seventeenth Century* (tr. F. W. Hugenholtz) (London, 1968), p. 16, speaks
of the formative "hydrographic" nature of the country.
3. DH, II, pp. 100–1.
4. In the summer of 1808 Louis visited the part of Gelderland abutting on the
Zuider Zee where funds for dyke and sluice maintenance were relatively meagre. He appropriated fl.20,000 for a new Orkmeerpolder and ensured the renovation of defences at
Nykerk and Harderwijk. DH, II, pp. 294–6; see also II, pp. 347ff.
5. *Ibid.*, III, p. 13.
6. See GS, V, pp. 70–1; DH, III, p. 17. For estimates of the damage done by the
flooding, see ARA, BZ 825–6.
7. From approximately fl.600,000 in 1804 to fl.1,800,000 in 1809 (AN, AF IV
1805).
8. Brugmans, *op. cit.*, p. 2.
9. *Ibid.*, p. 31 (data from the "Aperçu sur la Hollande" by Baron d'Alphonse, in
ARA BZ 1229).
10. *Memoriën en Correspondentiën* (Bijvoegsel), pp. 92–4.

11. See Appendix I.

12. F. Crouzet, *L'Économie brittanique et le blocus continentale 1806–1813* (Paris 1958), p. 99. Despite a more lively debate lately, this remains the outstanding work on this topic. The much older (1875) work by W. P. Sautijn Kluit on the same subject, *Geschiedenis van het Continentaal Stelsel*, provides some useful subsidiary information. For the data which follows on trade in agricultural, manufactured and colonial goods, see the Gogel *Bijvoegsel*, pp. 1–67.

13. DH, II, p. 167.

14. Crouzet, p. 228. It was a measure of the system's weakness that British colonial imports in the Netherlands were able to undercut French wares from similar provenance.

15. *Ibid.*, p. 129.

16. Source, Brugmans, *Pardekracht en Mensemacht*, pp. 29–31.

17. Crouzet, *op. cit.*, p. 227.

18. *Ibid.*, pp. 218–19.

19. *Ibid.*, p. 569–70.

20. *Ibid.*, p. 137.

21. See ARA, BuZ 167; the transport of gin to Britain was so well established and practised so openly that the burgemeester of Schiedam in February 1808 actually petitioned Gogel for exemption from the decree closing ports so that the freight should not go to competitors and interlopers! Gogel, GS, V, 235–6, was very ambivalent about violations of the blockade, being by nature a stickler for legality but very much wanting to avoid inflicting further gratuitous damage to Dutch commerce.

22. ARA, BuZ 165–6.

23. DH, I, p. 273.

24. See ARA, BuZ 119.

25. For these various cases, see GS, V, pp. 44, 55.

26. Crouzet, pp. 367–8, n. 30.

27. *Ibid.*, p. 443.

28. *Ibid.*, p. 447.

29. *Ibid.*

30. GS, V, pp. xxxix–xl.

31. GS, V, pp. 424, 427.

32. GS, V, pp. 685–6, 688, 692.

33. (October 23, 1807) Rocquain, p. lix. Louis on his side was incensed to discover French consuls in Holland giving Dutch certificates and licences to British cargoes destined for France and Italy!

34. The essential sources for gauging the degree of industrial deterioration in the Netherlands between the Goldberg material in 1800 and the report of the French prefects and "intendants" in 1811 are the landdrosten reports of 1808–10, covered (albeit imperfectly) in replies to circulars. These are to be found in ARA, BZ 783–6. Where not otherwise indicated, the data cited in this section are drawn from these files. See also the report on Holland, 1806, in GS, V, pp. 606–37.

35. BZ 783, 785.

36. GS, VI, p. 1322. The prefectoral reports for 1811 are to be found in ARA, BZ 1233, and were published by Colenbrander in GS, VI, pp. 1309–93.

37. ARA, BZ 785.

38. It was suggested, seemingly in all seriousness, that the smuggling in of British grand pianos had contributed further to the Amsterdam makers' difficulties. BZ 783.

39. For the Breda and Bergen op Zoom brewers' complaints, see ARA, BZ 786.

40. ARA, BZ 784. Schmidt's operation is more interesting for what, by Dutch standards, were advanced methods of advertisement marketing than for any technological sophistication of the product. His business was essentially an outgrowth of a simple candle-maker and -seller; and he introduced scented candles, special long-burning oils and waxes, and a night-light cum cooking oil for domestic use. I do not know whether his business subsequently prospered but he succeeded in introducing lines which became (and still are) an important minor industry in the country.

41. For an interesting general discussion of the problems facing the Dutch textile industry, see the *Mémoire* written by P. Klaarenbeek, a Haarlem dyer who had been on the revolutionary council of the city in 1795 and who had subsequently moved his business to Emmerik, just on the Cleves side of the border with Gelderland. GS, V, pp. 311–31; AN, AF IV 1801.

42. ARA, BZ 786; GS, VI, pp. 1461–2.

43. ARA, BZ 783.
44. GS, V, p. 3, 628n. In these circumstances it was all the more extraordinary that Louis, on transferring his capital to Amsterdam, should have contemplated a major project of public works and "beautification"; creating a new supply system for fresh water; removing the cemeteries outside the city; and transforming the not very salubrious quarter of Overtoom into a "beau quartier" complete with open air cafés, theatre, squares and fountains. The King would also have liked to complete the drainage of the Bijlemeer and to have rebuilt the overcrowded Jewish quarter around the Joodenbreestraat. GS, V, pp. 467–8.
45. ARA, GB 247; GS, V, p. 629. See also Z. W. Sneller, *Geschiedenis van de Nederlandsche Landbouw 1795–1940* (Groningen, 1951).
46. ARA, MF 847.
47. ARA, GB 247.
48. ARA, MF 847.
49. These figures are taken from the tables drawn up by the departmental administration in 1807, based on information received over the previous two years. The most important file is ARA, GB 72. Further data is accessible in GB 111–13 and 193–6.
50. ARA, GB 102.
51. For Dordrecht, see GB 102 and the very full protest in the "complaint against assessment" of 1809 in MF 847; for Delft, GB 111, 267; MF 847.
52. For The Hague, see GB 111, 267; the long report from Burgemeester Slicher in GB 102.
53. ARA, GB 267, 283, 194.
54. ARA, GB 72.
55. For Leiden, see ARA, GB 243, 247, 102, 72.
56. GS, V, pp. 279–81; AN, AF IV 1729.
57. ARA, BZ 784.
58. GS, V, pp. 313, 320.
59. ARA, BZ 267.
60. Aperçu (BZ 1229–30), pp. 490–4.
61. ARA, BZ, GB 102.
62. *Ibid.*
63. P. J. Blok, *Geschiedenis Eener Hollandsche Stad; Eene Hollandsche Stad in den Nieuweren Tijd* ('s Gravenhage, 1918), pp. 86–7; ARA, GB 111.
64. For Rotterdam, see ARA, GB 72, 102, 111, 243, 267, 193. For its economic condition, BZ 784, Goldberg 27.
65. For the history of the municipal poor house, see ARA, GB 72, a document giving important insight into attitudes towards poor relief in those straitened times: also GB 113, 193.
66. Similarly the report of the First Section of the Council of State, reporting on measures to be taken for poor relief in March 1808, allowed that as "good as were our traditional institutions for the poor . . . and justly admired . . . they can no longer be considered satisfactory for the present times." See ARA, Collectie Dassevael 50; also 92; 112.
This erosion of municipal autonomy through the burden of poor relief was not restricted to South Holland. In Alkmaar, for example, in 1811 (GS, VI, p. 835), the burgemeester mentioned that in a town of some 8,000 which before 1795 had paid on average some fl.3,000 towards poor relief, latterly paid fl.46,000 on this item. At the same time, income through holdings of public stock was becoming uncertain and delayed.
67. ARA, GB 194.
68. ARA, van Maanen, XXIII, 32.
69. DH, III, pp. 109, 117–18; Rocquain, p. lxxxii.
70. Rocquain, p. lxxxi.
71. GS, V, p. xxi.
72. For a Dutch view of the Walcheren expedition, see Colenbrander, *Schimmelpenninck*, pp. 171–7; Anthony Brett-James, "The Walcheren Failure," *History Today* (1963–4); DH, III, pp. 125ff; J. H. Deibel, *De Engelschen in Zeeland in 1809* (Middelburg, 1909).
73. GS, V, p. xviii. Zeeland, Napoleon commented (GS V, p. xx), could not be allowed to remain in the hands of a nation which did not know how to defend itself, for that put Antwerp at hazard.
74. GS, V, p. xviii. To la Rochefoucauld, the ambassador in Amsterdam, Napoleon

wrote that "after the events in Walcheren, it is impossible for Holland to preserve its independence." AE, Corr. Holl. 613.

75. DH, III, p. 172; Rocquain, p. lxxxvii.
76. GS, V, p. xix.
77. DH, III, p. 157.
78. Ibid., p. 179. Napoleon had already used this phrase in a letter to Champagny in November 1808 (Rocquain, p. xc) and it became a matter of public policy on December 3. It was the Minister of the Interior who used the famous phrase about the "alluvium." On January 16, 1813, writing to Louis, Napoleon referred to Holland as the "emanation de notre territoire" and "Holland is French forever." See also AE, Corr. Holl. 613.
79. (December 6, 1809) Theodorus Jorissen, De ondergang van het Koninkrijk Holland (Amsterdam, 1871), pp. 67–8.
80. December 21, 1809, DH, III, pp. 208–21.
81. Ibid., p. 213.
82. Ibid., p. 206.
83. Ibid., p. 199.
84. GS, V, pp. 720–3.
85. DH, III, pp. 184–5.
86. Rocquain, p. ci.
87. Ibid., p. ciii.
88. See AN, AF IV 1764; Louis Madelin, Fouché (Paris, 1901), pp. 175–83.
89. DH, III, pp. 200ff.
90. Th. Jorissen, Napoleon 1er et le roi de Hollande (Hague, 1868) p. 86.
91. ARA, Archief Mollerus 1810; Rocquain, p. cx, n.1.
92. For an account of Louis' last weeks as King, see GS V, pp. 145–9.
93. Mémoires du roi Jérôme (7 vols., Paris, 1861–6), IV, p. 404.
94. GS, V, p. 73.
95. DH, III, pp. 259ff.
96. GS, V, p. 739, n. 1. The crowd took few pains to disguise their pleasure at the affront.
97. Rocquain, p. 273.
98. DH, III, pp. 290–2.
99. GS, V, pp. 543–4.

CHAPTER 13: Babylon Undone . . .

1. GS, VI, p. 310.
2. Zappey, op. cit., p. 87.
3. Johanna W. A. Naber, Geschiedenis van Nederland tijdens de Inlijving bij Frankrijk (Haarlem, 1905), p. 127, n. 1.
4. GS, VI, p. 216.
5. Similarly the avenues in The Hague, the Lange Voorhout and Lange Vijverberg, became, respectively, the Cours Napoléon and the Cours de l'Impératrice. It was also planned to build a new town between Utrecht and Amsterdam, to be called "Austerlitz." See GS, VI, pp. 558–61, 1062; G. F. Gijsberti Hodenpijl, Napoleon in Nederland (Haarlem, n.d.).
6. GS, VI, p. 560.
7. See, for example, Odette Viennet, Napoléon et l'industrie française: la crise de 1810–11 (Paris, 1947); Eugene Tarlé, "Napoléon Ier et les intérêts économiques de la France," Le Revue du XIXe siècle, vols. 26–7 (1926); Bertrand de Jouvenel, Napoléon et l'économie dirigée: le blocus continental (Paris, 1942). For a general, if highly coloured, account of the terminal period of the Empire, see E. Driault, Napoléon et l'Europe, vol. V, La Chute de l'Empire (Paris, 1927).
8. GS, VI, p. 74.
9. Geoffrey Ellis, "Alsace and the Continental Blockade 1806–1813," unpublished paper read to Professor Richard Cobbs' graduate seminar in 1969, p. 9. I am most grateful to Dr. Ellis for permitting me to read the text of his paper and for the illuminating insights afforded by his work into the French attempt to impose its own goods and manufactures on Continental Europe, outre-Rhin, by political and military means. Parallels with similar experiences of occupation compensating for poor economic performance of the conqueror are inevitable.
10. GS, VI, pp. 1436–7.

11. *Ibid.*, p. 1454.

12. Naber, *de Inlijving*, pp. 26–7.

13. Alkmaar, for example, had half a million guilders tied up in public stock, the only dependable source of income with which to face its bloated poor relief commitments. GS, VI, pp. 835–6. For other similar predicaments, see AN, AF IV 1721.

14. GS, VI, pp. 822–3.

15. *Ibid.*, pp. 830–4.

16. Naber, *de Inlijving*, p. 58, n. 1.

17. *Ibid.*, p. 56, n. 1.

18. AN, AF IV 1721.

19. Identical practice in the Italian departments is confirmed by the research of Dorinda Outram in an unpublished Cambridge Ph.D thesis: *Education and the State in the Italian Departments Integrated into France Between 1802 and 1814.*

20. GS, VI, pp. 80–1.

21. ARA, BZ 1229–30.

22. *Ibid.*, pp. 185ff. D'Alphonse was much taken with the stories of legendary Dutch modesty; de Witt's habit of declining carriages; de Ruyter's one servant; and the Spanish ambassador who, during the twelve-year truce in The Hague, encountered a group of men dining on bread and beer, and when told they were "Members of the States of Holland" exclaimed, "My King can never conquer such people!"

23. *Ibid.*, GS, VI, pp. 1106–7.

24. *Ibid.*, p. 1057. D'Alphonse (*Aperçu*, pp. 483ff) was disturbed at the way in which hospices for the poor and aged were confused with hospitals for the treatment of the sick, a treatment, moreover, which he found was marred by mercenary motives "rather than pity and compassion."

25. See Sillem, *Gogel*, pp. 93ff; GS, VI, p. 1459.

26. GS, VI, pp. 26–7.

27. *Ibid.*, p. 1498.

28. *Ibid.*, p. 122.

29. *Ibid.*, p. 80.

30. *Ibid.*, pp. 177 (report of Réal); 976; 1119 (Kops); 1189; 1211.

31. *Ibid.* (ARA, BZ 1220).

32. The first "conscription" riots might be dated in 1809 when Louis' ill-judged attempt, partly successful, to conscript youths from orphanages was greeted with violence in Rotterdam and Amsterdam.

33. ARA, BZ 1073.

34. GS, VI, pp. 129–30.

35. *Ibid.*, p. 945.

36. *Ibid.*, p. 147.

37. *Ibid.*, p. 573.

38. *Ibid.*, p. 955.

39. *Ibid.*, p. 126.

40. AN, AF IV 1725 (June 1, 1812).

41. GS, VI, pp. 249, 623–5, 983.

42. Naber, *de Inlijving*, pp. 174–6.

43. GS, VI, p. 336. The man was not arrested but merely carefully tailed as a liberal source of information!

44. *Ibid.*, p. 372; also AN, FI, c[III] (de Stassart-Montalivet).

45. *Ibid.*, p. 973.

46. *Ibid.*, p. 987.

47. *Ibid.*, p. 607.

48. *Ibid.*, pp. 633–5. Santelaar's real crime was the common enough offence of his mouth being bigger than his wits.

49. For Stassart's account, see GS, VI, pp. 389–400; for Gogel's less agitated version, p. 1510–12.

50. *Ibid.*, p. 279.

51. *Ibid.*, pp. 240–5. Lebrun's sang-froid was somewhat shaken by evidence of an alleged plot, concocted by an Amsterdam tavern-keeper, Valentijn, to kidnap him. Abductions were becoming more common, particularly of coast guards, customs men and arsenal sentries (AN, FI, c[III]).

52. See Sillem, *Valckenaer*, II, pp. 324–5. This arrest was the brainwave of the confounding Devilliers Duterrage who, in desperation to find the "ringleader" of the seditious,

turned (as had his predecessors in 1796) to the unfortunate Valckenaer. It was only through the offices of his friend Maurits van Hall, the Amsterdam lawyer, that Valckenaer was released after a short stay in the Amsterdam House of Correction.

53. Naber, *de Inlijving*, p. 228, n. 1. In an interesting reversion to the vocabulary of the 1780's, Lebrun added. "Ce qu'on appelle patriote est essentiellement ennemi du gouvernement."

54. GS, VI, p. 313.
55. *Ibid.*, p. 1512.
56. *Ibid.*, p. 1513.
57. *Ibid.*, n. 2 (Canneman-Gogel).
58. *Ibid.*, pp. 927, 937. The disintegration of Imperial authority was further accelerated by the fact that, from the spring of 1813 onwards, there was virtually no money at all coming from Paris to pay senior officials, judges, predikants, schoolmasters or, most seriously, tax collectors.
59. GS, VI, pp. 459, 771–2.
60. Naber, *de Inlijving*, p. 260.
61. GS, VI, p. 57.
62. Louis Madelin, *Le Consulat et l'Empire* (2 vols., Paris, 1932–33), p. 281.
63. GS, VI, p. 298.
64. *Ibid.*, p. 321.
65. *Ibid.*, p. 297.
66. G. K. van Hogendorp, *Brieven en Gedenkschriften* (4 vols., 's Gravenhage, 1866–1887), IV, p. 234. For a detailed account of the uprising, see H. T. Colenbrander, *Inlijving en Opstand* (Amsterdam, 1911), pp. 174–246.
67. Quoted in Naber, p. 286.
68. GS, VI, pp. 300–1.
69. See H. T. Colenbrander (ed.), *Gedenkschriften van A. R. Falck* ('s Gravenhage, 1913).
70. GS, VI, pp. 301–2.
71. GS, VI, p. 1184.
72. GS, VI, p. 304.
73. *Ibid.*, p. 305.
74. Van Hogendorp, *Gedenkschriften*, VI, pp. 257–8.
75. GS, VI, p. 1526.
76. Kluit, *Van Maaner*, pp. 407–9.
77. GS, VI, pp. 1519ff.
78. *Ibid.*, p. 1529.
79. *Ibid.*, pp. 1538–9; Sillem, *Gogel*, pp. 112–19.
80. *Ibid.*, p. 135.

CHAPTER 14: Postscript

1. Paradoxically, van Stralen (who, however, tended to align with the more conservative group on the Council of Ministers) regained the post he had held under Schimmelpenninck at the same time that van Hogendorp was removed as Minister for Extrenal Affairs. A more permanent Minister of the Interior and solid ally of the reformers was Roëll, the ex-secretary of Louis Bonaparte and an accomplished exponent of cabinet politics. For the divisions and problems of these ministers, see de Wit, pp. 347ff; Zappey, pp. 93–133.
2. See de Vroede, *op. cit.*, pp. 327–84.
3. ARA, Gogel 5; Sillem, *Gogel*, p. 13.
4. Tulard, *art cit.*, p. 153.
5. See J. H. C. de Pater, "Groen's Beschouwing over het beloop der Franse Revolutie," in H. Smitskamp (ed.), *Groen's "Ongeloof en Revolutie"* ('s Gravenhage, 1949).
6. This is a point made, *en passant*, by L. G. J. Verberne, *In het Spiegel van het Verleden* (Utrecht, 1948).
7. AN, AF IV, 1816.
8. GS, V, pp. xxxvff.

Bibliography

(see Abbreviations at p. 657)

MANUSCRIPT SOURCES

Algemeen Rijksarchief (The Hague), 2nd Afdeeling (1795–1813)

STATE PAPERS

Archief van Binnenlandse Zaken: 182–3, 185–94, 195–202, 203–9, 217–20, 233–9, 330–2, 354–8, 362–6, 389–94, 502–14, 516–18, 522–37, 584, 635–40, 689–91, 713, 719, 731a–2, 733–7, 745–50, 776, 783–6, 796–7, 808–9, 812, 813–23, 825–6, 833–5, 844–9, 896–8, 901–3, 905–11, 999–1002, 1229–30, 1234–6, 2645–8, 2660–3, 2664–78, (1815–18).

Archief van Buitenlandse Zaken: 102–18, 119–25, 165–7, 200–19, 220–5, 231–2, 233–8, 337, 342, 394, 397–8, 420–1.

Archief, Wetgevende Collegiën: 182, 183–8, 223, 226, 360, 450–7, 463–4, 470–2, 476, 478, 488, 481, 492–4, 507–9.

Uitvoerend Bewind: 70–2, 195–202, 207–22, 230–1, 238–9, 240–2, 261, 269, 290, 355–9, 361–6, 370, 375, 380–6, 395, 482–5.

Staatsbewind: 230–1, 370, 400, 475, 501–18, 527, 529–30.

Raadpensionaris: 55–9, 61–5, 72, 87–8, 96.

Koninkrijk Holland: 322–3, 512–14, 635–40, 641–5.

Prins-Stedehouder: 11, 30–1.

Archief van Gewestelijke Bestuur (Holland): 226, 228, 229–31, 241–2, 243, 250, 282, 283–5, 286–8, 292, 347–8, 478, 501, 542, 545–6, 656, 749–50, 754, 756–9.

"Maasland": 72, 75, 77, 100–4, 107–8, 111, 113, 117, 193–6, 199, 242, 247, 267.

Archief van Financiën: 47–50, 52–62, 193, 210j–l, 270, 385, 390–a, 484a, 489jj–ll, 841, 843, 846, 854–69, 870–5, 1165.

Commissaris-Generaal voor onderwijs enz.: 2645, 2675, 2678.

PERSONAL PAPERS

Dumont-Pigalle: A, H, K, N, O, AA, CC, YYY, LLLL, PPPP, QQQQ, SSSS, TTTT, AAAAA, BBBBB, IIIII, NNNNN, OOOOO, PPPPP, QQQQQ, RRRRR, UUUUU, YYYYY, ZZZZZ.

Dassevael: 3–4, 8–9, 12–13, 43–4, 92–6, 98, 102–3, 108, 111–13, 125–6, 136, 148–9, 169; List II: 48; List III: 50.

Canneman: 1, 3–4, 6, 11, 15.

Fagel: 1857–8, 1868–9, 1871–3, 1882.

Gogel: 1–10, 14–17, 19, 21–2, 24–8, 30–5, 37, 39–41, 47, 54–5, 59–60, 76, 78–80,

85, 106, 110–14, 121–2, 128, 130–4, 136, 142, 145, 149–50, 164, 168–9, 170–4, 180, 186

Goldberg: 26–8, 37–8, 50, 59–65, 67, 71, 73, 75, 219, 223, 226.

Van Maanen, LXI, (Aanwinsten, 1895) XXIII (Aanwinsten, 1900): 33 and n.

Mollerus: 2, 22, 28.

Ockerse: 1–5.

Van de Spiegel: 250, 265, 272, 280, 373–7.

Wiselius: 1–5, 7–10, 13, 15–16, 19, 26, 28–9, 33, 40, 48, 53.

Verheyn: 7.

RIJKSARCHIEF IN GELDERLAND (Arnhem)

Schoolbestuur van den Rijn

RIJKSARCHIEF IN UTRECHT (Utrecht)

Archieven van Schoolbesturen in de provincie Utrecht (1801–57).

Archieven van de Districts schoolopzieners (1801–58).

GEMEENTE ARCHIEF UTRECHT: 1795–1810.

Archief van Stadssecretarie: 135, 49.

Archief van Almoezenierskamer Stadsrekeningen: 1800–10.

GEMEENTE ARCHIEF AMSTERDAM

No. 59: *Archief Felix Meritis:* 2, 8, 9, 34a–b, 66–9 (Notulen der vergaderingen), 87–8, 118–22, 125 (some printed).

No. 9: *Genootschap: Concordia et Libertate,* 5.

No. 211: *Archief, Maatschappij: Tot Nut van 't Algemeen:* 1–3, 59, 64–6, 183, 185, 188, 1179–90, 1366, 1406–9.

No. 311: *Gouverneur van Amsterdam* 1813–14.

No. 364: *Schutterij van Amsterdam,* 7, 16 (Onderboeken van de Burgerwacht, 1794–1801).

UNIVERSITY LIBRARY, LEIDEN

Collectie Luzac (Valckenaer correspondence).

Collectie Luzac (Valckenaer: 1031, 1032–40, 531, 885.

ARCHIVES NATIONALES (Paris)

FIC^III

AF III: 64, 69, 70.

AF IV: 1211, 1594, 1692, 1707–9, 1719, 1721, 1727, 1729, 1734–6, 1741, 1743–4, 1769–70, 1775, 1782, 1783, 1784–6, 1789–90, 1792–6, 1801, 1802–4, 1805–16, 1817, 1820, 1821, 1822–5, 1831.

ARCHIVES DU MINISTERE DES AF-
FAIRES ETRANGERES (Paris)
Correspondance de Hollande: 585, 592–8,
599–610, 612–15.

PRINTED SOURCES

PAMPHLETS, TREATISES, BROADSIDES, ETC.

It would be impractical here to cite in full
the titles and imprints of the hundreds of
political pamphlets consulted in the Koninklijke Bibliotheek, The Hague; the university libraries of Utrecht and Amsterdam; the Institute of Historical Research
and British Library, London. I list here
the numbers of the most illuminating,
principally in the period 1788–1806, corresponding to their enumeration in W.
P. C. Knuttel (abbrev. KN). *Catalogus
van de pamflettenverzameling berustende
in de Koninklijke Bibliotheek* (9 vols., 's
Gravenhage, 1899–1920). Where pamphlets are not included in this collection
they are cited in the general list below.

20368, 20404, 20576, 20669, 20743,
20797, 21050, 21741, 21750, 21751,
21768, 21769, 21820, 21842, 21843,
21919, 21975, 21980, 21981, 21985,
22059, 22118, 22119, 22136, 22165,
22185, 22198, 22199, 22200, 22202,
22204, 22205, 22206, 22207, 22209,
22213, 22255, 22260, 22273, 22277,
22278, 22303, 22324, 22327, 22328,
22335, 22337, 22344, 22365, 22371,
22375, 22376, 22377 (imprint, *Naz-
areth* 1794), 22380, 22417, 22464,
22472, 22483, 22485, 22492, 22501,
22502, 22503, 22508, 22513, 22515,
22518, 22522, 22524, 22538, 22540,
22551, 22556, 22575, 22576, 22577,
22581, 22587, 22595, 22599, 22601,
22603, 22605, 22606, 22613, 22618,
22619, 22623, 22631, 22635, 22642,
22643, 22644, 22645, 22650–8, 22664,
22677, 22702, 22703, 22704, 22855,
22862, 22863, 22864, 22871, 22874–6,
22884, 22885, 22891, 22892, 22893,
22904a, 22906, 22907, 22908a, 22941,
22953, 22988, 22993, 23006, 23010,
23013, 23013a, 23018, 23028, 23090,
23093–5, 23118, 23119–21, 23130,
23132, 23133, 23136, 23166, 23167,
23174, 23181, 23183, 23236, 23263,
23276, 23279, 23280, 23281, 23297,
23298, 23300, 23308, 23368.

CONTEMPORARY WORKS, PRINTED
DOCUMENTS, ETC.

van der Aa, C., *Geschiedenis van de jongst-
geeindigden Oorlog, tot op het sluiten*

van de vrede van Amiens (Amsterdam,
1804).
Adams, Charles Francis, (ed.) *The Works
of John Adams* (Vols. I, VII; Boston,
1851–2).
(Appelius, J. H.), *De Staatsomwenteling
van 1795. In haren aart loop, en gevolgen
beschouwd* (Leiden, 1801).
*Authentique Bijlagen tot de Gebeurtenissen
van den 12 Juny 1798* (Amsterdam,
1799).
*Authentique Bijlagen tot de Geschiedenis
der Omwenteling van 22 January 1798
en van het Arrest en Ontslag van 28
leden der Nationale Vergadering* (Amsterdam, 1799).
De Batavier (Leiden, 1784–7).
W. H. de Beaufort, *Brieven van en aan
Joan Derk van der Capellen tot de Poll*
(2 vols., Utrecht, 1879–93).
*Bijdragen betrekkelijk den staat en der ver-
beteringen van het schoolwezen in het
Bataafsch Gemeenebest* (Leiden, 1801–
9).
*Bijdragen ter bevordering van het onderwijs
en de opvoeding, voornamelijk met bet-
rekking tot de lagere scholen in Holland*
(5 vols., 1810–14).
Bonaparte, Louis, *Documents Historiques
et réflexions sur le gouvernement de la
Hollande* (3 vols., Paris, 1820).
Bosch, Bernardus, *Onze Verpligting, om tot
Nut van 't Algemeen te Werken* (Zaan-
dam-Amsterdam, 1794).
——, *Gedichten* (Leiden, 1803), III.
Brayer, J., *Coup d'oeil sur la Hollande*
(Paris, 1807).
Butterfield, L. H. (ed.), *The Diary and
Autobiography of John Adams* (Cambridge, 1961).
van der Capellen tot de Marsch, R. J., *Ad-
vijs . . . over de dringende noodzakelijk-
heid tot het formeeren van eene weder-
zijdsche defensieve alliance tussen den
Koning van Frankrijk en dezen staat* (Zutphen, 1789).
(van der Capellen tot den Pol, J.D.), *Aan
het volk van Nederland* (1781).
de Caraman, G., *Quelques mots sur les affaires de Hollande ar 1810* (Paris, 1856).
Carr, Sir John, *A Tour Through Holland
. . . in the Summer and Autumn of 1806*
(London and Philadelphia, 1807).
Cérisier, Marie-Antoine, *Tableau de l'historie générale des Provinces Unies* (10
vols., Utrecht, 1777–84).
——, *Le Politique Hollandais* (Amsterdam,
1781–4).
Colenbrander, H. T., "Aanteekeningen Betreffende de Vergadering van Vaderlandsche Regenten te Amsterdam 1783–7,"
BMHG, XX, (Amsterdam, 1899).

——, "Brieven van G. K. van Hogendorp, 1788–93," BMHG, xxxi (1910).

Condorcet, Marie Jean Antoine Nicholas de Caritat, marquis de, Aanspraak aan de Bataves (Dunkirk, 1792).

Cuvier, G. and Noël, F., Première partie du rapport sur les établissements d'instruction publique en Hollande (The Hague, 1816).

Cras, H. C., Verhandeling over de Gelijkheid der Menschen, en de Regten en Pligten, Welken uit die Gelijkheid Voortvloeijen (Haarlem, 1794).

——, Nagelatene Verhandelingen en Redevoeringen (2 vols., Amsterdam, 1822).

Dag verhaal der Handelingen van de Nationale Vergadering representeerende het Volk van Nederland (9 vols., The Hague, 1796–8).

Dagbladen van het verhandelde ter vergadering van de Provisionele Representanten van het volk van Holland (4 vols., The Hague, 1795–6).

Delprat, D. H., "Journal," in BMHG (1892).

De Democraten (Amsterdam, 1796–8).

"Demofilus" (Pieter Vreede?), De Zakboek van Neerlands Volk (Dordrecht, 1785).

Diderot, Denis, "Voyage de Hollande," Oeuvres (Paris, 1819), vol. VIII.

Dumouriez, Charles-François, Vie et mémoires (Paris, 1822–3).

De Eer der Nederlandsche Patriotten verdedigd door het Gezelschap Christenen (Holland, 1791).

Ellis, Sir George, History of the Late Revolution of the Dutch Republic (London, 1790).

Van den Ende, A., Geschiedkundige Schets van Neerlands School-Wetgeving (Deventer, 1847).

Etienne, E., Statistique de la Batavie (Paris, 1803).

Falck, A. R., Gedenkschriften (ed. H. T. Colenbrander) ('s Gravenhage, 1913).

Fell, R., A Tour Through the Batavian Republic During the Latter Part of the Year 1800 (London, 1801).

Fortescue, J. B., The Manuscripts of J. B. Fortescue Preserved at Dropmore (HMC Report, 13, London, 1892–1927).

Galdi, Matteo, Quadro politico delle rivoluzioni delle Provincie Unite e della Repubblica batava e dello stato attuale di regno di Olanda (2 vols., Milan, 1809).

Garat, Joseph, Mémoire sur la Hollande (Paris, 1806).

Gedenkstukken der Algemeene Geschiedenis van Nederland van 1789 tot 1840 (ed. H. T. Colenbrander) (10 vols. in 21 books, 's Gravenhage, 1905–22).

Gogel, I. J. A., "Over de nadeelen der buit-

enlandsche geldlichtingen," printed from De Democraten, 18 Augustus, 1796.

Gogel, J. M., Memoriën en Correspondentiën betrekkelijk den staat van 's Rijks geldmiddelen in den jare 1820, door I. J. A. Gogel (Amsterdam, 1844).

(Goldberg, J.), "Journaal der Reize van den Agent van Nationale Oeconomie der Bataafsche Republiek," Tijdschrift voor Staathuishoudkunde en Statistiek, vols. 18–19 (1859–60).

Grondwettige Herstelling van Nederlands Staatswezen . . . (2 vols., Amsterdam, 1784–6).

van Hamelsveld, Y., De Zedelijke Toestand der Nederlandsche Natie op het einde der XVIIIᵉ eeuw (2nd edn., Amsterdam, 1791).

Handelingen van het Comite Revolutionair in Amsteldam (Amsterdam, 1796).

Hanoteau, J., Mémoires de la reine Hortense (2 vols., Paris, 1927).

Hartog, J., De Spectatoriale Geschriften van 1741–1800 (Utrecht, 1872).

't Hoen, Pieter, Mars in boeijen. Of het herstel van den vrede (Arnhem, 1802).

van Hogendorp, D., Mémoires du General Dirk van Hogendorp, Comte de l'Empire, etc. (The Hague, 1887).

van Hogendorp, G. K., Brieven en Gedenkschriften (7 vols., 's Gravenhage, 1866–1903).

——, Gedagten over 's Lands Finantien Voorgedragen in Aanmerkingen op het Rapport tot een Stelsel van Algemeene Belastingen (Amsterdam, 1802).

van Hooff, J. F. R., Autobiografie van—— (ed. A. F. O. van Sasse van Ysselt, 's Hertogenbosch, 1918).

Huber, J. L., Brief . . . aan zyne Friesche Landgenooten (The Hague, 1797).

Hulshoff, Maria Aletta, Oproeping van het Bataafsche Volk (1806).

de Jonge, J. K. J., Documents politiques sur les révolutions de 1787 et 1795 (The Hague, 1857).

van der Kemp, F. A., Staatkundige Aanmerkingen . . . het gedrag van Israel en Rehoboam ten Spiegel van Volk en Vorst ('s Gravenhage, 1783).

Keuchenius, W. M., De Inkomsten en Uitgaven der Bataafsche Republiek Voorgesteld in Eene Nationale Balans (Amsterdam, 1803).

Korte Schets van den vorigen bloei, en het tegenwoordig verval van den koophandel, zeevaart etc., der Bataafsche Republicq, met aanstipping van eenige middelen tot herstel (Amsterdam, 1797).

van Linthorst, P., Verhandeling over de Politique Verschillen (1798–9).

te Lintum, C. (ed.), "Een Rotterdamsch

Gedenkschrift Uit den Patriottentijd en De Dagen der Revolutie," BMHG, XXXI (1910), pp. 97–232.

Loots, Cornelis, De algemeen vrede (Amsterdam, 1802).

Luzac, E., Hollands Rijkdom . . . behelzende den oorsprong van den Koophandel, en van de Magt van dezen Staat . . . (4 vols., Leiden, 1780–3).

Maaskamp, E., Voyage dans l'interieur de la Hollande fait clans, les années 1807–1817 (Amsterdam, 1813).

van der Marck, F. A., Redevoering van—over "De Liefde tot het Vaderland" (Deventer-Amsterdam, 1783).

——, Schets over de Rechten van den Mensch, het Algemeen Kerken-Staats-en Volkenrecht . . . (Groningen, 1798).

Metelerkamp, R., De Toestand van Nederland in Vergelijking met die van Eenige Andere Landen van Europa (2 vols., Amsterdam, 1804).

Mirabeau, Honoré Gabriel Riquéti, Comte de, Aux Bataves sur le Stadhoudérat . . . (Amsterdam, 1788).

Nieuw Nederlandsche Jaarboeken . . . (Leiden-Amsterdam, 1780–98).

Nieuwenhuizen, M., De Mensch. Een Gezang, uitgesprooken in de Maatschappij Felix Meritis (Amsterdam, 1789).

Paape, Gerrit, Aanspraak aan de Leden van het Genootschap van Wapenoeffening, onder de Spreuk: "Tot Herstel der Delftsche Schutterij voor Vrijjheid en Vaderland" (Delft, 1784).

——, Het Patriottismus (Rotterdam, 1787).

——, De Aristocraat en de Burger (Rotterdam, 1785).

——, De Knorrepot en de Menschenvriend (1795–6).

——, Het Verloste Nederland of de Nationale Conventie (Delft, 1796).

——, De Onverbloemde Geschiedenis van het Bataafsche Patriottismus (Delft, 1799).

——, De Bataafsche Republiek of Revolutionaire Droom (Delft, 1806).

J. C. H. de Pater, "Het Geheima Programma der Patriotten in 1782," Bijdragen voor Vaderlandse Geschiedenis en Oudheidkunde ('s Gravenhage, 1942), pp. 145–77.

Paulus, P., Het Nut der Stadhouderlijke Regering (Alkmaar, 1772–3).

——, Verklaring van de Unie der Utrecht (4 vols., Utrecht, 1775–7).

——, Verhandeling over de Vrage: In Welken zin kunnen de Menschen Gezegd worden Gelijk te Zijn? en welke zin de Regten en Pligten, die Daaruit Voordvloein? (Haarlem, 1793).

Pijman, G. J., Bijdragen tot de Voornaamste

Gebeurtenissen voorgevallen in der Republiek der Vereenigde Nederlanden 1778–1807 (Utrecht, 1826).

(H. A. le Pileur), Coup d'oeil sur l'état des lumières de l'instruction publique en Hollande depuis les temps les plus ancien jusqu'à nos jours (Paris, 1810).

van der Poel, Heren en Boeren, een Studie over de Commissiën van Landbouw (1805–1851) (Amsterdam, 1949).

De Politieke Blixem (Leiden, 1797–8).

De Burger Politieke Blixem (Leiden, 1800–1).

De Heer Politieke Blixem (1801–2).

De Politieke Kruijer (10 vols., Amsterdam, 1782–7).

De Politieke Opmerker (Amsterdam, 1795–6).

De Post van Neder Rijn (11 vols., Utrecht, 1781–7).

De Nieuwe Post aan de Nederrijn (Utrecht, 1795–9).

van der Pot, C. W., "Een Ontwerp-Staatsregeling van Gerhard Dumbar," Vereeniging tot Uitgaaf der Bronnen van het Oud-Vaderlandse Recht, Verslagen en Mededelingen, XI, 1–3 (1954–8), pp. 439–80.

Radcliffe, Anne, Journey through Holland (London, 1794).

Het Dagboek van Jacob Bicker Raye, 1732–1772 (ed. M. G. de Boer) (Amsterdam, n.d.).

Robinson, G. J., History of the internal affairs of the United Provinces from 1780 to 1787 (London, 1787).

Rocquain, Félix, Napoléon Ier et le roi Louis (Paris, 1875).

Rogge, C., Tafereel van de Geschiedenis der Jongste Omwenteling (Amsterdam, 1796).

——, Geschiedenis der Staatsregeling voor het Bataafsche Volk (Amsterdam, 1799).

——, Merkwaardige Brief van een Heer te Rotterdam aan zijnen vriend te Dordrecht (Rotterdam, 1783).

——, Request van Burgers en Inwoonders der Stad Rotterdam (Rotterdam, 1784?).

——, Aan de Burgers en Ingezetenen van Rotterdam (Rotterdam, 1784).

——, Memorie betreffende het Voorgevallene te Rotterdam. . . . (Rotterdam, 1784).

——, Echt Verhaal wegens het Bloedig Oproer . . . bevat in een Brief van Een Rotterdammer aan Zyn Vriend in Dordrecht (Rotterdam, 1784–5).

Scherenberg, R., Bedenkingen over de Armoede, en door welke middelen het aantal der armen in Nederland zoude kunnen worden verminderd . . . ('s Gravenhage, 1816).

Schimmelpenninck, R. J., De Imperio Pop-

ulari Caute Temperata (Leiden, 1784).

Smit, J., *Een Regentendagboek uit de 18de eeuw* (Assen, 1957).

van Swinden, J. H., *Advis over de Nationale Conventie* (The Hague, 1795).

Vaderlandsche Historie Vervattende de Geschiederissen der Vereenigde Nederlanden (*Vervolg van Wagenaar*, vols. 1-46; Amsterdam, 1788–1811).

(Valckenaer, J.), *Le Noeud gordien débrouillé du solution d'un grand problème politique* (Paris, Year III).

Verberne, L, G. J., "Gijsbert Karel van Hogendorp en Zijn 'Verklaring Aan het Staatsbewind,' 1801," *Bijdragen voor Nederlandsche Geschiedenis* (1950), pp. 31–62.

Verzameling van Authentique Stukken kunnende dienen tot Bijlagen voor de Nieuwspapieren van het jaaren 1793–6 (5 vols., Amsterdam, 1796?).

Verzameling van publicaties, reglementen enz. Departmentaal Bestuur 's Lands van Utrecht, 1802–6 (Utrecht, 1802–6).

Verzameling van Vaderlandsche Wetten en Besluiten Uitgevaardigd sedert 22 Januarij 1798 tot Julij 1810 . . . (ed. J. van de Poll) (Amsterdam, 1840).

(Vreede, P. and Fijnje, W.), *Ontwerp om de Republiek van binnen gelukkig en van buiten gedugt te maken* (3rd edn., Leiden, 1785).

de Vries, Johan, "Van de Spiegel's 'Schets tot een vertoog over de intrinsique en relative magt van de republyk' (1782)," *Economisch Historisch Jaarboek*, 26 (1958), pp. 81ff.

Wiselius, S. I., *De Staatkundige Verlichting der Nederlanden, in een wijsgeerig-historisch verhaal geschetst* (written 1793) (Brussels, 1828).

——, *Proeve over de Verschillende Regeeringsvormen in derzelver betrekking tot het maatschappij geluk* (written 1793) (Leiden, 1831).

——, *Beroep op het Bataafsche Volk* (Amsterdam, 1804).

——, *Oproeping van het Bataafsche Volk, om deszelfs en wil openlijk aan den dag te leggen tegen de overheersching door eenen vreemdeling waarmede het vaderland bedreigd wordt* ("Philos Patrios," Amsterdam, 1806).

de Witte van Citters, J., *Contracten van Correspondentie en Andere Bijdragen* . . . ('s Gravenhage, 1873).

Zappey, W. M. (ed.), J. Kops, "Levensberigt Betrekkelijk Mijne Werkzaamheden Voor Het Publiek en Hetgeen Hierop Invloed Had" (1839), in *Economisch-en Sociaal-Historisch Jaarboek*, 33 (1970), pp. 119–66.

Zillesen, C., *Wijsgeerig onderzoek, wegens Neerlands opkomst, Bloei en Welvaard; het Daarop Gevolgd Verval, en Wat de nog overgeblevene Middelen van Herstel Zijn* . . . (Amsterdam, 1796).

SECONDARY SOURCES

This must necessarily be a select bibliography. Of the books and articles consulted for this study, the most interesting or helpful are listed below.

For the nineteenth-century historiography, see in particular, J. Elias, *Bijdrage tot de Kennis van de Historiographie der Bataafsche Republiek* (Leiden, 1906).

GENERAL AND NARRATIVE WORKS

Blok, P. J., *History of the People of the Netherlands*, trans. O. A. Bierstadt and Ruth Putnam (5 vols., New York, 1898–1912).

Boxer, C. H., *The Dutch Seaborne Empire 1600–1800* (London and New York, 1965).

Colenbrander, H. T., *De Patriottentijd, hoofdzakelijk naar buitenlandsche bescheiden* (3 vols., 's Gravenhage, 1897–9).

——, *De Bataafsche Republiek* (Amsterdam, 1908).

——, "Napoleon en Nederland, 1799–1806," *De Gids*, (1908), pp. 100–25.

——, *Schimmelpenninck en Koning Lodewijk* (Amsterdam, 1911).

——, *Inlijving en Opstand* (Amsterdam, 1911).

Geyl, P., *Geschiedenis van de Nederlandse Stam* (3 vols., Amsterdam-Antwerp, 1958–9).

——, *Revolutiedagen in Amsterdam, Prins Willem IV en de Doelistenbeweging* ('s Gravenhage, 1936).

——, *De Patriottenbeweging 1780–1787* (Amsterdam, 1947).

——, "De Bataafsche Revolutie," in *Studies en Strijdschriften* (Groningen, 1958).

Hartog, J., *De Patriotten en Oranje van 1747–1787* (Amsterdam, 1882).

van Houtte, J. A., (ed.), *Algemene geschiedenis der Nederlanden* (13 vols., Brussels, 1944–58), vols. VIII, IX.

Jorissen, T., *De patriotten te Amsterdam in 1784* (Amsterdam, 1874).

——, *De overgave van Amsterdam in Januari 1795* (Amsterdam, 1884).

——, *De ondergang van het koninkrijk Holland* (Amsterdam, 1871).

——, *De omwenteling van 1813* (Amsterdam, 1867).

Legrand, L., *La révolution française en Hollande; La république Batave* (Paris, 1894).

Naber, J. W. A., *Geschiedenis van Neder-land tijdens de Inlijving bij Frankrijk, Juli 1810–November 1813* (Haarlem, 1905).

Palmer, R. R., "Much in Little: The Dutch Revolution of 1795," *Journal of Modern History*, XXVI (1954), pp. 15–35.

THE DUTCH IN EUROPE AND THE ATLANTIC

Bartstra, J. S., *Vlootherstel en Legeraug-mentatie, 1770–1780* (Assen, 1952).

Bruin, J. R., "Oranje in Engeland en de invasie van 1799," *T.v.G.*, 79 (1966), pp. 5–23.

Carter, Alice Clare, "How to Revise Treat-ies without Negotiating: Common Sense, Mutual Fears and the Anglo-Dutch Trade Disputes of 1759," in R. M. Hatton and M. S. Anderson (eds.), *Studies in Diplo-matic History* (London, 1970).

——, *The Dutch Republic in the Seven Years' War* (London, 1971).

——, *Neutrality or Commitment: The Evo-lution of Dutch Foreign Policy 1667–1795* (London, 1975).

Cobban, A., *Ambassadors and Secret Agents. The Diplomacy of the First Earl of Malmesbury at The Hague* (London, 1954).

Connelly, Owen, *Napoleon's Satellite King-doms* (New York, 1965).

Fehrmann, C. N., *Onze Vloot in de Franse Tijd* ('s Gravenhage, 1969).

Godechot, J., *La grande nation, l'expansion révolutionnaire de la France dans le monde 1789–1799* (2 vols., Paris, 1956).

Mackesy, Piers, *Statesmen at War, The Strategy of Overthrow 1798–1799* (Lon-don, 1974).

de Madariaga, Isabel, *Britain, Russia and the Armed Neutrality of 1780* (Oxford, 1938).

Mathiez, Albert, *La Révolution et les étrang-ers* (Paris, 1919).

Milo, T. H., *De geheime onderhandelingen tusschen de Bataafsche en Fransche Re-publieken van 1795 tot 1797 . . .* (den Helder, 1942).

Palmer, R. R., *The Age of Democratic Revolution: A Political History of Europe and America, 1760–1800* (2 vols., Prince-ton, N.J., 1959–64).

Sabron, F., *De Oorlog van 1794–5* (Breda, 1892).

Sciout, L., "La république française et la république batave," *Revue des questions historiques*, 47 (1896), pp. 537–81.

Smit, J. W., "The Netherlands and Europe in the Seventeenth and Eighteenth Cen-turies," in J. S. Bromley and E. H. Koss-mann (eds.), *Britain and the Netherlands in Europe and Asia* (London, 1968).

Sorel, Albert, *L'Europe et la Révolution française* (8 vols., Paris, 18 ?–1905).

Verhagen, D. R. G., *L'Influence de la Révolution française sur la Premiere Con-stitution Hollandaise du 23 avril 1798* (Utrecht, 1949).

Vreede, G. W., *Geschiedenis der diplo-matie van de Bataafsche Republiek* (2 vols., Amsterdam, 1863–5).

van Wijk, F. W., *De Republiek en Amerika 1776 en 1782* (Leiden, 1921).

IDEAS AND POLITICS

de Bosch Kemper, Ihr. J. de, *Letterkundige Aanteekeningen Betreffende de Geschied-enis van het Nederlandsche Staatsleven en Staatsregt* (Amsterdam, 1871).

Dirks, J., *De Uitgewekenen uit Nederland naar Frankrijk 1787–1795* (Amsterdam, 1868).

Fockema Andreae, S. J., "Montesquieu in Nederland," *De Gids*, CXII (1949), pp. 176–83.

van de Giessen, J., *De Opkomst van het Woord Democratie als Leuze in Neder-land* ('s Gravenhage, 1948).

Gobbers, W., *Jean-Jacques Rousseau in Hol-land—Een Onderzoek Naar de Invloed van de Mens en het Werk 1760–1810* (Gent, 1963).

Godechot, J., "Unita Batava e Unita Itali-ana all' Epoca del Dirretorio," *Archivo Storico Italiano* (1955), pp. 335–6.

Goslinga, A., *De beteekenis van de om-wenteling van 1795* (Amsterdam, 1927).

——, *De Rechten van den Mensch en Bur-ger, een Overzicht van Nederlandsche Geschriften en Verklaringen* ('s Graven-hage, 1936).

Haak, J., "Het nationaal besef bij G. K. van Hogendorp." *T.v.G.*, 79 (1966), pp. 407–17.

Hartog, J., "De Joden in het Eerste Jaar der Bataafsche Vrijheid," *De Gids*, (1875), pp. 116–52.

——, *De Spectatoriale Geschriften van 1741–1800* (Utrecht, 1890, 2nd edn.).

——, *Uit de Dagen der Patriotten* (Amster-dam, 1896).

Homan, G. D., "The *Staatsbewind* and the Freedom of the Press," *T.v.G.*, 1976, pp. 12–27.

Kossmann, E. H., *Verlicht Conservatisme: over Elie Luzac* (Groningen, 1966).

——, "The Crisis of the Dutch State, 1780–1813: Nationalism, Federalism, Unitar-ism," in J. S. Bromley and E. H. Koss-mann (eds.), *Britain and the Nether-lands*, vol. IV: *Metropolis, Dominion and Province* (The Hague, 1971), pp. 154–71.

de Lange, H., "De politieke actie van een

bewuste publieke opinie," *De Gids*, (1971).

——, "De Gemeenbestgezinde Burgersocieteit 1797–8," *Die Haghe* (1970).

——, "De politieke pers in de Bataafsche Revolutie," *Economisch-en Sociaal-Historisch Jaarboek*, 35 (1972), pp. 81–.

Leeb, I. Leonard, *The Ideological Origins of the Batavian Revolution. History and Politics in the Dutch Republic 1747–1800* (The Hague, 1973).

de Peyster, H. *Les Troubles en Hollande à la veille de la révolution française* (Paris, 1905).

Riker, W. H., "Dutch and American Federalism," *Journal of the History of Ideas*, XVII (1957), pp. 495–521.

Rogier, L. J., *Terugblik en Uitzicht, Verspreide opstellen* (Hilversum, 1964).

Roorda, D. J., *Partij en Factie* (Groningen, 1961).

Sautijn Kluit, W. P., "Janus; de Politieke Blixem; en beider gevolg," *Nederlandsche Spectator* (1867), pp. 347–52.

——, "De Politieke Kruyer," *Bijdragen voor Vaderlandsche Geschiedenis en Oudheidkunde*, 1 (1882).

——, "De Fransche Leidsche Courant," *Handelingen en Medelingen van de Maatschappij van Nederlandse Letterkunde* (1870).

Schutte, G. J., *De Nederlandse Patriotten en de koloniën. Een onderzoek naar hun denkbeelden en optreden 1770–1800* (Groningen, 1974).

Theissen, J. S., *Uit de voorgeschiedenis van het liberalisme in Nederland* (Groningen, 1930).

Thorbecke, J. R., *Historische Schetsen* ('s Gravenhage, 1872).

Vijlbrief, I., *Van Anti-Aristocratie tot Democratie, een bijdrage tot de Politieke en Sociale Geschiedenis der Stad Utrecht* (Amsterdam, 1950).

Vreede, G. W., *Bijdragen tot de Geschiedenis der Omwenteling van 1795 tot 1798* (2 vols., Amsterdam, 1847–51).

de Wit, C. H. E., *De Strijd Tussen Aristocratie en Democratie in Nederland: 1780–1848* (Heerlen, 1965).

——, *De Nederlandse Revolutie van De Achttiende Eeuw 1780–1787. Oligarchie en Proletariaat* (Oirsbeek, 1974).

BIOGRAPHIES

For brief but invaluable data, see in particular the *Nieuw Nederlandsch Biografisch Woordenboek* (eds. P. J. Blok and P. C. Molhuysen) (10 vols., Leiden, 1911–37).

Akerlaken, D. van, *Mr. Hendrik van Stralen, Aanteekeningen uit zijne nagelaten geschriften* ('s Gravenhage, 1878).

Byvanck, W. G. C., *Bataafsch Verleden ('Dorus' Droefheid)* (Zutphen, 1917).

Caumont de la Force, A. de, *L'Architrésorier Lebrun gouverneur de la Hollande 1810–1813* (Paris, 1907).

Davies, C. M., *Memorials and Times of Peter Philip Juriaan Quint Ondaatje* (Utrecht, 1870).

van Dijk, F. *Mr. Laurens Pieter van de Spiegel, Raad en Burgemeester van Goes* (Assen, 1963).

Duboscq, A., *Louis Bonaparte en Hollande, d'après ses lettres* (Paris, 1911).

van den Eerenbeemt, H. F. J. M., "Bernardus Bosch: Nutsfiguur, schrijver en politicus," *De Gids* (1971), pp. 489–97.

Fehrmann, C. N., "Mr. Jacob Abraham Uitenhage de Mist (1749–1823)," in *Overijsselse Portretten* (Zwolle, 1958).

Fockema Andreae, S. J., "Schimmelpenninck's Binnenlandse Bestuur," in *O.R.G.* (1949).

Goossens, Theodorus, *Mr. J. F. R. van Hooff, Een Brabants Patriot 1755–1816* (Nijmegen, 1943).

de Groot, A., *Leven en Arbeid van J. H. van der Palm* (Wageningen, 1960).

Hardenberg, H., *Etta Palm, een Hollandse Parisienne? 1743–1799* (Assen, 1962).

de Jong, M., *Joan Derk van der Capellen, Staatkundig Levensbeeld uit de Wordingstijd van de Moderne Democratie in Nederland*.

Kluit, M. E., *Cornelis Felix van Maanen tot Herstel der Onafhankelijkheid* (Groningen-The Hague, 1921).

Kraijenhoff, K. R. T., *Levensbijzonderheden van——* (ed. H. W. Tydeman) (Amsterdam, 1844).

Kroes-Ligtenberg, *Dr. Wybo Fijnje* (Assen, 1957).

Kronenburg, A. J., *Een en onder over Gerrit Paape en zijn tijd* (Deventer, 1886).

Labarre de Raillicourt, D., *Louis Bonaparte* (Paris, 1963).

van Limburg Brouwer, P., *Het leven van Mr. Samuel Iperuszoon Wiselius* (Groningen, 1846).

Mendels, I., *Herman Willem Daendels, voor zijne benoeming tot Gouverneur-Generaal van Oost Indië 1762–1807* ('s Gravenhage, 1890).

van der Meulen, J., *Studies over het Ministerie van Van de Spiegel* (Leiden, 1905).

(Paape, G.), *Leven en Ervaring van Gerrit Paape, Bijdragen tot de Kennis van het Volksleven op het laatst der Achttiende Eeuw* (Amsterdam, 1857).

van der Poel, J., *Te eere van mr. Jean Henri Appelius* (Deventer, 1954).

van der Pot, C. W., "De Twee Dumbars

1680–1744, 1743–1802," in C. N. Fehrmann (ed.), *Overijsselse Portretten* (Zwolle, 1958), pp. 123–43.

Rijndorp, J. L., "Gerrit Willem van Marle," in C. N. Fehrmann (ed.), *Overijsselse Portrotten* (Zwolle 1958), pp. 195–231.

Rogier, L. G., "Rutger Jan Schimmelpenninck . . ." *O.R.G.*, 77, (1962).

Schimmelpenninck, G., *Rutger Jan Schimmelpenninck en eenige Gebeurtenissen van Zijnen tijd* (2 vols., 's Gravenhage-Amsterdam, 1845).

Sillem, J. A., *De Politieke en Staathuishoudkundige Werkzaamheid van I. J. A. Gogel* (Amsterdam, 1864).

——, *Het Leven van Mr. Johan Valckenaer 1759–1821* (2 vols., Amsterdam, 1883).

——, *Dirk van Hogendorp, 1761–1822* (Amsterdam, 1890).

——, "Mr. Jacob Blauw," *De Gids*, (1875).

Spaans-van der Bijl, T., *Lodewijk Napoleon Koning van Holland* (Zaltbommel, 1967).

Surinagar, P. H., *Biographische Aanteekeningen betreffende Mr. Pieter Paulus* (Leiden, 1879).

Verberne, L. G. J., *Gogel en Uniteit* (Nijmegen, 1948).

Verhuell, Q. M. R., *Het Leven en Karakter van Karel Hendrik Graaf Ver Huell* (2 vols., Amsterdam, 1847).

Vreede, G. W., *Mr. Laurens Pieter van de Spiegel en zijne Tijdgenooten* (1737–1800 . . .) (4 vols., Middelburg, 1874–77).

de Vries, Theun, *Rutger Jan Schimmelpenninck, Republikein zonder republiek* (2nd edn., The Hague, 1965).

Wichers, L., *De regeering van Koning Lodewijk Bonaparte 1806–1810* (Utrecht, 1892).

Zappey, W. M., *De Economische en Politieke Werkzaamheid van Johannes Goldberg (1763–1828)* (Alphen aan den Rijn-Brussels, 1967).

PROVINCIAL AND LOCAL STUDIES

Bijleveld, H. J. J., *Verhandelingen over de geschillen met Frankrijk betrekkelijk Vlissingen sedert 1795* (Middelburg, 1865).

de Blécourt, A. S., *De organisatie der gemeenten gedurende de Jaren 1795–1851* (Haarlem, 1903).

Blok, P. J., *Geschiedenis Eener Hollandsche Stad, Eene Hollandsche Stad in den Nieuweren Tijd* (Leiden-'s Gravenhage, 1918).

de Boer, M. G., "Het Amsterdamsche stadsbestuur in moeilijkheiden," *T.v.G.*, 46 (1931), pp. 1–27.

Breen, J. C., "De regeering van Amsterdam gedurende den Franschen tijd," *Jaarboek Amstelodamum*, 12(1914), pp. 1ff.

Brugmans, H., *Het Nieuwe Amsterdam* (Amsterdam, 1925).

Bruinvis, C. W., *Uit Alkmaar's Verleden. Politieke afstraffing en zuivering in 1795–1798* (Alkmaar, 1905).

Driessen, F., *Leiden in den Franse Tijd (1794–1813)* (Leiden, 1913).

van der Eererbeemt, H. F. J. M., *'s Hertogenbosch in de Bataafse en Franse tijd 1794–1814* ('s Hertogenbosch, 1955).

Feith, E., *Bijdrage tot de geschiedenis der omwenteling van 1795 in de provincie Groningen* (Groningen, 1870).

van Gelder, H. E., "Onverbeterlijke Regenten"; "Die Regeering van 's Gravenhage 1795–1851," both in *Die Haghe* (1908), pp. 216–306.

Guibal, C. J., *Democratie en Oligarchie in Friesland tijdens de Republiek* (Assen, 1934).

van Hulzen, A., *Utrecht in de Patriottentijd* (Zaltbommel, 1966).

Lichtenauer, S., *Het bezoek van Napoleon aan Rotterdam in 1811* (Rotterdam, 1963).

van der Meulen, W. W., "De Beteekenis van de Haagsche Opstootjes in den Patriottentijd," *Die Haghe* (1909), pp. 79–112.

Pikkemaat, A. G., *Bataafse Vrijheid in Nijmegen 1794–5* (Nijmegen, 1963).

de Savornin Lohman, B. C., *De Bestuursinrichting van Gewest, Stad en Platteland van Utrecht gedurende de Bataafsche Republiek* (Utrecht, 1910).

Smit, J., *Den Haag in den Franschen Tijd* ('s Gravenhage, 1913).

Staats Evers, J. W., *Kroniek van Arnhem van 1789 tot 1868* (Arnhem, 1868).

——, *De Geldersche Achterhoek in 1799* (Winterswijk, 1879).

Theissen, J. S., *De omwenteling van 1795 in Staden Lande* (Groningen, 1916).

Theunisz, Joh., *Overijssel in 1795* (Amsterdam, 1943).

Vijlbrief, I. (Utrecht—see above, section on Ideas and Politics).

Vitringa, C. L., *Verhaal van het Oproer en de Burgergeschillen te Kampen 1795–1798* (Arnhem, 1862).

Vreede, G. W., *De vrijwoording van Noord-Brabant in 1795 Handelingen van het Provinciaal Genootschap van Kunst en Wetenschappen in Noord Brabant* (1859).

Westrate, H. A., *Gelderland in den Patriottentijd* (Arnhem, 1903).

SOCIAL AND ECONOMIC HISTORY

Baasch, E., *Holländische Wirtschaftsgeschichte* (Jena, 1927).

Bierens de Haan, J. A., *Van Oeconomische*

tak tot Nederlandsche Maatschappij voor Nijverheid en Handel, 1772–1952 (Haarlem, 1952).

de Boer, M. G., "De Ondergang der Amsterdamsche Gilden," *T.v.G.* (1932), pp. 230ff.

de Bosch Kemper, J., *Geschiedkundig onderzoek naar de armoede in ons vaderland, haare oorzaken en de middelen, die tot hare vermindering, zouden kunnen worden aangewend* (Haarlem, 1851).

Brink, E. A. B. J. ten, *Geschiedenis van het Nederlandse postwezen 1795–1810. Het ontstaan van een Rijksdienst onder de Bataafse Republiek en het Koninkrijk Holland* ('s Gravenhage, 1950).

Brugmans, I. J., *Paardenkracht en Mensemacht. Sociaal-economische geschiedenis van Nederland 1795–1840* ('s Gravenhage, 1961).

——, *Statistiek van de Nederlandse nijverheid uit de eerste helft der 19e eeuw* ('s Gravenhage, 1956).

Carter, Alice, "The Dutch and the English Public Debt in 1777," *Economica*, XX (May 1953), pp. 159–61.

——, "Dutch Foreign Investment 1738–1800," *Economica*, XX (November 1953), pp. 322–40.

Crouzet, F., *L'Économie britannique et le blocus continentale 1806–1813* (Paris, 1958).

van Dijk, H., and Roorda, D. J., "Sociale Mobiliteit onder regenten van de Republiek," *T.v.G.* (1971), pp. 306–28.

van Dillen, J. G., *Mensen en Achtergronden* (Utrecht, 1964).

——, *Van Rijkdom en Regenten* ('s Gravenhage, 1970).

van den Eerenbeemt, H. F. J. M., *'s Hertogenbosch* . . . (see above, section on Prov. and Local Studies).

——, "Streven naar sociale verheffing in een statische stad. Een kwart eeuw arbeid van de Maatschappij tot Nut van 't Algemeen in Bergen op Zoom 1791–1816," BGZN (Nijmegen), 1963

——, *De arme en het maatschappelijk welzijn in historisch perspectief* (Tilburg, 1961).

——, "Armoede en drankmisbruik in de Meijerij van 's Hertogenbosch," *Brabantia*, 7 (1958), pp. 310–20.

——, "In het spanningsveld der armoede," BGZN (1968)

——, "Oorzaken van het pauperisme in Nederland in de 18de Eeuw," *Economie, Tijdschrift voor algemeen economische bedrijfs-economische en sociaale vraagstukken*, 27 (1963), pp. 156–66.

——, "Het huwelijk tussen filantropie en economie; een patriotse en bataafse illusie," *Economisch-en Sociaal-Historisch Jaarboek*, 35, (1972), pp. 28–.

Elias, J., *De vroedschap van Amsterdam 1578–1795* (2 vols., Haarlem, 1903–5).

Faber, J. A., "Drie Eeuwen Friesland," *A-AG Bijdragen* 17 (Wageningen, 1972).

Faber, J. A., H. K. Roessingh, B. H. Slicher van Bath, A. M. van der Woude, and H. J. van Xanten, "Population Changes and Economic Developments in the Netherlands: A Historical Survey," *AAG Bijdragen* 12 (Wageningen, 1965).

Hovy, J., *Het Voorstel van 1751 tot Instelling Van Een Beperkt Vrijhavenstelsel in de Republiek* (Groningen, 1966).

Jansen, A. A., "De verhouding tussen Regenten en volk in de eerste helft der 18de Eeuw," *De Gids*, 1942, II, pp. 131–145.

de Jong, Thomas P. M. de, *De krimpende horizon van de Hollandse kooplieden. Hollands welvaren in het Caribisch zeegebied* (Assen, 1966).

——, "Sociale verandering in de Neergaande Republiek," *Economisch-er Sociaal-Historisch Jaarboek*, (1972), pp. 1–27.

de Jouvenel, B., *Napoléon et l'économie dirigée* (Paris, 1942).

Klein, P. W., "Stagnation économique et emploi du capital dans la Hollande des XVIIIe et XIXe siècles," *Revue du Nord*, LII, No. 204 (1970), pp. 33–41.

van der Kooy, T. P., *Hollands Stapelmarkt en Haar Verval* (Amsterdam, 1931).

Manger, J. B., *Recherches sur les relations économiques de la France et de la Hollande pendant la Révolution française* (Paris, 1923).

Melief, P. B. A., *De Strijd om de Armenzorg in Nederland 1795–1845* (Groningen, 1955).

van Nierop, L., "Eene Enquete in 1800. Eene bijdrage tot de economische geschiedenis van de Bataafsche Republiek," *De Gids*, LXXVII (1913).

——, "Amsterdam's scheepvaart in den Franschen tijd," *Jaarboek Amstelodamum*, XXI (1924).

van der Poel, J. M. G., "De Landbouw enquete van 1800," *Historia Agriculturae*, vols. I–III (1953).

Posthumus, N. W., *Geschiedenis van de Leidsche Lakenindustrie*, III ('s Gravenhage, 1937).

Riley, J. C., "Life Annuity-Based Loans on the Amsterdam Capital Market Toward the End of the Eighteenth Century," *Economisch- en Sociaal-Historisch Jaarboek*, 36 (1974), pp. 102–30.

Roessingh, H. K., "Beroep en Bedrijf op de Veluwe in het Midden van de 18de eeuw," *AAG Bijdragen* 13 (Wageningen 1966).

Schama, Simon, "The Exigencies of War and the Politics of Taxation in the Netherlands 1795–1810," in J. M. Winter (ed.), *War and Economic Development* (Cambridge, 1975).

Sickenga, F. N., *Geschiedenis der Nederlandsche belastingen, Tijdvak der omwenteling* (Amsterdam, 1865).

Sneller, Z. W., *Geschiedenis van der Nederlandsche landbouw 1795–1940* (Groningen, 1951).

Verberne, L. G. J., *Het Sociale en Economische Motief in de Bataafsche Tijd* (Tilburg, 1947).

de Vries, Johan, *De economische achteruitgang der Republiek in de achttiende eeuw* (Amsterdam, 1959).

——, "De Oeconomisch-Patriottisch Beweging," *De nieuwe stem*, 7 (1952), pp. 723ff.

Wilson, Charles, "Taxation and the Decline of Empires, An Unfashionable Theme," *BMHG*, 77 (1963), pp. 10–23.

——, *Anglo-Dutch Commerce and Finance in the Eighteenth Century* (Cambridge, 1941).

Wiskerke, *Der Afschaffing der Gilden in Nederland* (Amsterdam, 1938).

van Winter, P. J., *Het aandeel van den Amsterdamschen handel aan den opbouw van het Amerikaansche Gemeenebest* (2 vols., Ned. Econ. Hist. Archief, 1927–33).

van der Woude, "Het Noorderkwartier," *AAG Bijdragen* 16 (Wageningen, 1972).

——, "De Consumptie van Graan, Vlees en Boter in Holland op het Einde van de Achttiende Eeuw," *AAG Bijdragen* 9 (Wageningen, 1963), pp. 127–54.

Wright, H. R. C., *Free Trade and Protection in the Netherlands 1816–1830* (Cambridge, 1955).

Zappey, W. M. (see above, section on Biographies).

EDUCATIONAL, ADMINISTRATIVE AND LEGAL REFORM

Dodde, N. L., *Het Rijks-schooltoezicht in de Bataafse Republiek* (Groningen, 1968).

van Eysinga, W. J. M., "De Brug tusschen het Grondwettelijk Recht der Republiek der Vereenigde Nederlanden en dat van de Wedergeboorte," *MKAW* (1936).

Fockema Andreae, S. J., *Schimmelpenninck* . . . (see section on Biographies).

——, "Napoleon's bestuurshervorming in Nederland," *Publicatiën, Genootschap Napoleontisch Studiën*, 9 (1956).

van der Giezen, A. M., *De Eerste Fase van de Schoolstrijd in Nederland* (Assen, 1937).

Haak, J., "Tentatives bataves de régler la question des droits seigneuriaux," in *Annales historiques de Révolution française*, 1967 (1969).

van Hamel, G. A., "Koning Lodewijk en het crimineele wetboek van 1809," *Tijdschrift voor Strafrecht*, III (1899).

Hentzen, Cassianus, *De Politieke Geschiedenis van het Lagere Onderwijs in Nederland* (1920).

Langedijk, D., *Bibliographie van den Schoolstrijd 1795–1920* ('s Gravenhage, 1931).

Maas, W. J. M., *De Dijkwet van 1810* (1903).

Meylink, A. A. J., *Officiele Geschiedenis der Wet van 1806 voor het Lager Schoolwezen* ('s Gravenhage, 1857).

van der Pot, C. W., "Eerste Pogingen tot Staatshervorming in de Onderdeel der Bataafsche Republiek," *MKAW* (1947).

Schama, Simon, "Schools and Politics in the Netherlands 1796–1814," *Historical Journal*, XII, No. 4 (1970), pp. 589–610.

Index

Aachen, 8, 174; French occupation, 8, 11, 195

Abbema, Balthasar, 113, 144, 160, 362, 382, 420

Abercromby, General Sir Ralph, 392, 395–6, 398

absolutism, 652; of Kingdom of the United Netherlands, 648; of Schimmelpenninck regime, 464, 472–3

absolutist Règlements, 54–5, 75–6, 77, 78 85–6, 88, 103, 106, 115, 120, 122

Act of Advisorship (1766), 56, 106, 112

Act of Guarantee, 212

Act of Qualification (Amsterdam, 1787), 116–17

acts of indemnity, 429

Adams, John, 2, 59, 60, 61, 63, 104, 114, 424

Address to the Batavian People, 268, 285

admiralties, provincial, 26, 237–8

Advocaat van Nationale Vrijheid (newspaper), 248, 252, 256

d'Aelders, Etta, 150, 153, 156, 157

agency system of government, 319, 344, 362–3, 380–4, 474, 648; end of, 388, 430–1, 448

Agreed Constitutional Points (the "Points"), 303, 307–9, 314, 315, 317, 325

agriculture, 26, 28, 43, 220, 372, 504, 563, 577, 582–4, 622, 654; surveys, 380, 474–5

aldermen, 50, 54, 217, 531. See also *wethouders*

Alexander I, Tsar, 544, 636

Algemeen Spectator (weekly), 72

Alkmaar, 41, 82, 372; Batavian revolution, 217–18; British seizure of, 395–6; Patriot coup, 118; Restoration of Orange (1814), 642

Alma, Adrianus, 336

Almelo, 40, 221, 225, 578, 587

d'Alphonse, Baron, 617–19, 621, 623, 629, 655

American Revolution, 3, 6, 59–63, 81, 134; influence on Patriots, 59–61, 63

Amersfoort, 97, 104, 109–10, 119, 367, 475; States of Utrecht at, 75, 100, 103, 126, 130; textile industry, 371–2, 578; tobacco growing, 28, 579

Amiens, Peace of, 423, 436–9, 452–3

Amis de la Constitution (club), 148

amnesty of 1801, 413, 415, 422

Amstel (department), 363, 368

Amsterdam, 25, 30, 34, 75, 246, 307, 363, 470, 479, 544, 558, 582, 636; anti-French riots, 551, 621, 624–5, 627, 631, 636–40; 644; army augmentation opposed by, 57, 58, 113; bankruptcies of Imperial era, 614, 633; British troops in (1794), 176–7; Burgher Defence Council, 116; "Central Society" of clubs, 229, 230, 239; Council, 80, 103, 104, 109, 114–16, 190, 253–4; Council vs. Assembly of Holland, conflict over city sovereignty, 228–33, 242; Council elections (1796), 253; Council of 1798, 330; Council after 1801, 425; Doelisten unrest, 46, 52–3, 112; dykes, 493; economy, 39, 330, 405, 434; "English" vs. "French" factions, 36; financial centre, 34–7, 41, 51, 166–7, 407–8, 415, 434, 436, 516, 576; Free Corps, 84, 102, 114–16; 194; French in (1795), 191; French occupation of (1810), 555, 609–10; French regime in, 617; French retreat from, 637; "General Assembly" of *wijken*, 229, 231; guilds, 39, 378, 427–8, 525–7, 529; industries, 39, 40, 577–8, 581; inundation preparations (1809–10), 555, 604–5, 610; militia, 395, 551, 638–40; Napoleon in, 612–13; as national capital (1808), 586; Orange Societies, 117, 231; Orangist repression (1787), 166; Orangist Restoration of 1814, 642; Patriots of, 59, 60–1, 86, 103, 115–16, 141, 164, 173, 190–1; Patriot reading societies, 172, 174–5, 179, 194, 419; Patriot Regents of, and their goals, 112–14, 121; popular clubs and *wijken*, 227, 228–9, 246, 252, 253–4, 256, 267–8, 327, 329–30, 359, 651; population, 27, 372, 581; poverty and poor relief, 49, 372, 373, 492, 503, 545, 587, 590, 591; Provisional Representatives (1795), 190–1, 194, 212, 213, 228; Prussian seizure of, 129, 131–2; public finance, 492, 545; "reform party" and plot (1802), 432–3; regent office-holders, 48–52, 54–5, 67, 80, 86, 107, 109–10, 173; regents' equivocal stance in civil war, and offer to Orange, 111–15; regents ousted (1795), 190, 231, 254; regents restored, 425, 546; return of conservatives to government (1801), 420, 424–7; Revolutionary Committee, 163, 189–90, 218, 229; Rijksmuseum, 542; schools, 532–4, 538–9; in 1787 civil war, 109, 111–16; 1787 Patriot Revolution in, 115–16, 133; 1787 Patriot retreat to, 130; 1794 Patriot uprising quelled, 175–8, 179, 183, 188; 1795 revolution in, 188–90, 194, 212, 218, 228–9, 638; 1795 patrician goals and politics, 214–15, 228–31; 1796 cannoneers' mutiny,

clubs, *see* societies
Coalition powers, 277–8, 390. *See also* First
    Coalition; Second Coalition; Third Coali-
    tion
Cobban, Alfred, 131
Coburg, General Prince Friedrich Josias,
    159
Cochon de Lapperant, Charles, 201–2, 205,
    255, 275, 279
Code Napoléon, 543, 620
Colenbrander, H. T., 19, 20, 100, 101,
    102, 123, 132, 139, 140, 142, 143, 163,
    216, 246, 274, 286, 288, 303, 314, 318,
    414, 419, 460
collegiate system of administration, 77–8,
    89–91, 344, 417, 425, 430, 446, 545
colonies, Dutch, 207, 261, 278, 279, 436–7,
    439, 449, 550–1, 585; losses of, 281, 419,
    437, 568, 578, 585, 647; public expendi-
    tures for, 497
commissioners, departmental, 365–9, 380,
    648
Commission for Agriculture, 474–5
Commission for the Waterstaat, 475, 492
Committee for Finance, Batavian, 292, 293–
    4, 344
Committee for Foreign Affairs, Batavian,
    281–3, 292, 295, 301–2, 304, 309, 324,
    344
Committee for Insurrection (1794), 173,
    417, 499. *See also* National Revolutionary
    Committee
Committee for War, Batavian, 281
Committee of General Security, French, 10,
    196–7, 299, 307
Committee of Public Safety, French, 10,
    175, 181, 185, 186, 195–7, 198, 200–2,
    206, 235, 291, 356; Dutch peace terms of,
    203–7
Common Man's Weekly, 533
Common Sense (Paine), 168, 225
Condorcet, Marie Jean Antoine Nicholas de
    Caritat, Marquis de, 7, 10, 149, 151, 154,
    160, 168
Confederation of the Rhine, 481
Conrad, F. W., 493
conscription, 622–4, 627, 631–2; freedom
    from, 483, 485, 551; riots, 623–5
Constituent Assembly of 1798, 309, 314,
    316, 321, 325–6, 327–9, 335, 337–8,
    345–6; edicts of March 17 and May 4,
    338–9, 346, 347–8
constitutional commission, 239; of 1796
    ("commission of twenty-one"), 252, 256–
    7, 258, 263, 264, 267; of 1797–98, 291–2,
    303–4, 309, 313–14, 317–18, 320
constitutional plebiscites: abstentions counted
    as tacit affirmatives, 418, 467; of 1797,
    269–70; of 1798, 321, 329, 333–7, 353;
    of 1801, 418; of 1805, 467
Constitutional (Fundamental) Restoration
    (*Grondwettige Herstelling*), 113, 140,
    142, 214, 238, 414, 472, 651

Constitutioneele Vlieg (newspaper), 339–
    40, 345
Constitutioneele Vraag-al (newspaper), 339
constitutions, American: federal, 142, 398;
    states, 60–1
constitutions, Dutch, 20, 22, 67–8, 140–1,
    212, 236; Batavian Republic unitarist,
    (1798), 20, 95, 141, 304–5, 311–21,
    337, 356, 361, 364, 368–9, 374, 378–9,
    384–5, 388, 413–14, 429, 543, 544;
    Commonwealth unitarist (1805), 463,
    467–8, 470–3, 476, 483, 485; federalist
    (1801), 141, 363, 416–20, 423, 427,
    429, 448–9, 455, 458, 535; Holland
    provincial ("Regulation" of 1796),
    233; of Kingdom of Holland (1806),
    485; of Kingdom of the Netherlands
    (1848), 22, 95, 650; of 1788, 167;
    Union of Utrecht, 18, 170, 215, 461;
    Utrecht city Règlement, 88–93, 97–100;
—**drafts and proposals:** by Batavian Revo-
    lutionary Committee, 154; Gogel's views
    of 1804, 457–9, 460; Holland unitary
    plan of 1795, 237–9; Leiden Draft, 95,
    96, 141, 220, 315; Patriot reform pro-
    posal of 1787, 111–12; Patriot Regents'
    "programme" of 1782, 113, 140, 214,
    238, 414, 472, 651; "Points" of 1797–98,
    303, 307–9, 314, 315, 317; proposal for
    constitutional monarchy (Valckenaer,
    1791), 140, 142, 152, 162, 315; of
    1796–97, 258–9, 263–70, 271, 296, 311,
    316, 378; *Sketch for the General Re-
    form . . .* proposal of 1788, 142–3; "sym-
    bol" of Ducange and Delacroix (1797),
    300–3, 314; Utrecht provincial, of 1784,
    88–9
constitutions, French, 5, 143, 216; of 1791,
    5, 142; of 1793, 260, 265, 316; of 1795,
    11, 235, 265, 285, 300, 316; of 1799, 416
Continental system, 44, 464, 477, 480, 482,
    489, 553–4, 561–2, 568–77, 594, 602–3,
    612, 614, 622
contracts of correspondence, 50–1, 54, 546
Contrat Social (Rousseau), 68, 467
Coopmans, Georgius, 336, 364
Coote, Eyre, 598
Copes van Cattenburgh, 517, 649
Cornwallis, Charles, Earl of, 437–8
corporations: abolition of, 259–60, 378–9,
    427, 525–30; Jews barred from, 262, 529;
    law on (1808), 526–9. *See also* guilds
corruption, 47, 48–50, 85, 216, 374
Corruption of the Christian Religion (Priest-
    ley), 69
cottage industry, 373, 581, 584
cotton, 579; industry, 31, 39, 41, 578–9,
    587, 591; trade, 31, 59, 371, 451, 568,
    574–5
Council for Dutch Affairs (Paris), 617
Council of Finance, 445–6, 448, 497
Council of Ministers, 491, 605, 608,
    617

Wagenaar, Jan, 18, 57, 66, 81, 225
Wagram, Battle of, 596, 602
Walcheren, 119, 157, 158, 163, 174, 241, 366–7, 371, 438, 440, 492, 572; British invasion (1809), 523, 575, 595–8, 604; 1808 flood, 549, 557; French annexation threat (1795), 199; French occupation of (1810), 604, 608
van der Wall, P. H., 421, 424
Wallmöden, General, 187, 188
Washington, George, 31
Wassenaar van Starrenburg, Baron, 117
Waterloo, Battle of, 646
Waterstaat, 492–3, 560–1, 593; Ministry, 475, 492, 531, 559–60; public expenditures for, 497
Wattignies, Battle of, 160, 171
Webbers, Carel, 179
Weiland, Petrus, 473
Wellesley, Richard Colley, Marquis, 606
Welsman, J. G., 359
Wentholt (Patriot), 325
Werner (pamphleteer), 359
Wester, Hendrik, 533, 538
Westermann, General, 159, 160
West India Company, 54, 167
Westphalia, 40, 479, 580; Kingdom of, 481, 516, 635; Louis Bonaparte's campaign in, 551–2
Westphalia, Treaty of (1648), 156
wethouders, 516, 517, 531, 544, 547, 590, 593
Wickevoort Crommelin family, 246, 424, 426
Wijckerheid Bisdom, Dirk Rudolph, 426, 589
wijk (district) meetings, 217, 226–9, 231, 235, 275, 289, 327, 365, 650
van Wijn, Hendrik, 542
Wildrik, Barend, 338, 358
Wilhelmina, Princess of Orange, 56, 57, 105–6, 121–2, 125, 127–9, 132, 191, 284, 421, 452, 652
Wilhelmina, Queen of the Netherlands, 17
William I, King of the Netherlands, 380, 382, 494, 496, 502, 512, 530, 545–6, 561, 577, 580, 640–4, 647–9
William I, the Silent, Prince of Orange, 219, 586
William II, King of the Netherlands, 646
William II, Prince of Orange, 46, 58
William III, Prince of Orange, 46, 48, 54
William IV, Prince of Orange, 33, 46, 52–4, 55
William V, Prince of Orange, 2, 17, 55–7, 58–9, 61–3, 64, 71, 75–6, 80–1, 86–7, 93, 141, 150, 156, 161–2, 163, 172, 176, 178, 180, 183, 186–8, 283, 362, 394, 421, 545; death, 490; exile in England, 36, 191, 245; expulsion from The Hague, 104–5, 110; and Orange indemnity, 452–4; and Patriot Revolution, 104–10, 112, 115, 121–3, 124, 125, 128; Restoration

to power (1787), 129, 131, 166; trial in absentia, 324
Willink, Willem, 51, 415, 436, 516, 526–7, 546, 576–7, 639
Wilson, Charles, 35
Windham, William, 390
de Winter, Admiral Jan Willem, 278, 282, 284, 292, 335, 343, 408, 610, 613, 652
Wiselius, Samuel I., 169–70, 177, 215, 216, 229–32, 237, 239–40, 244, 256, 272–3, 295, 321, 327, 329–31, 356, 361–2, 382, 405, 460, 463, 467, 476, 487, 499, 620, 648–9, 651–3; on Asiatic Council, 449–50, 456, 653; and constitutional revision and regime of 1801, 414–16, 422–3, 432; and coup d'état and regime of 1798, 307–8, 310, 314, 337, 342, 345; on East India Committee, 250, 273, 303, 307, 329
Wiskerke (historian), 529
de Wit, Boudewijn, 425
de Wit, C. H. E., 22, 68, 274, 303, 361, 453, 460, 472
de Witt brothers (Cornelis and Jan), 17, 46, 48, 57, 323, 460
Wolff, Betje, 72
Wolff, Christian von, 69
Wolters van de Poll, Johan, 546, 606
wool, 579; industry, 39, 371, 578, 586, 587; trade, 37
work, right to, 260, 374, 378, 429
workhouses for poor, 373, 429, 434, 589, 591–2
van der Woude, A. M., 26, 27, 28, 29, 38, 41
Wouters, Willem, 404
Wright, H. R. C., 35

York, Frederick Augustus, Duke of, 175, 183, 395–6
Yorke, Sir Joseph, 57, 63
van der Yves, Franc, 546
d'Yvoy, Baron, 86, 92, 453–4

Zaandam, 30, 371, 577; anti-French riots, 624, 627–8, 630
Zakboek van Neerlands Volk, 96
van Zeebergh, Adriaan, 61, 103, 111–12
Zeeland, 75, 157, 158, 173, 174, 224, 363, 530, 533, 544, 546, 579, 580–1; Assembly of "People of Zeeland," 222; British occupation, 556, 575, 597; in federalism vs. unitarism debate, 230, 238–41, 243, 269, 320; fisheries, 503, 622; floods, 354, 557; French annexation threat, 204, 207; French annexation, 555, 595, 602–5, 608–9; and General Tax Plan, 512–13; industries, 371; local government, 51, 54, 222, 239, 366–7; Orangism, 54, 63, 104, 107, 119–20, 222, 238, 366; Orangist terror, 165; Orangists' return to office, 424; Patriots, 119, 164, 222, 239; poor relief, 376; public debt, 496; 1747–

A NOTE ABOUT THE AUTHOR

Simon Schama was born in London in 1945. He studied at Cambridge, where he was awarded a Starred First in History in 1966, and became a Fellow of Christ's College and Director of Studies in History. In 1976 he was made a Fellow of Brasenose College, Oxford, and Lecturer in Modern History. He is completing the volume on the History of the Jews for Alfred A. Knopf's History of Human Society Series, and is also at work on an account of the Rothschild family and their role in the Jewish settlement of Palestine.

A NOTE ON THE TYPE

The text of this book was set in Electra, a type face designed by William Addison Dwiggins for the Mergenthaler Linotype Company and first made available in 1935. Electra cannot be classified as either "modern" or "old-style." It is not based on any historical model, and hence does not echo any particular period or style of type design. It avoids the extreme contrast between thick and thin elements that marks most modern faces, and is without eccentricities that catch the eye and interfere with reading. In general, Electra is a simple, readable type-face that attempts to give a feeling of fluidity, power, and speed.

W. A. Dwiggins (1880–1956) began an association with the Mergenthaler Linotype Company in 1929 and over the next twenty-seven years designed a number of book types, including the Metro series, Electra, Caledonia, Eldorado, and Falcon.

The book was composed, printed, and bound
by The Haddon Craftsmen, Inc., Scranton, Pennsylvania.
Design by Leon Bolognese